DEMCO
W9-BHV-411

JACKSON COMMUNITY COLLEGE LRC

International Encyclopedia of the SOCIAL SCIENCES

International Encyclopedia of the SOCIAL SCIENCES

DAVID L. SILLS EDITOR

VOLUME 9

The Macmillan Company & The Free Press

LIBRARY OF CONGRESS CATALOG NUMBER 68–10023

MANUFACTURED IN THE UNITED STATES OF AMERICA

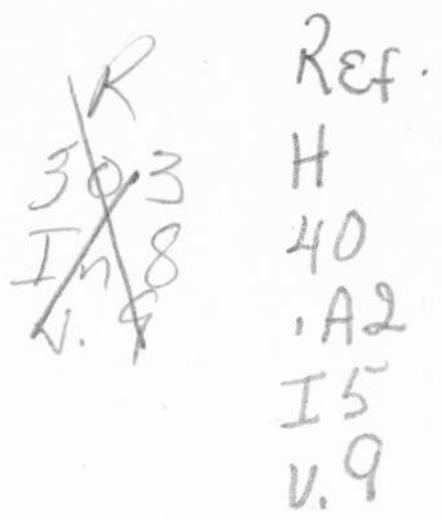

International Encyclopedia of the SOCIAL SCIENCES

[CONTINUED]

LANGUAGE

I. The Psychology of Language	*Charles N. Cofer*
II. Language Development	*Susan M. Ervin-Tripp*
III. Speech Pathology	*Jack Matthews*
IV. Language and Culture	*William Bright*

I
THE PSYCHOLOGY OF LANGUAGE

The psychologist tends to look at language in the first instance as he would look at any other problem area. Unique or special problems are confronted as they arise, but there is no unequivocal case for or against a special psychology—one created for language alone. The best, or, perhaps, the only way to discuss the psychology of language at this time is to describe how psychologists have been looking at it. Much of what can be said receives consideration in other articles in these volumes. The present one can serve as an introduction to the other articles, and it will be concerned, in part at least, with an attempt to set the framework which marks psychological studies of language. Certain more specific problems will also be treated—problems which represent some of the writer's special interests and which are unlikely to receive extended discussion elsewhere.

Early interests of psychologists in language

Studies of language—or, as psychologists prefer to call it, verbal behavior, which applies to both spoken and written forms—began very early in the postphilosophical period in psychology. Several themes may be identified (see Carroll 1953).

The "word-association experiment." First, Wilhelm Wundt, often called the first experimental psychologist, was interested in language—but more from a naturalistic than from an experimental point of view. However, workers in his laboratory early took an interest in the "word-association experiment," the origin of which is usually attributed to Sir Francis Galton. Galton's pioneering work was carried out with himself as subject: he wrote down stimuli on slips of paper and later looked at each slip (on more than one occasion) and recorded the thoughts that were thereby elicited. He also timed these reactions and noted the tendencies for the same or different thoughts to occur on the several occasions on which he looked at each slip (Warren 1921).

The "word-association experiment," despite its early entrance into the psychological laboratory (some of the results obtained are still cited today; see e.g. Woodworth [1938] 1960), soon figured more prominently in clinical diagnostic work than in the experimental laboratory. While the associations made by pathological subjects and by normal subjects were often found to differ, on the average, the association method never reached a dominant position in the armamentarium of clinical techniques, in the detection of "complexes," or, except in classroom demonstrations, in the detection of "guilty knowledge," although it was applied to all of these problems. It is safe to say that until about 1950 it had fallen into relative neglect. In the years since 1950, however, interest in association methods has reached a very high level because of the demonstrated value of measured associations in predicting other verbal behavior [*see* Marshall & Cofer 1963; Noble 1963; *see also* ANALYTICAL PSYCHOLOGY *and the biography of* JUNG].

Verbal learning. The study of verbal learning was begun in the laboratory almost as early as the word association method. Hermann Ebbinghaus reported the first experiments in a classic monograph in 1885. Ebbinghaus, however, was not really concerned with general questions of language or verbal behavior; he was interested instead in the formation of associations, and he attempted to prevent such factors as meaning, meaningfulness, and connectedness from influencing his results by inventing and using the nonsense syllable. A vast outpouring of work on verbal learning followed Ebbinghaus' pioneer efforts (see e.g. McGeoch [1942] 1952; Conference . . . 1961; Conference . . . 1963), but current opinion is that verbal learning cannot be divorced from features of the subject's usual language. [*See* LEARNING, *article on* VERBAL LEARNING; *and the biography of* EBBINGHAUS.]

Mediational processes. A third concern in psychology's study of verbal behavior is the role verbal processes may have in *mediating* between stimuli and responses. Quite early (in the 1890s) there was an interest in "mediate association," the notion that while two terms may not be related directly to one another they may be linked by a third term. Thus, justice and war may not be directly associated, but they may be related if, when one thinks justice, he also thinks peace. The latter may lead to the word "war," thus serving to mediate between justice and war.

Mediational processes, especially verbal ones, have provided a mechanism whereby objective and behavioristic psychologists can account for forms of thought, stimulus and response equivalence, and other phenomena which are otherwise refractory to a simple analysis in terms of stimulus and response (Goss 1961*a*). Much of the impetus to this way of thinking came from studies of semantic conditioning, both in Russia and in the United States (Osgood 1953; Jenkins 1963), in which verbal behavior is given an important role in the control of other behavior (Luriia 1961; Dollard & Miller 1950). There has also been great interest in the possibilities for altering verbal behavior itself (and thus perhaps its control over other behaviors) by means of reinforcement and nonreinforcement (Krasner 1958) or by other means (Cofer 1957; 1960).

Psycholinguistics. The fourth, and final, major trend appeared in the early 1950s and was a convergence of psychology (especially learning theory), descriptive linguistics, and information theory. This convergence was facilitated by the Social Science Research Council and the Carnegie Corporation (Carroll 1953). Essentially, it amounted to the bringing together of linguists and psychologists (see Osgood 1963; Osgood & Sebeok 1954) so that each group could become familiarized with the techniques and concepts of the other. As a result, an interdisciplinary "field"—psycholinguistics—has sometimes been identified, although its methods and concepts perhaps tend to be more aggregations than mergers of the concepts and methods of the disciplines. "Psycholinguisticians" tend to retain their primary identifications as linguists or as psychologists. The development of the notion of a "generative grammar" (Chomsky 1957) in linguistics may well alter the character of psycholinguistics. [*See* LINGUISTICS.]

It must be pointed out that what has been said implies very little concerning language as a process of interindividual communication. It is obvious that communication is a major function of language, but from the present vantage point it seems that matters other than communication per se have engaged the interests of the major psychological students of language or verbal behavior, although studies of communication processes do go on. Also neglected in the foregoing account is speech perception and speech pathology, the study of which can yield important and useful information on a variety of problems. [*See* LANGUAGE, *article on* SPEECH PATHOLOGY; PERCEPTION, *article on* SPEECH PERCEPTION.]

Viewpoints concerning mediational events

A major theoretical concern among psychologists interested in verbal behavior has been the implicit events which may accompany overt speech production or writing. Cofer and Foley (1942) suggested that a mediating response underlies cases of stimulus equivalence (or transfer or generalization) among stimuli which are physically dissimilar. Thus, if a response is learned to a word like "fashion" and it transfers, without further training, to the word "style" or "mode," the transfer cannot be explained on the basis of the visual appearance or the sound of the words. The argument advanced, in essence, was that each of these words elicits, as a result of prior experience, a common reaction. If this reaction occurs when fashion is presented, it will be associated with the new response being learned to fashion. Since style and mode also elicit the common reaction, its occurrence when they are presented would also result in the appearance of the response newly learned to fashion. The common reaction mediates the transfer. Cofer and Foley stressed the relation of synonymity among words as an indication of the existence of common mediating reactions among them, but they also spoke of interword associations in such a way as to suggest that associations, also, might serve as mediators.

Osgood's views—representational mediation. Osgood (1953; 1961) has made the mediating reaction the basis of a theory of meaning. Two words mean the same thing to the extent that they share the capacity to arouse the same *representational mediator*. The conception is that, with respect to an object, there is behavior, R_t (for total behavior). A sign, e.g., a word, may be acquired in relation to the object; but to have meaning with reference to the object the sign must arouse some representative part of the R_t made to the object. The representational part would ordinarily be those features of R_t which can readily be detached from the total and occur implicitly without interfering with other behavior.

This formulation led Osgood to make certain distinctions among word relations with respect to meaning. Thus, contrasting or opposite words (antonyms) cannot share common mediators and hence cannot have common meanings. This is because R_t with respect to objects or events must be very different in the case of antonyms. The representational mediators, in turn, would then be very different for antonyms. Thus, Osgood is forced to explain the fact that antonyms are often highly associated in word association tests (e.g., black–white, up–down) on the basis of a rote verbal habit rather than on the basis of common representational mediators. Similarly, he took the position that the existence of interword associations does not demonstrate, generally, the presence of common meanings. He also seemed to hold that transfer and generalization should ordinarily be predicated on common representational mediators rather than on common associations.

The semantic differential. As an index of a representational mediator, Osgood (see Osgood et al. 1957) emphasized the *semantic differential.* This is a technique by which a given word or concept (e.g., baby) is rated by a subject on each of a number of seven-point rating scales, the extremes of which are defined by polar adjectives. Thus, scales appear whose extreme points are designated by such adjective pairs as hot–cold, bad–good, active–passive, tense–relaxed. Factor analysis of the intercorrelations among such scales has usually yielded three more basic dimensions—evaluative (e.g., bad–good), activity (e.g., active–passive), potency (e.g., strong–weak). It is possible to describe a given word in terms of where its ratings fall in a semantic space defined by these three (and perhaps other) dimensions. As these dimensions are believed to characterize the representational mediator, they are an index of its meaning. Osgood has referred to this as connotative (or emotional) meaning in contrast to denotative meaning.

Among psychological investigators of verbal behavior, Osgood has perhaps been the leader in emphasizing that meaning is a critical factor in verbal behavior and that a satisfactory account of language must deal with it. Others have not been convinced. Skinner (1957) has written a psychology of language in which the concept of meaning does not enter and which treats verbal behavior as a case of the operant. Skinner is concerned with the analysis of this operant (and the classes into which it may be divided) in terms of the variables (reinforcement, stimulus control, deprivation, aversive conditions) which control its strength. This is essentially a descriptive or positivistic procedure, representing an extrapolation of notions developed in the animal laboratory.

Association in mediation. More closely associated with the mainstream of the psychological study of verbal behavior, however, have been the investigators who have emphasized interword associations as the important problem. They have insisted that the test of what is important is not whether a conception explains meaning. Rather, they have argued that the extent to which predictions can be made of the behavior of words in a variety of situations is critical. In other words, they have held forth not the criterion that a conception of verbal behavior explains (or ignores) meaning but the criterion that a theory of verbal behavior must accept measures and procedures which correlate well with other phenomena in the verbal realm.

To give this approach (it can hardly be called a theory) some concreteness, we may describe an experiment made a number of years ago at the University of Minnesota (see Jenkins 1963 for references and discussion). This experiment (and many others as well) was designed, in part, to determine whether meaning (in Osgood's sense) or association is a more effective variable in predicting transfer in certain situations. Before discussing the experiment, we may turn first to a discussion of contemporary procedures of association tests.

Association tests. The word association test, as it has been typically used, consists of a list of words to which a subject reacts, one at a time, by saying or writing down the first other single word that comes to mind when he sees or hears a list (stimulus) word. This process is called free association since no restriction is imposed on what response the subject can give, save that his response must be a single word and that repetitions of the stimulus word are prohibited. Despite its name, the procedure is not to be confused with the free association procedure as used in psychoanalysis: the two techniques differ widely.

The word association test is usually given to a number of subjects (from fifty to one hundred are considered a minimum for the establishment of norms), and their responses are tabulated for each stimulus. When such tabulations are made (and the stimuli used are relatively common words) the typical result is this: one word is given by a substantial number of subjects, another by somewhat fewer subjects, a third by still fewer subjects, and so on until words are found that are given by only one subject. An illustration will clarify this situation. Suppose the stimulus word is "length," and we obtain responses from 56 subjects. In such a sample the most frequent, or primary, response is width, occurring 18 times (32 per cent), the next is long, occurring 5 times (9 per cent), the next are height and measure, tied at 4 occurrences each, and there are 6 responses, each occurring twice—short, depth, foot, line, measurement, distance. In addition, there are 13 responses each occurring but a single time.

This set of associations, and others like it, is often termed an association hierarchy, because the responses differ and may be ordered in accordance with their frequencies of occurrence to the stimulus word. Such hierarchies may differ in a number of properties. Thus, the primary frequency may vary considerably (e.g., table elicits chair as a primary from about 75 per cent of a group of U.S. college students, in contrast to the 32 per cent indicated above), and the difference between the primary and other responses themselves may vary. Likewise, the number of different words given to a stimulus varies; usually the higher the primary frequency the fewer other words there are, a fact dictated by arithmetic if we are dealing with a constant sample size.

These differences in associative frequency have been taken as a measure of association or habit strength, not only for the group, but, by inference, for the individual. Though it is by no means a certain inference, there is evidence which justifies it (cf. Russell 1961). At any rate, a number of experiments have been predicated on this inference.

The dominant association to length, as we have seen, is width. The dictionary records a number of meanings for the word "length," but width is not among them; measure, measurement, and distance are, however, approximations to the dictionary statement of some of the meanings of length. We may say that width is a prominent *associative* meaning of length, if we wish to, but it certainly does not qualify in a dictionary or denotative sense as a meaning of length. This, of course, illustrates Osgood's argument that associations are not the same as meaning.

Predictive value of associations. The question, however, may still be raised whether the associations are effective in mediating transfer (and other phenomena) and, if they are, how they compare with synonyms in doing so. To answer this question, the following experiment was performed.

Two lists were constructed, each consisting of a series of word pairs. The subject was required to learn the two lists in succession, and the interest lay in the transfer effects of learning the first list upon learning the second list. Response members of the pairs in the two lists were related in two ways. Some responses were antonyms, but highly associated; since meaning has been ruled out by Osgood as a factor in the interrelation of antonyms, these pairs test the role of association. Other response members of the pairs were synonyms which, according to the word association test, were not associated. These test the capacity of meaning to mediate transfer without association. There were also control pairs, in which the response members of the two lists were neither synonyms nor associates. Table 1 shows the general experimental plan. When compared to control pairs in List 2, the pairs having associative and synonym relations with pairs in List 1 showed the effects of positive transfer in List 2. The associated pairs tended to be learned in a somewhat superior fashion than the synonymous pairs. In this experiment, then, both the postulated factors were effective. One can say that common meaning may effect transfer but that transfer can occur without it if suitable associations are present.

Table 1 — Experimental plan

CONDITION	LIST 1	LIST 2
Associated	eagle–sickness	eagle–health
Synonyms	mutton–long	mutton–tall
Controls	needle–king	needle–close

Many other experiments have been carried out which have explored and demonstrated the role of associations in a variety of situations. Among the situations studied have been free recall, list learning and recall, semantic generalization, recognition of words (in the context of other words) after very brief or inadequate presentations, verbal discrimination, transfer, and concept formation (for references see Deese 1961; Jenkins 1963; Cofer 1957; 1960; and Marshall & Cofer 1963). The role of meaning has also been studied in some of these situations, and some conflict has arisen over whether meaning or association is the better concept or whether one can be reduced to the other (see Bousfield 1961; Osgood 1961). Since the role of mediation is critical to this work, whether interpreted in terms of meaning or association, a good deal of effort has been devoted to basic mediational processes and mechanisms (Jenkins 1963).

Associations in other tasks. Two further areas of inquiry may be discussed to demonstrate the interest of psychologists in the role of associations in such tasks as concept identification and problem solving.

Underwood and Richardson (see Marshall & Cofer 1963) selected a large number of words, to each of which they obtained "sensory" associations from a large group of college subjects. The subjects were carefully instructed as to the kind of association they were to give; thus it was pointed out that to such a stimulus word as "apple" responses like red, sour, or round would be appropriate; responses like tree, fruit, or seed would not meet the criteria for a sensory association. To each stimulus, sensory associations were arranged in a hierarchy according to frequencies, called "dominance levels" by the investigators.

It is possible then to present several words to a new group of subjects, each word having a sensory associate in common with the other words of the set. The subject is asked what these words have in common. For example, one might present the words "chalk," "milk," "paste," and "shirt" and ask what they have in common or in what way they are similar. The instructions here would not mention or suggest sensory attributes. An answer for the set just mentioned might be that they are or can all be white. The subjects are more successful in finding the expected solution for sets with high dominance levels than for sets with low dominance levels.

This finding suggests that in tasks of this kind solution will be more likely if the instances suggest the answer than if they do not. More generally, it is consistent with the idea that problem solution often derives from responses to the materials available. If the materials suggest available and appropriate responses, solution will be quick; if they do not, or if they suggest inappropriate or incorrect responses, solution may be delayed, impeded, or prevented altogether.

A somewhat similar analysis may be made of an experiment by Judson and Cofer (see Cofer 1957). These investigators developed a number of four-word items; in each item, the subject was to exclude the word that did not go with or belong with the others. The critical items had two possible solutions. Thus, the item

skyscraper temple cathedral prayer

can be solved by excluding prayer, as it is not a building, or by excluding skyscraper, as it has nothing to do with religion. In the investigation carried out, an important factor found to determine solution was the word order of the item. As the item is shown above, prayer is excluded more often than skyscraper. If, however, the positions of prayer and skyscraper are interchanged in the item as presented, then skyscraper is excluded more often than prayer. Evidently, associations are initiated by the first word of the item and reinforced by the next two words (which are ambiguous in that they refer both to buildings and to religion) so that the last item is typically seen as not belonging. With highly religious persons, however (as measured by church attendance), the nonreligion item tends to be excluded no matter what its position is. Thus, while word order itself is important to the dominance of the concept to be identified (and thus to the word to be excluded), dominance can also arise from other, perhaps more personal, sources.

Associations should influence behavior over a period of time if their importance is great. A demonstration that is relevant was made by Judson and Cofer (see Cofer 1957). The procedure was divided into two parts, separated by a six-week interval. In part 1, each subject was asked to give ten free associations to each of ten stimulus words. Only one of these sets of associations was used later, however. Suppose one stimulus word was music and the first four associates given by one subject were tune, song, instrument, and melody. In part 2, for this subject, tune was presented on a card along with three other words (each on a card) that were new to the experiment. The subject was told to pick one of the four words. If he was "correct" (i.e., he chose tune) he was told that he was right. If he was "wrong" (i.e., he picked one of the other words), he continued to pick until he chose tune. After performing satisfactorily on this set of cards, he was then shown four more cards containing song and three new words. This time, he simply made a choice, with no information being given as to its correctness. Then he was shown four more cards, containing instrument and three new words and made a choice (without information); then melody with new words and so on until his sequence of ten associates was used up. The question was, would the subject choose more often the words that he had associated with music after the first response (tune in the example) was said to be correct than he would choose the new words which were not part of the associative chain? As compared to the control group, the subjects answered this question affirmatively, indicating that the chain established in part 1 was still intact and that subsequent choices were influenced by the designation of the first word of the chain as correct.

Another way of investigating the role of associations in problem-solving behavior was used by Cofer, Judson and Gelfand (see Cofer 1957). In this experiment, the subjects were asked to solve certain problems. Prior to attempting the problems, the subject was taught several short lists of words. One of the lists contained a sequence of words, which, if active in the subject's mind at the time of problem solving, could influence the kind of solutions used in solving the problems. The results were suggestive, if not definitive. That is, for male subjects at any rate, the frequency with which one particular solution appeared for each task was augmented (as compared to controls), and this solution was the one to which the word list was related.

These experiments on concept formation and problem solving do not cover the entire range of these phenomena but, so far as they go, they do suggest that verbal associative processes can have an important effect in these tasks. And experiments such as these illustrate very pointedly what is meant by the role of verbal responses in mediating and controlling other behaviors. [*See* CONCEPT FORMATION *and* PROBLEM SOLVING.]

Work of the kind we have just described illustrates the influence of association tests, learning theory, and the interest in mediation processes in the control of behavior. Our description should be clear on one point: much of what we have said has been concerned essentially with single words and their relations to one another. Language involves more complex arrangements of words than this, and in psychology some attention has been paid to these complexities. Both linguistics and information theory contribute knowledge and techniques to considerations of this problem of complexity.

Contributions of information theory

Information or communication theory has contributed, in addition to a model of the communication process and a means of measuring the amount of information transmitted, the important concept of redundancy. In successive segments of a sequence of words taken from normal English, there are or may be dependency on what has gone before. In such cases, the listener (or reader) can often predict accurately what is to come, and when it comes its occurrence does not contribute any information (i.e., resolve any uncertainty) over and above what the listener or reader already has. [*See* INFORMATION THEORY.] Some of this redundancy arises from structural features of the language; other aspects of it may arise from semantic (associative?) features. In the sentence "Tom went to the ____" there are many items (such as movie, play, concert, game, exhibit) which can be inserted in the blank with equal appropriateness. However, all of them are nouns; we cannot insert pronouns, adverbs, adjectives, verbs, conjunctions, and prepositions if only one word is to be placed in the blank and the sentence is to end with that word. This is an example of structural redundancy: our choice is limited to nouns in filling the blank. We cannot use just any word in the language to do so. As the noun class contains a very large number of items, we still have many choices but we are, nonetheless, restricted by the grammatical situation (here a prepositional phrase which contains an article before the blank) to selection among those words which have the privilege of occurrence in the situation.

In many situations, it is easier to fill in blanks when they stand for items that have chiefly structural rather than semantic significance. Thus, it is more likely that the blank in the following "Tom ____ going to the play" will be replaced with the word "is" or "was" than it is that the blank in the first version would be replaced by any of the noun alternatives listed. There is, we may say, more redundancy in the case of is or was than there is in the blank in the noun phrase, although there is redundancy there also. With content words (nouns, adjectives, verbs, or adverbs), the semantic or associative context often severely limits the possible choices. Thus, in the sentence "Tom went to read the part in the ____" few choices (play, drama, for example) remain to the reader or hearer; redundancy here is high.

One of the advantages for learning that connected discourse has over unconnected words is conferred by its redundancy, both structural and semantic (Deese 1961). The influence of structural redundancy is perhaps confined to strings of words in which some features, at least, of the language are preserved. Strings of unrelated words, however, may be associatively or semantically related; thus there may be some redundancy in such terms.

It is clear that redundancy is an important feature of language; it is probably essential to accurate communication (especially in noisy channels), and, for memory, it is very helpful that large amounts of material can be coded (thus reducing the load on memory) in terms of redundant features (Miller 1956). That language is often used to code or categorize (Brown 1958) the environment is perhaps a feature of the greatest importance to intellectual functioning and to the role of language in the control of behavior.

Contributions of linguistics

It is probably fair to say that linguistics has had its greatest impact on psychology because of its knowledge of the structure of language and the rules that govern the structure. Phonemic and morphemic analysis has been instructive, but morphology and syntax are perhaps more provocative.

There are at least two fundamental issues that morphology and syntax raise for a psychology of language. First, it is clear that no theory of verbal behavior which confines itself to semantic and associative relations among words alone is complete. Mechanisms must be developed to cope with semantic and associative changes that undoubtedly occur in the context of other words, and syntactic restraints must be an important aspect of this context. Furthermore, no psychological theory of morphology or syntax has been presented as yet. Analysis so far has largely been confined to specific cues in speech or writing which might elicit word inflections or specific syntactic forms (Goss 1961*b*).

The second issue arises from the fact that at a descriptive level it is clear that speech regularities appear very early in the development of the child (Brown & Fraser 1963). Furthermore, many rule-abiding features of speech are known to occur widely, even though the speakers are unaware of the rules or of the fact that they are following rules. Young children display the operation of a general rule when they pluralize goose incorrectly as gooses or form the past tense of the verb "take" as "taked." Perhaps more subtle examples are found in the speech of adults. We all recognize that there is something wrong with the expression "the sheer two silk stockings" and would prefer to say "the two sheer silk stockings." We would have difficulty in formulating the rule that makes one expression acceptable, the other not. Despite its semantic nonsense, we can recognize the grammatical correctness of Chomsky's (1957) famous sentence, "colorless green ideas sleep furiously," or make the appropriate substitutions of nouns, verbs, and modifiers in such strings as "the glibs duxed the neglan gojeys." Semantic factors are not essential to the identification of grammaticalness or to the identification of parts of speech.

The facts are, then, that morphological and syntactical principles govern much speech and writing behavior and that many of them cannot be verbalized by a large number of adults and appear in the speech behavior of young children without explicit instruction. These features suggest that a psychological theory or account of morphology and syntax may have to include concepts of a higher order than those of stimulus and response and that explicit coding responses cannot be invoked to mediate these phenomena of grammar.

Structural linguistics has provided descriptions of these phenomena and has described the regularities that prevail in language. However, it has not presented a theory of the behavior involved. Recently, Chomsky (1957) and Miller (1962) have argued for a new conception.

This conception holds that, in addition to a phrase-structure grammar, there is also a set of transformational rules which, when used, modifies a statement from one type to another including the necessary morphophonemic changes. Thus, a sentence model exists which appears to be the basic form (the kernel) of adult utterances, but it is transformed systematically, as needed, by the use of transformational rules like the interrogative, the passive, the negative, and so on. More than one rule may be applied, as when a simple declarative sentence becomes a passive interrogative negative. For example, "Tom hits the girl" would become "Is not the girl being hit by Tom?" by the application of the appropriate transformations.

Chomsky, a linguist, has been explicit in asserting that a simple stimulus–response formation and habit utilization theory cannot, in his opinion, cope with this conception of grammar. Miller, a psychologist, seems to agree, and while he thinks work on association is important, he believes that the mechanisms underlying the transformational grammar can hardly be of the associational kind. A psychological theory of the development and use of transformational grammar has not been formulated, but if these authors are correct it would presumably involve high-order processes not readily reducible to association or meaning.

We have surveyed some of the major interests and problems characterizing psychologists' work on language. Beginning with the historical trends in the psychological study of language, we have concentrated on mediational processes, conceived from both a meaning and a word-association point of view. While some progress on problems related to mediational processes has been made, many questions and further problems remain. Psychological understanding of language in the sense of connected words has not progressed very far, although concepts and methods of information theory and linguistics have been found useful. Whether the rule using that is evident in the verbal behavior of both children and adults, conceived either in terms of conventional morphology and syntax or in terms of transformational grammar, can be reduced to the concepts of contemporary learning theory is a question to be decided in the near future.

CHARLES N. COFER

[*Directly related are the entries* COMMUNICATION; LINGUISTICS; LITERATURE. *Other relevant material may be found in* INFORMATION THEORY; PERCEPTION, *article on* SPEECH PERCEPTION.]

BIBLIOGRAPHY

BOUSFIELD, W. A. 1961 The Problem of Meaning in Verbal Learning. Pages 81–91 in Conference on Verbal Learning and Verbal Behavior, New York University, 1959, *Verbal Learning and Verbal Behavior: Proceedings.* Edited by Charles N. Cofer. New York: McGraw-Hill.

BROWN, ROGER 1958 *Words and Things.* Glencoe, Ill.: Free Press.

BROWN, ROGER; and FRASER, COLIN 1963 The Acquisition of Syntax. Pages 158–197 in Conference on Verbal Learning and Verbal Behavior, Second, Ardsley-on-Hudson, N. Y., 1961, *Verbal Behavior and Learning, Problems and Processes: Proceedings.* Edited by Charles N. Cofer and Barbara S. Musgrave. New York: McGraw-Hill.

CARROLL, JOHN B. (1953) 1961 *The Study of Language: A Survey of Linguistics and Related Disciplines in America.* Cambridge, Mass.: Harvard Univ. Press.

CHOMSKY, NOAM 1957 *Syntactic Structures.* The Hague: Mouton.

COFER, CHARLES N. 1957 Reasoning as an Associative Process: III. The Role of Verbal Responses in Problem Solving. *Journal of General Psychology* 57:55–68.

COFER, CHARLES N. 1960 Experimental Studies of the Role of Verbal Processes in Concept Formation and Problem Solving. New York Academy of Sciences, *Annals* 91:94–107.

COFER, CHARLES N.; and FOLEY, JOHN P. JR. 1942 Mediated Generalization and the Interpretation of Verbal Behavior: I. Prolegomena. *Psychological Review* 49:513–540.

CONFERENCE ON VERBAL LEARNING AND VERBAL BEHAVIOR, NEW YORK UNIVERSITY, *1959* 1961 *Verbal Learning and Verbal Behavior: Proceedings.* Edited by Charles N. Cofer. New York: McGraw-Hill.

CONFERENCE ON VERBAL LEARNING AND VERBAL BEHAVIOR, SECOND, ARDSLEY-ON-HUDSON, N. Y., *1961* 1963 *Verbal Behavior and Learning, Problems and Processes: Proceedings.* Edited by Charles N. Cofer and Barbara S. Musgrave. New York: McGraw-Hill.

DEESE, JAMES 1961 From the Isolated Verbal Unit to Connected Discourse. Pages 11–31 in Conference on Verbal Learning and Verbal Behavior, New York University, 1959, *Verbal Learning and Verbal Behavior: Proceedings.* Edited by Charles N. Cofer. New York: McGraw-Hill.

DOLLARD, JOHN; and MILLER, NEAL E. 1950 *Personality and Psychotherapy: An Analysis in Terms of Learning, Thinking and Culture.* New York: McGraw-Hill. → A paperback edition was published in 1965.

GOSS, ALBERT E. 1961*a* Early Behaviorism and Verbal Mediating Responses. *American Psychologist* 16:285–298.

GOSS, ALBERT E. 1961*b* Acquisition and Use of Conceptual Schemes. Pages 42–69 in Conference on Verbal Learning and Verbal Behavior, New York University, 1959, *Verbal Learning and Verbal Behavior: Proceedings.* Edited by Charles N. Cofer. New York: McGraw-Hill.

JENKINS, JAMES J. 1963 Mediated Associations: Paradigms and Situations. Pages 210–245 in Conference on Verbal Learning and Verbal Behavior, Second, Ardsley-on-Hudson, N. Y., 1961, *Verbal Behavior and Learning: Problems and Processes: Proceedings.* Edited by Charles N. Cofer and Barbara S. Musgrave. New York: McGraw-Hill.

KRASNER, LEONARD 1958 Studies of the Conditioning of Verbal Behavior. *Psychological Bulletin* 55:148–170.

LURIIA, ALEKSANDR R. 1961 *The Role of Speech in the Regulation of Normal and Abnormal Behavior.* New York: Liveright.

MCGEOCH, JOHN A. (1942) 1952 *The Psychology of Human Learning.* 2d ed., revised by Arthur L. Irion. New York: Longmans.

MARSHALL, GEORGE R.; and COFER, CHARLES N. 1963 Associative Indices as Measures of Word Relatedness: A Summary and Comparison of Ten Methods. *Journal of Verbal Learning and Verbal Behavior* 1:408–421.

MILLER, GEORGE A. 1956 The Magical Number Seven, Plus or Minus Two: Some Limits on Our Capacity for Processing Information. *Psychological Review* 63:81–97.

MILLER, GEORGE A. 1962 Some Psychological Studies of Grammar. *American Psychologist* 17:748–762.

NOBLE, CLYDE E. 1963 Meaningfulness and Familiarity. Pages 76–119 in Conference on Verbal Learning and Verbal Behavior, Second, Ardsley-on-Hudson, N. Y., 1961, *Verbal Behavior and Learning, Problems and Processes: Proceedings.* Edited by Charles N. Cofer and Barbara S. Musgrave. New York: McGraw-Hill.

OSGOOD, CHARLES E. (1953) 1959 *Method and Theory in Experimental Psychology.* New York: Oxford Univ. Press.

OSGOOD, CHARLES E. 1961 Comments on Professor Bousfield's Paper. Pages 91–106 in Conference on Verbal Learning and Verbal Behavior, New York University, 1959, *Verbal Learning and Verbal Behavior: Proceedings.* Edited by Charles N. Cofer. New York: McGraw-Hill.

OSGOOD, CHARLES E. 1963 Psycholinguistics. Pages 244–316 in Sigmund Koch (editor), *Psychology: A Study of a Science.* Volume 6: Investigations of Man as Socius: Their Place in Psychology and the Social Sciences. New York: McGraw-Hill.

OSGOOD, CHARLES E.; and SEBEOK, THOMAS A. (editors) (1954) 1965 *Psycholinguistics: A Survey of Theory and Research Problems.* Bloomington: Indiana Univ. Press.

OSGOOD, CHARLES E.; SUCI, G. J.; and TANNENBAUM, P. H. (1957) 1961 *The Measurement of Meaning*. Urbana: Univ. of Illinois Press.

RUSSELL, WALLACE A. 1961 Assessment Versus Experimental Acquisition of Verbal Habits. Pages 110–123 in Conference on Verbal Learning and Verbal Behavior, New York University, 1959, *Verbal Learning and Verbal Behavior: Proceedings*. Edited by Charles N. Cofer. New York: McGraw-Hill.

SKINNER, B. F. 1957 *Verbal Behavior*. New York: Appleton.

WARREN, HOWARD C. 1921 *A History of the Association Psychology*. New York: Scribner.

WOODWORTH, ROBERT S. (1938) 1960 *Experimental Psychology*. Rev. ed. by Robert S. Woodworth and Harold Schlosberg. New York: Holt.

II
LANGUAGE DEVELOPMENT

Language development refers to the child's acquisition of his first language, usually under informal natural conditions. By the end of the first four years of life, children have mastered the essentials of this most distinctively human attribute. Given normal hearing and a normal brain, variations in rates of mastery are small. Indeed, so gifted in language learning are they that many children become skilled in more than one language in their early years. The evolution of a child's knowledge of his language is basic to his intellectual and social development, yet explanations of this process make demands on theories of human learning which have not yet been met.

Historical aspects. Studies of child language development in modern times fall into three phases. The first studies in the nineteenth century consisted primarily of parental diaries. Authors trained in linguistics (Gvozdev 1961; Leopold 1939–1949) have continued to use case studies. More than any other form of behavior, language reveals obvious internal patterning, and linguists have been loath to lose sight of these patterns by pooling quantitative measures of output. In the second phase of research, carried out by psychologists, standardized measuring methods of large samples were emphasized (McCarthy 1954). For the most part these studies have been atheoretical and have been concerned with variations in performance with age, sex, race, social class, and so on.

A landmark in modern research was Velten's (1943) application of Jakobson's (1941) theory of phonemic development. This theory proposed that changes in each child's linguistic system followed an orderly sequence of increasing differentiation of significant features; thus it related language development to perceptual development and provided a theoretical framework which made comparison of children in different linguistic environments possible.

Subsequent research, particularly on phonology and grammar, is a product of the mating of psychology and linguistics. The differences from the preceding phase lie in the later work's sensitivity to linguistic theories, respect for the systematic nature of the child's linguistic knowledge, and emphasis on inferences about the structures or rules which underlie the observed situational changes in verbal behavior.

Prelinguistic phase of infancy. By the end of the first year of life, the average child understands some adult speech and can execute some directions. At first, he merely responds to adult sounds by attention and then by making sounds himself. Later he comes to recognize gross differences between voices and may distinguish intonational contrasts. His gradual discrimination of the critical features in the speech of adults is probably the most important aspect of language learning, yet almost nothing is known about the growth of comprehension.

The infant at first makes sounds which are closely tied to feeding and breathing. His vocalizations become increasingly triggered by vocal stimulation from others. In the first three months cooing comes to be highly associated with vocal stimulation and can also be increased in frequency if followed by other forms of adult responsiveness. On the other hand, the actual sounds uttered seem to be autogenous, since the sounds of deaf children and of children who hear are indistinguishable before six months.

Cooing gradually gives way to the consonant–vowel sequences and repetitive patterns which sound to adults like the syllables of their own language. During the babbling period, there is a rich variety of vocal play by the normal child. Sometimes he persists in making sounds which are idiosyncratic and not present in the speech around him. Further, he readily produces sounds and sequences in the adult repertoire which he will be unable to produce again for years after he begins to use language.

The role of babbling in language development is controversial. A child who lives in a linguistically stimulating environment may babble a great deal, and he may be more fluent than average when language develops. Yet, contrary to popular belief, there is as yet no evidence that babbling is in any specific way practice for language development. Indeed, the formal properties of babbling and of speech are so different that they suggest somewhat distinct central processes in their production.

Semantic system

Early sentences. An average child uses meaningful utterances by the middle of the second year, and by the middle of the third year babbling virtually disappears in play except as a stylistic device.

At first these utterances vary considerably in both sound and meaning. They may be quite idiosyncratic. Because of the simplicity of the child's phonological system, there may be numerous homonyms if his vocabulary grows rapidly. Meanings are generalized readily, so that a given utterance might on various occasions mean "my coat," "my hat," "my baby carriage," "let's go for a walk," "bye-bye," and so on. Frequently there is a close integration with gesture.

If the first utterances are based on adult words, they may sometimes be very inclusive in reference ("bird") or very narrow ("Bobby"). Adult beliefs about the semantic contrasts needed by children may influence the words they use in talking with children. From the standpoint of adult meanings, the words used by children tend to refer to animal and human movements and to concrete items with characteristic shapes and sizes (Brown 1958). When the child's range of reference of a term is actually tested, it appears to depend on the variety of verbal contexts in which a word is heard and, to a lesser degree, on the variety of physical referents.

Conceptual changes. As the size of vocabulary increases, inevitably there is a change in the conceptual system. The number of semantic contrasts marked by vocabulary grows, and the referential range for each word must therefore narrow. A child might begin by calling all adults "papa," next use the word for his own father, and then later learn the word "adult," which has a similar referential range to the primitive "papa" (Leopold 1939–1949).

In this example, there has been more than a change in range. By the time the word "adult" is present, the child has a hierarchical system of superordinates. The criteria for each class have increased in specificity and changed in character, becoming less visual. Changes in the semantic system have in fact been only sketchily studied. They may include increases in the specificity of terms, increases in knowledge or in concept range as experience grows, a shift from sensorimotor to relational bases for concepts, and shifts in the verbal structure, so that antonyms, synonyms, superordinates, and other structural relations in the vocabulary reflect the critical contrasts employed in the language.

Studies of the deaf and other experimental research have suggested that conceptual development may have important nonverbal roots. Yet words give society a sure way of imposing its conceptual system. Societies differ considerably in the semantic contrasts marked by their vocabulary of kin, color, quantity, shape, time, space, and so on. The sanctions against deviant denotative use of these terms bring the child's comprehension, speech, and presumably his conceptual system into line with his language community.

Verbal relations. The basis of the child's system of relating words shifts by mid-primary school from sounds to meanings and grammatical features. The sound of a word is salient to the preschool child, who readily produces rhymes and alliterative sequences in word play. Words which sound alike are easily confused, leading to contaminations of meaning. On the other hand, children's greater interest in the sounds of words may facilitate the learning of a spelling system or the sound system of a second language. In contrast, adults, who tend to respond less to the sound and who are concerned more with meaning, are known to have greater difficulty with the phonology of a second language, although they may acquire vocabulary far more quickly.

As children mature, their vocabulary increasingly becomes organized in terms of grammatical and semantic replacement classes, and they become more able to isolate words from their situational and sentence contexts. Each word more readily elicits other words. Interverbal associations are more rapid, more fluent, more specific, and more predictable from the semantic and grammatical system. This high rate of mutual evocation of words may be a help in intelligence tests and in school tasks requiring verbal retention of information. Children vary considerably in their readiness to convert their experience—including nonverbal experience—into spontaneous verbal thought. This skill seems to be a consequence of the verbal milieu in which the child is reared, and hence is responsive to training (see Ervin-Tripp in Hoffman & Hoffman 1966).

Phonology

As soon as a child knows several meaningful utterances it is possible to study his phonological system. The units of this system are phonemes, which are constructs that represent the smallest distinguishable unit of speech and which account for the significant formal contrasts between utterances. A very primitive system is illustrated when a child has two words, such as "baba" and "tata." At this point there are three phonemes—one vowel and two consonants. Extrapolating from a small number of diary studies, we might expect the following changes to take place: (1) We might next find a system containing four consonant phonemes in which there is a contrast between the stop consonants and continuants. For example, the child might add /*m*/ and /*n*/, or /*f*/ and /*s*/ to the primitive system. At this point the consonant system would have two intersecting features—place of articulation (front versus back) and type of articulation (stop versus continuant). (2) In the vowels, probably a low versus high contrast will appear first, so the next vowel might be a single higher vowel, followed by a front–back contrast, as in /*i*/ versus /*u*/. (3) Typically, a contrast of position is followed by a voicing contrast. When voicing becomes significant, we might find both "dada" and "tata" with different meanings. (4) The consonant system will usually be more elaborate at the beginning of words, so that the number of contrasts may be greater there during the course of development. (5) Syllable repetitions, as in the example, usually decrease in the second year, and the length and variety of word-formation patterns increase. (6) Some sequential arrangements, such as consonant clusters (*ts*, *kr*, *pl*), are absent for a long time, even when the component phonemes are present (see Ervin-Tripp in Hoffman & Hoffman 1966).

This has been a description of the child's phonology in its own terms, but most observers are more likely to notice the mapping of the adult's system onto the child's when the child makes substitutions. Thus, in the above system with three phonemes and a *CVCV* syllable repetition pattern, any word acquired by the child must become either "tata" or "baba"—an extreme case to be sure. The most obvious substitution patterns are simple replacements, such as the mapping of both stops (*t*, *d*) and affricates (*ch*, *j*) onto stops when there is no stop–affricate contrast. The word formation pattern of the child may require omission of whole syllables or members of clusters. The conversion of "father" into "papa" is predictable for a child who has not yet developed a stop–fricative contrast (between /*p*/ and /*f*/), who has a *CVCV* syllable repetition rule, and who selects the adult stressed syllable.

The child with a simplified phonemic system sometimes has a preferred phonetic realization of a given phoneme and sometimes has random or free variation. In the first case, he might always say [*t*] and never use [*d*] in articulation of "tata." In the latter case, especially common for vowels, he may oscillate unpredictably. A third possibility is that he may use each predictably in a given context. For instance, he may use [*d*] at the beginning of words and [*t*] in the middle to realize a single phoneme (Velten 1943).

Although the number of phonemes in children's systems usually is less than in adults', their substitution rules are not always simple and may baffle parents or teachers unfamiliar with phonemic analysis. For instance, some children have a rule making an initial consonant nasal if there is a nasal consonant anywhere in the adult model word, producing imitations like /*ni*/ for "green." There may be phonemic contrasts in the child's system which are absent in the adult system. Assimilation is very common in children's word-formation patterns, so that neighboring phonemes or successive syllables may influence each other. Yet all of these are orderly rules. The factors producing these idiosyncratic patterns are as yet unknown.

What makes a child's phonemic system change? Perhaps the presence of numerous homonyms encourages change; yet some children tolerate extensive homonymy when they have a large vocabulary combined with a very simple phonemic system and restricted word-formation rules. Understanding or hearing a phonemic distinction is not a sufficient condition for producing it, although each process evidently facilitates the other. Thus, in adults, acoustic discrimination is much sharper when the listeners have learned a corresponding discrete articulation. The teaching of reading and spelling and the alteration of phonology when children learn to speak second dialects and second languages might be much easier if teachers knew more about phonological development [*see* PERCEPTION, *article on* SPEECH PERCEPTION].

Grammar

Languages differ considerably in their organization of basic grammatical devices, so it will be necessary to study children's language development in many types of languages to establish well-founded generalizations. For example, in English, the constituent order (e.g., subject–verb–object) has a high degree of regularity; deviations are significant; and the selection of entries in the subject and object position is semantically important. In Russian, on the other hand, there may be much more variability in constituent order, since inflectional suffixes mark the relations indicated by constituent order in English. Children learning both languages show order regularities before they use markers such as inflection or function words consistently, but children learning highly inflected languages have been reported to learn inflections much earlier (Gvozdev 1961).

Simple syntax. From the very beginning of multiword sentences, children usually reveal order regularities in speech. Certain frequent words may occupy fixed positions. For instance, "where," "there," and "this" may always be in antecedent position, and "up," "on," and "off" in last position. Other words and phrases, such as "broken," "blue," "truck," "the truck," "the broken," then could occupy either position in complement to the fixed items. On the basis of position alone, one can identify primitive word classes and usually a nominal phrase also, which can expand one of the complement classes. From the examples it can be seen that these classes are idiosyncratic and do not correspond exactly to adult classes (Bellugi & Brown 1964).

How do primitive classes develop? They cannot be based simply on imitation, since at this stage children's imitations are at least as simple as their own spontaneous speech, and classes appear even if the adult language has variable order (Gvozdev 1961). They reflect order regularities when they exist in adult language, and in part they reflect semantic features of adult classes (Brown 1958). In their idiosyncratic features they clearly reveal creative and analogizing activity by the child and cannot be based on rote learning. The study of the child's interpretation of what he hears may provide the key to this enigma. But as yet there have been no true experiments on grammatical acquisition in the very young. There is disagreement as to the character of "rules" in children's early grammar and as to the relation between the comprehension system and speech.

Inflections and function words. During the period of simple syntax, English-speaking children employ function words like "the" at random, and as their frequency increases such anomalous sentences may appear as "I see the Mary." The order of mastery of both function words and inflections is influenced by their semantic obviousness.

In English, inflectional suffixes such as plurals are randomly present at first, but in highly inflected languages, such as Russian, often a single form is used before the period of random variation. In many languages there are some irregular inflections, such as "go–went," which are preserved because of their high individual frequency. Children do not usually learn these first, as tense contrasts at least, even though they are frequent. Among English nouns and verbs, the largest variety of verbs have an inflectional suffix, such as "stop–stopped." It is these forms which are productive or generalized to new words by children. These analogies can be highly resistant to adult influence; typically, a form like "foots" can remain in a child's speech for months after he has learned the plural form.

Sometimes alternative inflections depend upon the preceding phoneme; for example, a plural is formed by "-s" in most cases, but by "-es" in some, as in "mats" versus "matches." Children use the most common form first, then both at random, before discovering the phonemic conditioning rule. During the period of random variation one finds forms such as "handses" and "toasteded" (Ervin-Tripp in Hoffman & Hoffman 1966).

Complex syntax. It is a common observation that children's sentences grow longer as they get older. This is a superficial effect of deeper changes. As we have seen, this increase is due in part to the systematic use of function words and suffixes. Some of the constituents which were optional in the simple grammars—such as verbs—may become obligatory in the more complex phrase structure. Potentially infinite expansions of coordinate and subordinate structures appear. These are all changes in the child's syntax itself; in addition, there may be increases in the amount of information a child can include in a given utterance. One might say that programming capacity increases with age.

In the course of these changes, it is not easy to establish criteria for mastery of the adult syntactic rules. Sometimes a given sentence in a child's speech has the appearance of an adult sentence, but it derives from a different syntax. For example, during the early stages in the development of negation, children commonly use "no" or "don't" as simple negativizing words, much like the plural. Later, as inflection of verbs appears, one may find "he doesn't goes." Eventually the child will arrive at the adult rule, which in the negative marks tense and person only in the auxiliary. The intermediate stages of the evolution of the negation rule can be inferred if one has appropriate tests or a sufficiently large text from a child and is willing to make such inferences.

At the age of six, there remain a number of constructions which are still absent in the speech of many children, such as nominalizations of simple verbs (Menyuk 1964). Some of these constructions may be rare in the colloquial speech used to children. Perhaps, on the other hand, they involve inherently more complex rules requiring conceptual maturation.

Children's syntactical rules are always inferred from behavior, but the study of comprehension, imitations, spontaneous speech, or other measures may give different results. Comparison of these varying measures may help in the analysis of such inferred processes. Each makes different demands on knowledge, much as recognition and recall make different demands on memory. Imitation, for example, requires phases of perceptions, storage, retrieval, and speech. At different ages imitations are structurally quite dissimilar. At first they appear to be markedly simplified by the child's speech production rules. Later, restrictions occur in the other phases of the process, but eventually the child can perceive and store even the mistakes which he hears (Ervin-Tripp in Hoffman & Hoffman 1966).

Language functions

Private functions. Vocalizing begins as an autogenous activity, and throughout life there exist varieties of speech in which listeners do not actively mediate the speaker's satisfactions. In babies these may include cooing, babbling, and at first, crying. Vocal play with sounds continues into the phase of organized speech. Babies vocalize when they see objects and when they engage in action, but around four and five such speech appears to have an implicit audience. Such monologues, for instance, decrease in isolation, are inhibited by strangers, and increase when difficulties are encountered (Vygotskii 1934). Eventually speech not only is a product of play but aids in its organization, perhaps being a precursor, as Vygotskii believed, of some aspects of covert thought.

Social functions. Social play—for example, in gestural games—may be at least as significant in the evolution of early language as demands for goods and services. Such play receives social rewards, and even a three-month-old infant may vocalize more if so reinforced. It thus becomes difficult to mark any point when one can say that vocalizing becomes intentional. The rhetorical question, ritual naming of objects, and many other vocal performances in the second year appear to be socially motivated and probably vary markedly according to milieu. True offering of information, addressed to lacunae in the listener's knowledge, demands mature social development, and difficulties can still be found in this function during the school years. Because of the heavy dependence of these different functions on social milieu, it is particularly difficult to establish any generalizations in the absence of experimental research.

Children's speech changes according to the audience, the function, and the setting. The most extreme adaptation occurs in multilingual children, who by three can usually distinguish their languages appropriately. Yet even within a language there may be formal alternations, as in the suffixes "-in" and "-ing" in English, which mark subtle style shifts in the speech of American children.

In many languages there is a special form of speech used in addressing infants, which may be called baby talk, and involves changes in phonology, vocabulary, and syntax. Children may employ baby talk as a stylistic device depending on the listener or the role during play. In languages such as Japanese there may be many changes in syntax or vocabulary according to the age or status of the listener, and these are acquired by children only gradually during the school years. Optional features of syntax, such as use of qualifiers and subordination, may be affected by audience or function. Conversations with adults or expository speech in the schoolroom may draw on syntactic skills not usually employed in conversations with other children.

Schooling. Schooling may indeed mark the most radical change in language functions encountered by children. In the home and among friends the function and form of speech may be quite different—briefer, situationally imbedded, narrative, repetitive, topically limited, aimed at solidarity or aggression. In school, there is a demand for precision, independence from the speech situation, exposition, novelty, breadth of topics, and transmission of information. The latter functions demand more abstract vocabulary and greater use of grammatical structures that signal analytic differentiations. Written language, since it is private, with neither audience nor situational support, is at the farthest remove from the colloquial practice children bring to school (Vygotskii 1934).

Knowledge of language increases, of course, after early childhood. The everyday vernacular of the peer group, not parents, in the preadolescent years remains as our spontaneous adult speech. We acquire new vocabulary from travel, reading, and the acquisition of skills. Later, as our social relationships become more complex we may come to control a greater range of the structural facilities of the language and its stylistic alternatives for such varied purposes as persuasive, expository, and aesthetic discourse. But these changes usually do not occur in children who lack any secondary education. While it is true that all normal children master the essentials of language before they enter school, variations in the language functions provided by the family and school milieu affect markedly the extent to which children go beyond these essentials.

SUSAN M. ERVIN-TRIPP

[*Directly related are the entries* LEARNING, *article on* VERBAL LEARNING; LINGUISTICS. *Other relevant material may be found in* DEVELOPMENTAL PSYCHOLOGY; HEARING.]

BIBLIOGRAPHY

BELLUGI, URSULA; and BROWN, ROGER W. (editors) 1964 *The Acquisition of Language.* Monographs of the Society for Research in Child Development, Vol. 29, No. 92. Univ. of Chicago Press.

BERKO, JEAN; and BROWN, ROGER W. 1960 Psycholinguistic Research Methods. Pages 517–557 in Paul Mussen (editor), *Handbook of Research Methods in Child Development.* New York: Wiley.

BROWN, ROGER W. 1958 *Words and Things.* Glencoe, Ill.: Free Press.

CARROLL, JOHN B. (1957) 1960 Language Development. Pages 744–752 in *Encyclopedia of Educational Research.* 3d ed. New York: Macmillan.

GVOZDEV, A. N. 1961 *Voprosy izucheniia detskoi rechi* (Problems in the Language Development of the Child). Moscow: Akademiia Pedagogicheskikh Nauk RSFSR.

HOFFMAN, MARTIN L.; and HOFFMAN, LOIS W. (editors) 1966 *Review of Child Development Research.* Volume 2. New York: Russell Sage Foundation. → See especially the article by Susan Ervin-Tripp on "Language Development."

JAKOBSON, ROMAN 1941 *Kindersprache, Aphasie, und allgemeine Lautgesetze.* Uppsala (Sweden): Almqvist & Wiksell.

LEOPOLD, WERNER F. 1939–1949 *Speech Development of a Bilingual Child: A Linguist's Record.* Studies in the Humanities, Nos. 6, 11, 18, 19. Evanston, Ill.: Northwestern Univ. Press.

LEOPOLD, WERNER F. 1952 *Bibliography of Child Language.* Evanston, Ill.: Northwestern Univ. Press.

LEWIS, MORRIS M. (1936) 1952 *Infant Speech: A Study of the Beginnings of Language.* 2d ed., rev. New York: Humanities.

LEWIS, MORRIS M. (1963) 1964 *Language, Thought and Personality in Infancy and Childhood.* New York: Basic Books.

MCCARTHY, DOROTHEA 1954 Language Development in Children. Pages 492–630 in Leonard Carmichael (editor), *Manual of Child Psychology.* 2d ed. New York: Wiley.

MENYUK, PAULA 1964 Syntactic Rules Used by Children From Preschool Through First Grade. *Child Development* 35:533–546.

TEMPLIN, MILDRED 1957 *Certain Language Skills in Children: Their Development and Interrelationships.* Institute of Child Welfare, Monograph No. 26. Minneapolis: Univ. of Minnesota Press.

VELTEN, H. V. 1943 The Growth of Phonemic and Lexical Patterns in Infant Language. *Language* 19:281–292.

VYGOTSKII, LEV S. (1934) 1962 *Thought and Language.* Cambridge, Mass.: M.I.T. Press. → First published as *Myshlenie i rech'.*

III
SPEECH PATHOLOGY

Speech pathology is a branch of communications dealing with disorders of speech and language. Speech pathologists concern themselves with diagnosis, treatment, and prevention of speech and language disorders. Although speech pathology in Europe was once a branch of medicine, today, throughout most of the world, the field has developed as an independent speciality, in somewhat the same fashion that clinical psychology has emerged as an area separate from psychiatry. As is the case with clinical psychology, most training programs in speech pathology in the United States are a part of the graduate program offered by colleges of arts and science. A limited number of training programs are affiliated with colleges of education or colleges of medicine.

Unlike the general field of speech, which is concerned with improving the normal and slightly subnormal, the area of speech pathology focuses on defects of speech and language. Speech is considered to be defective when any one or combination of the following conditions exists: speech is lacking in intelligibility; speech differs so much from normal that it calls undue attention to itself, often with the result that listeners pay more attention to the speech deviations than to what the speaker is saying; speech behavior leads to the development of negative attitudes by the speaker toward his own speech, which in turn often interfere with his over-all adjustment.

Speech and language problems can be described in terms of the acoustic end product perceived by listeners or in terms of the etiology of the problem.

Problems of the acoustic end product

From the standpoint of the acoustic end product, speech and language problems can be considered under five general headings: delayed speech and language, defects of articulation, defects of voice, defects of rhythm, defects of symbolic formulation.

Delayed speech and language. Most normal children are able to speak their first word at approximately age one. Language comprehension and production increase along with articulation ability. By age eight the majority of children have learned to articulate all sounds correctly. Speech pathologists use the term *delayed speech* to describe the speech of children who either do not talk or who perseverate habits and patterns of infantile speech. If there is vocabulary deficiency, inadequate formulation of ideas, or retarded sentence structure, the term *delayed language* may be employed (Matthews 1957*a*, pp. 394–395). A well-accepted listing of causes is provided by Van Riper (1963) and includes mental retardation, hearing loss, faulty coordination resulting from disease or paralysis, prolonged illness during infancy, lack of motivation for speech, improper teaching methods employed by parents, confused hand preference, necessity for learning two or more languages simultaneously, shock during the speaking act, emotional conflicts, and aphasia.

The treatment of delayed speech depends upon the significant etiological factors. The child with a hearing loss may need a hearing aid. Other causative factors should be removed or lessened. Van Riper describes therapy procedures for delayed speech. In general these procedures attempt to provide a stimulating environment in which the child is "bombarded" by speech and is taught to associate speech sounds with meaningful people and objects.

Defects of articulation. Defects of articulation in general can be divided into four types: substitution, distortion, omission, and addition. Substitution errors consist of the replacement of one sound with another. A common example is the substitution of *w* for *r*, as in "wed" instead of "red," "twuck" for "truck," and "dwink" for "drink." Other common substitution errors are *w* for *l*, as in "weave" for "leave"; *th* for *s*, as in "thick" for "sick"; and *d* for *th*, as in "dis" for "this."

The second type of articulation error involves sound distortion. This can be observed in the *s* sound when it is faultily produced with a whistling component, nasal air escape, or slushiness. Distortions in the pronounciation of the English *r* are often produced by speakers who have learned English as a second language.

The omission type of articulation error is illustrated by the individual who omits the *r* sound and says "ed abbit" instead of "red rabbit."

The addition type of articulation error is seen in the inclusion of an *r* sound where it is not called for, as in "idear" for "idea."

Articulatory disorders are sometimes classified as functional or organic in terms of possible causal factors. Matthews (1957*b*) has summarized the literature relating mental retardation and articulation disorders. A frequent cause of articulation disorders is faulty training resulting from inadequate speech environment. If a child's speech model is defective, he is likely to learn defective speech. (A detailed discussion of etiological factors in functional articulation disorders can be found in Van Riper 1963; Johnson et al. 1948; and Berry & Eisenson 1956.)

Although the majority of articulatory disorders are of functional origin, there are organic factors that can adversely affect articulation. West and his associates (1937) discuss in detail articulation disorders resulting from lesions of the central nervous system. Cleft palate, dental anomalies, structural disorders of the peripheral speech organs, and hearing loss can cause articulation disorders.

Where a structural abnormality contributes to an articulation disorder, the organic defect may need correction prior to speech therapy. Sometimes speech therapy may proceed in conjunction with the correction of the organic disorder. Often, complete correction of the structural anomaly is not possible but speech therapy may prove to be beneficial.

The correction of articulatory errors requires teaching the production and habitual use of sounds. As a rule the sound is taught first in isolation, then in combination with other sounds, and finally in words, sentences, and conversation. Milisen describes a variety of approaches to articulation therapy (Milisen et al. 1954).

Defects of voice. Defects of voice can include complete absence of voice as well as problems of pitch, volume, and quality. Voice may be lacking because of total or partial paralysis or removal of the vocal folds, or the vocal structures may be normal and the absence of voice may be a reflection of a hysterical condition.

Pitch may be inappropriate for the age and sex of the speaker. This would be illustrated by a male talking in an extremely high-pitched voice or a female talking with low pitch. Monotone consists of a sameness of pitch. The failure to vary pitch can not only result in a speech pattern that is dull and uninteresting to listen to; it can also interfere with speech intelligibility, inasmuch as certain aspects of meaning are conveyed by means of variations in pitch.

Just as pitch may be inappropriate, it is possible that volume, also, may be inappropriate. Volume may be so weak that it is difficult for listeners to hear what is being said, or it may be so loud that listeners experience a certain amount of discomfort. Normal speakers do not use exactly the same volume from beginning to end of a message. Just as there are normal variations in pitch, so there are normal variations in volume. The absence of these variations in volume would be considered a type of voice disorder.

The third general type of voice disorder consists of defects in quality. These defects are difficult to describe and should be heard to be fully appreciated. Defects of voice quality sometimes are labeled with such terms as "nasal," "hoarse," "husky," "breathy," "harsh," etc. The quality is considered defective when it is not only unpleasant to listen to but seriously detracts a listener's attention from the message of the speaker.

As is the case with articulatory disorders, there are both functional and organic causes of voice disorder. Imitation of poor speech models, psychological maladjustments, adolescent voice change, poor breathing habits, as well as laryngeal pathology, paralysis, and adenoidal obstructions, appear as causes of voice disorders.

In the case of any type of laryngeal pathology, voice therapy should not be attempted until a medical evaluation and laryngeal examination have been completed. Voice training often includes auditory training, to make the client aware of the differences, in both sound and "feel," between proper and improper use of the voice. Where the voice problem is related to emotional disturbances of any kind, psychological help may be necessary. In those instances where the vocal mechanism has been removed, the client may use an electrical or mechanical vibrator as a substitute for vocal-fold vibration or the client may learn esophageal speech, a technique that involves using air expelled from the esophageal tract as a source of sound vibration.

Defects of rhythm. Defects of rhythm can be described as repetitions, prolongations, or hesitations. Individual sounds, words, or phrases may be involved. Frequently the disruption in rhythm may be accompanied by facial grimaces, tics, or other bodily movements, which in time can become an intimate part of the disruptions of rhythm. Very frequently the disruptions in rhythm and the accompanying grimaces carry with them considerable fear and many negative attitudes on the part of the speaker. The speaker's fear that he will have problems with his speech often contributes to additional difficulties with speech rhythm.

Stuttering. More has been written on the topic of stuttering than on any other single disorder of speech. Matthews (1957*a*), in a brief summary of theories of stuttering, cites representatives of three broad theoretical viewpoints: (1) dysphemic theories, which suggest that stuttering is related to constitutional abnormality; (2) personality theories, which hold that stuttering is related to psychological maladjustment; and (3) developmental theories, which suggest that stuttering develops largely as the result of environmental conditions.

Therapy approaches are influenced by the therapist's theory concerning the etiology of stuttering. Those who view stuttering in terms of a general neurosis will employ some form of psychotherapy. A therapist who sees stuttering as the result of lack of cerebral dominance will seek ways of establishing a dominant gradient of excitation in the central nervous system. Environmental modification is the goal of many therapists, regardless of the theory of causation of stuttering they subscribe to. Van Riper (1963) not only summarizes much of the literature on etiology and treatment of stuttering but also outlines in detail a therapy approach widely employed in the United States. His therapy seeks to help the stutterer stop reinforcing his stuttering. An important aspect of this therapy consists of eliminating the stutterer's avoidance of feared situations and words.

Defects of symbolic formulation. The defects of symbolic formulation may be of both an expressive and a receptive type. Although defects of symbolic formulation are often categorized as either expressive aphasia or receptive aphasia, in actuality most patients who have difficulty with symbolic formulation have some difficulties in both the expressive and the receptive realm. Individuals with receptive aphasia may be able to hear a speaker say the word "chair" but will not be able to translate the sounds in this word into the concept of a piece of furniture on which a person may sit; they may be able to see and to recognize each of the five letters used in writing the word "chair" but be unable to translate the written letters into the concept of chair. The individual with an expressive type of aphasia may know what a chair is and be able to pronounce all of the sounds in the word "chair" but be unable to put these sounds together so they become a recognizable symbol of the concept "chair."

The treatment of aphasia involves re-education and retraining, which utilizes the past speech background of the patient as much as possible. A detailed discussion of therapy for aphasics can be found in Wepman (1951).

Negative attitudes and frustrations. Often the individual with a speech problem is handicapped by more than just the acoustic end product of his speech. Frequently the speaker's attitude toward his speech constitutes one of his most serious problems. In some instances the speaker may actually talk with a fairly high degree of intelligibility. However, if the speaker's attitude toward his own speech is apprehensive and fearful, he may experience a handicap far beyond what would normally result from the faulty articulation or faulty voice quality alone.

A speech problem not only can interfere with

defective communication in social development but also can lead to the frustration of not being able to make oneself understood and of constantly being made to feel different. Such feelings of frustration, difference, and inferiority can lead to personality problems and attitudes which may be more serious than the original speech problem itself. For this reason, speech pathologists must be interested in the total adjustment of the person who has a speech problem.

Etiology and therapy

If speech problems are examined from the standpoint of etiology, they can be categorized as organic or functional. In actuality it is extremely difficult to fit all speech problems neatly into one or the other of these two broad classifications. The two classifications are presented because they frequently appear in the literature.

Organic and functional factors. Speech problems arising from primarily organic causes would include speech associated with cleft palate, cerebral palsy, dental abnormalities, brain damage, hearing loss, or any other type of anatomical or neurological involvement affecting any of the mechanisms used in speech production.

Etiological factors of a nonorganic type would include lack of stimulation to speak, withdrawal tendencies associated with emotional disturbance, failure to have available good models of speech for imitation, mental retardation, faulty learning, etc. The organic and functional aspects frequently are intertwined. This can be seen in the individual who is aphasic because of brain damage. Because of his aphasia, he experiences considerable frustration. This frustration in turn leads to withdrawal behavior. Frustration and withdrawal behavior contribute to further deterioration of speech. Frequently it becomes difficult to separate the components of the speech problem that are of organic causation from those that represent some sort of functional overlay.

Therapy. The speech pathologist initiates therapy after a thorough diagnosis has been performed. This diagnosis often must include a medical examination, psychological assessment, and determination of hearing acuity. Dental and social-work information are often necessary before an adequate diagnosis can be made. Wherever possible, causative factors are removed or minimized. In the case of cleft palate, for example, surgical or dental procedures may be necessary to provide a mechanism adequate for speech production. In some instances it may be impossible to provide a mechanism that is completely normal. Under these circumstances methods must be found to compensate for the structural inadequacies. In the case of a severe hearing loss, it may be possible to provide sound amplification in the form of a hearing aid.

Articulatory disorders constitute the largest group of speech problems encountered in children. The majority of articulatory problems are not caused by anatomical, neurological, or other organic factors. Most articulatory problems can be traced to lack of stimulation, poor speech models, faulty learning, and other factors quite far removed from defects of the oral structures. An early step in treatment consists of describing adequately the nature of the speech deviation. The speech pathologist helps the individual with the speech problem to understand the detailed nature of the problem. In some cases this consists of the speech pathologist's helping a client become more aware of his speech errors. A client must learn to distinguish between the correct and incorrect speech productions. A wide variety of procedures will be employed to help the client articulate a sound correctly, to eliminate an undesirable component in voice quality, to produce a pitch level more appropriate to the age and sex of the client, etc. Frequently a client learns to make correct speech productions in isolated sounds or words but finds it difficult to carry over these new patterns into everyday speaking situations. Frequently the newly acquired speech skills result in a pattern of speech that sounds strange to the client. The speech pathologist often spends considerable time helping the client understand his feelings toward his speech problem, as well as his feelings toward the new speech patterns which he acquires. Often the attitude of a parent toward a child and toward the child's speech is a contributing factor. For this reason, speech pathologists frequently spend a good deal of their time in parent-counseling activities.

Because some voice disorders are associated with organic pathology, the speech pathologist may carry out some of his treatment procedures in cooperation with an otolaryngologist. Such collaborative therapy activities may be carried out with psychiatrists, clinical psychologists, plastic surgeons, and dentists, as well as classroom teachers. The speech pathologist cannot limit himself to a consideration of the mechanical aspects of sound production. His interest must be in the person with a speech problem. The modern practice of speech pathology makes comparatively little use of the tongue, lip, and jaw exercises that were prevalent in the field a decade ago.

Training in speech pathology. Standards for the training of speech pathologists have been established by the American Speech and Hearing Association. The association awards a certificate of clinical competence to individuals who successfully complete the requirements for a master's degree in the field of speech pathology. This graduate program includes didactic classroom instruction, supervised clinic practice, and four years of successful practice, under supervision, in an environment where speech and language problems are diagnosed and treated. Graduate training programs in speech pathology in the United States are accredited by the American Board of Examiners in Speech Pathology and Audiology of the American Speech and Hearing Association. The association is a clearinghouse for information regarding clinical facilities, training institutions, and other data relative to the field of speech pathology.

JACK MATTHEWS

[*See also* MENTAL DISORDERS, *article on* ORGANIC ASPECTS. *Other relevant material may be found in* HEARING; LANGUAGE, *article on* LANGUAGE DEVELOPMENT; MENTAL RETARDATION; PERCEPTION, *article on* SPEECH PERCEPTION.]

BIBLIOGRAPHY

BERRY, MILDRED F.; and EISENSON, JON 1956 *Speech Disorders.* New York: Appleton.

JOHNSON, WENDELL et al. (1948) 1956 *Speech Handicapped School Children.* Rev. ed. New York: Harper.

MATTHEWS, JACK 1957*a* Speech Defects. Pages 391–424 in Chauncey M. Louttit (editor), *Clinical Psychology of Exceptional Children.* 3d ed. New York: Harper. → First published in 1936.

MATTHEWS, JACK 1957*b* Speech Problems of the Mentally Retarded. Pages 531–551 in Lee E. Travis (editor), *Handbook of Speech Pathology.* New York: Appleton.

MILISEN, ROBERT et al. 1954 The Disorder of Articulation: A Systematic Clinical and Experimental Approach. *Journal of Speech and Hearing Disorders Monograph Supplements,* No. 4.

VAN RIPER, CHARLES 1963 *Speech Correction Principles and Methods.* 4th ed. Englewood Cliffs, N.J.: Prentice-Hall. → First published in 1939.

WEPMAN, JOSEPH M. 1951 *Recovery From Aphasia.* New York: Ronald Press.

WEST, ROBERT W.; ANSBERRY, MERLE; and CARR, ANNA (1937) 1957 *The Rehabilitation of Speech.* 3d ed. New York: Harper.

IV
LANGUAGE AND CULTURE

The key role of language in all human activities has made it perhaps inevitable that the field of linguistics should represent a mingling of several streams of interest. Modern linguistics has arisen from the philological tradition, concerned basically with the classical and modern written languages, and from the anthropological tradition, which has been concerned largely with preliterate peoples. The anthropologist has long recognized the importance of language, not only as a tool for more effective field work, but as a critical element of the cultural fabric which he studies. Thus we sometimes refer to "anthropological linguistics," which may be defined as the study of previously unknown speech varieties in the context of their cultures; the term contrasts the anthropological approach to language with philological, psychological, or philosophical approaches. Alternatively, we may wish to speak of "linguistic anthropology," focusing attention on language as one element of human culture; the term is analogous to "social anthropology," "economic anthropology," and the like. The older term "ethnolinguistics" may well be used to refer to the same area of interest.

All writers in this field have struggled with the expressions "language *and* culture" versus "language *in* culture," both of which are in common use as titles for university courses, scholarly symposia, etc. "Language and culture" seeems to imply a dichotomy, which we must then reject in the light of our position that language is *part* of culture. But if we speak of "language in culture," we then lack a separate name for all the other cultural areas whose relationship to language we wish to study. Perhaps the best solution is to give formal recognition to what has most often been done in practice and to use the word "culture" in two ways, on two different levels of a semantic hierarchy. Distinguishing these meanings by subscript numerals, $culture_1$, on the higher level of generality, constitutes learned patterns of human habitual behavior. Language is included along with everything else that contrasts with instinctive behavior. $Culture_2$, on a more specific level, is that part of "$culture_1$" which is *not* verbal communication; in this sense, "culture" contrasts with "language." In most cases, the context of discussion will make it clear whether we are referring to "$culture_1$" or "$culture_2$," just as context normally eliminates confusion between "man_1" (opposed to "animal") and "man_2" (opposed to "woman").

Taking the view that language is part of culture, linguistic anthropologists have been concerned with these basic questions: In what respects does language fit into the general conception of cultural systems, and in what ways is it distinguished from other components? What similarities are there between the internal structures of language and of other branches of culture? What role does language play in the over-all functioning of culture? In what way do language and culture reflect each other's structure at a given point in time or influence each other over the span of history? What techniques may we use to infer linguistic from nonlinguistic behavior, or vice versa, either in terms of predicting the future or of reconstructing the past? At this moment, most of these questions still lack definitive answers; the rapid growth of ethnolinguistics, however, suggests that the near future will bring, if not answers to all questions, at least a more unified framework for discussion.

The cultural nature of language. Language is assured a position as a branch of culture by its distinctively patterned nature, by its restriction to the human species, and above all because languages are learned, not transmitted genetically. In spite of the fact that race and language frequently have a historical connection—so that many people who share ancestors also share a common language—such connections are in no way necessary. The nongenetic transmission of languages is vividly demonstrated by the linguistic "melting pot" of the United States, in which people of the most diverse racial backgrounds share common standards of English usage. However, the fact that individual languages are transmitted culturally, not genetically, does not rule out the possibility that mankind has certain unique inborn capacities for linguistic behavior. For some purposes, we may distinguish between *language*, an inherited set of capabilities, and *languages*, particular structures which are built on those capabilities by culture.

The distinctiveness of language. Language obviously stands apart from other communication systems used by humans or animals because of the magnitude of its resources. It is especially impressive to consider that every normal child, by the age of four or five, is capable of using the language of his community to produce a literally infinite number of meaningful utterances. We are far from understanding all of the characteristics of language or of the human nervous system which make this possible. Two things, however, are clearly important—man's ability to invent *symbols* and the *duality of patterning* in linguistic structure.

If we understand a *sign* to be anything from which the existence of something else may be inferred, then we may define a symbol as a special kind of sign—one with arbitarary, conventionally assigned meaning. Thus, black clouds are a sign of rain, the relationship being intrinsic; but a particular weather flag, as a conventional sign of rain, is a symbol. By the same token, the word "rain" is a symbol; our use of this particular word is conventional and subject to change. Other animals may learn to respond to many arbitrary signals, including words of human language, but it is uniquely human to have the ability to assign arbitary meaning to signs, i.e., to *invent* symbols.

But language goes beyond other symbolic systems, such as those of gestures, in one very specific feature—the duality of patterning. The meaningful symbols of language—such as words and meaningful parts of words, called *morphemes*—are not indivisible, like a flag or a gesture, but are themselves built up of smaller units. These smaller units are the *phonemes* or sound units of spoken language, and they are meaningless in themselves. Every language uses a small number of these meaningless units—usually less than fifty—to build up a huge number of meaningful units. It is this two-level structuring which gives language a degree of efficiency that is qualitatively superior to, not merely quantitatively different from, other communication systems.

Similarities between language and culture. The identification of such building blocks of language as the phoneme and the morpheme has given linguistics great prestige among the branches of anthropology; it is sometimes said that linguists are the only social scientists to have identified the basic units of their subject matter. The method used in this process of identification is one which moves from the level of observation to the level of structure. First, raw data are classified in terms of a universal taxonomic grid; in studying sound systems, this is the phonetic classification. Then the investigator finds that some phonetic differences, in particular languages, are not associated with contrastive meaning; e.g., the meaning of the Spanish *día* ("day") is the same whether the initial *d* is pronounced as an occlusive (completely blocking the flow of air with the tongue and then releasing it), or as a fricative (letting air issue continuously between the tongue and the teeth). In every language, however, the linguist also finds that some phonetic differences *are* correlated with differences of meaning; e.g., the difference between occlusive and fricative, although nonsignificant in Spanish, is contrastive in English, serving to distinguish "day" from "they." The result of such observations is the replacement of phonetic classifications by phonemic classifications, unique for each language. The phoneme is defined simultaneously by the range of noncontrastive sound differences which it subsumes and by the contrasts which it displays with the other phonemes of the system.

This method of qualitative contrast, first applied in phonological study, has been successfully extended to the identification of morphemes, i.e., grammatical units; and many scholars have speculated about their applicability to other areas of culture. The terms *etic* and *emic* have been coined (after "phonetic" and "phonemic") to refer to the observational and structural levels, respectively, which might be distinguished in such areas as kinship, religion, music, art, and folklore. Such studies are still in their infancy, but they constitute one of the most interesting frontiers of anthropology, based as they are on the assumption that each branch of culture, or indeed culture as a whole, is, like language, an *internally cohesive* system.

The role of language in culture. Language is not merely one of several aspects of culture: it is, at the very least, *prima inter pares*, in that it makes possible the development, the elaboration, the transmission, and (particularly in its written form) the accumulation of culture as a whole. One can imagine handicrafts being taught by one generation to the next without the use of language; but social, legal, religious, political, or economic institutions are another matter. It is hard to imagine that a community of deaf-mutes (if they were deprived of such speech surrogates as writing) could carry on human social life.

But how, exactly, does language (or any other symbolic system) relate to experience? It is commonly said that symbols, like signs in general, "stand for" or "mean" something else. The definition of *meaning* itself clearly cannot be taken for granted. A variety of theoretical models for the concept of meaning, each one valuable for its own ends, has been proposed by philosophers, psychologists, and linguists of various persuasions. The model presented below is not intended to compete with others in defining the "real" nature of meaning, but it may be useful as a framework for ethnolinguistic discussion.

Structural linguists have customarily been extremely cautious in semantic matters, sometimes attempting to exclude them from linguistics altogether. Until very recently, a strictly behaviorist conception of meaning was much in vogue:

> We have defined the *meaning* of a linguistic form as the situation in which the speaker utters it and the response which it calls forth in the hearer. . . . The situations which prompt people to utter speech include every object and happening in their universe. In order to give a scientifically accurate definition of meaning for every form of a language, we should have to have a scientifically accurate knowledge of everything in the speaker's world. . . . We can define the names of minerals, for example, in terms of chemistry and mineralogy, as when we say that the ordinary meaning of the English word *salt* is "sodium chloride (NaCl)," . . . but we have no precise way of defining words like *love* or *hate*, which concern situations that have not been accurately classified. . . . (Bloomfield [1933] 1951, p. 139)

These statements seem to imply a model of linguistic function with just two parts—on the one hand, the linguistic form, and on the other hand, the associated nonlinguistic events (and, presumably, contextual linguistic events as well). Thus the definition of the word "salt" would be, at least in part, the actual substance NaCl. But Bloomfield seems to ignore the essentially arbitrary association between the word "salt" and the substance NaCl, in that his model has no place for the human individuals or the human cultures which have chosen this particular linguistic form.

A more satisfactory model was provided some two thousand years ago by the Hindu philosopher Patañjali: "Concentrate separately on the word, the meaning, and the object, which are mixed up in common usage"—which a modern commentator explicates with this example—"When we utter the word 'elephant,' we find that the word, the meaning and the object are mixed up; the word lives in air, the meaning lives in mind, the elephant lives by itself" (Patañjali, *Aphorism* . . .). It is indeed true that the word "lives in the air," in the sense that it is transmitted as vibrations of air molecules. It is equally true that the actual elephant "lives by itself," i.e., exists independently of all human conventions of nomenclature. The only way that these two isolates are related, then, is through the human mind; and we may define meaning not as a "thing," but rather as the *relationship* which associates word and object.

This three-part model is more adequate than Bloomfield's but still does not clarify the relation of language and culture. In order to do so, we may expand the model still further. First, a division may be made between the observational, or etic, universe, to which "word" and "object" belong, and the structural, or emic, universe, within the human mind. Second, we may distinguish linguistic behavior from its subject matter or content (though

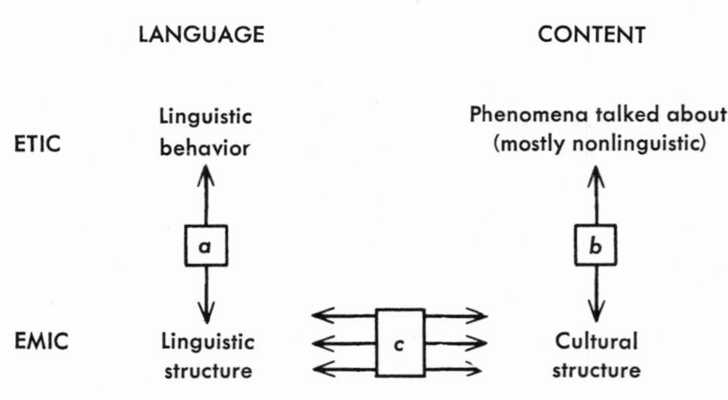

Figure 1 — The relation of language to culture

the subject matter may itself, as a special case, be linguistic behavior, as when linguists talk about language). The two dichotomies then intersect as shown in Figure 1.

In this figure, the arrows marked *a*, *b*, and *c* indicate relationships of importance to the ethnolinguist. Arrow *a* is the relationship which concerns him when he functions purely as a linguist: it may be thought of inductively, in terms of the process by which the investigator sets up a structure to account for his raw behavioral data, or deductively, as the process by which psychological patterns of linguistic competence give rise to observable linguistic performance. Arrow *b* is the analogous relationship that is investigated by the ethnographer: the actual objects and events which concern a particular human group are here linked, by induction or by deduction, to subjective patterns of organization. Finally, the set of arrows marked *c* represents the relationships to which we assign the term "meaning"; this is conceived of not as a direct connection between the utterance "elephant" and the flesh-and-blood *Elephas maximus*, but rather as a connection mediated by "elephant" as an item of the English lexicon and by "the elephant" as an item in the cultural inventory of English speakers.

There are two types of structural units which are linked by the relationships of meaning. The relevant linguistic units are not phonemes or morphemes, but units of a higher level, which are called *lexemes:* these are the minimum units which participate in arbitrary relationships of meaning. Thus, single morphemes like "green" and "house" are lexemes, but so also is the two-morpheme combination "greenhouse" (as opposed to "green house"), since it arbitrarily designates a particular kind of structure. There is still little agreement about structural units of cultural behavior; insofar as they can be identified, they are often called *sememes*. To be sure, there is not always a one-to-one correspondence between lexemes and sememes; people sometimes show culturally determined differences in behavior where their language provides no lexemic differentiation. However, the general regularity of lexeme–sememe correspondences reflects the close integration between language and the rest of culture, and it is in this way that language may be regarded as a key to culture as a whole.

Ethnosemantics. The study of vocabulary as a guide to the way in which members of a culture divide up their universe has received increasing attention, and the relativity of cultural classifications is emphasized with every new empirical study. Thus, where English vocabulary reflects its users' approach to spatial orientation with the four-way classification "north, south, east, west," the Indian languages of northwestern California reflect the functionally similar but incommensurable division "upriver, downriver, toward the river, away from the river." Anthropologists have begun to pay close attention to such lexemic systems, understanding that they reflect an emic view of the culture being studied, a view uncontaminated by the varying etic frameworks of outside observers. Various terms have been used to identify this study, such as "ethnoscience," "folk taxonomy," "structural semantics," and "ethnosemantics."

A further development in ethnographic semantics is generally known as "componential analysis." This method tries to answer the question, Given a particular set of taxonomic terms used by members of a culture, what are the criteria for applying the individual terms? Taking an example from kinship terminology, if some male collateral kin in generations above ego's are called "uncle" and some are called "cousin," what does one need to know in order to label a particular kinsman correctly? Attempts to answer such questions have resulted in the idea that terms may be conceived of as bundles of simultaneously occurring semantic components. Thus the term "uncle" is applied when the features of "maleness," "ascending generation," and "colineality" are simultaneously present. (A "colineal" in this case is a nonlineal kinsman all of whose ancestors are included in the ancestors of ego.) The term "cousin" is applied in a larger number of cases, but they include those where the features of "maleness," "ascending generation," and "ablineality" are simultaneously present. (An "ablineal" is a consanguineal kinsman who is neither a lineal nor a colineal.) This type of analysis, as applied to kin terms, results in definitions which are both more concise and more exact than the extensional definitions given in traditional ethnographies. Application of componential analysis to areas other than kinship holds great promise.

Language and world view. In addition to correspondences between vocabulary and cultural inventory, a much more controversial type of correlation between language and culture has been proposed. This involves, on one side, whole grammatical systems or subsystems, and, on the other side, whole philosophies or ways of life held to be characteristic of particular cultures (though often not brought to the level of conscious formulation). The interest of anthropologists was drawn to such correlations by Edward Sapir, who not only recognized a linguistic relativity, covarying with cultural relativity, but also postulated a linguistic determinism operating on culture:

Human beings do not live in the objective world alone, nor alone in the world of social activity as ordinarily understood, but are very much at the mercy of the particular language which has become the medium of expression for their society. . . . The fact of the matter is that the "real world" is to a large extent unconsciously built up on the language habits of the group. No two languages are ever sufficiently similar to be considered as representing the same social reality. The worlds in which different societies live are distinct worlds, not merely the same world with different labels attached. (Sapir [1910–1944] 1949, p. 162)

Benjamin Lee Whorf, a student of Sapir, continued the exploration of the matter, although with less emphasis on the tyranny of language over culture. His position has become known as the "Whorfian hypothesis," which holds that "language patterns [and] cultural norms . . . have grown up together, constantly influencing each other. But in this partnership the nature of the language is the factor that limits free plasticity and rigidifies channels of development in the more autocratic way" (Whorf [1927–1941] 1956, p. 156). The deterministic role of language is easy to understand when we consider how much of culture is transmitted through the linguistic medium. However, the Whorfian hypothesis is easier to accept intuitively than to prove in a rigorous way; in particular, no correlations can be traced between language and world view until specific world views are themselves defined in terms of observable behavior. Whorf shows that Hopi linguistic structure is compatible with a world view involving a peculiar relation between subjective and objective experience; but he tends to assume, rather than to demonstrate, that the Hopi actually hold such a view of the world. Pending the outcome of extensive, strictly controlled, cross-cultural testing of the Whorfian hypothesis, we may limit our acceptance to the following modified formulation: "Insofar as languages differ in the ways they encode objective experience, language users tend to sort out and distinguish experiences differently according to the categories provided by their respective languages. These cognitions will tend to have certain effects on behavior" (Carroll 1963, p. 12).

Language and society. While the studies mentioned above have regarded each language as a unified whole, another type of research has focused attention on the variation that exists within languages or within multilingual speech communities. Such variation, apart from that associated with geographical dialects or with the idiosyncrasies of individuals, is commonly found to be correlated with one or more socially defined factors, such as the social identity of the speaker, the addressee, or the person referred to, and the social context in which communication takes place. Study of the covariance between linguistic diversity and social structure thus constitutes the new field of sociolinguistics. The findings of this field are applicable, from the synchronic viewpoint, to the diagnosis and analysis of social encounters, and, from the diachronic viewpoint, to examination of the ways in which linguistic patterns and social systems each change under the influence of the other.

WILLIAM BRIGHT

[*Directly related are the entries* COGNITIVE THEORY; COMPONENTIAL ANALYSIS; LINGUISTICS; SEMANTICS AND SEMIOTICS; *and the biographies of* BLOOMFIELD; SAPIR; SAUSSURE; WHORF.]

BIBLIOGRAPHY

The most valuable reference that can be given for linguistic anthropology is Hymes 1964, *which contains not only a rich selection of papers in the field but also very extensive bibliographies.*

BLOOMFIELD, LEONARD (1933) 1951 *Language.* Rev. ed. New York: Holt.

CARROLL, JOHN B. 1963 Linguistic Relativity, Contrastive Linguistics, and Language Learning. *IRAL: International Review of Applied Linguistics* 1:1–20.

DIEBOLD, A. RICHARD JR. 1964 [Review of] Sol Saporta (editor), *Psycholinguistics. Language* 40:197–260. → An extensive review of the whole field of psycholinguistics, including many matters of interest to linguistic anthropology.

HAMMEL, EUGENE A. (editor) 1965 Formal Semantic Analysis. *American Anthropologist* New Series 67, no. 5, part 2 (Special publication).

HYMES, DELL H. (editor) 1964 *Language in Culture and Society: Reader in Linguistics and Anthropology.* New York: Harper.

NIDA, EUGENE A. 1964 *Toward a Science of Translating.* Leiden (Netherlands): Brill. → Chapter 5, "Referential and Emotive Meanings," summarizes recent work in ethnosemantics.

PATAÑJALI *Aphorisms of Yoga.* Translated into English with a commentary by Shree Purohit Swāmi. London: Faber, 1938.

ROMNEY, A. KIMBALL; and D'ANDRADE, ROY GOODWIN (editors) 1964 Transcultural Studies in Cognition. *American Anthropologist* New Series 66, no. 3, part 2 (Special publication). → Contains contributions by linguists, anthropologists, and psychologists to problems of ethnosemantics.

SAPIR, EDWARD A. (1910–1944) 1949 *Selected Writings in Language, Culture, and Personality.* Edited by David G. Mandelbaum. Berkeley: Univ. of California Press.

WHORF, BENJAMIN L. (1927–1941) 1956 *Language, Thought and Reality.* Edited by John B. Carroll. Cambridge, Mass.: M.I.T. Press.

LAPLACE, PIERRE SIMON DE

Pierre Simon de Laplace (1749–1827), renowned French mathematician, was born in Beaumont-en-Auge, a village 4 miles west of Pont l'Évêque in Normandy. He was the second of two children of Pierre de Laplace, a syndic of the parish, who owned and farmed a small estate. When Laplace arrived in Paris, barely twenty years old, he had finished his studies and begun his own research. His ability soon impressed d'Alembert, whose disciple he was to become. D'Alembert's patronage secured Laplace a position as a teacher at the École Royale Militaire, where he remained until changes in the organization brought his teaching there to an end. In 1783 he became an artillery inspector (Duveen & Hahn 1957), and in this capacity he made the acquaintance of the young Bonaparte. A mutual respect developed, and from then on Laplace enjoyed Bonaparte's increasingly powerful support. The two became colleagues at the Académie des Sciences; as first consul, Napoleon appointed Laplace minister of the interior, a position he gave up shortly afterward to become chancellor of the Sénat Conservateur. In 1814, however, he turned against Napoleon; he was eventually made a marquis by Louis XVIII, a surprising but not uncommon turn of events in those troubled times.

Laplace achieved distinction not only in mathematics; it was his literary style that won him election to the Académie Française in 1816. His famous sentence on the hidden determinism of natural laws is a good example of his style:

> If there were an intelligence that for a given instant could comprehend all the forces that animate nature and the condition of each being that composes it; if, moreover, this intelligence were sufficiently great to submit these data to analysis, it would create a single formula that would embrace both the movements of the vastest bodies of the universe and those of the smallest atoms: to this intelligence nothing would be uncertain, and the future, as the past, would be present to its eyes. ([1814] 1951, p. 4)

Although Laplace's work has literary elegance, his demonstrations are not always rigorous; often they are even obscure. He frequently wrote "it is clear that . . ." in place of long and difficult calculations.

Laplace presided over the famous Société d'Arcueil, one of the informal scientific societies that flourished in the nineteenth century. It took its name from Laplace's estate, where he and the great chemist Claude Louis Berthollet periodically received their students to discuss scientific questions in an informal atmosphere.

Although our primary concern here is with Laplace's contributions to probability and statistics, it is worth noting that the full scope of his work includes physics (the theory of capillary phenomena, the exact formula for the speed of sound), pure mathematics, and celestial mechanics (he was dubbed a "second Newton"). In probability and its applications Laplace systematized and further extended the scattered researches of his predecessors, bringing the subject to full flower in the third edition (1820) of his great treatise, *Théorie analytique des probabilités* (1812). This is why Todhunter wrote: "On the whole, the Theory of Probability is more indebted to him than to any other mathematician" ([1865] 1949, p. 464).

Laplace was not content to make important discoveries; he also thought it necessary to communicate them to a wide public. To this end he wrote two popular works addressed to the intelligent and educated general reader, *Exposition du système du monde* (1796) and *Essai philosophique sur les probabilités* (1814). Other French mathematicians have continued this practice; thus, Émile Borel thought it useful to write an analogous work, *Le hasard* (1914), which took into consideration the progress made since Laplace.

Generating functions and characteristic functions. Motivated by problems arising, for instance, in the mathematical treatment of games of chance, Laplace, in the epochal *Mémoire sur les suites* (1782), developed the general theory of a powerful power-series technique for solving finite-difference equations, or recurrence relations, which he termed the "method of generating functions" (*calcul des fonctions génératrices; ibid.*, p. 1). In Book 1, Part 1, of his *Théorie analytique des probabilités* (1812) he reproduced this *Mémoire* almost entirely, and in Book 2 he made repeated use of generating functions in solving a great variety of probability problems arising in the mathematical treatment of games of chance. The probability-generating function of a random variable, X—that is, the mean (or expected) value of t^X, where t is a "dummy" real variable—had already been used (without being named) by De Moivre, in studies of games of chance (1730, pp. 191–197; [1718] 1756, pp. 41–43), and by Simpson and Lagrange, in their studies of the distribution of the arithmetic mean of independent observations under various laws of error (Simpson 1756; 1757; Lagrange 1770–1773). However, it is Laplace's extensive discussion of generating functions (1782) and the applications of them in his *Théorie analytique des probabilités* that is the actual source of their widespread use in probability theory, combinatory analysis, and the solution of finite-difference equations and recurrence formulas (see David & Barton 1962; Feller 1950; Fréchet 1940–1943; Jordan 1939; Riordan 1958; Uspensky 1937). The invention of the characteristic function (*fonction caractéristique*) of the distribution of a random variable X (that is, the expected value of e^{itX}, where $i = \sqrt{-1}$) and the associated inversion formula for deducing the distribution function of a random variable from its characteristic function are often attributed to later writers, such as A. L. Cauchy, 1789–1857, and Henri Poincaré, 1854–1912. Laplace, however, introduced this very same (characteristic) function, without assigning it a name, and gave the associated inversion formula for the case of a discrete random variable, in article 21 of Book 1 of his *Théorie analytique des probabilités* (it also appears in *Oeuvres complètes*, vol. 7, pp. 83–84) and then employed such functions systematically in Book 2, Chapter 4 (cf. Molina 1930, arts. 3–4). The technical advantages possessed by the characteristic function permit simplification of many manipulations and proofs, although when X takes only integral values the generating function is usually adequate. [*See* PROBABILITY, *article on* FORMAL PROBABILITY.]

Bayesian inference. Laplace was apparently the first to have stated in a general form what is now called Bayes' theorem (*Théorie analytique* [1812] 1820, book 2, art. 1; Molina 1930, appendix I). Several scholars have deprecated Laplace's originality in this area of "probability of causes," or Bayesian inference. [*See* BAYESIAN INFERENCE *for a discussion of the probability of causes.*] But Laplace did introduce an essential innovation here. Bayes had considered only the case where the a priori probabilities are equal (as an evident hypothesis when one is ignorant of these probabilities); Laplace extended Bayes' theorem to cover the general case where these a priori probabilities are not necessarily equal. What has generally not been stressed enough is that Bayes' theorem—whether generalized or not—is really only an interpretation of a standard relationship for conditional probabilities. [*See* PROBABILITY, *article on* FORMAL PROBABILITY.] It is the interpretation of the formula itself that is important here. A discussion by Molina (1930) clearly establishes Laplace's position and demonstrates previous misunderstandings of it.

Normal distribution. Laplace should have the major credit for discovering and demonstrating the central role of the normal distribution in the mathematical theory of probability and for determining its principal mathematical properties [*see* DISTRIBUTIONS, STATISTICAL, *article on* SPECIAL CONTINUOUS DISTRIBUTIONS].

De Moivre in 1733 had shown how to employ integrals of the function $\exp(-t^2)$ to approximate sums of successive terms of the binomial expansion of $(a+b)^n$ when n is large, obtaining what we today call the normal approximation to the binomial probability distribution [*see* DISTRIBUTIONS, STATISTICAL, *article on* APPROXIMATIONS TO DISTRIBUTIONS]. (De Moivre's analysis is readily available in Smith [1929] 1959, pp. 566–575.) Laplace extended this approach in two important directions.

Approximations to the normal integral. He developed (1781) a general method for approximating an arbitrary definite integral by a series expansion in terms of integrals of the function $\exp(-t^2)$ and its derivatives, anticipating by a century the so-called Gram–Charlier Type A series expansion. He then utilized this technique to approximate various discrete and continuous probability distributions arising in games of chance and other problems in the calculus of probabilities. Remarking (1786*a*, p. 305) that the integral of $\exp(-t^2)$ arises so frequently that it would be useful to have a table of its values for a succession of limits of integration, Laplace provided (1785, sec. VI; 1805; [1812] 1820, book 1, art. 27) the now well-known power-series, asymptotic-series, and continued fraction expansions for integrals of the function $\exp(-t^2)$. These many results collectively constitute Laplace's first great contribution to the central role of the normal distribution today, and throughout their development the function $\exp(-t^2)$ seems to have been regarded exclusively as an approximating function —neither De Moivre nor Laplace appears to have regarded it or any corresponding expression as a law of error or even as a probability distribution in its own right.

Central limit theorem. Laplace's second great contribution to the establishment of the leading role of the normal distribution is his discovery and proof of what we today call the (classical) central limit theorem. De Moivre's result of 1733 is a special case of this theorem, as are many of Laplace's results in his papers of 1781, 1785, and 1786, but the theorem itself appears for the first time in the important *Mémoire* (1810, sec. VI), for the case of n independent errors from a common arbitrary symmetric discrete distribution on the interval $(-a, +a)$. Then (*ibid.*, sec. VI), by considering the discrete distribution corresponding to a fine subdivision of his double exponential law of error

(1774, sec. v), $\frac{1}{2}m \exp(-m|x|)$, he illustrated the extension of this important theorem to symmetric continuous distributions on the interval $(-\infty, +\infty)$. Gauss (1809, arts. 175–177) had deduced his law of error, $C \exp(-h^2x^2)$, and thence his development of the method of least squares, from the principle of the arithmetic mean. Laplace's central limit theorem provided an alternative justification, or "proof," of this law of error as the limit of the distribution of the sum of n independent random errors as $n \rightarrow \infty$ when the relative contribution of each to their sum tends to 0 as n increases, and thus he provided a valid basis for the method of least squares when the individual results involved "are each determined by a very large number of observations, whatever be the laws of facility of the errors of these observations," and hence "a reason for employing it in all cases" (1810, supplement, p. 353). [*See* DISTRIBUTIONS, STATISTICAL, *article on* SPECIAL CONTINUOUS DISTRIBUTIONS; *see also* LINEAR HYPOTHESES, *article on* REGRESSION.]

Laplace's proof had only the limited precision current in his time, but it was later made more rigorous and more general by Aleksandr Mikhailovich Liapunov, Paul Lévy, and others. Laplace's demonstration centers on the hypothesis that one deals with the *sum* of independent random variables, but in applications neither independence nor summation may be appropriate. Other functions of random variables can lead to other distributions; for example, if instead of a sum one deals with the greatest random variable, entirely different limit distributions can result (Fréchet 1927). One of these distributions has found application in flood protection, breaking strength of materials, and other areas (Gumbel 1958).

Estimation. Laplace's writings contain the seeds of ideas that have been carefully studied only in recent years: optimum point estimation, hypothesis testing, and confidence interval estimation. Laplace proposed (see 1774, sec. v) that when estimating a parameter, θ, one use that function $T = T(Y_1, Y_2, \cdots)$ of the observations $Y_1, Y_2, \cdots$ for which the mean (or expected) absolute error of estimation, $E[|T - \theta|]$, is a minimum for the given probability distribution of errors. For the case of three independent identically distributed observations he gave an explicit algorithm for finding such a function to use for estimating the location parameter of their common distribution, $f(y - \theta)$, when this is completely specified except for the value of θ. He subsequently extended (1781, sec. xxx) this procedure (which is the same as Pitman's method of "close estimation"—see Pitman 1939) to cover n independent observations in the one-parameter case. Gauss's reformulation (1821) of the method of least squares in terms of minimum mean-square error of estimation (i.e., min $E[(T - \theta)^2]$) stems directly from this earlier work of Laplace's.

Many modern statisticians see the problem of confidence intervals as one of providing a random interval that contains, with at least a specified probability, some parameter of the distribution sampled. Laplace, however, gave another—somewhat vague—interpretation of the interval (*Oeuvres complètes*, vol. 7, pp. 286–287). Major differences of opinion persist about the interpretation of such intervals. [*See* BAYESIAN INFERENCE; ESTIMATION, *article on* CONFIDENCE INTERVALS AND REGIONS; FIDUCIAL INFERENCE.]

Applications to demography. Laplace was not satisfied merely to describe useful statistical methods; he never stopped applying them, most particularly to demography. In this area he was preceded by the great naturalist Buffon, whose early career was in mathematics, although this is not generally known, and who solved the famous problem of the needle thrown onto a table covered with parallel lines. His "Essai d'arithmétique morale" of 1777 deals with demographic statistics; he notes, for example, the propensity that most people have to use round numbers in stating their age. Laplace, using more general and more precise mathematical methods and ideas, was able to treat demographic problems much more intensively. Buffon had already noted the general preponderance of male over female births; Laplace noted that during the years 1745–1785, 393,386 boys and 377,555 girls were born in Paris, and he proved that given certain natural hypotheses, the probability that the chance of a male birth would be more than $\frac{1}{2}$ is $1 - 1/N$; in this example N is a very large number, greater than 10^{72}. In an anomalous case cited by Buffon—the birth of 203 boys and 213 girls in the village of Vitteaux over a five-year period—the same probability is only about $\frac{1}{3}$. Laplace pointed out that there is no logical contradiction between the two cases, since it is only for large populations that the value of the sought probability is near unity—i.e., that the event is almost certain.

An exact census of the French population would have been a very difficult undertaking in Laplace's time, and he therefore tried to estimate the population indirectly, by a rather curious method. He used in the approximation the rough constancy of the ratio between total population and annual number of births, so that if the numerical value of the ratio is known, one need only multiply it by the number of births to obtain an estimate of the population. The government accepted his proposal that studies be made to determine annual births and total population for thirty *départements*, selecting in each *département* only those parishes whose mayors seemed sufficiently conscientious. On September 22, 1802 (the Republic's New Year's Day), the inhabitants of these parishes were counted, and the number of births in each of the three preceding years was also recorded. From the resulting ratio and an estimate of the total number of yearly births in France, Laplace estimated the population to be 25 million.

Laplace was also interested in statistics having to do with the duration of marriages and with life insurance. In addition, he studied the application of statistics to problems of social order, such as the validity of trial evidence and of court judgments, and the concept of "moral expectation." This concept, introduced by Daniel Bernoulli, is based on the observation that the richer a man is, the less concerned he is about any fixed moderate sum of money. Laplace added to this generalization the qualification "all other things being equal," meaning that the benefit to be calculated depends in general on an infinity of circumstances that are impossible to evaluate and that are relative to the individual who is calculating it [*see* UTILITY]. The work that Laplace did on trial evidence and court judgments has been especially controversial; J. L. F. Bertrand, in his caustic way, treated it with complete disdain, but Borel ([1914] 1948, pp. 251–262) felt that Bertrand was too harsh.

MAURICE FRÉCHET

[*Directly related is the entry* PROBABILITY. *Other relevant material may be found in* SOCIOLOGY, *article on* THE EARLY HISTORY OF SOCIAL RESEARCH; *and in the biographies of* GAUSS *and* MOIVRE.]

WORKS BY LAPLACE

1771 Recherches sur le calcul intégral aux différences infiniment petites, aux différences finies. Accademia delle Scienze di Torino, *Memorie* 4:273–375. → Volume 4 is dated "1766–1769."

(1774) 1891 Mémoire sur la probabilité des causes par les événements. Volume 8, pages 27–65 in Pierre Simon de Laplace, *Oeuvres complètes.* Paris: Gauthier-Villars. → Includes "Problème III: Déterminer le milieu que l'on doit prendre entre trois observations données d'un même phénomène" on pages 41–48.

(1781) 1893 Mémoire sur les probabilités. Volume 9, pages 383–485 in Pierre Simon de Laplace, *Oeuvres complètes.* Paris: Gauthier-Villars.

(1782) 1894 Mémoire sur les suites. Volume 10, pages 1–89 in Pierre Simon de Laplace, *Oeuvres complètes.* Paris: Gauthier-Villars.

(1785) 1894 Mémoire sur les approximations des formules qui sont fonctions de très grands nombres. Volume 10, pages 209–291 in Pierre Simon de Laplace, *Oeuvres complètes.* Paris: Gauthier-Villars.

(1786*a*) 1894 Suite du mémoire sur les approximations des formules qui sont fonctions de très grands nombres. Volume 10, pages 296–338 in Pierre Simon de Laplace, *Oeuvres complètes.* Paris: Gauthier-Villars.

(1786*b*) 1895 Sur les naissances, les mariages et les morts à Paris, depuis 1771 jusqu'en 1784, et dans toute l'étendue de la France, pendant les années 1781 et 1782. Volume 11, pages 35–46 in Pierre Simon de Laplace, *Oeuvres complètes.* Paris: Gauthier-Villars.

(1796) 1836 *Exposition du système du monde.* 2 vols. 6th ed. Paris: Bachelier.

(1805) 1880 Traité de mécanique céleste. Part 2: Théories particulières des mouvements célestes. Volume 4 in Pierre Simon de Laplace, *Oeuvres complètes.* Paris: Gauthier-Villars.

(1810) 1898 Mémoire sur les approximations des formules qui sont fonctions de très grands nombres et sur leur application aux probabilités. Volume 12, pages 301–345 in Pierre Simon de Laplace, *Oeuvres complètes.* Paris: Gauthier-Villars. → A supplement to the "Mémoire" appears on pages 349–353.

(1812) 1820 *Théorie analytique des probabilités.* 3d ed., rev. Paris: Courcier. → Also published as Volume 1 of *Oeuvres complètes de Laplace.*

(1814) 1951 *A Philosophical Study on Probabilities.* New York: Dover. → First published as *Essai philosophique sur les probabilités.*

Oeuvres complètes de Laplace. 14 vols. Paris: Gauthier-Villars, 1878–1912.

SUPPLEMENTARY BIBLIOGRAPHY

BOREL, ÉMILE (1914) 1948 *Le hasard.* New ed., rev. & enl. Paris: Presses Universitaires de France.

COLBERT-LAPLACE, A. 1929 Letter to Karl Pearson, Dated 16 February 1929. *Biometrika* 21:203–204.

DANTZIG, D. VAN 1955 Laplace, probabiliste et statisticien, et ses précurseurs. *Archives internationales d'histoire des sciences* 8:27–37.

DAVID, F. N. 1965 Some Notes on Laplace. Pages 30–44 in Jerzy Neyman and Lucien M. Le Cam (editors), *Bernoulli, 1713; Bayes, 1763; Laplace, 1813.* New York: Springer.

DAVID, F. N.; and BARTON, D. E. 1962 *Combinatorial Chance.* London: Griffin; New York: Hafner.

DUVEEN, DENIS I.; and HAHN, ROGER 1957 Laplace's Succession to Bézout's Post of Examinateur des Élèves de l'Artillerie. *Isis* 48:416–427.

EISENHART, CHURCHILL 1964 The Meaning of "Least" in Least Squares. *Journal of the Washington Academy of Sciences* 54:24–33.

FELLER, WILLIAM (1950) 1957 *An Introduction to Probability Theory and Its Applications.* Vol. 1. 2d ed. New York: Wiley.

FRÉCHET, MAURICE 1927 Sur la loi de probabilité de l'écart maximum. Polskie Towarzystwo Matematyczne, *Annales: Rocznik* 6:93–122.

FRÉCHET, MAURICE 1940–1943 *Les probabilités associées à un système d'évènements compatibles et dépendants.* Parts 1–2. Paris: Hermann.

GAUSS, CARL FRIEDRICH (1809) 1963 *Theory of Motion of the Heavenly Bodies Moving About the Sun in Conic Sections.* New York: Dover. → First published in Latin.

GAUSS, CARL FRIEDRICH (1821) 1880 Theoria combinationis observationum erroribus minimis obnoxiae. Pars prior. Volume 4, pages 1–26 in *Carl Friedrich Gauss Werke.* Göttingen (Germany): Dieterichsche Universitäts-Druckerei. → A French translation was published in Paris in 1855 under the title *Méthode des moindres carrés: Mémoires sur la combinaison des observations.*

GUMBEL, E. J. 1958 *Statistics of Extremes.* New York: Columbia Univ. Press.

JORDAN, CHARLES (1939) 1947 *Calculus of Finite Differences.* 2d ed. New York: Chelsea.

LAGRANGE, JOSEPH LOUIS (1770–1773) 1868 Mémoire sur l'utilité de la méthode de prendre le milieu entre les résultats de plusieurs observations; dans lequel on examine les avantages de cette méthode par le calcul des probabilités; et où l'on résout différents problèmes relatifs à cette matière. Volume 2, pages 173–234 in Joseph Louis Lagrange, *Oeuvres de Lagrange.* Paris: Gauthier-Villars.

LÉVY, PAUL 1925 *Calcul des probabilités.* Paris: Gauthier-Villars.

MACMAHON, PERCY A. 1915 *Combinatory Analysis.* Vol. 1. Cambridge Univ. Press.

MERRIMAN, MANSFIELD 1877 A List of Writings Relating to the Method of Least Squares, With Historical and Critical Notes. Connecticut Academy of Arts and Sciences, *Transactions* 4:151–232.

MOIVRE, ABRAHAM DE (1718) 1756 *The Doctrine of Chances: Or, a Method of Calculating the Probabilities of Events in Play.* 3d ed. London: Millar.

MOIVRE, ABRAHAM DE 1730 *Miscellanea analytica de seriebus et quadraturis. . . .* London: Tonson & Watts.

MOIVRE, ABRAHAM DE (1733) 1959 A Method of Approximating the Sum of the Terms of the Binomial $(a+b)^n$ Expanded Into a Series, From Whence Are Deduced Some Practical Rules to Estimate the Degree of Assent Which Is to Be Given to Experiments. Volume 2, pages 566–575 in David Eugene Smith, *A Source Book in Mathematics.* New York: Dover. → First published as "Approximatio ad summam terminorum binomii $(a+b)^n$ in seriem expansi."

MOLINA, E. C. 1930 Theory of Probability: Some Comments on Laplace's *Théorie analytique.* American Mathematical Society, *Bulletin* 36:369–392.

NEWMAN, JAMES R. 1956 Commentary on Pierre Simon de Laplace. Volume 2, pages 1316–1324 in James R. Newman (editor), *The World of Mathematics.* New York: Simon & Schuster.

PEARSON, KARL 1929 Laplace: Being Extracts From the Lectures Delivered by Karl Pearson. *Biometrika* 21:202–216.

PITMAN, E. J. G. 1939 The Estimation of the Location and Scale of Parameters of a Continuous Population of Any Given Form. *Biometrika* 30:391–421.

RIORDAN, JOHN 1958 *An Introduction to Combinatorial Analysis.* New York: Wiley.

SIMON, G. A. 1929 Les origines de Laplace: Sa généalogie, ses études. *Biometrika* 21:217–230.

SIMPSON, THOMAS 1756 A Letter to the Right Honourable George, Earl of Macclesfield, President of the Royal Society, on the Advantage of Taking the Mean of a Number of Observations, in Practical Astronomy. Royal Society of London, *Philosophical Transactions* 49:82–93.

SIMPSON, THOMAS 1757 An Attempt to Show the Advantage Arising by Taking the Mean of a Number of Observations in Practical Astronomy. Pages 64–75 in Thomas Simpson, *Miscellaneous Tracts on Some Curious, and Very Interesting Subjects in Mechanics, Physical-astronomy, and Speculative Mathematics.* London: Nourse.

SMITH, DAVID EUGENE (1929) 1959 *A Source Book in Mathematics.* 2 vols. New York: Dover.

TODHUNTER, ISAAC (1865) 1949 *A History of the Mathematical Theory of Probability From the Time of Pascal to That of Laplace.* New York: Chelsea.

USPENSKY, JAMES V. 1937 *Introduction to Mathematical Probability.* New York: McGraw-Hill.

WALKER, HELEN M. 1929 *Studies in the History of Statistical Method, With Special Reference to Certain Educational Problems.* Baltimore: Williams & Wilkins.

WHITTAKER, EDMUND 1949*a* Laplace. *Mathematical Gazette* 33:1–12.

WHITTAKER, EDMUND 1949*b* Laplace. *American Mathematical Monthly* 56:369–372.

WILSON, EDWIN B. 1923 First and Second Laws of Error. *Journal of the American Statistical Association* 18:841–851.

LASHLEY, KARL S.

Karl Spencer Lashley (1890–1958), American psychologist, was born in Davis, West Virginia, of middle-class English stock. His father, Charles Gilpin Lashley, was the manager of the family store in Davis and the founder of a small bank there; at various times he served in such political posts as mayor and postmaster. Lashley's mother, Maggie Blanche Spencer, was descended from Jonathan Edwards, the philosopher, theologian, and educator of American revolutionary times; she had been a country schoolteacher before her marriage. After that she continued to be an avid reader, amassing a personal library of more than 2,000 volumes, and was an informal "adult education" instructor in diverse subjects. She appears to have been responsible for cultivating Lashley's love of nature and of learning.

Except for four years, from 1894 to 1898, during which the family, afflicted with "gold fever," trekked to the west coast and Alaska, Lashley spent his early years in Davis. He showed signs of being a prodigy. During his elementary school years, his interest in nature and animal behavior was already evident in his collection of all sorts of plants and animals, including many pets. During this period, too, his marked mechanical aptitude became apparent; he expertly designed many gadgets, small and large, and made them in his own workshop.

Graduating from Davis High School at the age of 14, he entered the University of West Virginia, but because his high school was unaccredited he had to spend a year in preparatory work before becoming a freshman. Although vaguely inclined toward engineering, he enrolled, at his mother's wish, in a liberal arts program, intending to major in Latin or English. It was only to fill an unscheduled hour that he enrolled in a course in zoology taught by John Black Johnston (later dean at the University of Minnesota when Lashley taught there). This contact with Johnston crystallized his interest in zoology for, as he later wrote, "Within a few weeks in this class I knew that I had found my life's work" (Beach 1961).

After Lashley's freshman year Johnston left and was succeeded by Albert M. Reese, who appointed Lashley departmental assistant. In this role he found a fascinating Golgi series of frog brain sections and proposed to "draw all the connections between the cells." To his surprise, most of the cells were not stained and therefore not visible. He later commented, ". . . I think almost ever since I have been trying to trace those connections" (*ibid.*, p. 169). Lashley went on to take all the courses offered by Reese, the only zoologist on the faculty, but he got much of his education in zoology by independently working out projects for which Reese gave only the briefest instructions. Lashley's philosophy of education and handling of his own students reflected this experience with independent work.

In 1910, with a B.A. in zoology, Lashley went to work on a master's degree at the University of Pittsburgh, where he had been awarded a teaching fellowship in biology. It was here that he took his only formal course in psychology. This was a laboratory course in experimental psychology taught by Karl Dallenbach who later wrote, "Lashley was intensely interested and was the outstanding student in the class. . . . He showed in that course the promise that he later fulfilled" (*ibid.*, p. 170).

Lashley received his master's degree in June 1911 and went that summer to Cold Spring Harbor to do research on the variability in the number of cirri in the ciliate *Stylonychia.* (Cold Spring Harbor is a prominent Long Island center for biological research; during the summer months many outstanding academic biologists work there.) This research led to his appointment by H. S. Jennings as a teaching fellow in zoology at Johns Hopkins University. There Lashley worked with Jennings on paramecia and with S. O. Mast on the behavior of various invertebrates, taking his PH.D. in 1914 with a dissertation on inheritance in asexual reproduction of *Hydra.* During this period he also pursued his interest in psychology, working with Adolph Meyer, professor of psychiatry and director of the newly established Phipps Clinic, and with John B. Watson, then professor of psychology.

Watson's behavioristic approach had tremendous appeal for Lashley and led him to do postdoctoral work on vertebrate behavior. This work extended over three years, from 1914 to 1917, during which he slowly formulated and launched the rich program of research and writing he was to carry on for the rest of his life. The first two years he held successive appointments in zoology as Bruce fellow and Johnston scholar but worked with Watson on a variety of problems: field experiments on reproductive behavior of terns (in the Dry Tortugas), acquisition of human motor skills, color vision in birds, conditioning of the salivary reflex, and effects of strychnine and other drugs on maze learning in rats.

While pursuing these experiments, Lashley became interested in the work of Shepard Ivory Franz, who was examining the behavior of brain-injured patients at Saint Elizabeths Hospital in Washington, D.C. Franz was also inaugurating work on the behavioral effects of experimental brain lesions in animals. After frequent journeys to Washington to observe this work, Lashley was permitted to study neurological cases in the wards and to acquire the necessary surgical and histological skills for performing studies of the neural basis of learning. Here he got started solidly on the research career that eventually brought him eminence and recognition.

By the fall of 1917 the United States had entered World War I, and many psychologists were in the army or heavily involved in war-related activities, but Lashley's vision was too poor to meet army standards. Therefore, when he had completed his period of postdoctoral training, he accepted a post at the University of Minnesota arranged by Robert M. Yerkes, who was slated to become chairman there at the war's end but never did. Morale in the department was not high, and after one year Lashley, taking a leave of absence, accepted a position with the U.S. International Hygiene Board. Although he was working once again with Watson, this time in a program dealing with public education on the dangers of venereal disease, this assignment was not a productive one, and in 1920 R. M. Elliott, the new chairman of the department of psychology, prevailed on Lashley to return to the University of Minnesota as assistant professor.

Lashley's intellectual pre-eminence and prolific research on brain function brought him rapid promotion: in 1924, at the age of 34, he was made a full professor. In 1926 he left Minnesota for Chicago, at first serving as research psychologist with the Behavior Research Fund at the Institute for Juvenile Research and later, in 1929, moving to a professorship at the University of Chicago. In 1935 he went to Harvard University as professor and in 1937 was made a research professor in neuropsychology, a title he held until his retirement in 1955. However, in 1942, in a joint arrangement with Yale University and certain private foundations, he moved to Florida as director of the Yerkes Laboratories of Primate Biology.

It has been said of Lashley that he was an "inspiring teacher who described all teaching as useless" (Beach 1961, p. 163). He himself frequently asserted that "those who need to be taught can't learn, and those who can learn don't need to be taught" (*ibid.*, p. 182). He applied this principle by eschewing formal teaching, often raising artificial barriers to registration in his courses. Because his research was so excellent, he managed better than any other academic psychologist of his time to stay out of the classroom. The few lectures he did give were usually stimulating, often exciting. And in seminars he had few peers; he was an impressive scholar, with a pleasant wit and a fascinating intellect. Like Mark Hopkins, however, he was at his best "on a log." He was always available to graduate students and postdoctoral fellows in his laboratory, and for scores of psychologists their informal contacts with Lashley were to be the most significant periods of their education. In this way Lashley was a great teacher even though fewer students, probably, have studied under him formally than under any other psychologist of distinction.

One other related characteristic of Lashley's deserves mention. This was his "go-it-alone" attitude toward research. He had fewer collaborators and published fewer joint papers than most other comparable scientists. Except for very routine work, he did all his own research, "running" his animals, doing data analysis, making histological reconstructions, and writing his own papers. He expected the same of others working with him. He never directed but only advised when his advice was asked. He felt strongly that research of quality must be carried out by scientists of quality, not by a host of assistants and graduate students. It is easy, therefore, to understand his dismay at the increasingly large amounts of money being employed in organized research. Writing in 1953 to Watson, Lashley said, "The money available for research now is rather shocking. The man who doesn't have $20,000 per year for research is probably intellectually honest. There are not enough competent men to spend the money" (*ibid.*, p. 180).

Work on brain function. Lashley's most productive phase was launched in his work with Franz. At first he merely took for granted the connectionism of Watsonian behaviorism and looked for the neural basis of the connections. This, however, proved elusive, for in study after study in the 1920s he obtained data suggesting a field theory rather than a connectionist theory of brain function.

Lashley's reasoning and his findings in these studies should be briefly summarized. Connectionist theory holds that complex behavior is made up of conditioned reflexes, each forming a connection through the conditioning process. The connection, Lashley reasoned, should have a definite locus in the brain just as a connection in a telephone system does; he, therefore, tried to find a definite localization of these connections. His basic technique was to train an animal to run a maze or make a discrimination both before and after he had made lesions of different sizes in various areas of the cerebral cortex. He then tested for such effects of the lesion as a deficit in retention or learning ability. Except for certain specific visual discriminations discussed below, he found no localization of function. Deficits were found, indeed, but they were not specific to any particular cortical areas. Instead, the degree of deficit depended on the amount of cortex removed rather than upon its locus.

W. S. Hunter and others argued that Lashley's reasoning was faulty, and the present author agrees. Hunter pointed out that mazes involve many different cues, as others had shown by depriving animals of various senses, and complex motor responses. Quite specific localization of connections in the brain could well exist, but so many different connections would be involved in a habit like maze running that one could statistically expect the results Lashley obtained. Lashley's experiments, therefore, were not crucial to the issue. But Lashley felt otherwise and believed that his experiments did disprove the existence of specific connections and required explanation in terms of field-theory concepts.

Thus, Lashley came to propose two concepts (or principles) for which he became widely known and which had considerable influence on subsequent research. The two concepts were *mass action* and *equipotentiality*. Both were presented in his 1929 monograph *Brain Mechanisms and Intelligence*. By mass action he referred to his finding that learning, or at least certain kinds of learning, is mediated by the cerebral cortex as a whole. This principle is based mainly on his studies of maze learning which showed that the efficiency of learning depends roughly on the amount of cortex present and not on any particular cortical locus.

The related concept of equipotentiality came out of his studies of vision and applies primarily to sensory systems. It refers to the ability of certain parts of a system to assume the functions of its other parts. Lashley had found, for example, that a rat can relearn a visual discrimination after the discrimination has been destroyed by a lesion of the visual cortex; also, a rat can discriminate visual stimuli perfectly when only a small remnant of its visual cortex remains intact. From such results he concluded that various parts of a system are "equipotential" for the mediation of a learned visual discrimination.

Other investigators have, of course, pursued the problems raised by Lashley's work and his interpretations. Using more sophisticated physiological and behavioral techniques than Lashley had at his disposal and giving more attention to the brain of the primate, they have found more localization of function than the principle of mass action would lead one to expect. Indeed, in the primate brain there is considerable localization of learned functions. Still, Lashley was largely correct. The localization is far from precise, and within large areas of localized function there are mass-action effects. As for equipotentiality, later investigations bear out the presence of this phenomenon within sensory systems. It is the interpretation rather than the fact that is in question, and there are now complex alternative explanations available. The problem, however, remains far from solved and is in nearly the same state as Lashley left it.

Work on sensory functions. In another major phase of Lashley's work, the study of sensory functions, he made considerable contributions to the study of the generalization of learned visual discriminations, much of the work being planned as tests of connectionist versus field theories. He also made contributions to neuroanatomy. Concentrating at first on the visual system, he traced neural connections between the retina and the lateral geniculate nucleus of the thalamus and between this nucleus and the cerebral cortex. Later he extended this kind of neuroanatomic analysis to other sensory systems. His papers on thalamocortical connections (1941) and on the microscopic structure of the cortex are classics in their fields. In them he showed that although there are point-to-point projections in sensory systems, these systems cannot be rigidly compartmentalized. Later work, with more refined techniques, has borne him out.

Work on neural functions. The final major aspect of Lashley's work was an attempt to construct a general theory of neural function. Here he was frustrated; his grand design was to develop a theory of how the brain works in perception and learning. Having held earlier that other simple theories were untenable, he now turned to various forms of field theory. Many of his experiments and, particularly, his later papers were concerned with tests of such theories. In the end he felt he had succeeded only in exploding the theories proposed but not in devising one that would satisfactorily stand the test of experiment. He had to be content with the thought that he and his generation had only laid the groundwork for building a good theory at a later date. Despite his frustration in theory building, however, he adhered steadfastly to the belief that a satisfactory theory would some day be possible. In his last published article, "Cerebral Organization and Behavior," he made an impressive case for his claim that the study of "the organization [of] mental states does not reveal any operations which cannot be accounted for in principle by the mechanism of the brain" (1958, p. 15).

Not long after this was written, Lashley collapsed and died in Poitiers, France. He left over 100 papers of an experimental or theoretical nature, but no book—because he could never make a large-scale theory stand up. Without question, he was the twentieth-century pioneer in the experimental study of brain functions and behavior.

CLIFFORD T. MORGAN

[*For the historical antecedents of Lashley's work, see the biographies of* BROCA; FLOURENS; GALL. *The relevant work of Lashley's contemporaries is discussed in the biographies of* HUNTER; MEYER; WATSON; YERKES. *For discussion of the development of Lashley's ideas, see* NERVOUS SYSTEM; PSYCHOLOGY, *article on* PHYSIOLOGICAL PSYCHOLOGY; VISION.]

WORKS BY LASHLEY

1929 *Brain Mechanisms and Intelligence: A Quantitative Study of Injuries to the Brain.* Univ. of Chicago Press.

1930 Basic Neural Mechanisms in Behavior. *Psychological Review* 37:1–24.

1941 Thalamo-cortical Connections of the Rat's Brain. *Journal of Comparative Neurology* 75:67–121.

1958 Cerebral Organization and Behavior. Pages 1–18 in Association for Research in Nervous and Mental Disease, *The Brain and Human Behavior: Proceedings.* Baltimore: Williams & Wilkins.

The Neuropsychology of Lashley: Selected Papers. Edited by Frank A. Beach et al. New York: McGraw-Hill, 1960. → A posthumous collection containing papers published between 1915 and 1958.

SUPPLEMENTARY BIBLIOGRAPHY

BEACH, FRANK A. 1961 Karl Spencer Lashley: June 7, 1890–August 7, 1958. Volume 35, pages 163–204 in National Academy of Sciences, *Biographical Memoirs.* Washington: The Academy. → See pages 196–204 for a bibliography of Karl Lashley's works.

LASKI, HAROLD J.

Harold Joseph Laski (1893–1950), teacher, political scientist, and British Labour party leader, was born in Manchester, England, the second son of Nathan and Sarah Laski; his father was a prosperous cotton shipper, a prominent Liberal, and a leader of the orthodox Jewish community. The young Laski's intellectual gifts and his precocity were demonstrated by an article he wrote when he was 16 years old and still a student at the Manchester Grammar School. The article, "On the Scope of Eugenics," which appeared in the *Westminster Review* in July 1910, called forth a letter of congratulation from Sir Francis Galton. For six months after he left school, Laski pursued his interest in eugenics by studying with Karl Pearson at University College in London.

In the summer of 1911 he broke with his family by marrying a Gentile, Frida Kerry, who was eight years older than he, and in the fall of that year he began his undergraduate studies at New College, Oxford. After a year of reading science, he shifted to history; he studied under H. A. L. Fisher and Ernest Barker and was strongly influenced by the writings of F. W. Maitland. During his undergraduate days, Laski was active in the women's suffrage movement, in which his wife was deeply interested. In this connection he became a close friend of H. W. Nevinson and George Lansbury, then editor of the Labour newspaper, the *Daily Herald*. After receiving his degree in 1914, Laski spent the summer months writing articles for the *Herald* on Ireland and on constitutional issues that affected labor. When his attempt to enlist in the armed forces ended in medical rejection, he accepted a post as lecturer in history at McGill University in Montreal, Canada. While at McGill, he wrote his first book, *Studies in the Problem of Sovereignty* (1917).

Two years later, in 1916, as a result of a meeting with Felix Frankfurter, who became a lifelong friend, Laski accepted a post as instructor in history at Harvard University. For the next four years, Laski was a stimulating teacher and a lively member of the Harvard intellectual community. He wrote several books during this period, including *Authority in the Modern State* (1919) and *The Foundations of Sovereignty, and Other Essays* (1921); in these works he argued against the myth of the sovereign, omnicompetent state and defended the doctrine of political pluralism in a series of historical and analytical essays. The state, he maintained, is not the supreme association to whose will all other groups must bow, but is only one among many groups—corporations, unions, churches, societies of all kinds—with which it is engaged in a constant struggle for men's loyalty and obedience. Laski's pluralistic view of the state reflected the influence of Gierke, Maitland, and Figgis, as well as the antistatist and anti-idealist currents in political thought and action that were strong before and after World War I. Even at this period, Laski's primary concern was with the freedom of workers' organizations from control by the "sovereign state," and in October 1919, he gave striking evidence of this concern by a public defense of the Boston policemen who were then engaged in a strike that had outraged the leaders of the community [*see* PLURALISM].

In 1920 Laski left Harvard and his many American friends, chief among whom was, perhaps, Justice Oliver Wendell Holmes, with whom he maintained close touch until Holmes's death. Laski accepted a post at the London School of Economics and Political Science, where, in 1926, he succeeded Graham Wallas as professor of political science. Laski taught at the School until his death 24 years later; he was so well known and so influential among students that his name and the London School became almost synonymous terms in the minds of many people, especially of students from America and from Asia and Africa.

After his return to England, Laski became increasingly involved in politics and political discussions and in writing for the *Nation*. He was active in the election campaign of December 1923, which led to the first Labour minority government. Yet he found time for the teaching and counseling of students and for writing his most comprehensive study of politics, *A Grammar of Politics* (1925). In this work he moved away from his earlier pluralism and adopted a position that might be called "socialized Benthamism." He now accepted the view he had previously rejected, that the state was "the fundamental instrument of society," and he argued that its purpose was to "satisfy, or organize the satisfaction of, the wants of men on the largest possible scale." Yet he indicated that he retained a good deal of suspicion of political power by advocating a large measure of decentralization, consultation with organized groups, and restraints on governmental action. This suspicion of state power reflected his belief that in practice its incidence was heavily weighted in favor of the interests of the wealthy and powerful members of society. Laski, now committed to a democratic or Fabian socialism, urged that political democracy was virtually meaningless unless it led forward to "economic democracy" or socialism [*see* ECONOMIC THOUGHT, *article on* SOCIALIST THOUGHT].

From 1925 on, he began to express doubts that the necessary major reforms of the economic and social systems could be attained by the methods of political democracy. In his book *Communism* (1927), for example, he argued that since the workers no longer accepted capitalism or regarded it as legitimate, the only alternative to revolution was a series of major concessions by the ruling class—acceptance of nationalization of essential industries, sharp curtailment of inheritance rights, comprehensive regulation of private business, and guarantees of adequate wages, working conditions, and educational and welfare opportunities. He was not optimistic about the willingness of capitalists to accept these moves toward a more equal society and to abdicate from power peacefully, and in *Liberty in the Modern State* (1930) he warned that the price of social conflict is always the destruction of freedom.

With the advent of the great depression, the rise of fascism in Europe, the collapse of the British Labour government in 1931, and the defection of Ramsay MacDonald, Philip Snowden, and James H. Thomas from the party, which left it leaderless and bewildered, Laski's hopes for a peaceful and gradual transition to socialism grew dim, and his doubts about the possibility of achieving socialism by constitutional and democratic means became much more intense. In a series of works written during the 1930s, such as *Democracy in Crisis* (1933), *The State in Theory and Practice* (1935), *The Rise of European Liberalism* (1936), and *Parliamentary Government in England* (1938), he abandoned his Fabianism in favor of the Marxist view that the contradictions of capitalism were insoluble and that a democratic political system was incompatible with a capitalism in crisis. On the basis of British, French, German, and Italian experience, Laski now argued that once the operations of political democracy threatened the continued existence of capitalism and interfered with the pursuit of profits, the ruling class would destroy democracy and the labor movement and would initiate an authoritarian regime. The liberal and socialist alternatives to the communist doctrine of the necessity of violent revolution would then become untenable, and revolutionary socialism and fascism (the political form of capitalism in decay) would thus be left as the only serious contenders for power.

These were the years of Laski's most intense involvement in politics. From 1937 to 1949 he was a member of the National Executive of the Labour party, where he was often critical of the moderate views and tactics of the party's leaders. During the late 1930s his public influence probably reached its high point; this was the period of the Left Book Club, directed by Victor Gollancz, John Strachey, and Laski. During the Spanish Civil War he joined such left-wing Labourites as Sir Stafford Cripps and Aneurin Bevan in the Unity Campaign and the popular front movement of all antifascist groups, which was condemned by the Labour party leaders and by the party conference in 1937.

From the fall of 1938 to the end of the summer of 1939 Laski was in the United States, where he taught at the University of Washington and delivered at Indiana University the lectures that were later published as *The American Presidency* (1940). Shortly after his return to England the war began. The London School of Economics was evacuated to Cambridge, and during the war years Laski divided his time between teaching, assisting Clement Attlee after he became deputy prime minister under Churchill in 1940, and traveling around the country to address Labour party meetings and give lectures at military camps. Although overwork led to a serious nervous breakdown in 1943, he soon resumed his many activities and his writing. His major wartime publications were *Reflections on the Revolution of Our Time* (1943) and *Faith, Reason, and Civilization* (1944); in these books, and in many articles and speeches, he urged the leaders of the Labour party to insist that the Churchill coalition government commit itself during the war to a program of major social and economic reforms that would be carried out when peace was restored. In the unity of groups and classes and the patriotic enthusiasm of the war years he saw an opportunity, which would never be repeated, of achieving what he called "a revolution by consent." If this opportunity were missed because the Labour leaders were unwilling to threaten to resign from the coalition government, the postwar world would be neither any better nor more hopeful than the world of the 1920s and would again move toward the choice that had confronted Europe in the 1930s—reaction or revolution, fascism or communism. Laski was criticized by many people, including some of his friends in England and America, for his wartime attacks on Churchill and for his criticisms of the inadequacies and weaknesses of Attlee and other Labour party leaders.

Although the electoral victory of Labour in 1945 was a great satisfaction to Laski, the triumph was marred for him by the growing tensions on the international scene, particularly between the United States and the Soviet Union, and by his failure to win a libel action that he had instituted during the 1945 campaign, when several newspapers reported that he had made a speech in which he advocated violent revolution in Great Britain. He wrote a long book on American society and politics, *The American Democracy* (1948), which struck many observers, including some liberals, as a curiously doctrinaire and outdated portrait of the American scene. Early in 1949, Laski made his final visit to the United States; in the course of a five-week tour of the country he delivered, under the auspices of the Sidney Hillman Foundation, the series of lectures later published as *Trade Unions in the New Society* (1949). In these lectures he urged the American trade unions to move forward to the creation of a strong labor party in order to safeguard and develop the American democratic tradition.

Although he had resigned in 1949 from the national executive of the Labour party and was worn out and ill, Laski campaigned strenuously in the 1950 general election. He died suddenly, only a few weeks after the election, on March 24, 1950.

The influence that Laski exerted by his teaching and writing was probably greatest in the 1930s; during the years of depression and the growing menace of fascism and international war, he was an impassioned advocate of socialism who combined social and economic radicalism with a deep attachment to many traditional British and American institutions and values. In this period his influence among students in both Britain and the United States was particularly great. After World War II and especially since his death, his reputation as a political theorist and analyst has been higher among students and intellectuals in Asian and African countries than among similar groups in the West.

HERBERT A. DEANE

[*For the historical context of Laski's work, see* SOCIALISM *and the biographies of* FIGGIS; GIERKE; MAITLAND.]

WORKS BY LASKI

(1916–1935) 1953 HOLMES, OLIVER W.; and LASKI, HAROLD J. *Holmes–Laski Letters: The Correspondence of Mr. Justice Holmes and Harold J. Laski, 1916–1935.* Edited by Mark DeWolfe Howe, with a foreword by Felix Frankfurter. 2 vols. Cambridge, Mass.: Harvard Univ. Press. → A paperback edition was published in 1963 by Atheneum.

1917 *Studies in the Problem of Sovereignty.* New Haven: Yale Univ. Press.

1919 *Authority in the Modern State.* New Haven: Yale Univ. Press.

(1921) 1931 *The Foundations of Sovereignty, and Other Essays.* New Haven: Yale Univ. Press.

(1925) 1957 *A Grammar of Politics.* 4th ed. London: Allen & Unwin.

(1927) 1935 *Communism.* London: Butterworth.

(1930) 1961 *Liberty in the Modern State.* 3d ed. London: Allen & Unwin.

(1933) 1934 *Democracy in Crisis.* London: Allen & Unwin.

(1935) 1956 *The State in Theory and Practice.* London: Allen & Unwin.

(1936) 1958 *The Rise of European Liberalism: An Essay in Interpretation.* London: Allen & Unwin. → A paperback edition was published in 1962 by Barnes and Noble.

1938 *Parliamentary Government in England: A Commentary.* New York: Viking.

1940 *The American Presidency: An Interpretation.* New York: Harper. → A paperback edition was published in 1958 by Grosset and Dunlap.

1943 *Reflections on the Revolution of Our Time.* New York: Viking; London; Allen & Unwin.

1944 *Faith, Reason, and Civilization: An Essay in Historical Analysis.* New York: Viking.

1948 *The American Democracy: A Commentary and an Interpretation.* New York: Viking.

(1949) 1950 *Trade Unions in the New Society.* London: Allen & Unwin.

(1951) 1962 *Reflections on the Constitution: The House of Commons, the Cabinet [and] the Civil Service.* Manchester (England) Univ. Press.

SUPPLEMENTARY BIBLIOGRAPHY

DEANE, HERBERT A. 1955 *The Political Ideas of Harold J. Laski.* New York: Columbia Univ. Press.

ELLIOTT, WILLIAM Y. 1928 *The Pragmatic Revolt in Politics: Syndicalism, Fascism, and the Constitutional State.* New York: Macmillan.

MAGID, HENRY M. 1941 *English Political Pluralism: The Problem of Freedom and Organization.* Columbia University Studies in Philosophy, No. 2. New York: Columbia Univ. Press.

MARTIN, KINGSLEY 1953 *Harold Laski, 1893–1950: A Biographical Memoir.* New York: Viking; London: Gollancz.

LATENT STRUCTURE

A scientist is often interested in quantities that are not directly observable but can be investigated only via observable quantities that are probabilistically connected with those of real interest. Latent structure models relate to one such situation in which the observable or manifest quantities are multivariate multinomial observations, for example, answers by a subject or respondent to dichotomous or trichotomous questions. Models relating polytomous observable variables to unobservable or latent variables go back rather far; some early references are Cournot (1838), Weinberg (1902), Benini (1928), and deMeo (1934). These models typically express the multivariate distribution of the observable variables as a mixture of multivariate distributions, where the distribution of the latent variable is the mixing distribution [*see* DISTRIBUTIONS, STATISTICAL, *article on* MIXTURES OF DISTRIBUTIONS].

Lazarsfeld (1950) first introduced the term *latent structure model* for those models in which the variables distributed according to any of the component multivariate distributions of the mixture are assumed to be stochastically independent. (Thus a latent structure model of a subject's answers to 50 dichotomous questions—the latent class model of this article—assumes that subjects fall into relatively few classes, called latent classes, with the variable that relates the subject to his class being the latent variable. The distribution of this latent variable, that is, the distribution of the subjects among latent classes, is the mixing distribution. Within each class it is assumed that the responses to the 50 dichotomous questions are stochastically independent.) A basic reference for the general form of latent structure models is Anderson (1959).

The present article—restricted to the case of dichotomous questions—emphasizes the problems of identifiability and efficient statistical estimation of the parameters of latent structure models, points out difficulties with methods that have been proposed, and summarizes doubts currently held about the possibility of good estimation.

The simplest of the latent structure models and almost the only one in which the problem of parameter estimation has been carefully addressed is the *latent class model.* In this model, each observation in the sample is a vector $\boldsymbol{x}$ with p two-valued items or coordinates, conveniently coded by writing each either as 0 or as 1. The latent class model postulates that there is a small number m of classes, called *latent classes*, into which potential observations on the population can be classified such that within each class the p coordinates of the vector $\boldsymbol{x}$ are statistically independent. This is not to say that all identical observations in the sample are automatically considered as coming from the same class. Rather, associated with each class is a probability distribution on the 2^p possible vectors $\boldsymbol{x}$, such that the p coordinates of $\boldsymbol{x}$ are (conditionally) independent. An observation vector $\boldsymbol{x}$ thus has a probability distribution that is a mixture of the probability distributions of $\boldsymbol{x}$ associated with each of the latent classes.

An example of the above model comes from the study (Lazarsfeld 1950) of the degree of ethnocentrism of American soldiers during World War II. Because it is not known how to measure ethnocentrism directly, a sample of soldiers was asked the following three questions: Do you believe that our European allies are much superior to us in strategy and fighting morale? Do you believe that the majority of all equipment used by all the allies comes from American lend-lease shipment? Do you believe that neither we nor our allies could win the war if we didn't have each other's help?

Here $p = 3$ and $\boldsymbol{x}$ is the vector of responses to the three questions, with Yes coded as 1 and No coded as 0. A suitable latent class model would postulate that there are two latent classes (so that $m = 2$), such that within each class the answers to the three questions are stochastically independent. Postulating the existence of any more than two latent classes would, as will be seen later, lead to difficulties, since the parameters of such a latent class model could not be consistently estimated. The two latent classes would probably be composed of ethnocentric and nonethnocentric soldiers, respectively. However, this need not be the case, and in fact it may happen that the two latent classes will have no reasonable interpretation, let alone the hoped-for interpretation. This phenomenon of possible noninterpretability is characteristic not only of the latent class model but also of the factor analysis and other mixture-of-distributions models.

The latent class model. Let σ denote a subset (unordered) of the integers $(1, 2, \cdots, p)$, possibly the null subset ϕ. (Other subsets will, for concreteness, be denoted by writing their members in customary numerical order.) Let π_σ denote the probability that for a randomly chosen individual each coordinate of $\boldsymbol{x}$ with index a member of σ is a 1, and define $\pi_\phi = 1$. For example, $\pi_{2,7,19}$ is the probability that the second, seventh, and nineteenth coordinates of $\boldsymbol{x}$ are all 1, forgetting about—or marginally with respect to—the values of the other coordinates of $\boldsymbol{x}$.

Since the order of coordinates is immaterial for such a probability, one is justified in dealing with the 2^p unordered σ's, but a specific order in naming the subset is helpful for exposition. The π_σ's are notationally a more convenient set of parameters than what might be considered the 2^p natural parameters of the multinomial distribution of $\boldsymbol{x}$.

A concise description of the natural parameters of the distribution of $\boldsymbol{x}$ is the following. Let $\bar{\sigma}$ denote that subset of the integers $(1, 2, \cdots, p)$ which is the complement of σ. Let $\pi_{\sigma:\bar{\sigma}}$ denote the probability that for a randomly chosen individual each coordinate of $\boldsymbol{x}$ with index of a member of σ is a 1 and each coordinate of $\boldsymbol{x}$ with index a member of $\bar{\sigma}$ is a 0. The 2^p $\pi_{\sigma:\bar{\sigma}}$'s are the natural parameters of the multinomial distribution of $\boldsymbol{x}$, since they are the probabilities of each of the 2^p possible observation values. For example, in the ethnocentrism case, $\pi_{1,2:3}$ would be the probability that the first two questions are answered Yes, while the third question is answered No. The π_σ's and $\pi_{\sigma:\bar{\sigma}}$'s are related by a nonsingular linear transformation.

Let ν_α be the probability that the observation vector $\boldsymbol{x}$ is a member of the αth latent class, where

$\alpha = 1, 2, \cdots, m$ and $\sum \nu_\alpha = 1$. Let $\lambda_{\alpha\sigma}$ be the probability that if $\boldsymbol{x}$ is a vector chosen at random from the αth class, then each coordinate of $\boldsymbol{x}$ with index a member of σ is a 1. Clearly $\pi_\sigma = \sum_\alpha \nu_\alpha \lambda_{\alpha\sigma}$.

Let σ_i denote the ith member of σ, with the members of σ arranged in some order, say numerical. The fundamental independence assumption of the latent class model then says that for each α

$$\lambda_{\alpha\sigma} = \prod_{\sigma_i \epsilon \sigma} \lambda_{\alpha\sigma_i}$$

for all σ. That is, the probability (conditional on $\boldsymbol{x}$ being in the αth latent class) of any given set of coordinates of $\boldsymbol{x}$ being all 1's is the product of the probabilities of each of these coordinates being a 1. Then

$$\pi_\sigma = \sum_{\alpha=1}^{m} \nu_\alpha \prod_{\sigma_i \epsilon \sigma} \lambda_{\alpha\sigma_i}$$

for all σ. These equations are called the *accounting equations* of the latent class model. Thus the $m(p+1)$ parameters of the model are the *latent parameters* $\lambda_{\alpha i}$ and the ν_α, $\alpha = 1, \cdots, m$, $i = 1, \cdots, p$. These completely determine the 2^p *manifest parameters*, the π_σ, via the accounting equations.

Parameter estimation. Suppose that the number of latent classes, m, is known to the investigator. (This assumption is made because it underlies all the theoretical work on the estimation of parameters of the latent class model. In practice m is unknown, but a pragmatic approach is to assume a particular small value of m, proceed with the estimation, see how well the estimated model fits the manifest data, and alter m and begin again if the fit is poor.) Then a central statistical problem is that of estimating the parameters of the model, the ν's and λ's, from a random sample of n vectors $\boldsymbol{x}$. (The typical sample in survey work is a stratified rather than a simple random sample. However, the problem of estimating latent parameters from such samples is much more complicated, and as yet has hardly been touched.)

Let n_σ be the number of vectors in the sample with 1's in each component whose index is a member of σ, and let $p_\sigma = n_\sigma/n$. If the model were simply a multinomial model with parameters the π_σ's, then the p_σ's would be maximum likelihood estimators of the π_σ's. If for each set of 2^p π_σ's there is a unique set of latent parameters, ν_α's and $\lambda_{\alpha i}$'s, $\alpha = 1, \cdots, m$, $i = 1, \cdots, p$, then the ν's and λ's are functions of the π_σ's, and evaluating these functions at the p_σ's as arguments will yield estimators (actually consistent estimators) of the latent parameters. But the "if" in the last sentence is most critical; it *is* the identifiability condition, common to all models relating distributions of observable random variables to distributions of unobservable random variables. Consequently, most of the work on parameter estimation in latent class analysis is really a by-product of work on finding constructive procedures, that is, procedures that explicitly derive the unique latent parameters as function of the π's, for proving the identifiability of a latent class model associated with a given m and p. With such a constructive procedure available, one can replace the π's by their estimates, the p's, and use the procedure to determine estimates of the ν's and λ's. The following description of estimation procedures based on constructive proofs of identifiability will thus really be a description of the constructive procedure for determining the ν's and λ's from a subset of the π's.

Green's method of estimation. The earliest constructive procedure was given by Green (1951). Let $\boldsymbol{D}_i$ be the $m \times m$ diagonal matrix with $\lambda_{\alpha i}$, $\alpha = 1, \cdots, m$, on the diagonal, and let $\boldsymbol{L}$ be the $(p+1) \times m$ matrix with first row a vector of 1's and jth row $(j = 2, \cdots, p+1)$ the vector of $(\lambda_{1,j-1}, \cdots, \lambda_{m,j-1})$. Let $\boldsymbol{N}$ be the $m \times m$ diagonal matrix with ν_α, $\alpha = 1, \cdots, m$, on the diagonal. For σ a subset of $(1, 2, \cdots, p)$, define $\boldsymbol{D}_\sigma = \prod_{\sigma_j \epsilon \sigma} \boldsymbol{D}_{\sigma_j}$. Form the matrix $\Pi_\sigma = \boldsymbol{L}\boldsymbol{N}\boldsymbol{D}_\sigma\boldsymbol{L}'$, where the prime denotes the matrix transpose. The (i,j)th element of this matrix is

$$\sum_{\alpha=1}^{m} \nu_\alpha \lambda_{\alpha i} \lambda_{\alpha j} \prod_{\sigma_k \epsilon \sigma} \lambda_{\alpha\sigma_k}.$$

If $i \neq j$ and $i,j \notin \sigma$ then the (i,j)th element of this matrix is the manifest parameter $\pi_{ij\sigma}$. Otherwise the (i,j)th element of this matrix can formally be defined as a quantity called $\pi_{ij\sigma}$, where the subscript of π may have repeated elements. Since π's with repeated subscripts are not manifest parameters and have no empirical counterpart but are merely formal constructs based on the latent parameters, they are not estimable directly from the n_σ's. However, Green provided some rules for guessing at values of these π's (one rule is given below) so that the matrix Π_σ can be partly estimated and partly guessed at, given data.

Let $\Pi_0 = \boldsymbol{L}\boldsymbol{N}\boldsymbol{L}'$, $\boldsymbol{N}^{\frac{1}{2}}$ be the $m \times m$ diagonal matrix with $\sqrt{\nu_\alpha}$, $\alpha = 1, \cdots, m$, on the diagonal, $\boldsymbol{D} = \sum_{k=1}^{m} \boldsymbol{D}_k$, and $\boldsymbol{A} = \boldsymbol{L}\boldsymbol{N}^{\frac{1}{2}}$. Then $\Pi = \sum_k \Pi_k = \boldsymbol{A}\boldsymbol{D}\boldsymbol{A}'$. Under the assumptions that $m \leqslant p + 1$, rank $\boldsymbol{A} = m$, and all the diagonal elements of $\boldsymbol{D}$ are different and nonzero, the following procedure determines the matrices $\boldsymbol{L}$ and $\boldsymbol{N}$ of latent parameters.

Factor Π_0 as $\Pi_0 = \boldsymbol{B}\boldsymbol{B}'$ and Π as $\Pi = \boldsymbol{C}\boldsymbol{C}'$. (The matrices $\boldsymbol{B}$ and $\boldsymbol{C}$ are not unique, but any factorization will do.) Let $\boldsymbol{T} = (\boldsymbol{B}\boldsymbol{B}')^{-1}\boldsymbol{B}'\boldsymbol{C}$. A complete principal component analysis of $\boldsymbol{TT'}$ will yield an orthogonal matrix $\boldsymbol{Q}$, and it can be shown that $\boldsymbol{A} = \boldsymbol{BQ}$. Since the first row of $\boldsymbol{L}$ is a vector of 1's, the first row of $\boldsymbol{A}$ is an estimate of the vector $(\sqrt{\nu_1}, \cdots, \sqrt{\nu_m})$, so that $\boldsymbol{N}$ is easily determined. The matrix $\boldsymbol{L}$ is then just $\boldsymbol{AN}^{-\frac{1}{2}}$.

The major shortcoming of this procedure is the problem of how to guess at values of the π's bearing repeated subscripts. No one has yet devised a rule which, when applied to a set of p's, will yield consistent estimators of $\boldsymbol{L}$ and $\boldsymbol{N}$. For example, Green suggests using $p_{ii} = p_i^2 + \max_{j\neq i}(p_{ij} - p_ip_j)$ as a guess at π_{ii}. Yet in the case $m = 2$, $p = 3$ with latent parameters $\nu_1 = \nu_2 = .5$, $\lambda_{11} = .9$, $\lambda_{12} = .2$, $\lambda_{13} = .8$, $\lambda_{21} = .7$, $\lambda_{22} = .9$, $\lambda_{23} = .4$, if $i = 2$, $\max_{j\neq 2}(p_{2j} - p_2p_j)$ is a consistent estimator of $-.07$, so that p_{22} is a consistent estimator of something smaller than π_2^2. But $\pi_{ii} \geqslant \pi_i^2$, so that p_{22} is not a consistent estimator of π_{22}.

Determinantal method of estimation. A matricial procedure that does not have the above shortcoming, since it involves only estimable π's, was first suggested by Lazarsfeld and Dudman (see Lazarsfeld 1951) and independently by Koopmans (1951), developed by Anderson (1954), and extended by Gibson (1955; 1962) and Madansky (1960). For ease of exposition, the procedure will be described only for the cases treated by Anderson.

Assume that $p \geqslant 2m + 1$. In that case, $2m + 1$ different items can be selected from the p items (say, the first $2m + 1$) and the following matrices of π's involving only these items formed. Let

$$\Pi^* = \begin{bmatrix} 1 & \pi_1 & \cdots & \pi_m \\ \pi_{m+1} & \pi_{1,m+1} & \cdots & \pi_{m,m+1} \\ \vdots & \vdots & & \vdots \\ \pi_{2m} & \pi_{1,2m} & \cdots & \pi_{m,2m} \end{bmatrix}$$

and let $\tilde{\Pi}$ be the matrix Π^* with the 1 replaced by π_{2m+1} and all the π's having the additional subscript $2m + 1$. Let Λ_1 be an $(m + 1) \times (m + 1)$ matrix with the first row a vector of 1's and the jth row $(j = 2, \cdots, m + 1)$ the vector $(\lambda_{1,j-1}, \cdots, \lambda_{m,j-1})$, and let Λ_2 be an $(m + 1) \times (m + 1)$ matrix with first row a vector of 1's and the jth row $(j = 2, \cdots, m + 1)$ the vector $(\lambda_{1,m+j-1}, \cdots, \lambda_{m,m+j-1})$. Let $\boldsymbol{N}$ and $\boldsymbol{D}_{2m+1}$ be defined as above. Then $\Pi^* = \Lambda_1\boldsymbol{N}\Lambda_2'$ and $\tilde{\Pi} = \Lambda_1\boldsymbol{ND}_{2m+1}\Lambda_2'$. Thus, if the diagonal elements of $\boldsymbol{D}_{2m+1}$ are distinct and if Λ_1, $\boldsymbol{N}$, and Λ_2 are of full rank, then the diagonal elements of $\boldsymbol{D}_{2m+1}$ are the roots θ of the determinantal equation $|\tilde{\Pi} - \theta\Pi^*| = 0$.

Table 1

Parameter	Value	Asymptotic variance
ν_1	3/4	$1115.42/n$
λ_{11}	1/2	$39.00/n$
λ_{12}	1/3	$60.89/n$
λ_{13}	1/3	$4.96/n$
λ_{21}	1/4	$303.00/n$
λ_{22}	2/3	$611.53/n$
λ_{23}	1/4	$31.00/n$

If $\boldsymbol{Z}$ is the matrix of characteristic vectors corresponding to the roots $\theta_1, \cdots, \theta_m$, then the columns of $\Pi^*\boldsymbol{Z}$ are proportional to the columns of Λ_1, with the constant of proportionality determined by the condition that the first row of Λ_1 is a vector of 1's. A similar argument using the transposes of $\tilde{\Pi}$ and Π^* yields Λ_2, and $\boldsymbol{N}$ is determined by $\boldsymbol{N} = \Lambda_1^{-1}\Pi^*\Lambda_2'^{-1}$.

A difficulty with this procedure is that it depends critically on which $2m + 1$ items are chosen from the p items, on which of these $2m + 1$ is chosen to define Π^*, and on the allocation of the $2m$ items to the rows and columns defining Π^*. That is, it depends critically on the ordering of the items. There are no general rules available for an ordering of the items that will yield relatively efficient estimators of the latent parameters.

The most important shortcoming of this procedure and of its extensions (which involve more of the π's) is that there is no guarantee that when the procedure is used with a set of p's it will produce permissible estimates of the latent parameters, that is, estimates that are real numbers between 0 and 1. In four sampling experiments with $n = 1{,}000$, $m = 3$, and $p = 8$, Anderson and Carleton (1957) found that of 2,240 determinantal equations only 33.7 per cent had all roots between 0 and 1. Madansky (1959) computed the asymptotic variance of the determinantal estimates for the case $m = 2$, $p = 3$, a case in which these estimators, if permissible, are the maximum likelihood estimators of the latent parameters, and found the results presented in Table 1, where n is the sample size. Thus, sample sizes must be greater than 1,116 for the variance of the estimators of all the parameters to be less than 1.

Table 2

$$\begin{aligned}
\pi_{123;\phi} &= 10/192\\
\pi_{23;1} &= 14/192\\
\pi_{13;2} &= 17/192\\
\pi_{12;3} &= 22/192\\
\pi_{3;12} &= 19/192\\
\pi_{2;13} &= 34/192\\
\pi_{1;23} &= 35/192\\
\pi_{\phi;123} &= 41/192
\end{aligned}$$

Table 3

Response pattern	Number observed
123;ϕ	2
23;1	3
13;2	4
12;3	4
3;12	4
2;13	7
1;23	7
ϕ;123	9

Rounding error also affects the estimates greatly. The parameters of the multinomial distribution for the above model are given in Table 2.

For a sample of size 40, if one had actually observed the expected number of respondents for each of the response patterns (rounded to the nearest integer), then the sample would have the composition shown in Table 3. Table 4 shows the p_σ's based on these data (π_σ being given for comparison). The determinantal estimates of the latent parameters are given in the third column of Table 5. (The fourth column will be discussed below.)

Partitioning method of estimation. A third estimation procedure (Madansky 1959) looks at the problem in a different light. Since the latent classes are defined as those classes within which the p components of the vector $\boldsymbol{x}$ are statistically independent, one might (at least conceptually) look at all possible assignments of the n observations into m classes and find that assignment for which the usual χ^2 test statistic for independence is smallest. The estimates of the latent parameters would then just be the appropriate proportions based on this best assignment. They would always be permissible. Although for finite samples they would not be identical with minimum χ^2 estimates, they would have the same asymptotic properties and thus be asymptotically equivalent to maximum likelihood estimates.

Madansky (1959) introduced another measure of independence, simpler to compute than χ^2, and found that the asymptotic efficiency of the estimators of the latent parameters from this procedure, in the example described above, is about .91. The obvious shortcoming of this idea is that it is too time consuming to carry out all the possible assignments, even for moderate samples on an electronic computer. In the example described above, for a sample of size 40 it took four hours of computation on the IBM 704 to enumerate and assess all the assignments into two classes. The resulting estimates are shown in the fourth column of Table 5.

Table 4

σ	p_σ	π_σ
1	.425	.4375
2	.400	.4167
3	.325	.3125
12	.150	.1667
13	.150	.1406
23	.125	.1250
123	.050	.0521

Table 5 — Parameter estimates for two methods*

Parameter	Value	Determinantal estimate	Partitioning estimate
ν_1	.75	.23	.58
λ_{11}	.50	.82	.00
λ_{12}	.33	.23	.43
λ_{13}	.33	.42	.30
λ_{21}	.25	.30	1.00
λ_{22}	.67	.45	.35
λ_{23}	.25	.29	.35

* $n = 40$.

Source: Madansky 1959, p. 21.

Scoring methods. Current activity on estimation procedures for the latent class model (Henry 1964) is directed toward writing computer routines using the scoring procedure described by McHugh (1956) to obtain best asymptotically normal estimates of the latent parameters. The scoring procedure will yield estimators with the same large asymptotic variances as those indicated by the above example of the maximum likelihood estimators' asymptotic variances. Also, the scoring procedure has the same permissibility problem associated with it as did the determinantal approach described above. However, the problem can be alleviated for this procedure by using a set of consistent permissible estimators for initial values in the scoring procedure.

ALBERT MADANSKY

[*See also* SCALING. *Directly related are the entries* DISTRIBUTIONS, STATISTICAL, *article on* MIXTURES OF DISTRIBUTIONS; FACTOR ANALYSIS; STATISTICAL IDENTIFIABILITY.]

BIBLIOGRAPHY

ANDERSON, T. W. 1954 On Estimation of Parameters in Latent Structure Analysis. *Psychometrika* 19:1–10.

ANDERSON, T. W. 1959 Some Scaling Models and Estimation Procedures in the Latent Class Model. Pages 9–38 in Ulf Grenander (editor), *Probability and Statistics*. New York: Wiley.

ANDERSON, T. W.; and CARLETON, R. O. 1957 Sampling Theory and Sampling Experience in Latent Structure Analysis. *Journal of the American Statistical Association* 52:363 only.

BENINI, RODOLFO 1928 Gruppi chiusi e gruppi aperti in alcuni fatti collettivi di combinazioni. International Statistical Institute, *Bulletin* 23, no. 2:362–383.

COURNOT, A. A. 1838 Mémoire sur les applications du calcul des chances à la statistique judiciaire. *Journal de mathématiques pures et appliquées* 3:257–334.

DEMEO, G. 1934 Su di alcuni indici atti a misurare l'attrazione matrimoniale in classificazioni dicotome. Accademia delle Scienze Fisiche e Matematiche, Naples, *Rendiconto* 73:62–77.

GIBSON, W. A. 1955 An Extension of Anderson's Solution for the Latent Structure Equations. *Psychometrika* 20:69–73.

GIBSON, W. A. 1962 Extending Latent Class Solutions to Other Variables. *Psychometrika* 27:73–81.

GREEN, BERT F. JR. 1951 A General Solution for the Latent Class Model of Latent Structure Analysis. *Psychometrika* 16:151–166.

HENRY, NEIL 1964 The Computation of Efficient Estimates in Latent Class Analysis. Unpublished manuscript, Columbia Univ., Bureau of Applied Social Research.

KOOPMANS, T. C. 1951 Identification Problems in Latent Structure Analysis. Cowles Commission Discussion Paper: Statistics, No. 360. Unpublished manuscript.

LAZARSFELD, PAUL F. 1950 The Logical and Mathematical Foundation of Latent Structure Analysis. Pages 362–412 in Samuel A. Stouffer et al., *Measurement and Prediction.* Princeton Univ. Press.

LAZARSFELD, PAUL F. 1951 *The Use of Mathematical Models in the Measurement of Attitudes.* Research Memorandum RM-455. Santa Monica (Calif.): RAND Corporation.

LAZARSFELD, PAUL F. 1959 Latent Structure Analysis. Pages 476–543 in Sigmund Koch (editor), *Psychology: A Study of a Science.* Volume 3: Formulations of the Person and the Social Context. New York: McGraw-Hill.

MCHUGH, RICHARD B. 1956 Efficient Estimation and Local Identification in Latent Class Analysis. *Psychometrika* 21:331–347.

MCHUGH, RICHARD B. 1958 Note on "Efficient Estimation. . . ." *Psychometrika* 23:273–274. → This is a correction to McHugh 1956.

MADANSKY, ALBERT 1959 *Partitioning Methods in Latent Class Analysis.* Paper P-1644. Santa Monica (Calif.): RAND Corporation.

MADANSKY, ALBERT 1960 Determinantal Methods in Latent Class Analysis. *Psychometrika* 25:183–198.

WEINBERG, WILHELM 1902 Beiträge zur Physiologie und Pathologie der Mehrlingsgeburten beim Menschen. *Pflüger's Archiv für die gesamte Physiologie des Menschen und der Tiere* 88:346–430.

LATIN AMERICAN POLITICAL MOVEMENTS

The dominant characteristic of twentieth-century Latin America is the pressure for fundamental change—social, economic, and political change. In several nations, governments committed to such change have come to power. Even in many of the nations where conservative oligarchies maintain their hold, the pressures for change are such that few governments have believed it wise to ignore them completely. Dynamic forces are at work: population growth, urbanization, industrial development, growth of labor unions, the appearance and increasing influence of certain political parties, and an increasing demand on the part of the underprivileged and depressed mass of people for a better material life ("the revolution in rising expectations"). These forces have promoted, and to some degree have been promoted by, the emergence of several radical or reformist political movements during this century. The major ones are the Mexican revolution, the Uruguayan reforms (Batllism), the *Apristas*, Peronism, the Vargas movement, the Christian Democrats, and Castroism.

General characteristics and influences

Considerable similarity exists among these movements. They advocate development and various economic reforms, a strong government and a larger role for government, especially in the economic and social areas, and social reforms (e.g., increased literacy, expanded educational opportunities, social welfare programs). They appeal to and in varying degrees involve the masses. They urge either a breaking down or a modifying of traditional class lines and concomitantly urge broader mass participation in national life. In their economics most movements embrace some form of socialism. They are nationalistic and, either as an aspect of nationalism or as a separate ingredient, they inveigh against economic and political imperialism. Their anti-imperialism may be simply a negative, anti-United States sentiment, or it may be an aspect of a more positive phenomenon: a prohemispheric or pro-Latin American sentiment.

Numerous differences also exist among the movements. Some have a well-developed theoretical or philosophical base (especially the *Apristas* and the Christian Democrats); others are primarily pragmatic. They differ in the stress put on certain goals. Perhaps the major differences concern means of achieving desired changes and the kind of society that would be created. These differences are the effect of several factors: the level of social, economic, and political development; the political situation; and the variety of attitudes, inclinations, and estimations of the individuals who provide or have provided both intellectual and practical leadership for the movements.

The stress that twentieth-century movements put on change places them in sharp contrast with the political thought that previously dominated Latin America. That thought, primarily European in origin, was the monopoly of the small elite that had enjoyed political and economic power and high social status since independence. Reflecting the interests of the elite, the earlier thought either defended the *status quo* or urged relatively minor change, usually of a political nature (e.g., changes in electoral laws). In those instances where the principles advocated cannot be termed "minor" (e.g., matters in the area of church–state relations), they did not call for fundamental changes, nor were the changes called for intended to affect the masses. Where concerned with economic matters, the earlier thought proposed relatively moderate changes. Comtean positivism, the single most influential line of political thought in late nineteenth-century Latin America, emphasized a free secular society and the idea that the growth of knowledge gradually promoted political freedom and economic improvement. In short, the earlier political thought—still dominant in some of the nations—did not advocate a restructuring or reorganization of society; the newer political thought does.

This article will focus first on general factors influencing the new political thought, and then on each of the twentieth-century political movements and the methods it endorsed or employed to promote change.

The factors that have molded or influenced the movements may be classified as primarily material or primarily intellectual. These, in turn, may be classified as indigenous or nonindigenous, positive or negative influences.

Material influences. The most obvious and the single most important material influence is negative and indigenous: the reaction against prevailing economic conditions. Indeed, this is usually the main goal of all the movements, for other goals are seen to be directly related to it. The movements insist that conditions must be changed and advocate a massive, multipronged program of economic development. To some degree the desire for economic development may be attributed to the positive, nonindigenous influence of the world's mature economies, since economically less-developed nations desire to have the same level of economic well-being and diversity of economic activity. (This desire does not mean, however, that Latin America accepts the economic principles of the mature economies.)

A second influence, also negative and indigenous, is the reaction against prevailing social conditions. A large part, in some cases a majority, of the population is cut off from national life, living in a depressed condition without opportunity to achieve a better status. The movements pledge to improve the lot of this segment of the population and appeal to it for support.

Prevailing political conditions are a third negative, indigenous influence. Democratic forms (constitutions which are often modeled after that of the United States and provide for separation of powers, bills of rights, political parties, elections, and a variety of special devices to ensure democratic government) have long existed, but in many of the Latin American nations political practice has been quite undemocratic. Further, government, whether military or civilian, has been *by* and *for* the small elite, usually ignoring the needs of the masses. All of the movements advocate change in the political process. They may not agree on the kind of political system or how it should function, but they do agree that government by them and based on their principles will not be government devoted to promoting and protecting the interests of the elite. It will be government for (although not necessarily by) the masses.

Another negative influence, both indigenous and nonindigenous, on all of the movements (except perhaps Batllism) is the resentment against the economic and political influence the United States has long had and still has in Latin America. Limitation, if not elimination, of U.S. influence is a goal of the twentieth-century movements. Proposed means of accomplishing this end include controls on foreign capital, nationalization of some or all foreign investment, closer cooperation among Latin American nations, and creation of a new inter-American organization. The extent and intensity of efforts to reduce U.S. influence vary, of course, from movement to movement and from time to time.

Intellectual influences. For the most part the programs put forward by the movements are not borrowed ones. Rather, they are a response to local conditions. Nevertheless, various "outside" ideas and events have influenced all of the movements. European socialism, including Marxism, has had a tremendous impact on most of the movements. The same is true of French, British, and United States liberal thought. The notion of Latin American unification can be traced back to the liberator Simón Bolívar, and the ideal has been embraced by a host of persons in succeeding years. Similarly, the *Aprista* emphasis on the development of an Indian or Indo-American culture has some roots in Latin American thought.

The economic and social reforms of President Franklin D. Roosevelt (the New Deal) had an impact on several of the movements. The same can be said of the British Labour party and the development program "Operation Bootstrap" carried out by Muñoz Marín in Puerto Rico.

Since the end of World War II, the "new economics" of Raúl Prebisch and the United Nations

Economic Commission for Latin America has been the major influence on Latin American economic thought.

The major movements

The Mexican revolution and the Uruguayan reforms may be added to the list of general influences, since these movements preceded the others and have served as examples, if not as models. They will therefore be discussed first.

The Mexican revolution. The Mexican revolution, the foremost political movement of twentieth-century Latin America, began in 1910 under the leadership of Francisco I. Madero as a revolt against the dictatorship of President Porfirio Díaz. Its original objectives were entirely political, as epitomized by Madero's slogan, "Effective Suffrage! No Re-election!" As the revolt spread and its support increased, it became a full-blown social revolution. Economic and social objectives—land reform, economic development, restrictions on the church and foreign capital, integration of the Indians, destruction of the existing class structure and class barriers—were added to the political objectives. Civil war raged until 1916. Thereafter order was progressively restored, and implementation of the revolutionary program began on a nation-wide scale.

The revolutionary program. The revolution was pragmatic and evolutionary, not ideological. No master plan existed concerning the implementation of objectives. The revolution consisted of a series of acts, and often these acts were experiments. As Robert Scott says, "Mexico had no Marx to supply a theoretical, rational, and systematic model for its revolution. And somehow history failed to produce any single dominant personality who could perform this service. . . . Probably the movement was too big, too diverse, and too spontaneous to be identified with any one program or person" ([1959] 1964, p. 98). To answer the question "What was the Mexican revolution?" one must look at what was done.

The best place to begin is the constitution of 1917. That document expresses the objectives of the revolution and gives considerable insight into its philosophy. It is a hybrid, because ". . . it retained the ideals of liberalism while placing the interests of society and of the state above those of the individual" (Ross 1963, p. 89). Three articles are especially worthy of note. Article 3 assigns to the national government responsibility for providing free, public elementary education. The article reflects the importance attached to education by the revolutionary leaders and the anticlerical bent of the revolution. Article 27 deals with landownership and the rights of foreign capital, limits the size of agricultural holdings, and asserts the nation's control over the subsoil. Property is held to have a "social function," with the rights of private property subordinated to "social welfare." The article expresses several tenets of the revolution: hostility to the *hacienda*, commitment to agrarian reform, determination to overhaul the prerevolutionary class structure based on landownership, anticlericalism (for the church was a large landowner), opposition to foreigners, and nationalism. Article 123 assigns to the state the task of promoting, protecting, and regulating the labor movement and spells out the economic and social rights of labor. "The basic principle of Article 123 was that labor was a status, a way of life, for which the minimum essentials were now constitutionally guaranteed, rather than an economic commodity, subject to the market vagaries of supply and demand" (Cline 1953, p. 169). The article reflects the role—both the right and responsibility—assigned to the state in promoting social welfare, the effort to enhance the position of the working class, and concern with industrialization and the urban sector of the economy.

An extensive land reform program was begun in the early 1920s. Under this plan, land, either government-owned or taken from persons owning more than 5,000 hectares, was distributed to landless peasants. While some land was given outright to the peasants, most of it was given to village communities, *ejidos*. The *ejido* is not a collective farm; rather, it is a form of landholding with historical antecedents both in Spain and in pre-Hispanic Mexico. *Ejido* land is divided among the families of the community and is worked by them as individual units. Although the *ejidatario* cannot alienate his land, he can pass it on to his heir. By the mid-1960s, 40 to 50 per cent of the cropland was in *ejidos*, and about 30 per cent was in small and medium-size private holdings (Needler 1964, pp. 21–22).

During the early years of the revolution relatively little was done in the economic area apart from land reform, despite the declared objective of economic development. Admittedly some actions were taken that had economic effects (for example, nationalization of agricultural lands, railroads, and petroleum), but they were socially and politically, not economically, motivated (Cline [1962] 1963, p. 231). And the few economic programs that were attempted were unsuccessful.

The desire for economic independence, plus the adverse effects of the great depression and World

War II, dramatized the need for action and led to the inauguration of a development program. One part of this program was to increase the tempo of land reform. Another part, the key, was industrialization, and through various inducements a high rate of industrial development has been achieved. Industrialization is, in large part, the result of a shift in Mexican attitudes toward foreign capital; it is no longer rejected, but is welcomed. This shift in attitude is only one manifestation of a more general phenomenon: moderation of the revolution. (Such moderation is typical of radical movements once they have achieved power and consolidated their position.) However, the government is at least partially enforcing "Mexicanization" laws, which require that Mexicans must own 51 per cent of all business enterprises.

The economic and social programs accomplished fundamental change. The class structure was revamped and the prerevolutionary landowning elite was replaced by a new upper class whose wealth is in industry, commerce, and finance. A large, predominantly urban and industrial middle class has developed. The urban and rural masses have benefited, although the benefits have been limited. However, there has been much upward mobility of individuals *between* classes, and it is primarily through such individual mobility that substantial improvements in the real standard of living of the urban and rural proletariats can result (Needler 1964, p. 31).

The political objectives of the revolution have been implemented. Governmental stability has been achieved. "Effective Suffrage! No Re-election!" has been effected. A fairly high level of democracy prevails. Government is sensitive to citizen wants. Opposition groups are free to organize and operate. Civil liberties exist.

Mexico's foreign policy is based on the principles and experiences of the revolution: national sovereignty, juridical equality of nations, self-determination, and nonintervention. The Estrada doctrine, a Mexican contribution to international legal ideas, asserts that granting or withholding of diplomatic recognition at a government's discretion constitutes interference in the affairs of another state. Recognition should, therefore, be automatic.

Theory and philosophy. Although not an ideological movement, the revolution was not devoid of political thought. A list of writers would include (but not be limited to) Andres Molina Enríquez, Jesús Silva Herzog, Graciano Sánchez, Vincente Lombardo Toledano, Manuel Gamio, Gilberto Loyo, Fernando Gonzales Roa, Daniel Cosio Villegas, and Gómez Morin.

Uruguayan reform (Batllism). A much different but only slightly less important movement (Batllism) remade Uruguay during the first quarter of the twentieth century under the leadership of José Batlle y Ordónez. Like the Mexican revolution, Batllism was concerned with social, economic, and political problems. Also like the Mexican revolution, it was pragmatic, not ideological. Unlike the Mexican revolution it was a peaceful movement and did not touch the whole population; its impact was primarily urban.

The program. The actions taken under Batllism earned for Uruguay the reputation of being one of the world's most advanced laboratories for political, social, and economic experimentation (Fitzgibbon 1954, pp. 96–97).

The social and economic aspects of Batllism—which constituted a high degree of state socialism—can be described by citing what was done during Batlle's two presidential terms, 1903–1907 and 1911–1915. His proposal for an eight-hour working day and a weekly rest period was enacted, as were laws to protect the worker's life and health and to encourage labor union activity. During Batlle's presidency elementary education was made obligatory and education at all levels was made free. New schools were constructed; a women's university was established. Foreign professors and technicians were brought to Uruguay, and scholarships were given for study abroad.

Various social service measures were also enacted. Laws were passed giving protection to women, children, the sick, and the elderly. Women were emancipated. Divorce was legalized. Tax was abolished on the earnings of the lowest-paid public officials and on the smallest pensions.

Furthermore, steps were taken to stimulate industry. Immigration was encouraged. A state insurance monopoly was created. The Bank of the Republic was nationalized. Several government-owned and government-operated industries were established to provide certain basic products at a low price and to reduce dependence on imports. Railroads, power facilities, meat-packing plants, and some other businesses were nationalized.

Although Batllism focused attention on urban, industrial problems, some attention was also given to the agricultural sector. Stock raising and agriculture received governmental assistance. Rural credit facilities were established. Agricultural research was promoted. Import duties on agricultural tools and machinery were removed. To some degree, the agricultural programs may have been a means of "buying" rural toleration, for Batlle was detested and opposed by the large landowners.

From the perspective of the second half of the twentieth century, Batlle's reforms may seem extremely mild, but for the first quarter of the twentieth century they were radical.

The political reforms were equally radical. Batlle saw a Uruguay plagued with political problems, e.g., dictatorship, instability, and civil strife. He blamed these problems on the domination and abuses of past presidents. To overcome the problems, Batlle proposed the abolition of the presidency and the establishment of a nine-member executive council (modeled on the Swiss collegial executive) with three of the seats assigned to the minority party. Further, he proposed that congressional elections be conducted on a proportional representation system. The proposal met with hostility, especially from his own party, and was not adopted until 1919 (after Batlle was out of office) —and then in limited form. The bi-partisan collegial executive was abandoned in 1933 but reestablished, and in the form Batlle envisioned, in 1951. Batlle's political reforms are largely responsible for the high level of democracy that prevails in Uruguay.

Theory and philosophy. Very little theoretical writing is associated with Batllism. Batlle's ideas are expressed in his articles in *El Día*, his newspaper. But the articles "do not form a very systematic whole, since he did not generally concern himself with the philosophical base of ideas" (Davis 1958, p. 103).

The "Apristas." Between the two world wars Peru produced a distinctive ideological party, the Alianza Popular Revolucionaria Americana (APRA), whose ideology was popularly known as *aprismo* and whose members were called *Apristas.* The party dates back to 1914, but it was not formally organized until 1931. Led by Victor Raúl Haya de la Torre, the *Apristas* have had an almost hemisphere-wide influence, and *Aprista*-type parties have been founded in these areas and countries: in Cuba, Partido Revolucionario Cubano (Auténtico); in Venezuela, Acción Democrática; in Costa Rica, Liberación Nacional; in Paraguay, Partido Febrerista; in Haiti, Mouvement Ouvrier et Paysan; and in Puerto Rico, the Popular Democratic Party. However, there was little contact between the *Aprista* parties during their formative years.

Aprismo was begun by a group of students at Lima's University of San Marcos who led a successful effort to reform the school. Their next step was to establish night schools for adults, in order to raise the economic and social level of the illiterate (Kantor 1953). The government suppressed the schools and exiled the student organizers, who then decided that political action was necessary and developed the *Aprista* ideology.

The ideology. *Aprismo* is a blend of ideas and ideals about the uniqueness of Latin America and democratic socialism. The aim is to create a "new" Peru and a "new" Latin America. The basic thesis is that Latin America is unique; it is different from the United States and Europe, and must cease imitating their institutions and create its own Indo-American culture. (The thesis is related to Haya's historical space–time theory, which holds that there is no single theory or explanation of history valid for all societies.) Its over-all plan consists of two parts: a "maximum program" for all Latin America and a "minimum program" for Peru only. The principles of the maximum program are integration or assimilation of the Indian population, opposition to imperialism, unification of the Latin American nations, a planned economy including nationalization of land and business, and democratic government.

Aprista thinkers stress the need to integrate the Indian into society. To the *Apristas*, Latin America will not realize its economic or political potential until the Indian has been integrated. Two conflicting cultures are said to exist in Latin America, one European, the other indigenous, or Indian. The result is instability. A stable society will be possible in Latin America only when the two clashing cultures are merged. The *Apristas* believe that their program would amalgamate the Indian and Europeanized sections and produce a *new*, integrated Indo-American culture containing elements from both (Kantor 1953). Integration would not be easy or quick, and to achieve it several actions would be necessary: free, state-controlled education, including technical education; agrarian reform (formation of cooperative farms, government authority to regulate land purchases and sales, programs to increase productivity, and dissemination of technical information); and laws to enhance the position of labor (wage and hour laws, retirement benefits, employment services, organization of unions).

Anti-imperialism is another major tenet. Indeed, the *Apristas* believe that the most important problem facing Latin America is that created by imperialistic penetration. Imperialism, held to be economic in nature, is explained in the following terms:

> Outward expansion is inevitable in a highly industrialized country based on the capitalist system of production. As the *Apristas* see the process, capitalism forces an industrially developed country to seek raw

materials in the underdeveloped areas of the world. At the same time, an industrial country must seek markets for the manufactured goods which cannot be consumed at home. (Kantor 1953, pp. 37–38)

And in an alliance with local elites, foreign capital gained control of the Latin American economies. However, the *Apristas* do not reject foreign capital; they recognize that it has made a contribution and can continue to do so. But foreign capital must be controlled to ensure that it plays a "useful role." Without eliminating their opposition to imperialism, *Aprista* leaders have over the years moderated their statements on this subject.

The *Apristas* hold that unification of Latin America is the only means of combating imperialism and strengthening Latin America. They see Latin America as a single "natural unit." Existing boundaries have no justification, being mere carry-overs from the colonial period that perpetuate economic feudalism. *Apristas* insist that unification would not be difficult. There are, they say, more similarities than differences among the hemisphere's people. Unification is necessary for defense. Further, realization of increased economic and political strength should be sufficient to overcome any hurdles that may exist. Two strong but not insurmountable forces—U.S. imperialism and the elite—work against unification. Although opposed to U.S. imperialism, the *Apristas* are not anti-United States. They desire to cooperate with the United States, seeing cooperation as a benefit to both parties. And Latin American unification is seen as a means of promoting cooperation by putting Latin America and the United States on an equal footing.

Economic development is a goal. Originally nationalization of industry and land was posited as the ideal form of economic organization. However, nationalization was a long-range goal, and the means of achieving it was spelled out. Nationalization is another area in which *Aprista* doctrine has changed; a mixed economy is now envisioned.

Haya de la Torre and other Peruvian *Aprista* leaders insist that the political process must be democratic, and they refuse to use force to obtain power. One author states that the most conspicuous weakness of the Peruvian *Apristas* is their neglect of the means of achieving power (Kantor 1953, p. 1). Asked why the *Apristas* have not used force, Haya replied ". . . that although the *Apristas* were not pacifists, they were convinced that the experience of history demonstrated that the use of violence in politics exposed its users to the danger of degenerating into complete dependence upon violence . . ." (Kantor 1953, p. 56). However, not all *Aprista*-type parties have refused to use force. In Venezuela, Acción Democrática joined with segments of the military to overthrow a government, and when it came into power, established a democratic political process.

The Peruvian *Apristas* endeavor to make their movement more than a political party, seeing themselves as soldiers in a crusade and as seekers of educational purification which will transform Peru into a modern, democratic nation. They want to establish a high standard of living, but even more important than that, they want to see a spiritual renovation within Peru which will create a new country based on a morally changed people (*ibid.*, p. 61). In short, they seek to make *aprismo* a way of life.

Theory and philosophy. The theory and philosophy of *aprismo* is expressed in countless works and by numerous writers. Of the writers, Haya de la Torre stands out. Others who should be mentioned include Manuel Seoane, Luis Alberto Sánchez, Alfredo Saco, and Carlos Mariategui (a founder of *aprismo* who later embraced international communism).

Peronism. Argentina's Peronist movement began in 1945: the following year the movement's leader, Juan D. Perón, was elected president of Argentina; he and his program then dominated the nation until mid-1955. Although Peronism wrought change, the change was not as fundamental as in the Mexican revolution and Batllism or in the *Aprista* program. Nevertheless, Peronism had a tremendous impact on Argentina, and despite the dictatorial, corrupt nature of Perón's regime and its eventual collapse, its impact has not been eradicated—probably cannot be eradicated.

Some have labeled Peronism as fascism (Lipset 1960, pp. 173–176). Still others reject the label (Silvert 1963, pp. 361–366), and the latter individuals may have the better case. Granted Perón may have been favorably impressed by Franco's Spain and Mussolini's Italy and some of his statements had fascist or profascist overtones. But Peronism differed from European fascism in fundamental ways. Actually, Peronism was nonideological, despite the appearance of *justicialismo*—the so-called ideology of the movement. The term *justicialismo* did not appear until 1949 (Blanksten 1953), and the *justicialist* ideas were propounded after that. *Justicialismo*—the "balancing of forces" or "Third Position"—never passed beyond being whatever Perón did or said.

The program. Peronism advocated the "economic independence of Argentina," and to this end a primarily industrial development program was pursued to free the country from dependence on agriculture, imports, and foreign capital. As part of the development program, and as part of the nationalism that characterized Peronism, the government nationalized some industries and took over foreign-owned transportation and communications facilities. In typical twentieth-century Latin American fashion, private property was held to have a "social function" and was subordinated to state regulation.

The heart of Peronism was the program of "social justice." That program was directed toward the great mass of workers (the *descamisados*), who lived in ignorance and poverty and whose minimum wants and needs were ignored by the privileged members of society (Edelmann 1965, p. 354). A large body of social and labor legislation was enacted. The social and economic rights of the masses were written into the 1949 constitution. The *descamisados* were molded into a political force and a source of support by Perón, who, in return, rewarded them with social and economic benefits, a voice in government, and a government that was sympathetic to their needs and wants. (Perón's wife, Evita, played a major role in the program of "social justice.") The benefits were achieved at a price in addition to their financial cost: a loss of freedom of action.

Perón attempted to export his movement, or at least his influence, through labor attachés in Argentine embassies in Latin America, through general publicity, and through contacts with military leaders in other Latin American nations. And although Peronist governments did not come to power elsewhere in Latin America, Perón's efforts had some political impact in other Latin American nations.

The program was, however, very limited. The land tenure system was not changed. Wealth was not redistributed. The pre-Perón social class structure was not overthrown. And a question may be raised if Peronism was anything more than a typical Latin American dictatorship. Davis, for example, says Peronism was simply "a shrewd mixture of militarism, economic planning, and a demagogic appeal to the underprivileged [cemented with] a long overdue program of labor and social legislation" (1958, p. 112). Certainly Perón "governed internally by juggling already existing power centers in a fashion typical of states in immediately prenational situations, and . . . the regime even toppled in traditional . . . Latin American style" (Silvert 1963, p. 366). The power centers referred to were the army, the church, the oligarchy, "foreign imperialists," the interior, the *porteños*, and a new one, labor.

But the importance of Peronism must not be underestimated. The workers saw a government aware of their needs that allowed them a certain degree of participation in the political process, and, perhaps equally important, even the integrated middle and upper classes were finally willing to admit the alienation of some of their fellow citizens. Most of all, Peronism convinced the workers that much *could* be done by government to improve their lot. As a result, Peronism—even without Perón—remains a political force in Argentina.

Theory and philosophy. Peronism, a pragmatic movement, at first borrowed from the Neo-Thomism of Nicolas Desiri, an Argentine priest and philosopher, and from the ideas of Hernán Benítez, whose writings appeared in the *Revista de la Universidad de Buenos Aires.* After 1949, Peronism sought to develop its own ideology, *justicialismo.* Three men in particular endeavored to make it a social and political philosophy: Raúl A. Mende, Julio Claudio Otero, and Luis C. A. Serras. However, it is in the speeches of Péron and his wife that one finds most of the ideas of Peronism.

The Vargas movement. The major twentieth-century political movement in Brazil was that of Getulio Vargas, who headed the government from 1938 to 1945 and from 1950 to 1954. In many respects, the Vargas and Perón movements are of the same species. Originally Vargas relied for support on the *tenentes* (a group of young officers and civilians), but gradually he expanded his base through appeals to the discontented. Shortly before the 1938 election, Vargas promulgated a new constitution (the *estado novo* constitution) with features resembling Portuguese corporatism and Italian fascism. But the resemblance "was rather superficial; . . . the *estado novo* . . . is better understood as the product of Brazilian social and political elements" (Davis 1958, p. 109).

The program. Vargas pushed economic development. The government built highways and railroads. A development commission was established to promote industry and commerce—Vargas' principal objective. Education was promoted. Social and labor measures were enacted. Of all the decisions made by Vargas, probably none had greater political implications than his determination to bring the working groups into the political arena. Vargas retained their approval through elaborate welfare programs and by imposing restrictions and obligations on business and management. At the same time he maintained strict federal control over the labor movement as a guarantee to the business community that labor would not be permitted to get out of hand (Johnson 1958, pp. 167–168).

The movement contained a strong element of nationalism. One expression of this nationalism was the law providing that two-thirds of the workers in every enterprise had to be Brazilian. Another expression, the most dramatic, was construction of the Volta Redonda steel plant.

The importance of the movement did not end with Vargas' death in 1954. The forces activated or promoted by him retain much political influence.

Theory and philosophy. The Vargas movement evolved no political theory of its own. Vargas' speeches were pragmatic and opportunist, not theoretical. Francisco Campo's *O estado nacional,* published in 1940, was widely but wrongly viewed as the regime's fascist theory (Loewenstein 1942).

The Christian Democrats. The Latin American political movement growing most rapidly in strength and influence is Christian Democracy. The movement is not new. The first Christian Democratic party was established in 1910 (in Uruguay), and since then Christian Democratic parties have been established in all the nations except Cuba, Haiti, Honduras, and Paraguay (Edelmann 1965, p. 355). Its growing influence is, however, a recent development (Szulc 1965). In 1958, a Christian Democratic party, COPEI, became the second largest party in Venezuela. In 1964, the Christian Democratic candidate, Eduardo Frei, was elected president of Chile, and the following year the party gained control of the lower house of congress.

The movement possesses a well-developed ideology, of European origin, adapted to fit the Latin American scene. It was greatly influenced by the writing of the Catholic philosopher Jacques Maritain, a spokesman for liberal Thomism. Frei is the leading Latin American spokesman of the movement.

The ideology. Christian Democracy is based on the Christian ethic. More specifically, it is based on the tenets of Roman Catholicism, especially the encyclical *Rerum novarum,* issued by Pope Leo XIII in 1891. That encyclical, the so-called Magna Carta of labor, declared that laborers had the right to organize and the employer had an obligation to pay a fair wage.

Latin American Christian Democracy is reformist, and left of center or leftist. Its leaders are committed to achieving a social revolution through evolutionary means. Their objective is a society of social and Christian justice for all. They are committed to democracy—a political system *by* and *for* all the people. "Democracy," Frei writes, "will not be saved by those who, praising it as it now exists, petrify its abuses. Much less will it be saved by those who see only its defects and not its infinite possibilities. . . . Our task is to realize the possibilities of democracy" (see statement in Pike 1964, p. 213). Frei argues that democracy does not in fact exist when a sizable portion of the population is not incorporated into society—a common phenomenon in Latin America. "In order to acquire and preserve the precious gifts of democracy it is necessary," Frei declares, "to incorporate this proletariat into the national existence" (*ibid.*, p. 217).

The programs of Latin American Christian Democratic parties differ from nation to nation. Some general comments may be made about the Chilean party, not because it is a "typical" Christian Democratic party but because of its political power. The Chilean Christian Democrats reject both capitalism and communism. They condemn capitalism as "merciless" and "degrading of human dignity" and brand communism as "totalitarian" and "undemocratic" (Bray 1965, p. 24).

They advocate a middle way, a "communitarian society," characterized by labor's involvement in management and ownership, and government action to prevent "economic concentration" (Sigmund 1963, p. 309). The 1963 Chilean Christian Democratic platform advocated a mixed economy, control of foreign investment, agrarian reform, and government reform. In the international sphere, the Chilean Christian Democrats desire to cooperate with the United States. At the same time, they insist that Latin America should have a stronger voice in world affairs and a broader range of international relations. Further, they urge the Latin American nations to cooperate among themselves. Frei is endeavoring to expand Chilean contacts with Europe. Also, he supports Latin American economic integration and is urging the creation of a common market for all of Latin America.

Theory and philosophy. As noted earlier, a large measure of the Christian Democratic ideology is drawn from European sources. In addition to Frei, Latin Americans who have contributed to the ideology include Jaime Castillo, Jacques Chonchol, Julio Silva, Máximo Pacheco Gómez, Bernardo Leighton, Radomiro Tomic, and Rafael Caldera.

Castroism. On New Year's Day, 1959, the Batista dictatorship in Cuba collapsed and Fidel Castro came to power. The victors, who had waged a guerrilla war since December 1956, were determined that "this was to be a thorough-going revolution. The institutions and groups which possessed sufficient power to block such a revolutionary course were to be neutralized and, if necessary, destroyed. Above all, the United States was not going to be able to impose limitations upon change" (Schneider 1964, pp. 27–28). And for the first time in Cuban history, a group of revolutionaries, after achieving power, began a full-scale social revolution instead of rewarding themselves with the spoils of government.

The program. A social revolution is a complex of actions. Only a few of the Cuban actions can be cited here.

The Agrarian Reform Law was passed just four months after Batista's fall. It had three objectives: to Cubanize and socialize the sugar industry, to give land to the landless, and to diversify agricultural production. The law provided for three types of holdings: state farms, sugar cooperatives (now scheduled to be converted into state farms), and small peasant properties. At present more than 70 per cent of the land is state owned.

Decrees during 1960 nationalized all large businesses, both Cuban and foreign. Since then additional businesses have been nationalized and a collective economy has emerged.

Beginning in 1962, emphasis was put on industrial expansion. However, after Castro's trip to Moscow in May 1963, Cuba accepted the principle of the international socialist division of labor, which led to a reversal of the revolution's original emphasis on agricultural diversification and industrialization (Hennessy 1964, p. 203). Now, as before 1959, emphasis is on sugar production.

Education has also received attention. An imaginative attack was made on adult illiteracy through the 1961 *alfabetismo* campaign. The public education system was reformed; teaching was nationalized; and private schools were suppressed. Emphasis in university education was placed on science and technology.

Evolution of Castroism. The Cuban revolution became a communist revolution. This statement is based on the view that "Castro was not a Communist for all practical purposes before he took power but decided to cast his lot with the Communists sometime afterward" (Draper 1965, p. 3).

Castro's "History Will Absolve Me" speech at his 1953 trial and the succeeding pamphlet provided the first insight into his objectives. He promised restoration of the 1940 constitution, a popularly elected government, and a relatively limited land reform program. "The most radical note in the speech . . . was perhaps a brief reference to the 'nationalization of the U.S.-owned electric and telephone companies'" (*ibid.*, p. 6). The "History Will Absolve Me" program was within the scope of traditional left-wing Cuban politics. The same judgment applies to the several pronouncements issued during the guerrilla war.

On December 2–3, 1961, Castro made his "I Am a Marxist–Leninist" speech. The speech was preceded by a host of actions indicating an increasing closeness between Castro and the communist bloc. Relations between Castro and the Cuban communists had not always been cordial; in the early 1950s they were strained. However, after Castro gained power, the communists not only supported him but also gave him the assistance of their trained cadres. At the same time Castro was gradually alienated from his moderate supporters, who consistently called for a slowing down of his efforts to turn society inside out (Burks 1963, p. 82).

With the "I Am a Marxist–Leninist" speech, Castroism obtained an ideology or philosophy. In and of itself Castroism was an armed struggle, not an ideology, and Castro gave very little attention to developing one for the movement. Rather, the movement borrowed or attached itself to existing ideologies and could change attachments (although it may no longer be able to do so).

Castro's identification with Marxism–Leninism put the Cuban revolution in a very different category from the other Latin American movements and led Castro to adopt means different from those used by the other movements. It also affected Cuban relations with the outside world. The identification with communism and the declared intention of exporting Castro-style revolutions have, more than anything else, made the United States and many Latin Americans hostile to Cuba.

Theory and philosophy. The numerous speeches and articles of Fidel Castro and his closest associates are the best source of the ideas or ideology of Castroism. Many of the speeches and articles have appeared in the Cuban periodicals *Cuba socialista, Revolución, Hoy,* and *Verde olivo.*

This article has focused on movements for relatively sharp reform or revolution. A more comprehensive treatment of significant political elements and groups would include an analysis of elements supporting the *status quo*, even though these elements perhaps do not constitute "movements." Hopefully, however, the article shows both the essence and the variation of the major twentieth-century Latin American political movements. In a very real sense, the essence is far greater than the variation. Furthermore, the movements, in their goals as well as in their means, resemble those found in other developing regions, and even the diversity of movements found in Latin America is similar to the diversity found in the new nations of Asia and Africa.

The ideas embodied in the twentieth-century movements stand in sharp contrast with the bulk of Latin America's nineteenth-century political thought. Nineteenth-century thought was nonindigenous, primarily imitative of European thought. The current movements are rooted in local social–economic–political conditions; hence, they are more realistic and practical as means of solving Latin American problems and restructuring Latin American society.

JAMES D. COCHRANE

[*See also* CARIBBEAN SOCIETY; CAUDILLISMO; MIDDLE AMERICAN SOCIETY; MODERNIZATION; REVOLUTION; SOCIAL MOVEMENTS; SOUTH AMERICAN SOCIETY.]

BIBLIOGRAPHY

ALEXANDER, ROBERT J. (1951) 1965 *The Perón Era.* New York: Russell.

BLANKSTEN, GEORGE I. 1953 *Perón's Argentina.* Univ. of Chicago Press.

BRAY, DONALD W. 1965 Chile Enters a New Era. *Current History* 48:21–25, 52.

BURKS, DAVID 1963 The Future of Castroism. *Current History* 44:78–83, 116.

CLINE, HOWARD F. (1953) 1963 *The United States and Mexico.* Rev. & enl. ed. New York: Atheneum; Cambridge, Mass.: Harvard Univ. Press.

CLINE, HOWARD F. (1962) 1963 *Mexico: Revolution to Evolution, 1940–1960.* New York: Oxford Univ. Press.

DAVIS, HAROLD E. 1958 Political Movements and Political Thought. Pages 94–118 in Harold E. Davis (editor), *Government and Politics in Latin America.* New York: Ronald.

DRAPER, THEODORE 1962 *Castro's Revolution: Myths and Realities.* New York: Praeger.

DRAPER, THEODORE 1965 *Castroism: Theory and Practice.* New York: Praeger.

EDELMANN, ALEXANDER T. 1965 *Latin American Government and Politics: The Dynamics of a Revolutionary Society.* Homewood, Ill.: Dorsey.

FITZGIBBON, RUSSELL H. (1954) 1966 *Uruguay: Portrait of a Democracy.* New York: Russell.

HENNESSY, C. A. M. 1964 Cuba: The Politics of Frustrated Nationalism. Pages 183–205 in Martin C. Needler (editor), *Political Systems of Latin America.* Princeton, N.J.: Van Nostrand.

JOHNSON, JOHN J. 1958 *Political Change in Latin America: The Emergence of the Middle Sectors.* Stanford Studies in History, Economics, and Political Science, Vol. 15. Stanford Univ. Press.

KANTOR, HARRY 1953 *The Ideology and Program of the Peruvian Aprista Movement.* California, University of, Publications in Political Science, Vol. 4, No. 1. Berkeley: Univ. of California Press.

LIPSET, SEYMOUR M. 1960 *Political Man: The Social Bases of Politics.* Garden City, N.Y.: Doubleday.

LOEWENSTEIN, KARL (1942) 1944 *Brazil Under Vargas.* New York: Macmillan.

NEEDLER, MARTIN C. 1964 Mexico: Revolution as a Way of Life. Pages 1–33 in Martin C. Needler (editor), *Political Systems of Latin America.* Princeton, N.J.: Van Nostrand.

PIKE, FREDERICK B. (editor) 1964 *The Conflict Between Church and State in Latin America.* New York: Knopf. → See especially Part 3, dealing with Roman Catholic social action and Christian democracy.

ROSS, STANLEY R. 1963 Mexico: Cool Revolution and Cold War. *Current History* 44:89–94, 116–117.

SCHNEIDER, RONALD M. 1964 Five Years of Cuban Revolution. *Current History* 46:26–33.

SCOTT, ROBERT E. (1959) 1964 *Mexican Government in Transition.* Rev. ed. Urbana: Univ. of Illinois Press.

SIGMUND, PAUL E. (editor) 1963 *The Ideologies of the Developing Nations.* New York: Praeger.

SILVERT, KALMAN H. 1963 The Costs of Anti-nationalism: Argentina. Pages 347–372 in American Universities Field Staff, *Expectant Peoples: Nationalism and Development.* Edited by Kalman H. Silvert. New York: Random House.

SZULC, TAD 1965 Communists, Socialists, and Christian Democrats. American Academy of Political and Social Science, *Annals* 360:99–103.

LATIN SQUARES

See EXPERIMENTAL DESIGN.

LAUDERDALE, JAMES MAITLAND

James Maitland, eighth earl of Lauderdale, (1759–1839) was a product of the famous Scottish educational system that flourished in the second half of the eighteenth century. He was a pupil of the great John Millar, of whom it was said that "to hear his lectures . . . students resort hither (i.e., to Glasgow) from all quarters of Britain." Among his contemporaries in Glasgow and Edinburgh Lauderdale numbered James Mill, Sydney Smith, Francis Jeffrey, Thomas Chalmers, Francis Horner, and Henry Brougham—to name but a few members of that amazing generation. Politically he allied himself with the Whig opposition to Pitt, a policy that long kept him from high government office, an honor he would without doubt have achieved had he been of the government party. Following his teacher he was a staunch defender of democratic principles at a time when the holocaust of the French Revolution encouraged an extreme reaction in England. However, it would be a mistake to place Lauderdale in the radical tradition; he advocated limited democracy, and he lived to oppose—in a rather inexplicable *volte face*—the moderate innovations suggested in the 1832 Reform Bill.

Lauderdale has a rightful place in the history of economics, although not perhaps as a major figure. This is a position comparatively recently achieved and is a consequence, as with so many reevaluations in the history of economics, of quite recent developments in economic analysis.

Lauderdale's most original contributions are to be found in his *Inquiry Into the Nature and Origin of Public Wealth* (1804). The frame of reference for this work is Adam Smith's *Wealth of Nations*, and in an important sense Lauderdale's *Inquiry* may be regarded as a commentary on Smith's classic. It is important to remember this when considering Lauderdale's position in the development of economic thought. Lauderdale is often regarded as being in basic opposition to the orthodox English classical school and as representing an entirely separate, although contemporary, stream of development. While there is an element of truth in this, Lauderdale's work should not be considered too far outside the mainstream of economic thought: he did have certain criticisms of Smith's orthodoxy, but in terms of policy—the belief in the competitive order and the minimization of interference with economic systems—Lauderdale was part of the classical school.

The central theme of the *Inquiry*—the nature of relations between individual and public well-being—is not as pathbreaking as Lauderdale thought. He was worried by the fact that a rise in total spending on a commodity might be accompanied by a decline in the physical volume of purchases. We would now consider the problem in terms of index numbers of output. Lauderdale, however, was forced to consider it in terms of the demand schedule and what is now called the elasticity of the schedule, and did so in a way that was highly sophisticated for the time. His emphasis on the role of utility in the determination of relative prices places him much more with the subjective school (Condillac, Say, A. Walras, S. Bailey) than with the classical writers.

Lauderdale also applied his analysis to the question of overproduction. He argued, in opposition to the central classical position—often described as a belief in Say's Law—that saving could, nationally, be carried too far and result in an over-all excess supply of goods. It is for this reason that some contemporary economists, like Alvin Hansen or H. L. McCracken, consider Lauderdale as an early forerunner of Keynes. This is a mistaken view: since Lauderdale assumed the equality of *planned* saving and investment, oversaving was for him the mere production of capital equipment. This is certainly not what is normally understood as the Keynesian dilemma of capitalism. However, it must be acknowledged that when Lauderdale applied his analysis to the economic effects of national debt policy he came very close to a modern understanding of the question.

Lauderdale also wrote on monetary questions and gave an early statement of the bullionist position in *Thoughts on the Alarming State of the Circulation and on the Means of Redressing the Pecuniary Grievances in Ireland* (1805). Later on he defended the Bullion Report—he was a member of the committee that prepared it—and pressed for the early resumption of cash payments. Rather paradoxically, he combined these orthodox monetary views with vivid fears of underconsumption.

BERNARD CORRY

[*For the historical context of Lauderdale's work, see the biography of* SMITH, ADAM; *for much later development of his ideas, see* INCOME AND EMPLOYMENT THEORY *and* UTILITY.]

WORKS BY LAUDERDALE

(1804) 1819 *An Inquiry Into the Nature and Origin of Public Wealth, and Into the Means and Causes of Its Increase.* 2d ed., enl. Edinburgh: Constable.

1805 *Thoughts on the Alarming State of the Circulation and on the Means of Redressing the Pecuniary Grievances in Ireland.* London: Longman; Edinburgh: Constable.

(1829) 1965 *Three Letters to the Duke of Wellington, on the Fourth Report of the Select Committee of the House of Commons, Appointed in 1828 to Enquire Into the Public Income and Expenditure of the United Kingdom.* New York: Kelley.

SUPPLEMENTARY BIBLIOGRAPHY

CANNAN, EDWIN (1893) 1953 *A History of the Theories of Production and Distribution in English Political Economy From 1776 to 1848.* 3d ed. London and New York: Staples.

CORRY, B. A. 1962 *Money, Saving and Investment in English Economics, 1800–1850.* New York: Macmillan.

PAGLIN, MORTON 1961 *Malthus and Lauderdale: The Anti-Ricardian Tradition.* New York: Kelley.

LAUNHARDT, WILHELM

Carl Friedrich Wilhelm Launhardt (1832–1918) was by training and profession a transportation engineer, but he is now remembered chiefly for his pioneer work in the application of mathematical techniques to economic problems. He lived and worked virtually all his life in Hanover, Germany, as professor of highway, railroad, and bridge construction at the Polytechnical College. He received an honorary engineering doctorate in 1903 from the Institute of Technology at Dresden in recognition of basic work done on the technical and economic problems of transportation, in particular, of railroads. Not all his economic thinking was original, of course; on questions of capital and interest, for example, his ideas in general followed those of Léon Walras and Stanley Jevons. But he made important contributions to welfare economics, to pricing policies for public utilities, to industrial-location and market-area analysis, and to transportation-engineering economics in the narrow sense as well as doing original work on the labor-supply function (1885, pp. 88–97).

Welfare economics. Much of Launhardt's writing in the area of welfare economics, although embedded in price theory, often delves into side areas that anticipate recent developments. For instance, his treatment of "repeated exchange" and "exchange with continually changing prices" in its dependence on the number of market participants (1885, pp. 35–53) foreshadows the basic theme, if not the results, of Oskar Morgenstern's demand theory (1948) rather than being simply a version of Walrasian *tâtonnement.*

Knut Wicksell (1901) implied that Launhardt had supplied a pseudo proof of the proposition that pure, perfect competition leads to the greatest social income. However, Launhardt explicitly disagreed with this proposition; in fact, in criticism of Walras, he branded such a conclusion as a "grave error" (1885, pp. 27–33, 42–44).

Public utility pricing policies. Launhardt's analysis of railroad costing and pricing (e.g., 1885, pp. 189–205), while in the spirit of Walras and Jevons, has been acclaimed for its originality and clarity. His analysis is marred by the spurious definiteness that results from his assumption of specific function forms. He opposed private ownership of railroads, since he favored marginal-cost pricing and differential freight rates, and believed that overhead costs should be paid out of general taxation in a manner dictated by over-all fiscal policies. Similar studies had been done both by Jules Dupuit and by Émile Cheysson and Clément Colson. The latter two were contemporaries of Launhardt's and, like him, combined engineering with economics.

Industrial location and market area. In the words of Walter Isard (1956, pp. 143, 160), Launhardt "presented the first significant treatment of industrial location theory" and "the earliest systematic treatment of the division of the market-area among competing firms" (see Launhardt 1885, pp. 149–214). Although Johann Heinrich von Thünen had previously discussed industrial location, varying the circumstances more than Launhardt was to do, still Launhardt's location theories contain the germs of ideas later developed by Alfred Weber, Tord Palander, and more recent theorists. For example, he sketched the pole principle: a geometric construction for finding locational equilibrium points (Isard 1956, pp. 254–287). In the Launhardt–Hotelling problem, however, Launhardt did not simultaneously vary price and location; that remained for Harold Hotelling (1929) to do.

Transportation-engineering economics. In the field of transportation-engineering economics, which lay closer to his main occupation, Launhardt investigated such matters as the influence of gradients and curves on railroad operating costs (1877) and the location-dependent "rentability" of highways and railroads.

EBERHARD M. FELS

[*For the historical context of Launhardt's work, see the biographies of* JEVONS; THÜNEN; WALRAS; *for discussion of the subsequent development of his ideas, see* SPATIAL ECONOMICS; WELFARE ECONOMICS; *and the biography of* WEBER, ALFRED.]

WORKS BY LAUNHARDT

1877 Die Betriebskosten der Eisenbahnen in ihrer Abhängigkeit von den Steigungs- und Krümmungsverhältnissen der Bahn. Supplement to Volume 4 of Edmund Heusinger von Waldegg (editor), *Handbuch für specielle Eisenbahn-technik.* Leipzig: Engelmann.

1882 Die Bestimmung des zweckmässigsten Standortes einer gewerblichen Anlage. *Zeitschrift des Vereines deutscher Ingenieure* 26: cols. 105–116.

1885 *Mathematische Begründung der Volkswirthschaftslehre.* Leipzig: Engelmann.

SUPPLEMENTARY BIBLIOGRAPHY

HOTELLING, HAROLD 1929 Stability in Competition. *Economic Journal* 39:41–57.

ISARD, WALTER 1956 *Location and Space-economy: A General Theory Relating to Industrial Location, Market Areas, Trade and Urban Structure.* Cambridge, Mass.: Technology Press of M.I.T.; New York: Wiley.

MORGENSTERN, OSKAR 1948 Demand Theory Reconsidered. *Quarterly Journal of Economics* 62:165–201.

SCHNEIDER, ERICH 1959 Wilhelm Launhardt. Volume 6, pages 533–534 in *Handwörterbuch der Sozialwissenschaften.* Stuttgart (Germany): Fischer.

WICKSELL, KNUT (1901) 1951 *Lectures on Political Economy.* Volume 1: General Theory. London: Routledge. → Translated from the third Swedish edition.

LAW

The articles under this heading deal mainly with the study of law, and with the relationship between law and society, as do also JURISPRUDENCE; LEGAL REASONING; PSYCHIATRY, *article on* FORENSIC PSYCHIATRY; PUBLIC LAW. *The articles listed under* LEGAL SYSTEMS *discuss and compare the major modern systems. Other branches of the law are dealt with in* ADMINISTRATIVE LAW; CANON LAW; CRIMINAL LAW; CONFLICT OF LAWS; CONSTITUTIONAL LAW; INTERNATIONAL LAW; MILITARY LAW. *The creation of law and its relations with political institutions are discussed in* ADJUDICATION; CONFLICT OF INTERESTS; JUDICIAL PROCESS; JUDICIARY; LEGISLATION; POLITICAL JUSTICE. *Relevant to the development of modern jurisprudence are the biog-*

raphies of AUSTIN; BLACKSTONE; BRANDEIS; CARDOZO; COKE; DUGUIT; EHRLICH; FRANK; GIERKE; GROTIUS; HAMILTON, WALTON H.; HAURIOU; HOLMES; JELLINEK; KANTOROWICZ; KELSEN; LLEWELLYN; MAINE; MAITLAND; MOORE; JOHN BASSETT; POUND; RADBRUCH; SAVIGNY; SCHMITT; VATTEL. *For a discussion of law and related problems in preliterate societies see* POLITICAL ANTHROPOLOGY; SANCTIONS.

I
THE SOCIOLOGY OF LAW

The broad aim of legal sociology is the extension of knowledge regarding the foundations of a legal order, the pattern of legal change, and the contribution of law to the fulfillment of social needs and aspirations. The special interest of sociology in these matters rests on the basic assumption that law and legal institutions both affect and are affected by the social conditions that surround them.

Within sociology, the study of law touches a number of well-established areas of inquiry. In criminology attention is given to the changing character of penal law, the assumptions upon which it rests, and the social dynamics of law enforcement and corrections. The sociology of law shares with political sociology a concern for the nature of legitimate authority and social control, the social bases of constitutionalism, the evolution of civic rights, and the relation of public and private spheres.

The roots of legal sociology lie mainly in jurisprudence rather than in the autonomous work of sociologists. In legal theory a "sociological school" emerged out of the work of such jurists as Rudolf von Jhering, Oliver Wendell Holmes, Léon Duguit, Eugen Ehrlich, and Roscoe Pound, all of whom felt the need to look beyond the traditional confines of legal scholarship. The sociologists Émile Durkheim, Max Weber, E. A. Ross, and W. G. Sumner, among others, contributed to the development of a sociological orientation among students of jurisprudence, in some cases by direct influence on legal writers such as Duguit and Pound.

Historical perspectives

Four basic motifs have been prominent in the intellectual history of legal sociology: historicism, instrumentalism, antiformalism, and pluralism.

Historicism. Historicism emphasizes the tracing of legal ideas and institutions to their historical roots; patterns of legal evolution are seen as unplanned outcomes of the play of social forces. Important illustrations of this approach are Henry Maine's *Ancient Law*, Oliver Wendell Holmes's *Common Law*, and the treatments of legal typologies and evolution in Émile Durkheim's *Division of Labor in Society* (1893) and various writings by Max Weber (see especially 1922*a*). The historicist emphasis has had two implicit objectives. First, historical study is a way of identifying legal anachronisms, especially in the reasoning behind a received rule or concept. Second, the analysis of an underlying historical trend (e.g., Maine's thesis regarding the movement of "progressive societies" from status to contract) can provide an illuminating context for the interpretation of contemporary issues.

Instrumentalism. The instrumentalist approach, associated with the names of Jeremy Bentham and Rudolf von Jhering, among nineteenth-century writers, as well as Roscoe Pound, calls for the assessment of law according to defined social purposes. It thus invites close study of what the law is and does in fact. The chief significance of instrumentalism is that it encourages the incorporation of social knowledge into law. For if laws are instruments, they must be open to interpretation and revision in the light of changing circumstances. Moreover, law is seen as having more than one function; not only is it a vehicle for maintaining public order and settling disputes, but it also facilitates voluntary transactions and arrangements, confers political legitimacy, promotes education and civic participation, and helps to define social aspirations.

Antiformalism. Sociological jurisprudence has gained much of its vitality from attacks upon the "unrealistic" nature of legal rules and concepts. A jurisprudence that emphasizes the purity of law as a formal system is fallible on two counts. First, legal rules are necessarily abstract and general; there is always a considerable gap between a system of general rules and its implementation, if only because the rules are applied by human agencies that have their own interests and problems. Second, any view of the legal order as an isolated system wrongly detaches it from the environment in which it is implicated. Failure to take account of the historical and cultural forces impinging upon the law not only distorts reality but gives the legal order an excessive dignity, insulates it from criticism, and offers society inadequate leverage for change. In pressing its criticism of legal abstractions, the antiformalist approach leads readily to a derogation of the importance and effectiveness of legal norms.

While antiformalism is congenial to an instrumentalist assessment of the legal tradition, it is out of sympathy with the more narrowly utilitarian image of man as an isolated, goal-seeking actor guided by a hedonic calculus. Instead, it encourages a fuller awareness of the *nonrational* springs of action, of human dependency on social support, and of the emergence of social systems that have a viability of their own. The antiformalist theme is prominent in the work of Eugen Ehrlich and of the American legal realists, but almost every analyst of the social or psychological foundations of law has struck the same note, albeit with varying emphasis.

Pluralism. In the history of legal sociology, "pluralism" refers to the view that law is located "in society"—that is, beyond the official agencies of government. Sociological skepticism of state law has led some legal scholars, notably Ehrlich, to deny that law is solely or even mainly made by government. Ehrlich held that law is endemic in custom and social organization; it is in the actual regularities of group life that we find the "living law." In context, this approach is more than an appeal to bring law into closer relation with social practice; it is an assertion that *authoritative* legal materials are to be found in the realities of group life. In other words, it questions the claim of the state to be the sole receptacle of legal authority.

The pluralist motif was further enhanced by the central place Ehrlich gave to the "inner order of associations" as a font of law; here his work recalls Otto von Gierke's treatment of the law of associations. Gierke stressed the reality of the autonomous collectivity, and in doing so he criticized not only the atomistic view of society and legal order as based upon individual will but also the legal notion of the association as a juridical fiction. Related ideas are found in the writings of Maurice Hauriou, who sought a legal reality in "the institution"—that is, in the association or enterprise (private as well as public) that has its own established authority and appropriate procedures.

The sociological approach. These intellectual tendencies have helped open up the boundaries of the legal order. They have enlarged the relevance of nonlegal ideas and findings to law and legal reasoning. On the other hand, they have had the common outcome of downgrading formal legal systems as significant social realities. In an important sense, the sociological school has been antilegal. It has sought to put law in its place by emphasizing the primacy of the social context and by seeking "the legal" outside of its conventional sphere. In so doing, the sociological perspective runs the risk of dissolving the concept of law into the broader concepts of social control and social order; the idea of a "living law," encompassing all the regularities of group life, offers no touchstone for the distinctively legal. Whatever the merits of the sociological school in having called attention to the need for a more realistic jurisprudence, the failure to offer a theory of the distinctively legal has been its cardinal weakness.

The distinctively legal

According to Max Weber, the distinctively legal emerges when "there exists a 'coercive apparatus,' i.e., that there are one or more persons whose special task it is to hold themselves ready to apply specially provided means of coercion (legal coercion) for the purpose of norm enforcement" ([1922*a*] 1954, p. 13). In other words, a legal norm is known by the probability that it will be enforced by a specialized staff. Thus Weber offers an operational definition of law that is meant to exclude all value judgments in the assessment of what is or is not law. Although he emphasizes coercion, Weber is careful to point out that the threat of physical force is not essential to legal action, for coercion may consist in the threat of public reprimand or boycott. Thus Weber's definition does not limit law to the political community; it allows for "extrastate" law, such as ecclesiastical law or the law of any other corporate group that is binding on its own members.

Weber's approach does have a certain rough utility, and it has the special virtue of being general enough to encourage the study of law in private associations. However, he offers no satisfactory theoretical ground for identifying the requirements of a legal order as he does. The availability of a specialized staff for the enforcement of norms may be highly correlated with the existence of a legal order and thus may serve as a reliable *indicator* of norms that have been selected for special treatment. However, it does not follow that this is what basically distinguishes legal from nonlegal norms and institutions.

Authoritative norms. An adequate theory of law must identify the distinctive *work done* by law in society, the special *resources* of law, and the characteristic *mechanisms* that law brings into play. In the quest for such a theory, little is gained from formulas that place coercive enforcement of norms at the center of legal experience. The key word in the discussion of law is *authority*, not coercion. The fundamental problems of jurisprudence stem from the puzzles and ambiguities associated with identifying the sources of authoritative rules, the authoritative application of rules, and the nature of authoritative change in existing rules.

Although the legal requirement of paying a tax certainly has some connection with the coercive consequences of refusal to pay, the character of the obligation is more decisive. A tax is *illegal* if it violates an authoritative order, and it is *nonlegal* if it lacks appropriate authority, regardless of whether the probability of coercion exists. Hence legality presumes the emergence of authoritative norms whose status as such is "guaranteed" by evidence of other, consensually validated, rules.

H. L. A. Hart has argued that, in stepping "from the pre-legal to the legal world," a society develops special rules for curing the defects of a social order based on unofficial norms (1961, p. 91). A regime of unofficial norms has a number of inherent limitations, including the difficulty of resolving uncertainties as to the existence or scope of a norm. No criterion or procedure is available for settling such issues. The distinctively legal emerges with the development of "secondary rules," that is, rules of authoritative determination. These rules, selectively applied, raise up the unofficial norms and give them a legal status.

The elementary legal act is this appeal from an *asserted* rule, however coercively enforced, to a *justifying* rule. This presumes at least a dim awareness that some reason lies behind the impulse to conform; furthermore this reason is founded not in conscience, habit, or fear alone but rather in the decision to uphold an authoritative order. The rule of legal recognition may be quite blunt and crude: The law is what the king or priest says it is. But this initial reference of a historically given social norm to a more general ground of obligation breeds the complex elaboration of authoritative rules that marks a developed legal order.

Resources of legal institutions. The special work of law is to identify claims and obligations that merit official validation or enforcement. This may consist of nothing more than the establishment of a public record invested with a special claim upon the community's respect as a guide to action. When institutions emerge that do this work we can speak of a legal order. These institutions need not be specialized, and they may have no resources for coercive enforcement; it is essential only that their determinations affecting rights and duties are accepted as authoritative.

An authoritative act asserts a claim to obedience, and the reach of that claim determines whether and to what extent a legal system exists. Although a weak legal order rests on a narrow base of consent, it may be able to mobilize very large resources of intimidation and thus command wide, if grudging, submission. A strong legal order is the product of a more substantial consensus and summons more willing obedience; it is correspondingly less dependent on the machinery of coercion. There is thus an important difference between the strength of a *regime* and the strength of a *legal order*, although the sheer persistence of the former may greatly influence acceptance for its claim to speak with authority. Of course, coercion is an important and often indispensable *resource* for law, but so are education, symbolism, and the appeal to reason. Coercion does not make law, though it may indeed establish an order out of which law may emerge.

In much of his work Max Weber saw quite clearly the intimate relation of the legal and the authoritative. For example, his theory of authority and legitimacy contrasts the charismatic, the traditional, and the "rational legal," thus placing law in a context of evolving forms of authority (1922*b*, pp. 328 ff. in 1947 edition). In this analysis Weber views fully developed law as a system of governance by rules; he sees the distinctively legal obligation as a component of an impersonal order that exhibits a strain toward rationality. Thus when Weber actually used the concept of law, especially in his theory of bureaucracy, he greatly modified the significance of coercion.

Social foundations of legality

The view of law just sketched highlights the place of authority, consensus, and rationality in the legal order. In a developed legal order, authority transcends coercion, accepts the restraints of reason, and contributes to a public consensus regarding the foundations of civic obligation. To the extent that law is "the enterprise of subjecting human conduct to the governance of rules" (Fuller 1964, p. 106), it can be said that law aims at a moral achievement; the name of that achievement is *legality* or "the rule of law." Its distinctive contribution is a progressive reduction of the arbitrary element in positive law and its administration.

As an intellectual discipline, the sociology of law has a far broader compass than the study of "the requirements of justice which lawyers term principles of legality" (Hart 1961, p. 202). Not every society gives equal weight to the ideal of "control by rule" as against other ideals; and there is much else to be said about law in society. Still, law is so intimately associated with the realization of these special values that study of "the rule of law" must be a chief preoccupation of legal sociology. Indeed, a considerable amount of contemporary research, as we shall note below, falls within this topic.

The sociological study of legality presumes that the potential of law for realizing values is at best unevenly fulfilled. Legal decision making is carried on by living men in living institutions, who are subject to all the external pressures and constraints and all the inner sources of recalcitrance that frustrate the embodiment of abstract ideals in action. At the same time, some patterns of group life are more congenial than others to the rule of law. To discover which social conditions are congenial to the rule of law and which undermine it, and in what ways, is the main task of scientific inquiry in this field. Four topics provide a framework in which research on legality can be pursued: the transition from legitimacy to legality; rational consensus and civic competence; institutionalized criticism; and institutionalized self-restraint. While these topics are suggested by the experience of the Western world, their relevance is universal.

Legitimacy and legality. The existence of legality presumes that the power exercised by public officials is "legitimate" power. This means that an appeal is made to some principle as a source of right—the right to dispose of community resources in a certain way and especially the right to issue orders and enforce them. Many different principles of legitimacy are possible—for example, divine will, democratic election, private property, hereditary succession, seniority, and special competence. What principle of legitimacy will be accepted depends on the nature of the group, its cultural heritage, and special historical circumstances. To trace the rise and decline of various principles of legitimacy is to touch on major themes of political and social history.

Legitimate power tends to be restrained. It is inherent in legitimacy that the will of the ruler, including the majority will of a democratic assembly, is not completely free. Nevertheless, many regimes properly classified as legitimate retain a very large amount of arbitrary rule. Legitimacy is only a first step toward legality. It can begin in a quite primitive fashion, meaning little more than unconscious acceptance of another's authority because he is thought to have communication with the gods or special magical powers or because he belongs to a noble family. Authority is primitive when power is legitimated by no more than a historically given public sentiment supporting a claim to rightful rule.

But legitimacy carries the lively seed of legality, implanted by the principle that the exercise of power must be justified. From this it is but a step to the view that reasons must be given to defend official acts. Reasons invite evaluation, and evaluation requires the development of public standards. At the same time, implicit in the fundamental norm that reasons should be given is the conclusion that where reasons are defective, authority is to that extent weakened and even invalidated.

The transition from legitimacy to legality requires the recognition that official acts can be questioned and appraised. The test is not whether the ruler is wise or good but whether his acts are justified by an explicit or implied grant of power. Most important, *legality goes beyond a gross justification of the right to hold office;* it gains strength and focus in proportion as the criterion of legitimacy is used to decide whether particular acts meet public standards of validity. For example, if conservation of natural resources is the purported foundation of rule making by a government agency, then that publicly acknowledged objective becomes available as a basis for criticizing specific rules and decisions.

Clearly some principles of legitimacy are more competent than others to sustain the ideal of legality. If power is justified on the basis of tradition, proprietorship, kinship, or hereditary succession, it is difficult to find the leverage for continuous, reasoned criticism. When prescriptive right gives way to an abstract principle, as in the case of justification by popular will, social utility, trusteeship, or even divine right, then the principle of legitimacy can be analyzed and acts assessed. The way is then open for an appeal to reason.

Rational consensus and civic competence. Legality requires that the principles of legitimacy be firmly established in the community's habits of thought; hence the study of both the content and the *quality* of consensus has a special bearing on the social bases of the rule of law. Strictly speaking, there can be no purely rational consensus. However, it may be approximated under two related conditions: if the historically given, nonrational sentiments are themselves supportive of rational conduct, for example, when received modes of apprehending man and society encourage self-restraint and tolerance of ambiguity; and if there is broad opportunity for the emergence of a public opinion founded in the free play of interests and ideas. In other words, rational consensus presupposes a genuine public opinion rather than agreement based on manipulation, withholding of information, or unmitigated appeals to tradition.

Whatever contributes to rational consensus provides social support for legality. Decision making in the light of legality requires the continuous exercise of discriminating judgment, especially in the balancing of values, the elaboration of defensible rules, and the application of abstract principles to changing circumstances. While this work is largely carried on by a relatively small group of professionals, the capacity of the professionals to sustain and extend the ideals of legality depends on a parallel development of the public mind. The legal profession itself is not immune to influences that may undermine its commitment to the rule of law.

The consensus that sustains legality entails deepened public understanding of the complex meaning of freedom under law. This goes beyond passive belief or even commitment. It is an extension of civic competence—the competence to participate effectively in a legal order. This is manifested, for example, in an increased capacity to be patient with procedural niceties in the face of a desire to punish, to exercise impartial judgment, and to use principles of criticism against even the most favored leaders of government.

In a vital legal order something more is wanted than submission to law. A military establishment places very great emphasis on obedience to lawful commands, yet such a setting is hardly a model of the development of legality. So, too, a conception of law as the manifestation of awesome authority encourages a posture of submission and is fully compatible with arbitrary rule. In a community that aspires to a high order of legality obedience to law is not submissive compliance. The obligation to obey the law should be closely tied to the defensibility of the rules themselves and of the official decisions that enforce them.

Institutionalized criticism. If the ideals of legality are to be fulfilled, the capacity to generate and sustain reasoned criticism of the rules and of official discretion must be built into the machinery of lawmaking and administration. To this end, the Anglo–American legal tradition has relied heavily upon the availability of counsel, upon the adversary concept of the legal process, and upon the freedom of the judiciary and other officials to adopt a critical stance toward received law, both statutory and judge-made.

Sociological research in this area confronts the ideals of due process with the realities of institutional life. For example, the availability of counsel may be limited for large sectors of the population; the independence and objectivity of officials may be weakened by their social origins and commitments; and limitations of competence and resources may inhibit the judiciary from effective criticism of rule making in private and public agencies. The possibility of effective criticism may largely depend upon the availability of *group* resources. The lone individual seeking justice—especially if he is poor and if his claim is subject to routine processing—has little opportunity to press for new interpretations of law or of administrative regulations. Group-based counsel, on the other hand, can develop specialized expertise as well as work out a strategy for legal change.

In the Anglo–American tradition, the adversary principle has a special place as a vehicle of institutionalized criticism. It lends legitimacy to partisan advocacy within the legal process, allowing and even encouraging the zealous pursuit of special interest by means of self-serving interpretations of law and evidence. The assumptions underlying the adversary principle have not been fully analyzed or tested, nor have variations or functional surrogates in other societies been adequately studied. Moreover, there is evidence that partisan advocacy is weakened by certain factors that are becoming increasingly common in "administered" societies. Among these are the commitment of tribunals to a positive outcome, as in family conciliation proceedings; reliance on experts and investigators who serve the court directly; the mandate to temper justice with treatment, as in juvenile hearings; and the routine handling of a large number of cases.

No doubt these new problems and contexts will lessen reliance on the adversary principle in some areas; more important, however, will be the development of new forms of advocacy and critical dialogue. Administrative agencies, both criminal and civil, are increasingly recognized as active centers for making laws and dispensing justice, although the visibility of such decisions is often quite low. Sociological study of organizations can trace the actual course of decision making and can identify the opportunities available, within the social structure of the agency, for increasing the visibility of decisions and developing new forms of institutionalized criticism.

Institutionalized self-restraint. Every officer of the law—policeman, president, legislator, attorney, judge, licensing commissioner, draft board member—is in some degree a magistrate. He exercises discretion and thereby affects the rights of citizens. The rule of law requires that this discretion be restrained, yet it also asks for independent judgments in the assessment of fact, the assignment of moral culpability, and the application of legal rules to particular circumstances. To achieve restrained discretion, more is needed than criticism of authority and pressure upon it. The system depends heavily on *self*-restraint and thus on social mechanisms for building in appropriate values and rules of conduct.

Historically, legal self-restraint has been supported by public consensus on the nature and limits of authority, professionalization of lawyers and other officials, and the evolution of clearly defined roles, such as that of the judge. But there is considerable variation in that achievement, and under modern conditions there is a need for more attention to the *organizational* sources of self-restraint as distinguished from mechanisms of socialization. Ethical conduct is mainly found in settings that nourish and sustain it, that is, where such conduct makes sense for the official in the light of the realistic problems he faces. To design such settings is properly the chief aim of the architect of legal institutions. As applied to the legal profession, this principle has been documented in a recent study of the New York City bar (Carlin 1966).

Law and social change

The preceding discussion of the social foundations of legality emphasizes the conditions that strengthen or weaken the rule of law. The same problem may be approached historically, placing the evolution of legality in a context of broad social change and relating it to the development of other social institutions, including culturally defined conceptions of authority and justice. Thus Max Weber was interested in the emergence of rationality as a principle of organization and decision making; he saw rationality as the key to modernization and traced its effects in many fields, including law.

In modern Western society the extension of legality to new institutions and settings occurs mainly *within* government, encompassing wider circles of officials and agencies, subjecting more decisions to review, and raising the standard of what constitutes fair procedure. The Scandinavian ombudsman, an official to whom the citizen can appeal directly when he feels wronged by a government agency, is a symbol of the demand for new modes of redress against a large and opaque government apparatus. Also evident is a tentative movement toward legal restraint of arbitrary decision in nongovernmental institutions, especially those that serve a general public, such as colleges, trade unions, and large business firms. These developments, fostered in large measure by the work of associations formed to advance group interests, reflect a growing public sensitivity to legal rights. The legal profession itself, both by scholarship and by the official statements of its professional organizations, has contributed to the critical assessment of official procedures. Nor should it be overlooked that modern organizations, as part of their greater effectiveness and rationality, have an increased capacity to support the machinery of due process.

There is, however, an underlying conflict between administration and legality. In the first place, procedural safeguards are costly in time, energy, and the risk that action will be inhibited. In the United States, for instance, the police must carry out their traditional tasks of surveillance and apprehension subject to many new legal rulings affecting search, arrest, and detention. Any organization that has a job to do, yet must meet standards of fairness, faces this tension. Second, an official who is preoccupied with the fair application of general rules—equal treatment under law—finds it difficult to deal with each problem or case on its merits, taking account of special circumstances and needs and adapting policies to desired outcomes. The modern quest, and one that requires much supportive research, is for variable standards of fairness, embodying basic principles of procedural justice with due regard for the distinctive needs of specialized institutions and programs.

Incipient law. The antiformalist posture of legal sociology has encouraged interest in the problem-solving practices and spontaneous orderings of business or family life. While this approach has tended to depreciate formal law, in principle it just as easily supports an emphasis on the *emergence* of formal law out of the realities of group life. Incipient law is implicit in the way in which public sentiment develops or in any increasingly stabilized pattern of organization; it refers to a compelling claim of right or a practice so viable and so important to a functioning institution as to make legal recognition in due course highly probable. Thus some of the private arrangements worked out in collective bargaining agreements, especially seniority rights and protection against arbitrary dismissal, may be seen as incipient law. However, the location of incipient law cannot rest solely on the prevalence of a practice or even the urgency of a claim; two parallel assessments are required. First, the social viability of the practice in question—its functional significance for group life and especially for new institutional forms—must be considered. Second, the contemporary evolution of relevant legal principles must be assessed to see whether the new norm can be absorbed within the received but changing legal tradition.

A focus on incipient legal change bridges the concepts of law and social order without confounding the two; it assumes that law does indeed have its distinctive nature, however much it may rely on social support or be responsible to social change. On the other hand, some law is seen as *latent* in the evolving social and economic order. For example, the trend toward strict liability for harm caused by defects in manufactured goods (weakening or eliminating the need to prove negligence) reflects changing technology, both in manufacture and distribution, as well as the increased capacity of large firms to absorb the attendant costs either by increasing productivity or by passing them on to the general public. Similarly, the growing importance of large-scale organizations carries with it the likelihood that new claims of right will emerge, based upon a new perception of organizational membership as a protectable status.

Law as a vehicle of social change. For the most part, legal sociology has viewed law as a passive rather than active agent in social change. Law "responds" to new circumstances and pressures. However, especially in recent years the great social effects of legal change have been too obvious to ignore. The question is no longer whether law is a significant vehicle of social change but rather *how* it so functions and what special problems arise.

One way of approaching these problems is to consider the relative significance for social change of *legislation*, *administration*, and *common law*. Each has its special competence, and each has been dominant as a mode of change at different periods and in different branches of the law. In this context "common law" is not restricted to the Anglo–American legal tradition. Rather, it refers to any pattern of legal decision and evolution that relies on judicial creativity. Although this form of legal development is most explicitly recognized in what are called the "common-law" jurisdictions, in fact such creativity is inherent in the judicial process and plays an important part in the "code" jurisdictions of continental Europe (Friedmann [1944] 1960, pp. 483–486).

The common-law approach relies heavily upon tradition and the authority of the tribunal as sources of legitimacy. Judicial elaboration of abstract ideas, including reasoning by analogy, fits new departures into a received system of concepts and rules. "Realist" criticism of common-law concepts has sometimes overlooked this social function of abstractions. Legal ideas are indeed often distant from the realities of social practice, but their very generality is useful for making new adaptations while preserving a sense of continuity and therefore of legitimacy.

The common-law method of change is mainly piecemeal and gradual. It can safeguard a precarious consensus by avoiding radical or sweeping change and by relying on studied indirection rather than unambiguous confrontation. On the other hand, judges who have the authority to interpret a basic statute, such as a written constitution, can provide leadership in some branches of the law, as United States history has shown. In such a case, public commitment to the statute reinforces the legitimacy of judicial decision.

The great weakness of common-law empiricism is the difficulty of working out comprehensive attacks on new problems, such as urban land use, industrial accidents, or labor–management relations. The common-law approach seems to work best when basic policy is settled and the need is for refinement of distinctions and adaptation of the policy to new settings.

Legislation is the most obvious way of bringing political will to bear for the purpose of effecting social change through law. Unlike courts, which are tied to tradition, legislatures are commonly perceived as legitimate agencies for innovation; they can muster better means of inquiry, and they can create administrative agencies to execute and elaborate legislative policy.

There are important continuities, as well as tensions, in the relation between legislation and common law. Where these continuities and tensions occur, jurisprudential problems of law and social change arise. For example, a series of statutes can be viewed as creating a new "field" of law (such as labor law or welfare law), with the result that authoritative concepts and doctrines emerge which go beyond the letter of the statutes and form starting points for legal reasoning. This work of interpretation and elaboration, using a common-law perspective, is carried on by administrative agencies as well as courts. Its effect is to institutionalize the statutory policy.

Although politics and legislation are the basic *sources* of legal change in modern society, the administrative agency is a characteristic and potent *vehicle* of that change. It can summon material and human resources, including moral dedication and professional zeal, for turning legislative policy into social reality. An administrative agency can contribute to law by detailed rule making, its own adjudications, the patterned course of discretion it adopts, the practical effect it has on the social structure, and the initiative it may take in proposing statutory changes. However, agencies differ markedly in their capacity to influence law and society. Much depends on whether the agency conceives of itself as active or passive; this in turn reflects the nature of its special constituency, if any, as well as the newness and popular appeal of the program, the initial resources it is given, and the relations it may develop with other agencies. Some agencies are captives of their constituencies, including groups they are supposed to regulate, and contribute little to legal development.

Perhaps the most basic resource of the law for fostering and guiding social change is the set of legal principles that can be invoked to justify action in their name. This is especially true of constitutional principles that contain ideals of civic right. Such ideals are usually only imperfectly embodied in the operative rules of a given time and place. For long periods the gap between the legal ideal and the legal reality may be accepted with passivity and even good will, but social change may bring with it new opportunities for more perfect embodiment of the ideal in practice and a quickened awareness of this possibility. The result is twofold: Energy for social change is enlarged by a sense of legitimacy, and those who attempt to defend the *status quo* are made vulnerable and placed on the defensive. Thus law both contributes to rising expectations and may, in due course, provide vehicles for their realization.

Major trends. Several large-scale social changes have contributed to a vast increase in the tasks that must be assumed by a modern legal order. As kinship, fixed status, and community have declined as sources of social control, the drift has been toward a mass society marked by high rates of mobility, fragmented social experience, rising demands for short-run gratification, and more active participation by large numbers in hitherto insulated areas of social life. This trend has resulted in greatly increased pressure on formal agencies of regulation and service. A related development has been the emergence of the large organization as the representative institution of modern society; it depends upon, and also summons, mass participation in economic, political, and cultural life. A new "corporatism" brings with it many new problems for the law, including assessment of the social responsibilities of private associations, blurring of the distinction between private and public law, concern for the rights of association members, and regulation of competition and conflict when self-governing market mechanisms break down (Friedmann 1959).

A third significant trend has been the ascendance of social interests over parochial interests. The increasing interdependence of existence in modern society and correlative changes in values have weakened the claims of private interests and stimulated the quest for criteria of social worth. This is the foundation of what has been called the "socialization of law." As described by Pound (1959), the socialization of law is manifested in a growing tendency to impose limitations on the use and disposition of property, on freedom of contract, and on the power of creditors to exact satisfaction; in the movement toward liability without fault; and in many other legal rules and concepts. While this trend undermines the concept of the individual as a holder of abstract rights, it tends strongly to make the *person* an object of social and legal concern. This is reflected in much welfare legislation, which often begins as a way of solving a social problem and increasingly turns attention to the needs of persons.

Social research

Recent efforts to encourage the sociology of law have emphasized the need for empirical research and for a corresponding sense of relevance to contemporary social problems. The newer work is less interested in showing the limitations of law relative to other forms of social control than in bringing the expertise of social science to bear on the analysis of specific problems. It is likely that in the future legal sociology will be characterized by an affirmation of law rather than by a downgrading of it. This is especially true of research on the administration of justice. Studies of tribunals and other legal agencies may be narrowly concerned with efficient use of scarce resources, but they also tend to compare the ideal and the reality. As the "morality of law" (Fuller 1964) becomes a subject for empirical research, there will be a natural tendency to stress the contribution law can make to a moral order.

In line with this emphasis, much current research centers on social aspects of the administration of justice, as in studies of the jury (Kalven & Zeisel 1966; Simon 1967), patterns of law enforcement (Lindesmith 1965; Skolnick 1966), juvenile justice (Tappan 1947; Matza 1964), and the legal profession. Most of this work is normative as well as factual: It seeks out the conditions and processes that undermine or support procedural fairness and the recognition of basic rights. There is an implicit demand for fulfillment of legal ideals.

A more ambiguous attitude toward the moral significance of law is found in the sociology of deviance. Here the recent emphasis is on the law's role in *creating* deviance (Becker 1963). This occurs in two ways. First, the definition of what is "criminal" is a social process; and in borderline crimes, where consensus is weak, large numbers of people may find themselves classified as "criminals" as a result of political action by moralists. When this occurs, there is a strong tendency for illicit activity to continue, for that activity to take on more determinate criminal form, and for the quality of law enforcement to suffer. Second, a casual offender may be transformed into a committed deviant by the legal "processing" to which he is exposed, especially when he is systematically treated as a deviant and stigmatized as such. Under these circumstances law breeds illegality. The normative lesson is: To preserve the integrity of law it should be used with restraint in the control of personal conduct, especially where the specific harm is problematical and may be exceeded by the social costs of ineffective enforcement (Schur 1965).

Other research includes studies of public opinion and law (Cohen et al. 1958), legal forms and economic realities (Berle 1959; Macaulay 1963), judicial values and perspectives (Schubert 1960), the extension of legal or quasi-legal rights to members of "private governments," such as the large corporation (Eels 1962), and social history of legal ideas and institutions (Friedman 1965; Hall 1935; Hurst 1950; 1960; 1964). The comparative study of law and society is being stimulated by scholarly interest in the "developing" nations (Anderson 1963; Lev 1965), by the assessment of changes in communist society (Berman 1950; Hazard 1953; 1960), and by a marked tendency among some students of comparative law to take fuller account of social and political contexts (Von Mehren 1963).

The major problem of legal sociology remains the integration of jurisprudence and social research. Unless jurisprudential issues of the nature and functions of law, the relation of law and morals, the foundations of legality and fairness, and the role of social knowledge in law are addressed by modern investigators, the sociology of law can have only a peripheral intellectual importance.

PHILIP SELZNICK

BIBLIOGRAPHY

ANDERSON, JAMES N. D. (editor) 1963 *Changing Law in Developing Countries*. New York: Praeger.

ARENS, RICHARD; and LASSWELL, HAROLD D. 1961 *In Defense of Public Order: The Emerging Field of Sanction Law*. New York: Columbia Univ. Press.

BECKER, HOWARD S. 1963 *Outsiders: Studies in the Sociology of Deviance*. New York: Free Press.

BERGER, MORROE (1952) 1954 *Equality by Statute: Legal Controls Over Group Discrimination*. New York: Columbia Univ. Press.

BERLE, ADOLF A. 1959 *Power Without Property: A New Development in American Political Economy*. New York: Harcourt.

BERMAN, HAROLD J. (1950) 1963 *Justice in the U.S.S.R.: An Interpretation of Soviet Law*. Rev. & enl. ed. Cambridge, Mass.: Harvard Univ. Press. → First published as *Justice in Russia: An Interpretation of Soviet Law*.

CARLIN, JEROME E. 1962 *Lawyers on Their Own: A Study of Individual Practitioners in Chicago*. New Brunswick, N.J.: Rutgers Univ. Press.

CARLIN, JEROME E. 1966 *Lawyers' Ethics: A Survey of the New York City Bar*. New York: Russell Sage Foundation.

COHEN, JULIUS; ROBSON, REGINALD A. H.; and BATES, ALAN 1958 *Parental Authority: The Community and the Law*. New Brunswick, N.J.: Rutgers Univ. Press.

DAVIS, F. JAMES et al. 1962 *Society and the Law: New Meanings for an Old Profession*. New York: Free Press.

DICEY, ALBERT V. (1905) 1962 *Lectures on the Relation Between Law and Public Opinion in England, During the Nineteenth Century*. 2d ed. London and New York: Macmillan. → A paperback edition was published in 1962.

DURKHEIM, ÉMILE (1893) 1960 *The Division of Labor in Society*. Glencoe, Ill.: Free Press. → First published as *De la division du travail social*.

DURKHEIM, ÉMILE (1950) 1958 *Professional Ethics and Civic Morals*. Glencoe, Ill.: Free Press. → First published, posthumously, as *Leçons de sociologie: Physique des moeurs et du droit*.

EELS, RICHARD 1962 *The Government of Corporations*. New York: Free Press.

EHRLICH, EUGEN (1913) 1936 *Fundamental Principles of the Sociology of Law*. Translated by Walter L. Moll with an introduction by Roscoe Pound. Cambridge, Mass.: Harvard Univ. Press. → First published as *Grundlegung der Soziologie des Rechts*.

EVAN, WILLIAM M. (editor) 1962 *Law and Sociology: Exploratory Essays*. New York: Free Press.

FRIEDMAN, LAWRENCE M. 1965 *Contract Law in America: A Social and Economic Case Study*. Madison: Univ. of Wisconsin Press.

FRIEDMANN, WOLFGANG (1944) 1960 *Legal Theory*. 4th ed. London: Stevens.

FRIEDMANN, WOLFGANG 1959 *Law in a Changing Society*. Berkeley: Univ. of California Press.

FULLER, LON L. 1964 *The Morality of Law*. New Haven: Yale Univ. Press.

GEIGER, THEODOR (editor) 1964 *Vorstudien zu einer Soziologie des Rechts*. Berlin and Neuwied: Luchterhand. → See especially "Internationale Bibliographie der Rechtssoziologie" by Paul Trappe.

Gurvitch, Georges D. (1940) 1947 *Sociology of Law.* Preface by Roscoe Pound. London: Routledge. → First published in French.

Hall, Jerome (1935) 1952 *Theft, Law and Society.* 2d ed. Indianapolis, Ind.: Bobbs-Merrill.

Hart, H. L. A. 1961 *The Concept of Law.* Oxford: Clarendon.

Hazard, John N. 1953 *Law and Social Change in the U.S.S.R.* London: Stevens.

Hazard, John N. 1960 *Settling Disputes in Soviet Society: The Formative Years of Legal Institutions.* New York: Columbia Univ. Press.

Hurst, James W. 1950 *The Growth of American Law: The Law Makers.* Boston: Little.

Hurst, James W. 1960 *Law and Social Process in United States History.* Ann Arbor: Univ. of Michigan Law School.

Hurst, James W. 1964 *Law and Economic Growth: The Legal History of the Lumber Industry in Wisconsin; 1836–1915.* Cambridge, Mass.: Harvard Univ. Press.

Kalven, Harry; and Zeisel, Hans 1966 *The American Jury.* Boston: Little.

Lev, Daniel S. 1965 The Lady and the Banyan Tree: Civil-law Change in Indonesia. *American Journal of Comparative Law* 14:282–307.

Lindesmith, Alfred R. 1965 *The Addict and the Law.* Bloomington: Indiana Univ. Press.

Llewellyn, Karl N. (1928–1960) 1962 *Jurisprudence: Realism in Theory and Practice.* Univ. of Chicago Press.

Llewellyn, Karl N. 1960 *The Common Law Tradition: Deciding Appeals.* Boston: Little.

Macaulay, Stewart 1963 Non-contractual Relations in Business: A Preliminary Study. *American Sociological Review* 28:55–67.

Mannheim, Hermann 1946 *Criminal Justice and Social Reconstruction.* London: Routledge.

Matza, David 1964 *Delinquency and Drift.* New York: Wiley.

Pound, Roscoe 1959 *Jurisprudence.* 5 vols. St. Paul, Minn.: West. → Volume 1: *Jurisprudence: The End of Law.* Volume 2: *The Nature of Law.* Volume 3: *The Scope and Subject Matter of Law.* Volume 4: *Application and Enforcement of Law.* Volume 5: *The System of Law.* Volume 1 reviews the main literature of sociological jurisprudence.

Renner, Karl (1929) 1949 *The Institutions of Private Law and Their Social Functions.* London: Routledge. → First published as *Die Rechtsinstitute des Privatrechts und ihre soziale Funktion: Ein Beitrag zur Kritik des bürgerlichen Rechts.*

Schubert, Glendon 1960 *Quantitative Analysis of Judicial Behavior.* Glencoe, Ill.: Free Press.

Schur, Edwin M. 1965 *Crimes Without Victims.* Englewood Cliffs, N.J.: Prentice-Hall.

Simon, Rita (James) 1967 *American Jury—The Defense of Insanity.* Boston: Little.

Simpson, Sidney P.; and Stone, Julius (editors) 1948–1949 *Cases and Readings on Law and Society.* 3 vols. St. Paul, Minn.: West.

Skolnick, Jerome H. 1966 *Justice Without Trial.* New York: Wiley.

Tappan, Paul W. 1947 *Delinquent Girls in Court: A Study of the Wayward Minor Court of New York.* New York: Columbia Univ. Press.

Timasheff, Nicholas S. 1939 *An Introduction to the Sociology of Law.* Cambridge, Mass.: Harvard Univ., Committee on Research in the Social Sciences.

Vinogradoff, Paul 1920–1922 *Outlines of Historical Jurisprudence.* 2 vols. Oxford Univ. Press. → Volume 1: *Introduction; Tribal Law.* Volume 2: *The Jurisprudence of the Greek City.*

Von Mehren, Arthur T. (editor) 1963 *Law in Japan: The Legal Order in a Changing Society.* Cambridge, Mass.: Harvard Univ. Press.

Weber, Max (1922*a*) 1954 *Max Weber on Law in Economy and Society.* Edited, with an introduction and annotations by Max Rheinstein. Cambridge, Mass.: Harvard Univ. Press. → First published as Chapter 7 of *Wirtschaft und Gesellschaft.*

Weber, Max (1922*b*) 1957 *The Theory of Social and Economic Organization.* Edited by Talcott Parsons. Glencoe, Ill.: Free Press. → First published as Part 1 of *Wirtschaft und Gesellschaft.*

II
THE LEGAL SYSTEM

The comparative analysis of the social structures of legal systems has its historical roots in the study of comparative law. It is possible to draw an analytical distinction between the two disciplines. Comparative structural analysis is a sociological endeavor. Its subject matter is the organization of legal activity and the variable character of the groups and social roles involved in the legal process; its primary goal is the discovery and explanation of regularities in institutional structure and development. Comparative law, on the other hand, is a jurisprudential study. Its practitioners are interested in the normative content of various systems of law and are often motivated by a desire to seek the fairest and most effective means of ordering the legal relations between men. Nevertheless, the intimate connection between the two fields should not be overlooked. In one branch of comparative law the sociological element is particularly strong: students of comparative legal history have generally accepted the proposition that legal concepts and modes of legal thought reflect an underlying framework of social organization. Thus, legal historians have often viewed the normative content of law from a sociological perspective.

Origins of the structural approach

The sociological perspective is at least as old as the Enlightenment and Montesquieu's classic, *De l'esprit des lois* (1748). Montesquieu found the sources of law in climate and geography and in the social institutions and national character of a people.

The concept of national character pervades the work of Friedrich Karl Savigny, who is generally regarded as the founder of historical jurisprudence (Stone [1946] 1950, chapter 18). Savigny wrote in the context of a national debate regarding the proposed codification of German law. He argued that codification would destroy the peculiarly Germanic character of German law and that the loss of national distinctiveness would be disastrous because any system of law must truly reflect the spirit and genius of the institutions of a people. To document his views, he produced a series of scholarly volumes on Roman and German law that were designed to demonstrate the close correspondence between social and legal development in those nations.

From here it is but a short, logical step to our contemporary interest in the relation between the "positive" norms of the law of the state and the *de facto* norms which emerge from the institutions of the larger society. In American sociology this concern has independent roots in William Graham Sumner's interest in the mores, the folkways, and the stateways (1906), and in E. A. Ross's emphasis on social control (1901; see also F. J. Davis et al. 1962, chapters 1, 2). On a global scale, however, the dominant transitional figure was the Austrian jurist Eugen Ehrlich (1913).

The proposition that laws *ought* to reflect the peculiar character of a nation's social institutions is easily transformed into the closely related view that such a correspondence is desirable but has not been achieved. Ehrlich became disturbed by the failure of the conceptual apparatus of positive law to adequately reflect the "living law." For Ehrlich the living law is the *de facto* normative pattern that develops as competing social interests are resolved within the many groups and institutions constituting the "inner order" of a society.

In the English-speaking world the works of Sir Henry Sumner Maine (1861) had a profound impact on jurists and social scientists alike, since Maine attempted to trace both the evolutionary development of legal concepts and the social developments that produced them. Maine's posthumous influence extended to the Continent, where it played a role in shaping the thought of scholars within the emerging discipline of sociology.

Weber's comparative studies. Among those Continental scholars, Max Weber (1922) formulated the most comprehensive accounts of comparative legal structure. Weber's investigations were carried out as a part of his inquiries into the causes and consequences of the "rationalization" of the Western world. "Rationalization" in this context refers to the process by which an institution becomes systematically and logically elaborated according to general, analytical, and calculable principles.

Weber developed one of his characteristic ideal typologies for distinguishing the various types of legal thought found in the history of juristic development. He then elaborated one of Maine's fundamental ideas by showing that each type of legal thought is associated with a given form of legal organization and particularly with the structural location of legal specialists. Thus, for example, the logical rationality of Continental European conceptual jurisprudence is attributable to the influence of university-based professors who turned their philosophically trained intellects to the task of expounding the Roman law as a logically closed, abstract system.

Weber also examined the impact of variation in the structure of both governmental institutions and power relations among elite groups. He pointed out that the forms of legal development fostered by the university-based Romanists appealed to the interests of monarchs and bureaucrats in systematic administration and to the concerns of the rising capitalist class with the predictable protection of private rights.

Weber's account of comparative legal structure must also be seen in the context of his general interest in the rise and development of capitalist economic structure. His analysis of the role of law in capitalist development is effectively summarized in his treatment of the change in the concept of "special law." We may speak of special law when legal obligations apply differentially to different groups of people. According to Weber, special law originated in the differentiation of society into various status groups each with its traditional code and a degree of feudal independence from regulation by agents of the larger society. By contrast, the modern law of the centralized, bureaucratic state permits the different units of society to enter into legally binding contracts with each other. Thus, the power of the state is made to support bodies of special law created *de novo* by capitalists with interdependent interests.

Durkheim's theory of sanctions. Weber's theory converges with the ideas of the French sociologist Émile Durkheim (1893), who, following in a direct line of influence from Maine, was interested in the transition to a social order based upon contract.

Durkheim speculated that differences in legal structure so closely reflect underlying differences in social structure as to constitute indices of types of societies. In primitive societies the bonds of cohesion are formed by the global, undifferentiated norms of the "common conscience." In such a society, law is repressive; it operates through sanctions designed to obliterate offenses to the common conscience and heal its wounds. Over time, as social solidarity comes to depend more and more upon the interdependence of specialized units, the legal order also becomes differentiated. Bodies of specialized norms develop, which are backed by *restitutive* sanctions designed to restore the balance of interests between competing but interdependent social groups. The new type of law permits private groups to negotiate within the context of general normative limitations and to contractually create for themselves viable systems of enforceable legal obligations.

Thus, Durkheim and Weber converged in a common recognition of an important dimension of structural variation in legal systems, namely, the extent of reliance on private action to create legal obligation. At the same time, both recognized the critical importance of the problem of the articulation of the authority of the larger society with private legal obligations.

Problems of structural analysis

Given Western legal values, one problem area stands out as the central concern of comparative structural analysis: What are the various ways that "legal system." This is a notoriously difficult prob- and in particular, what are the structural correlates of legal independence?

Defining the system. The first problem is to establish an analytical boundary between the legal system and its environment by defining the term "legal system." This is a notoriously difficult problem. Not the least of the difficulties stems from the fact that definitions that are adequate to the task of defining law in modern states fail to include the law of societies in which legal relations are inextricably entangled in other institutional contexts. One solution is to define the legal system functionally, so that its existence is not made to depend upon a structurally distinct set of roles or upon groups such as courts or police.

Many functional definitions rely upon the concept of social control (F. J. Davis et al. 1962, chapter 2). Law is defined as a type of social control that relies on a particular form of enforcement, usually enforcement through the legitimate use of force. Parsons (1962) and others would rather treat enforcement as a political function, external to the legal system. The advantage of this strategy is that it focuses attention on the variable structural arrangements through which legal systems come to have access to sources of coercive power.

In this view, the peculiar province of law is interpretation. Social integration is often attributed to normative controls. However, social norms are not sufficiently specific to provide authoritative guides to conduct. Further, consensus about norms is often accompanied by dispute about the facts to which norms are to be applied. Accordingly, procedures develop for issuing authoritative versions of ambiguous situations of conflict and for propounding binding rules tailored to the particularities of these situations. Enforcement, on the other hand, is a political problem, a problem of mobilizing sufficient power to implement legal decisions.

Those who insist on including enforcement within the legal system can reply that interpretation is a necessary component of any act of enforcement. Interpretation could never be isolated in any single differentiated institution. A viable research strategy must guard against the fallacy of neglecting the fact that consequential interpretive decisions are continually being made at many points in the social structure.

System and environment. However the boundaries of the legal system are drawn, the problem of conceptualizing relations with the environment remains. There are a variety of ways of viewing this problem, but in Western thought one approach has dominated analysis. The problem has been defined as one of accounting for the independence of the legal system. Western political philosophy has accorded a high place to the "rule of law." From a sociological perspective, the rule of law refers to a society with a differentiated legal system, free from domination by any other institutional complex. Where the rule of law prevails, the legal process is subordinate only to established, known, and universalistic rules. Given this value concern, the task of comparative sociology is to account for the social basis of the rule of law.

To this end, we may distinguish four types of relations between the legal system and its social environment. First, the legal system may be *undifferentiated*, that is, it may have no differentiated structural home. Thus, legal functions are performed only as a by-product of activity within other institutions. For example, among the Eskimos socially enforceable interpretations are implicitly made in the context of public curing ceremonies and popular assemblies and in ritualized combat of various sorts, but there are no specialized procedures for formally proclaiming enforceable decisions (Hoebel 1954, chapter 5).

Second, a system may be *subordinate*. In this case specialized formal procedures, involving specially designated personnel, are present but legal activities are controlled by other institutions. For example, justice may be dispensed by the king's ministers, as in ancient Egypt, or by priests subject to sacerdotal discipline, as in Sumer and Babylonia.

Third, a system may be *autonomous*. The legal practitioners may become so insulated from external controls as to become unresponsive to demands from other quarters. In these circumstances a legal system will develop according to an inner dynamic reflecting the dominant concerns of the practitioner group. Thus, for example, religious scholars may treat the law as a logical elaboration of theological concepts. The outstanding example of this is the development of the Semitic legal tradition.

The fourth category is the most complicated, as well as the most highly prized, in legal philosophy. Legal systems may be called *partially independent* when they are sufficiently insulated to permit independence in some spheres but not so protected as to prevent adaptive responses to the needs of other sectors of the society. The "ideal" form of partial independence is *procedural* independence. In this case, insulating mechanisms protect the day-to-day operation of the legal system and the interpretive process but do not make the system unresponsive to social interests, as formulated into general policies by legislatures and organized public opinion.

The concept of procedural independence must not be confused with the discredited idea that the judicial process can be purely mechanical or logical. American political science and legal realism have effectively shown that legal decisions necessarily involve choices between alternative policies. The difference between autonomy and procedural independence is that in the latter case adjudicators are responsive to policy premises originating outside the legal system.

Procedural independence is not only highly valued; it is also a crucially important case for sociological theory. Theorists as divergent as Weber (1922) and Engels (Marx & Engels 1848–1898, pp. 447–448 in 1949 edition) have stressed that procedural independence may contribute to the interests of particular social classes or institutions. An independent legal system, operating through the universalistic interpretation of established rules, is an efficient vehicle for legitimizing political domination. Further, such a system provides a set of stable expectations that facilitate economic calculation. A degree of procedural independence may emerge as a response to the conditions of stable economic relations, even in the face of considerable political domination of the legal process. For instance, contractual arbitration in the Soviet Union became subject to the rule of law in order to foster accountability and stability in the relations between economic units (Berman 1950).

Law as social institution

The demand for stabilization of economic rights is only one of the forces supporting procedural independence. It is the task of comparative analysis to explicate the various structures and mechanisms that either insulate legal systems or make them vulnerable to external demands. Many protective devices are quite familiar; judicial tenure, judicial review, constitutional limitation, and judicial control over enforcement officials are obvious sources of judicial power. But from a sociological point of view the important question is, How are these mechanisms institutionalized? that is, How are they supported by concrete social arrangements?

A number of components of social structure are involved in the patterning of the relations between legal systems and other social institutions, but one factor has seemed especially important to sociologists. Comparative analysts have been particularly interested in the impact of the structure of professional specialization.

Legal specialists. The significance of the structural location and internal organization of professional groups is implicit in what has already been stated. Undifferentiated legal systems, having no specialized legal procedures, lack persons with special legal functions. Once a differentiated legal system develops, its character is profoundly affected by the social characteristics of its associated professionals. Indeed, one of the central propositions of comparative legal sociology is that autonomous and independent legal systems are supported by tightly organized professional groups, with an independent power base, whereas subordinate legal systems reflect the dependency and weakness of legal specialists.

Apart from this general proposition, it may also be asserted that specific characteristics of legal systems may be derived from attributes of professional groups. To take an obvious example, when adjudication is controlled by religious functionaries, then law is likely to have religious overtones.

Four major categories of legal specialists can be distinguished for present purposes. The first group may be broadly designated *adjudicators* and includes judges, magistrates, arbitrators, referees, hearing examiners, and similar functionaries. The second group consists of professional *advocates* of legal causes. The third group consists of legal *advisers*, such as the familiar English solicitor. Notaries, conveyancers, and other draftsmen, also, belong in this category, and their significance should not be underestimated. As Weber ([1922] 1954, pp. 72–201, 210) has shown, where private elements are strong in the legal system, these "auxiliary" jurists assume special importance. When the state assures the bindingness of private agreements, the drafters of legal documents may become legal innovators who play an important role in shaping legal development.

The fourth group consists of the legal *scholars* —the teachers, writers, historians, and commentators whose contributions have been very important in both the Roman and civil law and in many non-Western traditions as well.

The four categories of legal specialists may or may not be differentiated from each other in practice, and the type and degree of internal differentiation is one of the important structural features of a legal system. Another of Weber's hypotheses is that the intensely practical and empirical character of the common law reflects the fact that it developed at a time when teaching was not differentiated from legal practice; there were no specialized scholars to impart an abstract ideological content to the law.

Professional organization. The internal differentiation of the legal profession is only one organizational element among many within the profession. Patterns of professional recruitment and advancement, the organization of professional training, and the organization and control of professional practice may have important consequences for the operation of the legal system. The explanatory potential of these variables is illustrated in Ulf Torgersen's study of the small and declining political role of the Norwegian Supreme Court (1963). The relative insignificance of judicial review is attributable to the patterns of recruitment to the court, which has been increasingly dominated by career bureaucrats rather than private attorneys.

Tight professional control over recruitment, training, advancement, and practice, founded upon a monopoly of access to technical legal knowledge and a monopoly of the right to legal advocacy, is one major source of independence and autonomy. However, there are other sources of legal power. The independence of legal specialists may be supported by the sponsorship of representatives of other powerful groups. Thus, adjudicators may be insulated from the domination of economic interests by the sponsorship of governmental power, or vice versa.

Symbolic factors are often especially powerful in the legal sector. Legal specialists have rivaled religious functionaries in their capacity to assert successfully claims of special access to the sources of truth and right. Such claims have been supported by a variety of symbolic paraphernalia, ranging from magic and ritual to the more subtle trappings of modern judicial dignity. Ritualistic practices should not be discounted, but in modern liberal democracies the most important bulwark of legal independence has been the capture of the right to symbolically represent the limitation of governmental power. In this sense, the rule of law has supported itself; the independent professionals, who provide its social foundation, derive their influence in part from their symbolic embodiment of the normative regulation of power.

The legal process. Another approach to the articulation of the legal system and its social environment would eschew the abstract analysis of the structural location and internal organization of legal specialists in order to concentrate on the concrete transactions between legal specialists and representatives of other spheres.

These transactions include such processes as litigation, professional consultation, judicial enforcement, appointment or election to adjudicative office, and complaint to legal authorities.

According to this view, the proper strategy for comparative analysis is to study the structural arrangements that pattern interaction between legal specialists and others. The structural framework of legal transactions shapes their content and often provides leverage for either the legal system or its potential adversaries.

For example, one of the functions of formal legal procedure is to compel the parties to legal disputes to mold their concrete conflicts into issues subject to normative settlement. In so doing, the parties are forced to isolate normative issues and eliminate extraneous power factors. Power factors come to be defined as being outside of the scope of inquiry, and the adjudicator thus gains leverage on his clients.

On the other hand, the process of litigation is structured by the characteristics of cases that are preshaped by social organization before they come to the attention of legal authorities. Social structure generates a variety of types of conflict. Some conflict situations are channeled to the legal system; others are resolved in other contexts. Ready access to the legal system may depend upon a preferred position in the social order. Further, even among those who have ready access to the legal system, litigation is a strategic alternative to a variety of other modes of pressing interests. In consequence, legal officials are not always in a position to control the types of issues that come before them or the structural context within which issues are presented. Thus, litigation can be conceived of as a series of transactions between the legal system and other social components, which are structured in part by the legal system and in part by external factors. Other transactions are subject to similar analysis.

Evolution of legal systems

A third approach to comparative analysis may be described as evolutionary: How, and in what sequence of steps, have differentiated legal systems emerged?

In this respect, Durkheim's thought runs counter to Weber. Weber was concerned with the emergence of the modern state from its feudal predecessors, and in this context he stressed the lack of centralized machinery of enforcement in many preindustrial societies. Durkheim, in his insistence on the importance of repressive sanctions in primitive society, seems to assume that the existence of societal enforcement mechanisms is not problematical. The anthropologists and historians who are students of legal evolution cannot agree with him. They continually search for the analogues to the legal process in "stateless" societies and trace the development of differentiated legal systems based upon a state monopoly of legitimate enforcement power.

The gradual development of central legal machinery in Europe has been known to legal historians for some time (F. J. Davis et al. 1962, chapter 2; Wigmore 1928). Scholarly interest in the evolution of legal procedure has been reawakened recently, in part because of concern for the problems of world legal order. The sequence of development from primitive self-help to central enforcement of norms through a universalistic, normatively regulated procedure has intrigued those who are interested in the possibility of a similar development at the world level [*see* INTERNATIONAL LAW].

R. D. Schwartz and J. C. Miller (1964), in a cross-cultural study of 51 societies, have shown that three structural attributes of legal procedure combine in a systematic pattern that can be described as a cumulative scale. The representation of interests by third parties is found only in societies with both special police forces and third-party mediation of disputes. Police and mediation sometimes occur in the absence of representation, and sometimes mediation is found in the absence of any police to carry out the orders of mediating agencies. In some societies none of these procedural devices is present. The authors also found that the elaboration of legal procedure as measured by position on the cumulative scale is associated with measures of societal complexity, suggesting an evolutionary sequence of development. The sequence suggested is consistent with Western legal development as it has been pieced together by juristic scholars. The earliest legal systems are barely legal. The closest approximations to legal institutions are the rules governing kin-organized feuding and the sets of traditional compensations for wrongs. Later, regular procedures for submitting feuds to arbitration develop, but even then the parties may need to resort to self-help for enforcement. With the monopolization of legitimate force in the hands of the state, the legal system may rely on a specialized police force for enforcement of adjudicative orders. Finally, given a forum for binding and enforceable arbitration, the stage is set for the full development of professional advocacy.

Growth of legal pluralism. Historians have paid particular attention to the first two steps in the process. Law is said to appear in fully differentiated form once there is centralized enforcement of binding adjudication. From the perspective of comparative structural analysis the third step, also, is crucial, for with the appearance of institutionalized representation comes powerful support for procedural independence. For the first time there exists a set of legal specialists whose interests are not identical with the interests of mediators. It is possible that the new representer group will be captured by a particular set of interests, but theoretically the requisite social supports are present for the introduction of pluralism into the structure of the legal system. Professional representation can bring to the day-to-day administration of justice effective legal advocacy of the full range of interests present in society.

One step to pluralism is the creation of a market for professional services, so that legal representation can be purchased without regard to the content of the claims one wishes to advance. This requires either a high degree of professional neutrality or heterogeneity in the backgrounds and interests of recruits to professional service.

The establishment of a market for legal services is not a sufficient condition for pluralism, since the professional market will reflect the imperfections and inequalities of the economic structure of society. Since the inequalities of the marketplace may be overcome by various procedural devices and by effective organization for legal advocacy, the variable organization of access to representation is one of the most important elements in the comparative study of modern legal systems.

Administrative law

In many instances ready access to the legal system has been promoted through the creation of administrative remedies, which permit rights to be secured by direct application to administrative agencies of government. Traditional courts and their sometimes cumbersome procedures are bypassed. At the same time, in their judicial activities the administrative agencies operate in at least a quasi-judicial fashion, preserving many of the forms of law and subjecting themselves to the rule of law. Administrative procedure tends to be more informal than traditional legal procedure, and is less likely to involve formal adversaries. It can therefore permit the adjudicator a relatively free hand to shape solutions that take into account the particularities of a given case. Yet, administrative procedure is normatively regulated, and the standards of impartiality and decision according to law apply.

The tremendous burgeoning of administrative law in the twentieth century is the most recent chapter in legal evolution. On this count, Durkheim's sense of evolutionary development fared well, for he successfully foretold the growth and elaboration of administrative law. For Durkheim administrative law was an integral part of the restitutive approach to law; the moral order, as represented by the common conscience, seemed to him less important than effective administration of a complicated network of obligations.

From this perspective, the growth of administrative law should be interpreted as consisting in the legalization of administration. It is simply an aspect of the process of bureaucratization that accompanies economic development. The increasing involvement of government in large-scale economic and welfare projects has been a worldwide phenomenon. The requirements of efficient administration and the interests of bureaucratic officials have combined to create pressure for the stabilization of rights and obligations.

Important as it is, the legalization of administration does not entirely account for the increasing domination of administrative law, for there has been a corresponding and converging development on the legal side. Many administrative tribunals have been created to operate in areas that have been exclusively within the jurisdiction of courts. Numerous boards, commissions, and authorities have sprung up to deal with various criminal actions and tort claims.

Again one may invoke the argument of efficiency. The administrative tribunal has numerous practical advantages: it is less costly to litigants; it permits a high volume of litigation; it permits adjudication by specialists who are both technically skilled in particular areas and well acquainted with the concrete, practical problems of administration; it permits individualized treatment of complicated situations. But efficiency is not a sufficient explanation, unless one can show that particular groups have an interest in efficient administration. In this context, the growth of democracy is crucial (Evan 1962). Populist governments are responsive to demands for efficient administration of programs designed to produce public welfare and economic development. In the United States, for example, the growth of administrative law has been stimulated by a tendency for social welfare legislation to become bogged down in courts and by a movement to temper all legal administration by the application of a philosophy of social welfare.

Despite its humanitarian credentials, the growth of administrative law is often viewed with alarm in countries with a strong legal tradition. It is not surprising that administrative law should be surrounded by controversy, for its emergence is a classic case of a process that is usually associated with social strain. Whenever a group claims that special expertise or special familiarity with problems gives it a right to perform functions that were traditionally handled at other social locations, conflict ensues. Conflict is heightened when the technical specialist claims that his expertise frees him from some of the normative restraints that have governed performance of the function in the past. Yet this is exactly the claim of emergent administrative systems. The very differentiation of the legal function appears threatened as legal systems lose functions to substantively specialized but multifunctional enforcement agencies. All these processes have still to be adequately studied by students of contemporary social organization.

LEON MAYHEW

[*Directly related are the entries* ADMINISTRATIVE LAW; CRIMINAL LAW; LEGAL SYSTEMS; POLICE; PUNISHMENT; SOCIAL CONTROL. *Other relevant material may be found in* JURISPRUDENCE; LEGAL REASONING; *and in the biographies of* BECCARIA; BLACK-

STONE; COKE; DURKHEIM; EHRLICH; HAURIOU; MAINE; MONTESQUIEU; SAVIGNY; WEBER, MAX.]

BIBLIOGRAPHY

BERMAN, HAROLD J. (1950) 1963 *Justice in the U.S.S.R.: An Interpretation of Soviet Law*. Rev. & enl. ed. Cambridge, Mass.: Harvard Univ. Press. → First published as *Justice in Russia: An Interpretation of Soviet Law*.

DAVIS, E. EUGENE 1962 Legal Structures in a Changing Society. Pages 196–226 in F. James Davis et al., *Society and the Law: New Meanings for an Old Profession*. New York: Free Press. → Summarizes, from a lawyer's point of view, the administrative problems of the contemporary United States court system.

DAVIS, F. JAMES et al. 1962 *Society and the Law: New Meanings for an Old Profession*. New York: Free Press. → A symposium in which sociologists collaborated with lawyers. Chapter 1, "The Sociological Study of Law," is especially useful for its summary of sociological interest in law in the United States since 1900.

DURKHEIM, ÉMILE (1893) 1960 *The Division of Labor in Society*. 2d ed. Glencoe, Ill.: Free Press. → First published as *De la division du travail social*.

EHRLICH, EUGEN (1913) 1936 *Fundamental Principles of the Sociology of Law*. Translated by Walter L. Moll with an introduction by Roscoe Pound. Cambridge, Mass.: Harvard Univ. Press. → First published as *Grundlegung der Soziologie des Rechts*.

EVAN, WILLIAM M. (editor) 1962 *Law and Sociology: Exploratory Essays*. New York: Free Press. → See especially "Public and Private Legal Systems," pages 165–184. Argues that the modern democratic state contains a plurality of legal orders.

HOEBEL, E. ADAMSON 1954 *The Law of Primitive Man: A Study in Comparative Legal Dynamics*. Cambridge, Mass.: Harvard Univ. Press.

MAINE, HENRY J. S. (1861) 1960 *Ancient Law: Its Connection With the Early History of Society, and Its Relations to Modern Ideas*. Rev. ed. New York: Dutton; London and Toronto: Dent. → A paperback edition was published in 1963 by Beacon.

MARX, KARL; and ENGELS, FRIEDRICH (1848–1898) 1962 *Selected Works*. Volume 2. Moscow: Foreign Languages Publishing House.

MONTESQUIEU (1748) 1962 *The Spirit of the Laws*. 2 vols. New York: Hafner. → First published as *De l'esprit des lois*.

PARSONS, TALCOTT 1962 The Law and Social Control. Pages 56–72 in William M. Evan (editor), *Law and Sociology: Exploratory Essays*. New York: Free Press.

ROSS, EDWARD A. 1901 *Social Control: A Survey of the Foundations of Order*. New York and London: Macmillan.

SCHWARTZ, RICHARD D.; and MILLER, JAMES C. 1964 Legal Evolution and Societal Complexity. *American Journal of Sociology* 70:159–169.

STONE, JULIUS (1946) 1950 *The Province and Function of Law: Law as Logic, Justice, and Social Control; a Study in Jurisprudence*. Sydney: Associated General Publications; Cambridge, Mass.: Harvard Univ. Press.

SUMNER, WILLIAM G. (1906) 1959 *Folkways: A Study of the Sociological Importance of Usages, Manners, Customs, Mores, and Morals*. New York: Dover. → A paperback edition was published in 1960 by the New American Library.

TORGERSEN, ULF 1963 The Role of the Supreme Court in the Norwegian Political System. Pages 221–244 in Glendon A. Schubert (editor), *Judicial Decision-making*. New York: Free Press.

WEBER, MAX (1922) 1954 *Max Weber on Law in Economy and Society*. Cambridge, Mass.: Harvard Univ. Press. → First published as Chapter 7 of Max Weber's *Wirtschaft und Gesellschaft*, published posthumously; Weber died in 1920. His earliest contributions to the sociology of law date from the 1890s, and the topic was rarely absent from his subsequent writings.

WIGMORE, JOHN H. (1928) 1936 *A Panorama of the World's Legal Systems*. 3 vols. Washington: Washington Law Book. → A historical survey of 16 legal systems.

III
THE LEGAL PROFESSION

The legal profession encompasses all those who in view of their special competence in matters of law assume a distinctive responsibility in the administration of a legal order. The nature and extent of this responsibility may vary, and its locus may be found in one or in several social roles: judges, advocates, counselors, draftsmen, teachers, scholars. Because of special issues connected with it, the topic of the judiciary is treated more extensively under other headings [*see* JUDICIAL PROCESS].

The legal profession attracts the interest of both students of the professions and students of law and government. Political scientists, legal scholars, historians, and political sociologists are mainly concerned with the role of lawyers in politics and in the administration of justice. Recent sociological writings approach the bar from the perspective of the study of professions, focusing on such problems as professional independence, ethics, careers, recruitment, and relations with clients. The sociology of law draws on all these approaches.

The profession and the law

Whatever approach one takes to the study of the legal profession, it cannot be fully understood unless it is seen in the light of the special functions it performs for law and legal institutions. Indeed, the development and character of a legal profession are closely related to the growth and orientations of the legal order which it serves and within which it operates.

Where law is simply an expedient for the settlement of disputes or the accommodation of conflicting interests, the work of the lawyer involves little more than mastery of some techniques of social adjustment. The legal profession develops most fully when law is viewed as an embodiment of values. Society then requires specialized group energies for the protection of its legal heritage and may find them in that occupation whose interests are identified with the preservation of legal skills and values. In this process, the legal craftsmen are transformed into a legal elite and assume the critical mission of maintaining the legal order and determining its subsequent development. Although values are at stake, a legal elite may not be necessarily called for when, as in ancient Greece or in imperial China, the values of law are not seen as distinct from the morality of the polity. In Athens the legal tasks of counsel and judge were performed by experienced citizens in the absence of any specialized legal profession. But the more the distinctiveness of law is emphasized and the more society aspires to legality, the greater is the need for an autonomous profession. The profession will require more or less independence and authority, depending upon the relative strength of community commitment to legal values.

While its role is partly fashioned in response to social needs, the legal profession carries much autonomous power over the orientations of the legal and social order. It may shape many features of a legal tradition. The growth of Roman law can thus be traced to the way in which *pontifices* and, later, praetors declared the law in private cases: by developing and extending formulas to be used as bases for actions at law, they created a system that allowed a continuing and highly pragmatic elaboration of legal ideas. The legal profession may also succeed in imprinting the value of law upon the community, as American arbitrators have done in the relations between labor and industry. It may even give a color of legality to moral norms and religious doctrines as did the rabbis in the Talmudic period and, in a different way, the canonists in the Roman Catholic church. Similarly, the inner weaknesses of the profession may breed corresponding weaknesses in the quality and authority of the legal order. This occurs when the profession becomes captured by the special interests it serves or when it so insulates itself as to weaken its participation in and responsibility for the solution of social problems. How competent the profession is to perform its role and what institutional means secure this capability are critical issues in the assessment of the legal profession.

Thus, the more developed a legal order, the more demands and responsibilities are placed upon its legal profession. The lawyer is called to bring a set of distinctive skills to his task. His special competence may be defined as an *expertise in the assessment of authoritativeness;* this follows from the special character of law as an authoritative order. Whatever kind of activity he may be involved in, the lawyer's distinctive contribution lies in his ability to formulate or criticize the *reasons* upon which the authority of claims, decisions, policies, or actions rests. This ability is not confined to the evaluation of lawfulness; it includes a capacity to unravel issues, to scrutinize the rationale of policies, and to explore the firmness and test the relevance of evidence and inferences. The true lawyer is a generalist: he conveys this quality in his very posture of self-confidence and in the forthrightness of his style (Riesman 1954). To what extent such skills can be developed, of course, always remains problematic. This will vary partly with the richness of the resources a legal tradition makes available in its techniques of reasoning and criticism and partly with the capacity of the profession itself to instill this competence in some, if only a few, of its members. But some expertise of that nature is essential if the lawyer is to perform his task: that is, to add to social and legal institutions this strain toward the rational and the justified, which is the source of growth and strength of the legal order (Kadish 1961).

Typical legal roles. The legal profession is historically associated with the performance of some typical roles involving particular applications of this general expertise.

The *adjudicator* is responsible for making authoritative decisions on issues of right and responsibility in the light of legal principles. As the normative dimensions of adjudication rather than the mere settlement of disputes become more salient, there tends to be more pressure to reserve access to, and control of, this role to the legal profession.

The *advocate*, as a legal representative, carries out the task of pressing for the official recognition of claims of right. This role is closely tied to the adjudicative process, especially when the latter rests upon the adversary presentation of claims, as in the Anglo–American tradition. The significance of advocacy may however extend beyond the sphere of adjudication, especially when the law assumes a positive role in the fulfillment of human aspirations. The advocate may then acquire more direct functions in the formation of law; as a result new forms of advocacy will tend to develop in new institutional settings. The role of advocate is marked by conflict between the lawyer's responsibilities as an officer of the law and his commitment to the interests of his client. This is a source of strains not only for the lawyer, who may cope with them in a variety of ways, but also for the legal system as a whole. Different systems vary in the way they balance these conflicting duties, as well as in the degree to which they tolerate this ambivalence and allow for the free development of advocacy. Whereas partisanship has been a cornerstone of common-law procedure, Soviet Russian law has until recently tended to restrict the right to counsel, and to insist on the advocate's primary loyalty to the courts and the public interest (Hazard 1960).

The *counselor* or *draftsman* has the special burden of assisting in the solution of social and human problems, while at the same time preserving the ideals of the legal order. The more emphasis that is placed on law as a creator of opportunities, the more this role is likely to develop. Thus, the notaries of northern Italy became pioneers in the fashioning of the law merchant, or commercial law, and the creation of negotiable instruments; their influence can be compared to that of modern lawyers in the growth of corporate enterprise. This development has been particularly significant in the United States, where business counseling became a primary focus of law practice to a much greater extent than in any European country.

The *jurist* or legal scholar is in charge of the systematic analysis and criticism of legal doctrine. One characteristic of law, as compared with other systems of norms, is that it contains its own built-in principles of criticism; the extension and refinement of these principles is a major task of the jurist. He may also share with the practitioners the role of training future lawyers. Jurists provide the profession with an instrument of self-scrutiny. The authority of their opinions varies, being generally higher in continental European than in Anglo–American law. One of the most important sources of law in imperial Rome lay in the *responsa prudentium*, that is, opinions in which famous scholars answered difficult questions of law. Under Hellenic influence, these jurists founded a tradition of formal legal analysis and teaching, which contributed to the progressive systematization and codification of Roman law; the Valentinian Law of Citations in A.D. 426 conferred legal authority on their writings. The revival and reception of Roman law in the Middle Ages was also the work of a school of jurists, the glossators of northern Italy, later followed by the scholastic postglossators in France and Italy. The German school of *usus modernus pandectarum* continued this tradition and, until the end of the nineteenth century, adapted the Roman doctrines to provide Germany with a workable common law; much of this work was incorporated in the German civil code of 1900.

Jurisprudence also attempts to clarify the ideals and perspectives of the legal order, a function that may be more effectively performed when jurists are not too closely bound to the practicing profession. There is, however, no clear evidence on this point, although the case of American law schools may be suggestive. Because of weak ties to universities and a tendency to recruit teachers from the ranks of practitioners, American law schools have generally been oriented to the practical interests of the profession, with little concern for jurisprudence and broader issues pertaining to the quality and needs of the legal order.

Lawyers have also been called to assume many other roles, such as mediators, managers in private business, politicians, and public administrators. How extensively they participate in such roles, especially in government, may both affect and reflect the authority of the law. Of special importance is the character of their participation. Their only contribution may lie in the ability to accommodate interests and manipulate social structures, a kind of activity in which they would not significantly differ from any trained politician (Eulau & Sprague 1964). Or they may bring to public life some of their own distinctive commitments and competence and help evolve, in both private and public government, an orientation to orderly procedure and the ideals of legality.

Structure of the profession

To analyze the structure of the legal profession is to ask how the social organization of the profession affects the role it performs in the legal order. The focus here is on internal and external sources of weakness or strength.

Legal education. By controlling access to the profession and the training of future lawyers, legal education has an important bearing on the character of the profession and the orientations of the law. Whether the law becomes the property of a privileged class or of the whole polity depends to some extent upon criteria of access to the profession. When admission is limited to a narrow segment of society, the services of the profession may be oriented primarily to this clan. The more the legal career is viewed as an avenue to political power and social status, the more efforts will be made to keep access open, especially where there is strong antipathy toward the establishment of governmental elites. This has been evident in the United States (Hurst 1950). Although wide accessibility may make the law responsive to a larger range of interests, it may also create problems for the profession in its endeavor to preserve standards of quality. American attempts to raise educational standards of admission to the bar have met only limited success: the shift from apprenticeship to academic training has been accompanied by the development of a highly stratified system of education, with only relatively few high-standard university law schools at the top. The bottom consists of a large number of low quality, part-time schools that have weak or no university ties and seek merely to prepare the student for the bar examination.

Methods of legal training affect the skills and perspectives lawyers bring to their practice and thereby shape many features of the law. Max Weber has noted the relation between apprenticeship and the pragmatic responsiveness of the common law, as contrasted with the more intellectual and formalistic treatment of the law arising from university education in Europe (1922). Orientations to law are thus created, which confer on the legal order more or less rigidity or flexibility. Some can better preserve the "open texture" of the law, allowing law to incorporate social change while retaining its continuity; the Anglo–American system has been remarkable in this respect. Other orientations are apt to freeze the structure of legal rules and to paralyze processes of legal change; the academism of legal education in Europe—a tradition that dates back to the glossators—tends to promote this rigidity. Social reforms are then more likely to be sought by means outside the law, thus arousing critical problems for the stability of both the legal and the political order. This tendency can be observed in some civil-law countries, especially in South America.

In a more direct way, legal education may become a source of law. In the very act of ordering legal materials for pedagogical purposes, law is divided into branches, and these are organized around governing concepts. The institutes of Roman law were originally purely pedagogical instruments; however, by systematizing the principles of Roman law, they started a movement toward codification and became an authoritative source of the *Corpus juris civilis*. In the process of being taught, law is thus given a structure which reflects the changing emphases of positive law and the needs of the practitioners. But this structure also provides ideas and perspectives which may affect the capacity of the law to cope with social change. Thus, the disappearance of the law of persons as a separate branch of legal study tends to impoverish the resources of American law for recognizing new forms of status.

Even more significant for the legal order is the role of legal education in providing lawyers with distinctive modes of analysis and reasoning. The case method, as practiced in American law schools, may be peculiarly competent to impart these skills. It may also tend, however, to create a perspective in which law appears as an outcome of controversies rather than a way of implementing values. More importantly, by identifying the main locus of law in appellate decisions, it may promote a restricted conception of the legal. Attention is diverted from the variety of ways and settings in which law can emerge and be administered. Even in its empirical focus on decisions, the case method overstresses the role of the judiciary, neglecting legislation and administrative decision making. It may thus limit the capacities of legal education to prepare lawyers for a period such as the present, when the role of law is being extended beyond its traditional confines.

Professional autonomy. The integrity of the law depends in part upon its ability to respond to political demands while maintaining its commitment to reason and impartiality. A continuing problem for the practicing lawyer is to remain sensitive to social needs and interests without becoming their captive and to preserve his autonomy without withdrawing himself from practical concerns.

Captivity may, of course, take a crude form, as when a political regime seizes control over the profession in order to neutralize a potential source of criticism (Kirchheimer 1961). It can, however, develop in more subtle forms where the profession is otherwise left free to serve. The lawyer can become the captive of his clients' interests: an insecure practice, for example, makes it harder for him to resist pressures from clients for fear of losing them to competitors. This condition arises when the demand for legal services remains weak and intermittent, as it is among the lower classes, or when there is intense competition from other lawyers or from such groups as realtors and accountants, who encroach upon areas of practice requiring only low level and standardized skills (Carlin 1962). Captivity can also result from too intimate involvement in the affairs of particular clients. Lawyers may thus tie themselves to a small number of institutional clients who demand extensive and continuing services, or as "house counsel" (members of a legal department) they may become too closely identified with or too submissive toward the enterprise or agency which employs them.

Professional integrity may also be undermined in the lawyer's dealings with courts and government agencies. The lower the standards of these institutions or the more open they are to outside political influences, as lower courts often are, the more they create opportunities and pressures which may attenuate norms of professional conduct. Continual practice before an agency may also lead the lawyer to share the perspectives of its administrators.

A common consequence of captivity is to deprive the lawyer of his special identity: he is transformed into a manipulator of social and economic structures who is no longer committed to the use of distinctively legal methods or resources. In this process, he tends to become indistinguishable from the politician or the business operator. Law is then made to appear as simply an expedient for the promotion of special interests, and the distinction between law and politics is lost.

The lawyer can resist pressures by avoiding involvement or insecurity, but such avoidance entails its own difficulties. A too rigid insistence upon independence and distinctiveness may divorce the lawyer from his clients' problems and needs, thus weakening the contribution law might make to their solution. The lawyer may then find himself confined to the passive role of providing technical help in the event of legal trouble. Under such conditions, law tends to evolve into legalism. A special view of law is conveyed which stresses the formalism of the legal order and the obstacles it creates to effective problem solving. Law may thus be emptied of its moral and political significance and reduced to its purely technical and positivistic aspects. Paradoxically, in seeking to protect his autonomy the lawyer may so insulate himself as to weaken both his own authority and the authority of the law, perhaps eventually becoming a docile servant of corporate or political power. The history of the legal profession in Nazi Germany illustrates this process.

Organization of the bar. The profession has evolved a number of structural arrangements which can be more or less successful in securing a viable autonomy. Apart from its effectiveness in this regard, the social organization of the bar may also influence patterns of development in the law.

One organizational device is to create within the profession an elite specially charged with the protection of legal ideals. While this segment insulates itself from outside pressures, others in the profession are left free to respond to and accommodate the variety of demands that are made on the legal order. The British system has achieved this differentiation by developing a small and specialized class of barristers, who enjoy a monopoly of practice in the higher courts and deal with clients only through solicitors. The latter do most of the client counseling and take care of cases in the lower courts and government agencies (Jackson 1940). In the United States, the large law firms have developed a very high level of technical proficiency in legal work, have restricted their practice to the most stable and secure clientele, and have limited their contacts to the top levels of government and the judiciary (Smigel 1964). Special training institutions, such as the Inns of Court in Britain and the American Ivy League law schools, help to strengthen these elites, while sharing in their trusteeship for the legal order.

The services of the elite bar tend to benefit those most competent to pursue their interests through use of the legal process. Thus, a critical issue is whether the elite can preserve its loyalty to legal institutions and its responsibility for the law as a whole, for it runs the risk of becoming so identified with the aims of a special clientele as to restrict its concerns to those areas of the law that best serve these aims. This encourages a highly selective development of the law and impairs recognition of legal demands arising from other segments of society. Large American law firms have thus been strongly criticized for their too exclusive services to corporate interests and their loss of concern for general legal values (Berle 1933). Moreover, in the United States the large metropolitan bar is highly stratified, with little mobility or communication between the upper and lower strata (Carlin 1966). The more the elite is cut off from the lower levels of the profession and of government, the more difficult it becomes to incorporate in the legal order the demands that are brought to these levels.

Formal associations. The weaker the sense of common purpose is within the bar and the more threatening the conditions under which it operates, the more pressing is the need for instruments of self-scrutiny and control. The practicing profession has traditionally been organized into guildlike associations, such as the Inns of Court in Britain and the Ordre des Avocats in France, which have often been quite powerful in regulating the practice of law. In the United States, the organization of the bar used to consist exclusively of small local and voluntary associations with little cohesion and authority. It still remains today highly fragmented, and primarily concerned, even in the exercise of disciplinary control, with the protection of the profession against public intervention and lay encroachments. A movement of reform, starting in the 1870s, led to the establishment of state bar associations and later to the integration of some of these. In states which have an "integrated bar," membership is compulsory for all practitioners in the state, and the association can thus enjoy greater security and larger resources. The American Bar Association was created in 1878 and progressively developed into a federation of state and local groups. It has assumed a prominent role in the bar as a whole, elaborating standards of admission and canons of ethics and recommending reforms in the law and the administration of justice. In legal reform it collaborates with two specialized organizations of the profession, the American Judicature Society and the American Law Institute. The latter undertook to codify American common law in a "Restatement of the Law." This work is still in progress. Contributions of the Institute include the drafting of model acts and codes in various branches of the law.

Types of practice. The practice of law may take a variety of forms, some of which have already been mentioned. Lawyers may work on their own or associate in firms of various size. They may serve mainly discrete individuals or organizations and businesses; the role of family lawyers, such as attorneys in the field of probate and estate, tends to decline as the family loses its economic functions.

Not all areas of legal practice allow the same quality of work. For instance, workmen's compensation and, frequently, personal injury call mainly for mass production and standardized legal techniques. In other fields, such as criminal law and domestic relations, "marriage counseling" and political manipulation are often more salient than legal craftsmanship (O'Gorman 1963). The lawyer is then likely to feel frustrated and threatened in his professional identity. The character of the market for services may also affect professional integrity: lawyers can more easily preserve their dignity when they can count on a secure and regular clientele. Others, however, especially those with low-status clients, have to keep continually searching for business, establishing connections, and resorting to such expedients as "ambulance chasing," through which potential clients are located and advantage is taken of whatever claims and speculations can be aroused. In this very process they become deprofessionalized (Carlin 1962).

A new type of practice has begun to develop as organized groups, such as labor unions and trade associations, assume the function of providing to their members the services of their retained counsel. The special contribution of these groups lies in their ability to aggregate common interests and to articulate legal demands. Resources can then be mobilized to press these claims in a systematic way and thereby promote legal change.

The practice of law has become more specialized: lawyers specialize according to the class of clients they serve, the agencies with which they deal, or the branch of the law they handle. In the United States, this trend has been facilitated by the expansion of law firms (Smigel 1964). Specialization is particularly significant for the growth of legal doctrine in undeveloped areas of the law and where special government institutions must be made accountable and sensitive to social demands. Specialized lawyers have thus played an important role in the development of administrative law and labor law and in the extension of constitutional rights in the United States.

The explosion of advocacy

Modern social transformations tend to place new demands on the legal order and the legal profession. Government—public and private—is asked to perform tasks and satisfy needs that were formerly taken care of in more informal settings. Thus, in contrast to a rather passive role in the past, law and legal institutions are being summoned to participate more positively in the task of fulfilling human aspirations and accomplishing social purposes.

The effectiveness of law in this new role depends upon considerable expansion of social resources for legal criticism. Modern times may thus witness what has been termed an "explosion of advocacy," with corresponding demands for critical changes in the services of the legal profession. The lawyer is called upon to relinquish his passive stance and assume an active role in the transformation of privileges into rights and in the development of rationality and competence in government institutions (Cahn & Cahn 1964).

This enlarged responsibility will require greater initiative on the part of the profession in scrutinizing the variety of social settings where decisions are made affecting established or incipient rights. The traditional role of law schools and professional associations will need re-evaluation in this respect. More positive responsibilities may fall upon legal departments, in view of their growing role in public and private organizations. Special agencies, similar to the Scandinavian office of ombudsman, may also be designed to carry out this task of legal criticism.

Wherever government relies upon self-help for the assertion of claims and interests, the viability of the system will ultimately depend upon the legal competence of the citizenry, that is, its capacity to make effective use of the legal machinery. To promote this competence is one of the major tasks of the legal profession. One requirement is that the provision of legal services be extended.

Pressures on the profession to broaden its availability have been heightened by social demands for equality and political enfranchisement. It is unlikely, however, that the enlarged need for legal services can be fully met with existing institutions, such as legal aid and public defender offices. Serious limitations of available organized services can be seen in their dependence upon traditionally restricted sources of support, their routine treatment of cases, and their view of legal assistance as a form of public welfare ("The Availability of Counsel . . ." 1965).

As legal institutions become increasingly used and crowded, a new burden falls on the lawyer. The working of both law offices and tribunals comes to depend upon establishing standardized methods for the mass processing of cases. Thus the operation of rules and procedures tends to become a routine which escapes criticism and blocks adaptation to unusual cases and new experiences. Special efforts are then required of the lawyer in continually subjecting procedures to re-evaluation and in opening them to challenge and change.

However, more than a simple extension of legal services may be needed. The traditional model of individual representation and counseling may prove inadequate to the task of developing legal competence. New types of legal services must be evolved. Thus, the older emphasis on serving individual clients may have to be supplemented and in part replaced by *organizational advocacy:* here legal services are provided to an organization representing the common interests of a group or they are made available to members of the group through intervention by the organization. This transformation has already taken place in American industry, where organized labor has secured the services of specialized labor lawyers to support the legal interests of its constituents. Group services will have to expand if legal assistance is to be made effectively available ("The Availablity of Counsel . . ." 1965). Experience has shown that persons who are insecure and lack social support for the assertion of their claims need a representative organization to lend them its strength and resources. Neighborhood law firms and defense organizations such as the National Association for the Advancement of Colored People and the American Civil Liberties Union constitute a step in this direction. As these changes proceed, new specializations will develop within the legal profession, thus promoting the growth of new, still inchoate, fields of law.

Together with the growth of group representation, there is a drift away from the passive acceptance of individual cases as they come. This traditional approach is consistent with an adversary system in which the presentation of legal issues depends upon the development of specific controversies between defined interests. This system tends to divert attention from structural sources of injustice. As individual demands become organized, *strategic advocacy* develops: the lawyer can select and possibly generate issues for the purpose of challenging practices and pressing recognition of new rights (Cahn & Cahn 1964). In this process, adjudication becomes less dependent upon disputes and can address itself more directly to issues of policy and the broader interests at stake. Adversariness is then used as a way of clarifying policy problems; at the same time, the role of the *amicus curiae* develops, and there is greater reliance upon forms of declaratory relief, where questions of law are clarified without the necessity of deciding on the outcome of a particular dispute. More importantly, the growth of the law tends to be less contingent upon the more or less random occurrence of cases and to proceed along lines of more systematic planning.

PHILIPPE NONET AND
JEROME E. CARLIN

[*Directly related are the entries* JUDICIAL PROCESS; JUDICIARY; LEGAL SYSTEMS. *Other relevant material may be found in* CANON LAW; JURISPRUDENCE; LEGAL REASONING; LEGISLATION.]

BIBLIOGRAPHY

The Availability of Counsel and Group Legal Services: A Symposium. 1965 *U.C.L.A. Law Review* 12:279–463. → Contains a foreword and eight articles.

BERLE, A. A. JR. 1933 Modern Legal Profession. Volume 9, pages 340–346 in *Encyclopaedia of the Social Sciences*. New York: Macmillan.

BLAUSTEIN, ALBERT P.; and PORTER, CHARLES O. 1954 *The American Lawyer: A Summary of the Survey of the Legal Profession*. Univ. of Chicago Press. → Valuable as a bibliographical source.

CAHN, EDGAR S.; and CAHN, JEAN C. 1964 The War on Poverty: A Civilian Perspective. *Yale Law Journal* 73:1317–1352.

CARLIN, JEROME E. 1962 *Lawyers on Their Own: A Study of Individual Practitioners in Chicago*. New Brunswick, N.J.: Rutgers Univ. Press.

CARLIN, JEROME E. 1966 *Lawyers' Ethics: A Survey of the New York City Bar*. New York: Russell Sage Foundation.

EULAU, HEINZ; and SPRAGUE, JOHN D. 1964 *Lawyers in Politics: A Study in Professional Convergence*. Indianapolis, Ind.: Bobbs-Merrill.

HAZARD, JOHN N. 1960 *Settling Disputes in Soviet Society: The Formative Years of Legal Institutions*. New York: Columbia Univ. Press.

HURST, JAMES W. 1950 *The Growth of American Law: The Law Makers*. Boston: Little.

JACKSON, RICHARD M. (1940) 1964 *The Machinery of Justice in England.* 4th ed. Cambridge Univ. Press.

KADISH, SANFORD H. 1961 The Advocate and the Expert—Counsel in the Peno-Correctional Process. *Minnesota Law Review* 45:803–841.

KIRCHHEIMER, OTTO 1961 *Political Justice: The Use of Legal Procedure for Political Ends.* Princeton Univ. Press.

LASSWELL, HAROLD D.; and MCDOUGAL, MYRES S. 1943 Legal Education and Public Policy: Professional Training in the Public Interest. *Yale Law Journal* 52:203–295.

O'GORMAN, HUBERT J. 1963 *Lawyers and Matrimonial Cases: A Study of Informal Pressures in Private Professional Practice.* New York: Free Press.

PLUCKNETT, THEODORE F. T. (1929) 1956 *A Concise History of the Common Law.* 5th ed. London: Butterworth. → See especially pages 79–289, "The Courts and Profession."

POUND, ROSCOE 1953 *The Lawyer From Antiquity to Modern Times: With Particular Reference to the Development of Bar Associations in the United States.* St. Paul, Minn.: West.

RIESMAN, DAVID 1954 *Individualism Reconsidered, and Other Essays.* Glencoe, Ill.: Free Press. → See especially pages 440–466, "Toward an Anthropological Science of Law and the Legal Profession."

SCHACHT, JOSEPH (1950) 1959 *The Origins of Muhammadan Jurisprudence.* Oxford: Clarendon.

SMIGEL, ERWIN O. 1964 *The Wall Street Lawyer: Professional Organization Man.* New York: Free Press.

WEBER, MAX (1922) 1954 *Max Weber on Law in Economy and Society.* Edited, with an introduction and annotations by Max Rheinstein. Cambridge, Mass.: Harvard Univ. Press. → First published as Chapter 7 of Max Weber's *Wirtschaft und Gesellschaft.*

IV
LAW AND LEGAL INSTITUTIONS

More scholarship has probably gone into defining and explaining the concept of "law" than into any other concept still in central use in the social sciences. Efforts to delimit the subject matter of law—like efforts to define it—usually fall into one of several traps that are more easily seen than avoided. The most naive beg the question and use "law" in what they believe to be its common-sense, dictionary definition—apparently without looking into a dictionary to discover that the word "law" has six entries in Webster's second edition, of which the first alone has 13 separate meanings, followed by five columns of the word used in combinations. German and French have even more complex ambiguities, since their comparable words (*Recht, droit*) include some dimensions for which English uses other words.

Sophisticated scholars, on the other hand, have been driven either to write treatises on the art and pitfalls of definition (Cohen & Hart 1955) or, like Stone (1964), to realize that in relation to a noetic unity like law, which is not represented by anything except man's ideas about it, definition can mean no more than giving the reader a set of mnemonics to remind him what has been talked about. It was Kant who said, "The lawyers are still seeking a definition of their concept of law." A century and a half later Stone stated that " 'law' is necessarily an abstract term, and the definer is free to choose a level of abstraction; but by the same token, in these as in other choices, the choice must be such as to make sense and be significant in terms of the experience and present interest of those who are addressed" (1964, p. 177).

Definitions of "law"

Even if we agree with Hart (1954) that the searches for definition and the concomitant search for security that they represent became serious only in the time of Austin (and Kant's remark would seem to belie this), it is apparent that schools of jurisprudence have risen, battled, and fallen on bastions erected on one meaning or another. Austin has permanently affected British jurisprudence by emphasizing the command aspect of a law and pointing out that the law is a command of the "sovereign" (itself an ambiguous concept). Since then lawyers have for generations and without signal success been arguing whether Austin's stipulations applied only to developed systems of "municipal" law and whether he himself really gave the point of command such primacy.

The American "realists" clustered around Oliver Wendell Homes's dictum that law is a prediction of what a court will enforce. Continental scholars tended to be more concerned with the moralistic "right" and "ought" aspects of the rules of law and have gone deeply into moral philosophy.

In the effort to define "law," some modern scholars like Hart (1954) conclude that there are three "basic issues": (1) How is law related to the maintenance of social order? (2) What is the relation between legal obligation and moral obligation? (3) What are rules and to what extent is law an affair of rules? Others (Stone 1966) describe several sets of attributes that are usually found associated with law. Accordingly, law is (1) a complex whole, (2) which always includes social norms that regulate human behavior. These norms are (3) social in character, and they form (4) a complex whole that is "orderly." The order is (5) characteristically coercive and (6) institutionalized. Law has (7) a degree of effectiveness sufficient to maintain itself. Anthropological studies of law in the non-Western world have followed a similar course. To cite one of the most vivid and orderly presentations, Pospisil (1958) examined several attributes of the law—the attribute of authority, that of intention of universal application, that of *obligatio* (the right–obligation cluster), and that of sanction. In his view, the "legal" comprises a field in which custom, political decision, and the various attributes overlap, though each may be found extended outside that overlapping field, and there is no firm line, but rather a "zone of transition," between that which is unquestionably legal and that which is not.

It was Kantorowicz (1958) who pointed out that there are many subjects, including some of a nonlegal nature, that employ a concept of law. He perceived that each needs a different definition of "law" if it is to achieve its purposes. He then proceeded to a more questionable point: it is for "general jurisprudence" to provide a background to make these differing definitions sensible—in short, it is the task of jurisprudence to elicit meaning from this cacophony of attempted definitions. Kantorowicz's method in jurisprudence is very like Pospisil's in anthropology. Instead of trying to find points for definition of law, Kantorowicz examined some characteristics of law that are vital to one or more of the specific definitions. Law is thus characterized by having a body of rules that prescribe external conduct (it makes little immediate difference to the law how one feels about it—the law deals in deeds). These rules must be stated in such a way that the courts or other adjudging bodies can deal with them. Each of the rules contains a moralizing or "ought" element—and Kantorowicz fully recognized that this "ought" element is culturally determined and may change from society to society and from era to era. Normative rules of this sort must, obviously, also be distinguished from the real uniformities by which men (sometimes with and sometimes without the help of courts and lawyers) govern their daily round of activity. Law is one of the devices by means of which men can reconcile their actual activities and behavior with the ideal principles that they have come to accept, and can do it in a way that is not too painful or revolting to their sensibilities and in a way which allows ordered (which is to say predictable) social life to continue. No act is wholly bad if it is "within the law"; no law is wholly good if it condones "immoral" action.

Rules. Custom is a body of more or less overt rules which express "ought" aspects of relationships between human beings and which are actually followed in practice much of the time. Law has an additional characteristic: it must be what Kantorowicz calls "justiciable," by which he means that the rules must be capable of reinterpretation, and be actually reinterpreted, by one of the legal institutions of society so that the conflicts within nonlegal institutions can be adjusted by an outside "authority."

It is widely realized that many peoples of the world can state more or less precise "rules" which are, in fact, the ideals in accordance with which they think they ought to judge their conduct. In all societies there are allowable lapses from rules, and in most there are more or less precise rules (sometimes legal ones) for breaking rules.

Legal institutions. In order to make the distinction between law and other rules, it has been necessary to introduce furtively the word "institution." We must now make an honest term of it. A social institution can be defined as a group of people who are united (and hence organized) for some purpose; who have the material and technical means of achieving that purpose or at least of making rational attempts at it; who support a value system, ethics, and beliefs validating that purpose; and who repeat more or less predictable activities and events in the carrying out of the purpose (Malinowski 1945). With this rubric, all human activity can be viewed either as institutionalized or as random (and the degree of random behavior may be the most diagnostic feature of any society). It need hardly be added that "institutionalized" does not necessarily mean "approved" by the people who participate in the institutions.

With these ideas it is possible to distinguish legal institutions from nonlegal ones. A legal institution is one by means of which the people of a society settle disputes that arise between one another and counteract any gross and flagrant abuses of the rules of the other institutions of society. Every ongoing society has legal institutions in this sense, as well as a wide variety of nonlegal institutions.

It can be pointed out that some nonlegal institutions—the priestly, the psychiatric, and the like—serve the function of settling disputes. To make the distinction between legal and nonlegal, social scientists generally invoke the doctrine of coercion and use of force. Such a settlement is sensible because the legal institutions with which modern Western lawyers deal are usually associated with a political unit of which the state is one type. A political organization *ipso facto* supplies theorists with a "sovereign" of Austinian type and the "enforcement" predicated by Holmes and others. From this point of view, then, legal institutions must have two defining criteria: (1) they must settle the disputes that arise in other (nonlegal) institutions, and (2) they must be associated with (or even constitute) some sort of political organization. Obviously, for some purposes—particularly in the study of less-developed legal systems—the second criterion can and must be dropped; for most purposes of Western jurisprudence, just as obviously, it is probably necessary to retain it.

In carrying out the task of settling difficulties in the nonlegal institutions, legal institutions must have specific ways to (1) disengage the difficulties from the institutions of origin which they now threaten, (2) handle the difficulties within the framework of the legal institution, and (3) set the new solutions back within the processes of the nonlegal institutions from which they emerged. Indeed, the presence of such characteristics is a vivid index of the presence of a political organization.

There are, thus, at least two aspects of legal institutions that are not shared with other institutions of society. First, legal institutions alone must have some regularized way to interfere in the malfunctioning (and, perhaps, the functioning as well) of the nonlegal institutions in order to disengage the trouble case. Second, there must be two kinds of rules in the legal institutions—those which govern the activities of the legal institution itself (called "adjectival law" by Austin and "procedure" by most modern lawyers) and those which are substitutes for, or modifications or restatements of, the rules of the nonlegal institution that has been invaded (called "substantive law"). The above are only the minimal aspects that are shared by all known legal institutions.

Seen in this light, the distinction between law and custom is fairly simple. Customs are rules (more or less strict and with greater or less support of moral, ethical, or even physical coercion) about the ways in which people must behave if social institutions are to perform their tasks and society is to endure. All institutions (including legal institutions) develop customs. Some customs in some societies are *re*institutionalized at another level: they are restated for the more precise purposes of legal institutions. When this happens, therefore, law may be regarded as a custom that has been restated in order to make it amenable to the activities of the legal institutions. In this sense one of the most characteristic attributes of legal institutions is that some of these "laws" are about the legal institutions themselves, although most are about the other institutions of society, such as the familial, economic, political, and ritual.

Malinowski, by his little book *Crime and Custom in Savage Society* (1926), has widely influenced lawyers with a faulty mode of distinguishing law from nonlaw. His idea was a good one; he claimed that law is "a body of binding obligations regarded as right by one party and acknowledged as the duty by the other, kept in force by the specific mechanism of reciprocity and publicity inherent in the structure of . . . society." His error was in equating what he had defined with the law. It is not law that is "kept in force by . . . reciprocity and publicity" ([1926] 1961, p. 58). It is custom as we have defined it here. Law is better thought of as "a body of binding obligations regarded as right by one party and acknowledged as the duty by the other" *which has been reinstitutionalized within the legal institution so that society can continue to function in an orderly manner on the basis of rules so maintained.* In short, reciprocity is the basis of custom; but the law rests on the basis of this double institutionalization.

Rights. One of the best ways to perceive the doubly institutionalized norms, or "laws," is to examine the smaller components as they attach to persons (either human individuals or corporate groups) and so to work in terms of "rights" and their reciprocal "obligations." In the framework of rights and duties, the relationships between law and custom, law and morals, law and anything else can be seen in a new light. Whether in the realm of kinship or contract, citizenship or property rights, the relationships between people can be reduced to a series of prescriptions with the obligations and the correlative rights which emanate from these prescriptions. In fact, thinking in terms of rights and obligations of persons (or role players) is a convenient and fruitful way of investigating much of the custom of many institutions. Legal rights are only those rights which attach to norms that have been doubly institutionalized; they provide a means for seeing the legal institutions from the standpoint of the persons engaged in them.

The phenomenon of double institutionalization of norms and therefore of legal rights has been recognized for a long time, but analysis of it has been only partially successful. Legal rights have their material origins in the customs of nonlegal institutions but must be *overtly restated* for the specific purpose of enabling the legal institutions to perform their tasks.

Sanctions. Many scholars, in comparative studies, have focused attention on the sanction for purposes of determining what is to be included in the "legal" field. Use of the term "sanction" has the advantage of allowing the scholar to beg the question of the Austinian sovereign. Sanction is generally understood to mean what the law itself says will or may happen to one found guilty of having transgressed a legal rule. The word is often used in common parlance to mean "the teeth in the law." When it is used as a verb, its true ambivalence becomes apparent. "To sanction" something is in ordinary usage not to interfere with someone's doing it; yet jurists also use it to mean "visit an evil on doing it," and social scientists have extended the word "sanction" far beyond its technical meaning for modern law. Radcliffe-Brown (1934*a*) described positive and negative sanctions for behavior, embracing not only penalization of nonconformity but also rewarding of conformity—and all this without specifying precisely who confers rewards or inflicts punishments.

The problem of sanction would seem to be better summarized in terms of legal institutions which, in some situations, apply specific types of correction to adjudged breaches of law. That is, the "sanction" is the body of rules according to which legal institutions interpose themselves for the purpose of maintenance of a social system so that living in it can be comfortable and predictable.

Law and social science

It is apparent that we must examine two further factors. First, what sort of definitions of law may be needed by the social sciences? Second, and related to this, how can social scientists go about investigating the legal institutions and the legalization of rights in any specific culture or in any concatenation of cultures?

The kernel of the social scientist's concept of law must be found, I believe, in the phenomenon of double institutionalization of rights: once within customary institutions, then again within the legal institutions. Therefore he is required absolutely to study both the legal institutions and the social institutions on which they feed—and only in this way can he ever make any progress with the thorny problem of the relationship between law and society.

The social scientist studying law is quite right when he considers the law a type of social superstructure to be judged by criteria or values of the social sciences. He is, however, quite wrong if he extends this position to mean that he need not consider what is known about the law on its own ground. The determining variables of the law may be considered as part of a social field; but equally so, the social field must be considered by jurisprudence. In short, what is required is a sort of stereoscopic vision, looking at data with the lens of jurisprudence in one eye and the lens of social science in the other.

Seen thus stereoscopically, a legal right (and, with it, a law) is the restatement, for the purpose of maintaining peaceful and just operation of the institutions of society, of some but never all of the recognized claims of persons within those institutions; the restatement must be made in such a way that these claims can be more or less assured by the total community or its representatives. Only by so viewing legal rights can the moral, religious, political, and economic implications of law be fully explored.

In fact, a primary problem of all legal studies may be the intersecting of the law and the other institutions of society. This relationship is no mere reflection of society in the law: it must be realized, rather, that the law is always out of phase with society, specifically because of the duality of the statement and restatement of rights. Indeed, the more highly developed the legal institutions, the greater the lack of phase, which not only results from the constant reorientation of the primary institutions but is magnified by the very dynamics of the legal institutions themselves (Stone 1964, chapter 1, sec. 1).

Thus, it is the very nature of law and its capacity to "do something about" the primary social institutions that create the lack of phase. Moreover, even if one could assume perfect legal institutionalization, change within the primary institutions would soon jar the system out of phase again. What is less obvious is that if there were ever to be perfect phase between law and society, then society could never repair itself, grow and change, flourish or wane. It is the fertile dilemma of law that it must always be out of step with society but that people must always (because they work better with fewer contradictions, if for no other reason) attempt to reduce the lack of phase. Custom must either grow to fit the law or it must actively reject it; law must either grow to fit the custom or it must ignore or suppress it. It is in these interstices that social growth and social decay take place.

Social catastrophe and social indignation and resultant changes in custom are sources of much new law. With technical and moral change new situations appear that must be "legalized." This truth has particular and somewhat different applications to developed and to less highly developed legal systems. In developed municipal systems of law, in which means for institutionalizing behavior on a legal level are already traditionally concentrated in political decision-making groups such as legislatures, there is a tendency for the legal institution not to reflect custom so much as to shape it. As developed nations put more faith in their legislatures, nonlegal social institutions sometimes take a very long time to catch up with the law. On the other hand, in less-developed legal systems, it may be that little or no popular demand is made on the legal institutions, and therefore little real contact exists or can be made to exist between them and the primary institutions (Stone 1966, chapter 2, sec. 17). Law can become one of the major sources of innovation in society.

The social scientist's first task, then, is the analysis of the legal institutions to be found and their interrelationships with the nonlegal institutions of society. There may be courts as in some parts of indigenous Africa or indigenous Europe; there may be self-help, oracles, moots, town meetings, contests, and certain types of feuds (although most feuds do not correct the difficulty and feed the corrected situation back into the nonlegal institutions of society). The social scientist can examine the particular types of customs that are legalized in any particular society. He can begin the process of comparing the customs of mating and child rearing with the laws of marriage; the customs of trading with the laws of contract; the customs of interpersonal relations with the law of tort; the customs of approved behavior with criminal law.

And what will he find? He will find that the practice of law is a force by itself, a force for preserving and molding society that both has its roots irrevocably in social institutions and must supersede any particular historicoethnographic phase of them.

The social scientist's next task is the reporting and comparison of legal institutions *in the terms of the people who participate in those institutions* and the subsequent comparison of those terms with the terms in which other people live in analogous or similar institutions.

His third task is the exposition of what Hoebel (1954) has called the "postulates" of that people's law: the assumptions held about the "natural" ways of the world, most often without even a possibility of overt statement, by the people who live by a custom and a law. These postulates lie behind the law as they lie behind every other aspect of that people's activity. They are those "values," or unquestioned premises, on which a people bases not merely its behavior (including law) but its moral evaluation of behavior (including ethics). The postulates behind a legal system are congruent with the postulates behind the accompanying economic or religious system. What may seem blatant discrepancies and contradictions and, indeed, hypocrisies (as between Sunday school and the market place) are in fact no more than inadequate analyses of the postulates. A postulate lying behind Anglo–American law is that the human body is inviolably private unless marriage or certain contracts have been entered into; a postulate behind Eskimo law is that life is hard and that kinship, amity, or love between individuals cannot be allowed to override the welfare of the society. The postulates underlying a people's law also underlie the rest of its culture. Law cases provide one of the best mechanisms by which the ethnographer can capture these postulates and make them overt.

PAUL BOHANNAN

[*See also* JUDICIAL PROCESS; POLITICAL ANTHROPOLOGY; SANCTIONS.]

BIBLIOGRAPHY

ALLEN, CARLETON K. (1927) 1958 *Law in the Making.* 6th ed. Oxford Univ. Press.

BOHANNAN, PAUL 1957 *Justice and Judgment Among the Tiv.* Published for the International African Institute. Oxford Univ. Press.

COHEN, JONATHAN; and HART, H. L. A. 1955 Symposium: Theory and Definition in Jurisprudence. Pages 213–264 in Aristotelian Society, *Proceedings,* Supplementary Volume 29: Problems in Psychotherapy and Jurisprudence. London: Harrison.

COHEN, MORRIS R. 1950 *Reason and Law: Studies in Juristic Philosophy.* Glencoe, Ill.: Free Press. → A paperback edition was published in 1961 by Collier.

EHRLICH, EUGEN (1913) 1936 *Fundamental Principles of the Sociology of Law.* Translated by Walter L. Moll with an introduction by Roscoe Pound. Cambridge, Mass.: Harvard Univ. Press. → First published as *Grundlegung der Soziologie des Rechts.*

GLUCKMAN, MAX 1955 *The Judicial Process Among the Barotse of Northern Rhodesia.* Manchester Univ. Press; Glencoe, Ill.: Free Press.

HAAR, BAREND TER (1939) 1948 *Adat Law in Indonesia.* Translated and edited with an introduction by E. Adamson Hoebel and A. Arthur Schiller. New York: Institute of Pacific Relations, International Secretariat. → First published as *Beginselen en stelsel van het adatrecht.*

HART, H. L. A. 1954 Definition and Theory in Jurisprudence. *Law Quarterly Review* 70:37–60.

HART, H. L. A. 1961 *The Concept of Law.* Oxford: Clarendon.

HOEBEL, E. ADAMSON 1954 *The Law of Primitive Man: A Study in Comparative Legal Dynamics.* Cambridge, Mass.: Harvard Univ. Press.

JONES, HARRY W. 1962 Law and the Idea of Mankind. *Columbia Law Review* 62:753–772.

KANTOROWICZ, HERMANN 1958 *Definition of Law.* Edited by A. H. Campbell. Cambridge Univ. Press. → Published posthumously.

KANTOROWICZ, HERMANN; and PATTERSON, EDWIN W. 1928 Legal Science: A Summary of Its Methodology. *Columbia Law Review* 28:679–707.

LLEWELLYN, KARL N.; and HOEBEL, E. ADAMSON 1941 *The Cheyenne Way: Conflict and Case Law in Primi-*

tive Jurisprudence. Norman: Univ. of Oklahoma Press.

MALINOWSKI, BRONISLAW (1926) 1961 *Crime and Custom in Savage Society.* London: Routledge. → A paperback edition was published in 1959 by Littlefield.

MALINOWSKI, BRONISLAW 1945 *The Dynamics of Culture Change: An Inquiry Into Race Relations in Africa.* New Haven: Yale Univ. Press. → A paperback edition was published in 1961.

POSPISIL, LEOPOLD 1958 *Kapauku Papuans and Their Law.* Yale University Publications in Anthropology, No. 54. New Haven: Yale Univ., Department of Anthropology.

RADCLIFFE-BROWN, A. R. 1934*a* Sanction, Social. Volume 13, pages 531–534 in *Encyclopaedia of the Social Sciences.* New York: Macmillan. → Reprinted in the author's *Structure and Function in Primitive Society.*

RADCLIFFE-BROWN, A. R. 1934*b* Law, Primitive. Volume 9, pages 202–206 in *Encyclopaedia of the Social Sciences.* New York: Macmillan.

RADIN, MAX 1940 *Law as Logic and Experience.* New Haven: Yale Univ. Press.

STONE, JULIUS 1964 *Legal System and Lawyers' Reasonings.* Stanford Univ. Press.

STONE, JULIUS 1966 *Social Dimensions of Law and Justice.* Stanford Univ. Press.

TIMASHEFF, NICHOLAS S. 1939 *Introduction to the Sociology of Law.* Cambridge, Mass.: Harvard University, Committee on Research in the Social Sciences.

WILLIAMS, L. GLANVILLE 1945 International Law and the Controversy Concerning the Word "Law." *British Year Book of International Law* 22:146–163.

WILLIAMS, L. GLANVILLE 1945–1946 Language and the Law. *Law Quarterly Review* 61:71–86, 179–195, 293–303, 384–406; 62:387–406.

LAW ENFORCEMENT

See CRIME; PENOLOGY; POLICE; PUNISHMENT; SOCIAL CONTROL.

LAW, JOHN

John Law of Lauriston (1671–1729), economist, banker, merchant, and statesman, founded the first Bank of France and is generally held responsible for the Mississippi Bubble. He was born in Edinburgh, the son of a prosperous goldsmith–banker, who died when Law was only 13. However, his mother, who was distantly related to the duke of Argyll, saw to it that Law studied both theoretical and applied economics. Law was a handsome man with an engaging personality and the ability to make a favorable impression on important people. Nevertheless, he spent many years as a fugitive from British justice, having been sentenced to death in 1694 for killing a man in a duel. It was not until 1717 that he was pardoned by George I, and his extensive travels during his exile enabled him to study diverse economic institutions and conditions abroad.

Law's early interest in money and banking may well have been intensified by the adoption of William Paterson's plan for the Bank of England in 1694, since Paterson was a fellow Scot. Over the next 20 years Law was to spend much time and energy making proposals for the establishment of banks, both in Scotland and on the Continent, and these efforts eventually culminated in the founding of the first Bank of France.

The original proposal was outlined in two drafts for a privately owned Bank of France, which he sent in 1702 to Madame de Maintenon, the morganatic wife of Louis XIV. In a brief theoretical introduction, Law enumerated as components of the money supply: Bank of England stock, stock in the English and Dutch East India companies, exchequer notes, and Dutch government bonds—a concept of money supply that was destined to lead to his most calamitous mistakes in monetary policy. Each province of France would have a branch of the Bank, with a fixed allotment of capital, and notes payable to bearer would be redeemed at the parent Bank in Paris or at any one of the branches. Law argued that the Bank of France, like the Bank of Amsterdam and the Bank of England, would increase the money supply, lower the rate of interest (thereby raising the price of land and stimulating economic activity), reduce losses from fire and theft, eliminate shipments of specie from the provinces to Paris, and, through its notes, provide a safe and convenient medium of exchange for travelers. Law's project was not accepted: the French finance minister, Michel Chamillart, was also war minister and was preoccupied with military problems, and Madame de Maintenon's prejudice against Protestants and foreigners did not predispose her to support Law.

But Law did not have to wait long for another opportunity to propose a banking scheme. He was in Edinburgh in the summer of 1704, when Scotland was suffering a depression subsequent to the failure of William Paterson's Darien expedition. The suspension of specie payments by the Bank of Scotland in December 1704 intensified the crisis, and this stimulated Law to propose to the Parliament of Scotland in 1705 that a land bank be created. The proposal was published anonymously, as *Money and Trade Considered: With a Proposal for Supplying the Nation With Money.* At least 15 other tracts with surprisingly similar titles appeared in the same year or early in 1706. Law and the authors of the other tracts all attributed the crisis to scarcity of money, but Law was the only one who carefully formulated the theory underlying his proposal. He explained that value is determined by supply and demand and that the value of money is only a special case in value theory. The key to his monetary thought is his assumption of a state of disequilibrium, with large masses of idle factors of production, as a starting point for analysis.

Law presented at least 24 numerical examples to show that if the money supply were increased by notes issued for productive loans, employment and output (and, implicitly, the demand for money) would rise proportionately and the value of money would remain stable. He also argued that the notes of the land bank would have other advantages over metallic money in that they would be easier to transport, store, and count, while being equally divisible without loss of value and equally capable of receiving a stamp as metallic money. Moreover, the supply of bank notes, unlike that of metallic money, would be perfectly elastic. Yet another advantage that Law attributed to his scheme was that it would prevent any adverse effect on the balance of trade. Assuming that the international demand for goods was perfectly inelastic, he argued that debasing the coinage and marking up coins would render the balance of trade unfavorable and induce an outflow of specie, while the introduction of notes would avoid this consequence. Nor would the notes, unlike debasement of the coinage, create inflation. Although Law's scheme was favored by the duke of Argyll, the lord high commissioner, and the earl of Islay, it won active support from only two members of the Scottish Parliament.

Back in France, in 1706 Law submitted to Chamillart his "Treatise on Money and Commerce" ("Mémoire touchant les monnoies et le commerce"). It was dated November 28, 1706, and has remained not only unpublished but unused even by scholars; yet it is the best single presentation of Law's monetary theory. A most interesting aspect of the document is Chamillart's extensive and often shrewd commentary in the margins; these comments are noteworthy because they show that Chamillart detected the error in Law's argument that debasing or marking up the coinage would render the balance of trade unfavorable. Law's proposals that France adopt paper money, as superior to gold and silver, led to his expulsion from that country. Allegations that he was banished because of his success as a gambler are unfounded.

In the winter of 1712 Law was in Turin and presented several tracts on money and banking to Vittorio Amadeo II, duke of Savoy, who was deeply impressed by Law's intellectual power and monetary knowledge but who decided against a bank. Later the duke urged Law to return to Turin, presumably to establish a bank, but Law declined.

In December 1713 Law returned to Paris and was soon again plying the French government with proposals for a bank. In July 1715 he came very close to convincing Desmarets, then finance minister, who rejected his project only because he could not stomach a bank that would be as completely dominated by one man as, he sensed, the proposed one would be dominated by Law. After the death of Louis XIV, Law convinced the duke of Orleans, the regent, of the desirability of a royal bank, and encountered his last defeat when the proposal was rejected by the Council of Finance on October 24, 1715. Shifting to the concept of a privately owned institution, Law obtained a charter for the General Bank, on May 2, 1716. It was the first Bank of France and the opening wedge for his System. The charter for the Bank was granted to "Mr. Law and his Company." Law drafted the charter and subscribed for one-fourth of the stock. As Desmarets had anticipated, the bank was completely dominated by Law—more so than any other national or central bank has ever been dominated by one man.

From the outset the General Bank was conservatively managed. There is no evidence that it ever failed to meet an obligation. During the 31 months of its operation its notes raised the money supply only about 3 per cent, and its deposits were infinitesimal. The General Bank discounted accepted bills of exchange drawn on Paris at 6 per cent from June 1716 through March 1718, when the rate was reduced to 4 per cent. While the Bank's discount rate was 6 per cent, the modal market rate on secured loans at Paris was 5 per cent, and the average rate was a trifle lower. From April to December 1718 the market rate moved irregularly downward but did not reach 4 per cent. The General Bank may have exerted some slight downward pressure on the rate of interest, but it did not end "usury."

In the beginning the business of the Bank was confined to Paris; but in the summer of 1716 custodians of public revenue in the provinces were instructed to accept and redeem Bank notes, and on October 7 they were ordered to remit to Paris exclusively in these notes. Consequently, even in the Bank's first year, notes were circulating in distant provinces, and the Bank achieved a national circulation far more quickly than did any other public bank in Europe before the nineteenth century.

It was early in 1717 that Law first became involved in the financial scheme eventually known as the Mississippi Bubble (Louisiana being commonly called Mississippi then). The financier Antoine Crozat, a neighbor and friend of Law's, decided to give up his Louisiana concession, having lost 1.25 million livres in four years. Convinced that only a company could raise the necessary capital, the government made no effort to dissuade Crozat. It was attempting to withdraw paper money from circulation; since this currency lessened confidence in Bank notes, Law favored deflating it. He thereupon devised a scheme to solve the government's financial problem and at the same time promote colonial trade—he proposed to establish a company to take over Louisiana and sell its stock for government paper money, to be converted into *rentes* and destroyed.

In August 1717 his Company of the West was chartered. Its shares were in denominations of 500 livres, and the capital was ultimately fixed at 100 million livres, payable in government paper money depreciated by about 60 per cent. Business was far better than in 1716, when the General Bank had been chartered, and many people believed that Louisiana offered possibilities of rich rewards. But they also knew that West India companies chartered under Richelieu and Colbert had failed miserably and that Crozat, one of the ablest and richest financiers in France, had just relinquished his Louisiana concession. Hence the stock was not fully subscribed until July 1718.

Thereafter the company's fortunes rose. In September 1718 it outbid all rivals for the lucrative monopoly on the importation, manufacture, and sale of tobacco, and in November it purchased the property and privileges of the Senegalese Company. Law was on his way. On May 26, 1719, the Company of the West absorbed the French East India Company and the China Company, thereby forming the Company of the Indies. In June the Africa Company was acquired.

Meanwhile, on December 4, 1718, the General Bank had been nationalized and its name changed to Royal Bank; nationalization was actually only a formality, since the crown had already bought 100 per cent of the stock. Control over the Bank remained in Law's hands, subject to approval by the regent (as had been the case up to that time). But notes could be issued only by royal decree and were guaranteed by the crown. In July 1719 the Company of the Indies was granted the right to farm the mints for nine years, and 25 of the 26 mints, the sole exception being the one at Lyons, became virtual branches of the Bank. In August, Law took over the general farm of indirect taxes, and in October he arranged for the Company of the Indies to refund the remaining public debt of 1,500 million livres at 3 per cent. On January 5, 1720, after having been "publicly" converted to Catholicism, Law became finance minister.

Law's System was complete, and he stood at the pinnacle of his power. After his fall he often said that he had had more power than any other uncrowned person had ever exercised in Europe, and he may have been right; for he controlled the colonial trade, the Royal Bank, the tobacco monopoly, the public debt, indirect taxes, and more than half of what is now the United States (excluding Alaska). In addition to being finance minister, he was the principal economic adviser and favorite of an absolute prince.

Law's India shares rose fiftyfold in about two years, most of the rise in the last half of 1719, when France experienced the greatest speculative orgy she has ever had. The first impetus to this speculative rise was the substantial profit from the tobacco monopoly; more important was Law's acquisition of the tax farm, since it was well known that many of the great fortunes in France had been made through tax farming. From the beginning Law encouraged speculation, and his advice was widely taken. Traders rushed in from the provinces and from many foreign countries. Hitherto prudent Frenchmen and even some families in other countries liquidated real property to buy Law's stock, and the mania extended down to the very poor, who staked their patrimonies and life savings on small fractions of shares. The *Nouveau mercure* of November 1719 reported that "some stockholders have died from surprise, others from joy, [while still others] have gone mad from calculating their profits." Law converted much of his own great fortune—most of which was a capital gain on his stock—into magnificent rural estates and town houses, thus advertising his wealth and whetting the public appetite for his shares. The speculative boom rested heavily on hopes of gain from the exploitation of Louisiana.

It was not only the exaggerated estimate of the natural riches of Louisiana that constituted an essential weakness of Law's System but also his conviction, which went back to at least 1702, that shares of stock are money. Believing this, Law pegged the price of his stock at 9,000 livres when it began falling in January 1720, thus not only monetizing the stock but making it a monetary standard. Sales of stock to the Bank far exceeded purchases, and the quantity of Bank notes in circulation rose so sharply that they occasionally fell below par in specie. On Law's initiative, pegging was discontinued by the stockholders on February 22, but a considerable decline in the price of Law's stock led to its resumption on March 20. Inflation was disastrous: from March 26 to May 1 note circulation increased by 1,470 million livres, or about 125 per cent, and during May the note issue reached a peak of 2,696 million livres. Pegging the stock cost more than the equivalent of half the public debt. (The government admitted in 1725 that the second round of pegging was ordered by the regent.) Commodity prices had risen more than 50 per cent in the major cities, and money wages lagged far behind.

Law then made a mistake that again derived from his erroneous belief that stock is money: he chose to deflate, rather than remove the peg on his stock. Although this deflation has been widely attributed to his enemies, a decree lowering the price of stock to 8,000 livres as of May 22, 1720, and by stages to 5,000 livres on December 1, was drafted by Law himself and corrected in his own hand. Bank notes were to be marked down 20 per cent on May 22 and by stages to 50 per cent by December 1. Consternation and panic reigned, intensified by an attempt by the Bank to collect all loans on stock. Yielding to the clamor of the populace, the regent dismissed Law, but this only increased the uncertainty. On May 27 the deflationary decree was repealed and the old rating of the Bank's notes restored, while the peg on stock was removed. The restoration of Law, at the end of May, to his former position in the Bank and the company was not accompanied by any restoration of public confidence, and his System was doomed.

From June to September of 1720, Law and the regent strove desperately to rehabilitate the System through drastic deflation of the Bank's notes. But the notes steadily lost favor, and by December the country had returned to a specie basis. In mid-December Law was permitted to leave France, and his tottering System collapsed.

Even Law's worst enemies and severest critics recognized that France had been suffering one of the worst crises in her history in June 1716, when the General Bank opened its doors. Commodity prices had been falling disastrously for a year and a half. Unemployment, bank failures, commercial bankruptcies, agricultural distress, and social unrest were rife. Pessimism filled the air. Law was at the head of a national bank and in a position to influence strongly the economic policy of an absolute prince. No other "Keynesian" economist has ever had such a golden opportunity.

What did Law accomplish? He not only ended unemployment but even induced a labor shortage and overfull utilization of plant capacity. Public and private obligations, hitherto chronically in arrears, were paid promptly. Despair gave way to optimism. The population of Louisiana rose almost tenfold; the burden of taxation was lightened; sinecures were reduced; and many fetters to trade were removed.

Many of Law's achievements were lasting. There was feverish construction of buildings—including a substantial number of magnificent structures in the Place Vendôme in Paris erected by Law himself. Large numbers of skilled workers and technicians were brought from abroad to establish new industries and improve old ones. The books of the tax farm were rationalized, subfarming was largely eliminated, and the administration was simplified and unified. Reform of the tax system was one of Law's most durable achievements. Dreams of wealth from Louisiana focused attention on the New World. Reflections on a new people and a new culture enlarged horizons, bred tolerance, and prepared the way for the Enlightenment.

But these gains were not without cost. During the boom commodity prices rose about 100 per cent in Paris and Bordeaux; 170 per cent in Marseilles, afflicted in 1720 by one of the worst plagues in French history; and 140 per cent in Toulouse, also affected by the plague. Creditors, pensioners, and other holders of passive rights suffered cruel losses, and the average decline of daily real wages in Paris, Marseilles, and Toulouse was 25 per cent. Holders of the Bank's notes and of shares of the Company of the Indies presented more than half a million claims (nearly four-fifths of which were from the provinces) to the commission that liquidated the System, and losses in the liquidation ran as high as 95 per cent. (Even for those who could prove they had exchanged coins for notes at the Bank the loss was two-thirds.) Many families were ruined; most were hurt. A surprising number of very poor people suffered crushing losses on small fractions of shares. Thousands of noble and well-to-do families in foreign countries lost major portions of their fortunes.

Law made serious mistakes in theory and practice and undertook far more than anyone should have. However many of his ideas have stood the test of time, and his integrity has withstood all assaults.

Earl J. Hamilton

WORKS BY LAW

(1705) 1966 *Money and Trade Considered: With a Proposal for Supplying the Nation With Money.* New York: Kelley.

Oeuvres complètes. Edited by Paul Harsin. 3 vols. Paris: Sirey, 1934. → Contains much previously unpublished material.

Oeuvres de J. Law. Translated from the English by Étienne de Sénovert. Paris: Buisson, 1790.

SUPPLEMENTARY BIBLIOGRAPHY

BUVAT, JEAN 1865 *Journal de la régence (1715–1723).* Edited by Émile Campardon. 2 vols. Paris: Plon. → Published posthumously.

DUTOT (1738) 1935 *Réflexions politiques sur les finances et le commerce.* 2 vols. Liége, Université de, Faculté de Philosophie et Lettres, Bibliothèque, Vol. 66–67. Paris: Droz.

FAIRLEY, JOHN A. 1925 *Lauriston Castle: The Estate and Its Owners.* Edinburgh: Oliver & Boyd.

[FORBONNAIS, FRANÇOIS V. D. DE] 1758 *Recherches et considérations sur les finances de France, depuis l'année 1595 jusqu'à l'année 1721.* 2 vols. Basel: Cramer. → Published anonymously.

HAMILTON, EARL J. 1936 Prices and Wages at Paris Under John Law's System. *Quarterly Journal of Economics* 51:42–70.

HAMILTON, EARL J. 1937 Prices and Wages in Southern France Under John Law's System. *Economic History* 3:441–461.

HEINRICH, PIERRE 1908 *La Louisiane sous la Compagnie des Indes, 1717–1731.* Paris: Guilmoto.

LA JONCHÈRE, ÉTIENNE LESCUYER DE 1720 *Système d'un nouveau gouvernement en France.* 4 vols. Amsterdam: Le Bon.

LEVASSEUR, ÉMILE 1854 *Recherches historiques sur le système de Law.* Paris: Guillaumin.

LÜTHY, HERBERT 1959–1961 *La banque protestante en France, de la révocation de l'Édit de Nantes à la Révolution.* 2 vols. Paris: S.E.V.P.E.N.

MANN, FRITZ K. 1913 Die Vorgeschichte des Finanzsystems von John Law. *Schmollers Jahrbuch für Gesetzgebung, Verwaltung und Volkswirtschaft im Deutschen Reiche* 37:1165–1229.

[MARMONT DU HAUTCHAMP, BARTHÉLEMI] 1739 *Histoire du système des finances, sous la minorité de Louis XV. pendant les années 1719 & 1720.* 6 vols. The Hague: Hondt. → Published anonymously.

[MARMONT DU HAUTCHAMP, BARTHÉLEMI] 1743 *Histoire générale et particulière du visa fait en France. . . .* 4 vols. The Hague: Scheurleer. → Published anonymously.

[MELON, JEAN-FRANÇOIS] (1734) 1739 *A Political Essay Upon Commerce.* Dublin: Woodward & Cox. → First published anonymously in French.

P. C. 1722 *Het leven en caracter van den heer Jan Law.* Amsterdam. → Published under this pseudonym.

[PARIS DUVERNEY, JOSEPH] 1740 *Examen du livre intitulé* Reflexions politiques sur les finances et le commerce. 2 vols. The Hague: Prevôt. → Published anonymously.

WOOD, JOHN P. 1824 *Memoirs of the Life of John Law of Lauriston, Including a Detailed Account of the Rise, Progress, and Termination of the Mississippi System.* Edinburgh: Black.

LAWS, CONFLICT OF

See CONFLICT OF LAWS.

LE BON, GUSTAVE

Although Gustave Le Bon (1841–1931) is most generally known for his book *The Crowd,* his career in fact had three overlapping phases, the successive focuses of his interest being anthropology and archeology, experimental and theoretical natural science, and only finally social psychology.

Le Bon received a doctorate of medicine without any vocation for the profession. He began his adult life with travels in Europe, north Africa, and Asia. From these travels there resulted a half-dozen books, chiefly on anthropology and archeology. The last of the works on these subjects, *Les monuments de l'Inde*, appeared in 1893, when Le Bon was 52.

However, when he was in his late thirties Le Bon's interests began to shift radically: he invented recording instruments (exhibited in 1878), studied racial variations in cranial capacity, analyzed the composition of tobacco smoke, published a photographic method for making plans and maps, as well as a treatise that put the training of horses on an experimental basis, and, finally, devoted more than ten years to research on black light, intra-atomic energy, and the equivalence of matter and energy. During this period, furthermore, Le Bon began the work in social psychology that was to become the predominant concern of the final phase of his career. *The Crowd* appeared in 1895, when he was 54.

It is, of course, chiefly by virtue of the works of this third phase that Le Bon belongs to the history of social science. But these works in social psychology have links not only with the books of the period of his travels but also with those of what might be called his scientific phase. Thus, when Le Bon dealt with pedagogy and politics, he carefully transposed to children and peoples what he had earlier learned about horses. Similarly, he claimed to support his ideas on the psychological hierarchy of races and sexes with material from his study of the variations in the volume of the brain.

Before sketching the main outlines of the doctrine underlying all of Le Bon's psychological work, one trait of this work—perhaps at the time the most original—should be stressed. He selected extremely concrete problems for study—for example, the socialist movement, the organization of education, colonial policy, the French Revolution, and World War I—but always sought to treat these problems in terms of scientific generalizations at the highest level of abstraction. This was nothing less than an attempt to synthesize Comte and Spencer with Michelet and Tocqueville. Le Bon was convinced that contingent events as well as social behavior are guided by eternal laws (1912, p. 322).

The unconscious. One of these eternal laws that Le Bon constantly invoked is the futility of rationality in the affairs of society: an idea does not prevail because it is true, but by virtue of psychological mechanisms that have nothing to do with reason, such as repetition and "mental contagion." These mechanisms permit an idea to penetrate into the unconscious, and it is only when an idea does become part of the unconscious that it becomes effective for action. This rudimentary theory of learning was first formulated when he was studying the training of horses and then extended to human education and to politics. His watchword was: let the conscious become the unconscious.

The principle that only the unconscious produces effective action applies, according to Le Bon, not only to individuals but also to whole peoples (or races, so long as it is well understood that what is meant are "historical races," created by the events of history, and not races in the anthropological sense). Thus a people, or a civilization, or a race, properly so-called, must have a national soul, that is, shared sentiments, shared interests, and shared ways of thinking. The national soul is produced by such nonrational mechanisms as suggestion and heredity; all metaphysical, religious, political, and social beliefs are so rooted in the national soul of each people. It is these deeply-rooted beliefs that govern institutions (*not* the inverse, as Tocqueville had imagined).

The vital implication of this theory for politics is that laws are illusory and ineffective if they lack a basis in the national psychology. Moreover, according to Le Bon, it is these fundamental beliefs that produce lack of understanding and intolerance between peoples and groups and thus account for the irreducibility of what may be called ideological conflicts and the inevitability of civil strife and international wars.

Hierarchies. Le Bon was perennially establishing hierarchies. Thus he asserted the existence of a hierarchy of races, based on psychological criteria (such as degree of reasoning ability, power of attention, mastery over instinctual drives; see the *Psychology of Peoples* 1894) and confirmed on anatomical grounds by the alleged greater differentiation of the superior races and the greater consequent incidence of individuals who rise above the mean. As a specific instance of such hierarchical ordering, Le Bon repeatedly compared the mental constitution of the Anglo–Saxon race with that of the Latin peoples, and down to World War I he considered the Anglo–Saxons superior in every way. He established a hierarchy of the sexes using the same kind of criteria. According to his system of evaluation, animals, the insane, socialists, children, degenerates, and primitives were inferior beings.

The crowd. He postulated another, very interesting kind of inferiority: this is the inferiority of the crowd, or of man in the crowd. Le Bon believed that the psychology of men in a crowd differs essentially from their individual psychology; they become simple automata, instances of a sort of new being. Their spirit is that of the crowd which, like every spirit, is part of the unconscious; but this is a very low-level part of the unconscious, archaic or primitive from a historical point of view and medullar from a physiological one.

The psychological characteristics of crowds, as analyzed at length in the celebrated *The Crowd*, may be grouped around three themes. The first and most general characteristic attributed by Le Bon to crowd behavior is that of unanimity; he called this the law of the mental unity of crowds and asserted it as a dogma. He saw this mental unity accompanied by an awareness of unanimity that has important consequences: dogmatism and intolerance, a feeling of irresistible power, and a sense of irresponsibility. The second characteristic of crowd behavior is its emotionality: the actions of the crowd are sudden, simple, extreme, intense, and very changeable, so betraying the feminine nature of crowds. The third descriptive theme is that the intellectual processes of crowds are rudimentary and mechanical: crowds are very credulous, their ideas are schematic, and their logic is infrarational and ignores the principle of noncontradiction.

How, then, does it happen that in a crowd situation even the most rational of men are transformed into brutes? Le Bon, like Tarde, who wrote on the same topic at the same time, offered two explanations: mental contagion and the role of leaders, who are often, but not always, described as agitators. But what do these explanations amount to? "Contagion is a phenomenon that is readily observed, but has not yet been explained, and had best be related to the phenomena of hypnotism . . ." (1895, p. 17). "The unconscious minds of the charmer and the charmed, the leader and the led, penetrate each other by a mysterious mechanism" (1910, p. 139). These tautologous passages suggest that on occasion Dr. Le Bon knew how to resort to the technique of the doctors in Molière.

To concentrate criticism on this particular problem of explanation would be misleading, for these theories of mental contagion and of the role of leaders are no more gratuitous, no more confused, and no more based on obsolete psychology than is the entire core of Le Bon's system. They may even have special merit, for it was precisely such arbitrary assertions of Le Bon that contained his happiest insights. He believed that "the action of a group consists mainly in fortifying hesitant beliefs. Any individual conviction that is weak is reinforced when it becomes collective" (1912, p. 102); or that, during World War I, "isolated individuals regained their military value when they rejoined a familiar group, but not when they were merged into other groups" (1916, p. 243). These are sentences that would not surprise us if they appeared in *The People's Choice* or in *The American Soldier*.

The fact remains that these two sentences went unnoticed. It was by the most reckless, the most false, and the most harmful of his theories that Le Bon exerted his greatest influence, in France and even more so abroad. In particular, the "law of the mental unity of crowds" was widely accepted and taught, and perhaps still is. Ironically, the fame of some men is based on their mistakes and thereby confronts their critics with a painful dilemma: either to blame such a man for the very things that made him popular or to praise him for contributions that would not have existed were it not for the mistakes.

JEAN STOETZEL

[*For the historical context of Le Bon's work, see the biographies of* TARDE; TOCQUEVILLE. *For discussion of the subsequent development of his ideas, see* COLLECTIVE BEHAVIOR.]

WORKS BY LE BON

1892 *L'équitation actuelle et ses principes: Recherches expérimentales.* Paris: Firmin-Didot.

1893 *Les monuments de l'Inde.* Paris: Firmin-Didot.

(1894) 1898 *The Psychology of Peoples.* New York: Macmillan. → First published as *Lois psychologiques de l'évolution des peuples.*

(1895) 1947 *The Crowd.* New York: Macmillan. → First published as *Psychologie des foules.* Translation of extract was provided by the editors. A paperback edition was published in 1960 by Viking.

(1898) 1965 *Psychology of Socialism.* New York: Fraser. → First published as *Psychologie du socialisme.*

1902 *Psychologie de l'éducation.* Paris: Flammarion.

1910 *Psychologie politique et la défense sociale.* Paris: Flammarion.

1911 *Les opinions et les croyances.* Paris: Flammarion.

(1912) 1913 *The Psychology of Revolutions.* London: Allen & Unwin. → First published as *La révolution française et la psychologie des révolutions.* Translation of extract in the text provided by the editors.

1913 *Aphorisme du temps présent.* Paris: Flammarion.

1916 *The Psychology of the Great War.* London: Allen & Unwin. → First published in the same year as *Enseignements psychologiques de la guerre européenne.* Translation of extract in the text provided by the editors.

WORKS ABOUT LE BON

MERTON, ROBERT K. (1960) 1963 The Ambivalences of Le Bon's *The Crowd.* Pages v–xxxix in Gustave Le Bon, *The Crowd.* New York: Viking.

PICARD, EDMOND 1909 *Gustave Le Bon et son oeuvre.* Paris: Mercure de France.

LE PLAY, FRÉDÉRIC

Frédéric Le Play (1806–1882), French sociologist, is best remembered for his development of a method of research and data presentation known as the monographic method and for his classification of families into patriarchal, stem, and unstable types. His ideas had an important influence on European sociology from about 1860 to 1940, and his work is still a major inspiration to Roman Catholic sociologists. Many concepts developed by Durkheim can be found in their initial crude form in Le Play's work.

Le Play was born in Normandy, the son of a petty customs officer. His father died when Le Play was only five, and shortly afterward he went to live with a rich uncle in Paris. Here, as he grew up, he became an avid listener to the intellectual discussions that took place in his uncle's salon. Le Play, however, was never to forget the harbor town of his birth. He seems to have greatly idealized the frugal existence his family led during the difficult years of the Napoleonic blockade; this may help to explain why, when he came to consider such problems as the maintenance of order, the avoidance of violence, and the demoralization of the poor, it was not in the increase of the standard of living that he saw the solution but in the strengthening of family ties.

Social philosophy

Le Play wrote his main work, *Les ouvriers européens* (1855), between 1829 and 1855. At that time a large section of the bourgeoisie had developed a fairly durable synthesis of aristocratic and bourgeois values. Abandoning Voltairean skepticism, it had adopted a largely ceremonial Catholicism, tempered by mild anticlericalism and theological indifference. The only dynamic elements in this outlook were respect for hard work and a stress on the need for rootedness (*enracinement*) in the locality of one's birth—a rootedness consecrated by the ownership of private property.

Few counterinfluences disturbed this prevailing climate of thought. The followers of Saint-Simon still constituted a very articulate intellectual minority, and it was in reaction to one of them, with whom Le Play traveled through Europe, that Le Play was led to develop and systematize the beliefs and attitudes instilled by his upbringing. For the Saint-Simonians, centralist and deductive in their approach, social disorder and pauperism were to be solved through the complete reintegration of society around the industrial order. Property was to be controlled by the industrialists (the creators of wealth), rather than by inheritors, and the industrialists were to be helped—"guided," Auguste Comte would say—by the priests of the positive science of society. The problem of power relations would be solved by the obviousness of right reason. Reason would organize the world, control nature, and promote progress, with the happiness of the individual following naturally from the welfare of society.

Le Play rejected this technocratic and optimistic view. He decided that there is no such thing as unilinear social progress—there can only be cycles of prosperity and corruption, the former inevitably engendering the latter. People in simple societies, like the fishermen of his childhood or the gentle folk of the Harz, may attain peace and contentment, but people in complex societies cannot escape strife and misery. Le Play believed that man has always known that the supreme good lies in social peace, on the one hand, and moral conduct, on the other; this was codified once and for all in the Decalogue. How, then, can one speak of inevitable progress when the principles of the Decalogue may have been followed in earlier periods of history only to be ignored in later ones? The best that could happen would be a revival of what has always been acknowledged to be the truth. The happiness of man does not reside in increased comforts and education but in recognizing the soundness of these principles of good conduct, in spite of the seductiveness of false doctrines, and in conforming his life to them.

It is interesting to note the dual orientation of Le Play's thought. There is, on the one hand, the importance of having the right ideas—a typical French approach, which culminated in the concept of the idea-force of the late-nineteenth-century psychologists and which was not without influence even on Durkheim. And yet, on the other hand, there is the belief in the effectiveness of sheer coercion when practiced by the righteous to preserve lesser men from temptation. It reflects the Roman Catholic oscillation between the stress on individual free will and the need for the church to protect man from himself. The function of the social scientist is to fight against false doctrines and through the use of the scientific method to prove the soundness of the simple eternal truths. Another interesting aspect of Le Play's thought, differentiating it from Saint-Simon's, Comte's, or Tocqueville's, is its resolutely homocentric quality: he focused upon the problem of individual happiness—or salvation, as a Puritan might say—rather than upon the "utility of the community," as Pareto was to phrase it. The use of the word "happiness" (*bonheur*) is not accidental either, and Durkheim used this concept later in his discussion of anomie: *bonheur* is a state of inner harmony, with a definite sensualist tonality, rather than an external goal, like salvation. And *bonheur* is to be gained through control over man's essentially base nature (Durkheim would later speak, more neutrally, of the animal nature of man in contrast to his social nature). To achieve this control, man has as allies a divine force, the grace of God, and a social force, the family. When population size and density reach a certain level, thereby creating more complex problems of control (the exact terms of the equation are left unclear, but the critical level seems related to a more complex division of labor), the church and the state are to assist the family in its task. Insofar as men acting collectively can have any impact upon the happiness of the individual, they can do so only through the strengthening of the family.

Since industrialization had created pauperism and a rootless, marginal type of working class, the members of which were at the mercy of their base passions, the control and reintegration of that working class into the community of the righteous would be secured only by the consolidation of the working-class family and, more immediately, by its assimilation into the entrepreneur's family through the institution of patronage. Then the individual worker and his kin would have once more an opportunity for *bonheur*. Where Durkheim was to offer the professional organization as a means of alleviating the anomie that prevailed in economic life—a recommendation commonly made by French intellectuals, unless they belonged to the somewhat marginal Manchesterian group of Molinari—Le Play offered the family firm, in which the sting of the power relationship was removed by the fusion, in paternal-type relationships, of power with love. The rootlessness of the urban working class might be overcome through the device of permanent labor contracts and the fostering of property ownership by workers.

Le Play's theoretical interest in the variety of income sources in the workingman's budget (see Parsons et al. 1961, pp. 457–459) not only shows he rejected on empirical grounds the definition of working-class status as the nonownership of the means of production but also suggests his concern for a program of social action. The budgets itemized by Le Play often show the worker's family securing "profits" from home industries of which family members are the sole customers (owning a cow, rather than buying milk on the open market). Ideally, instead of private property being abolished, as advocated by the socialists, its ownership should be diffused, and more immediately, the workers should be encouraged and assisted by the entrepreneur in securing home ownership, since the latter is strategic to family stability.

Le Play's conception of the way in which the industrial world should be organized fitted very well with the romanticized version of the French family firm. He believed that in return for fealty and a nonbargaining approach to the labor contract, the family firm protected the worker from the vagaries of the market, through a conservative investment and sales policy—restricting expansion in times of boom and stretching out employment in times of depression, protecting the worker's family from want by provision of easily purchased homes and gardens and free social services.

The function of the employer, according to Le Play, was not so much to raise the standard of living of the worker as to provide him with moral leadership, help him acquire private property, and stimulate in him "the respect of the laws governing the family" (1864, vol. 2, p. 28). Property, in this context, whether house, land, or factory, is a visible symbol of the family, of its continuity and its moral fervor, rather than a mere means of production. Complete testamentary freedom is necessary to permit the transmission of family property, in its entirety, to the most deserving heir and, even more important, to prevent the destruction of the stability of the family itself. Not only may a parceled-out homestead be economically unviable but the breaking up of the estate will foster a break in the sibling solidarity, so indispensable to the preservation of the sound family structures, i.e., the patriarchal family and the stem family (for definitions, see below).

Le Play realized that the preservation of integral estates, the moral importance of which he had established, was in conflict with rules of the Code Civil, which enforce practically equal division among heirs. In his opinion, families faced with this dilemma had resolved it through a reduction in their fecundity, so that equal division would not destroy completely the holdings accumulated through years of hard work and thrift. This is his explanation for the decline of the French birth rate.

This deceptively simple mechanism—a bad decision by jurists may have widespread consequences for the reproduction policy of millions of families—underlines Le Play's belief in the power of good or bad political decisions to effect broad changes in the society in a one-way causal chain. Although this attribution of far-reaching demographic consequences to the Code Civil became widely popular, it was, in the main, erroneous. The tendency to divide estates equally had existed in French families prior to the enactment of the Code Civil. Even aristocratic families, before the French Revolution, as Le Play's disciple Paul de Rousiers showed in the history of his own family (1934), tended to give equal shares to their children: Equal love for one's children must be symbolized by equal shares of property. Therefore, it was not inheritance laws that were responsible for the restriction of fecundity—such laws could be bypassed by any father who was able to make his children internalize his own conception of the importance of integral estates—but instead the relatively high degree of social mobility present in French society after the revolution.

Nevertheless, we can readily understand the great success of Le Play's ideas among the provincial aristocracy and among that section of the bourgeoisie which aspired to assimilate aristocratic patterns and protect its dynasties from the vagaries of the market and the competition of "upstarts." Strictures against the growth of central state power, suspicion of intellectuals, respect for local notables, belief that men are born unequal in their capacity to resist evil or do good—all this was highly pleasing to the *bien-pensants*. No wonder that for a century Le Playism has been a basic ideology for that group, becoming a major element in the development of one brand of Christian socialism; it is a most plausible version of conservative mythology, and its influence extended to Russia, Great Britain, Holland, Germany, and French Canada.

Le Play's sociology

So far we have dealt only with the ideological component in Le Play's work. But important though this is, it should not be allowed to obscure Le Play's major contributions to the growth of sociology as a science. These contributions cover three major areas: the theory of social control, the theory of social change, and research methodology.

Social control. For Le Play, the family is the chief agency of socialization and social control. The chances for the abuse of power that are inherent in any system of social control are here limited by the love of the parents for their children, who, in return, endure frustration more easily when it is meaningfully related to the family's welfare. The church and the state can at best only assist or complete the work done by the family in checking the base impulses of the child's raw nature. Indeed, the weaker the central government, the better is the opportunity for the family to develop its authority and improve its performance.

Le Play distinguished three main types of family structure: the patriarchal family; the unstable family; and an intermediate type, the stem family. In the patriarchal family the father characteristically keeps near him all his married sons and exercises supreme authority over them and their children. Property remains communal. The patriarch directs all work and accumulates whatever savings can be gathered once the traditional needs of all family members have been satisfied. Le Play saw this type of family as common among the pastoral peoples of the Orient, the Russian peasantry, and the Slavs of central Europe.

Le Play's unstable family resembles what is today called the isolated nuclear family. It is unstable because it has little resiliency in the face of economic hardship. It is typical of the industrial working class and is also to be found among the upper classes, mainly because of successional laws that compel the division of estates among heirs. Although this type of family permits a brilliant individual to gain great success, it compounds the risk of failure for the untalented.

The stem family is a type of patriarchal family in which only one of the heirs is retained in the family homestead; the others receive some form of dowry that enables them to establish themselves elsewhere. Nevertheless, for those who leave, the family homestead remains a ceremonial center, as well as a port in a storm. Thus, the stem family combines some of the flexibility and recognition of talent of the unstable family with the continuity and security of the patriarchal family.

Social change. Le Play's theory of social change is essentially dualistic. On the one hand, he attached enormous importance to beliefs and ideas; on the other, he seemed to stress a sort of technological determinism, rooted in the geographic environment.

Religious belief was given an especially important part in Le Play's theory of social change, although differences between individual doctrines were of little consequence to him. All human societies, he asserted, accept some form of the Decalogue, belief in which is a fundamental condition for the maintenance of order and solidarity. When these beliefs weaken, the society suffers—and when they vanish, the society vanishes with them. The diffusion of areligious and/or antireligious doctrines by intellectuals was, therefore, a major source of social disorganization; so were erroneous laws regarding succession, which made it difficult for families to maintain the continuity of the family estate; or political decisions such as those of Louis XIV regarding the centralization of the French state; or beliefs, such as Rousseau's, in the inherent goodness of human nature. Such errors only show man incapable, of his own free will, of availing himself of the wisdom contained in the Decalogue. But these errors are a contingent factor, like the presence or absence of elite personalities—Plato's "divine men"—who create peace and order around them (and whom Le Play thought to be the best sources of information for the researcher). What can be taken for granted is that men will remain vulnerable to these errors, as well as remaining unequal in their capacity to create harmony around them.

The only causal process in history of which Le Play was certain was that prosperity always leads to the corruption of the elites, which leads in turn to the corruption of society. Corrupt social orders are purged by wars, which permit the more virtuous populations to assume political control over the more corrupt ones. The measure of this corruption is essentially the decline of paternal authority and the move away from the patriarchal and stem forms of family pattern toward the unstable form. Le Play's theory of social change belongs with the pessimistic, cyclical theories rather than with the optimistic, unilinear ones.

In contrast to the religious factor in social change or the impact of leadership and prosperity—which are essentially unpredictable in their incidence, if not in their consequences—the relationship between the family and its physical environment, as mediated by work patterns, seems to provide causal regularities susceptible of scientific inquiry. Steppe areas tend to produce stable patriarchal families; coastal fishing areas, stem families; and forests, unstable families (unless there happens to be rational exploitation of timber resources). Agriculture, if combined with proper succession laws, permits patriarchal families but usually produces stem families. The factory system, on the other hand, encourages unstable families among its workers, especially if the entrepreneurs do not fulfill their obligations of patronage. This was a major source of corruption in the prosperity engendered by industrialization.

Methodology. The monographic method is usually considered to be Le Play's unique contribution to the development of social science. Indeed, this method marks a twofold departure from the prevailing type of social science writing: first, it stresses immediate contact with the field data, collected with an eye to measurement, rather than relying on historical data or shrewd observations, as did Tocqueville or Taine; second, as Sorokin pointed out (1928, pp. 63–98), it introduces a selective principle for the collation and presentation of data that is derived from a theoretical schema—the primacy of family relationships in controlling behavior, the dependence of family relationships upon certain aspects of the environment and especially upon those which determine the type of work the family engages in, and the belief that all crucial family activities express themselves in a monetary form, which can be represented as a budget item.

No doubt the monographic method developed from the type of systematic reports that students of the School of Mines were supposed to make on their field trips, with emphasis upon those items which could be tabulated and counted. Another intellectual influence was the surveys and inquiries which were commissioned by the parliaments of France and Great Britain. And about the same time Le Play began his field work, Villermé was conducting his inquiries on poverty in French cities.

The unique thing about Le Play's method is that his work contains the beginning of statistical techniques which *later* led to sampling, as well as the beginning of index construction. (The family budget was used because it permitted accurate computation, and the rigorous itemization of budgets is probably the reason why the *Ouvriers européens* received a prize from the Académie des Sciences in 1855). However, the monographic method, as Le Play used it, was in fact a rejection of the system building of Saint-Simon and Comte, rather than an effective commitment to inductive and experimental thought. Le Play was turning the positivist approach against its inventors because he believed that in his day only scientific descriptions of social realities would render self-evident the one way to social harmony and individual happiness. For him social science was not a cumulative body of theoretical propositions; it was simply a way to make evident the eternal laws of social peace. If abstract reasoning should lead to statements that contradict these laws, then the reasoning must be false. And although Le Play at one time seemed to draw an analogy between fact gathering and parliamentary representation, he did not see the necessity for systematic sampling, because he felt that a few monographs were sufficient to convince the reader of the correctness of these basic moral laws. The accumulation of data is more a rhetorical device than an attempt at inductive proof. In order to verify the results of direct observation, one should consult with local leaders, who are best equipped to describe and interpret local customs and events.

The paradox of Le Play's methodology is that it is the invention of an antiempiricist. This inherent contradiction may explain why it failed to make as significant an impact upon scientific sociology as one might have expected.

Diffusion of Le Play's ideas

After the *Ouvriers européens*, Le Play turned essentially to propagandizing for social reform. Although he invoked the authority of the scientific method, rather than its logic, it is likely that he did render social science an important service by making the field of study a respectable one for the gentleman scholar, even though it meant contact with the lower classes in a context that precluded appropriate deference.

Le Play's follower Henri de Tourville was to complete the monographic method in 1886 by drawing up a "nomenclature"—a sort of sequential check list for describing the relationship of the family to its social and physical environment. The items to be covered were place, work, property system, forms of wealth, remuneration, savings, and the major social categories and organizations with which the family must deal—neighborhood, formal organizations, community, city, province, state, racial group—in essence, the outline of what was to become known as the community study.

However, the duality of Le Play's thought—idealist in its emphasis upon religious values, positivist in its emphasis upon geography and technology—led in 1886 to a split between his followers. The idealist component was developed into a predicating type of analysis, most notably by Charles de Ribbe, and again, more recently, into a philosophical–æsthetic type of essay writing, best exemplified by the work of Jean Lacroix.

The positivist group, represented by Tourville, de Rousiers, Robert Pinot, and Edmond Demolins, focused much more on the elements of a theory of the social system that were already implicit in the famous "nomenclature." Some, like Demolins, became much more openly positivist and stressed the geographical aspect of Le Play's theory of social change. They refused to condemn the industrial order as the source of social disorganization and came to challenge the belief that the stem family was the highest form of moral life. For them the model family was the "particularist" type, which they saw predominating in Scandinavian and Anglo-Saxon countries and which is essentially an optimistic version of what we would now call the isolated nuclear family. De Rousiers in particular, who visited the United States, gave the American family a good share of the credit for American enterprise and progress (see 1892). The analysis made by the positivist group of the relations between family type, on the one hand, and forms of government, types of economy and managerial policies, general styles of formal and informal organizations, and the school system, on the other, are often amazingly insightful and modern in content.

Neither wing of the Le Play school, however, had much impact upon French academic sociology, which was controlled by middle-class, anticlerical Durkheimians. The Le Play school was Roman Catholic and upper class in orientation. In fact, many of its members were aristocrats, for whom the field techniques of the monographic method, far from implying a threat to their social status, represented both a novel way of reaching out benevolently to the masses and an endorsement of the "facts," rather than a submission to the "theories" of bureaucrats or professors. The method fitted the antirational ideology of the traditional French upper classes, as displayed, for instance, in their predilection for the metaphysical philosophy of Henri Bergson.

This rejection of theory was the key weakness of the monographic method. It accumulated data which are supposed to speak for themselves but which, in the absence of comparative perspectives, say relatively little. However, the contemporary sociologist who wishes to compare these data with present-day equivalents will find in the monographs of the Le Play school a rich lode of "sociological fossils."

Influences on the literature. The first edition of the *Ouvriers européens* was published in 1855. "In order to avoid upsetting public opinion," it was published as a limited luxury edition, and the government presses in Paris handled the printing. The second edition was published in Tours in 1879, by the Mame publishing company, well known in France for its specialization in Roman Catholic literature.

The books that Le Play published after the *Ouvriers européens* are fundamentally works of special pleading, although claiming to be based on his past empirical research. The main ones are *La réforme sociale en France* (1864), *L'organisation du travail* (1870; an English translation appeared in 1872), *L'organisation de la famille* (1871*a*), *La paix sociale après le désastre* (1871*b*), *La constitution de l'Angleterre* (1875), and *La réforme de l'Europe et le salut en France* (1876). Part of Le Play's correspondence was published under the title *Voyages en Europe, 1829–1854: Correspondance* (1899).

A fairly extensive bibliography of Le Play's works can be found in *Textes choisis* (1947, pp. 59–60). Partial translations of the *Ouvriers européens* into English are to be found in Zimmerman and Frampton's *Family and Society* (1935, pp. 359–595). Extracts have been translated and reproduced in Riley's *Sociological Research* (1963, vol. 1, pp. 80–90) and in Parsons and his associates' *Theories of Society* (1961, pp. 457–459).

In 1856 the Société Internationale des Études Pratiques d'Économie Sociale was founded, with L. R. Villermé as its first president. It published a bulletin of its proceedings and in 1857 brought out ten volumes of "monographies" under the title: *Les ouvriers des deux mondes*. The bulletin of the society became in 1881 a review called *La réforme sociale*. This journal was conservative, Catholic, and largely anti-industrial. One of the better representatives of that tendency was de Ribbe, whose *La famille et la société en France avant la Révolution* (1873) is fundamentally a work of moralizing ideology.

Dissatisfied with the orientation of *La réforme sociale*, a group composed of Demolins, Tourville, de Rousiers, and Robert Pinot broke away in 1886 and founded *La science sociale*, under the editorship of Demolins. (In 1935 *La réforme sociale* and *La science sociale* merged to become *Les études sociales*.)

Among the works of the *Science sociale* group one may cite Demolins's *Les grandes routes des peuples: Essai de géographie sociale, comment la route crée le type social* (1901–1903). A more popular book by the same author was translated into English in 1898 (see 1897), with the title *Anglo-Saxon Superiority: To What It Is Due*; it ascribes the putative superiority of the Anglo-Saxons over the collectivistic societies of France and Germany to the particularistic family system and its stress upon self-reliance, progressive education, a responsible elite, and a noninterfering government. A crucial interest of Demolins was indeed education, which he wanted to reform along the lines of the English public school system. He founded the only successful progressive school that France has known, and it is described in his *L'éducation nouvelle: L'École des Roches* (1898).

Tourville was the theoretician of the *Science sociale* group. His most important work, besides the refinement of Le Play's nomenclature, was translated into English in 1907 as *The Growth of Modern Nations: A History of the Particularist Form of Society* (1905).

One of the most interesting writers of the *Science sociale* group was de Rousiers. He wrote one of the best statements of the group's position in his article "La science sociale," published in the

Annals of the American Academy of Political and Social Science (1894). His *American Life* (1892) and *The Labour Question in Britain* (1895) are among the best products of the Le Play school. In *The Labour Question* the monographic method reaches a new level of sophistication, through effective comparisons between the families of wage earners in different industries and between different types of productive organizations. Note also de Rousier's *Hambourg et l'Allemagne contemporaine* (1902), which brings a needed correction to Demolins's strictures on Germany as a collectivistic society, and *Une famille de hobereaux pendant six siècles* (1934).

Sociologists who wish to use monographies for a comparative historical perspective will consult with profit the extensive bibliography in Ferré's *Les classes sociales dans la France contemporaine* (1936, pp. 231–262), in particular the works of Jacques Valdour, who used participant–observer techniques. An addition to the Ferré bibliography should be the white-collar budgets in Henry Delpech's *Recherches sur le niveau de vie et les habitudes de consommation (Toulouse 1936–1938)* (1938).

One of the more fruitful uses of the budget method was made by the Durkheimian Maurice Halbwachs and is summarized in his work *L'évolution des besoins dans les classes ouvrières* (1933).

The most interesting offshoot of the Le Play school has been the work of Philippe Ariès, who has attempted to synthesize its approach with that of the Durkheim school, using a comparative historical approach rather than a strictly monographic one. His most important works are *Histoire des populations françaises* (1948) and *L'enfant et la vie familiale sous l'ancien régime* (1960), which was published in English as *Centuries of Childhood: A Social History of Family Life* in 1962.

Among commentaries on Le Play and his school must be cited Sorokin's *Contemporary Sociological Theories* (1928, pp. 63–98), *Recueil d'études sociales publié à la mémoire de Frédéric Le Play* (1956), and "Les cadres sociaux de la doctrine morale de Frédéric Le Play," by Andrée Michel (1963).

JESSE R. PITTS

[*For the historical context of Le Play's work, see the biographies of* COMTE *and* SAINT-SIMON; *for discussion of the subsequent development of Le Play's ideas, see* ANTHROPOLOGY, *article on* THE ANTHROPOLOGICAL STUDY OF MODERN SOCIETY; GEOGRAPHY, *article on* SOCIAL GEOGRAPHY; MODERNIZATION, *article on* SOCIAL ASPECTS; *and the biographies of* DURKHEIM *and* TOURVILLE.]

WORKS BY LE PLAY

(1855) 1877–1879 *Les ouvriers européens.* 2d ed. 6 vols. Tours: Mame. → Volume 1: *La méthode d'observation appliquée . . . à l'étude des familles ouvrières.* Volume 2: *Les ouvriers de l'Orient et leurs essaims de la Méditerranée.* Volume 3: *Les ouvriers du nord et leurs essaims de la Baltique et de la Manche.* Volumes 4–6: *Les ouvriers de l'Occident.* Part 1: *Populations stables.* Part 2: *Populations ébranlées.* Part 3: *Populations désorganisées.*

(1864) 1878 *La réforme sociale en France.* 2 vols. 6th ed. Tours: Mame.

(1870) 1872 *The Organization of Labor in Accordance With Custom and the Law of the Decalogue: With a Summary of Comparative Observations Upon Good and Evil in the Regime of Labor.* Philadelphia: Claxton. → First published in French.

(1871*a*) 1907 *L'organisation de la famille: Selon le vrai modèle signalé par l'histoire de toutes les races et de tous les temps.* 5th ed. Tours: Mame.

1871*b* *La paix sociale après le désastre.* Tours: Mame.

1875 *La constitution de l'Angleterre.* Tours: Mame.

1876 *La réforme en l'Europe et le salut en France.* Tours: Mame.

1899 *Voyages en Europe, 1829–1854: Correspondance.* Paris: Plon.

Textes choisis. Preface by Louis Baudin. Paris: Dalloz, 1947.

SUPPLEMENTARY BIBLIOGRAPHY

ARIÈS, PHILIPPE 1948 *Histoire des populations françaises.* Paris: Société d'Éditions Littéraires Françaises.

ARIÈS, PHILIPPE (1960) 1962 *Centuries of Childhood: A Social History of Family Life.* New York: Knopf. → First published as *L'enfant et la vie familiale sous l'ancien régime.*

DELPECH, HENRY 1938 *Recherches sur le niveau de la vie et les habitudes de consommation (Toulouse 1936–1938).* Paris: Sirey.

DEMOLINS, EDMOND (1897) 1898 *Anglo-Saxon Superiority: To What It Is Due.* New York: Scribner. → First published as *À quoi tient la supériorité des Anglo-Saxons.*

DEMOLINS, EDMOND 1898 *L'éducation nouvelle: L'École des Roches.* Paris: Firmin-Didot.

DEMOLINS, EDMOND 1901–1903 *Les grandes routes des peuples: Essai de géographie sociale, comment la route crée le type social.* 2 vols. Paris: Firmin-Didot.

FERRÉ, LOUISE 1936 *Les classes sociales dans la France contemporaine.* Paris: Hachette.

HALBWACHS, MAURICE 1933 *L'évolution des besoins dans les classes ouvrières.* Paris: Alcan.

MICHEL, ANDRÉE 1963 Les cadres sociaux de la doctrine morale de Frédéric Le Play. *Cahiers internationaux de sociologie* 34:47–68.

PARSONS, TALCOTT et al. (editors) (1961) 1965 *Theories of Society: Foundations of Modern Sociological Theory.* New York: Free Press.

Recueil d'études sociales publié à la mémoire de Frédéric Le Play. 1956 Paris: Picard.

RIBBE, CHARLES DE (1873) 1879 *La famille et la société en France avant la Révolution.* 4th ed. Tours: Mame.

RILEY, MATILDA W. (editor) 1963 *Sociological Research.* 2 vols. New York: Harcourt.

ROUSIERS, PAUL DE 1892 *American Life.* Translated by A. J. Herbertson. Paris: Firmin-Didot. → Published in French in the same year.

ROUSIERS, PAUL DE 1894 La science sociale. American Academy of Political and Social Science, *Annals* 4, no. 4:620–646.

ROUSIERS, PAUL DE (1895) 1896 *The Labour Question in Britain.* London and New York: Macmillan.

ROUSIERS, PAUL DE 1902 *Hambourg et l'Allemagne contemporaine.* Paris: Colin.

ROUSIERS, PAUL DE 1934 *Une famille de hobereaux pendant six siècles.* Paris: Firmin-Didot.

SOCIÉTÉ D'ÉCONOMIE SOCIALE, PARIS *Les ouvriers des deux mondes.* → Published from 1857 to 1908.

SOROKIN, PITIRIM A. 1928 *Contemporary Sociological Theories.* New York: Harper. → A paperback edition was published in 1964 as *Contemporary Sociological Theories Through the First Quarter of the Twentieth Century.*

TOURVILLE, HENRI DE (1905) 1907 *The Growth of Modern Nations: A History of the Particularist Form of Society.* London: Arnold. → First published as *Histoire de la formation particulariste: L'origine des grands peuples actuels.*

ZIMMERMAN, CARLE C.; and FRAMPTON, MERLE E. 1935 *Family and Society: A Study of the Sociology of Reconstruction.* London: Williams & Norgate; Princeton, N.J.: Van Nostrand.

LEADERSHIP

I PSYCHOLOGICAL ASPECTS

The concept of leadership, like that of general intelligence, has largely lost its value for the social sciences, although it remains indispensable to general discourse. There is a great variety of ways in which one individual stands out from others in social situations and in which the one may be said, therefore, to be "leading" the others. So diverse are these ways that any one concept attempting to encompass them all, as "leadership" does, loses the specificity and precision that is necessary to scientific thinking. To call someone a leading artist may mean only that as writer or painter he enjoys greater public acclaim and probably greater sales than do others similarly engaged; but it may also mean that others are aware of him and that in subtle ways he exercises an influence upon them. In general, it is an essential feature of the concept of leading that influence is exerted by one individual upon another, or more commonly, that one or a few individuals influence a larger number. Influence, however, is itself a nonspecific term. One may be influenced by another's disapproved-of behavior to act antagonistically toward him or in a direction quite contrary to that he represents or advocates. It is usual in such circumstances to say that one is driven to act thus, rather than led. "Leading" implies a shared direction, and this, in turn, often implies that all parties to the leadership relation have a common goal or at least similar or compatible goals; and as Hollander and Julian (1964) say, "leader influence suggests a positive contribution toward the attainment of these goals." Thus, any act of leading implies an interindividual relationship, and leading is one form of interindividual influence. Definition of the simplest unit of analysis in leadership as "the act of leading" has led to the identification of four basic elements in the relationship: (1) the *leader*, with his characteristics of ability and personality and his "resources relevant to goal attainment" (Hollander & Julian 1964); (2) the *followers*, who also have relevant abilities, personality characteristics, and resources; (3) the *situation* within which the relationship occurs; and (4) the *task* with which the interacting individuals are confronted. The nature of the leader–influence relationship and the characterization of the act of leading are to be understood in terms of interaction between these four sets of variables, each of which requires modest amplification.

The leader. Acts of leading may be very brief and of varying importance for long-term interaction, but the concept of leader implies a role relationship of some duration, although this duration is not so great or the role so unvarying as is often thought. A leader, however, is one who is repeatedly perceived to perform acts of leading. As Sherif (1962) points out, generally the leader position is occupied for a considerable time by the same individual. While what has been said thus far holds equally for animal and for human social action, the greater complexity of human interaction and our more detailed knowledge of the communication processes involved in it enable us to pursue this discussion more deeply if particular attention is paid to human interaction.

The group. It is appropriate here to introduce the concept of groups and to discuss leading as action occurring in groups.

The term "group" refers to two or more individuals interacting in the pursuit of common or compatible goals in such a way that the existence of many is utilized for the satisfaction of some needs of each (Cattell 1951; Gibb 1954). Leading may therefore be said to occur only within groups, and a leader may be seen to occupy a position within a group and to fulfill a group role. The principal characteristic of this role is that its occupants are accorded a high proportion of the group's resources of time and attention and are expected to perform a high proportion of initiating, decision-making, or leading acts; there is a disposition to "follow" them. Given agreement with these principles, there is still room for a variety of approaches to the identification of leaders in specific groups. Fortunately these different approaches do not frequently lead to identification of different leaders in a given group at a given time, but they do represent different emphases. One widely used approach, which owes much to the work of Hemphill (e.g., 1949), identifies leaders in terms of the relative frequency with which they perform defined acts of leading. This approach recognizes the fact that groups develop leadership hierarchies and that differentiation between successive levels is primarily in terms of frequency of leading. Only rarely, and then in highly structured organizations, does such an approach identify "the leader." Most groups have many leaders, and differentiation between leaders and followers is a question of drawing an arbitrary line on a frequency continuum.

A second approach seeks those who exercise influence (in a shared direction) over other individuals. It has been shown (Gibb 1950) that leaders may be reliably identified in terms of the extent of such influence, and this form of definition has been employed frequently. In an unpublished study Seeman and Morris (1950) suggested one possible definition of leadership that emphasizes the aspect of influence: leadership acts influence other persons in a shared direction. The position of leader is then defined in terms of relative degrees of influence.

One of the earliest definitions, still widely adopted, is that of Pigors (1935), who indicated that leadership is a concept applied to the personality–environment relation to describe the situation when a personality is so placed in the environment that his "will, feeling and insight direct and control others in the pursuit of a common cause."

An important variant of the influence criterion has been proposed by Cattell (1951). It is his suggestion that the measure of a leader's influence is to be sought not so much in his influence on other group members but in his influence upon total group locomotion or group "syntality" (characteristics, nature, or quality, analogous to individual personality), which is judged from the effectiveness of total performance of the group as group. While this view has important implications, it does not necessarily lead to different leader identification than the other approaches.

The source of power. Cutting across these considerations in the identification of leaders in a group, and contributing significantly to the definition of the concept of leading, is the essential question of the source of the power to influence. The point at issue here will be understood most readily if thought is given to a group within a larger organization. Power within such a group frequently resides, in whole or in part, in a person appointed by the parent organization to exercise a power delegated to him by that organization. That such a person exercises influence over other group members, there can be no question; but the sources of the power, the nature of the relevant and effective sanctions, and the nature of the relation between influence agent and recipient are in this case qualitatively very different from those to be observed in a voluntary group or association. There seem to be specific advantages for clarity in maintaining this distinction (Pigors 1935) and in using the term "headship" for the former, reserving "leadership" for the latter only. While many characteristics differentiate headship and leadership (Gibb 1954), most basically these two forms of influence differ with respect to the source of the authority. In Sherif's words, "the leadership status itself is within a group and not outside of it" (1962). The leader's authority is spontaneously accorded him by his fellow group members, the followers. The authority of the head derives from some extragroup power that he has over members, who cannot meaningfully be called his followers. They accept his influence on pain of punishment derived from the larger organization, rather than following him in the promise of positive satisfaction derived from the achievement of mutually compatible goals. It is not suggested, of course, that headship and leadership are mutually exclusive, but neither are they coincident, as so much popular thinking suggests. It is a most significant consideration that, as Sherif (1962, p. 17) recognizes, "the leader is not immune from group sanctions if he deviates too far from the bounds of acceptable behavior prevailing in the group," while a head is independent of sanctions applied by the group, though he will in turn, of course, be subject to those applied by the larger organization to its members occupying this particular status. Thus, there is a sensitivity to the interaction between leader and followers that is not necessarily present in that between head and subordinates.

The followers. Probably the most important thing to be said about the concept of followers is that they, too, fulfill active roles. They are not to be thought of as an aggregation minus the leaders. It is part of the intention of the group concept to imply that all members actively interact in the course of movement in a common direction. Leaders and followers are collaborators. The concepts of leading and following define each other. There can be no leading without following, and of course, no following without leading. Not all members of any given group will, at any particular time and with a particular leadership, be followers, but all members will at some times, under some conditions, be followers or they will forfeit their membership. Neither are followers exclusively confined to this role, any more than leaders are exclusively and always engaged in acts of leading. In fact, leaders and followers frequently exchange roles (Hollander 1961), and observation has shown that the most active followers often initiate acts of leading. Hollander and Julian (1964) suggest that it is an error to speak of an influence agent and an influence recipient as if they were distinct from one another, and this is well supported. The expectations of the follower and the acceptance he accords the leader may be as influential in the production of the act of leading as are the resources of the leader himself. This relation, although rather more subtle and less well taught, may be quite as important as the reciprocal sex roles so readily observable in any society.

The situation. The term "situation" is used here to mean "the set of values and attitudes with which the individual or the group has to deal in a process of activity and with regard to which this activity is planned and its results appreciated. Every concrete activity is the solution of a situation" (Thomas & Znaniecki [1918] 1947, p. 76). The elements of the situation are (1) the structure of interpersonal relations within a group; (2) the characteristics of the group as group and taken as a unit; (3) the characteristics of the larger culture in which the group exists and from which group members have been drawn; (4) the physical conditions within which the group finds itself constrained to act; and (5) the perceptual representation, within the group and among its members, of these elements and the attitudes and values engendered by them. The situation is especially liable to modification through changes in interpersonal relations, the entrance of new members and departures of others, changes in physical conditions, and the like, which alter action possibilities and, consequently, the perceived probabilities of goal attainment or assessments of costs. Research (Stogdill 1948; Gibb 1954) has shown that a person does not become a leader solely by virtue of any particular pattern of personality traits but rather by possession of any attribute that, by virtue of its relevance to the situation and its situationally determined evaluation by other group members, establishes a relation of leading–following.

The task. While the task must, in many respects, be regarded as an additional element of the situation, its separate significance in defining acts of leading is probably sufficient to justify separate identification. Research has not yet succeeded in establishing a taxonomy of tasks, even for small groups, that would permit exploration of the relation between task characteristics and other leadership variables. However, Carter (1953) has shown that as far as the differentiation of leaders is concerned, tasks are not discrete but may be grouped in "families." In his experiments, using the same groups, leading in intellectual tasks fell to quite different members than leading in tasks calling for the manipulation of physical objects. More recently Hemphill, during an investigation of motivation to lead, observed, "Group tasks set widely different demands or requirements for leadership. The nature of the task thus becomes an important consideration in the complex of motivational factors related to the attempt to lead. A task that repeatedly presents occasions where a decision must be made produces many attempted leadership acts" (1961, p. 212). Certainly it has been repeatedly observed that as a group moves from one task to another, the situational demands alter in such a way that different forms of participation assume leading qualities, and different members may, depending on the complex interaction of all the elements now under discussion, become influence agents and leaders.

To some degree the nature of the interaction of these elements has already been explicitly discussed or clearly implied, and little more need be said of it until particular theoretical formulations are discussed below. It will be clear, also, that any suggestion that leadership can be reduced to some specific ability or to a set of personal attributes has been abandoned (Lang 1964). The quality of leadership inheres, not in an individual, but in a role that is played within some specified social system. A satisfactory summary statement is that of Zaleznik and Moment:

> Identifying leadership [or leading] as a particular kind of interaction event, rather than as a particular set of characteristics of a person, conforms to the temporal, sequential and patterned aspects of role performance. The individual who engages in leadership events becomes a sometimes leader. Thus, the group leader would be the person or persons who engaged in more leadership events than others. We would use the term *influence* as synonomous [*sic*] with leadership only when the term *intended* preceded it. Behavioral analysis describes the ways in which all members of an

interacting group influence one another; we identify as leadership only those interaction events in which *intended* influences are consummated. (1964, p. 414)

Leadership as group function

It is now common for social psychologists and sociologists, without any real or implied contradiction of the above analysis of acts of leading, to view leadership as a characteristic of a group rather than of individuals or individual acts. "Leadership is probably best conceived as a set of functions which must be carried out by the group" (Gibb 1954). As Cartwright and Zander suggest, the contemporary view of leadership, which ". . . stresses the characteristics of the group and the situation in which it exists, . . . seeks to discover what actions are required by groups under various conditions if they are to achieve their goals or their valued states, and how different group members take part in these group actions. Leadership is viewed as the performance of those acts which help the group achieve its preferred outcomes" (1953, p. 492). As Secord and Backman (1964) then recognize, such an orientation to leadership has the clear implications (1) that acts of leading will almost inevitably be very varied indeed, depending upon the situation, the task, interpersonal evaluations, and perceptions and interactions of all of these; and (2) that acts of leading may be performed by any or all members of a group and that there is no force in the nature of the leadership relation itself, making for "focused" rather than "distributed" leadership. Furthermore, since groups have two primary "needs"—for goal achievement or achievement of "valued states" and for maintenance of the group—it is to be expected that two primary categories of acts of leading exist and that, in turn, two primary modes of leadership appear. Empirical evidence for this was offered by Bales (1953), who found in small goal-oriented discussion groups both "instrumental" and "social–emotional" leaders. Strong theoretical and empirical support for this view exists.

On this view, the provision of leadership in a group is a complex but limited aspect of the more general process of role differentiation, by which a group develops "specialists" in the performance of recurring functions. The complex of functional roles that characterizes leadership has been more fully studied than have other and probably comparable complexes—for example, that of political figure or ambassador—but it is, perhaps, questionable whether a more complete understanding of role will not supersede particular concern with leadership.

Current psychological theories

Two recent attempts (Berelson & Steiner 1964; Collins & Guetzkow 1964) to set out systematically what is known of leadership have indicated the limitation of this knowledge, and this is especially true with respect to an understanding of the process by which roles are differentiated and status or position established. Gibb (1949) observed that in newly formed groups some degree of leadership emerged within the first few minutes of interaction. The enigma of this phenomenon has still not been elucidated. While it can be confidently asserted (Collins & Guetzkow 1964) that "the greater the personal attraction of other group members to a single individual, the greater the power of that individual," there remains little understanding of the sources and nature of differential personal attraction.

Sociometry. A very large proportion of the research in leadership has made use of the sociometric method. This technique has developed greatly since the first valuable lead given by Moreno (1934) and the first sociometric study of leadership by Jennings (1943). It provides an easily accessible, relatively objective means of assessing interpersonal attitudes within a group, and by way of such linkages, it offers a means of mapping the interpersonal structure of a group [*see* SOCIOMETRY].

The simple but important recognition that different choice criteria could be incorporated in the sociometric question has led to very significant insights into the leadership of groups. The value of Jennings' varying the criteria from choices among group tasks to quite informal friendship choices (1947) cannot be overestimated. Role criteria in the study of leadership are now numerous, and the use of different criteria has shown that members of a group do often distinguish between those they like as friends and those they would wish to have as leaders (Hollander 1961, p. 34). The sociometric method has also demonstrated that interpersonal designation of leaders varies in any group from time to time as goals, tasks, and internal structure change.

In an attempt to explain the importance of sociometric technique to the study of leadership, Hollander (1961) has said that social interaction leads to an implicit interpersonal assessment, which the perceiver reaches by comparing task-related elements and behavior with some social standard. Parsons (1952) was responsible for a very significant advance when he indicated that persons interacting are objects to each other in an evaluational process, the elements of which are cognitive (what the object is) and cathectic (what the object means in an emotional sense). Leadership is such an evaluational relationship; the cognitive component is perception of another individual's instrumentality in need satisfaction, and an emotional tone derives from the as yet not understood processes of interpersonal attraction.

The principal theories of leadership are based in some sense upon the sociometric method. Of these, mention should certainly be made of interaction theory, of Hollander's work on "idiosyncrasy credit," and of Fiedler's "contingency theory."

General interaction theory. The important aspects of interaction theory have been stated as follows (Gibb 1958). First, groups are mechanisms for achieving individual satisfactions, and conversely, persons interact with other persons for the achievement of group satisfactions. Second, role differentiation, including that complex called leadership, is part and parcel of a group's locomotion toward its goals and, thus, toward the satisfaction of needs of individual members. Third, leadership is a concept applied to the interaction of two or more persons when the evaluation of one or some of the parties to the interaction is such that he or they come to control and direct the actions of the others in the pursuit of common or compatible ends. Any group is a system of interactions. Within this system a structure emerges as a result of the development of relatively stable sets of expectations for the behavior of each member, and these expectations are an expression of the member's interaction with all other members. Thus, the particular role an individual member achieves within the group is determined both by the functional or role needs of the group in a situation and by the member's particular attributes of personality, ability, and skill, which differentiate him perceptually from others in the group. Leadership is basically a function of personality and social system in dynamic interaction. Fourth, evaluation of one party to interaction by another is itself an integration of perceptual and emotional relationships; it is a product of perception of instrumentality in need satisfaction and of emotional attachment. This form of conceptualization leads to a recognition of a complex of emotional relationships, which in turn define a variety of leadership relations. Among these may be identified (1) patriarchal leadership, in which the person upon whom the members perceive themselves to be dependent is both loved and feared; (2) tyrannical leadership, where the emotional relationship is dominated by fear; and (3) "ideal," or charismatic, leadership, in which the interpersonal relationship is characterized by love or affection. Insofar as attention is given only to the momentary capacity of a group to mobilize its resources for a particular task, the emotional quality of the relations to a leader may be irrelevant. But if the time dimension is admitted, then the cathexis of the parties of the interaction to one another seems inevitable. It is a part of this theory, then, that even if consideration is given only to those groups in which the sources of all influence and control are within the group (i.e., if headship situations are ignored), the concept of leadership still embraces a wide variety of interactional relationships, all of which must be expected to have quite different effects in terms of group behavior. This view of social interaction gives rise to a number of hypotheses concerning leadership for which there is already some evidence in sociological observations and in the findings of psychological experimentation. Among these is the observation that, under different conditions, a leader can have varying degrees of influence on the "locomotion" of his group.

Fiedler's contingency theory. Some aspects of interaction theory have been systematically elaborated and investigated by Fiedler and his associates (Fiedler 1964). The starting point of these investigations was the widely recognized fact that while one form of leadership was associated with effective group performance in one set of circumstances, there were circumstances in which a quite contrary form seemed most effective. For example, a number of studies had shown that human-relations-oriented, considerate, or democratic leader behavior promoted high morale and productively effective behavior in a wide variety of work groups. Yet, other studies had shown task-oriented, instrumental, or authoritarian leadership to be associated with productive efficiency in experimental groups. Further examination of this research revealed that "the prediction of group performance on the basis of these leader attributes is contingent upon the specific, situational context in which the leader operates" (*ibid.*, p. 154).

Fiedler chose to measure, as predictors of leadership effectiveness, "assumed similarity between opposites" (ASo) and "esteem for the least preferred co-worker." These rather esoteric measures acquire general meaning and significance by virtue of the fact that each can be shown to bear some relation to the rather more widely acceptable variables of "task-orientation" and "consideration." Individuals who differentiate sharply between their most and least preferred co-workers (low ASo) tend to be more oriented toward the task and more punitive. A person who sees even a poor co-worker in a relatively favorable manner (high ASo) is likely to behave in a way that shows consideration for others and promotes member satisfaction; he is also likely to be less directive.

In an early study Fiedler (1955) was able to show that the leaders' ASo scores and the performance of army and air-force crews were negatively associated for crews in which the leader sociometrically endorsed his "keyman" (e.g., the gunner on a tank-gunnery task) and were positively associated for crews in which the leader sociometrically rejected his keyman. Subsequently, Fiedler demonstrated that "The relationship between ASo scores and crew effectiveness . . . seemed to be contingent upon the sociometric choice pattern within the crew" (1964, p. 156).

Fiedler has also suggested that group situations may be described in terms of three dimensions: (1) affective leader–group relations; (2) task structure; and (3) position power. There is reason to believe that task structure and position power are not independent (1964, p. 162), and further elaboration of this model is sure to follow. The first of these dimensions reflects the extent to which the leader feels accepted by his group members. Task structure is defined in terms of four scales, developed by M. E. Shaw, which refer to the degree to which the correctness of a decision can be demonstrated, the clarity to members of the requirements of the task, the restriction of procedures by which the task may be accomplished, and the uniqueness of the "correct" solution. By "position power" is meant the extent to which the leader may dispense rewards, punishments, and sanctions, generally by virtue of authority given him by the organization within which the group operates, by tradition, or by any other formally recognized institution.

By dichotomizing each of these dimensions into high and low, Fiedler obtains eight descriptively different group-task situations. The results from many studies are then called upon to reveal the relationship between leadership style and group performance in each of these different situations. "In very favorable conditions, where the leader has power, informal backing [i.e., good leader–member relations], and a relatively well-structured task, the group is ready to be directed on how to go about its task" (*ibid.*, p. 165), as is shown by the fact that the correlations between ASo scores and group effectiveness are large and negative. In other words, the controlling, managing, and directive leaders perform best in these conditions. And under very unfavorable conditions, where leader–member relations are poor, the task is unstructured, and the leader lacks power, the managing, controlling leadership style also proves most effective. It is in moderately favorable conditions, where the group faces an unstructured or ambiguous task or where the leader's relations with group members are tenuous, that permissive, considerate leadership is most effective. It is probably not unimportant that the situation where the leader position is weak, the task ambiguous, but the leader well liked is characterized by considerate, permissive leadership; and, alternatively, when the leader is not well liked but the task is clearly structured and his position is strong, the leadership is generally authoritarian and task oriented. This fact suggests a need for further consideration of the summary concept of favorableness of the situation. However, there is reason enough to accept Fiedler's general hypothesis that "the type of leader attitude required for effective group performance depends upon the degree to which the group situation is favorable or unfavorable to the leader" (1964, p. 164).

Fiedler and Meuwese (1963) have also shown that a leader's ability scores correlate highly with group performance only if the leader is sociometrically accepted or liked, and this finding contains the essence of the contingency theory. The fact that a person may be identified as a leader in an uncohesive group and that the correlation between his ability and group performance may be negative suggests that when the group perceives its major task to be group maintenance, the identified leader will be one who attends primarily to the performance of maintenance functions rather than to the overt task.

Hollander's idiosyncrasy credit. Within the context of an interaction theory that sees social behavior as dependent upon individual attributes, conditions of the situation, and "inputs to a dynamic system arising from their interaction," Hollander (1958) proposed a mediating construct of "idiosyncrasy credit," to explain the fact that leaders must conform to the norms of the group led and also must be a force for innovation. Basically this is made possible through the achievement of status, which is primarily a matter of the leaders' being perceived to conform to group expectancies in the areas of both high individual task performance and generalized characteristics (e.g., pleasant appearance). To the extent that a person is positively evaluated in both task competence and status external to the group, he accumulates "idiosyncrasy credit."

> This represents an accumulation of positively disposed impressions residing in the perceptions of relevant others; it is defined operationally in terms of the degree

to which an individual may deviate from the common expectancies of the group. In this view, each individual within a group—disregarding size and function, for the moment—may be thought of as having a degree of group-awarded credits such as to permit idiosyncratic behavior in certain dimensions *before* group sanctions are applied. (Hollander 1958, p. 120)

Against this credit, such deviant behavior as the individual indulges in is to be seen as a debit. For any given individual, then, the extent to which he is allowed to innovate will depend upon his status. So long as he does nothing to negate the perception of himself as task competent, motivated to belong to the group, and loyal to others' expectations of him, he may enjoy sufficient credit to challenge and change prevailing social patterns in the group. But Hollander (1961) points out that "in attaining this level, the particular expectancies applicable to him will have undergone change," so there is no guarantee that it will be appropriate or possible for him to continue in innovation; in fact, the converse is more likely to obtain.

This "mediating concept" of idiosyncrasy credit is consistent with and helps to explain leader rotation in the group as task and other features of the situation alter, for as Hollander says, "the task competent follower who conforms to the common expectancies of the group at one stage may become the leader at the next stage. And, correspondingly, the leader who fails to fulfill the expectancies associated with his position of influence may lose credits among his followers and be replaced by one of them" (*ibid.*, p. 45).

Summary of current theories. The principal insistence of interaction theories in any of these forms is that the major variables in terms of which leadership might be understood are (1) the leader's personality; (2) the needs, attitudes, and problems of followers; (3) the group itself, in terms of both interpersonal structure and syntality; and (4) the situation in terms of both the physical circumstances and the group task. Further, it is clearly understood that the investigator needs to deal with the perception of each of these variables by the leader and by other group members.

Personality and leadership

In the context of interaction theories there is room for a thorough exploration of the extent to which attributes of the leader are related to the process of leadership and to group performance. Probably the earliest "explanation" of leadership phenomena was given in terms of personal qualities that, while partially modifiable and learnable, characterized the individual and established his dominance of and influence in any situation. For a time during the late 1940s, reaction against this view was so marked that psychology seemed to some to be in danger of offering a thoroughly "situational" view of leadership phenomena. The major influences in this reaction were Gibb's report of the situational shifting of leadership in small groups (1947) and Stogdill's study of the literature of personality traits (1948), which revealed that those personality traits which were leadership traits depended upon the situation and the requirements of the group. Each of these papers, however, was interactional rather than situational in theoretical orientation. And the interactional approach has opened the way for understanding the relation between personality and leadership, while at the same time ending the quest for generalized "leadership traits."

The early tendency to lean heavily to the side of situational determinacy in this process was most effectively checked by Carter and Nixon (1949), who showed that when the emergence of leadership was studied in a carefully controlled way, through tasks which fell into three distinct "families," the leadership varied considerably from task family to task family but that within families it was relatively stable and appeared to be determined by other, probably personality, factors. In the years since 1950 many studies have provided evidence that personality factors contribute to the emergence and maintenance of leadership status. This has been especially true of those studies in which the situational variance has not been relatively great.

Representative studies. As examples, four of these studies may be mentioned.

(1) Bass (1960, p. 172) reports that in initially leaderless discussion groups extremely authoritarian personalities, as measured by the California *F* scale, are least likely to exhibit successful leadership behavior. On the other hand, in these groups he observed a positive correlation between successful leadership and perceptual flexibility. But probably the most telling is the finding of Klubeck and Bass (1954) that persons who do not naturally exhibit successful leadership in such groups are unable to profit from brief coaching as to how to behave as leaders, and the conclusion that these persons seem to be limited by personality and would need to undergo change, probably through major psychotherapy, before they could be freed to behave as leaders.

(2) Borgatta, Couch, and Bales have presented findings that they describe as relevant to a "great man" theory of leadership (1954). They varied the composition of three-man groups working on the same tasks and showed that individuals who scored

high on a composite of intelligence, leadership ratings by fellow participants, participation rate, and sociometric popularity in one group were also high in three subsequent group sessions, where they interacted with different persons. Those who scored highest on this composite criterion in one group did so consistently, and it was evident that "great men" selected on the basis of their first session continue to have an influence on the relatively superior performance of the groups in which they subsequently participate. However, as Hollander comments, "the task setting was essentially constant with only the participants varying across sessions" (Hollander and Julian 1964).

(3) In somewhat similar vein Cattell and Stice (1954) offered four formulas for selecting leaders on the basis of personality. They differentiated four kinds of leaders: "persistent momentary problem solvers" or technical leaders, identified in terms of the frequency with which nonparticipant observers had judged the individual to have influenced the group; salient leaders, picked by the observers as most powerfully influencing the group in at least one of the 22 situations presented; sociometric leaders, identified by choice by fellow members; and elected leaders, who were named after formal election on one or more occasions in the course of the experimental interaction.

The personality profiles of leaders were compared with those of nonleaders, and eight personality factors showed differences in the same direction for all four categories. These were *C*, emotional maturity, or ego strength; *E*, dominance; *G*, character integration, or superego strength; *H*, social adventurousness; *N*, shrewdness; *O* (negative), freedom from anxiety; Q3, deliberate will control; and Q4 (negative), absence of nervous tension. Differences between leader types were that technical leaders had higher general intelligence, *B*, and elected leaders were higher in *F*, surgency. Discussing these results, the authors indicate that the relationships revealed are consistent with both technical and nontechnical thinking about leadership and the influence process. For example, the timid, withdrawn, hesitant behavior associated with a low *H* score would not be conducive to leadership in any of the categories. The anxious, worrying cautiousness in dealing with people represented by high *O* would not inspire confidence. And where conscience is considered to be the "will of the group"—a regard for superindividual values—the selection of leaders with high *G* represents a gain for the group. [*See* TRAITS.]

(4) Some confirmation of this finding is to be found in a study by Borg (1960). He derived four factor scores from a variety of tests that were primarily measures of personality variables and related these to sociometric measures of six small-group roles. Twelve of his 24 correlation coefficients were significant at the .01 level. The predictor factor "assertiveness" was the most successful. A correlation of .46 was found between assertiveness scores and a composite leadership role derived from individual role measures of assertiveness, creativity, and leadership. It is interesting to observe that the predictor factor "power orientation" is consistently unassociated with this leadership composite and that a third predictor, "rigidity," dependent primarily on the California *F* scale, is consistently and significantly negatively associated with leadership, thus confirming Bass's results. As Borg himself points out (p. 115), his success in predicting especially the leadership-role scores may mean that even more can be achieved in this area if predictor instruments are further developed.

Summary of the literature. Despite the common promise of these studies and others like them, it cannot at this time be said that there is evidence for a predominant personality component in leadership. The best review of the literature in this area to date is that of Mann (1959). In the course of examining a number of relationships between the personality characteristics of the individual and the way he behaves or is perceived to behave in small groups, Mann presents a summary of the relationships between some aspects of personality and leadership, as follows.

Intelligence. After examination of 28 independent studies, the positive association of intelligence and leadership in small groups seems to be beyond doubt, although the median correlation is only .25; no reported coefficient exceeded .50; and just half of the results examined failed to establish the significance of this trend.

Adjustment. The association of personal adjustment and leadership was found in 22 studies. Again the over-all trend is clearly positive, with a median correlation of approximately .15 and no single correlation coefficient greater than .53.

Extraversion–introversion. Twenty-two different studies have suggested a median correlation between extraversion and leadership of .15, and the highest correlation reported is .42. Despite some difficulty in ensuring the real similarity of scales of similar title, there is evidence for the conclusion that "those individuals who tend to be selected as leaders are more sociable and outgoing."

Dominance. On the evidence of 12 studies, dominance, as measured by personality scales, is positively associated with leadership, having a median correlation around .20 and a highest reported correlation of .42. "Although the trend is not very strong, these data suggest that dominant or ascendant individuals have a greater chance of being designated leader."

Conservatism. Seventeen studies reveal that in general there is a negative association between conservatism and leadership. Mann found that the California *F* scale had been used ten times in the prediction of leadership and that on each occasion authoritarian persons had been rated lower on leadership.

Interpersonal sensitivity. The measurement of interpersonal sensitivity, or empathic ability, has been subject to much attention. Some caution is needed in attempting to summarize the 15 studies relating it to leadership, and Mann duly qualifies his summary judgment that "there appears to be a low but clearly positive relationship between interpersonal sensitivity and leadership."

Evaluation and other techniques. A further and even more important qualification of these results is made by Mann in pointing out that leadership is variously determined by one of three popular techniques: peer ratings, criterion measures, and observer ratings. The relationship of some of the above personality variables differs when these different measuring techniques are used for leadership. While the relationship between intelligence and leadership is independent of the technique of identifying leadership, that between adjustment and leadership is more closely associated with peer ratings or informal leadership than with either of the other forms; extraversion is more likely to characterize formal leaders determined by criterion measures. Further, Mann observes that "extraverted individuals are no more likely than introverted individuals to be rated as informal leaders by their peers." To a large extent the significance of this observation by Mann, based upon a careful scrutiny of the literature, is that it confirms, in principle at least, the Cattell and Stice proposal of different regressions of personality measures upon different measures of leadership.

The evidence of research to date is clear in demanding that future research attempting to relate personality variables to the exercise of influence in groups must make use of more refined concepts than that of leadership, and close attention must be given to the techniques used to assess both personality and influence relationships.

Leadership in the enduring group

Implicit in the recognition that leadership is situation contingent is the understanding that leader behavior varies with such group factors as organization structure and pattern of communication. Probably the most prominent determinant of variation in these structural respects is the duration of the group. Much of the research in the psychology of leadership has employed newly formed groups of short duration, while a great many of the groups with which social science generally concerns itself are those that endure for a considerable period and either have or achieve a significant history. Sherif and Sherif (1948) have done much to establish the fact that enduring groups develop an organization and structure that becomes a considerable determinant of group-related behavior; and, indeed, they discuss leadership within the context of such structures. Secord and Backman (1964) properly indicate that "in groups that have functioned long enough to develop stable structures and a certain routine much of the stability in leader personnel can be explained" in terms other than those of personality–situation interaction. [*See* GROUPS, *article on* GROUP FORMATION.]

In enduring groups it is patent that formal office structure usually remains relatively stable, continuing from one situation to another throughout a formal term. This cannot always be regarded as continuing leadership. Primarily because of the complex values of stable structure and because there is a culture-carried expectation that offices will be filled for predetermined periods, groups maintain a status structure even if it no longer corresponds to functional demands. One result of this culture-carried expectation of persisting organization is that the nature or emotional–relational quality of leadership will change. In the early stages of group development persons emerge as organizational leaders by virtue of their control over problem-related resources or they emerge as positively cathected leaders by virtue of both their command of resources and the readiness members show to relate themselves emotionally to others on the basis of first impressions (Gibb 1949; 1958). As interaction persists, structure is stabilized for a variety of reasons. With time, the early congruence of the cognitive relation to the person controlling resources and the positive cathexis of that same person is reduced. When stability of structure, then, is formalized so that offices are held for a stated time without reference to contemporary contributory strength in problem solving, leadership becomes less functional and the officeholder is supported by structural rigidity. His leadership may now be said to have become headship, and the dynamics of the group will almost certainly have become complicated by the emergence of new leaders, thrown up by the complex of forces, which now includes, of course, the behavior of the formal officeholders. The officeholders strive to maintain the satisfactions of office, whether these be simply of status or more complex, and in doing so their behavior becomes more coercive. Frequently this implies the establishment of power cliques or bureaucracies. Under such conditions the emotional quality of relations to the leader or head becomes less positive and the nature of the influence has changed. [*See* BUREAUCRACY.]

However, in other, simpler, and more direct ways, too, the time dimension, or history, has been seen to affect leadership. Klein (1956) has suggested that communication structure may become habitual and independent of the problem to be solved. A structure that has been successful repeatedly because problems have been similar will, she suggests, be persisted in even when problems become dissimilar, because of a preference for orderliness and routine. Bass (1960) has shown that the perceived status an individual brings into a group by virtue of past interaction in the group or in another, mutually known group directly affects his willingness to make attempts to lead and the success of such attempts. As Secord and Backman (1964) observe, the communication and status structures mutually reinforce each other and together constitute strong forces determining leadership. One's position in group structure, whether in the communication net or in the mutually perceived status hierarchy, greatly affects his opportunities and abilities to exercise influence. Obviously communication centrality and status position are not independent. Hopkins (1964) adduces considerable evidence for the proposition that "for any member of a small group, the higher his rank, the greater his influence."

Two final points of some significance have also been made by Secord and Backman (1964). First, once having achieved success in leadership, and through it having attained centrality and status, which in turn tend to establish their leadership, these leaders have the best opportunity to develop leadership skills, which further accentuate their positive evaluation. Second, because of the community value placed upon status and leadership directly, established leaders are highly motivated to maintain their roles, while reciprocally, their success spells satisfaction for their followers, whose involvement may be correspondingly reduced.

CECIL A. GIBB

[*Directly related are the entries* ELITES; POWER. *Other relevant material may be found in* ATTITUDES, *article on* ATTITUDE CHANGE; AUTHORITY; GROUPS, *especially the article on* GROUP FORMATION; ORGANIZATIONS; PERSUASION; POLITICAL ANTHROPOLOGY, *article on* POLITICAL ORGANIZATION; POLITICAL MACHINES; POLITICAL PROCESS; ROLE; *and in the biography of* LEWIN.]

BIBLIOGRAPHY

BALES, ROBERT F. 1953 The Equilibrium Problem in Small Groups. Pages 111–161 in Talcott Parsons et al., *Working Papers in the Theory of Action.* Glencoe, Ill.: Free Press.

BASS, BERNARD M. 1960 *Leadership, Psychology, and Organizational Behavior.* New York: Harper.

BERELSON, BERNARD; and STEINER, GARY A. 1964 *Human Behavior: An Inventory of Scientific Findings.* New York: Harcourt.

BORG, WALTER R. 1960 Prediction of Small Group Role Behavior From Personality Variables. *Journal of Abnormal and Social Psychology* 60:112–116.

BORGATTA, EDGAR F. et al. 1954 Some Findings Relevant to a Great Man Theory of Leadership. *American Sociological Review* 19:755–759.

BROWNE, CLARENCE; and COHN, THOMAS S. (editors) 1958 *The Study of Leadership.* Danville, Ill.: Interstate Printers & Publishers.

CARTER, LAUNOR F. 1953 Leadership and Small-group Behavior. Pages 257–284 in Conference in Social Psychology, University of Oklahoma, 1952, *Group Relations at the Crossroads.* Edited by Muzafer Sherif and M. D. Wilson. New York: Harper.

CARTER, LAUNOR F.; and NIXON, MARY 1949 Ability, Perceptual, Personality, and Interest Factors Associated With Different Criteria of Leadership. *Journal of Psychology* 27:377–388.

CARTWRIGHT, DORWIN; and ZANDER, ALVIN (editors) (1953) 1960 *Group Dynamics: Research and Theory.* 2d ed. Evanston, Ill.: Row, Peterson; New York: Harper. → See especially pages 487–510, "Leadership and Group Performance: Introduction."

CATTELL, RAYMOND B. 1951 New Concepts for Measuring Leadership in Terms of Group Syntality. *Human Relations* 4:161–184.

CATTELL, RAYMOND; and STICE, GLEN F. 1954 Four Formulae for Selecting Leaders on the Basis of Personality. *Human Relations* 7:493–507.

COLLINS, BARRY E.; and GUETZKOW, HAROLD 1964 *A Social Psychology of Group Processes for Decision-making.* New York: Wiley.

FIEDLER, FRED E. 1955 The Influence of Leader–Keyman Relations on Combat Crew Effectiveness. *Journal of Abnormal and Social Psychology* 51:227–235.

FIEDLER, FRED E. 1964 A Contingency Model of Leadership Effectiveness. Volume 1, pages 149–190 in *Advances in Experimental Social Psychology.* Edited by Leonard Berkowitz. New York: Academic Press.

FIEDLER, FRED E.; and MEUWESE, W. A. T. 1963 Leader's Contribution to Task Performance in Cohesive and Uncohesive Groups. *Journal of Abnormal and Social Psychology* 67:83–87.

GIBB, CECIL A. 1947 The Principles and Traits of Leadership. *Journal of Abnormal and Social Psychology* 42:267–284.

GIBB, CECIL A. 1949 *The Emergence of Leadership in Small Temporary Groups of Men.* Publication No. 1392. Ann Arbor, Mich.: University Microfilms.

GIBB, CECIL A. 1950 The Sociometry of Leadership in Temporary Groups. *Sociometry* 13:226–243.

GIBB, CECIL A. 1954 Leadership. Volume 2, pages 877–920 in Gardner Lindzey (editor), *Handbook of Social Psychology.* Cambridge, Mass.: Addison-Wesley.

GIBB, CECIL A. 1958 An Interactional View of the Emergence of Leadership. *Australian Journal of Psychology* 10:101–110.

HEMPHILL, JOHN K. 1949 *Situational Factors in Leadership.* Monograph No. 32. Columbus: Ohio State Univ., Bureau of Educational Research.

HEMPHILL, JOHN K. 1961 Why People Attempt to Lead. Pages 201–215 in Luigi Petrullo and Bernard M. Bass (editors), *Leadership and Interpersonal Behavior.* New York: Holt.

HOLLANDER, E. P. 1958 Conformity, Status, and Idiosyncrasy Credit. *Psychological Review* 65:117–127.

HOLLANDER, E. P. 1961 Emergent Leadership and Social Influence. Pages 30–47 in Luigi Petrullo and Bernard M. Bass (editors), *Leadership and Interpersonal Behavior.* New York: Holt.

HOLLANDER, E. P.; and JULIAN, J. W. 1964 Leadership. Unpublished manuscript.

HOPKINS, TERENCE K. 1964 *The Exercise of Influence in Small Groups.* Totowa, N.J.: Bedminster Press.

JENNINGS, HELEN H. (1943) 1950 *Leadership and Isolation: A Study of Personality in Inter-personal Relations.* 2d ed. New York: Longmans.

JENNINGS, HELEN H. 1947 *Sociometry of Leadership, Based on the Differentiation of Psychegroup and Sociogroup.* Sociometry Monograph No. 14. New York: Beacon House.

KLEIN, JOSEPHINE 1956 *The Study of Groups.* London: Routledge; New York: Humanities.

KLUBECK, STANLEY; and BASS, BERNARD M. 1954 Differential Effects of Training on Persons of Different Leadership Status. *Human Relations* 7:59–72.

LANG, KURT 1964 Leadership. Pages 380–381 in Julius Gould and William L. Kolb (editors), *A Dictionary of the Social Sciences.* New York: Free Press.

MANN, RICHARD D. 1959 A Review of the Relationships Between Personality and Performance in Small Groups. *Psychological Bulletin* 56:241–270.

MEREI, FERENC 1949 Group Leadership and Institutionalization. *Human Relations* 2:23–39.

MORENO, JACOB L. (1934) 1953 *Who Shall Survive? Foundations of Sociometry, Group Psychotherapy and Sociodrama.* Rev. & enl. ed. Sociometry Monograph No. 29. Beacon, N.Y.: Beacon House.

PARSONS, TALCOTT (1952) 1953 The Superego and the Theory of Social Systems. Pages 13–29 in Talcott Parsons et al., *Working Papers in the Theory of Action.* Glencoe, Ill.: Free Press.

PETRULLO, LUIGI; and BASS, BERNARD M. (editors) 1961 *Leadership and Interpersonal Behavior.* New York: Holt.

PIGORS, PAUL 1935 *Leadership or Domination.* Boston: Houghton Mifflin.

ROSS, MURRAY G.; and HENDRY, CHARLES E. 1957 *New Understandings of Leadership: A Survey and Application of Research.* New York: Association Press.

SECORD, PAUL F.; and BACKMAN, CARL W. 1964 *Social Psychology.* New York: McGraw-Hill.

SEEMAN, MELVIN; and MORRIS, R. T. 1950 A Status Factor Approach to Leadership. Unpublished manuscript.

SHERIF, MUZAFER (editor) 1962 *Intergroup Relations and Leadership: Approaches and Research in Industrial, Ethnic, Cultural, and Political Areas.* New York: Wiley.

SHERIF, MUZAFER; and SHERIF, CAROLYN W. (1948) 1956 *An Outline of Social Psychology.* Rev. ed. New York: Harper.

STOGDILL, RALPH M. 1948 Personal Factors Associated With Leadership. *Journal of Psychology* 25:35–71.

STOGDILL, RALPH M. 1962 Intragroup–Intergroup Theory and Research. Pages 48–65 in Muzafer Sherif (editor), *Intergroup Relations and Leadership.* New York: Wiley.

THOMAS, WILLIAM I.; and ZNANIECKI, FLORIAN (1918) 1947 The Definition of the Situation. Pages 76–77 in Society for the Psychological Study of Social Issues, *Readings in Social Psychology.* New York: Holt. → Reprinted from Volume 1 of W. I. Thomas and F. Znaniecki, *The Polish Peasant in Europe and America.*

VERBA, SIDNEY 1961 *Small Groups and Political Behavior: A Study of Leadership.* Princeton Univ. Press.

ZALEZNIK, ABRAHAM; and MOMENT, DAVID 1964 *The Dynamics of Interpersonal Behavior.* New York: Wiley.

II
SOCIOLOGICAL ASPECTS

To most sociological writers leadership is the exercise of power or influence in social collectivities, such as groups, organizations, communities, or nations. This power may be addressed to any or all of three very general and related functions: establishing the goals, purposes, or objectives of the collectivity; creating the structures through which the purposes of the collectivity are fulfilled; and maintaining or enhancing these structures. Sociological studies have emphasized the last function, in part because it seems more amenable to empirical investigation, particularly in bureaucratic settings, where much of the research on leadership is conducted. This emphasis has implied an interest in the role of leadership in maintaining the integrity and viability of the collectivity against threats, both internal and external, in maintaining collective order and unity, in minimizing dissension and conflict, and in motivating members and fostering their acceptance of the collectivity, of its goals, and of leadership itself. Thus, most theories of leadership are conservative in that they are addressed to the maintenance of social systems rather than to their change. Although this is not an exclusive emphasis, it is consistent with a major concern in contemporary sociology with the problems of social order and stability.

The exercise of power or influence implies "making things happen" through others. Leaders may engage in a number of activities in furthering this purpose. They may coordinate, control, direct, guide, or mobilize the efforts of others. A recent focus on the leaders' role in motivating members implies that they may counsel, support, help, persuade, or elicit the participation of others in some degree of

goal setting. Leaders may also cajole, manipulate, entice, reward, coerce, or harangue, although some writers exclude some of these activities from the definition of leadership. "Strictly speaking," according to Schmidt (1933, p. 282), "the relation of leadership arises only where a group follows an individual from free choice and not under command or coercion and, secondly, not in response to blind drives but on positive and more or less rational grounds."

Many of the above activities of leaders are concerned with the details of interpersonal relations. Leaders may also wield power in representing the collectivity in its external relations. Or they may make decisions and formulate policies on a broad scale without becoming directly involved in the details of their execution. Selznick (1957) applies the term "institutional statesman" to those organization leaders who look beyond questions of routine administration and productive efficiency to the broader philosophic implications of the collectivity and its role in the larger society. Organization statesmen assume responsibility for defining policy values and for developing a plan of organization that embodies these values. Similarly, Harbison and Myers (1959) employ the term "organization builders" for those leaders who devote themselves to *creating* organizations. These leaders are concerned as much with innovation as with collective stability. Leaders in developing nations, in particular, are concerned with change, with defining new collective goals and creating structures appropriate to these goals. Many of these leaders must also undertake the difficult task of establishing new social values in the context of traditional philosophies (Fourastié & Vimont 1956, p. 57).

Leadership defines, initiates, and maintains social structure. The social system is, so to speak, "programmed" through leadership. Understanding leadership, then, should be a simple and parsimonious approach to understanding the larger social system. Leadership can have consequences for the lives and welfare of large numbers of people, and, therefore, those who are concerned with the practical consequences of human actions must be concerned with leadership.

Important social values are also frequently associated with leadership conceptions, and attempts are made to legitimate social systems in terms of particular theories or ideologies of leadership. The drama of leadership can be seen in its consequences and in the behavior of some well-known leaders. History is personalized and dramatized through stories of leadership, and the names of famous or infamous leaders elicit strong feeling. But the drama associated with leadership, together with its apparent theoretical and practical import, gives it an appeal that may sometimes be deceptive. The "great man theory," according to which outstanding leaders determine the course of history, is one expression of this appeal. Models of ruling elites, which explain whole social systems in terms of power concentrated in the hands of relatively small and exclusive leadership groups, are similarly appealing in their simplicity and drama. "The whole history of civilized mankind," according to Mosca, "comes down to a conflict between the tendency of dominant elements to monopolize political power and transmit possession of it by inheritance . . ." ([1896] 1939, p. 65). The United States, according to Mills's more contemporary analysis (1956), is dominated by a "power elite" that is in command of the major organizations of society.

Sociological treatments of leadership have leaned heavily on conceptions applying to elites, to autocratic systems, and to rigid class or caste societies. Almost all of the literature on leadership, according to Bell, stems from the works of Aristotle and Machiavelli and is committed to "the image of the mindless masses and the image of the strong-willed leader" (1950, p. 396). Classical models of bureaucracy share with these elite conceptions an authoritarian bias in their emphasis on the exclusive prerogative of leaders to command and the unquestioning obligation of subordinates to obey (Weber 1922*a*).

According to Michels (1911), leadership and democracy are incompatible. Leadership inevitably becomes oligarchic, even in political organizations that start democratically and are committed to a democratic ideology. Leaders themselves are incapable of deflecting this historic process; democratic and idealistic leaders succumb eventually to the corruption inherent in power. Michels cites a number of arguments in support of the tendency toward oligarchy in social systems. First, the masses, through incompetence and apathy, cannot and do not want to participate actively in the political process; they prefer to be led. Second, democracy is structurally impossible in large and complex social systems; there is no way of arranging the systems so that the views of the many individual members can be heard and taken into account. The impracticality of democracy is especially apparent in organizations or nations undergoing conflict with others. Especially during periods of crisis, organizations need firm leadership and precise adherence to orders. Finally, the tendency toward oligarchy results from the character of leaders themselves and of the role they must play. Because of their cultural and educational superiority over the masses, leaders form a distinct elite. The status, perquisites, and privileges associated with the leadership role serve further to separate the leaders from the masses. In labor unions and socialist parties, for example, the life of the leaders becomes that of the petty bourgeois. Leaders therefore develop a vested interest in their positions, which they must protect. Furthermore, a personal lust for power, which is characteristic of leaders, intensifies their efforts to enhance their power, and leaders will resort to ulterior devices toward this end. In "democratic" parties leaders will employ emotional and demagogic appeals to manipulate the gullible masses. They will control the party press, using it to describe themselves in the most favorable light, while deriding their opposition within the party. They will exploit their special information and knowledge of the organization to outmaneuver opponents. And if, despite these tactics, the leaders should be overthrown, the new officeholders in their turn will undergo the inevitable "transformation which renders them in every respect similar to the dethroned tyrants. . . . The revolutionaries of today become the reactionaries of tomorrow" (Michels 1911, p. 195 in 1962 paperback edition).

Changes in the character of leadership

Many of the classical conceptions of leadership, including those in Weber's work on bureaucracies and in Michels' on political organizations, have proven valuable in analyses of contemporary social systems. Nonetheless, the changing character of societies over the years, and of leadership itself, has made apparent some of the limitations of these older conceptions. The emphasis in contemporary sociology on quantitative research has also contributed to changes in interpretations of the leadership process because of the need to develop conceptions that are operationally feasible as well as theoretically meaningful. At the same time, research findings themselves have led to reinterpretations of older conceptions.

The increasing numbers and complexity of organizations in modern industrial societies require large numbers of persons with high levels of technical and administrative expertise to play leadership roles. The demand for expert leaders reduces the suitability of those recruited on the basis of social status or of family connections. Achievement thus replaces ascription as the basis for placing leaders, and their recruitment spreads to all strata of society. Similarly, political criteria prevalent as the basis of recruitment during early stages in newly independent countries and in revolutionary societies become less important in highly industrialized societies. Training centers for leaders are established in universities, business schools, and training institutes, and the possibility for careers in industrial leadership are opened to large numbers of persons. Management becomes professionalized. While these developments are most apparent in business and industrial organizations and in some agencies of government, they are also occurring in other organizations, including military establishments and labor unions (see Kerr et al. 1960).

Most of these changes imply a rationalization of leadership in organizations that is consistent with Weber's (1922*a*) model of bureaucratic leadership. However, further changes in the way leaders exercise control are likely to accompany this rationalization, and these represent a divergence from the classical bureaucratic model. For example, leaders may rely on discussion and persuasion rather than exclusively on command. Attempts may be made to elicit cooperation, sometimes by having organization members participate in the making of decisions that affect them in the work place. The rising level of education of the work force contributes to this trend. Furthermore, professional managers are more inclined than their predecessors to consider the results of social research, which have supported the growth of "human relations" approaches to leadership in organizations. At the same time, political developments, particularly in some European countries, have led to the introduction of schemes for co-management and of workers' councils, with varying degrees of success (Emery & Thorsrud 1964; Meister 1964; Sturmthal 1964). These developments may not be fully consolidated in any contemporary society, but at least incipient support can be found in many organizations for less autocratic approaches to leadership than those that were customary in the past. A survey in 14 industrialized and developing nations, for example, shows that managers overwhelmingly subscribe at least to the idea of participation in decision making, although they express skepticism about workers' capacities to assume the responsibilities consonant with democratic leadership (Haire et al. 1963).

Taken together, these developments imply the growth—actual in some places, potential in others—of new types of leadership in addition to those prevalent in the past. Partly as a consequence of this trend and of developments in research, sociological conceptions have been broadened. This can be observed in a number of related issues.

Leader power. Many of the limitations of traditional leadership conceptions stem from assumptions about the social context within which leadership operates and about the character of power, which is the essence of leadership. One such assumption is that the context is one of conflict, in which the relative power of leaders and others is at stake. It is further assumed that the total amount of power in a social system is a fixed quantity and that leaders and followers are engaged in a "zero-sum game"—that is, an increase in the power of one party must be accompanied by a corresponding decrease in the power of the other. Contemporary social scientists are more inclined than their predecessors to question the generality of these assumptions (Likert 1961; Parsons 1963; Tannenbaum 1966, pp. 95–100). The total amount of power in a relational system may grow, and leaders and followers may therefore enhance their power jointly. Total power may also decline, and all groups within the system may suffer corresponding decreases.

Another view common to traditional analyses argues that the leadership process is unilateral: one either leads or is led, is strong or is weak, controls or is controlled. Georg Simmel, in spite of his general adherence to the traditional conflict view of leadership, noted a more subtle interaction underlying the appearance of "pure superiority" on the part of the leader and the "purely passive being led" of the follower: "All leaders are also led; in innumerable cases the master is the slave of his slaves" ([1902–1917] 1950, p. 185; contrast *ibid.*, p. 193). Contemporary analyses of leadership are more likely than earlier ones to consider relationships of mutual as well as unilateral power, of followers influencing leaders as well as vice versa.

An accompanying change has taken place in analyses of the bases of leaders' power. Coercion has played a prominent role in traditional analyses, consistent with the presumed conflict between leaders and followers. According to the traditional view, leaders are obeyed out of fear of punishment or out of hope for reward. Machiavelli, for example, advised his prince concerning the proper balancing of injuries and benefits to subjects. The leader who finds it necessary to commit injuries should do so quickly in order to minimize resentment. On the other hand, he should dispense rewards in small doses over time so that their effects will be enjoyed longer.

Weber, however, argued that the stability of social systems depends on acceptance by followers of the right of leaders to exercise control. This implied *legitimate* authority; and Weber (1922*b*) defined three types, all of which share a prominent position in sociological analyses of leadership. The first type is *charismatic authority*, according to which leaders are thought to be endowed with extraordinary, sometimes magical powers. Charisma on the part of a leader elicits obedience out of awe. It is illustrated in its pure form by the prophet, the warrior hero, and the great demagogue. Second, *traditional authority* appertains to those who possess the right to rule by virtue of birth or class. The traditional leader is obeyed because he or members of his class or family have *always* been followed. Its pure type is illustrated by certain patriarchs, monarchs, and feudal lords. The third type, *legal authority*, applies to those who hold leadership positions because of demonstrated technical competence. Legal authorities act impersonally, as instruments of the law, and they are obeyed impersonally out of a sense of duty to the law. Leadership in the ideal-type bureaucracy is based exclusively on legal authority.

The character of leadership envisioned within Weber's framework is still consistent with many of the traditional analyses; his leaders are prophets, warriors, demagogues, patriarchs, lords, and bureaucrats. More recent analyses have stressed bases of power in addition to those outlined by Weber.

Simon, for example, points to the importance of *social approval*. Approval and disapproval represent forms of reward and punishment, but they deserve special consideration, since they are frequently dispensed not only by the designated leader but by others as well (1957, pp. 105–106). Thus, a subordinate may obey a leader not so much because of the rewards and punishments meted out by the leader as because of the approval and disapproval given by the subordinate's own peers. *Confidence* may represent a further basis for acceptance of leaders' authority (*ibid.*, p. 106): a subordinate may trust the judgment, and therefore accept the authority, of a leader in areas where the leader has great technical competence. French and Raven (1959) make a further distinction between influence of a leader based on confidence by subordinates in the leader's expert knowledge, on the one hand, and "informational influence" based on acceptance by subordinates of the logic of the arguments which the leader offers, on the other. An expert leader, then, may be followed not simply because he is an acknowledged authority but because his decisions, being based on expertise, are manifestly logical, appropriate, and convincing; that is, subordinates are persuaded that the decisions are correct. This view is related to human relations approaches, which stress control by facts as opposed to control by men. Such "fact control" relies on *understanding*, and it is illustrated by the participative leader who influences subordinates by helping them understand the facts of a situation so that they may jointly arrive at a course of action consistent with their own interests and that of the collectivity. Some of these conceptions represent radical departures from many traditional ones, assuming as they do an overriding community of interests between leaders and followers.

Leaders and followers. The term "leader" has traditionally implied a person clearly distinguished from others in power, status, visibility, and in any of a number of character traits, such as decisiveness, courage, integrity, and intelligence. However, contemporary changes in assumptions, in the direction of recognizing both mutual influence between leaders and followers and the possibility of increasing total power, have led to some lack of clarity in the lines of demarcation between leaders and others. Human relations and participative approaches to leadership, which de-emphasize status and stress the community of interests among all members of the collectivity, also blur the conceptual distinction between leaders and followers. The results of research have added to this ambiguity.

First, little evidence has been found for the existence of universal character traits that define the essential and distinguishing qualities of leadership. This has strengthened the position of those "situationalists" who argue that the relevance of a trait will depend on the specific situation in which leadership occurs. Furthermore, while leaders in similar situations may share *some* relevant characteristics, they are also very likely to differ on others, so that their total personalities will certainly differ. Research also suggests that traits (e.g., intelligence) that may suit an individual to some leadership roles are likely to be distributed continuously in a population rather than dichotomously. Nor is there any basis for assuming that the traits pertinent to many leadership roles are so rare that large numbers of persons differing widely in total personalities would be ineligible for leadership positions.

As a group, therefore, leaders need not be alike, nor need they be distinguished sharply from followers. These conclusions are consistent, in some of their implications, with the changing character of leadership itself, in which the broad recruitment and trainability of leaders is stressed. Leadership abilities need not be an exclusive possession of narrowly defined types or classes of individuals. Many persons, given proper training, can perform a wide range of leadership functions.

Research has had a further effect on the conceptual distinction between leaders and followers. In terms of the operational criteria used to define and measure leadership behavior, many presumed followers are found to act in some degree like leaders and vice versa. Furthermore, the *same* individual may manifest different degrees of leadership behavior. He may be a leader at one point in time, not at another. He may be a leader relative to certain areas of collective action, not others. Leadership, then, is best understood as a matter of degree; it may be distributed in varying degrees throughout a social system. These interpretations call attention to leadership as a social function rather than simply as a property of an individual. While persons who perform leadership functions must have appropriate skills and qualities of character if they are to perform well, the *distribution* of leadership in collectivities and the variety of situations in which leadership occurs suggest some variety in the types of persons who can fulfill leadership functions [*see* GROUPS, *article on* ROLE STRUCTURE].

The concept of leadership should be understood as encompassing a wide range of activities. It applies to the running of small groups and the governing of nations. It may concern the relatively diffuse process of influence in establishing norms of style or opinion—or it may involve specific orders in a chain of command. It includes supervision and statesmanship, routine administration and organization building. Interpretations of leadership as a sociological concept have changed over the years. The total effort of sociologists can be seen as an attempt to develop conceptions that apply to a variety of social systems, including those that prevailed in the past as well as those now emerging. The need for more general conceptions is also felt as a need to understand leadership within the widely differing social and political contexts that exist in the modern world.

ARNOLD S. TANNENBAUM

[*Directly related are the entries* DIFFUSION, *article on* INTERPERSONAL INFLUENCE; INDUSTRIAL RELATIONS; ORGANIZATIONS, *article on* THEORIES OF ORGANIZATIONS. *Other relevant material may be found in* ADMINISTRATION; AUTHORITY; DEMOCRACY; *and in the biographies of* MACHIAVELLI; MICHELS; MILLS; MOSCA; SIMMEL; WEBER, MAX.]

BIBLIOGRAPHY

For definitions, reviews, and discussions of leadership see Schmidt 1933; Gouldner 1950; Gibb 1954; Rouček 1947. Bass 1960 *provides a thorough review of laboratory research as well as the research on leadership in organizations. For a classic expression of the great man theory of leadership, see* Carlyle 1841. Plekhanov 1898 *offers a critique of the great man view. Critiques of elite theories can be found in* Dahl 1958 *and in* Harbison & Myers 1959, *which also presents a detailed discussion of changes in industrial management and in social and political leader-*

ship brought about by industrialization. Bendix 1956 *provides a review of traditional and more recent leadership ideologies as applied to industrial management in western and eastern Europe and the United States.* Dahrendorf 1957 *and* Parsons 1963 *discuss the issue of power in collectivities as a zero-sum game. Leadership under conditions of mutual influence and increasing total power (non-zero-sum) is illustrated by the principles of "co-optation"* Selznick 1949; *"participative management"* March & Simon 1958; *"interaction influence system"* Likert 1961; *"organic" as opposed to "mechanistic" organization* Burns & Stalker 1961; *and by the concept of high "total control"* Tannenbaum & Kahn 1957 *and* Tannenbaum 1966. *The trait theory of leadership remains controversial.* Rainio 1955, *in a review of some of the American and European literature, lists 99 traits that are presumed by various authors to represent the essential qualities of leadership. See* Bogardus 1934 *and* Urwick 1957 *for illustrations of the trait approach; see* Bavelas 1960 *for a critique.*

BASS, BERNARD M. 1960 *Leadership, Psychology, and Organizational Behavior.* New York: Harper.

BAVELAS, ALEX 1960 Leadership: Man and Function. *Administrative Science Quarterly* 4:491–498.

BELL, DANIEL 1950 Notes on Authoritarian and Democratic Leadership. Pages 395–408 in Alvin W. Gouldner (editor), *Studies in Leadership: Leadership and Democratic Action.* New York: Harper.

BENDIX, REINHARD 1956 *Work and Authority in Industry: Ideologies of Management in the Course of Industrialization.* New York: Wiley.

BOGARDUS, EMORY S. 1934 *Leaders and Leadership.* New York: Appleton.

BURNS, TOM; and STALKER, GEORGE M. 1961 *The Management of Innovation.* London: Tavistock.

CARLYLE, THOMAS (1841) 1928 *On Heroes, Hero-worship and the Heroic in History.* London: Oxford Univ. Press.

CARTWRIGHT, DORWIN 1965 Influence, Leadership, Control. Pages 1–47 in James G. March (editor), *Handbook of Organizations.* Chicago: Rand McNally.

DAHL, ROBERT A. 1958 A Critique of the Ruling Elite Model. *American Political Science Review* 52:463–469.

DAHRENDORF, RALF (1957) 1959 *Class and Class Conflict in Industrial Society.* Rev. & enl. ed. Stanford Univ. Press. → First published as *Soziale Klassen und Klassen-Konflikt in der industriellen Gesellschaft.* See especially pages 165–173 for a discussion of the issue of power in collectivities as a zero-sum game.

EMERY, FREDERICK E.; and THORSRUD, E. 1964 *Industrielt demokrati.* Oslo: Universitets-forlaget.

FOURASTIÉ, JEAN; and VIMONT, CLAUDE 1956 *Histoire de demain.* Paris: Presses Universitaires de France.

FRENCH, JOHN R. P.; and RAVEN, BERTRAM 1959 The Bases of Social Power. Pages 150–167 in Dorwin Cartwright (editor), *Studies in Social Power.* Research Center for Group Dynamics, Publication No. 6. Ann Arbor: Univ. of Michigan, Institute for Social Research.

GIBB, CECIL A. 1954 Leadership. Volume 2, pages 877–920 in Gardner Lindzey (editor), *Handbook of Social Psychology.* Cambridge, Mass.: Addison-Wesley.

GOULDNER, ALVIN W. (editor) 1950 *Studies in Leadership: Leadership and Democratic Action.* New York: Harper.

HAIRE, MASON; GHISELLI, EDWIN E.; and PORTER, LYMAN W. 1963 An International Study of Management Attitudes and Democratic Leadership. Pages 101–104 in International Congress for Scientific Management, Thirteenth, New York, 1963, *Proceedings.* New York: Council for International Progress in Management.

HARBISON, FREDERICK H.; and MYERS, CHARLES A. 1959 *Management in the Industrial World: An International Analysis.* Princeton University, Industrial Relations Section. New York: McGraw-Hill.

KERR, CLARK et al. 1960 *Industrialism and Industrial Man: The Problems of Labor and Management in Economic Growth.* Cambridge, Mass.: Harvard Univ. Press. → A second edition was published in paperback in 1964 by Oxford Univ. Press.

LIKERT, RENSIS 1961 *New Patterns of Management.* New York: McGraw-Hill.

MARCH, JAMES G.; and SIMON, HERBERT A. 1958 *Organizations.* New York: Wiley. → Contains an extensive bibliography.

MEISTER, ALBERT 1964 *Socialisme et autogestion: L'expérience yougoslave.* Paris: Éditions du Seuil.

MICHELS, ROBERT (1911) 1959 *Political Parties: A Sociological Study of the Oligarchical Tendencies of Modern Democracy.* New York: Dover. → First published as *Zur Soziologie des Parteiwesens in der modernen Demokratie.* A paperback edition was published in 1962 by Collier.

MILLS, C. WRIGHT 1956 *The Power Elite.* New York: Oxford Univ. Press.

MOSCA, GAETANO (1896) 1939 *The Ruling Class (Elementi di scienza politica).* New York: McGraw-Hill. → First published in Italian.

PARSONS, TALCOTT 1963 On the Concept of Political Power. American Philosophical Society, *Proceedings* 107:232–262.

PLEKHANOV, GEORGE (1898) 1940 *The Role of the Individual in History.* New York: International Publishers. → First published in Russian.

RAINIO, KULLERVO 1955 Leadership Qualities: A Theoretical Inquiry and an Experimental Study on Foremen. Suomalainen Tiedeakatemia, Helsingfors, *Toimituksia: Annales* Series B 95, no. 1.

ROUČEK, JOSEPH S. (1947) 1956 *Social Control.* 2d ed. Princeton, N.J.: Van Nostrand.

SCHMIDT, RICHARD 1933 Leadership. Volume 9, pages 282–287 in *Encyclopaedia of the Social Sciences.* New York: Macmillan.

SELZNICK, PHILIP 1949 *TVA and the Grass Roots: A Study in the Sociology of Formal Organization.* University of California Publications in Culture and Society, Vol. 3. Berkeley: Univ. of California Press.

SELZNICK, PHILIP 1957 *Leadership in Administration: A Sociological Interpretation.* Evanston, Ill.: Row, Peterson.

SIMMEL, GEORG (1902–1917) 1950 *The Sociology of Georg Simmel.* Edited and translated by Kurt H. Wolff. Glencoe, Ill.: Free Press.

SIMON, HERBERT A. 1957 Authority. Pages 103–118 in Industrial Relations Research Association, *Research in Industrial Human Relations: A Critical Appraisal.* New York: Harper.

STURMTHAL, ADOLF F. 1964 *Workers' Councils: A Study of Workplace Organization on Both Sides of the Iron Curtain.* Cambridge, Mass.: Harvard Univ. Press.

TANNENBAUM, ARNOLD S. 1966 *Social Psychology of the Work Organization.* Belmont, Calif.: Wadsworth.

TANNENBAUM, ARNOLD S.; and KAHN, ROBERT L. 1957 Organizational Control Structure: A General Descriptive Technique as Applied to Four Local Unions. *Human Relations* 10:127–140.

Urwick, Lyndall 1957 *Leadership in the 20th Century.* New York: Pitman.

Weber, Max (1922*a*) 1957 *The Theory of Social and Economic Organization.* Edited by Talcott Parsons. Glencoe, Ill.: Free Press. → First published as Part 1 of *Wirtschaft und Gesellschaft.*

Weber, Max (1922*b*) 1961 The Three Types of Legitimate Rule. Pages 4–14 in Amitai Etzioni (editor), *Complex Organizations: A Sociological Reader.* New York: Holt. → First published in German.

III
POLITICAL ASPECTS

By the middle of the twentieth century, in new nations and old, social and economic changes had imposed on all regimes new demands that resulted in greatly augmenting the power of executive leaders. Prime ministers and presidents, not legislators, were asked to supply the innovation and integration that these situations demanded.

In democratic regimes the executive is no longer merely an arm of government but has become the organizing center of the political system itself. A parliamentary regime in France was transformed into Charles de Gaulle's executive rule. West German politics were stabilized by Konrad Adenauer's shrewd balancing. British politics, in the opinion of some, has been transformed from cabinet government to prime-ministerial government. In the United States the president and the presidential corps have become the fulcrum of politics.

In many emerging nations, democratic forms of government, which have only recently been instituted, are precariously sustained by dramatic executive leaders who rule by mass appeal and the exercise of broad political powers. Fragile identifications with the new national entities are nurtured by mass loyalty to the leader. By personifying the new national values and giving a relentless drive to development, executive leaders energize the mobilized advance of these societies.

Twentieth-century social thought has expressed the paradox that leadership is a solution to the problems of both excessive and insufficient political power. Strong executive leadership was offered as a solution to two general and characteristic maladies of political systems. First, the ideologists of authoritarian movements and regimes proposed strong leadership as a substitute for atrophied traditional primary-group identifications—community, church, family, etc. The breakdown of traditional norm-fostering groups, they argued, leaves society open to conflicts that could be overcome or avoided by strong identification with political leaders. This was a seminal explanation of fascist and communist movements in Western industrial systems and of nationalist movements in preindustrial, developing countries.

Another ideological premise was that only effective leadership can furnish integrative direction and action as a cure for the stalemated pluralism endemic to Western democratic systems. Competing interests wear down consensus and paralyze national decision making. The pathology of political pluralism, the argument ran, is *immobilism.* Under such conditions, only strong executive leadership can furnish decisive national purpose. The most striking recent illustration has been the ideological justification surrounding the presidency of de Gaulle in France. Weaker but nonetheless insistent echoes of this ideology reverberate in the justifications for increasing the powers of other democratic chief executives—the American president, the British prime minister, and the German chancellor.

This integrative function of leadership is fulfilled by two political role types. One is the national hero—the chief executive as personification and representative of the "general will" or "higher interest" of the nation. De Gaulle and the leaders of many emerging nations exemplify this type. Like Rousseau's legislator, such populist figures stand above politics and particular interests. The second is the executive as political broker or artful synthesizer, exemplified by Franklin D. Roosevelt, that is, the expert manager of interests and builder of coalitions.

These two roles are distinct but not mutually exclusive. Each has its relevance in different political systems at particular times. The "general will" spokesman is called into power when national consensus becomes problematical; the "broker" comes to power when a viable consensus exists, unthreatened by polarizing and uncompromisable conflicts—when the management of interest conflicts is the compelling need. To some extent every chief executive must fulfill both roles.

Leadership theory and political executives

The principal functions of chief executives may vary, but all are responses to leadership demands and expectations by the led. Hence, understanding of executive behavior depends in large measure on understanding the phenomenon called leadership.

Historically, the concept of leadership was derived from leadership in a religious sectarian setting or in groups of primary relationships. Sectarian followings inspired by prophetic figures have been at the genesis of many religious movements. Moses, Muhammad, Jesus, Calvin, and many others are illustrative. The solitary, dramatic personality who mobilized and inspired masses to new goals and methods of religious salvation became an important prototype of leadership.

This conceptual view was reinforced by research on historical and primitive governmental institutions, e.g., tribal chiefs and leaders of small city-states, vested with absolute authority. Such studies also contributed the notion of status and hierarchy to the concept of leadership. Power was vested in the *status*, as well as in the person, of a ruler. The personalization of leadership was thus further reinforced.

By the twentieth century several intellectual trends had already effected a change in this conception of leadership. First, the democratic revolution of the eighteenth and nineteenth centuries depersonalized the concept of authority. Power, prescribed and defined in constitutions and law, was vested in the *office*, not the person. The scope and jurisdiction of public officials were given limits in law, so that arbitrary power could be prevented. Rules about leadership succession were specified, to check seizures of power by violence. Office set boundaries to personal influence, and the institutionalization of the executive was firmly implanted.

Second, the positivistic influence of the social sciences drastically modified the concept of political leadership. The traditional "hero" disappeared in the face of new views of psychology. The prevailing instinct-and-trait psychology gave way before the critiques of Mead, Cooley, Dewey, and others and their conceptions of a variable human behavior molded by social interaction. Leadership came to be viewed, not as a set of fixed traits and attributes, biologically peculiar to some individuals, but as a role that satisfies mutual expectations of leaders and followers.

Building on this new, interactional emphasis, research in the social sciences (invigorated by experimental emphasis) added increasing sophistication to the concept of leadership. Situational and group components were strongly emphasized. The leadership role was found to vary with situations. Leaders are always, covertly or overtly, "preselected" by their supporters according to the situational needs of the group. Leadership is a nexus of need fulfillments that binds situational demands and group membership. Thus, during crisis situations groups are likely to select leaders who diagnose problems quickly and act decisively. During less critical periods, leaders who can maintain cohesion and regularity of group performance may be preferred.

Another factor was given emphasis: group goals. Leadership is a differentiated role that enables group purposes to be realized. Where a group is task oriented, leadership integrates the members so that individual needs and group performance can be enhanced. Groups with other purposes choose leaders of another type.

Much insight on leadership is derived from experimentation with and observation of small groups. However, problems arise when such "micro" research is elevated to the "macro" level of many political science concerns. Can insights about leadership that are derived from small-group situations be extrapolated to large units or systems as a whole? Certainly, small-group situations are not replications of nation-state political systems. The danger of such extrapolations has been widely recognized, but general agreement exists that small-group leadership can provide suggestive simulations and simplifications for studying larger units. [*See* GROUPS.]

Characteristics of executive leadership. Analysis of the leadership of chief executives or of national political executives poses special problems to the social science analyst. In contrast to leadership in small-group situations, executive leadership is distinguishable by at least the following: (1) it is leadership at a distance; (2) it has a multirole character; (3) it has a corporate character; (4) it functions in an institutional framework.

If leadership is an interactional relationship, then the relationship between the chief executive of a modern state and his public supporters has the unique character of being leadership at a distance, where neither leader nor follower has *direct* impact upon the other. The relationship is mediated by mass communications, organized groups, and individuals. The leader is linked to his supporters by people who play many roles on various levels of the political system. The relationship between followers and leader is at some remove and therefore indirect. When Harry Truman ordered an atomic bomb dropped on Hiroshima, he could not see the consequences of his decision on the victims nor could he receive the immediate feedback.

Executive behavior is multirole conduct, fulfilling a variety of expectations that flow from various clienteles—from those immediately around the executive, from political parties and political associations, from the various bureaucracies and their political networks, and from the general public. One of the major tasks facing a chief executive is maintaining these different roles in balance. Role expectations are met by various techniques of reconciliation, e.g., by assigning priorities to various roles, minimizing some and stressing others; by insulating incompatible ones from each other; by delegating some and reserving others. What we have come to call the "style" of leadership has its referents in patterns of role management.

Modern executive leadership is an organizational process. The American presidency, the French presidency, and the British office of prime minister are corporate entities, consisting of a sizable staff. In such an organizational context, "leadership" may be attributed to an individual but it is in reality a collective product of organizational activity. It is generically distinct from the leader–led relationships of small-scale situations.

In its organizational context, executive leadership presents a complex face. The chief executive today has become a symbolic individual, whose many roles are collectively filled by several men. If the chief executive is expected to make programmatic statements in some policy area, then corps of experts and speech writers are grouped to produce such a statement. Before the executive makes decisions, various people, playing specific and general roles, define the situation and its alternatives for him. His manifold duties are all largely carried out *in his name by others*. Executive leadership has become institutionalized.

This inner leadership group or staff may be called the executive elite. All executives are dependent upon such a collective formation to perform their tasks. In the United States, for example, it is composed of several groups, some formally organized and some informal. Included among these are the White House staff, the Bureau of the Budget, the Council of Economic Advisors, the National Security Council, and many specialists and *ad hoc* committees. Various presidents have organized and used these cadres in different ways, depending on their interpretations of their roles. In Great Britain, Churchill instituted the so-called Statistical Section, the prime minister's brain trust. Numerous cabinet committees have been established, as well as staff agencies to coordinate the work of the prime minister and the cabinet.

Finally, executive leadership is a process that operates within an institutional framework. At any given time there are prescribed norms that bound and define the scope of authority and the channels of its exercise. These limits are fairly elastic. The chief executive, by the style of his operation, stretches or contracts the boundaries of the position. When the boundaries are exceeded, crisis exigency must justify the practice. At other times, executive boundary aggrandizement is resisted and can be accomplished only by skillful political bargaining on the part of the chief executive.

Because of its corporate and institutional character, the office itself is not wholly dependent upon its occupant. A cumulative heritage of decision and expectation has established precedents that make much of an executive's conduct predictable. This cumulative institutionalization of the office supplies continuity to all executive positions. Cases of sudden death or disability of the chief executive have demonstrated that the office functions in the absence of its principal. Such situations dramatically illustrate the fact that, while in normal times the corporate entity called executive leadership is sensitive to situational demands, it also has a degree of trained "insensitivity" and routine which gives it stability and continuity.

Some doubts have been raised as to whether this cumulative institutionalization might jeopardize executive capacity for decision. The growth in personal agents and *ad hoc* groups testifies to the vigor with which executives strive to prevent overencumbrance by bureaucratization.

Legitimations of executive behavior

The structure of executive leadership is complex because of its multirole, organizational, and institutional context. This complex structure relies on diverse legitimations for support. [*See* LEGITIMACY.] Generally, the democratic chief executive is legitimated by his identification with the central values of his social system, both nonpolitical and political; by the manner in which he is recruited; by the symbolic and effective representation he bestows; and by his decision-making performance.

Societal and political values. Chief executives are legitimated by their identification with the most pervasive goals in society—that is, their embodiment of a national consensus. Thus, Adenauer personified rebirth of the German republic, in keeping with a pre-Nazi, republican past. De Gaulle was in part legitimized by his absorption with a romantic restoration of French glory and power. The sacred values of the system, those beyond dispute, must be expressed and epitomized by the chief executive.

The *political* goals of the executive must conform to the traditional political value system. Even the most innovating and precedent-shattering presidents and prime ministers affirm their adherence to the traditional substantive political values of the system. In Western democracies the chief executives must also affirm their adherence to procedural values—popular consent, parliamentary representation, majority rule, and civil liberties. They must profess respect for, and act in accordance with, the traditional continuities of the system.

Recruitment. The manner in which executives are recruited and elected provides an important basis of their legitimation. In normal times their nomination and election reflect their acceptability to party elites and the general public. Recruitment methods chart career paths and provide a test of the skills regarded as requisite. Most American presidents have been middle-class professionals, usually chosen from the echelon of governors of the leading states. The path to the post of British prime minister has been open to those of a certain social status, educational background, and parliamentary and cabinet career. The path of political mobility reaffirms the central values of the system. [*See* POLITICAL RECRUITMENT AND CAREERS.]

In the United States, as an expression of American egalitarian beliefs, it was expected that a president should rise from humble origins. He would thus embody the American ideal of success by achievement and competence rather than because of family status. The same ethos influences presidential appointments to staff and cabinet.

During periods of crisis or stalemate, recruitment patterns are disrupted. Then chief executives may be co-opted from outside conventional grooves and without the usual political experience, as was the case with de Gaulle in France. Such deviations from established patterns are legitimated by crisis needs and have themselves become a "tradition."

Symbolic and effective representation. The chief executive must represent or appear to represent the public at large *and* its various component segments. He does this in several ways. A common method is the appointment of spokesmen of various groups to his cabinet and to leading offices. Another method gives group representation through an executive staff accessible to various interests.

Another facet of representation by a chief executive may be called "apparent" representation. This is expressed in the many subtle forms of symbolic recognition bestowed by the chief executive upon various groups in the population. When the prime minister of England sends messages to conventions and when the president of the United States greets group delegations of many kinds, they are conferring status and symbolic recognition.

Both apparent and effective representation by the executive are important, because there are general expectations of access and status. The chief executive's audience and clientele must be (at least in a symbolic way) *all* the consensual groups in the system. [*See* REPRESENTATION.]

Decision making. Finally, the chief executive is legitimated by his decision-making performance. Despite overarching "sacred" authority, the effective influence of the chief executive is tested by his capacity to carry out certain policies. The failure or success of his leadership depends upon his effectiveness in knitting together political influence so that it responds to functional demands of the system. It is to this decision-making aspect of executive leadership that the greatest analytical attention has been devoted in recent years. [*See* DECISION MAKING, *article on* POLITICAL ASPECTS.]

Dilemmas of legitimation. The more chief executives are expected to perform, the greater the contradictory pressures which confront them. Crises of legitimation arise when acute tensions develop between several levels of legitimation. A political position that is legitimized by sacred values for what it "is" encounters dilemmas when it is called upon to "do." Despite the secularizing separation between politics and religion, overmoralization of politics makes political tasks delicate. The holders of public office carry the burden of excessive expectations of rectitude and exemplary conduct, yet they are also expected to behave expediently in order to be responsive to public demands.

Another dilemma that confronts chief executives arises from the gap between the executive elite and the public. They must bridge the social and political distance between their special knowledge and the need for responsiveness by the public. The executives must wear different faces at different stages of the policy-making process: when they formulate policies; when they settle for those that are acceptable; and when they implement the accepted ones.

Another dilemma arises out of the conflict between the expectations of the status or position and the political capabilities to fulfill such expectations. Often the public simplifies and exaggerates expectations of executive action. Yet the modern executive in democratic societies is limited by law, administrative organization, group resistances, and the climate of opinion from fulfilling such expectations. Status and influence are not equivalents, and many chief executives fail because their power is not commensurate with their status.

Efforts to resolve these dilemmas of legitimation generate new roles for members of the executive elite. Executives need "buffers" and "catalysts," expert bargainers whose freewheeling, unofficial conduct, is screened off from usual scrutiny. The appearance of rectitude can be maintained as long as the occupational "dirty work" is performed by executive agents.

Dilemmas are also resolved by the executive's efforts to control public expectations. The modern chief executive has become a direct communicator with the public, in order to manage and control public attitudes effectively. The skillful use of the press, radio, and television by chief executives invites identification, which can then be used as a political weapon against resistant and parochial bureaucracies, groups of legislators, or group interests.

Research on executive behavior

Some twenty years ago a shock of realization occurred among students of executive behavior with the discovery that executive behavior deviated from its institutional prescriptions and descriptions. The rigid compartmentalization of government action implied in the separation of powers was found not to exist in fact. This principle, regarded by Montesquieu and Locke as a cardinal check to absolute power, did not realistically describe what occurred. Executive and legislative action closely interpenetrated. Moreover, the modern nation-state more and more demanded the closer integration of these functions, rather than their separation.

Dichotomous categories such as "politics" and "administration" were found to be inaccurate and insufficient for the explanation of decision making. "Administrative" behavior was found to be, not a discrete type of behavior, distinct from "political" activity, but part of a continuous stream of action in a large-scale organizational environment. [*See* ADMINISTRATION.]

While such older categorizations were thus discredited, newer concepts and models were developing, of deeper and more empirical explanatory power. Decision making and systems theory were two such models. Herbert Simon, Richard Snyder, and others elaborated decision-making models that dissected the individual, organizational, and situational components of decision making and linked them together in causal propositions. The focus of analysis shifted away from the policies themselves toward the complexities of the processes of policy making. The "how" of decisions gave more significant clues to the organization of influence in modern governmental structures than the metaphysical "what."

Not all effort was bent on model building. Much analysis of executive behavior took the form of case studies. Many of these were narrative and descriptive, designed to illustrate and depict the variegated paths of policy formation. Some contended that many of these case studies relied on recollection, hearsay, and other questionable evidence and therefore could not be considered more than illustrative. They were also criticized for their overemphasis on the idiosyncratic and the unique, a fragile basis for theory building. Despite such limitations, in the building stages of more systematic analysis, case studies communicated a sense of executive milieu that contributed to suggestive hypotheses. [*See* PUBLIC ADMINISTRATION.]

Another approach in analyzing executive behavior proceeded from institutional frameworks and demonstrated how executive behavior departed from such institutional presumptions. The work of Richard Neustadt and Don Price, among others, exemplified this category. This type of analysis was rich in insight about the interplay between the less formal and more formal factors which condition and influence executive authority.

Situational analysis. Still another way of analyzing executive behavior stressed situational factors. It proceeded from the multirole character of executive behavior in its organizational context as it confronted characteristic problem situations. Illustrative of this are the following situational typologies, derived from American governmental experience.

Executive decisions may be divided into three situational types: (1) crisis situations; (2) programmatic situations; (3) anticipatory situations. In each situation interest groups, the executive, and the presidential elite play varying roles.

Crisis situations. Under crisis conditions, public opinion is more aware of the situation, but legislative and interest-group involvement is less than in programmatic or anticipatory situations; and in these stress situations, executive discretion is greatest.

Crisis situations, which have become quite frequent in the post-1945 world, can be categorized as follows: bargaining crises (e.g., industrial disputes); legitimacy crises (e.g., the dismissal of MacArthur); crises of norms (e.g., scandals of various kinds, such as the Profumo affair); and, by far the most frequent and serious, national defense crises (situations which acutely threaten resources regarded as essential to national safety, e.g., the Cuban missile standoff and the Berlin airlift).

In crisis situations each system, in varying degrees, loses some of its pluralistic safeguards as the executive assumes broad discretion. The executive acquires exclusive control in defining the situation and in directing the appropriate measures. The normal institutional workings of decision making are reduced to an executive directorate consisting of a handful of people. The public is anxiously alert but little informed, while the legislative bodies and interest groups assume passive roles. In sum, crisis situations bring structural changes in the system that give the broadest of authority to the executive. [*See* CRISIS; CRISIS GOVERNMENT.]

Programmatic situations. Programmatic situations demand long-range and broad-gauge policies. They require strategic determinations of ends and means. When programmatic issues are faced, a moderate degree of legislative and bureaucratic involvement results and executive discretion is limited. The Marshall Plan of the United States and the European Defense Community decisions by European governments are examples.

Anticipatory situations. Anticipatory situations concern eventualities, not immediate situations. The likelihood of occurrence may not be great, but should the situation occur, a course of action will have been decided upon. Of all situations, these evoke the greatest legislative debate, the least public awareness, and the greatest interest-group concern. Executive discretion is severely limited under these conditions, because the costs of inaction are difficult to foretell and the consequences are not close at hand.

Anticipatory situations are the result of previous crises. For example, the depression of the 1930s gave rise both to legislation and to administrative policies that anticipated a recurrence and were therefore designed to come into play when economic danger signals appeared. Programs such as the federal insurance of deposits in savings banks and the public works agendas to be used when unemployment reaches certain levels were created.

Problems of executive behavior

Within the three situational configurations described above, there are problems of executive behavior which flow from certain structural features of the system itself. Insufficient recognition has been given to the subgroups within the executive. It is traditional to think of the executive and governmental bureaucracy in hierarchic terms. In this view, the president or prime minister stands at the pinnacle of the executive, and below him are the administrators, ranged in a descending order of subordination. The enlargement of executive scope gave rise to centrifugal tendencies that diffused executive influence. The bureaucracies, which ostensibly enlarge executive jurisdiction, in fact dilute and disperse executive influence. These bureaucratic groups have their own biases and often act autonomously and at variance with executive policies.

As a result, a problem that executives face is the "horizontal bargaining" *within* the executive. Not uncommonly the executive has to negotiate with his nominally subordinate agencies. Governmental bureaucracy is pluralistic, so that each bureaucracy has its own subvalues. Out of the long-accrued interdependence between the bureaucracies and legislative and economic interests, the bureaucrats have gained considerable independence of executive authority, and a growing political division occurs between the executive and the governmental bureaucracies normally under his jurisdiction. The internal politics of the executive in decision making has, perhaps, become more significant than executive–legislative relations. [*See* BUREAUCRACY *and* CIVIL SERVICE.]

At the outset of this article, the integrating and innovating functions of executive leadership in all political systems were stressed. These functions are closely related to the expectations of executive programs, i.e., the definition of broad political goals and specific legislative and administrative measures necessary to their fulfillment. Broad and consistent national programs for economic stability and growth, foreign policy strategy, defense postures, and welfare goals are expected of the chief executive. It is through these that the executive defines the situation for all the political actors.

The winning of acceptance for these programs demands accommodation to various political subgroups, whose focus is less on the general societal effects of legislative and administrative proposals than on the special effects these have upon their particular interests. This accommodation to specialized publics and interests is a serious executive problem. The "politics" of executive behavior is largely a matter of finding some synthesis, i.e., identity of interest or complementarity of roles, between the general viewpoint of the executive and the particular perspective of various groups.

In sum, despite institutionalized continuities, executive decision making forms not a single pattern but several situational patterns, in which the roles of bureaucracies, interest groups, parties, and legislators vary. The increase of both secular and acute crises has more sharply differentiated these modes of executive decision making.

The study of executive decision making reveals the several configurations of political systems as they respond to situational demands. In an era so prone to crisis as the present, the far-reaching consequences of crisis decision making deserve fuller attention than they have yet received. As we have seen, crisis decision making is not merely a slight shift but a change in configuration of the system itself. Studies are needed, both of these structural changes and of certain secondary effects, such as changes in elite recruitment, responses of the various bureaucracies, and capabilities of the executive for prompt decision making.

The subject of leadership and executive behavior in general should draw the increasing attention of social scientists. The gap between the significance of executive behavior and current explanatory methods calls for greater research attention. The wide use of aggregate data about executive behavior and of direct empirical studies of executives in various systems has not seriously begun. If executive centralization is the trend, it must be carefully analyzed so that its processes and consequences are better understood.

LESTER G. SELIGMAN

[*See also* POLITICAL EXECUTIVE. *Other relevant material may be found in* GOVERNMENT; POLITICAL BEHAVIOR; POLITICAL PROCESS; PRESIDENTIAL GOVERNMENT; PUBLIC POLICY.]

BIBLIOGRAPHY

ACHESON, DEAN 1956 Legislative–Executive Relations. *Yale Review* New Series 45:481–495.

BROWNLOW, LOUIS 1949 *The President and the Presidency.* Chicago: Public Administration Service.

BURNS, JAMES M. (1956) 1962 *Roosevelt: The Lion and the Fox.* New York: Harcourt.

CORWIN, EDWARD S.; and KOENIG, LOUIS W. 1956 *The Presidency Today.* New York Univ. Press.

FENNO, RICHARD F. JR. 1958 President–Cabinet Relations: A Pattern and a Case Study. *American Political Science Review* 52:388–405.

HERRING, E. PENDLETON 1940 *Presidential Leadership.* New York: Farrar & Rinehart.

HOBBS, EDWARD H. 1954 *Behind the President: A Study of Executive Office Agencies.* Washington: Public Affairs Press.

HOLCOMBE, ARTHUR M. 1954 Presidential Leadership and the Party System. *Yale Review* New Series 43: 321–335.

KAUFMAN, HERBERT 1956 Emerging Conflicts in the Doctrines of Public Administration. *American Political Science Review* 50:1057–1073.

KOENIG, LOUIS W. 1944 *The Presidency and the Crisis: Powers of the Office From the Invasion of Poland to Pearl Harbor.* New York: King's Crown Press.

LIPSON, LESLIE 1939 *The American Governor From Figurehead to Leader.* Studies in Public Administration, No. 9. Univ. of Chicago Press.

LITWAK, EUGENE 1961 Models of Bureaucracy Which Permit Conflict. *American Journal of Sociology* 67: 177–184.

LONGAKER, RICHARD P. 1956 The President as International Leader. *Law and Contemporary Problems* 21: 735–752.

MILTON, GEORGE F. (1944) 1965 *The Use of Presidential Power, 1789–1943.* New York: Octagon.

NEUSTADT, RICHARD E. 1955 Presidency and Legislation: Planning the President's Program. *American Political Science Review* 49:980–1021.

NEUSTADT, RICHARD E. 1956 The Presidency at Midcentury. *Law and Contemporary Problems* 21:609–645.

PROTHRO, JAMES W. 1956 Verbal Shifts in the American Presidency: A Content Analysis. *American Political Science Review* 50:726–739.

RANSONE, COLEMAN B. 1956 *The Office of Governor in the United States.* University: Univ. of Alabama Press.

REDFORD, EMMETT S. 1952 *Administration of National Economic Control.* New York: Macmillan.

ROSSITER, CLINTON L. (1956) 1960 *The American Presidency.* 2d ed. New York: Harcourt.

SCHUBERT, GLENDON 1957 The Public Interest in Administrative Decision-making: Theorem, Theosophy, or Theory? *American Political Science Review* 51: 346:368.

SELIGMAN, LESTER G. 1955 Developments in the Presidency and the Conception of Political Leadership. *American Sociological Review* 20:706–712.

SELIGMAN, LESTER G. 1956*a* The President Is Many Men. *Antioch Review* 16:305–318.

SELIGMAN, LESTER G. 1956*b* Presidential Leadership: The Inner Circle and Institutionalization. *Journal of Politics* 18:410–426.

SELIGMAN, LESTER G. 1956*c* The Presidential Office and the President as Party Leader. *Law and Contemporary Problems* 21:724–734.

SELVIN, HANAN C. 1960 *The Effects of Leadership.* Glencoe, Ill.: Free Press.

SILVA, RUTH C. 1956 Presidential Succession and Disability. *Law and Contemporary Problems* 21:646–662.

SMITH, M. BREWSTER 1952 Social Psychology and Group Processes. *Annual Review of Psychology* 3: 175–204.

SOMERS, HERMAN M. 1950 *Presidential Agency: OWMR, the Office of War Mobilization and Reconversion.* Cambridge, Mass.: Harvard Univ. Press.

STOGDILL, RALPH M. 1948 Personal Factors Associated With Leadership: A Survey of the Literature. *Journal of Psychology* 25:35–71.

STOKE, HAROLD W. 1941 Executive Leadership and the Growth of Propaganda. *American Political Science Review* 35:490–500.

TURNER, HENRY A. 1951 Woodrow Wilson: Exponent of Executive Leadership. *Western Political Quarterly* 4:97–115.

VERBA, SIDNEY 1961 *Small Groups and Political Behavior: A Study of Leadership.* Princeton Univ. Press.

WILDAVSKY, AARON B. 1964 *The Politics of the Budgetary Process.* Boston: Little.

LEARNING

In addition to the general articles under this heading, broad fields of learning phenomena are reviewed in FORGETTING; IMITATION; IMPRINTING; THINKING. *More specific concepts relevant to learning are discussed in* CONCEPT FORMATION; DRIVES; FATIGUE; INTELLIGENCE AND INTELLIGENCE TESTING; MOTIVATION; PROBLEM SOLVING; REASONING

AND LOGIC. *The role of learning in personal development is discussed in* DEVELOPMENTAL PSYCHOLOGY; INTELLECTUAL DEVELOPMENT; LANGUAGE, *article on* LANGUAGE DEVELOPMENT; MORAL DEVELOPMENT; SENSORY AND MOTOR DEVELOPMENT; SOCIALIZATION. *The role of learning in society is treated in* ADULT EDUCATION; EDUCATION; EDUCATIONAL PSYCHOLOGY; INTELLECTUALS; KNOWLEDGE, SOCIOLOGY OF; LITERACY; TEACHING; UNIVERSITIES. *The importance of learning is also emphasized in* MENTAL DISORDERS, TREATMENT OF. *Theories of learning are discussed in* GESTALT THEORY; INFORMATION THEORY; LEARNING THEORY; MODELS, MATHEMATICAL. *Some applications of learning are discussed in* BRAINWASHING; COMMUNICATION, MASS; COMMUNICATION, POLITICAL; PERSUASION; PROPAGANDA. *The measurement of learning is discussed in* ACHIEVEMENT TESTING; INTELLIGENCE AND INTELLIGENCE TESTING; RESPONSE SETS. *Of direct relevance to learning are the biographies of* BEKHTEREV; GUTHRIE; HULL; MONTESSORI; PAVLOV; SECHENOV; TOLMAN; WATSON.

I
INTRODUCTION

Learning has been defined (Kimble 1961) as a relatively permanent change in a behavioral tendency, which occurs as a result of reinforced practice. One purpose of this definition, as with any definition, is to delimit as precisely as possible a particular realm of discourse. Thus, a word or two appears to be in order with respect to topics that this definition specifically includes and excludes.

Changes in behavior occur as a result of many processes, not all of which are forms of learning. The above definition succeeds in eliminating most if not all of these changes. Behavioral changes occurring as a result of maturation are ruled out by the requirement of dependence upon practice. Changes resulting from motivational fluctuations are temporary and are eliminated by the reference to a permanent change. Changes in behavior that come under the heading of forgetting and experimental extinction are excluded by the reference to reinforced practice. Learning necessitates the appropriate use of reward or punishment. If these operations, collectively called reinforcement, are omitted, learning disappears; experimental extinction or "unlearning" takes place. The reference to reinforced practice is necessary to exclude such changes from the definition of learning.

Turning now to matters that the definition does not exclude, it should be noted that the definition says nothing about the kinds of behavioral changes that qualify as learning. There is, for example, no suggestion that learning always leads to an improvement in behavior: bad habits as well as good habits are encompassed by the definition. Similarly, acquired motives, attitudes, and values come within the scope of the definition as easily as do changes in language habits and motor skills. Finally, the use of the term "tendency" allows the definition to cover cases in which the products of learning do not immediately appear in performance. In this way the definition covers the numerous cases in which an individual learns something that may not be put to practical use for years. Someone might learn as a boy scout that moss typically grows on the north side of trees and that this information may be used to find one's way out of a forest when lost, but not actually perform any responses based on this information until much later, if ever. The distinction implicit in the previous statements, that between learning and performance, is basic to the psychology of learning. In general, learning refers to the establishment of tendencies; performance refers to the translation of these tendencies into behavior.

Historical background. Although ideas basic to the modern psychology of learning have existed for millennia, especially in the associationistic philosophies, the immediate antecedents of the scientific study of learning are to be found in the work of three scientists writing in the late nineteenth and early twentieth centuries: the German Ebbinghaus, the Russian Pavlov, and the American Thorndike [*see* EBBINGHAUS; PAVLOV; THORNDIKE].

Ebbinghaus. Ebbinghaus fathered the study of verbal rote learning (1885). As materials, he used meaningless three-letter, consonant–vowel–consonant, sequences, which have come to be called nonsense syllables. GOC, TER, and BIV are examples. Ebbinghaus constructed lists of these materials of various lengths, memorized them under various conditions, and attempted to recall them after various amounts of time. He discovered many of the laws of such learning, which remain valid today. It is of incidental interest that Ebbinghaus also appears to have been the first psychologist to make use of the ideas of statistics and probability.

Pavlov. Using dogs as subjects, Pavlov studied the simple form of learning that we now call classical conditioning (1927). The Pavlovian procedure consisted of presenting the dog with food or an acid solution, which made the animal salivate, shortly after the presentation of some neutral stimulus, such as a tone or light, which did not. After several such pairings, the dog came to salivate at the presentation of the neutral stimulus as if that stimulus had somehow become a substitute for food or acid. Pavlov was able to demonstrate many of the basic phenomena of conditioning. He also developed a quasi-neurological theory to account for such learning.

Thorndike. Thorndike also worked with lower animals, such as dogs, cats, and chickens, and studied what we now call instrumental learning. The most famous of Thorndike's studies were those in which cats learned to operate a latch to escape from a puzzle box and to obtain a bit of fish outside (Thorndike 1898–1901). On the basis of his observations in these studies, Thorndike was led to develop an influential theory of learning in which three hypotheses were central: (1) learning consists of the formation of connections between stimuli and responses; (2) learning is a gradual rather than a sudden or insightful process; and (3) learning depends not just upon practice but also upon reward and punishment. This last hypothesis Thorndike called the law of effect.

Taxonomy of learning

As these historical materials indicate, the scientific study of learning involves the use of widely different procedures. It is useful, in fact, to differentiate forms of learning in addition to those described above. The most important of these are considered here.

Classical conditioning. Many investigators make a distinction between forms of learning in which the subject's reactions lead to reward or punishment and those in which such events take place independently of the subject's behavior. The former arrangement defines instrumental learning; the latter identifies classical conditioning. The four most important aspects of the classical conditioning experiment may be described by referring to the example of Pavlovian conditioning mentioned above.

(1) *Unconditioned stimulus* (*US*)—any stimulus that at the outset of an experiment produces a regular reaction. In the typical Pavlovian experiment the *US* is food.

(2) *Unconditioned response* (*UR*)—the consistent reaction evoked by the *US* just referred to. In the Pavlovian experiments this was the salivation.

(3) *Conditioned stimulus* (*CS*)—a neutral stimulus paired with the *US* for experimental purposes. In the typical Pavlovian experiments, this was a light, buzzer, bell, or ticking metronome.

(4) *Conditioned response* (*CR*). After several pairings of the *CS* and *US*, a response resembling the *UR* may be elicited by the conditioned stimulus. This is the conditioned response, conditioned reaction, or conditioned reflex.

Studies of the conditioned reflex show that such learning is a very general process. Reactions that have been conditioned, in addition to salivation, include the galvanic skin response, the eyeblink, a blocking of the alpha rhythm of the brain, pupillary dilation, vasodilation and constriction, and secretion of various internal organs. It has also been demonstrated that the range of neutral stimuli to which such conditioning may take place is wide and includes all of the stimuli that the organism ordinarily perceives and some that it ordinarily may not perceive.

In discussing classical conditioning, two items of interpretation appear to be important. First, as the responses listed above suggest, the reactions modifiable by classical conditioning are often emotional reactions. Thus, classical conditioning appears to be the mechanism by which hopes, fears, attitudes, and other emotionally toned reactions are established. Second, it is important to restrict the application of the term "conditioning" to classical conditioning. The extension of the concept of conditioning to almost every form of learning, as some authors have done, leads to confusion.

Simple instrumental learning. Most learning situations differ from classical conditioning in that the organism's reactions are instrumental to the securing of reward or the avoidance of punishment —hence the name "instrumental learning." In purely physical terms, there are four possible relationships between a given response and reward and punishment: the response in question may (1) produce reward, (2) avoid a punishment, (3) lead to punishment, or (4) lead to the withholding of reward. The great majority of experimental work in simple instrumental learning involves the first two of these, reward learning and avoidance learning. We shall discuss reward learning here, postponing the treatment of avoidance learning until later.

A common device for the study of reward learning is the Skinner box. A representative version of this apparatus might consist of a chamber about one foot on a side. A lever extends into the box on one side. If the rat (the species most commonly studied in the Skinner box) presses the lever, a bit of food or a small dipper of water is automatically presented.

Investigations of simple instrumental learning employ two general procedures: free responding and discriminative. In the latter method a distinctive signal such as a light or tone or the insertion of the lever into the box is used to indicate when reward is available. If the animal presses the bar in the presence of the discriminative stimulus, reward occurs. Bar pressures at other times go unrewarded. In the free-responding situation, there is no discriminative stimulus to indicate when reward is available.

Schedules of reinforcement. Most investigations of learning in the Skinner box employ the free-responding procedure and some version of a partial-reinforcement schedule. The rat does not receive reward for every bar depression but is reinforced on a schedule that is defined either in terms of a temporal interval or in terms of a specified number of responses. Thus, there are both interval and ratio schedules of reinforcement. Moreover, the number of responses required for reinforcement or the temporal interval separating reinforcements may be fixed (regular) or variable (irregular). The combinations of these physical arrangements generate four basic schedules of reinforcement: (1) fixed interval, (2) variable interval, (3) fixed ratio, and (4) variable ratio. In the fixed interval schedule the animal is reinforced for the first response after a standard period of time, perhaps one minute. In the variable interval schedule the animal is rewarded for the first response after some average amount of time, such as one minute, but the intervals separating successive reinforcements vary widely around this average value. Similarly with ratio schedules, the fixed ratio schedule is one in which the animal is reinforced for the *n*th (for example, the fifteenth) response and the variable ratio schedule provides reward after some average, but varying, number of bar depressions. These schedules of reinforcement produce characteristic behavioral patterns that cannot be described within the scope of this article. The interested reader is referred to Skinner (1938), Ferster and Skinner (1957), or to any standard book on learning (for example, Hall 1966; Kimble 1961). One practical consequence of any partial reinforcement schedule is the establishment of great persistence in behavior. This is particularly true of the variable interval schedule. This schedule, therefore, is widely used in experiments in which many tests must be conducted. The investigation of stimulus generalization, which we shall discuss later, and the influence of drugs upon behavior are important examples.

Complex instrumental learning. The simple experimental situations typified by the Skinner box are relatively recent in the history of the scientific study of learning. Earlier investigations tended to use more complex situations, the multiunit maze being, by far, the most popular. The general abandonment of these procedures probably resulted from two difficulties: the complex instrumental learning situations were difficult to subject to automation; and, more importantly, the learning that takes place in such situations is so complex as to defy analysis. On the other hand, investigations of complex instrumental learning did lead to a preliminary statement of certain laws of learning and to the development of certain important concepts. One of the most important items in the first category was suggested by the fact that mazes tend to be learned in a backward order; the correct turns near the goal are learned first, and those near the starting point are learned last. This fact implies the existence of a *goal gradient* or delay of reinforcement gradient, which means that responses followed immediately by reward are learned more rapidly than those for which reward is delayed.

Habit family hierarchy. The most useful general concept to come from the study of complex instrumental learning is that of habit family hierarchy. Investigators of maze behavior, for example, noticed that the initial behavior of the rat in the maze was not merely random wandering but revealed certain dependabilities. The rat might show a consistent tendency to turn right rather than left, to proceed straight ahead rather than to make a turn at all, to prefer dim alleys to those more brightly illuminated, and to choose paths leading in the general direction of the home cage over those that lead in the opposite direction. Such observations suggested the general proposition that the learner comes to the learning situation with a repertoire of responses (habit family) that vary in strength (hierarchy). This made it possible to view complex instrumental learning as a reorganization of the habit family hierarchy.

Acquisition of motor skill. At the human level, an important form of learning is the acquisition of motor skill. Improvements in handwriting, baseball pitching, piano playing, and bicycle riding are familiar examples. The only caution that should be urged is that it is important to distinguish between skills that emerge as a result of learning and those that appear as a result of maturation. In the young child, walking is an example of the latter type of skill. Although we speak of "learning to walk," experimental studies have shown that this skill is almost entirely the result of maturation and that practice has relatively little to do with it.

As is the case in all other areas of learning, laboratory study has led to a refinement in methods and to the use of relatively standardized procedures. A very commonly used device for the study of motor learning is the pursuit rotor (rotary-pursuit apparatus). The pursuit rotor resembles a phonograph turntable. Its main feature is a motor-driven disc, which usually turns at the rate of 60 rpm. At a distance of four or five inches from the center, there is a small target approximately the size of a dime. The subject's task is to keep the point of a hinged stylus in contact with the target while the disc rotates. The measure of performance is the amount of time the subject keeps the point of the stylus in contact with the target.

Massed versus distributed practice. Some of the most important results obtained from pursuit rotor studies deal with the spacing of practice trials. In one investigation (Kimble & Shatel 1952), subjects received fifteen 50-second trials per day for ten days (see Figure 1). One group learned under conditions of massed practice, in which the trials were separated by 10-second rest pauses. The other group learned under conditions of distributed (spaced) practice, the trials being separated by rest pauses of 70 seconds. The results of the investigation were as follows: (1) Massed practice produces a serious interference with the acquisition of pursuit rotor skill. (2) Under either condition of practice, improvement continues for a long time. In Figure 1, it can be seen that even after 150 trials, the subjects under both conditions of practice still continue to show improvement. (3) The initial trials on any day's session show certain interesting characteristics. One of these is the phenomenon of warm-up, which is most conspicuously displayed in the later sessions of the subjects who learn under distributed practice. The first trials are quite inferior to the final trials of the preceding day, and it may take six or eight trials for the warm-up process to be complete and for the level of performance of the previous day to be reached. (4) Under conditions of massed practice, a different effect may appear at the beginning of each practice. This is an improvement in performance that apparently occurs as the result of rest and the disappearance of a fatiguelike state produced by massed practice. This phenomenon is most obvious in the early sessions under massed practice. In Figure 1 the straight lines through the massed-practice functions are fitted curves used to estimate what performance would have been on the first trial of a particular session if a day's rest had not intervened (open circles) and what it would have been on that same trial if there had been no need to warm up (filled circles). The difference between the open and closed circles is a measure of this improvement, technically called reminiscence. It is of interest that in this experiment reminiscence disappears late in learning. (5) If these subjects, who practice with their preferred hand, are tested for performance with their nonpreferred hand and if appropriate control procedures are employed, it is possible to demonstrate that the performance of the nonpreferred hand benefits considerably from practice with the preferred one. This characteristic of motor learning, called transfer of training, is very conspicuous in motor skills.

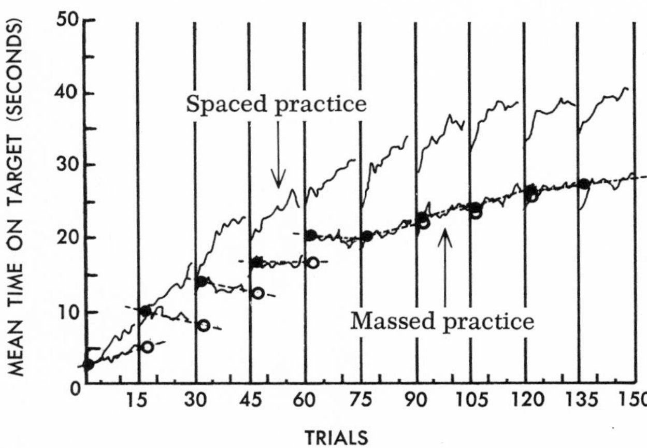

Figure 1 — Learning curves for a pursuit rotor task under spaced and massed practice

Source: Kimble & Shatel 1952, p. 356.

Rote verbal learning. As was mentioned at the outset of this article, one of the earliest forms of learning to receive scientific study was verbal learning, which Ebbinghaus began to investigate in the late nineteenth century. In its modern form the study of verbal learning takes two major forms, serial learning and paired-associate learning. Serial learning involves the memorization of lists, typically lists of nonsense syllables; paired-associate learning, as the name implies, involves the learning of pairs of items in the way one learns a foreign language vocabulary.

Both of these forms of rote learning are influenced in the same way by certain variables: (1) The manipulation of distribution of practice

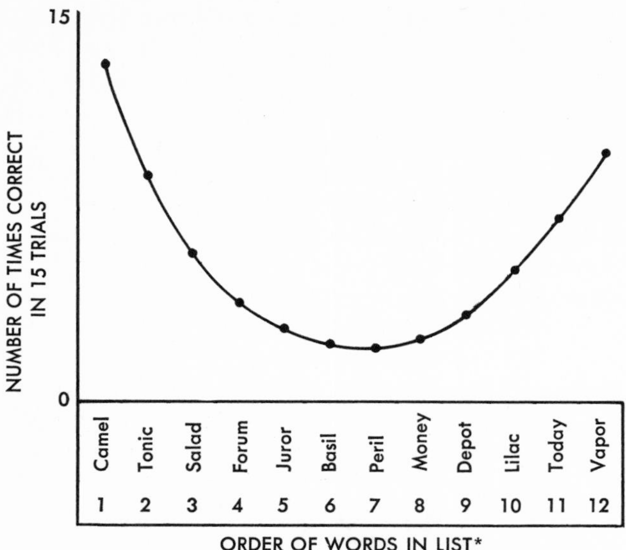

Figure 2 — A characteristic serial position function

* For purposes of illustration the words are listed along the base line.

leads, as in motor learning, to better performance under spaced practice than under massed practice; but typically the effect is of a much less impressive magnitude than in motor learning. (2) Both proceed much more rapidly with meaningful materials (for example, a list containing the words *house*, *robin*, *wagon*, *money*, *uncle*, etc.) than with nonsense materials (for example, a list containing the items TOZ, LUN, GIB, VUR, DEG).

Studies of serial learning have revealed characteristic differences in the ease of learning different portions of the list. The very first items are easiest; those at the end are next easiest; the most difficult items are those just after the middle of the list. This phenomenon, illustrated in Figure 2, may be referred to as a serial position function.

Interference phenomena. The paired-associate learning procedure has been particularly useful in the study of interferences of the kind thought to be responsible for normal forgetting. Suppose a subject learns the following pairs of words:

table–bright
dozen–forest
value–camel
willow–stone
label–graze

He then learns these pairs:

table–lozenge
dozen–tempest
value–blister
willow–horse
label–trial

Note that the stimulus words are the same in the two lists but that the responses are different. Referring to the stimulus and response words in the first list as *A* and *B*, respectively, the items in the second list can be referred to as *A* and *C*. This *A–B*, *A–C* relationship leads to great difficulty in remembering the *A–B* associations. The establishment of such interferences is commonly thought by psychologists of verbal learning to be the essential condition for forgetting.

Learning to learn. If subjects are required to learn a series of lists of verbal materials, they show a steadily improving ability as a function of the number of lists previously committed to memory (unless, as just noted, the lists are constructed to interfere with each other). The results typically obtained in experiments on learning to learn appear in Figure 3. Among the most important experimental demonstrations of this fact are the investigations of Harlow (1949). Harlow taught monkeys a series of several hundred discrimination

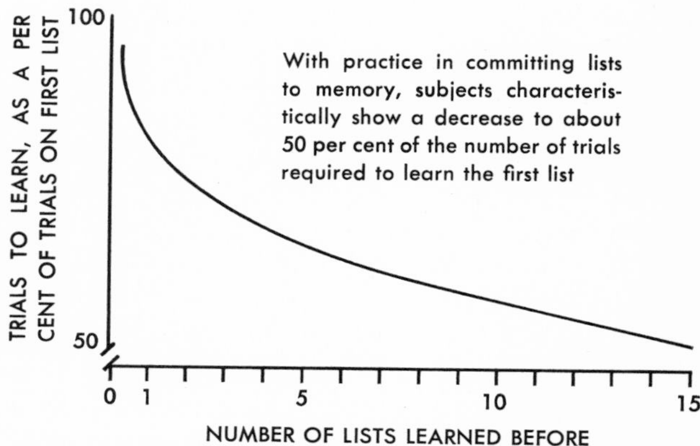

Figure 3 — Hypothetical function depicting "learning to learn" in a typical rote learning situation

problems. During the course of this experiment, the subjects improved to the point where they were solving new discriminations after just one trial.

Basic phenomena of simple learning

Most students of learning assume that the variety of forms of learning considered in the previous section all obey the same basic laws. For this reason, it has seemed expedient to most such students to study the basic properties of learning in simple situations, often with lower organisms as subjects. Thus, realistic presentations of what are regarded as the basic phenomena of learning (this section), as well as of its most fundamental laws (next section), must depend heavily upon studies of classical conditioning and simple instrumental learning.

Acquisition and the learning curve. During the course of practice, a subject's performance changes in a direction that indicates an increase in the strength of the underlying process. The phenomenon of habit acquisition is often represented in the form of a learning curve. The shape and direction of such functions depend upon the particular measure of learning employed. Idealized but typical functions appear in Figure 4. In what follows, we shall limit ourselves to a report of investigations where increases in the measure plotted reflect increases in the strength of a habit.

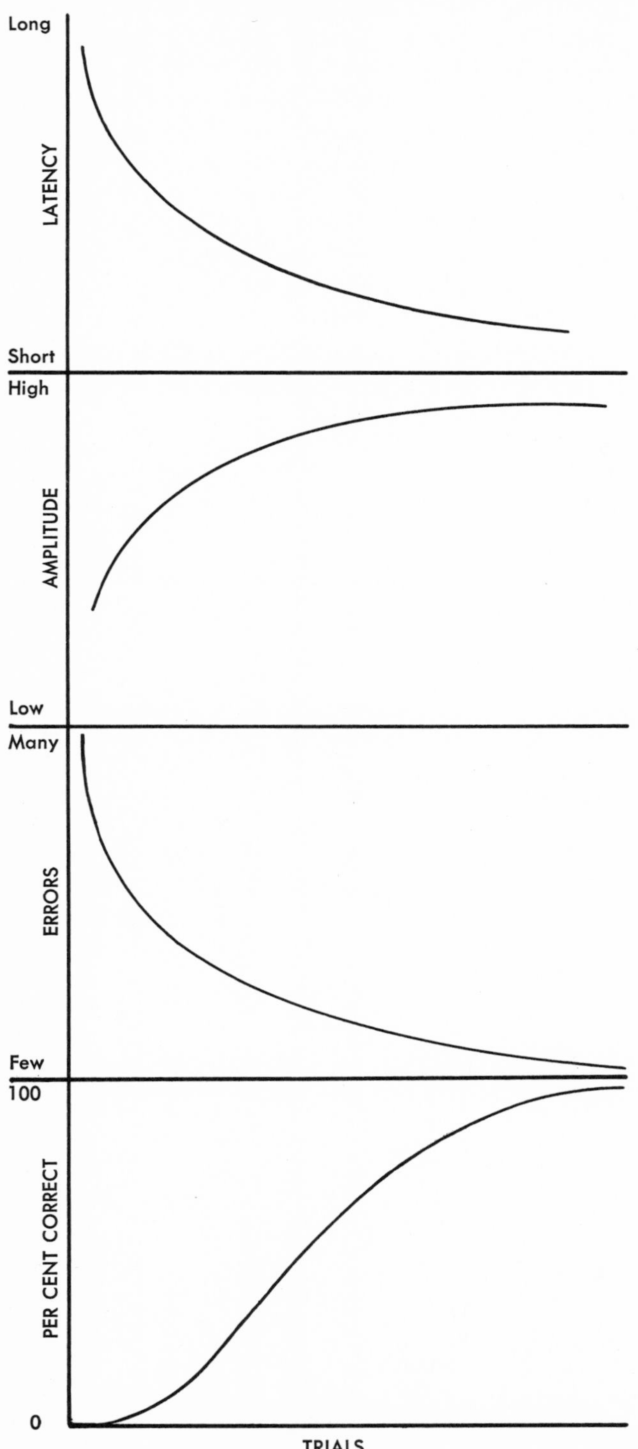

Figure 4 — Characteristic forms of learning curves for four different measures of performance

Extinction. As mentioned earlier, and as will be developed in more detail later, learning requires the use of reinforcements; for example, allowing the subject the opportunity to obtain food or avoid punishment for performing the response to be learned. The omission of reinforcement leads to a reduction in performance that Pavlov called experimental extinction and is now more often referred to simply as extinction.

Spontaneous recovery. If, following extinction, the subject is allowed a period of rest, there frequently occurs a spontaneous increase, or spontaneous recovery, in the strength of the previously extinguished response. This increase resembles the increase called reminiscence, which occurs in motor learning. Many theorists (for example, Hull 1951) regard both as reflecting the dissipation of some type of inhibitory process. What next happens to the strength of the spontaneously recovered response depends upon whether or not it is reinforced. The reintroduction of reinforcement leads to the rapid re-establishment of the full strength of the response. Omission of reinforcement leads to re-extinction. Figure 5 provides a graphic summary of the phenomena described.

Stimulus generalization. Ordinarily, in a conditioning experiment the conditioned stimulus is precisely controlled. If the response is tested with other stimuli, the conditioned reaction may occur but in diminished strength. For example, Guttman and Kalish (1958) trained pigeons to peck at a disc illuminated with a light of 550 $m\mu$ and tested the reaction of the pigeon to lights of other colors. The measure of response strength employed was the rate of pecking. These investigators obtained results indicating that there is a generalization gradient (Figure 6 illustrates these findings). In general, such a gradient shows the transfer of response strength to stimuli similar to the training stimulus and a reduction in strength that is proportional to the difference between the training and test stimuli.

Discrimination. The tendency for a response to generalize means that the subject fails to discriminate between similar stimuli. Discrimination between two stimuli may be obtained by presenting the two stimuli either together (allowing the organism to choose one) or in succession (allowing the organism to respond or not) and reinforcing responses to one stimulus and withholding reinforcement for responses to the other, provided that the organism's sensory mechanisms can detect the difference. Following such training, the subject

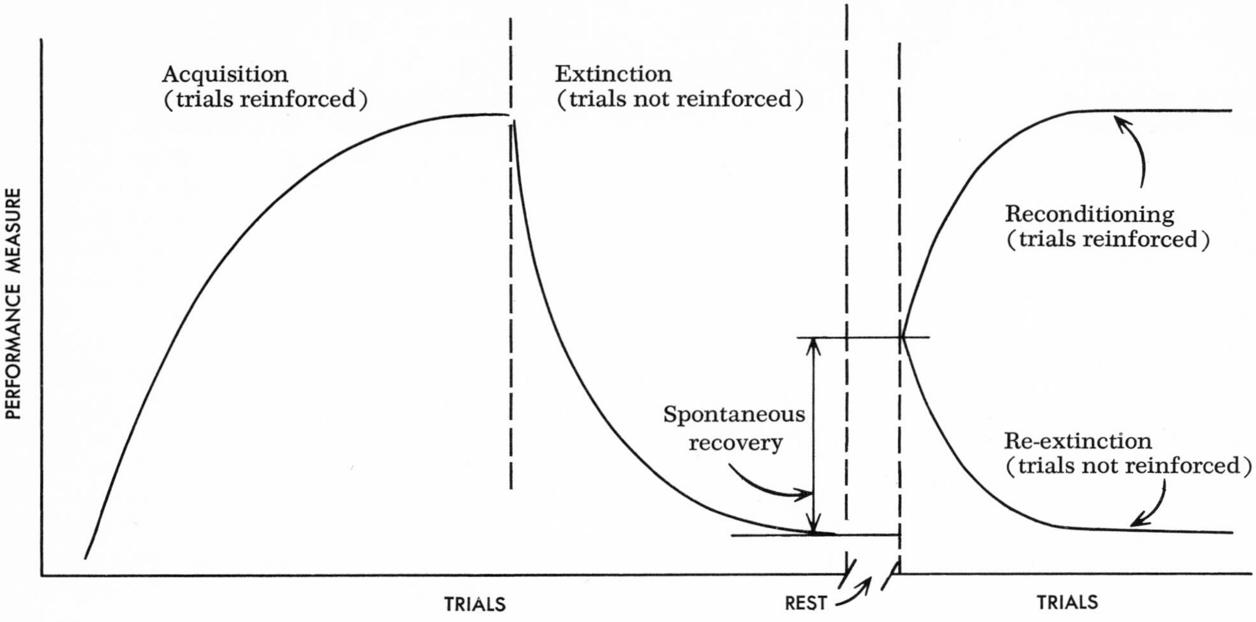

Figure 5 — Summary graph depicting acquisition, extinction, spontaneous recovery, reconditioning, and a second extinction

typically learns to respond to the reinforced stimulus but not to the other. It is clear that the establishment of a discrimination involves all of the basic phenomena discussed so far: Responses to the reinforced stimulus are *acquired* and then *generalized* to the nonreinforced stimulus. These latter responses are *extinguished* by nonreinforcement but presumably are subject to spontaneous recovery.

Concept formation. At a level much more complex than that of simple learning, it seems very likely that the formation of concepts entails a process of discrimination learning. A concept obviously involves a tendency to treat diverse things as identical (generalization) but to limit the extent of such indiscriminate reaction.

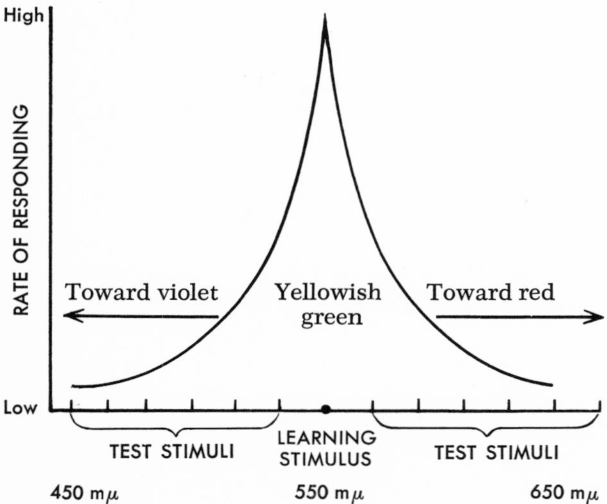

Figure 6 — A generalization gradient

The laws of learning and performance

The major preoccupation of students of learning has been with the experimental manipulation of a variety of variables in an effort to determine their lawful relationship to learned changes in behavior. As we shall see, it is easy to list variables that have powerful effects upon performance in the learning situation. What is not so easy is to determine with certainty whether the effect is upon learning or performance. To illustrate this difficulty, suppose that two groups of rats learn a maze under conditions that are exactly alike except that one group learns after having been deprived of food for 24 hours and the other group learns after having been deprived of food for only 2 hours. The learning curves obtained on these two groups of subjects would surely be very different (see Figure 7). But is this difference a difference in learning or performance—or both? The obvious way to find out is to subdivide each group at some point when an impressive difference in behavior has been established, testing some previously very hungry animals when they are only moderately hungry and some previously moderately hungry animals when they are very hungry. Under controlled conditions and with the change in motivation, the performance of both groups changes immediately to what it would have been if the new condition of motivation had prevailed from the beginning (see Figure 7). In short, there is no evidence that motivation has any effect upon learning in an experiment of this sort. The influence, which is a powerful one, is entirely upon performance.

The difficulty in the experiment just described exists for every other variable that might be manipulated. Thus, in the sections to follow, we shall present several important regularities emerging from the experimental study of learning; but, except in connection with the first of these, we shall not return to the question whether the effect is on learning or performance. It will be sufficient to say that the current trend in the thinking of psychologists of learning is to assign more and more of these variables a role as determiners of performance rather than of learning.

Number of practice trials. By definition, learning depends upon practice; and it is obvious that the amount of practice must figure in some way in determining the amount of learning. There is considerable argument, however, about the kind of law involved (Kimble 1961, pp. 109–136). Some psychologists have maintained that all learning is, in some sense, insightful and occurs in just one trial; others have insisted that all learning represents the gradual strengthening of some underlying process. The learning–performance issue is a concern chiefly of the theorists who maintain that all learning is basically insightful, for the fact of the matter is that most learning curves reflect gradual improvements in performance. The general way out of this paradox taken by insight theorists has involved the assumption that learning involves numerous subskills that are acquired suddenly but after different amounts of practice, producing the appearance of gradual learning.

Amount of reinforcement. Obviously a practice trial, among other things, provides an occasion for the administration of reinforcement. Several of the best established laws of learning relate to reinforcement in some way. It is known, for example, that the amount of reinforcement is an

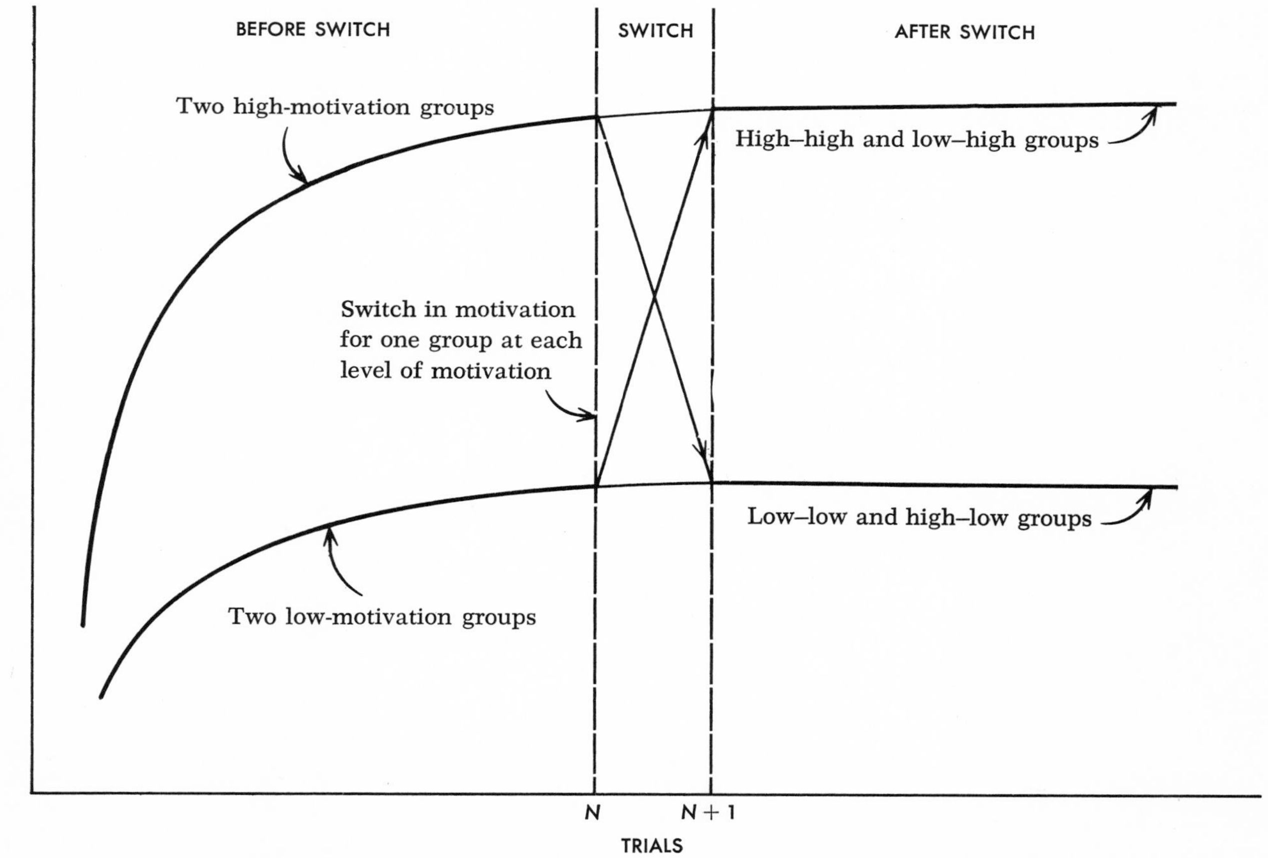

On trial $N + 1$ one low-motivation group is switched to high motivation and one high-motivation group is switched to low motivation

Figure 7 — Hypothetical learning curves showing that the effect of motivation is on performance, not on learning

important variable. Up to some limit, increasing amounts of reinforcement lead to improvements in performance, the characteristic function being negatively accelerated. The same results have been obtained for quality of reinforcement. Subjects learn more rapidly for a highly desirable reinforcer than for a less desirable one.

Delay of reinforcement. It is now well established that the time separating a response and its reinforcer is a very powerful variable in determining the progress of behavioral change in a learning situation. In general, the longer reinforcement is delayed following the execution of the response, the slower the rate of such change. What is most surprising in the results of such studies is that when extraneous sources of reinforcement are eliminated (for example, Grice 1948), it has been found that little if any learning occurs with delays greater than four or five seconds.

Secondary reinforcement. This last fact, of course, raises the question of what mechanisms have been at work in experiments in which subjects have learned with a fairly long delay of reinforcement. The commonly accepted answer is in terms of secondary reinforcement. A discussion of the details of secondary reinforcement would lead us far afield, but fortunately a nontechnical presentation of the argument will suffice. Suppose a rat runs a maze and at the end is restrained in a delay chamber for five minutes before being allowed access to the food used as a reinforcer. Suppose, further, that the rat learns the maze under these conditions, which obviously involve a delay of reinforcement much greater than the four or five seconds mentioned above. How are these two sets of facts to be brought into harmony? The argument in terms of secondary reinforcement goes this way: Cues in the delay chamber come to stand for food because they are always present just before food becomes available. Since these cues stand for food, they have some of the same characteristics as food, including the important characteristic of functioning as (secondary) reinforcers. Thus, the cues in the delay chamber serve as immediate (secondary) reinforcers and promote the progress of learning. The obvious implication of this argument is that if the cues preceding reinforcement varied from trial to trial, so that no stable association could be formed, there would be a serious disruption in the progress of learning.

The delay of reinforcement gradient is basic to the theoretical interpretation of a variety of phenomena in learning. For example, the backward order of elimination of blinds in a complex maze referred to earlier probably reflects the operation of this gradient. A gradient with all the features of the delay of reinforcement gradient also seems to apply to punishment. Miller (for example, 1959) has developed a theory of approach–avoidance conflict that is based on simultaneous operation of gradients based on reward and punishment.

The interstimulus interval. The experiments on delay of reinforcement described in the preceding section were all experiments in instrumental learning. A related variable in classical conditioning is the time between conditioned and unconditioned stimuli, often referred to as the interstimulus interval. Studies of this variable have produced relatively consistent results, which Figure 8 presents graphically. Two features of the interstimulus interval are important: (1) Backward conditioning, in which the unconditioned stimulus precedes the conditioned stimulus, leads to little or no conditioning. (2) The function for forward conditioning, in which the conditioned stimulus precedes the unconditioned stimulus, displays a conspicuous optimal interval; intervals either longer or shorter than the optimum produce inferior conditioning. For many response systems the optimal interval is in the neighborhood of .5 second. Recent investigations suggest that this optimal interval is more limited than was once thought. These studies (for example, Noble & Adams 1963; Noble & Harding 1963) have tended to indicate (1) that for lower animals the optimal interval is longer than .5 second and (2) that its duration may be different at different points in practice.

Other variables. The variables described above are representative of those studied in investigations of simple learning. A complete catalogue of such variables is beyond the scope of this report. Thus, we shall supplement the foregoing review by

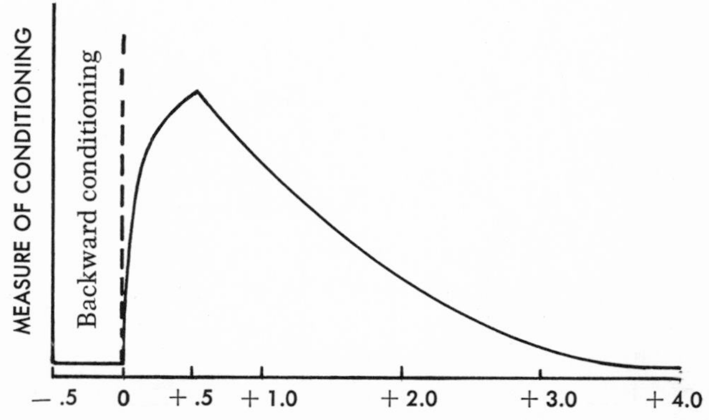

Figure 8 — A characteristic interstimulus interval function

simply mentioning certain other variables and only briefly indicating their effect upon performance.

Motivation. As we have seen, motivation ordinarily facilitates performance in the learning situation. In some circumstances, however, motivation may energize tendencies that interfere with the response to be learned. Under these circumstances, motivation, particularly very strong motivation, may appear to interfere with learning.

Distribution of practice. As we have also seen, distribution of practice usually favors rapid learning. In some complex tasks, however, massed practice may aid in the elimination of initial errors and briefly speed the progress of learning.

Intensity of the unconditioned stimulus. The intensity of the unconditioned stimulus in classical conditioning behaves as the amount of reinforcement does in instrumental learning; the greater the intensity of the unconditioned stimulus, the more rapidly conditioning proceeds.

Intensity of the conditioned stimulus. The intensity of the conditioned stimulus usually has little effect on the speed of conditioning; but recent studies (Grice & Hunter 1964) show that when strong and weak conditioned stimuli are used in the same experiment with the same subjects, the effectiveness of this variable increases considerably.

A final point is that the effects of the variables mentioned in this and the preceding section interact; that is, the effect of one depends upon the values of the others. The precise nature of the interactions remains to be worked out for almost all combinations of variables.

The nature of reinforcement

The major theoretical issues in the psychology of learning are traceable to the opinions of E. L. Thorndike. As mentioned earlier, from Thorndike's studies of cats in a simple instrumental learning situation, Thorndike developed three important hypotheses about the nature of learning: learning is gradual rather than sudden; learning consists in the formation of stimulus–response connections; and at bottom, reinforcement entails the operation of rewards and punishments. This last idea is the one that we shall develop most fully in this section. As Thorndike put it:

> The Law of Effect is that: Of several responses made to the same situation, those which are accompanied or closely followed by satisfaction to the animal will, other things being equal, be more firmly connected with the situation, so that, when it recurs, they will be more likely to recur; those which are accompanied or closely followed by discomfort to the animal will, other things being equal, have their connections with that situation weakened, so that, when it recurs, they will be less likely to occur. The greater the satisfaction or discomfort, the greater the strengthening or weakening of the bond. ([1898–1901] 1911, p. 244)

This statement came in for severe criticism on two particular counts: (1) It was criticized as subjective and unscientific in that the terms "satisfaction" and "discomfort" appeared to entail commitments to a mentalism that the psychology of 1911 was struggling to escape. Thorndike, however, was on safer methodological ground than his critics realized for he offered a means of objectifying these terms that we find perfectly acceptable today. "By a satisfying state of affairs is meant one which the animal does nothing to avoid, often doing such things as attain and preserve it. By a discomforting or annoying state of affairs is meant one which the animal commonly avoids or abandons" ([1898–1901] 1911, p. 245).

(2) The law of effect was criticized as circular: that is, learning to approach some object (for example, food) could define an object as a satisfier that, in turn, could be used to explain the learning that served to define it as a satisfier in the first place. Although Thorndike himself was not particularly clear on how to deal with this criticism, later advocates of his general point of view (for example, Miller & Dollard 1941) provided an answer. In general, this answer is that the transparent circularity in the example above disappears when it is understood that the definition of a satisfier in a defining experiment of the type proposed by Thorndike establishes the object as a general satisfier that will function as a reinforcer in a variety of learning situations. That is, given that food functions as a reinforcer in one situation, it is possible to predict with a fair degree of certainty that it will function in a similar way in a host of others. The law of effect has survived these criticisms and now has become the position by which other interpretations of reinforcement are usually defined.

The law of effect. Before proceeding further with this discussion, it is important to make a distinction between empirical and theoretical versions of the law of effect. The empirical law of effect involves nothing more than the simple factual statement that there are objects, such as food, water, and escape from punishment, that function dependably as reinforcers. The theoretical law of effect, on the other hand, states (using Thorndike's terminology) that these events are reinforcers because they are satisfiers. Because of its factual status, the empirical law of effect is not an object of dispute. Arguments about the nature of reinforcement involve the theoretical law of effect.

The statement that all reinforcers are satisfiers or annoyers is merely one of several proposals that have been offered as to the ultimate nature of reinforcement. For purposes of exposition, it is convenient to identify three general classes of such proposals, which we shall call tension-reduction theory, stimulational theory, and reactional theory.

Tension-reduction theory. Tension-reduction theory maintains that the essential condition of reinforcement is the alleviation of a state of physiological or psychological tension. In the past, tension-reduction theory was so closely tied to Thorndike's theory that current usage tends to identify the law of effect with this position and often erroneously equates tension-reduction theory with reinforcement theory.

At different times, and in the hands of different authors, need-reduction, drive-reduction, and drive-stimulus–reduction theories of reinforcement have been offered. Need-reduction theory identifies reinforcement with the satisfaction of some physiological need (for example, food, water, or sex) that if not attained means that the individual or its species will perish. Although this theory is attractive because of its affinity to biological processes, certain facts make its acceptance impossible: (1) There are many rewards that appear to correspond to no biological need. These include rewards that satisfy such acquired motives as those for affection, dominance, and accomplishment. (2) Certain biological needs appear to involve no correlated reinforcer. One of these is the need for oxygen, which is present at very high altitudes but which does not seem to create a state of tension or drive. There is no evidence that the administration of oxygen under these circumstances is a reward.

Difficulties such as these led certain theorists (Hull 1943) to distinguish between need (a physiological condition) and drive (the psychological experience associated with needs) and to suggest that reinforcement is drive reduction rather than need reduction. We shall apply this distinction presently.

The drive-stimulus–reduction theory of reinforcement (Miller & Dollard 1941) suggests that drives are always intense stimuli and that drive reduction (assumed to be reinforcing) is a matter of stimulus reduction.

Stimulational theory. Stimulational theory maintains that particular stimuli are reinforcing and distinguishes itself from tension-reduction theory in these terms. Thus, food is a reinforcer because of its taste (not because it reduces hunger), and water is a reinforcer because of the stimulational aspects of drinking (not because it reduces thirst).

Reactional theory. Reactional theory stands in opposition to both tension-reduction theory and to stimulational theory and holds that it is the act of eating or drinking, rather than taste or drive reduction, that is essential to reinforcement.

Experimental tests. Disagreements among these various interpretations of reinforcement have led, over the years, to a wide variety of experimental tests designed to establish the validity of one particular interpretation. Typically, tension-reduction theory has provided the point of departure, and adherents of opposing theories have attempted to strengthen their theoretical positions by discrediting tension-reduction theory. For example, Sheffield and Roby (1950) demonstrated that rats will learn to run a simple maze for a reward consisting of saccharine dissolved in water. The significance of this finding derives from the fact that saccharine has no nutritional value, being eliminated from the body chemically unchanged. This suggests that it must be either the sweet taste of saccharine (stimulational theory) or the act of ingestion (reactional theory) that provides for reinforcement. Advocates of tension-reduction theory, however, were able to point out that although saccharine produces no reduction in need it may produce a reduction in drive. Thus, Miller (1963) reported that rats that were allowed to drink a saccharine solution subsequently ate less food than the control subjects, which were allowed to drink only water. Miller's interpretation was that the consumption of saccharine had led to a reduction of the hunger drive although obviously it had not altered the rats' need for food.

Similar problems for tension-reduction theory were provided by demonstrations that the opportunity to explore or to manipulate the environment is rewarding for lower animals. For example, Butler (1953) was able to show that rhesus monkeys will learn a discrimination for no other reward than the opportunity to see out of their normally closed cage. Other investigators (Harlow, Harlow, & Meyer 1950) demonstrated that monkeys learned to distinguish between manipulable and nonmanipulable objects apparently for no other reward than the opportunity to manipulate them. Still others (Kish 1955) showed that rats will learn a bar-pressing response to turn on a dim light or that they will learn a simple maze for the opportunity to explore a novel environment. For some of these demonstrations, but not all, tension-reduction theorists were able to deal with the problem by the postulation of a motive to explore or to manipulate and by the assumption that learning depended on the reduction of these drives. Obviously there are certain difficulties with such explanations in that they open the possibility of postulating a new motive for every demonstrable type of reward. On the other hand, it is known that some of these motives, for example, the exploratory motive, increase in strength with deprivation, as many other motives do. Such evidence makes the interpretation somewhat more acceptable in that it lends credence to the concept of an exploratory motive by providing independent evidence for it.

A special threat to tension-reduction theory has recently come in the form of demonstrations that rats will learn a variety of responses (the most common response is bar pressing) for a weak electrical stimulation of a variety of areas of the brain stem. The simplest interpretation of such a result is that such stimulation is somehow pleasant for the rat, and such demonstrations have been interpreted as a support for stimulational theory. On the other hand, Olds (1958) has shown that the effectiveness of brain stimulation depends in part upon the level of the rat's hunger and sex drives. This opens the possibility that brain stimulation reduces these and other motives.

At the same time that tension-reduction theorists were dealing with these attacks upon their position, they were also providing more positive evidence in support of their own position. A typical experiment is that of Miller and Kessen (1952). These investigators demonstrated that rats learned a simple discrimination for a reward provided by the introduction of food directly into the stomach by way of a fistula. Such learning took place in the absence of taste stimulation emphasized by stimulational theory and ingestive behavior emphasized by reactional theory. This appears to leave the alleviation of hunger (tension reduction) as the only remaining mechanism of reinforcement.

It is apparent that the variety of experimental tests described above did not succeed in establishing any particular theory as the obviously correct theory of reinforcement. This state of affairs has had two important consequences. One consequence is that certain theorists, most notably Collier (see, for example, Collier & Myers 1961), have made a strong case for the view that reinforcement entails a variety of mechanisms, probably all of those emphasized by the more specialized theories of reinforcement.

The other important consequence is the increased appeal of multiprocess theories of learning. Such theories propose that learning itself involves a number of subtypes and that the mechanisms of reinforcement differ for the various forms of learning.

Multiprocess theories. The most popular form of multiprocess theory is a two-process theory that maintains that the mechanisms of reinforcement are different for classical conditioning and instrumental learning. The position is that instrumental learning occurs as a result of reinforcement provided by tension reduction, whereas for classical conditioning all that is necessary is the contiguous occurrence of conditioned and unconditioned stimuli (or, in some versions, conditioned stimulus and unconditioned response).

One of the appealing features of two-process theory is the readiness with which it can be applied to avoidance learning, which is difficult to understand in terms of any single principle of reinforcement. Suppose we consider the following experimental arrangement: A rat is placed in a Skinner box and on each trial a light comes on and five seconds later an electric shock is applied to the animal's feet through an electrifiable grid in the floor, unless, in the meantime, the rat presses the bar. Rats are able to learn this response quite quickly. Two-process theory deals with this learning as follows. On the early trials, before the rat has learned to press the bar and avoid the shock, light and shock are paired on every trial as in classical conditioning. This pairing leads to a conditioning to the light of a fear reaction. On subsequent trials, the appearance of the light arouses fear in the subject, and this, in turn, leads to a heightened level of activity. In the course of such activity, sooner or later the animal presses the bar, terminating the light, reducing fear, and also avoiding the shock. The reduction in fear, which is contingent upon the cessation of the light, provides reinforcement for the bar-pressing reaction.

Psychopathology. Applications of learning theory to psychopathology, for example, those attempted by such theorists as Dollard and Miller (1950), have made important use of a two-process explanation in their descriptions of neurotic symptomotology. Phobias are often interpreted as direct or symbolic representations of classically conditioned fear reactions; and neurotic behavior is viewed as avoidance behavior motivated by fear and reinforced by fear reduction.

GREGORY KIMBLE

[*See also* FORGETTING. *Other relevant material may be found in* ACHIEVEMENT TESTING; DRIVES; MOTIVATION; NERVOUS SYSTEM, *article on* BRAIN STIMULATION; STIMULATION DRIVES.]

BIBLIOGRAPHY

BUTLER, ROBERT A. 1953 Discrimination by Rhesus Monkeys to Visual-exploration Motivation. *Journal of Comparative and Physiological Psychology* 46:95–98.

COLLIER, GEORGE; and MYERS, LEONHARD 1961 The Loci of Reinforcement. *Journal of Experimental Psychology* 61:57–66.

DOLLARD, JOHN; and MILLER, NEAL E. 1950 *Personality and Psychotherapy: An Analysis in Terms of Learning, Thinking, and Culture.* New York: McGraw-Hill. → A paperback edition was published in 1965.

EBBINGHAUS, HERMANN (1885) 1913 *Memory: A Contribution to Experimental Psychology.* New York: Columbia Univ., Teachers College. → First published as *Über das Gedächtnis.* A paperback edition was published in 1964 by Dover.

FERSTER, C. B.; and SKINNER, B. F. 1957 *Schedules of Reinforcement.* New York: Appleton.

GRICE, G. R. 1948 The Relation of Secondary Reinforcement to Delayed Reward in Visual Discrimination Learning. *Journal of Experimental Psychology* 38: 1–16.

GRICE, G. R.; and HUNTER, J. J. 1964 Stimulus Intensity Effects Depend Upon the Type of Experimental Design. *Psychological Review* 71:247–256.

GUTTMAN, NORMAN; and KALISH, HARRY L. 1958 Experiments in Discrimination. *Scientific American* 198, no. 1:77–82.

HALL, JOHN F. 1966 *The Psychology of Learning.* Philadelphia: Lippincott.

HARLOW, HARRY F. 1949 The Formation of Learning Sets. *Psychological Review* 56:51–65.

HARLOW, HARRY F.; HARLOW, M. K.; and MEYER, D. R. 1950 Learning Motivated by a Manipulation Drive. *Journal of Experimental Psychology* 40:228–234.

HILLMAN, BEVERLY; HUNTER, W. S.; and KIMBLE, G. A. 1953 The Effect of Drive Level on the Maze Performance of the White Rat. *Journal of Comparative and Physiological Psychology* 46:87–89.

HULL, CLARK L. 1943 *Principles of Behavior: An Introduction to Behavior Theory.* New York: Appleton.

HULL, CLARK L. 1951 *Essentials of Behavior.* New Haven: Yale Univ. Press.

KIMBLE, GREGORY A. 1961 *Hilgard and Marquis' Conditioning and Learning.* 2d ed., rev. New York: Appleton. → First published in 1940 as *Conditioning and Learning,* by Ernest R. Hilgard and Donald G. Marquis.

KIMBLE, GREGORY A.; and SHATEL, R. B. 1952 The Relationship Between Two Kinds of Inhibition and the Amount of Practice. *Journal of Experimental Psychology* 44:355–359.

KISH, GEORGE B. 1955 Learning When the Onset of Illumination Is Used as Reinforcing Stimulus. *Journal of Comparative and Physiological Psychology* 48:261–264.

MILLER, NEAL E. 1959 Liberalization of Basic *S–R* Concepts: Extensions to Conflict Behavior, Motivation and Social Learning. Volume 2, pages 196–292 in Sigmund Koch (editor), *Psychology: A Study of a Science.* New York: McGraw-Hill.

MILLER, NEAL E. 1963 Some Reflections on the Law of Effect Produce a New Alternative to Drive Reduction. Volume 11, pages 65–112 in *Nebraska Symposium on Motivation.* Edited by Marshall R. Jones. Lincoln: Univ. of Nebraska Press.

MILLER, NEAL E.; and DOLLARD, JOHN 1941 *Social Learning and Imitation.* New Haven: Yale Univ. Press; Oxford Univ. Press.

MILLER, NEAL E.; and KESSEN, M. L. 1952 Reward Effects of Food Via Stomach Fistula Compared With Those of Food Via Mouth. *Journal of Comparative and Physiological Psychology* 45:555–564.

NOBLE, MERRILL; and ADAMS, C. K. 1963 Conditioning in Pigs as a Function of the Interval Between *CS* and *US.* *Journal of Comparative and Physiological Psychology* 56:215–219.

NOBLE, MERRILL; and HARDING, G. E. 1963 Conditioning in Rhesus Monkeys as a Function of the Interval Between *CS* and *US.* *Journal of Comparative and Physiological Psychology* 56:220–224.

OLDS, JAMES 1958 Effects of Hunger and Male Sex Hormone on Self-stimulation of the Brain. *Journal of Comparative and Physiological Psychology* 51:320–324.

PAVLOV, IVAN P. (1927) 1960 *Conditioned Reflexes: An Investigation of the Physiological Activity of the Cerebral Cortex.* New York: Dover. → First published as *Lektsii o rabote bol'shikh polusharii golovnogo mozga.*

SHEFFIELD, FRED D.; and ROBY, THORNTON B. 1950 Reward Value of a Non-nutritive Sweet Taste. *Journal of Comparative and Physiological Psychology* 43:471–481.

SKINNER, B. F. 1938 *The Behavior of Organisms: An Experimental Analysis.* New York: Appleton.

THORNDIKE, EDWARD L. (1898–1901) 1911 *Animal Intelligence: Experimental Studies.* New York: Macmillan.

II
CLASSICAL CONDITIONING

Classical (or Pavlovian, respondent, or type-S) conditioning refers to any of a group of specific procedures that, when applied to an organism under appropriate conditions, result in the formation of the type of learned behavior known as the conditioned response. The term also refers to phenomena and relationships discovered through experiments using classical conditioning procedures. The adjective "classical" is used to distinguish these procedures from the more recently developed instrumental, or operant, conditioning procedures, which also lead to the formation of conditioned responses.

The Russian physiologist I. P. Pavlov was primarily responsible for the development of the methods and nomenclature of classical conditioning, and he discovered and described many of the most important associated phenomena (Pavlov 1927). The early writings of Pavlov had a profound influence on the development of behaviorism by John B. Watson, who considered classical conditioning to be the basis of acquisition of all learned behavior. The wide acceptance of behaviorism by American psychologists and the availability of two English translations of Pavlov's *Lectures on Conditioned Reflexes* (1923) in the late 1920s were followed by an increased and sustained output in the United States of published research on conditioning. However, most of this research was conducted by psychologists who used instrumental techniques more often than they used classical conditioning. Although Pavlov's methods and data were behavioral in nature, he treated them as bearing directly upon the physiology of the cerebral cortex. His theory of conditioning is, therefore, a theory of brain function. (The present article, however, will deal mainly with its more behavioral aspects.) The Russian work on conditioning since Pavlov has very largely followed the pattern set by him.

Characteristics. The following characteristics are principal features of classical conditioning. A response already within the repertory of the experimental subject is designated the unconditioned response (*UR*) and the stimulus that evokes it is called the unconditioned stimulus (*US*). Another stimulus, one that does not elicit the *UR* or any response similar to it, is designated the conditioned stimulus (*CS*). The *CS* and the *US* are presented repeatedly to the subject, either simultaneously or with the *CS* preceding but overlapping the *US* in time. A response similar to the *UR* that develops to the *CS* is called the conditioned response (*CR*). The change in this response to the *CS* from an initial zero magnitude or frequency to a positive magnitude or frequency following practice constitutes a learned acquisition that is called conditioning.

Pavlov and his collaborators used the dog as their experimental subject. Salivation was the *UR* to the *US* of food or dilute acid. The *CS*s were lights, sounds, or pressures systematically applied to the skin, and the *CR* was salivation. But Pavlov discovered that the sights and sounds produced accidentally by the experimenter and his apparatus might also become *CS*s or interfere with the process of conditioning. He found it necessary to develop techniques and apparatus for collecting and measuring the magnitude and latency of the salivary *CR*s and *UR*s and for controlling the duration, magnitude, and time relations of the *CS*s and *US*s. These and similar procedures for isolation of the experimental subject and for control of the environment and measurement of responses are part of the technical procedures of classical conditioning.

Generality. Classical conditioning has very great generality. There is no apparent limit to the kinds of responses that can be conditioned in this manner or to the kinds of events that can serve as *CS*s. Any response that is evoked consistently by the *US* can be conditioned, and any stimulus that passes the initial test of neutrality can serve as a *CS*. Many stimuli fail this test, particularly when human beings are the subjects.

The generality of classical conditioning can be viewed also in terms of the level in the phyletic series and the chronological age of the organism in which conditioning first occurs. The few reports of classical conditioning of one-celled organisms have not been confirmed, and there is serious doubt that it is possible to achieve conditioning in these organisms. The evidence on conditioning of the worm is in similar confusion, and it is very doubtful that organisms without a true nervous system can be conditioned. With organisms higher in the phyletic series, who have a true nervous system, there is little question that they can be conditioned. Conditioning of infants of many species, including the human being, has been reported. There have also been reports of successful classical conditioning of the human fetus in the age range of 6.5–8.5 months.

Parameters of classical conditioning. It is possible to measure the latency, duration, and amplitude of a *CR* and also the frequency of its occurrence within a specified period of time. Ordinarily, only one or perhaps two of these measurements will be made concurrently, and whatever measure is applied to the *UR* will be applied also to the *CR* as a basis for comparison. Similar but not identical assessments of conditioning are obtained when different measures are used.

As conditioning develops over practice trials, the latency of the *CR* decreases, while the duration, the amplitude or magnitude, and the frequency of the *CR* increase. Eventually, each of these measures approaches an asymptotic level and does not change with further conditioning trials. The rates at which such asymptotic levels are approached vary with the measures used. It is common practice in experiments on classical *CR*s either to give all subjects an equal number of conditioning trials or to continue conditioning training until the same performance level has been attained by every subject. In the former case, individual differences between subjects show up in the variable level of conditioning attained, and in the latter case the differences appear in variations in the number of training trials required to reach the performance criterion. There are advantages and disadvantages to each of these procedures, but the results of any given experiment will depend upon this methodological consideration as well as upon the measurement procedures.

Temporal contiguity of stimuli. The rate or amount of conditioning and its relative difficulty are functions of the time relations between the *CS* and the *US*. Different names have been given to conditioned responses that are established under different time relations of the conditioned and unconditioned stimuli.

Simultaneous conditioning. The simultaneous conditioned response is developed when the *CS* and the *US* are coincident or when the onset of the *CS* precedes the onset of the *US* by an amount of time just sufficient for the *CR* to occur. Exact simultaneity makes it impossible to follow the course of conditioning over each trial since there is no way to distinguish between the *CR* and the *UR*. If occasionally the *CS* is presented alone, the *CR* can be measured—but then these trials are extinction trials and interfere with conditioning. Since the acquisition process cannot be measured precisely in the simultaneous situation, it is standard procedure for the onset of the *CS* to precede the onset of the *US* and for the *CR* to be considered a simultaneous *CR*. The length of the interval between the onset of the *CS* and onset of the *US* that defines the simultaneous *CR* depends on the latency of the *UR*. For very fast striated-muscle responses, this interval ranges from a quarter of a second up to several seconds. For slow, or long-latency, responses, such as those of smooth muscle and glands, the interval varies from a few seconds up to thirty or more seconds.

Delayed conditioning. With the delayed conditioned response the interval between the onset of the *CS* and the onset of the *US* is longer than it is for the simultaneous *CR*, and the delayed *CR* also has a longer latency. Delayed *CR*s are subclassified into short delay and long delay *CR*s, depending upon the interval between onset of the *CS* and onset of the *US*.

Trace conditioning. The trace conditioned response is very similar to the delayed *CR*. The time relations for onset of the *CS* and onset of the *US* are identical. The time relations differ only with respect to the termination of the *CS*. For delayed conditioning, the *CS* overlaps the *US* and terminates either with it or some time after its onset. In trace conditioning the *CS* lasts as long as a *CS* in simultaneous conditioning, but it terminates a considerable time before the onset of the *US*. The trace *CR* has the same latency as the delayed *CR*, but because of the short duration of the *CS* it occurs in the time interval between the termination of the *CS* and the onset of the *US*. Since it is assumed in classical conditioning that no response occurs in the absence of a stimulus, it is assumed in this situation that there is a *trace* of the *CS* to which the *CR* is made.

Temporal conditioning. With the temporal conditioned response the *US* is presented alone at a constant rate. The time interval between successive presentations of the *US* functions as a *CS*. The *CR* occurs just prior to the time at which the *US* is to be presented.

Backward conditioning. For the backward conditioned response, onset of the *CS* occurs after termination of the *US* and the *UR*. The *CR* occurs, of course, to the *CS*, after the prior occurrence of the *US* and the *UR*.

Pseudo conditioning. The pseudo conditioned response occurs without any impaired training trials of the *CS* and the *US*. First the *US* is presented alone for a series of trials. Then, after a short interval of time, the *CS* is presented alone. If a response similar to the *UR* occurs to the *CS*, it is called a pseudo conditioned response.

Effects of temporal variations. The simultaneous *CR* is acquired most rapidly and with the greatest ease. The first *CR* may occur on the second or third trial. Delayed and trace *CR*s are acquired with about equal difficulty if the time between the onset of the *CS* and that of the *US* is equal for both. Both are more difficult to establish than the simultaneous *CR*. For simultaneous, delayed, and trace conditioning the difficulty of conditioning increases as the time between the onset of the *CS* and that of the *US* increases. With long delay or long trace conditioning it is impossible to develop a *CR* unless a simultaneous *CR* is established first and training trials are then arranged in which the time interval between onset of the *CS* and onset of the *US* is gradually increased.

The temporal *CR* for short intervals of time is more readily established than the simultaneous *CR*. It may be acquired even when the interval between presentations of the *US* is as great as thirty minutes. It has not been studied extensively, but because it can be so easily acquired in standard simultaneous conditioning, it is necessary to vary the intervals between trials in a random sequence in order to prevent the occurrence of temporal conditioning.

The backward *CR* is more difficult to establish than are forward *CR*s. The difficulty of backward conditioning increases as the interval beween termination of the *US* and onset of the *CS* increases. The range over which this relation holds is small, since there is no evidence of backward conditioning for the longer time intervals between the onset of the *US* and the onset of the *CS* that are possible in delayed or trace forward conditioning.

Pseudo conditioning appears to depend upon the use of a very-high-intensity *US* that produces a large-magnitude, diffuse, emotional *UR*. The pseudo *CR* is neither as readily established nor as stable as a *CR* based upon equivalent practice with simultaneous conditioning procedures. Pseudo conditioning may be treated as a variant of backward conditioning, since presentation of the *US* precedes presentation of the *CS*. The efficiency of the method is low.

Other factors affecting conditioning. The study of other variables that affect the rate or speed of acquisition has been conducted primarily with simultaneous *CR*s. However, what evidence there is suggests that the effects of these variables on other types of *CR*s are similar. Distribution of practice, magnitude of the *US*, deprivation condition of the organism, physiological condition, neural condition, intensity of the *CS*, and the number of trials are independent variables that are well established as relating to acquisition.

Distributed versus massed practice. Some degree of distribution of practice provides the most rapid conditioning. The particular optimal distribution depends upon other variables, such as time relations, nature of the *US* and *CS*, and nature of the organism. The results universally show massed practice to be inferior to some form of distributed practice in speed of conditioning.

Magnitude of the unconditioned stimulus. Speed of conditioning increases with the magnitude of the *US* up to a point and thereafter declines with further increases in the magnitude of the *US*. This has been well established for *CR*s for which the *US* is food or electric shock.

Deprivation. The deprivation condition of the organism interacts with the magnitude of the *US* when the *US* is food. With very large magnitudes of *US* and fairly low degrees of deprivation, after only a few conditioning trials the subject may have received its total daily intake and become satiated. When the *US* is held constant at relatively small magnitudes and the period of deprivation increases, speed or amount of acquisition increases up to a point and then declines with further increase. This relation holds separately for food and for water, but there is probably an interaction between the two.

Deprivation is sometimes treated as a particular physiological condition, but physiological condition usually refers to endocrinological, biochemical, or drug conditions, and the effects of these on conditioning are complex.

Neural conditions. The effects of neural conditions are studied through application of the *CS* and *US* at different levels of the nervous system or through the use of conditioning procedures on organisms when varying levels of the nervous system are rendered functionless. Conditioning is possible if the *CS* is electrical stimulation of the sensory cortex or of the sensory tracts in the spinal cord. There is much evidence that conditioning will not occur if the *US* is direct stimulation of the motor cortex. The decorticate animal can be conditioned, but the weight of evidence is against the possibility of conditioning the spinal animal.

Stimulus intensity and complexity. Conditioning increases in rate and magnitude as the *CS* is increased in intensity from the stimulus threshold to the middle range of intensity but not to greater intensities. Conditioning at very high *CS* intensities has not been tested. Conditioning occurs at a greater magnitude and faster rate with compound *CS*s than with any one of the single component stimuli, whether the *CS*s are from the same or from different sense modalities. Variation in the characteristics of *CS*s makes it possible to study sensory thresholds and discriminations by conditioning procedures.

Transfer. Many instances of positive and negative transfer have been found in studies of classical conditioning. Transfer is usually positive when it is measured as a difference between performances under conditions that involve acquisition procedures. It is most often negative when it is measured as a difference between performance at a terminal level of acquisition and a subsequent performance that results from alteration of some variable present during acquisition. Positive transfer occurs for any subsequent *CR* elicited by a new *CS*, by a new *US*, or by both at the same time. The only instances of negative transfer under the above conditions occur when the *UR* and *CR* for the second treatment are the reverse of or are incompatible with those of the first conditioning treatment.

Stimulus generalization, response generalization, and incentive generalization are forms of positive transfer. Stimulus generalization refers to the occurrence of the *CR* to stimuli similar to the *CS* in the absence of specific training with those stimuli. Stimulus generalization declines as the degree of similarity along a given dimension (such as frequency of a tone in cycles per second) decreases. The form of stimulus-generalization gradients is not known because of serious technical difficulties in measuring stimulus generalization. Cross-modal stimulus generalization occurs only rarely. Response generalization can be studied only in limited fashion, such as from right to left side of body, but may also involve opposing responses when the *CR* is prevented from occurring. Incentive generalization refers to positive transfer of a *CR* that occurs following variation in the *US*, such as in the kind of food or in the frequency or locus of application of electric shock.

Extinction. The most striking transfer phenomenon is experimental extinction. This form of negative transfer occurs when, after acquisition, the *US* is omitted and the *CS* is presented alone under the same schedule as that used during acquisition. There is a progressive decrement in the magnitude and frequency of occurrence of the *CR* to the zero level. This phenomenon has led to a conception of reinforcement of the *CR* by the *US*. Empirical nonreinforcement refers to nothing more than the decrement of conditioning when the *US* is absent from the training procedure, and empirical reinforcement refers to nothing more than the original acquisition of the *CR* when the *US* is present in the training procedure and the reinstatement of the *CR* by reintroduction of the *US* following extinction. The theoretical views of reinforcement are many, and much of the study of extinction has been directed toward discovery of the reinforcement functions of the *US*.

With classical conditioning, there appears to be a positive relation between strength of conditioning and resistance to experimental extinction. The greater the amount of conditioning training and the larger the measures of *CR* magnitude, the greater the resistance to extinction. Any variable that increases the strength of a *CR* also increases its resistance to extinction. As the degree of extinction training is increased, the amount of training required to re-establish the *CR* is increased. There is even continued "silent" extinction beyond the zero level of *CR*: a greater amount of conditioning training is required to re-establish the *CR* than that required when just the zero extinction level is attained. If there is successive alternation of conditioning and extinction, each reversal requires fewer training trials, until a single trial of either the conditioning or the extinction procedure is sufficient to provide consistent response or response failure to the *CS*. Speed of extinction is greater for massed extinction trials than it is for distributed extinction trials. Extinction of a *CR* to one *CS* will increase the rate of extinction of the *CR* to a second *CS* that has not been given extinction training. This is called secondary extinction and is evidence of a generalization of extinction. Delay, trace, and pseudo *CR*s show more rapid extinction than do simultaneous *CR*s.

Although reintroduction of the *US* to the training procedure is the most efficient way to reverse experimental extinction, there are three other procedures that will also produce reversal. If the subject is removed from the experimental room at the time a zero level of extinction has been reached and is returned at a later time, the *CS* will evoke a *CR*. This recovery of the conditioned response is called spontaneous recovery. However, with sufficient extinction training there is no spontaneous recovery.

It is possible also to produce recovery of conditioning following extinction by presenting the *US* alone for a few trials. The *CR* will then be evoked by the *CS* presented alone.

Recovery of the *CR* following experimental extinction may also be produced by disinhibition. This occurs when a novel stimulus is presented in the laboratory at the termination of an extinction series. Disinhibition is a temporary phenomenon, and its magnitude is a function of the extent of extinction and the intensity of the disinhibiting stimulus.

Retention. The retention of classical *CR*s has received little study. What evidence there is indicates very high degrees of retention in animals who have experienced no conditioning for several years.

W. J. BROGDEN

[*Directly related are the biographies of* PAVLOV *and* WATSON. *Other relevant material may be found in* FORGETTING.]

BIBLIOGRAPHY

HILGARD, ERNEST R.; and MARQUIS, DONALD G. (1940) 1961 *Hilgard and Marquis' Conditioning and Learning.* Revised by Gregory A. Kimble. 2d ed. New York: Appleton. → First published as *Conditioning and Learning.*

PAVLOV, IVAN P. (1923) 1928 *Lectures on Conditioned Reflexes: Twenty-five Years of Objective Study of Higher Nervous Activity (Behavior) of Animals.* New York: International Publishers. → First published as *Dvadtsatiletnii opyt ob'jektivnogo izucheniia vysshei nervnoi deiatel'nosti (povedeniia) zhivotnykh.*

PAVLOV, IVAN P. (1927) 1960 *Conditioned Reflexes: An Investigation of the Physiological Activity of the Cerebral Cortex.* New York: Dover. → First published as *Lektsii o rabote bol'shikh polusharii golovnogo mozga.*

RAZRAN, G. 1961 The Observable Unconscious and the Inferable Conscious in Current Soviet Psychophysiology: Interoceptive Conditioning, Semantic Conditioning, and the Orienting Reflex. *Psychological Review* 68:81–147.

STEVENS, S. S. (editor) 1951 *Handbook of Experimental Psychology.* New York: Wiley.

III
INSTRUMENTAL LEARNING

The concept of instrumental learning is a powerful one, primarily because it assists psychologists in their goals of predicting and controlling, or modifying, behavior. The concept is based on an empirically derived functional relationship between the probability of a response and the previous consequences of that response: while battles between theoreticians have not yet been fully resolved, it is generally useful to consider that the probability of a response to a stimulus situation is particularly likely to be strengthened if the response is followed by what may loosely be called a satisfying state of affairs.

This presentation will be chiefly concerned with applications and implications of instrumental, or operant, learning that may be of more general interest to social scientists; the technical aspects are covered elsewhere [*see* LEARNING, *article on* REINFORCEMENT].

Adherents of this position have maintained that most of the forms of behavior exhibited by infrahuman animals can be effectively analyzed in instrumental terms. A dog approaches when its name is called, horses respond to signals from their riders, cats "know" where to go for food, and cattle avoid an electrified fence, all because of the consequences of previous relevant behavior. Applying the techniques of instrumental conditioning in laboratory settings, experimental psychologists have succeeded in eliciting behavior of great complexity. B. F. Skinner has trained pigeons to engage in behavior that strikingly resembles table tennis. He and his colleagues have also, by reinforcing aggressive behavior, converted usually placid birds into "vicious" killers. The familiar reverse procedure, taming, is also accomplished by instrumental conditioning. Discriminations between colors, shapes, tones, and so forth, can be taught by differential application of reinforcements. For example, an animal can readily be trained to approach a green disc when a low-pitched tone is presented and to approach a red disc in response to a tone of higher frequency. A procedure as simple as this provides a most reliable means of ascertaining sensory capacities of animals. If, say, a food-deprived rat is given food whenever it presses a blue lever but is given no reinforcement when it presses a yellow lever of equal brightness, then equal rates of pressing the two levers would lead us to conclude that the animal cannot distinguish between the two colors. For the sake of simplicity this example has ignored both the possibility that in this instance reinforcement is not effective and the important finding that the kinesthetic and other stimulation resulting from a lever press may itself be reinforcing; recent studies indicate that almost any form of nonnoxious stimulation may possess, under certain specifiable conditions, extremely important reinforcing properties. [*See* LEARNING, *article on* DISCRIMINATION LEARNING.]

In terms of potential for generalization, few consequences of the learning process are more influential than what Harry F. Harlow (1949) has called "learning to learn." A monkey that has learned to make a particular discriminative response in a particular stimulus situation (e.g., to the "odd" stimulus in a three-stimulus array) has apparently learned not only that a particular response is rewarded in this situation but also that situations may have embedded in them stimulus properties which, if reacted to appropriately, lead to reinforcement. Thus, if "oddness" ceases to be relevant or reinforcing in this or other situations, a new principle will be sought (e.g., the largest object or the object on the far left of the array). Furthermore, this principle will be discovered far more readily if the animal has previously learned the value of learning.

There is good reason to believe that even some of the most "basic" forms of animal behavior are acquired through and maintained by instrumental conditioning. Copulation, for example, at least in those mammalian species in which it has been carefully studied, is apparently a product of learning. Rhesus monkeys without previous sexual experience have been observed to engage in considerable trial and error—males mounting males, and so on—before arriving at the usual preference for heterosexual intercourse. It is clear that "normal" sexual behavior becomes preferred simply because, for anatomical reasons, it is most likely to be reinforced. Statistically deviant forms of sexuality can be explained in exactly the same way: homosexual or autoerotic activity will tend to be repeated to the extent that it has been positively reinforced. A critical period for learning may exist: learning during a particular portion of the animal's life may be more influential than learning that takes place either earlier or later. Such a possibility would seem to hold greater promise for future research than speculations about the "mental health" of the deviant animals. [*See* IMPRINTING; SEXUAL BEHAVIOR.]

In a similar vein is the finding by Melzack and Scott (1957) that escaping from pain is a function of particular stimulus dimensions present early in life. It is apparently no longer safe to assume that if a stimulus–response bond is of sufficient biological importance, it is genetically transmitted. [*See* PAIN.]

As a final example of operant conditioning in infrahuman animals, let us consider what has been called "neurotic" behavior. After an animal has learned that a particular response (e.g., turning left in a T maze) is followed by positively reinforcing stimulation, the experimenter arranges for a strong electric shock, or other negative reinforcer, to be contingent upon the same response. If the experimenter has skillfully controlled his variables, he will have induced conflict. The frustrated animal will display fairly stereotyped behavior: going round in circles, "freezing," or showing other signs of acute and stressful indecision. Even if the shock apparatus is disconnected, the animal will continue to exhibit this behavior (which presumably serves to reduce anxiety) and may even starve to death unless "therapeutic" measures are taken. It is the compulsive self-destructive nature of the behavior and its origin in conflict that may justify the designation of "neurotic." Generalization to the human level must, of course, be undertaken with great caution. It should be noted that neurotic behavior can also be elicited by classical procedures. [*See* CONFLICT, *article on* PSYCHOLOGICAL ASPECTS.]

Instrumental conditioning in humans

B. F. Skinner chose to give to his seminal 1938 book the general title *The Behavior of Organisms.* No new principles, he suggests, need be invoked in order to study human behavior. There is good reason to believe that the human equivalents of the types of behavior described above are also attained, or at least maintained, by means of operant conditioning. Thus, for example, while a definitive experiment will probably never be conducted, it seems reasonable to assume that all forms of sexual behavior are learned by trial and error, by imitation, or by instruction. And both the tendency to imitate and the tendency to follow instructions can themselves be understood as functions of the organism's reinforcement history [*see* IMITATION].

Language. Perhaps the most important human skill from the standpoint of psychology is language. The initial babblings of the infant are random or semirandom; some sounds, like "ma," are easier to produce than others and will therefore be emitted at a relatively higher base rate. These babblings are differentially reinforced. Differential reinforcement simply means, in this case, that the mother —or other socializing agent—will find certain sounds more reinforcing than others and will behave in such a way as to increase the frequency of these sounds. "Ma," as a response, is strengthened; "ka" and "la" are not. The infant next learns that "ma" is reinforced only under certain conditions. Under other conditions (e.g., when only the father is present), "ma" is either ignored or is negatively reinforced. More complicated utterances can be built up in similar fashion. Thus, while the development of a repertoire of sounds and sound combinations that serve as responses to specific external or internal stimulus situations may be a prodigious feat, it is not a particularly mysterious one (Skinner 1957). Not all language is learned in this rather inefficient fashion. Many utterances result from imitation or from intentional instruction.

Recent experiments have revealed that the verbal behavior of adults can likewise be manipulated. Rates of emission, particular sounds, parts of speech, sentence length, and content are responsive to operant-conditioning procedures in which a smile or a nod provides quite effective reinforcement (see, for example, Portnoy & Salzinger 1964). It might also be pointed out here that operant conditioning is now being used by Lilly (1963) in an effort to teach bottle-nose dolphins to use the English language "intelligently." [*See* LANGUAGE, *article on* LANGUAGE DEVELOPMENT.]

Creativity. Another important kind of activity, creativity, is also susceptible to analysis in these terms. Here the key psychological, as distinguished from sociological, variable is novelty of response to a stimulus situation. Numerous studies (e.g., Maltzman et al. 1960) have demonstrated that the individual will learn to make novel responses if he is rewarded for doing so. A "motive" for originality is thus instilled just as readily as the "motive" for conformity is instilled in most of our educational institutions. The learned tendency to produce "original" responses, combined with the learned tendency to view one's productions critically, may be enough to explain even the highest achievements of human creativity. The fact that computer-type machines can be programmed to "create" music in a large variety of styles points in the same direction. [*See* CONFORMITY; CREATIVITY.]

Emotional behavior. Operant conditioning also provides a useful framework for studying those most complicated psychological processes, the emotions. Whether they are subjective states or physiological events, or both, emotions may be viewed as (*a*) responses to antecedent stimuli and (*b*) stimuli for consequent responses. As responses, emotions are learnable. It is extremely doubtful that the newborn infant has any emotions at all; he almost definitely is not afraid of the dark, or of falling, or of snakes; he does not love his mother, nor does he feel inferior. How are these emotions learned? It appears that no new principles need be invoked. A child observing his mother's frightened reactions to a thunderstorm may exercise his acquired tendency to imitate by manifesting similar signs of fright. These signs are reinforced by maternal solicitude. Studies indicate high correlations between the fears of children and of their parents (Hagman 1932).

As an extended hypothetical example, consider what is generally called love. The child may learn that the words "I love you" are often followed by more tangible rewards and that his own manifestations of "loving" behavior are followed by rewards from people in his environment. Consequently he may learn to seek out circumstances in which it is appropriate for such kinds of behavior to occur. He wants to love and be loved. The rewards of establishing a love relationship, which go far beyond the food and tactile stimulation that probably served as initial reinforcement, may include temporary freedom from corporal punishment, victory in a sibling rivalry, or erotic stimulation. With such a multitude of possible reinforcements, the child may readily learn those forms of behavior that elicit "loving" behavior from the people in his environment. And one particularly effective method for achieving this is to engage in "loving" behavior oneself. But since the well-socialized child has also probably learned that there are negative reinforcements for deceptive behavior, he must get himself to actually "feel" the emotion he is expressing. This necessary internal state is conditionable, but a classical conditioning model is probably more useful here than the operant model. [*See* AFFECTION; EMOTION; MORAL DEVELOPMENT; PERSONALITY, *article on* PERSONALITY DEVELOPMENT.]

Religiosity. One's religious convictions may likewise be regarded as nothing more than a complex set of learned responses to a complex set of stimuli. The objection that man is born with a knowledge of and reverence for God receives its strongest rebuttal from the practices of the major religions, whose emphasis on Sunday school and other forms of religious instruction seems at odds with such concepts as revelation or innate knowledge. The combination of formal religious training, informal parental inculcation (e.g., answering "God did it" to difficult questions in the natural sciences), and ubiquitous social pressures (e.g., the motto "In God We Trust" on U.S. currency) makes clear why so many children engage in religious behavior. Whether the mediator in such cases is the learned motive to conform or the learned motive to imitate, religious utterances and other religious activities tend to be positively reinforced. The intense emotionality that so often accompanies or defines the "religious experience" may result from the capacity of religion to satisfy such needs as dependency, affiliation, and (perhaps) erotic gratification, needs that may themselves be products of instrumental learning. Thus, to the extent that religiosity is inferred from behavior, principles of conditioning appear to be sufficient for a complete explanation. [*See* RELIGION.]

Mental illness. As a final example of the widespread applicability of these principles, we may consider those forms of behavior that characterize "mental illness." It is possible to regard the disordered or undesired behavior simply as a set of responses that have become progressively stronger because of their reinforcing consequences. This formulation holds true even if the behavior (nail-biting, cigarette smoking, destructive interpersonal relationships, self-degrading activities) appears to have negative consequences. The "reward" in such cases may be temporary relief from anxiety, satisfaction of abnormally strong learned needs to conform or not conform, to confirm a self concept, and so on. There may be a wide gap in complexity between a rat that makes the correct choice in a T maze and an accident-prone human, but it is possible to understand the behavior of both animals in terms of the same principles. [*See* MENTAL DISORDERS; NEUROSIS.]

Practical applications

In most sciences, including psychology, the goals of prediction and control, or modification, are inextricably related. While the foregoing paragraphs have emphasized the prediction of responses, the following examples refer specifically to the possibility of response modification or control.

Programmed instruction. The widespread adoption of "teaching machines" and other programmed instructional devices in schools all over the world attests to the ability of operant methods to establish the repertoire of stimulus–response bonds deemed necessary by society. Instead of the primary reinforcement of a pellet of food, so often used to control or shape the behavior of infrahuman animals, it has been found that such secondary reinforcers as "the feeling of success" are extremely effective for human students of all ages. There is nothing mysterious about these secondary reinforcers; their emergence can be predicted—or arranged—by virtue of their frequent association with primary rewards. So long as teacher shortages exist, programmed instructional devices will continue to be useful adjuncts to more conventional pedagogic techniques. But these devices are of far more than ancillary value. They provide advantages that are uniquely their own. Each student is permitted to proceed at his own rate and thus avoids either the boredom or the frustration that may result from the single-level approach so often necessary in crowded classrooms. Furthermore, the use of programmed materials largely does away with extrinsic rewards, such as grades and teacher-approval, by relying primarily on the reinforcing nature of the learning process itself. While many of their potentialities remain to be developed, it is difficult to conceive of any academic subject matter that cannot be taught, and taught effectively, by means of these methods. [*See* LEARNING, *article on* PROGRAMMED LEARNING.]

Behavior therapy. Principles of operant conditioning have also been found to be extremely useful in the modification of undesirable behavior. The behavior in question, whether it involves an isolated S–R connection (e.g., fear-responses to heights) or a complex pattern of behavioral tendencies from which some clinicians infer "neurosis" or "psychosis," can be altered by extinguishing the undesired response while building up a desired response (or set of responses) to the same stimuli. For example, homosexuality—a form of behavior that is notoriously resistant to traditional varieties of psychotherapy—often responds quite favorably to what is called behavior therapy (see, for example, Feldman & MacCulloch 1964). Procedures differ widely, but the following outline of treatment may be of illustrative value. The "patient" (a term which is particularly inappropriate in this context) is requested by the therapist to have a homosexual fantasy. When he signals that the fantasy has reached a peak of excitement, the individual receives a painful electric shock. This procedure is repeated over several sessions, with the result that in subsequent interviews, when it is clear to the patient that shock will not occur, he reports that homosexual thoughts and behaviors are gradually being extinguished. During the extinction process, heterosexual motives and activities are strengthened by means of familiar techniques of reinforcement. Early in the treatment, for example, the individual is directed to masturbate while engaging in heterosexual fantasies; before very long, an association develops between having an orgasm and visualizing a partner of the opposite sex. Within one year most individuals exposed to this form of treatment are behaving in ways acceptable to society and to themselves outside the therapist's office. New forms of undesirable behavior do not appear, and the proportion of "relapses" is far smaller than that encountered in other forms of treatment. [*See* MENTAL DISORDERS, TREATMENT OF, *article on* BEHAVIOR THERAPY; SEXUAL BEHAVIOR, *article on* HOMOSEXUALITY; *see also* Feldman & MacCulloch 1964.]

Obviously, behavior therapy is not simply symptom removal. Starting with the premises that the undesired behavior has been learned and that whatever has been learned can be unlearned, the method proceeds to instill new learnings as efficiently as possible. As a by-product of this counterconditioning, we may expect a reduction in the anxiety engendered by the behavior in question. This reduction, as measured, for example, by the galvanic skin reflex, will, in turn, tend to lower the frequency of pathological behavior. Alternatively the therapist may choose to attack the anxiety more directly by viewing it as a learned response to specifiable interpersonal or other stimuli. [*See* ANXIETY; PERSONALITY, *article on* THE FIELD.]

There appears to be no qualitative difference between the treatment of a simple self-destructive habit and of the most complex of neurotic constellations. Although some critics might accuse them of unjustified reductionism, proponents of behavior therapy would allege that the more conventional methods of treatment take longer and have a lower success rate because the necessary learning process is managed inexpertly, being incorrectly regarded as little more than an epiphenomenon of insight, catharsis, and so on.

The apparent therapeutic effectiveness of Skinnerian methods should not blind the reader to the equally stimulating applications of Pavlovian methodology to behavior therapy. The cautionary note should also be added that the number of individuals, the number of conditions treated, and the duration of follow-up studies are not yet sufficient to justify unreserved acceptance of the new methodology. Still, unlike certain other recent innovations in therapy, the use of conditioning is firmly based on a mass of quite unequivocal laboratory data. [*See* MENTAL DISORDERS, TREATMENT OF.]

Implications

As has been indicated, the principles and practices of instrumental conditioning provide useful tools for the prediction and control of behavior. This practical utility leads to a consideration of a number of quite crucial questions.

First, can a science of psychology exist entirely on the basis of prediction and control, without regard to the task of *understanding* behavior? The question virtually answers itself if the goals of understanding are made explicit. Although the wish to understand is, for some, based largely on intellectual curiosity rather than on the desire for practical applications, there are only two ways that one can persuasively confirm, test, or demonstrate understanding: by predicting or by controlling the phenomena he claims to understand. Furthermore, some psychologists wish to understand primarily because they wish to predict and control. It might also be pointed out here that the individual who wishes to apply psychological principles to his own betterment can do so by means of, and perhaps only by means of, that intelligent arrangement of stimulus–response contingencies called self-control. Clearly, the specification of empirical regularities in the occurrences of stimuli and responses eliminates the need for prior "understanding." The thoroughgoing adherent of the instrumental point of view might also claim that explanations of behavior in terms of the functioning of the central nervous system are likewise unnecessary.

Second, are there any forms of behavior that do not make sense within the framework of instrumental learning? Some writers have argued that behavior which is very complex requires a more complicated explanatory model; but complex behavior—including behavior that involves language—yields readily to instrumental analysis. Such analysis of a phenomenon is not, of course, logically identical to a valid causal explanation of it. Some also maintain that there are forms of complex behavior (referred to as "instinctive") that are genetically determined, but the realm of instinct seems to dwindle as more and more alleged instances yield to analysis in terms of prenatal or early postnatal conditioning. Certainly at the human level the concept of instinct seems no longer useful. On the other hand, there is no need to deny the existence of genetically transmitted unconditioned reflexes. [*See* GENETICS, *article on* GENETICS AND BEHAVIOR; INSTINCT.]

Perhaps the best objection to what might be called instrumental imperialism is that many kinds of behavior fit more readily into the framework of classical, rather than operant, conditioning. But it may be that these two categories are not really distinct from each other. To give a somewhat oversimplified example, Pavlov's dogs may have learned to salivate to the initially neutral stimulus because the response of salivation was "paid off" by the presentation of food.

A final consideration has to do with the ancient problem of free will versus determinism. If behavior is nothing but responses to stimuli, and if the stimuli determine the responses, then the concept of free will ceases to be necessary. The fact that different people may respond differently to the same stimulus is, of course, beside the point. The stimulus may not be the "same" at all, being contingent upon receptors, thresholds, and previous conditioning. And even if the stimuli *are* viewed as identical, response differences would be explicable by virtue of individual differences in reinforcement histories or physical abilities.

Because of the number and the complexity of the determining variables, some behavior may be, practically speaking, "unpredictable." But this practical limitation in no way justifies an explanation of such acts in terms of free will. Analogously, the result of a coin flip, while usually attributed to "chance," is the inevitable outcome of a set of variables: air currents, the force of the flip, the distance the coin is permitted to drop, and so on. While these variables can be ascertained only with great difficulty, we do not conclude that the coin has manifested free will. The same line of reasoning may be raised against those who invoke the physicists' principle of indeterminacy in support of the free-will position.

In short, as the instruments, methods, and concepts in the science of psychology become increasingly sophisticated, the number of unpredictable and uncontrollable human acts appears to be shrinking proportionately. The widespread application of conditioning procedures is not without its dangers. But the possible abuses of this powerful tool should not obscure the recognition of its potential advantages. It does not seem unrealistically optimistic to view instrumental conditioning as a way, perhaps *the* way, to elicit from human beings those forms of creative, satisfying, and socially useful behavior that the less-systematic educational methods have so conspicuously failed to obtain.

Instrumental conditioning is by no means a *new* method of behavioral development. Indeed, if its principles are valid, they were operating long before they were formulated. But the recent advances that have been reviewed herein suggest that these principles will play an increasingly pivotal role in twentieth-century psychology.

LAWRENCE CASLER

BIBLIOGRAPHY

FELDMAN, M. P.; and MACCULLOCH, M. J. 1964 A Systematic Approach to the Treatment of Homosexuality by Conditioned Aversion: Preliminary Report. *American Journal of Psychiatry* 121:167–171.

HAGMAN, ELMER R. 1932 A Study of Fears of Children of Pre-school Age. *Journal of Experimental Education* 1:110–130.

HARLOW, HARRY F. 1949 The Formation of Learning Sets. *Psychological Review* 56:51–65.

LILLY, JOHN C. 1963 Productive and Creative Research With Man and Dolphin. *Archives of General Psychiatry* 8:111–116.

MALTZMAN, IRVING et al. 1960 Experimental Studies in the Training of Originality. *Psychological Monographs* 74, no. 6.

MELZACK, RONALD; and SCOTT, T. H. 1957 The Effects of Early Experience on the Response to Pain. *Journal of Comparative and Physiological Psychology* 50:155–161.

PORTNOY, STEPHANIE; and SALZINGER, KURT 1964 The Conditionability of Different Verbal Response Classes: Positive, Negative and Nonaffect Statements. *Journal of General Psychology* 70:311–323.

ROGERS, CARL; and SKINNER, B. F. 1956 Some Issues Concerning the Control of Human Behavior. *Science* 124:1057–1066.

SKINNER, B. F. 1938 *The Behavior of Organisms: An Experimental Analysis.* New York: Appleton.

SKINNER, B. F. 1953 *Science and Human Behavior.* New York: Macmillan.

SKINNER, B. F. 1957 *Verbal Behavior.* New York: Appleton.

IV
REINFORCEMENT

The principle of reinforcement is not new. One form of that principle, the law of effect, dates back to Thorndike (1898–1901), who was one of the first systematic experimenters to observe that the development and maintenance of new instrumental performances are closely controlled by their environmental consequences. Thorndike theorized that an organism's behavior was "stamped in" when it was followed by a satisfying state of affairs. By a satisfying state of affairs, Thorndike meant a condition that the animal did nothing to avoid, and whose maintenance and renewal the animal sought. Although our language has developed in the interest of greater scientific objectivity, and our experimental methods have progressed in the direction of greater precision and analytical prowess, Thorndike's early observations on trial-and-error learning represent the foundations of modern effect, or reinforcement, theory.

In contrast to the trial-and-error, or instrumental, learning studied by Thorndike, Pavlov (1927) worked with classical conditioning procedures. Perhaps the best known example of Pavlov's work is salivary conditioning. A stimulus which does not initially elicit salivation (the conditioned stimulus: a bell or metronome, for example) is presented in close temporal conjunction with a substance that does elicit salivation when placed in the mouth (the unconditioned stimulus: food powder or dilute acid, for example). After several paired presentations of the conditioned and unconditioned stimuli —provided sufficient attention is given to the details of the conditioning procedure—the conditioned stimulus gains the power to elicit salivation as a conditioned response. Because the development and maintenance of the conditioned response are closely dependent upon presentation of the unconditioned stimulus, the latter has been called a reinforcing stimulus.

Generalizing from the above considerations, it can be said that both instrumental, or Thorndikean, and classical, or Pavlovian, reinforcers may be looked upon as critical events in a learning episode. Just as the occurrence of reinforcement "strengthens" behavior, so the omission of reinforcement "weakens" behavior. In both instrumental and classical conditioning, the elimination of behavior by removing the reinforcer responsible for its maintenance is called *extinction.* Space does not permit a detailed comparison between instrumental and classical conditioning procedures. The reader is referred to Kimble's revision of Hilgard and Marquis' *Conditioning and Learning* (1940).

While this discussion has stressed the importance of reinforcement in learned behavior, it should be noted that not all psychologists agree on this point. E. R. Guthrie (1935), for example, developed a theoretical system in which learning does not depend on reinforcement. Although Guthrie agreed with Thorndike that learning consists of the bonding or conditioning of responses to stimuli, Guthrie maintained that simple temporal contiguity of response and stimulus is sufficient. Thorndike, it will be recalled, stated that reinforcement, that is, the satisfying state of affairs, was necessary in addition to stimulus–response contiguity. Perhaps the most extensive stimulus–response reinforcement theory was developed by C. L. Hull (1943). The similarities and differences among the various theories of learning constitute a study in themselves—Hilgard's *Theories of Learning* (Hilgard & Bower 1948) should be consulted as a general reference. An indication of the type of research evolving from a theoretical concern with the nature of reinforcement is provided by Birney and Teevan's *Reinforcement* (1961), a collection of original papers—some classics—by prominent experimentalists.

Instrumental or operant behavior

Particularly important in the development of knowledge regarding the dynamics of reinforcement has been the work of B. F. Skinner (1938; 1953) and his colleagues. Skinner has adopted a nontheoretical, descriptive approach in his analysis of behavior, and the results of his work have had great practical and systematic significance. The methodology characteristic of Skinner's work has been analyzed and discussed by Sidman (1960) in his book *Tactics of Scientific Research.*

Instrumental, or operant, behavior may be defined as behavior that is under the control of its environmental consequences. Opening a door, walking across the street, speaking, etc., are examples of operant behaviors. When the consequence of a behavior serves to increase the frequency or probability of occurrence of the behavior, we refer to the consequence as *reinforcement. Positive reinforcement* involves the onset of some stimulus as the reinforcing consequence; *negative reinforcement* involves stimulus termination as the reinforcing consequence. Negatively reinforcing stimuli are often called aversive stimuli; it has been found that the onset of an aversive stimulus contingent upon a behavior will often decrease the probability of occurrence of that behavior. The reinforcement relationships just described are actually quite complex, and no simple statement will adequately summarize all of the detailed facts regarding positive and negative reinforcement. However, types of reinforcers and the ways in which they have been manipulated provide for some of the well-known behavioral paradigms.

Reward training. In reward training a positive reinforcer is contingent upon the occurrence of a response. Thorndike's experimental situation is a case in point; modern versions of the procedure involve such arbitrarily selected experimental behaviors as lever pressing, running in mazes and alleys, turning a wheel, jumping a gap, and, in humans, verbal behavior. Typical reinforcers that have been employed are food and water, for an animal appropriately deprived; the opportunity to engage in sexual activity or to explore a novel environment, money, praise, etc., have been used with humans.

Escape training. Negative reinforcement involves the termination of an aversive stimulus. The behavior which terminates that stimulus is called escape behavior. Arbitrarily selected behaviors like those mentioned above have been used to study the properties of negative reinforcement. The most frequently used negative reinforcer has been electric shock, although reproof, social isolation, etc., have been used with humans.

Avoidance training. While an escape-training paradigm involves the presentation of the aversive stimulus independent of the organism's behavior, a paradigm can be arranged in which some arbitrary response postpones or avoids the delivery of the aversive stimulus. Any response which does so is an avoidance response. Often a warning stimulus, such as a light or a buzzer, precedes by some predetermined period of time the scheduled occurrence of the aversive stimulus. In this arrangement, called discriminated avoidance, a response occurring between the onset of the warning stimulus and the scheduled onset of the aversive stimulus is the avoidance response. Typically, a response occurring during that interval terminates the warning stimulus and results in the avoidance of the aversive stimulus. Sidman (1953) has carefully studied an avoidance procedure, called nondiscriminated avoidance, in which no warning stimulus occurs. Instead, the aversive stimulus, such as electric shock, is scheduled to occur on a purely temporal basis. A response recycles a timer, and the shock is postponed. Ordinarily, more than one temporal interval is involved in this kind of experiment.

Punishment training. Punishment training involves the onset of an aversive stimulus contingent upon the occurrence of a response. An effective procedure for studying punishment has been employed by Azrin and is described by Azrin and Holtz (1965). Animals are trained to respond through the use of positive reinforcement. A punishment is then applied, and the local, transient, and permanent effects of punishment are studied.

This outline is necessarily brief and cannot do justice to the many detailed findings in the control of behavior through reinforcement contingencies. In order to explore further some of those findings, however, we may consider in more detail the positive reinforcement of operant behavior.

Reinforcement and chaining

Some of the important facts regarding reinforcement can be displayed by considering a laboratory example where a pigeon is trained to step on a treadle in the rear of an experimental chamber, then to peck on an illuminated plastic disk or key on the wall, and, finally, to approach and eat from a grain tray. The first step is the adaptation of a hungry pigeon to the experimental chamber. After the bird is in the chamber for several minutes, the food tray is raised, with the grain illuminated by a small overhead light. The tray is held in place until the bird sees and eats some grain. After the bird has eaten for several seconds, the tray is dropped away, out of reach of the bird, and the light is turned off. The procedure is repeated until the bird responds immediately to the lifting of the tray and the illumination of the grain. By temporally spacing tray presentations, we provide for the extinction of approach behavior when the tray is not in the lifted position.

For the next step, we illuminate the translucent plastic disk on the wall. The pigeon is trained to stay in the vicinity of the disk by means of a procedure known as *successive approximation.* In this procedure each movement of the bird is noted, and as soon as a movement occurs that brings him a little closer to the disk, the grain tray is immediately lifted for a few seconds and the bird is allowed to eat. When the bird is near the disk his finer movements are observed, and, again by successive approximation, we bring his beak closer and closer to the disk until he pecks it. Each closer approximation to the desired response of pecking the disk is immediately followed by, that is, *reinforced* with, access to the grain tray. Next, we darken the disk and permit the pigeon to peck. The grain tray is not lifted. Soon the key is illuminated and a peck is followed by the grain tray's being lifted. Several pecks at the dark disk are allowed, but none of them is reinforced with food. When the disk is illuminated, a peck produces grain. This procedure (that is, *discrimination training*) results in a rapid decrease in the frequency of pecking at the dark disk, with the maintenance of a high probability of pecking at the illuminated disk. In the final step, another example of successive approximation, we start with a dark disk. A movement by the pigeon in the direction of the treadle is immediately followed by illumination of the disk. The pigeon is allowed to peck the disk and eat from the tray. As before, when he pecks at the dark disk, the grain tray is not lifted. By the illumination of the disk, contingent on some preselected aspect of the bird's behavior, we get him closer and closer to, and finally stepping on, the treadle. The behavior sequence is complete. The pigeon steps on the treadle; the disk is illuminated; the pigeon pecks the disk; the grain tray is immediately raised for a few seconds; the pigeon approaches the tray, and sees and eats the grain.

Paradigm of behavior chain. The behavior chain may be written symbolically, as follows ("$S_x : R_x \longrightarrow$" indicates the stimulus, S_x, in the presence of which a specified response, R_x, will have a specified effect, that is, $\longrightarrow$, the production of a new stimulus):

S_4	:	R_4	$\longrightarrow$	S_3	:	R_3	$\longrightarrow$	S_2	:	R_2	$\longrightarrow$	S_1	:	R_1
sight of treadle		step on treadle		key illuminated		peck at key		grain tray rises		approach tray		sight of grain		eat

If the behavioral chain in question is "free running," that is, if the bird is permitted to run it through over and over (a recycling chain), we might specify another stimulus event, S_0. The dropping away of the grain tray, S_0, is "produced" by (more exactly, correlated with) R_1. Thus, S_0 becomes the stimulus event in the presence of which the bird emits R_0, approach to the treadle. The approach response R_0 produces S_4. Thus the chain is closed, forming a continuous behavioral sequence that might be expected to continue as long as deprivation (motivational) variables are effective, all else being equal.

Conditioned and primary reinforcers. In analyzing the sequence of events that we have just described, it is important to notice that the actual reinforcers maintaining the specific responses are light and sound rather than the ingestion of food. This is the distinction between *conditioned* and *primary* reinforcement. While the primary reinforcement, that is, the ingestion of food, is a necessary condition for maintaining the bird's over-all performance, the conditioned reinforcers are made instantaneously and precisely contingent on the exact form of behavior that we wish to maintain. Virtually all operant behavior is maintained by conditioned reinforcers such as sounds and lights analogous to those described above, rather than directly by primary reinforcers such as food, water, oxygen, etc.

Principles of reinforcement. The preceding demonstration illustrates the following important principles pertinent to the operation of reinforcement:

(1) The strength of the several components of the response chain—stepping on the treadle, pecking the key, approaching the food tray—is maintained by their immediately reinforcing consequences. This fact can be demonstrated by performing extinction operations within the chain. Suppose we permit the pigeon to step on the treadle; but now, unlike the previous situation, we do not illuminate the disk when the pigeon responds in this way. Since the disk is not illuminated, the pigeon does not peck at it; but ceasing to illuminate the disk also constitutes the removal of conditioned reinforcement for the initial chain link, that is, stepping on the treadle. As a consequence of that removal of reinforcement, we may note first an increase and then certainly a decrease in the disposition of the bird to step on the treadle. The chain has been broken at its initial link. As a matter of fact, we could have broken the chain at any of its links by the simple expedient of removing the immediately reinforcing consequences of any of the responses making up the chain.

(2) Experiments of the kind just described demonstrate clearly the essential relationship among the several reinforcers of the chain. Food, the primary reinforcer that occurs at the end of the behavior sequence, is necessary to maintain the entire chain in strength, but each one of the several arbitrary links is closely controlled by the conditioned reinforcer that it immediately produces.

(3) A stimulus such as the illuminated response key serves a double function. Not only is it a reinforcer for the immediately preceding behavior, but it sets the occasion for the next response in the required sequence. Illumination of the key not only reinforces stepping on the treadle, but it also sets the occasion (that is, serves as a *discriminative stimulus*) for which a peck at the key will be reinforced. Implicit in the discriminative control by the illuminated disk is the corollary fact that when the disk is not illuminated, responses to it will have no further effect; the animal cannot progress any further in the chain. Since the animal's behavior is under the specific control of each stimulus element in the chain, it is this discriminative control by each stimulus element in the chain that keeps the sequential emission of the chain going.

(4) The chain is constructed by starting with its final component. After the final component

is securely developed, the next to the final one is added. When this is securely developed, another is added, and so on. In other words, the chain is built in a backward sequence. The reason for this procedure is readily appreciated if we take note of the fact that at the beginning of our training procedure we have at our disposal a single strong reinforcer, namely, the grain. The other events that finally serve as the conditioned link reinforcers are initially neutral and arbitrary events, such as light and sound. In order to establish such stimuli as conditioned reinforcers, it is necessary to associate them with already established reinforcers. Therefore, the compound stimulus, consisting of a flash of light illuminating the grain and the slap of the tray being raised, is established as a reinforcer through its association with the grain. It is thus capable of strengthening and maintaining peck responses on the illuminated disk. Note, however, that the illuminated disk is now correlated with the flash of the feeder light and the sound of the tray. By virtue of this association, the illuminated disk itself becomes a conditioned reinforcer and can be used to strengthen and maintain still an earlier member in the chain. Thus, practical considerations dictate the backward development of the sequence of conditioned reinforcers, and it is this development that makes advisable the backward development of a behavioral chain. A detailed review of positive conditioned reinforcement has been published by Kelleher and Gollub (1962).

Kinds of control through reinforcement

Continuous versus intermittent reinforcement. For many years the typical laboratory experiment involved the *continuous reinforcement* of the criterion response. Continuous reinforcement refers to a schedule of reinforcement in which the behavior in question is reinforced each time it occurs. It is clear that an analysis of behavior restricted to this experimental program can have limited applicability to the affairs of men. Men live in complicated societies. Their behaviors are not reinforced by automatic "grain trays," but are subject rather to the possible whims and fancies of such agencies of society as government bureaus, social groups, religious groups, and, perhaps most important for the day-to-day existence of most of us, other individuals at home, at work, and at play. If there is any outstanding characteristic of people either in groups or as individuals, it is that their behavior is complexly determined. As a consequence of this complex determination, behavior is reinforced on an intermittent basis when individuals interact. For this reason, the general problem of intermittent reinforcement must occupy a central and crucial place in the experimental analysis of behavior, if the latter is to come to grips with the problems of human performance.

Intermittent reinforcement refers to the case where some of, rather than all, the occurrences of the specified response are followed by a reinforcer. The phrase *schedule of reinforcement* refers to the particular rule by which reinforcement is made contingent upon some occurrence of a response. Broadly speaking, there are two general schemes whereby reinforcers can be related to response emission. Within either of these schemes, not to mention those cases where they are combined, there are literally thousands of different schedules. Many of the simpler ones and some of the more complex ones have been extensively studied in the laboratory using both animal and human subjects.

Interval and ratio schedules. When a rule specifying the contingency between a response and its reinforcement involves the passage of time, we speak of *interval schedules*. For example, we may specify that reinforcement will occur on the first response following a fixed period of elapsed time since the last reinforcement. Such a schedule is referred to as a *fixed interval* schedule of reinforcement. On the other hand, when the contingency involves some number of responses we speak of *ratio schedules*. We may specify that reinforcement will occur following the emission of the *n*th response since the last reinforcement. This rule, specifying a fixed number of responses, is ordinarily referred to as a *fixed ratio* schedule of reinforcement. These are simple cases, but they exemplify the two broad classifications of response–reinforcement contingencies referred to as "interval" and "ratio" schedules. These two broad classifications of reinforcement contingencies produce behaviors that have markedly different properties.

Characteristics of ratio schedules. Fixed ratio schedules are generally characterized by high rates of response emission. As the reinforcer is made contingent upon successively higher and higher response requirements, sharp breaks in responding ordinarily develop. Initially, these breaks appear following a reinforcement and preceding the next ratio run. Later, when the ratio requirement has reached some relatively high number, breaks may occur at various places during the ratio run. An outstanding characteristic of ratio performance is that the organism is either not responding (pausing) or is responding at a relatively constant rate. If the ratio requirement is increased still further, responding becomes relatively sporadic; we refer to this condition as ratio strain.

It is no secret that a type of gambling machine, the slot machine, is designed in accordance with the principles of ratio behavior. The payoff frequency must be great enough so that the gambling behavior does not show marked strain. On the other hand, the exact ratio contingency must not be defined by the emission of a *fixed* number of responses. If that were the case, we would observe potential gamblers waiting for the other fellow to play until, of course, $N-1$ coins had been fed the machine. Then there would ensue a dash to the machine in order to make the payoff response. Instead, the slot machine is programmed according to a *variable ratio* schedule of reinforcement. In this case, reinforcement is again contingent upon the emission of a number of responses, but the number of responses required differs from reinforcement to reinforcement. A variable ratio schedule of reinforcement is less susceptible to the development of ratio strain. Although very large numbers of response occurrences may be required for some instances of reinforcement, other instances occur after very few responses. Through judicious selection of a sequence of ratio sizes in a variable ratio program, the slot machine may be made to show a consistent profit.

Characteristics of interval schedules. The properties of interval schedules are different from those of ratio schedules. Interval schedules often show intermediate rates of responding. In the fixed interval case mentioned earlier, one frequently observes a relatively smooth transition from a zero rate of responding immediately after a reinforcement to a fairly high rate of responding preceding the next reinforcement. The characteristic shape of the fixed interval, cumulative-response graph is referred to as a *fixed interval scallop.* As in the case of variable ratio reinforcement, we can specify a rule that defines the *variable interval* case. In a variable interval schedule of reinforcement, reinforcement availability is again made contingent upon elapsed time, but, unlike the fixed interval case, the periods of time that must elapse between the reinforcements vary in a random sequence around some selected value. By the careful selection of interval sizes and their exact order of occurrence, one can produce a nearly uniform rate of responding, if one desires to do so. In fact, there have been variable interval response graphs that were so regular, a straightedge would be required to detect deviations from regularity. It can be seen, then, that the schedule of reinforcement, to a considerable extent, serves to control the rate and pattern of response emission. Schedules also serve to determine the characteristics of extinction, when reinforcements are no longer obtainable. A schedule of continuous reinforcement produces a relatively brief extinction curve, whereas a schedule of intermittent reinforcement may produce a protracted extinction curve characterized by a gradual transition from a high rate of responding to a zero rate after variable interval reinforcement, or gradually increasing periods of no responding punctuated by response bursts at a constant rate after ratio reinforcement.

Motivation. Schedules of reinforcement, to a large extent, account for some of the properties of behavior that are often referred to as "motivational." Individuals characterized as highly motivated or "driven" may in fact be individuals who are capable of sustaining high ratio requirements without obvious signs of strain. On the other hand, people who are characterized as lazy or indolent may be, in fact, individuals who are not capable of sustained performance on even a modest ratio requirement. While such characterizations must not be accepted on the basis of face validity, they do have the merit of suggesting methods of changing the behaviors of such individuals. In this way, the research of the animal laboratory can be brought to bear on the problems of human behavior. The reader interested in the details of reinforcement schedules should consult *Schedules of Reinforcement* by Ferster and Skinner (1957). [*See* DRIVES; MOTIVATION.]

Differentiation of new response forms. It has been seen that schedules of reinforcement can be utilized to control the rate and pattern of response emission. Another major function of reinforcement is to create "new" behavior. By the creation of new behavior, we do not mean the creation of something out of nothing, but rather the transition from one form of behavior into another. There are many examples from the world of human affairs. The powerful and accurate play of the professional golfer is created from the fumbling, awkward movements of the beginner. The changes characterizing such a transition in behavior are not simply quantitative in the sense that a change in response rate is quantitative. The professional golfer does not simply move faster or swing his club more often. Rather, his performance is qualitatively different from that of the beginner. It may be seen that the development of new behavior is often a problem in the acquisition of skills. We have already specified the essential process by which skills are acquired; that is, successive approximation. Once we can specify the form of the final behavior that we desire, we can, starting with almost any arbitrary performance, bring about the desired behavior by stages. The instructor, teacher, therapist, or any other individual who is concerned with the creation of new behavior in others must be capable of recognizing closer and closer approximations to the desired performance. In addition to recognizing these closer and closer approximations, he must have at his disposal a conditioned reinforcer that may be presented immediately upon the appearance of an acceptable intermediate performance. Verbal reinforcers such as "good" or "now you have it" are often used with humans. Improved control over the immediacy of reinforcement was one of the major considerations in the development of the new and very promising technique of programmed instruction or, as it is often called—with misplaced emphasis on the hardware—"teaching machines."

Differential reinforcement. The critical procedure in the development of new behavior involves a process known as *differential reinforcement.* Differential reinforcement refers to a procedure in which reinforcement is administered upon the occurrence of some behaviors and withheld upon the occurrence of other behaviors. The extremely powerful and precise control that may be gained over behavior through differential reinforcement is responsible for the success of the successive approximation technique. Since reinforcement may be made contingent upon either a qualitative or intensive property of a response, the procedure may be used to change the topographical characteristics of the response or its intensity.

Consider the example of a young child ignored by his parents. In searching for attention, he may emit a wide range of specific behaviors, differing enormously with respect to topography. Any of these behaviors that succeeds in gaining attention from the parents will be strengthened to some extent and become prepotent over the others. Attention is reinforcing. By the process of differential reinforcement, the parents can create a new and strong behavior pattern in the young child. It is no accident that in the practical case the new behavior pattern typically involves some element of aversiveness for the parent. The parent, after all, is a reinforceable organism. Termination of the child's aversive behavior serves to reinforce the parent's behavior, which, as we have noted, may likewise serve to reinforce the behavior of the child. It may be readily appreciated how a vicious feedback system may be developed. In order to gain attention from the parent, the child raises his voice or generally displays some other form of temperamental behavior. Because this behavior is aversive to the parent, the parent terminates it by responding to the child. The attention thereby shown to the child reinforces the temperamental display. Through a process of adaptation to the aversive properties of the child's behavior, or simply because the parent may not want to "give in" so readily, attention may be withheld on some specific instance of a temperamental display. Since an increase in the intensity of a temperamental display will ordinarily establish a new level of aversiveness, it is likely that the parent will respond to that new level with immediate attention. As a result, a more intense form of the temperamental display is differentially reinforced. The end result of such a feedback system is one that most of us have seen at one time or another. The fundamental mistake made by the parent at the outset is to respond to (that is, reinforce) any form of behavior that has aversive properties for him. By withholding reinforcement under these conditions and responding with attention when some form of nonaversive behavior is emitted by the child, the whole problem can be avoided. On the other hand, starting with a child who has already developed in strength some form of aversive behavior, the principle of differential reinforcement may be used in order to short-circuit the development of the feedback system. Simple withholding of reinforcement on all temperamental displays by the child will produce eventual extinction of that form of behavior. Perhaps a more positive approach would be to combine extinction of intense forms of temperamental display with deliberate reinforcement of less and less intense exhibitions by the child. Ultimately, the child will have learned that attention, and hence satisfaction of his needs, will be forthcoming only when his request is stated moderately.

The dynamic properties of reinforcement

We have stressed the importance of immediacy in the effective use of reinforcement. A reinforcement that is delayed after the occurrence of the criterion behavior will ordinarily occur in close temporal proximity to some other behavior. Although there might be some tendency for the criterion behavior to be strengthened, maximal strengthening will occur with respect to the intervening behavior.

Superstition and uncontingent reinforcement. If the intervening behavior that is maximally strengthened is incompatible with the criterion behavior, we might, in fact, note a decrease in the strength of the criterion behavior. Perhaps the most dramatic example of the effect of uncontingent reinforcement is the well-known "superstition" experiment (Skinner 1948).

A hungry pigeon is placed in an experimental chamber, and the grain tray is operated at fairly frequent intervals, but independent of the animal's behavior. After a period of time, we note the development of some rather strong behavioral patterns during the intervals between reinforcement. Frequently, these behavior patterns appear quite bizarre. The pigeon, for example, may hop about on one leg while fluttering a wing, or the bird may dance furiously from one side of the box to the other while stretching its neck. The important point is that these behaviors have developed as a function of the uncontingent reinforcement: *Simply because the reinforcement has not been made experimentally contingent upon some specified response does not mean that the reinforcement was without effect.* In fact, what will always happen is the strengthening, by the reinforcement, of some chance behavior. By the process of differential reinforcement, the behavior that is accidentally reinforced may show some slow drift in topography. After a period of time, we actually might note a completely different topography from that which we observed earlier. As a general principle, we may state that the more immediate the reinforcement is with respect to the criterion response, the more highly stereotyped the criterion response is likely to be. Less immediate reinforcement will produce somewhat looser control, with a noticeable tendency for the criterion response to change in time. We may, as a matter of fact, make an experimental prediction about the superstition experiment just described. If the uncontingent reinforcers are presented at fairly frequent intervals, we will note the relatively rapid development of some arbitrary and perhaps bizarre behavior that will be fairly resistant to drift, that is, it will maintain a roughly similar topography over long periods of time. If the uncontingent reinforcements are delivered at less frequent intervals, we will note a susceptibility to change and drift in the accidentally reinforced behavior. In the extreme, if the uncontingent reinforcers are delivered at widely spaced intervals, then the drift becomes such a dominating characteristic of the behavior that we fail to notice a long-range strengthening effect of the reinforcement at all. Our conclusion, therefore, is that for reinforcement to be maximally effective it must follow the to-be-reinforced response without delay.

Reinforcement and deprivation. A second dynamic property of reinforcement is its relationship to deprivation. Some environmental events will be effective as reinforcers only if the organism has been deprived of some commodity. Food, for example, is effective in controlling the behavior of an animal only if that animal has been made hungry through food deprivation. Similarly, water can be used as a reinforcer only if the animal has been deprived of water. Other kinds of reinforcers, even at the level of lower organisms, can be effective in the absence of deprivation. Electric shock, for example, can serve as a very powerful negative reinforcer without the organism having been deprived of any commodity such as food or water. It is no accident that negative reinforcement is the most popular form of behavior control employed by the average person. It is easy to dispense in its varied forms, and it does not depend for its effect on some prior operation not under the control of the punisher, such as deprivation of the punishee. Many of us have met individuals who through some quirk of behavioral development are themselves positively reinforced by their own dispensation of negative reinforcement.

Novelty as a reinforcer. There is now evidence to indicate that even at the level of the rat, a novel situation may serve to reinforce positively and to maintain exploratory behavior (Montgomery 1954). It is clear, however, that deprivation-independent reinforcers become more important as one ascends the phylogenetic scale. It has been demonstrated quite clearly that at the level of the monkey, behavior may be reinforced and maintained if the monkey has a brief opportunity to look out from an experimental chamber into a room that is occupied by other monkeys or by people (Butler 1953). Curiosity, then, is a motive in higher animals, and curiosity satisfaction is a potent reinforcer.

Generalized reinforcers. Reinforcers such as food and water and oxygen are of obvious importance in the control of lower animals. Of course they can also serve to control the behavior of higher animals. Ordinarily, however, the behavior of higher animals is under the control of nonhomeostatic reinforcers. A child, for example, can be powerfully reinforced by some particular play activity or by some manipulatable novel object, such as a brightly colored toy or a plastic ring. Adult humans can be powerfully reinforced by a wide range of reinforcers that we refer to as *generalized* reinforcers. These may be defined as specific events or objects that can be used to reinforce a wide range of different behaviors across many motivational systems, both homeostatic and nonhomeostatic. In the life of human beings, the most obvious example of a generalized reinforcer is money. More subtle, but nonetheless just as powerful, are such reinforcers as praise, attention, and improvement in living standard and working conditions. It is interesting to note that "improvement in working conditions" can serve as a reinforcer for the behavior of lower animals also. It has been demonstrated, for example, that a pigeon will peck at one key when the sole consequence of behavior on that key is to change the schedule of reinforcement to a more favorable one on a second key (Findley 1958). A more favorable schedule may be defined either by a higher rate of reinforcement or less work per reinforcement.

Physiological mechanisms. Finally, a recent finding offers considerable promise for the laboratory study of the physiological mechanisms of reinforcement. It has been demonstrated by Olds and Milner (1954) that such animals as rats and cats will work to produce weak electrical stimulation of certain brain loci. The technique holds great promise for the study of the neural substrates of reward. Olds (1962) has recently summarized most of the studies on reward by electrical stimulation of the brain.

STANLEY S. PLISKOFF
AND CHARLES B. FERSTER

[*Other relevant material may be found in* DRIVES; MOTIVATION; NERVOUS SYSTEM, *article on* BRAIN STIMULATION; STIMULATION DRIVES; *and in the biographies of* GUTHRIE; HULL; PAVLOV; THORNDIKE.]

BIBLIOGRAPHY

AZRIN, N. H.; and HOLTZ, W. C. 1965 Punishment. Pages 380–447 in Werner K. Honig (editor), *Operant Behavior: Areas of Research and Application.* New York: Appleton.

BIRNEY, ROBERT C.; and TEEVAN, RICHARD C. (editors) 1961 *Reinforcement, an Enduring Problem in Psychology: Selected Readings.* Princeton, N.J.: Van Nostrand.

BUTLER, ROBERT A. 1953 Discrimination Learning by Rhesus Monkeys to Visual-exploration Motivation. *Journal of Comparative and Physiological Psychology* 46:95–98.

FERSTER, C. B.; and SKINNER, B. F. 1957 *Schedules of Reinforcement.* New York: Appleton.

FINDLEY, JACK D. 1958 Preference and Switching Under Concurrent Scheduling. *Journal of the Experimental Analysis of Behavior* 1:123–144.

GUTHRIE, EDWIN R. (1935) 1960 *The Psychology of Learning.* Rev. ed. Gloucester, Mass.: Smith.

HILGARD, ERNEST; and BOWER, GORDON H. (1948) 1966 *Theories of Learning.* 3d ed. New York: Appleton. → Ernest Hilgard was sole author of the previous editions.

HILGARD, ERNEST R.; and MARQUIS, DONALD G. (1940) 1961 *Hilgard and Marquis' Conditioning and Learning.* 2d ed., revised by Gregory A. Kimble. New York: Appleton.

HULL, CLARK L. 1943 *Principles of Behavior: An Introduction to Behavior Theory.* New York: Appleton.

KELLEHER, ROGER T.; and GOLLUB, LEWIS R. 1962 A Review of Positive Conditioned Reinforcement. *Journal of the Experimental Analysis of Behavior* 5:543–597.

MONTGOMERY, K. C. 1954 The Role of Exploratory Drive in Learning. *Journal of Comparative and Physiological Psychology* 47:60–64.

OLDS, JAMES 1962 Hypothalamic Substrates of Reward. *Physiological Reviews* 42:554–604.

OLDS, JAMES; and MILNER, PETER 1954 Positive Reinforcement Produced by Electrical Stimulation of Septal Area and Other Regions of Rat Brain. *Journal of Comparative and Physiological Psychology* 47:419–427.

PAVLOV, IVAN P. (1927) 1960 *Conditioned Reflexes: An Investigation of the Physiological Activity of the Cerebral Cortex.* New York: Dover. → First published as *Lektsii o rabote bol'shikh polusharii golovnogo mozga.*

SIDMAN, MURRAY 1953 Avoidance Conditioning With Brief Shock and No Exteroceptive Warning Signal. *Science* 118:157–158.

SIDMAN, MURRAY 1960 *Tactics of Scientific Research: Evaluating Experimental Data in Psychology.* New York: Basic Books.

SKINNER, B. F. 1938 *The Behavior of Organisms: An Experimental Analysis.* New York: Appleton.

SKINNER, B. F. 1948 "Superstition" in the Pigeon. *Journal of Experimental Psychology* 38:168–172.

SKINNER, B. F. 1953 *Science and Human Behavior.* New York: Macmillan.

THORNDIKE, EDWARD L. (1898–1901) 1911 *Animal Intelligence: Experimental Studies.* New York: Macmillan.

V
DISCRIMINATION LEARNING

Discrimination learning, or the acquisition of ability to respond differentially to objects in the environment, is of continuing interest to psychologists for both empirical and theoretical reasons. Its study provides an opportunity for exploring the sensory capacities of the nonverbal organism, as well as the possibility of relating the fields of learning, perception, and attention, a possibility that has motivated much of the theoretical speculation available on this subject. Before attempting to evaluate the progress made in this direction, however, it is helpful to outline the most common procedures used in studying the learning of discriminations, most of which have employed laboratory animals.

Simultaneous discrimination procedure. In a simultaneous discrimination procedure, the animal is usually confronted with two stimulus objects on each trial. These objects normally are alike in all respects except for variation on some given attribute such as brightness, color, or shape. The animal indicates its choice between them by some reaction such as picking one up, approaching one, or the like. A "correct" choice is rewarded with something desirable, perhaps a pellet of food. An incorrect choice is nonrewarded or even punished.

Initially, of course, the animal shows only a chance level of accuracy because it has no prior knowledge of which object is related to reward and which to punishment. With continued training, the percentage of successful choices may increase to the point where it is clear the animal has mastered the problem. When the appropriate experimental controls have been used, such performance is clear evidence that the animal is sensitive to the stimulus attribute under investigation. The experimenter may then decrease the difference between the two objects. As he continues to do this, the animal's accuracy again approaches a chance level. From these data, it is possible to determine the animal's differential sensitivity to values on this stimulus attribute.

Successive discrimination procedure. In a successive discrimination procedure, only one of the two stimulus objects is presented on a given trial, but each occurs equally often in a sequence of such trials. In a T maze, for example, the stimulus object is displayed at the choice point, and the animal has the alternatives of turning into either the right or left alley. If turning left is the correct and rewarded response to one of the objects, then turning right is the correct and rewarded response in the presence of the second object. Thus, a different reaction must be related to each of the two stimulus objects in order to master the successive discrimination.

Alternatively, the animal's choice may be between reacting and not reacting. In classical conditioning procedures, for example, the animal is required to make the conditioned response in the presence of one object, the positive stimulus, and to inhibit this response in the presence of a different object, the negative stimulus. This technique has been valuable in determining absolute thresholds, that is, the minimum amount of an attribute that the animal can detect. Once the discrimination is established, the intensity or amount of the positive stimulus is gradually reduced until the animal no longer responds to it.

Generalization and discrimination. Theoretical interest in discrimination learning has tended to concentrate on two opposing tendencies that the animal shows during training. If it has been trained to respond in some definite manner to one stimulus, it will generalize or transfer this tendency to respond to a wide variety of other similar stimuli. This occurs spontaneously, without any specific training with these new stimuli. This tendency to generalize is of considerable interest to the theorist because it is one obvious basis for the transfer of training. But at the same time it poses a problem for him. He must not only indicate the conditions under which this tendency to generalize is aroused, but he must also explain why this generalization occurs for certain new stimuli but not for others.

An opposing tendency, however, is also evident during discrimination training. Using the procedures described above, the animal can be taught to make differential responses to two very similar stimuli, that is, stimuli that would otherwise evoke quite similar responses in accordance with the generalization tendency. But during the course of discrimination training this generalization tendency is suppressed. The animal now acts as though the two stimuli were perceived as being distinctly different. Thus, a focal problem for a theory of discrimination learning is to explain the disappearance or suppression of the tendency to generalize as a result of the training procedures used.

Hull's theory. One of the more influential accounts of discrimination learning was developed by Clark Hull (1943). This formulation has two unique features. First, it does not attempt to explain the tendency to generalize; instead it assumes that it is an innate and universal characteristic of all organisms. Second, it accounts for the partial suppression of this tendency during discrimination learning by postulating a second and opposing form of generalization.

Hull's basic formulation is that every time an animal's response to a stimulus object is followed by a reward, there is an increase in the probability that the animal will respond in the same way to that stimulus object the next time it is presented. This is the excitatory tendency, the tendency to respond. This excitatory tendency, however, is not specific to the rewarded stimulus. It generalizes or spreads to other stimuli in direct proportion to the degree of similarity they have to the rewarded stimulus. This differential spread is conceived of as a generalization gradient. The amount of excitatory tendency is greatest for the rewarded stimulus, but this amount diminishes along a continuum of decreasing stimulus similarity. Basically, this conception is a description of what is empirically observed in transfer-of-training studies.

The suppression of this generalization tendency during discrimination training is accounted for by postulating an opposing tendency. It is assumed that each time the animal's response to a stimulus is not rewarded there is an increase in the strength of an inhibitory tendency, the tendency to withhold or suppress the response in the presence of that stimulus. This inhibitory tendency also generalizes. It forms a gradient that has a maximum value at the nonrewarded stimulus and that diminishes in magnitude along a continuum of decreasing stimulus similarity.

In these terms, a conditioned discrimination can be conceived of in the following way. On some trials the animal is confronted by one stimulus and on the remainder of the trials by a second, similar stimulus. If it responds appropriately to the first stimulus, the positive one, it is rewarded. Thus, some amount of the excitatory tendency is associated with this stimulus and generalizes, although to a lesser degree, to the second stimulus. However, if the animal responds in the same way when this second or negative stimulus is presented, no reward is given. This results in a certain amount of inhibitory tendency becoming associated with the negative stimulus. This in turn generalizes, although to a lesser degree, to the positive stimulus. It is assumed that these successive interactions between excitatory and inhibitory processes continue during discrimination training until the following two conditions occur: (1) the excitatory tendency associated with the positive stimulus clearly outweighs the inhibitory tendency that has generalized to this stimulus, and (2) the converse is true for the negative stimulus. At this point the animal shows clear-cut discrimination behavior by responding appropriately on each trial to the positive stimulus and withholding that response to the negative one.

When stated more exactly, this formulation has a wide range of implications concerning the rates of learning to be expected in various discrimination tasks, the types of transfer or transposition behavior that should occur, and the like. A sufficient number of these implications have received empirical support to justify considerable faith in this approach. At the same time, these empirical studies have indicated a number of weaknesses in the basic concepts of the formulation. Perhaps the most important of these weaknesses is the absence of any means of defining the degree of similarity between two stimuli independently of the observed generalization behavior of the animal. This suggestion of circularity in the system has led in large part to a number of alternative formulations of discrimination learning.

The concept of similarity. In the psychological literature, stimulus similarity has been treated as a response-inferred construct. This means that the degree of similarity between two stimulus objects can be inferred only from the behavior of the animal with respect to them. If the stimuli are equivalent in the sense of producing comparable reactions, then, psychologically, they are highly similar for that animal. Phrased in this way, a theoretical account of the concept of similarity must state the conditions under which the animal will treat two stimulus objects as though they were equivalent. This can be done either in terms of assumptions about the make-up of the organism or in terms of the physical properties of the stimulus objects.

Organismic attributes. One possible approach to this concept of similarity stems from the early work of Pavlov (1927). He claimed that similarity was largely a function of the neurological organization of the animal's cortex. Whether an animal perceives two stimuli as similar, as inferred from the generalization of behavior from one to the other, depends upon the spatial proximity of the sensory projections associated with these stimuli. If these are close together, considerable interaction or generalization can occur. With wider separations, the stimulus objects are perceived as independent or nonsimilar units. These neurological assumptions about the basis of similarity continue to have some influence in the physiological literature but have had little influence on psychological theorizing.

Stimulus attributes. Recent theoretical interest has centered on the possibility of defining similarity in terms of overlap or of common elements in the two stimulus objects. This approach was prominent in the writings of Thorndike ([1913] 1921, chapter 4) and Guthrie (1935) but has been given a much more precise formulation in statistical learning theory (Estes 1959). The basic notion in this approach is that each stimulus object, plus the stimulus context in which it appears, is to be conceived of as potentially a population, or large set, of stimulus elements rather than as a single, unanalyzable unit. On a given trial the animal experiences only a randomly selected sample, or subset, of this potential population of elements that constitutes the object. This trial-to-trial variability in the sample of elements experienced is due to a number of factors; it stems in part from the impossibility of exactly reproducing the physical stimulus situation, in part from moment-to-moment variation in the state of an organism, in part from changes in the postural orientation of the animal with respect to the stimulus object, and so on. In order for the animal to experience all the elements in the population, it must be exposed repeatedly to the same stimulus object.

With two stimulus objects, of course, there are two populations of stimulus elements. Some of these elements may be common to the two populations, the rest being specific to one or the other. The proportion of common elements to the total number of elements in the combined populations is one possible measure of the degree of similarity between the two stimulus objects. The greater the proportion of overlapping elements, the greater is the degree of similarity.

The unique feature of this conception of similarity is that it does away with the need to assume that the animal has an innate tendency to generalize its learned behaviors. If an animal does transfer such a response from a training stimulus to a new one, it is because the populations of elements constituting the two objects have elements in common. These common elements were associated with the learned response during training with the first stimulus object. Consequently, there is a definite probability that they will evoke that same response when they again occur in the context of the new stimulus object. The probability that this generalization will occur increases as the proportion of overlapping elements in the two populations increases; the larger this degree of overlap, the more likely it becomes that any one sampling from the new stimulus object will contain a large number of them.

The assumptions underlying this conception of similarity have been stated mathematically in several recent formulations of statistical learning theory, making possible much more precise statements as to when generalization will occur and the amount of such transfer to be expected. As these predictions have considerable empirical support, it would appear that a real advance has been made in understanding the basis for psychological similarity.

Paradoxically, however, the success of this approach in predicting generalization has led to an impasse in attempting to apply the same assumptions to discrimination learning. If taken in its most literal form, this conception of similarity as being due to overlapping stimulus elements implies that an animal can never achieve a perfect discrimination between two similar stimulus objects, since their common elements would always be associated with each of the different responses, an implication that is clearly at variance with empirical observation.

Consequently, if this conception of similarity in terms of common elements is to apply to discrimination learning, as well as to generalization situations, additional assumptions must be made concerning these stimulus populations. One possibility is that their composition of elements is modified during discrimination training. In some sense the number of common elements is reduced, or at least their control over choice behavior is minimized [*see* GUTHRIE; THORNDIKE].

Selective attention. In a different context, the idea that the effective stimuli for behavior are modified or transformed during the course of learning has been discussed under the heading of selective attention. Two conceptualizations of this transformation process have been suggested. One of these involves the enrichment of, or additions to, the effective stimulus; the other emphasizes a reduction in the content of the stimulus.

Enrichment of the effective stimulus. The enrichment idea was clearly formulated by William James (1890, pp. 508 ff. in volume 1 of 1950 edition). He denied that the immediate sensory input from the stimulus object is the direct elicitor of choice behavior. Instead, he suggested that the effective stimulus is the complex of ideas, emotions, and other reactions that are associated with this sensory input. The main implication of this formulation is that the complexes associated with two stimulus objects may have proportionately less overlap and fewer common elements than do the immediate sensory experiences that give rise to them. Consequently, the tendency to generalize is reduced as these differentiating complexes develop during the course of learning. In more recent discussions of discrimination learning, this notion has been formulated somewhat more explicitly in terms of the concept of the "acquired distinctiveness of cues" (Miller & Dollard 1941).

Elimination of irrelevant cues. A more popular approach to the problem, however, is to view the stimulus transformation process as one in which the initial sensory inputs are gradually stripped of all irrelevant or nondifferentiating aspects. Only the differentiating, nonoverlapping aspects remain as the effective stimulus for the choice behavior. The simplest of these formulations postulates the learning of receptor-orienting behaviors. If, for instance, an animal looks at the top halves of two stimulus objects, the sensory input from them is likely to be quite different than if the animal looks at the bottom halves. Consequently, the animal may learn that certain receptor orientations lead to a more accurate discrimination than would be otherwise possible insofar as these sensory inputs contain a minimum number of common aspects and a maximum number of differentiating aspects. Learned orienting behaviors of this sort undoubtedly are involved in many types of discrimination, but the concept would seem to be of quite limited usefulness in situations where there is minimal need or opportunity for visual search procedures.

Stimulus coding. A number of alternative mechanisms have been proposed to account for the selective aspects of attention. These are variously referred to as "filter theory" (Broadbent 1961), "analyzer mechanisms" (Sutherland 1959), or "stimulus coding behaviors" (Lawrence 1963).

While these differ in many details, the general approach can be illustrated in terms of stimulus coding behaviors.

The stimulus coding formulation recognizes that the sensory input at any moment depends as much on the behavior of the organism as it does on the characteristics of the external stimulus object. For instance, the tactual sensations from a piece of sandpaper are quite different depending upon whether the individual merely places a finger tip on it or draws a finger rapidly across the surface. Thus, the effective stimulus to which the individual reacts is a joint function of his own behavior and the characteristics of the stimulus object.

In order to allow for both of these factors in determining the effective stimulus, the stimulus coding formulation assumes that the total sensory input from the discrimination situation is functionally divided into two parts. The first part corresponds to the stable, recurring aspects of the situation and the second part to the changing, variable aspects. In a successive discrimination, the stable part of the input may correspond to the characteristics of the room, the apparatus, and the like; the variable aspects may correspond to the characteristics of the stimulus objects to be discriminated.

It is assumed that the stable aspects of the situation become associated with, and control, an implicit, inferred coding response. When this coding response is elicited, it reacts on, or interacts with, the sensory input from the stimulus object. As a result of this interaction, a new input is generated which is called the "coded stimulus." When, as in discrimination learning, there are two different stimulus objects but only one coding response, two different coded stimuli are produced. These control the choice behavior.

In this schema, the characteristics of the coded stimuli change whenever there is a change in the coding response even though the stimulus objects remain constant. The coded stimuli are resultants from an interaction between a coding response and the immediate sensory inputs. A change in either the coding response or the immediate sensory inputs modifies the coded stimuli. The range of values the coded stimuli can assume, however, is limited by the actual properties of the sensory inputs. These latter are members of the interaction, and therefore the resultants cannot be independent of them. The implication is that these coded stimuli correspond to parts of, relationships within, or other limited aspects of the sensory input. But even with this restriction, the coded stimuli can vary greatly with changes in the coding response.

To complete the formulation, it is assumed that the coding response varies in a trial-and-error fashion during the initial stages of discrimination learning. Gradually, however, it shifts in that direction which tends to minimize the confusion and overlap between the coded stimuli. This is, of course, the direction that maximizes the accuracy of the discrimination. Thus, a dual learning process is always involved in a discrimination procedure: The animal must discover a coding response that produces highly distinctive coded stimuli, and at the same time learn which overt choice reactions are appropriate to these coded stimuli.

Formulations of this type offer a mechanism that permits the effective stimulus for behavior to be continuously modified throughout the course of learning. They permit the animal to react initially to the total stimulus input including the common, or overlapping, aspects. Thus, there can be the broad generalization characteristic of such situations. But with experience, the effective stimulus shifts in the direction that corresponds to the differentiating, nonoverlapping aspects of the stimulus objects. This ensures a high level of accuracy for the discrimination and offers a solution to the dilemma encountered in statistical learning theory. On the other hand, it is obvious that these formulations once again make stimulus similarity a direct function of the animal's own behavior.

Additional aspects. It should be emphasized, however, that even more precise and powerful theories of this type would not do justice to the wide range of empirical effects found during discrimination learning. The experimental literature contains many suggestions of changes in response selectivity, of heightened motivational effects, and of conflict resolution that largely fall outside the bounds of any of the theoretical approaches so far mentioned.

A clear example of changes in response selectivity is provided by the studies on learning set (Harlow 1959). These demonstrate that an animal can solve simultaneous discriminations with incredible rapidity after repeated experience with this class of problems. A sophisticated monkey requires only one or two information trials to reach a high level of mastery, whereas initially it required a prolonged training period to solve an equivalent problem. An analysis of this type of learning suggests that the increase in efficiency is in part due to the elimination of the response biases so prominent in the naive animal, for example, such biases as position preferences, alternation tendencies, or tendencies toward perseveration in a given response.

Motivational changes are apparent in studies on

contrast effects. Pavlov first demonstrated these in his studies on positive and negative induction. He found that once a successive discrimination was established by conditioning procedures, a series of presentations of the positive or rewarded stimulus object tended to strengthen and maintain the inhibitory tendencies evoked by the negative stimulus object. This was true even though the negative stimulus object was now followed by reward. Conversely, a series of presentations of the negative or nonrewarded stimulus object tended to strengthen and maintain the excitatory tendency evoked by the positive stimulus object, even though this was no longer rewarded. Descriptively, it is as though the animal has built up a set of contrasts as the result of discrimination training; experience with the positive stimulus object increases the undesirability of the nonrewarded behavior, and experience with the negative stimulus object enhances the desirability of the rewarded behavior. Comparable phenomena have been demonstrated with other types of discrimination training.

Related to these contrast effects are any number of phenomena that can be grouped in terms of conflict resolution. Perhaps the most dramatic of these is the change in behavior that occurs in experimental neurosis (Liddell 1956). After a successive discrimination is well established, the two stimulus objects are made more and more similar until the animal is unable to discriminate between them. Occasionally, under these conditions, the animal begins to show agitated and highly emotional behavior. This emotionality persists for long periods of time both in the experimental situation and in other contexts. Equally impressive are the abortive and stereotypic behaviors exhibited by animals who have been frustrated by being forced to respond in an unsolvable discrimination situation (Maier 1949).

This brief and highly selected survey of the many behavioral changes that occur during discrimination learning is sufficient to indicate the limitations of present theories on this subject. These formulations have been primarily concerned with developing appropriate concepts to deal with generalization phenomena, stimulus similarity, and selective attention. They obviously have not dealt adequately, as yet, with the phenomena of response selectivity, motivational changes, and conflict resolution.

DOUGLAS H. LAWRENCE

[*Other relevant material may be found in* ATTENTION; CONCEPT FORMATION; MODELS, MATHEMATICAL; PERCEPTION, *article on* PERCEPTUAL DEVELOPMENT; *and in the biography of* HULL.]

BIBLIOGRAPHY

ATKINSON, RICHARD C.; and ESTES, WILLIAM K. 1963 Stimulus Sampling Theory. Volume 2, pages 121–268 in R. Duncan Luce, Robert R. Bush, and Eugene Galanter (editors), *Handbook of Mathematical Psychology.* New York: Wiley.

BROADBENT, D. E. 1961 Human Perception and Animal Learning. Pages 248–272 in W. H. Thorpe and O. L. Zangwill (editors), *Current Problems in Animal Behaviour.* Cambridge Univ. Press.

ESTES, WILLIAM K. 1959 The Statistical Approach to Learning Theory. Volume 2, pages 380–491 in Sigmund Koch (editor), *Psychology: A Study of a Science.* New York: McGraw-Hill.

GUTHRIE, EDWIN R. (1935) 1960 *The Psychology of Learning.* Rev. ed. Gloucester, Mass.: Smith.

HARLOW, HARRY F. 1959 Learning Set and Error Factor Theory. Volume 2, pages 492–537 in Sigmund Koch (editor), *Psychology: A Study of a Science.* New York: McGraw-Hill.

HULL, CLARK L. 1943 *Principles of Behavior: An Introduction to Behavior Theory.* New York: Appleton.

JAMES, WILLIAM (1890) 1962 *The Principles of Psychology.* 2 vols. New York: Smith.

LAWRENCE, DOUGLAS H. 1963 The Nature of a Stimulus: Some Relationships Between Learning and Perception. Volume 5, pages 179–212 in Sigmund Koch (editor), *Psychology: A Study of a Science.* New York: McGraw-Hill.

LIDDELL, HOWARD S. 1956 *Emotional Hazards in Animals and Man.* Springfield, Ill.: Thomas.

MACKINTOSH, N. J. 1965 Selective Attention in Animal Discrimination Learning. *Psychological Bulletin* 64: 124–150. → A more recent and more easily accessible account of N. S. Sutherland's viewpoint and a review of the experimental evidence bearing on it.

MAIER, NORMAN R. F. 1949 *Frustration: The Study of Behavior Without a Goal.* New York: McGraw-Hill. → A paperback edition was published in 1961.

MILLER, NEAL E.; and DOLLARD, JOHN C. 1941 *Social Learning and Imitation.* New Haven: Yale Univ. Press; Oxford Univ. Press.

PAVLOV, IVAN P. (1927) 1960 *Conditioned Reflexes: An Investigation of the Physiological Activity of the Cerebral Cortex.* New York: Dover. → First published as *Lektsii o rabote bol'shikh polusharii golovnogo mozga.*

SUTHERLAND, N. S. 1959 Stimulus Analysing Mechanisms. Volume 2, pages 575–609 in Teddington, England, National Physical Laboratory, *Mechanisation of Thought Processes: Proceedings of a Symposium.* London: H.M. Stationery Office. → This is paper No. 2, session 4A, of the National Physical Laboratory Symposium No. 10. Reprinted in 1961.

THORNDIKE, EDWARD L. (1913) 1921 *Educational Psychology.* Volume 2: The Psychology of Learning. New York: Columbia Univ., Teachers College.

VI
AVOIDANCE LEARNING

In avoidance learning the organism comes to behave in an anticipatory or foresightful manner in order that unpleasant events no longer will occur. It learns to respond to certain cues or danger signals before painful or frightening stimuli can occur, and it performs acts that usually prevent the painful events from occurring. In the following account empirical generalizations are emphasized to demonstrate the wide variety of variables operating in avoidance learning. In some cases these generalizations are not very well established, and so they represent only the current state of affairs and are always subject to change as more experiments are reported. Avoidance learning represents an empirical focus today, and hundreds of experiments each year are completed in this area of science. Empirical findings have clearly outstripped adequate theoretical accounts of the avoidance learning process.

Avoidance training experiments of a scientific sort have, for obvious humanitarian and ethical reasons, been confined mainly to animal subjects. There have been few experiments in which human subjects were studied, and those experiments have yielded results quite similar to those obtained in animal experiments. There is every reason to believe that the variables in control of animal avoidance learning are not very different across mammalian species.

Two different types of training

Active avoidance. Imagine, if you will, a white rat placed by an experimenter (*E*) into a small training box. The floor of the box is an electrifiable grid of metal rods. At a height of 10 inches above the floor and hinged as a shelf to the side of the box is a small platform. The lid of the box is a transparent plastic plate, and above it is suspended a 60-watt lamp. *E* allows his subject *S*, the rat, to explore the box for a few minutes. Then training begins. *E* switches on the light above the rat box for a 30-second period. *S* continues his sniffing and exploring during the switching on and off of the light. *E* repeats the procedure 5 times, noting that *S* does not jump onto the platform. Then *E* switches on the light, waits for 5 seconds, and turns on the power supply which electrifies the metal grid floor of the box and shocks *S*. *S* squeals, rushes about, leaps into the air, and then, 12 seconds after the shock is turned on, jumps onto the platform where there is no shock. As *S* lands, *E* turns off the light. One minute later, the hinged shelf is momentarily lowered, dropping *S* onto the grid again. Then 2 minutes later, a second training trial is begun. The light goes on, and 5 seconds later the shock goes on. The rat leaps onto the platform 4 seconds after the shock goes on.

The rat's performance has improved in two trials of training. We say he is learning to *escape* from shock. After several escape training trials have gone by, *S* eventually will respond directly to the onset of the light, and he will jump onto the platform without the stimulus of shock. This jump is called an *avoidance* response. By this response, *S* *avoids* the shock, and since the light is turned off when he jumps onto the platform, he also *escapes* the light.

S has learned to respond in an anticipatory fashion in such a way that if he jumps quickly at the onset of the light he will never again receive the shock. This type of process is called *active* avoidance learning. *S* is taught *what to do* to minimize pain and distress. Note that he is punished for doing everything else but jumping onto the platform whenever the light goes on. He is, therefore, not being taught anything specific that he should *not do*. In the active avoidance training procedure, the light is usually called the *discriminative stimulus* (S^d), *cue*, or *signal;* the shock is called the *unconditioned stimulus* (*US*). Because the escape responses are instrumental in terminating the shock and the light and because the avoidance responses are instrumental in preventing the shock and terminating the light, they are often called *instrumental* responses. They change the environment in such a way as to make it more acceptable to the subject. They *operate* on the environment and so are often called *operants*.

Passive avoidance. A somewhat different yet very important avoidance training procedure produces *passive* avoidance learning. Passive avoidance training corresponds to our everyday conception of *punishment*. In this procedure *S* is taught specifically *what not to do*, but he is not taught *what to do*.

Imagine now that another white rat is placed by *E* on the platform of the small training box. This *S* is hungry, and *E* has placed a food pellet for him on the grid floor. After some hesitation, *S* scrambles down from the platform and eats the food pellet. *E* then picks *S* up and places him on the platform again. This time *S* jumps down more quickly than he did on the first trial, and he again eats a food pellet. After many trials, *S* shows stable food-getting behavior; he jumps down quickly and uniformly on each training trial. Now *E* can get rid of this instrumental response (jumping off the platform) by means of *passive* avoidance training. *E* electrifies the grid whenever *S* jumps down to get a pellet. Eventually, *S* will stay on the platform rather than jump down. *S* has learned to avoid shock by avoiding specific action. What *S* does when on the platform is *not* being specified by the training procedure, and so *anything* he does, as long as it does not lead him to the grid floor, goes unpunished.

Active and passive avoidance learning can take place under a wide variety of training procedures, and the characteristics of learning depend heavily on the type of procedure *E* uses.

Variants of the two types of training

Active avoidance. Six important variants of the active avoidance procedure warrant discussion.

The method of gradual emergence. By use of the general training conditions described under active avoidance, it can be shown that *S* will learn avoidance responses either very suddenly or very gradually by varying the training techniques. For example, when small movements or reflexive responses are selected by *E* to be the active avoidance responses, learning is slow and tortuous. Forepaw flexion responses in the dog often require several hundred training trials in order to establish them as reliable avoidance responses. The same is true of a tiny toe movement in human *S*s. In contrast, massive movements that change the *S*'s environment are quick to emerge as reliable avoidance responses. Requiring a rat to jump onto a platform, as described above, requiring a dog to jump from one compartment of a box to another, or requiring a human *S* to push a knob a distance of 2 feet—all three are examples of efficient situations for producing sudden and reliable avoidance learning. A way of interpreting these findings is that medium-probability operants make the best avoidance responses, while high-probability, short-latency respondents (reflexes) make the poorest avoidance responses.

A characteristic of some avoidance responses is their persistence. In general, those training conditions leading to efficient learning also lead to a high degree of resistance to extinction. Such responses as the jumping onto a platform described above can persist over hundreds of trials without a shock being administered. This is not likely to be true of responses like forelimb flexion or toe flexion. The persistence of avoidance responses, as an empirical phenomenon, has extensive implications for studies of human neuroses. Long-lasting phobias, obsessive and compulsive behavior, and neurotic defenses of many types can be fruitfully analyzed in terms of the special experimental conditions that established such behavioral rigidity. Sometimes therapeutic treatments are deduced from such analyses. [*See* OBSESSIVE–COMPULSIVE DISORDERS; PHOBIAS.]

Other variables influencing the ease of active avoidance learning and, inversely, the ease of extinction are the S^d–US time interval, the intensity of the *US*, the similarity of the S^d to the *US*, the immediacy of termination of the *US* and the S^d after the performance by *S* of the avoidance response, and the occurrence of events arousing responses that are incompatible with the required avoidance response. Usually, there is an optimum S^d–US interval for each type of avoidance response. If an avoidance response is a long-latency, complex operant, a long S^d–US interval of perhaps 5 to 10 seconds will be optimal. For short-latency, reflexive types of avoidance responses, short S^d–US intervals of around 1 to 2 seconds will be optimal. Usually, for a given type of avoidance response, lengthening the S^d–US interval beyond the optimal interval will facilitate extinction of the response when shock is no longer administered.

Shock intensity complexly influences avoidance learning. There is an optimum intensity for each type of response, and intensities lower or higher than the optimum will retard learning and facilitate extinction. The optimum intensity decreases as the complexity of the avoidance response increases. This is known as the Yerkes–Dodson law. When the S^d is frightening, learning is more rapid than when it is neutral. Thus, a mild shock used as an S^d will facilitate learning, as will a frightening buzzer. A nonfrightening light may be less efficient in controlling stable avoidances. Delaying either the termination of shock following an escape response, or the termination of the S^d following an avoidance response, or both, will retard avoidance learning, and even short delays of about 5 seconds may make it impossible for *S* to learn. Finally, some avoidance responses are incompatible with the innate fear responses of *S* and can interfere with correct responses as fear increases. For example, when *S* is a rat, we have to try to eliminate innate "freezing" reactions that often occur when the S^d becomes fear-arousing as a result of its association in time with the painful *US*. Often a rat will "freeze" when the S^d goes on and thus fail to avoid during the S^d–US time interval. He may escape easily as soon as the shock goes on if the shock is of an appropriate intensity for vigorous behavior arousal. One way of eliminating freezing is to decrease *US* intensity. Another way is to increase the S^d–US interval. Quite often, however, *S* fails to avoid in many experimental situations, and these failures have not yet been analyzed sufficiently by psychologists. Rather, they tend to be ignored as accidents or are attributed to unspecified individual differences. They represent an area of ignorance.

Most successful avoidance learning in the method of gradual emergence is characterized by a high level of fear and emotionality early in learning, when shocks are still being administered, followed by declining emotionality when the avoidance responses become reliable. Along with these correlated events, the topography of the avoidance responses themselves becomes stereotyped. When this stereotypy occurs, extinction is not easy to produce by constant elicitation of the responses.

The method of prior response shaping. In the method of prior response shaping, the *S* is first trained to escape the *US* without a signalizing S^d. After *S* is an expert escaper, the warning signal or S^d is paired with the *US*. Using this method, the avoidance responses are very much like the escape responses. In contrast, the method of gradual emergence often produces avoidance responses different in appearance from the escape responses from which they were derived.

Escape with short S^d–US interval. When the S^d–*US* interval is too short to allow avoidances, except on test trials when the S^d is presented without the *US*, very poor avoiding is produced along with reliable and short-latency escaping. The *S* is usually very fearful and emotionally disturbed.

The method of prior fear conditioning. In the method of prior fear conditioning, the S^d and *US* are paired closely in time on each trial, but there is at first no escape or avoidance response available to *S*. He merely learns to fear the S^d. After many trials, *S* is then allowed to terminate the S^d by means of a response in his repertory. If such a response is emitted in the presence of the S^d, the response is quickly adopted by *S* as a reliable avoidance response. On the other hand, *S* often does not make the required response, and so he never learns. Failures of this type are frequently produced by this method. Extinction of avoidance responses appears to occur more readily by this method than by the method of gradual emergence. This method is sometimes called the "acquired drive" experiment.

The Pavlovian method. In the Pavlovian procedure, *E* presents *S* with an S^d–*US* sequence repeatedly, but *S* cannot do anything either to prevent or to terminate the painful *US*. Instead, the *US* is omitted on test trials, and sometimes the *S* will demonstrate a consistent type of anticipatory or preparatory response pattern. Russian physiologists call this method "motor conditioning." When many test trials are run, we note that the *US* does not occur no matter what anticipatory responses may be evoked by the S^d. Thus, such trials are like avoidance-response trials in other methods. Despite this, very unstable learning occurs. Often the response consists of constantly varying struggling and diffuse emotional expressions.

The Sidman method. In the Sidman procedure, no S^d is used (although one can be used). Instead, the *US* is regularly presented if *S* does not perform a particular response desired by *E*. If *S* does perform the required response, the *US* is delayed for a fixed time interval. The avoidance response thus "buys" shock-free time for *S*. Note that the *US–US* interval can be varied independently of the response–*US* interval. If an S^d is used, it can come anywhere in the *US–US* interval or in the response–*US* interval. This method can produce very stable avoidance responding and high resistance to extinction. There are, however, many individual failures of rats to learn. These failures can be reduced if the avoidance response is capable of terminating the *US*. This method is especially interesting because *S*s often develop stable response rates, with the avoidance responses appearing at regular intervals. The responses appear to be under the control of some type of "internal time mechanism" that serves as an S^d substitute. As long as this mechanism elicits responses at interresponse time intervals less than the response–shock interval, *S* never receives a shock. The method is often viewed as revelatory of the build-up in time of "conditioned anxiety"; whenever the anxiety becomes intolerable during the response–shock interval, *S* makes another response. The similarity of this phenomenon to human compulsive neuroses is often pointed out.

Passive avoidance. Two major variants of the passive avoidance procedure will be discussed.

Punishment methods. There are two general types of punishment techniques. One technique used in the punishment method is illustrated by the general example given above to describe passive avoidance training in the rat. The rat is presented with a painful *US* contingent upon each jump from the platform to the grid floor of the training box.

The second technique, called the secondary aversive stimulus technique, establishes a previously neutral stimulus as an aversive *CS* (conditioned stimulus) by pairing it in time with several presentations of a painful or frightening *US*. When the *CS* evokes an acquired fear or anxiety reaction, called the "conditioned emotional response" (*CER*), the *CS* is then used to punish a specific type of behavior. The example we used above to illustrate passive avoidance learning would have been a secondary aversive stimulus technique if the rat, instead of being shocked for jumping down to the food, had been presented with a *CS* previously paired with shock.

Punishment procedures may be applied in an attempt to eliminate at least five different types of behavior: (1) an *instrumental* response previously established by rewards, illustrated by punishing the rat for jumping off the platform to get food; (2) an *instrumental* response previously established by punishment, illustrated by punishing a shock avoidance response with another frightening stimulus; (3) a *consummatory* response, such as eating, drinking, or copulating; (4) a complex, *instinctive* response pattern, such as nest building in birds; and (5) a simple *reflexive* reaction, such as an eyeblink. The results obtained by punishment procedures differ for each of these five categories.

First, when an instrumental response that has been previously established by rewards is punished, the outcome depends heavily on: (1) *duration* of the punishing stimulus—short-duration punishments that are presented after the response has occurred usually produce temporary suppression of the response and are followed by recovery of the response (sometimes to supernormal levels), while long-duration stimuli often suppress the punished behavior for long time intervals; (2) *intensity* of the punishing stimulus—low-intensity punishing stimuli will suppress behavior temporarily, but the behavior recovers, often to a level more vigorous than that prior to the use of punishment, but high-intensity punishing stimuli will often suppress behavior for long periods of time; (3) *delay* of punishment—the sooner the punishing stimulus is applied after an unwanted response has occurred the more effective will the punishment be, giving us what is known as the "temporal gradient of delay of punishment"; (4) *repeated exposure*—Ss often show some adaptation to repeated punishments, and, therefore, new punishments are often more effective than familiar ones, provided of course that their duration and intensities are equal; (5) *reward–punishment habituation*—if a response is simultaneously rewarded and punished and if the punishment is of low intensity and duration, sometimes the punishment will not only be ineffective in suppressing the response but will also be able to serve as a reward in its own right (this is similar to masochism in neurotic disturbances); (6) existence of a *rewarded alternative*—if alternative response A is punished and alternative B is quickly rewarded, the punishment will be very effective in suppressing A, but when there is no rewarded alternative to A, the response will recover more quickly from the suppressing effects of punishment; (7) *temporal discriminative alternatives*—the housebroken dog learns to urinate under condition A (outdoors) and never to urinate under condition B (indoors), provided that frequent punishment for B is followed quickly in time by no punishment for A (this is often referred to as "impulse control" training); (8) *temporal order* of reward and punishment—when a reward is followed regularly by punishment, the behavior leading to the reward is often suppressed, but if exactly the same behavior is evoked by punishment and then rewarded, the behavior can be strengthened, and S may come to tolerate the punishment or even to seek it out; (9) *species-specific* characteristics—a toy snake can be used to punish behavior in monkeys, but it does not bother a rat, for example; (10) the *resistance to extinction* of the response being punished—responses which would normally be extinguished quickly in the absence of reward will be suppressed more readily by punishment than will responses normally having a high resistance to regular extinction procedures.

Second, when an instrumental response that has been previously established as an active avoidance response is punished, the outcome is hard to predict. Sometimes the response intended by *E* to be suppressed by the punishment is actually energized. Probably this facilitation is produced most reliably when the punishing stimulus is very similar to or the same as that which was used as the *US* in the earlier avoidance training procedure. A good deal of ignorance exists in this field of study.

Third, when a consummatory response is punished, the suppression is very often long-lasting and emotionally disturbing. Punishment seems to be more effective when applied to this type of behavior than it is when used to suppress instrumental responses, for reasons that are at present quite mystifying.

Fourth, when punishment is used to suppress complex, species-specific, instinctive behavior patterns, the results are often confusing. Sometimes displacement occurs; that is, *S* shows behavior characteristics of another behavior pattern. Frightening an animal for courting behavior may induce nest-building behavior or other inappropriate acts.

Finally, little is known of the effects of punishment for specific reflexive behavior. This contingency happens frequently in everyday affairs, as when an involuntary act annoys others, but the phenomenon has not been studied systematically in the laboratory.

The CER method. The *CER* procedure differs from the punishment procedure in a subtle but evidently important way. No specific passive avoidance response is established. Thus, this method is similar to the punishment method. But, in contrast to the punishment method, the *CER* method does not apply a punishment to a specific response. Instead, a frightening, secondary aversive stimulus is added to the general surroundings of *S* for limited periods of time. Often the usual behavior in that environment is depressed in rate, or amplitude, or quickness. A typical example is as follows: a rat is trained to press a lever when he is hungry in order to obtain food pellets. After this lever pressing occurs at a reliable rate, the *CER* procedure is introduced. A previously neutral stimulus is now associated with shock in a special shock box (repeated *CS–US* pairings, with no escape or avoidance possible) and evokes a *CER*. When the *CER* stimulus is presented in the lever box, the lever-pressing rate often decreases. The *CER* stimulus is not presented contingent upon *S*'s lever-pressing response. Rather, it occurs without regard to the behavior being rewarded by food. Despite this, the instrumental behavior is often suppressed. Indeed, the *CER* technique may often produce suppression as effectively as does the punishment method.

One major value of the *CER* procedure has been in the assessment of psychologically active drugs. Often, tranquilizers have been shown to minimize the response suppression attendant on the *CER* stimulus, and the special characteristics of behavior during the suppression period in drugged *S*s can be of value in analyzing the action of the drug. The method has also been used to assess the level of fear controlled by a *CS*, assuming that the more the ongoing, appetitive, and instrumental behavior is suppressed, the more fear arousing is the *CS*. This dependent variable can then be related to events taking place during fear conditioning or to those occurring during avoidance training in which the same *CS* is used. For example, the S^d in avoidance training in situation A may not suppress appetitive behavior in situation B—thus leading to the conclusion that the S^d no longer arouses much fear. This finding has been correlated with observations of declining fear during stereotyped avoidance responding and with the finding that conditioned heart-rate elevation decreases during late phases of successful avoidance responding as the behavior becomes stereotyped. Thus, active and passive avoidance procedures can be combined to yield significant interrelationships between emotional reactions and instrumental responding.

Two of the most pressing questions concerning avoidance learning are theoretical ones. What mechanism produces the first avoidance response? What mechanism reinforces avoidance responses? Here, we are still in the dark. One explanatory scheme is cognitive. It argues that *S* comes to anticipate shock by virtue of S^d–*US* pairings and that *S* comes to know how to terminate shock by virtue of escape responses. Then, by an insightful inference, *S* terminates the S^d by performing an avoidance response. Another explanatory scheme depends heavily on the James–Lange theory of emotion. It argues that the S^d–*US* pairings lead to conditioned fear (*CER*) in the presence of the S^d. When the *CER* is intense enough to be as arousing as the shock itself, then *S* does in the presence of the S^d what he has learned to do in the presence of the shock. He performs the escape response during the S^d–*US* interval, and so he comes to avoid. Avoidance responses remove the S^d, thus reducing the anxiety level, and so avoidances are reinforced by anxiety reduction. Finally, another explanatory scheme depends heavily on proprioceptive feedback arising from skeletal movements. It argues that *S* learns to avoid movements associated with shock, thus leaving *S* to perform only movements not associated with shock. Certain proprioceptive stimulus patterns acquire aversive properties during the escape training phase or, as in the Sidman method, during the phase of learning wherein the *US* is frequently presented. Avoidance of aversive proprioceptive stimulus patterns gradually "shapes up" the avoidance behavior. At the moment there seems to be no decisive evidence that would allow us to choose among the major explanatory alternatives. However, many current experiments are being aimed at the theoretical systems to probe their strengths and weaknesses in predicting important variables and phenomena.

RICHARD L. SOLOMON

[*Other relevant material may be found in* ANXIETY; DEFENSE MECHANISMS; ELECTROCONVULSIVE SHOCK; STRESS.]

BIBLIOGRAPHY

BRADY, JOSEPH V.; and HUNT, HOWARD F. 1955 An Experimental Approach to the Analysis of Emotional Behavior. *Journal of Psychology* 40:313–324.

DINSMOOR, JAMES A. 1954 Punishment: I. The Avoidance Hypothesis. *Psychological Review* 61:34–46.

ESTES, WILLIAM K. 1944 An Experimental Study of Punishment. *Psychological Monographs* 57, no. 3.

FERSTER, CHARLES B. 1958 Control of Behavior in Chimpanzees and Pigeons by Time Out From Positive Reinforcement. *Psychological Monographs* 72, no. 8.

GIBSON, ELEANOR J. 1952 The Role of Shock in Reinforcement. *Journal of Comparative and Physiological Psychology* 45:18–30.

GWINN, GORDON T. 1949 The Effects of Punishment on Acts Motivated by Fear. *Journal of Experimental Psychology* 39:260–269.

HOLZ, WILLIAM C.; and AZRIN, NATHAN H. 1961 Discriminative Properties of Punishment. *Journal of the Experimental Analysis of Behavior* 4:225–232.

KAMIN, LEON J. 1959 The Delay of Punishment Gradient. *Journal of Comparative and Physiological Psychology* 52:434–437.

KAMIN, LEON J.; BRIMER, C. J.; and BLACK, A. H. 1963 Conditioned Suppression as a Monitor of Fear of the CS in the Course of Avoidance Training. *Journal of Comparative and Physiological Psychology* 56:497–501.

KEEHN, J. D. 1959 On the Non-classical Nature of Avoidance Behavior. *American Journal of Psychology* 72:243–247.

LICHTENSTEIN, P. E. 1950 Studies of Anxiety: I. The Production of Feeding Inhibition in Dogs. *Journal of Comparative and Physiological Psychology* 43:16–29.

MASSERMAN, JULES H.; and PECHTEL, CURTIS 1953 Neuroses in Monkeys: A Preliminary Report of Experimental Observations. New York Academy of Sciences, *Annals* 56:253–265.

MILLER, NEAL E. 1960 Learning Resistance to Pain and Fear: Effects of Overlearning, Exposure, and Rewarded Exposure in Context. *Journal of Experimental Psychology* 60:137–145.

MOWRER, ORVAL H. 1960 *Learning Theory and Behavior*. New York: Wiley.

SHEFFIELD, FRED D. 1948 Avoidance Training and the Contiguity Principle. *Journal of Comparative and Physiological Psychology* 41:165–177.

SIDMAN, MURRAY 1953 Avoidance Conditioning With Brief Shock and No Exteroceptive Warning Signal. *Science* 118:157–158.

SOLOMON, RICHARD L. 1964 Punishment. *American Psychologist* 19:239–253.

SOLOMON, RICHARD L.; and BRUSH, ELINOR S. 1956 Experimentally Derived Conceptions of Anxiety and Aversion. Volume 4, pages 212–305 in Marshall R. Jones (editor), *Nebraska Symposium on Motivation*. Lincoln: Univ. of Nebraska Press.

SOLOMON, RICHARD L.; KAMIN, LEON J.; and WYNNE, LYMAN C. 1953 Traumatic Avoidance Learning: The Outcome of Several Extinction Procedures With Dogs. *Journal of Abnormal and Social Psychology* 48:291–302.

SOLOMON, RICHARD L.; and WYNNE, LYMAN C. 1954 Traumatic Avoidance Learning: The Principles of Anxiety Conservation and Partial Irreversibility. *Psychological Review* 61:353–385.

TURNER, LUCILLE H.; and SOLOMON, RICHARD L. 1962 Human Traumatic Avoidance Learning. *Psychological Monographs* 76, no. 40.

YERKES, R. M.; and DODSON, J. D. 1908 Relation of Strength of Stimulus to Rapidity of Habit Formation. *Journal of Comparative Neurology and Psychology* 18: 459–482.

VII
NEUROPHYSIOLOGICAL ASPECTS

How the brain changes as a result of an organism's experiences, how it maintains its altered state through time, and how it influences future behavior in a modified but systematic manner are some of the most intriguing mysteries facing modern biology. Direct experimental study of this problem started shortly after the turn of the century, a time when substantial neuroanatomical knowledge had already accumulated, although the electrical techniques that evolved into those of modern day neurophysiology were then in their simplest, primitive stages. By the 1920s, two pioneering behavioral scientists, Lashley (1929) in the United States and Pavlov (1927) in Russia, were well along with their classical studies of learned behavior in animals and were attempting to relate their findings to the function of the brain.

Lashley, studying instrumental behavior in rats with experimentally created brain lesions, and Pavlov, theorizing about brain function from his studies of conditioned behavior in dogs, both focused their attention on the uppermost layer of the brain—the neocortex. The cortex, as it is more commonly called, gained early attention because of its greater size in man and the other higher animals. This anatomical fact suggested that the cortex might be particularly concerned with such complex neural processes as learning. It was not until the 1950s that investigations concerned with the physiology of the process of learning started to disengage themselves from the belief that the neocortex is exclusively responsible for the fixation of experience that permits new behavior patterns to be acquired.

From the standpoint of the nervous system, experience is some temporospatial pattern of transitory electrical activity in the nerve cells (neurons) of the brain. The basic neurophysiological question, then, is how can this evanescent neural activity modify the circuits of the brain so that they remain uniquely altered after the initiating physiological event has vanished. Any final understanding of this process requires answers to a number of interrelated and interlocking questions. First of all, how are the stimulus events that are to be learned electrophysiologically coded for introduction into the nervous system and transmission throughout the complex pathways of the brain? In what parts of the brain are the relevant coded messages integrated and stored for future use? How do electrical neural events, arising transitorily during initial learning, manage to induce a patterned and relatively permanent change in the brain, a change that is presumed to be chemical or structural? Finally, what is the physical nature of this semipermanent brain cell change, which can persist in neural tissue for years despite the active metabolic turnover in neurons, and how does this cellular change selectively modify the brain's subsequent functioning so that the organism's behavior can be an adaptive synthesis of past experience and current environmental demands? These are questions that have dominated research in the neurophysiology of learning.

Electrophysiological aspects

The nerve impulse. Any speculation about the physical basis of learning has of course been heavily influenced by the existing state of neurophysiological knowledge. The conspicuous electrical event that was first observed in the early studies of peripheral nerves was the nerve impulse, action potential, or spike, as it is variously called. This bioelectric activity is crucial in neural functioning and can be recorded from the stringlike extensions (fibers or axons) of all nerve cells. It is the nerve impulse, propagated along nerve fibers as the result of rapidly shifting chemical changes, that allows one neuron to influence the activity of other neurons with which it is in contact. At these points of contact (synapses), it is now known that the traveling nerve impulse induces the secretion of minute amounts of biochemical compounds (neurotransmitters) that, in turn, can influence the electrophysiological state of the next neuron in line. In this way, a nerve impulse can be initiated in the adjoining nerve cell.

It was early recognized that the basic nerve impulse was an all-or-none process. If the activation of a nerve cell reaches a given threshold, a spike of a predetermined size will be propagated at a given speed along the cell's axon. Further, once such a spike has developed and subsided (in several milliseconds at most), either in the initially stimulated neuron or in adjoining neurons via synaptic connections, there ensues a sequence of physiological changes (after potentials) that systematically influences the "firing" threshold of the cells for a brief time period. Over the span of about a tenth of a second, it is first more difficult and then easier to initiate a second spike. These were the primary facts of high-speed neural function that were available to behavioral scientists of the 1930s and early 1940s as they contemplated the overwhelming plasticity and long-term memory of the complex, multisynaptic brain.

Reverberating circuits and synaptic change. The first attempts to define the neurophysiological mechanisms that might provide the basis of learning were developed from these simple basics of brain function. Many more facts about the functioning of the central nervous system are now available, but the broad outlines of the generally accepted neurophysiological mechanism of learning have not changed in principle. It is still thought that nerve impulses, bombarding some combination of synapses in a pattern that is somehow appropriate to the task to be learned, bring about a change in the functional characteristics of the synapses and, thereafter, that particular pattern of nerve impulses will induce the response sequence that occurred during the original learning. Reverberating neuron circuits are thought capable of supplying the time necessary for the electrical activity to lead to some form of permanent synaptic change that would account for the long-term behavioral changes that can follow a learning experience. Possibly the best-known statement of this point of view was that of the Canadian psychologist Donald O. Hebb, who suggested that the permanent neural changes might be based on the structural growth of appropriate axon endings at the synapse (Hebb 1949). His specific suggestion has yet to be proved or, for that matter, disproved.

Brain waves and electroencephalography. With improved electronic techniques that permit the direct study of brain activity, a variety of characteristics of brain function have been discovered. Neurophysiologists, for example, are looking with increased interest at the variety of slowly shifting electrical potentials that can be recorded throughout the central nervous system. Whereas the small spike of a primary nerve impulse, for example, can subside in less than a millisecond, these larger potentials can oscillate as slowly as several times a second. There are also even slower shifts of D.C. voltage, lasting seconds or even minutes. Certain of these slow potentials oscillate spontaneously even in the resting or sleeping brain. These are the brain waves seen in the well-known electroencephalogram (EEG). Although independently discovered in lower animals by R. Caton in England and A. Beck in Poland in 1875 and 1890, respectively, the EEG did not receive widespread attention until 1935, when the German psychiatrist Hans Berger reported that the same slow electrical rhythms were also evident in the human brain. The EEG remained largely a clinical tool, little used in behavioral research, until some of its neural and behavioral correlates started to be better understood because of the classic study made by the Italian neurophysiologist Giuseppe Moruzzi and his American collaborator, H. W. Magoun, in 1949. These investigators, together with many that followed them, showed that the EEG could serve as an indicator of arousal (or the lack of it) in the cortex as a whole or in restricted centers within the brain (Magoun 1958). As we shall see, behavioral scientists have subsequently started to use the EEG to evaluate the level of activity in various brain centers during different stages of learning.

Horizontal versus vertical organization

Aside from the more specific question of which particular structures within the brain may be necessary for learning, there is the prior but related question concerning the general flow of brain activities during complex behavior in general and learning in particular. General attitudes concerning this matter have shifted considerably during the half century or so since the beginning of direct laboratory study of brain mechanisms and learning.

Horizontal organization—association areas. The earliest point of view, and still the most common oversimplification of the facts, placed almost exclusive faith in the importance of the multilayered neocortex, which is conveniently located at the top of the central nervous system. As we have seen, the pattern of the phylogenetic development of the brain conspicuously pointed to the increased size of the cortex as the most likely source of control for such higher mental processes as learning. In its most traditional form, this corticocentric frame of reference also emphasized the horizontal organization of the neural substrate of learning, which is presumed to take place in the transcortical pathways that connect the sensory and motor areas of the neocortex. The so-called association areas, located between the sensory-input and motor-output areas, were assumed to supply pools of synapses where changes in transmission characteristics could afford new patterns of transcortical connections that would provide for the changing patterns of learned behavior. The highly influential Pavlovian theory of learning was like this in general form, the transcortical effects being visualized as irradiating neural influences between sensory and motor areas in the cortex.

Vertical organization. Along with the recent growth of interest in the role of subcortical structures in all varieties of behavior, there has developed a newer point of view, which emphasizes the vertical organization of the brain and the recurrent interactions between neural centers at all levels of the central nervous system, including the cortex. Possibly the most convincing evidence of the importance of extracortical pathways in learning has been reported from studies of animal conditioning in which the training was managed exclusively with direct electrical stimulation of sensory and motor areas in the cortex. After suitable pairing of sensory stimulation (*CS*) and motor stimulation (*US*), activation of the sensory electrode by itself led to the limb movement (now the conditioned response) that had occurred originally only when the motor electrode was stimulated (Doty 1961). Cutting transcortical connections between the two electrodes did not eliminate the conditioned response. That transcortical pathways are not necessary for such a newly developed neural circuit was further confirmed by studies in which similar electrophysiological conditioning was accomplished even though the sensory electrode was in one cerebral hemisphere, the motor electrode in the other, and the interhemispheric connections (corpus callosum) completely severed (Doty & Giurgea 1961). While the cortex is certainly involved, in one way or another, in a variety of kinds of learned behavior, it appears to be substantially dependent on vertical interconnections that exist at all levels of the central nervous system.

Geography of the learning process

The recording of spontaneous EEG rhythms during simple learning situations, usually one form or another of classical conditioning, has shown that various parts of the brain are differentially active throughout successive stages of learning.

Alpha rhythm and alpha blocking. The use of brain wave changes to trace the shifts of brain activity during learning was initiated by an accidental observation of the French neurophysiologists G. Durup and A. Fessard in 1935. These investigators were studying the EEG alpha rhythm, a moderately slow wave form that can be recorded from the visual cortex of a resting animal during periods of reduced visual stimulation. This slow brain wave is arrested (alpha blocking) and replaced with a faster, lower voltage pattern following the onset of a bright light. This faster EEG pattern is what has since come to be known as the arousal pattern and, as discussed previously, is thought to indicate increased activity in the brain area concerned. Durup and Fessard were photographing examples of alpha blocking when they noticed that the click of the camera shutter started to induce the blocking even before the bright light was presented. They recognized that the click, by virtue of being paired with the light, had acquired the ability to influence the alpha waves. The conditioning-like properties of these paired sensory events attracted the attention of investigators throughout the world, and, with many modifications and elaborations, the study of spontaneous EEG changes during various conditioning procedures has since received widespread study (Morell 1961*a*, pp. 444–451).

Localization of the arousal pattern. Early in conditioning, an EEG arousal pattern is seen widely throughout all levels of the brain. With further pairing of the conditioned and unconditioned stimuli, however, these generalized electrical changes start receding to areas, particularly cortical ones, that are related to the unconditioned stimulus and, finally, to areas concerned with the conditioned response. Since the arousal type of EEG is taken to mean that patterned or potentially integrating neural activity is taking place, widespread circuits apparently are active, or available, for use early in learning; as learning progresses, the cells and pathways involved become more localized along with the differentiation and refinement of the conditioned response.

Slow wave changes. During the early period of diffuse brain activity, a subcortical EEG arousal pattern has been particularly noted in the reticular formation and limbic system and is thought by some to be related to attentional and motivational priming of the central nervous system, preparatory to learning, when the organism finds itself facing a novel situation. Two Hungarian investigators, K. Lissák and A. Grastyán, reported (1960) a specific type of slow wave change (theta) in the subcortical hippocampus during learning. They believe that this change, which arises during early training and subsides shortly before conditioning is complete, represents a suppression mechanism that damps distracting activity, both neural and behavioral, during the time that the learned response is being developed. When conditioning is complete, the EEG arousal pattern is seen most consistently in those connections between the thalamus and the neocortex that are topographically appropriate to the final learned response.

"Tagged" brain-wave changes. Comparable findings have been reported recently from a similar, although slightly more elegant, experimental procedure in which tagged brain-wave changes, as they are called, are recorded during conditioning. In this type of study, a flashing or flickering light is used as the conditioned stimulus. If the flicker rate is not too divergent from the 10-per-second rate of the brain's alpha rhythm, EEG oscillations at about the same rate as the conditioned stimulus can be detected as they shift among different brain structures at various stages of the learning. While such a procedure was first reported about twenty years ago by M. N. Livanov and K. Poliakov in connection with a standard conditioning study, it has recently been put to more elaborate experimental use by the American research team of E. R. John and K. F. Killam (1960). These investigators recorded such frequency-specific EEG changes, as they are called, while cats were learning a differential discrimination problem in which two lights, flashing at different rates, were the positive and the negative stimulus. There were thus two frequency-specific changes to be sought in the brain wave record. The cats had to learn to perform an avoidance response to one flicker rate but not to the other. Under these conditions, the general sequence in which the tagged EEG changes appear in different brain structures during training was much the same as already discussed above. John and Killam, however, discovered one new phenomenon of considerable interest. They found that when the flicker rate of the stimulus, and thus the tagged EEG rhythm seen in the visual cortex, matched the frequency of the EEG pattern recorded from certain subcortical structures, a correct response was more apt to be made. Discordance between the EEG frequencies at these two sites, on the other hand, was commonly correlated with either an error of omission or commission. It is as though the way the animal "reads" the stimulus or, for one reason or another, is "set" to respond to it is represented by the subcortical frequency, while the temporal events in the visual cortex are tied, of course, to the actual flickering stimulus being presented. The importance of an organism's expectancies or response set in conditioning situations is not a new idea (Sperry 1955), although it is presently receiving renewed consideration.

Evaluation of evidence. While these bioelectric events indicate something about the widely shifting focuses of neural activity that occur during the course of even a simple learning experience, there is no compelling reason to believe that EEG changes of the type just discussed, no matter how meaningful their localization may appear to be, represent electrical changes that are necessarily associated with stimulus recognition or the eventual fixation of memory. For example, when EEG arousal occurs in its immediate vicinity, an individual cortical neuron may show increased transmission of nerve impulses, decreased transmission, or neither (Jasper et al. 1960). While conditioning systematically brings about statistical changes in the activities of single cells in particular brain areas, an invariant relation between the occurrence of a conditioned response and activity in a specific neuron thus far has not been reported. It may be, of course, that the performance of even a specific learned response by a particular subject does not always involve precisely the same individual neurons.

The hippocampus and memory. Although much that we have considered indicates the diffuse nature of the neural substrate of learned behavior, scientists in several disciplines have become interested recently in the possibility that one subcortical structure, the hippocampus, contributes uniquely to the memory process. The hippocampus is in the rhinencephalon, the primitive portion of the forebrain. Recent interest in the hippocampus arose as the result of memory losses observed in human patients who had sustained damage to this brain structure as the result of either surgery or disease (Milner 1959). Such findings in man are particularly convincing since, in contrast to lower animals, one can be more confident that the deficit is in memory per se and not in some performance capacity that simply leaves the animal subject unable to demonstrate what has in fact been remembered. These neurological patients show a striking loss of recent memory, particularly if they are distracted while trying to memorize or have had no chance for repetitious practice. Retrograde amnesia for as long as a year prior to hippocampal damage is also seen in people with this type of brain lesion.

While no details are known about the manner in which the hippocampus might contribute to memory, one group of investigators discovered that electrophysiological activity in the hippocampal area of the cat did differ with correct and incorrect choices in a maze (Adey et al. 1960). The majority of studies employing hippocampally damaged animals, however, have failed to find the expected loss in learning ability when the operated subjects were measured on discrimination tasks or conditioned avoidance tests. It could be, however, that the failure to demonstrate a memory loss in animals with hippocampal lesions is due to the fact that tests of animal learning are typically the type that measure learning across a series of practice trials. This is the kind of repetitious training that, based on human studies at least, might minimize evidence of the surgically produced memory deficit. This explanation receives some support from the fact that mice, with chemically induced hippocampal damage, showed dramatic losses of recent memory when they were tested with a very simple learning task that they could have mastered in only a few practice trials (Flexner et al. 1963).

Mechanisms of memory storage

A variety of behavioral experiments support the notion that the early and late stages of the process of memory fixation are probably based on different physiological mechanisms (Gerard 1961). There is an early stage, which lasts for less than an hour and is easily disrupted by a variety of physiological insults to the brain, such as lowering its oxygen supply, cooling it, or bombarding it with electric current (Glickman 1961). Thereafter, the memory trace, or engram as it is sometimes called, becomes more rigidly fixed and cannot be disassembled so easily. As already discussed, these facts are usually taken to mean that the first evanescent steps in memory fixation are electrical in nature and then subsequently become anchored in some biochemical or structural alteration, most commonly presumed to be at the synapse.

Aside from these two well-recognized stages of memory fixation, sometimes called the dynamic and static stages of memory, there may be two additional critical time periods in the sequence of physical changes that underlie memory fixation. For one thing, chemical interference in the hippocampal area can eliminate a newly learned habit as long as a week after the original learning but not thereafter (Flexner et al. 1963). Finally, generalized brain trauma, such as a concussion, can disrupt the memory for events extending back for months and years prior to the injury. Yet, memory commonly remains intact for the stretch of years preceding this period of retrograde amnesia. There thus could be at least four successive steps in the process of memory storage: (1) an acute process, initiated at the time of learning and completed before an hour has passed; (2) a semiacute second process, at least in the hippocampal area, requiring some number of days; (3) a slowly developing third stage, completed over a period of months or years; and (4) a final, static stage of memory, which is not commonly open to disruption by either experimental or clinical influences. As Deutsch (1962) has pointed out, however, it is not clear that all these stages necessarily involve different physiological processes; they could represent, in part, different degrees of development in some common process. Finally, since it is not uncommon for the memories lost in retrograde amnesia to be retrieved when the patient recovers, it may well be that long-term memories are never really eliminated by generalized trauma to the brain but are only made unavailable for current use.

Dominant focus and postpolarization memory. In 1953, V. S. Rusinov discovered an electrophysiological procedure by which he was able to produce new temporary connections between sensory and motor cells in the cortex. He applied a mild anodal current to a small area of motor cortex in the rabbit and found, during this period of polarization, that a previously indifferent sensory stimulus, such as a novel tone, induced a discrete skeletal movement that was related topographically to the part of the motor area that was polarized. The polarizing current is thought to lower the excitability threshold of the motor cells that it influences and thus permit sensory activity in widespread brain areas to "drain," so to speak, through the polarized area and initiate motor activity appropriate to the polarized motor cells. Using a term originally suggested by A. A. Ukhtomskii in 1926, such an area of elevated excitability is called a dominant focus.

If a dominant focus is induced in the part of the motor area that, for example, initiates response pattern *A* (e.g., right foreleg flexion), the focus will help maintain previous conditioning if the conditioned response was pattern *A*. On the other hand, a conditioned response of pattern *B* is suppressed by the induction of dominant focus *A*. Such findings suggest that something like a dominant focus might be involved during the early stages of conditioning. The effect of a dominant focus persists for about thirty minutes after the anodal current is removed (postpolarization period), which matches reasonably well the time course of the early dynamic stage of memory as it is reported by some workers.

Frank Morrell (1961*b*), an American investigator, studied the activity of individual motor cells within the area of a dominant focus and started to analyze the fiber pathways, which are critical for this interesting phenomenon. He demonstrated, further, a degree of specificity for the 30-minute "memory" in the area of a previous dominant focus; the motor area can be activated during this postpolarization period only by a stimulus that has been presented during the period of polarization. Both transcortical and subcortical pathways were found to be necessary for the activation of the dominant focus by an effective stimulus event. Finally, perseverating activity of nerve impulses was not detected during the postpolarization period in the area of the dominant focus. This is contrary to what might have been expected if reverberating circuits of nerve impulses were responsible for the short-term maintenance of memory in the area. If the short-term phase of memory really is electrical in nature, this finding suggests that the process might be based on persistent graded potentials rather than on propagated nerve impulses. It is still possible, of course, that the early memory process is based on some other fragile biological process, which is possibly chemical and which is not apparent to the recording electrode of the neurophysiologist.

RNA and long-term memory. The physical basis of long-term memory is no better understood than the case of recent memory. As we have seen, the most popular idea is that some permanent change of a structural, or at least chemical, nature takes place at the synapses, and thereafter the routing or patterning of nerve impulse transmission is altered. No specific structural change at a synapse, associated with learning, has ever been demonstrated experimentally. In recent years, however, there has been growing interest in the possibility that changes in the ribonucleic acid (RNA) molecules of the nerve cell might be responsible for structural changes, at the synapse or elsewhere, that could then serve the purpose of long-term memory. This possibility, suggested by Joseph J. Katz and Ward C. Halstead in 1950, now has received some indirect experimental support, although definite proof of such a mechanism is still lacking (Dingman & Sporn 1964). The general idea is that patterns of neural activity, impinging on a particular nerve cell, would shape the structure of complex RNA molecules within the cell. The RNA, as a regulator of protein synthesis in the cell, would thereafter perpetuate chemically coded protein molecules, thus rendering the cell, for example, maximally sensitive to the temporospatial pattern of neural activity that had originally induced the structural change in the RNA (Hydén 1962). How electrical neural activity could modify the structural pattern of RNA or how structurally coded RNA might then influence the synaptic characteristics of its neuron is still entirely speculative. Nevertheless, changes both in the concentration of RNA and in the specific chemical structure of RNA have been demonstrated in specific brain centers that have been subjected to high levels of neural activity or, more interestingly, have been involved in the learning of new patterns of behavior.

ROBERT A. MCCLEARY

[*Other relevant material may be found in* NERVOUS SYSTEM; PSYCHOLOGY, *article on* PHYSIOLOGICAL PSYCHOLOGY; SENSES, *article on* CENTRAL MECHANISMS; STIMULATION DRIVES; *and in the biographies of* FLOURENS *and* LASHLEY.]

BIBLIOGRAPHY

ADEY, W. R.; DUNLOP, C. W.; and HENDRIX, C. E. 1960 Hippocampal Slow Waves: Distribution and Phase Relationships in the Course of Approach Learning. *A.M.A. Archives of Neurology* 3:74–90.

DEUTSCH, J. A. 1962 Higher Nervous Function: The Physiological Bases of Memory. *Annual Review of Physiology* 24:259–286.

DINGMAN, WESLEY; and SPORN, MICHAEL B. 1964 Molecular Theories of Memory. *Science* New Series 144:26–29.

DOTY, R. W. 1961 Conditioned Reflexes Formed and Evoked by Brain Stimulation. Pages 397–412 in Daniel E. Sheer (editor), *Electrical Stimulation of the Brain: An Interdisciplinary Survey of Neurobehavioral Integrative Systems.* Austin: Univ. of Texas Press.

DOTY, R. W.; and GIURGEA, C. 1961 Conditioned Reflexes Established by Coupling Electrical Excitation of Two Cortical Areas. Pages 133–151 in Council for International Organizations of Medical Sciences, *Brain Mechanisms and Learning: A Symposium.* Oxford: Blackwell; Springfield, Ill.: Thomas.

FLEXNER, JOSEFA B.; FLEXNER, L. B.; and STELLAR, E. 1963 Memory in Mice as Affected by Intracerebral Puromycin. *Science* New Series 141:57–59.

GERARD, R. W. 1961 The Fixation of Experience. Pages 21–35 in Council for International Organizations of Medical Sciences, *Brain Mechanisms and Learning: A Symposium.* Oxford: Blackwell; Springfield, Ill.: Thomas.

GLICKMAN, STEPHEN E. 1961 Perseverative Neural Processes and Consolidation of the Memory Trace. *Psychological Bulletin* 58:218–233.

HEBB, DONALD O. 1949 *The Organization of Behavior: A Neuropsychological Theory*. New York: Wiley.

HYDÉN, H. 1962 A Molecular Basis of Neuron–Glia Interaction. Pages 55–69 in Francis O. Schmitt (editor), *Macromolecular Specificity and Biological Memory*. Cambridge, Mass.: M.I.T. Press.

JASPER, H. H.; RICCI, G.; and DOANE, B. 1960 Microelectrode Analysis of Cortical Cell Discharge During Avoidance Conditioning in the Monkey. *Electroencephalography and Clinical Neurophysiology* (Supplement 13): 137–155.

JOHN, E. R.; and KILLAM, K. F. 1960 Studies of Electrical Activity of Brain During Differential Conditioning in Cats. Pages 138–148 in Society of Biological Psychiatry, *Recent Advances in Biological Psychiatry*. New York: Grune.

LASHLEY, KARL S. 1929 *Brain Mechanisms and Intelligence: A Quantitative Study of Injuries to the Brain*. Univ. of Chicago Press.

LISSÁK, K.; and GRASTYÁN, E. 1960 The Changes of Hippocampal Electrical Activity During Conditioning. *Electroencephalography and Clinical Neurophysiology* (Supplement 13): 271–277.

MAGOUN, HORACE W. (1958) 1963 *The Waking Brain*. 2d ed. Springfield, Ill.: Thomas.

MILNER, BRENDA 1959 The Memory Defect in Bilateral Hippocampal Lesions. *Psychiatric Research Reports* 11:43–58.

MORRELL, FRANK 1961*a* Electrophysiological Contributions to the Neural Basis of Learning. *Physiological Reviews* 41:443–494.

MORRELL, FRANK 1961*b* Effect of Anodal Polarization on the Firing Pattern of Single Cortical Cells. New York Academy of Sciences, *Annals* 92:860–876.

PAVLOV, IVAN P. (1927) 1960 *Conditioned Reflexes: An Investigation of the Physiological Activity of the Cerebral Cortex*. New York: Dover. → First published as *Lektsii o rabote bol'shikh polusharii golovnogo mozga*.

SPERRY, R. W. 1955 On the Neural Basis of the Conditioned Response. *British Journal of Animal Behaviour* 3:41–44.

VIII
VERBAL LEARNING

Research in the area of verbal learning is concerned with the experimental analysis of the acquisition and retention of verbal habits. The major emphasis in both experimentation and theory construction has been on rote learning, that is, the mastery of verbal materials in a prescribed arrangement. Studies of rote learning have provided the central body of empirical facts, analytic tools, and theoretical concepts dealing with verbal learning.

Historical developments

Early experimental studies. The first systematic experimental investigation of rote learning was carried out by the German psychologist Hermann Ebbinghaus, whose treatise *Memory* (1885) occupies an undisputed position as a classic in the field. Ebbinghaus set out to show that higher mental processes such as memory could be studied under strictly controlled experimental conditions and that they could be precisely measured. His conception of the processes of learning and memory was heavily influenced by the British empiricist doctrine of association by contiguity. In a monumental series of experiments, which were carried out with himself as the only subject, Ebbinghaus introduced procedures and methods of analysis which provided the point of departure for the subsequent development of the entire area of verbal learning. The large majority of Ebbinghaus' experiments were concerned with the acquisition and retention of series of discrete verbal units. In an effort to develop standardized materials that could be used interchangeably in a large variety of learning tasks, Ebbinghaus devised the nonsense syllable as the unit to be used in the construction of verbal series. (A nonsense syllable is a consonant–vowel–consonant combination devoid of dictionary meaning.) While such materials turned out to be far from equal in difficulty, the introduction of these materials was the first step toward the standardization and classification of the verbal units used in studies of rote learning. To provide a uniform standard of attainment with respect to which differences among tasks and conditions of practice could be evaluated, Ebbinghaus established the concept of a criterion of performance, for example, the errorless reproduction of an entire series. The number of repetitions or the amount of time required to reach this criterion could then be related to such variables as the length of the series or the temporal distribution of practice periods. A fixed criterion of performance also made it possible to evaluate retention after the cessation of practice; specifically, Ebbinghaus measured the amount of retention in terms of the amount of time saved in relearning a series relative to the time required for original acquisition. Using these methods of analysis, Ebbinghaus established a number of basic principles of acquisition and retention. His findings included evidence that the amount of practice time per item increases with the length of the series and that a strong positive relationship exists between the number of repetitions of a task and the degree of retention. Another famous product of Ebbinghaus' investigations is the classical curve of retention, which is characterized by a steep initial drop in retention immediately upon the end of learning, followed by more gradual losses thereafter.

Ebbinghaus' approach was soon adopted in other laboratories, and additional techniques for the study of rote verbal learning were developed rapidly. Among the early German investigators, G. E. Müller deserves special mention. In Müller's laboratory the first systematic studies of the processes of interference in retention were carried out. He was also responsible for many refinements in experimental technique, such as the use of an automatic exposure device for the presentation of learning materials (the prototype of the contemporary memory drum). Within less than two decades after the appearance of Ebbinghaus' pioneer investigations, the study of rote verbal learning had become a standard procedure in laboratories of experimental psychology.

American functionalists. In the United States the development of the area of verbal learning is historically tied to the functionalist movement, which helped to make the experimental study of learning a central concern of contemporary experimental psychology and which emphasized the application of psychological principles to problems of education. Although those working in the functionalist tradition put the discovery of empirical laws ahead of formal theory construction, there was a strong predilection for the analysis of the learning process in terms of principles of association. A discussion of the influence of the functionalist movement on the psychology of learning is provided by Hilgard ([1948] 1956, chapter 10). The associationist orientation permitted a ready translation of theoretical concepts and experimental operations into the language of stimulus–response psychology, which became widely accepted under the influence of behaviorism. Thus, the prevalent approach to problems of verbal learning became that of an associationistic stimulus–response psychology. With some important exceptions to be noted later, there was no strong commitment to formal theories of behavior.

A pragmatic orientation is apparent in the writings of the experimental psychologists who had a major influence on the development of the field of human learning. An exposition of the prevailing theoretical approach was given in Edward S. Robinson's *Association Theory Today* (1932). The broad definition of *association* as "the establishment of functional relations among psychological activities and states in the course of individual experience" (p. 7) was designed to accommodate the pursuit of a wide range of empirical questions within a common associationist framework. Robinson stressed the multiplicity of the laws of association and the necessity of reformulating such laws as functional relations between these multiple antecedent conditions on the one hand and measures of associative strength on the other.

The emphasis on functional relations led to the formulation of a program of *dimensional analysis* as a guide to experimental investigation. The essential objectives of such a program were first outlined by McGeoch (1936); a later systematic exposition of this approach may be found in an important article by Melton (1941). Learning situations vary continuously with respect to a manifold of descriptive characteristics or dimensions, and learning tasks can be ordered along these dimensions to provide the framework for the exploration of quantitative functional relations. Among the major axes of reference is the verbal–motor dimension; purely verbal tasks define one extreme and predominantly motor ones the other. A second dimension is defined by the degree to which the subject must discover the correct response and ranges from the acquisition of rote series to problem-solving situations. A third dimension refers to the degree to which mastery of a task requires a response to relational rather than to absolute properties of the stimuli.

Influence of conditioning theory. While dimensional analysis has provided a thread of continuity in empirical research, there have been important attempts to conceptualize the facts of verbal learning within the framework of general psychological theory. During the period between the two world wars an important landmark was the publication of the *Mathematico–Deductive Theory of Rote Learning* by Clark L. Hull and his associates (1940). In this analysis, the basic phenomena of serial rote learning are deduced from a set of postulates that were derived largely from the theory of classical conditioning. The effective strength of the associations linking the members of a verbal series was conceived as representing the balance of excitatory and inhibitory potentials, in accord with the dual-process interpretation of Pavlovian conditioning. With the aid of assumptions about the conditions governing the growth and decline of excitatory and inhibitory tendencies, specific quantitative predictions were made concerning the shape of the serial-position curve (level of performance as a function of the position of an item in a series), the effects of the temporal distribution of practice trials, and other properties of serial learning. Some of these predictions were confirmed experimentally; however, the scope of the theory is limited, and its influence has been declining with the rapid accumulation of empirical findings that fall outside its boundary conditions.

Another systematic application of principles of classical conditioning to verbal learning was proposed by Eleanor J. Gibson (1940). Gibson's analysis centered on the concepts of stimulus generalization and differentiation, which were adopted from conditioning theory. Stimulus generalization refers to the tendency for the conditioned response to be elicited by stimuli similar to the conditioned stimulus. The amount of generalization describes a gradient, that is, it is directly related to the degree of similarity between the training stimulus and the test stimulus. Differentiation refers to the reduction of generalization as a consequence of reinforcement of responses to the training stimulus and nonreinforcement of responses to other test stimuli. According to Gibson's analysis, speed of acquisition is determined by the rate at which differentiation among the stimulus items is achieved during practice. Thus, speed of learning should vary inversely with the degree of interstimulus similarity. In general, the experimental facts are consistent with this prediction. The theory also predicts, in accordance with principles of conditioning, that generalization tendencies recover spontaneously over time, with a consequent loss of differentiation. It follows that long-term retention, like speed of acquisition, should vary inversely with interstimulus similarity. However, this prediction has consistently failed to be confirmed. This lack of support for one of the critical deductions from the theory necessarily calls into question the validity of the basic postulates. The analytic power of the theory is also limited by the failure to consider the role of response generalization along with that of stimulus generalization. A comprehensive evaluation of the theory, which has exerted considerable influence on research in verbal learning ever since its publication, is provided by Underwood (1961).

Gestalt psychology. Although there has been wide agreement among investigators of verbal learning on the usefulness of associationist concepts in the formulation of empirical questions and theoretical issues, such agreement has been by no means general. A quite different approach is represented by exponents of the gestalt school of psychology, whose work in verbal learning was directed primarily at the validation of general principles of their theory. An exposition of this approach may be found in Koffka (1935, chapters 10–13). From the point of view of gestalt theory, learning and retention are governed by the same principles of organization that govern the formation of perceptual units. In the acquisition of verbal tasks, relationships such as similarity and proximity between the component items are considered critical in determining the readiness with which the organization required for mastery is achieved. The organizations developed during learning are, in turn, assumed to be preserved in the nervous system as memory traces, whose subsequent development is likewise governed by principles of organization. Re-exposure to part of an organized pattern activates the trace of the pattern and thus permits the recall of other component parts. Association is, therefore, interpreted as a special case of organization. Experimental studies initiated by gestalt psychologists have sought to demonstrate the applicability to verbal learning and memory of principles of perceptual organization. An example is provided by the studies of the effects of perceptual isolation. When a unique item is embedded in an otherwise homogeneous series, the unique or "isolated" item is recalled better than the average member of the homogeneous series. According to gestalt theory, the traces of the homogeneous items suffer assimilation and lose their identity, whereas the trace of the unique item remains distinctive and accessible. This dependence of recall on the relationship between items is interpreted as analogous to the salience of a perceptual figure against a homogeneous background. Alternative interpretations have been offered, for example, the differential susceptibility of isolated and homogeneous items to generalization. The conditions determining the isolation effect are still under investigation. This example illustrates the fact that crucial experiments permitting a clear-cut decision between gestalt and associationist interpretations have often been difficult to design. [*See* GESTALT THEORY.]

Recent developments. The two decades since the end of World War II have witnessed a rapid growth of activity in the field of verbal learning, with several new developments adding greatly to the diversity of experimental methods and theoretical concerns. Perhaps the most important trend is the convergence on common problems of research in psycholinguistics and in verbal learning. This development is reflected in the increased emphasis on the role of natural language habits in the analysis of verbal learning. A large amount of work has centered on the assessment of the effects on acquisition and retention of the associative hierarchies that are developed through linguistic usage. The method of free association (in which the individual is required to respond to each stimulus word with the first other word that comes to mind) and related normative techniques have been used to determine the structure of verbal associations characteristic of a given speech community. Learning tasks constructed on the basis of such norms are then used to evaluate the influence of pre-existing associative patterns on the formation of new verbal habits. Within this problem area a focus of special concern has been the study of mediational processes, that is, of the ways in which pre-existing associations serve to facilitate the establishment of connections between initially unrelated terms (see Jenkins 1963). The influence of contemporary linguistic analysis is also reflected in the growing number of investigations concerned with the role of grammatical habits in the acquisition and performance of verbal tasks. Largely under the influence of George A. Miller (e.g., 1962), much of the recent work has been directed at the exploration of the psychological processes suggested by the principles of transformational grammar.

In the experimental study of memory processes, several influences have converged to produce an upsurge of interest in short-term retention. Any a priori distinction between short-term and long-term memory is, of course, arbitrary; in practice the operational difference is between retention intervals of the order of seconds or minutes on the one hand and of hours, days, or weeks on the other. Rapid developments in the theory of communication and in the study of man–machine interaction have brought to the fore the question of man's capacity to process and to store continuously changing inputs of information; for example, in the performance of monitoring tasks incoming information has to be retained for critical periods of time to permit effective action. Thus, the study of short-term memory is an integral part of the analysis of the nervous system as a limited-capacity channel for the transmission of information. This general approach is well represented by the work of Broadbent (1958), who has introduced a number of influential new techniques for the measurement of short-term memory. The availability of the analytic methods of information theory has, of course, been of considerable value in bringing order to measures of immediate memory that are obtained with a wide variety of materials. Short-term memory also has continuing systematic significance for theories of the physiological basis of memory. A central concept of several influential theories is that of a transitory memory trace, which is assumed to fade or decay rapidly unless it is restored by repetition or rehearsal. The assumption of a short-lived immediate trace is characteristically supplemented by the postulation of a separate and distinct mechanism of long-term storage. A considerable amount of effort is being devoted to experimental tests of the dual-process conception. A systematic question on which agreement does not appear to be in sight as yet is whether the principles governing short-term and long-term memory are continuous or discontinuous. [*See* FORGETTING.]

Recent developments in verbal learning, as in several other special fields of psychology, include the construction of mathematical models for the description of circumscribed sets of data. Among the most influential approaches have been the stochastic models that treat acquisition as a probabilistic process. Very briefly, it is assumed that on any given learning trial (*a*) the organism samples the environmental events which constitute the stimulus situation; (*b*) all the stimulus elements sampled become connected to the response occurring contiguously with them; and (*c*) such association by contiguity occurs in an all-or-none fashion, that is, reaches maximal strength on a single trial. The probability of occurrence of the response increases as more and more stimulus elements are connected with it. While the most important applications of these models have been to discrimination learning and conditioning, the models have also been used for the acquisition of verbal associations as well. A point of major theoretical significance is the assumption made by stochastic models that association by contiguity occurs in an all-or-none fashion. If verbal stimuli function as single elements, it follows that associations are not built up gradually as a function of practice but, instead, change in probability from zero to one after a single occurrence. The assumption that associations may vary continuously in strength and are built up gradually through practice has been explicit or implicit in associationist interpretations of verbal learning. This assumption, which has been designated as the incremental hypothesis, has been challenged in recent years by exponents of the all-or-none position. Experimental tests to decide between these alternative conceptions have focused on the question of whether there is a growth in associative strength on practice trials prior to the first correct response. While it is fair to say that the evidence thus far has favored the incremental position, the issue cannot be regarded as finally settled (for a review see Postman 1963). The emergence of this controversial issue illustrates the recent trend toward the consideration of hypotheses about the nature of association and memory in the context of studies of verbal learning. [*See* MODELS, MATHEMATICAL.]

A brief survey of some representative experimental methods and findings in the area of verbal learning now follows. The evidence is grouped under the headings of acquisition, transfer of training, and retention. Detailed reviews and discussions of the relevant literature may be found in McGeoch (1942) and in the collections of papers edited by Cofer (Conference on Verbal Learning . . . 1961), Cofer and Musgrave (Conference on Verbal Learning . . . 1963), and Melton (Symposium . . . 1964).

Acquisition

It will be convenient to consider the analysis of the process of acquisition with reference to specific experimental procedures, each of which focuses on a different type of verbal performance.

Paired-associate learning. In the paired-associate method, the subject's task is to learn a prescribed response to each of a list of stimulus terms (much as in vocabulary learning). The characteristics of the stimulus and response terms can be varied independently. An important analytic advantage of the method is, therefore, that it permits the assessment of stimulus and response functions in the acquisition of associations. Progress in this task will depend on the extent to which the following requirements are met: (*a*) the stimulus terms are differentiated from each other; (*b*) the prescribed responses are available as integrated units in the subject's repertoire; and (*c*) stable associative connections are developed between the appropriate stimulus and response terms.

It is apparent that the requirements of the task with respect to the stimulus and response terms are not the same. Whereas the response terms must be recalled as prescribed, the stimulus terms need only be discriminated from each other and recognized as the occasions for the performance of the appropriate responses. The subject is free, therefore, to attend to only those characteristics of the stimulus which are minimally essential for the placement of the correct responses, that is, the subject can practice "stimulus selection." Recognition of this fact has led to the distinction between nominal and functional stimuli (Underwood 1963). The nominal stimulus refers to stimulus terms as specified by the experimenter for presentation to the subject; the functional stimulus refers to those characteristics of the stimulus which actually function as cues for the learner. The available evidence indicates that stimulus selection does, in fact, occur within the limits permitted by the requirements of the task; for example, when the stimulus is a compound composed of elements which vary in meaningfulness, there is a strong tendency to select the more meaningful element as the functional cue.

The analysis of the components of the paired-associate task makes it useful to conceive of the total acquisition period as divided into two successive stages, namely, a response-learning stage and an associative stage (Underwood & Schulz 1960, pp. 92–94). During the former, the prescribed responses are established as integrated units available for performance; during the latter, the responses are linked to the appropriate stimuli. If the responses are items in the subject's pre-experimental repertoire, for example, familiar words, the response-learning stage reduces to a response-recall stage during which the subject learns to restrict his responses to the units in the list. The two stages certainly overlap in time. The distinction is, however, useful in the analysis of the conditions which influence performance in paired-associate learning.

Of the task variables which influence speed of acquisition, two will be singled out on the basis of the magnitude and reliability of their effects. These are (*a*) meaningfulness and (*b*) intralist similarity. In current usage, the term "meaningfulness" refers to several scaled characteristics of verbal units, such as the probability of a unit evoking an association within a limited period of time, the number of different associations evoked by the unit, etc. These indices tend to be closely related to each other and to the frequency of occurrence of the unit in the language (for a survey of measures of meaningfulness see Underwood & Schulz 1960). Intralist similarity may be either formal or semantic. Formal similarity is defined by the degree to which overlapping elements, such as letters, are used in the construction of different units included in a list; this variable is characteristically manipulated in lists composed of nonsense items. Semantic similiarity refers to the degree of synonymity and applies to lists composed of words.

Meaningfulness. The speed of paired-associate learning varies widely as a function of meaningfulness, but the relationship is much more pronounced when responses rather than stimuli are varied in meaningfulness (Underwood & Schulz 1960). From the point of view of the two-stage analysis of acquisition, it is clear that meaningfulness decisively influences the response-learning stage: the more fully a response unit conforms to prior linguistic usage the more readily it enters into association with new stimuli. There are two factors which may serve to reduce the effectiveness of the variable of stimulus meaningfulness: (*a*) stimulus selection may counteract the differences that exist in the nominal stimuli; (*b*) increases in stimulus meaningfulness may facilitate not only the formation of associative linkages with the prescribed responses but also the development of inappropriate associations with other responses. Thus, associative facilitation and interference may increase concurrently as a function of stimulus meaningfulness.

Intralist similarity. The effects of intralist similarity also differ depending on whether stimuli or responses are manipulated. In general, speed of acquisition varies inversely with the degree of similarity of the stimulus terms. As stimuli become less discriminable, the associative phase of learning is retarded. Variations in response similarity, on the other hand, have only small effects on the rate of learning, except for units of low meaningfulness. The usual absence of a large effect is attributable to the balance between two opposed influences: As responses become more similar, the amount of response learning is reduced; at the same time, individual responses become less discriminable from each other and the associative phase is prolonged.

Serial learning. Serial-learning tasks require the reproduction of a series of items in a prescribed order. The experimental procedure typically consists of the paced presentation of the successive members of the series, with the subject required to anticipate each item before it appears. Speed of acquisition varies reliably as a function of the ordinal position of the item in the series. The initial items are usually acquired first, the terminal items next, and the central items last. Thus, when percentage of correct responses during learning is plotted against serial position, a typical bow-shaped curve is obtained. Classical interpretations of serial learning (for example, that of Hull mentioned earlier) were based on the assumption that an individual member of the series serves a dual function during acquisition: it is the response to the immediately preceding item and the stimulus for the immediately following one. The bow-shaped serial position curve was attributed to interferences from incorrect associations among nonadjacent members of the series. Given certain assumptions about the number and strength of such remote associations, it can be shown that the total amount of interference should first increase and then decrease as a function of serial position. Recent experiments have, however, served to call the classical conception of serial learning into question. Some of the critical evidence comes from experiments in which the subject first learns a serial list and immediately thereafter a paired-associate list in which the pairs are composed of adjacent members of the serial list. If the mastery of the serial list depends on the establishment of a chain of sequential associations, pronounced facilitation should be found in the acquisition of the paired-associate list. A conclusive test of this prediction has proved difficult. Performance on the critical transfer task appears to be complexly determined and sensitive to procedural variations. The difficulties encountered by the classical hypothesis have raised questions about the nature of the functional stimulus in serial learning; for example, it has been suggested that each member of the series is associated to its ordinal position in the series rather than to the preceding item. This problem is receiving considerable experimental attention at the present time (Underwood 1963).

Free learning. The two methods discussed above require the establishment of prescribed links between verbal units, and, thus, they focus on the development of sequential associations. By contrast, the method of free learning yields information about the ordering and reproduction of verbal units when no sequential constraints are placed upon the subject. Under this method, a list of items, such as words, is presented to the subject, and he is then permitted to reproduce them in whatever order they occur to him (free recall). The method is useful in the investigation of pre-experimental habits of classifying verbal units and of the process of recall (for general discussions see Deese 1961; Postman 1964). The major determinants of the amount of free recall are (*a*) the total learning time prior to the test of recall and (*b*) the number and strength of the pre-experimental associations between the units in the list. The total learning time is the product of the list and the presentation time per item. The number of items recalled after a single exposure of a list remains approximately invariant with total learning time, that is, the number of items recalled increases with the length of the list and with the amount of study time per item, but a decrease in the value of one of these variables can be compensated for by an increase in the other. Thus, it is the total amount of time available for practice which is critical rather than the length of the task or the exposure rate per se. With length and rate held constant, the number of words recalled varies with the average degree of associative connection between the items in the list (as determined, for example, by the method of free association). In the absence of external constraints, recall performance reflects pre-existing associations and relations between the component units of the list. As free learning continues beyond a single presentation and recall, stable groupings of items are likely to be formed which are carried over from one test of recall to the next.

Transfer of training

Transfer of training refers to the influence of prior learning on the acquisition of new habits. The transfer effects may be positive or negative, depending on whether the earlier training facilitates or inhibits the mastery of the later task. In studies of verbal learning it has been conventional to distinguish between specific and general transfer effects. Specific transfer effects are those attributable to known similarity relations between successive tasks; general transfer effects represent the development of skills which cannot be ascribed to known similarity relations between tasks. General effects will be considered first.

General effects. When unrelated verbal lists are learned in the laboratory, the speed of acquisition typically increases, sharply at first and more gradually thereafter. Such progressive practice effects have been demonstrated for both paired-associate and serial learning. When learning sessions are held daily, the gains in performance are considerably greater within sessions than from one session to the next. A common interpretation of this finding is that the gains within a session are largely a matter of warm-up, that is, the development of postural adjustments, rhythms of responding, and other components of a set appropriate to the learning task. Such adjustments to the requirements of the task may be expected to be lost once the subject leaves the experimental situation. The changes which persist from one session to the next are attributed to "learning-to-learn," that is, the acquisition of higher-order habits or modes of attack which are relatively stable and persistent. According to this analysis, warm-up both develops and declines more rapidly than do the habits which constitute learning-to-learn. The possibility cannot be ruled out, however, that perceptual–motor adjustments are conditioned to the experimental situation and that components of learning-to-learn are forgotten.

Specific effects. The principles of specific transfer have been investigated primarily as a function of the similarity relations between the stimulus terms and/or the response terms of successive tasks. One general principle is that the amount of transfer, whether positive or negative, increases as the stimulus terms in successive tasks become more similar; stimulus identity is, therefore, the condition of maximal transfer. At a given level of similarity, the sign (positive or negative) and degree of transfer vary with the similarity, or strength of pre-existing associative connection, between successive responses. A large array of experimental findings may be subsumed under the following general principle: as the responses become increasingly dissimilar, the transfer effects shift from positive to negative. Thus, positive transfer is obtained when the successive responses learned to identical or similar stimuli are associatively related; negative transfer results when new unrelated responses are learned to old stimuli. These principles are, however, subject to modification by other factors, such as the readiness with which successive tasks can be differentiated from each other. For example, when old stimuli and old responses are re-paired, there is considerable negative transfer; even though the repertoire of responses remains the same, the identity of both stimuli and responses makes differentiation between successive tasks extremely difficult (for a discussion of methods and designs in the study of transfer see McGeoch 1942).

Retention

Retention refers to the persistence over time of changes produced by practice. It is apparent that retention is an integral component of acquisition; a habit can be mastered only if there is retention from one practice trial to the next. In the present context, however, the term retention refers to measurements of performance which are made after the end of a period of formal practice. The operational distinction between measures of acquisition and of retention is a convenient and, indeed, an essential one for investigation of the conditions of forgetting. The amount of retention is, of course, always inferred from specific measures of performance; the absolute level of performance will vary with the specific method of testing. Thus, after a given amount of practice, tests of recognition usually yield higher retention scores than do tests of recall, although the degree of discrepancy may vary widely as a function of the specific conditions of recall and recognition.

The basic empirical fact which theories of retention have sought to account for is the progressive decline in performance that occurs as a function of time after the end of practice. The position now held most widely attributes forgetting to the interference that develops between successively learned habits. Two major types of interference are distinguished, namely, retroactive inhibition and proactive inhibition. Retroactive inhibition refers to the interference produced by the acquisition of new habits between the end of practice and the test of retention; proactive inhibition occurs when earlier habits interfere with the retention of a more recent task. In both cases, the amount of interference varies with the similarity relations between successive tasks; specifically, the amount of interference is governed by the same conditions of intertask similarity as is negative transfer. Thus, negative transfer in acquisition, retroactive inhibition, and proactive inhibition are complementary manifestations of habit interference. Retroactive and proactive inhibition differ with respect to the development of interference effects over time. Whereas retroactive inhibition is present to its full extent immediately after acquisition of the interfering task, proactive inhibition develops gradually over time. Several specific mechanisms responsible for the observed interference effects have been identified experimentally. These include (*a*) the unlearning, in the sense of reduced availability, of old associations during the acquisition of new ones; (*b*) competition between incompatible responses at the time of recall which may cause performance to be blocked or a dominant error to displace a correct response; and (*c*) failure to differentiate between the members of alternative response systems at the time of recall (for a review of interference theory see Postman 1961).

The principles of retroactive and proactive inhibition have been established in experimental situations in which the conditions of interference can be fully controlled. Interference theory assumes that the same principles apply to forgetting outside the laboratory. For example, the forgetting of a verbal task would be attributed to interference from other verbal habits acquired both prior and subsequent to that task. Proactive inhibition is likely to play a larger role than retroactive inhibition to the extent that the number and strength of prior habits exceed those of subsequent habits.

Regardless of theoretical interpretation, certain facts about the long-term retention of verbal tasks are well supported by the experimental evidence. The single most important determinant of the amount of long-term retention is the degree of original learning, with resistance to forgetting a direct function of the degree of overlearning. It is essential, therefore, to hold the degree of original learning constant whenever the influence of other variables, such as meaningfulness or intratask similarity, on retention is to be evaluated. The evidence available thus far shows that the effects of such variables are minor relative to the sheer degree of original learning. The practical implication is that overlearning provides the most certain means of insuring the long-term stability of verbal habits.

LEO POSTMAN

[*See also* FORGETTING; LANGUAGE; *and the biographies of* EBBINGHAUS; HULL; MÜLLER, GEORG ELIAS.]

BIBLIOGRAPHY

BROADBENT, DONALD E. 1958 *Perception and Communication.* Oxford: Pergamon.

CONFERENCE ON VERBAL LEARNING AND VERBAL BEHAVIOR, NEW YORK UNIVERSITY, *1959* 1961 *Verbal Learning and Verbal Behavior: Proceedings.* Edited by Charles N. Cofer. New York: McGraw-Hill.

CONFERENCE ON VERBAL LEARNING AND VERBAL BEHAVIOR, SECOND, ARDSLEY-ON-HUDSON, N.Y., *1961* 1963 *Verbal Behavior and Learning; Problems and Processes: Proceedings.* Edited by Charles N. Cofer and Barbara S. Musgrave. New York: McGraw-Hill.

DEESE, JAMES 1961 From the Isolated Verbal Unit to Connected Discourse. Pages 11–31 in Conference on Verbal Learning and Verbal Behavior, New York University, 1959, *Verbal Learning and Verbal Behavior: Proceedings.* Edited by Charles N. Cofer. New York: McGraw-Hill.

EBBINGHAUS, HERMANN (1885) 1913 *Memory: A Contribution to Experimental Psychology.* New York: Columbia Univ., Teachers College. → First published as *Über das Gedächtnis.* A paperback edition was published in 1964 by Dover.

ESTES, WILLIAM K. 1959 The Statistical Approach to Learning Theory. Volume 2, pages 380–491 in Sigmund Koch (editor), *Psychology: A Study of a Science.* New York: McGraw-Hill.

GIBSON, ELEANOR J. 1940 A Systematic Application of the Concepts of Generalization and Differentiation to Verbal Learning. *Psychological Review* 47:196–229.

HILGARD, ERNEST R. (1948) 1956 *Theories of Learning.* 2d ed. New York: Appleton.

HULL, CLARK L. et al. 1940 *Mathematico–Deductive Theory of Rote Learning: A Study in Scientific Methodology.* New Haven: Yale Univ. Press; Oxford Univ. Press.

JENKINS, JAMES J. 1963 Mediated Associations: Paradigms and Situations. Pages 210–245 in Conference on Verbal Learning and Verbal Behavior, Second, Ardsley-on-Hudson, N.Y., 1961, *Verbal Behavior and Learning; Problems and Processes: Proceedings.* Edited by Charles N. Cofer and Barbara S. Musgrave. New York: McGraw-Hill.

KOFFKA, KURT 1935 *Principles of Gestalt Psychology.* New York: Harcourt.

MCGEOCH, JOHN A. 1936 The Vertical Dimensions of Mind. *Psychological Review* 43:107–129.

MCGEOCH, JOHN A. (1942) 1952 *The Psychology of Human Learning.* 2d ed., rev. New York: Longmans.

MELTON, ARTHUR W. 1941 Learning. Pages 667–686 in Walter S. Monroe (editor), *Encyclopedia of Educational Research.* New York: Macmillan.

MILLER, GEORGE A. 1962 Some Psychological Studies of Grammar. *American Psychologist* 17:748–762.

POSTMAN, LEO 1961 The Present Status of Interference Theory. Pages 152–179 in Conference on Verbal Learning and Verbal Behavior, New York University,

1959, *Verbal Learning and Verbal Behavior: Proceedings.* New York: McGraw-Hill.

POSTMAN, LEO 1963 One-trial Learning. Pages 295–335 in Conference on Verbal Learning and Verbal Behavior, Second, Ardsley-on-Hudson, N.Y., 1961, *Verbal Behavior and Learning; Problems and Processes: Proceedings.* Edited by Charles N. Cofer and Barbara S. Musgrave. New York: McGraw-Hill.

POSTMAN, LEO 1964 Short-term Memory and Incidental Learning. Pages 145–201 in Symposium on the Psychology of Human Learning, University of Michigan, 1962, *Categories of Human Learning.* Edited by Arthur W. Melton. New York: Academic Press.

ROBINSON, EDWARD S. 1932 *Association Theory Today.* New York: Century.

SYMPOSIUM ON THE PSYCHOLOGY OF HUMAN LEARNING, UNIVERSITY OF MICHIGAN, *1962* 1964 *Categories of Human Learning.* Edited by Arthur W. Melton. New York: Academic Press.

UNDERWOOD, BENTON J. 1961 An Evaluation of the Gibson Theory of Verbal Learning. Pages 197–223 in Conference on Verbal Learning and Verbal Behavior, New York University, 1959, *Verbal Learning and Verbal Behavior: Proceedings.* Edited by Charles N. Cofer. New York: McGraw-Hill.

UNDERWOOD, BENTON J. 1963 Stimulus Selection in Verbal Learning. Pages 33–75 in Conference on Verbal Learning and Verbal Behavior, Second, Ardsley-on-Hudson, N.Y., 1961, *Verbal Behavior and Learning; Problems and Processes: Proceedings.* Edited by Charles N. Cofer and Barbara S. Musgrave. New York: McGraw-Hill.

UNDERWOOD, BENTON J.; and SCHULZ, RUDOLPH W. 1960 *Meaningfulness and Verbal Learning.* Philadelphia: Lippincott.

IX
TRANSFER

The phrase "transfer of learning," or "transfer of training," refers to a class of phenomena that are aftereffects of learning. When some particular performance has been learned by an individual, the capability established by that learning affects to some extent other activities of the individual. The effects of the learning are said to transfer to these other activities. Having learned some performance, the individual may thereby be enabled to exhibit some additional, different performance that he could not do prior to learning. As more commonly used, transfer of training means that the individual is able to learn something else more readily than he could prior to the original learning (positive transfer) or that he is able to learn something else less readily than he could before the original learning (negative transfer).

Transfer of learning, since it is virtually always present as a learning effect, may reasonably be considered an essential characteristic of the learning process. Accordingly, it may be shown to play a role in a wide variety of human activities, including the learning of language, social customs, values, and attitudes and the acquisition of the human skills and knowledge that underlie practically all types of vocational activity. Transfer of learning is of particular importance in formal education. In the opinion of many educators, education should have transfer of learning, or "transferability of knowledge," as a recognized goal. It is generally agreed that the assessment of outcomes of education and training should include measures of transfer in addition to more direct measures of learning.

In studying the phenomenon of transfer of learning, investigators have employed a wide variety of situations and techniques. The work of experimental psychologists includes the exploration of such questions as (1) the degree of transfer resulting from the establishment of conditioned responses; (2) the specificity and limitations to transfer in the learning of simple perceptual and motor acts; (3) the occurrence of transfer between learned actions performed by different body members, such as the hand and foot; (4) the extent of bilateral transfer, as between actions performed by the left and right hands; (5) the occurrence of positive and negative transfer (called interference) in connection with the learning of verbal associates and sequences; (6) the positive transfer to a variety of specific novel situations resulting from the learning of principles; (7) the acquisition of a capability for transfer to novel discrimination problems in monkeys and human beings; and (8) the relation of transfer to the mediating effects of language in children. An interesting line of investigation has been undertaken by neurophysiologists in determining the conditions of transfer of training in animals with "split brains."

Educational aspects. In the field of educational research, studies have been concerned with the broad question of transfer of learning among the component subjects and topics that make up the school curriculum. Older studies arose from controversies over the doctrine of formal discipline, which held that certain subjects of the curriculum, such as Latin, geometry, and logic, derived a great part of their value from the general (that is, transferable) discipline they imparted to the mind, thus facilitating the learning of other subjects (Thorndike 1924). While this doctrine is probably quite true in the sense that certain capabilities acquired in school are much more widely transferable than others, the rationale for the choice of particular subjects was not a convincing one. At any rate, educational studies in the older tradition were concerned with such questions as whether transfer of training could be measured from the study of Latin to the study of English or from that of geometry to other fields necessitating the use of logical thinking.

More modern studies of educational transfer have concerned themselves with such questions as the extent to which certain kinds of within-subject learning transfer positively to advanced topics, such as the concept of the numberline to later mathematical topics, the discrimination of language sounds to the learning of foreign language utterances, etc. Additionally, there has been concern with the possibilities of negative transfer between the learning of such activities as the formal statements of verbal definitions and the later learning of advanced mathematical principles and between the learning of letter sounds and the acquisition of reading skill. Finally, there is an increasing interest in the exploration of the possibility of designing instruction to develop such highly transferable individual characteristics as thinking strategies, curiosity, and even creativity.

Observing and measuring transfer

The simplest observations of transfer of learning occur in the following ways. The individual is known to have learned a new performance, such as spelling the word *nation* in response to the oral direction, "Spell nation." It may now be found that the same child is able to learn to spell such words as *motion* and *lotion* much more rapidly than he learned to spell *nation*. The inference is that the child learns to spell *motion* more rapidly than he would have if he had not first learned to spell *nation*. Besides the specific outcome of the original learning, the performance of spelling *nation*, there has been another aftereffect of learning: some residual capability, which shows itself in the speeding up of the learning to spell a different word. A different example, illustrating negative transfer, is the following. An individual has moved to a new location and must learn two new telephone numbers, those of his office and his home. One is 643-2795, and the other is 297-6534. He has learned single telephone numbers previously, without a great deal of difficulty. But he now finds that he makes many errors in trying to learn these two numbers, tending to substitute one portion of one number for another portion of the other number. Over a period of time, he finds that, in his experience, learning these two new numbers turns out to be more than twice as difficult as learning any one number has been. There appears to be interference between the two learning tasks; in other words, the inference is made that the learning of one number produces a negative transfer effect, which slows down the attainment of recalling the other number.

Design of transfer experiments. While neither of these sequences of observation and inference is unreasonable, it is apparent that certain variables are uncontrolled, and this generates a requirement for a more painstaking method of observing transfer in an experimental sense. Returning to the example of learning to spell, it is clear that for any given individual we do not really know how long it should take him to learn to spell either *nation* or *motion* because we do not know where learning begins. Possibly some peculiarity of his past learning makes *nation* a difficult word and *motion* an easy one. Accordingly, an experimental design for the measurement of transfer typically includes a pretest to measure the initial capabilities of the individual before learning begins. Still another possibility must be considered: perhaps the increase of facility at the second task (spelling *motion*) is engendered partly by increased motivation, partly by a "set" to learn, or partly by "warm-up" factors (Thune 1950), rather than by the specific effects of learning the first task (spelling *nation*). As a consequence, it is usually considered necessary to include in a transfer experiment a control condition for this set of "general" factors.

The typical schema for experimental study of transfer that results from these control requirements is one that uses two groups of individuals, either assumed or shown to be equivalent at the beginning of learning. Table 1 provides an example.

Table 1

Transfer group	*Control group*
1. Takes pretest on task 2	1. Takes pretest on task 2
2. Learns task 1	2. Learns a task of a sort very different from tasks 1 and 2 but requiring the same amount of time as task 1
3. Learns task 2	3. Learns task 2

When this design is used, an average difference in the ease of learning (often, the time to learn) of task 2 in the two groups is taken to be an indication of "specific" transfer of training from the learning of task 1 to the learning of task 2. This and other experimental designs for the study of transfer are discussed by Murdock (1957).

Quantification. The amount of transfer of learning is usually expressed as a percentage (Gagné et al. 1948). Should it be found that a second performance is learned no more readily than if the learning of a first performance had never occurred, transfer is said to be zero, or 0 per cent. If the second performance is found to be fully learned after the first performance has been learned, transfer is 100 per cent. Amounts between these extremes are, of course, often found. It is also possible to express negative transfer in this way; if a second performance takes half again as long to learn following initial learning of a first performance, the amount of transfer can be expressed as −50 per cent. The use of percentages in expressing amount of transfer is, however, largely a matter of convenience and has no particular systematic significance for an understanding of the phenomenon.

Conditions of positive and negative transfer

The occurrence of transfer of training depends, by definition, on the occurrence of previous learning. For certain performances, such as the learning of a set of verbal associates, the evidence indicates that the amount of positive transfer obtained is directly related to the amount of initial learning (Gagné & Foster 1949; Mandler & Heinemann 1956). As for negative transfer, a somewhat more complex relationship has been found to hold: the amount of interference exhibited in the second task increases as the amount of practice on the initial task is increased to some intermediate amount (McGeoch 1952, pp. 335–339). As practice of the initial task continues, however, the interference with the second task decreases and may under some conditions come to yield positive transfer (Mandler 1954).

Effects of similarity. As a general rule, the amount of transfer (positive or negative) is influenced by the similarity of the performance initially learned to the second performance in which the occurrence of transfer is observed. For example, when a conditioned response is established to a tone of 1,000 cycles, the amount of positive transfer exhibited to tones differing in pitch from this original stimulus bears a direct relation to the degree of physical similarity of the second tone to the original one (Hovland 1937). According to Gibson's study (1941), when the two performances are such that negative transfer is found, the amount of such interference increases with the degree of similarity between the stimuli of the first and second tasks. There is an apparent paradox to these findings, whose resolution seems to depend upon a careful definition of what aspects of the two performances are being compared in similarity. According to Osgood (1949), the prediction of the direction of transfer (positive or negative) depends upon the differential specification of the stimuli of the two tasks and of their responses. A brief and partial summary of Osgood's conclusions may be given as follows. When tasks 1 and 2 contain identical responses, transfer is increasingly positive as the similarity of the stimuli of the two tasks increases. When tasks 1 and 2 contain identical stimuli, transfer is increasingly negative as the similarity of the responses of the two tasks decreases.

Despite the clarifying analyses that have been made, it is nevertheless apparent at the present time that the relation of transfer to the similarity of learned performances remains a perplexing and essentially unsolved problem. Two practical situations may serve as bench marks in consideration of what has yet to be understood about this relationship. (1) An individual first learns to drive a standard-shift automobile with the gearshift attached to the floor. A later model car comes equipped with the same type of transmission but with the gearshift attached to the steering column, so that first gear is now down rather than back, second gear is now up rather than forward and so on. Under these circumstances of apparent difference, the two tasks would nevertheless be judged as similar by almost any driver, and in fact the amount of positive transfer is close to 100 per cent. (2) The second situation is one in which a later model car comes equipped with a four-speed transmission; the gearshift, which is on the floor, must be pushed forward for first gear, backward for second gear, and so on. The situation in the second task is not only dissimilar; it may also be judged to have in it certain elements of reversal relative to the first task. It is a common experience that a considerable amount of negative transfer occurs under these conditions. Reversal of stimulus–response relationships has also been shown in laboratory tasks to produce large amounts of negative transfer (Lewis & Shephard 1950).

Mediational processes. Other limitations of the similarity principle in its present state of development are also shown by studies in which the performance acquired depends upon the learning of a mediational process.

Concept formation. The studies of Kendler and Kendler (1961) have shown that the performance of seven-year-old children who are required to learn a reversal of a discrimination task is markedly superior to the performance of four-year-olds on the same reversed task. These findings suggest that transfer occurs to the second task, which is dissimilar to the original task to the extent of requiring an opposite choice (the choice of a white square as opposed to a black one), because the older children are able to provide an implicit verbal mediator (such as "the opposite"); whereas the amount of transfer for the younger children is very small because they are unable to do this. Logically related are Harlow's studies of learning in monkeys (1949). These animals, over many practice periods, were able to acquire the capability of choosing "the odd one" of three objects, even though the particular objects used may have been highly dissimilar in physical appearance to those used during the original learning.

Acquisition of principles. The importance of mediational processes for transfer of training is also illustrated by a number of studies concerned with transfer of principles. Principles, whether verbally stated or not, relate classes of stimuli to classes of performance; accordingly, they remove the control of performance from the specific stimuli of the situation. If a principle is learned in connection with some particular performance, then it is to be expected that this principle will make possible broad transfer to an entire class of problem situations. In connection with card-trick and matchstick problems, as well as with other tasks, Katona (1940) showed that the acquiring of principles led to high degrees of transfer to classes of problems that differed from those of original learning in physical appearance. In contrast, learning to solve the original problems without acquiring such principles resulted in only small amounts of transfer to new problems. One meaning of "teaching for transfer" in educational settings appears to be the encouragement of principle learning as opposed to rote learning on the part of pupils.

Mechanisms of transfer

Although referred to by a single class name, it is fairly certain that the various phenomena called transfer of training represent several different kinds of events. The differences among them are to be found in the specific conditions that generate them and, consequently, in the kinds of mechanisms that may be inferred to account for them.

Stimulus generalization. When a conditioned response is established to a signaling stimulus, it is found that the same response, diminished in frequency or strength, is given to other stimuli differing from the initial one along some physical dimension. This finding, the phenomenon of stimulus generalization, has been obtained many times, and the previously cited results of Hovland (1937) are typical. The underlying mechanism in this case appears to be a fairly dependable characteristic of the functioning central nervous system. The effects of stimulation on the nervous system are not highly specific but are generalized. The amount of this generalization may be markedly reduced by further conditioning contrasting stimulation that is positive in its effects with stimulation that is negative, a procedure referred to as discrimination training.

Transfer in associative learning. An association of words like *ready–joyful* or *small–klein* is frequently described by psychologists as an *S–R* (stimulus–response) association, in which the first member of the pair is called the stimulus member; through learning, this first member comes to elicit the second, or response, member. This form of learning has an extensive literature of its own that cannot be thoroughly summarized here (see McGeoch 1952; Underwood 1964). The following conclusions, which come from these investigations, however, have particular relevance to the phenomenon of transfer of training and to suggested underlying mechanisms.

One of these conclusions is that under many conditions, positive transfer occurs in the learning of verbal associates when previous learning "predifferentiates" the stimulus members (Gibson 1940; Gannon & Noble 1961). A second finding is that positive transfer is also a common occurrence when the response members of the paired associates have been made familiar through previous learning (Underwood & Schulz 1960). The mechanism of transfer suggested by these two findings is that the learning of paired associates is *not* simply a matter of associating an *S* and an *R*; it is better conceived as the "linking" of two performances, the first of which may be called "recognizing the stimulus member" and the second "uttering the response member." The thorough learning of these two different performances apparently transfers positively to the subsequent learning of the completed linking, or "association."

A third finding throws additional light on the process of association. Positive transfer in paired-associate learning is generated by previously learned mediating responses, which appear to serve the function of "coding" the stimulus member into the response member (McGuire 1961; Jenkins, 1963). The associate *hand* to the French word *main* may, for example, be mediated by the previously learned word *manual.* Still a third kind of previously learned performance, then, appears to be responsible for positive transfer; the ease of learning pairs of associates is markedly affected by the prior learning of what may be called a "coding performance."

The fourth conclusion that may be drawn from studies of associative learning has, in one form or another, been the subject of hundreds of experimental investigations. Negative transfer (interference) results when the learning of a pair of associates *A–B* is followed by the learning of the pair *A–C*, which has the same stimulus member but a different response member (Postman 1961; Underwood 1964). Although there is a great deal of evidence for this and related findings, it remains true at present that the mechanism by means of which such interference occurs has not been clearly delineated. The idea that there is "response competition" (Postman 1961) is a widely accepted view but seems little more than a renaming of the phenomenon of interference itself. A more promising possibility is the suggestion that the learning of a second response member also requires the complete erasure of the first from memory, that is, it extinguishes it after the fashion of extinction in a conditioned response (Barnes & Underwood 1959).

A quite different sort of hypothesis concerning the nature of negative transfer as it occurs in associative learning is receiving increasing attention. This is the proposition that the interference of a first task with a second (as in the arrangement *A–B*, then *A–C*) does not affect the learning of the second task at all but only its retention (Tulving 1964). This idea is consistent with the more general notion that the learning of each associate occurs in a single trial. Such a view, carried to its logical conclusion, would lead to the belief that negative transfer is essentially a process that reduces the probability of recall of learned associates in the phenomena called proactive interference and retroactive interference.

Transfer by means of concepts. The learning of relational concepts like "middle," "below," and "the odd one" and object concepts like "tree" and "door" has the effect of freeing performances from specific stimulus control. Having acquired a concept through learning, the individual is able to deal with a great variety of specific instances of the class that the concept represents. Particularly, it is true that the individual's performance can be correctly mediated by a concept, even though the specific instance to which he must respond has never been encountered during learning (cf. Kendler 1964; Gagné 1965). Concepts, therefore, are intimately bound with transfer of training. In order to demonstrate that an individual has learned a concept, one must show that the effects of the learning will apply to not previously encountered members of the class of stimuli that are denoted by the concept's name. The mechanism by means of which the central nervous system accomplishes this feat of generalization is not well understood at present. This kind of capability is, of course, not restricted to human beings, although human conceptual behavior seems often to involve the use of language (Kendler 1964).

Transfer from principles. If principles are thought of as combinations of concepts, then for a similar reason they too provide the basis for transfer of training from the specific instances of learning to a large class of performances. The learning of a principle must be demonstrated by means of a test of transfer of training; it must be possible to show that the individual is able to apply the principle in a variety of situations that have not been specifically presented during learning (Gagné 1964). Hendrickson and Schroeder (1941) showed that the direct teaching of a principle in verbal form to high school students resulted in positive transfer to the task of hitting a target under water and that the transfer was greater than that produced by direct practice. Katona's findings (1940) concerning the transfer value of learning principles in the solution of card-trick and matchstick problems have been verified and elaborated by Hilgard and his colleagues (1953). To these laboratory studies concerning the effectiveness of principle learning for transfer must be added a great mass of unrecorded observations of teachers, who do not hesitate to assert that a principle such as is implied by the expression $a \cdot b + a \cdot c = a(b + c)$ accomplishes the job of knowledge transfer better than almost any number of specific examples like $2 \cdot 3 + 2 \cdot 4 = 2 \cdot 7$.

Transferability of learning

There are, then, a number of ways in which transfer can come about in behavior, ranging from the relatively specific stimulus generalization of a conditioned response to the very broad applicability of a principle. Whatever particular objective learning may have, it is reasonable to state that it will always be accompanied by an additional outcome of transfer of learning. So far as formal education is concerned, and even more broadly for the functioning of the human individual in society, the transferability of acquired knowledge and skill is often considered a more important goal than any number of specific learning accomplishments. For it is such transfer that makes it possible for the individual to solve new problems, to adjust to new situations, and to make novel inventions. Enthusiasm for transferability as an educational goal needs to be tempered by the reflection that transfer depends upon prior learning.

ROBERT M. GAGNÉ

[*Other relevant material may be found in* CONCEPT FORMATION; FORGETTING; RESPONSE SETS.]

BIBLIOGRAPHY

BARNES, JEAN M.; and UNDERWOOD, BENTON J. 1959 "Fate" of First-list Associations in Transfer Theory. *Journal of Experimental Psychology* 58:97–105.

GAGNÉ, ROBERT M. 1964 Problem Solving. Pages 293–323 in Symposium on the Psychology of Human Learning, University of Michigan, 1962, *Categories of Human Learning.* New York: Academic Press.

GAGNÉ, ROBERT M. 1965 *Conditions of Learning.* New York: Holt.

GAGNÉ, ROBERT M.; and FOSTER, H. 1949 Transfer to a Motor Skill From Practice on a Pictured Representation. *Journal of Experimental Psychology* 39:342–354.

GAGNÉ, ROBERT M.; FOSTER, H.; and CROWLEY, M. C. 1948 The Measurement of Transfer of Training. *Psychological Bulletin* 45:97–130.

GANNON, DONALD R.; and NOBLE, CLYDE E. 1961 Familiarization (*n*) as a Stimulus Factor in Paired-associate Verbal Learning. *Journal of Experimental Psychology* 62:14–23.

GIBSON, ELEANOR J. 1940 A Systematic Application of the Concepts of Generalization and Differentiation to Verbal Learning. *Psychological Review* 47:196–229.

GIBSON, ELEANOR J. 1941 Retroactive Inhibition as a Function of Degree of Generalization Between Tasks. *Journal of Experimental Psychology* 28:93–115.

HARLOW, HARRY F. 1949 The Formation of Learning Sets. *Psychological Review* 56:51–65.

HENDRICKSON, GORDON; and SCHROEDER, WILLIAM H. 1941 Transfer of Training in Learning to Hit a Submerged Target. *Journal of Educational Psychology* 32: 205–213.

HILGARD, ERNEST R.; IRVINE, R. P.; and WIPPLE, J. E. 1953 Rote Memorization, Understanding, and Transfer: An Extension of Katona's Card-trick Experiments. *Journal of Experimental Psychology* 46:288–292.

HOVLAND, CARL I. 1937 The Generalization of Conditioned Responses: I. The Sensory Generalization of Conditioned Responses With Varying Frequencies of Tone. *Journal of General Psychology* 17:125–148.

JENKINS, JAMES J. 1963 Mediated Associations: Paradigms and Situations. Pages 210–257 in Conference on Verbal Learning and Verbal Behavior, Second, Ardsley-on-Hudson, N.Y., 1961, *Verbal Behavior and Learning: Problems and Processes, Proceedings.* New York: McGraw-Hill.

KATONA, GEORGE 1940 *Organizing and Memorizing.* New York: Columbia Univ. Press.

KENDLER, HOWARD H. 1964 The Concept of the Concept. Pages 211–236 in Symposium on the Psychology of Human Learning, University of Michigan, 1962, *Categories of Human Learning.* New York: Academic Press.

KENDLER, HOWARD H.; and KENDLER, TRACY S. 1961 Effect of Verbalization on Reversal Shifts in Children. *Science* 134:1619–1620.

LEWIS, DON; and SHEPHARD, ALFRED H. 1950 Devices for Studying Associative Interference in Psychomotor Performance: IV. The Turret Pursuit Apparatus. *Journal of Psychology* 29:173–182.

MCGEOCH, JOHN A. 1952 *The Psychology of Human Learning.* 2d ed., rev. New York: Longmans. → The first edition was published in 1942 by Longmans.

MCGUIRE, WILLIAM J. 1961 A Multiprocess Model for Paired-associate Learning. *Journal of Experimental Psychology* 62:335–347.

MANDLER, GEORGE 1954 Transfer of Training as a Function of Degree of Response Overlearning. *Journal of Experimental Psychology* 47:411–417.

MANDLER, GEORGE; and HEINEMANN S. 1956 Effect of Overlearning of a Verbal Response on Transfer of Training. *Journal of Experimental Psychology* 52: 39–46.

MURDOCK, BENNET B., JR. 1957 Transfer Designs and Formulas. *Psychological Bulletin* 54:313–326.

OSGOOD, CHARLES E. 1949 The Similarity Paradox in Human Learning: A Resolution. *Psychological Review* 56:132–143.

POSTMAN, LEO 1961 The Present Status of Interference Theory. Pages 152–179 in Conference on Verbal Learning and Verbal Behavior, New York University, 1959, *Verbal Learning and Verbal Behavior: Proceedings.* New York: McGraw-Hill.

THORNDIKE, EDWARD L. 1924 Mental Discipline in High School Studies. *Journal of Educational Psychology* 15: 1–22; 83–98.

THORNDIKE, EDWARD L.; and WOODWORTH, ROBERT S. 1901 The Influence of Improvement in One Mental Function Upon the Efficiency of Other Functions. *Psychological Review* 8:247–261; 384–395; 553–564.

THUNE, LELAND E. 1950 The Effect of Different Types of Preliminary Activities on Subsequent Learning of Paired-associate Material. *Journal of Experimental Psychology* 40:423–438.

TULVING, ENDEL 1964 Intratrial and Intertrial Retention: Notes Towards a Theory of Free Recall Verbal Learning. *Psychological Review* 71:219–237.

UNDERWOOD, BENTON J. 1964 The Representativeness of Rote Verbal Learning. Pages 47–78 in Symposium on the Psychology of Human Learning, University of Michigan, 1962, *Categories of Human Learning.* New York: Academic Press.

UNDERWOOD, BENTON J.; and SCHULZ, RUDOLPH W. 1960 *Meaningfulness and Verbal Learning.* Philadelphia: Lippincott.

X
ACQUISITION OF SKILL

In the scientific inquiry into the nature of skill, which has been largely conducted by experimental psychologists, operational definitions of skill are generally stated in terms of overt responses and controlled stimulation. Responses are subdivided into three types: verbal, motor, and perceptual, which typically stress speaking, moving, and judging, respectively. Common verbal tasks require the memorization of a list of words; motor tasks demand precise movements of the limbs and body; and perceptual tasks require discrimination of sensory information. Responses are evaluated or scored by means of errors, rates, pressures, amplitudes, time sharing, and information transmitted. Stimuli, on the other hand, are energy inputs to the operator and are expressed in units, such as frequency, length, time, and weight.

The study of skill has largely been confined to a relatively few laboratory tasks and trainers. The inquiry has been directed far less to the arts, the shop, and the playing field than to identifying variables that cut across many jobs and finding general laws that stand for many specific tasks. For example, practice, rest, feedback, and transfer are prominent variables.

The work of the skills psychologist may be divided into two parts. In his basic research, he seeks relevant variables, discovers empirical laws of relations between variables, and constructs theories to account for the laws. In his applied work, he takes part in selecting personnel for special jobs, helps to design display and control stations, and prescribes some of the training rules of educational programs.

World War II provided the impetus for an accelerated study of motor skill. It was necessary to select from hundreds of thousands of men a limited number to fly airplanes, aim gunnery equipment, etc. A battery of tests to determine psychomotor abilities was developed containing eight apparatus tests: tracking moving targets, setting dials, etc. A candidate's performance rank on these devices turned out to be very much related to his proficiency during later training for aircrew stations in air force schools. The devices used in the apparatus tests did not resemble air force or civilian hardware, yet they brought out basic learning and performance factors, such as reaction time, speed of movement, and pattern discrimination common to operable equipment. The great success of the apparatus tests in predicting later behavior led to the accelerated growth of both theoretical and applied studies of skills. One of the specific accomplishments was to provide an impetus to the laboratory study of what skills are and of how they are learned.

Tasks involving continuous responses. The major components of a typical research device involving continuous responses include (1) a visual display station, such as an oscilloscope; (2) a mechanical or electronic means for programming the display, such as the movement of a pip of light in some prescribed way; (3) a station with a control, such as an airplane stick, for the operator to compensate for pip movement; and (4) a means of measuring the operator's response output with respect to the stimulus input. Appropriate stick responses for spatial coordinates x and y balance or neutralize the programmed displacements, and the pip remains quiet, centered, and under control. Ordinarily, several groups of operators or subjects are trained, each group under a special condition. One set of conditions may involve change in the properties of the apparatus; another set may involve change in the methods of training. Obvious *display* variations are changes in target speed and path complexity; simple *control* variations involve resistance to movement and amount of pip movement per unit of stick displacement. These and other variations have led to the discovery of quantitative relationships between responses and the conditions of practice. In addition, all of these variations are often treated by a systems approach in which the output of men and machines is expressed as a function of the input. Examples of maturing areas of application are the piloting of aircraft and submarines and target detection and identification in radar.

The training expert gives advice on schedules of practice: when, how long, how often. He decides on practice matters pertaining to individual tasks: their relative emphases and staging. He makes important recommendations on the operator's data-processing abilities and need for training aids. The operator may be in for long periods of vigilance, and he ought to detect faint or occasional signals; in addition, the operator is expected to make suitable decisions in the available time and to select and execute the proper response for the system. The expert's most critical analyses center on feedback (information about past performance) and the manner of its representation, since any solution for coding the feedback (which is essential) necessitates selecting a sensory modality and temporal, spatial, and numerical schedules of transformation.

Tasks involving discrete responses. One major premise underlying tasks involving discrete responses is that the next response (R) depends upon the knowledge of results of previous responses (KR), that is, $R = f(KR)$. The relations between KR and R are arbitrary, and transformations always obtain. For example, if a blindfolded person were directed to "Draw a 3-inch line," he need not be informed of his error after each and every attempt, nor are we compelled to report a $+\frac{1}{8}$ inch error as "too far by $\frac{1}{8}$ inch." It is possible, of course, to report any numerical error at any time.

As the line-drawing example shows, targets and responses need not be in continuous motion, although the variables of continuous and discrete types of tasks are quite similar. The task of learning to move levers and knobs through a critical distance has afforded a simple situation for studying the conditions regulating learning and performance. In these simple tasks, the simplest train of events is R_1, KR_1, R_2, KR_2, $\cdots$, R_n, KR_n; the timing can be anything at all. A few illustrations of typical findings will suffice: (1) the massing of trials produces faster learning than does spacing; (2) the occasional omission of *KR* does not prejudice the effect of a later *KR* on the following *R*; and (3) even day or week intervals between *R* and *KR* do not necessarily impair the learning of *R*. The learning of *R*, however, is seriously handicapped by (1) *KR*s which are vague ("You didn't do very well") and (2) *KR*s displaced from their normal position by another *R*, that is, R_1, R_2, KR_1, R_3, etc. Some investigators interpret the primary role of *KR* as reinforcing in much the same way that food can be used to shape the behavior of the hungry animal. Others interpret the primary role of *KR* as informational and treat it as a stimulus variable that serves as a representational code for the response or its effect.

Work tasks. A man's output is dependent upon his recent and remote history of responding. His rate of work, for example, depends upon such obvious variables as work periods, rests, and loads. Rate also depends upon anticipated conditions of practice, rest, and load. According to the reactive inhibition theory of work decrement, decrement in performance is attributable to the build-up of reactive inhibition, and recovery in performance is attributable to the decay of inhibition. This theory is quite elaborate and effective; indeed, it explains a great deal more decrement data than do physiological-fatigue theories.

Among work tasks that have been studied are prolonged efforts at cranking, canceling letters of the alphabet, and packing small objects. The investigation of vigilance, a related topic, arose with the introduction of radar—watching radar is associated with infrequent, but critical, stimulation and with losses in performance at the critical moment. Losses in proficiency, however, may be caused by other means, a prominent one being response overload. Overload can be readily brought about by requiring reactions to more than one task. The breakdown in monitoring the incoming signals is intensified by increasing their number, complicating their constitution, or raising their frequency.

Forgetting. A learned series of skilled procedures, such as an instrument check-out sequence, is much more susceptible to forgetting than a response that requires muscular coordination. The forgetting of a motor skill that may occur over periods of extended disuse is quickly overcome by comparatively few trials of retraining. Still, forgetting of even simple motor skills has been demonstrated, the phenomenon being more readily observed in changes in variance than in means.

Recent analyses of a person's ability to remember a list of words have shown that a person is far less likely to forget than experiments since the 1890s have led us to believe. Recent work on verbal retention has made more use of meaningful material—one word per subject and normative information on word-association structures—and more use of recalling under conditions of controlled retention environments. Retrieval of words from memory seems to depend strongly on free-association processes. Cultural norms have been tabulated which show the probability (p) of any response word to a stimulus word, for example, for the stimulus word *thirsty*, the $p(R_1)$ for *water* (the most frequent response) is .35, the $p(R_2)$ for *drink* (the second most frequent response) is .30, etc. If a naïve student is taught the word *drink* (as one of several words in a list), later, in the presence of the word *thirsty*, if *drink* is not recalled, *water* is likely to intrude instead. The illustration shows the effects of language habits established some time ago on present recall behavior (Bilodeau 1966*a*).

The explanations of forgetting are nearly all related to interference theory, either retroactive or proactive. If the reader cannot quite recall the items of yesterday's breakfast, it may be that this morning's fare intrudes or otherwise interferes (*retroaction*); if the failure to recall can be traced to breakfasts prior to yesterday, then *proactive* agents are to blame. The bulk of the literature favors retroaction as the mechanism of forgetting, but proaction is favored by present-day investigators.

Transfer of training. An individual is never tested or required to perform under the very same conditions which constituted training. There is always at least a small difference; sometimes there is a large one. The inquiry into the effects of these differences is called transfer of training. The objective of any training program is to maximize the amount of transfer, although examination of actual instructional programs might make us wonder. The student might be trained to read to himself, but when tested he might be required to read orally; another's training might be characterized by his watching, testing by his performing. Generally, it is found that learning almost anything (referred to as Task *A*) facilitates the learning of almost anything similar (Task *B*). That is, the transfer is ordinarily positive in sign. Generally, it is less than 100 per cent in quantity. In order to obtain more than 100 per cent transfer, a training trial in Task A must be superior to a training trial in Task B when subsequently evaluated by the skill shown on Task B. Strictly speaking, more than 100 per cent transfer is most difficult to find. It appears that if Task B performance serves as the criterion, it is better to train at B and, if possible, avoid Task A from the start. Task B, however, in the hands of the novice may involve elements of danger or excessive expense, and so Task A may be substituted for Task B after all. For example, though it is probably true that the best training for helicopter piloting involves learning to fly the helicopter itself, the craft is dangerous and costly to operate. The ground trainers are inefficient, but if ten hours in them are actually worth five hours in the air, the 50 per cent transfer figure works to advantage.

The findings on negative transfer (detrimental effect of Task A upon the subsequent performance of Task B) are fairly clear. When Task A interferes with B, the interference is usually small and disappears quickly with additional practice on B. Indeed, there is even evidence to show that reversed forms of the same task involve the same psychomotor factors, and, further, there is no evidence for an individual trait of susceptibility to negative transfer. It can be speculated that to immunize oneself against negative transfer, or even to accelerate the normal processes of positive transfer, an exposure to any and many tasks is desirable. On the other hand, if a small amount of negative transfer includes one fatal error, the small amount should be considered most carefully.

Most psychologists believe that learning is an incremental process which could not take place without transfer. The number of constituent elements in two adjacent learning trials (A_1 and A_2) and the number of elements in common is believed to determine the amount of transfer. Because the events of training and education are never exactly reproduced in later life, a knowledge of the principles of transfer is of top priority for all users of applied skills research.

Composition rules. Skills have been analyzed and then synthesized by methods of probability, correlation, and geometry. A probability and a correlation model are sketched below to show how the reduction of skill to its components is accomplished in principle.

Probability model. Imagine that an operator views two meters whose pointers continually wander from center and that the pointers can be recentered by means of cranks for the left and right

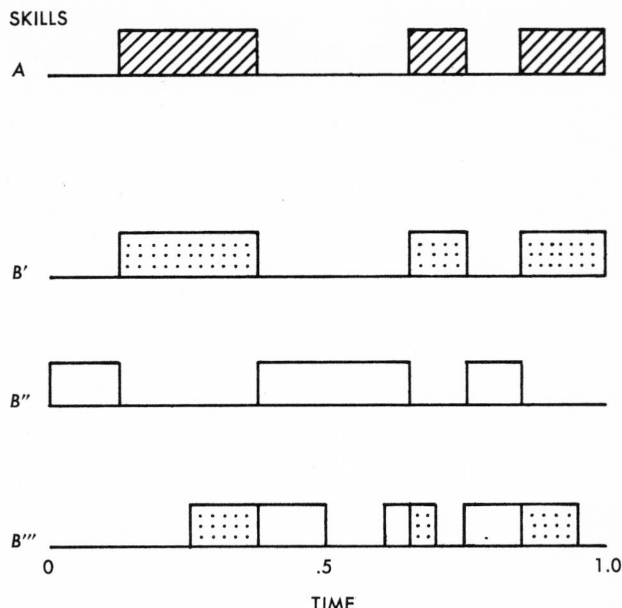

The stippled portions of the instances of B (that is, B', B'', B''') represent the temporal overlap of A and B, the time during which both hands are on target simultaneously. If A and B are fixed at probabilities of .5, time sharing is maximum (.5) for B', minimum (0) for B'', and at chance (.25) for B'''.

Figure 1 — An illustration of three levels of coordination between skills A and B

hands. Figure 1 represents a polygraph record of the on–off target time for hands A and B. The total time represented is unity and, for simplicity only, the probability (p) for each hand's being on-target is arbitrarily fixed at .5. Three special cases of coordination are shown: for A and B' the time that both hands are on the target at the same time is maximum (.5); for A and B'' it is minimum (0); and for A and B''' it is at the level of chance (.25). In each of these three cases, the hands are equally coordinated in the sense of equal proficiency at their separate tasks (.5); but in the sense of time sharing, the probability of the joint event $p(AB)$ ranges widely from 0 to .5. Somewhat surprisingly, many training situations yield results resembling B''' or chance time sharing, whatever the value of p. As a rule of thumb, the multiplicative formula $p(A) \times p(B)$ for independent events is used to produce a very good estimate of $p(AB)$. A better-than-chance score, then, is a show of positive coordination.

The multiplicative formula has a number of applications. If it is generalized to a three-part profile where, for example, $A = .90$, $B = .90$, and $C = .20$, the following predictions of their joint occurrence [$p(ABC)$] are possible: the best prediction is

.90 × .90 × .20 = .16; instant improvement may be dramatically obtained through any increase in the poorest part at the expense of a better part, .70 × .90 × .40 = .25; the maximum possible score is $[\frac{1}{3}(.90 + .90 + .20)]^3 = .30$; the worst possible score in a rearranged profile is .00. The training objective now becomes one of raising the value of $p(ABC)$. The most common way is to raise the sum of the part probabilities through additional standard practice. A second possibility is to make a change in the profile of the component parts, while holding their sum constant. Still a third method would strive to break the multiplicative rule and replace it with better-than-chance pairing of events.

The correlation model. Another method of skills analysis intercorrelates the scores from (1) within a single task but from different stages of practice and (2) different tasks at the same or different stages of practice. The two techniques reveal the amounts of variance (the statistic σ^2) common to two or more variables and establish the degree of relationship. The questions at issue involve abilities, pre-experimental experience, integration of components into total task, and training procedures. To date most of this work has involved the correlations among length of time scores, such as time on target in tracking tasks.

Intratask analyses show relationships between (1) the first trial and successive later ones to be progressively lower and (2) adjacent trials to grow progressively larger. These patterns mean that the underlying composition of skill becomes simpler with increasing proficiency, for example, fewer abilities contribute to sophisticated than to naïve performance. Intertask analyses show that (1) predictor tests can provide better estimates for final than for initial criterion trials when the operator is skilled at both tasks; and (2) final level of criterion performance can be better predicted by extratask measures than by earlier levels of skill on the criterion-learning task.

EDWARD A. BILODEAU

[*Other relevant material may be found in* ATTENTION; CYBERNETICS; FATIGUE; FORGETTING.]

BIBLIOGRAPHY

ADAMS, JACK A. 1964 Motor Skills. *Annual Review of Psychology* 15:181–202.

ANDREAS, BURTON G. 1960 *Experimental Psychology.* New York: Wiley. → A college text; an introduction to the laboratory analysis of learning.

BILODEAU, EDWARD A. 1966*a* Retention. Pages 315–350 in Edward A. Bilodeau (editor), *Acquisition of Skill.* New York: Academic Press.

BILODEAU, EDWARD A. (editor) 1966*b* *Acquisition of Skill.* New York: Academic Press. → The book contains a survey of motor and verbal skills learning by a number of leading contributors to the field.

BILODEAU, EDWARD A.; and BILODEAU, INA MCD. 1961 Motor-skills Learning. *Annual Review of Psychology* 12:243–280.

FITTS, PAUL M. 1964 Perceptual–Motor Skill Learning. Pages 243–285 in Symposium on the Psychology of Human Learning, University of Michigan, 1962, *Categories of Human Learning.* New York: Academic Press. → Definitions, taxonomies, models and other issues with a communication–computer flavor.

FLEISHMAN, EDWIN A. 1962 The Description and Prediction of Perceptual–Motor Skill Learning. Pages 137–175 in Robert Glaser (editor), *Training Research and Education.* Univ. of Pittsburgh Press. → A survey of work involving correlation and factor analysis.

SCOTT, MYRTLE G. (1942) 1963 *Analysis of Human Motion: A Textbook in Kinesiology.* 2d ed. New York: Appleton.

XI
LEARNING IN CHILDREN

Learning may be defined broadly to encompass relatively permanent behavior changes that result from experience. The experiential requirement usually implies that for the learning organism some changes in the associative properties of certain stimuli have taken place in such a way that the stimuli produce response effects that are different after training than before. Two general classes of empirical investigations in the area of children's learning may be cited. One type involves experimental manipulation of variables through laboratory investigation. Such studies have varied the number of conditioning trials, schedules of reinforcement, delay and magnitude of reinforcement, and motivational factors and have measured the resulting change in response or some attribute of response (Bijou & Baer 1960; Spiker 1960; Lipsitt 1963; White 1963; Rheingold & Stanley 1963; Munn 1946). The second category includes investigations of such training variables as familial or parental practices pertaining to feeding, toilet training, and effects of deprivation in infancy or in early childhood (McCandless 1961). The concepts of imprinting and trauma are not alien to this type of study, although little solid research with children is available on such matters.

Basic learning processes

Many of the experimental procedures used with animals and human adults have been adapted to the study of child behavior at all age levels. These studies generally indicate that for both classical (Pavlovian) conditioning and operant (Skinnerian) learning processes, the various parameters pertinent to conditioning in animals also control the occurrence and rate of conditioning in children.

Classical conditioning. It has been demonstrated that in classical conditioning in children, the time interval between the initially neutral stimulus (the conditioned stimulus, *CS*) and the initially effective response-producing stimulus (the unconditioned stimulus, *UCS*) is pertinent to the rapidity and strength of conditioning: there is an optimal interval of approximately half a second that varies somewhat with age and the nature of the response. A positive relationship has also been demonstrated between the drive or arousal level of the child and the rate of classical conditioning where that level has been variously defined by measures of muscular tension, tests of anxiety, or instruction-induced stress states. As in other organisms, it has been shown that the sensory modalities to which the *CS* and *UCS* are directed are pertinent to the conditioning process, as are the number of paired *CS–UCS* trials administered, and the nature of the tests used to measure the presence and strength of conditioning. In fact, the conclusion that conditioning has occurred often depends on the nature of these tests, including such procedural technicalities as whether interspersed test trials were administered among the training trials, whether conditioning was measured solely during extinction, or whether the response-recording apparatus permitted detection of subtle aspects of the reaction. In short, classical conditioning in the infant and child is a well-documented phenomenon, although knowledge of the variables affecting the phenomenon, including the age of the child, requires additional and extensive investigation. At present it appears quite likely, for instance, that there is an interaction between the age of the child and certain other parameters pertinent to the speed and strength of conditioning. One suggestion is that a younger child may require longer *CS–UCS* intervals for optimal conditioning than an older one.

Several investigators have recently established classical conditioning in neonates under rather well-controlled experimental conditions. Conditioning of appetitive responses is apparently obtained somewhat more easily than is classical conditioning of avoidance responses, at least under the levels of noxious stimulation that have been utilized. Some investigators have pointed out that fetal response to oral stimulation is developed neurophysiologically very early and that this response, and presumably its conditionability, has great survival value for the organism and the species. It can be pointed out, however, that certain withdrawal reactions to aversive stimuli also develop early and, under adverse circumstances, could play an important role in the survival of the organism. Again, investigations involving both appetitive and aversive processes in infants are much needed.

It may be added that the behavioral phenomenon of habituation has been well documented in infants and children, just as it has been with a wide variety of infrahuman organisms. Habituation is a progressive diminution of response that occurs as a result of repetitive presentation of a given stimulus. There may be, in fact, several different response–decrement phenomena, resulting from different conditions of stimulus presentation and varying histories of the organism, only one or some of which might be properly classified as learning processes.

Operant conditioning. Operant conditioning has also received considerable attention from investigators of child behavior. The systematic reinforcement of a response initially low in the child's hierarchy of responses importantly affects the rate at which that response will subsequently occur. Operant conditioning may involve the presentation of a "positive" event contingent on the desired response. Examples of such positive reinforcers would be the awarding of candy or the introduction of a signal indicating correctness of response. Alternately, "negative" reinforcement involves termination of an aversive stimulus contingent on occurrence of a response to be learned. Both kinds of reinforcement ultimately yield increases in the response to which the reinforcement is addressed. A third type of response-contingent event is the withdrawal of a positive reinforcer on the occasion of an undesired response. Automatic obliteration of a motion picture, for instance, has been shown to be most effective in terminating or suppressing undesired behavior, such as thumb sucking in children. The operant technique capitalizes on the well-known law of effect and has been shown under many experimental arrangements to exert powerful control over various kinds of behavior, including imitative responses, smiling, emission of expressions of courtesy, and language. It has been found that different types of reinforcement schedules (e.g., intermittent versus continuous) tend to produce different response patterns in children; these patterns result in differential susceptibility to extinction when the reinforcer is ultimately withdrawn.

Discrimination learning. Discrimination learning studies are another type of conditioning investigation having to do with effects of reinforcement in maintaining or generating certain kinds of behavior. These studies typically involve discrete trial procedures rather than techniques that permit the subject to respond at any time. In discrimination learning, the child is rewarded for choosing the correct manipulandum, or correct stimulus, among multiple opportunities present. Numerous parameters have been shown to influence the occurrence and rate of children's discrimination learning, including some variables that are unique to the articulate organism and, therefore, affect learning differently at different ages and in children of varying intelligence and social circumstances. Such studies of children's discrimination learning have contributed importantly to the development and extension of behavior theory; this seems to be particularly true in the areas of verbal learning and mediational (cognitive) effects upon performance.

It has been demonstrated in children that presenting the discriminative stimuli simultaneously generally produces more rapid learning than presenting the same stimuli successively, particularly if the response required is directed at or involves the manipulation of those stimuli. However, successive presentation and simultaneous presentation do not produce very different effects if the response is to be made to a locus removed from the stimulus source, such as buttons that are some distance away from the stimuli. Although psychophysical scaling of discriminative stimuli would be required for a meaningful comparison of the ease of discrimination learning in one sense modality with another, it appears that learning is more easily achieved when the discriminative cues involve variations in stimulus size and less easily achieved when the stimuli vary in color. Solid (stereometric) objects tend to be discriminated more rapidly than do two-dimensional representations of the same figures. Greater magnitudes of reward (including more preferred rewards) and lesser delays of reward produce more rapid learning than their opposites; recent data, however, suggest that the relationship may not be a monotonic one and that greater delays may result in better retention. Studies are needed of interactions of such incentive attributes of rewards as size and delay with factors affecting drive or arousal level, such as frustration. In some circumstances, increased delay of reward, for instance, may lead to poorer performance; but in other circumstances it is possible that such delay could increase frustration, which may in turn facilitate some aspect of performance, particularly those responses that are already prepotent.

Much new research on children's discrimination learning has dealt with effects of variables that have been historically of great interest to the general experimentalist but that only recently have been selected for extensive study by child psychologists. Some of these, for instance, pertain to the relative importance of positive and negative stimuli (i.e., reinforcement versus nonreinforcement) with most results indicating that both types of trial enhance performance.

Orientation behavior. White (1963) has noted that orientation behavior of children, or "observing responses," has been neglected by most experimenters, perhaps partly because this aspect of behavior is seldom included in formal learning theories. Because visual scanning of stimuli increases sharply at the onset of criterion performance in discrimination learning, an attentional shift important to the production of criterion or solution behavior is not unlikely. Studies of attentional behavior in discrimination learning as well as studies of observing behavior per se are becoming more frequent. In particular, a marked interest has recently arisen in the orientational behavior of human infants, wherein children from birth onward are provided with visual (and other) stimulation to which their reactions are recorded. It has been demonstrated that neonates respond differently to visual stimuli, depending primarily on the complexity of those stimuli, and that shifts in interest (defined in terms of length and frequency of fixation) occur with increasing age and experience. Since visual fixation occurs very early in life and is seemingly controlled by at least crudely specifiable stimulus attributes, there exists the intriguing possibility that attentional responses may be trained or conditioned very early through systematic reinforcement. Some writers, moreover, have suggested that visual orienting behavior of infants and the early changes in such behavior may be analogous to imprinting behavior found in lower organisms. Although much of this remains to be studied, the implication is that young human beings may "reach out" and follow with their eyes much as lower animals fixate upon and remain with objects that they encounter early [*see* ATTENTION; IMPRINTING].

Transfer of learning. Much work in children's discrimination learning has dealt with transfer of training. The phenomenon principally involved is that of generalization, whereby learning a certain response to a given stimulus predisposes the organism to respond to other similar stimuli, and proportionately so the greater the similarity.

Two general types of transfer of training, i.e., nonspecific and specific, have been extensively studied in children. Both of these are pertinent to the generalization of learning from one situation to another, whether from one laboratory situation to another, from the laboratory to "real life," or from one "real life" situation to another. Nonspecific transfer, variously referred to as "warm-up" or "learning to learn" depending upon the conditions used to induce it, refers to the subject becoming "set" to perform in certain prescribed ways. This type of transfer has to do with the skills involved in manipulating the response objects, viewing the stimuli properly, or merely relaxing and awaiting instructions. Quite possibly, such warm-up may impair as well as facilitate subsequent performance depending upon the requirements of the subsequent task. Specific transfer may also either facilitate or impair performance, and it refers to the influence of earlier task requirements on subsequent task performance, particularly to whether the previously learned task is similar or not to the subsequently learned task.

Many studies of specific transfer in both verbal and motor discrimination learning have been done with children. Much of the paired associate work with children has concentrated on the negative transfer phenomenon, created by retraining the subject to make new responses to stimuli to which other responses had been previously learned. Many of these paired associate studies, however, have dealt with verbal mediation that can produce either positive or negative transfer depending on the specific stimuli and responses involved. Some of these studies of proactive facilitation or interference deal with the phenomena of acquired distinctiveness or acquired equivalence. Acquired equivalence studies have demonstrated that children have more difficulty learning differential responses to stimuli to which they have previously learned similar names, whereas acquired distinctiveness studies have shown that if children have previously learned different names for the discriminative stimuli any subsequent learning of differential responses to the stimuli will be easier.

Transposition and verbal mediation. Considerable attention has focused on a special kind of training transfer in children—that known as transposition behavior. Typically, the child is first trained to select one of two or more stimuli simultaneously presented, such as the larger of a pair of circles; transposition is said to have occurred if the child, when confronted with a transfer task involving presentation of the larger stimulus together with a still larger one, chooses the largest rather than the specific stimulus to which response has been previously reinforced. Lower animals often show transposition when the transfer pair is very similar to the training pair but a breakdown in such transposition when the test pair is more dissimilar. Several studies have shown that the same is true for young children, but total transposition tends to occur with older or more articulate children. Presumably, possession of a concept, such as "larger than," accounts for extension of transposition to the very dissimilar stimuli. Transposition attracts developmental interest because transposition behavior clearly tends to change with increasing chronological and mental age and because language skill seems to bear an important relationship to the phenomenon.

Corroborative evidence for the importance of verbality in discrimination learning is found in studies comparing "reversal shift" with "nonreversal shift" procedures. The typical experiment involves the presentation of stimuli varying in two dimensions, with one of these dimensions providing the cues pertinent to making the correct response. For instance, both size and brightness might be varied, the child being required to respond to the dark rather than the bright stimulus, regardless of size. A reversal shift would involve a change to making a bright response correct, while a nonreversal shift would make size the pertinent dimension. Nonreversal shift has been found easier for animals and young children; reversal shift is easier for adults and more articulate (or older) children. Presumably, verbal mediational factors, such as the subject informing himself covertly of the pertinent dimension, are crucial [*see* CONCEPT FORMATION].

The study of children's cognitive processes has been approached recently by many students of paired associate learning and verbal mediation. While much exploration remains to be done on the mechanisms by which verbal or symbolic responses mediate and control behavior, it has become increasingly apparent that children are excellent subjects for such study. Work with children should enable extensions of behavior theory that would not be possible otherwise. There is the interesting and not unlikely possibility, moreover, that studies of verbal learning in children, including the phenomena of associative clustering, free association, and other aspects of verbal expression, will illuminate important personality processes and anomalies. The suggestion does not seem amiss, for instance, that self-concepts (the responses that humans make to themselves about themselves) may be viewed as covert verbal responses which are learned according to the principles by which other responses are learned and that these self-conceptualizations may act as mediational responses to affect subsequent learning.

Effects of early experience

The study of children's learning and the lasting effects of such learning necessarily includes any documentation of sequelae of "crucial" life circumstances. Thus, any studies relating parent–child variables or institutional factors as antecedents to behavior of children fall within the scope of the present topic. Effects of traumatic experiences and psychodynamic hypotheses about such effects ultimately refer to learned changes in behavior that reflect familial or other social circumstances. One of the difficulties inherent in the study of the relationship between such early experiences and later behavior is that the behavioral phenomena must occur *in natura* to be the subject of study, since it is impossible or undesirable to produce such behavior deliberately. Consequently, factors other than those specifically investigated have the opportunity of producing effects on the behavior studied. For instance, it has been demonstrated that infants who were rated as being permissively fed engaged in more "reality play" at preschool age, whereas children who were rated as being rigidly fed engaged in more fantasy. While such a finding is interesting and suggestive and does support clinically held presuppositions about the influences of feeding schedules on children's behavior, the possibility exists that both rigidity in feeding and the occurrence of fantasy behavior in children are products of a common type of parenthood. This possibility necessarily attenuates the cause–effect relationship one would wish to infer from the data.

The same methodological weakness lies in the cross-cultural approach to collecting developmental data on effects of early-experience factors. For instance, it has been shown that there is a rather high negative correlation between the age of weaning and intensity of guilt feelings among members of a large number of cultures. While it is tempting, on the basis of such data, to conclude that guilt is produced by early weaning or oral frustration, it is possible that those cultures which reinforce guilt responses are also those which happen to wean early. Perhaps both guilt and early weaning are behavioral phenomena produced by some third causative factor. Another study related oral pessimism and optimism to age of weaning (whether before or after four months of age), and found that the oral pessimists tended to have been weaned earlier. A number of studies exist that, like those cited, implicate the age and style of weaning as causatively pertinent social determinants of later behavior, but few of these studies permit more than conjectural conclusions.

Toilet training. Another area of children's social training which involves a great investment of parental time and produces considerable conflict and anxiety is toilet behavior. Just as certain crucial interactions between parent and child may occur around oral activities when the child is in infancy, so later may the child's excretory activities become the focus of much parental attention. Studies suggest that toilet-training practices do constitute an important "arena" within which parents and children interact, often unpleasantly, to produce potentially lasting developmental effects. The earlier toilet training starts, the longer it takes to complete. Also, the earlier such training starts, the more annoying, frustrating, and generally unpleasant experiences there are likely to be between the parties involved. Rigid toilet training, along with a constellation of other restrictive parental attributes, seems to be associated with slower development, and mothers who are high in anxiety tend to start toilet training earlier than more relaxed mothers.

Deprivation of social stimulation. While effects of institutionalization and, in general, deprivation of social stimulation remain to a certain extent controversial, the bulk of evidence suggests that such experiences often produce serious emotional and intellectual deficits. The effects are not as controversial as is the specification of the real antecedent events producing these effects, e.g., whether the pertinent variable is separation from a mother or sheer reduction in human or environmental contacts. It does seem reasonable to assume that institutional and deprivational effects consist largely of sequelae to previous unfortunate learning circumstances [*see* INFANCY, *article on* THE EFFECTS OF EARLY EXPERIENCE].

LEWIS P. LIPSITT

[*See also* DEVELOPMENTAL PSYCHOLOGY; INTELLECTUAL DEVELOPMENT. *Other relevant material may be found in* INFANCY; INTELLIGENCE AND INTELLIGENCE TESTING; LANGUAGE, *article on* LANGUAGE DEVELOPMENT; PERCEPTION, *article on* PERCEPTUAL DEVELOPMENT; READING DISABILITIES; SENSORY AND MOTOR DEVELOPMENT; SOCIALIZATION; STIMULATION DRIVES.]

BIBLIOGRAPHY

BIJOU, SIDNEY W.; and BAER, DONALD M. 1960 The Laboratory–Experimental Study of Child Behavior. Pages 140–197 in Paul H. Mussen (editor), *Handbook of Research Methods in Child Development.* New York: Wiley.

LIPSITT, LEWIS P. 1963 Learning in the First Year of Life. Volume 1, pages 147–195 in Lewis P. Lipsitt and Charles C. Spiker (editors), *Advances in Child Development and Behavior.* New York: Academic Press.

MCCANDLESS, BOYD R. 1961 *Children and Adolescents: Behavior and Development.* New York: Holt.

MUNN, NORMAN L. (1946) 1954 Learning in Children. Pages 374–458 in Leonard Carmichael (editor), *Manual of Child Psychology.* 2d ed. New York: Wiley.

RHEINGOLD, HARRIET L.; and STANLEY, WALTER C. 1963 Developmental Psychology. *Annual Review of Psychology* 14:1–28.

SPIKER, CHARLES C. 1960 Research Methods in Children's Learning. Pages 374–420 in Paul H. Mussen (editor), *Handbook of Research Methods in Child Development.* New York: Wiley.

WHITE, SHELDON H. 1963 Learning. Pages 196–235 in National Society for the Study of Education, Committee on Child Psychology, *Child Psychology.* Yearbook, Vol. 62, part 1. Univ. of Chicago Press.

XII
PROGRAMMED LEARNING

The term "programmed learning" is used to describe an instructional situation in which materials presented in a controlled sequence require the learner to respond in a way that meets specified criteria of the program objectives. Terms often used synonymously are "programmed instruction," "automated instruction," "automatic tutoring," or even "teaching machines."

Because of the control over responses and sequence of presentation, the materials are referred to as a "program." The responses made by the learner may be completing a statement with a word or words, writing an answer to a question, making a selection in a multiple-choice situation, imitating auditory or visual stimuli with oral or motor responses, stating agreement or disagreement, or solving a problem. The program may be presented to the learner through a mechanical device, known as a teaching machine, or in a book, known as a programmed textbook. The materials are programmed so that a tutorial situation is approximated without the immediate presence of a human tutor.

Programmed learning is viewed as a technological advancement in education and training developed in order to meet the increasing complexities in nearly all areas of human learning endeavor. In education, these complexities include the numbers to be educated, the rapidly expanding body of knowledge to be taught, and the special cases within a population—e.g., the intellectually gifted, the retarded, the delinquent, and the illiterate. Problems in management development and training–retraining associated with automation are concerns in business and industry to which the techniques of programmed learning are applicable.

History

Sidney L. Pressey. A device that could administer and score tests automatically was exhibited by Sidney L. Pressey in 1924. In a description of the uses of this device in his educational psychology classes at Ohio State University, Pressey also described the effectiveness of this machine for drill and recitation ([1926] 1960, pp. 35–41). The machine, which looked like a four-key typewriter, presented multiple-choice questions to the student. After the student had completed instruction through lectures and text reading, the machine was used to test his retention. The key corresponding to the student's choice for each item was pressed. If the student made the correct choice, the machine would present the next question; however, if the student chose incorrectly, the machine would not advance. The machine recorded the total number of key presses for the entire test. The immediate bringing into awareness of the correctness of a response provided more effective application of several of Thorndike's principles of learning than could the normal behaviors of the human teacher. Pressey observed that students who were tested by machine for weekly units of work showed higher achievement than students who took conventional tests.

Educators and trainers gave almost no consideration to the work done by Pressey and some of his students with the machine. After several years of effort modifying the device and applying it to several types of courses at different age levels, Pressey stopped working on the device and stated that education could not stay in a "crude handicraft stage" but would have to begin "quantity production methods" ([1932] 1960, pp. 47–51). He also predicted that new instruments and materials would be developed to facilitate research and sweeping advances in education and learning. Whether because of cultural inertia or other reasons, automated instructional devices failed to become established among educators and psychologists.

B. F. Skinner. More than twenty years later, in the 1950s, B. F. Skinner (1954, pp. 86–97) pointed out that education as a technology of learning did not approximate in its practice those principles observed and confirmed in learning research. Skinner stated that there were two principles of the learning process that had to be considered by those involved in teaching and training. The first, "contingencies of reinforcement," he described as a serious application of Thorndike's "law of effect" since it makes certain that desired responses appear in the student's behavior and that these responses are immediately reinforced. The second principle maintains that reinforcement should be arranged or "scheduled" so that the learner continues to make responses, i.e., so that the material keeps him interested. Responses that successfully approximated the criteria of learned behavior should be emitted by the learners, and any other responses would be considered a faulty arrangement of the stimuli presented to the learners.

On the basis of these principles Skinner stated that anyone wishing to control the learning situation so that the desired changes in behavior would occur must consider the following questions: (1) What responses are desired to meet the criterion of learning? (2) What sort of successive approximations in emitted responses will lead to the desired behavior? (3) What reinforcers are available in the particular situation? (4) How can the reinforcements be arranged so that behavior can be maintained in necessary strength?

It was obvious to Skinner that educational practice would have to change radically to be able to construct an instructional situation that would meet these requirements. For example, almost no provision was made for each learner to emit successive approximations of the desired behavior, nor was there any provision for the desired responses to be frequently and immediately reinforced. He observed that the reinforcements used in education *were* usually indirectly related, at best, to the responses desired for learning and that the contingencies of reinforcement, if considered at all, *are* arranged most haphazardly. The teacher as the primary reinforcing agent certainly was not adequate in most instructional situations. Some sort of device was needed.

A number of studies followed in which programs and machines were developed and tested, applying the principles described by Skinner. Programs in the areas of physics, remedial reading and vocabulary building, spelling, German, arithmetic, algebra, and psychology were involved. Various machines were designed and built for these programs. Much of this work was done under Skinner's direction and influence and reported by him a few years later (Skinner 1958, pp. 969–977).

The mechanism, or machine, had a number of features differing from Pressey's. The learner was required to compose his answer rather than select one from alternatives. Skinner argued that in step-by-step approximations plausible alternative choices presented to the learner can potentially strengthen unwanted responses. The machine would present only one frame, or item, to which the learner responded, and all other frames were out of sight. The machine would not advance to the next frame until the learner responded correctly on the current frame. Coding the correct answers into the machine made this feature automatic. With older subjects it was felt that the learner could himself make the comparison between his response and the correct one and that precoded answers might make the program too rigid. These frames were on a disc, which revolved on a turntable; the frames were exposed one at a time, and the learner composed his answer on a strip of paper exposed in another opening. After making his response, he raised a lever that caused his response to move under a transparent cover and at the same time exposed the correct answer. Lowering the lever caused the disc to expose the next frame. The machine could only control the presentation of the program. This control is most vital in the learning situation, but it is the program or material being exposed that teaches.

The characteristics of this learning situation can be described as follows: (1) The student is forced to be active in the learning situation. Unlike less-controlled situations, such as lectures, text reading, movies, or television, he is forced to make responses to stimuli as they are presented to him. (2) He must give the correct response before proceeding further. Again, this differs from techniques where the next stimulus can be presented whether or not the student is ready to proceed. (3) Through the step-by-step approximation, it is apparent when the learner is ready for the next step. (4) With hints, suggestions, and promptings the program helps the learner to make the correct response. (5) Immediate reinforcement is given to each appropriate response. The exposure of the answer is reinforcement, and this immediate feedback is sufficient to maintain the strength of the behavior, i.e., "keep him going."

Norman A. Crowder. Somewhat different approaches to automated instructional devices began to appear in 1958. These differed from Skinner's mainly in what was termed *intrinsic* programming: it was not so important that errors be completely omitted from the learner's responses but that the program should adjust to the correct or incorrect response. Examples of this type of programming are the Tab Item, digital computers that adjust problems automatically according to the learner's responses, and Crowder's automatic tutoring devices. Since Crowder and Skinner represent the two major approaches to automated instruction in the developmental period, the comparison will be made between what Crowder has described as intrinsic programming and what has been discussed concerning Skinner's approach.

Crowder's intrinsic program goes beyond "knowledge of results" to an evaluation of the communication process between the learner and the program. Crowder stated that it is impossible to understand the learning process with specific material so completely that perfect step-by-step approximation can be constructed. To overcome this handicap he built into the program an evaluation of the learner's responses in order to make corrections when the learner does not adequately understand each step. A simple example of how this is done is Crowder's "TutorText" (1960, pp. 286–298). A problem is introduced and the learner makes a choice among the answers that are presented at the bottom of the page in a multiple-choice arrangement. Along with each choice is a page number to which he is referred on the basis of that answer. If his answer is a correct one, he is informed of that fact and is presented with the next step. If his answer is incorrect, his error will be pointed out and explained, and he is referred to the original problem again. The "AutoTutor" is a more complex mechanism, which presents microfilm, motion picture film, or both and records responses and response time on a paper tape. Crowder described what he calls greater flexibility both within and between program steps. "Within-step flexibility" refers to each item of a page or screen presentation, and this is a larger amount of material than is presented in one frame on Skinner's program. Crowder states that this larger amount of material, or flexibility, is necessary because of the complexity of the material and the complexity of the learners. The "between-items flexibility," sometimes referred to as "branching," is necessary because all incorrect responses represent a communication failure that needs correcting, and this can be done only by repeating some items or introducing special items to clear the misunderstanding.

Another major difference between the approaches of Skinner and Crowder is the question of response mode. Skinner emphasizes the necessity of the subject constructing his response rather than responding to a multiple-choice situation. Related to this difference is the fact that the steps from one frame to the next represent a wide jump in Crowder's intrinsic programming as opposed to the small steps in Skinner's linear programming.

Programmed learning criteria

Regardless of the differences between what has been described as linear programming and intrinsic programming, certain criteria can be established for both, which distinguish programming from other techniques and devices of instruction.

(1) Stimuli to which the learner must respond are presented to him. Active participation is required of the learner in contrast to the situations of the lecture, textbook, and audio–visual aids.

(2) The sequence of the material presented is highly controlled as a result of prior observation of its content within and between steps.

(3) A two-way communication is established, since immediate feedback is given by the program to the learner's response. The learner is aware of his progress at all times.

(4) Reinforcement or reward (usually this is immediate feedback) is used to keep the learner responding or interested.

(5) The learner responds to the program at his own rate; this then is similar to a tutorial situation.

(6) Learning occurs without a human instructor in the immediate situation.

Another way of contrasting the techniques of automated instruction with the more traditional educational methods is in the emphasis on what pays off for the learner rather than for the instructor. The lecturer, textbook writer, and the director of various audio–visual aids make use of those techniques which work for each in his own medium. In building a program the emphasis is on the learner's behavior at each step from beginning to end.

Research and development

The first reports of the use of programs in instruction began to appear in 1958, and most of the early reports were based on programs and machines developed and tested under Skinner's direction and influence. Much of this early effort was reported by Skinner in an article in *Science* which received a wide audience and gave impetus to the teaching-machine movement (Skinner 1958). In fact, the article was titled "Teaching Machines," and this was the first time these devices were given this label; the continued use of the term is an indication of the impact of that article.

Effectiveness of programmed instruction. The earliest research yielded some rather dramatic results that indicated a superiority of programmed instruction to more conventional techniques. This superiority was demonstrated in the significant differences found in the amount of time spent in learning and in learner performance.

The research and development in the next few years was phenomenal—a commentary on the value of this early effort and the tremendous need that many scholars felt existed for work in this direction. By 1964 more than two hundred research reports in programming appeared, directed toward the questions of whether programs do teach and, if so, which of the significant variables in the teaching–learning situation are under the control of the program.

The evidence leaves no doubt whether the programs teach: they do. Results of programs developed that use the models of Skinner, Crowder, or Pressey, as well as recent variations or combinations of these, contribute to this conclusion. Furthermore, learning occurs whether the program is presented by machine or in a text format. Learners varying in age from preschool to adult and in ability from the retarded and adult illiterate to advanced graduate student and practicing professional have been the subjects of these observations of program effectiveness. Programs have been used to teach motor, verbal, and perceptual skills at nearly every level of difficulty.

The question of whether programs teach more efficiently and effectively than other possible techniques was one of the first asked in research; in fact, most of the early research was concerned with a comparison of programmed instruction with conventional instruction. All but a few of these studies showed either a significant difference in favor of the program or no difference between the two. These observations were made with programs using the Skinnerian linear, or "shaping" model, the Crowder "intrinsic," or communication model, and the automated test model of Pressey. Although most of the programs constructed for these studies were of the linear type, enough programs employing the techniques of other models were used to indicate no inherent superiority of a particular set of techniques. It should be pointed out that these studies lacked the precision and thoroughness to warrant much confidence in them; the programs in most cases covered relatively small amounts of instructional material and generally were too crude and hastily developed to be exemplary of a desirable programming technology. Nevertheless, the results were such that most researchers felt that programs provided effective instruction, and because of the control over the teaching–learning situation inherent in the programming approach, their efforts were directed toward isolating those variables which make the instructional situation effective.

Analysis of the learning process. Most of the research has been done by psychologists and educational psychologists with the objective of basing a description of the learning process in instructional situations upon psychological principles of learning. Not since Thorndike had experimental psychologists interested in learning directed a concerted effort toward the application of learning principles in instruction. Because of techniques of behavioral analysis developed by Skinner and because of the respected position he enjoys among experimental psychologists, a great number of psychologists were attracted to analysis of instruction through techniques of behavioral analysis developed in the laboratory. It was the application of the methodology to the applied situations in education and training, rather than a comparison of new and conventional instructional techniques, that attracted most psychologists. The major research, then, was concerned with isolating and describing the critical variables in the teaching–learning situation, using the method of behavioral analysis.

It was natural that many researchers began by attempting to replicate in modified form the earlier learning laboratory experiments and that the first of these were directed toward those variables found to be significant in Skinner's techniques of behavioral analysis. The techniques to be used for shaping the learner's responses, the effect of errors on this shaping process, the characteristics of the responses to be made by the learner, and the identification of the reinforcers in these learning situations were the problems covered in the early research; namely, how should the stimulus material be presented to the learner, in what mode and in what relationship to the stimulus should the learner's response be made, is confirmation of correct responses a reinforcement, and what effect does a high error rate have on learning?

Amount of information. A number of studies have focused upon varying the amount of information to which the learner is to respond. This amount ranged in scope from short statements to one or two paragraphs or even several pages of written material. The results of these studies are not easy to interpret; the amount of information is difficult to measure in terms of length alone and is not independent of the type of information transmitted. Generally the results favor smaller amounts, especially in the early steps of instruction. Since most of the studies used short programs involving a relatively small amount of information, critical tests of this question have yet to be made.

Sequence of information. Related to amount of information is the problem of how the information is to be sequenced. Should the information be arranged according to "expert" understanding of the specific material? Is there some logical pattern underlying the learning task that can be used in sequencing the material for instruction? Several experiments have failed to show any difference between ordered or random sequencing of the material, but these have been with short programs. A few studies that have been concerned with analyzing the material to identify categories of learning tasks for instructional sequencing appear as the major effort in attacking this area. By basing the instruction on the learner's present repertory and then proceeding through the material that has been sequenced according to the characteristic responses to be learned, the studies have made a major contribution to the technology of programmed learning.

Mode and importance of response. A relatively large number of experiments have been concerned with the response mode, i.e., overt responses, covert responses, multiple-choice responses, or reading the same material with no required response. In the great majority of studies no difference has been found between the three types of active responses, and evidence does not clearly indicate that active responding is superior to merely reading the material. The results, however, do show a relationship between errors during learning and some criteria of performance at the end of instruction. When response errors are made in the program, evidence suggests that those students required to make a correct response before proceeding further, ultimately perform at a higher level. Obviously, a short program with a low error probability would not yield much difference, especially if the performance criteria were not particularly sensitive.

In addition to the mode of response, the question of the relationship of the response to the material has been investigated, i.e., is the response critical to the material presented by the stimulus? Although only a few studies have been directed toward this question, the evidence indicates superior results from those programs in which critical response is required.

The nature of reinforcement. The research area receiving the major emphasis in the early work in programmed learning has been the application of the principle of reinforcement. What is reinforcing in the programming situation? Confirmation of correct responses is not clearly a reinforcer in all programming situations; the responses of some students do extinguish in the presence of confirmation while those of others fail to extinguish in the absence of confirmation. In several studies the effects of prompting—the correct response being shown to the learner, who is then required to repeat it—have been compared to those of confirmation, and in most of these studies prompting led to higher performance than confirmation. Obviously, reinforcement in the programming situation is related to the incentive conditions under which the learner is responding. One study suggests that the appearance of the frame in the machine is itself reinforcing. Other efforts to control responses have made highly desirable behaviors contingent upon making responses in a program. For example, a peer–tutor situation makes use of this by requiring the student to learn in order to teach another student. This has been most successful in teaching adult illiterates to read and write. Nevertheless, the complex relationship of intrinsic and extrinsic reinforcers present in human learning situations makes the task of identifying effective reinforcers extremely difficult indeed.

Errors. One of the clearest results of the research has been recognition of the relationship between the number of errors and performance criteria. Programs with a lower probability of response errors tend to be related to ultimately higher criterion performance. The cause of a high rate of error obviously cannot be separated from other variables in the instructional situation; therefore, attempts to solve this particular problem become somewhat circular. There has been no adequate analysis of the effect of errors in intrinsic programs except an awareness that a learner's attitude tends to be negative when the error rate is high. Regardless of the type of program, the evidence indicates that errors need to be corrected immediately before proceeding.

Evaluation. Since the beginning of concerted research effort to describe the significant variables in the area of programmed learning, one is struck by the high proportion of studies in which no differences have been observed. It is clear that the variables involved in effective instruction have not been isolated and described. Many studies that have registered observable differences are counterbalanced by contradictory evidence in other research or lack sufficient replication to allow extrapolation to general instruction procedure. While the effort has been considerable, the period during which this work has occurred has been a brief one, the programs have covered only small amounts of material, and the instruments for evaluation have lacked precision.

Potential

Although positive contributions to an instructional technology from specific research efforts are few, the fact remains that never has the teaching–learning situation received the attention of so many experimentalists interested in human learning. Programmed learning represents an application of behavioral analysis techniques to the learning of meaningful material. The controlled observations possible through programmed learning are making possible more precise descriptions of behavior in the instructional situation than at any time previously. The necessity of evaluating instruction with stated objectives in behavioral terms and the effectiveness of the principles of active response and immediate reinforcement to instruction have been successfully demonstrated. From these beginnings a technology can be expected to develop which translates, in a systematic and highly generalizable way, the specified terminal behaviors into the form and sequence of the instructional task.

To many psychologists and educators the attraction of programming, and certainly the success of the approach thus far, has been the attention to laboratory research in learning. As noted earlier, however, the research in programming has been concerned with showing the influence of learning variables studied in the laboratory to applied learning situations; in general, the results of this research have been somewhat equivocal. Gagné (1962, pp. 85–86) has noted that the identification and arrangements of task components are more important in developing efficient and effective instructional situations than many of the variables studied in the learning laboratory, e.g., reinforcement, meaningfulness, distribution of practice, and so forth. Also, Melton (1959, pp. 100–101) has stated that laboratory research has not produced sufficient knowledge of different learning areas to allow an integration of possible generalizations to be highly useful in application. Melton also stated that there is yet no satisfactory taxonomical scheme to describe specific tasks that humans perform.

It is apparent that a number of factors are contributing to the absence of any rapid integration of a science of learning with an educational technology. The limited development of a science of learning, a taxonomy that allows placement of learning tasks in a dimensional matrix, the mutually exclusive efforts of the experimental and educational psychologists beween the 1930s and late 1950s, and the complex interaction of variables in an educational learning situation are some of the obstacles that have held back such an integration. By the mid-1960s, however, these obstacles seemed to be disappearing. Experimental psychologists were introducing into the laboratory problems from applied instructional situations, and experimental and educational psychologists were cooperating on research projects at an increasing rate. Programmed learning introduced a methodology for observing and controlling behavior in an instructional situation which attracted the experimentalist, and the programming technique proved to be an effective instructional instrument which attracted the educational psychologist. Clearly the effort was made to build an educational technology from a science of learning just as an engineering technology was built from basic sciences. Equally clear was the necessity for an area of transitional research to develop a taxonomy of tasks useful to technology and the science of learning.

Breadth of application. By 1965 there were more than a thousand programs published and available for purchase in the United States. Of these, approximately two-thirds were educational programs for courses or units within courses at all levels—elementary through graduate school. Programs were available for teaching beginning reading skills, mathematics at all levels, second-language reading and listening skills, spelling, grammar, punctuation, economic concepts, music fundamentals, statistics, genetics, biology, medicine, and physics. Many more programs were being developed or had been developed and were being used for limited objectives in specific classes. Programs were being used in other special situations, such as educational and vocational counseling, marriage counseling, interpersonal relationships, and the teaching of recreational skills.

Nearly three hundred programs in the field of business and industry were published and available by 1965; these included programs in areas of secretarial skills, management skills, bank teller skills, salesman training, and consumer training. Many more programs had been developed for the exclusive training of personnel of a particular company. Also, the military and the U.S. Public Health Service have developed a large number of programs to train their personnel.

Except in those cases in which the material presented or the response required demands a mechanical device, most programs are available in a text format. Language-listening skills, pitch discrimination, or the control of the responses of a small child are examples of such specific demands. The text format has provided economy and flexibility advantageous to programming's extended use in education, but the format probably has had a restraining effect on making broader application of the programming technique in education.

Use outside the United States. Because of the development of the programming technique in the United States, most research has taken place and the largest number of programs have been published there, but considerable effort in the research and development of programmed materials has been made in other countries. Considerable use of the techniques has been made in many European and Latin American countries, particularly in Great Britain, Germany, Sweden, the Soviet Union, the Netherlands, and Brazil. Much of the work has been done in these countries by following models of efforts in the United States. With the exception of the Soviet Union, a science of learning has not developed in other countries to the extreme that it has in the United States, a fact which has limited the use of the programming model elsewhere. Because of a highly developed psychology of learning and its differences from that in the United States, the Russians might be expected to make significant contributions to the programming field.

In 1963, two UNESCO-sponsored workshops, one in Nigeria and the other in Jordan, introduced programmed instruction to areas of the world where it may have special significance. The necessity for more efficient and effective methods of education and training is especially great in the so-called developing countries, but this necessity is compounded by the world-wide scarcity of teachers. The self-instruction feature of programming makes its potential obvious.

There is little doubt that programmed learning represents a significant union of the science of learning with the practical problems of learning management. Effective teaching and training devices have been constructed. These early devices undoubtedly are extremely crude in comparison to what may appear in the future. The limit and potential of the use of programming in education and training are far from being determined in this early stage of development. The more important contribution of programmed learning to teaching and training is the introduction of a technique for an experimental analysis of behavior. Through the technique the practical problems of learning management can be brought under control so that careful observation and precise descriptions of learner responses to stimulus materials in an instructional situation can be made.

RUSSELL W. BURRIS

[*Other relevant material may be found in* EDUCATIONAL PSYCHOLOGY; SIMULATION, *article on* INDIVIDUAL BEHAVIOR; *and in the biography of* THORNDIKE.]

BIBLIOGRAPHY

CENTER FOR PROGRAMED INSTRUCTION, NEW YORK 1962 *The Use of Programed Instruction in U.S. Schools: Report of a Survey of the Use of Programed Instructional Materials in the Public Schools of the United States During the Year 1961–1962.* New York: The Center. → Compiled and produced by the Center's Research Division in cooperation with the U.S. Department of Health, Education and Welfare.

CONFERENCE ON APPLICATION OF DIGITAL COMPUTERS TO AUTOMATED INSTRUCTION, WASHINGTON, D.C., *1961* 1962 *Programmed Learning and Computer-based Instruction: Proceedings.* New York: Wiley. → See especially John E. Coulson's contribution, "A Computer-based Laboratory for Research and Development in Education," on pages 191–204.

CROWDER, NORMAN A. 1960 Automatic Tutoring by Intrinsic Programming. Pages 286–298 in Arthur A. Lumsdaine and Robert Glaser (editors), *Teaching Machines and Programmed Learning: A Source Book.* Washington: National Education Association, Department of Audio–Visual Instruction.

GAGNÉ, ROBERT M. 1962 Military Training and Principles of Learning. *American Psychologist* 17:83–91.

GAGNÉ, ROBERT M. 1965 *The Conditions of Learning.* New York: Holt.

GALANTER, EUGENE (editor) 1959 *Automatic Teaching: The State of the Art.* New York: Wiley.

GLASER, ROBERT (editor) 1962 *Training Research and Education.* Univ. of Pittsburgh Press.

GREEN, EDWARD J. 1962 *The Learning Process and Programmed Instruction.* New York: Holt.

HOLLAND, JAMES G. 1960 Teaching Machines: An Application of Principles From the Laboratory. *Journal of the Experimental Analysis of Behavior* 3:275–287.

LUMSDAINE, ARTHUR A. 1961 *Student Response in Programmed Instruction: A Symposium on Experimental Studies of Cue and Response Factors in Group and Individual Learning From Instructional Media.* Washington: National Academy of Sciences–National Research Council.

LUMSDAINE, ARTHUR A.; and GLASER, ROBERT (editors) 1960 *Teaching Machines and Programmed Learning: A Source Book.* Washington: National Education Association, Department of Audio–Visual Instruction.

MAGER, ROBERT F. 1961 *Preparing Objectives for Programmed Instruction.* San Francisco: Fearon.

MELTON, ARTHUR W. 1959 The Science of Learning and the Technology of Educational Methods. *Harvard Educational Review* 29:96–106.

PRESSEY, SIDNEY L. (1926) 1960 A Simple Apparatus Which Gives Tests and Scores—and Teaches. Pages 35–41 in Arthur A. Lumsdaine and Robert Glaser (editors), *Teaching Machines and Programmed Learning: A Source Book.* Washington: National Education Association, Department of Audio–Visual Instruction. → First published in Volume 23 of *School and Society.*

PRESSEY, SIDNEY L. (1932) 1960 A Third and Fourth Contribution Toward the Coming "Industrial Revolution" in Education. Pages 47–51 in Arthur A. Lumsdaine and Robert Glaser (editors), *Teaching Machines and Programmed Learning: A Source Book.* Washington: National Education Association, Department of Audio–Visual Instruction. → First published in Volume 36 of *School and Society.*

PRESSEY, SIDNEY L. 1963 Teaching Machine (and Learning Theory) Crisis. *Journal of Applied Psychology* 47:1–6.

SCHRAMM, WILBUR L. 1962 *Programmed Instruction, Today and Tomorrow.* New York: Fund for the Advancement of Education.

SCHRAMM, WILBUR L. 1964 *The Research on Programed Instruction: An Annotated Bibliography.* U.S. Office of Education, Bulletin No. 35. Washington: U.S. Department of Health, Education and Welfare, Office of Education.

SKINNER, B. F. 1954 The Science of Learning and the Art of Teaching. *Harvard Educational Review* 24:86–97.

SKINNER, B. F. 1958 Teaching Machines. *Science* 128: 969–977.

LEARNING THEORY

Since its emergence as a relatively distinct topic, learning theory has played a central role in psychology. Historically, many psychologists interested in the scientific understanding of behavior have worked with learning phenomena, while psychologists with major interests in areas other than learning, as well as workers in related disciplines, have considered learning to be a pervasive process that enters into quite diverse aspects of behavior. Widespread interest in learning theory has followed the recognition that the theoretical integration of facts and laws is an integral part of what is meant by scientific understanding and that theory serves useful organizational and conceptual functions. Objections to the theory aspect of learning theory have generally reflected disagreement concerning the schedule of the theorizing relative to the empirical development of the field, rather than questions of the ultimate desirability of theorizing about learning.

At the present time the kinds of activities subsumed under the rubric of learning theory present a rapidly changing and expanding pattern of interests. Because of this situation it is impossible to define or specify learning theory in any simple way. Indeed, neither "learning" nor "theory" is a term that is used with consistent meaning by those active in the area. Commonly, learning has been considered to be a process which results from practice and which is reflected as a more or less permanent change in behavior. In many traditional learning theories, learning has been carefully specified to be some sort of associationist process as distinguished from motivational, maturational, inhibitory, and fatigue processes. While learning is thus defined in some cases, even a cursory survey of those systems called learning theories reveals that they include motivational and inhibitory factors. In most such formulations, with the exception of mathematical theories of learning, consideration of motivational variables greatly overshadows concern with the more narrowly defined learning process itself. Thus, many learning theories are in reality theories of behavior, with the term "learning" more or less limiting the range of behavior included.

Similarly, the word "theory" is used in many ways, with an even greater range of meaning than is the case with "learning." At one extreme are theories which represent nonspecific verbal systems that better serve the "psychology of discovery" of the theorist than satisfy the basic requirement of theories with respect to the integration of data or generation of testable predictions. In this respect, it should be noted that the present discussion applies the term "theory" to a wide variety of formulations, without requiring that they meet criteria of testability, usefulness, or scope. At the other extreme are very specific uses of the term deriving from its usage in mathematical logic. In more restricted uses of the term, there are theories which represent, in varying degrees of quantitative elaboration, hypotheses about the interrelationships of systems of constructs, such as those of the intervening variable type. Further complicating the picture is the increasing use of the term "model" (Lachman 1960), which has a similar variable meaning.

It is obvious that no simple classification of learning theory is possible, and instead of an attempt to develop an arbitrary classificatory scheme attention will be directed, first, toward the development of learning theory and, second, toward a characterization of present approaches and formulations.

The development of learning theory

In the United States, systems or theories specifically concerned with learning and motivation began to emerge in the late 1930s and early 1940s. Coming from a background of "schools" of psychology, for example, structuralism, functionalism, gestalt psychology, and behaviorism, learning theory took the form of systematic positions organized around individuals who promulgated systems of constructs, principles, and research strategies in attempts to account for varying ranges of learning phenomena. Closely connected with this development were the controversies which arose about the basic nature of learning and reinforcement. These controversies, which came to dominate much of the activity in learning at that time, furthered the establishment and growth of the individualistic systems.

Major systems. The major systematic positions were the subject of Hilgard's influential book *Theories of Learning* (1948), the book itself being instrumental in establishing the term "learning theory" in common usage. Among the systems described by Hilgard were Thorndike's early connectionism, Guthrie's emphasis on contiguous conditioning as a basic principle of learning, Hull's attempt to develop a highly rigorous quantitative theory based on data from simple learning situations, and Tolman's cognitive, gestalt-influenced theory, which stressed "sign-learning." The contributions of Pavlov and Bekhterev certainly must be listed here also because of their tremendous influence on the development of learning theory and because of the importance of present-day neo-Pavlovian theory in the Soviet Union. [*See the biographies of* BEKHTEREV *and* PAVLOV.]

The learning theories of this period were characterized by Spence (1951) as being divided on two major issues: first, the nature of the concepts used to represent the hypothetical changes taking place in learning, and, second, the conditions believed to be necessary for these changes to take place.

Sign–significate versus stimulus–response. With respect to the first of these issues the comparison was between those (for example, Koffka, Köhler, Lewin, Tolman) who considered learning to reflect some kind of a perceptual reorganization or restructuring of the subject's cognitive field which corresponded to the stimulus relationships present in the environment; and those (for example, Guthrie, Thorndike, Hull) who conceived learning to be a modification of the strength of associations, habits, or response tendencies. The former were called *S–S* (sign–significate) theorists, the latter *S–R* (stimulus–response) theorists. The emphasis was directed, respectively, toward the effects of field conditions and other variables on perceptual organization and the relations between sensory events and toward the factors influencing the strength of associations, whether the associations were represented as empirical functional relationships or defined theoretical constructs. [*See the biographies of* GUTHRIE; HULL; LEWIN; THORNDIKE; TOLMAN; WATSON.]

Reinforcement versus contiguity. The second division was termed the reinforcement–contiguity issue. Here the distinctions concerned whether or not environmental aftereffects of behavior operated in some manner to change the strength of the learning process. Also involved were issues about the usefulness of special theories of reinforcement that attempted to identify the nature of the reinforcement or the manner in which the learning association was changed. Mention must also be made of two factor theories that generally postulated a classical–instrumental or autonomic–skeletal breakdown in which different kinds of learning were involved. These dual theories, which became increasingly popular, were held at various times by B. F. Skinner, Harold Schlosberg, O. H. Mowrer, and Kenneth Spence, among others. While many variations were proposed, contiguity principles were commonly paired with classical conditioning or with the conditioning of autonomic-nervous-system responses, and reinforcement theory was usually paired with instrumental–skeletal responses.

Learning controversies. The learning theories and issues discussed above resulted in a great many disputes and controversies regarding the nature of learning, especially discrimination learning. Absolute and relational views of discrimination learning represented one such issue. The absolute position held that discrimination learning involves the strengthening or weakening of the response of approaching different aspects (discriminanda) of the total stimulus configuration, as a function of reinforcement and nonreinforcement; the relational position viewed discrimination learning as depending upon inherent perceptual-organizing tendencies, with the response always being to certain relational properties inherent in the stimulus configuration. This distinction also appeared in views of the nature of generalization and in analyses of transposition phenomena.

Another important controversy of the period centered on continuity and noncontinuity interpretations of discrimination learning, interpretations that were concerned with the question of whether an animal learns about environmental events which are being differentially reinforced but to which he is not responding differentially. The continuity position's answer to this question was, Yes; the noncontinuity answer, No. Interest in the problem declined because of the difficulty in testing the alternative positions that developed, although in a modified and less controversial form the general question of attention in discrimination learning remains an active area of interest. Finally, mention should be made of disputes regarding "latent learning," place (cognitive) versus response learning, and insight versus trial and error learning. [*See* LEARNING, *article on* DISCRIMINATION LEARNING; PERCEPTION, *articles on* PERCEPTUAL DEVELOPMENT *and* DEPTH PERCEPTION.]

The shift from major systems. It must be recognized that these positions and controversies occupied the major attention of learning theorists for a relatively long period during the growth of interest in learning phenomena and that much of the research of this time was in the context of these issues. Thus, the shift away from these formulations that began to be evident in the early 1950s marked a distinct change in both the direction and content of learning theory. This transition, which is clearly evident in a comparison of Hilgard's first (1948) and second (1956) editions of *Theories of Learning,* was due to a number of factors. Without detracting from the historical importance of these approaches or the recognition of their essential contribution to all aspects of current learning theory, it can be recognized that the problems and limitations of the systematic and controversy-oriented theory of that period were such as to lead to change. As psychology became more sophisticated about applying testability criteria to theories, the demand increased that concepts and constructs (or the systems and models into which they were incorporated) should have empirical reference. It became obvious that many of the positions and controversies that had been the focal points of debate were not formulated in a way that would provide clear-cut empirical predictions. In other words, with some exceptions these were systems at the verbal level that could not be translated into the clear-cut experimental manipulations necessary for unambiguous testing. While adequately representing general approaches and serving certain heuristic functions, many of the systems did not serve a desired function of theories—that of integrating and predicting laws. It was also recognized that one possible reason for their lack of specificity was the range of behavior included. It was found that with the existing state of empirical knowledge, learning, as an area, was much too complex to be adequately handled by these broad approaches.

By and large the systems were concerned with simple learning situations; for example, classical conditioning, instrumental learning, and simple discrimination learning. While many learning psychologists recognized the strategy of building from the simple to the complex, they were not satisfied with the pace, were skeptical of the system–controversy aspect of the activity, or felt that important variables were being neglected. These workers, therefore, applied some of the techniques and concepts to other areas of interest or became involved in different kinds of theorizing. The changes as they have developed have represented a distinct turn toward "smaller" theories that are more closely tied to empirical data and that often deal with a single or closely related group of phenomena. Thus, these "smaller" theories have not been based on the theoretical predictions of a few dominant theorists, instead, they have proliferated as phenomena or areas of investigation have been developed or have caught the interest of investigators. Concurrently, there has come a great increase in the use of the model and in the utilization of mediation process notions in all areas of theory construction.

Current learning theory. Current activity in learning theory cannot be simply classified along orthogonal dimensions, such as type of theorizing employed, type of learning phenomena involved, or experimental situations used. Rather than attempting to develop and justify a complex classificatory system, the following section will use broad categories that are intended only to serve a loose organizing function. Considered first are more general theories that have a relatively close relationship to the older systems; second, those which deal with classes of behavior or specific variables. In addition, theoretical activity concerned with traditional experimental learning situations, for example, classical conditioning, instrumental conditioning, discrimination learning, and verbal learning, is discussed, along with a brief consideration of more complex learning situations. It should be recognized that considerable overlap exists between these divisions and that many individual theories and areas of theoretical activity are omitted.

General approaches

While it is obvious that present-day learning theory is not primarily engaged in the elaboration of the theoretical structures of previous systems, the influence of older formulations is clearly represented in current work, and some theoretical activity has been rather directly derived from the "classical" positions. The latter has been the case more for *S–R* theory than for *S–S* approaches. There are several theoretical systems that are closely related to Hullian theory, and, similarly, the relationship of stimulus-sampling models to Guthrie's position is obvious. On the other hand, the influence of *S–S* theory is primarily evident in approaches that stress perceptual and cognitive variables, for example, perceptual models of discrimination learning and notions of cue utilization.

Modifications of *S–R* approaches. *Miller.* The changes in *S–R* approaches are exemplified by Miller's discussion of the "liberalization of *S–R* theory" (1959), which includes a consideration of the application of *S–R* concepts to central processes and the role of cybernetic-type feedback systems and attentional mechanisms in behavior. While admitting that postulation of central processes within an *S–R* framework reduces the difference between *S–R* and cognitive theory, Miller describes the *S–R* position as one that tends to apply the same laws to central processes as to peripheral stimuli and responses; this is in contrast to cognitive theory, which is characterized as being less specific about the laws involved. A characteristic of Miller's work has been his attempt to apply laboratory-developed theories and concepts to complex social-behavior situations, the application of his theory of approach–avoidance conflict behavior to diverse and complex human behavioral situations being a case in point. In a sense this is a "model" approach, since the attempt is to find isomorphism between the systems developed in simple animal learning situations and complex human behavior. This approach is to be contrasted with that which attempts to expand theories dealing with a restricted range of simple phenomena by gradually integrating variables and laws from other behavioral situations. [*See* CONFLICT, *article on* PSYCHOLOGICAL ASPECTS; CYBERNETICS.]

Spence. Spence's theory (e.g., 1956) developed from early collaborative work with Hull. Starting with a quantitative *S–R* account of discrimination learning, Spence has developed in his later work a system that is more systematic than Hull's theory and much more closely tied to empirical data. In contrast to Hull's broader, less empirically based approach, is Spence's detailed concern with such topics as (1) the fractional anticipatory goal response, which is proposed as the mechanism underlying incentive; (2) the role of frustration in partial reinforcement and extinction; and (3) his theory of emotionally based drive. A major objective of Spence's theorizing has been to develop formulations that would allow for the derivation of empirical relationships found in a variety of learning situations and that could, with the addition of "composition rules," extend to more complex learning phenomena. [*See* DRIVES, *article on* PHYSIOLOGICAL DRIVES.]

Mowrer. Another theorist to be considered in this section is Mowrer. His most recent formulation (1960) assigns a central role to the classical conditioning of implicit responses or emotional states, which are called hope, disappointment, fear, or relief, depending upon the nature of the reinforcer (positive or negative) and the relation of the stimulus to the reinforcer (signaling its presence or imminent onset, or absence or approaching cessation). Mowrer is one theorist who does not follow the trend toward more restricted theorizing; rather, he proposes that his basic explanatory principles will encompass a wide range of human learning phenomena.

Mathematical theories. Perhaps the most rapidly expanding area of learning theorizing is that of mathematical (stochastic) theories of learning. Two principal lines of development have generally been distinguished. Statistical learning theory, or stimulus-sampling theory, has used conceptions of the environmental stimulus situation to obtain learning axioms and theorems about the changes that occur in response probabilities as a consequence of environmental events. Operator models, on the other hand, have been primarily concerned with those properties of response sequences that are a result of various transformation rules; assumptions about outcome effects and response classes appear in the nature of the particular model. Both approaches share similar features, such as the assumptions that the environmental outcomes associated with response alternatives change the distribution of choice probabilities and that probabilistic mechanisms govern response selections. Mathematical representations of learning have been quite successful in handling the data from some learning situations. Often, however, these situations have been specifically arranged to lend themselves to mathematical treatment and do not represent paradigms commonly used by other theorists. Further problems have been the relative difficulty of deciding when a particular formulation is appropriate and the fact that there are often a number of alternative assumptions or models that lead to essentially the same results. While promising advances have been made, the future of this approach will be determined by its success in overcoming obstacles and arriving at transsituational mathematical representations of basic learning processes. [*See* MODELS, MATHEMATICAL; *for a survey of this area, see* Sternberg 1963.]

Phenomena-centered theories

Turning to theories which tend to deal more with certain kinds of behaviors or classes of variables, brief mention will be made of several areas in which the general shift toward phenomena-centered theorizing is evident.

Curiosity behaviors and reinforcement. One trend that has developed since the 1950s has been the increasing attention directed toward exploratory, manipulatory, and curiosity behaviors; and it is not surprising to find corresponding theoretical formulations which attempt to integrate the data of this area. One such theory is represented by the work of Berlyne (1960), who considers four variables to be of primary importance in stimulus-selection processes: novelty, uncertainty, degree of conflict, and complexity. The organism is presumed to direct attention both by central processes and by exploratory behavior (orienting responses, locomotor exploration, and investigatory responses) that alters the stimulus field. These variables are integrated with arousal-level concepts and further tied to reinforcement, for example, in that arousal reduction may be reinforcing. [*See* ATTENTION; STIMULATION DRIVES.]

Concern with the nature of the reinforcing event is characteristic of formulations dealing with the effects of novelty, exploratory behavior, curiosity, and similar stimulus variables and response patterns. To a large extent this concern has represented dissatisfaction with the tendency of older theories to expand their motivational and reinforcement notions from a single drive or drive mechanism and with their disposition to concentrate upon a few biogenic drives, for example, hunger. Also contributing to this interest has been the demonstration of the high reinforcing value of visual and manipulatory exploration. This work, in which Harlow has played a major role, has forced learning to attend to a new class of variables in a manner similar to the way in which gestalt psychology focused attention on a previously ignored set of perceptual phenomena. While theory concerned with novelty, curiosity, and similar variables has generally not reached the degree of specificity associated with some other areas of theorizing, it is an active and promising area that will undoubtedly become integrated with theories that presently do not deal with these variables to any great extent.

A similar situation exists with respect to investigations of the orienting reflex. Starting with Pavlov's original work, the orienting reflex has proved a rich topic for research in the Soviet Union and has been the focus of a great increase of interest in the United States. The orienting reflex, which is considered to be a functional, centrally organized and integrated system of somatic, visceral, and cognitive reactions, is evoked by changes in stimulation or "novel" stimuli. Sokolov, the most prominent worker in this field, has elaborated a neuronal model concerned with the properties of the orienting reflex (1960).

Verbal processes. Of similar interest is the concern with the role of verbal processes in learning. While these processes play a major role in some theories of discrimination learning, interest in verbal processes also serves as a more general framework within which many theoretical formulations are being made. Work in the Soviet Union is particularly noteworthy in this respect. Coming from the separate but related traditions of Pavlov and L. S. Vigotski, Soviet researchers have increasingly been concerned with the second (verbal) signaling system and its relationship to learning. Luria (1961) among others has been quite active in theorizing about the verbal regulation of behavior, especially voluntary movements, with an emphasis on developmental factors both in normal and abnormal children. Note should also be made of the growing interest in relating conceptions of orienting reflex and feedback to theories of the development of voluntary action. [*See* CONCEPT FORMATION; LEARNING, *article on* VERBAL LEARNING.]

Punishment. Another area that has seen a large increase in theoretical activity is that concerned with the effects of punishment on behavior. It has become clear that punishment can have a wide variety of facilitatory, inhibitory, or suppressive effects depending upon the behavioral, situational, and punishment parameters involved, and a number of theorists have attempted to integrate these effects into existing theoretical structures or to develop principles which will link the various experimental findings. Thus, some theorists have discussed the conditioning of anticipatory punishment cues or have considered punishment to be a special case of avoidance learning, while others have emphasized the role of fear, the nature of the skeletal responses elicited by the punishment, or the stimulus properties of punishment. [*See* LEARNING, *article on* AVOIDANCE LEARNING.]

Developmental psychology. Another increasingly active area with import for learning theory is developmental psychology. The recent trend in this area has been a de-emphasis of normative, naturalistic observation and an increasing use of the experimental method. Correspondingly, there has been a turning away from the "grand" developmental theories as theories, although their utilization as a source of ideas continues. Thus, the conceptual framework and insightful observations of Piaget have occasioned intense interest in developmental psychology, and considerable effort is underway to translate the system and specific ideas into experimentally testable form. As this sort of experimental activity continues, developmental psychology seems destined to have closer ties to other areas of psychology. Indeed, those working in various content areas have also been moving toward developmental concepts. It appears obvious that learning theory must utilize, include, or become integrated with specific experimentally based developmental theory if it hopes to make significant progress in the future. [*See* DEVELOPMENTAL PSYCHOLOGY.]

Neurophysiology. Brief mention should also be made of the current work on the neurophysiological basis of learning. Although learning theory of the past has not emphasized physiological constructs to any great extent, this situation may well change as progress is made in understanding the neural basis of learning. It should also be noted that physiological theorizing has generally taken the form of hypotheses about the nature of the physiological or biochemical mechanisms involved. This is in contrast to learning theory in the United States, which has been much more inclined toward the use of systems involving defined concepts or constructs. Theorizing in both areas has felt the impact of the "model" approach, and some rapprochement may occur because of this. Learning theory in the Soviet Union has been much more closely tied to neurophysiological concepts. [*See* LEARNING, *article on* NEUROPHYSIOLOGICAL ASPECTS; NERVOUS SYSTEM.]

Other phenomena. Examples of theorizing can also be seen with learning phenomena of more limited scope. Thus, the effects of partial reinforcement in acquisition and extinction have served to trigger the development of "small" theoretical formulations that attempt to isolate the effective parameters in the experimental situation and to derive the effects from more basic learning phenomena, for example, stimulus generalization, or as special cases of more general learning theories. In some cases, empirical findings that have countered common sense expectations or the simple derivations of theory have served as the focal points of theoretical activity.

In these examples the phenomena-centered nature of current learning theory is evident, in contrast to the older formulations which tended to start with general principles or postulates concerning the nature of the learning or reinforcement process.

Current work in traditional areas

Classical conditioning. Contemporary theories concerned with classical conditioning have been summarized by Grings (1963). With some exceptions, for example, Razran's detailed schema, the primary theoretical work has been directed more toward various aspects of the conditioning process than toward the development of a general explanatory system of classical conditioning per se. Much of the interest in classical conditioning has been in its postulated role in other, presumably more complicated, kinds of behavior; for example, theorizing regarding incentive variables, such as the fractional anticipatory goal response, has made use of classical conditioning processes, or as Lachman (1960) discusses it, classical conditioning provides the model, that is, the inference rules, for fractional anticipatory goal response theory. Similar theorizing has developed with respect to (1) the consequences of frustration, with frustration being defined either as the blocking of an ongoing response or as the omission of a reward, as in partial reinforcement or extinction; and (2) behavioral situations involving the use of punishment. Thus, in many situations where events are conceptualized to mediate overt behavior, classical conditioning is postulated to play some role or to serve as an inference model for the mediation theory. It should be noted that this use of conditioning is in the *S–R* rather than the cognitive tradition. [*See* DRIVES, *article on* PHYSIOLOGICAL DRIVES; LEARNING, *article on* CLASSICAL CONDITIONING.]

Soviet work. In the Soviet Union, theorizing about classical conditioning has remained a major interest since the pioneering work of Pavlov (e.g., see Anokhin 1955). The characteristics of Pavlov's theorizing are well known, and while many of his specific notions regarding physiological structure and function have been abandoned or modified considerably, present-day learning theory in the Soviet Union retains a physiological orientation. The current Soviet emphasis on interoceptive conditioning, semantic conditioning, and the orienting reflex is reviewed in detail by Razran (1961). Especially noteworthy, in the present context, has been the theoretical development coming from Soviet interests in configural conditioning, the role of conditioning in verbal behavior, and the ontogenetic implications of their work.

Instrumental conditioning. Theorizing involving instrumental conditioning has taken several forms. The effects of various parameters upon instrumental learning have been of interest to theorists who have attempted to integrate empirical relationships into a more comprehensive theory, or who have tried to use the laws obtained in these simple situations to develop formulations which would make it possible to derive the data previously obtained from more complicated selective-learning paradigms. The relative simplicity of instrumental conditioning has been attractive to those who have found the more complicated situations difficult to analyze in a precise manner. Phenomena-centered theorizing is quite evident here, as in other behavioral situations. To mention only two such efforts: certain partial reinforcement effects in acquisition and extinction have been of theoretical interest, and Abram Amsel's analysis (1962) of frustrative nonreward effects has been based on data from instrumental conditioning. [*See* LEARNING, *article on* INSTRUMENTAL LEARNING.]

Avoidance learning. Perhaps the greatest amount of theorizing concerning instrumental behavior has taken place with respect to avoidance learning. These theoretical formulations have generally been concerned with the mediating role of anxiety or fear in avoidance behavior and with the reinforcement principles operating in the dual learning processes of (1) fear or anxiety and (2) the instrumental skeletal response. A comprehensive overview of this area is presented by Solomon and Brush (1956). More recent theorizing has been concerned with specific avoidance phenomena, again demonstrating the trend toward more molecular theorizing. [*See* LEARNING, *article on* AVOIDANCE LEARNING.]

Selective learning. The original work in selective (discrimination) learning was largely concerned with controversies regarding the nature of learning and reinforcement processes. While some of this type of work is still found, current interest has largely shifted to the various processes—attentional, verbal, etc.—which presumably mediate the learning. A closely related development has been the emphasis on phylogenetic and ontogenetic considerations, in terms of discrimination-learning performance and the relative use of the postulated mediational mechanisms. One of the most important developments in the discrimination-learning area has been the learning-set work of Harlow (1959). This research focused attention on discrimination procedures, demonstrated the relevance of this sort of research for more complex learning (for example, concept formation), and provided behavioral techniques that have proved useful in comparing human and infrahuman learning. Theoretical activity has been concerned with the nature of interfering tendencies or error factors.

A great deal of current activity is concerned with discrimination-learning "transfer" situations. A number of paradigms have been used to (1) compare the learning processes in human and infrahuman organisms, (2) explicate the nature of postulated mediating mechanisms, and (3) examine the mediational processes ontogenetically. Theoretical approaches that should be mentioned here include those of Luria (1961) and Kendler and Kendler (1962), both of which have tended to identify mediational processes with verbal behavior, and that of Zeaman and House (1963), which has developed from work with retarded children and which, although mathematical in nature, emphasizes the importance of attentional responses to stimulus dimensions. These formulations demonstrate several trends in discrimination-learning theory. First, the use of multistage mediational models to account for the data; second, the increasing use of normal and retarded children as subjects; and third, as in the case of Zeaman and House, the emphasis on observing or attentional responses. Other theories proposed for selective learning include the observing–response formulation of Wyckoff (1952) and the analyzer-mechanism approach of N. S. Sutherland (1959). A succinct phrase which describes the basic process of concern in a number of these formulations is "selective attention," which can be conceived of in terms of stimulus–response relationships and laws or perceptual–cognitive processes. Approaches which attempt the integration of verbal-behavior relationships with discrimination-learning processes are also popular.

Verbal learning. An excellent discussion of the nature of theory in verbal learning is available in a paper by Gough and Jenkins (1963). These authors point out that verbal learning—the "rote" learning of material under laboratory conditions—did not develop from the learning theories of the 1940s but from the work of Ebbinghaus and the functionalist school of psychology. As an area, verbal learning has always been very closely tied to empirical data and methodological considerations, with little in the way of broad systematic theory. The theories that have developed have been concerned with specific verbal learning or retention phenomena and, as Gough and Jenkins point out, often have been called "analyses" rather than "theories." This lack of broad systematic formulations has led to the development of "small" testable theories, which have been quickly modified to reflect new experimental evidence. A listing of some recent theoretical formulations or analyses gives the flavor of the work. It has been proposed by Underwood and Schulz (1960) that paired-associate verbal learning can best be considered as a two-stage process involving response learning and stimulus–response associative stages. A considerable amount of research has demonstrated the usefulness of this conceptualization. Underwood (1957) has demonstrated that the role of proactive interference in laboratory learning is much greater than was previously assumed, an advance that has contributed to the understanding of forgetting and has led to important changes in methodology. Finally, the development of the interference theory of retroactive inhibition has witnessed the introduction of the concepts of differentiation or the discrimination of list membership and unlearning or extinction to account for discrepancies between interference theory and the obtained data. The close interplay between data and theory is apparent. [*See* FORGETTING; LEARNING, *article on* VERBAL LEARNING.]

Complex learning situations. Concept learning, skill learning, and problem solving are areas that have generally been considered to be more complex and harder to handle in terms of theory than those previously discussed. There are several dimensions of this complexity, for example, the ease or difficulty of dealing with discrete units of behavior or a limited number of basic processes and the necessity of considering sequential relationships. Until relatively recently, theorists were reluctant to deal with these situations, as demonstrated by the early discarding of problem-box situations for the simpler classical-conditioning and instrumental-learning procedures. The resurgence of interest in and of theorizing about these more complex areas has led to attempts to extend *S–R* and cognitive approaches to these phenomena, and, in some cases, it has led to new conceptual frameworks which bear little obvious relationship to traditional learning approaches.

Concept learning. Concept learning has, perhaps, remained closer to conventional learning research than the other areas mentioned. Kendler (1964) has pointed out that various learning models have been applied to concept learning. He lists *S–R* conceptions, operant conditioning, clustering, Piaget's methods of investigation, computer simulation of cognitive processes, and mathematical models as methods and models for the analysis of concept learning. [*See* CONCEPT FORMATION.]

Skill learning. In comparison to concept learning, theoretical activity regarding skill learning has been more removed from traditional learning theorizing. While issues such as the relative role of specific associations or cognitive sets in skill learning seem closely related to learning theory, the conceptual framework is not. Thus, the language of many models of skill learning is couched in terms of communication models, involving (1) notions of information processing, with subcategories of information translation, transmission, reduction, collation, and storage; (2) control-system models emphasizing feedback systems; and (3) adaptive-system models, with programs and memory systems which allow changes in the characteristics of the model with experience. [*See* LEARNING, *article on* ACQUISITION OF SKILL; *see also* Fitts 1964.]

Problem solving. Problem solving has long represented an area of controversy with *S–R* oriented theorists opposing gestalt-cognitive approaches. The *S–R* approach attempts to use such concepts as mediated generalization, response hierarchies, verbal mediators, and fractional anticipatory goal responses to account for problem-solving phenomena. Gestalt theory, on the other hand, emphasizes perceptual reorganization processes within the problem. One recent formulation or suggested framework, more in the gestalt than in the *S–R* tradition, has been the ahistorical, relatively rationally derived notions of Miller, Galanter, and Pribram (1960), which involve informational and feedback processes. [*See* PROBLEM SOLVING.]

The question as to what extent new language and methodological approaches are needed for theorizing in these complex areas remains to be determined. It seems evident, however, that information processing and feedback concepts of some sort will greatly influence learning theorizing in the future.

LEONARD E. ROSS

[*Directly related is the entry* LEARNING, *especially the articles on* CLASSICAL CONDITIONING, INSTRUMENTAL LEARNING, REINFORCEMENT. *Other relevant material may be found in* DRIVES; GESTALT THEORY; MOTIVATION.]

BIBLIOGRAPHY

AMSEL, ABRAM 1962 Frustrative Nonreward in Partial Reinforcement and Discrimination Learning: Some Recent History and Theoretical Extension. *Psychological Review* 69:306–328.

ANOKHIN, P. K. (1955) 1961 Features of the Afferent Apparatus of the Conditional Reflex and Their Importances for Psychology. Pages 75–103 in N. O'Connor (editor), *Recent Soviet Psychology.* New York: Liveright.

BERLYNE, D. E. 1960 *Conflict, Arousal, and Curiosity.* New York: McGraw-Hill.

FITTS, PAUL M. 1964 Perceptual–Motor Skill Learning. Pages 243–285 in Symposium on the Psychology of Human Learning, University of Michigan, 1962, *Categories of Human Learning.* New York: Academic Press.

GOUGH, PHILIP B.; and JENKINS, JAMES J. 1963 Verbal Learning and Psycholinguistics. Pages 456–474 in Melvin H. Marx (editor), *Theories in Contemporary Psychology.* New York: Macmillan.

GRINGS, WILLIAM W. 1963 Classical Conditioning. Pages 495–526 in Melvin H. Marx (editor), *Theories in Contemporary Psychology.* New York: Macmillan.

HARLOW, HARRY F. 1959 Learning Set and Error Factor Theory. Pages 492–537 in Sigmund Koch (editor), *Psychology: A Study of a Science.* Volume 2: General Systematic Formulations, Learning, and Special Processes. New York: McGraw-Hill.

HILGARD, ERNEST R. (1948) 1956 *Theories of Learning.* 2d ed. New York: Appleton.

KENDLER, HOWARD H. 1964 The Concept of the Concept. Pages 211–236 in Symposium on the Psychology of Human Learning, University of Michigan, 1962, *Cate-*

gories of *Human Learning*. New York: Academic Press.

KENDLER, HOWARD H.; and KENDLER, TRACY S. 1962 Vertical and Horizontal Processes in Problem Solving. *Psychological Review* 69:1–16.

KOCH, SIGMUND (editor) 1959 *Psychology: A Study of a Science*. Volume 2: General Systematic Formulations, Learning, and Special Processes. New York: McGraw-Hill.

LACHMAN, ROY 1960 The Model in Theory Construction. *Psychological Review* 67:113–129.

LURIA, ALEKSANDR R. 1961 *The Role of Speech in the Regulation of Normal and Abnormal Behavior*. New York: Liveright.

MILLER, GEORGE A.; GALANTER, E.; and PRIBRAM, K. H. 1960 *Plans and the Structure of Behavior*. New York: Holt.

MILLER, NEAL E. 1959 Liberalization of Basic S–R Concepts: Extensions to Conflict Behavior, Motivation and Social Learning. Pages 196–292 in Sigmund Koch (editor), *Psychology: A Study of a Science*. Volume 2: General Systematic Formulations, Learning, and Special Processes. New York: McGraw-Hill.

MOWRER, ORVAL H. 1960 *Learning Theory and Behavior*. New York: Wiley.

RAZRAN, GREGORY 1961 The Observable Unconscious and the Inferable Conscious in Current Soviet Psychophysiology: Interoceptive Conditioning, Semantic Conditioning, and the Orienting Reflex. *Psychological Review* 68:81–147.

SOKOLOV, EUGENE N. 1960 Neuronal Models and the Orienting Reflex. Pages 187–276 in *The Central Nervous System and Behavior: Transactions of the Third Conference*. Edited by M. A. B. Brazier. New York: Macy Foundation.

SOLOMON, RICHARD L.; and BRUSH, ELINOR S. 1956 Experimentally Derived Conceptions of Anxiety and Aversions. Volume 4, pages 212–306 in Marshall R. Jones (editor), *Nebraska Symposium on Motivation*. Lincoln: Univ. of Nebraska Press.

SPENCE, KENNETH W. 1951 Theoretical Interpretations of Learning. Pages 690–729 in Stanley S. Stevens (editor), *Handbook of Experimental Psychology*. New York: Wiley.

SPENCE, KENNETH W. 1956 *Behavior Theory and Conditioning*. New Haven: Yale Univ. Press.

STERNBERG, SAUL 1963 Stochastic Learning Theory. Volume 2, pages 1–120 in R. Duncan Luce et al. (editors), *Handbook of Mathematical Psychology*. New York and London: Wiley.

SUTHERLAND, N. S. 1959 Stimulus Analysing Mechanisms. Volume 2, pages 575–609 in Teddington, England, National Physical Laboratory, *Mechanisation of Thought Processes: Proceedings of a Symposium*. London: H.M. Stationery Office.

UNDERWOOD, BENTON J. 1957 Interference and Forgetting. *Psychological Review* 64:49–60.

UNDERWOOD, BENTON J.; and SCHULZ, RUDOLPH W. 1960 *Meaningfulness and Verbal Learning*. Philadelphia: Lippincott.

WYCKOFF, L. B. 1952 The Role of Observing Responses in Discrimination Learning. Part 1. *Psychological Review* 59:431–442.

ZEAMAN, DAVID; and HOUSE, BETTY J. 1963 The Role of Attention in Retardate Discrimination Learning. Pages 159–223 in Norman R. Ellis (editor), *Handbook of Mental Deficiency*. New York: McGraw-Hill.

LEAST SQUARES

See ESTIMATION *and* LINEAR HYPOTHESES.

LEGAL EVIDENCE

See PSYCHIATRY, *article on* FORENSIC PSYCHIATRY; STATISTICS AS LEGAL EVIDENCE.

LEGAL PROFESSION

See under LAW.

LEGAL REASONING

In countries like the United States and England, where thought about law has focused primarily on adjudication, legal reasoning is often identified with the intellectual processes by which judges reach conclusions in deciding cases. In countries like France and Germany, on the other hand, where thought about law has focused primarily on codification—that is, the creation of a complex and harmonious body of legal rules and concepts—legal reasoning is often identified with the intellectual processes by which the rationality and consistency of legal doctrines are maintained and justified. Since, as we shall see, both these types of reasoning are closely related to each other, we would define legal reasoning broadly enough to include them both; and indeed, we propose to broaden the definition still further to include also the types of reasoning used in other kinds of legal activity, such as making laws, administering laws, the trial (and not merely the decision) of cases in court, the drafting of legal documents, and the negotiation of legal transactions.

When legal reasoning is conceived of in these broader terms, it is seen to involve not only, and not primarily, the application of rules of formal logic but also other methods of exposition. To reason, according to dictionary definitions, may mean to give grounds (reasons) for one's statements, to argue persuasively, or to engage in discourse. Law, insofar as it has a distinctive subject matter and is founded on distinctive principles and purposes, has not only its own kinds of *logic* but also its own kinds of *rhetoric* and its own kinds of *discourse*, which are, of course, similar to the logic, rhetoric, and discourse of other social institutions and other scholarly disciplines but which nevertheless have certain distinctive characteristics.

In seeking to identify these distinctive characteristics, we must keep in mind that legal reasoning is not identical in all societies and that, in addition, the degree of its distinctiveness is not identical in all societies. In a theocracy, for example, legal reasoning may be closely related to sacerdotal reasoning; at one time the high priests of Israel found the law by consulting the breastplates which they wore (the Urim and Thummim) —that is, their legal decisions were justified in terms of divine revelation. In a society that is undergoing a political revolution, such as the Soviet Union in the first years after 1917, legal reasoning may dissolve into the reasoning of politics and class struggle. These variations strongly suggest that in any society there is an intimate connection between the logic, rhetoric, and discourse of law and the dominant beliefs of the society concerning religion, politics, and other aspects of social life, including its beliefs about the nature of reasoning itself. Legal reasoning seems to be most distinctive in those societies that have experienced the emergence of a special professional class of lawmen, with its own special professional traditions and institutional values; here special modes of logic, rhetoric, and discourse seem to have as part of their functions the preservation and further development of the legal profession's traditions and values, although at the same time even in such societies the intimate connections between legal reasoning and other types of reasoning must be maintained if the legal profession is to retain the respect of the community as a whole.

Legal logic. Many Western jurists of the eighteenth and nineteenth centuries sought to make legal reasoning conform to syllogistic logic. The rules of law declared by legislatures, courts, and legal scholars were viewed as major premises, and the fact situations of particular cases or the terms of particular legal problems were viewed as minor premises. The decision of a case, or the resolution of a legal problem, was thought to follow inevitably from a proper juxtaposition of the major and minor premises. Given a rule or doctrine defining burglary, or contract, or any other basis of legal duty, it was thought only to be necessary to determine whether or not a particular act fell within the definition in order to determine whether or not legal responsibility should attach to it. It was supposed by many that if the entire body of law could be summarized in a set of rules, the sole remaining task of law would be to classify particular facts under one rule or another.

This mechanical model of the application of rules to facts did not go unchallenged even in its heyday. In Germany, Rudolf von Jhering ridiculed a "jurisprudence of concepts" (*Begriffsjurisprudenz*) and called for a conscious legal policy of evaluating the social and personal interests involved in the legal resolution of conflicts (*Interessenjurisprudenz*). Similarly, in the United States, Oliver Wendell Holmes, Jr., in some of his writings, viewed the logical form in which judges announced their conclusions as a veil covering their views of public policy. The life of the law has not been logic; it has been experience, Holmes stated in 1881. By "logic" Holmes indicated he meant "the syllogism" and "the axioms and corollaries of a book of mathematics"; by "experience" he meant "considerations of what is socially expedient."

However useful syllogistic logic may be in testing the validity of conclusions drawn from given premises, it is inadequate as a method of reasoning in a practical science such as law, where the premises are not given but must be created. Legal rules, viewed as major premises, are always subject to qualification in the light of particular circumstances; it is a rule of English and American law, for example, that a person who intentionally strikes another is civilly liable for battery, but such a rule is subject, in legal practice, to infinite modification in the light of possible defense (for example, self-defense, defense of property, parental privilege, immunity from suit, lack of jurisdiction, insufficiency of evidence, etc.). In addition, life continually presents new situations to which no existing rule is applicable; we simply do not know the legal limits of freedom of speech, for example, since the social context in which words are spoken is continually changing. Thus legal rules are continually being made and remade.

Also the "minor premises"—the facts of particular cases or the terms of particular legal problems —are not simply "there" but must be perceived and characterized, and this, too, requires interpretation and evaluation. Indeed, the legal facts of a case are not raw data but rather those facts that have been selected and classified in terms of legal categories.

Finally, the conclusion, that is, the application of the rule to the particular case or problem, since it is a responsible decision directly affecting particular people in particular situations, is never mathematically inevitable but always contingent upon the exercise of judgment. In the telling words of Immanuel Kant, "there is no rule for applying a rule"; that is, there are no rules that can tell us in advance, with certainty, how a particular judge (legislator, administrator, etc.) ought to resolve a concrete case or problem that is before him—and this would be true even though we were able to say in advance what rules are relevant to such a resolution. Once a legal conclusion is reached, it may often be stated in syllogistic form; but in the process of reaching it, the determination of the major and minor premises may have come last.

To say that legal reasoning cannot be reduced to the classical rules of formal logic is not, however, to deny that it has logical qualities. It is characteristic of legal reasoning that it strives toward consistency both of legal rules and of legal judgments; such a striving for consistency is implicit in the belief that law should apply equally to all who are subject to it and that like cases should be decided in a like manner. Even the judgments of the ancient Greek oracles were believed to reflect a hidden consistency. It is also characteristic of legal reasoning that it strives toward continuity in time; it looks to the authority of the past, embodied in previously declared rules and decisions, and it attempts to regulate social relations in such a way as to preserve stability. Finally, legal reasoning is dialectical reasoning; it is characteristically concerned with the weighing of opposing claims, whether expressed in legislative debate, in forensic argument, or the like. These three basic characteristics of legal reasoning impose upon it certain logical requirements.

The most pervasive form of legal logic is that of *analogy*, in the broad sense of the comparison and contrast of similar and dissimilar examples. Analogical reasoning is implicit in the striving for consistency; the striving for continuity (that is, historical consistency) also involves analogical reasoning, the analogies being found in past experience; similarly, the dialectical quality of legal reasoning involves comparison and contrast between the examples put forward by the opposing sides. (It should be noted that the term "analogy" also has a technical legal meaning, signifying the extension of a legal category to a situation which is "similar to" but not "the same as" those situations which the category "logically" includes; in contrast, we use the term "analogy" here more broadly and include under it the process by which it is determined that one situation is "the same as" another.)

In a legal system such as that of England or the United States, which stresses the authority of past judicial decisions (precedents), analogical reasoning in adjudication characteristically takes the form of (*a*) comparison of the fact situation before the court with the fact situations of previously decided cases in order to find a previously decided case whose fact situation is comparable; (*b*) extraction from the previously decided comparable case of the principle upon which that case was decided; and (*c*) application of that principle to the case at hand. It is generally recognized that each of these three steps is dependent upon the other two. Moreover, the second step—the extraction of the principle of the previous case—is complicated by the fact that the principle expressly relied on by the court in deciding the previous case is not necessarily binding upon future courts. Even under a strict doctrine of precedents, at least as understood in the United States, a court, although bound by the decisions in previous cases, may reject the reasons previously given for those decisions—as, for example, where much broader reasons were given than were required. In technical terms, the court is not bound by (may treat as mere *dictum*) any statement made in a previous comparable case which was not necessary to the decision in that case; and even a reason stated by the previous court as the necessary ground for its decision may be treated as dictum, and not binding, if the later court considers that the same decision could have been reached on other (better) grounds. Thus what is binding on future courts—the "holding" of the case—is determined in part by its subsequent application to similar fact situations.

Reasoning by *analogy of precedents* has been called by one writer "the basic pattern of legal reasoning." However, another characteristic method of legal reasoning—especially (but not exclusively) in legal systems that do not recognize the binding force of precedents—is to decide cases or resolve particular legal problems by *analogy of doctrines* expressed in statutes and in other forms of legal rules. To give an American example: in the latter part of the nineteenth century, most states enacted statutes giving married women the right to own their separate property, to make contracts, and to sue and be sued. Using the authority of such married women's acts, many courts overruled various earlier precedents which made a wife and husband incompetent to testify for or against each other, which made a husband liable for his wife's torts, which made one spouse not liable to conviction for stealing from the other, etc. These matters, although not dealt with specifically by the married women's acts, were sufficiently similar to the matters with which the married women's acts did deal that the policy of those acts was considered to be applicable. Such use of analogy of statute (or of legal doctrine) is especially prevalent in those countries of Europe in which the law is largely found in codes and in which the writings of leading legal scholars in interpreting the codes have more authority than judicial decisions.

Analogical reasoning, and especially reasoning

from analogy of decided cases, is sometimes said to be "inductive," as contrasted with "deductive" reasoning from legal rules. Such a characterization presupposes that the facts of cases are first analyzed and then legal principles are "inferred" from such facts. However, the distinction between the facts of a legal case and the legal principle governing those facts is not the same as the distinction sometimes drawn between the facts of a laboratory experiment and the hypothesis offered by the scientist to explain the facts. The facts of a legal case do not have an existence independent of the theory of liability applied to them. A collision between X and Y may be a "fact" which natural science can "explain"; but whether or not X should be legally liable to Y, or Y to X, depends on whether or not X or Y was "negligent" or was carrying on an "extrahazardous activity" or was otherwise engaged in liability-creating conduct. Thus, as suggested earlier, the same kind of judgment that is required to determine the applicable legal principle (liability for harm caused by negligence, liability for harm caused by extrahazardous activity) is also required to characterize the legally operative facts (X drove negligently, X was engaged in an extrahazardous activity). To contend that since liability is imposed in situation A (for example, harm caused by collision of aircraft with ground structures, regardless of fault, air travel being considered an extrahazardous activity), and since situation B (for example, harm caused by automobile travel) is (or is not) comparable to situation A, therefore liability should (or should not) be imposed in situation B is an example neither of deductive nor of inductive reasoning, although it contains elements of each. It is an example of reasoning applied to reach decisions for action and, like the reasoning of a physician or an engineer or a politician, is based on a very large variety of considerations, many of which cannot be fully articulated.

Although reasoning by analogy is the primary form of legal logic, it is not sufficient in itself to compel particular legal results. There is, indeed, a large area of indeterminacy in all analogical reasoning, since the criteria for selecting similarities and differences are left open to debate. A rigid definition confining the term "logic" to those propositions that necessarily follow from given premises might therefore exclude analogy altogether. According to an old proverb, " 'For example' is not proof." Yet analogical reasoning, despite its flexibility, does impose limits upon legal results even if it does not in itself compel them. In each society some similarities and differences are so strongly felt that they cannot be denied. Moreover, particular legal doctrines often restrict the range within which analogies may be found. Most modern legal systems, for example, require that a criminal statute be interpreted much more "strictly" than a statute imposing only civil obligations; similarly, courts are generally more reluctant to extend analogies under rules of commercial law than under rules of personal injury law, since commercial rules are relied on in business transactions where a high degree of stability and predictability is desired. In addition, each legal system establishes procedures and methods for drawing analogies—such as adversary and investigative procedures or the method of precedent and the method of codification—and these procedures and methods are designed to prevent analogical reasoning from becoming arbitrary.

Analogical reasoning is, of course, a universal mode of reasoning and by no means unique to law. What is distinctive about law, in this respect, is the degree of emphasis placed upon the use of analogy and the development of special legal rules, procedures, and methods for drawing analogies. For law the method of analogy has the special virtue—as compared with syllogistic reasoning—of exposing the examples by which consistency, continuity, and the weighing of opposing claims and defenses are tested.

Legal rhetoric. We define rhetoric, following Aristotle, as referring not only to the art of persuasion through appeals to emotions but also to the art of public deliberation through appeals to reason and hence as a mode of reasoning. At the same time rhetoric is distinguished from logic, since logic is concerned with indicative statements that are considered to be either true or false ("propositions"), whereas rhetoric is concerned with subjunctive, normative, and imperative statements uttered in order to influence thought or action. The classical formula of logic: All men are mortal, Socrates is a man, therefore Socrates is mortal—might be rendered in rhetorical form as: If you would be a man, O Socrates, you must prepare yourself for death!

Legal rules, being stated usually in the indicative mood, give the deceptive appearance of being only logical propositions; yet on closer analysis it is apparent that they have a rhetorical significance at least equally as great as their logical significance. The statement, for example, that the intentional premeditated killing of a person with malice aforethought constitutes the crime of murder in the first degree and is punishable by life imprisonment or death is not only a "true proposition" concerning what *is* murder (assuming it has been authoritatively declared); it is also a warning to potential murderers, an assurance to potential victims, a mandate to law enforcement officials, and, in general, an expression of the desires and beliefs of the political community. Legal reasoning with respect to the crime of murder consists, therefore, not only in the logical analysis of its definition, involving the comparison of various kinds of homicide (for example, homicide committed from motives of mercy, in self-defense, in the heat of passion, negligently, etc.); it also consists in both legislative and forensic rhetoric ("the death penalty should be abolished"; "the defendant is not a murderer") as well as in other, less formal types of argumentative speech (for example, "a person should certainly not escape responsibility for murder just because he believed his act would benefit society").

As the logical aspect of legal reasoning focuses attention on legal *rules* and on the principles to be derived from decisions in analogous cases, so the rhetorical aspect of legal reasoning focuses attention on legal *activities*. As many writers have emphasized, law itself is not simply, or primarily, a body of rules but an activity, an enterprise. A principal purpose of this enterprise is to subject human conduct to the governance of rules (Fuller 1964); but for that purpose rules must be drafted, debated, voted, published, interpreted, obeyed, applied, enforced—all of which legal activities involve the use of rhetoric and not only of logic. Moreover, apart from activities connected with rule making, it is also a purpose of the legal enterprise to render decisions, as by the casting of votes, the issuance of orders, the handing down of judgments; and the rendering of such decisions, like the making of legal rules, is both a product and an expression of rhetorical utterance. In addition, legal reasoning is directed to the negotiation of legal transactions, the making of petitions or recommendations, the writing of legal opinions, the issuance of legal documents, and to a variety of other types of legal activities, all of which involve the use of language to induce a response in those to whom the language is addressed.

As the use of analogy is a characteristic and pervasive form of legal logic, so the appeal to authority is a characteristic and pervasive form of legal rhetoric. The nature of the authority to which appeal is made differs in different legal systems. It is said, for example, that in traditional Muslim law the authority of the Koran is decisive and that only a literal interpretation of its provisions is permissible. In Judaic law, on the other hand, with the development of the Talmud, there emerged the authority of leading rabbis who interpreted the Torah. In Roman law a similar authority was vested in leading jurists. We have already referred to the authority of judicial precedents in English and American law and of codes in modern continental European law. Probably the highest authority governing judicial decisions in most contemporary legal systems is that of statutes enacted by the legislature, although in the United States and some other countries the authority even of statutes must yield to that of constitutional provisions.

The appeal to authority in legal reasoning is not necessarily limited, however, to an appeal to legislation (whether embodied in statutes, codes, an authoritative book, or in a constitution), to judicial precedents, or to juristic commentaries on such legislation or precedents. In many legal systems—and perhaps in all—some room, at least, is left for appeal also to custom (that is, what is commonly done and what is commonly believed ought to be done) and to a sense of justice. Thus it is often said that there are four sources of law: legislation (including rules made by administrative authorities), precedent, custom, and equity. These four sources may also be viewed as four dimensions of law—legislation (and administrative rules) being directed to what should be done in the future, precedent being directed to what has been done in the past, custom being directed to outer social patterns and norms of behavior, and equity being directed to the inner sense of justice or fairness. Different legal systems, and different branches within a particular legal system, emphasize one or another of these four dimensions or sources or types of authority, and hence legal rhetoric is not uniform as between different legal systems or even within a single system. In American law, for example, the legislation-based rhetoric of a traffic regulation ("parked cars will be towed away") differs from the precedent-based rhetoric of a judicial decision ("this court has consistently held that the manufacturer is not liable to retail purchasers unless he is shown to have been negligent"); and both of these differ from the custom-based rhetoric of a negotiable instrument ("pay to the order of John Jones $1,000") or the equity-based rhetoric of a divorce decree ("the father may have the child visit him four times a year for a week at a time").

Legal discourse. It is apparent that legal logic is itself a form of legal rhetoric. Legal rhetoric, in turn, is a form of legal discourse, whose functions go beyond that of influencing immediate thought and action and include the preservation and development of the legal traditions and values of the entire political–legal community as well as the traditions and values of the legal profession itself in societies where a legal profession exists.

The distinctive characteristics of legal discourse arise principally from the institution of *the hearing*, which is the basis of all legal activities, including not only adjudication but also legislation, administration, negotiation of legal transactions, and other legal activities. It is the opportunity of both sides to be heard that principally distinguishes adjudication from vengeance. Similarly, it is, above all, the opportunity to debate pending enactments that distinguishes legislation from mere commands, and it is the opportunity to petition for relief that distinguishes lawful administration from bureaucratic fiat. Even a unilateral legal act such as the writing of a will requires the draftsman to put himself in the position of third persons who might be called upon to interpret the will in the light of a dispute over its validity or meaning.

A legal hearing involves two qualities of discourse that are not necessarily present in nonlegal procedures of listening and speaking. The first quality may be described as formality, that is, the use of a deliberate and ceremonial form of discourse, which usually is reflected in a formal presentation of claims and defenses, formal deliberation of the court or other tribunal, and the formal rendering of a decision. The formalities of the hearing help to secure its objectivity, that is, its impartiality, internal consistency, restraint, and authority.

A second distinctive quality of discourse characteristic of a legal hearing is the tendency to categorize the persons and events that are involved. The specific, unique qualities of the dispute are named in general terms. John Jones is called "the plaintiff"; Sam Smith is called "the defendant"; the defendant is alleged, for example, to have broken a "lease" by causing certain "damage" to the leased "premises." These are the "legally operative facts." The "real" facts—Smith's obnoxious personal habits, the neighbors' gossip, the family feud, etc.—are excluded unless they can be brought into relevant legal categories. This helps to secure the generality of the hearing. For the issue is not whether John Jones or Sam Smith is the better man but rather whether the rights of a lessor, rights established by the law of the community, have been violated by a lessee.

The formulation of the dispute or problem in terms of general categories, and thus the viewing of the concrete facts *sub specie communitatis*, is organically derived from the hearing, although it is logically distinct from it. The dispute or the problem has challenged the existing legal rules; the parties have invoked a reformulation of them in the light of the concrete facts; and the court (if it is a judicial proceeding), or legislature (if it is a proposed statute), or administrative agency (if it is a new regulation that is sought), or lawyer (if it is a contract that is being negotiated or a will that is being drawn) is asked to reinterpret the existing rules or to create new rules in the light of the new dispute or new problem. Categorization of the specific, unique facts, carried out in the context of a deliberate and ceremonial presentation of claims and defenses with a formal procedure for interrogation, argument, and decision, helps to secure the generality and objectivity not only of the hearing but also of the reinterpreted or newly created rules and hence their acceptance by the community. At the same time, the legal vocabulary and techniques that are generated in this process provide a professional shorthand or jargon that is designed to contribute to the efficiency of legal procedures or to the fraternity of the legal profession, or to both, although it often has the effect of making both law and lawyers seem alien to the society that has produced them.

The circularity of legal reasoning. If law is seen, in the first instance, not as rules but as the enterprise of hearing, judging, prescribing, ordering, negotiating, declaring, etc., then it becomes possible to give a satisfactory explanation of what Jeremy Bentham called the tautology and circuity of legal terms and what H. L. A. Hart calls the "great anomaly of legal language—our inability to define its crucial words in terms of ordinary factual counterparts" (1953, p. 41). It is, indeed, true that legal reasoning characteristically appears to be circular. When it is said, for example, that a man has a "right" to something because someone has an "obligation" to transfer it to him, the "right" of the one and the "obligation" of the other seem to be merely two different terms for the same thing. Similarly, the word "crime" and the word "law" themselves seem to be only alternative ways of saying "right," "obligation," etc. Bentham wrote:

> Each of these words may be substituted the one for the other. . . . The law directs me to support you—it imposes upon me the *obligation* of supporting you—it grants you the *right* of being supported by me—it converts into an *offence* the negative act by which I omit to support you—it obliges me to render you the *service* of supporting you. . . . This, then, is the connexion between these legal entities: they are only the law con-

sidered under different aspects; they exist as long as it exists; they are born and they die with it. . . . The legal terms seem to have no "empirical referents"—no "things" to which they "correspond." (*Bentham's Theory of Fictions*, pp. cxxix–cxxx)

The proliferation of interdependent legal terms referring to the same thing is due to the fact that the terms are not supposed to "refer" to "things" but instead to regulate a complex interrelationship of people engaged, actually or potentially, in legal activities of various kinds. From the standpoint of the child, support is a "right"; from the standpoint of the parent, it is an "obligation"; from the standpoint of the prosecutor, failure to fulfill the obligation may be a "crime." It is true that if there were no right there would be no obligation and no crime, and if there were no crime there would be no obligation and no right (or at least a different kind of obligation and right). But these (and many other) terms are needed to identify the complexity of the relationship between the child, the parent, and the state; they are needed especially when the relationship is described in abstract terms. The decision of the court may be simple enough: "Pay $25 a week for support of the child or go to jail."

It may seem senseless for courts or writers to go (as they sometimes do) from right to obligation to penalty as if in a logical sequence. Yet what may be senseless as a logical proposition may be sensible as a means of identifying the parties to a dispute and the nature of the disputed issue. To attack legal rules as question-begging is itself to beg the question of their function. Indeed, in some cases it is the function of judicial tautology and circularity to avoid giving a reason for a decision in a situation in which it is better to give no reason than to give the real reason. This is apt to be especially true of legal fictions, which are legal doctrines that state a legal result in terms of assumed facts that are known to be nonexistent. Here what are understood to be only analogies are consciously treated as identities, in order to preserve consistency of doctrine in the face of an unexplained inconsistent result. For example, a battery is traditionally defined as an unpermitted blow which the defendant intended to inflict on the plaintiff, but the courts nevertheless give a recovery to a person whom the defendant struck unintentionally while intending to strike another, applying the fiction that the defendant's intent to strike the third person is "transferred" to the person whom he in fact struck. Thus the original definition is preserved in form but its consequences are changed. In most cases, however, legal tautologies and circularities are not intended to change the consequences of legal rules but are primarily a means of specifying the various aspects of legal relationships, often for procedural reasons. In any event, not only circular but also other "unscientific" qualities of law may often be understood if they are seen as part of the logic of analogy, the rhetoric of appeals to authority, and the discourse of formality and categorization that are the distinguishing characteristics of legal reasoning.

Legal reasoning and social science. Despite important insights into the nature and functions of legal reasoning contributed by such classical sociologists as Émile Durkheim and Max Weber (both of whom were legally trained), modern social science has left the subject largely to legal scholars. However, recent sociological studies of the professions have, following Weber, related legal reasoning to the need of the legal profession to have its own professional language; and in the last two decades many American political scientists have attempted to debunk legal reasoning as a disguise for judicial decisions reached on the basis of nonlegal considerations. More important, probably, at least in the long run, are studies by social scientists not of legal reasoning as such but of legal institutions, such as the jury system, civil rights legislation, criminal law enforcement, collective bargaining, the antitrust laws, etc., since such studies provide a necessary foundation for any generalizations about the relationship of legal reasoning to other types of reasoning. In the meanwhile, studies of legal reasoning by legal scholars —who are also social scientists—will continue to benefit from social science theories and methods directed to the study of social institutions generally, including legal institutions. Indeed, social science theories and methods sometimes have a direct impact on legal reasoning itself when they are introduced into legal proceedings through, for example, legislative hearings and, occasionally, court cases in which social scientists are called in as experts.

Social sciences other than law may, however, have more to learn from an understanding of legal reasoning than they have to contribute to such an understanding. Since law is a practical social science, in which principles of order and justice accepted by a given society are applied to the reaching of reasoned decisions for action, the legal profession (including legislators, judges, administrators, and legal scholars, as well as practicing lawyers) is highly sensitive to the relationship between theory and practice, and, more specifically, to the relationship between reasoning and the social context in which it takes place. Thus legal experience not only provides a wealth of data for investigation by social scientists but also has much to teach them concerning the nature of social science. Indeed, legal reasoning challenges the belief that any social science can properly avoid the question of its applicability to society; it challenges, therefore, the theory of a "value-free" social science based upon the methods of the physical sciences or of mathematics. Such a challenge is inherent in the emphasis which law places on the connection between what is said and the role of the speaker, as well as in the assumption implicit in law that a judgment affecting persons is not merely an observation or measurement of external facts but also a response to the language addressed to the person making the judgment, and that a proper judgment is itself addressed to the participants in the proceedings in which it is made.

HAROLD J. BERMAN

[*See also* ADJUDICATION; JUDICIARY; JURISPRUDENCE; LAW; LEGAL SYSTEMS; *and the biographies of* CARDOZO; COHEN; DURKHEIM; WEBER, MAX.]

BIBLIOGRAPHY

BENTHAM, JEREMY *Bentham's Theory of Fictions*. Introduction by C. K. Ogden. London: Routledge, 1932. → A selection of Bentham's unpublished writings.

BERMAN, HAROLD J. 1958 *The Nature and Functions of Law: An Introduction for Students of the Arts and Sciences*. New York: Foundation Press.

EVAN, WILLIAM M. (editor) 1962 *Law and Sociology: Exploratory Essays*. New York: Free Press.

FULLER, LON L. 1930–1931 Legal Fictions. *Northwestern University Law Review* 25:363–399, 513–546, 877–910.

FULLER, LON L. 1964 *The Morality of Law*. New Haven: Yale Univ. Press.

GENY, FRANÇOIS (1889) 1962 *Méthode d'interprétation et sources en droit privé positif: Critical Essay*. 2d ed. St. Paul, Minn.: West.

HART, HERBERT L. A. (1953) 1954 Definition and Theory in Jurisprudence. *Law Quarterly Review* 70:37–60.

HART, HERBERT L. A. 1961 *The Concept of Law*. Oxford: Clarendon.

LEVI, EDWARD H. 1949 *An Introduction to Legal Reasoning*. Univ. of Chicago Press.

LLEWELLYN, KARL N. 1960 *The Common Law Tradition: Deciding Appeals*. Boston: Little.

PERELMAN, CHAIM (1962) 1963 *The Idea of Justice and the Problem of Argument*. New York: Humanities. → First published in Hebrew.

PERELMAN, CHAIM; and OLBRECHTS-TYTECA, L. 1958 *Traité de l'argumentation: La nouvelle rhétorique*. 2 vols. Paris: Presses Universitaires de France.

ROSENSTOCK-HUESSY, EUGEN 1956–1958 *Soziologie*. 2 vols. Stuttgart (Germany): Kohlhammer. → Volume 1: *Die Übermacht der Räume*. Volume 2: *Die Vollzahl der Zeiten*.

STONE, JULIUS 1964 *Legal System and Lawyers' Reasonings*. Stanford Univ. Press.

VIEHWEG, THEODOR (1953) 1963 *Topik und Jurisprudenz*. 2d ed. Munich: Beck.

VON MEHREN, ARTHUR T. 1957 *The Civil Law System: Cases and Materials for the Comparative Study of Law*. Englewood Cliffs, N.J.: Prentice-Hall.

LEGAL SYSTEMS

I
COMPARATIVE LAW AND LEGAL SYSTEMS

Laws are different in different countries and often within the same country. This fact has given rise to that branch of jurisprudence which is known as comparative law (*Rechtsvergleichung; droit comparé*).

Precursors

While laws have been different through the ages, sustained scholarly concern about their diversity is hardly one hundred years old. An occasional interest in the diversity of laws has, of course, been shown every now and then, but systematic studies had their origin in the 1860s.

Comparative law could not be developed as a field of learning before the various local laws had come to constitute subject matters of academic learning. On the continent of Europe that was not the case until the high Middle Ages; in England it did not occur until the nineteenth century. But even the development of scholarly pursuits in the several legal systems did not immediately result in their comparative treatment. In fact, the way legal learning developed on the European continent constituted a hindrance to comparative observation.

The legal learning of the Roman Empire was lost in the barbarian invasions. In the course of the Middle Ages the crude customs of the Germanic invaders developed into bodies of law of considerable complexity and refinement, but they developed as customs of local courts of manifold kinds rather than as bodies of law that would be cultivated and elaborated by scholars. In England, the only medieval country where, in consequence of the Conquest, the growth of the law began to be centralized in the courts of the king, the law specialists were craftsmen rather than academic teachers and scholars. Only canon law, the law of the church, was given some attention by the scholars who came to gather in the emerging universities. A change occurred when Roman law was rediscovered and, from the twelfth century on, made the subject matter of academic teaching and writing, first in Bologna and then in the other rapidly growing and increasing universities. By the successive schools of the glossators (twelfth century) and post-glossators (thirteenth and fourteenth centuries), the humanists (sixteenth century), the Dutch and French jurists of the seventeenth and eighteenth centuries, the rationalist school of natural law, and, ultimately, the German Pandectists of the eighteenth and nineteenth centuries, the Roman law was transformed into the so-called civil law, which was taught in all the universities and was elaborated in scholarly treatises and dissertations, but which was not practiced anywhere in the form in which it was taught. The law that was actually applied in the courts was an amalgam of the civil law and local customs and statutes. The civil law of the scholars was thought of as a body of rules and principles of universal validity. The law in action differed from place to place. It was rarely regarded as worthy of the attention of the scholars. The law with which they were concerned was uniform. There was nothing with which to compare it. If views of the law differed, only one of them could be right. The actual laws that could have been compared were too limited in their spheres of application. What little comparative attention was paid to them was limited to a dry enumeration of differing rules. Even the great codifications of private law in Denmark–Norway (1683–1687), Sweden (1734), Prussia (1791–1794), and Austria (1811) evoked little interest on the part of the scholars. In France, on the other hand, Napoleon's codes (1804–1810) established themselves so firmly as the subject matter of professional treatment that the old civil law disappeared from the curriculum. The same concentration on new nationwide unified laws took place in consequence of the later codifications in Germany (1896), Switzerland (1907), Italy (1865–1942), and other countries. The vast task of expounding and elaborating the contents of the new codes absorbed the energies of the scholars. In each country legal science came to be nationalized in the sense of being nationally isolated. Scholars would look beyond the national borders only insofar as the national codification had been modeled upon that of another nation. French legal learning was thus looked to in Italy, the Netherlands, Spain, Latin America, and those other countries in which Napoleon's codes had served as models. German legal learning was influential where the local codes or laws had come under the influence of German scholarly writing, as in Austria, Switzerland, Scandinavia, and Japan.

In both periods, that of the civil law and that of the codes, Continental legal learning was primarily interested in "dogmatics." Starting with an authoritative text—in the civil-law epoch that of the corpus juris and in the later period that of the respective national code—the scholars busied themselves with the "interpretation" of these texts. The law laid down in the texts was regarded as being complete, that is, as providing the answer to every problem that would ever arise, provided one would only read and understand the text in the right way. Legal science was the science of properly interpreting the texts, just as theology consisted in the interpretation of the Scriptures. Under such an approach there was as little room for, and interest in, comparison of laws as there was in the comparison of religions.

In England the situation was similar but for different reasons. The centralized, well-organized, and politically powerful English bar had succeeded in resisting the onslaught of the Roman law. In the royal courts at Westminster, the various local customs were welded into the common law of England. The elaborators of the law were the practitioners, especially the judges. They were craftsmen, not academicians. English law was hardly taught in the universities; one learned it in apprentice fashion, by doing. To learn the practice of some outlandish law, say, of Scotland, was for the English lawyer of as little interest as it would have been for a shoemaker to learn carpentry.

Lawyers are not the only people interested in law. The law also attracts the interest of theologians, philosophers, and those who in English-speaking countries have come to be called jurists, that is, scholars who know the law and yet are interested in it not from the strictly professional point of view but from that of one who looks upon the law, so to speak, from the outside. The jurist is the man who is interested in the law's growth in history, in the values which it protects and promotes, in the machinery through which it functions, in the structure of its body, and in its role and functions in society. It was among philosophers and jurists that interest in comparative law was first exhibited. It is among sociologists, anthropologists, and political scientists that such interest is presently growing; but attitudes are changing also among the lawyers, especially the legal scholars. They have begun to develop a new jurisprudence within which comparative law is coming to play a constantly increasing role.

Among the precursors of modern comparative law students one might mention Aristotle, who engaged in the comparison of the constitutions of the Greek city-states. In the Middle Ages some canonist, legist, or theologian every now and then engaged in comparative observation of secular law and canon law. In later times the peculiar features of the law merchant attracted some attention.

Suddenly there appeared Montesquieu, almost without predecessor—and also to be without immediate successors. In *The Spirit of the Laws* (1748), the law is treated as a social phenomenon and the diversity of the laws is seen as being caused by diversities of the natural, historical, ethnical, political, and other factors of the social setting. In the early part of the nineteenth century, Montesquieu's ideas reappeared in the thinking of Hugo, Savigny, Eichhorn, and the other writers of the German historical school. In reaction to the natural-law jurists' belief in the possibility and desirability of a system of law that could be developed by reason and would be valid universally, they again emphasized the dependency of the laws upon the surrounding conditions, especially the peculiar spirit of each nation (the *Volksgeist*). Divided into the two hostile camps of Romanists and Germanists, the men of the historical school endeavored to replace the amalgam of Roman and Germanic traditions that characterized the *usus modernus pandectarum* by new systems of revitalized Roman or Germanic law. Comparisons between these two systems were, of course, incidental to the heated debates, and some attention had to be paid to the law of France, in which Germanic traditions had survived to a larger extent than in Germany, and to the laws of England and Scandinavia, where no wholesale reception of Roman law had taken place. Institutions of English public law had attracted attention ever since their praises had been sung by Montesquieu, and they were widely imitated on the Continent in the course of the revolutionary movements that were sparked by the events of 1789.

Montesquieu's insight into the interdependency of the law and other social factors was applied again by Sir Henry Maine, who was struck by similarities between the laws of ancient Rome and of India and by parallels in their development. Influenced by the Darwinist thought of his time, he ventured in his *Ancient Law* (1861) to formulate his famous "law" of universal sociolegal development from status to contract.

Modern comparative law

The interest of lawyers rather than jurists in the field of modern comparative law began with the foundation of the Société de Législation Comparée in 1869, the establishment of the Comité de Législation Comparée in the French Ministry of Justice in 1876, and the founding of the English Society of Comparative Legislation in 1898. The movement had its origin in practical considerations. It was believed that the ideas and experiences of foreign countries, especially new foreign legislation, should be made available for one's own national law making, which in the spirit of the time was identified with legislation. Translation and discussion of new foreign codes and laws thus constituted the principal field of activity of the small circle of interested specialists.

Comparative law rather than comparative legislation came to appeal to a widening circle of scholars in connection with the late nineteenth century's optimistic belief in the desirability and possibility of large-scale international unification of private law. Along with public and private international law, comparative law thus figured among the topics discussed at the annual meetings of the Institut de Droit International. The ideal of international legal unification also was the inspiring motive of the great international Congress of Comparative Law, held in Paris in 1900. With its large assembly of scholars from all over the world, the congress lived in the memories of the participants as the high point of what is nostalgically called *la belle époque du droit comparé*. From then on the work in the field grew more realistic. The development is reflected in the life work of Édouard Lambert, whose institute of comparative law at the University of Lyon (founded in 1920) constituted for some decades the center of painstaking, detailed research.

Practical interest in knowledge of law for purposes of legislation, international unification, and everyday law practice in international transactions, commercial and otherwise, continued to stimulate steadily increasing interest in the study of foreign laws. There also grew up new theoretical interest. The desire to discover the beginnings of the development of law as a general social phenomenon —a development which was widely regarded as having proceeded more or less unilineally—drew attention beyond Roman, Greek, or Germanic law to laws of more archaic character, as well as to the customs of primitive peoples. This new interest in "ethnological jurisprudence" and related matters was given a focus in the *Zeitschrift für vergleichende Rechtswissenschaft* (begun in 1878).

The more comparative law assumed the character of a social science, that is, a pursuit of systematic knowledge about law as a social phenomenon the study of which would have to reach beyond national boundaries, the more the workers in the field became aware of its difficulties. Where could one find a library containing all the necessary materials? What human mind could retain and organize them? A decisive step was taken in 1917 with the establishment of Ernst Rabel's institute of comparative law at the University of Munich and, nine years later in Berlin, the Kaiser Wilhelm (now Max Planck) institutes for foreign and international private law (now in Hamburg) and also for foreign and international public law (now in Heidelberg). At these institutes a comprehensive library was established, and there was assembled a team of specialists, who under Rabel's direction would advise drafters of new legislation and participants in international legal life and who would systematically observe legal developments the world over in order to gain theoretical insights and develop new methods of legal thinking and research. The impact of the innovation has been far-reaching. The establishment of the comparative law institutes coincided with and strengthened the change in method of German legal thought from conceptual–analytical jurisprudence to the new method of jurisprudence of interests with its emphasis upon knowledge of the facts of social life and of socially current evaluations of conflicting interests. Under such a method, limitation of scholarly concern to the phenomena of one's own nation is no longer possible.

The simultaneous shift in legal method that occurred in the United States was a principal cause of the rapid growth of American interest in comparative law or, as it is now frequently called, international legal studies. The growing involvement of the United States in world affairs, political and commercial, was another powerful motive.

Scholars like Roscoe Pound, John H. Wigmore, Ernst Freund, and H. W. Millar had been working since the turn of the century at breaking through "Mainstreetism" toward world-mindedness in legal learning. Their breadth of learning is reflected in the scope of their own work as well as in the Legal Philosophy Series, the Continental Legal History Series, and the Modern Criminal Science Series, which they promoted and edited. Effectively supported by the Ford Foundation, international legal studies have, since World War II, come to constitute an essential part in the curriculum and the research programs of American university law schools. Cooperation with sociologists, economists, political scientists, anthropologists, and historians is being sought by the law scholars. What is still lacking in the United States is a great research institute on the pattern of the German Max Planck institutes.

In the United Kingdom, the study of comparative law was pioneered by Harold C. Gutteridge. It is now finding its place in the universities, where academic teaching of the law has come at a rapidly increasing pace to supplement, or to take the place of, the old-fashioned apprenticeship training. A center for research is provided at the Institute of Advanced Legal Studies in London, established in 1948.

In France, courses on the great legal systems of the world are offered at the university law schools; research is promoted through institutes, especially in Paris, Lyon, and Toulouse. In Italy, interest in comparative law is vigorously cultivated at a number of universities. Institutes and university faculties in Spain, Latin America, Scandinavia, Japan, Yugoslavia, and other countries are also active. In the Soviet Union, foreign legal developments are closely observed in the law institute of the Academy of Sciences.

Comparative law, being supranational, calls for international cooperation. An organizational instrument for cooperation is provided by the International Association of Legal Science, which is affiliated with UNESCO, and through its directorate, the International Committee of Comparative Law. International meetings of comparatists are sponsored by the International Academy of Comparative Law. Instruction is offered by the International Faculty for the Teaching of Comparative Law, which has its seat in Strasbourg, and the International University of Comparative Sciences in Luxembourg.

Methods and scope

In comparative legal research one may distinguish between micro-comparison and macro-comparison. The latter is concerned with the comparison of entire legal systems, such as the Anglo–American common law and the so-called civil law, or, within the civil law, the family of the so-called Romanist laws, that is, those based on the French and German patterns. Micro-comparison is concerned with detailed legal rules and institutions. The two approaches, of course, shade into each other, especially in the comparison of methods of procedure and of legal thought.

Micro-comparison. In the earlier phase of the study of comparative law one tended to start out from particular institutions. One would, for instance, compare contract in Anglo–American and in civil law, or possessions in French and in German law, or the common-law doctrine of consideration and the civil-law concept of *causa.* In such a process one made two important discoveries: first, that seemingly identical terms rarely have the same meaning in different legal systems; second, that the same, or seemingly same, institution might perform different functions in different surroundings. The meaning of the Anglo–American term "contract," for instance, was found to differ in several respects from the term "contractus" of Romanist terminology and its modern counterparts. The institution of damages for tort was found to have a strictly compensatory function in German law, but both a compensatory and a punitive function in the common law. Thus, comparatists have increasingly come to incline toward the functional approach. Instead of starting with any particular rule or institution, one starts with a social problem and seeks to discover the rules or institutions by means of which the problem is resolved. What devices are, for instance, employed in different laws to provide for the orderly payment of the debts of a dead person, or to provide relief for the victims of unfair or sharp practices in business deals, or to provide for the security of title of purchasers of real estate? Such investigations are likely to indicate that, on the one hand, devices of considerable variety have been and can be used to achieve more or less identical purposes but, on the other hand, that the catalogue of technical devices available to legal designers is not unlimited.

Macro-comparison. Macro-comparison of entire legal systems has sought, in the rare case of Max Weber or in such modern surveys as that of René David, to cover the world. Mostly, however, it has been concerned with the two great systems of Western civilization, the Anglo–American common law and the civil law.

Common law versus civil law. Close inspection has shown that the characteristic differences between common law and civil law ought not to be expressed in the frequently used antitheses of codified versus uncodified law, or of statute law versus judge-made law, and even less in that between authoritarian versus libertarian law. Large sections of the law of civil-law countries, for example, the bulk of French or German administrative law, are neither codified nor even expressed in statutes, while big portions of English and American law have been brought together in comprehensive statutory codifications, as, for instance, the maritime and commercial laws of the United Kingdom or, in the United States, the uniform commercial code and the U.S. code of internal revenue. There exist, it is true, differences in the judicial attitudes toward such codifications, but they have their basis in that difference between the two great systems which is essential, namely, the difference between methods of legal thought.

The role of judicial precedent also differs less in the two systems than it was commonly believed to do. In theory, a common-law judge is bound by precedent, while a civil-law judge is not only free to ignore it but is supposed to take a fresh look at every individual case. In fact, judges in France or Germany pay such careful attention to precedent that entire sections of the law are judge-made, such as the French law of torts or that large body of German law which determines in great detail the commands of good faith and fairness which contracting parties are to observe toward each other. The older the code—the French civil code is 160 years old, the German civil code is about 70—the greater is the weight of the judicial gloss by which the text is overlaid. Common-law judges, on their side, are as well versed as their Continental brethren in the fine art of distinguishing upon the facts a new case from an unconformable precedent. Besides, in contrast to British courts, American courts no longer shy away from openly overruling a precedent that is regarded as no longer suitable.

As to the alleged contrast between civil-law authoritarianism and common-law espousal of liberty, it suffices to indicate that Switzerland is a civil-law country and Ghana is a common-law one, as was England in the days of Cromwell. And finally, it is a myth, though apparently an ineradicable one, that in civil-law criminal procedure the accused has to prove his innocence.

The essential difference between common law and civil law lies in the technical structure of court procedure, in the different conceptual framework within which legal thought moves, and in the underlying cause of these differences: the diversity of the personnel by which the machinery of the administration of justice is handled and guided.

Perhaps the most far-reaching discovery that has been made in comparative law research is Max Weber's observation that the climate of a society's legal system is ultimately determined by the kind of people by whom it is dominated, that is, as Weber calls them, the *honoratiores* of the law (1922). It makes a difference whether a legal system is dominated, as that of classical Rome, by gentlemen of leisure and high-ranking administrators, or, as the Islamic, by theologians, or, as the classical Chinese, by philosopher-bureaucrats. The common law grew up as the law of one set of centralized courts that was staffed with a small elite judiciary; this judiciary, in turn, was linked to that closely knit centralized bar from which it was drawn. The resulting common law reflects these surroundings: the mode of reasoning is that of analogy—policies are not always followed with consistency, nor are concepts always clean-cut; the law is thought of less as a body of norms of social conduct than as a set of rules of decision for the relatively few disputes that cannot be settled extrajudicially. Occasional obsolescence is not necessarily regarded as a serious evil, but, in general, those ex-barristers who occupy the bench are close to the course of affairs and know how to decide a concrete case that is presented to the court in oral contradictory trial by the members of a highly experienced bar.

What was decisive on the Continent was the absence of one central court. If the law was to keep abreast of changing conditions and to preserve a minimum of uniformity, guidance had to be exercised by the university law faculties, whose members for centuries constituted a supralocal community. Interpreting the book that was thought to constitute the theoretical basis of *the* law, they tended toward systematic arrangement, the elaboration of great principles, the logic of the syllogism, consistency of terminology, and an occasional remoteness from life. Efforts to adapt the law to changing social conditions were apt to be hidden behind controversies as to what should be the right interpretation of the authoritative text. Law being thought of as a set of rules of human conduct, it tended toward paternalistic guidance by those who would know best—the professors and the high-ranking officers in the service of the princes.

Today the scene has changed. On the Continent the establishment of central national courts has given great power to the judiciary, with a corresponding decline of the once leading role of learned doctrine. In the United States, on the other hand, the influence of the professors of the national law schools has come to be powerful in those branches of the law for which no uniform case law is created by a court of nationwide jurisdiction, that is, for all law other than that of the constitution of the United States and the body of federal statute law. With the breakdown of the centralized appellate jurisdiction of the Judicial Committee of the Privy Council, a similar development has occurred in Britain. Legal education is being taken over by the universities, and their professors are becoming guides for the judges of the courts of England and the Commonwealth countries. These courts are now as independent of each other as the state supreme courts in the United States are and as the courts of the small jurisdictional units of the Continent once were. Subtle changes in the character of the law, substantive and procedural, are the consequence of these developments in both systems.

Socialist law. In macro-comparison of legal systems, much attention has recently been paid to the laws of the socialist countries, especially the Soviet Union. Western observers have raised the question of whether these laws constitute a legal system of their own or whether they should be regarded as a branch of the civil-law system. The answer depends upon what test one applies. If one looks to the content of the legal rules and the machinery by which they are administered, one will agree with the Soviet jurists that their laws constitute a system of their own, even if one regards the difference between socialist law and "bourgeois law" as less enormous than it is made to appear in Soviet theory. After all, the welfare-state idea has taken hold in Western countries. If, on the other hand, one looks to the conceptual framework of the law, especially as it appears in the codes, or if one is interested in the basic features of court organization and procedure, a lawyer trained in French, German, or Swiss law will find his way more easily than one trained in the common law. If one looks to the personnel of the administration of justice, he will observe attitudes considerably different from those of Western judges and lawyers, but he can also observe among his Eastern brethren a steadily growing tendency to look upon themselves as guardians of individual rights against arbitrariness.

The tasks of comparative law

The careful analysis of legal systems that is now being elaborated has resulted in a distrust of timeworn clichés. Even the distinction between common law and civil law must, we have learned, not be overestimated. It is a difference more in method and traditions than in content. Also, it applies more to private than to public law. The forms of democratic government and the legal devices to secure the citizen's participation in government and his protection against abuses of governmental power, democratic or authoritarian, are independent of the historical background of legal development.

Comparative law impressively demonstrates the unity of Western civilization, which has spread over the world and is transforming the once different civilizations of the East. Western laws have come to be the laws of Asia and Africa. They are influencing even family law, in which non-European traditions have held out longest. Except for disappearing traditions of family law and matters related thereto, there is now in the world not a single country whose law would not belong to one of the three systems of Western origin: civil law, common law, socialist law.

In both micro-comparison and macro-comparison, the comparatist has to do more than merely ascertain differences and similarities of legal norms and institutions. If he wishes to learn about the reasons he must investigate the social conditions under which the norms and institutions of the law have originated, under which they operate, and which they influence. The legal comparatist must become a social scientist. The difficulties of the task, which are already formidable in a strictly formal comparison, are multiplied. No wonder that performance has been lagging. However, beginnings have been made in micro-comparative as well as in macro-comparative studies, especially of subjects of private law and procedure.

The great creators of law have always been observers of social reality. The classical Roman jurists who patiently elaborated the legal norms which are necessary for the smooth functioning of an economic order of free enterprise were consistently engaged in what we today call social research. Medieval canonists sound like modern sociologists when they observe that papal efforts to suppress blood feuds by means of law had to fail because such means conflicted with the mores of the people. The ever-recurrent tendency of lawyers to regard law as a self-sufficient body of rules was carried *ad absurdum* by Montesquieu, Savigny, and such more recent legal scholars as Rudolf von Jhering, Henry Maine, Frederic W. Maitland, Otto von Gierke, and François Gény.

In the new jurisprudence of the mid-twentieth century, as it has been developed simultaneously in the United States (Roscoe Pound, John H. Wigmore, Karl Llewellyn), in Germany and Austria (Eugen Ehrlich, Max von Rümelin, Philipp von Heck), and in Scandinavia (Anders Vilhelm Lundstedt), and which is now tending to become as universal as the jurisprudence of concepts was in the latter part of the nineteenth century, the science of law has become a social science.

MAX RHEINSTEIN

[*See also* JURISPRUDENCE; LAW; PUBLIC LAW; *and the biographies of* EHRLICH; GIERKE; LLEWELLYN; MAINE; MAITLAND; MONTESQUIEU; POUND; SAVIGNY.]

BIBLIOGRAPHY

A concise but comprehensive discussion of comparative law, its background, and its problems is Gutteridge 1946. *For a bibliography of books and articles published in English see* Szladits 1955–1962 *and annual supplements; for non-English periodical literature, see the* Index to Foreign Legal Periodicals.

AMERICAN JOURNAL OF COMPARATIVE LAW 1961 *XXth Century Comparative and Conflicts Law: Legal Essays in Honor of Hessel E. Yntema.* Leiden (Netherlands): Sythoff.

American Journal of Comparative Law. → Published since 1952.

DAVID, RENÉ 1964 *Les grands systèmes de droit contemporains: Droit comparé.* Paris: Dalloz.

GUTTERIDGE, HAROLD C. (1946) 1949 *Comparative Law: An Introduction to the Comparative Method of Legal Study and Research.* 2d ed. Cambridge Univ. Press.

Index to Foreign Legal Periodicals. → Published since 1960.

INTERNATIONAL ASSOCIATION OF LEGAL SCIENCE, INTERNATIONAL COMMITTEE OF COMPARATIVE LAW, *Bulletin d'information.* → Published since 1955.

International and Comparative Law Quarterly. → Published since 1952.

Introduction à l'étude du droit comparé: Recueil d'études en l'honneur d'Edouard Lambert. 3 vols. 1938 Paris: Société Anonyme du Recueil Sirey.

MAINE, HENRY J. S. (1861) 1960 *Ancient Law: Its Connection With the Early History of Society, and Its Relations to Modern Ideas.* Rev. ed. New York: Dutton; London and Toronto: Dent. → A paperback edition was published in 1963 by Beacon.

MONTESQUIEU (1748) 1962 *The Spirit of the Laws.* 2 vols. New York: Hafner. → First published in French.

Rabels Zeitschrift für ausländisches und internationales Privatrecht. → Published since 1927.

Revue internationale de droit comparé. → Published since 1949.

SCHLEGELBERGER, FRANZ (editor) 1927–1939 *Rechtsvergleichendes Handwörterbuch für das Zivil- und Handelsrecht des In- und Auslandes.* 7 vols. Berlin: Vahlen.

SCHNITZER, ADOLF F. (1945) 1961 *Vergleichende Rechtslehre.* 2 vols., 2d ed., rev. & enl. Basel: Verlag für Recht und Gesellschaft.

SZLADITS, CHARLES 1955–1962 *A Bibliography on Foreign and Comparative Law: Books and Articles in English.* Published for the Parker School of Foreign and Comparative Law, Columbia University. 2 vols. Dobbs Ferry, N.Y.: Oceana. → Volume 1 contains a bibliography up to 1953, published in 1955; Volume 2, from 1953 to 1959, published in 1962. Supplemented annually.

WEBER, MAX (1922) 1954 *Max Weber on Law in Economy and Society.* Edited, with an introduction and annotations by Max Rheinstein. Cambridge, Mass.: Harvard Univ. Press. → First published as Chapter 7 of Max Weber's *Wirtschaft und Gesellschaft.*

Zeitschrift für ausländisches öffentliches Recht und Völkerrecht. → Published since 1929.

Zeitschrift für vergleichende Rechtswissenschaft. → Published since 1878.

II
COMMON LAW SYSTEMS

The term "common law" is used in a number of different senses. In medieval English law it denoted that law which was administered by the king's courts and which was, in principle at least, common to the whole realm. The common law, in this sense, was to be distinguished from the law administered in the local, county courts or in the feudal, barons' courts, which tended to be specialized or particularized by region; and it was also to be distinguished from autonomous bodies of law, like the law merchant, which were peculiar to certain classes of persons.

In another sense, however, the common law is set in opposition to statute law. The common law is rendered concrete and explicit in, and derives its juridical efficacy from, decisions of courts; whereas statute law, or legislation, is an emanation of the will of the sovereign parliament or legislature. In this same specific sense, the common law is also distinguished from codified law or code law (civil law). The common law is conceived of as a body of principles originally derived from customs which are either reflected in the judgments of the highest national courts or else contained in piecemeal statutes passed *ad hoc* to correct or extend those same decisions. Thus it is opposed to those systems of law which have been reduced to more or less permanent written form and organization through a single comprehensive piece of legislation or codification.

Insofar as the English-speaking countries have generally been able to resist comprehensive codification of their laws, we are led into the broadest and most popular meaning of the term common law—the law of the English-speaking countries as opposed to the (generally codified) civil law of continental Europe and of those countries in Latin America, Asia, and Africa that were politically influenced by, and whose legal systems were shaped by, continental Europe.

In yet another sense, the common law is opposed to equity—that body of law, distinct from the common law, which was administered by the lord chancellor, as "keeper of the king's conscience," through the chancery courts, in order to correct or ameliorate the harshness or rigidities of the common law as administered by the regular courts. Equity started as a series of principles and rules, reflecting considerations of fairness and natural justice, which were, in medieval times, of such flexibility and range as to warrant the latter-day charge that equity was "as long as the chancellor's foot." By the early nineteenth century, however, it had jelled into a fairly rigid system of precedents and judicial authorities distinguishable from the common law mainly in that it was administered by a separate judicial hierarchy, the chancery courts. The Judicature Acts of 1873–1875, which effected a wholesale organization of the English judicial structure, abolished the special chancery courts, and equity was formally fused with the common law into a single system of precedents administered by one system of courts.

Last, the term common law is sometimes used to denote the private law, i.e., that body of law governing relationships of private citizens *inter se* in which the public or state interests are normally minimal or else only peripheral (for example, the law of contracts, torts, personal property), in contradistinction to constitutional law and public law generally (for example, administrative law, labor law, antitrust law) in which the public interests are normally pervasive. This distinction is ceasing to be really meaningful in modern terms, as the state increasingly intrudes into areas of law originally considered as involving personal interests only.

Diffusion of the common law. It is true of the common law that English settlers proceeding overseas to found new colonies carry with them the law of England existing at the time of the first settlement, except insofar as that law may be obviously inapplicable to the new area. For example, the old common law rule of "ancient lights" might be considered inappropriate or unnecessary in newly settled areas without any tall buildings and therefore inapplicable and not automatically "received" as law on settlement. Through this device, whereby new content and meaning were poured into old formulas, the common law became the basic law of the United States and of those Commonwealth countries founded by settlement. In the case of those parts of the British colonial empire acquired by military conquest and already having a local population (indigenous people or non-British settlers), different principles were applied, usually involving the maintenance of the local private law, as, for example, in the case of India, South Africa, and the Province of Quebec.

Once the English common law was "received" into an overseas colony, it continued in force until such time as it was repealed, altered, modified, or added to by appropriate constitutional authority—whether by the British Parliament as the supreme imperial legislative authority, or by the Privy Council sitting in Westminster as the final appellate tribunal for the overseas empire, or by the colonial legislature and colonial courts acting within their respective jurisdictional limits and competence and subject to appropriate control by imperial constitutional agencies. These imperial controls disappeared, in the case of the American colonies, with the Declaration of Independence; and they virtually disappeared in the case of the self-governing Commonwealth countries with developing constitutional custom and convention. This was partly confirmed and recognized in statutory form with the Statute of Westminster (1931), a British statute, although some members of the Commonwealth (Australia and New Zealand, for example) still retain, by their choice, an appeal from their courts to the Privy Council. Insofar as the common law remains the basic private law of the various English-speaking countries today, it is by those countries' own decisions to maintain and even extend their historical legal inheritance. For these purposes it becomes necessary to consider the juridical institutions and techniques whereby the common law is applied and developed in these countries.

Institutions and techniques. The key element in the continued viability of the common law today is undoubtedly the existence of the *doctrine of precedent*. This doctrine establishes, first, the obligation of court jurisdictions to adhere to and apply the decisions of tribunals that are superior to them in the judicial hierarchy; and, second, the principle that the highest court in the land is bound by its own decisions. The first aspect seems obvious enough, since it is a natural consequence of the pyramidal structure of court organization in England and has the practical utility of ensuring uniformity and predictability of decisions by inferior and intermediate tribunals. The second aspect—the principle of *stare decisis* in the strict sense—although often regarded as a truism of common law jurisprudence, was actually formulated as a binding principle of the English common law only in 1898, in the London Tramways case decision. Since that time, however, it has been one of the major preoccupations of common law legal theory.

Quite apart from the issue of whether courts ought to be bound by past decisions, the "legal realist" school, which was very influential in American law schools in the period between the two world wars, raised the issue of whether courts, as a matter of *fact*, did bind themselves by past decisions. Led by such brilliant young scholars as Judge Jerome Frank and Karl Llewellyn in the early 1930s, the legal realists pointed to the substantial devices or stratagems available to courts to mitigate the effects of unwanted judicial decisions from earlier eras. Among these devices the legal realists identified the practice of "distinguishing" prior cases: focusing on assertedly new or different fact situations in the case before the court, in contrast to the fact present in those earlier cases that established the now unwanted principles of law. The legal realists also pointed to the widespread judicial inclination toward "shading" of earlier decisions, that is, giving some more weight than others by categorizing them as the decisions of "strong courts" or by focusing on individual judicial opinions, separate and distinct from the official opinion of the court, in cases in which more than one judicial opinion is filed. These individual opinions could be special concurring opinions or even dissenting opinions in the case of "prestige" jurists like Oliver Wendell Holmes of the United States Supreme Court. Opinions of the intellectual caliber and clarity of Holmes's great dissent in the Lochner case in 1905 became appeals to the future and were later expressly vindicated by United States Supreme Court majorities, as in *West Coast Hotel Company* v. *Parrish Company* (300 U.S. 379) in 1937.

It must be admitted that "distinguishing" prior decisions is immensely facilitated by the proliferation of individual opinion writing on final appellate tribunals in the common law world. Only the Privy Council, among these courts, still resolutely adheres to its practice of filing only a single *per curiam* opinion in each case.

The "distinguishing" of cases is also assisted by the plethora of separate common law jurisdictions of the present day, each turning out its own decisions. Consider the problem in the federal states of the English-speaking world. In the United States there are 50 autonomous private law jurisdictions; each is theoretically independent and separate from the other, and the supreme court of each state is the final appellate tribunal for cases arising there (except insofar as those cases also raise issues involving federal jurisdiction). Although the decisions of any one state supreme court are not, of course, binding on any other state, they may have a certain persuasive authority, and it is frequently possible to find lines of opposing decisions from different state supreme courts, thus opening up the way for a creative judicial choice—judicial policy making. Notwithstanding the 50 separate, and at times competing, state private law jurisdictions there are countervailing forces that point toward the unity of the common law in the United States. There is, first, the *Restatement of the Law* prepared by the American Law Institute (1953–1965). Although not "official," it brought together the best experts available (law professors, judges, and lawyers) and soon achieved a quasi-official status. The *Restatement* tried to present the consensus of private law among the then 48 states and thus performed an important unifying function among the 48 jurisdictions. It still enjoys high respect in most state courts. Another important unifying factor is the existence of great "national" law schools (Yale, Harvard, Columbia, Chicago, etc.), which consciously avoid stressing the law of their own particular state and can thereby teach a genuinely "national" common law that can draw on the best principles of the jurisprudence of the 50 separate state systems.

Emphasis upon the "distinguishing" of cases on the facts directs attention to the crucial role of facts in contemporary common law decision making. It is not merely that the orthodox view of the principle of a case (or *ratio decidendi*) is the rule enunciated by the judge plus the material facts in the case (Goodhart 1931). It is also that, under the influence of legal realist teachings, courts, in accepting the desirability and inevitability of judicial policy making (or judicial legislation) at the final appellate level, have increasingly accepted the desirability of having an adequate factual record in aid of such judicial legislation. This new emphasis has perhaps received its fullest outlet in American jurisprudence in the so-called "Brandeis Brief" method of adducing constitutional facts to the notice of the United States Supreme Court; but it has also had its effects in the private law.

It is in American constitutional law, of course, that the direct and avowed departure from the principle of *stare decisis* has been most marked, prompting Judge Owen Roberts to comment ruefully, on the overruling of earlier United States Supreme Court decisions, that this trend to court flexibility tended to "bring adjudications of this tribunal into the same class as a restricted railroad ticket, good for this day and train only" (*Smith* v. *Allwright*, 321 U.S. 649, 1944).

The common law and social change. The contemporary judicial disposition to depart from *stare decisis*—either by directly overruling past decisions or by "distinguishing" cases—emphasizes movement and growth in the positive law as the society in respect to which the positive law is to operate itself changes.

The American school of sociological jurisprudence, led by Roscoe Pound, was strongly influenced by the pragmatist teachings of William James and John Dewey. Sociological jurisprudence preached the necessary and proximate relationship, or symbiosis, between law and society—that is to say, the notion that the criteria for evaluating and appraising the positive law at any time must include (1) the extent to which that positive law in fact reflects the complex of interests pressed in society at that time, and (2) the extent to which the positive law has changed in measure with that society. The values to which a sophisticated legal system must give effect include both the interest in a reasonable stability of settled legal expectations and the interest in mobility and change in law, lest the positive law, if too unimaginatively and rigidly applied, should act as a brake on future social development.

The legal realists charged that in attempting to balance these two opposing principles the common law systems, certainly until the 1930s, overemphasized the interest in stability and predictability of legal relationships and forgot the maxim that "the life of the law has not been logic, but experience" (see, for example, the writings of Karl Llewellyn and Jerome Frank). The theories of most legal realists emphasized the law-making role of appellate judges. The recent emphasis on the more dynamic elements in law (see the work of Myres McDougal, Harold Lasswell, and others) represents, in addition, a return to an earlier common law philosophy, a philosophy which had, after all, so successfully transformed the common law from crude and unrefined custom, in the closed medieval society, into an instrument of social control amply suited to the resolution of conflicts and tensions in modern complex industrial civilization.

EDWARD MCWHINNEY

[*See also* JURISPRUDENCE; LAW. *Directly related are the biographies of* BLACKSTONE; BRANDEIS; CARDOZO; COKE; FRANK; HOLMES; LLEWELLYN; POUND.]

BIBLIOGRAPHY

AMERICAN LAW INSTITUTE 1953–1965 *Restatement of the Law Second: Conflict of Laws.* Tentative Draft Nos. 1–13. Philadelphia: The Institute.

CARDOZO, BENJAMIN N. (1921) 1960 *The Nature of the Judicial Process.* New Haven: Yale Univ. Press.

DICEY, ALBERT V. (1885) 1959 *Introduction to the Study of the Law of the Constitution.* 10th ed. New York: St. Martins.

FRANK, JEROME (1930) 1949 *Law and the Modern Mind.* New York: Coward.

FRANK, JEROME 1949 *Courts On Trial.* Princeton Univ. Press. → A paperback edition was published in 1963 by Atheneum.

GOODHART, ARTHUR L. 1931 *Essays in Jurisprudence and the Common Law.* Cambridge Univ. Press.

HOLMES, OLIVER WENDELL (1881) 1963 *The Common Law.* Cambridge, Mass.: Harvard Univ. Press.

LLEWELLYN, KARL 1931 Some Realism About Realism: Responding to Dean Pound. *Harvard Law Review* 44: 1222–1264.

McDougal, Myres S.; Lasswell, Harold D.; and Vlasic, Ivan A. 1963 *Law and Public Order in Space*. New Haven: Yale Univ. Press.

Maitland, Frederic W. 1908 *The Constitutional History of England*. Cambridge Univ. Press.

Maitland, Frederic W. (1909*a*) 1936 *Equity*. Cambridge Univ. Press.

Maitland, Frederic W. (1909*b*) 1936 *The Forms of Action at Common Law*. Cambridge Univ. Press.

Plucknett, Theodore F. T. (1929) 1956 *A Concise History of the Common Law*. 5th ed., enl. & entirely rewritten. London: Butterworth.

Pound, Roscoe (1922) 1954 *An Introduction to the Philosophy of Law*. Rev. ed. New Haven: Yale Univ. Press.

Stone, Julius (1946) 1950 *The Province and Function of Law: Law as Logic, Justice, and Social Control; a Study in Jurisprudence*. Cambridge, Mass.: Harvard Univ. Press.

III
CODE LAW SYSTEMS

The term "code-law systems" is usually employed, as a legal term of art, with two different, if related, meanings. First, "code" refers to the reduction of the laws customarily observed by a particular people to a more or less permanent, organized, and written form through a comprehensive piece of legislation or *codification*. Strictly speaking, a "code" may denote a constitution or similar public-law enactment of fundamental laws; but more usually the term is limited to compilations of the private law (contracts, torts, property, agency, marriage, matrimonial property, and related matters), although many countries also have codifications of their criminal law, criminal procedure, civil procedure, and commercial law. It is in the general sense of there being a collection in a single, comprehensive statute of particular national laws on one or more main subjects that the code-law systems are normally opposed to uncodified, or common-law, systems. In the latter systems, in general, the private law at least remains an uncodified body of what were originally custom-derived rules or principles that purport to be reflected in the judgments of the highest national courts and in piecemeal statutes that may be passed *ad hoc* to correct or extend those judicial decisions.

In a second and more popular sense, the term "code-law systems" denotes the body of continental European civil law, which, as represented principally in the two major acts of codification of modern times, the French civil code (or Code Napoléon) of 1804 and the German civil code (Bürgerliches Gesetzbuch, or B.G.B.) of 1900, has spread throughout the world. The German civil code of 1900 had a decisive influence on the drafting and adoption of the present Japanese civil code and on the precommunist Chinese code. The Code Napoléon has been widely copied or borrowed from in the codifications of the Middle East, former French Africa, and Latin America generally.

It is in this particular sense of referring to the substantive civil-law content of the two great western European acts of codification that the term "code-law systems" is normally distinguished from the common law of the English-speaking countries. The common law of England was carried by process of conquest, occupation, or settlement, to the original American states and to the British colonies overseas. With some modifications based on deference to existing local, customary law, in the case of certain countries having an indigenous, predominantly non-English or non-European population, the common law has remained in these countries even after British political power has formally and practically disappeared. Thus the common law is today the basic private law of Great Britain, the Commonwealth countries, and the United States. The term "common law" applies both where the common law has itself been codified—as is the case in most of the English-speaking countries in regard to commercial law and criminal law—and even where the law was originally Romanist (as in South Africa and Ceylon) and, while still formally uncodified, was transformed by successive decisions of the Privy Council in London into a semblance of the common law, case law system of precedents. An act of codification is always something of a revolutionary step in the sense that it represents a certain intellectual break with the past. Although all the codes purport to be merely a restatement of the old, pre-existing law, most of the great codifying commissions have used the opportunity to make innovations and changes in the old law; and the act of codification itself, in the sense that it involves reducing a large and hitherto unorganized mass of materials to comprehensive form, necessarily involves a certain clarification and streamlining of the existing law.

The great codifying projects have usually coincided with eras of great political or social change or upheaval, probably because in such periods it may be easier to obtain that minimum degree of consensus among the decision-making elite necessary to force such projects through to completion. It may be only in such periods that the conflicting pressures for stability and change can be satisfactorily reconciled to the point of reducing the laws to a single, comprehensive enactment. The French civil code was adopted in the wake of years of revolutionary turmoil in France and was one of the first projects of the Emperor Napoleon, who personally guided it through to completion, to the point of sometimes presiding himself at the sessions of the codifying commission. In Germany the codification movement only really got under way and received official blessing after the achievement of German political union, in federal form, in 1871; and codification was then looked upon as an instrument for assisting and furthering the spirit of national unity.

In the case of Quebec, the civil code of 1866 was adopted at the time of the pending political incorporation of French-speaking Roman Catholic Lower Canada into a Canadian confederation in which French Canadians would be heavily outnumbered by English-speaking Protestants: the codification of French Canada's civil law was viewed as a defensive measure to protect the distinctive social values and institutions of Quebec (for example, the family law, with its emphasis on the family unit with paternal control, the absence of any divorce, and the institution of the joint matrimonial property system) against the encroachment, after confederation, of an alien common law that was viewed as incorporating Anglo-Saxon Protestant values.

The modern Japanese and Chinese civil codes, with their large German civil law influences and derivations, were adopted as part of a deliberate policy of modernization or "Westernization" of basic social institutions, with a view to speeding large-scale industrialization and development.

The Soviet Russian civil code of 1922 was adopted at a time when governmental pressures in the Soviet Union were all for stability, clarity, and certainty in law, after the disastrously chaotic experiences in the era of free law finding from 1917 to 1921. During that period, the tsarist codes and laws had been largely swept away and Soviet judges and administrators were often bound by a no more sure and reliable criterion for decision than their own "spirit of revolutionary consciousness." The year 1922 also marked the introduction in the Soviet Union of the New Economic Policy, with an official relaxation of controls on economic activity and a new encouragement of entrepreneurial business activity and of foreign trade and investment in the country. It was, therefore, argued that a fixed and definite civil code—which manifestly, in its structure and organization and in a great deal of its substantive principles, too, did not depart too much from the main continental European civil-law stream—would be an invaluable asset in promoting a more liberal Soviet official image, both at home and abroad.

Individual national codes differ widely, depending principally upon whether their makers have looked to the French or to the German civil code for their main intellectual inspiration. The Code Napoléon is direct, lucid, and often sparkling in structure and in language, reflecting perhaps both the inherently graceful qualities of the French language and the personality and techniques of its original drafting commission, whose members, essentially practicing lawyers, under some prodding from the Emperor Napoleon produced their final code in a matter of several months. The B.G.B., by contrast, is heavy, pedantic, and profuse, both in language and in drafting, reflecting in measure the essentially professorial and bureaucratic character of its main drafters and the years of research, public debate, and criticism that preceded its final adoption; for although the actual project for codification was put under way in 1874, with the appointment of the members of the codifying commission, it was not until 1896 that the final draft was completed and approved, to take effect from 1900. The Emperor Napoleon had said that his aim was to have the code so simple and convenient in its arrangement that the French peasant, reading it in its single, slim, pocket-book form by candlelight, would be able to know his legal rights; and so successful has the code been, from the viewpoint of legal writing, that Stendhal is said to have read a few pages of it each day to improve his literary style. The German code, by contrast, remains essentially a legal technician's code, without any particular claims to literary elegance or refinement of style.

This reference to a distinctive national psychology or personality—or *Volksgeist*, as Savigny called it—and its relationship to individual acts of national codification calls attention to the question of whether there are any particular periods in a nation's history that are especially ripe for codification, and perhaps it also poses the even more basic question of why some countries have achieved codes and others have not. In 1814, in reaction against the various French invasions and military occupations of the revolutionary and Napoleonic eras, Anton Thibaut and the German nationalist movement urged the immediate codification of German laws. Savigny, who opposed these pressures, argued that since a code existed primarily as a restatement or concretization of a nation's law it would act as a brake on national development if any nation should seek to codify its laws before it had reached its full political, social, and economic maturity. Savigny added a nationalistic argument to his injunction against any "premature" codification. He stated that, given the condition of German law at the opening of the nineteenth century, when only the loose, diffuse, and prolix Prussian code of 1794—an original project of Frederick the Great acting under the impulse of French rationalism—was available as a strictly Germanic model, any German act of codification, unless it were to be a reproduction in terms of the Code Napoléon, which had been carried into the Rhineland and other parts of Germany by Napoleon's armies, would require legal talents and resources beyond the then existing intellectual capacities of the German university law faculties.

It was far better, in Savigny's view, to keep the existing patchwork quilt of German law. In the Rhineland states, for example, the Code Napoléon would be retained; in Prussia and the areas under its control, the code of 1794; in the other states, the uncodified common law, or "received Roman law." The absorption of this uncodified law into Germany had taken place over the course of the fourteenth, fifteenth, and sixteenth centuries. In the process of that absorption and in the subsequent intensive study in the university law schools, it was progressively refined and restated. There is a particular irony in Savigny's argument against codification by appeal to *German* nationalistic traditions, since the received Roman law, which dominated so much of Germany at the opening of the nineteenth century, became ultra-*Roman* in content and character. Even the Code Napoléon, for example, while drawing heavily on the Roman law of southern France (or the *pays de droit écrit*), was still greatly influenced as to its substantive principles by the Germanic customary law of the northern provinces of France (or *pays de coutumes*).

A good part of the dynamics of a codification movement certainly comes from the spirit of rationalism. There have been powerful codification movements in both Great Britain and the United States. Bentham and his disciples, as part of their general law-reform movement in the early nineteenth century, launched a codifying project designed, in Bentham's own words, to render the law "cognoscible" to the layman. But the movement, except for some sustained influence in certain specialized areas of law, especially the criminal law and commercial law, and in the British colonies overseas, had largely petered out by the middle and late nineteenth century, probably because of the tenacious resistance of the vested professional interests of the judiciary and the practicing bar. The intellectual thoughtways of these special skill groups were attuned to that pragmatic, problem-by-problem development of legal principles inherent in the case-law system, and they were firmly opposed to any a priori postulation of principles through an act of codification. Since university teaching of law in England was very weak and largely unorganized until well into the nineteenth century, the practicing profession's influence was dominant in legal education through the Inns of Court, and this acted as a further intellectual barrier to codification.

In the United States the codification movement had its impact, represented in the great Field–Carter debate of the mid-nineteenth century; but the influence of codification has been very slow and, outside the commercial sphere, limited in area of impact. On the other hand, some factors have been very conducive to uniformity in the development of American private law, notwithstanding the existence of fifty formally separate and autonomous state jurisdictions. Especially important are the Restatements of American Law and the influence of the prestigious "national" law schools of the pattern of Yale and Harvard, which purport to teach a truly national, as distinct from a particularist or local law.

Once they have been drafted, there is a certain tendency for codes to become invested with a great deal of the seeming permanence, rigidity, and immutability of constitutions or similar fundamental laws. This particular truth, which had been observed by Savigny, seemed to be amply vindicated by the detailed history of the interpretation and application of the Code Napoléon during the nineteenth century. In France a highly conservative judiciary, aided by a strict and literal "grammatical" construction or exegesis of the text of the code, insisted on confining its practical application to a highly individualistic laissez-faire philosophy, at a time when France as a whole, speaking in social and political terms, had experienced a full-scale industrial revolution and had largely accepted collectivist or social democratic ideas. Yet, by the close of the nineteenth century the judiciary, aided by the work of a brilliant group of text writers and commentators, had begun systematically to reinterpret the Code Napoléon to take account of the new climate of an advanced industrial civilization, in which the code must operate. The operational tools for this transformation of the code were the new techniques of teleological interpretation (or interpretation in terms of social purposes), themselves products of Gény's call (1889) for free scientific research in law (*la libre recherche scientifique*). These developments in French code law in action parallel and anticipate the later realist and sociological emphases in North American jurisprudence.

Codes, like constitutions, if they are to be viable, must change with the society in which they operate; and this preferred relationship, or symbiosis, between law and society is assisted by the use of broad general formulas in drafting them. When the German Social Democrats were disposed to challenge the draft B.G.B. because of its alleged liberal, individualistic bias, the great jurist Rudolf Stammler was able to assure them that the lapidarian quality of the code's general provisions would make it continually adjustable to the community's own acceptance of social democratic ideas. The very generality of a code's key provisions—like the "due process" clauses in the fifth and fourteenth amendments to the United States constitution—enables new content to be poured into the old formulas. Thus the process of interpretation can serve to effect change and innovation in the law while avoiding the apparently radical step of direct legislative amendment.

EDWARD MCWHINNEY

[*See also* CONSTITUTIONS AND CONSTITUTIONALISM; JURISPRUDENCE; LAW; *and the biographies of* MONTESQUIEU *and* SAVIGNY.]

BIBLIOGRAPHY

AMERICAN JOURNAL OF COMPARATIVE LAW 1961 *XXth Century Comparative and Conflicts Law: Legal Essays in Honor of Hessel E. Yntema.* Edited by Kurt H. Nadelmann, Arthur T. Von Mehren, and John N. Hazard. Leiden: Sythoff.

DAVID, RENÉ; and DE VRIES, HENRY P. (1957) 1958 *The French Legal System: An Introduction to Civil Law Systems.* Dobbs Ferry, N.Y.: Oceana.

DAVID, RENÉ et al. 1960– *Le droit français.* Paris: Libraire Générale de Droit et de Jurisprudence. → Two volumes have been published to date.

GENY, FRANÇOIS (1889) 1962 *Méthode d'interprétation et sources en droit privé positif: Critical Essay.* 2d ed. St. Paul, Minn.: West.

GREAT BRITAIN, FOREIGN OFFICE 1950–1952 *Manual of German Law.* 2 vols. London: H.M. Stationery Office.

HAZARD, JOHN N.; and SHAPIRO, ISAAC 1962 *The Soviet Legal System: Post-Stalin Documentation and Historical Commentary.* 3 vols. Dobbs Ferry, N.Y.: Oceana.

MCWHINNEY, EDWARD 1958 *Canadian Jurisprudence: The Civil Law and Common Law in Canada.* Toronto: Carswell.

SAVATIER, RENÉ 1948 *Les métamorphoses économiques et sociales du droit civil d'aujourd'hui.* Paris: Dalloz.

SAVIGNY, FRIEDRICH KARL VON (1814) 1840 *Vom Beruf unserer Zeit für Gesetzgebung und Jurisprudenz.* 3d ed. Heidelberg (Germany): Mohr.

SCHLESINGER, RUDOLF B. 1950 *Comparative Law: Cases and Materials.* New York: Foundation Press.

VON MEHREN, ARTHUR T. 1957 *The Civil Law System: Cases and Materials for the Comparative Study of Law.* Englewood Cliffs, N.J.: Prentice-Hall.

IV
SOCIALIST LEGAL SYSTEMS–SOVIET LAW

Despite its stormy history, the Soviet legal system has acquired a definite character and gives evidence of being permanently established. Many of its features derive from prerevolutionary Russian origins and are therefore similar to those of other legal systems (especially the German and French), from which Russia borrowed in the nineteenth century. Other features, however, are peculiarly Soviet, reflecting the needs of a one-party state, a planned economy, and a social order directed toward a communist morality.

Development

In the first two decades after the Communist seizure of power, in 1917, Soviet legal institutions had to contend with the official Marxist–Leninist theory that law (like the state) is essentially a capitalist institution destined to wither away (literally, "die out") once socialism is established. This theory derived from the premise that the apparatus of political authority (the state) and the formal procedures and general rules enforced by such apparatus (law) are essentially instruments of domination by the ruling class. They would have to be retained during the period of proletarian dictatorship but would not be needed in the future classless society, which would regulate itself, like a family or a kinship society, by customary standards, by morality and common sense, and by a recognition of the identity of individual and social interests.

In the period of War Communism, 1917–1921, the new Soviet regime made strenuous efforts to eliminate the legal institutions of the prerevolutionary period and to usher in the new classless society as rapidly as possible. The formal political and legal institutions that were introduced were quite primitive in character and were thought to be very temporary. By 1921, however, the entire economy was at a standstill, and Lenin introduced the New Economic Policy (NEP); private trade was restored, foreign firms were invited to do business on the basis of "concessions," and the peasants were encouraged to sell the produce of their private holdings in the open market. The restoration of a certain degree of capitalism was thought to require also a restoration of law, and Lenin therefore sent his jurists to the prerevolutionary Russian codes, as well as to western European legal systems, to copy their provisions and adapt them to the new Soviet conditions.

In the 1920s there were promulgated codes of criminal law, criminal procedure, civil law, civil procedure, land law, labor law, and family law. These codes, as interpreted and developed by the judiciary, the bar, the Procuracy, the Ministry of Justice, and legal scholars, gave the Soviet Union a system of law comparable in its techniques and main outlines to those of Western countries. The system was hedged about, however, with provisions designed to prevent its being used contrary to the interests of the proletarian dictatorship.

Thus, article 1 of the Civil Code stated that the rights declared in the code should be protected by law "except in instances when they are exercised in contradiction to their social–economic purpose." Similarly, the Criminal Code, rejecting the "bourgeois" principle of *nullum crimen sine lege,* provided that an act not made punishable by a specific article of the code may, if it is socially dangerous, be punished under articles relating to analogous acts (the doctrine of analogy).

Other features of the law of the NEP that reflected a "proletarian" or "Leninist" orientation included severe limitations upon rights of private ownership, civil liability for causing personal injury regardless of the absence of fault on the part of the defendant, an administrative procedure for divorce by unilateral repudiation, and heavy penalties for "counterrevolutionary" acts or utterances. In addition, the legal system as a whole was rendered somewhat precarious by the theory that it was only part of a transition toward a socialist society in which law would die out.

With the end of the NEP in 1928, the introduction of the first Five-Year Plan, and the collectivization of agriculture, there came a return to the nihilistic and apocalyptic spirit of the earlier period of War Communism. Now, however, a more positive content was given to the notion of the dying out of state and law. These were to be replaced, it was declared, by the plan. The legal institutions of the NEP, although not formally abolished, now became in many respects obsolete. Communist party directives and police terror replaced law in many areas of economic and social life, and Stalin, in that period, built his personal machine for governing.

The spirit of Soviet law in the early 1930s was reflected particularly in the writings of E. B. Pashukanis, the leading jurist of that period, who in his "General Theory of Law and Marxism" (1927) had expounded the view that law in its very nature is based on the concept of reciprocal exchange of goods and hence is essentially a product of a market economy. In the early 1930s Pashukanis foresaw the imminent disappearance of law and argued that such law as continued to exist in the period of construction of the planned economy should have maximum political elasticity. "The utmost dynamic force is essential," he wrote in 1930. "Revolutionary legality is for us a problem which is ninety-nine per cent political" (*Soviet Legal Philosophy* 1951, pp. 279–280).

In the mid-1930s, however, there was once again a reaction against excessive dynamism. Stalin, in his "Report on the Draft Constitution," 1936, called for "stability of laws." With the adoption of the constitution in December 1936, socialism was declared to have been achieved; class antagonisms were said no longer to exist within the Soviet Union; but at the same time the new socialist era was said to require the strictest legality together with the strongest possible state power. The dying out of state and law was now postponed until the final stage of communism, after the end of "capitalist encirclement"—that is, when the whole world would be communist.

To this postponement Stalin added the "dialectical" doctrine that in order to pave the way for its own abolition the state must in the meanwhile become stronger and stronger. Thus the increase of terror against internal enemies—called agents of foreign imperialism—was given a theoretical justification, while at the same time the stabilization of the legal system could be promoted in those areas of social and economic life where terror was not considered necessary.

The dual system of law and terror that Stalin established in the mid-1930s is well symbolized by the fact that Pashukanis' nihilistic theories of law were denounced and he himself was shot as a counterrevolutionary. He was replaced as dean of the Soviet legal profession by Andrei Ia. Vyshinskii, who laid down the new party line about law in a series of articles and in a book on Soviet public law (1938). While defending party supremacy and the use of force against "enemies of the people," Vyshinskii attacked Pashukanis and other Soviet jurists for their attempt to reduce law to economics or to politics. He asserted that law has an "active, creative role" to play in the Soviet planned economy and that the reduction of law to politics would signify the ignoring of those tasks that stand before law, such as the tasks of legal protection of personal, property, family, testamentary, and other rights and interests (1938).

Under Vyshinskii's aegis the whole vocabulary of "rights," "duties," "legality," "contract," "ownership," "inheritance," "fault," "independence of the judiciary," "right to counsel," "burden of proof," and the like was carried over from the NEP period and rebaptized as "socialist both in form and in content." Moreover, the escape clauses of the NEP codes, such as article 1 of the Civil Code and the doctrine of analogy in criminal law, were greatly restricted in their application. In criminal law the element of personal guilt was emphasized as an essential element of crime. Liability for personal injury was now to be based on fault rather than on mere causation. A judicial procedure for divorce was introduced. Freedom of testation was increased, and the maximum 90 per cent inheritance tax was eliminated and replaced by a maximum 10 per cent notarial fee.

At the same time, "counterrevolutionaries" and "enemies of the people" were generally dealt with in secret administrative trials by the Special Board of the Ministry of Internal Affairs (MVD) or in a special secret procedure in the military courts. (The great purge trials of 1936–1938 were an exception to this rule.) Indeed, Vyshinskii developed theories to justify the application of special legal doctrines in political cases—for example, the theory that confessions have special evidentiary force in cases of counterrevolutionary crimes, since no person would confess to such a crime unless he were actually guilty!

The restoration of law as a positive feature of Soviet socialism was part of a general stabilization of social relations that occurred in the mid-1930s. It was related to the restoration of historical traditions, the re-emphasis of family stability, and the stress on Soviet patriotism, as well as to the recognition of the need for personal material incentives and for greater regularity and calculability in the administration of the economy. In the sphere of constitutional law, however, including choice of leaders, the legislative process, and civil liberties, "socialist legality" was largely a facade for Stalin's personal despotism.

After Stalin's death, in 1953, his successors denounced his "violations of socialist legality" and restricted very substantially the use of terror. They abolished the Special Board of the MVD and the special procedures in military courts for counterrevolutionary crimes. Hundreds of thousands of persons who had been convicted of counterrevolutionary crimes were released from labor camps and rehabilitated. Confessions were deprived of special evidentiary value, and the burden of proof was placed squarely on the prosecution in all criminal cases. The doctrine of analogy was eliminated from criminal law. New laws provided for the publication of all statutes and executive decrees having "general significance." There was also a slight narrowing of the law on counterrevolutionary crimes (renamed "state crimes"), although it remained a crime to defame the Soviet political and social system or even to possess written materials of such defamatory nature for the purpose of weakening Soviet authority. The regime in the labor camps (renamed labor colonies) was substantially reformed.

Even apart from political crimes, Soviet law underwent substantial liberalization in the years after Stalin's death. There was a re-examination of virtually every branch of law and a weeding out of most of the harshest features. Between 1958 and 1962 "Fundamental Principles" were enacted by the U.S.S.R. Supreme Soviet in the fields of criminal law, criminal procedure, civil law, civil procedure, and judicial administration. On the basis of these Fundamental Principles the various Soviet republics have begun to enact new codes in these fields. Draft "fundamental principles" of labor law were published in 1959 and were still under discussion in 1965, with new Fundamental Principles of family law in preparation as of that date. The new basic legislation has effected not only a general liberalization of the pre-existing law but also a significant systematization and rationalization.

Characteristics

Among the distinguishing features of the Soviet legal system is the institution of the Procuracy, which was established by Lenin in 1922 on the model of the old Russian Procuracy established by Peter the Great. The procurator-general of the U.S.S.R. and his subordinates at all levels have the function not only of indicting and prosecuting criminals but also of supervising legality generally. "General supervision" includes "protesting" administrative abuses to higher administrative authorities, as well as "protesting" erroneous judicial decisions to higher courts. Any citizen may complain about an abuse of his rights to the Procuracy, which is required to investigate and reply to the complaint and in proper instances to "protest" it. Thus, the Procuracy exercises a "watchdog" function, without having administrative powers of its own (apart from the power to indict for crime). It is a legal institution peculiarly adapted to a political system in which there is a high degree of central administrative regulation.

A second characteristic Soviet legal institution is the system of administrative adjudication of contract disputes between state economic enterprises and organizations. So-called *Arbitrazh* tribunals hear such disputes and resolve them on the basis of contract law, administrative regulations, and state economic plans. Where plans require enterprises to enter into contracts for supply of goods and the enterprises cannot agree on the terms, *Arbitrazh* tribunals will hold hearings and resolve the dispute. Most of the several hundred thousand cases decided annually by *Arbitrazh* involve, however, not these "pre-contract" disputes, but suits for specific performance or for damages for breach of contract.

A third distinguishing feature of the Soviet legal system is its heavy stress on the educational role of law. Both substantive and procedural law, in virtually all fields, is oriented toward the guidance, training, and disciplining of Soviet citizens to be loyal, responsible, and devoted to the aims of the society as formulated by the Communist party. A specific manifestation of this "parental" philosophy is the law of official crimes, which makes administrative and managerial personnel of state organizations criminally liable for intentional malperformance or negligent performance of their official duties.

The emphasis on the educational role of law is connected with the theory of the dying out of state and law once communism is achieved. In 1961 the achievement of the first stage of communism was promised within twenty years. At the same time the Stalinist theory that the state must get stronger and stronger in order to create the conditions for its demise was rejected. The 1961 Communist party program declared that the period of proletarian dictatorship was over and that Soviet society would take immediate (although very gradual) steps to replace the coercive machinery of the state by the persuasive, voluntary processes of popular social action. In accord with this theory, various paralegal bodies have been established—notably, informal "comrades' courts" in factories and apartment houses, which mete out reprimands and light fines for minor offenses, as well as "people's patrols" (*druzhiny*), which act as volunteer auxiliary police. In addition, people who lead an "antisocial, parasitic way of life" and "live on unearned income" are tried by collectives of workers or by the courts in a special administrative procedure and are subject to "resettlement" for two to five years in places where they must take socially useful jobs.

The adoption of these "antiparasite" laws in the major republics in 1961 coincided with a general increase in harsh penalties for serious crimes. Thus, in 1961 the death penalty was introduced for large-scale economic crimes, counterfeiting, and illegal transactions in foreign currency. In 1962 repeated bribery of officials, rape committed by a group, and attempted homicide of a policeman or volunteer auxiliary policeman (*druzhinnik*) were added to the list of capital offenses. (Prior to 1961, only certain political crimes—treason, espionage, banditry, wrecking, terrorist acts—and murder committed under aggravating circumstances were subject to the death penalty in time of peace, and in 1958 the maximum period of confinement had been reduced from 25 to 15 years.)

Thus, as of the early 1960s there was a certain ambivalence in the Soviet legal system. On the one hand, many of Vyshinskii's theories justifying the use of terror were denounced, and socialist legality was proclaimed to extend to all spheres of Soviet life. On the other hand, the dualism of law and terror was replaced by a dualism of law and informal social pressure, and law itself, although applied with greater objectivity than ever before in Soviet history, reflected increased harshness in some areas and increased leniency in others. Soviet jurists rejected Vyshinskii's definition of law as a coercive instrument of state domination (embodying, Vyshinskii added, the will of the people); yet they were unable to find a new definition that corresponded to Marxist–Leninist theory, to the new conditions of Soviet life, and to the aspirations toward a communist society in which social influence and persuasion would replace formal rule and command.

HAROLD J. BERMAN

[*See also* COMMUNISM; MARXISM.]

BIBLIOGRAPHY

The major "classics" of Soviet legal theory in the period prior to Stalin's death have been translated in part by Hugh W. Babb in **Soviet Legal Philosophy 1951.** *No one has emerged to replace Vyshinskii as dean of Soviet jurisprudence (1938). Among those scholars, formerly associated with Vyshinskii, who have been in the forefront of the reform movement since 1955 are M. S. Strogovich, S. A. Golunskii, A. A. Piontkovskii, and S. N. Bratus. Of the younger jurists who first came to prominence in the middle 1950s, O. S. Ioffe is perhaps the most outstanding. An extensive bibliography of Soviet legal writings may be found in* **Hazard & Shapiro 1962.**

BERMAN, HAROLD J. (1950) 1963 *Justice in the U.S.S.R.: An Interpretation of Soviet Law.* Rev. & enl. ed. Cambridge, Mass.: Harvard Univ. Press. → Originally published as *Justice in Russia: An Interpretation of Soviet Law.*

BERMAN, HAROLD J. (compiler) 1966 *Soviet Criminal Law and Procedure: The R.S.F.S.R. Codes.* Cambridge, Mass.: Harvard Univ. Press.

GRZYBOWSKI, KAZIMIERZ 1962 *Soviet Legal Institutions: Doctrines and Social Functions.* Ann Arbor: Univ. of Michigan Press.

Gsovski, Vladimir 1948–1949 *Soviet Civil Law: Private Rights and Their Background Under the Soviet Regime.* 2 vols. Ann Arbor: Univ. of Michigan Press.

Hazard, John N. 1960 *Settling Disputes in Soviet Society: The Formative Years of Legal Institutions.* New York: Columbia Univ. Press.

Hazard, John N.; and Shapiro, Isaac 1962 *The Soviet Legal System: Post-Stalin Documentation and Historical Commentary.* 3 vols. Dobbs Ferry, N.Y.: Oceana.

Pashukanis, E. B. 1927 *Obshchaia teoria prava i marksizm* (General Theory of Law and Marxism). Moscow: Izdatel'stvo Kommunisticheskoi Akademii. → For a partial English translation see *Soviet Legal Philosophy,* 1951.

Schlesinger, Rudolf (1945) 1951 *Soviet Legal Theory: Its Social Background and Development.* 2d ed. London: Routledge.

Soviet Legal Philosophy. 1951 Cambridge, Mass.: Harvard Univ. Press; Oxford Univ. Press. → A collection of major classics by V. I. Lenin and others, translated by Hugh W. Babb and published under the auspices of the Association of American Law Schools.

Vyshinskii, Andrei Ia. (editor) (1938) 1948 *The Law of the Soviet State.* New York: Macmillan. → First published in Russian.

LEGENDS

See Folklore.

LEGISLATION

I NATURE AND FUNCTIONS

The term "legislation," in its narrowest modern usage, denotes the enactment of rules of law by specialized State agencies endowed with high authority and fairly representative of the general population; the term also denotes the rules that result from this process. In a wider sense, legislation includes, in addition, rules of general application enacted by executive, by subordinate administrative, by regional, and by local authorities. Rules of this kind are also known as secondary, or subordinate, or delegated legislation. At times, the term is used in a still broader meaning, in relation to rules stemming from other than State authorities (e.g., church or international legislation).

Legislation, thus understood, presupposes a fair degree of political and legal differentiation. It requires, first, a well-understood distinction between general norms intended to govern human conduct in an indefinite number of future instances and individual norms or commands intended to apply in a specific instance or in a strictly limited number of specific instances only. It requires, second, a well-established distinction between institutions authorized to issue general norms and those not authorized to do so; and more particularly, the setting up of a *central* agency equipped with this authority—the legislature in the proper sense of the word. It requires, third, a fair degree of consensus that norms thus enacted rank above most other legal rules found in the society. In more primitive legal systems, where such differentiation has not taken place and where society is largely regulated by rules to which metaphysical or customary origin is ascribed and which are regarded as beyond deliberate change by man-made institutions, one can hardly speak of legislation. And in those modern societies where differentiation of functions disappears in the plenitude of power wielded by an individual or by a small collective group—notably in some dictatorships—the concept of legislation as a distinct function suffers a serious setback.

Development of the concept

The term "legislation" derives from the Latin *lex.* The *lex,* once Roman law emerged from its primitive stage, was a distinct kind of legal rule of overriding authority and mainly of general application, expressly enacted by the people or on their behalf by some highly placed institutions (monarch, senate), singly or in combination. The same institutions were also regarded as entitled to modify or abrogate a *lex* once passed. It was therefore a term narrower than *ius*—the sum total of rules presumed to govern human conduct, whatever their authority, scope, or procedure of formation. It was, more precisely, an especially authoritative rule of the *ius civile* in the original meaning of the expression (i.e., the law which the State-organized society, *civitas,* provided for the regulation of conduct within itself), of what is called today "positive law" (i.e., imposed by the State) and of the *ius scriptum* (written, or enacted, law). Within this area of written positive law, the *lex* is a specific rule attributed to the highest lawmaking authority, which thus becomes *the* legislative authority par excellence. By definition, any other rule of positive law is viewed as subject to the *lex,* and if it acquires a status equal to a *lex,* it is said, in the language of Justinian's *Institutes* (I, II, 4), to "have the force of a lex" (*legis habet vigorem*).

Whether "nonpositive" law, which claims derivation from religion, from nature, from ethics, from reason, or from various ideological assumptions, is also subject to State-made legislative rules or, on the contrary, represents a "higher law" that states may not transgress, has remained a point of controversy in theory and still more in practice, ever since antiquity. Even custom and judge-made law were often regarded as immune from legislative interference, and not until the seventeenth century in England was the supremacy of legislation over the common law definitely acknowledged.

Several terms in various European languages—*loi*, *legge*, *ley*, *Gesetz*, *zakon*, and in English *a law* (as distinct from *the law*), but more precisely *statute*, *Act of Parliament*, *Act of Congress*—were coined to conform more or less to the historically developed meaning of *lex*. Upon closer observation, the criterion of generality appears in all of these to be rather incidental. The Romans had already noted that there are personal laws not intended to establish binding standards for future conduct (*leges . . . personales quae nec ad exemplum trahuntur*). Indeed, individual and special laws continue to form a considerable part of the legislative output in most civilized states. The decisive criterion for identifying legislation as a process and laws as the product of the process is increasingly the formal criterion of the identity of the enacting agency. In a curious reversal of roles, instead of legislation being explained as the activity which aims at the enactment of laws, we tend today to hold as laws those rules which are arrived at by the process of legislation.

Neither in antiquity nor in later times did specialists, let alone general usage, adhere strictly to the above meanings of the terms. In Rome *lex* was often used instead of *ius* to denote a whole area of jural regulation (e.g., *lex mancipi*, *lex commissoria*); and even another part of Justinian's codification (*Digest* I, III, 1) defines *lex* in a far broader manner than does his *Institutes*. *Lex* apparently had already become a highly popular expression, as overworked and used as indiscriminately as *law* in the English language today. In some other modern languages, the distinctiveness of the term is better preserved because, like Latin, they have a second term at their disposal (*loi–droit*, *legge–diritto*, *Gesetz–Recht*, *zakon–pravo*); but there, too, confusion is not unknown.

With the emergence of the Roman emperor and his appointees as the center of all governmental functions, a special legislative agency and its specific product, the *lex*, though maintained in theory, lost all practical importance. Different rules now stemmed largely from the same sources and from the same motivations; it hardly seems worthwhile, therefore, to pay much attention to formal differences between them. The influence of theology on juristic theory in the centuries after Constantine's conversion to Christianity made the distinction even less meaningful. The three systems of the *ius naturale*, *ius gentium*, and *ius civile*, which the Romans were at such pains to keep distinct, tended to coalesce, the law of the church proper was added to them, and all four claimed ultimate legitimation by the same authority. Both enacted and customary rules of municipal law were occasionally described as *leges*, but so were the asserted principles of *ius gentium* and of *ius naturale*, as well as rules which claimed none but divine authority. Feudalism, too, contributed to this development. A device for maintaining social organization in the face of a weakened central power, it preserved no specific function as that power's sole prerogative but opened all of them, including the enactment of general rules, to the interplay of bilateral feudal relations; agreement and custom tended to rank above enactment in the legal structure. *Lex* and its plural *leges*, though at times used in contradistinction to *consuetudines*, extended beyond the particular rule and embraced a whole body of rules, being used in this sense concurrently with *jus*. *Lex Salica*, *lex Romana*, *lex civilis*, *leges Langobardorum*, and in private international law, *lex fori* and *lex contractus*, became technical expressions in which *lex* stood for *jus*.

From the eleventh century on, the revival of the original concept was stimulated by the universities, where Roman law dominated the jurists' thinking. The strengthening of the State at the expense of feudalism, which followed soon after, again lent reality to the distinction between higher-ranking and lower-ranking rules, and between individual and general ones. The *statutum* was defined as a written, general enactment, and the authority to enact statutes as the *potestas statuendi*. When exercised by the supreme political authority, it became the *potestas legis ferendi*. The *legis lator*, an expression known already in Rome and used there, as was the Greek *nomothetes*, mainly to denote an individual leader endowed with charisma or exceptional wisdom, like Moses or Solon or Lycurgus, appeared in a French source of the fourteenth century in its modern institutionalized meaning.

Further developments were again intimately connected with the gradual differentiation between the functions of various State agencies. As long as different rules emanating from the prince enjoyed similar status in the legal system, there was not much point in drawing formal distinctions between them. No doubt, certain restrictions were considered binding upon the princes of continental Europe, and some acts called in theory for the consent of representative assemblies. But in actual practice, most of these representative assemblies lost their powers, and the absolute power of the princes became prevalent, sweeping away before its authority all distinctions between basic and subordinate rules. Where, however, the representatives played an active part in the law-making machinery, e.g., in England, the Netherlands, Poland, the Italian and Hanseatic city-republics, and the Swiss cantons, the differentiation between rule-enacting agencies sharpened the differences between the resulting sets of rules. A rule which could be made only with the consent of a representative assembly and had to be modified in the same way was considered higher law than that enacted by mere executive authority. In monarchical countries such as England, the Netherlands, and Poland, this conception was somewhat blurred by the existence of the prince's "own right" or "prerogative"—a rival system of law impenetrable to the powers of the representative body. Nevertheless, there too the rules enacted by consent of representative bodies emerged as rules of higher authority, both in the consciousness of the population and in juristic practice. These were the rules that became increasingly identified as legislation, first in England and then in continental Europe.

In England special authority was early attributed to enactments agreed upon by the king and an assembly, soon to be divided into two houses. Thus arose the Act of Parliament, the first modern legislative act. The identity of the body which, in addition to the king, participated in the enactment; the procedure of this participation; and the social consensus symbolized by it lent special significance to the enactment. The contents of the act were of minor importance. Quite often its scope was general, but even where the same procedure was observed with respect to a measure of limited scope or applicability, the measure still enjoyed the same high degree of authority. Down to the seventeenth century there were many attempts to contest the special status of Acts of Parliament, to attribute a similar status to certain measures enacted on the king's sole authority, and to dispute the authority of Acts of Parliament to deviate from the common law; but by the end of that century the superiority of these acts over both king and common law stood unchallenged.

This concept of legislation, identified by the participation of a representative body in the enacting process and given a pre-eminent position in the State's scale of norms, remained virtually unchanged until the end of the eighteenth century. Both Continental and English philosophers and jurists adopted it and helped to spread it among the growing literate stratum of the population. A change ensued when the United States, followed by France, inaugurated the era of formal constitutions. These, wherever adopted, have displaced the ordinary laws, enacted through the legislative process, from their theoretical and moral pre-eminence in the legal structure, and—to the extent that the supremacy of the Constitution was accompanied by judicial or other sanctions—the displacement was of practical legal significance as well. Otherwise, legislation and its products—the laws, in the narrow meaning of the word—remained in their place, at or near the apex of the legal structure.

Secondary legislation

The stress of modern conditions has resulted in complications connected with (*a*) the complexities inherent in an industrial society, (*b*) a closer relationship between executive and legislature, (*c*) a generalized pattern of self-governing units, (*d*) the problem of meeting emergencies, and (*e*) the growth of modern dictatorships.

The complexities of modern society, combined with the increased social welfare purposes of the modern State, call for a vastly increased intervention by public authorities in areas of social relations which in former times had been regarded as lying outside the authorities' field of interest. Both administrative convenience and an increased sensitivity to the "rule of law" and the principle of equal treatment militate against exclusive reliance on *ad hoc* decisions, demanding instead regulation by general rules. But the very number of the general rules required, the complexity of their subject matter, and the specialized knowledge needed for their formulation make it difficult for the legislature to solve the problems incidental to their enactment. Willy-nilly, legislatures acquiesce nowadays to the enactment by administrative agencies of general rules, which but a few decades ago would have been regarded as reserved to legislation proper. [*See* DELEGATION OF POWERS.]

This trend was greatly assisted by a major change that has taken place in most countries of the world in the relations between legislatures and the top layers of the executive arm. No longer do these institutions represent two different principles of legitimacy and two different social groupings, often with opposing interests and credos and generally suspicious of each other's objectives, one centering on the prince, the nobility and the top bureaucracy; the other, on a broader group not intimately associated with the day-to-day conduct of public affairs. Nowadays the government, the top layer of the bureaucracy, and the legislature all trace their authority to the same source—the "people" (whatever the measure of reality or fiction behind this attribution)—and to a large extent share or reflect identical social interests. In those countries where some variety of the parliamentary regime prevails (i.e., one in which the heads of the executive are permanently answerable to the legislature and may be dismissed at the latter's discretion), it is the practice to place the direction of executive affairs in the hands of a group of persons who not only are for the most part members of the legislature enjoying the confidence of a majority of their fellow members, but are actually the leaders of that majority. In the circumstances, despite disagreements and mutual jealousies which still persist between executive and legislature, their conflicts can in no way be compared in intensity to those which marked the relations between the two in the days when they represented opposing principles of government and divergent social forces. In the modern State a large degree of basic unity of purpose and outlook between the legislature and the executive leadership replaces the fundamental lack of confidence which formerly existed between them.

This new situation explains why parliaments have largely abdicated their policy-making function to governments, whose lead they now tend to accept, but it explains more particularly why the former parliamentary reluctance to let executive agencies enact far-reaching general norms has considerably weakened. Many a statute is no more than an *enabling statute* authorizing the president, the cabinet, the minister, the subordinate executive department or officer to issue general rules within a very wide range of discretion. At times, special statutory provisions are aimed at exempting such rules and the decisions based on them from effective judicial review. Other general rules are issued by the executive without express authorization by statute, in the exercise of its powers under the Constitution, or of its police powers, or under the theory of the implied powers of government; and the legislature, as long as it does not disagree with the government on major questions of composition or policy, does not generally object. Action which in the former days of struggle between prince and parliament would have been resisted by the latter as usurpation of power, is now accepted as normal, inevitable, or even desirable, in the interest of good government.

This state of affairs is not without its influence on the judiciary and on academic jurisprudence: courts have accepted it, and so have universities. In theory as well as in practice, the border line between legislation and regulations has become blurred, and regulations with more or less general contents are increasingly referred to as "secondary" or "subsidiary" or "delegated" legislation. Statutes passed by a parliamentary body are no longer the only form of legislation; they are distinguished merely by being "primary legislation." And the body itself is no longer the sole legislator; it is but the "primary legislator." In Britain this development has been most pronounced and, despite occasional protests from the traditionalist legal profession, is growing stronger. Other countries influenced by English law follow suit, and so do countries of the civil law tradition. In the United States, "delegation of legislative powers" is still rejected in principle, and the country's courts attempt to enforce this prohibition. But the factors that made for the practice elsewhere are active in the United States as well, and though the character of "legislation" is denied them, far-reaching general norms without much statutory guidance are becoming the rule.

Another kind of "secondary legislation," widespread in the modern world, is that indulged in by local authorities when making general rules within the scope of their jurisdiction. This trend goes back to medieval towns, many of which had representative institutions at a time when states were still governed autocratically, a circumstance which facilitated the conception of a difference between rules enacted by representative authorities and those made by executive authorities alone. Indeed, the very term "statute" was largely used to denote acts of self-governing local or regional authorities. But while, in premodern times, the jurisdiction of local authorities was often based on special arrangements and charters, it now conforms to a general State-wide pattern. In this pattern, the local authority consists of a predominantly elected representative body and of administrative personnel headed by an individual (mayor) or a small committee of officeholders with departmental responsibilities. Within this structure, the bifurcation into "higher" rules issued by the larger representative body and the acts of the "executive," bound by those rules, resembles the legislative–executive relationship within the State and justifies the designation by analogy of the "higher" local body as legislature and its output of general rules as legislation. In relation to the State, though, the rule-enacting activity in question is, of course, limited by State agencies and is subject to a variety of controls both before and after enactment. By no means can this activity pretend to "high" status within the total legal structure, however valued the principle of local self-government may be in current political thinking. At most, these acts too could be considered a kind of "secondary legislation" in the British sense. The special designation of "bylaws" points both to the analogy these rules bear to legislation and to the difference between them. [*See* LOCAL GOVERNMENT.]

The discussion of near-legislative activities by local authorities applies equally to representative regional authorities. The size of a regional entity, the scope of its authority, and the over-all status it enjoys in the politico-legal scheme of things do not theoretically affect the situation as described. In the United States this holds true of the school district as well as of the county, in England of the parish as well as of the county, in France of the *arrondissement* as well as of the *département* and the *région*.

It even holds true, to some extent, of regional entities in a federation which by courtesy, tradition, or formal enactment are accorded the dignity of statehood, whatever their precise designation (*states* in the United States, Australia, India, and Mexico; *republics* in the Soviet Union and Yugoslavia; *provinces* in Canada; *Länder* in Austria and the German Federal Republic; *cantons* in Switzerland). The scope of jurisdiction of these units is usually much wider, and within that scope they are much freer or altogether free from central controls; their status is anchored in the constitution and is often entrenched against interference by the federal legislature; and tradition or the letter of the constitution may describe them as "sovereign." Nevertheless, theirs too is an authority derived from a body politic larger than their own. Often there is the added limitation that in case of conflict, a federal statute will prevail over the product of the "member-state" legislation, thus relegating the latter to a clearly subordinate plane.

A further phenomenon which complicates the legislative picture is the emergency regulation. The ordinary regulation (variously known also as executive order, *décret*, *Verordnung*) and any action undertaken pursuant to it are characterized by being quite often an execution of a specific statute and, in any case, subject to statutory and constitutional provisions; this, as well as the sanction of judicial control of all regulatory activities, is the principal concomitant of the *rule of law*. However, genuine emergency conditions are apt to arise —mainly in connection with wars, internal disorders, severe economic crises, and major disasters —which make it imperative to allow for measures that would be free from the time-consuming procedures accompanying modern legislation and yet might deviate from statutory and perhaps even from constitutional provisions. The proclamation by the executive of martial law, of a state of emergency, or of a state of siege has variously served in the past to justify such deviation from the normal rule of law pattern and is still occasionally resorted to, but whether or not accompanied by such proclamation, the emergency regulation (or emergency order) has become the main form of such exercise of executive powers in the twentieth century. Where war was concerned, Great Britain (until 1920) and the United States have found it possible to postpone the enactment of a suitable legal framework of emergency powers until the emergency has actually arisen and to do so by means of *ad hoc* legislation. Thus the British Defence of the Realm Act and the American Emergency Powers Act were passed in these countries in connection with the two world wars. In many other countries, however, where there are good grounds to fear a more instantaneous emergency, provision for such powers has been made ahead of time as part of the country's permanent structure, and even Great Britain now has the permanent Emergency Powers Act. The abuse of emergency powers that occurred in central Europe, notably in Germany, in the 1930s has made countries more cautious and has caused them to place emergency powers under increased parliamentary and judicial control. Nevertheless, even regulations passed under this conception of emergency powers approach legislation in the narrow sense of the word: they are not strictly bound by pre-existing statutory law; they enjoy a position of pre-eminence roughly approximating that of statutes; and they are held in check but little by judicial review. It is even more difficult than in the case of ordinary "secondary legislation" to ensure that the essential distinction between emergency regulations and parliamentary legislation be properly observed. [*See also* CRISIS GOVERNMENT.]

The previously noted complications arise even where the individuals and groups in control of the executive are willing to abide by the limitations placed on their powers and do not seek to overthrow the rule of law. Where this condition does not apply, the difficulties noted are aggravated, and the observer encounters a wholesale and deliberate trespassing by those who control the executive on what would be regarded as the normal domain of the legislature. Like those earlier regimes where power was highly concentrated, modern dictatorships, whether ideologically motivated or merely ambition-driven, whether totalitarian in their policies or fairly liberal, tend to obliterate the distinction between legislation and other procedures of law making. Representative legislative institutions are either abolished, or reduced in authority, or transformed into mere instruments whose composition and deliberations are wholly managed by the wielders of executive power. In either case the intrinsic importance of legislation and the distinction between it and other rules of law are diminished. [*See* TOTALITARIANISM.]

Structure of legislatures

The foregoing observations have shown that the body regarded specifically as the legislature bases its claim to higher legitimation on its being more fully representative than other public authorities. The actual mode of determining that body's composition, as well as the relative weight of the circles and interests thought worthy of representation, vary in accordance with the views prevailing at the time in the given society generally and among those who occupy the centers of power especially. A common characteristic of all properly differentiated legislatures is that they are *collective* bodies —an elementary device which makes fuller representativeness more likely and an excessive concentration of power less likely than would be possible in the case of a one-man legislature. *Appointment*, whether for a given period, for life, or even to a hereditary seat, was often practiced as a suitable mode of composing the legislature along with or instead of *election*, and this mode is still found in the mid-twentieth century in a number of "upper chambers," e.g., in Afghanistan, Canada, Ethiopia, Jordan, Luxembourg, the United Kingdom, and the Republic of South Africa.

Historically, the division of legislatures into two houses or chambers is a survival from the strongly estate-conscious medieval society, when deliberative bodies with partly legislative functions were organized by estates or groups of kindred estates. With the weakening of the estate as the prime integrating group and the strengthening of the direct links between the individual and the State, the "lower" chamber, based on some system of fairly wide and, most recently, near-universal adult suffrage, became the principal vehicle of mass representation, while the "upper" chamber was used to add an element of conservatism, moderation, or stability to the legislature. Conditions of eligibility and of voting were formulated more strictly in upper chamber elections, indirect elections were resorted to in the hope that they would screen out radical elements and make for a higher level of expertness, and appointment was often practiced. All these methods could ensure weighted representation to social groups and interests favored by the regime. In federations, the device of the upper house is generally used to secure special representation of the federated entities, sometimes on the basis of equality irrespective of population numbers, thus affording the smaller autonomous units additional protection against encroachment by the larger ones. With the continuous growth of the idea that election by a larger proportion of the population furnishes the elected body a fuller measure of legitimate authority, the political importance and the formal attributes of upper houses gradually declined, except in some federal unions where they are regarded as the guardians of the federal principle. Several countries have dispensed with upper houses altogether, and the tendency seems to be spreading. In 1963, the list of countries with unicameral legislatures embraced a number of Latin American states, all unitary states with communist regimes, most of the new states in Africa and Asia, and Cyprus, Denmark, Finland, Greece, Israel, Lebanon, New Zealand, and Norway.

The shift from legislation

Legislation has constituted the principal business of parliamentary bodies almost from the beginning, a circumstance which so impressed political philosophers of the seventeenth and eighteenth centuries, especially Locke and Montesquieu, that they saw the creation of a specialized representative agency as principal participant in the legislative process to be a prominent characteristic of a well-ordered State. With modifications, this conception, an intrinsic part of the separation-of-powers doctrine, became the predominant practice, and representative parliaments became associated in the popular mind with the legislative power as such. In fact, however, this identity is by no means complete. In this article, some of the reasons have been set out which made parliaments lose much of their decisive role in the legislative process. In addition, parliaments in a number of countries occasionally share the legislative function with binding or advisory plebiscitary procedures (Australia, Austria, Denmark, France, Germany during the Weimar Republic, Italy, New Zealand, Norway, Switzerland, and—quite often—member states in federations) or with heads of State who may grant or withhold consent to a pending bill (United States, most other presidential republics, and constitutional monarchies of the nonparliamentary type). Nor can the representative character of parliaments always stand scrutiny. The not-quite-representative character of many an upper house has already been commented upon. Elections in which only part of the adult population was given the franchise and individual votes were given unequal weight were quite common until 1918. Since then, both practices have become less frequent, except in the form of assigning larger representation to rural than to urban constituencies—a practice still widespread. [*See* APPORTIONMENT.]

A newer problem is posed by parliamentary bodies in countries with communist, "popular-democratic," "guided-democratic," *caudillo*-type, and fascist regimes. There, parliaments are encountered which, though elected on an extremely broad suffrage basis and sometimes with an unusually large participation of voters, have their election process so encumbered with formal and factual restrictions on free discussion of issues and free choice of candidates, in an atmosphere so dominated by governmental and reigning-party pressure, that their representative character is doubtful in the extreme. The weaker a parliament's claim to be widely representative, the less foundation there is for its claim to have a preponderant part in legislation.

But even aside from these particular weaknesses, the significance of parliaments as legislative agencies has generally decreased. The connection between this development, the complexities involved in modern law making, and the greater unity of outlook between modern legislatures and executives, has been set out earlier. Even in the United States, where legislative activity proper is carried out more fully and more jealously by Congress and by the state legislatures than in most other countries, the national or state administrations initiate an ever-increasing portion of the more important bills. The American legislature is still in a position to deny clearance to a legislative measure desired by the administration, but less and less frequent are the cases in which, overriding a president's or a governor's veto, a legislature is able to enact a measure to which the administration objects. [*See* PRESIDENTIAL GOVERNMENT.] In other countries, to the extent to which parliaments are the expression of the voters' choice rather than of the governing group's pressure, legislation conforms to an even greater extent to the executive's desires. The executive's subordination to parliament is expressed mainly in the former's composition, so constituted as to ensure that the latter will confidently accept its guidance. Where parliamentary regimes are concerned, it is also expressed in formal votes denoting continuance or discontinuance of this confidence. But as long as a government enjoys a parliament's confidence, executive guidance of legislative business is accepted as a matter of course. [*See* PARLIAMENTARY GOVERNMENT.]

Nonetheless, parliaments, other than single-party ones, continue to exercise considerable influence on the specific contents of legislation. Bills introduced on the initiative of the government quite often undergo radical change as a result of discussion on the floor and in the committees of the legislature, and of public debate. Furthermore, bills are often introduced by the government or on its behalf as a result of opinions expressed in the legislature and of similar bills proposed by the opposition.

In matters of budgetary and finance legislation, special procedures have grown to hinder parliaments from seeking to please the voters by simultaneously advocating increased expenditures and decreased taxes—a double treatment necessary at times but dangerous when used indiscriminately. In several countries such devices were adopted as limiting parliament's opportunity to propose expenditures over and above those suggested by the government, making such increases conditional upon simultaneous provision for added revenues, or providing for a lengthened legislative procedure (such as an authorization and an appropriation act in the United States; the financial resolution in Great Britain). Long-term financial provisions such as the British Consolidated Fund, multiyear plans involving financing and enacted in advance, and authorization of economic activities controlled by the government and carried on through the intermediary of public corporations have further reduced the significance of the annual budgets handled by parliaments as part of their legislative routine. [*See* BUDGETING.]

Not only has the part of parliaments in the over-all legislative picture become smaller. Legislation has also become a less important, though not necessarily less time-consuming, part of parliamentary business. Its place has been taken largely by two other functions: the day-to-day control of governmental operation and the formalized, highly resonant expression of the grievances and aspirations of groups within the population. Speeches on the floor and in committee, interventions by members with appropriate ministers and their officials, questions or "interpellations," "points of order" and motions of different kinds ascending in intensity to the (British) motion of censure and the (continental European) motion of nonconfidence serve these various purposes. In the United States, some of these forms are not used, but their place is taken no less effectively by the formalized procedure of open hearings in legislative committees and the informal contact which members of the legislatures maintain with the press and other mass media so as to mobilize the latter in the service of causes to be supported or fought. Legislatures and their members thus become highly sensitive parts of the machinery of government, attuned to currents of popular opinion, capable of broadcasting their own moods to the population, and constantly pressing the resulting views on the administration.

If modern parliaments are still regarded largely as the legislative agencies par excellence and legislation is still represented as their principal business, this is, to some extent, an echo from the past, perhaps a reminder of a weapon parliaments hold in reserve to be used against the executive in some future contingency but hardly a fair description of the actual state of affairs. Those "legislatures" which have been deprived of the dynamic role of daily controllers and gadflies of the administration because of the utter subservience of their membership to the executive, and which have been reduced largely to legislative activity—again in an atmosphere of such subservience—lead but a shadowy existence. For obvious reasons, opposition groups and members in parliaments—wherever genuine opposition is allowed—are much freer from executive dominance than are groups and members that support the government of the day, both in their legislative and in their gadfly activities, and they appear by and large as the more dynamic part of the legislature. Only where party discipline is lax do members of the group pledged to support the government make themselves strongly felt in the conduct of parliamentary affairs. This is the case to a very marked extent in the United States and to some extent in Italy; such was the case in France during the Third and Fourth republics, and with respect to a few individualistic members of other parliaments (e.g., in Britain, Winston Churchill and Leopold Amery among the Conservatives; Stafford Cripps and Aneurin Bevan among Labour party members). [*See* Parties, political.]

Legislative techniques

Typical of modern legislation is the elaborate procedure intended to avoid drafting errors and hasty decisions. Both the guiding ideas and the actual text of the original proposal may be suggested by an individual member of the legislature, by a group of members, by a partisan body, by an outside group primarily interested in the issue, by a government agency, or by experts to whom the task has been entrusted by one of the foregoing. Where formal introduction of bills by the government or a government minister is allowed, the role of the individual legislator in initiating legislation has been on the decrease, and so have his chances to have his bills considered on their merits or adopted. Legislative counsel, legislative reference services, and experts attached to specific legislative committees are growing in importance as media for assembling information, drafting documents, or otherwise assisting members and committees of the legislature. With the formal introduction of a text for consideration as a proposed piece of legislation, the text becomes a *bill*. In most legislatures, either members or the government (in the United States only members) are authorized to introduce bills.

Though subject to serious modification in detail, the legislative process commonly involves four stages. Upon formal introduction in parliament, the bill is either automatically turned over for consideration to an appropriate committee or first briefly discussed in plenary session (first reading) with a view to dismissal or to retention for further consideration. In Britain and some countries that closely follow British procedure, the next stage (second reading) takes the form of a debate in plenary session, which, in turn, is followed by consideration in committee (usually a smaller body chosen *ad hoc* or generally entrusted with matters of that kind, but in Britain often the "Committee of the Whole House"—i.e., the entire membership of the chamber proceeding in a less formal manner). In most other countries, consideration in a smaller committee comes first; and the second reading in the plenary session, with opportunity for detailed discussion and vote on individual sections of the bill, takes place only after it has been "reported out" by the committee or (in the United States) after the committee has been "discharged" from further consideration of it. (The discharge procedure is a remedy against undue dilatoriness on the part of the committee or the committee chairman.) Representatives of the government are usually heard by the committee, and in most countries other interested parties may also be heard (in the United States predominantly in open hearings, in other countries mainly behind closed doors). During the committee stage, especially when proceedings are held behind closed doors and do not involve the prestige of individual members, of parties, and of the government in the same measure as in public session, considerable changes are often introduced into the original text in response both to argument and to pressure. The last stage (third reading) usually involves a brief debate and, in most countries, concludes with a vote on the bill as a whole, although under British procedure the debate is more extensive and opportunity is given to decide on various amendments that have arisen out of committee proceedings.

Ordinarily, intervals of several days, weeks, or months separate these stages. Indeed, such intervals are regarded as desirable in order to permit thorough deliberation and to enable public reaction to make itself felt. But in emergencies legislatures resort to a "suspension of the rules," limiting debate, shortening the accepted intervals between stages, dispensing with committee consideration, and even passing the entire measure in the course of a single day.

Other decisions taken by legislatures are not to be confused with legislation proper. These include elections; votes of confidence, nonconfidence, and censure; votes of impeachment; expressions of approval or disapproval of administrative measures that require such action; procedural decisions of various kinds (including the determination of rules of procedure, or standing orders, under which the legislature operates); and especially declaratory resolutions of different kinds which may be morally and politically significant but have no binding force in strict law. In the United States Congress, it is important to distinguish between "joint resolutions," which are tantamount in their effect to statutes, and "concurrent resolutions," which in themselves have no legal effects. Where legislative agencies also have constitution-making and constitution-amending functions, procedures governing them should be distinguished from those involved in "ordinary" legislation.

Voting procedures differ greatly among the legislatures of the world and, depending upon circumstances, even in the same legislature. The vote may be taken by an informal estimate of the strength of the voiced (*viva voce*) approval and disapproval, by a "show of hands" or a "rising vote" estimated or actually counted, or by more formal counting ("division" in the British Parliament), by roll-call votes registered by name, or even by secret ballot. A simple majority of those voting, with abstentions not taken into account, is usually decisive, and most legislatures require either a low proportion of members to be present at deliberations or votes (quorum) or no quorum at all. The British House of Commons requires a quorum of only 40 members (out of 630 in 1963); the quorum requirements of both houses of the United States Congress of a majority of all members are among the strictest. There are, however, legislative and other decisions which require, to become effective, an absolute or an even higher majority of all members voting, of members present, or of the total membership.

Participation of other bodies in the formal legislative process is secondary in the modern State. Formal consultation of economic councils of various kinds takes place in some countries. Under some newer constitutions, an appropriate judicial or semijudicial body may be requested for its opinion if the constitutionality of the measure is doubtful (in Iran the Council of Ulemas, i.e., religious dignitaries, passes on the religious orthodoxy of the measure), and, if necessary, the bill is returned to the legislature. More widespread is the opportunity given to the head of state to withhold his consent to the bill, thereby either preventing its passage into law (absolute veto) or requiring its consideration anew by the legislature (suspensive veto).

Except in very special circumstances, publicity is a mark of modern legislative procedure. This publicity serves to enable public opinion and that of interested groups to make their weight felt before the final decision is taken, as well as to rally the public around the decision's results. The bill, after having been given the assent of all those whose participation is required, is certified, proclaimed (promulgated), and published, thus becoming *a law*, a statute.

Interpretation and codification of statutes

In most cases, a statute is restricted to a single subject matter, though this may be quite involved, present many aspects, and require subdivision into several sections or articles. As a rule, the adoption of a statute does not invalidate previous statutes, save insofar as they are expressly invalidated. But where a provision of an earlier statute is inconsistent with the provision of a later statute, the *later* rule should be applied (*lex posterior derogat priori*), unless the earlier rule is a special and the later a general one, in which case the special rule will prevail (*lex specialis derogat generali*). These and other principles of statutory interpretation are generally left to the courts, which follow certain traditional criteria and their own precedents; where statutes themselves contain rules of interpretation, these are to be followed, of course, but in no case are executive agencies to prescribe rules for the interpretation of statutes in states where the rule of law or the *principe de la légalité* prevails. [*See* JUDICIAL PROCESS.]

Where partial modification of an existing statute is desired, this is done mainly by an *amending* statute. When this has been done a number of times, or when provisions relating to a given subject matter are dispersed over several statutes (and perhaps over statutes, secondary legislation, and various forms of customary law), a patchwork pattern ensues which makes it difficult to grasp the exact requirements of the law. In the interest of clarification, *consolidated* statutes may then be adopted by the legislature or an up-to-date revision of the statutory material, to be done by experts, authorized by it. When the consolidation of the legal material is done in a particularly systematic and comprehensive manner and purports to regulate fully a very broad sector of social relations, the process is known as *codification* and the resulting product as a *code*. Codification may contain restatement of pre-existing statutory, customary, and judge-made law in diverse proportions, but also newly formulated rules that differ materially from the law previously in force. Several Oriental, Latin American, and European countries have adopted, virtually unchanged, codes that were previously enacted elsewhere, the most frequent models being the French, German, Italian, and Swiss codes. Such wholesale reception of foreign codes represents a variant of the well-known phenomenon of the reception of foreign law in general.

In its continental European meaning, a code, upon coming into force, is meant to displace all pre-existing law relating to the subject, thus rendering unnecessary inquiry into older sources and precedents, and simplifying access to the law. But in the United States pre-existing law, especially rules derived from the common law and from equity, continue to be regarded as in force, unless specifically conflicting with or expressly repealed by the code. In time, even consolidated and revised statutes as well as codes cease to be up to date: social changes and political aspirations result in partial amendments of the enacted material, and so do technical deficiencies in the original text as revealed in the course of its application. Furthermore, the best-planned and most detailed code or comprehensive statute is overgrown in time by judicial interpretation, even if—as in the case of countries outside of the common law sphere—its interpretation in the light of precode material is discouraged.

The above difference between English-speaking countries and others in regard to codification is related to the different attitudes which legal practitioners and scholars traditionally assume toward the relative places of enacted law and of customary law authoritatively formulated by a succession of judicial decisions. In civil law countries, legal thought considers law primarily the product of general enactments made by the legislators; custom is but one of the factors which the legislators may take into account; judicial decisions, however important in applying the law to concrete situations, are of merely interstitial significance in classifying, specifying, and sometimes stretching (by analogy, for instance) the general principles of the enactment to cover unforeseen combinations of circumstances—all of this under the guise of interpretation. In common law countries, law is primarily thought of as the body of rules evolved from a succession of judicial decisions on the basis of real or alleged custom, whereas legislation comes in interstitially, to fill the lacunae of the judge-made law or to adjust it to changing demands of society. The formal supremacy of the legislative rule is but reluctantly recognized in the English-speaking world, and wherever possible its significance is reduced by the tendency to interpret the enacted rule in the light of the common law. The difference is further accentuated by the tendency in civil law countries to interpret the enacted rule broadly, so as to bring under its sway as many concrete situations as possible, whereas common law countries tend to interpret the enacted rule narrowly and to continue applying judge-made law outside that narrow area. Basically, the common law attitude reflects the belief that the legislator is inherently a political agent interested in furthering his interests at the expense of true law, somehow related to "natural" law, of which the judge is the guardian, whereas civil law thinking has resigned itself to the acceptance of the legislator as the foremost exponent of the law. [*See* LEGAL SYSTEMS.]

Legislation and natural law

The foregoing section brings us back to the question of the relation of legislation, as the outstanding instance of a positive, i.e., State-imposed, law, to norms of human conduct which claim validity independently of State action. Where the role of legislator is entrusted to an elected assembly on a broad basis or to direct popular vote, the element of consensus enters the picture, and it is society as a whole that is assumed to impose the law on individual members and groups; still, there is a deliberate act of imposing a rule of conduct which previously could claim no validity. The question arises, in what relation the legislated rule, and positive law generally, stands to *natural law* or morality, that vague but intensely felt body of principles which in human consciousness divides the *just* from the *unjust*. In this confrontation, positive law enjoys great advantages: its contents are far more ascertainable, its formulators are tangible and certain, its sanction is secured by an organized and generally efficient machinery—all unlike the rules of natural law, the precise contents of which are doubtful, the originators and formulators of which are diffuse in the extreme, the sanctions of which are indefinite and uncertain. [*See* JUSTICE; NATURAL LAW.]

And yet, for all their weaknesses, natural law concepts—closely intertwined as they are with social *mores*, with rationalized interests and desires, with theological postulates, with individual conscience, and with the ensuing pattern of ethics accepted in society—exercise a permanent influence on positive law in general and on legislation in particular. Enacted rules of law are quite often a reflection of those natural law concepts which prevail at the time. And when positive law appears to one group or another to deviate from natural law, to be *unjust*, it is in the name of natural law, of justice, that changes in positive law are advocated and brought about more often than in the name of any other principle. This applies to partial changes in positive law, which can be accomplished in the forms provided for by the positive law itself, i.e., through the ordinary channels of new or amending legislation, of reglementation, of judicial interpretation, and of constitutional amendments. But it applies no less to such wholesale changes of the existing positive legal structure as are accomplished in disregard, even in violation, of these channels, i.e., to *revolutions*. Most revolutions which have a widely acknowledged ideological basis claim to be methods of adjusting the positive law to the true natural law as seen by the revolutionaries.

BENJAMIN AKZIN

[*See also* ADMINISTRATION; GOVERNMENT; INTEREST GROUPS; PARTIES, POLITICAL; POLITICAL EXECUTIVE; POLITICAL PROCESS; REPRESENTATION. *A guide to other relevant material may be found under* LAW.]

BIBLIOGRAPHY

AHMAD, MUSHTAQ 1959 *Legislatures in Pakistan.* Lahore: Univ. of the Panjab Press.

ALLEN, CARLETON K. (1927) 1964 *Law in the Making.* 7th ed. Oxford: Clarendon.

ALLEN, CARLETON K. (1945) 1956 *Law and Orders: An Inquiry Into the Nature and Scope of Delegated Legislation and Executive Powers in English Law.* 2d ed. London: Stevens.

AMELLER, MICHEL (editor) (1961) 1966 *Parlements: Une étude comparative sur la structure et le fonctionnement des institutions.* 2d ed., enl. Paris: Presses Universitaires de France.

ANDRADA, B. 1962 *Parlamentarismo e a evolução brasileira.* Belo Horizonte (Brazil): Alvarez.

BERMAN, DANIEL M. (1964) 1966 *In Congress Assembled: The Legislative Process in the National Government.* New York: Macmillan.

CAMPION, GILBERT F. (1929) 1958 *An Introduction to the Procedure of the House of Commons.* London: Macmillan.

CAMPION, GILBERT F.; and LIDDERDALE, D. W. S. 1953 *European Parliamentary Procedure: A Comparative Handbook.* London: Allen & Unwin.

CLAPP, CHARLES L. (1963) 1964 *The Congressman: His Work as He Sees It.* Garden City, N.Y.: Doubleday.

CRAIES, WILLIAM F. (1906) 1963 *Statute Law.* 6th ed. London: Sweet.

DAHL, ROBERT A. 1950 *Congress and Foreign Policy.* New York: Harcourt.

FINER, HERMAN (1932) 1961 *The Theory and Practice of Modern Government.* 4th ed. London: Methuen.

FRIEDMANN, WOLFGANG G. (1944) 1960 *Legal Theory.* 4th ed. London: Stevens.

FRIEDRICH, CARL J. (1937) 1950 *Constitutional Government and Democracy: Theory and Practice in Europe and America.* Rev. ed. Boston: Ginn. → First published as *Constitutional Government and Politics: Nature and Development.*

GALLOWAY, GEORGE B. 1953 *The Legislative Process in Congress.* New York: Crowell.

GRIFFITH, ERNEST S. (1951) 1961 *Congress: Its Contemporary Role.* 3d ed. New York Univ. Press.

GROSS, BERTRAM M. 1953 *The Legislative Struggle: A Study in Social Combat.* New York: McGraw-Hill.

HANSON, ALBERT H.; and WISEMAN, H. V. 1962 *Parliament at Work: A Case-book of Parliamentary Procedure.* London: Stevens.

HARRIS, JOSEPH (1964) 1965 *Congressional Control of Administration.* Garden City, N.Y.: Doubleday.

HART, H. L. A. 1961 *The Concept of Law.* Oxford: Clarendon.

HÅSTAD, ELIS 1957 *The Parliament of Sweden.* London: Hansard Society for Parliamentary Government.

HÖJER, CARL H. 1946 *Le régime parlementaire Belge de 1918 à 1940.* Stockholm: Almqvist & Wicksell.

ITALY, PARLAMENTO 1964 *Il parlamento nella storia d'Italia: Antologia storica della classe politica.* Edited by Giampiero Carocci. Bari (Italy): Laterza.

JENNINGS, W. IVOR (1939) 1960 *Parliament.* 3d ed. Cambridge Univ. Press.

KELSEN, HANS (1934) 1960 *Reine Rechtslehre.* With Supplement: Das Problem der Gerechtigkeit. 2d ed., rev. & enl. Vienna: Deuticke.

KING-HALL, STEPHEN; and ULLMANN, RICHARD K. 1954 *German Parliaments.* London: Hansard Society for Parliamentary Government.

LAPONCE, J. A. 1961 *The Government of the Fifth Republic: French Political Parties and the Constitution.* Berkeley: Univ. of California Press.

LEIBHOLZ, GERHARD (1929) 1960 *Das Wesen der Repräsentation und der Gestaltswandel der Demokratie im 20. Jahrhundert.* 2d ed. Berlin: Gruyter.

LIDDERDALE, D. W. S. 1951 *The Parliament of France.* London: Hansard Society for Parliamentary Government.

LOEWENSTEIN, KARL (1957) 1962 *Political Power and the Governmental Process.* Univ. of Chicago Press.

MCCRACKEN, J. L. 1958 *Representative Government in Ireland: A Study of Dáil Éireann 1919–48.* Oxford Univ. Press.

MAXWELL, PETER B. (1875) 1962 *The Interpretation of Statutes.* 11th ed. London: Sweet.

MORE, S. S. 1960 *Practice and Procedure of Indian Parliament.* Bombay: Thacker.

MORRIS-JONES, WYNDRAETH H. 1957 *Parliament in India.* Philadelphia: Univ. of Pennsylvania Press.

Parliamentary Affairs. → Published since 1947 by the Hansard Society for Parliamentary Government, London.

POLLARD, ALBERT F. (1920) 1964 *The Evolution of Parliament.* 2d ed. London: Longmans; New York: Russell.

POUND, ROSCOE 1959 *Jurisprudence.* 5 vols. St. Paul, Minn.: West. → Volume 1: *Jurisprudence: The End of Law.* Volume 2: *The Nature of Law.* Volume 3: *The Scope and Subject Matter of Law.* Volume 4: *Application and Enforcement of Law.* Volume 5: *The System of Law.*

RAALTE, E. VAN 1959 *The Parliament of the Kingdom of the Netherlands.* London: Hansard Society for Parliamentary Government.

ROSS, ALF (1953) 1959 *On Law and Justice.* Berkeley: Univ. of California Press. → First published in Danish.

STONE, JULIUS (1946) 1950 *The Province and Function of Law: Law as Logic, Justice, and Social Control; a Study in Jurisprudence.* Cambridge, Mass.: Harvard Univ. Press.

SUTHERLAND, JABEZ G. (1891) 1943 *Statutes and Statutory Construction.* 3d ed. 3 vols. Chicago: Callaghan.

WAHLKE, JOHN C.; and EULAU, HEINZ (editors) 1959 *Legislative Behavior: A Reader in Theory and Research.* Glencoe, Ill.: Free Press.

WHEARE, KENNETH C. 1963 *Legislatures.* New York: Oxford Univ. Press.

II
LEGISLATURES

If legislation may be defined as making new rules of general applicability for the future, it should be evident that most, if not all, agencies of government legislate. The judge was probably the first public official to "discover" law, while the legislature, as a self-conscious lawmaking body, is a relatively late creation. The pressures of change induced by the industrial, technological, and scientific revolutions have made even the legislature inadequate, requiring it to lay down broad policy directives and delegate to administrative agencies the power to make actual rules.

If the legislature has no monopoly on legislation, it does at least have a distinct character of its own. Generally it is composed of one or two relatively large bodies of people who, technically at least, are peers. Their authority customarily is derived from some scheme of representation, most often the population living in a delimited geographical area, although there may be some other basis, such as class, or function performed in the system. Because all members are on the same footing and issues are decided by a majority vote, members tend to be or to become generalists, whatever their previous vocation. Except in some upper houses based on class, members are politicians forced to face the recurrent hazards of the ballot box. These facts are important: they shape the institutional life of the legislature and the attitudes of its members, just as the bureaucracy and the judiciary are shaped institutionally by their own methods of recruitment and advancement and by the materials and methods of decision making on which they must rely.

Legislative structure

The structure of a legislature obviously affects its decision making, although structure is not necessarily the most important influence. There are essentially two models of legislative structure, the parliamentary and the congressional–presidential (referred to hereafter as the "congressional").

The parliamentary model. The crucial element in the parliamentary model is that the executive is selected by the legislature from among its own members. Presumably, then, the executive is responsible to the legislature. This responsibility may be enforced if the executive is allowed to stand only so long as it has the support of the legislature. The executive may in turn have the power to force the dissolution of the house to which it is responsible, thus requiring a new election. It should be obvious that this kind of responsibility is difficult to maintain toward more than one house. In England, where cabinet government emerged, the powers of the House of Lords withered away or were taken away by the House of Commons, as logically they should have been, until convention would not allow a lord to be prime minister (though he might still sit in the cabinet). There are systems, nevertheless, in which some responsibility falls to a second house, as it did in the French Third Republic and still does in some other systems, with predictable difficulties.

Most national legislatures in continental Europe are relatively recent creations or fairly complete overhauls of feudal institutions. In France, for instance, the States-General lay dormant for two centuries during the reigns of divine right monarchs; the National Assembly was a creature of revolution. The only legislature to survive to the present, adapting its procedures and distribution of powers without changing ancient forms, is the English Parliament. When William of Normandy conquered England in 1066, he imposed Norman feudal institutions, including the Curia Regis, a court of nobles who attended and advised him, and the Curia Regis Magnae, a great council that met usually three times a year to give counsel and present petitions. The permanent bureaucracy emerged from the former, while the seeds of Parliament took root in the latter. Knights first came to the Great Council in 1213, and virtually all elements were represented, after a fashion, in the Model Parliament of Edward I in 1295. The knights, burgesses, and lesser clergy, who represented the communities, met separately from the barons—who were summoned by name—and came in time to be the House of Commons.

It would be pleasant to relate that the members of Commons set about asserting themselves and followed a rational sequence of development to a system of responsible cabinet government—pleasant but not true. Actually, Commons frequently gave away its own tools, and the cabinet developed as a leadership group through necessity, because George I neglected his job. What has emerged nevertheless is a prototype of parliamentary government. The crown reigns but does not rule. The House of Lords sits and talks without power to bother anybody very much. In Commons the government is supreme, initiating legislation, controlling debate, and determining outcomes with the support of its disciplined majority, even when its margin of numerical superiority is quite thin. The notion that the House of Commons will overthrow a government that has lost its confidence is now a fiction. So, apparently, is the description of the prime minister as "first among equals"; a rather weak prime minister, Harold Macmillan, demonstrated that he could shuffle the membership of his cabinet without interference. It is also true, of course, that party leadership in England must consider the sentiments of its parliamentary members and of the country at large, as it probably must in any system and certainly must in a democratic one.

The government nevertheless can be responsible to the electorate because it is in fact in power: controlling the majority party. Its dominance is safeguarded by procedures that deny to the individual member an opportunity to build a personal following that might support him against his party's leadership, and the electorate demonstrates its understanding of the system by retiring the occasional rebel who tries. [*See* PARLIAMENTARY GOVERNMENT.]

Needless to say, there may be no end of variations on the parliamentary model. In Norway and the Netherlands and in the French Fifth Republic, ministers are prohibited from being members of parliament. They may have been members, they may run again when they are not ministers, but so long as they are in the government, they may be physically in the chamber but may not vote.

Structural differences may have less profound impact, however, than those induced by other variables in the system. Among the most important of these is the character of the party system. When more than two or three parties elect members to parliament and none has a majority, the coalition cabinet that, perforce, must be formed is likely to lack the stability and poise of a leadership confident of support. In the French Third Republic, where multiple parties could play musical chairs with cabinet seats without having to face a general election, governments fell with boring regularity. The fact that successive cabinets had little actual change of personnel was a consolation to the politicians but did little to increase the prestige of the system. In Germany under the Weimar Republic more than thirty parties reduced the regime to such impotence that the minority National Socialist party easily took power.

The problems faced by a multiparty parliament are enormously enlarged when one or more parties are antidemocratic in ideology and, thus, are determined to bring an end to the democratic game. Hemmed in at both ends of the political spectrum, the democratic parties are forced to mute legitimate differences if the system itself is to stand. Parliamentary government faced this problem in the French Third Republic, as it has in Italy since WORLD WAR II [*see* PARTIES, POLITICAL, *article on* PARTY SYSTEMS].

The congressional model. The daily operations of the U.S. Congress show a strong influence of British forms and procedure. For example, a speaker presides over the House of Representatives. The constitutional stipulation that revenue bills must originate in the lower house reflects hard British experience, as do the privileges and immunities which members take for granted. But such resemblances are superficial; the constitution fashioned a structure of power unlike the British one, and the forces of American life have strengthened and extended the differences. For example, the American speaker is as partisan as the British speaker is neutral.

The makers of the American constitution followed Locke and Montesquieu in attributing a separation of powers to the British system. More important, their colonial experience encompassed a more or less representative lower house pitted against the executive—the king's representative. Thus, they wrote into the constitution a prohibition against any person's serving simultaneously in both executive and legislative branches. This did not quite accomplish a separation of powers—the constitution provided for a certain commingling of powers, and in practice there has been even more.

Institutions, however, were separated with clean finality. When the Founding Fathers then gave the president and members of both houses fixed but different terms of office, they established conditions making continuous bargaining and compromise an imperative of the system.

British members of Parliament look to the bureaucracy for information, because its ministers are their own men; the same is not true for members of Congress. Congress recognized early that if it were to maintain its independence of, and a semblance of equality with, the executive, it must develop its own research tools. The answer was a system of standing committees, each, in time, coming to have a fairly clear subject-matter jurisdiction, which made it a little legislature within its own sphere of competence. Woodrow Wilson's observation at the end of the nineteenth century that "congressional government is committee government" is still true and seems likely to remain so, barring really fundamental changes in Congressional procedures. Each bill that becomes law must pass the committee test in each house; it may be the subject of hearings, debate, and amendment, or it may die without consideration. If it goes to the floor of either house, it will be promoted there by committee leaders, who also sit in conference with their counterparts of the other body of Congress, to compromise differences written into the bill by the respective houses. Committee chairmen, who gain their eminence through seniority on their committees and retain it so long as they are members, are thus powerful men indeed. Party leaders negotiate with them in a relationship that has more than a superficial resemblance to that of a medieval king and his feudal barons.

Power is further fragmented in Congress by the separation of the legislative and appropriations processes. The expenditure of public funds must first be authorized by legislation considered by the appropriate subject-matter committee in each house. No money can be spent, however, until there has been an appropriation, which is considered not by the legislative committees but by the two appropriations committees. Inasmuch as they may reduce the amount requested or deny funds altogether, they (and their subcommittees) exercise power and enjoy prestige not rivaled by many of the legislative committees.

Power vested in committee chairmen might still be harnessed to party purposes (the chairmen might sit on a party policy committee, for instance, and advance its program in their respective committees) if it were not for the localism of American politics. The constitution requires members of Congress to be residents of the states they represent, and in nearly all cases representatives reside in their districts. The major parties are not truly national; they are federations of state and local parties, held together by the exigencies of presidential politics, unable to help or hurt members of Congress very much. The individual member's constituency therefore is usually paramount; it can end his political life or furnish him a secure base independent of national party leadership. His policy preferences therefore tend to be an amalgam of interests; he may vote with a majority of his party on most issues because there is no conflict but reserve the right to proceed independently when he chooses. Thus, there are very few straight party-line votes in either house, and the president's floor leaders must learn to put together majorities however they can. Interest groups are in the thick of every fight, knowing full well that each contest is in a sense a new one [*see* PRESIDENTIAL GOVERNMENT].

Problems for research

Legislative–executive relations. The relationship of the legislature and the executive is crucial in any political system; yet analysis of it has not gone very deep. In England the House of Commons may harass its own minister through the question hour, but how much control can a minister who spends so much time on the floor exercise over his department? Indeed, how much does the legislature affect the performance of the bureaucracy in any country? In the republics of France the bureaucrats paid little heed to parliamentary charades. In the United States the oversight of administration is supposed to be a primary function of committees, but not much is known about the complex patterns of relationships that actually exist. Some committees apparently exercise no supervision; others participate as virtual partners in the most important decisions. Indeed, there probably is no more richly varied or complicated political relationship anywhere than that between the president and his establishment, on the one hand, and Congress, on the other. The initiative in legislation has passed over to the executive, but members of Congress share in it. Administration, the responsibility of the executive, is subjected to a variety of Congressional pressures, with results that defy measurement.

Answers to questions concerning legislative–executive relations had to wait for research interest to turn in that direction. In the early twentieth century students of the legislature were likely to devote themselves to formal descriptions of the institution and its procedures or to legal analyses of its powers and its relations with other organs of government. In the United States such writing was often value-laden; scholars could draw up "model" legislatures because they knew what a good legislature was like and what it should do. This willingness to prescribe, which extended to other public institutions as well, was a product of an earlier generation more confident of the efficacy of reform through structural change. And this trend has not by any means disappeared from American academic scholarship.

Legislative decision making. Beginning roughly with the 1930s, however, attention turned more and more to the political forces that shape legislative decisions—pressure groups, parties, constituencies; this research trend was to manifest itself somewhat later in other countries, particularly England. More recently, legislative research has begun to pry into the internal structure and group life of the legislative body and its subsystems.

A popular tool for this more behavioralistic approach was the case study of some slice of legislative life—the passage of a bill, say, or the activity of an interest group. The case study often gave fresh insights and, at its best, hypotheses worth more rigorous investigation. At its worst, it served as a substitute for analysis, piling up sterile recitals of what happened, which had no cumulative value. Other scholars turned to the public act of decision, the recorded vote, which had the virtue of being a quantifiable unit. With various indices (e.g., liberalism–conservatism, party cohesion, party loyalty) attempts were made to measure the relative weight of contending influences on Congressional decisions. These efforts increased in sophistication with the use of scaling, which tested whether a single attitudinal dimension (e.g., liberalism–conservatism) was in fact being tested, and cluster-bloc analysis, which made possible comparison of the votes of every member of the body on a set of issues with those of every other member.

Needless to say, a fatal flaw of the roll call vote is that it does not reveal vast portions of the legislative process. What finally happens on the floor may be simply the ratification of treaties negotiated elsewhere through bitter disputes. Students of this process face an array of fascinating problems—the relations of the leadership with the rank and file; the internal life of subsystems, such as committees, state delegations, friendship groups, and "classes" of legislators who enter the legislature at the same time; the influence of rules and procedures on legislative outcomes; the legislator's perceptions of himself, other political actors, and the process; the relations of legislators with outsiders in the bureaucracy, press, interest groups, constituency; and many others. A host of impressions are easy to come by; what is necessary is that some patterns of behavior, individual and group, be identified and some hypotheses as to their relationships be formulated.

Whether they tried to answer such questions or merely sought to get the "feel" of the legislature, political scientists by the mid-1950s were going in person to the legislative chambers and offices. The days were past when a gifted scholar like Woodrow Wilson could write a classic on the American Congress from nearby Baltimore without ever having laid eyes on either house in session. In the United States especially, internships liberally financed by foundations provided for participant observation of national and state legislatures. They led in turn to the actual employment of academic scholars in legislative staff jobs. Interviewing became a popular technique. Usually this was unstructured and relatively informal, but, increasingly, highly structured schedules of questions yielding quantifiable results were used with success.

Questions on process shifted their focus to include analysis of the legislative product as well. Were legislative outcomes actually affected differentially by changes in rules and procedures? Relating process to product suggested a different question: Does the legislature go about settling different categories of policy problems in systematically different ways?

Theory construction. As legislative research increased in systematic rigor and sophistication, the troubling question remained: Does it add up to anything? The testing of isolated hypotheses and the posing of problems for further research lead nowhere unless findings can be related to some tenable theory, even one of the "middle range" (to use Robert K. Merton's term). Theoretical endeavors were obstructed, however, by the difficulties posed by the data. On the one hand, roll call votes were so numerous that even a modest study of one Congress could be costly in time and money. To go back even a few congresses, sort out the votes by parties and other significant categories, and relate them to an evaluation of the significance of the votes was quite beyond the resources of research largely performed by individuals. Moreover, except for recorded votes there were few reliable records. Basic information, such as biographical and political data about members and analyses of the meaning of issues, was lacking altogether or hard to uncover. Tentative generalizations therefore lacked the crucial historical dimension, which could be supplied only by costly cooperative efforts to discover and store essential data and provide for easy retrieval.

Even if those tasks were accomplished and a reasonably useful theoretical model of a legislature constructed, there would still be no certainty that it had analytical value beyond the legislatures in a single system. A legislature is a part of a political system that in turn is a component of a larger social system. No model that ignored these relationships would make much sense. Obviously it matters what tasks the system assigns to the legislature. Again, the history of a people is important; it determines the level of their political sophistication and the kinds of divisions among the people the political process must bridge. Revolutions, civil wars, military defeats, are hard to assimilate. If the United States can see no end, a century later, to the passions stirred by its one civil war, how much of the difficulties of France should be attributed not to its governmental structure but to its tortured past?

Comparative analysis. If it should prove feasible and profitable to study political systems comparatively, can the same be said for political institutions like legislatures? Have developments in different countries been similar enough to suggest that there is an endemic need in a modern political system for such institutions? Do they perform similar enough functions for the system, do they affect the behavior of their members in ways enough alike, to make a comparative study of legislatures worthwhile? The same questions might be asked about parties, interest groups, bureaucracies, and so on; the issue is fundamental. Whatever the answer, research on legislatures has been almost wholly confined to single systems, with only some tentative comparisons of local legislatures within a system.

The role of modern legislatures

How effective is the modern legislature? This question has been asked earnestly and repeatedly in the twentieth century. The answer usually is that it is not very effective, that it has lost much ground to the executive. In the United States the criticism has been continuous and bitter. Ironically, the British Parliament, which is dominated by the executive and exercises little independent judgment compared to Congress, usually is discussed in deferential terms even by its critics. In any case, the common judgment is that the legislature was better suited to an earlier, more leisurely day and that its appropriate task now is to react to executive initiative.

The question can be answered analytically only by relating the legislature to the political system of which it is a part. What functions does the legislature perform for the system—that is, what does it do that contributes to the adjustment or adaptation of the system, that is necessary to the maintenance of the system? It is self-evident that a legislature passes laws, but what is there about the enactment of legislation that is functional to the system? When the question of function is raised, it becomes apparent that to be a mere debating society is not contemptible if the debate is necessary to political education or stability. Performing routine chores for constituents is not degrading if the chores serve as a vital link between citizens and government. Legislation that does not accomplish its avowed purpose is not necessarily a sign of impotence; it may provide a symbolic victory for interests not strong enough to prevail. The lonely champion of a hopeless cause has not cried out in vain if he is the champion of the hopeless. Some of the legislative functions may be manifest, in the sense that their objective consequences for the system are intended and identified; some are latent, having unintended and unrecognized consequences. Whether manifest or latent, these functions contribute to the stability and maintenance of the system. It may be that there are common functions that all legislatures perform for their respective systems. If so, it seems likely also that there are functions performed by each legislature that are the products of the unique relationship between the particular institution and the system it serves.

RALPH K. HUITT

[*See also* ADMINISTRATION, *article on* THE ADMINISTRATIVE PROCESS; ELECTIONS, *article on* ELECTORAL SYSTEMS; JUDICIAL PROCESS; PARLIAMENTARY GOVERNMENT; PRESIDENTIAL GOVERNMENT; REPRESENTATION, *article on* REPRESENTATIONAL SYSTEMS.]

BIBLIOGRAPHY

BEER, SAMUEL H.; and ULAM, ADAM B. (editors) (1958) 1962 *Patterns of Government: The Major Political Systems of Europe.* 2d ed. New York: Random House.

FINER, HERMAN (1932) 1961 *The Theory and Practice of Modern Government.* 4th ed. London: Methuen. → See especially Part 4, "Legislatures," pages 367–572.

JENNINGS, W. IVOR (1939) 1960 *Parliament.* 3d ed. Cambridge Univ. Press.

KEEFE, WILLIAM J.; and OGUL, MORRIS L. 1964 *The American Legislative Process: Congress and the States.* Englewood Cliffs, N.J.: Prentice-Hall.

LIDDERDALE, D. W. S. 1951 *The Parliament of France.* London: Hansard Society.

TAYLOR, ERIC (1951) 1958 *The House of Commons at Work.* 3d ed. Harmondsworth, Middlesex (England): Penguin.

WHEARE, KENNETH C. 1963 *Legislatures.* New York: Oxford Univ. Press.

WILLIAMS, PHILIP 1954 *Politics in Post-war France: Politics and the Constitution in the Fourth Republic.* London: Longmans.

YOUNG, ROLAND A. 1958 *The American Congress.* New York: Harper.

III
LEGISLATIVE BEHAVIOR

In its most general connotation, "legislative behavior" refers to the activities of members of any representative body; in its commonest usage, however, it refers to activities of members of public representative bodies constituted by popular election.

Objectives and methods of study

The earliest relevant literature is the work of certain political philosophers prescribing various rules which they thought proper to guide legislators' actions, generally deduced from their conceptions of the proper functions of legislative institutions. Such literature includes Edmund Burke's familiar strictures concerning the desirability of representatives' being "free agents" instead of ambassadors from local interests (1774), numerous principles of behavior deduced by Jeremy Bentham from his conception of political and legislative functions (1817; 1843), and John Stuart Mill's arguments concerning the desirability of having representatives merely accept or reject proposals formulated by other agencies, or of responding to "free-forming" constituencies created by proportional-representation elections (1861).

Much current legislative behavior study is still concerned primarily with the functioning of legislative institutions, but in quite a different way. Instead of deducing norms of behavior from normative assumptions about legislatures' functions, it tends to discover, describe, and explain actually observable patterns of behavior which presumably are relevant to those functions. A. Lawrence Lowell, in the first modern empirical study of legislative behavior (1902), examined party-line voting in the British Parliament, the U.S. Congress, and several American state legislatures and based his work on implicit assumptions about the relationship between party voting and responsible legislative functioning. Julius Turner (1952), in comparing party with constituency factors in congressional voting, was more explicit about this functional relationship, and David B. Truman (1959) not only explored the patterns of such influences in the U.S. Congress in still greater depth and precision but also sought more explicitly than previous investigators to identify and secure data concerning the legislative functions in question. A number of contemporary investigators, particularly Duncan MacRae, Jr. (1958), have explored overt and latent bases of cleavage and consensus underlying legislative voting, relating these either explicitly or implicitly to decision-making and value-allocating patterns characterizing the over-all legislative process.

The development of the "political behavior approach" influenced legislative behavior study as early and as much as it influenced any branch of political science. In the 1920s Stuart A. Rice (1928) and Herman C. Beyle (1931) had already suggested legislative roll calls as a fertile field of data to be explored by new, quantitative methods of analysis devised by them. The previously mentioned works of Turner and Truman, in fact, relied heavily on the methods of Rice and Beyle, respectively. E. Pendleton Herring's pioneering study of group representation in Congress (1929) and the "noninstitutional," "realistic" process studies stimulated in part by it (e.g., McKean 1938; Schattschneider 1935; Zeller 1937), while not precisely focused on legislators' behavior as such, nevertheless impelled attention to it by questioning the adequacy of purely formal and legal descriptions. The principal concern of these and many later writers, however, is still essentially "institutional," that is to say, related to questions about the structure and functions of the legislature or of the wider set of political institutions. They deal not so much with legisla*tors*' behavior as with legisla*tures*' activities, with legislative decisions rather than with legislators' choices. Their dependent variables tend to be process variables (e.g., characteristic ways of handling issues in different legislatures) or "output" variables (e.g., characteristic types of legislation produced under different circumstances). The behavioral indexes of such variables may be the aggregate voting of legislators on relevant roll calls, but the problem treated is that of relating the aggregate behavioral variable to some ecological, demographic, political, or other characteristic of the political or social system rather than explaining variations in behavior among individual legislators.

Of course, legislative decisions are definable only in terms of their component individual actions, so the behavior of individual legislators has in a sense had the theoretical status of 'intervening variable" between social, political, and other determinants of individual behavior (as independent variables) and legislative output and functioning (as dependent variables). But preoccupation with the aggregate of individual actions, the legislative decision, long inhibited scholars even from classifying legislators' behavior in terms of analytic concepts relevant to the explanation of individual behavior. The common practice was to make descriptive classifications in terms of those overt actions—above all the roll call vote—most directly and obviously related to the aggregate legislative decision. Even other categories of behavior which relate almost as clearly and directly to this function as do roll call votes (e.g., initiation or introduction of proposals, floor speeches, and actions in legislative committees) rarely were used to describe legislative behavior systematically.

Instead of inquiring into the antecedents of legislators' behavior, most research proceeded rather uncritically from assumptions about the bases of behavior, which were almost never made explicit. A simple *rationalistic model* pictured the legislator's activity as the outcome of individual means–ends calculations on his part. According to its simplest version, a legislator, knowing what "the public interest" is, acts in an effort to promote it. More complex versions envisage more demanding information-seeking and analytical efforts by him to discover what the "public interest" requires in specific instances and to assess the relative utility of various means of furthering it [*see* PUBLIC INTEREST]. The *group pressure model*, on the other hand, pictured the legislator acting primarily in response to specific cues or orders from external agencies—constituents, executives, pressure groups, lobbyists, political party agents, friends, relatives, and many others. These pressuring agencies might act out of selfish desire, out of reasoned conviction about the public interest, or other motives. And the legislator's motives for responding to the "pressure" might vary from plain fear to agreement in principle with the pressuring agent. But legislators' actions will in any case be seen as an arithmetic sum of the amounts and directions of the different pressures on them [*see* POLITICAL GROUP ANALYSIS]. Sometimes, particularly in normatively oriented works, these two models have been treated as the ideal and the perverse extremes of legislative behavior, with the actually observable behavior of "real" legislators in each case presumably lying somewhere between.

The inadequacy of such frameworks for the investigation of individual legislators' behavior was implied by one of the first types of behavioral study, the tabulation of various social, economic, and political "background characteristics" of the individual legislators. This line of investigation, suggested as early as Lowell's time (Orth 1904), was pursued particularly by Charles S. Hyneman and his students (Hyneman 1940; Hyneman & Lay 1938), who made extensive inquiries into the occupation, political career, legislative tenure, and other characteristics of legislators in a number of American states over considerable time periods. Although, as Hyneman himself explicitly pointed out, there were few hypotheses and no clear theory about the relationship between background characteristics and legislative behavior, the assumption that some relationship did exist was made quite explicit. And it seemed clear to most scholars that this assumption fitted poorly with either rationalistic or group-pressure conceptions.

At the same time, increasing sophistication in more general conceptions of political structures and functions led to increasing awareness of hitherto neglected aspects of legislative behavior. For example, the many, varied "errand-boy" activities performed by legislators in many systems, informal but structured relationships among legislators (friendship, etc.), and numerous other aspects were seen to be as important for understanding the functioning of legislatures as were roll call votes. The importance of attitudinal dimensions of legislative behavior was emphasized by studies which viewed legislators' conceptions of themselves and their legislative jobs as the proximate indicators, if not the determinants, of their behavior (Silverman 1954).

It rapidly became accepted, therefore, that legislative behavior is social behavior in a particular institutional context, not atomistic rational calculation or mechanical reaction to mechanical impulsion or pressure. Increasingly the effort has been to conceptualize and explain legislative behavior more fully, both with respect to the amount and manner of its effect (as an independent variable) on legislative functioning and output and with respect to its relationship (as dependent variable) to other varieties or more general principles of human behavior. Recent studies, for example, have sought to relate the behavior of legislators to the group life of the society and to the role concepts of legislators as individuals (Patterson 1958) and to explain significant aspects of the observed behavior of legislators in terms of role theory (Wahlke et al. 1962), reference-group behavior (Michel 1964), or other social-psychological and psychoanalytical premises (Barber 1965).

Advances have also been made in surmounting

some of the methodological limitations which characterized earlier legislative behavior research. One limitation has been the failure to encompass the universe of public representative bodies. American social scientists, who have been responsible for most of this research, have generally confined their attention to American legislatures. Of the relatively few studies dealing with behavior in non-American legislatures, a disproportionate share are the product of American scholars (e.g., Aydelotte 1963; MacRae 1963). Although studies of behavior in American state legislatures and city councils are increasingly frequent (e.g., Zisk et al. 1965), research in America, as in other countries, has tended to concentrate on the national rather than on local or intermediate levels of government. There have been some important studies of behavior in international or supranational bodies, but they are relatively few (Alker & Russett 1965).

Moreover, despite the example of comparative analysis set by Lowell's pioneering venture, research has more often than not taken the form of case studies. There are numerous important exceptions, but, quantitatively speaking, the literature to date offers primarily studies of single legislatures rather than comparative studies, either of different legislatures or of single legislatures at different points in time. Research has often attempted to explain the historically unique features of particular events, decisions, or policy problems in a particular legislature. As a result, it is relatively difficult to establish generalizations by cumulating findings about legislative behavior even in a particular legislature, despite the qualitative richness of many available studies.

Another methodological limitation has been the tendency to utilize only the most obviously available types of data. Official documents, such as legislative journals and reports of debates, committee reports, newspaper accounts, and similar records provide a seemingly rich mine of data for a number of national legislatures, including the U.S. Congress, the British Parliament, the French National Assembly, and others, as well as for the United Nations General Assembly. Where such data have been readily available, a number of studies have been based on them. But, except for numerous roll call analyses, these studies have been more intuitive than systematic. Rarely have such data been subjected to content analysis or other objective techniques. Roll call analysis, however, has been developed with considerable methodological sophistication, so that various types of scalogram, factor, and other mathematical analyses of roll call data are by now familiar (Anderson et al. 1966). Another frequently used type of documentary data is the legislative "blue book," or regularly published summary of memberships, legislative assignments, and limited biographical and other related information. A number of social background and recruitment studies have been based at least in part on these (e.g., Finer et al. 1961; Hyneman 1940; Hyneman & Lay 1938; Matthews 1954; 1960).

The most important methodological development in legislative behavior research since the beginnings of roll call analysis has been the use of new sources of data and new methods of gathering them. Systematic interviewing of whole legislative memberships or samples of them is perhaps the most widely used such method (e.g., Wahlke et al. 1962; Barber 1965). But direct observation, systematic surveillance, and participant observation, frequently in combination with systematic interviewing, have also produced some interesting findings (Crane 1959; Patterson 1958). Increasingly sophisticated methods of observing, recording, and analyzing data obtained by these methods promise further fruitful results.

Perhaps the most persuasive sign of methodological maturity in the field of legislative behavior research is the increasing frequency of efforts to combine many types of data, subjected to various types of analysis, in comprehensive assaults on theoretically important problems. Miller and Stokes (1963), for example, have combined survey and other data, utilizing imaginative statistical techniques, to investigate the problem of representation. Bauer, Pool, and Dexter (1963) have explored policy formulation in a broad context, also using a variety of data and techniques. It is fair to say, therefore, that by the middle 1960s legislative behavior had become an identifiable field of research and study, part of the mainstream of empirical political and social research; that scholars in the field were contributing their share of methodological innovations as well as utilizing techniques developed in other fields; and that research was becoming productive of findings relevant to theoretical interests well beyond the historical events and personages of the particular legislatures serving as research sites.

Dimensions of legislative behavior

The most striking characteristic of current legislative behavior research is the number of dimensions of behavior it envisages. Reference was made above to the categories of activity examined in legislative research. One important new category was revealed by the theoretical recognition (or recollection) that legislatures are, after all, political institutions. As such, legislatures in general are essentially patterns of behavior, and each specific legislature is a particular institutionalized group by virtue of the specific behavioral uniformities exhibited by each legislative generation and passed on from it to the next.

The uniformities which constitute the legislative institution have their roots in the constitutional and statutory definitions of legislative functions and tasks, but they go well beyond the formally prescribed behaviors. "Folkways" or "rules of the game," which include not only direct norms of behavior but also sanctions against violators, have been identified in a number of different representative bodies (Matthews 1960; Wahlke et al. 1962; Kornberg 1964). They prescribe such behavior as respect for fellow members' rights in the legislature and in politics; engaging in debate only when informed on a subject, and then with due restraint; standing ready to compromise rather than holding dogmatically to fixed positions; and so on. They have been shown to serve the functions of promoting cohesion and solidarity of the legislative group, channeling and restraining conflict, expediting the conduct of legislative business, etc. [*see* RULES OF THE GAME].

These norms enter into legislative behavior as major elements of the legislators' conceptions of the legislative role. They are the behaviors expected of individuals associated with the office or position of legislator, by legislators themselves and by their fellows. Besides "rules of the game" the legislative role includes norms concerning (1) the legitimate purpose of legislative activity (identifying social problems and inventing solutions to them, acting as broker between competing groups and interests, etc.), (2) the representational focus of the legislators' actions (the community collectively served by the whole legislature, the local community or constituency which elected the legislator, etc.), and (3) the style of representational judgment ("independent judgment," orders or advice from party leaders or powerful constituents, etc.). The legislature collectively gets work done because the job of legislator is perceived by all legislators in terms of such categories (even though there may be variation among members' conceptions of them).

Moreover, legislatures tend to develop roles obviously related to legislative task performance, to which the same principles apply. The positions of formal and semiformal leaders (speaker, committee chairmen, party leaders, whips, and so on) have role behaviors associated with them. In most legislatures there are also highly informal specialized roles that play an important part in the legislative process. One of these is the role of "subject-matter specialist," a status recognized by legislators, who tend to accept the advice or recommendations of such specialists not on the basis of their party affiliation, personal friendship, or political identification, but directly on the basis of their recognized "expertise" as knowledgeable, though nonprofessional, specialists. It has been demonstrated that such "experts" make their influence felt not just within their own party but among members of other parties as well (Wahlke et al. 1962, pp. 193–215).

Certain other relationships among legislators play a part in their legislative behavior even though they may be peripheral or irrelevant to legislative purposes and legislative roles as such. Friendship groups and cliques, for example, have been found to influence voting, debating, and other categories of behavior. Such groups may be based on affective social ties (*ibid.*, pp. 216–235; Patterson 1959), on membership in a common state delegation (Truman 1959), or other nonlegislative social bases. These groups, which are never large (a dozen or more is unusual), tend to form within parties more than across party lines. There is an even stronger tendency for veteran legislator groups to be relatively impervious to newcomer legislators (who, as might therefore be expected, tend to form friendship groups among themselves).

Like social roles in general, legislative roles are conceived in terms of behavior appropriate for an individual in relation to some specific "significant other." In the case of the above-described rules of the game, the legislator's "significant other" comprises all his fellow legislators. But the legislative system (a network somewhat wider than just the legislature itself) includes numerous other classes of "significant others" with whom legislators interact with sufficient regularity to generate other components of the legislator's role. In most legislatures today these classes would include the chief executive and his representatives and aides, administrators, party officials (both within the legislative party leadership and in the broader party organization outside), lobbyists and other pressure-group representatives, and different categories of constituents.

One important dimension of legislative behavior, then, is the number of different categories of behavior which have analytically been found to be subsumed in legislative role concepts and manifested in legislative role behavior, and the amount and type of variation in these respects found empirically to occur between members of a given legislature and between patterns found in different legislatures.

A closely related dimension involves the synthesis of these components by individual legislators and its consequences for collective legislative action. The aggregative and individual behavior approaches intersect at this point. The aggregative approach sees it as a problem of assessing the relative significance of competing determinants of legislative decisions (e.g., parties versus pressure groups versus constituents). The individual approach sees it as a problem of determining which role cues have most salience for various legislators, which role sectors (e.g., expectations vis-à-vis executive agents, political party agents, lobbyists, etc.) will prevail where there may be role incongruity, or what cognitive and affective structure of individual attitudes will operate under what conditions. On this crucial point relatively little is known. With respect to individual legislative behavior, a beginning has been made at detecting, describing, and classifying individual role orientations in various role sectors—e.g., "trustee," "delegate," and "politico" orientations with respect to representational style (Wahlke et al. 1962)—and styles of conceiving and performing the legislative job in more general terms—e.g., "lawmakers," "advertisers," "spectators," and "reluctants" (Barber 1965). From the aggregative viewpoint, a number of assessments have been made of the degree of influence in particular instances of party, constituents, and other factors—e.g., the many investigations of party cohesion in roll call voting, beginning with Lowell's. There are as yet no instruments and measures for accurately determining the relative influence of such factors or the relative salience of different role concepts and their impact on behavior. Equally important is the theoretical need for more precise and comprehensive conceptualization in this area. It is, therefore, impossible to say with assurance why parties (or constituencies, or other agencies or factors) seem to affect legislative behavior enormously in one system but much less so in another, or even to determine the magnitude of such differences with any precision.

A final dimension, which has yet to receive much attention in research, is that of time—the duration of uniformities of behavior for individual legislators, as well as among groups of them, and the patterns and process of change and development over time. Secular trends in aggregate patterns have been shown to exist in many instances (Buchanan 1963; MacRae 1958), but stability in the behavior of individuals whose behavior constitutes the aggregate picture at any given moment has generally had to be assumed (Aydelotte 1963; Truman 1959). There is now some reason to believe that blocs and coalitions manifest themselves in a much smaller proportion of legislative business than has generally been believed (Riker & Niemi 1962). But the temporal mechanics of legislative behavior, whether in aggregate or individual terms, is another subject requiring considerable study.

Bases of legislative behavior

To account for variations in behavior along the dimensions described above obviously requires consideration of the mechanics and antecedents of individuals' behavior. Interpretation of behavior patterns identified in various cases is difficult without understanding this. For example, party cohesion was long explained in terms of party discipline, in the sense of more or less coercive activities by leaders, whips, and so on. But studies by Epstein (1960) of the British Parliament, by Dahl (1950) and Truman (1959) of Congress, and by others, point to the conclusion that disciplinary activity by party organizations is much less significant in this respect than are individual legislators' sentiments of party identification. The latter phenomenon must be comprehended within the same framework, to begin with, as the party identification of voters in general. Although it seems clear that other factors also enter in, it is by no means clear how or to what extent. Thus, there is conflicting evidence concerning whether American state legislators are more likely to cohere with their party if they are from safe or from competitive districts (Froman 1963; Sorauf 1963), and some evidence that deviation from party positions by CDU members in the West German Bundestag is traceable to the way in which the structure of interest groups in the party influences its nominations for proportional-representation, as against single-member, district seats (Rueckert & Crane 1962).

It does seem clear that legislators acquire basic elements of the legislative role conception as part of their general political socialization, and not from specific socialization into the legislative group, since all members of all legislatures so far examined on this point appear to recognize and conform to legislative expectations remarkably quickly and dependably upon entry into the legislature. It is not clear, however, whether this is because only certain types of persons, who, for reasons that are not yet known, will already have acquired the particular knowledge in question, are recruited for legislative service, or because general political socialization processes equip practically all members of a given culture with relevant norms that remain latent until called rapidly to consciousness by recruitment into the legislature. Socialization and recruitment studies to date offer little more than descriptive data about the occupational and social origins of legislators and their prelegislative political experience. [*See* POLITICAL RECRUITMENT AND CAREERS; SOCIALIZATION, *article on* POLITICAL SOCIALIZATION.]

The factors offered to account for variations in behavior fall into several identifiable classes, despite the paucity of theory and hypotheses about the exact linkages between the variables and the behavior to be explained.

Ecological and demographic characteristics of salient political units or environments of the legislator have long been presumed to affect his behavior. Reference has already been made to party competition in legislative districts as a possible influence on party identification and cohesion. The socioeconomic character of such units has also been considered an important factor of this kind. In American legislative research it has usually been assumed that the urban–rural character of the unit is the important characteristic in this respect, whereas in other systems the presumption has been that it is differences in social class (workers, businessmen, etc.) which are important. [*See* PARTIES, POLITICAL, *article on* PARTY UNITS.]

In neither case has it ever been made clear just how these variables are linked to legislative behavior. Social background and recruitment studies of the characteristics of legislators themselves sometimes imply that legislators individually tend to embody the ecological characteristics described. On the other hand, there is considerable evidence that, at least in American legislative bodies, legislators will in various ways reflect ecological and demographic characteristics of their districts, whatever their own individual backgrounds (Crane 1959). In any case, there is very little evidence for a simple deterministic view of the connection between individual socioeconomic background and individual legislative behavior.

From findings like those concerning the relationship between partisanship and party competition, it may well be inferred that structural and situational political variables have a great deal to do with variations of behavior among legislators. The finding in most American legislatures that constituents and constituency interests seem to have primary salience for most legislators similarly points to the importance of such factors. But there is no accepted theory or model of legislative behavior describing the mechanism by which such variables affect the individual legislators. And there is certainly no accepted explanation for the gross difference in such respects between legislatures.

Despite the fears of some early critics of behavioral studies of legislatures, it does seem that the unique personality and character of the individual legislator must be taken into account. An early, never replicated study in one American state (McConaughy 1950), for example, strongly suggested the psychological normality or well-adjustedness of legislators as compared with a matched sample of laymen. Barber (1965) has identified some differences of a psychological order among legislators. And Froman (1963) has shown that the unique "individuality" of Congressmen—elements of personality, outlook, style, etc., as well as views on issues and ideological orientations (if any)—leaves detectable traces in their legislative behavior.

The tasks of future legislative behavior research, then, include the elaboration of theories and concepts which will encompass the institution-forming uniformities of behavior within legislatures, the corollary differences and similarities between legislatures in these respects, and the differences in behavior among members within a legislature. Social-psychological frameworks such as role and reference-group theory appear to offer the most promise as guides to these tasks. But it seems clear from work to date that such guides will not by themselves provide answers to the important questions subsumed under the organizing questions—Why do legislators behave as they do, and what difference does it make in the legislative process?

JOHN C. WAHLKE

[*See also* COALITIONS; ELECTIONS; INTEREST GROUPS; LOBBYING; PARTIES, POLITICAL; REPRESENTATION, *article on* REPRESENTATIONAL BEHAVIOR. *Other relevant material may be found in* POLITICAL BEHAVIOR; POLITICAL PARTICIPATION; POLITICAL RECRUITMENT AND CAREERS; PUBLIC INTEREST; *and in the biographies of* KEY; LOWELL; RICE.]

BIBLIOGRAPHY

ALKER, HAYWARD R. JR.; and RUSSETT, BRUCE M. 1965 *World Politics in the General Assembly.* New Haven: Yale Univ. Press.

ANDERSON, LEE F.; WATTS, MEREDITH W.; and WILCOX, ALLEN R. JR. 1966 *Legislative Roll-call Analysis.* Evanston, Ill.: Northwestern Univ. Press.

AYDELOTTE, WILLIAM 1963 Voting Patterns in the British House of Commons in the 1840s. *Comparative Studies in Society and History* 5, no. 2: 134–163.

BARBER, JAMES D. 1965 *The Lawmakers.* New Haven: Yale Univ. Press.

BAUER, RAYMOND A.; POOL, ITHIEL DE SOLA; and DEXTER, L. A. 1963 *American Business and Public Policy: The Politics of Foreign Trade.* New York: Atherton.

BENTHAM, JEREMY (1817) 1818 *Plan of Parliamentary Reform: In the Form of a Catechism* . . . . London: Wooler.

BENTHAM, JEREMY (1843) 1962 Essay on Political Tactics. Volume 2, pages 291–373 in Jeremy Bentham, *Works.* Edited by John Bowring. New York: Russell.

BEYLE, HERMAN C. 1931 *Identification and Analysis of Attribute–Cluster–Blocs: A Technique for Use in the Investigation of Behavior in Governance. . . .* Univ. of Chicago Press.

BUCHANAN, WILLIAM 1963 *Legislative Partisanship: The Deviant Case of California.* Berkeley: Univ. of California Press.

BURKE, EDMUND (1774) 1920 *A Letter to the Sheriffs of Bristol.* Cambridge Univ. Press.

CRANE, WILDER W. 1959 The Legislative Struggle in Wisconsin: Decision-making in the 1957 Wisconsin Assembly. Ph.D. dissertation, Univ. of Wisconsin.

DAHL, ROBERT A. 1950 *Congress and Foreign Policy.* New York: Harcourt.

EPSTEIN, LEON D. 1960 British M.P.s and Their Local Parties: The Suez Cases. *American Political Science Review* 54:374–390.

EULAU, HEINZ; and SPRAGUE, JOHN D. 1964 *Lawyers in Politics: A Study in Professional Convergence.* Indianapolis, Ind.: Bobbs-Merrill.

FINER, SAMUEL E.; BERRINGTON, H. B.; and BARTHOLOMEW, D. J. 1961 *Backbench Opinion in the House of Commons,* 1955–59. New York: Pergamon.

FROMAN, LEWIS A. 1963 *Congressmen and Their Constituencies.* Chicago: Rand McNally.

GLEECK, L. E. 1940 96 Congressmen Make Up Their Minds. *Public Opinion Quarterly* 4:3–24.

HERRING, E. PENDLETON 1929 *Group Representation Before Congress.* Washington: Brookings Institution.

HYNEMAN, CHARLES S. 1940 Who Makes Our Laws? *Political Science Quarterly* 55:556–581.

HYNEMAN, CHARLES S.; and LAY, HOUSTON 1938 Tenure and Turnover of the Indiana General Assembly. *American Political Science Review* 32:51–67, 311–331.

KORNBERG, ALLAN 1964 The Rules of the Game in the Canadian House of Commons. *Journal of Politics* 26:358–380.

KORNBERG, ALLAN 1966 Caucus and Cohesion in Canadian Parliamentary Parties. *American Political Science Review* 60:83–92.

LIJPHART, AREND 1963 The Analysis of Bloc Voting in the General Assembly: A Critique and a Proposal. *American Political Science Review* 57:902–917.

LOWELL, A. LAWRENCE 1902 The Influence of Party Upon Legislation in England and America. American Historical Association, *Annual Report* [1901] No. 1: 319–542.

MCCONAUGHY, JOHN B. 1950 Certain Personality Factors of State Legislators in South Carolina. *American Political Science Review* 44:897–903.

MCKEAN, DAYTON D. 1938 *Pressures on the Legislature of New Jersey.* New York: Columbia Univ. Press.

MACRAE, DUNCAN JR. 1958 *Dimensions of Congressional Voting: A Statistical Study of the House of Representatives in the Eighty-first Congress.* California, University of, Publications in Sociology and Social Institutions, Vol. 1, No. 3. Berkeley: Univ. of California Press.

MACRAE, DUNCAN JR. 1963 Intra-party Division and Cabinet Coalitions in the Fourth French Republic. *Comparative Studies in Society and History* 5, no. 2:164–211.

MATTHEWS, DONALD R. 1954 *The Social Background of Political Decision-makers.* Garden City, N.Y.: Doubleday.

MATTHEWS, DONALD R. 1960 *U.S. Senators and Their World.* Chapel Hill: Univ. of North Carolina Press.

MELLER, NORMAN 1960 Legislative Behavior Research. *Western Political Quarterly* 13:131–153.

MELLER, NORMAN 1965 Legislative Behavior Research Revisited: A Review of Five Years' Publications. *Western Political Quarterly* 18:776–793.

MICHEL, JERRY B. 1964 Legislative Decision Making: A Case Study of Reference Behavior. Ph.D. dissertation, Univ. of Texas.

MILL, JOHN STUART (1861) 1962 *Considerations on Representative Government.* Chicago: Regnery. → A reprint of the original edition.

MILLER, WARREN E.; and STOKES, DONALD E. 1963 Constituency Influence in Congress. *American Political Science Review* 57:45–56.

NAMIER, LEWIS B. (1929) 1957 *The Structure of Politics at the Accession of George III.* 2d ed. London: Macmillan; New York: St. Martins. → A paperback edition was published in 1961 by St. Martins.

ORTH, SAMUEL P. 1904 Our State Legislatures. *Atlantic Monthly* 94:728–739.

PATTERSON, SAMUEL C. 1958 Toward a Theory of Legislative Behavior: The Wisconsin State Assemblymen as Actors in a Legislative System. Ph.D. dissertation, Univ. of Wisconsin.

PATTERSON, SAMUEL C. 1959 Patterns of Interpersonal Relations in a State Legislative Group: The Wisconsin Assembly. *Public Opinion Quarterly* 23:101–109.

RICE, STUART A. 1928 *Quantitative Methods in Politics.* New York: Knopf.

RIKER, WILLIAM H.; and NIEMI, DONALD 1962 The Stability of Coalitions on Roll Calls in the House of Representatives. *American Political Science Review* 56:58–65.

ROBINSON, JAMES A. 1962 *Congress and Foreign Policy-making: A Study in Legislative Influence and Initiative.* Homewood, Ill.: Dorsey.

ROUTT, GARLAND C. 1938 Interpersonal Relationships and the Legislative Process. American Academy of Political and Social Sciences, *Annals* 195:129–136.

RUECKERT, GEORGE L.; and CRANE, WILDER W. 1962 CDU Deviancy in the German Bundestag. *Journal of Politics* 24:477–488.

SCHATTSCHNEIDER, ELMER E. 1935 *Politics, Pressures, and the Tariff: A Study of Free Private Enterprise in Pressure Politics, as Shown in the 1929–1930 Revision of the Tariff.* Englewood Cliffs, N.J.: Prentice-Hall.

SILVERMAN, CORINNE 1954 The Legislators' View of the Legislative Process. *Public Opinion Quarterly* 18:180–190.

SORAUF, FRANK J. 1963 *Party and Representation: Legislative Politics in Pennsylvania.* New York: Atherton.

TRUMAN, DAVID B. 1959 *The Congressional Party: A Case Study.* New York: Wiley.

TURNER, JULIUS 1952 *Party and Constituency: Pressures on Congress.* Johns Hopkins University Studies in Historical and Political Science, Series 69, No. 1. Baltimore: Johns Hopkins Press.

WAHLKE, JOHN C.; and EULAU, HEINZ (editors) 1959 *Legislative Behavior: A Reader in Theory and Research.* Glencoe, Ill.: Free Press.

WAHLKE, JOHN et al. 1962 *The Legislative System: Explorations in Legislative Behavior.* New York: Wiley.

ZELLER, BELLE 1937 *Pressure Politics in New York: A Study of Group Representation Before the Legislature.* Englewood Cliffs, N.J.: Prentice-Hall.

ZISK, BETTY H.; EULAU, HEINZ; and PREWITT, KENNETH 1965 City Councilmen and the Group Struggle: A Typology of Role Orientations. *Journal of Politics* 27: 618–646.

LEGITIMACY

Legitimacy is the foundation of such governmental power as is exercised both with a consciousness on the government's part that it has a right to govern and with some recognition by the governed of that right.

The concept of usurpation as the opposite of legitimacy has accompanied the concept of legitimate government since early medieval times and has helped to clarify it. Usurpers, after seizing power, have often tried to strengthen their positions by giving their governments a legitimate form, and these attempts to clothe a usurping power with legitimacy, whether successful or not, have often revealed what the standards of legitimacy are for a given society or civilization.

Revolutions, unlike usurpation or *coups d'état*, are not necessarily illegitimate. If they succeed they introduce a new principle of legitimacy that supersedes the legitimacy of the former regime. Under such circumstances recognition by the people will often be acquired only as the new government begins governing, and the process of becoming legitimate may include violence and terror. Foreign diplomatic recognition, while not essential, may help internal consolidation and therefore speed acceptance of the new pattern of legitimacy.

Governments, whether following traditional principles of legitimacy or establishing revolutionary ones, may lose their legitimacy by violating these principles. The desire for legitimacy is so deeply rooted in human communities that it is hard to discover any sort of historical government that did not either enjoy widespread authentic recognition of its existence or try to win such recognition. Because it is so universal a phenomenon, however, legitimacy is continuously endangered by the plurality of its patterns and sources. Rivals for power often automatically consider themselves legitimate and their opponents illegitimate. It is therefore difficult to talk about legitimacy in general terms; the different types must be discussed separately and specific examples given.

Types of legitimacy

The numerous historical types of governmental legitimacy may be classified into two broad groups: numinous and civil.

Numinous legitimacy. The dominion of a *god-king*, of which ancient Egypt offers perhaps the most impressive example, is the theological doctrine according to which every pharaoh is himself (among other things) the god Horus, son of Osiris. The doctrine seems to go back to the very origin of the empire. The underlying myth of the birth of Horus, repeated, as it were, in every accession to the throne, provided the Egyptian kingship with a powerful guarantee of identity and continuity, the appearance of eternity. The pharaoh is, as Henri Frankfort (1948) put it, the epiphany of the god, as distinct from the Hellenistic or late Roman institution of the apotheosis granted to an individual emperor (for example, Alexander the Great). The pharaoh's empire is god's empire. Obedience is not merely a political necessity but a religious obligation. Obviously, legitimacy of this sort is a matter of might rather than of right and transcends all juridical explanation.

The *godly origin* of the king, more specifically the king being the son of god, is a concept close to that of the godliness of the king. The early pharaoh was, indeed, both god and son of god. The phenomenon of being the son of god does not belong to antiquity alone, however; it constitutes an essential element of the Christian faith.

Divine vocation as a principle of legitimate government (whether temporal or spiritual) must be distinguished from divine origin. *Dominus noster Jesus Christus nos ad regnum vocavit* ("Jesus Christ our Lord called us to the throne"), claimed Henry IV in his struggle against Pope Gregory VII, and this understanding of the foundation of his office, and of his personal rulership as well, strictly followed the traditional pattern of the medieval Roman emperors. Charlemagne had considered himself as *a Deo coronatus* ("crowned by God"), and he also seems to have been the first king to attribute to himself the famous formula of *Dei gratia* ("by the grace of God"). The Christian *sacerdotium* ("priesthood") derived its legitimacy, and still does, from a source very similar to that of the *regnum* ("kingship"); according to official doctrine, the papal office is based on Christ's designation of St. Peter, which continues to sanctify and legitimize the rule of every successive pope. For centuries both king and priest were considered the embodiment of the institution of the vicariat. The controversy between them was not about their respective legitimacy as such, but rather about the question whether priestly coronation and consecration were of constituent or merely affirmative significance for the *regnum*.

Inspiration is a numinous basis of legitimate government that has not produced lasting governmental institutions to the degree the three previous bases have. Moses is the foremost example of numinous inspiration, and his name is cited in Christian political philosophy whenever government by inspiration and revelation is discussed. The later prophets of ancient Israel could be considered as performing the function in government that has since come to be called the opposition. Time and again prophecy (in the sense of a mission based on direct revelation of a superior will) has inspired powerful political movements, often of a revolutionary kind. The Puritan revolution is a prominent example. Such superior will is not necessarily of a divine nature; Marx, for example, refers to history, and the Bolshevik party is guided by the will of history, of which the party claims to have a (quasi-theological) scientific knowledge.

Civil legitimacy. Civil legitimacy exists when a system of government is based on agreement between equally autonomous constituents who have combined to cooperate toward some common good. The polis is one paradigm, especially if understood in accordance with Aristotle, who defines it as "an aggregate of citizens, or in other words, of men possessing access to office and therefore either actual or possible rulers" (*Politics* III, 130). Medieval confederacies, viewed not as aggregates of citizens but as aggregates of autonomous estates, form another type of commonwealth, deriving their legitimacy from agreement, or *conjuratio*. Switzerland is an example of this type of commonwealth, the confederacy having survived Switzerland's transformation into a federal state. The institution of assemblies of estates (as for example, the French États Généraux, the old German Reichstag, or the unreformed English Parliament) is another example of an aggregate of autonomous entities, although it is of a very different structure and importance from the confederacy. Finally, every modern constitutional system, or more specifically, every system of representational government is founded either on a basic agreement to follow certain rules or at least on a justifiable assumption that a basic agreement to follow certain rules exists. These rules include the government's obligation to protect civil rights and liberties and to pursue the common good.

Modern constitutional government makes one characteristic of civil legitimacy particularly clear: governmental offices are ordered by trust rather than exercised by dominion. This characteristic is expressed in the institution of periodic elections. In recent times popular elections have become so predominant a criterion of legitimacy that almost every nation feels obliged to pay lip service to the institution of elections, no matter what its system of government [*see* ELECTIONS].

History and interpretations of the concept

Etymology. The word *legitimus* is classical Latin, while *legitimitas* seems to occur first in medieval texts, and, even then, only rarely. The Roman form means lawful, according to law. While the word was used in all spheres of juridical relations, there are definite political overtones: Cicero uses *legitimum imperium* and *potestas legitima* in the sense of powers or magistrates constituted by law. His concept of the *justus et legitimum hostis* ("enemy by right and by law") is revealing; this enemy is to be distinguished from a robber or pirate and is *legitimus* because treaties are concluded with him, and concluding treaties constitutes a common ground of law (*De officiis* III, 108). Occasionally Cicero's usage seems to approach the meaning of hereditary succession: he wrote of dominions given by the tyrant Dionysius to his son, as *quasi justam et legitimam potestatem* ("his by right and by law") (*De natura deorum* III, 84).

The medieval meaning is very different: *legitimus* is what conforms to ancient custom and to customary procedure. The word begins to be applied to persons: *electi sunt quatuor legitimi viri communi assensu* ("four duly constituted men were chosen by common consent") (from a monastery charter, quoted in Du Cange's *Glossarium mediae et infimae latinitatis*) which means qualified persons (*boni homines*) who can testify and guarantee some juridical action to which they give lawlike validity by their very presence, as custom requires. There is, indeed, something to be said for interpreting the medieval *lex* as indicating the particular customary procedure of an appropriate council or assembly composed of members of the family or the judiciary whose resolution or assent gives legitimacy to the respective decisions. *Legitima auctoritas* ("legal authority") is thus sometimes opposed to *regale preceptum* ("royal warrant") just as *legitima potestas* ("legal power") is opposed to *tyrannica usurpatio* ("dictatorial seizure of power"). In these cases the word legitimate points to the element of constituted rule and order, but included in the meaning is the assembly itself to which the rule refers. The 1338 Bavarian electoral law of Emperor Louis states that he who is elected by the electors *ex sola electione censeatur . . . pro vero et legitimo imperatore* ("by the sole process of election he shall be constituted . . . emperor in truth and in law") instead of having to wait for papal consecration and other sanctifying ceremonies. Here the meaning of *legitimus* appears to come very close to its modern sense by adding the element of consent to the original *veritas* of the elected emperor. This idea of consent is precisely the element of meaning which remains in modern usage. Popular consent, although not the whole essence of legitimate government, is one of its most important criteria.

Because the word legitimacy has had so many

different meanings, the kinds of problems considered relevant to a discussion of legitimacy have also varied. For example, Plato's idea of justice bears on the problem of legitimacy. The same is true of Aristotle's concept of the best constitution and his distinctions between good and bad forms of monarchy, aristocracy, and democracy (*Politics* III). In the course of the medieval revival of interest in Aristotle, his discussion of king and tyrant became particularly important. Later, Thomas Aquinas drew a much sharper line between king and tyrant than Aristotle had done and thus came close to a theory of legitimate and illegitimate government. (The king is pursuing the *bonum commune*, the tyrant his *bonum proprium.*)

Augustine. Augustine declared that it was impossible for any community or government outside the City of God to be legitimate. Empires, he stated (*De civitate Dei* IV, 4), are big gangs of robbers. By turning Cicero's definitions against him, he claimed to prove that the Roman Empire had never been a *civitas* ("state") or *res publica* ("commonwealth") in the true meaning of those terms. He traced the origin of temporal government back to either Cain—the murderer—or Abel—a citizen of God's city. The two *civitates*, he insisted, share only a mutual enmity. There is one respect in which the worldly *civitas* seems to be justified: its desire for peace is a *bonum* ("good"), which through its imperfection points to the perfect and eternal peace of the heavenly city. Since legitimacy thus applies exclusively to the City of God, kingdoms must demonstrate that their subjects are Christ's people, just as kings must demonstrate that they are Christ's vicars. This need, which existed from the time of Augustine on through the Middle Ages, may explain a good deal of medieval political theology and "christology" (Kantorowicz 1957). It may also explain the similarity of claims made by the Roman church and the Roman Empire: *Extra civitatem Dei nulla legitimitas* ("No laws are binding save those of the City of God") [*see* AUGUSTINE].

Marsilius of Padua. Marsilius rediscovered the concept of the polity as an autonomous entity not in need of spiritual approbation or interpretation. His *Defensor pacis* (1324) represented a bold revolution in political thought. He denied the church any right of dominion, and he based *regnum* and *imperium*, like any *principatus* ("civil power") on the constitution of the human society and the consent of the people, using Aristotle's explanation of the polis as his main source. His astonishing book served the cause of Louis of Bavaria in his struggle with Pope John XXII but did so in a completely novel way: the foundation of imperial legitimacy was neither God's institution and vocation nor the theory of *translatio imperii* ("imperial succession") but, instead, constitutional election. Marsilius thereby cut the bond of theological legitimation that had united church and empire for over five hundred years [*see* MARSILIUS OF PADUA].

John Locke. Locke, the great revolutionary political thinker of seventeenth-century England, was, like Marsilius, an Aristotelian and a developer of a novel theory of civil legitimacy. While Marsilius' polemical attack was directed at papal domination and intervention, Locke's analysis of the nature of government started with an attack on the divine right of kings. He used Robert Filmer's *Patriarcha* as his text and demolished its arguments one by one in the first part of *Two Treatises of Government* (1690). Having destroyed the theory of the divine right of kings, he went on to build a totally different theory of government, according to which kingship was an office created by human agreement that served the common good of those agreeing to create it. Certainly, Locke's celebrated compact, from which political society originates, is concluded in order to preserve the natural rights of the contracting parties, but what matters more with regard to the question of legitimacy is that monarchy, as indeed all political institutions, is based on agreement and on the consent of the people. Locke served the cause of the Whig party and its Glorious Revolution against the Stuarts as Marsilius had served the Imperial party against the pope [*see* LOCKE].

Joseph de Maistre. De Maistre was a leading nineteenth-century advocate of legitimism and a prime opponent of Locke and his revolutionary views. He argued that Locke's concept of law was actually the outcome of human agreement and not of natural right. Condemning Locke's interpretation, he claimed that man cannot make a constitution because *toute constitution est divine dans son principe.* De Maistre conceived of the divine right of kings in a dynastic sense; it is the royal *family* rather than the royal *office* that has been chosen by God. He gave no explanation of the origin of a given dynasty's power, other than through the paradoxical process of *usurpation légitime.* Royal families exist, he stated, and this fact is the most telling sign of their legitimacy. In this view hereditary succession is an essential element of legitimate rule. *Des constitutions politiques* (1809) served the cause of the Bourbon restoration and, more specifically, of Talleyrand's introduction of legitimist doctrine into Europe. Although legitimism as a political force ended in France with the

July revolution of 1830, legitimist ideas dominated nineteenth-century discussions of legitimacy.

Modern discussions

Modern scholarly discussions of legitimacy can best be covered by reviewing three writers who dealt with the general notion of legitimacy: Max Weber, Carl Schmitt, and Guglielmo Ferrero. (From this selection of a sociologist, a lawyer, and a historian, it is apparent that the problem of legitimacy is of concern to many disciplines other than political science.)

Max Weber. Weber was the first to discover the universal applicability of the notion of legitimacy and therefore the first to use the term for classifying and comparing a great number of sociopolitical phenomena. The legitimists' preoccupation with dynastic succession had narrowed the meaning of the word "legitimacy," and this narrow usage had continued for almost a century. Weber's use of legitimacy helped deprive it of this specific historical connotation. Weber's typology of modes and sources of legitimacy forms part of his sociology of dominion (*Herrschaftssoziologie*) and is to be found in that monumental fragment *Wirtschaft und Gesellschaft* (1922). Legitimate dominion is not distinguished from illegitimate dominion. Instead, within the general framework of a value-free description of social patterns, the plurality of legitimacies becomes apparent. Weber seemed to assume that in legitimate dominion of any type, legitimacy is based on belief and elicits obedience. However, he did not discuss the general sense of legitimacy and instead concentrated on the pure types of legitimacy: the traditional, the charismatic, and the rational. His three types together cover the whole range of such phenomena. (Although these terms have provided the impetus for much empirical research, whether they provide the best classification of the empirical material they have helped unearth is still questionable.) By traditional legitimacy Weber understood mainly patriarchal and feudal forms of order and dominion. Here the objection may be made that the sanction of tradition plays its part in almost every kind of legitimacy, from constitutional systems to charismatic ones. Weber's notion of charisma is so closely associated with the uniqueness of prophets, heroes, and other leaders that it is difficult to understand the striking durability of certain historical systems based on the charisma either of kinship or of office. Weber himself had some doubts about the rationality of the third type: rational legitimacy. However, he never described the precise nature of the belief in legality which he placed at the bottom of legal and bureaucratic dominion. There is almost no place left in his system for civil government in its proper sense. Democratic legitimacy occurs only as a reversion of charismatic leadership and is another concept that cannot be handled in his system. Whether laws are granted or agreed upon did not basically affect Weber's defiant and somewhat bitter "realism" [*see* WEBER, MAX].

Carl Schmitt. The problem of democratic legitimacy was, for obvious reasons, urgently discussed in the late years of the Weimar Republic. Schmitt's contribution to the discussion was his largely polemical treatise, *Legalität und Legitimität* (1932). The distinction between legality and legitimacy goes back to the French legitimist writers and is most sharply made in M. de Bonald's *Essai analytique sur les lois naturelles de l'ordre social* (1800). Although Schmitt did not define the terms of his title, he seemed to say that the state with parliamentary legislation lacks legitimacy altogether. "Fifty-one percent of parliamentary votes make for law and legality," he stated somewhat sarcastically, without ever asking why the remaining 49 per cent accept the majority decision, although this acceptance is, after all, the basic prerequisite of any constitutional system. Schmitt considered the plebiscitary elements of the Weimar constitution to be legitimizing factors, and he therefore pleaded that these factors be made the basis of an amended constitution. Schmitt's critics pointed out that his caesarist version of democracy was just as formalistic and neutral as to values as the parliamentary majority rule which he attacked (Kirchheimer & Leites 1932/1933). Schmitt's treatise both mirrored the lack of basic consent that characterized the Weimar Republic and was responsible for increasing that lack of consent [*see* SCHMITT].

Guglielmo Ferrero. Neither Weber's pattern of rationality and legality nor Schmitt's notion about the plebiscitary legitimation of democratic leadership answered the basic question: What is the core of democratic legitimacy? One significant solution was offered by Ferrero, who described democratic legitimacy as resting on two "pillars": majority and minority, or government and opposition. His formula broke the spell of the Rousseauean fiction of a general will (*volonté générale*) and avoids the dangerous drawbacks of considering majority rule as the essence of democracy. Hopefully this illuminating concept will be tested by comparative studies.

Apart from the particular problems already mentioned, there are many important questions about legitimacy that deserve further study. Among them are the partly logical question of the universality of the concept and the partly ethical question of how to resolve conflicts of legitimacies both in theory and in practice.

DOLF STERNBERGER

[*See also* CHARISMA; DEMOCRACY; GENERAL WILL; MONARCHY; POLITICAL THEORY; SOCIAL CONTRACT.]

BIBLIOGRAPHY

BALON, JOSEPH 1959–1960 *Jus medii aevi.* 4 vols. Namur (France): Godenne. → See especially Part 2, "Lex jurisdictio."

BONALD, LOUIS GABRIEL AMBROISE DE (1800) 1817 *Essai analytique sur les lois naturelles de l'ordre social: Ou, du pouvoir, du ministre et du sujet dans la société.* 2d ed. Paris: Le Clère.

BRIE, SIEGFRIED 1866 *Die Legitimation einer usurpierten Staatsgewalt.* Heidelberg: Emmerling.

BRUNNER, OTTO 1962 Bemerkungen zu den Begriffen "Herrschaft" und "Legitimität." Pages 116–133 in *Festschrift für Hans Sedlmayr.* Munich: Beck.

CARLYLE, ROBERT W.; and CARLYLE, A. J. 1903–1936 *A History of Mediaeval Political Theory in the West.* 6 vols. New York: Barnes & Noble; London: Blackwood.

FERRERO, GUGLIELMO 1942 *The Principles of Power: The Great Political Crises of History.* New York: Putnam.

FIGGIS, JOHN N. (1896) 1922 *The Divine Right of Kings.* 2d ed. Cambridge Univ. Press. → First published as *The Theory of the Divine Right of Kings.* A paperback edition was published in 1965 by Harper.

FRANKFORT, HENRI 1948 *Kingship and the Gods: A Study of Ancient Near Eastern Religion as the Integration of Society and Nature.* Univ. of Chicago Press.

FRIEDRICH, CARL J. 1961 Political Leadership and the Problem of Charismatic Power. *Journal of Politics* 23: 3–24.

GIERKE, OTTO VON (1881) 1954 *Das deutsche Genossenschaftsrecht.* Volume 3: Die Staats- und Korporationslehren des Altertums und des Mittelalters und ihre Aufnahme in Deutschland. Graz (Austria): Akademische Druck- und Verlagsanstalt.

HECKEL, JOHANNES 1953 *Lex charitatis: Eine juristische Untersuchung über das Recht in der Theologie Martin Luthers.* Abhandlungen der Bayerischen Akademie der Wissenschaften, Phil-hist. Klasse, New Series, vol. 36. Munich: The Academy.

KANTOROWICZ, ERNST H. 1957 *The King's Two Bodies: A Study in Mediaeval Political Theology.* Princeton Univ. Press.

KERN, FRITZ (1914) 1939 *Kingship and Law in the Middle Ages.* Oxford: Blackwell. → First published as *Gottesgnadentum und Widerstandsrecht im früheren Mittelalter.*

KIRCHHEIMER, O.; and LEITES, N. 1932/1933 Bemerkungen zu Carl Schmitts *Legalität und Legitimität. Archiv für Sozialwissenschaft und Sozialpolitik* 68: 457–487.

LOCKE, JOHN (1690) 1960 *Two Treatises of Government.* Cambridge Univ. Press.

MCILWAIN, CHARLES H. (1940) 1947 *Constitutionalism: Ancient and Modern.* Rev. ed. Ithaca, N.Y.: Cornell Univ. Press. → A paperback edition was published in 1958.

MAISTRE, JOSEPH DE (1809) 1959 *Des constitutions politiques et des autres institutions humaines.* Edited by Robert Triomphe. Univ. of Strasbourg, Faculté des Lettres, Publications, Series 2, Fasc. 21. Paris: Belles Lettres.

SCHMITT, CARL 1932 *Legalität und Legitimität.* Munich and Leipzig: Duncker & Humblot.

SCHRAMM, PERCY E. 1929 *Kaiser, Rom und Renovatio: Studien und Texte zur Geschichte des römischen Erneuerungsgedankens vom Ende des Karolingischen Reiches bis zum Investiturstreit.* 2 vols. Leipzig: Teubner.

STERNBERGER, DOLF 1962 *Grund und Abgrund der Macht: Kritik der Rechtmässigkeit heutiger Regierungen.* Frankfurt am Main: Insel-Verlag.

TAEGER, FRITZ 1957–1960 *Charisma: Studien zur Geschichte des antiken Herrscherkults.* 2 vols. Stuttgart: Kohlhammer.

WEBER, MAX (1922) 1956 *Wirtschaft und Gesellschaft* 4th ed., 2 vols. Tübingen: Mohr. → Part 1 has been translated as *The Theory of Social and Economic Organization* and published by the Free Press in 1957; Chapter 7 has been translated as *Max Weber on Law in Economy and Society* and published by Harvard University Press in 1954.

WINCKELMANN, JOHANNES 1952 *Legitimität und Legalität in Max Webers Herrschaftssoziologie.* Tübingen: Mohr.

WOLZENDORFF, KURT (1916) 1961 *Staatsrecht und Naturrecht in der Lehre vom Widerstandsrecht des Volkes gegen rechtswidrige Ausübung der Staatsgewalt.* Aalen: Scientia.

LEISURE

Some authors hold that leisure has existed in all civilizations at all periods. This is not the view that will be taken in this article. Time-out is of course as venerable an institution as work itself. But leisure has certain traits that are characteristic only of the civilization born from the industrial revolution.

In the earliest known societies, work and play alike formed part of the ritual by which men sought communion with the ancestral spirits. Both these activities, although their functions differed at the practical level, had the same kind of meaning in the essential life of the community. Religious festivals embodied both work and play. Moreover, work and play were often combined. Conflict between them was either inconsequential or nonexistent, since play entered into work and became part of it. However, it would be going too far to view the shamans or witch doctors, who were exempted from ordinary labor, as a primitive form of "leisure class" in Veblen's sense. Shamans and witch doctors undertake to perform magical or religious functions that are regarded as essential to the community. "Leisure" is not a term that can be applied to societies of the archaic period.

Nor was leisure, in the modern sense, to be found in the agrarian societies of recorded history.

The working year followed a timetable written in the very passage of the days and seasons; in good weather work was hard, in bad weather it slackened off. Work of this kind had a natural rhythm to it, punctuated by rests, songs, games, and ceremonies; it was synonymous with the daily round, and in some regions began at sunrise to finish only at sunset. After work came relaxation; but even then, it was hard to tell where one ended and the other began. In the temperate zones of northern Europe, during the long winter months, the period of hard work would give way to a kind of semiactive existence during which the struggle for survival was nearly always hard. The deadly cold was regularly accompanied by famine and disease. Inactivity, under such circumstances, was something to be endured; followed (as it too often was) by a train of misfortunes, it certainly had none of the characteristics of leisure as we understand it today.

The cycle of the year was also marked by a whole series of sabbaths and feast days. The sabbath belonged to religion; feast days, however, were often occasions for a great investment of energy (not to mention food) and constituted the obverse or opposite of everyday life. But the ceremonial aspect of these celebrations could never be disregarded; they stemmed from religion, not leisure. Accordingly, even though the major European civilizations knew more than 150 workless days a year, we cannot use the concept of leisure to analyze their use of time. Let us take the example of France. In his *Projet d'une dîme royale* (a revolutionary proposal for impartial direct taxation, which was published in 1707 and immediately suppressed) Sébastien Le Prestre de Vauban used the term "unemployed" to denote these workless days; among them he singled out the "holidays"; such days were often imposed by the church, against the will of the peasants and artisans, in order to promote the carrying out of spiritual obligations. Thus the poor man in one of La Fontaine's fables ("Le savetier et le financier") is made to complain that Monsieur le Curé "is always burdening us with a sermon on some new saint" (*ll.* 28–29). In France at the beginning of the eighteenth century, there were 84 "holidays" of this sort, and to these should be added an average of about 80 days a year on which work was impossible because of "illness, frost, or personal business" (Vauban [1707] 1943, p. 18). Thus by the end of the seventeenth century, according to Vauban, French peasants and artisans (some 95 per cent of the labor force) had to reckon with 164 workless days a year. In those poverty-stricken times the majority of such days were not chosen; rather, they were imposed either by religious requirements or by lack of work.

Aristocratic and courtly leisure. Some authors, of whom de Grazia (1962) is representative, trace the origins of leisure to the way of life enjoyed by certain aristocratic classes in the course of Western civilization. But, in my opinion, neither the idle state of the ancient Greek philosophers nor even that of the gentry in the sixteenth century can be given the name of leisure. Such financially and socially privileged classes, cultured or not, paid for their own idleness with the work of their slaves, peasants, or servants. Such idleness cannot be defined in terms of its relation to work, since it neither complements nor rewards work but rather takes the place of work altogether. Of course, the aristocratic way of life has contributed in no small measure to the refinement of human culture; its ideal man was freed from work so that none of his capacities, physical or mental, should fail to be developed to the highest level. In ancient Greece, philosophers associated this ideal with wisdom; Aristotle himself argued that the work of slaves (that is, almost any form of manual labor) was incompatible with nobility of mind, and it is significant that the Greek word for having nothing to do (*scholē*) also meant "school." The courtiers of Europe, after the end of the Middle Ages, both invented and extolled the ideal of the humanist and the gentleman. The idleness of the nobility never lost its connection with the very highest values of civilization, even though many of the nobles themselves might have been mediocrities or scoundrels. Nevertheless, "leisure" is not a suitable term for referring to the activities of these idle elites, since leisure in the modern sense presupposes work.

Modern leisure. For leisure to become possible in the life of the great majority of workers, two preconditions must exist in society at large. First, society ceases to govern its activities by means of common ritual obligations. At least some of these activities (work and leisure, among others) no longer fall under the category of collective rites but become the unfettered responsibility of the individual, even though the individual's choice in the matter may still, of course, be determined by more impersonal social necessities. Second, the work by which a man earns his living is set apart from his other activities; its limits are no longer natural but arbitrary—indeed, it is organized in so definite a fashion that it can easily be separated, both in theory and in practice, from his free time.

These two necessary conditions exist only in

the social life of industrial and postindustrial civilizations; their absence from archaic and traditional agrarian civilizations means the absence of leisure. When the concept of leisure begins to infiltrate the rural life of modern societies, it is because agricultural labor is tending toward an industrial mode of organization and because rural life is already permeated by the urban values of industrialization. The same can be said of the agrarian societies of the "third world," which are in the process of raising themselves to the preindustrial level.

Definition of leisure

Having outlined the nature of leisure in general, we can now proceed to a more specific definition, since the numerous studies of leisure made during the last thirty years allow us to describe with some exactitude how the concept may and may not be applied. In the first place, leisure should be distinguished from free time, that is, time left free not only from regular employment but also from overtime and from time spent in travel to and from the work place. Free time includes leisure, as well as all the other activities that take place outside the context of gainful employment. The personal needs of eating, sleeping, and caring for one's health and appearance, as well as familial, social, civic, and religious obligations, must all be attended to in one's free time. Leisure, by contrast, will be described here as having four basic characteristics, two of which can be called negative, since they refer to the absence of certain social obligations, and two positive, since they are defined in terms of personal fulfillment. In a 1953 survey of concepts of leisure based on a sample of French laborers and white-collar workers, it was found that, in nearly every case, these four characteristics were closely associated in the mind of the respondent.

Freedom from obligations. Leisure is the result of free choice. To be sure, leisure is not the same thing as freedom, and it would be wrong to say that obligations have no part in leisure at all. However, leisure does include freedom from a certain class of obligations. It must, of course, be conceded that leisure, like other social phenomena, is subject to the operation of social forces. In the same way, since it is an activity, it must depend, like every activity, on social relationships and therefore on interpersonal obligations such as contracts or even agreements to meet at a certain time and place. It is likewise subject to the obligations that may be imposed by any of the groups and organizations, from athletic teams to film societies, that minister to its needs. But leisure does imply freedom from those institutional obligations that are prescribed by the basic forms of social organization. With respect to these institutional obligations, the obligations arising from leisure, considered as a form of social organization, always have a secondary character from society's viewpoint, regardless of how heavy they may be. To employ a dialectical mode of reasoning, leisure both implies and presupposes the existence of the fundamental obligations that are its opposite; the latter must cease before the former can begin, and each can be defined only in terms of the other.

Leisure, then, consists first and foremost in freedom from gainful employment in a place of business; similarly, it implies freedom from study that is part of a school curriculum. Leisure also includes freedom from the fundamental obligations prescribed by other basic forms of social organization such as the family, the community, and the church. Let us call this class of institutional obligations "primary obligations." Conversely, when a leisure activity becomes part of one's job (like sport to an amateur turned professional), one's studies (like a film show that all members of the school must attend), one's family life (like a Sunday walk), or one's religious or political obligations (like a political mass rally), then its nature, from a sociological point of view, undergoes a change even when its technical content has not changed at all and it affords the same satisfactions as before.

Disinterestedness. The disinterested character of leisure is the corollary, in terms of means and ends, of its freedom from primary obligations. Leisure is not motivated basically by gain, like a job; it has no utilitarian purpose, as do domestic obligations; unlike political or spiritual duties, it does not aim at any ideological or missionary purpose. True leisure precludes the use of any physical, artistic, intellectual, or social activity—in short, of any form of play—to serve any material or social end whatsoever, even though leisure, like any other activity, is subject to the laws of physical and social necessity.

It follows that, if leisure is governed in part by some commercial, utilitarian, or ideological purpose, it is no longer wholly leisure. Such leisure retains only part of its nature; we will therefore call it "semileisure." Under these conditions it is as if the circle of primary obligations partially obscured the circle of leisure; semileisure is the area where the two circles intersect. This situation exists when the athlete is paid for some of his appearances, the angler sells part of his catch, the gardener with a passion for flowers plants a few vegetables for his own consumption, or the ardent handyman repairs his own house; it can even happen when someone attends a municipal function more for the show than the ceremony, or when an office worker reads a highbrow novel so that he can let the head of his department know that he *has* read it.

Leisure and diversion. We have defined what leisure is *not* by stating its relationship to the obligations and limits imposed by the basic forms of social organization. In order to define what leisure *is*, it is necessary to state its relationship to the needs of the individual, even when the individual fulfills these needs as a willing member of a group. In nearly all the empirical studies, leisure appears to be distinguished by a search for a state of satisfaction—a state that is sought as an end in itself. This activity is of a pleasure-seeking nature. To be sure, happiness is not simply a matter of leisure, since one can be happy while carrying out basic social obligations. But the search for contentment, pleasure, and delight is one of the fundamental characteristics of leisure in modern society. In this connection, Martha Wolfenstein (1951) has spoken of "fun morality." When the desired state of satisfaction either passes or begins to wear off, the individual tends to give up the activity in question. Nobody is tied to a leisure activity by material need or by moral or legal obligations, as is the case with the activities of getting an education, earning a living, or carrying out civic or religious ceremonies. Although social pressure or habit may run counter to his decision to give up, the question of whether or not he is contented weighs more heavily with the individual in his leisure than in any other form of activity. The prime condition of leisure is the search for a state of contentment; it is enough to say "That interests me." This state can consist in the denial of all tension, study, or concentration; but it can just as well consist in voluntary effort or even in the deferment of gratification. Whether the avocation involves battling against the elements, against a competitor, or against oneself, the effort of perfecting one's performance or one's wisdom can be greater than that spent on one's regular occupation and may even approach the intensity of religious discipline. But it is an effort and a discipline that is chosen voluntarily, in the expectation of an enjoyment that is disinterested. The search for diversion is so fundamental to leisure that when the expected delight or enjoyment fails to materialize, leisure itself is denatured—a situation that is summed up by such remarks as "It was boring" or "It wasn't entertaining." Leisure, in such cases, is no longer wholly itself, but suffers impoverishment.

Leisure and personality. All the manifest functions of leisure, to judge from their effect on the persons concerned, answer to individual needs, as distinguished from the primary obligations imposed by society. Thus leisure is directly associated both with the possibility that the individual may deteriorate (for instance, if he becomes an alcoholic), and with the fact that the individual is free to defend the integrity of his personality against the attacks of an urban industrial society that is becoming less and less natural and more and more regimented and run by the clock. It is associated with the realization, whether encouraged or discouraged, of unbiased human potentialities —in short, with the whole man. Such realization, whether or not it accords with social needs, is conceived as an end in itself.

The positive functions of leisure can be summed up as follows. (1) It offers the individual a chance to shake off the fatigue of work that, because it is imposed, interferes with his natural biological rhythms. It is a recuperative force, or at least an opportunity to do nothing. (2) Through entertainment, whether of a sort permitted or forbidden by society, leisure opens up new worlds, both real and imaginary, in which the individual can escape from the daily boredom of performing a set of limited and routine tasks. (3) Finally, leisure makes it possible for the individual to leave behind the routines and stereotypes forced on him by the workings of basic social institutions, and to enter into a realm of self-transcendence where his creative powers are set free to oppose or to reinforce the dominant values of his civilization. Leisure in the truest sense of the word fulfills all three of these basic functions and satisfies the human need that corresponds to each. Leisure that fails to offer all of these three kinds of choice at any time is leisure that, with regard to the needs of the human personality in modern society, must be considered seriously defective.

The sociology of leisure

The importance of leisure in the development of our civilization was foreseen by social thinkers from the very beginning of industrial society. In some contexts Marx treated work in itself as the first need of man, but in others he qualified this statement by adding that work would become fit for man only when it had been transformed by collective ownership, automation, great increases in free time, and the transcending of the antithesis between work and leisure by the creation of the unalienated "whole man." Comte and Proudhon differed from Marx in their conceptions of the society of the future, but all three attached great importance to conquering leisure by means of technological progress and social emancipation. And they all associated the growth of leisure with raising the workers' level of education and increasing the part played by them in public life.

The realities of leisure in the twentieth century, as sociologists have observed them in both socialist and capitalist societies, have turned out to be more complex and less easily defined. The first modern pamphlet in favor of leisure for the worker was written in Europe by Paul Lafargue (1883), who was a militant socialist; its title was *Le droit à la paresse* ("The Right to Be Lazy"). But it was in the United States that the foundations were laid for the sociology of leisure by Thorstein Veblen's *The Theory of the Leisure Class* (1899). Veblen analyzed the different types of idlers that he found among the bourgeoisie; he exposed the conspicuous consumption indulged in by the bourgeoisie in its quest for social status. But it was not until the 1920s and 1930s that there appeared, both in Europe and in the United States, the first empirical studies of leisure by sociologists. The introduction of the eight-hour day awakened both the hopes and the anxieties of social reformers, who wondered whether the extra free time would be used for self-improvement or for dissipation. In the U.S.S.R., the work of Strumilin (1925) inspired research on the "time budgets" of individuals, at the same time that the Soviet government developed an official policy on the organization of leisure. In 1924 the International Labor Office organized the first international conference on the free time of the worker; it was attended by 300 delegates from 18 nations. There was a general feeling that as the time spent on work decreased, leisure activities would have to become more organized (*International Labour Review* 1924). Research projects were launched in the United States; the most famous of them, by Robert and Helen Lynd (1929; 1937), devoted much space to the study of leisure activities, both traditional and modern, and to the way in which they were organized. In 1934 George A. Lundberg, in a study that has since become a classic, defined leisure as the *opposite* of those activities that are on the whole instruments to other ends rather than ends in themselves (Lundberg et al. 1934).

After World War II the sociology of leisure took on a new dimension and new levels of meaning. The United States was beginning to grapple with the problems of mass society, namely, mass consumption and mass culture. In this new context the paradox of leisure nourished a whole new crop of studies. In 1950 David Riesman's *The Lonely Crowd* appeared, a work of which nearly one million copies have been printed and which has had a great influence not only in the United States but in every part of the world. Riesman argued in favor of the hypothesis that modern man, viewed in terms of his social character, has known only two revolutions. The first began with the Renaissance, when the "tradition-directed" man whose social character had been derived entirely from the community began to be governed by the norms and values of the family and so became "inner-directed." Finally, about the middle of the twentieth century, the second of these revolutions appeared in those countries that had entered the stage of mass consumption and mass culture. In this period man has begun to be governed by the norms and values conveyed by the mass media of communication on the one hand and by peer groups on the other. Under such circumstances man becomes "other-directed." Reflections on mass leisure were therefore central to Riesman's theoretical perspective. A few years later there appeared the first collections of readings on the topic of "mass leisure" (Larrabee & Meyersohn 1958; Rosenberg & White 1957). Finally, decisive progress was made in the empirical verification of these new ideas on the relationship of leisure and culture in mass society (see especially Havighurst & Feigenbaum 1959; Wilensky 1964).

In Europe, during the same period, the sociology of leisure has made almost equally remarkable progress; the work of Georges Friedmann, in particular, gives a special place to the role of leisure in "relocating" man in a civilization dominated by technology. In England B. S. Rowntree and G. R. Lavers' *English Life and Leisure* (1951) has inspired a whole series of sociological monographs and research studies that have evoked considerable response in other countries, especially Holland. Large-scale public-opinion polling from 1954 onwards on the way in which young people spend their leisure is beginning to result in vigorous government programs stressing character building and the provision of facilities for leisure. With these problems in mind, in 1953 Joffre Dumazedier began the research that finally resulted in *Vers une civilisation du loisir?* ("Towards a Civilization of Leisure?" 1962) and in *Le loisir et la ville* ("Urban Leisure") (Dumazedier & Ripert 1966).

In the socialist countries, likewise, the study of leisure has undergone expansion. For instance, in the U.S.S.R. during the period 1956–1962 the gradual replacement of the eight-hour working day by one of seven hours stimulated renewed inquiry, in the tradition of Strumilin, into time budgets and leisure-time activities (Prudenskii 1964; Petrosian 1965). The first empirical study of leisure in a socialist setting that made use of the very latest sociological research methods took place in Yugoslavia (Ahtik 1963). The empirical study of sociology has also taken remarkable strides forward in Poland, thanks to the efforts of the Center for the Study of Mass Culture, which is affiliated with the Polish Academy of Sciences.

Applications. The sociology of leisure has made it possible, for the first time, to draw empirical comparisons between the working class culture of different or contrasting political and economic systems. In 1956 the first comparative study of leisure in Europe was launched, dealing with the leisure of workers in six European cities, each in a different country. The countries included in the survey were Yugoslavia, Poland, France, Finland, Denmark, and the German Federal Republic.

The vitality of the sociology of leisure has given rise to a number of problem-oriented approaches. Leisure has been studied in its relation to work (Friedmann 1958; Riesman 1964), the family (Scheuch 1960; Anderson 1961), religion (Pieper 1948), politics (Lipset et al. 1956), and culture (Kaplan 1960; Dumazedier 1962; Wilensky 1964). It has been treated as a temporal framework (Prudenskii 1964; Petrosian 1965; Szalai 1966), a complex of activities (Littünen 1962), a system of values (de Grazia 1962), and in several other ways.

The sociology of leisure also exhibits great methodological variety; it is not marked by adherence to any particular method, but by use of any and all available methods. Thus, although empirical studies are more common, we find a strong historical tradition, from Veblen to Riesman and de Grazia. The most important project now in progress concerns time budgets; it is a comparative study, using national samples from the German Federal Republic, Belgium, Austria, France, Hungary, Poland, and the U.S.S.R., directed by Alexander Szalai, a Hungarian scholar, under the auspices of the European Center for Coordination of Research and Documentation in the Social Sciences.

It is to be expected that in the future the different industrial and preindustrial societies will stand in increasing need of research, especially in order to: (1) measure the effective limitations of time, distance, money, and so on, that are preventing the transformation of free time into genuine leisure in the life of numerous classes and categories of workers; (2) evaluate the resources available for leisure in the cultural development of whole societies.

In the postindustrial societies now entering the phase of mass consumption, specific problems have arisen, and will continue to arise with even greater intensity. It is the ambivalence of leisure values in popular culture that will pose the greatest problems to sociologists. Will commitment to leisure values be balanced by commitment to occupational, associational, political, and spiritual values, or will leisure threaten all these other values, thus placing in jeopardy the active participation of citizens in directing the future of their society? Finally, since leisure values are themselves diverse, will the values of entertainment and unfettered personal development join forces to create a new ideal of individual happiness and social well-being? Or, on the contrary, will the values of entertainment, artificially hypertrophied by an irresponsible commercial system, come to play, in certain countries, the role of a new "opiate of the people," while in certain other countries a unilateral and oppressive government policy for leisure activities risks truncating the complex phenomenon of leisure, encouraging boredom and malingering by way of reaction? In the last analysis, the whole future of man in industrial and postindustrial civilization is bound up with the answers to these questions. Today, they are the most important questions facing the sociology of leisure.

JOFFRE DUMAZEDIER

[*Directly related are the entries* LABOR FORCE, *article on* HOURS OF WORK; TIME BUDGETS. *Other relevant material may be found in* AUTOMATION; COMMUNICATION, MASS; GAMBLING; INDUSTRIAL RELATIONS; TIME; WORKERS; *and in the biographies of* LUNDBERG; MARX; VEBLEN.]

BIBLIOGRAPHY

AHTIK, VITO 1963 Participation socio-politique des ouvriers d'industrie yougoslaves. *Sociologie du travail* 5:1–23.

ANDERSON, NELS 1961 *Work and Leisure.* New York: Free Press.

CAILLOIS, ROGER (1958) 1961 *Man, Play and Games.* New York: Free Press. → First published as *Les jeux et les hommes.*

DE GRAZIA, SEBASTIAN 1962 *Of Time, Work and Leisure.* New York: Twentieth Century Fund.

DUMAZEDIER, JOFFRE 1962 *Vers une civilisation du loisir?* Paris: Éditions du Seuil.

DUMAZEDIER, JOFFRE; and RIPERT, A. 1966 *Le loisir et la ville.* Paris: Éditions du Seuil.

FRIEDMANN, G. 1958 *Le travail en miettes: Spécialisation et loisirs.* Paris: Gallimard.

HAVIGHURST, ROBERT J.; and FEIGENBAUM, KENNETH 1959 Leisure and Life-style. *American Journal of Sociology* 64:396–404.

HUIZINGA, JOHAN (1938) 1949 *Homo ludens: A Study of the Play-element in Culture.* London: Routledge. → First published in Dutch.

International Labour Review [1924], 9, no. 6.

KAPLAN, MAX 1960 *Leisure in America: A Social Inquiry.* New York: Wiley.

LAFARGUE, PAUL (1883) 1917 *The Right to Be Lazy, And Other Studies.* Chicago: Kerr. → First published as *Le droit à la paresse.*

LARRABEE, ERIC; and MEYERSOHN, ROLF (editors) (1958) 1960 *Mass Leisure.* Glencoe, Ill.: Free Press.

LIPSET, SEYMOUR M.; TROW, MARTIN A.; and COLEMAN, JAMES S. 1956 *Union Democracy: The Internal Politics of the International Typographical Union.* Glencoe, Ill.: Free Press. → A paperback edition was published in 1962 by Doubleday.

LITTÜNEN, YRJÖ 1962 Activity and Social Dependence. Unpublished manuscript. → Paper delivered before the World Congress of Sociology, Fifth, Washington, D.C., September 2–8, 1962.

LUNDBERG, GEORGE A. et al. 1934 *Leisure: A Suburban Study.* New York: Columbia Univ. Press.

LYND, ROBERT S.; and LYND, HELEN M. (1929) 1930 *Middletown: A Study in Contemporary American Culture.* New York: Harcourt. → A paperback edition was published in 1959.

LYND, ROBERT S.; and LYND, HELEN M. 1937 *Middletown in Transition: A Study in Cultural Conflicts.* New York: Harcourt. → A paperback edition was published in 1963.

MARX, KARL; and ENGELS, FRIEDRICH (1875–1891) 1959 *Critique of the Gotha Programme.* Moscow: Foreign Languages Publishing House. → Written by Marx in 1875 as "Randglossen zum Programm der deutschen Arbeiterpartei." First published with notes by Engels in 1891.

PETROSIAN, G. S. 1965 *Vnerabochee vremiia trudiashchikhsia v SSSR* (The Leisure Time of Workers in the USSR). Moscow: Ekonomika.

PIEPER, JOSEF (1948) 1960 *Leisure: The Basis of Culture.* New York: Pantheon. → First published as *Musse und Kult.*

PRUDENSKII, GERMAN A. 1964 *Vremia i trud* (Time and Work). Moscow: Mysl.

RIESMAN, DAVID 1950 *The Lonely Crowd: A Study of the Changing American Character.* New Haven: Yale Univ. Press. → An abridged paperback edition was published in 1960.

RIESMAN, DAVID 1964 *Abundance for What? And Other Essays.* Garden City, N.Y.: Doubleday.

ROSENBERG, BERNARD; and WHITE, DAVID M. (editors) 1957 *Mass Culture: The Popular Arts in America.* Glencoe, Ill.: Free Press.

ROWNTREE, BENJAMIN S.; and LAVERS, G. R. 1951 *English Life and Leisure: A Social Study.* London: Longmans.

SCHEUCH, ERWIN K. 1960 Family Cohesion in Leisure Time. *Sociological Review* 8:37–61.

STRUMILIN, STANISLAV G. 1925 *Problemy ekonomiki truda* (Problems of Labor Economy). Moscow: Izdatel'stvo "Voprosy Truda."

STRUMILIN, STANISLAV G. 1961 *Problemy sotsializma i kommunizma v SSSR.* Moscow: Izdatel'stvo Ekonomicheskoi Literatury.

SZALAI, ALEXANDER 1966 Trends in Comparative Time-budget Research. *American Behavioral Scientist* 9, no. 9:3–8.

VAUBAN, SÉBASTIEN LE PRESTRE DE (1707) 1943 *Projet d'une dîme royale.* Paris: Guillaumin. → Published in English in 1708 as *A Project for a Royal Tythe, or General Tax.*

VEBLEN, THORSTEIN (1899) 1953 *The Theory of the Leisure Class: An Economic Study of Institutions.* Rev. ed. New York: New American Library. → A paperback edition was published in 1959.

WILENSKY, HAROLD L. 1960 Work, Careers, and Social Integration. *International Social Science Journal.* 12: 543–560.

WILENSKY, HAROLD L. 1961 Social Structure, Popular Culture and Mass Behavior: Some Research Implications. *Studies in Public Communication* 3:15–22.

WILENSKY, HAROLD L. 1964 Mass Society and Mass Culture: Interdependence or Independence? *American Sociological Review* 29:173–197.

WOLFENSTEIN, MARTHA (1951) 1960 The Emergence of Fun Morality. Pages 86–96 in Eric Larrabee and Rolf Meyersohn (editors), *Mass Leisure.* Glencoe, Ill.: Free Press.

LENIN

Vladimir Il'ich Ul'ianov (who in 1901 began to call himself Lenin) was born on April 22, 1870, in Simbirsk, now Ul'ianovsk, a provincial town on the Volga, one of six children in an educated middle-class family. When he died on January 21, 1924, near Moscow, he was acclaimed as "the greatest genius of mankind, creator of the Communist Party of the Soviet Union, founder of the Union of Soviet Socialist Republics, the leader and teacher of the peoples of the whole world." In different measure the events of his personal life, his intellectual life, and his active political life contributed to this metamorphosis.

His father, of lower middle-class origin, was a graduate of the university in Kazan and for many years taught mathematics and physics in secondary schools in the Volga region. In 1869 he was appointed a school inspector and, shortly afterward, director of the "people's schools" in Simbirsk province, thus earning the rank of nobleman. Ul'ianov's mother was a woman of indomitable character. Daughter of a country doctor with little money and a large family, she had received her schooling at home. The boy Vladimir, the second son, was an intelligent and conscientious student, and a good swimmer, skater, and chess player. He was much impressed by his father's talk of the "darkness" of life in the villages and of the arbitrary treatment of peasants by officials. A voracious reader, Ul'ianov became well acquainted at an early age with the writings of the great Russian authors, from Pushkin through Turgenev to Tolstoi, and was especially interested in the works of Nekrasov; he was also aware of such protorevolutionary writers as Belinskii, Herzen, Chernyshevskii, Pisarev, and Dobroliubov. But there was no hint in these early intellectual activities that he would become a revolutionary.

The first blow to young Ul'ianov's happy existence was the death of his father in 1886. An even worse shock was the arrest, in March 1887, of his elder brother, Alexander, whose brilliant research on worms at the university in St. Petersburg had promised a bright future but who, unknown to his family, had been active in terrorist revolutionary circles. Alexander was executed for having plotted the assassination of the tsar. The Ul'ianov family, shunned by local society, moved to a village not far from Kazan. Ul'ianov was admitted to the university in Kazan, though only on the strength of a character reference from the director of the Simbirsk Gymnasium, father of Alexander Kerenskii, the man Lenin was later to overthrow.

Ul'ianov was arrested in December 1887 for his part in a student demonstration against a university rule that enjoined students from forming organizations. Expelled from the university and forbidden to go abroad for study, he threw himself into preparation for external examinations and was finally permitted to take these in the spring of 1891, thus winning a first-degree diploma from the law faculty of the university in St. Petersburg. For two years he held a job in a Samara law office; at the same time he was studying Marxism and engaging in open criticism of the *narodniki*, activities which he continued in St. Petersburg, where he went in 1893 "in quest of the proletariat." By the spring of 1895 he had become well enough known to be sent by his comrades to visit Georgii Plekhanov, the "grandfather of Russian Marxism," in Geneva. Before his return he met Paul Lafargue, son-in-law of Karl Marx, and the veteran German Marxist Wilhelm Liebknecht but was unable to see the dying Friedrich Engels.

That fall young Ul'ianov joined with L. Martov (pseudonym of Iulii O. Tsederbaum) and a handful of other intellectuals to form the so-called Union of Struggle for the Emancipation of the Working Class, which planned to publish an illegal newspaper, *Rabochee delo* ("The Workers' Cause"). The first issue was confiscated, and Ul'ianov was among those arrested. Imprisonment prevented him from participating in the vigorous strike movement of 1896, but with the aid of books borrowed from the leading libraries of the capital he was able to continue his study and writing. In February 1897 he was released to make his arrangements for a three-year period of exile at the Siberian village of Shushenskoe in Yenisei province, near the modern coal basin of Kuznetsk. There he lived in a peasant hut, his main source of income being the government allowance of 8 rubles a month. A year later Nadezhda Krupskaia, whom he had met in St. Petersburg in 1894, arrived with her mother for a visit and was permitted to remain in Siberia on the condition that she and Ul'ianov be formally married.

In Siberia, he continued his feverish literary activity, in particular pursuing his study of the spread of capitalist relations in the peasant villages. Aware of serious gaps in his education, he undertook a systematic study of quite diverse philosophical views, while also broadening his knowledge of the writings of Marx and Engels. He completed his first major work, *The Development of Capitalism in Russia* (1899*a*), published under the pseudonym Vladimir Il'in. It was at this time also that he read Eduard Bernstein's *Die Voraussetzungen des Sozialismus und die Aufgaben der Sozialdemokratie* ("The Prerequisites of Socialism and the Tasks of Social Democracy"). Bernstein's thesis, revising some basic tenets of Marxism, shocked Ul'ianov profoundly, and he was no less outraged by the *Credo* of the "Economists." He issued his own *Protest* (1899*b*) against this penetration of Russia by the revisionist heresy, and it was adopted by a conference of exiles in Siberia (meeting ostensibly to celebrate a child's birthday).

Political achievements

From this time on, Ul'ianov's consuming passion was the organization of a disciplined Russian Marxist party capable of effectively combating all revisionist tendencies. To this end, he felt, it was necessary to found an all-Russian Marxist newspaper. Released from exile at the beginning of 1900 but forbidden to reside in either of the two capitals or in university or major industrial towns, he promptly applied for permission to go abroad and in July was able to leave for Switzerland. In Geneva, Plekhanov's insistence on controlling the proposed newspaper so offended Ul'ianov that the project almost fell through. However, a compromise was reached whereby Ul'ianov was permitted to arrange for the publication of *Iskra* ("The Spark") in Munich; there Krupskaia joined him in April 1901. The first number was printed (in Leipzig) in January 1901, and a monthly periodical, *Zar'ia* ("Dawn"), followed in December. It was in the course of this year that he began to sign his articles "Lenin."

It was in 1901 also that Lenin began to write his second—and most significant—major work, *What Is to Be Done?*, published at Stuttgart in March 1902. Meanwhile, disagreements between Lenin and his editorial colleagues in Switzerland multiplied; in particular, Lenin's insistence on emphasizing the "dictatorship of the proletariat" in connection with the formulation of an agrarian program irritated Plekhanov, who opposed Lenin's "polemics."

Mainly at Lenin's insistence it was decided to call the Second Party Congress to create an all-Russian party, a task at which the Minsk Congress of 1898 had failed. Lenin himself devoted immense effort, by voluminous correspondence with *Iskra* agents in Russia, to guarantee a workable majority of reliable delegates. The congress met in Brussels in the summer of 1903 but found it expedient to move to London. It was attended by 43 delegates, assigned 51 votes; of these, 44 could be counted on to support the *Iskra* position. With the support of his colleagues on the *Iskra* editorial board Lenin won adoption of his draft program, though two Economist delegates fought hard to include a reference to class consciousness as a precondition to establishment of the "dictatorship of the proletariat." However, a split developed among *Iskra* supporters over Lenin's effort to secure adoption of his version of the first paragraph of a party statute, embodying his conception of the dominance of a revolutionary elite. Despite the somewhat unexpected support of Plekhanov, Lenin's formulation was defeated; Martov's broader definition of party membership was adopted by a vote of 28–22, with one abstention. The subsequent withdrawal from the congress, over other issues, of the five delegates of the Jewish Bund and of two Economists changed the balance of strength. By vigorous caucusing Lenin was able to whip together a fairly solid bloc of 24 votes, which enabled him to carry the election of his candidates to the new editorial board of *Iskra* (now confirmed as the new party's "central organ") and to the new central committee. It was by virtue of these votes, not of the statistics of later party allegiance, that Lenin's followers for decades boasted the name *bol'sheviki* ("majority men").

Lenin's triumph was brief. Plekhanov soon abandoned Lenin's "hard" *Iskra* line, and control of the party and of its central committee passed to the *men'sheviki* ("minority men"). Lenin found himself doomed to years of bitter wrangling with his former colleagues. In the revolution of 1905 he was able to exercise almost no influence. He did not return to Russia until, with the October Manifesto, the autocracy had apparently surrendered. In Russia, he continued to denounce all socialists who would not follow him, and all liberals. After some wavering he supported boycott of the elections to the Duma, and he gave his blessing to, though he did not participate in, an abortive armed uprising in Moscow. After a few months of underground existence, of shifting from one hiding place to another, Lenin withdrew to the relative security of Finland. Pained by his failure to dominate the Fourth ("Unity") Congress of the Russian Social Democrats, in Stockholm (April–May 1906), he took some comfort from his successes at the Bolshevik-organized Fifth Congress in London (May 1907) and was considerably heartened by participation in the Stuttgart Congress of the Second International (August 1907), the first international congress he had ever attended. At the end of 1907 he abandoned his base in Finland and slipped back to Switzerland.

The next ten years were the bitterest and most difficult of Lenin's life. He became wholly occupied not with the direct struggle to combat capitalism and tsarism but with a preliminary, many-faceted battle to destroy the influence of all those who professed devotion to the cause of the proletariat, as he did, but who formulated its task in ways he considered unacceptable. Although Lenin was always ready to score a point at the expense of his rivals, he loudly and insistently denounced "opportunism" as the greatest brake on the progress of the socialist revolution. Thus, he worked himself into a position of almost total isolation within the revolutionary movement. This position, however, was ultimately to prove most advantageous to him. His name became one of the best known among the revolutionaries; but he was dissociated from all the failures of the other leading figures and thus was able, at a crucial moment, to offer fresh hope to the despairing.

In 1912, Lenin's Bolshevik adherents in Russia secured permission from the tsarist government to publish a newspaper called *Pravda* ("Truth"). Lenin at once moved from Switzerland to Cracow and then to Poronino, near the Austrian–Russian border. Here he could hope to keep in maximum contact with, and direct the policy of, the new organ. He could also supervise the activities of the "Bolshevik six" in the newly elected Fourth Duma. Lenin selected Roman Malinovskii to be their spokesman, unaware that he was on the police payroll. Although Bolsheviks from abroad were regularly arrested on their arrival in Russia, Lenin long remained obdurately blind to this circumstance, despite repeated protests from more sensitive friends.

On the outbreak of war in 1914 Lenin was arrested by the Austrian police on suspicion of espionage. The absurdity of the charge facilitated his release on condition that he return to Switzerland. There he remained, in devastating impotence, attending international socialist conferences at Zimmerwald and Kienthal, only to see the meager fruits of his vigorous efforts ruined by the subsequent defection of his allies. It is to this period that belongs the work of which Bolsheviks have remained most proud, *Imperialism, the Highest Stage of Capitalism*, completed in the summer of 1916.

At the end of January 1917, Lenin consoled himself—and all who would still heed him—with the thought that the tsar, fearing the outbreak of a bourgeois revolution in Russia, would not dare make a separate peace with Germany. Therefore, the war would continue, enormously enhancing the chances that Europe (*not* Russia) would begin the socialist revolution. Six weeks later, on March 15, 1917, to his surprise and delight Lenin learned from the Swiss newspapers that the Russian autocracy had collapsed and that a "Provisional Government" had been set up. A new danger loomed—the possibility that all elements in Russia might rally to the new regime. Lenin felt it was an urgent necessity that he reach Russia and prevent the Bolsheviks from making fools of themselves. The German government was likewise persuaded that Lenin's presence in Russia was an urgent need, though not for the same reasons. It was arranged, through Swiss intermediaries, that Lenin and other Russian exiles in Switzerland, whatever their political complexion, be permitted to travel incommunicado (on the "sealed train") across Germany. Via Sweden and Finland, Lenin reached Petrograd on the evening of April 16, 1917. From that moment, one might say, Lenin had no personal life, for his biography and the further history of the Russian Revolution became inextricably intertwined.

Lenin acknowledged that "Russia is now the freest country in the world"; yet he refused to take any part in enabling the new regime to establish itself. Instead he watched for every opportunity to overthrow it in the name of a new absolutism, "the dictatorship of the proletariat." He did seize power successfully on November 7, 1917, and thereafter, notwithstanding frequent vigorous opposition from tried associates, Lenin was in fact able to guide the ever-shifting policies of the new "Soviet" regime until he was incapacitated in May 1922 by a paralytic stroke. Sufficiently recovered to partially resume his duties, he was rendered wholly impotent by a second stroke and remained so for almost a year before his final, fatal stroke.

Major writings

The explanation of Lenin's political success cannot be found in his intellectual achievements, for he was of no significance as an abstract thinker. His most scholarly work, *The Development of Capitalism in Russia* (1899*a*), was simply a tract to prove definitively the folly of the *narodnik* concept of the role of the peasantry in Russia. He showed that the peasantry was ceasing to be a uniform mass and was splitting into capitalist and proletarian sectors (a development of which Witte and Stolypin became aware independently). In Lenin's view this process should be encouraged by the abolition of landlordism, which was slowing the development of capitalist relations in the village. Thus, the proletarian, "depeasantized," element in the countryside would strengthen the urban proletariat, whose lack of numbers was compensated for by its concentration, fitting it to lead a mass movement of the village poor to overthrow tsarism and capitalism together.

In *What Is to Be Done?*—directed against the *narodniki*, and against the Economists as well—Lenin developed the thought that the working class, left to its own spontaneous strivings, would never become socialist. Only the conscious effort of "educated representatives of the propertied classes," i.e., the Marxists, would be able to "*divert* the labor movement, with its spontaneous trade-unionist striving, from under the wing of the bourgeoisie, and to bring it under the wing of revolutionary Social-Democracy." This viewpoint was embodied in the program adopted by the Second Congress, in preparation for which *What Is to Be Done?* had been published. It continued to dominate all Lenin's thinking and actions and is perhaps the very essence of "Leninism" as distinct from Marxism.

Imperialism, the Highest Stage of Capitalism has been hailed as "the most outstanding contribution to the treasury of creative Marxism" and as evidence of Lenin's stature as "a scholar of genius, a most conscientious researcher, and the greatest fighter for revolution" (Moscow [1960] 1963, p. 274). It did indeed assert as a scientific prediction that imperialism spells the doom of capitalism and, because it creates the objective conditions for world revolution, also represents the eve of socialist revolution. In other writings at this time, however, Lenin suggested that the "law of uneven development" might make possible the victory of socialism in a single country.

Even less original than *Imperialism* was his other famous tract, *State and Revolution* (1917*a*), written after the failure of the July uprising as a blueprint for the immediate future. He argued that the existing "hypocritically democratic" regime was merely a "dictatorship of the bourgeoisie" and must be replaced by a "dictatorship of the proletariat," a term that Lenin never ceased to think of as meaning dictatorship of the Bolsheviks. He was careful to emphasize the distinction between the two stages, "socialism" ("from each according to his abilities, to each according to his labor") and "communism" ("from each according to his abilities, to each according to his needs"), a distinction that Stalin was later to cause to be written into the 1936 constitution. Lenin believed that although social inequalities would persist under "socialism," it was impossible to attain to "communism" without an indefinitely prolonged period of "socialism."

Political realism

Lenin's forte was an extraordinary ability, found also in men such as Bismarck, to analyze a given practical situation and to give things an unexpected push in the general direction in which he wished them to move. He did not rely on abstract ideas as guides to policy; he attacked Trotsky for using "abstract (and therefore empty) words." Although, like many other Russian middle-class youths of his generation, he was impressed by the grandiose aspects of Marxism, he never fully committed himself to their implications as worked out in western Europe. On the morrow of his return to Russia in 1917 he denounced " 'Bolshevik' prerevolutionary antiques" on the grounds that they failed to grasp the "incontestable truth that a Marxist must take cognizance of real life, of the true facts of *reality*, and not cling to a theory of yesterday, . . . which like all theories . . . only *comes near* to embracing life in all its complexity. Theory . . . is grey, but green is the eternal tree of life" ([1917*b*] 1964, p. 45).

His leadership of the Bolsheviks during the revolution and in the still more chaotic years that ensued involved a shrewd following of events rather than a genuinely creative initiative. With the definite goal of seizure—and retention—of power in mind, he showed true realism, even adopting positions that to many seemed at the moment completely unrealistic.

His initial demand, in the "April Theses" (announced to his party colleagues the day after his arrival in Petrograd: see 1917*c*), for "all power to the Soviet" surely seemed ridiculous, for the Bolsheviks were only a small minority in the Petrograd Soviet. Yet it turned out to be the only way to save the Bolsheviks from joining the Soviet majority in support of the Provisional Government and thus to absolve them from responsibility in the eyes of the masses later when discontents and disappointments had accumulated. (To be sure, this demand involved the Bolsheviks in the premature July uprising, from whose consequences they were rescued, however, by the Kornilov affair.)

It was realism, too, that prompted Lenin to insist on an armed uprising in November rather than wait for the "uncertain voting" at the Second Congress of Soviets. He was aware, as some of his associates were not, that the masses were not swinging to active support of the Bolsheviks, that disappointments and weariness had bred tremendous apathy, and that there was no likelihood of serious opposition to any group that would act with vigor, particularly if it could wrap itself in the cloak of the soviets and would promise speedy convocation of the long-dreamt-of Constituent Assembly.

His extrication of Russia from the war, similarly, was not the realization of a plan thought out in advance; it was the result of realistic yielding to facts as they gradually became obvious to him. The initial "Appeal to the Peoples and Governments of All Warring Countries" (1917*d*) simply called for a general armistice (Lenin then rejected a separate one) and conclusion of the "democratic peace" that had been proposed by the Provisional Government. Only after weeks of silence on the part of the Allies did Lenin approve of separate negotiations with the Central Powers, and only on the same "democratic" terms. When it became clear that the Central Powers would not make a separate peace on the basis of no annexations and no indemnities, Lenin addressed pointed questions to a congress of army representatives: If negotiations were broken off, would the Germans, despite the winter weather, launch an offensive? If they did, could the army fight or would it flee in panic? Lenin was tempted by Wilson's Fourteen Points address, of January 8, 1918, to contemplate renewal of the war with practical assistance from the Allies. Even in the face of a German ultimatum, Lenin advised dragging out the negotiations in the hope that the expected German revolution would break out and save Russia. Only when Trotsky's defiant "no war, no peace" declaration precipitated the final rupture of the negotiations did Lenin begin to insist on immediate acceptance of the German terms, arguing that, no matter how onerous the

Brest-Litovsk terms were, they would leave the Bolsheviks in control of an amputated Russia, with a "breathing spell" to consolidate their power in preparation for the inevitable "revolutionary war" against the whole capitalist world.

This same realism showed in his handling of the peasant question. Rejecting as irrelevant the criticism that the original Bolshevik decree on the land problem meant scrapping the established Bolshevik program in favor of the policy advocated by the Socialist Revolutionaries, Lenin had exclaimed, "We must follow life." If the Bolsheviks were to remain in power, the peasant masses must be acquiescent; otherwise there would be no food for the towns. When, however, the peasants had clearly tired of accepting worthless Bolshevik paper in exchange for their surplus grain, Lenin promptly abandoned his principle that "the general and basic source of any right to the use of agricultural land is individual labor." He called for a crusade—not, of course, against the peasantry but against the "village bourgeoisie"—to "carry the class war into the countryside" with the aid of the "village poor" (*Polnoe sobranie sochinenii*, vol. 36, pp. 368–369).

His attitude toward the Constituent Assembly also reflected keen appraisal of the realities of the moment rather than any previously elaborated ideological position. At the moment of the seizure of power, when the Bolsheviks still needed the semblance of democracy and there was at least some hope that the Bolsheviks and their Left Socialist Revolutionary allies might win a slender majority, Lenin had been willing to gamble on permitting the election of a Constituent Assembly. When, however, despite Bolshevik control of the power centers, the elections went overwhelmingly against the Bolsheviks and their allies, he flatly declared, "The Soviets are superior to any parliament, to any Constituent Assembly" (*ibid.*, vol. 35, p. 140). After it had met for one night, Lenin announced, "We will not give up Soviet power for anything in the world," and the assembly was dissolved (*ibid.*, vol. 36, p. 242).

Wherever one turns in examining the various policies for which at various times he fought so vigorously, the same theme recurs. Never did Lenin argue for action on the basis of ideas he had advanced in his major theoretical works. In combating the "Left Communists" (April 1920), he wrote them off as "doctrinaires of revolution," adding that "God himself has ordained that for a time the young should talk such nonsense." In advocating the abandonment of the policy of confiscating all surplus grain, the basic step in the introduction of the New Economic Policy, he argued: "We know that only agreement with the peasantry can save the socialist revolution in Russia, unless revolution begins in other countries. . . . [The] peasantry is not content with the form of relations we have established with it . . . and will not go on living this way. . . . [We] are sober enough politicians to say right out: 'Let's reconsider our policy in relation to the peasantry' " (*ibid.*, vol. 43, p. 59). In demanding at the Third Congress of the Third International that that body switch from the aggressive position he had urged on it a year earlier, he acknowledged:

> When we began the international revolution . . . [it] seemed clear to us that without the support of international world revolution the victory of a proletarian revolution was impossible. . . . In other large, capitalistically more developed countries the revolution has not broken out even yet. . . .
>
> What must we do now? We need fundamental preparation of the revolution and deep study of its concrete development in advanced capitalist countries. . . . As for our Russian Republic, we must take advantage of this brief breathing spell to adapt our tactics to the zigzag line of history. (*ibid.*, vol. 44, pp. 36–37)

In celebrating the fourth anniversary of the seizure of power, Lenin admitted:

> We thought—or, it would be more accurate to say, we assumed without adequate consideration—that by direct orders of the proletarian state we could get state production and state distribution of products going on a communistic basis in a land of petty peasants. Life showed us our mistake. . . . Not directly on the basis of enthusiasm, but . . . on the basis of *personal* interest, on the basis of *individual* [or *personal*; in Russian, *lichnyi*] incentive, on the basis of economic calculation, will you labor to construct the first solid footbridge leading in a land of petty peasants by way of state capitalism to socialism; you will not otherwise attain to communism. . . . This is what life has told us. This is what the objective course of development of the revolution has told us. (*ibid.*, vol. 44, p. 151, italics added)
>
> . . . It is individual incentive that raises production; we need increase in production above all and no matter what. (*ibid.*, vol. 44, p. 152)

This "lesson in tactics," far more than his so-called testament penned in the interval between his first and second strokes, was the real guideline Lenin left to his successors.

JESSE D. CLARKSON

[*For the historical context of Lenin's work, see* MARXISM *and* SOCIALISM; *and the biographies of* MARX *and* TROTSKY. *For discussion of the subsequent development of Lenin's ideas, see* COMMUNISM *and* IMPERIALISM.]

WORKS BY LENIN

The writings of Lenin listed below were first published in Russian.

(1899*a*) 1960 The Development of Capitalism in Russia: The Process of the Formation of a Home Market for Large-scale Industry. Volume 3, pages 23–607 in Vladimir I. Lenin, *Collected Works.* 4th ed. Moscow: Foreign Languages Publishing House.

(1899*b*) 1960 A Protest by Russian Social-Democrats. Volume 4, pages 167–182 in Vladimir I. Lenin, *Collected Works.* 4th ed. Moscow: Foreign Languages Publishing House.

(1902) 1961 What Is to Be Done? Volume 5, pages 347–529 in Vladimir I. Lenin, *Collected Works.* 4th ed. Moscow: Foreign Languages Publishing House.

(1916) 1964 Imperialism, the Highest Stage of Capitalism: A Popular Outline. Volume 22, pages 185–304 in Vladimir I. Lenin, *Collected Works.* 4th ed. Moscow: Progress.

(1917*a*) 1964 The State and Revolution: The Marxist Theory of the State and the Tasks of the Proletariat in the Revolution. Volume 25, pages 381–492 in Vladimir I. Lenin, *Collected Works.* 4th ed. Moscow: Progress.

(1917*b*) 1964 Letters on Tactics. Volume 24, pages 42–54 in Vladimir I. Lenin, *Collected Works.* 4th ed. Moscow: Progress.

(1917*c*) 1964 The Tasks of the Proletariat in the Present Revolution. Volume 24, pages 20–91 in Vladimir I. Lenin, *Collected Works.* 4th ed. Moscow: Progress. → This article contains Lenin's famous "April Theses."

(1917*d*) 1964 Report on Peace, October 26 (November 8). Volume 26, pages 249–253 in Vladimir I. Lenin, *Collected Works.* 4th ed. Moscow: Progress.

(1920) 1952 *"Left-wing" Communism: An Infantile Disorder.* Moscow: Foreign Languages Publishing House.

Collected Works. 4th ed. Vols. 1—. Moscow: Foreign Languages Publishing House; Progress, 1960—.

Polnoe sobranie sochinenii (Complete Works). 5th ed. Vols. 1–55. Moscow: Gosudarstvennoe Izdatel'stvo Politicheskoi Literatury, 1958–1965. → Translations in the text provided by Jesse D. Clarkson.

Selected Works. 12 vols. New York: International Publishers, 1935–1938.

SUPPLEMENTARY BIBLIOGRAPHY

Balabanov, Angelica 1961 *Lenin.* Hanover (Germany): Literatur und Zeitgeschichte.

Bukharin, Nikolai I. 1925 *Lenin as a Marxist.* London: Communist Party of Great Britain.

Haimson, Leopold H. 1955 *The Russian Marxists and the Origins of Bolshevism.* Cambridge, Mass.: Harvard Univ. Press.

Krupskaia, Nadezhda K. (1924) 1942 *Memories of Lenin (1893–1917).* London: Lawrence & Wishart. → First published in Russian.

Lefebvre, Henri 1957 *La pensée de Lénine.* Paris: Bordas.

Lukács, György 1924 *Lenin: Studie über den Zusammenhang seiner Gedanken.* Vienna: Malik.

Moscow, Institut Marksizma–Leninizma (1960) 1963 *Vladimir Il'ich Lenin: Biografiia.* 2d ed. Moscow: Gosudarstvennoe Izdatel'stvo Politicheskoi Literatury.

Trotsky, Leon (1924) 1925 *Lenin.* New York: Blue Ribbon Books.

LESLIE, T. E. CLIFFE

T. E. Cliffe Leslie (1827–1882), Irish sociologist and economist, was born in County Wexford and educated at Trinity College, Dublin. After graduation in 1847 he studied law in London, where he attended the lectures of Sir Henry Maine and was influenced by Maine's emphasis on the historical approach to an understanding of institutions. He was a member of Lincoln's Inn and of the Irish bar, but he never practiced. In 1853 he was appointed to the chair of jurisprudence and political economy at Queen's College, Belfast, a post he held until his death. His academic duties required his presence in Belfast for only a few weeks in the year, and the larger part of the time he resided in London.

Leslie was a prolific writer of essays, most of which were reprinted. He never published a full-length book, and after his death a biographical sketch reported that while traveling on the Continent he had lost a partially completed manuscript of a comprehensive work on English economic and legal history. His first publication, in 1851, "Self-Dependence of the Working Classes Under the Law of Competition," read before the Dublin Statistical Society, was a youthful performance along conventional lines. It stressed the force of competition and showed none of the originality or break with conventional economics which marked his later writing. In 1856 appeared the only one of his professorial lectures to be printed as such: *The Military Systems of Europe Economically Considered,* a defense of voluntary enlistment as against compulsory military service. His concern with military problems, both in their narrower economic aspects and in their broader historical and sociological bearing, continued for over a decade.

Beginning in the late 1860s Leslie's writings were concentrated for several years on the land problem, particularly in Ireland. He opposed home rule for Ireland but championed land reform and was critical of what he called "insolent theories of race." Drawing upon observations from several visits to the Continent, which brought him in close touch with the French economist and politician Léonce de Lavergne, he stressed the advantages of small agriculture holdings. In his views of the land problem he generally defended laissez-faire policies, and his emphasis was on elimination of legislative abuses in taxation and property rights rather than on positive policies of social welfare. He attacked entail and primogeniture, urged taxation more equitable to workers, and supported extension of the political franchise.

In the 1870s Leslie's main interest turned to economic methodology, apparently as an outgrowth of a cross-fertilization between his studies of the land problem and the ideas of Sir Henry Maine. Leslie had, however, already attacked prevailing theory: in connection with a discussion of Irish conditions (1870*a*), he had repudiated the wages fund doctrine, and he repeatedly criticized it as not squaring with the historical facts of wage determination. He criticized the "vicious abstraction that has done much to darken economic inquiry" (1879*a*, p. 385), and he urged the importance of historical studies for an understanding of the workings of an economic system. In particular, he stressed that competition had not brought about the equalization that theory assumed, and he documented his thesis by repeated citations of geographical differences in agricultural wages in England and Ireland.

Leslie was an acute critic and a careful observer who was quick to see facts that did not square with the theories of classical economics. He did little, however, to present an organized alternative approach or to consider what modification of theory might explain these individual situations. Leslie is sometimes referred to as spokesman of the historical approach to economics in England, but this does not mean that he was part of an organized movement like the German historical school. His wide-ranging criticism of classical economics and his emphasis on the importance of institutions have much in common with the work of Thorstein Veblen.

Numerous references to Leslie by neoclassical economists in the 1880s and 1890s—in particular Henry Sidgwick, John Neville Keynes, and Alfred Marshall—suggest that he had some influence in softening the rigidity of the deductive economics of the classical tradition then dominant in England. His essays on the land problem are still important for the history of the controversy over the economic difficulties of Ireland, and his stimulating criticisms of the purely deductive approach to economics have timeless relevance.

FRANK W. FETTER

[*Directly related are the entries* ECONOMIC THOUGHT, *articles on* THE HISTORICAL SCHOOL *and* THE INSTITUTIONAL SCHOOL. *Other relevant material may be found in the biographies of* KEYNES, JOHN NEVILLE; MARSHALL; SIDGWICK.]

WORKS BY LESLIE

1856 *The Military Systems of Europe Economically Considered.* Belfast: Shepherd & Aitchison.

1870*a* *Land Systems and Industrial Economy of Ireland, England, and Continental Countries.* London: Longmans.

(1870*b*) 1881 The Land System of France. Pages 291–312 in Cobden Club, *Systems of Land Tenure in Various Countries.* New York and London: Cassell.

(1871) 1872 Financial Reform. Pages 189–263 in Cobden Club, *Cobden Club Essays. Second Series.* 2d ed. London: Cassell.

1879*a* *Essays in Political and Moral Philosophy.* Dublin: Hodges & Figgis; London: Longmans.

(1879*b*) 1888 *Essays in Political Economy.* Dublin: Hodges & Figgis; London: Longmans.

SUPPLEMENTARY BIBLIOGRAPHY

KEYNES, JOHN N. (1890) 1955 *The Scope and Method of Political Economy.* 4th ed. New York: Kelley.

MARSHALL, ALFRED (1890) 1961 *Principles of Economics.* 9th ed. New York and London: Macmillan.

MILL, JOHN STUART (1870) 1875 Professor Leslie on the Land Question. Volume 5, pages 95–121 in John Stuart Mill, *Dissertations and Discussions: Political, Philosophical, and Historical.* New York: Holt. → First published in Volume 13 of the *Fortnightly Review.*

Politico–Economical Heterodoxy: Cliffe Leslie. 1883 *Westminster Review* 120:470–500.

SIDGWICK, HENRY 1879 Economic Method. *Fortnightly Review* New Series 25:301–318.

LEVASSEUR, ÉMILE

Émile Levasseur (1828–1911) was the father of modern economic history in France. He was born into a family of jewelers in Paris, and he himself worked at the jeweler's trade. It was this experience which aroused his interest in economic history. After the revolution of 1848, as he put it, "I became interested in political and social problems and, with the eagerness of youth I embraced the republican idea" (quoted in Hauser 1911, p. 88).

He received his secondary schooling in a Paris *lycée* and then attended the École Normale Supérieure and passed the *agrégation des lettres*; it may be worth noting that he never received a degree in history. He advanced rapidly in his academic career. Initially he taught rhetoric at Alençon and Besançon, but in 1868 he was asked to introduce economic history into the curriculum of the Collège de France, and in 1872 a chair of economic history and geography was created for him. In 1871 he succeeded Louis Wolowski at the Conservatoire des Arts et Métiers, and in the very same year he founded, with Émile Boutmy and Ernest Renan, the École Libre des Sciences Politiques, where he taught until his death.

Levasseur's concern with incorporating the material, concepts, and methods of the social and economic sciences into the study of history represented a break with the historical tradition of his time. And not only did he broaden the traditional concept of history; he also brought history into the field of economics, following in the footsteps of the German historical school of economists in general and of Wilhelm Roscher in particular. Until the publication of Levasseur's *Recherches historiques sur le système de Law* (1854) and his *Histoire des classes ouvrières . . . avant 1789* (1859), political economy in France had been an abstract and speculative science; after Levasseur it became an area of historical research. He substituted historical criticism for theorizing and replaced abstractions with data derived from documents and the analysis of statistics.

To be sure, Levasseur made a fundamental distinction between what he called pure political economy, or economic science, and applied political economy, or "economic art"; his own sphere, economic history, was economic art. However, he saw the two aspects of political economy as interrelated: "Economic history is one of the branches of the history of civilization; it protects economic science from the errors of judgment that can result from abstraction, just as experience is a safeguard against the dangers of the mathematical method. In a way, economic history is political economy in action; it teaches, more or less clearly, the lesson of experience, and it is also ancillary to theory" (see Liesse 1914, pp. 348–349). Thus defined, political economy becomes a moral science, focused on man as the center of the whole economic process; he is both active principle and goal.

Of all the related sciences that Levasseur brought to bear on economic history, he singled out statistics as the most important. The publication of *La population française* (1889–1892) was, therefore, an even more important event in historiography than that of *Histoire des classes ouvrières*. For Levasseur, the object of statistics as a science was to make numerical data available to historians and economists. Indeed, he believed that statistics had become an indispensable tool for the historian.

Geography was another discipline Levasseur wished to see more closely connected with history. More than that, he made important contributions to the reorientation of the discipline and is considered one of the precursors of the great French geographers of the beginning of the twentieth century. In place of nomenclature and description, he substituted analysis of both present and future conditions. His 1879 report on the prospects of the proposed Panama Canal, made at the request of Ferdinand de Lesseps, is characteristic of this type of analysis: he calculated the traffic that could be expected and estimated the financial returns.

Finally, Levasseur considered what is now called sociology to be indispensable to the historian.

Levasseur made the following programmatic statement about the ways in which the economic historian should proceed:

> Economic history, using documents from the past, statistics, archival material, and the descriptions of contemporaries, etc. aims to explain either a single aspect of the economy of a particular nation, or successive manifestations of such a single aspect in the economies of several nations, or else to present a comprehensive picture of all aspects of a particular national economy. . . . Economic history enables us to observe and follow the progress of economic phenomena in their social milieu, and to determine as accurately as possible the causes and effects of each nation's economic activity. . . . It shows how economic development is an integral part of the general evolution of all societies. (1898, pp. 25–26)

Levasseur's conception of economic history was humanistic, rather than mechanistic. Thus, in a lecture at the Collège de France in 1898, he considered the reasons why once-flourishing empires declined. The soil and climate had remained the same. It was man who had changed. Either he no longer had the skill to raise the produce that had made him rich, or social conditions had diverted him from his original goal. Levasseur explored this humanistic and synthetic concept in the five volumes of his *Histoire des classes ouvrières et de l'industrie* (1867*a*), which is his masterpiece and which after a century remains in large part valid.

Levasseur's economic concepts are no longer accepted, and sociology and statistics have undergone rapid transformations since his death. However, Levasseur was an important innovator and one who laid the groundwork for, and to some degree directly inspired, such important scholars as François Simiand, Henri Hauser, Marc Bloch, and Ernest Labrousse. French economic historians today still revere him.

CLAUDE FOHLEN

[*For the historical context of Levasseur's work, see* ECONOMIC THOUGHT, *article on* THE HISTORICAL SCHOOL; HISTORY, *article on* ECONOMIC HISTORY; *and the biography of* ROSCHER; *for discussion of the subsequent development of Levasseur's ideas, see the biographies of* BLOCH *and* SIMIAND.]

WORKS BY LEVASSEUR

1854 *Recherches historiques sur le système de Law.* Paris: Guillaumin.

1858 *La question de l'or: Les mines de Californie et d'Australie, les anciennes mines d'or et d'argent, ...* Paris: Guillaumin.

(1859) 1900–1901 *Histoire des classes ouvrières et de l'industrie en France avant 1789.* 2d ed., 2 vols. Paris: Rousseau. → First published as *Histoire des classes ouvrières en France depuis la conquête de Jules César jusqu'à la Révolution.*

1865 *La France industrielle en 1789.* Paris: Durand.

1866 *La prévoyance et l'épargne.* Paris: Hachette.

(1867*a*) 1903–1904 *Histoire des classes ouvrières et de l'industrie en France de 1789 à 1870.* 2d ed., 2 vols. Paris: Rousseau. → First published as *Histoire des classes ouvrières en France depuis 1789 jusqu'à nos jours.*

1867*b* *Du rôle de l'intelligence dans la production.* Paris: Hachette.

(1869) 1892 *Géographie de la France et de ses colonies (cours moyen).* 12th ed. Paris: Delagrave.

1872 *L'étude et l'enseignement de la géographie.* Paris: Delagrave.

1879 *Rapport sur le commerce et le tonnage relatifs au canal interocéanique.* Paris: Martinet.

1885 *La statistique officielle en France: Organisation, travaux, et publications des services de statistique des différents ministères, précédée d'un aperçu historique.* Nancy (France): Berger-Levrault.

1889–1892 *La population française: Histoire de la population avant 1789 et démographie de la France comparée à celle des autres nations au XIXe siècle, précédée d'une introduction sur la statistique.* 3 vols. Paris: Rousseau.

(1898) 1900 *The American Workman.* Baltimore: Johns Hopkins Press. → First published as *L'ouvrier américain: L'ouvrier au travail, l'ouvrier chez lui, les questions ouvrières.*

1899 *L'organisation des métiers dans l'Empire Romain.* Paris: Giard & Brière.

1901 *L'enseignement de l'économie politique au Conservatoire des Arts et Métiers.* Paris: Chevalier-Marescq.

1902 *Les études sociales sous la Restauration: Saint-Simon et le saint-simonisme, Fourier et le fouriérisme.* Paris: Giard & Brière.

1907 *Questions ouvrières et industrielles en France sous la Troisième République.* Paris: Rousseau.

1911–1912 *Histoire du commerce de la France.* 2 vols. Paris: Rousseau. → Volume 1: *Avant 1789.* Volume 2: *De 1789 à nos jours.*

SUPPLEMENTARY BIBLIOGRAPHY

HAUSER, HENRI 1911 Émile Levasseur. *Revue historique* 108:88–91.

LÉVY, RAPHAËL-GEORGES 1911 Levasseur. *Revue des deux mondes* 5:96–131.

LIESSE, ANDRÉ 1914 Notice sur la vie et les travaux de M. Émile Levasseur. Académie des Sciences Morales et Politiques, *Séances et travaux* 181:337–361.

La vie scientifique: P. É. Levasseur. 1911 *Revue économique internationale* 3:396–418. → Contains a comprehensive bibliography.

LÉVY-BRUHL, LUCIEN

Lucien Lévy-Bruhl (1857–1939), French anthropologist, was born in Paris. He received a *doctorat ès lettres* from the École Normale Supérieure, and entered upon a brilliant university career, which was crowned by his nomination to the chair of history of modern philosophy at the Sorbonne in 1904. His lectures there were the basis of several of his books, notably those on Jacobi (1894) and Auguste Comte (1900). His lasting contributions, however, are his book *Ethics and Moral Science* (1903) and especially the six volumes he devoted to the study of what he called the primitive mentality.

Lévy-Bruhl's work is highly original, and it is hard to define precisely the influences on his thinking. His stress on the role of the emotions in psychic life may have derived from his studies of Jacobi. In the sociological aspects of his thought he was influenced by the ideas of Émile Durkheim. Yet Lévy-Bruhl also rejected some of Durkheim's ideas and carried on spirited controversies with Durkheim, who then dominated the French sociological school. Lévy-Bruhl could not accept all the implications of Durkheimian rationalism, but he did learn much from Durkheim's *Rules of Sociological Method.* In general, one might say that Lévy-Bruhl was influenced more in a negative than in a positive sense. He was nobody's disciple; indeed, he often defined his thinking by contrasting it to that of others, for instance, to that of the theorists of animism (Frazer, Tylor, and Spencer). But he was not indifferent to criticisms made of his theories, especially the objections of such sociologists as Durkheim and Mauss or of an anthropologist like Evans-Pritchard. His responsiveness to these criticisms caused changes in the orientation of his thought. Three major stages may be distinguished in his intellectual development: the first was marked by his work on morality; the second by his theories on the primitive mentality; and the third by the revisions and changes that he himself made in these latter theories.

Moral philosophy. In *Ethics and Moral Science* Lévy-Bruhl began by showing that all theoretical moralities (whether of metaphysical or scientific origin) are doomed to failure, because theory can be applied only to what is, not to what ought to be. They suffer also from the fact that they fail to take into account the variation of human nature in various civilizations. Morals do vary with time and place, and Lévy-Bruhl advocated that they be studied objectively and that their laws be discovered. On the basis of such scientific knowledge, a rational art and rules of conduct may be set up that will be valid solely in a specified sociological situation rather than claiming the universal validity of the theoretical moralities. Thus, already in this book Lévy-Bruhl was making a direct attack on the postulate of the unity of human nature and laying the foundations of a relativistic and pluralistic sociology.

The theory of the primitive mentality. Lévy-Bruhl's pluralism led him to suppose that several types of mentality can exist among men, that is, that their methods of thinking may vary basically from one society to another. The surest way to prove this, he believed, was to begin by comparing the mentality of civilized man with the mentality furthest removed from it.

He therefore studied the mental functions in so-called primitives, collecting and classifying a large number of documents on this subject. His first conclusion was that the mentality of primitives and that of people living in modern Occidental civilization differ not in nuance or degree but rather in kind. The anthropologists of the English animist school had believed that primitive peoples think or reason in the same way as civilized ones, although they may reason from mistaken premises. For Lévy-Bruhl the primitive man's very reasoning processes differ from ours; the primitive mentality is not simply a rudimentary or pathological form of the civilized. What makes for these differences is not the thought of the individual but collective representations. Ideally, the social scientist would establish the particular collective psychology of each society. Instead, in order to describe the primitive mentality Lévy-Bruhl took his documentation from all preliterate societies.

To the objections of those, like Marcel Mauss, who argued that these societies are not all alike, Lévy-Bruhl answered that for his purpose it was enough that they all share a characteristic that distinguishes them from us. When Evans-Pritchard reproached him with taking his examples from the books of travelers or missionaries, whose observations had not been made in conformity with the best ethnographical methods, he replied that it sufficed for him if the mentality of the peoples studied had been well understood. Evans-Pritchard did get Lévy-Bruhl to admit that he sometimes made savages appear more irrational than they actually are; he maintained, however, that it was not his intention to give a complete description of the life of primitive peoples but to highlight the differences between their mentality and ours.

The collective representations of primitives, he asserted, are essentially mystical, since they imply belief in forces or influences that are imperceptible to the senses. Mysticism pervades all their perceptions. Further, the primitive mentality is not governed exclusively by our laws of logic. Although it is not generally opposed to these laws, it does not shrink from violating especially the law against contradiction. This is why Lévy-Bruhl designated it as prelogical. The connections made by the primitive mind that fall outside of our principles of logic are governed by a principle that Lévy-Bruhl called the law of participation. According to this principle, a being or object can be both itself and at the same time something else. Participation cannot be explained by animism.

The conception of this mystical mentality based on participation led Lévy-Bruhl to more detailed analyses supported by a large number of concrete examples. He showed the effects of this mentality on the language of primitive peoples and on their way of conceiving the world. He described their occasionalist notion of causality and their way of looking at the human personality, distinguishing neither the human being (*l'être même*) from its "appurtenances," nor the body from the spirit or soul.

Between the primitive mind, which directly exhibits participation, and the civilized mind Lévy-Bruhl found intermediate stages in which participation can no longer be perceived directly but is represented or symbolized. He thus seems to have placed his dualism in an evolutionist perspective. But he took care to state that the mystical and prelogical mentality is never completely supplanted by the undisputed reign of logic. He held that in every human mind there is always some rational thought and some mystical thought. Reason alone cannot completely satisfy man. Lévy-Bruhl did not accept the charge that his was a doctrine of prelogicism. For him there are not two mentalities that exclude one another; prelogical thought is not a stage antedating logical thought. Thus, such philosophers as Émile Bréhier maintained that Lévy-Bruhl's theory is actually more structuralist than evolutionist. And the phenomenologist Van der Leeuw interpreted it as postulating the mystical mentality and the logical mentality as two permanent structures of the human mind. In primitive man, the first dominates the second; in civilized man, it is the contrary.

Revisions in the theory. Lévy-Bruhl's first books on mental functions in primitive societies provoked a vigorous reply from Durkheim in his *Elementary Forms of the Religious Life* of 1912. Many further criticisms appeared in 1926–1927, in particular those of Larguier des Bancels, Raoul Allier, and Olivier Leroy. Lévy-Bruhl examined these objections seriously and was led to sharpen and revise his thought. As a result between 1931 and 1938 he published three further books on the same subject. He now became more demanding as to the sources of his documentation, relying more frequently on the work of the best ethnographers. Also, without completely abandoning any of the basic concepts of his first analysis (mysticism, prelogical character, participation, occasionalism), he inverted their order of importance, putting mysticism ahead of the prelogical character. And, above all, he introduced a new principle of explanation that tended to dominate all the others, which he called "the affective category of the supernatural." He still maintained, to be sure, that primitive peoples are sometimes insensitive to contradiction, but he strongly affirmed that "the fundamental structure of the human mind is the same everywhere." Primitive men have concepts, but their knowledge is not rationally classified and organized, which leaves the field clear for "mystical preconnections" when the emotional, affective element supplements logical generalization. This colors their entire thinking, since for them ordinary experience is pervaded by mystical experience; similarly, for them the supernatural world, although different from the natural world, is not separate from it, and they pass unaware from one to the other. The prelogical is therefore explained by the mystical and this in turn by the predominance of affectivity over reason. Indeed, affectivity gives a special tonality to primitive representations, and it thus has that element of generality that makes it a category of thought.

In his last works Lévy-Bruhl reduced the study of primitive mentality entirely to an analysis of the mystic experience and the affective category of the supernatural that characterizes and explains it. He showed how this experience of the supernatural emerges mainly in the face of the unusual. He devoted other chapters to the various representations and beliefs marked by this affective category, for example, occult influences, beings and objects that bring bad or good luck, various rituals, magic, revelations as to the secret nature of things and animals, dreams, visions, the presence of the dead, and all of mythology and the techniques for participating in the mythical world.

In these books Lévy-Bruhl was also concerned with transitions between the primitive and the modern mentalities. He found such transitions especially in the development of prereligion into elaborated religion, or of myth into tale and folklore; but at the same time he emphasized more and more that both mentalities persist.

Hence the theory that at the outset seemed to postulate a principle of radical difference between the thinking of primitive and civilized peoples became more flexible. This evolution continued in the notes that Lévy-Bruhl was writing toward the end of his life and that probably would have become a book had he lived longer. These notes were collected and published after his death in a small book entitled *Les carnets de Lévy-Bruhl* (1949). In it he stated that he was prepared to give up the term "prelogical," and he even questioned the specificity of the characteristics he had attributed to the primitive mentality.

Influence of Lévy-Bruhl. In addition to the phenomenological and structuralist extensions of Lévy-Bruhl's theory, mentioned above, the important influence it has had on the Jungian psychoanalysts should be pointed out: Aldrich (1931) has related the primitive mind to the archetypes of the unconscious. As for the fundamentals of the doctrine, however, few contemporary authors seem to accept a difference in kind between the primitive and the civilized mind. Lévy-Bruhl himself was on the point of giving it up, as may be seen in his posthumously published notebooks. But his analyses of participation play an important part in the thought of many philosophers and sociologists, for example, Przyluski (1940) and Roger Bastide (1953). Again, the advocates of a pluralist sociology, like Georges Gurvich, applaud Lévy-Bruhl's undermining of the classical unitary conception of the universality of modes of thinking. Lévy-Bruhl's doctrine may have few faithful disciples, but at least it compelled anthropologists to reflect on certain problems and in that sense gave a new direction to the study of primitive peoples.

JEAN CAZENEUVE

[*For the historical context of Lévy-Bruhl's work, see the biographies of* DURKHEIM; FRAZER; MAUSS; SPENCER; TYLOR. *For discussion of the subsequent development of his ideas, see* POLLUTION; RELIGION, *article on* ANTHROPOLOGICAL STUDY.]

WORKS BY LÉVY-BRUHL

1884 *L'idée de responsabilité.* Paris: Hachette.

1890 *L'Allemagne depuis Leibniz.* Paris: Hachette.

1894 *La philosophie de Jacobi.* Paris: Alcan.

(1900) 1903 *The Philosophy of Auguste Comte.* New York: Putnam; London: Sonnenschein. → First published in French.

(1903) 1905 *Ethics and Moral Science.* London: Constable. → First published as *La morale et la science des moeurs.*

(1910) 1926 *How Natives Think.* London: Allen & Unwin. → First published as *Les fonctions mentales dans les sociétés primitives.*

(1922) 1923 *Primitive Mentality.* New York: Macmillan. → First published as *La mentalité primitive.*

(1927) 1928 *The "Soul" of the Primitive.* New York: Macmillan. → First published as *L'âme primitive.*

(1931) 1935 *Primitives and the Supernatural.* New York: Dutton. → First published as *Le surnaturel et la nature dans la mentalité primitive.*

1935 *La mythologie primitive.* Paris: Alcan.

1938 *L'expérience mystique et les symboles chez les primitifs.* Paris: Alcan.

1949 *Les carnets de Lévy-Bruhl.* Paris: Presses Universitaires de France. → Published posthumously.

SUPPLEMENTARY BIBLIOGRAPHY

ALDRICH, CHARLES R. 1931 *The Primitive Mind and Modern Civilization.* New York: Harcourt.

ALLIER, RAOUL 1927 *Le non-civilisé et nous.* Paris: Payot.

BASTIDE, ROGER 1953 Contribution à l'étude de la participation. *Cahiers internationaux de sociologie* 14: 30–40.

BLONDEL, CHARLES 1926 *La mentalité primitive.* Paris: Stock.

BRÉHIER, ÉMILE 1949 Originalité de Lévy-Bruhl. *Revue philosophique* 139:385–388.

CAZENEUVE, JEAN 1961 *La mentalité archaïque.* Paris: Colin.

CAZENEUVE, JEAN 1963 *Lucien Lévy-Bruhl: Sa vie, son oeuvre, avec un exposé de sa philosophie.* Paris: Presses Universitaires de France.

DAVY, GEORGES (1931) 1950 *Sociologues d'hier et d'aujourd'hui.* 2d ed. Paris: Presses Universitaires de France.

ESSERTIER, DANIEL 1927 *Les formes inférieures de l'explication.* Paris: Alcan.

LEROY, OLIVIER 1927 *La raison primitive.* Paris: Geuthner.

PRZYLUSKI, JEAN 1940 *La participation.* Paris: Presses Universitaires de France.

SHAREVSKAIA, B. 1958 O metodologicheskoi i terminologicheskoi putanitse v voprosakh pervobytnogo myshleniia (Methodological and Terminological Confusions in the Question of the Mentality of Primitive Peoples). *Sovietskaia etnografiia* 6:61–75.

VAN DER LEEUW, G. G. 1940 *L'homme primitif et la religion.* Paris: Presses Universitaires de France.

LEWIN, KURT

Kurt Lewin (1890–1947) was born in Mogilno, Prussia. After studying at the universities of Freiburg and Munich, he completed his doctorate in philosophy at the University of Berlin in 1914. He taught in Berlin from 1921 to 1933, at which time he left Germany. In the United States he was a visiting professor at Stanford and at Cornell before becoming professor of child psychology in the Child Welfare Research Station of the State University of Iowa in 1935. In 1945 he left Iowa to found the Research Center for Group Dynamics at the Massachusetts Institute of Technology. He also served as a visiting professor at the University of California in Berkeley and at Harvard.

During his thirty years of scientific work, Lewin's theoretical interests and the focuses of his research shifted several times. At first he was concerned with the study and analysis of the cognitive processes of learning and perception; with the dynamics of individual motivation and emotion; and with the interpersonal processes of reward and punishment, conflict, and social influence. In his next phase, he conducted and stimulated research on group phenomena such as leadership, social climate, group standards, and values. Finally, he was led to an examination of the social restraints imposed on groups by technology, economics, law, and politics. Although his interests changed and developed, he nevertheless carefully adhered to a central theoretical tenet: that to represent and interpret faithfully the complexity of concrete reality situations requires continual crossing of the traditional boundaries of the social sciences, rather than a progressive narrowing of attention to a limited number of variables.

The theory that requires this interdisciplinary approach to psychological and social reality has at various times been referred to, by Lewin himself and by others, as "dynamic theory," "topological psychology," and "field theory." Field theory was Lewin's final preference. Briefly stated, it holds that events are determined by forces acting on them in an immediate field rather than by forces acting at a distance. Field theory may be characterized as a method of analyzing causal relations and building scientific constructs, that is, a theory about theory building, or a metatheory. At the same time, Lewin's field theory is a set of constructs, developed through empirical research, for describing and interpreting psychological and social phenomena.

Field theory as metatheory. The major tenets of field theory as metatheory for social science have been identified by Cartwright (1959, p. 7).

(1) The full empirical reality of human experience and behavior—not just certain abstract aspects that are most accessible or easy to manipulate—must be comprehended in a scientific manner. The observation of behavior in a real-life setting (what has been called naturalistic observation) and phenomenological analysis are procedures that may prevent scientific formalization from focusing on trivial aspects of human behavior.

(2) The language of concepts that is developed must be "two-faced," providing both a rigorous terminology for describing the behavioral events of the real world and a set of theoretical constructs that can be related to each other logically in the formulation of lawful regularities about the causation of behavioral events.

(3) The concepts must "fit" the nature of psychological phenomena, which they will not do if they are simply borrowed from physical or biological science. Presuppositions about the ultimate unity of science should not be allowed to distort the development of concepts that are intended to describe psychological phenomena (emotions, hopes, fears, illusions) rather than biological or physical processes.

(4) Lewin's *principle of concreteness* states that effects "can be produced only by what is 'concrete,' i.e., by something that has the position of an individual fact which exists at a certain moment" (1936, p. 32). From this important principle Lewin derived several of his basic ideas: that every behavioral event must be viewed as caused by several interdependent features of the total concrete situation of that moment; that the dynamics of a behavioral event cannot be adequately comprehended by the specialized concepts of a particular discipline or scientific specialty, for example, cognition, learning, economics, or political science; that the "life space" or concrete field of all coexisting psychological facts is quite different from the quantified dimensions of that situation; that causation is a contemporary process—"Since neither the past nor the future exists at the present moment it cannot have effects at the present" (*ibid.*, p. 35).

(5) Mathematics provides basic tools for developing a formal systematic theory of psychological processes, but this does not mean that all phenomena can be treated quantitatively. Non-Euclidean geometry seemed to Lewin the most appropriate mathematical tool for treating many empirical aspects of human behavior in terms of psychological space.

(6) Basic research that is generated by the need to develop field theoretical concepts should be of great practical value in the world of action. To Lewin this meant that there "is nothing as practical as a good theory." He demonstrated this again and again in his own contributions to the understanding of many critical social problems, such as autocracy, self-hatred, scapegoating, intergroup conflict, industrial inefficiency, conservative food habits, and child rearing. [*See* PREJUDICE.]

Experimental research. In his search for a comprehensive conceptual grasp of significant psychological events and processes Lewin instigated and led many research programs. Often they were carried on by his students after he himself had turned his attention to new problems.

His first research sequence began with an experimental critique of the work of Ach (1910) on "associative bonds" in the process of remembering. Lewin moved beyond structural concepts of remembering to such notions as intention to recall and expectation about events. Basic work was done by Ovsiankina (1928) and Zeigarnik (1927), who demonstrated experimentally that the tendency to recall interrupted tasks is stronger than the tendency to recall completed tasks and that there are forces acting toward resuming and completing interrupted activities.

This work on psychological interruption and on the forces acting toward resumption and completion led directly to another program of research that represents an early experimental investigation of motivational concepts. The research sought to discover whether the completion of a task different from the interrupted one can reduce the tendency to resume the interrupted one. In other words, can one task have substitute value for another? Lewin's students Lissner (1933) and Mahler (1933) demonstrated that tasks of different degrees of similarity and different degrees of reality have different types of substitute value. An important series of studies by Adler (1939), Cartwright (1942), and Sliosberg (1934) further developed this area of inquiry.

Lewin's interest in the internal dynamics of motivation led him to initiate another series of studies on the psychological process of satiation. Karsten (1928) and other students (Freund 1930; Kounin 1941; Seashore & Bavelas 1942) discovered that the time it takes to become satiated with a task depends on the over-all meaning context of the activity, on ego involvement in the activity, on the physiological state of the person, and on the degree of rigidity of interpersonal psychological systems.

Another important series of studies of motivational dynamics dealt with frustration and regression. Again, Lewin's plan of research was primarily carried out by others. Dembo's initial work in Berlin (1931) consisted of careful observational studies of the symptoms of emotional tension as contrasted to the symptoms of task- or problem-solving tension that occurred when subjects were assigned impossible tasks. The symptoms observed included anger, aggression, regression, substitution, and flight from reality. Later studies by Barker, Dembo, and Lewin (1941) and by Wright (1942) established important connections between frustration and intellectual regression as measured by the developmental level of play activity before and after frustration situations.

Dembo (1931) and Hoppe (1931) did valuable research on the concept of level of aspiration, and again other research developed from it. After Jerome Frank, one of Lewin's students, presented a summary in English of the German research (1935*a*; 1935*b*), a flood of studies by American investigators followed. The early research indicated that the experience of success or failure depends to a very significant degree upon the person's aspiration rather than upon some objective standard of performance. There was also clear evidence that the motivation for success or achievement of individuals leads them to set levels of aspiration that do not guarantee easy success. This line of inquiry has been the springboard for much of the current advanced theoretical work on social comparison processes, self-evaluation, and discrepancies between ideal self and actual self. [*See* ACHIEVEMENT MOTIVATION.]

The phenomena of decision making and conflict resolution were the focuses of another important series of investigations by Lewin and his students. These inquiries demonstrate the effect on decision making of the strength of the valences of the alternatives, the reality level of the choice situation, the difference in a choice between negative and positive alternatives, and attitudes of cautiousness and risk taking.

As Lewin's interests changed from individual to social psychology, his approach to decision making and conflict also changed. His famous series of studies of group decision making (1953) demonstrates the influence on individual behavior of participation in group discussions and decisions. Group discussion affects such phenomena as parental behavior, eating habits, and amount of effort on the production line. Later work on patterns of intergroup conflict derived from this work on individual decision making.

As he moved into social psychology, Lewin's research interests focused on the phenomena of social perception, social values, social influence, cooperation, and competition. In all these areas he instigated important research. His students demonstrated experimentally that the expectation or perception that another person is "warm" or "cold," high or low in power, or an insider or outsider greatly influences interpersonal attitudes and behavior (Kelley 1950; Pepitone 1950; Thibaut & Riecken 1955). [*See* PERCEPTION, *articles on* PERSON PERCEPTION *and* SOCIAL PERCEPTION.]

His move from Germany to the United States stimulated Lewin's interest in the comparative analysis of personal values as they relate to cultural differences and social norms. Several of Lewin's papers ([1935–1946] 1948, pp. 3–68) deal with the development of a definition of values and with approaches to change in cultural values. This was perhaps the beginning of his focus on the theory of planned change and social action, which became increasingly important in the later years of his career. His work on values moved from methodological work on the content of values (as developed in Kalhorn 1944; White 1951) to work on the development of the value of "fairness," which he conducted by means of experimental situations with children of different ages, and then to an important series of studies on the development and functioning of group standards or group norms. The experimental field studies of the influence of group standards on work output in a factory (Coch & French 1948) and on behavior of residents in a housing project (Festinger et al. 1950) led to a basic theoretical paper in 1947 by Lewin (see in [1939–1947] 1963, pp. 188–237) on the quasi-stationary equilibrium as a tool for conceptual analysis of the field of forces determining behavior in a given social setting and situation. [*See* MORAL DEVELOPMENT.]

Perhaps Lewin's best-known contributions to social psychology and group dynamics are those focusing on authority and social influence. Initially, a series of children's groups were studied to see what effect different styles of leadership might have on the social–emotional atmosphere of a group, on its work productivity, and on the personal adaptation of members. There followed basic work on social influence, with laboratory studies of status hierarchy and communications channels; field studies of behavioral contagion and influence structures; and studies of the patterns and bases of influence in military units and in the working relations among the members of professional teams, such as those composed of psychiatrists, clinical psychologists, or social workers. [*See* LEADERSHIP.]

In the later years of his career, Lewin and his co-workers became interested in the problem of what they called psychological ecology. Thus, in his work on the maintenance and change of food habits (1943), Lewin constructed a theory of social channels and "gatekeepers" to account for the ecological processes by which particular foods reach the table and come in contact with the consumer. He showed that a number of cultural, economic, and technological factors combined to influence this series of decisions. This approach has been greatly developed and extended by Lewin's student and co-worker Barker, in his series of field studies of the psychological ecology of children and adults in a number of communities and a variety of social settings (Barker & Wright 1954).

Major concepts. In all his work, Lewin maintained an active interplay between the construction of theory and the concrete analysis of human behavior in all its complexity. It is possible here to indicate only briefly some of the concepts that became important in Lewin's comprehensive conceptual system. Probably the most widely known Lewinian concept is that of *psychological life space.* This fundamental notion refers to the totality of events or facts that determines the behavior of an individual at a given time. It is related to the basic tenet that causation is a contemporary process, and it has, therefore, created much active controversy in the field of psychotherapy. Defending the importance of this concept, one psychoanalyst (Ezriel 1956, p. 32) has asserted that the unconscious structures the analyst uncovers in working with a patient are *active in the present* and are not necessarily replicas of past realities and reactions.

The life space includes two major components: the person and the psychological environment. The latter is conceived to be the environment as it exists for the individual. Lewin assumed that an understanding of the interaction between the person and the psychological environment would permit the understanding and prediction of the person's behavior.

The concepts that Lewin developed to deal with the psychological and social processes of the life space can be classified as *structural* concepts, having to do with the arrangement and relationship of the parts of the life space, and *dynamic* concepts, dealing with tendencies toward change or resisting change. The basic structures of the life space are region and boundary, and derived from these are degree of differentiation, centrality, path, and psychological distance. The principal dynamic processes are interdependence, tension, force, field of forces, equilibrium, and power. Lewin also introduced two dimensions of the life space: a vertical dimension of degrees or levels of reality and a horizontal dimension of time perspective. Lewin's studies demonstrated that psychological processes vary with different levels of reality: the processes involved in assessing facts or expectations are different from those involved in fantasies or wishes. The use of the concept of time perspective was related to Lewin's field-theoretical stress on the interpretation and prediction of behavior in ahistorical terms.

When he first made contributions to social psychology, Lewin was content to treat the facts of interpersonal relations as social facts in the life space of each individual. For example, the fact of group membership and its implications for behavior then seemed quite satisfactorily represented as regions in the life space of the person. But as he added such new problems as group goals, group decision making, and group problem solving, it became necessary to relate life spaces to one another, that is, to construct a *social space* or a social field in which social, economic, political, and physical facts have objective, or at least intersubjective, reality, rather than only individual psychological reality. In some of his final papers ([1939–1947] 1963, pp. 170–237), Lewin was beginning to grapple with the challenging problems of defining social space and social field-theory and of relating these concepts to those of psychological space. He was indicating some of the ways in which the behavioral sciences might go beyond empirical unity to the achievement of conceptual unity.

Social action and social problem solving. Lewin had a deep sensitivity to social problems and a commitment to use his resources as a social scientist to do something about them. Thus, in the early 1940s, he drew a triangle to represent the interdependence of research, training (or education), and action in producing social change. He saw every practical problem as requiring basic conceptual analysis, research, and a "change experiment." The concept of action-research as a method of planned social change was developed and clarified in the period when he was helping found the Commission on Community Interrelations of the American Jewish Congress and establishing the Research Center for Group Dynamics at MIT.

Lewin may well have been a bit optimistic when he asserted in 1945 that "leading practitioners" in government, agriculture, industry, education, and community life seemed to have an increasing awareness of the need for a "scientific level of understanding" and that they seemed to accept the dictum that "nothing is as practical as a good theory." Yet the success of the National Training Laboratories, which he helped establish in 1946 and 1947, does seem to vindicate his optimism. First held at Bethel, Maine, the summer after Lewin's death, these sessions have since expanded into a nationwide network serving the needs of professional men. They provide a link between these professional men and the resources of the behavioral sciences and the growing technology of re-education of attitudes, values, and behavior.

Persisting influence. Current research directly derived from Lewin's work is being carried on by Cartwright and his colleagues, who are working on the development and use of mathematical concepts that are coordinated with life-space phenomena; at the Research Center for Group Dynamics at the University of Michigan (it was founded by Lewin at MIT and moved to Michigan after his death) and at university centers founded by some of his students, for example, by Festinger, Schachter, Deutsch, Thibaut, and Kelley; by Barker and his colleagues, working on psychological ecology; by French, Bavelas, Marrow,

Cook, and others, who are coordinating organizational field experiments; and by Lippitt and his colleagues at the Center for Research on Utilization of Scientific Knowledge, the title of which is a key to its activities.

RONALD LIPPITT

[*See also* FIELD THEORY. *Other relevant material may be found in* DEVELOPMENTAL PSYCHOLOGY; GESTALT THEORY; GROUPS; SYSTEMS ANALYSIS, *article on* PSYCHOLOGICAL SYSTEMS; THINKING, *article on* COGNITIVE ORGANIZATION AND PROCESSES.]

WORKS BY LEWIN

1917 Die psychische Tätigkeit bei der Hemmung von Willensvorgängen und das Grundgesetz der Assoziation. *Zeitschrift für Psychologie* 77:212–247.

(1935–1946) 1948 *Resolving Social Conflicts: Selected Papers on Group Dynamics.* New York: Harper.

1936 *Principles of Topological Psychology.* New York: McGraw-Hill.

(1939–1947) 1963 *Field Theory in Social Science: Selected Theoretical Papers.* Edited by Dorwin Cartwright. London: Tavistock.

1941 BARKER, ROGER; DEMBO, TAMARA; and LEWIN, KURT *Frustration and Regression: An Experiment With Young Children.* University of Iowa Studies in Child Welfare, vol. 18, no. 1. Iowa City: Univ. of Iowa Press.

1943 Forces Behind Food Habits and Methods of Change. National Research Council, *Bulletin* 108:35–65.

(1945) 1948 LEWIN, KURT; and GRABBE, PAUL Conduct, Knowledge, and Acceptance of New Values. Pages 56–68 in Kurt Lewin, *Resolving Social Conflicts: Selected Papers on Group Dynamics.* New York: Harper. → First published in Volume 1 of the *Journal of Social Issues.*

1953 Studies in Group Decision. Pages 287–301 in Dorwin Cartwright and Alvin Zander (editors), *Group Dynamics: Research and Theory.* Evanston, Ill.: Row, Peterson. → Selections from writings first published between 1943 and 1947.

SUPPLEMENTARY BIBLIOGRAPHY

ACH, N. 1910 *Über den Willensakt und das Temperament: Eine experimentelle Untersuchung.* Leipzig: Quelle & Meyer.

ADLER, D. L. 1939 Types of Similarity and the Substitute Value of Activities at Different Age Levels. Ph.D. dissertation, State Univ. of Iowa.

BARKER, ROGER G.; and WRIGHT, HERBERT F. 1954 *Midwest and Its Children.* Evanston, Ill.: Row, Peterson.

CARTWRIGHT, DORWIN 1942 The Effect of Interruption, Completion and Failure Upon the Attractiveness of Activities. *Journal of Experimental Psychology* 31: 1–16.

CARTWRIGHT, DORWIN 1959 Lewinian Theory as a Contemporary Systematic Framework. Volume 2, pages 7–91 in Sigmund Koch (editor), *Psychology: The Study of a Science.* New York: McGraw-Hill.

COCH, LESTER; and FRENCH, JOHN R. P. JR. 1948 Overcoming Resistance to Change. *Human Relations* 1: 512–532.

DEMBO, TAMARA 1931 Der Ärger als dynamisches Problem. Untersuchungen zur Handlungs- und Affektpsychologie, 10. *Psychologische Forschung* 15:1–144.

DEUTSCH, MORTON 1954 Field Theory in Social Psychology. Pages 181–222 in Gardner Lindzey (editor), *Handbook of Social Psychology,* Volume 1: Theory and Method. Cambridge, Mass.: Addison-Wesley.

ESCALONA, SIBYLLE 1954 The Influence of Topological and Vector Psychology Upon Current Research in Child Development: An Addendum. Pages 971–983 in Leonard Carmichael (editor), *Manual of Child Psychology.* 2d ed. New York: Wiley.

EZRIEL, H. 1956 Experimentation Within the Psychoanalytic Session. *British Journal for the Philosophy of Science* 7:29–48.

FESTINGER, LEON; SCHACHTER, STANLEY; and BACK, KURT (1950) 1963 *Social Pressures in Informal Groups: A Study of Human Factors in Housing.* Stanford Univ. Press.

FRANK, JEROME D. 1935*a* Individual Differences in Certain Aspects of the Level of Aspiration. *American Journal of Psychology* 47:119–128.

FRANK, JEROME D. 1935*b* The Influence of the Level of Performance in One Task on the Level of Aspiration in Another. *Journal of Experimental Psychology* 18: 159–171.

FREUND, ALEX 1930 Psychische Sättigung im Menstruum und Intermenstruum. Untersuchungen zur Handlungs- und Affektpsychologie, 7. *Psychologische Forschung* 13:198–217.

HOPPE, FERDINAND 1931 Erfolg und Misserfolg. Untersuchungen zur Handlungs- und Affektpsychologie, 9. *Psychologische Forschung* 14:1–62.

KALHORN, JOAN 1944 Values and Sources of Authority Among Rural Children. Pages 99–152 in Kurt Lewin et. al., *Authority and Frustration.* University of Iowa Studies in Child Welfare, vol. 20. Iowa City: Univ. of Iowa Press.

KARSTEN, ANITRA 1928 Psychische Sättigung. Untersuchungen zur Handlungs- und Affektpsychologie, 5. *Psychologische Forschung* 10:142–254.

KELLEY, HAROLD H. 1950 The Warm–Cold Variable in First Impressions of Persons. *Journal of Personality* 18:431–439.

KOUNIN, JACOB S. 1941 Experimental Studies of Rigidity: 1–2. *Character and Personality* 9:251–282. → Part 1: The Measurement of Rigidity in Normal and Feeble-minded Persons. Part 2: The Explanatory Power of the Concept of Rigidity as Applied to Feeblemindedness.

LEEPER, ROBERT W. 1943 *Lewin's Topological and Vector Psychology: A Digest and a Critique.* Eugene: Univ. of Oregon.

LISSNER, KATE 1933 Die Entspannung von Bedürfnissen durch Ersatzhandlungen. Untersuchungen zur Handlungs- und Affektpsychologie, 18. *Psychologische Forschung* 18:218–250.

MAHLER, WERA 1933 Ersatzhandlungen verschiedenen Realitätsgrades. Untersuchungen zur Handlungs- und Affektpsychologie, 15. *Psychologische Forschung* 18: 27–89.

OVSIANKINA, MARIA VON 1928 Die Wiederaufnahme unterbrochener Handlungen. Untersuchungen zur Handlungs- und Affektpsychologie, 6. *Psychologische Forschung* 11:302–379.

PEPITONE, ALBERT 1950 Motivational Effects in Social Perception. *Human Relations* 3:57–76.

SEASHORE, HAROLD C.; and BAVELAS, ALEX 1942 A Study of Frustration in Children. *Pedagogical Seminary and Journal of Genetic Psychology* 61:279–314.

SLIOSBERG, SARAH 1934 Zur Dynamik des Ersatzes in Spiel- und Ernstsituationen. Untersuchungen zur Handlungs- und Affektpsychologie, 19. *Psychologische Forschung* 19:122–181.

THIBAUT, JOHN W.; and RIECKEN, HENRY W. 1955 Some Determinants and Consequences of the Perception of Social Causality. *Journal of Personality* 24:113–133.

WHITE, RALPH K. 1951 *Value-analysis: The Nature and Use of the Method.* Glen Gardner, N.J.: Society for the Psychological Study of Social Issues.

WRIGHT, M. ERIK 1942 Constructiveness of Play as Affected by Group Organization and Frustration. *Character and Personality* 11:40–49.

ZEIGARNIK, BLUMA 1927 Das Behalten erledigter und unerledigter Handlungen. Untersuchungen zur Handlungs- und Affektpsychologie, 3. *Psychologische Forschung* 9:1–85.

LEXIS, WILHELM

Wilhelm Lexis (1837–1914), a German statistician and economist, made major contributions to the theory of statistics and its application, particularly in population research and economic time series. As a mathematician Lexis was deeply skeptical about the state of mathematical economics in his time. His criticism of certain contemporary work in mathematical economics led him to some fundamental observations on economic events and their interdependence.

Lexis was born in Eschweiler, near Aachen, Germany. His studies were widespread, and his interests ranged from law to the natural sciences and mathematics. He graduated from the University of Bonn in 1859, having written a thesis on analytical mechanics; he also obtained a degree in mathematics. For some time he did research in Bunsen's chemical laboratories in Heidelberg. In 1861, Lexis went to Paris to study the social sciences, and his studies led to his first major publication (1870), a treatise on French export policies. This work displays the feature that characterizes his later economic writings: a skepticism toward "pure economics" and toward the application of supposedly descriptive mathematical models which have no reference to economic reality. Even in this early work he insisted that economic theory should be founded on quantitative economic data. In Lexis' view an elaborate general economic equilibrium analysis, whose main problem was to match the unknowns with an equal number of equations, could make no contribution to the understanding or solution of economic problems and therefore should not be taken too seriously. He was one of a number of mathematically trained students of economics who, in the second half of the nineteenth century, became alienated from that discipline; another, more famous one was Max Planck, who, after attempting to read Marshall's work, threw it away and changed his course of study for good (see Schumpeter 1954, pp. 957–958).

Lexis was appointed to the University of Strassburg in 1872. While there, he wrote his introduction to the theory of population (1875). From Strassburg he went to Dorpat in 1874, as professor of geography, ethnology, and statistics, and then to Freiburg in 1876, as professor of economics. His major contributions to statistics were made while he was at Freiburg (1876; 1877; 1879*a*), and he also published papers on economics at this time (1879*b*; 1881; 1882*a*; 1882*b*). After an interlude at the University of Breslau from 1884 to 1887, he was appointed professor of political science at the University of Göttingen.

Lexis' activities in his later years were remarkably diverse. An editor of the *Handwörterbuch der Staatswissenschaften*, the major German economic encyclopedia, he was also an active contributor, and he was director of the first institute of actuarial sciences in Germany. In the 1890s he published and edited several volumes pertaining to education, particularly to the university system (1893; 1901; 1902; 1904*a*; 1904*b*). Lexis' works on population research, economics, and statistics during the subsequent decade bring together and refine some of his earlier arguments (see 1903; 1906*a*; 1906*b*; 1908; 1914). He died in Göttingen during the very first days of World War I.

Statistics

Lexis' major contributions were in statistics. His statistical work originated in problems he encountered in population research (1875; 1879*b*; 1891; 1903), sociology (1877), and economics (1870; 1879*a*; 1908; 1914). In connection with his studies of social mass phenomena (1877) and the time series encountered in several of the social sciences (1879*b*), Lexis came upon problems concerning statistical homogeneity which apparently had been neglected up to then, although, as Bortkiewicz pointed out (1918), Dormoy (1874; 1878) developed similar ideas at about the same time. (Other possible forerunners of Lexis were Bienaymé [1855], Cournot [1843], and R. Campbell [1859].) Lexis credited Dormoy with having anticipated some of his ideas; nevertheless, it was Lexis who more or less independently gave a new direction to the analysis of statistical series and led statisticians in the shift of emphasis from the purely mathematical approach, with which Laplace is associated, to an empirical or inductive approach (see Keynes 1921, pp. 392 ff.). He also initiated the analysis of dispersion and variance in his attempts to develop statistics with which to evaluate qualitative changes in populations over time (see Keynes 1921; Pólya 1919).

Lexis showed that in the universe of social mass phenomena the conditions of statistical homogeneity (random sampling from a stable distribution) are seldom, if ever, fulfilled (1877; 1879*a*; 1879*b*). The underlying probability structure may well differ from one part of the sample to another because of special circumstances related to dispersion in space, time, or other factors. A universe in which individual samples are drawn from potentially different populations is now known as a *Lexis universe* (see, for example, Herdan 1966). To some extent Lexis' work was a reaction to the uncritical assumptions of homogeneity made in statistical work before his time—for instance, by Quetelet. As Keynes (1921) pointed out, Quetelet and others simply asserted, with little evidence, the probabilistic stability from year to year of various social statistics.

Lexis' work centered on the dispersion of observations around their local means and on the behavior of the means and dispersions over time. He devised statistics to measure the degree of stability of such time series and arrived at the useful generalization that these statistics would either confirm statistical homogeneity, indicating a *Bernoulli series*, or diverge from it, indicating a *Poisson series* or a *Lexis series*. (This terminology was developed by C. V. L. Charlier; see A. Fisher 1915, p. 117).

Lexis considered only dichotomous variates (male–female, living–dead, etc.), but the argument he advanced holds equally for numerical variates in the ordinary sense (see also Pólya 1919). In the following, Lexis' ideas are given in a generalized form.

Let x_{ij} ($i = 1, \cdots, n$, $j = 1, \cdots, m$) be a set of n samples with m observations each, and let the arithmetic mean of the x_{ij} in sample i be $\bar{x}_i$ and the arithmetic mean of the x_{ij} over all n samples be $\bar{x}$. Similarly, let $a_{ij} = E(x_{ij})$, the expectation of x_{ij}, so that $\bar{a}_i = E(\bar{x}_i)$ and $\bar{a} = E(\bar{x})$. Lexis considered the following quadratic forms which measure dispersion in three different senses:

$$s_w^2 = \frac{1}{nm} \sum_i \sum_j (x_{ij} - \bar{x}_i)^2,$$

$$s_b^2 = \frac{1}{n} \sum_i (\bar{x}_i - \bar{x})^2,$$

$$s^2 = \frac{1}{nm} \sum_i \sum_j (x_{ij} - \bar{x})^2,$$

where s_b^2 has rank (degrees of freedom) $r_b = n - 1$, s_w^2 has rank $r_w = n(m - 1)$, and s^2 has rank $r = r_b + r_w = nm - 1$. (The subscripts "*w*" and "*b*" are used to indicate that s_w^2 comprises within sample dispersion and s_b^2 between sample dispersion.) Furthermore,

$$s^2 = s_b^2 + s_w^2.$$

If the n samples of m objects each are drawn at random from the same population, then the expected value of each observation equals the expected value of the sample mean and the expected value of the mean of all observations, that is,

$$a_{ij} = \bar{a}_i = \bar{a},$$

and statistical homogeneity is present. Repeated independent measurements of a distance and $n \times m$ drawings of balls from an urn with each ball returned after it is drawn are examples of such series. In this case the three quadratic forms, multiplied by appropriate constants, have the same expectations. Specifically, when statistical homogeneity holds,

$$E\left(\frac{n}{r} s^2\right) = E\left(\frac{n}{r_b} s_b^2\right) = E\left(\frac{n}{r_w} s_w^2\right),$$

and the common value is $1/m$ times the variance of the underlying population. A set of samples drawn under such conditions is known as a Bernoulli series (see, e.g., A. Fisher 1915).

It may, however, be the case that statistical homogeneity holds within the samples ($a_{i1} = a_{i2} = \cdots = a_{im}$) but not between samples—that is, the n samples may be random samples from different populations. In this case a Lexis series is generated (a supernormal series, in Lexis' terminology). Such a series is expected when, for example, each set of balls (one sample) is drawn from a different urn. Other examples of such series explain further the importance of the Lexis series: m observations made at time t_0, another m observations made at time t_1, and so forth, up to t_n, will give rise to a *time series* of $m \times n$ observations, where the ith sample (covering one period, t_i) may well come from a single population but where between different periods such changes occurred that statistical homogeneity is no longer preserved—that is, the samples come from different populations.

Similarly, social or economic samples of m observations drawn from n different geographical regions (nations) are likely to come from different statistical populations, although in each region (nation) the m observations of the sample come from the same distribution (*interregional series, in-*

ternational series). In short, if the over-all dispersion is caused not only by chance variations about a constant but also by trends and other systematic factors varying between samples, then a Lexis series will be generated. (A comprehensive and elementary treatment of Lexis series is given in Pólya 1919.)

We expect in this case that the variance between the samples will contribute relatively more to the over-all variance of the $m \times n$ observations than will the variance within the samples and that the expected value of an observation will equal the sample mean, whereas the sample mean is expected to differ from the mean of all observations. Further, although $a_{ij} = \bar{a}_i$, $\bar{a}_i \neq \bar{a}$ for at least some i, and

$$E\left(\frac{n}{r_w} s_w^2\right) < E\left(\frac{n}{r} s^2\right) < E\left(\frac{n}{r_b} s_b^2\right).$$

Statistical homogeneity is not preserved.

Much less realistic, but a formal complement to the Bernoulli and Lexis series, is the Poisson series (a subnormal series, in Lexis' terminology). The Poisson model was developed as one that would generate higher within sample than between sample variability. In this case the jth observation of each sample is drawn from a fixed population, but the populations differ according to j. In short, $a_{1j} = a_{2j} = \cdots = a_{nj}$, but for a fixed i the a_{ij} are not all equal. Hence $\bar{a}_i = \bar{a}$, and there is no between sample variability coming from the a's. It follows that

$$E\left(\frac{n}{r_b} s_b^2\right) < E\left(\frac{n}{r} s^2\right) < E\left(\frac{n}{r_w} s_w^2\right).$$

Other kinds of models leading to subnormal dispersion have also been considered.

Lexis proposed a statistic, based on the above quadratic forms, to describe the extent to which a given series is homogeneous, supernormal, or subnormal. The statistic, called the Lexis quotient, is

$$L = \frac{s_b^2/r_b}{s^2/r},$$

a monotone increasing function of another statistic, $(s_b^2/r_b)/(s_w^2/r_w)$, which might be used alternatively. A. A. Chuprov showed later (1922) that in the case of statistical homogeneity, $E(L) = 1$ and the variance of L is approximately $2/(n-1)$.

A further elaboration of this leads to significance tests. A first step in that direction is made by adding to and subtracting from the expected value of L its standard error, obtaining $1 \pm \sqrt{2/(n-1)}$. If L lies within the boundaries thus calculated, one may conclude with confidence of approximately two out of three that the statistical mass is homogeneous; if L is significantly larger than 1, one may conclude that the series was drawn from a Lexis universe; and if L is significantly smaller than 1, one may conclude that the series is Poisson.

The relevance and connections of the Lexis series and Lexis' L to the analysis of variance and the chi-square distribution were later shown by many authors. The formal connection between L and the χ^2 statistic of Pearson was elaborated by R. A. Fisher. Fisher showed that in the case of a $2 \times n$ classification the χ^2 statistic is just nL. [*See* COUNTED DATA; *see also* R. A. Fisher 1928; Gebelein & Heite 1951.]

The relation of the L-statistic to the F-statistic is very direct, and we may say that Lexis anticipated the F-statistic (see Coolidge 1921; Rietz 1932; Geiringer 1942*a*; 1942*b*; Gini 1956; Herdan 1966). Whereas in L one compares the variance between the samples to the variance of all $n \times m$ observations, that is,

$$L = \frac{s_b^2/r_b}{s^2/r},$$

in the F-statistic one compares the variance between the samples to the variance within the samples, that is,

$$F = \frac{s_b^2/r_b}{s_w^2/r_w}.$$

Furthermore,

$$L \gtreqless 1 \quad \text{if and only if} \quad F \gtreqless 1.$$

This concurrence is based on the previously stated equality

$$s^2 = s_b^2 + s_w^2.$$

Although the asymptotic distribution of the F-statistic as $m \to \infty$ was established by R. A. Fisher (1925, p. 97) and by W. G. Cochran (1934, p. 178) and generalized by M. G. Madow (1940), the same distribution was established for Lexis' L as early as 1876 by F. R. Helmert, using the method of characteristic functions.

Bortkiewicz extended the application of Lexis' theory of dispersion, and Chuprov (1922) extended Lexis' theory and gave it the most comprehensive treatment. Others influenced by Lexis were J. von Kries, H. Westergaard, and F. Y. Edgeworth, the only Anglo–American scholar closely familiar with statistical work on the Continent at that time (see Keynes 1921).

Economics

Lexis' contributions to economic theory were less appreciated than were his contributions to statistics; many economists, including Schumpeter, largely ignored them. Such a negative assessment of Lexis' work proves to be not entirely justified after closer examination of the reasons that led him to criticize certain aspects of the mathematical and "pure" economics of his contemporaries. His main contribution was a valid criticism of the work done at his time, particularly that of the Austrian school and the Lausanne school. His criticism was informed in part by the outlook of the historical school, which was prevalent in Germany, and accordingly he believed that it was necessary to incorporate in any theory of value and demand the element of time as well as the phenomenon of the recurrence of wants.

Lexis accepted Gossen's analysis of human behavior because Gossen appreciated all the shortcomings of any such theory. The criticisms Lexis made of the Austrian school seem contradictory but are only superficially so: he deplored the lack of mathematics in the work of some authors, especially Carl Menger, and found fault with the application of inappropriate mathematics in the work of others, especially Auspitz and Lieben.

Lexis regarded the concept of utility as being rather vague, since utility cannot be measured. He argued that to say that the utility of a good (set of goods) is equal to, larger than, or less than the utility of some other good permits a partial or complete preordering of utilities. Complementarity and substitution effects imply, however, subadditivity and superadditivity of utilities, which render futile any attempt to aggregate utilities and demand correspondences. Lexis questioned the convexity and continuity assumptions of preference orderings.

The controversy then raging over how to determine total utility given the marginal utility correspondences (a controversy between E. von Böhm-Bawerk and F. von Wieser) was correctly interpreted by Lexis and led him to a discussion of Gossen's other laws, most notably the equalization of marginal utilities. Any such theorem, he believed, must be hedged by a number of qualifications; it is particularly important to consider the time element connected with demand and consumption. Want and satisfaction are both felt and exercised over time. At one and the same time only a limited set of wants can be satisfied. One can eat, drink, sleep, and work, but these activities are to some extent mutually exclusive. Thus, the individual has to decide what sequence to follow in satisfying his set of wants. This sequence will be determined, according to Lexis, by the intensity of wants and by their periodicity, the most fundamental rhythms being the day, the year, and one lifetime. The demand of an individual will be classified and exercised accordingly. Intensive wants will be satisfied first, on a daily, yearly, or other basis, depending on the periodicity of recurrence of wants. Other, less intensive wants will be satisfied after full satisfaction of the intensive wants has been achieved. The implications are far-reaching but perhaps misleading; they have not been accepted by subsequent economists. Individual demand correspondences have to be defined by the period to which they relate, which in turn requires a reformulation of the theory of demand and implies the necessity of defining the demand for (consumption of) each good at different times as quantitatively different. This entails no theoretical difficulties in a general mathematical equilibrium analysis, but it does prevent the theory from having any operational value.

The concept of preferential ordering over time induced Lexis to observe that certain more intensive wants will be saturated whereas other, less intensive wants will be satisfied partially, implying satisfaction of zero marginal utility for the first set of wants and some positive marginal utility for the second. Lexis supported this conclusion by referring to economic reality. However, his statement about the equalization of marginal utilities turns out ultimately to be incorrect if we allow for errors of judgment, evaluations of uncertainties and risks, and diversity of attributes of each good for any individual.

Thus, Lexis' skepticism about the potential of the marginal utility theory in economics was based on the difficulty of measuring utility, the existence of subadditivities and superadditivities in utility correspondences, and the impossibility of aggregating individual preferences. The introduction of the time element into the theory of value and demand adds interesting arguments to general equilibrium analysis which imply, according to Lexis, obvious refutations of the equalization of marginal utilities. As a consequence of his skepticism, Lexis turned, in the rest of his economic work, to a rather dry description of economic events, which failed to be attractive to more speculative minds.

KLAUS-PETER HEISS

WORKS BY LEXIS

1870 *Die französischen Ausfuhrprämien im Zusammenhange mit der Tarifgeschichte und Handelsentwicklung Frankreichs seit der Restauration.* Bonn: Marcus.

1875 *Einleitung in die Theorie der Bevölkerungsstatistik.* Strassburg: Trübner.

1876 Das Geschlechtsverhältniss der Geborenen und die Wahrscheinlichkeitsrechnung. *Jahrbücher für Nationalökonomie und Statistik* 27:209–245.

1877 *Zur Theorie der Massenerscheinungen in der menschlichen Gesellschaft.* Freiburg im Breisgau: Wagner.

(1879*a*) 1942 *Über die Theorie der Stabilität statistischer Reihen (The Theory of the Stability of Statistical Series).* Minneapolis, Minn: WPA. → First published in Volume 32 of *Jahrbücher für Nationalökonomie und Statistik.*

1879*b* Gewerkvereine und Unternehmerverbände in Frankreich. Verein für Socialpolitik, Berlin, *Schriften* 17:1–280.

1881 *Erörterungen über die Währungsfrage.* Leipzig: Duncker & Humblot.

(1882*a*) 1890 Die volkswirthschaftliche Konsumtion. Volume 1, pages 685–722 in *Handbuch der politischen Oekonomie.* 3d ed. Edited by Gustav Schönberg. Tübingen: Laupp.

(1882*b*) 1891 Handel. Volume 2, pages 811–938 in *Handbuch der politischen Oekonomie.* 3d ed. Edited by Gustav Schönberg. Tübingen: Laupp.

1886 Über die Wahrscheinlichkeitsrechnung und deren Anwendung auf die Statistik. *Jahrbücher für Nationalökonomie und Statistik* 47:433–450.

1891 Bevölkerungswesen, II: Bevölkerungswechsel, 1: Allgemeine Theorie des Bevölkerungswechsels. Volume 2, pages 456–463 in *Handwörterbuch der Staatswissenschaften.* Jena: Fischer.

1893 *Die deutschen Universitäten: Für die Universitätsausstellung in Chicago 1893.* 2 vols. Berlin: Asher.

(1895*a*) 1896 *The Present Monetary Situation.* American Economic Association, Economic Studies, Vol. 1, No. 4. New York: Macmillan. → First published as *Der gegenwärtige Stand der Währungsfrage.*

1895*b* Grenznutzen. Volume 1, pages 422–432 in *Handwörterbuch der Staatswissenschaften: Supplementband.* Jena: Fischer.

1901 *Die neuen französischen Universitäten.* Munich: Academischer Verlag.

1902 LEXIS, WILHELM (editor) *Die Reform des höheren Schulwesens in Preussen.* Halle: Waisenhaus.

1903 *Abhandlungen zur Theorie der Bevölkerungs- und Moralstatistik.* Jena: Fischer. → Contains reprints of 1876 and 1879*a*.

1904*a* LEXIS, WILHELM (editor) *Das Unterrichtswesen im Deutschen Reich.* 4 vols. Berlin: Asher.

1904*b* *A General View of the History and Organisation of Public Education in the German Empire.* Berlin: Asher.

1906*a* Das Wesen der Kultur. Pages 1–53 in *Die allgemeinen Grundlagen der Kultur der Gegenwart.* Die Kultur der Gegenwart, vol. 1, part 1. Berlin: Teubner.

1906*b* *Das Handelswesen.* 2 vols. Sammlung Göschen, Vols. 296–297. Berlin: Gruyter. → Volume 1: *Das Handelspersonal und der Warenhandel.* Volume 2: *Die Effektenbörse und die innere Handelspolitik.*

1908 Systematisierung, Richtungen und Methoden der Volkswirtschaftslehre. Volume 1, pages I:1–45 in *Die Entwicklung der deutschen Volkswirtschaftslehre im neunzehnten Jahrhundert.* Leipzig: Duncker & Humblot.

(1910) 1926 *Allgemeine Volkswirtschaftslehre.* 3d ed., rev. Die Kultur der Gegenwart, vol. 2, part 10, section 1. Berlin and Leipzig: Teubner.

(1914) 1929 *Das Kredit- und Bankwesen.* 2d ed. Sammlung Göschen, Vol. 733. Berlin: Gruyter.

SUPPLEMENTARY BIBLIOGRAPHY

BAUER, RAINALD K. 1955 Die Lexissche Dispersionstheorie in ihren Beziehungen zur modernen statistischen Methodenlehre, insbesondere zur Streuungsanalyse (Analysis of Variance). *Mitteilungsblatt für mathematische Statistik und ihre Anwendungsgebiete* 7: 25–45.

BIENAYMÉ, JULES (1855) 1876 Sur un principe que M. Poisson avait cru découvrir et qu'il avait appelé loi des grands nombres. *Journal de la Société de Statistique de Paris* 17:199–204.

BORTKIEWICZ, LADISLAUS VON 1901 Über den Präcisiongrad des Divergenzkoëffizienten. Verband der Österreichischen und Ungarischen Versicherungs-Techniker, *Mitteilungen* 5:1–3.

BORTKIEWICZ, LADISLAUS VON 1909–1911 Statistique. Part 1, Volume 4, pages 453–490 in *Encyclopédie des sciences mathématiques.* Paris: Gauthier-Villars.

BORTKIEWICZ, LADISLAUS VON 1915 Wilhelm Lexis [Obituary]. International Statistical Institute, *Bulletin* 20, no. 1:328–332.

BORTKIEWICZ, LADISLAUS VON 1917 Wahrscheinlichkeitstheoretische Untersuchungen über die Knabenquote bei Zwillingsgeburten. Berliner Mathematische Gesellschaft, *Sitzungsberichte* 17:8–14.

BORTKIEWICZ, LADISLAUS VON 1918 Der mittlere Fehler des zum Quadrat erhobenen Divergenzkoëffizienten. Deutsche Mathematiker-Vereinigung, *Jahresbericht* 27: 71–126.

BORTKIEWICZ, LADISLAUS VON 1930 Lexis und Dormoy. *Nordic Statistical Journal* 2:37–54.

BORTKIEWICZ, LADISLAUS VON 1931 The Relations Between Stability and Homogeneity. *Annals of Mathematical Statistics* 2:1–22.

CAMPBELL, ROBERT 1859 On the Probability of Uniformity in Statistical Tables. *Philosophical Magazine* 18:359–368.

CHUPROV, ALEKSANDR A. 1905 Die Aufgaben der Theorie der Statistik. *Jahrbuch für Gesetzgebung, Verwaltung und Volkswirtschaft im Deutschen Reich* 29: 421–480. → The author's name is given its German transliteration, Tschuprow.

CHUPROV, ALEKSANDR A. 1922 Ist die normale Stabilität empirisch nachweisbar? *Nordisk statistisk tidskrift* 1:369–393. → The author's name is given its German transliteration, Tschuprow.

COCHRAN, W. G. 1934 The Distribution of Quadratic Forms in a Normal System, With Applications to the Analysis of Covariance. Cambridge Philosophical Society, *Proceedings* 30:178–191.

COOLIDGE, JULIAN L. 1921 The Dispersion of Observations. American Mathematical Society, *Bulletin* 27: 439–442.

COURNOT, ANTOINE AUGUSTIN 1843 *Exposition de la théorie des chances et des probabilités.* Paris: Hachette.

DORMOY, ÉMILE 1874 *Théorie mathématique des paris de courses.* Paris: Gauthier-Villars. → Also published in Volume 3 of *Journal des actuaires français.*

DORMOY, ÉMILE 1878 *Théorie mathématique des assurances sur la vie.* 2 vols. Paris: Gauthier-Villars.

EDGEWORTH, F. Y. 1885 Methods of Statistics. Pages 181–217 in Royal Statistical Society, London, *Jubilee Volume.* London: Stanford.

FISHER, ARNE 1915 *The Mathematical Theory of Probabilities and Its Application to Frequency Curves and Statistical Methods.* Vol. 1. London: Macmillan.

FISHER, R. A. 1925 Applications of "Student's" Distribution. *Metron* 5, no. 3:90–104.

FISHER, R. A. 1928 On a Distribution Yielding the Error Functions of Several Well Known Statistics. Volume 2, pages 805–813 in International Congress of Mathematicians (New Series), Second, Toronto, 1924, *Proceedings.* Univ. of Toronto Press.

GEBELEIN, HAND; and HEITE, H.-J. 1951 *Statistische Urteilsbildung.* Berlin: Springer.

GEIRINGER, HILDA 1942*a* A New Explanation of Nonnormal Dispersion in the Lexis Theory. *Econometrica* 10:53–60.

GEIRINGER, HILDA 1942*b* Observations on Analysis of Variance Theory. *Annals of Mathematical Statistics* 13:350–369.

GINI, C. 1956 Généralisations et applications de la théorie de la dispersion. *Metron* 18, no. 1/2:1–75.

HELMERT, F. R. 1876 Ueber die Wahrscheinlichkeit der Potenzsummen der Beobachtungsfehler und über einige damit im Zusammenhange stehenden Fragen. *Zeitschrift für Mathematik und Physik* 21:192–218.

HERDAN, G. 1966 *The Advanced Theory of Language as Choice and Chance.* New York: Springer.

KEYNES, JOHN MAYNARD (1921) 1952 *A Treatise on Probability.* London: Macmillan. → A paperback edition was published in 1962 by Harper.

KRIES, JOHANNES VON (1886) 1927 *Die Principien der Wahrscheinlichkeitsrechnung: Eine logische Untersuchung.* 2d ed. Tübingen: Mohr.

MADOW, WILLIAM G. 1940 Limiting Distributions of Quadratic and Bilinear Forms. *Annals of Mathematical Statistics* 11:125–146.

PÓLYA, GEORG 1919 Anschauliche und elementare Darstellung der Lexisschen Dispersionstheorie. *Zeitschrift für schweizerische Statistik und Volkswirtschaft* 55: 121–140.

RIETZ, H. L. 1932 On the Lexis Theory and the Analysis of Variance. American Mathematical Society, *Bulletin* 38:731–735.

SCHUMPETER, JOSEPH A. (1954) 1960 *History of Economic Analysis.* Edited by E. B. Schumpeter. New York: Oxford Univ. Press.

VON MISES, RICHARD 1932 Théorie des probabilités: Fondements et applications. Paris, Université de, Institut Henri Poincaré, *Annales* 3:137–190.

LIBERALISM

Liberalism is the belief in and commitment to a set of methods and policies that have as their common aim greater freedom for individual men. Early liberalism was identified with political parties or social classes and often with specific programs. Today, although some parties in Europe, Great Britain, and elsewhere bear the title Liberal, in contemporary usage the term "liberalism" refers to a system of thought and practice that is less specific than a philosophical doctrine and more inclusive than party principle. Liberalism is also too ecumenical and too pluralistic to be called, properly, an ideology. Contemporary liberalism is the product of centuries of development and of attitudes and responses widely shared among individuals. It can be described as: (1) a valuing of the free expression of individual personality; (2) a belief in men's ability to make that expression valuable to themselves and to society; and (3) the upholding of those institutions and policies that protect and foster both free expression and confidence in that freedom.

The term "liberal" probably first acquired its modern political connotation from the Liberales, a Spanish party that supported for Spain a version of the French constitution of 1791. As a coherent system of ideals and practical goals, however, liberalism first developed in England in the seventeenth and eighteenth centuries. Thereafter, liberal parties and liberal views, developing independently or derived from the English model, appeared in Europe, several British colonies, and elsewhere in the world.

Liberal thought and practice have stressed two primary themes. One is the dislike for arbitrary authority, complemented by the aim of replacing that authority by other forms of social practice. A second theme is the free expression of individual personality. Liberal movements and liberal thought have usually emphasized one theme more than the other, though seldom one to the virtual exclusion of the other. Much of liberal political and social theory has, in fact, been devoted to reconciling these two aims, especially with respect to their philosophical and practical implications.

Early liberalism emphasized freedom *from* arbitrary authority. One mode of attack was the assertion of free conscience and the demand for religious tolerance. Liberals have often been nonconformists in religion, secularists, skeptics, and even antireligious. In place of traditional authority they have supported the authority of reason and of demonstrated, rather than revealed, truth. Liberalism has stressed also the desirability of impersonal social and political controls: the rule of law and the market. Liberals have usually been individualists and pluralists and have supported local and group liberties and the methods of consent and persuasion.

Also vital to liberalism has been the goal of an active freedom, the ideal that the individual has the opportunity and the capacity for free expression. To this end, liberals have supported a more equal distribution of liberty, the abolition of monopolies, the destruction of aristocratic privilege, and a law that was general and founded upon rational principles. Liberals have argued also for the expansion of opportunity, including state intervention to equalize and increase the opportunities open to individuals. For all these reasons, liberalism has usually been "progressive," i.e., concerned with economic and social progress and favorable to science, technology, and pragmatic experimentalism.

The two most important objectives of liberalism —noninterference and enfranchisement—support each other but also conflict. The first objective, pursued to an extreme, would leave the individual at the mercy of nature, society, and group and economic power. The second, followed alone, leads ultimately to statism and technocracy. Liberalism is neither of the extremes. It is a reconciliation of the two goals, with the relation between them determined by the needs of a society and the means available to it. Thus, liberalism does not, in fact, include such disparate figures as Rexford G. Tugwell, John Dewey, and Ludwig von Mises. Each is in part illiberal. Liberalism requires a rational and conscientious reconciliation of two essential goals.

The heritage of liberalism

Liberalism, in both its classical and its more contemporary, or "revisionist," forms, is essentially a modern phenomenon. It is the heir of a rich tradition. Liberty, constitutionalism, and toleration were known to the ancient world, and the Western liberalism of England, Europe, and America is the beneficiary of several religious traditions, of Greek philosophy and literature, of Roman law and constitutionalism. In the ancient world, however, liberty was closely associated with religion, ethnic culture, and citizenship. Liberalism itself did not exist as a separate and self-sustaining tradition. Moreover, the line of descent from ancient to modern liberty is not a direct one. The liberalism that developed in England and Europe in the eighteenth and nineteenth centuries was, at that time, a unique occurrence, resulting from the convergence of social and political tendencies peculiar to a specific time and environment.

Liberalism benefited from medieval constitutionalism and from the religious traditions of the church and Western Christianity. English liberalism, because of the common law, the parliamentary tradition, and the peaceful character of the English Reformation, drew much from this background, a fact illustrated by the works of John Fortescue, Richard Hooker, and Edward Coke. On the Continent the same materials proved less usable, but they served in a limited way to legitimate ancient liberties, a measure of toleration, and the rule of law.

The Renaissance and the Reformation were important in fostering liberalism, especially through the contribution they made to individualism. The Protestant doctrine that each believer could communicate directly with God, without dependence upon priest or churchly hierarchy, was an important anti-institutional influence and therefore favorable to individualism. Ideals of personal sanctification and inwardness of moral life that earlier had been restricted to orders of monks, knights, and burghers were democratized during the fifteenth and sixteenth centuries. In addition, the Reformation and the Counter Reformation, by stressing internal energy, individual responsibility, and the need for reconstructing the worldly order, greatly stimulated individualism, despite the intentions of Luther and Calvin or St. Ignatius and Pope Paul III.

Political changes, especially during and after the Reformation, contributed ultimately to the rise of liberalism. Wars decimated nobilities, broke down settled relations between lord and commoner, engaged new groups in collective activity. The domestic and international policies of monarchs brought to prominence bureaucrats of common or seminoble status, lawyers, town merchants, military adventurers, and scholars and scientists. The new nation-states fostered changes in law, in the economy, and in personal relations that increased commerce and the circulation of money, and the numbers of merchants, masters, and artificers. Not to be ignored is the further fact that many of these political changes entailed taxation, intervention, oppression, and suppression, which were important issues in later constitutional struggles and liberal protests.

From the policies of modern states, from economic change, and from a diffusion of culture and literacy came the small self-conscious middle class, which was the most important vehicle for liberal doctrine. Scientific discovery and technological innovation, capitalist methods of economic venture, modified legal concepts, and new forms of property worked reciprocally, especially from the sixteenth through the eighteenth centuries, to provide both the opportunity and the incentives for individual and group initiative. The consequence was the increase not only of a small commercial and industrial middle class but, even more important, the spread of attitudes hospitable to individual enterprise and to the creed of individual responsibility.

A comparatively rapid and wide diffusion of enlightened and cosmopolitan attitudes among social and political elites, as well as among burghers, professional men, merchants, and country gentry, was of enormous importance to the development of liberalism, especially in the later seventeenth and eighteenth centuries. This development depended upon and grew from the earlier humanism and enlightenment of the Renaissance and Reformation. But the earlier tradition had been restricted largely to the court, the city, and the clergy. During the eighteenth century the arts and the sciences, political life, and a comparatively sophisticated culture became accessible to a much wider circle. Many more read; many more discussed.

Liberalism, viewed in historical perspective, was the culmination of several broad social and political trends. It involved a change in the scope of individual aspirations and, perhaps more important, in the people who had them. Prior to the nineteenth century these aspirations were restricted to an elite of birth and wealth. Social environment, individual aspiration, and consciousness of capacity combined to produce, in the nineteenth century, a widely shared and politically potent liberal faith.

Classical liberalism

Liberalism, both as a doctrine and as a political program, developed most fully in England between the Glorious Revolution (1688) and the Reform Act of 1867. Liberalism was first a limited appeal for constitutional guarantees and individual rights. It became a positive theory of economic and political organization and a political program with broad national appeal extending to many groups and classes. Neither on the Continent nor in the United States did early liberalism develop in a similar fashion. The experience of England stands alone; and the term "classical liberalism" is ordinarily used with reference to England.

Liberalism in England first took the form of a demand for religious liberties and toleration, constitutionalism, and political rights. During the Puritan revolution and the Commonwealth, written constitutions were proposed and pamphlets published demanding a number of liberties. Digger and Leveller tracts, the pamphlets of John Lilburne, the more reflective *Commonwealth of Oceana* of James Harrington, and Milton's exalted defense of free speech in *Areopagitica* not only illustrate the scope of the constitutional controversy but also afford a sample of the political literature of the period. The revolution of 1688, the first "liberal revolution" in history, consolidated and gave definite constitutional form to the liberal gains of that century. The liberalism recognized and vindicated in 1689 was essentially negative in character, protecting groups and individuals *from* government, especially from the prerogatives of the crown. It was also aimed at securing chiefly political rather than economic objectives. Among those political objectives are some of the most important principles of liberal constitutionalism: the right of opposition, the rule of law, and the separation of powers. The settlement also included a recognition of important civil liberties by acts securing toleration, in 1688, and liberty of the press, in 1695. Locke's *Second Treatise of Government* and the American Declaration of Independence stand as the great monuments of this phase of liberalism. [*See* CONSTITUTIONS AND CONSTITUTIONALISM; *and the biography of* LOCKE.]

The constitutional settlement and civil peace gave enormous impetus to a second theme of classical liberalism: the theory and practice of economic liberty. The English liberal economists, led by Adam Smith, were neither the first nor the only group to erect a theory upon the postulate of laissez-faire, but they were the most influential. Their ideals were: in the juridical sphere, free contract and the rule of law; in the economic sphere, a self-regulating market, unrestrained either by monopoly or political intervention; and in the social sphere, voluntarism and collaboration for mutual benefit. The laissez-faire doctrine and the practical organization of the economy that the classical economists advocated greatly strengthened liberalism. They did so, first of all, because they broadened and democratized the values of liberalism, extending them to mercantile, commercial, and laboring classes. Second, they did so because they encouraged forms of social and economic activity that could substitute for more compulsive and bureaucratic techniques of regulation. Thus, the point of Adam Smith's "obvious and simple system of natural liberty" was not only that it was "free" and "impersonal" but—equally important—that it was a "system" allowing men to exert their energies both to their own and to the common benefit [*see* LAISSEZ-FAIRE; SMITH, ADAM].

The English utilitarians and their political allies completed the edifice of classical liberalism. Jeremy Bentham and James Mill accepted the market economy and especially the ideals it served. They accepted, for the most part, the aims but not the methods of the liberalism of 1689. They brought the two species of liberalism together by applying the concepts of utility and the market to politics and the tasks of constitutionalism. Arguing from the hedonistic calculus and the principle of equality, they advocated "the greatest good of the greatest number." They insisted in law and politics upon general rules that provide for a maximum of free choice and practical liberty for all, or as many as consonant with general utilitarian maxims. And they argued that only education and free speech, inclusive representation and an expanded suffrage, and the regular accountability of the governors to the governed—politics organized on the model of the free economy—could provide constitutional security and good government. English utilitarianism, as propounded by Bentham and James Mill, provided a philosophical foundation for political liberalism. It also unified economic liberalism with a theory of positive political action. Properly, this utilitarian doctrine deserves the title of the first comprehensive liberal philosophy [*see* BENTHAM; MILL; UTILITARIANISM].

Classsical liberalism in England owed much of its success to the fact that three liberal traditions—constitutionalism, economic liberalism, and utilitarianism—each developing in a different historic period and having a different group appeal, could be effectively joined in practical politics. Liberalism in England became a party with a broad appeal and sustained its appeal for many years. At the time of the corn law repeal (1846) liberalism in England had its broadest support, including many Whigs, Cobden and Bright liberals, utilitarians, and middle-class and working-class adherents. Probably this alliance marked the natural limits of the older liberalism. It also occupied the common meeting ground of several varieties of liberal program and ideology. Liberalism at this point in England achieved a maximum synthesis of its two competing themes: noninterference and enfranchisement.

Liberalism in Europe and America

Two vital conditions for a classical liberal synthesis existed only in England—a broad liberal movement and a powerful liberal party. In the United States the second condition was missing; on the Continent, the first.

In the United States classical liberalism did not exist, partly because conservatism in the European sense did not exist either. From Europe, Americans inherited the libertarian precepts of the Puritan revolution, the Whig settlement of 1689, and some liberal economic values. These were "received" in the colonial tradition and figured in the American Revolution, the Constitutional Convention, and, broadly, in the politics and jurisprudence of the developing nation. But they were a part of the national heritage and the spirit of the laws, not the self-conscious creed of a party or a class. Liberalism as such did not need to be vindicated, nor did it have a specific role to play. Moreover, liberalism was mixed with other issues of democracy and equality, as, for instance, in the eras of Jefferson and Jackson. When, in the late nineteenth and early twentieth centuries, social Darwinism and natural-rights jurisprudence were erected into a creed of noninterference and supposed liberty, they were already "ideology" and not "utopia." America was, then, in large measure the unreflective inheritor of classical liberalism, especially the Lockean variety. Conscious or self-conscious liberalism in America came with the second phase of liberal development—the transition to a modern liberalism.

The classical liberal synthesis was sought in Europe but never fully achieved. Instead of developing into a broad and powerful movement and a comparatively effective political party, European liberalism remained fragmented and sectarian. Civil and religious strife and the slow development of commerce and industry contributed to this result. So did war. The state and the traditions of authority were too strong, liberalism too divided and weak, at the time when a liberal synthesis might have been realized. As a consequence, classical liberalism did not fully develop in Europe; instead several leading liberal creeds arose, which were usually doctrinaire in social philosophy and narrowly based in group support.

In Europe the primary task of securing and protecting the rule of law and constitutionally sanctioned liberties was more difficult. That task tended to become, for some European liberals, almost an end in itself, creating a liberal philosophy that Guido de Ruggiero (1925) has called "guarantism." Unfortunately, what needed to be guaranteed in the interests of constitutionalism were often ancient liberties and privileges that because of their oligarchic origins and reactionary tendency worked against a more common liberty and the general good. Consequently, one species of European liberalism was decidedly aristocratic, supporting not only liberty but also the inequitable privileges of localities, corporations, and social and religious groups. Montesquieu and Benjamin Constant afford good illustrations of aristocratic liberalism in political theory. The Restoration and the July Monarchy in France and the revolt of 1848 in Germany are historic tragedies of this divided heritage of European liberalism.

Rationalistic and utilitarian liberalism found expression, during the age of reason and afterward, primarily in an appeal for reform from above. The *philosophes* in France and German liberals such as Goethe and Herder adopted the goals of individualism, widened liberty, and a rational code of laws. They did not associate these objectives with political liberty or popular participation. For some the ideal was enlightened despotism and utilitarian standards, whatever the cost to particular and historic liberties or a constitutional tradition. The reform of civil and administrative institutions for liberal ends took precedence over the liberal method. And the liberal tradition was further divided within itself: some liberals espoused a despotic method, and others such as Rousseau, Fichte, and Mazzini sought the liberal spirit in a "general will" or "the people." Louis Bonaparte in France and Bismarck in Germany built much of their power upon this division.

In Europe there were liberal economic theorists, such as Jean Baptiste Say, Frédéric Bastiat, and Friedrich von Hermann; there were also middle-class political movements and parliamentary factions supporting laissez-faire and free trade. But Europe lacked the well-grown middle class and the economic, legal, and political environment needed to make the cause of economic freedom effective and, more important, to give liberalism a central direction. As a consequence, economic liberalism remained too long the creed of a part of the bourgeoisie and an intellectual preoccupation for scholars and a few publicists. Later, when economic liberalism was both possible and widely adopted—for instance, in the French Third Republic and in unified Italy—that policy served less fully the original liberal objectives of expanding liberty and equalizing opportunity. Economic circumstances made laissez-faire, as socialists protested, not a service to liberty as a whole but to the interests of a comparatively small number of economically advantaged individuals.

At an early stage, in Europe, liberalism failed because it was weak and divided. In the later decades of the nineteenth century it was "too late" for classical liberalism. This is not to say that liberalism was not a vitally needed political and doctrinal element of European society: it was. But liberalism had to appeal to a radically changed world, one in which democracy or republicanism, nationalism, and socialism were the popular gospels.

Modern liberalism

In the late nineteenth and early twentieth centuries classical liberalism and the traditions of thought and policy closely related to it were progressively modified. Later liberalism—especially in Great Britain and the United States, but to some extent almost everywhere in the modern world—has emphasized the positive rather than the negative aspect of liberty: the opportunity to form and accomplish self-appointed goals, rather than freedom from the state. Along with this shifting of proximate goals of liberalism came an adoption of new methods. The central value of the liberated individual, of man as far as possible his own sovereign, did not change; the understanding of that value and of the means for achieving it did.

An important cause of this revision was the success of liberalism itself: the securing of a considerable measure of political and economic liberty and the conversion of liberalism from a sectarian demand for noninterference into a program of political and economic organization. Success raised not only the question, What next? but also, Liberty for whom? Aristocrats and the bourgeoisie now had substantially the bundle of rights they needed. The franchise gave them the means of self-defense. But the same concessions—even when granted—were not enough for the peasant or the worker. Effective liberty for them required more positive action by the state, a fact that conservatives, Catholic social theorists, and Marxian and other socialists pointed out emphatically.

Liberal reorientation came partly through challenge and response, from a need to meet political and philosophical criticism. Liberalism was itself a philosophical and reasonable doctrine and therefore responsive to the new theories of man and society announced by nineteenth-century scientists and made popular by parliamentary inquiry, governmental commissions, and the newspapers. Politics was also important. The varied appeals of Tory Democracy in England, Louis Bonaparte's imperialism in France, and monarchical socialism in Germany were political forces that could not be ignored. Nor could a liberalism that served principally the bourgeoisie of the French Second Republic or the textile manufacturers of Manchester prosper in an age of the expanded franchise, effective mass communications, and social consciousness. The liberalism that survived after 1848 had, perforce, to accommodate itself to democratic, nationalist, and socialist sentiment.

The growth of cities, of industry, and of national and world-wide commerce also forced revisions of the liberal position. Earlier liberal theory, with its individualistic premises, had contrived a model of man, his institutions, and society that minimized the facts of organizational power, of community cost and benefit, and of national history and common fate. Time progressively falsified that model, especially after the growth of the modern corporation and industrial technology. Great inequalities in market power made one man's economic freedom another's oppression. Similarly, free trade in commodities—such as child labor, slum housing, poisoned meat, and bad gin—made the common benefit of regulation obvious. Liberals split among themselves. One group argued for a remedy of abuses other than those perpetrated by the state. Another group clung to the dogmas of nonintervention and free trade. They made the means of liberalism into ends in themselves and liberalism itself into a conservative ideology. Thus, one heir of Bentham and Adam Smith is John Stuart Mill, and another is Herbert Spencer [*see* SPENCER].

With consciousness of changed circumstances came a major reassessment of the means to liberty. Later liberals assigned greater importance to the social environment within which liberty had to be realized. Their revision of liberalism followed from a recognition that certain forms of coercion and obstacles to liberty arise from society itself rather than the activities of officials. The revision had another important foundation. A society of great economic and social interrelatedness makes access to culture, the capacity to participate, and membership and status in natural and artificial groups increasingly important both to the pursuit of liberty and to its defense. Rousseau and Hegel, and, later, T. H. Green and John Dewey, all argued this theme. Man is in society, the point at which many impinging groups, institutions, and cultural influences intersect. Seldom can he effectively withdraw. He can realize and defend his liberty only by participation. But a live option of participation does not simply happen: it is a social product depending upon education, incentive, opportunity, and a supporting system of political and social values. Modern liberalism tends necessarily, therefore, to be closely associated not only with social reform but with democracy and popular participation.

The modern liberal's view of the individual is also different from the classical description. It was not merely that the life and goals that suited a Bentham or an English merchant would distress a Coleridge, a Cardinal Newman, and, indeed, even a John Stuart Mill. The earlier liberal view of human nature was two dimensional and overly rationalistic. Nineteenth-century sociology and psychology destroyed that view thoroughly. Modern liberalism has assimilated much of the critique. Liberals today see man not only as an individual in society but as a person with a continuing need for self-expansion and reintegration. For this reason the emphasis of modern liberalism is less upon external impediments to motion and more upon the individual person's subjective feeling of freedom and those circumstances that give to this feeling an objective reality in the experience of the individual. If a man does not feel free, he is not free. [*See* PERSONALITY, POLITICAL.]

One question that arises is whether modern, or "revised," liberalism can still appropriately be called liberalism. Liberty and equality, rights and powers are not the same things. Modern liberalism advocates collectivist means, invoking the state in aid of individuals and disadvantaged groups. It has adopted much of the program of democratic and socialist movements. Is modern liberalism still "liberal"? Three considerations argue that this query be answered with a qualified affirmative. In the first place, modern liberalism retains the same end of the autonomous individual that has guided all true liberalism. The means to that end and proximate ends have changed, but the final end remains the same. Second, those changes in method and policy that most writers identify with the expansion and modernization of liberalism have served not only to reduce arbitrary compulsion but also to extend the scope, equalize the distribution, and enrich the liberty enjoyed by individuals. Third, constitutional rights and the rule of law not only survive in the mixed regime of liberty, democracy, and the administrative state but have in some ways grown stronger. They are stronger to the extent that the mixed regime is a representative one—in which the state cannot be used as a tool for the purposes of any *one* group or class but must serve and be responsive and accountable to *all*. Certainly, modern liberalism invokes the coercive power of the state. In relation to the state itself men are, in some ways, less free to do with their own as they please. For this reason it is important that the options open to men be many and that the relations of state, society, and individual afford alternate ways of suiting means to essential ends. Pluralism, decentralization, and a variety of relations between the state and society answer to these needs. They probably afford men, given an established welfare state, a better marginal choice in distributing their energies and opting for one of several modes of liberty than ever before in history. [*See* WELFARE STATE.]

The future of liberalism

Although liberalism has been important to Western civilization, it may not continue to be so. Since the two world wars, many argue, liberalism has been in decline. Liberalism means less, so the argument runs, to the developing nations, to the semi-socialist states of western Europe, to a world menaced with war and preoccupied with material benefit. Liberal parties and liberal ideology, it could also be argued, have served their function. The programs they supported have been adopted by others who have gone further. Historic liberalism survives only as a temper or mood of politics.

Liberal parties and liberal movements have been on the wane. In the British Commonwealth and Europe they have not fared well since World War II. Some maintain their electoral following, but mainly by altering their liberal stance. Specific movements, such as the neoliberalism of Germany and the Low Countries or the Mouvement Republicain Populaire of France, show an attrition of membership, unity, and purpose. The conclusion that liberalism as an *organized* party or self-conscious movement is for the present in decline is warranted by the facts. In no place, presently, are liberal parties or liberal movements gaining significantly in organized power or appeal.

Liberal policies have also received scant support among developing nations struggling for independence and material prosperity. The conditions that made Adam Smith's strategy of liberty suitable for England are missing today. Even such countries as Mexico and India, which seem determined to save liberty, are far from classical liberalism and even from more modern versions of liberalism. They are nationalistic and socialistic in many of their policies and are so by conscious intent and design.

The cold war has also weakened liberalism. In the short run, the communist challenge threatens liberty and constitutionalism directly. In the longer run, the danger is more insidious: external threats evoke response; and response demands collective effort. That effort is stimulated by nonliberal incentives and appeals: appeals to national purpose and common action and the incentives of a war economy. Liberty is not broken; but it shrinks. Liberalism is not vanquished; but it is not pursued. If, as John Stuart Mill said, "things left to themselves inevitably decay," the threat is greater than at first sight it appears. The danger to liberalism is not that it will be openly destroyed but that it will be forgotten or perverted.

From these facts it does not follow that liberalism is unimportant for the future. The importance of the liberal temper and of liberal principles applied to politics has not diminished; probably it has increased. Liberalism thrives on material prosperity, social peace, and common enlightenment. In the programs of the nations of western Europe immediately after World War II liberalism did not have a prominent place, nor has it been important in the programs of the developing nations. These nations have been engaged in creating the conditions of material prosperity and economic security. Hopefully, their labor will eventually bear fruit in comparatively stable, pluralistic democracies and welfare economies capable of providing security and abundance for their populations. Such developments would not make liberalism outmoded. They would, in fact, make it possible and profitable: for they make it possible to realize liberty along with abundance and social justice; and they make the finer qualities of human relations increasingly accessible and valuable to all.

DAVID G. SMITH

[*See also* CONSERVATISM; CONSTITUTIONS AND CONSTITUTIONALISM; DEMOCRACY; EQUALITY; FREEDOM; LAISSEZ-FAIRE; UTILITARIANISM; WELFARE STATE; *and the biography of* MILL. *Other relevant material may be found in* ECONOMIC THOUGHT *and* POLITICAL THEORY.]

BIBLIOGRAPHY

DEWEY, JOHN (1927) 1957 *The Public and Its Problems.* Denver: Swallow.

GIRVETZ, HARRY K. (1950) 1963 *The Evolution of Liberalism.* Rev. ed. New York: Collier. → First published as *From Wealth to Welfare: The Evolution of Liberalism.*

HALÉVY, ÉLIE (1901–1904) 1952 *The Growth of Philosophic Radicalism.* New ed. London: Faber. → First published in French.

HARTZ, LOUIS 1955 *The Liberal Tradition in America.* New York: Harcourt.

HAYEK, FREDERICK A. VON 1960 *The Constitution of Liberty.* Univ. of Chicago Press; London: Routledge.

HOBHOUSE, LEONARD T. (1911) 1945 *Liberalism.* Oxford Univ. Press. → A paperback edition was published in 1964.

HUGHES, EMMET J. 1944 *The Church and Liberal Society.* Princeton Univ. Press.

KEYNES, JOHN M. 1926 *The End of Laissez-faire.* London: Woolf.

LASKI, HAROLD J. (1936) 1958 *The Rise of European Liberalism: An Essay in Interpretation.* London: Allen & Unwin. → A paperback edition was published in 1962 by Barnes & Noble.

LOCKE, JOHN (1689) 1963 *A Letter Concerning Toleration: Latin and English Texts. . . .* The Hague: Nijhoff. → First published as *Epistola de tolerantia.*

LOCKE, JOHN (1690) 1960 *Two Treatises of Government.* Cambridge Univ. Press.

MILL, JOHN STUART (1859) 1963 *On Liberty.* Indianapolis, Ind.: Bobbs-Merrill.

POLANYI, KARL 1944 *The Great Transformation.* New York: Farrar. → A paperback edition was published in 1957 by Beacon. Also published in 1945 by Gollancz under the title *Origins of Our Time.*

RUGGIERO, GUIDO DE (1925) 1927 *The History of European Liberalism.* Oxford: Collingwood. → First published as *Storia del liberalismo europeo.* A paperback edition was published in 1959 by Beacon.

WATKINS, FREDERICK 1948 *The Political Tradition of the West: A Study in the Development of Modern Liberalism.* Cambridge, Mass.: Harvard Univ. Press.

LIBERTY
See FREEDOM.

LIBIDO
See PSYCHOANALYSIS.

LIBRARIES
See under INFORMATION STORAGE AND RETRIEVAL.

LICENSING, OCCUPATIONAL

In labor markets in which the rule of free choice prevails, individuals may enter and leave occupations without securing the consent of private or public authorities. Occupational licensing limits the range within which free choice governs. Occupational licensing occurs where a profession, trade, or occupation may be legally practiced only by those who have been authorized to do so by some agency of government.

Occupational licensing should be distinguished from certification. In the former case, the law permits only licensed persons to practice; in the latter, anyone may practice but only certified persons may use the relevant occupational title in notifying the public that their services are available. It is also different from the licensing of businesses, although that sometimes involves occupational licensing implicitly.

Occupational licensing is extensive in the United States, where the licensing authorities are usually agents of the states or of municipalities, rather than of the federal government. The practice of a few occupations does require a federal license. Gellhorn (1956, p. 106) found that state licenses were required in one or more states for the practice of some eighty occupations. State legislatures and municipal legislative organs routinely receive proposals that additional occupations be licensed. In countries other than the United States, licensing is apparently less common but it does occur.

Justification. When legislatures enact occupational licensing legislation, they usually do so on grounds that the public health, safety, or morals are being protected. In the absence of provision for licensing, it is reasoned, incompetent practitioners will offer their services. Prospective buyers of these services are said not to be able to distinguish between qualified and unqualified persons, and this is considered to be especially true if consumers buy services of the particular kind only at infrequent intervals. Where the consequences of the employment of unqualified persons can be expected to be seriously adverse to the purchaser, and especially where the consequences of incompetently rendered service are irreversible, it is thought to be desirable that the state administer some examining or other procedure to determine who are qualified to practice, and prevent those who are unqualified from offering their services. The average quality of those permitted to practice is raised, and by the exclusion of "quacks" and incompetents the public is protected from the error of employing them.

Thus, occupations that are licensed are concentrated in the tertiary sector of the economy, in which self-employment is common and services are purchased by any given buyer only infrequently. Information about professional competency that is produced by employment over a long period is not easily available in such cases to would-be purchasers. (A sophisticated exposition of the reasons for licensing in the special case of medical care can be found in Arrow 1963.)

While there are some licensed occupations for which the foregoing line of reasoning is sensible, there are others for which it seems far-fetched.

Certification, although it permits anyone to practice, nevertheless diminishes uncertainty, as does licensing, by informing prospective buyers which of those in the occupation have successfully passed the state examination and which have not. Neither licensing nor certification reduces uncertainty to zero, because there is variance in the competency of those who are licensed or certified and consumers must still search out additional information.

The requests that come to legislatures that an occupation be licensed or that the qualifying standards of an already-licensed occupation be raised rarely come from coalitions of consumers but almost always from associations of practitioners of the occupation. These requests are almost always accompanied by the proposal that those who have already entered and are practicing the occupation be qualified *pro forma* and exempted from examination. Such a "grandfather clause" often appears in occupational licensing legislation; only those desiring to enter the occupation are subjected to the qualifying tests. It is also common for states and municipalities to appoint already-licensed practitioners to examining boards that determine whether applicants for entry into licensed trades and professions are qualified. In addition, professional and trade associations of those in licensed occupations are the most watchful and aggressive in preventing others from performing services the associations believe to be exclusively comprehended by their particular occupation.

The circumstances just described could reflect the desire of practitioners to assure consumers that they will secure only competent services. However, it is more likely that they reflect the hopes of practitioners for higher incomes, for licensing frequently causes the price of service and the earnings of practitioners in licensed occupations to be higher than they would be if the occupations were unlicensed.

Economic effects. Whether economic effects occur depends upon the nature of the qualifying rules. If these do not check entry into the occupation, prices and earnings will be left unaffected. If entry is checked, they will be higher than they would have been had there been no licensing. The magnitude of the difference is determined by the degree to which the qualifying rules of licensure check entry and by the extent of change in the quantities of the relevant services that sellers are willing to sell and buyers are willing to buy as their prices change—that is to say, by the price elasticities of supply and demand. An estimate of the relative income effects of licensure in medicine and dentistry in the United States for the period 1929 to 1934 was made by Friedman and Kuznets (1945, chapter 4). The Friedman and Kuznets estimate is discussed by Lewis (1963, p. 114 ff.), who also makes a similar estimate for a more recent period.

Not all occupational licensing causes prices and earnings to rise, because in some licensed occupations almost all qualify and entry is not checked. This is the case if licenses are granted to all who are "of good moral character." Licensing arrangements of this kind are usually adopted in order to facilitate the administration of some standard of conduct by practitioners. Illustratively, a rule that in massage parlors men clients are to be separated from women clients can be conveniently enforced by the revocation of the licenses of masseurs who violate the rule. Most occupational licensing, however, does check entry, by imposing either explicit or implicit costs of entry in addition to those which would be incurred in the absence of licensing.

Explicit additional entry costs may include required general schooling, of some specified level; vocational or professional schooling, for some period or containing a specified content; successful performance upon written or oral examination; and employment for some period as an apprentice, with relatively low earnings. The explicit costs are the sum of tuition charges and other fees paid for schooling, and the income forgone that might have been earned if other employment had been taken during the required period of schooling and apprenticeship.

Implicit entry costs are, for example, a minimum-age qualification or a limitation on the number of licenses that will be issued. For those who do not qualify under such rules, the implicit cost of entry into the occupation is infinite.

Not infrequently, persons seeking to be licensed in some occupation are examined in subject matter that has no immediate relevance to the skills that will be ordinarily performed in it. In this way specialization in the acquisition of skill is discouraged. This is done, apparently, in order to prolong the period of training in preparation for the examination, thus increasing the cost of new entry into the occupation.

If the cost of entry is raised—either because incremental costs are imposed by licensure or for any other cause—fewer people will make themselves available to that occupation at every hypothetical level of relative earnings in it. In the conventional graphic representation of market schedules, a rise in entry costs shifts the supply schedule of labor in that occupation to the left. The point of intersection of the supply and demand schedules, which determines the price paid to labor in the occupation and (to a first approximation) the number who are employed in it, is now such that earnings in the trade will be higher and the number who are employed in it will be less than if there had been no increase in the cost of entry.

This is not to say that there are necessarily monopoly gains for those who are employed in the occupation. In principle, the rise in earnings will be just sufficient to compensate for the rise in entry costs. Those who have incurred the increased costs of entry will receive earnings that, when adjusted for the higher cost of entry, will just equal the earnings of those who are in similar occupations which are freely entered and for which licensure has not created an additional increment to the cost of entry.

But there will be monopoly gains—rents—for those in a licensed occupation who have *not* been required to incur the extra entry costs imposed by licensure or by higher qualifying standards. It is therefore understandable that practitioners in unlicensed occupations frequently propose that their occupations be licensed—with grandfather clauses that will qualify them *pro forma*—and that practitioners in licensed occupations propose higher qualifying standards for entry than those they were required to satisfy when they entered. Any increase in entry costs will check entry into the occupation and cause earnings to rise. This will produce rents for those already in the occupation, who are exempted from incurring the additional cost.

Rationing problem. If the licensing rules impose entry costs, a smaller number will be employed in the occupation than if there had been no licensing. But if licensing rules permit *all* who meet the qualifying standards to enter an occupation, there will be no explicit rationing problem. The number employed will be determined by the point of intersection of demand and supply schedules; the number making themselves available in the occupation will be just equal to the number whose services buyers want to buy, and the market will clear.

This may not be true, however, when explicit limits are put upon the number of licenses to be issued by the public authorities. This arrangement occurs in a minority of cases. In these cases, rationing may be necessary when, given the cost of entry and relative earnings in the licensed occupation, more qualify and seek to enter it than there are licenses available. Here the relevant agency of government must act on some principle that distinguishes those who will be granted a license from those who will be rejected. The rule may be of a first-come-first-served type—as when available licenses are issued to those who have waited longest for one—or it may be of some other nature. If the authorities, having predetermined the number of licenses they will issue, sell them by some auction procedure to the highest bidders, market processes will, of course, determine the distribution of licenses among prospective entrants to the occupation and the market will clear.

In some cases the authorities, after numerically limiting licenses to be issued for some occupation and rationing them among applicants for a nominal charge, have permitted these licenses to be privately transacted. Here the licenses, which give access to employment in the occupation exclusively to those who hold them, are capital assets whose values depend upon the time-discounted stream of monopoly rents (net earnings, over time, that exceed those that would be attached to the occupation if there were free access to it). The capital value of these licenses—that is to say, the prices at which they are transacted—may rise or fall in successive transactions. If their prices do change, it is because the future has not been perfectly foreseen by sellers or buyers in prior transactions with respect to any one or a number of relevant variables that affect the monopoly gains associated with the possession of a license.

Licensing checks on entry into an occupation only rarely use the strategy of explicit numerical limitation of licenses to be issued; the alternative device of imposing new entry costs is much more commonly employed. The latter device can be associated with the raising of standards of performance and qualification in the trade. The enforcement of numerical limits, on the other hand, can be defended only on the ground that unlimited entry will have adverse effects on third parties, for example, that unlimited numbers of taxis, competitively racing for customers, will cause accidents. Legislatures seem to find the defense-of-standards argument more attractive. If requirements for acquisition of the license exclude those who fall below some prescribed minimum of capacity or knowledge relevant to the service rendered in an occupation, the mean standard of performance by legal practitioners of a licensed occupation will, of course, be higher than if the occupation were unlicensed. In such a case, the mean quality of this service that is purchased by consumers will usually also be higher. But this result does not always occur. Whether it does depends on the substitute to which consumers have recourse when the law denies them access to low-priced, low-quality professional services.

The number of persons in licensed occupations is still a small proportion of all employed persons in the United States, but their relative numbers seem to be increasing as more and more legislatures respond to the overtures of practitioners and more and more occupations are licensed.

SIMON ROTTENBERG

[*See also* OCCUPATIONS AND CAREERS; PROFESSIONS.]

BIBLIOGRAPHY

ARROW, KENNETH J. 1963 Uncertainty and the Welfare Economics of Medical Care. *American Economic Review* 53:942–973.

FRIEDMAN, MILTON; and KUZNETS, SIMON 1945 *Income From Independent Professional Practice.* National Bureau of Economic Research, General Series, No. 45. New York: The Bureau.

GELLHORN, WALTER 1956 *Individual Freedom and Governmental Restraints.* Baton Rouge: Louisiana State Univ. Press.

LEWIS, H. G. 1963 *Unionism and Relative Wages in the United States: An Empirical Inquiry.* Univ. of Chicago Press.

ROTTENBERG, SIMON 1962 The Economics of Occupational Licensing. Pages 3–20 in Universities–National Bureau Committee for Economic Research, Conference, Princeton, N.J., 1960, *Aspects of Labor Economics.* National Bureau of Economic Research, Special Conference Series, No. 14. Princeton Univ. Press.

LIEBEN, RICHARD

See AUSPITZ, RUDOLF, AND LIEBEN, RICHARD.

LIFE CYCLE

The observer of life is always immersed in it and thus unable to transcend the limited perspectives of his stage and condition. Religious world views usually evolve pervasive configurations of the course of life: one religion may envisage it as a continuous spiral of rebirths, another as a crossroads to damnation or salvation. Various "ways of life" harbor more or less explicit images of life's course: a leisurely one may see it as ascending and descending steps with a comfortable platform of maturity in between; a competitive one may envision it as a race for spectacular success—and sudden oblivion. The scientist, on the other hand, looks at the organism as it moves from birth to death and, in the larger sense, at the individual in a genetic chain; or he looks at the cultural design of life's course as marked by rites of transition at selected turning points.

The very choice of the configuration "cycle of life," then, necessitates a statement of the writer's conceptual ancestry—clinical psychoanalysis. The clinical worker cannot escape combining knowledge, experience, and conviction in a conception of the course of life and of the sequence of generations—for how, otherwise, could he offer interpretation and guidance? The very existence of a variety of psychiatric "schools" is probably due to the fact that clinical practice and theory are called upon to provide a total orientation beyond possible verification.

Freud confessed only to a scientific world view, but he could not avoid the attitudes (often in contradiction to his personal values) that were part of his times. The original data of psychoanalysis, for example, were minute reconstructions of "pathogenic" events in early childhood. They supported an orientation which—in analogy to teleology—could be called *originology*, i.e., a systematic attempt to derive complex meanings from vague beginnings and obscure causes. The result was often an implicit fatalism, although counteracted by strenuously "positive" orientations. Any theory embracing both life history and case history, however, must find a balance between the "backward" view of the genetic reconstruction and the "forward" formulation of progressive differentiation in growth and development; between the "downward" view into the depth of the unconscious and the "upward" awareness of compelling social experience; and between the "inward" exploration of inner reality and the "outward" attention to historical actuality.

This article will attempt to make explicit those psychosocial insights that often remain implicit in clinical practice and theory. These concern the individual, who in principle develops according to predetermined steps of readiness that enable him to participate in ever more differentiated ways along a widening social radius, and the social organization, which in principle tends to invite such developmental potentialities and to support the proper rate and the proper sequence of their unfolding.

"Cycle" is intended to convey the double tendency of individual life to "round itself out" as a coherent experience and at the same time to form a link in the chain of generations from which it receives and to which it contributes both strength and weakness.

Strategic in this interplay are developmental crises—"crisis" here connoting not a threat of catastrophe but a turning point, a crucial period of increased vulnerability and heightened potential, and, therefore, the ontogenetic source of generational strength and maladjustment.

The eight stages of life

Man's protracted childhood must be provided with the psychosocial protection and stimulation which, like a second womb, permits the child to develop in distinct steps as he unifies his separate capacities. In each stage, we assume a new drive-and-need constellation, an expanded radius of potential social interaction, and social institutions created to receive the growing individual within traditional patterns. To provide an evolutionary rationale for this (for prolonged childhood and social institutions must have evolved together), two basic differences between animal and man must be considered.

We are, in Ernst Mayr's terms (1964), the "generalist" animal, prepared to adapt to and to develop cultures in the most varied environments. A long childhood must prepare the newborn of the species to become specialized as a member of a pseudo species (Erikson 1965), i.e., in tribes, cultures, castes, etc., each of which behaves as if it were the only genuine realization of man as the heavens planned and created him. Furthermore, man's drives are characterized by instinctual energies, which are, in contrast to other animals, much less bound to instinctive patterns (or inborn release mechanisms). A maximum of free instinctual energy thus remains ready to be invested in basic psychosocial encounters which tend to fix developing energies into cultural patterns of mutuality, reliability, and competence. Freud has shown the extent to which maladaptive anxiety and rage accompany man's instinctuality, while postulating

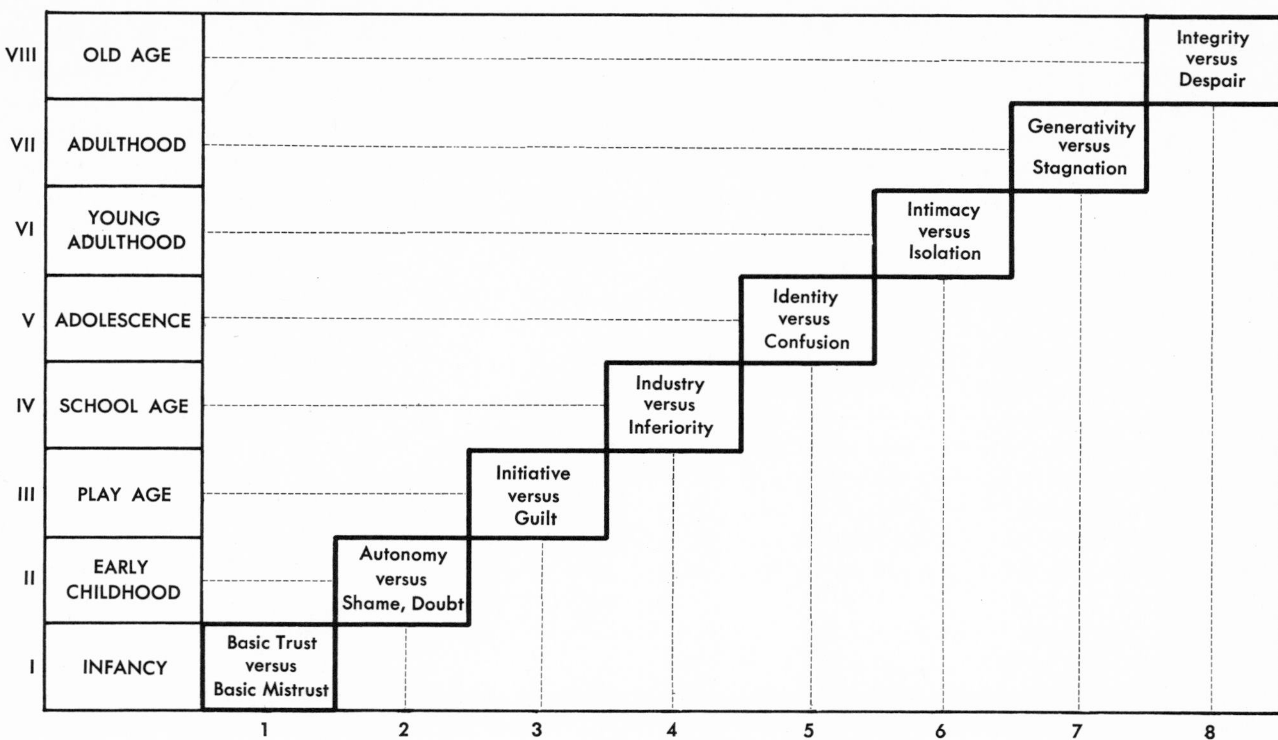

Figure 1 — Psychosocial crises in the life cycle

Source: Adapted from *Childhood and Society*, by Erik H. Erikson, Copyright 1950, © 1963 by W. W. Norton & Company. Reproduced with permission of W. W. Norton & Company, Inc. and Hogarth Press, Ltd.

the strength of the ego in its defensive and in its adaptive aspects (see Freud 1936; Hartmann 1939). We can attempt to show a systematic relationship between man's maladjustments and those basic strengths which must emerge in each life cycle and re-emerge from generation to generation (Erikson 1964).

In Figure 1, above, the various psychosocial crises and thus the ontogenetic sources of adaptation and of maladjustment are arranged according to the epigenetic principle. The diagonal signifies a successive development and a hierarchic differentiation of psychosocial strengths.

If a favorable ratio of basic trust over basic mistrust is the first step in psychosocial adaptation, and the second step a favorable ratio of autonomy over shame and doubt, the diagram indicates a number of fundamental facts. Each basic psychosocial trend (1, 2, etc.) meets a crisis (I, 1; II, 2; etc.) during a corresponding stage (I, II, etc.), while *all* must exist from the beginning in some form (broken line) and in later stages (solid lines) must continue to be differentiated and reintegrated with newly dominant trends. An infant will show something like autonomy from the time of birth (I, 2), but it is not until the second year (II, 2) that he is ready to experience and to manage the critical conflict of becoming an autonomous creature while continuing to be dependent. At this time those around him will convey to him a cultural and personal version of the ratio of autonomy and dependence. The diagonal thus indicates a necessary sequence of such encounters but leaves room for variations in tempo and intensity.

The epigenetic pattern will have to be kept in mind as we now state for each stage: (*a*) the psychosocial crisis evoked by social interaction, which is in turn facilitated and necessitated by newly developing drives and capacities, and the specific psychosocial strength emanating from the solution of this crisis; (*b*) the specific sense of estrangement awakened at each stage and its connection with some major form of psychopathology; (*c*) the special relationship between all of these factors and certain basic social institutions (Erikson 1950).

Infancy (basic trust versus mistrust—hope). The resolution of the first psychosocial crisis is performed primarily by maternal care. The newborn infant's more or less coordinated readiness to incorporate by mouth and through the senses meets the mother's and the society's more or less coordinated readiness to feed him and to stimulate his awareness. The mother must represent to the child an almost somatic conviction that she (his first "world") is trustworthy enough to satisfy and to regulate his needs. But the infant's demeanor also inspires hope in adults and makes them wish to give hope; it awakens in them a strength which they, in turn, are ready and needful to have confirmed in the experience of care. This is the ontogenetic basis of hope, that first and basic strength which gives man a semblance of instinctive certainty in his social ecology.

Unavoidable pain and delay of satisfaction, however, and inexorable weaning make this stage also prototypical for a sense of abandonment and helpless rage. This is the first of the human estrangements against which hope must maintain itself throughout life.

In psychopathology, a defect in basic trust can be evident in early malignant disturbances or can become apparent later in severe addiction or in habitual or sudden withdrawal into psychotic states.

Biological motherhood needs at least three links with social experience—the mother's past experience of being mothered, a method of care in trustworthy surroundings, and some convincing image of providence. The infant's hope, in turn, is one cornerstone of the adult's faith, which throughout history has sought an institutional safeguard in organized religion. However, where religious institutions fail to give ritual actuality to their formulas they may become irrelevant to psychosocial strength.

Hope, then, is the first psychosocial strength. It is the enduring belief in the attainability of primal wishes in spite of the anarchic urges and rages of dependency.

Early childhood (autonomy versus shame, doubt —will power). Early childhood sets the stage for psychosocial autonomy by rapid gains in muscular maturation, locomotion, verbalization, and discrimination. All of these, however, create limits in the form of spatial restrictions and of categorical divisions between "yes and no," "good and bad," "right and wrong," and "yours and mine." Muscular maturation sets the stage for an ambivalent set of social modalities—holding on and letting go. To hold on can become a destructive retaining or restraining, or a pattern of care—to have and to hold. To let go, too, can turn into an inimical letting loose, or a relaxed "letting pass" and "letting be." Freud calls this the anal stage of libido development because of the pleasure experienced in and the conflict evoked over excretory retention and elimination.

This stage, therefore, becomes decisive for the ratio of good will and willfulness. A sense of self-control without loss of self-esteem is the ontogenetic source of confidence in free will; a sense of overcontrol and loss of self-control can give rise to a lasting propensity for doubt and shame. The matter is complicated by the different needs and capacities of siblings of different ages—and by their rivalry.

Shame is the estrangement of being exposed and conscious of being looked at disapprovingly, of wishing to "bury one's face" or "sink into the ground." This potentiality is exploited in the "shaming" used throughout life by some cultures and causing, on occasion, suicide. While shame is related to the consciousness of being upright and exposed, doubt has much to do with the consciousness of having a front and a back (and of the vulnerability of being seen and influenced from behind). It is the estrangement of being unsure of one's will and of those who would dominate it.

From this stage emerges the propensity for compulsive overcompliance or impulsive defiance. If denied a gradual increase in autonomy of choice the individual may become obsessed by repetitiveness and develop an overly cruel conscience. Early self-doubt and doubt of others may later find their most malignant expression in compulsion neuroses or in paranoiac apprehension of hidden critics and secret persecutors threatening from behind.

We have related basic trust to the institutions of religion. The enduring need of the individual to have an area of free choice reaffirmed and delineated by formulated privileges and limitations, obligations and rights, has an institutional safeguard in the principles of law and order and of justice. Where this is impaired, however, the law itself is in danger of becoming arbitrary or formalistic, i.e., "impulsive" or "compulsive" itself.

Will power is the unbroken determination to exercise free choice as well as self-restraint in spite of the unavoidable experience of shame, doubt, and a certain rage over being controlled by others. Good will is rooted in the judiciousness of parents guided by their respect for the spirit of the law.

Play age (initiative versus guilt—purpose). Able to move independently and vigorously, the child, now in his third or fourth year, begins to comprehend his expected role in the adult world and to play out roles worth imitating. He develops a sense of initiative. He associates with age-mates and older children as he watches and enters into games in the barnyard, on the street corner, or in the nursery. His learning now is intrusive; it leads him into ever new facts and activities, and he becomes acutely aware of differences between the sexes. But if it seems that the child spends on his play a purposefulness out of proportion to "real" purposes, we must recognize the human necessity to simultaneously bind together infantile wish and limited skill, symbol and fact, inner and outer world, a selectively remembered past and a vaguely anticipated future—all before adult "reality" takes over in sanctioned roles and adjusted purposes.

The fate of infantile genitality remains determined by the sex roles cultivated and integrated in the family. In the boy, the sexual orientation is dominated by phallic-intrusive initiative; in the girl, by inclusive modes of attractiveness and "motherliness."

Conscience, however, forever divides the child within himself by establishing an inner voice of self-observation, self-guidance, and self-punishment. The estrangement of this stage, therefore, is a sense of guilt over goals contemplated and acts done, initiated, or merely fantasied. For initiative includes competition with those of superior equipment. In a final contest for a favored position with the mother, "oedipal" feelings are aroused in the boy, and there appears to be an intensified fear of finding the genitals harmed as punishment for the fantasies attached to their excitability.

Infantile guilt leads to the conflict between unbounded initiative and repression or inhibition. In adult pathology this residual conflict is expressed in hysterical denial, general inhibition, and sexual impotence, or in overcompensatory exhibitionism and psychopathic acting-out.

The word "initiative" has for many a specifically American, or "entrepreneur," connotation. Yet man needs this sense of initiative for whatever he learns and does, from fruit gathering to commercial enterprise—or the study of books.

The play age relies on the existence of some form of basic family, which also teaches the child by patient example where play ends and irreversible purpose begins. Only thus are guilt feelings integrated in a strong (not severe) conscience; only thus is language verified as a shared actuality. The "oedipal" stage thus not only results in a moral sense restricting the horizon of the permissible, but it also directs the way to the possible and the tangible, which attract infantile dreams to the goals of technology and culture. Social institutions, in turn, offer an ethos of action, in the form of ideal adults fascinating enough to replace the heroes of the picture book and fairy tale.

That the adult begins as a playing child means that there is a residue of play acting and role playing even in what he considers his highest purposes. These he projects on a larger and more perfect historical future; these he dramatizes in the ceremonial present with uniformed players in ritual arrangements; thus men sanction aggressive initiative, even as they assuage guilt by submission to a higher authority.

Purpose, then, is the courage to envisage and pursue valued and tangible goals guided by conscience but not paralyzed by guilt and by the fear of punishment.

School age (industry versus inferiority—competence). Before the child, psychologically a rudimentary parent, can become a biological parent, he must begin to be a worker and potential provider. Genital maturation is postponed (the period of latency). The child develops a sense of industriousness, i.e., he begins to comprehend the tool world of his culture, and he can become an eager and absorbed member of that productive situation called "school," which gradually supersedes the whims of play. In all cultures, at this stage, children receive systematic instruction of some kind and learn eagerly from older children.

The danger of this stage lies in the development of a sense of inadequacy. If the child despairs of his skill or his status among his tool partners, he may be discouraged from further learning. He may regress to the hopeless rivalry of the oedipal situation. It is at this point that the larger society becomes significant to the child by admitting him to roles preparatory to the actuality of technology and economy. Where he finds, however, that the color of his skin or the background of his parents rather than his wish and his will to learn will decide his worth as an apprentice, the human propensity for feeling unworthy (inferior) may be fatefully aggravated as a determinant of character development.

But there is another danger: If the overly conforming child accepts work as the only criterion of worthwhileness, sacrificing too readily his imagination and playfulness, he may become ready to submit to what Marx called a "craft-idiocy," i.e., become a slave of his technology and of its established role typology.

This is socially a most decisive stage, preparing the child for a hierarchy of learning experiences which he will undergo with the help of cooperative peers and instructive adults. Since industriousness involves doing things beside and with others, a first sense of the division of labor and of differential opportunity—that is, a sense of the technological ethos of a culture—develops at this time. Therefore, the configurations of cultural thought and the manipulations basic to the prevailing technology must reach meaningfully into school life.

Competence, then, is the free exercise (unimpaired by an infantile sense of inferiority) of dexterity and intelligence in the completion of serious tasks. It is the basis for cooperative participation in some segment of the culture.

Adolescence (identity versus identity confusion—fidelity). With a good initial relationship to skills and tools, and with the advent of puberty, childhood proper comes to an end. The rapidly growing youths, faced with the inner revolution of puberty and with as yet intangible adult tasks, are now primarily concerned with their psychosocial identity and with fitting their rudimentary gifts and skills to the occupational prototypes of the culture.

The integration of an identity is more than the sum of childhood identifications. It is the accrued confidence that the inner sameness and continuity gathered over the past years of development are matched by the sameness and continuity in one's meaning for others, as evidenced in the tangible promise of careers and life styles.

The adolescent's regressive and yet powerful impulsiveness alternating with compulsive restraint is well known. In all of this, however, an ideological seeking after an inner coherence and a durable set of values can be detected. The particular strength sought is fidelity—that is, the opportunity to fulfill personal potentialities (including erotic vitality or its sublimation) in a context which permits the young person to be true to himself and true to significant others. "Falling in love" also can be an attempt to arrive at a self-definition by seeing oneself reflected anew in an idealized as well as eroticized other.

From this stage on, acute maladjustments due to social anomie may lead to psychopathological regressions. Where role confusion joins a hopelessness of long standing, borderline psychotic episodes are not uncommon.

Adolescents, on the other hand, help one another temporarily through much regressive insecurity by forming cliques and by stereotyping themselves, their ideals, and their "enemies." In this they can be clannish and cruel in their exclusion of all those who are "different." Where they turn this repudiation totally against the society, delinquency may be a temporary or lasting result.

As social systems enter into the fiber of each succeeding generation, they also absorb into their lifeblood the rejuvenative power of youth. Adolescence is thus a vital regenerator in the process of social evolution, for youth can offer its loyalties and energies to the conservation of that which it feels is valid as well as to the revolutionary correction of that which has lost its regenerative significance.

Adolescence is least "stormy" among those youths who are gifted and well trained in the pursuit of productive technological trends. In times of unrest, the adolescent mind becomes an ideological mind in search of an inspiring unification of ideas. Youth needs to be affirmed by peers and confirmed by teachings, creeds, and ideologies which express the promise that the best people will come to rule and that rule will develop the best in people. A society's ideological weakness, in turn, expresses itself in weak utopianism and in widespread identity confusion.

Fidelity, then, is the ability to sustain loyalties freely pledged in spite of the inevitable contradictions of value systems. It is the cornerstone of identity and receives inspiration from confirming ideologies and "ways of life."

Young adulthood (intimacy versus isolation—love). Consolidated identity permits the self-abandonment demanded by intimate affiliations, by passionate sexual unions, or by inspiring encounters. The young adult is ready for intimacy and solidarity—that is, he can commit himself to affiliations and partnerships even though they may call for significant sacrifices and compromises. Ethical strength emerges as a further differentiation of ideological conviction (adolescence) and a sense of moral obligation (childhood).

True genital maturity is first reached at this stage; much of the individual's previous sex life is of the identity-confirming kind. Freud, when asked for the criteria of a mature person, is reported to have answered: *"Lieben und Arbeiten"* ("love and work"). All three words deserve equal emphasis.

It is only at this stage that the biological differences between the sexes result in a full polarization within a joint life style. Previously established strengths have helped the two sexes to converge in capacities and values which enhance communication and cooperation, while divergence is now of the essence in love life and in procreation. Thus the sexes first become similar in consciousness, language, and ethics in order then to be maturely different. But this, by necessity, causes ambivalences.

The danger of this stage is possible psychosocial isolation—that is, the avoidance of contacts which commit to intimacy. In psychopathology isolation can lead to severe character problems of the kind which interfere with "love and work," and this often on the basis of infantile fixations and lasting immaturities.

Man, in addition to erotic attraction, has developed a selectivity of mutual love that serves the need for a new and shared identity in the procession of generations. Love is the guardian of that elusive and yet all-pervasive power of cultural and personal style which binds into a "way of life" the affiliations of competition and cooperation, procreation and production. The problem is one of transferring the experience of being cared for in a parental setting to an adult affiliation actively chosen and cultivated as a mutual concern within a new generation.

The counterpart of such intimacy, and the danger, is man's readiness to fortify his territory of intimacy and solidarity by exaggerating small differences and prejudging or excluding foreign influences and people. Insularity thus aggravated can lead to that irrational fear which is easily exploited by demagogic leaders seeking aggrandizement in war and in political conflict.

Love, then, is a mutuality of devotion greater than the antagonisms inherent in divided function.

Maturity (generativity versus stagnation—care). Evolution has made man the teaching and instituting as well as the learning animal. For dependency and maturity are reciprocal: mature man needs to be needed, and maturity is guided by the nature of that which must be cared for.

Generativity, then, is primarily the concern with establishing and guiding the next generation. In addition to procreativity, it includes productivity and creativity; thus it is psychosocial in nature. From the crisis of generativity emerges the strength of care.

Where such enrichment fails, a sense of stagnation and boredom ensues, the pathological symptoms of which depend on variations in mental epidemiology: certainly where the hypocrisy of the frigid mother was once regarded as a most significant malignant influence, today, when sexual "adjustment" is in order, an obsessive pseudo intimacy and adult self-indulgence are nonetheless damaging to the generational process. The very nature of generativity suggests that the most circumscribed symptoms of its weakness are to be found in the next generation in the form of those aggravated estrangements which we have listed for childhood and youth.

Generativity is itself a driving power in human organization. For the intermeshing stages of childhood and adulthood are in themselves a system of generation and regeneration given continuity by institutions such as extended households and divided labor.

Thus, in combination, the basic strengths enumerated here and the structure of an organized human community provide a set of proven methods and a fund of traditional reassurance with which each generation meets the needs of the next. Various traditions transcend divisive personal differences and confusing conditions. But they also contribute to a danger to the species as a whole, namely, the defensive territoriality of the pseudo species, which on seemingly ethical grounds must discredit and destroy threateningly alien systems and may itself be destroyed in the process.

Care is the broadening concern for what has been generated by love, necessity, or accident—a concern which must consistently overcome the ambivalence adhering to irreversible obligation and the narrowness of self-concern.

Old age (integrity versus despair—wisdom). Strength in the aging and sometimes in the old takes the form of wisdom in its many connotations—ripened "wits," accumulated knowledge, inclusive understanding, and mature judgment. Wisdom maintains and conveys the integrity of experience, in spite of the decline of bodily and mental functions. Responding to the oncoming generation's need for an integrated heritage, the wisdom of old age remains aware of the relativity of all knowledge acquired in one lifetime in one historical period. Integrity, therefore, implies an emotional integration faithful to the image bearers of the past and ready to take (and eventually to renounce) leadership in the present.

The lack or loss of this accrued integration is signified by a hidden fear of death: fate is not accepted as the frame of life, death not as its finite boundary. Despair indicates that time is too short for alternate roads to integrity: this is why the old try to "doctor" their memories. Bitterness and disgust mask such despair, which in severe psychopathology aggravates senile depression, hypochondria, and paranoiac hate.

A meaningful old age (preceding terminal invalidism) provides that integrated heritage which gives indispensable perspective to those growing up, "adolescing," and aging. But the end of the cycle also evokes "ultimate concerns," the paradoxes of which we must leave to philosophical and religious interpreters. Whatever chance man has to transcend the limitations of his self seems to depend on his full (if often tragic) engagement in the one and only life cycle permitted him in the sequence of generations. Great philosophical and religious systems dealing with ultimate individuation seem to have remained (even in their monastic establishments) responsibly related to the cultures and civilizations of their times. Seeking transcendence by renunciation, they remain ethically concerned with the maintenance of the world. By the same token, a civilization can be measured by the meaning which it gives to the full cycle of life, for such meaning (or the lack of it) cannot fail to reach into the beginnings of the next generation and thus enhance the potentiality that others may meet ultimate questions with some clarity and strength.

Wisdom, then, is a detached and yet active concern with life in the face of death.

Conclusion

From the cycle of life such dispositions as faith, will power, purposefulness, efficiency, devotion, affection, responsibility, and sagacity (all of which are also criteria of ego strength) flow into the life of institutions. Without them, institutions wilt; but without the spirit of institutions pervading the patterns of care and love, instruction and training, no enduring strength could emerge from the sequence of generations.

We have attempted, in a psychosocial frame, to account for the ontogenesis not of lofty ideals but of an inescapable and intrinsic order of strivings, which, by weakening or strengthening man, dictates the minimum goals of informed and responsible participation.

Psychosocial strength, we conclude, depends on a total process which regulates individual life cycles, the sequence of generations, and the structure of society simultaneously, for all three have evolved together.

Each person must translate this order into his own terms so as to make it amenable to whatever kind of trait inventory, normative scale, measurement, or educational goal is his main concern. Science and technology are, no doubt, changing essential aspects of the course of life, wherefore some increased awareness of the functional wholeness of the cycle may be mandatory. Interdisciplinary work will define in practical and applicable terms what evolved order is common to all men and what true equality of opportunity must mean in planning for future generations.

The study of the human life cycle has immediate applications in a number of fields. Paramount is the science of human development within social institutions. In psychiatry (and in its applications to law), the diagnostic and prognostic assessment of disturbances common to life stages should help to outweigh fatalistic diagnoses. Whatever will prove tangibly lawful about the cycle of life will also be an important focus for anthropology insofar as it assesses universal functions in the variety of institutional forms. Finally, as the study of the life history emerges from that of case histories, it will throw new light on biography and thus on history itself.

ERIK H. ERIKSON

[*Directly related are the entries* ADOLESCENCE; AGING; DEVELOPMENTAL PSYCHOLOGY; EVOLUTION, *articles on* HUMAN EVOLUTION, CULTURAL EVOLUTION, *and* SOCIAL EVOLUTION; INFANCY. *Other relevant material may be found in* IDENTITY, PSYCHOSOCIAL; PSYCHOANALYSIS; SELF CONCEPT; SOCIALIZATION.]

BIBLIOGRAPHY

BÜHLER, CHARLOTTE (1933) 1959 *Der menschliche Lebenslauf als psychologisches Problem.* 2d ed., rev. Leipzig: Hirzel.

BÜHLER, CHARLOTTE 1962 *Values in Psychotherapy.* New York: Free Press.

ERIKSON, ERIK H. (1950) 1964 *Childhood and Society.* 2d ed., rev. & enl. New York: Norton.

ERIKSON, ERIK H. 1958 *Young Man Luther.* New York: Norton.

ERIKSON, ERIK H. 1964 *Insight and Responsibility.* New York: Norton.

ERIKSON, ERIK H. 1965 The Ontogeny of Ritualisation in Man. Unpublished manuscript.

FREUD, ANNA (1936) 1957 *The Ego and the Mechanisms of Defense.* New York: International Universities Press. → First published as *Das Ich und die Abwehrmechanismen.*

FREUD, ANNA 1965 *Normality and Pathology in Childhood: Assessment of Development.* New York: International Universities Press.

HARTMANN, HEINZ (1939) 1958 *Ego Psychology and the Problem of Adaptation.* Translated by David Rapaport. New York: International Universities Press. → First published as *Ich-Psychologie und Anpassungsproblem.*

MAYR, ERNST 1964 The Evolution of Living Systems. National Academy of Sciences, *Proceedings* 51:934–941.

WERNER, HEINZ (1926) 1965 *Comparative Psychology of Mental Development.* Rev. ed. New York: International Universities Press. → First published as *Einführung in die Entwicklungspsychologie.*

LIFE TABLES

The life table (also referred to as the mortality table) is a statistical device used to compute chances of survivorship and death and average remaining years of life, for specific years of age. The concept of the life table is applicable not only to humans (Spiegelman 1957) and other species of life (Haldane 1953; Ciba Foundation 1959) but also to items of industrial equipment (Dublin, Lotka, & Spiegelman [1936] 1949) and other defined aggregates subject to a measurable process of attrition. Life tables can also be developed further for computing the chances of other vital events in human life, such as marriage and remarriage, the birth of children, widowhood, illness and disability, and labor force participation and retirement (Spiegelman 1957); and they enter into a wide variety of annuity and life insurance computations (Hooker & Longley-Cook 1953–1957; Jordan 1952).

The conventional life table

The conventional form of a life table for the general population is illustrated in Table 1. The original data are recorded deaths and the census of population classified according to age (this step is not shown on the table). From these data were computed the *rates of mortality*, conventionally designated as q_x, for each year of age, x. These rates show the proportion of deaths occurring within the year of age among those who attain that age; the rates are usually shown per thousand ($1{,}000q_x$). For example, Table 1 shows that of every 1,000 who just attained age 0 (the newly born), 23.55 died before reaching their first birthday; similarly, of every 1,000 who attained age six, 0.53 died within that year of age. Typically, mortality rates for a general population start at a high point in the first year of life, fall rapidly to a minimum at about age ten, and then rise with advance in years. The rise is gradual to about age 40, and then becomes increasingly rapid; since the maximum attainable age for human beings is in the neighborhood of 110 years, life tables seldom go beyond that point.

Once one knows the mortality rates at each age of life, it becomes possible to compute the number of *survivors* (column l_x of the life table) and also the number of *deaths* (column d_x). It is usually most convenient to start the population life table with a base (radix) of 100,000 newborn individuals. In the example presented here, where there is a death rate of 23.55 per 1,000 at age 0, among the 100,000 newly born there must be 2,355 deaths in the first year of life. The number of survivors to attain age 1 is then $100{,}000 - 2{,}355 = 97{,}645$. With a mortality rate of 1.89 per 1,000 at age 1, among the 97,645 who attained that age there are

$$97{,}645 \times \frac{1.89}{1{,}000} = 185 \text{ deaths.}$$

The number of survivors to age 2 is then calculated in the same way:

$$97{,}645 - 185 = 97{,}460.$$

This procedure is continued to the end of the life table. Obviously, the number in the survivorship column, l_x, at any attained age is equal to the sum of the deaths in the d_x column for that and all higher ages.

To compute the *expectation of life* ($\mathring{e}_x$), or average future lifetime, for any attained age, it will be assumed that deaths, d_x, are uniformly distributed over the year of age, x. Equivalent to this is the

Table 1 — Life table for white females, United States, 1949–1951[a]

Year of age	RATE OF MORTALITY PER 1,000: Number dying between ages x and x + 1 among 1,000 living at age x	OF 100,000 BORN ALIVE: Number surviving to exact age x	Number dying between ages x and x + 1	Number of years lived by the cohort between ages x and x + 1	Total number of years lived by the cohort from age x on, until all have died	Average number of years lived after age x per person surviving to exact age x[b]
x	$1{,}000q_x$	l_x	d_x	L_x	T_x	$\mathring{e}_x$
0	23.55	100,000	2,355	97,965	7,203,179	72.03
1	1.89	97,645	185	97,552	7,105,214	72.77
2	1.12	97,460	109	97,406	7,007,662	71.90
3	0.87	97,351	85	97,308	6,910,256	70.98
4	0.69	97,266	67	97,233	6,812,948	70.04
5	0.60	97,199	59	97,169	6,715,715	69.09
6	0.53	97,140	52	97,114	6,618,546	68.13
7	0.48	97,088	46	97,065	6,521,432	67.17
8	0.44	97,042	43	97,020	6,424,367	66.20
9	0.41	96,999	39	96,980	6,327,347	65.23
⋮	⋮	⋮	⋮	⋮	⋮	⋮
100	388.39	294	114	237	566	1.92
101	407.52	180	73	143	329	1.83
102	426.00	107	46	84	186	1.74
103	443.67	61	27	48	102	1.66
104	460.76	34	16	26	54	1.59
⋮	⋮	⋮	⋮	⋮	⋮	⋮

a. Based upon recorded deaths in the United States during the three-year period 1949–1951, recorded births for each year from 1944 through 1951, and the census of population taken April 1, 1950; for details, see U.S. Public Health Service 1959, pp. 149–158.

b. Represents complete expectation of life, or average future lifetime.

Source: U.S. Public Health Service 1954–1955, p. 18.

assumption that each of the persons dying lived one-half year after the last birthday. Thus, among the 294 in Table 1 who attained age 100, there were 114 deaths during that year of age, and these individuals lived $\frac{1}{2} \times 114$ years after their last birthday. Similarly, the 73 who died at age 101 lived $1\frac{1}{2}$ years each after attaining age 100, and the 46 who died at age 102 lived $2\frac{1}{2}$ years each after attaining age 100, and so on, to the last death. Altogether, the total number of years of life lived from age 100 on by the 294 who attained that age is $(\frac{1}{2} \times 114) + (1\frac{1}{2} \times 73) + (2\frac{1}{2} \times 46) + (3\frac{1}{2} \times 27) + \cdots = 566$. This is the figure for age 100 in the column headed T_x. Since the 294 who attained age 100 lived a total of 566 years from their 100th birthday until the death of the last survivor, the average remaining lifetime was

$$566 \div 294 = 1.92 \text{ years.}$$

This is more commonly known as the expectation of life, $\mathring{e}_x$; as an average, it is not applicable to any specific individual.

In Table 1 the life table symbols at the head of each column are defined by the terms above them. Reference has already been made to each, except L_x, which denotes the total number of years lived within the year of age by the number, l_x, who attain that age. It has been assumed that each of the persons dying lived only one half year after the last birthday. Accordingly, among the number, l_x, who attain age x, the years of life lived by those dying during that year of age is $\frac{1}{2}d_x$. The years of life lived by the survivors is l_{x+1}, which is equal to $l_x - d_x$. The sum of $\frac{1}{2}d_x$ and $l_x - d_x$ is the total number of years lived within that year of age. Thus,

$$L_x = l_x - \tfrac{1}{2}d_x .$$

Since T_x is the total number of years lived from age x on by those who attain age x, it follows that

$$T_x = L_x + L_{x+1} + L_{x+2} + \cdots$$

and also that

$$T_x = L_x + T_{x+1} .$$

It should be recognized that except for the mortality rates, which represent an actually observed situation, *all other columns of figures in the life table represent a hypothetical situation.* Thus, the survivorship column and the column of life table deaths show only the expected number of survivals and deaths for successive ages, on the assumption that the mortality rates observed during the specified calendar period continue without change over time. The same assumption underlies the column of figures for expectation of life.

Life table formulas. It will be seen from the preceding discussion that the construction of life tables rests upon a small number of elementary assumptions, which can be summarized in the following formulas:

$$l_x - l_{x+1} = d_x ,$$

$$q_x = \frac{d_x}{l_x} .$$

Moreover, it is evident that if p_x denotes the probability of surviving one year after attaining age x, then

$$p_x = \frac{l_{x+1}}{l_x} = \frac{l_x - d_x}{l_x} = 1 - q_x .$$

Similarly, if ${}_np_x$ denotes the probability of surviving n years after attaining age x, then

$${}_np_x = \frac{l_{x+n}}{l_x} = 1 - {}_nq_x ,$$

where ${}_nq_x$ is the probability of dying within n years after attaining age x. Thus,

$${}_nq_x = 1 - {}_np_x = \frac{l_x - l_{x+n}}{l_x} .$$

Another measure of mortality is the "force of mortality." This measure takes into account the fact that mortality varies continually with advance in age. In this sense, the rate of mortality in the brief instant after attaining exact age x will be different from that for the brief instant just before leaving age x to attain exact age $x + 1$. The force of mortality, μ_x, is the annual rate of loss of lives, corresponding to the loss, at any instant of time, per head surviving at that time. In terms of the calculus,

$$\mu_x = -\frac{1}{l_x} \cdot \frac{dl_x}{dx} = -\frac{d \log l_x}{dx} ,$$

where d/dx denotes the derivative of the specified function with respect to x.

The force of mortality at age x may be approximated by

$$\mu_x = \frac{l_{x-1} - l_{x+1}}{2l_x}$$

or, more closely, by

$$\mu_x = \frac{8(l_{x-1} - l_{x+1}) - (l_{x-2} - l_{x+2})}{12l_x} .$$

The relevant approximation formulas have been discussed by Jordan (1952, pp. 19–21).

Life table computation. The first task to be carried out in computing a life table for any specific population is to convert the *central death* *rate*, m_x—that is, the average annual death rate for persons of a given age—into a *mortality rate*, q_x, such as has already been described. A means of doing this is illustrated as follows. In any specified community, let D_x denote the number of deaths recorded within a calendar year of individuals at age x on last birthday (or average annual deaths for a calendar period). Also, let P_x denote the number of people at age x on last birthday on the mid-date of the calendar year or period; this is an approximation to the average number living and, therefore, to the number of years of life lived within the year of age. Then the central death rate at age x for the community is

$$m_x = \frac{D_x}{P_x}.$$

The problem is to convert the central death rate, m_x, into a mortality rate, q_x.

In the life table the number of years of life lived during the year of age x is L_x and deaths during age x number d_x, so that the central death rate m_x is

$$m_x = \frac{d_x}{L_x} = \frac{d_x}{l_x - \frac{1}{2}d_x}.$$

Since $d_x = l_x \cdot q_x$,

$$m_x = \frac{l_x \cdot q_x}{l_x - \frac{1}{2}l_x q_x} = \frac{q_x}{1 - \frac{1}{2}q_x}.$$

Solving for q_x yields

$$q_x = \frac{m_x}{1 + \frac{1}{2}m_x}.$$

In terms of the recorded (observed) deaths and population,

$$q_x = \frac{D_x/P_x}{1 + \frac{1}{2}D_x/P_x} = \frac{D_x}{P_x + \frac{1}{2}D_x}.$$

In practice, however, the mortality rates at the very early ages are usually computed on the basis of a population estimated from recorded births and deaths, since census data for this stage of life are usually unreliable. The risk of mortality in infancy is highest in the first month following birth, and decreases rapidly thereafter; accordingly, the assumption of a uniform distribution of deaths is not valid for the first year of age. For the terminal ages of life, the basic data are usually meager and unreliable; various artifacts are therefore used to compute these mortality rates. The mortality rates for the broad range of intervening ages are generally subjected to mathematical procedures of interpolation and graduation in order to produce a smooth progression of figures (Spiegelman 1955, p. 72). A complete life table shows the figures in each column for every age of life. An abridged life table shows figures for only selected ages, such as every fifth or tenth year of age.

Life tables directly from census data

Where death data are grossly inadequate or lacking, a life table may be approximated from the age distributions of population in two consecutive censuses, as in the following simplified example.

Assume two censuses, five years apart, with correct reporting of ages and with no migration. Then, clearly, the population at age $x + 5$ in the second census, P''_{x+5}, consists of survivors of the population five years younger at the time of the first census, P'_x. The ratio of P''_{x+5} to P'_x accordingly is a five-year survivorship rate for a population at age x last birthday. Assuming a uniform distribution of population over the year of age, this population is approximately at an average attained age $x + \frac{1}{2}$. Thus,

$${}_5p_{x+\frac{1}{2}} = \frac{P''_{x+5}}{P'_x}.$$

Having arrived at a series of values of ${}_5p_{x+\frac{1}{2}}$ according to age, it is possible to work back to a series of mortality rates, q_x. In using this method, allowance may be made for migration (Mortara 1949).

There is also a method of life table estimation that can be used when a population age distribution is available from only one census (Stolnitz 1956). If there is good reason to believe that the size of the population of a community has been virtually stationary over time and that mortality according to age has remained essentially unchanged over time, then its age distribution is clearly very much like that of the life table column L_x. In other words, the number living, P_x, at age x last birthday is proportionate to L_x. Thus,

$${}_5p_{x+\frac{1}{2}} = \frac{P_{x+5}}{P_x} = \frac{L_{x+5}}{L_x},$$

and q_x may be estimated, as in the case with two consecutive censuses.

Consider now a population that may be regarded as stable, in the sense that it is growing at a constant annual rate, r, and that mortality at each age is also constant over time. This growth results solely from an excess of births over deaths each year; there is no migration. Then, for an interval of five years,

$$P''_x = P'_x(1 + r)^5.$$

Likewise, P''_{x+5} consists of survivors of P'_x as before. It follows that

$${}_5p_{x+\frac{1}{2}} = \frac{P''_{x+5}}{P'_x} = \frac{P''_{x+5}}{P''_x/(1 + r)^5} = \frac{P''_{x+5}(1 + r)^5}{P''_x},$$

so that use is made of the population at the second census only. Stolnitz generalized this approach by tracing the populations P''_{x+5} and P''_x from their respective births, $x + 5$ and x years previously, namely B_{x+5} and B_x. For this, he introduced survival factors to the same attained age x last birthday, namely S'_x and S''_x, and made use of the five-year survivorship ratio, ${}_5p_{x+\frac{1}{2}}$. Thus,

$$\frac{P''_{x+5}}{P''_x} = \frac{B_{x+5}}{B_x} \cdot \frac{S'_x}{S''_x} \cdot {}_5p_{x+\frac{1}{2}} .$$

Stolnitz shows how the birth ratio and the ratio of survival factors may be estimated from other experiences. With such estimates it becomes possible to compute ${}_5p_{x+\frac{1}{2}}$ from the age distribution of a single census.

Model life tables for developing areas. In the developing areas the problem is to estimate a life table for a population with scanty mortality data or from data gathered in a special survey. Since the mortality rate in infancy or the first few years of life is frequently indicative of the general level of mortality, such a rate may be used as the basis for estimation of life table values. Such an observed mortality rate, with suitable adjustment to enhance its validity, is used as a key to select one of a series of life table mortality rates (q_0, ${}_4q_1$, and ${}_5q_x$ for x at five-year intervals) from 40 theoretical model series (United Nations 1955*a*). These models were derived from a study of the patterns of mortality rates in existing life tables. For refinement, the series of life table mortality rates may be selected by interpolating among the models on the basis of the key rate. Further refinement is possible by computing from the equations used to derive the models. Although these model life tables of the United Nations have been subject to technical criticisms, they are widely used (Gabriel & Ronen 1958; Kurup 1966). A more extensive set of model life tables, prepared at Princeton University, takes into account variations in the patterns of mortality between four broad geographic regions, defined as East, West, North, and South, in addition to variations in the level of mortality within each region (Coale & Demeny 1966).

Life tables directly from death data

As pointed out before, in a population that is virtually stationary, with mortality rates essentially unchanged over time, the age distribution corresponds closely to that in a life table. Only in such a situation is it feasible to cumulate the distribution of deaths according to age, starting with the highest age and noting the total for each age, running back to birth, in order to approximate the survivorship column of the life table. This approach is not applicable in any other situation, since the age distribution of deaths will be influenced by the age distribution of the population. Thus, a population with a large proportion of aged persons will have a large proportion of its deaths at the older ages, irrespective of the level of its mortality rates.

Multiple decrement tables

In a multiple decrement table, the survivorship column of the life table is split, in passing from one age to the next, into two or more component parts, on the basis of changes in status or of newly acquired characteristics (Jordan 1952, pp. 237, 251; Bailey & Haycocks 1946). One example is the case where the survivorship column is split, on the basis of marriage rates according to age, to distinguish those who marry from those who remain single. In another example, shown in Table 2, the

Table 2 — Example of a double decrement table, with decrements by death and by disability

				Of 100,000 born alive[a]						
	RATE OF MORTALITY PER 1,000		DISABILITY RATE PER 1,000[b]	NUMBER SURVIVING TO EXACT AGE x			ACTIVE LIVES DISABLED	NUMBER DYING BETWEEN AGES x AND x + 1		
Year of age, x	Among active lives	Among disabled lives	Among active lives	Total	As active lives	As disabled lives[c]	Between ages x and x + 1	Total	Among active lives	Among disabled lives
15	7.55	267	0.587	66,949	66,949	0	40	511	505	6
16	7.47	254	0.584	66,438	66,404	34	39	509	496	13
17	7.40	241	0.581	65,929	65,869	60	38	507	487	20
18	7.40	229	0.578	65,422	65,344	78	38	506	484	22
19	7.40	217	0.575	64,916	64,822	94	38	504	480	24
⋮	⋮	⋮	⋮	⋮	⋮	⋮	⋮	⋮	⋮	⋮

a. The radix in the source (100,000 at age 10) was changed to 100,000 at birth.
b. Per 1,000 active lives at exact age x.
c. Assuming no lives were disabled before age 15.

Source: Adapted from Hunter et al. 1932, p. 92.

Table 3 — Example of select and ultimate table, showing probabilities of remarriage during widowhood

Age at widowhood	Years elapsed since husband's death: 0	1	2	3	4	5 or more	Attained age
35	0.0201	0.0490	0.0386	0.0376	0.0230	0.0163	40
36	0.0184	0.0449	0.0354	0.0345	0.0211	0.0149	41
37	0.0169	0.0412	0.0324	0.0316	0.0193	0.0137	42
38	0.0155	0.0377	0.0297	0.0290	0.0177	0.0126	43
39	0.0142	0.0345	0.0272	0.0266	0.0162	0.0115	44
	SELECT TABLE					ULTIMATE TABLE	

Source: Adapted from Myers 1949, p. 73.

survivorship column of the life table is split to show those who become permanently disabled lives apart from those who remain as active lives. This table shows, in addition to the numbers surviving to successive ages as active lives and as permanently disabled lives, the rates of mortality for each of these categories and the rates at which active lives become permanently disabled. The column of life table deaths is also split to show the number of deaths among the permanently disabled separately from that among the active. It is assumed that the number of newly disabled lives in any year of age is uniformly distributed over that year; consequently, they are exposed to the mortality rate of the disabled for an average of one half of a year.

Select tables

The life table has been described in terms of rates of mortality dependent only upon attained age; in describing multiple decrement tables, reference was made to rates of disability and of marriage according to attained age. In select tables, rates of mortality (or other rates) are shown on the basis of both the age at acquisition of a new characteristic and the duration since that acquisition (Jordan 1952, p. 26). This two-way classification constitutes a select table, since some selective process is present at the time of acquisition. For example, mortality rates for permanently disabled lives may be shown not only for the age at which disablement occurred but also separately for each subsequent year of disability. Another example of a select table is the two-way classification of rates of remarriage for widows, in relation to both age at widowhood and years since that event. Such a two-way classification of rates is shown in Table 3. In that table, remarriage rates after the fifth year of widowhood are shown only on the basis of attained age, since duration in this case is only of minor influence upon the rates. The table as a whole is known as a select and ultimate table. That portion showing rates according to duration since widowhood is the select table; the ultimate table is that portion showing rates only according to attained age, since duration is no longer of any importance. Select and ultimate tables are used in life insurance mortality investigations. The choice of the number of durations to be shown for the select period is a matter of study in each experience.

Cohort or generation life tables

In the foregoing account of the conventional life table and the related multiple decrement and select tables, the rates of mortality and other rates of attrition were based upon observations during some specified year or other period. The hypothetical nature of the conventional life table with respect to the time period of observation has already been indicated. A realistic picture of the mortality and survivorship experience of a cohort traced from birth is obtained by observing these events each year in a generation born at the latest 100 years ago. In that way, a record would be obtained of the number surviving to successive ages in successive years and also of the corresponding number of deaths at each age; the mortality rates according to age in successive years may then be computed. After the last death, it would be possible to compute the average length of life of the generation and the average years of life remaining after each age. Such a table is called a generation life table, since it reflects the actual mortality rates of a cohort as it ages in successive years. The table derived from mortality rates for a calendar year or period is called a current life table (Dublin, Lotka, & Spiegelman [1936] 1949, p. 174; Jacobson 1964). Thus, the expectation of life computed from mortality rates observed in 1850 will understate the average length of life of the generation born that year, because of the reductions in mortality since then. In general, with the trend toward lower mortality, the expectation of life at birth computed from a current life table understates the average length of life of a newly born generation.

Further applications

In addition to the applications of the life table that are mentioned in the opening paragraph of this article, increasing use is being made of it as an analytic tool in social and economic problems. Several interesting and important examples may be cited in the field of demography (for references to examples, see Spiegelman 1955; 1957). John Durand (1960) made use of the United Nations model life tables, cited previously, as an adjunct in arriving at estimates of expectation of life at birth for the western Roman Empire. The life table is fundamental in the stable-population theory developed by A. J. Lotka (Dublin & Lotka 1925) and also in Lotka's work on the structure of a growing population (1931). In the field of education E. G. Stockwell and C. B. Nam (1963) prepared school life tables to show the joint effects of death and school dropouts on school attendance patterns. B. C. Churchill (1955) studied the mortality and survival of manufacturing, wholesale trade, and retail trade firms in the United States; in similar fashion A. J. Jaffe (1961) has used data from the censuses of manufactures in Puerto Rico to prepare survival curves according to the age of the establishment.

MORTIMER SPIEGELMAN

[*See also* MORTALITY; POPULATION; VITAL STATISTICS; *and the biographies of* GRAUNT; LOTKA.]

BIBLIOGRAPHY

A very elementary account of the essentials of the life table is given in Dublin, Lotka, & Spiegelman [1936] 1949. *A wholly nontechnical account of the life table, including double decrement and select tables, with brief descriptions of applications, will be found in* Spiegelman 1957. *The beginner in graduate study who has a nonmathematical background but a sense of arithmetic will find the chapter on the life table in* Barclay 1958 *a good introduction to the subject. A corresponding account of the life table, with some further development, is contained in* Pressat 1961. U.S. Bureau of the Census 1951 *provides step-by-step directions for elementary life table construction, as well as exercises for the beginning student. More technical is the exposition of the life table in* Benjamin 1959. *The student with a background in the calculus seeking a more comprehensive understanding of the life table, double decrement tables, and select tables may start with* Hooker & Longley-Cook 1953–1957; Jordan 1952. *The theoretical aspects of double and higher-order decrement tables are discussed in* Bailey & Haycocks 1946. *A firm understanding of the techniques of life table construction requires a good background in the means for estimating the exposed-to risk, as given in* Gershenson 1961, *and also for a grasp of the elements of graduation and interpolation, as given in* Miller 1946. *The principal techniques used in the construction of life tables are described in* Spiegelman 1955, *which also treats, in detail, the special situations at the early ages, where the assumption of a uniform distribution of deaths over the year of age is not applicable, and at extreme old age, where artifacts are used to complete the column of mortality rates.*

BAILEY, WALTER G.; and HAYCOCKS, HERBERT W. 1946 *Some Theoretical Aspects of Multiple Decrement Tables.* Edinburgh: Constable.

BARCLAY, GEORGE W. 1958 *Techniques of Population Analysis.* New York: Wiley.

BENJAMIN, BERNARD (1959) 1960 *Elements of Vital Statistics.* London: Allen & Unwin; Chicago: Quadrangle Books.

BRASS, WILLIAM 1963 The Construction of Life Tables From Child Survivorship Ratios. Volume 1, pages 294–301 in International Population Conference, New York, 1961, *Proceedings.* London: International Union for the Scientific Study of Population.

CHIANG, CHIN L. 1960 A Stochastic Study of the Life Table and Its Applications: 2. Sample Variance of the Observed Expectation of Life and Other Biometric Functions. *Human Biology* 32:221–238.

CHURCHILL, BETTY C. 1955 Age and Life Expectancy of Business Firms. *Survey of Current Business* 35, no. 12:15–19, 24.

CIBA FOUNDATION 1959 *Colloquia on Aging.* Volume 5: The Lifespan of Animals. Boston: Little.

COALE, ANSLEY J.; and DEMENY, PAUL 1966 *Regional Model Life Tables and Stable Populations.* Princeton Univ. Press.

DUBLIN, LOUIS I.; and LOTKA, ALFRED J. 1925 On the True Rate of Natural Increase. *Journal of the American Statistical Association* 20:305–339.

DUBLIN, LOUIS I.; LOTKA, ALFRED J.; and SPIEGELMAN, M. (1936) 1949 *Length of Life.* Rev. ed. New York: Ronald Press. → The 1936 edition was written by Dublin and Lotka only; citations in the text refer to the 1949 edition.

DURAND, JOHN D. 1960 Mortality Estimates From Roman Tombstone Inscriptions. *American Journal of Sociology* 65:365–373.

GABRIEL, K. R.; and RONEN, ILANA 1958 Estimates of Mortality From Infant Mortality Rates. *Population Studies* 12:164–169.

GERSHENSON, HARRY 1961 *Measurement of Mortality.* Chicago: The Society of Actuaries.

GREVILLE, T. N. E. 1966 *Methodology of the National, Regional, and State Life Tables for the United States: 1959–61.* Washington: National Center for Health Statistics.

HALDANE, J. B. S. 1953 Some Animal Life Tables. Institute of Actuaries, London, *Journal* 79:83–89.

HOOKER, PERCY F.; and LONGLEY-COOK, L. H. 1953–1957 *Life and Other Contingencies.* 2 vols. Cambridge Univ. Press.

HUNTER, ARTHUR et al. 1932 *Disability Benefits in Life Insurance Policies.* 2d ed. Actuarial Studies, No. 5. Chicago: Actuarial Society of America.

JACOBSON, P. H. 1964 Cohort Survival for Generations Since 1840. *Milbank Memorial Fund Quarterly* 42: 36–53.

JAFFE, A. J. 1961 The Calculation of Death Rates for Establishments With Supplementary Notes on the Calculation of Birth Rates. *Estadistica: Journal of the Inter-American Statistical Institute* [1961]:513–526.

JONES, J. P. 1962 *Remarriage Tables Based on Experience Under OASDI and U.S. Employees Compensation Systems.* Actuarial Study No. 55. Washington: U.S. Social Security Administration.

JORDAN, CHESTER W. 1952 *Society of Actuaries' Textbook on Life Contingencies.* Chicago: The Society of Actuaries.

KEYFITZ, NATHAN 1966 A Life Table That Agrees With the Data. *Journal of the American Statistical Association* 61:305–312.

KURUP, R. S. 1965 A Revision of Model Life Tables. Unpublished manuscript. → Paper presented at the second World Population Conference.

LOTKA, ALFRED J. 1931 The Structure of a Growing Population. *Human Biology* 3:459–493.

MILLER, MORTON D. 1946 *Elements of Graduation.* Chicago: Actuarial Society of America.

MORTARA, GIORGIO 1949 *Methods of Using Census Statistics for the Calculation of Life Tables and Other Demographic Measures.* Population Studies, No. 7. Lake Success, N.Y.: United Nations, Department of Social Affairs.

MYERS, ROBERT J. 1949 Further Remarriage Experience. Casualty Actuarial Society, *Proceedings* 36:73–104.

PRESSAT, ROLAND 1961 *L'analyse démographique.* Paris: Presses Universitaires de France.

SIRKEN, MONROE G. (1964) 1966 *Comparison of Two Methods of Constructing Abridged Life Tables.* Rev. ed. Series 2, No. 4. Washington: National Center for Health Statistics.

SPIEGELMAN, MORTIMER 1955 *Introduction to Demography.* Chicago: The Society of Actuaries. → See the references in Chapter 5 for materials on life tables.

SPIEGELMAN, MORTIMER 1957 The Versatility of the Life Table. *American Journal of Public Health* 47:297–304. → Contains a list of references.

STOCKWELL, EDWARD G.; and NAM, CHARLES B. 1963 Illustrative Tables of School Life. *Journal of the American Statistical Association* 58:1113–1124.

STOLNITZ, GEORGE J. 1956 *Life Tables From Limited Data: A Demographic Approach.* Princeton Univ., Office of Population Research.

UNITED NATIONS, DEPARTMENT OF SOCIAL AFFAIRS 1955*a* *Age and Sex Patterns of Mortality: Model Life Tables for Under-developed Countries.* Population Studies, No. 22. New York: United Nations.

UNITED NATIONS, DEPARTMENT OF SOCIAL AFFAIRS 1955*b* *Methods of Appraisal of Basic Data for Population Estimates.* New York: United Nations.

U.S. BUREAU OF THE CENSUS 1951 *Handbook of Statistical Methods for Demographers.* Washington: Government Printing Office.

U.S. PUBLIC HEALTH SERVICE 1954–1955 [Life Tables for 1949–1951.] U.S. National Office of Vital Statistics, *Vital Statistics: Special Reports* 41, no. 1; no. 2.

U.S. PUBLIC HEALTH SERVICE 1959 [Life Tables for 1949–1951.] U.S. National Office of Vital Statistics, *Vital Statistics: Special Reports* 41, no. 5:149–158.

U.S. PUBLIC HEALTH SERVICE 1961 *Guide to United States Life Tables, 1900–1959.* Bibliography Series, No. 42. Washington: Government Printing Office.

LIFE TESTING

See under QUALITY CONTROL, STATISTICAL.

LIKELIHOOD

The *likelihood function* is important in nearly every part of statistical inference, but concern here is with just the *likelihood principle,* a very general and problematic concept of statistical evidence. [*For discussion of other roles of the likelihood function, see* ESTIMATION; HYPOTHESIS TESTING; SUFFICIENCY.]

The likelihood function is defined in terms of the probability law (or density function) assumed to represent a sampling or experimental situation: When the observation variables are fixed at the values actually observed, the resulting function of the unknown parameter(s) is the likelihood function. (More precisely, two such functions identical except for a constant factor are considered equivalent representations of the same likelihood function.)

The likelihood principle may be stated in two parts: (1) the likelihood function, determined by the sample observed in any given case, represents fully the evidence about parameter values available in those observations (this is the *likelihood axiom*); and (2) the evidence supporting one parameter value (or point) as against another is given by relative values of the likelihood function (likelihood ratios).

For example, suppose that a random sample of ten patients suffering from migraine are treated by an experimental drug and that four of them report relief. The sampling is binomial, and the investigator is interested in the unknown proportion, p, in the population of potential patients, who would report relief. The likelihood function determined by the sample is a function of p,

$$\binom{10}{4} p^4(1-p)^6, \qquad 0 \leqslant p \leqslant 1,$$

whose graph is shown in Figure 1. This likelihood function has a maximum at $p = .4$ and becomes very small, approaching 0, as p approaches 0 or 1. Hence, according to the likelihood principle, values of p very near .4 are supported by the evidence in this sample, as against values of p very near 0 or 1, with very great strength, since the corresponding likelihood ratios $(.4)^4(.6)^6/p^4(1-p)^6$ are very large.

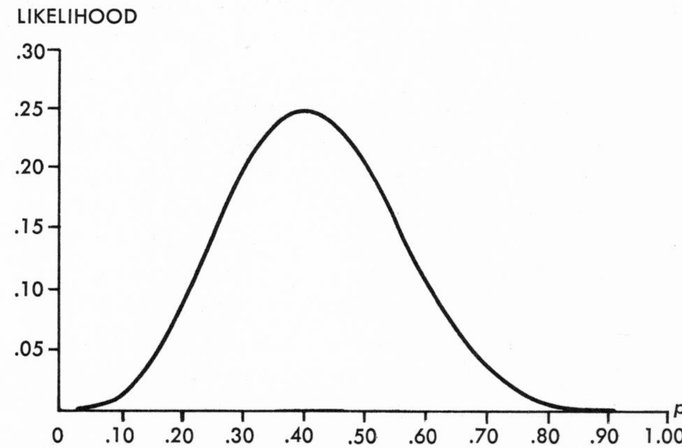

Figure 1 — The likelihood function $\binom{10}{4} p^4 (1-p)^6$

A different rule for sampling patients would be to treat and observe them one at a time until just four had reported relief. A possible outcome would be that just ten would be observed, with six reporting no relief and of course four reporting relief. The probability of that observed outcome is

$$\binom{9}{3} p^4(1-p)^6, \qquad 0 \leqslant p \leqslant 1.$$

This function of p differs from the previous one by only a constant factor and hence is considered to be an alternative, equivalent representation of the *same* likelihood function. The likelihood principle asserts that therefore the evidence about p in the two cases is the same, notwithstanding other differences in the two probability laws, which appear for other possible samples.

Relation to other statistical theory. The likelihood principle is incompatible with the main body of modern statistical theory and practice, notably the Neyman–Pearson theory of hypothesis testing and of confidence intervals, and incompatible in general even with such well-known concepts as standard error of an estimate and significance level [*see* ESTIMATION; HYPOTHESIS TESTING].

To illustrate this incompatibility, observe that in the example two distinct sampling rules gave the same likelihood function, and hence the same evidence under the likelihood principle. On the other hand, different determinations of a lower 95 per cent confidence limit for p are required under the respective sampling rules, and the two confidence limits obtained are different. The likelihood principle, however, is given full formal justification and interpretation within Bayesian inference theories and much interest in the principle stems from recently renewed interest and developments in such theories [*see* BAYESIAN INFERENCE].

Finally, on grounds independent of the crucial and controversial Bayesian concepts of prior or personal probability, interest and support for the likelihood principle arises because most standard statistical theory fails to include (and clearly implicitly excludes) any precise general concept of evidence in an observed sample, while several concepts of evidence that many statisticians consider appropriate have been found on analysis to entail the likelihood axiom. Some of these concepts have become part of a more or less coherent widespread body of theory and practice in which the Neyman–Pearson approach is complemented by concepts of evidence often left implicit. Such concepts also appear as basic in some of Fisher's theories. When formulated as axioms and analyzed, these concepts have been discovered to be equivalent to the likelihood axiom and hence basically incompatible with, rather than possible complements to, the Neyman–Pearson theory.

General concepts of statistical evidence. The central one of these concepts is that of *conditionality* (or *ancillarity*), a concept that appeared first in rather special technical contexts. Another somewhat similar concept of evidence, which can be illustrated more simply here and which also entails the major part of the likelihood axiom, is the *censoring axiom:* Suppose that after interpretation of the outcome described with the second sampling rule of the example, it is discovered that the reserve supply of the experimental drug had been accidentally destroyed and is irreplaceable and that no more than ten patients could have been treated with the supply on hand for the experiment. Is the interpretation of the outcome to be changed? In the hypothetical possible case that seven or more patients reported no relief before a fourth reported relief, the sampling plan could not have been carried through even to the necessary eleventh patient: The change of conditions makes unavailable ("censored") the information whether if an outcome were to include more than six patients reporting no relief, that number would be seven, or eight, or any specific larger number. But in fact the outcome actually observed was a physical event unaffected, except in a hypothetical sense, by the differences between intended and realizable sampling plans. Many statisticians consider such a hypothetical distinction irrelevant to the evidence in an outcome. It follows readily from the general formulation of such a concept that the evidence in the observed outcome is characterized by just the function $\binom{9}{3}p^4(1-p)^6$, $0 \leqslant p \leqslant 1$. More generally this censoring concept is seen to be the likelihood axiom, slightly weakened by disallowance of an arbitrary constant factor; the qualification is removable with adoption of another very weak "sufficiency" concept concerning evidence (see Birnbaum 1961; 1962; Pratt 1961).

Interpreting evidence. The only method proposed for interpreting evidence just through likelihood functions, apart from Bayesian methods, is that stated as part (2) of the likelihood principle above. The briefness and informality of these statements and interpretation are typical of those given by their originator, R. A. Fisher (1925; 1956), and their leading proponent, G. A. Barnard (1947; 1949; 1962). "Likelihood ratio" appears in such interpretations as a primitive term concerning statistical evidence, associated in each case with a nonnegative numerical value, with larger values representing qualitatively greater support for one parameter point against the other, and with unity (representing "no evidence") the only distinguished point on the scale. But likelihood ratio here is not subject to definition or interpretation in terms of other independently defined extramathematical concepts.

Only in the simplest case, where the parameter space has but two points (a case rare in practice but of real theoretical interest), are such interpretations of likelihood functions clearly plausible; and in this case they appear to many to be far superior to more standard methods, for example, significance tests. In such cases the likelihood function is represented by a single likelihood ratio.

In the principal case of larger parameter spaces, such interpretations can be seriously misleading with high probability and are considered unacceptable by most statisticians (see Stein 1962; Armitage 1963). Thus progress in clarifying the important problem of an adequate non-Bayesian concept of statistical evidence leaves the problem not only unresolved but in a positively anomalous state.

Another type of argument supporting the likelihood principle on non-Bayesian grounds is based upon axioms characterizing rational decision making in situations of uncertainty, rather than concepts of statistical evidence (see, for example, Cornfield 1966; Luce & Raiffa 1957).

Likelihoods in form of normal densities. Attention is sometimes focused on cases where likelihood functions have the form of normal density functions. This form occurs in the very simple and familiar problem of inferences about the mean of a normal distribution with known variance (with ordinary sampling). Hence adoption of the likelihood axiom warrants and invites identification with this familiar problem of all other cases where such likelihood functions occur. In particular, the maximum likelihood estimator in any such case is thus related to the classical estimator of the normal mean (the sample mean), and the curvature of the likelihood function (or of its logarithm) at its maximum is thus related to the variance of that classical estimator. In similar vein, transformations of parameters have been considered that tend to give likelihood functions a normal density shape (in problems with several parameters as well as those with only one). (See, for example, Anscombe 1964.)

Likelihoods in nonparametric problems. In nonparametric problems, there is no finite set of parameters that can be taken as the arguments of a likelihood function, and it may not be obvious that the likelihood axiom has meaning. However, "nonparametric" is a sometimes misleading name for a very broad mathematical model that includes all specific parametric families of laws among those allowed; hence in principle it is simple to imagine (although in practice formidably awkward to represent) the extremely inclusive parameter space containing a point representing each (absolutely) continuous law, and for each pair of such points a likelihood ratio (determined as usual from the observed sample).

ALLAN BIRNBAUM

[*Other relevant material may be found in* DISTRIBUTIONS, STATISTICAL, *articles on* SPECIAL CONTINUOUS DISTRIBUTIONS *and* SPECIAL DISCRETE DISTRIBUTIONS.]

BIBLIOGRAPHY

ANSCOMBE, F. J. 1964 Normal Likelihood Function. Institute of Statistical Mathematics, *Annals* 26:1–19.

ARMITAGE, PETER 1963 Sequential Medical Trials: Some Comments on F. J. Anscombe's Paper. *Journal of the American Statistical Association* 58:384–387.

BARNARD, G. A. 1947 [Review of] *Sequential Analysis* by Abraham Wald. *Journal of the American Statistical Association* 42:658–664.

BARNARD, G. A. 1949 Statistical Inference. *Journal of the Royal Statistical Society* Series B 11:116–149.

BARNARD, G. A.; JENKINS, G. M.; and WINSTEN, C. B. 1962 Likelihood Inference and Time Series. *Journal of the Royal Statistical Society* Series A 125:321–375. → Includes 20 pages of discussion.

BIRNBAUM, ALLAN 1961 On the Foundations of Statistical Inference: I. Binary Experiments. *Annals of Mathematical Statistics* 32:414–435.

BIRNBAUM, ALLAN 1962 On the Foundations of Statistical Inference. *Journal of the American Statistical Association* 57:269–326. → Includes 20 pages of discussion. See especially John W. Pratt's comments on pages 314–315.

CORNFIELD, JEROME 1966 Sequential Trials, Sequential Analysis and the Likelihood Principle. *American Statistician* 20:18–23.

COX, D. R. 1958 Some Problems Connected With Statistical Inference. *Annals of Mathematical Statistics* 29:357–372.

FISHER, R. A. (1925) 1950 Theory of Statistical Estimation. Pages 11.699*a*–11.725 in R. A. Fisher, *Contributions to Mathematical Statistics.* New York: Wiley. → First published in Volume 22, Part 5 of the Cambridge Philosophical Society, *Proceedings.*

FISHER, R. A. (1956) 1959 *Statistical Methods and Scientific Inference.* 2d ed., rev. New York: Hafner; London: Oliver & Boyd.

LUCE, R. DUNCAN; and RAIFFA, HOWARD 1957 *Games and Decisions: Introduction and Critical Survey.* A Study of the Behavioral Models Project, Bureau of Applied Social Research, Columbia University. New York: Wiley.

PRATT, JOHN W. 1961 [Review of] *Testing Statistical Hypotheses* by E. L. Lehmann. *Journal of the American Statistical Association* 56:163–167.

STEIN, CHARLES M. 1962 A Remark on the Likelihood Principle. *Journal of the Royal Statistical Society* Series A 125:565–573. → Includes five pages of comments by G. A. Barnard.

LIMITED WAR

Limited war is a subjective and relative term that has gained currency chiefly to distinguish certain conflicts from wars fought for ends and by means that have impressed men as extreme. Limited wars are as old as the history of mankind. They have occurred among the most primitive and the most advanced peoples and in every civilization. The great majority of all international wars have been fought for ends far short of domination or annihilation and by means far short of the complete destruction of the enemy's armed forces or his society. In these respects even the two so-called total wars of this century—World War I and World War II—were significantly limited.

The *concept* of limited war is also old and ubiquitous in history. Primitive tribes, as well as the knights of the Middle Ages, have been conscious of explicit customs and rules of mutual restraint in the conduct of warfare. In ancient China, as well as eighteenth-century Europe, there were laws explicitly formulated to regulate warfare.

Yet the consciousness of limited war as a distinct kind of warfare, with its own theory and doctrine, has emerged most markedly in contrast to three major wars, waged between several major states, in behalf of popular national and ideological goals, by means of organized conscripted forces and massive firepower: the Napoleonic Wars, World War I, and World War II.

The detailed elaboration of a strategic doctrine of limited war, the formulation of specific plans for carrying out this doctrine, and the combined efforts of government, the military establishment, and private analysts and publicists to translate the doctrine into particular weapons and forces are developments peculiar to the nuclear age. They are products of the profound fear of nuclear war and the belief that the limitation of war must be carefully contrived, rather than left to inherent limitations upon military capabilities.

The principal exponents of limited war in the eighteenth century were (1) the principal military tacticians of wars of fortification and maneuver, like Vauban and Marshal de Saxe; (2) proponents of international laws to regulate and civilize war, like Vattel, who drew upon the principles of Grotius; and (3) political theorists like Rousseau and Fénelon, who saw war as a necessary, if rather indecisive, instrument for preserving a balance of power. In the latter half of the nineteenth century legal and balance-of-power theorists were somewhat overshadowed by the exponents of modern military power and glory, like Marshal Foch. Most of the leading military thinkers, with the notable exception of Karl von Clausewitz, were prophets of blitzkrieg and wars of annihilation. After World War I, proponents of international order, in their search for collective security and disarmament as methods of avoiding war, generally ignored the problem of limiting war. Liddell Hart, virtually the only exponent of a military strategy of limited war between the two world wars, applied his prescriptions chiefly to Britain's situation.

After World War II, however, there was a great resurgence of interest in limited war among civilian analysts as well as military experts, particularly in the United States after the Korean War. The new exponents of limited war advocated the systematic control of military potential and of war as a useful, carefully restricted instrument of policy. On the most fundamental level they drew their inspiration from Clausewitz, who in expounding the theory of war as a continuation of diplomacy had related the scope and intensity of war to its political context with a profundity appreciated equally by Lenin and Mao Tse-tung. [*See the biography of* CLAUSEWITZ.]

A limited war is now broadly defined as a war that is fought for ends far short of the complete subordination of one state's will to another's and by means involving far less than the total military resources of the belligerents, leaving the civilian life and the armed forces of the belligerents largely intact and leading to a bargained termination. More narrowly, it is defined as a local nonnuclear war. Limited war is therefore a matter of degree. It is also a matter of perspective, since a war that is limited for one belligerent might be close to total for another. Furthermore, a limited war may be restricted in some respects and not in others. Thus, a civil war or insurrection may be fought by limited means for the total stake of controlling a government.

Yet despite the impossibility of defining limited war by simple and absolute criteria, it is not difficult, historically, to distinguish limited wars from wars of great scope and intensity.

Limited wars in history

The eighteenth century. The middle of the eighteenth century stands out as the first notable period of limited warfare in the history of the modern state system. In marked contrast to the preceding religious wars and the general wars revolving around Louis XIV's struggle for hegemony and to the subsequent French Revolution and Napoleonic Wars, the wars of this period generally consisted of short, duellike battles of maneuver fought for limited dynastic and territorial objectives, within a system where rough equilibrium of power was maintained by about five major states. The wars left civilian life relatively unaffected and altered the international status of the major countries only minimally or gradually.

The limited character of war in this period must be attributed largely to the economic and technological obstacles preventing the major states from destroying each other's armed forces and devastating or occupying each other's homelands. This in turn reflected the limited capacity of monarchies to organize armed forces and mobilize military potential. Furthermore, warfare was limited by the great role of sea power and by the fact that sea war did not ravish the land.

The limited warfare of the eighteenth century, however, cannot be attributed solely to the nature of military technology, since the technology was not very different then from that of the preceding and following periods of general war. It must also be attributed to the limited nature of the political ends for which states fought; to the equilibrium of power between the major participants, which restrained them from pushing an advantage too far; to the stilted, drill-field military tactics suited to keeping expensive and untrustworthy troops under control; to a general respect for laws of war distinguishing between combatants and noncombatants, belligerents and nonbelligerents; and to the prevailing social and political system, which made these political, legal, and military constraints congenial to the homogeneous ruling classes of Europe. Beyond these factors, the limitation of eighteenth-century warfare can be explained simply by the desire of rulers and ruled to avoid the chaos of the religious wars.

The nineteenth century. The Napoleonic period removed many of the political and social conditions of limited war. In undermining the *ancien régime* and introducing the concept of the "nation in arms," it prepared the way for a popular nationalism far less congenial to the limitation of war than the pragmatic *Realpolitik* of the eighteenth century.

Napoleon demonstrated the capacity of states to generate popular enthusiasm for war by nationalistic and ideological appeals and to translate this enthusiasm into unprecedented military power through mass conscription and the mobilization of industry and technology. By reconciling military discipline with individual initiative, he enabled states to use new tactics of camouflage, mobility, and destructive pursuit that gave war a new dynamism. He showed that where such decisive force could be exerted on land, sea war would cease to be a limiting factor and instead would become, through blockade and the destruction of commerce, a forerunner of total war against civilian life.

Nevertheless, the rest of the nineteenth century —notably from 1854 to 1870—was, again, a period of limited war, thanks largely to the absence of wars between the several major states (except the Crimean War, which was fought in a peripheral location). The latter half of the nineteenth century saw the unprecedented development in peacetime of war plans, conscription, military logistics, and communications (notably railroads and telegraph) and a rapidly advancing military technology. Yet, the new potentialities of destruction inherent in these developments were not fully exploited or generally appreciated until World War I, although the American Civil War should have been a grim warning. Instead, Prussia's quick, limited victories in 1866 (against Austria) and 1871 (against France) were believed to be the models of future wars.

The two world wars. World War I was not deliberately undertaken as a general war. It became a world war because of diplomatic miscalculations, the interlocking network of alliance commitments, the inflexibility of mobilization plans and war plans, the prevailing assumption among the military that a general war was inevitable, the weakness of civilian control over the military, and the failure of the initial German offensive, followed by a war of attrition and stalemate that national animosities, fed by popular sentiment, made it difficult to terminate without victory. Consequently, even if the will to avoid general war had been stronger, war would have become general and extremely destructive without a systematic effort by governments to subject military planning and operations to over-all political direction under a strategy of limited war.

Yet few drew any such lessons from that shocking experience. Rather, it was generally assumed that unless war could be avoided by collective security and disarmament there would soon be another and even more devastating world war. The rise of the expansionist totalitarian powers, the fascist glorification of war, and the perfection and proliferation of more destructive weapons, including aerial bombardment, seemed to make this inevitable.

Actually, the fascist states preferred to satisfy their ambitions through intimidation and through quick, limited aggressions against negligible opposition; but the failure of the democratic states to contain these aggressions at the outset by limited means and their unwillingness to use force for limited ends assured the fulfillment of the prophecies of total war when the democratic states, contrary to Hitler's calculations, belatedly offered resistance in 1939 and when Japan, confronted with the American oil embargo and rearmament, launched what it regarded as a limited, preventive attack on Pearl Harbor.

The nuclear age. In the aftermath of World War II, the invention of nuclear weapons and the onset of the cold war raised a general feeling that only the United Nations and disarmament could prevent another total war. Yet, within a decade this opinion had been modified by the widespread conviction that the potential destructiveness of a nuclear war would deter a total war and by a concomitant surge of private and official interest in meeting a purported danger of limited wars.

This new attention to limited war has been justified by the occurrence of more than fifty limited wars of various kinds within twenty years after World War II. All of them were fought outside Europe, with the exception of the Greek civil war in 1945–1949 and the Hungarian rebellion in 1956. The great majority were internal wars; that is, wars that arose and were fought largely within the boundaries of a single state. Several of these were full-scale civil wars: in Greece; China in 1945–1949; Bolivia in 1949; Algeria in 1954–1962; Cuba in 1958–1959; the Congo in 1960–1963; Vietnam from 1959; and Indonesia in 1966.

A number of internal wars were, in communist parlance, "national liberation wars," supported from outside by the Soviet Union, Communist China, or other communist countries: in Greece; French Indochina in 1946–1954; Burma in 1948–1954; Malaya in 1948–1960; the Philippines in 1946–1954; and Vietnam. And one should add to this list two abortive rebellions against Soviet and Communist Chinese domination: in Hungary, and Tibet in 1956–1957. Although internal, most of these wars were major international political events because they determined the status of colonial holdings and/or affected the balance of power in the cold war.

Several of the approximately fifty limited wars arose from a direct invasion of the territory of one state by another state: the Korean War in 1950–1953; the Guatemalan war in 1954 (which, however, had many characteristics of an internal war); the Israeli–Egyptian war and the British–French invasion of Suez in 1956; and the Indian conquest of Goa in 1961. One might also categorize the Quemoy–Matsu conflict in 1954–1958 as an aborted interstate war. Like most of the internal wars, these interstate wars reflected the major political issues in the world since World War II: the national–colonial conflict and the communist–noncommunist conflict.

There were, also, a few interstate wars fought primarily by subversive means, but all of these except the war in Vietnam were low-level conflicts arising from indigenous national rivalries: Somalia–Ethiopia in 1960, Indonesia–Malaya in 1963, and Algeria–Morocco in 1963.

Some of the civil and internal wars were quite destructive—as in Greece, China, and Algeria—and total, rather than limited, in the sense that different regimes competed for complete control of a country. The Korean War, although limited from the American and Chinese standpoint, was virtually total from the standpoint of the North and South Korean regimes. Yet, all of these wars were strictly limited in geographical extent, the number of countries directly involved, and the scope and intensity of violence. Although a number of them involved either the United States or the Soviet Union, none involved both powers directly and simultaneously.

The limited nature of these wars can be partly explained by a variety of conditions that helped limit wars in previous periods of history: the limited or local nature of political issues at stake, the tactics of internal warfare, the limited military capacity of the belligerents, the one-sided nature of the contest, the pressure by allies for constraint, the fear of overcommitment at the expense of protecting prior interests elsewhere. The notable feature of this period, however, is that despite the global nature of the cold war and the depth and intensity of the over-all conflict of interests and aims, and despite the immense destructive power that the principal adversaries could inflict upon each other, the major communist and democratic powers did not bring their full military power to bear upon each other. Only in the Korean War did major Western and communist powers employ their armed forces in direct combat with each other. Therefore, the limitation of warfare since World War II must be largely attributed to the military abstinence and restraint practiced by the principal adversaries in the cold war.

A large part of the explanation of this military abstinence and restraint lies in the deterrent effect of the very capacity for mutual destruction that would make another general war so catastrophic. This deterrent effect, combined with a number of other military and political factors conducive to limitation, was most marked in the Korean War, where, contrary to all previous expectations in the West, an American–Communist Chinese conflict remained local and limited, with each side deliberately refraining from military actions that threatened to expand the war and both sides agreeing to an inconclusive termination.

The limited war in Vietnam is as notable an example as the Korean War of studied application by the United States of ascending gradations of limited force toward the achievement of a negotiated settlement on limited terms. It was even more notable, however, for evoking widespread popular approval of and insistence upon such limits.

The modern concept

The Korean War in time stimulated a new concept and strategic doctrine of limited war, which received additional impetus from the growth of Soviet nuclear striking power, the introduction of thermonuclear bombs and long-range missiles in Soviet and American arsenals, and the communists' explicit emphasis in the 1960s on national liberation wars.

According to this concept, the stability of the bipolar nuclear balance, resulting from the reluctance of the nuclear powers to use nuclear weapons except in retaliation against nuclear weapons, could not be relied upon to deter communist powers from supporting limited aggressions and might, in fact, encourage such aggressions because the United States might be deterred from using nuclear weapons first when it had no effective means of conventional resistance. Furthermore, if involved in a local conventional conflict, the United States and its allies might not be capable of controlling the escalation or expansion of such a war but would have to choose between defeat and a nuclear catastrophe. To deter such aggressions or to fight local wars effectively without incurring an intolerable risk of nuclear war, the United States, according to this thesis, would have to develop a capacity to fight different kinds of small wars successfully, with a diversified arsenal of conventional capabilities appropriate to various constraints upon weapons, targets, and the zone of combat, while holding open the lines of diplomatic communication to facilitate the termination of combat, probably short of a clear-cut military or political victory. This new concept of limited war was explicitly based on the principle, drawn from Clausewitz, that the conduct of war should be scrupulously disciplined by over-all political considerations, so that war will be an effective instrument of policy rather than an instrument of maximum destruction.

The concept of limited war did not find official favor with American Secretary of State Dulles; only in the last years of the Eisenhower administration were some concessions made to the idea. Instead, the administration stressed the alleged economic and military necessity of avoiding future Koreas by depending primarily on the American capacity to meet local conventional aggressions with strategic and tactical nuclear retaliation to deter little and big wars alike. This strategy—loosely called massive retaliation—was also adopted by allies of the United States in the North Atlantic Treaty Organization (NATO), who were equally anxious to substitute nuclear firepower for conventionally armed man power following their brief rearmament effort during the Korean War period.

In this period, however, a movement for strategic revision arose within the United States Army and Navy and among academic analysts and research organizations interested in military questions. According to this revisionist movement, the dependence of the West on nuclear weapons was increasingly incredible as a deterrent against the most likely forms of aggression; it would be ineffective or disastrous if deterrence should fail or be inapplicable; and it was inadequate as an instrument of policy in conflicts short of war (in which the Soviet Union could confront the United States and its allies with the choice between acquiescence and thermonuclear holocaust).

When President Kennedy and Secretary of Defense McNamara took office in 1961, they explicitly adopted the concept of limited war, which had emerged as a criticism of the prevailing strategy. Moreover, they instituted a far-reaching program to revise military policies so as to support a strategy of limited war. They created "special forces" to handle guerrilla warfare, urged a build-up of NATO's conventional capabilities in order to raise the threshold of effective resistance without resorting to nuclear war, and increased the capacity of the United States to transport armed forces by air to prevent or deter local wars. The key phrase used to describe this revised strategy was "flexible and controlled response."

The concept of flexible and controlled response, however, was applied beyond local nonnuclear war. It also embraced the concept of deliberately planning for the "option" of using nuclear weapons in a limited fashion, under constraints upon their number, type, and targets and in response to effective central political direction. Thus, the concept of limited war came to include even a controlled strategic "counterforce" war, in which the United States would try to confine nuclear exchanges to such military targets as missile bases, holding back its capacity to devastate Soviet cities, as an inducement to the Soviet Union not to attack American cities.

Whether or not a nuclear war could be kept limited, the unwillingness of the American government to relinquish this possibility was a striking indication of growing inhibitions against resorting to unlimited war or depending entirely on the "balance of terror" to deter armed conflict. It signified increasing reluctance to depend for deterrence upon a military response that it would not be rational to carry out.

There were signs that the nuclear-missile age had induced similar attitudes in Soviet civilian and military leaders. Premier Khrushchev led Soviet spokesmen in avowing that thermonuclear weapons, by deterring the "capitalist–imperialist" powers, had overruled the Marxist–Leninist dictum that the dictatorship of the proletariat could come about only by a violent clash of arms precipitated by imperialist desperation. Such a clash, he said, was no longer "fatalistically inevitable." On numerous occasions he and other Soviet leaders stressed the immense and intolerable damage that communist as well as "imperialist" powers would suffer in a nuclear war.

Although Chinese spokesmen did not disagree with this view, they differed with Soviet spokesmen in being more confident that the United States would be deterred by Soviet nuclear power from escalating national liberation wars and particularly from initiating the use of nuclear weapons.

Whether for effect or out of conviction, Soviet spokesmen continued to assert that any war between the Soviet Union and the United States would result in nuclear war and continued to deny the possibility that either a strategic or tactical nuclear war could be limited, but in the mid-1960s some Soviet military men began to publish criticisms and qualifications of these views.

Furthermore, communist doctrine had always emphasized political constraints on war and the cautious, flexible use of force. Mao Tse-tung's strategy of revolutionary war, which dominated Chinese thinking and remained the leading rationale of unconventional war, was suffused with concepts of limited war although its aim was total. By 1961 both Soviet and Chinese strategy emphasized the necessity of supporting "national liberation wars" (that is, internal wars promoting a communist takeover) and acknowledged the possibility of "local wars" outside Europe (that is, geographically restricted wars between states, which might or might not be limited in weapons) as a contingency to be deterred or frustrated.

Continuing problems

In the United States there emerged during the 1960s a broad consensus supporting the strategy of flexible and controlled response. America's European allies largely accepted the strategy as it applied outside Europe, but they were generally far more skeptical about the feasibility or utility of fighting a limited conventional war, let alone a limited nuclear war, in Europe. Their skepticism reflected differences of geography and was not likely to yield to American persuasion. Accordingly, they remained reluctant to build up NATO's conventional capabilities and were fearful that the emphasis on a strategy of limited conventional war would undermine the credibility of nuclear deterrence. France went furthest in openly criticizing the doctrine of flexible and controlled response and in acclaiming a doctrine of extended nuclear deterrence as a substitute for conventional resistance. Despite the German Federal Republic's twelve divisions and the six American divisions, the capacity of NATO's European-based forces to withstand the Soviet Union's forces in eastern Europe for more than a few days remained in doubt. France's withdrawal from NATO's integrated commands in 1966 only highlighted this situation.

The United States in the mid-1960s became increasingly preoccupied with the war in Vietnam. There the addition of concentrated firepower (including heavy strategic and tactical bombing) and regular ground warfare to guerrilla warfare and civic action fitted none of the previous concepts of limited war. Except for more detailed attention in the United States to the process of escalation, strategic thought about limited war seemed to have passed its phase of innovation.

Strategic quiescence, however, did not resolve outstanding differences in the West about the particular forces and strategies needed for deterrence, resistance, and the support of policy in crises short of war. What should be the purpose of NATO's conventional forces in Europe: to provide merely a "screening force" to detect an attack or to be a "tripwire" to sound the alarm for nuclear retaliation? to prevent an unopposed limited territorial grab? to force the enemy to pause long enough to consider the risk of a nuclear war? to withstand Soviet forces in Europe conventionally for days? months? Under what conditions, if any, should the West use nuclear weapons first? If nuclear weapons were used, how, if at all, could a bilateral nuclear war, especially one in Europe, be significantly limited in geographical extent, targets, and duration? What should be the function of tactical (that is, battlefield) weapons as opposed to longer-range nuclear weapons? Could either tactical or strategic nuclear exchanges be confined to "bargaining and demonstration"? How could such exchanges be kept under effective central command and political control?

The most hopeful thing about these unanswered and necessarily conjectural questions was that their very imponderability made a potential aggressor uncertain about the response to his incursions, and this uncertainty, combined with his awareness of the intolerable penalties of miscalculation, would itself be a powerful deterrent to rash moves. Indeed, notwithstanding the Korean War, throughout the cold war both the communist powers and the United States and its allies have exercised great caution in avoiding a direct military encounter with each other, afraid that any such encounter might expand into a thermonuclear war. Approaches to the brink of war, such as the Formosa Strait crisis in 1958, the Berlin crises in 1948–1949 and 1958–1962, and the Cuban crisis in 1962, show that this caution does not preclude dangerous tests of will and nerve, under the shadow of war. Yet, through such tests the major adversaries in the cold war seem to have learned the acceptable limits of pressure and counterpressure short of war. If the *détente* that developed after the Cuban missile crisis should last, it will be largely due to this mutual understanding, toward which the American doctrine and forces of limited war made a major contribution by bolstering American resolve to accept the risks of war in crises.

One of the serious questions for the future, however, is whether the deterrents that have developed in an essentially bipolar world would persist in a world in which there might be a number of additional significant centers of political decision and military power both inside and outside the two blocs. A more decentralized structure of international power and interests might weaken the existing deterrents against aggression and war and increase the danger of limited wars breaking out and expanding into major wars, especially if the initial belligerents owned nuclear weapons. In the light of this danger, the most challenging problem of limiting warfare in the future might be to extend to an eroding bipolar or multipolar world methods and concepts of deterring, confining, and restraining warfare that would be as effective as those that emerged in the first two decades after what one must hope was the last, and not just the latest, world war.

ROBERT E. OSGOOD

[*See also* DETERRENCE; NUCLEAR WAR; STRATEGY. *Other relevant material may be found under* INTERNATIONAL RELATIONS; MILITARY; WAR.]

BIBLIOGRAPHY

ARON, RAYMOND (1963) 1965 *The Great Debate: Theories of Nuclear Strategy.* Garden City, N.Y.: Doubleday. → First published as *Le grand débat: Initiation à la stratégie atomique.*

CLAUSEWITZ, KARL VON (1832–1834) 1943 *On War.* New York: Modern Library. → First published in German as *Vom Kriege,* in three volumes.

EARLE, EDWARD MEAD (editor) 1943 *Makers of Modern Strategy: Military Thought From Machiavelli to Hitler.* Princeton Univ. Press.

GARTHOFF, RAYMOND L. 1966 *Soviet Military Policy: A Historical Analysis.* New York: Praeger.

HALPERIN, MORTON H. 1963 *Limited War in the Nuclear Age.* New York: Wiley.

HSIEH, ALICE L. 1962 *Communist China's Strategy in the Nuclear Era.* Englewood Cliffs, N.J.: Prentice-Hall.

HUNTINGTON, SAMUEL P. (editor) 1962 *Changing Patterns of Military Politics.* New York: Free Press.

KAHN, HERMAN 1965 *On Escalation.* New York: Praeger.

KAUFMANN, WILLIAM W. 1964 *The McNamara Strategy.* New York: Harper.

KISSINGER, HENRY A. 1957 *Nuclear Weapons and Foreign Policy.* New York: Harper.

KISSINGER, HENRY A. 1965 *The Troubled Partnership: A Re-appraisal of the Atlantic Alliance.* New York: McGraw-Hill.

LIDDELL HART, BASIL H. (1929) 1954 *Strategy: The Indirect Approach.* New York: Praeger. → First published as *The Decisive Wars of History: A Study in Strategy.*

OSGOOD, ROBERT E. 1957 *Limited War: The Challenge to American Strategy.* Univ. of Chicago Press.

OSGOOD, ROBERT E. 1962 *NATO: The Entangling Alliance.* Univ. of Chicago Press.

ROPP, THEODORE 1959 *War in the Modern World.* Durham, N.C.: Duke Univ. Press. → A paperback edition was published in 1962 by Collier.

ROSENAU, JAMES N. (editor) 1964 *International Aspects of Civil Strife.* Princeton Univ. Press.

SCHELLING, THOMAS C. 1960 *The Strategy of Conflict.* Cambridge, Mass.: Harvard Univ. Press.

SOKOLOVSKII, VASILII D. (editor) (1962) 1963 *Military Strategy: Soviet Doctrine and Concepts.* Introduction by Raymond L. Garthoff. New York: Praeger. → First published in Russian.

VAGTS, ALFRED 1956 *Defense and Diplomacy: The Soldier and the Conduct of Foreign Relations.* New York: King's Crown.

WOLFE, THOMAS W. 1964 *Soviet Strategy at the Crossroads.* Cambridge, Mass.: Harvard Univ. Press.

WRIGHT, QUINCY (1942) 1965 *A Study of War.* 2d ed. Univ. of Chicago Press.

LINDSAY, A. D.

Alexander Dunlop Lindsay, Lord Lindsay of Birker (1879–1952), a political philosopher, was born in Scotland but spent most of his life in England as fellow and then as master of Balliol College, Oxford. After his retirement, he became the first principal of the University College of North Staffordshire (now the University of Keele). Because of his services to the Trades Union Congress and the Labour party, he was elevated to the peerage in 1945 and took the title of Baron Lindsay of Birker. In many ways, Lindsay's life followed the pattern originated by such Oxford idealist philosophers as T. H. Green; in other ways, he followed the lead of Benjamin Jowett, perhaps the most famous of Lindsay's predecessors as master of Balliol. Like Green, he attempted to combine the teaching of philosophy with the obligations imposed by citizenship—participation in actual administration as well as aiding the poor and teaching the disadvantaged; like Jowett, he thought that the first purpose of a university is to train public servants by sharpening their intellects and developing their will to control events. Lindsay also continued Balliol's Victorian tradition in that he preached in the college chapel and derived his politics as much from religion as from philosophy.

In the face of the assaults upon idealism made by Bertrand Russell, G. E. Moore, and Ludwig Wittgenstein, who redirected philosophical inquiry, Lindsay tacitly abandoned the traditional idealist attempt to base political ideas upon firm metaphysical grounds (for his specific criticism of modern British philosophy, see Lindsay 1951). Rather, he paraphrased idealist political ideas in terms derived from common sense, practical politics, and the language of classical political theory. The result was a persuasive statement of the "operative ideals" of modern constitutional democracies. Although Lindsay's work added little to what had already been said by Green and Bosanquet, he did prolong their influence by his restatement, which he based upon the points that had originally persuaded many people of the superiority of idealism over Victorian positivism and scientism, whether of the utilitarian or the social Darwinian varieties. As Talcott Parsons has indicated, idealism was an important source of modern sociology and political science. Idealist philosophers emphasized the importance of human groups, of collective representations, and the place of values in social action. No less important were idealist polemics against theories of human behavior that stress individual decisions taken on purely rational and self-interested grounds.

Lindsay's antipathy to doctrines stressing egotism was rooted in his family background. Both his parents were descended from Scottish families, aristocratic in origin but active in social work and in movements for the reform of religion and politics. His father was T. M. Lindsay, a distinguished church historian and principal of the United Free Church College at the University of Glasgow. Lindsay's first degree was from Glasgow University. Despite his failure to win a Snell exhibition at Balliol, he obtained a first class degree in greats and was elected president of the Oxford Union. Even as an undergraduate he was a member of the Fabian Society. After holding fellowships in philosophy at Glasgow and Edinburgh and assisting Samuel Alexander, professor of philosophy at Manchester, Lindsay was elected in 1906 to a fellowship at Balliol. In the period before World War I, he translated Plato's *Republic* (1907), wrote a number of prefaces to philosophical volumes in the Everyman's Library series, published short books on Henri Bergson (1911) and Kant (1913), and contributed to the influential volume, *Property: Its Duties and Rights* (1914), published by the Christian Social Union, an organization led by those of Green's students who combined high-church theology with distaste for economic inequality. Lindsay married in 1907 and had two sons and a daughter.

After his service in World War I, Lindsay returned to Balliol and took an important part in establishing the new undergraduate degree in philosophy, politics, and economics. In 1922 he was elected professor of moral philosophy at Glasgow but returned to Oxford when he was elected master of Balliol in 1924. Although increasingly drawn into administration and university politics (he served a term as vice-chancellor of Oxford), he taught philosophy and preached in the Balliol chapel. Lindsay was among the few heads of Oxford colleges who supported the Labour party (1949). Probably the cause he cared for most was the Workers' Educational Association. In 1939 he was the Labour party candidate for a seat in Parliament that was won by Quinton Hogg, who had defended the Munich settlement of the previous year. During World War II, Lindsay often spoke on the radio and finished the first and, as it turned out, the only volume of his *Modern Democratic State* (1943), a work that displayed him at his best and was certainly preferable to his long book on Kant (1934*a*). After retiring as master of Balliol in 1948, he did much as first principal at Keele to institute a curriculum that put its stress on general education rather than on the specialized studies that until then were characteristic of English universities.

Lindsay's conception of political theory depended upon a series of distinctions that was designed to maintain the autonomy and, indeed, the primacy of ideas and values in the analysis of political action. Retreating from the metaphysical arguments of idealism, he nevertheless denied that the study of politics should center exclusively upon actual institutions or behavior. For Lindsay claimed that his position was neither metaphysical nor historical. He rejected the distinction between the state as studied by political theorists (in the form it ideally should have) and the state as studied by political scientists (in its actual form). Lindsay argued that these two views of the state are analytically and empirically inseparable.

Every state, he thought, is a historically conditioned association whose members share certain purposes, although these purposes need not be consciously recognized or fully realized. The laws, institutions, and moral and political practices of a society record its "operative ideals," that is, what it most values in its common life. Such preferences will be found to vary in the different historical types of states, such as the classical Greek democracies or medieval constitutional monarchies. What, in Lindsay's view, distinguishes the modern democratic state from all other types is the fact that in it the political organization that exercises a monopoly of organized force has as its function neither the creation of operative ideals nor their enforcement by coercion alone. The power of the state is properly used when, and only when, it corrects anomalies and harmonizes conflicts. The purpose of the state is to remove hindrances to the kinds of spontaneity and freedom that are compatible with the common purposes of society. It is significant that when Lindsay made this central argument in his two major works (1929; 1943) he did so by paraphrasing Bosanquet:

> What Bosanquet seems to have done in his account of the general will is to have developed a hint of Rousseau's into a masterly account of the elaborate system of institutions and mutual relations which go to make up the life of society, to have insisted on its complexity and richness and vitality, its transcendence of what any one individual can conceive or express. This, he declares, in all its elaborateness and multifariousness *is* the community. It is less than that. That is the standard of legislation and what we ordinarily call state action. The business of politics is to take this elaborate complex of individuals and institutions for granted . . . and . . . [to] seek to remove the disharmonies which are threatening its life and checking its vitality. ([1943] p. 244 in 1947 edition)

The state, in the narrow political sense, is, according to Lindsay, the hinderer of hindrances. The aim of its compulsion and the criterion of the success of that compulsion is the setting free of the spontaneity which is inherent in the life of society. Political machinery, general elections, legislatures, judges, and executives are endeavoring or ought to be endeavoring to express the spirit of a common social life.

Thus, Lindsay accepted certain distinctions that Bosanquet also had considered essential: the distinction between state and society, with primacy given to society; and that between the state, as an organization to which all must belong, and voluntary societies. These voluntary societies, traced by Lindsay to Puritan congregations, have the great merit of permitting individuals to have, within a limited sphere, real initiative, spontaneity, and liberty. But in the nature of things all such associations have purposes limited to the interests of their members. Voluntary associations, if left to themselves, come into conflict. It is the purpose of the state to eliminate such conflicts and to reconcile disagreements by reference to the operative ideals of society.

Lindsay, then, followed earlier idealists in a number of ways: he attempted to rescue by paraphrase and dilution a position that was essentially religious; he favored reconciliation and synthesis of the interests of different groups, rather than the admission of persisting conflicts and harsh choices between such interests; he refused to distinguish fact from value and argued that the social arrangements and moral practices of a society provide a meaningful guide to future decisions, both by conscientious individuals seeking to determine their obligations and by the state seeking to determine the proper sphere of its action. From this mode of analysis, however, Lindsay drew socialist conclusions, thus distinguishing his position from those of Green and Bosanquet.

MELVIN RICHTER

[*For the historical context of Lindsay's work, see* DEMOCRACY; PLURALISM; STATE; *and the biographies of* BOSANQUET *and* GREEN.]

WORKS BY LINDSAY

(1907) 1942 Introduction. In Plato, *Republic of Plato.* Translated by A. D. Lindsay. London: Dent; New York: Dutton.

1911 *The Philosophy of Bergson.* London: Dent.

(1913) 1914 *The Philosophy of Immanuel Kant.* London: Jack.

(1914) 1915 The Principle of Private Property. Pages 65–81 in *Property: Its Duties and Rights, Historically, Philosophically and Religiously Regarded.* 2d ed. London: Macmillan.

(1925) 1937 *Karl Marx's* Capital: *An Introductory Essay.* Oxford Univ. Press.

1927 *The Nature of Religious Truth: Sermons Preached in Balliol College Chapel.* London: Hodder & Stoughton.

1928 *General Will and Common Mind.* London: Hodder & Stoughton.

(1929) 1951 *The Essentials of Democracy.* 2d ed. Oxford Univ. Press.

1934*a* *Kant.* London: Benn.

1934*b* *The Churches and Democracy.* London: Epworth.

1940 *I Believe in Democracy: Addresses Broadcast in the B.B.C. Empire Programme on Mondays From May 20th to June 24th 1940.* Oxford Univ. Press.

(1943) 1959 *The Modern Democratic State.* Volume 1. Oxford Univ. Press.

1945 *The Good and the Clever.* Cambridge Univ. Press.

1949 The Philosophy of the British Labour Government. Pages 250–268 in Filmer S. C. Northrop (editor), *Ideological Differences and World Order: Studies in the Philosophy and Science of the World's Cultures.* New Haven: Yale Univ. Press.

1951 Philosophy as Criticism of Standards. *Philosophical Quarterly* 1:97–108.

SUPPLEMENTARY BIBLIOGRAPHY

GALLIE, W. B. 1960 *A New University: A. D. Lindsay and the Keele Experiment.* London: Chatto & Windus.

RICHTER, MELVIN 1964 *Politics and Conscience: T. H. Green and His Age.* Cambridge, Mass.: Harvard Univ. Press. → Provides a background for A. D. Lindsay's politics and philosophy.

LINEAGE

See KINSHIP.

LINEAR HYPOTHESES

I. REGRESSION — *E. J. Williams*
II. ANALYSIS OF VARIANCE — *Julian C. Stanley*
III. MULTIPLE COMPARISONS — *Peter Nemenyi*

I
REGRESSION

Regression analysis, as it is presented in this article, is an important and general statistical tool. It is applicable to situations in which one observed variable has an expected value that is assumed to be a function of other variables; the function usually has a specified form with unspecified parameters. For example, an investigator might assume that under appropriate circumstances the expected score on an examination is a linear function of the length of training period. Here there are two parameters, slope and intercept of the line. The techniques of regression analysis may be classified into two kinds: (1) testing the concordance of the observations with the assumed model, usually in the framework of some broader model, and (2) carrying out estimation, or other sorts of inferences, about the parameters when the model is assumed to be correct. This area of statistics is sometimes known as "least squares," and in older publications it was called "the theory of errors."

In the regression relations discussed in this article only one variable is regarded as random; the others are either fixed by the investigator (where experimental control is possible) or selected in some way from among the possible values. The relation between the expected value of the random variable (called the dependent variable, the predictand, or the regressand) and the nonrandom variables (called regression variables, independent variables, predictors, or regressors) is known as a regression relation. Thus, if a random variable Y, depending on a variable x, varies at random about a linear function of x, we can write

$$Y = \beta_0 + \beta_1 x + e,$$

which expresses a linear regression relation. The parameters β_0 and β_1 are the regression coefficients or parameters, and e is a random variable with expected value zero. Usually the e's corresponding to different values of Y are assumed to be uncorrelated and to have the same variance. If η denotes the expected value of Y, the basic relation may be expressed alternatively as

$$E(Y) = \eta = \beta_0 + \beta_1 x.$$

The parameters in the relation will be either unknown or given by theory; observations of Y for different values of x provide the means of estimating these parameters or testing the concordance of the simple linear structure with the data.

Linear models, linear hypotheses. A regression relation that is linear in the unknown parameters is known as a linear model, and the assertion of such a model as a basis for inference is the assertion of a linear hypothesis. Often the term "linear hypothesis" refers to a restriction on the linear model (for example, specifying that a parameter has the value 7 or that two parameters are equal) that is to be tested. The importance of the linear model lies in its ease of application and understanding; there is a well-developed body of theory and techniques for the statistical treatment of linear models, in particular for the estimation of their parameters and the testing of hypotheses about them.

Needless to say, the description of a phenomenon by means of a linear model is usually a matter of convenience; the model is accepted until some more elaborate one is required. Nevertheless, the linear model has a wide range of applicability and is of great value in elucidating relationships, especially in the early stages of an investigation. Often a linear model is applicable only after transformations of the independent variables (like x in the above example), the dependent variable (Y, above), or both [*see* STATISTICAL ANALYSIS, SPECIAL PROBLEMS OF, *article on* TRANSFORMATIONS OF DATA].

In its most general form, regression analysis includes a number of other statistical techniques as special cases. For instance, it is not necessary that the x's be defined as metric variables. If the values of the observations on Y are classified into a number of groups—say, p—then the regression relation is written $E(Y) = \beta_1 x_1 + \beta_2 x_2 + \cdots + \beta_p x_p$, and x_i may be taken to be 1 for all observations in the ith group and 0 for all the others. The p x-variables will then specify the different groups, and the regression relation will define the mean value of Y for each group. In the simplest case, with two groups,

$$E(Y) = \beta_1 x_1 + \beta_2 x_2,$$

where $x_1 = 1$ and $x_2 = 0$ for the first group, and vice versa for the second.

The estimation of the population mean from a sample is a special case, since the model is then just

$$E(Y) = \beta_0,$$

β_0 being the mean of the population.

This treatment of the comparison of different groups is somewhat artificial, although it is important to note that it falls under the regression rubric. Such comparisons are generally carried out by means of the technique known as the analysis of variance [*see* LINEAR HYPOTHESES, *article on* ANALYSIS OF VARIANCE].

When a regressor is not measured quantitatively but is given only as a ranking (for example, order in time of archeological specimens, social position of occupation), it may still provide a regression relation suitable for estimation or prediction. The simplest way to include such a variable in a relation is to replace the qualitative values (rankings) by arbitrary numerical scores, equally spaced (see, for example, Strodtbeck et al. 1957). More refined methods would use scores spaced according to some measure of "distance" between successive rankings; thus, in some instances the scores have been chosen so that their frequency distribution approximates a grouped normal distribution. Since any method of scoring is arbitrary, the method that is used must be judged by the relations based on it as well as by its theoretical cogency. Simple scoring systems, which can be easily understood, are usually to be preferred.

When both the dependent variable and the regression variable are qualitative, each may be replaced by arbitrary scores as indicated above. Alternative methods determine scores for the dependent variable that are most highly correlated (formally) with the regressor scores or, if the regressor scores for any set of data are open to choice, choose scores for both variables so that the correlation is maximized. The calculation and interpretation of the regression relations for such situations have been discussed by Yates (1948) and by Williams (1952).

Regression, correlation, functional relation. The regression relation is a one-way relation between variables in which the expected value of one random variable is related to nonrandom values of the other variables. It is to be distinguished from other types of statistical relations, in particular from correlation and functional relationships. [*See* MULTIVARIATE ANALYSIS, *articles on* CORRELATION.] Correlation is a relation between two or more random variables and may be described in terms of the amount of variation in one of the variables associated with variation in the other variable or variables. The functional relation, by contrast, is a relation between the *expected values* of random variables. If quantities related by some physical law are subject to errors of measurement, the functional relation between expected values, rather than the regression relation, is what the investigator generally wants to determine.

Although the regression relation relates a random variable to other, nonrandom variables, in many situations it will apply also when the regression variables are random; then the regression, conditional on the observed values of the random regression variables, is determined. Here the *expected value* of one random variable is related to the *observed values* of the other random variables. For a discussion of the fitting of regression lines when the regression variables are subject to error, see Madansky (1959). When more than one variable is to be considered as random, the problem is usually thought of as one of multivariate analysis [*see* MULTIVARIATE ANALYSIS].

History. The method of least squares, on which most methods of estimation for linear models are based, was apparently first published by Adrien Legendre (1805), but the first treatment along the lines now familiar was given by Carl Friedrich Gauss (1821, see in 1855). Gauss showed that the method gives estimators of the unknown parameters with minimum variance among unbiased linear estimators. This basic result is sometimes known as the Gauss–Markov theorem, and the least squares estimators as Gauss–Markov estimators.

The term "regression" was first used by Francis Galton, who applied it to certain relations in the theory of heredity, but the term is now applied to relationships in general and to nonlinear as well as to linear relationships.

The linearity of linear hypotheses rests in the way the parameters appear; the x's may be highly nonlinear functions of underlying nonrandom variables. For example,

$$\eta = \beta_0 + \beta_1 x_1 + \beta_2 x_1^2 + \beta_3 x_1^3$$

and

$$\eta = \beta_1 e^{x_1} + \beta_2 \tan x_1$$

both fall squarely under the linear hypothesis model, whereas

$$\eta = \beta_1 e^{\beta_2 x_1}$$

does not fit that model.

There is now a vast literature dealing with the linear model, and the subject is also treated in most statistical textbooks.

Application in the social sciences. There has been a good deal of discussion about the type of model that should be used to describe relations between variables in the social sciences, particularly in economics. Linear regression models have often been considered inadequate for complex economic phenomena, and more complicated models have been developed. Recent work, however, indicates that ordinary linear regression methods have a wider scope than had been supposed. For example, there has been much discussion about how to treat data correlated in time, for which the residuals from the regression equation (the e's) show autocorrelation. This autocorrelation may be the result of autocorrelation in the variables not included in the model. Geary (1963) suggests that in such circumstances the inclusion of additional regression variables may effectively eliminate the autocorrelation among the residuals, so that standard methods may be applied.

Further discussion of the applicability of regression methods to economic data is given by Ezekiel and Fox (1930, chapters 20 and 24) and also by Wold and Juréen (see in Wold 1953).

Investigators should be encouraged to employ the simple methods of regression analysis as a first step before turning to more elaborate techniques. Despite the relative simplicity of its ideas, it is a powerful technique for elucidating relations, and its results are easily understood and applied. More elaborate techniques, by contrast, do not always provide a readily comprehensible interpretation.

Assumptions in regression analysis. A regression model may be expressed in the following way:

$$E(Y) = \eta = \beta_0 + \beta_1 x_1 + \cdots + \beta_p x_p,$$
$$Y = \eta + e,$$

where Y is the random variable, η is its expected value, the x's are known variables, the β's are unknown coefficients, and e is a random error or deviation with zero mean. In the notation for variables, either fixed or random, subscripts are used only to distinguish the different variables but not to distinguish different observations of the same variable. The context generally makes the meaning clear. Thus, the above expression is an abbreviated form of

$$E(Y_j) = \eta_j = \beta_0 + \beta_1 x_{1j} + \beta_2 x_{2j} + \cdots + \beta_p x_{pj}, \quad j = 1, 2, \cdots, n;$$
$$Y_j = \eta_j + e_j.$$

This model is perfectly general; however, in estimating the coefficients, it is usually assumed that the e_j are mutually uncorrelated and are of equal variance (homoscedastic).

If there is no regressor variable that is identically one (as in the two-sample situation described earlier), the β_0 term might well be omitted. This is primarily a matter of notational convention.

The additional assumption that the errors are normally distributed is convenient and simplifies the theory. It can be shown that, on this assumption, the linear estimators given by least squares are in fact the maximum likelihood (m.l.) estimators of the parameters. In addition, the residual sum of squares $\sum(Y - \hat{\eta})^2$ (see below) is the basis for the m.l. estimator of the error variance (σ^2).

Apart from the theoretical advantages of the assumption of normality of the e's, there are the practical advantages that efficient methods of estimation and suitable tests of significance are relatively easy to apply and that the test statistics have well-known properties and are extensively tabulated. The normality assumption is often reasonable in applications, since even appreciable departures from it do not as a rule seriously invalidate regression analyses based upon normality [*see* ERRORS, *article on* EFFECTS OF ERRORS IN STATISTICAL ASSUMPTIONS].

Some departures from assumptions may be expected in certain situations. For example, if some of the measurements of Y are much larger than others, the associated errors, either errors of measurement or errors resulting from uncontrolled random effects, may well be correspondingly larger, so that the variances of the errors will be heterogeneous (the errors are heteroscedastic). Again, with annual data it is to be expected that errors may arise from unobserved factors whose influence from year to year will be associated, so the errors will not be independent (but see Geary 1963). It is often possible in particular cases to transform the data so that they conform more closely to the assumptions; for instance, a logarithmic or square-root transformation of Y will often give a variable whose errors have approximately constant variance [*see* STATISTICAL ANALYSIS, SPECIAL PROBLEMS OF, *article on* TRANSFORMATIONS OF DATA]. This will amount to replacing the linear model for Y with a linear model for the transformed variable. In practice this often gives a satisfactory representation of the data, any departure from the model being attributed to error.

The method of least squares determines, for the parameters β_i in the regression equation, estimators that minimize the sum of squares of deviations of the Y-values from the values given by the equation. This sum of squares is

$$\sum(Y - \eta)^2 = \sum(Y - \beta_0 - \beta_1 x_1 - \cdots - \beta_p x_p)^2.$$

In the following discussion the estimated β's are denoted by b's, and the corresponding estimator of η is denoted by $\hat{\eta}$, so that

$$\hat{\eta} = b_0 + b_1 x_1 + \cdots + b_p x_p$$

and the minimized sum of squared deviations is $\sum(Y - \hat{\eta})^2$.

The method has the twofold merit of minimizing not only the sum of squares of deviations but also the variance of the estimators b_i (among unbiased linear estimators). Thus, for most practical purposes the method of least squares gives estimators with satisfactory properties. Sometimes such estimators are not appropriate—for example, when errors in one direction are more serious than those in the other—but those cases are usually apparent to the investigator.

The method of least squares applies equally well when the errors are heteroscedastic or even correlated, provided the covariance structure of the errors is known (apart from a constant of proportionality, which may be estimated from the data). The method can be generalized to take account of the general correlation structure or, equivalently, a linear transformation of the observations may be used to reduce the problem to the simpler case of uncorrelated homoscedastic errors. (Details may be found in Rao 1965, chapter 4.)

When the correlation structure is unknown, the method of least squares may still be applied. If the data are analyzed as though the errors are uncorrelated and homoscedastic, the estimators of the parameters will be unbiased, although they will be less precise than if based on the correct model.

On the other hand, if the assumed linear model is incorrect—for example, if the relation is quadratic in one of the variables but only a linear model is fitted—then the estimators are liable to serious bias.

Since the form of the underlying model is almost always unknown there is usually a corresponding risk of bias. This problem has been studied in various contexts, but there is still much to be done; see Box and Wilson (1951), Box and Andersen (1955), and Plackett (1960, chapter 2).

Simple linear regression

In the simple linear regression model the expected value of Y is a linear function of a single variable, x_1:

$$E(Y) = \eta = \beta_0 + \beta_1 x_1.$$

The parameter β_0 is the intercept, and the parameter β_1 is the slope, of the regression line. This model is a satisfactory one in many cases, even if a number of variables affect the expected value of Y, for one of these may have a predominating influence, and although the omission of variables from the relation will lead to some bias, this may not be important in view of the increased simplicity of the model.

In studying the relation between two variables it is almost always desirable to plot a scatter diagram of the points representing the observations. The x-axis, or abscissa, is usually used for the regression variable and the y-axis, or ordinate, for the random variable. If the regression relation is linear the points should show a tendency to fall near a straight line, though if the variation is large this tendency may well be masked. Although for some purposes a line drawn "by eye" is adequate to represent the regression, in general such a line is not sufficiently accurate. There is always the risk of bias in both the position and the slope of the line. Because there is a tendency for the deviations from the line in both the x and y directions to be taken into account in determining the fit, lines fitted by eye are often affected by the scales of measurement used for the two axes. Since Y is the random variable, only the deviations in the y direction should be taken into account in determining the fit of the line. Often the investigator, knowing that there may be error in x_1, may attempt to take it into account. It should be understood that this procedure will give an estimate not of the regression relation but of underlying structure, which often differs from the regression relation. Another and more serious shortcoming of lines drawn by eye is that they do not provide an estimate of the variance about the line, and such an estimate is almost always required.

The method of least squares is commonly used when an arithmetical method of fitting is required, because of its useful properties and its relative ease of application. The equations for the least squares estimators, b_i, based on n pairs of observations (x_1, Y), are as follows:

$$b_1 = \sum Y(x_1 - \bar{x}_1) / \sum (x_1 - \bar{x}_1)^2,$$
$$b_0 = \bar{Y} - b_1 \bar{x}_1.$$

Here the summation is over the observed values, $\bar{x}_1 = \sum x_1/n$, and $\bar{Y} = \sum Y/n$. (Note that the observations on x_1 need not be all different, although they must not all be the same.) The estimated regression function is

$$\hat{\eta} = b_0 + b_1 x_1.$$

The minimized sum of squares of deviations is

$$\begin{aligned}\sum (Y - \hat{\eta})^2 &= \sum (Y - \bar{Y})^2 - b_1^2 \sum (x_1 - \bar{x}_1)^2 \\ &= \sum (Y - \bar{Y})^2 - b_1 \sum Y(x_1 - \bar{x}_1).\end{aligned}$$

The standard errors (estimated standard deviations) of the estimators may be derived from the minimized sum of squares of deviations. Two independent linear parameters have been fitted, and it may readily be shown that the expected value of this minimized sum of squares is $(n-2)\sigma^2$, where σ^2 is the common variance of the residual errors. Consequently, an unbiased estimator of σ^2 is given by

$$s^2 = \sum (Y - \hat{\eta})^2 / (n - 2),$$

and this is the conventional estimator of σ^2. (The m.l. estimator of σ^2 is $\sum (Y - \hat{\eta})^2/n$.) The sum of squares for deviations is said to have $n-2$ degrees of freedom, representing the number of linearly independent quantities on which it is based.

The estimated variances of the estimators are est. var $(b_1) = s^2/\sum(x_1-\bar{x}_1)^2$ and est. var $(b_0) = s^2\sum x_1^2/[n\sum(x_1-\bar{x}_1)^2]$, and the estimated covariance is est. cov $(b_0, b_1) = -s^2\bar{x}_1/\sum(x_1-\bar{x}_1)^2 = -\bar{x}_1$ var (b_1).

Separate confidence limits for the parameters β_0 and β_1 may be determined from the estimators and their standard errors, using Student's t-distribution [*see* ESTIMATION, *article on* CONFIDENCE INTERVALS AND REGIONS]. If $t_{\alpha;n-2}$ denotes the α-level of this distribution for $n-2$ degrees of freedom, the $1-\alpha$ confidence limits for β_1 are $b_1 \pm t_{\alpha;n-2}\, s/\sqrt{\sum(x_1-\bar{x}_1)^2}$. Confidence limits for the intercept, β_0, may be determined in a similar way but are not usually of interest. In a few cases it may be necessary to determine whether the estimator b_0 is in agreement with some theoretical value of the intercept. Thus, in some situations it is reasonable to expect the regression line to pass through the origin, so that $\beta_0 = 0$. It will then be necessary to test the significance of the departure of b_0 from zero or, equivalently, to determine whether the confidence limits for β_0 include zero.

When it is assumed that $\beta_0 = 0$ and there is no need to test this hypothesis, then the regression has only one unknown parameter; in such a case the sum of squares for deviations from the regression line, used to estimate the residual variance, will have $n-1$ degrees of freedom.

When the parameters β_0 and β_1 are both of interest, a joint confidence statement about them may be useful. The joint confidence region is usually an ellipse centered at (b_0, b_1) and containing all values of (β_0, β_1) from which (b_0, b_1) does not differ with statistical significance as measured by an F-test (see the section on significance testing, below). [*The question of joint confidence regions is discussed further in* LINEAR HYPOTHESES, *article on* MULTIPLE COMPARISONS.]

Choice of experimental values. The formula for the variance of the regression coefficient b_1 shows that it is the more accurately determined the larger is $\sum(x_1-\bar{x}_1)^2$, the sum of squares of the values of x_1 about their mean. This is in accordance with common sense, since a greater spread of experimental values will magnify the regression effect yet will in general leave the error component unaltered. If accurate estimation of β_1 were the only criterion, the optimum allocation of experimental points would be in equal numbers at the extreme ends of the possible range. However, the assumption that a regression is linear, although satisfactory over most of the possible range, is often likely to fail near the ends of the range; for this and other reasons it may be desirable to check the linearity of the regression, and to do so points other than the two extreme values must be observed. In practice, where little is known about the form of the regression relation it is usually desirable to take points distributed uniformly throughout the range. If the experimental points are equally spaced, this will facilitate the fitting of quadratic or higher degree polynomials, using tabulated orthogonal polynomials as described below.

Confidence limits for the regression line. The estimated regression function is

$$\begin{aligned}\hat{\eta} &= b_0 + b_1x_1\\ &= \bar{Y} + b_1(x_1 - \bar{x}_1),\end{aligned}$$

and corresponding to any specified value, x_{1*}, of x_1, the variance of $\hat{\eta}$ is estimated as

$$\text{est. var}\,(\hat{\eta}) = s^2\left(\frac{1}{n} + \frac{(x_{1*}-\bar{x}_1)^2}{\sum(x_1-\bar{x}_1)^2}\right).$$

Thus, for any specified value of x_1, confidence limits for η can be determined according to the formula

$$Y_L = \hat{\eta} \pm t_{\alpha;n-2}\, s\sqrt{\left(\frac{1}{n} + \frac{(x_{1*}-\bar{x}_1)^2}{\sum(x_1-\bar{x}_1)^2}\right)}.$$

The locus of these limits consists of the two branches of a hyperbola, lying on either side of the fitted regression line; this locus defines what may be described as a confidence curve. A typical regression line fitted to a set of points is shown in Figure 1 with the 95 per cent confidence curve shown as the two inside upper and lower curves, Y_L.

The above limits are appropriate for the estimated value of η corresponding to a *given* value of x_1. They do not, however, set limits to the whole line. Such limits are given by a method developed by Working and Hotelling, as described, e.g., by Kendall and Stuart ([1943–1946] 1958–1966, vol. 2, chapter 28). [*See also* LINEAR HYPOTHESES, *article on* MULTIPLE COMPARISONS.] As might be expected, these limits lie outside the corresponding limits for the same probability for a single value of x_1. The limits may be regarded as arising from the envelope of all lines whose parameters fall within a suitable confidence region. These limits are given by

$$Y_{WH} = \hat{\eta} \pm s\sqrt{2F_{1-\alpha;2,n-2}\left(\frac{1}{n} + \frac{(x_{1*}-\bar{x}_1)^2}{\sum(x_1-\bar{x}_1)^2}\right)},$$

where $F_{1-\alpha;2,n-2}$ is the tabulated value for the F-distribution with 2 and $n-2$ degrees of freedom at confidence level $1-\alpha$. These limits, for a 95 per cent confidence level, are shown as a pair of broken lines in Figure 1.

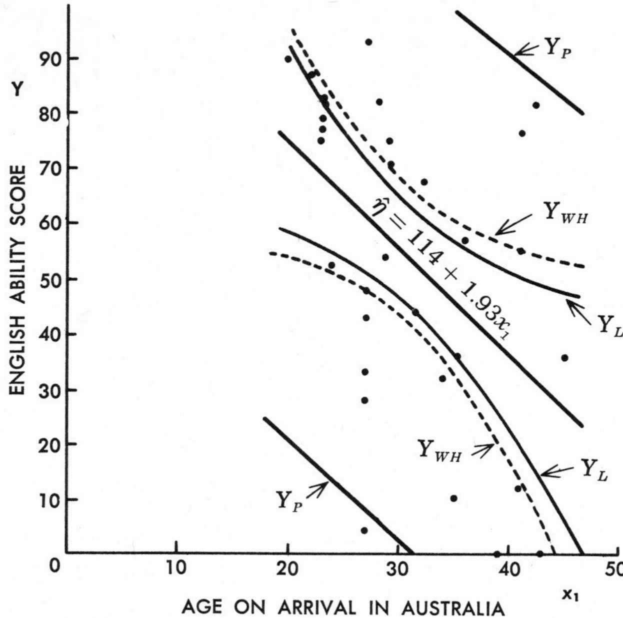

Figure 1 — Regression line and associated 95 per cent confidence regions*

* The Y_P curves, although they appear straight in the figure, are hyperbolas like the other Y curves.

Source of data: Martin, Jean I., 1965, *Refugee Settlers: A Study of Displaced Persons in Australia.* Canberra: Australian National University.

The user of the confidence limits must be clear about which type of limits he requires. If he is interested in the limits on the estimated η for a particular value x_{1*} or in only one pair of limits at a time, the inner limits, Y_L, will be appropriate, but if he is interested in limits for many values of x_{1*} (some of which may not be envisaged when the calculations are being made), the Working–Hotelling limits, Y_{WH}, will be needed.

Application of the regression equation. The regression equation is usually determined not only to provide an empirical law relating variables but also as a means of making future estimates or predictions. Thus, in studies of demand, regression relations of demand on price and other factors enable demand to be predicted for future occasions when one or more of these factors is varied. Such prediction is provided directly by the regression equation. It should be noted, however, that the standard error of prediction will be greater than the standard error of the estimated points ($\hat{\eta}$) on the regression line. This is because a future observation will vary about its regression value with variance equal to the variance of individual values about the regression in the population. When standard errors are being quoted, it is important to distinguish between the standard error of the point $\hat{\eta}$ on the regression line and the standard error of prediction. The estimated variance of prediction is

$$\text{est. var } (\hat{\eta}_P) = s^2\left(1 + \frac{1}{n} + \frac{(x_{1*} - \bar{x}_1)^2}{\sum(x_1 - \bar{x}_1)^2}\right).$$

The outside upper and lower curves in Figure 1 are confidence limits for prediction, Y_P, based on this variance. Clearly, for making predictions of this sort there is little point in determining the regression line with great accuracy. The major part of the error in such cases will be the variance of individual values.

The formula for the standard error of $\hat{\eta}$ or $\hat{\eta}_P$ shows that the error of estimation increases as the x_1-value departs from the mean of the sample, so that when the deviation from the mean is large the variance of estimate can be so great as to make the estimate worthless. This is one reason why investigators should be discouraged from attempting to draw inferences beyond the range of the observed values of x_1. The other reason is that the assumed linear regression, even though satisfactory within the observed range, may not hold true outside this range.

Inverse estimation. In many situations the investigator is primarily interested in determining the value of x_1 corresponding to a given level or value, η_*. Thus, although it is still appropriate to determine the regression of the random variable Y on the fixed variable x_1, the inference has to be carried out in reverse. For example, if a drug that affects the reaction time of individuals is being tested at different levels, the reaction time Y will be a random variable with regression on the dose level x_1. However, the purpose of the investigation may be to determine a dose level that will lead to a given time of reaction on the average. The experimental doses, being fixed, cannot be treated as random, so that it is inappropriate to determine a regression of x_1 on Y, and such a pseudo regression would give spurious results. In such situations the value of x_1 corresponding to a given value of η has to be estimated from the regression of Y on x_1.

The regression equation can be rearranged to give an estimator of x_1 corresponding to a given value, η_*,

$$\hat{X}_* = (\eta_* - b_0)/b_1.$$

The approximate estimated variance of the estimator is

$$\text{est. var } (\hat{X}_*) \cong \frac{s^2}{b_1^2}\left(\frac{1}{n} + \frac{(\hat{X}_* - \bar{x}_1)^2}{\sum(x_1 - \bar{x}_1)^2}\right)$$
$$= \frac{s^2}{b_1^2}\left(\frac{1}{n} + \frac{(\eta_* - \bar{Y})^2}{b_1^2\sum(x_1 - \bar{x}_1)^2}\right).$$

A more precise method of treating such a problem is to determine confidence limits for η given x_1 and to determine from these, by rearranging the equation, confidence limits for x_1. For the regression shown in Figure 1, the 95 per cent confidence curves (the inner curves, Y_L, on either side of the line) will in this way give confidence limits for x_1 corresponding to a given value of η. The point at which the horizontal line $Y = \eta$ cuts the regression line gives the estimate of x_1; the points at which the line cuts the upper and lower curves give, respectively, lower and upper confidence limits for x_1. This may be demonstrated by an extension of the reasoning leading to confidence limits. [*See* ESTIMATION, *article on* CONFIDENCE INTERVALS AND REGIONS.]

Sometimes, rather than a hypothetical regression value, η_*, a single observed value, y_* (not in the basic sample), is given, and limits are required for the value of x_1 that could be associated with such a value. The estimator $\hat{X}_*$ is given by

$$\hat{X}_* = (y_* - b_0)/b_1,$$

and its approximate estimated variance (which must take into account the variation between responses on Y to a given value of x_1) is

$$\text{est. var}\,(\hat{X}_*) \cong \frac{s^2}{b_1^2}\left(1 + \frac{1}{n} + \frac{(\hat{X}_* - \bar{x}_1)^2}{\sum(x_1 - \bar{x}_1)^2}\right).$$

Using this augmented variance, confidence limits on x_1 corresponding to a given y_* may be found. For more precise determination of the confidence limits for prediction, the locus of limits for y_* given x_1 may be inverted to give limits for x_1 given y_*. In Figure 1, the outer curves are these loci (for the 95 per cent confidence level); the 95 per cent limits for x_1 will be given by the intersection of the line $Y = y_*$ with these confidence curves for prediction.

Multiple regression

In many situations where a single regression variable is not adequate to represent the variation in the random variable Y, a multiple regression is appropriate. In other situations there may be only one regression variable, but the assumed relation, rather than being linear, is a quadratic or a polynomial of higher degree. Since both multiple linear regression and polynomial regression relations are linear in the unknown parameters, the same techniques are applicable to both; in fact, polynomial regression is a special case of multiple regression. The number of variables to include in a multiple regression, or the degree of polynomial to be applied, is to some extent a matter of judgment and convenience, although it must be remembered that a regression equation containing a large number of variables is usually inconvenient to use as well as difficult to calculate. With the use of electronic computers, however, there is greater scope for increasing the number of regression variables, since the computations are routine.

Consider the multiple regression equation

$$E(Y) = \eta = \beta_0 + \beta_1 x_1 + \cdots + \beta_p x_p,$$

with p regression variables and a constant term. The estimation of these $p + 1$ unknown parameters can be systematically carried out if β_0 is also regarded as a regression coefficient corresponding to a regression variable x_0 that is always unity. As in simple regression, the method of least squares provides unbiased linear estimators of the coefficients with minimum variance and also provides estimators of the standard errors of these coefficients. The quantities required for determining the estimators are the sums of squares and products of the x-values, the sums of products of the observed Y with each of the x-values, and the sum of squares of Y. The method of least squares gives a set of linear equations for the b's, called the *normal equations*:

$$\begin{array}{ccccc} b_0 t_{00} + b_1 t_{01} + \cdots + b_p t_{0p} = u_0 \\ b_0 t_{10} + b_1 t_{11} + \cdots + b_p t_{1p} = u_1 \\ \vdots \quad \vdots \qquad \vdots \quad \vdots \\ b_0 t_{p0} + b_1 t_{p1} + \cdots + b_p t_{pp} = u_p \end{array}$$

where $t_{hi} = t_{ih} = \sum x_h x_i$ and $u_i = \sum Y x_i$. These equations can be written in matrix form as

$$\boldsymbol{Tb} = \boldsymbol{u},$$

where $\boldsymbol{T} = (t_{hi})$ and $\boldsymbol{u}$ is the vector of the u_i. The solution requires the inversion of the matrix $\boldsymbol{T}$, the inverse matrix being denoted by $\boldsymbol{T}^{-1}$ (with typical element t^{hi}). The solution may be written in matrix form as

$$\boldsymbol{b} = \boldsymbol{T}^{-1}\boldsymbol{u}$$

or in extended form as

$$b_0 = t^{00}u_0 + t^{01}u_1 + \cdots + t^{0p}u_p,$$

and so forth.

The variance of b_i is $t^{ii}\sigma^2$, and the covariance of b_i and b_j is $t^{ij}\sigma^2$. It should be remarked that in the special case of "regression through the origin"—that is, when the constant term β_0 is assumed to be zero—the first equation and the first term of each other equation are omitted; the constant regressor x_0 and its coefficient β_0 thus have the same status as any other regression variable.

When the constant term is included, computational labor may be reduced and arithmetical accuracy increased if the sums of squares and products are taken about the means. That is, the t_{hi} and u_i are replaced by

$$t'_{hi} = t_{hi} - \sum x_h \sum x_i / n = \sum (x_h - \bar{x}_h)(x_i - \bar{x}_i)$$

and

$$u'_i = u_i - \sum Y \sum x_i / n,$$

respectively. All the sums of products with zero subscripts then vanish, and the sums of squares are reduced in magnitude. The constant term has to be estimated separately; it is given by

$$\begin{aligned} b_0 &= \bar{Y} - b_1\bar{x}_1 - b_2\bar{x}_2 - \cdots - b_p\bar{x}_p \\ &= (\sum Y - b_1\sum x_1 - b_2\sum x_2 - \cdots - b_p\sum x_p)/n. \end{aligned}$$

The computational aspects of matrix inversion and the determination of the regression coefficients are dealt with in many statistical texts, including Williams (1959); in addition, many programs for matrix inversion are available for electronic computers.

Effect of heteroscedasticity. When the error variance of the dependent variable Y is different in different parts of its range (or, strictly, of the range of its expected value, η), estimators of regression coefficients ignoring the heteroscedasticity will be unbiased but of reduced accuracy, as already mentioned. The calculation of improved estimators may then sometimes be necessary.

There are some problems in taking heteroscedasticity into account. Among them is the problem of specification: defining the relation between expected value and variance. Often, with adequate data, the estimated ($\hat{\eta}$) values from the usual unweighted regression line can be grouped and the mean squared deviation from these values for each group used as a rough measure of the variance. The regression can then be refitted, each value being given a weight inversely proportional to the estimated variance. Two iterations of this method are likely to give estimates of about the accuracy practically attainable. If an empirical relation between expected value and error variance can be deduced, this simplifies the problem somewhat; however, the weight for each observation has to be determined from a provisionally fitted relation, so iteration is still required.

To calculate a weighted regression, each observation Y_j $(j = 1, 2, \cdots, n)$ is given a weight w_j instead of unit weight as in the standard calculation. These weights will be the reciprocals of the estimated variances of each value. Then, if weighted quantities are distinguished by the subscript w,

$$\begin{aligned} t_{whi} &= \sum w x_h x_i, \\ u_{wi} &= \sum w Y x_i, \end{aligned}$$

and the normal equations are

$$b_{w0}t_{w00} + b_{w1}t_{w01} + \cdots + b_{wp}t_{w0p} = u_{w0}$$

and so on, or in matrix form

$$\boldsymbol{T}_w \boldsymbol{b}_w = \boldsymbol{u}_w.$$

The solution is

$$\boldsymbol{b}_w = \boldsymbol{T}_w^{-1} \boldsymbol{u}_w,$$

and the variances of the estimators b_{wi} are approximately $t_w^{ii}\sigma^2$.

When the weights are estimated from the data, as in the iterative method just described, some allowance has to be made in an exact analysis for errors in the weights. This inaccuracy will somewhat reduce the precision of the estimators. However, for most practical purposes, and provided that the number of observations in each group for which weights are estimated is not too small, the errors in the weights may be ignored. (For further discussion of this question see Cochran & Carroll 1953.)

Estimability of the coefficients. It is intuitively clear in a general way that the $p + 1$ regression variables included in a regression equation should not be too nearly linearly dependent on one another, for then it might be expected that these regression variables could be approximately expressed in terms of a smaller number.

More precisely, in order that meaningful estimators of the regression coefficients exist, it is necessary that the variables be linearly independent (or, equivalently, $\boldsymbol{T}$ must be nonsingular). That is, no one variable should be expressible as a linear combination of the others or, expressed symmetrically, no linear combination of the variables vanishes unless all coefficients are zero. Clearly, if only $p - r$ of the variables are linearly independent, then the regression relation may be represented as a regression on these $p - r$, together with arbitrary multiples of the vanishing linear combinations. From the practical point of view, this lack of estimability will cause no problems, provided that the regression on a set of $p - r$ linearly independent variables is calculated. Estimation from the equation will be unaffected, but for testing the significance of the regression it must be noted that the regression sum of squares has not $p + 1$ but $p - r$ degrees of freedom, and the residual has $n - p + r$.

However, if the lack of estimability is ignored, the calculations to determine the $p + 1$ coefficients either will fail (since the matrix $\boldsymbol{T}$, being singular, has no inverse) or will give misleading results (if an approximate value of $\boldsymbol{T}$, having an inverse, is used in calculation and the lack of estimability is obscured).

When the regression variables, although linearly independent, are barely so (in the sense that the matrix $\boldsymbol{T}$, although of rank $p+1$, is "almost singular," having a small but nonvanishing determinant), the regression coefficients will be estimable but will have large standard errors. In typical cases, many of the estimated coefficients will not differ with statistical significance from zero; this merely reflects the fact that the corresponding regression variable may be omitted from the equation and the remaining coefficients adjusted without significant worsening of the fit.

In this situation, as in the case of linear dependence, these effects are not usually important in practice; however, they may suggest the advisability of reducing the number of regression variables included in the equation. [*For further discussion, see* STATISTICAL IDENTIFIABILITY.]

Conditions on the coefficients. Sometimes the regression coefficients β_i are assumed to satisfy some conditions based on theory. Provided these conditions are expressible as linear equations in the coefficients, the method of least squares carries through and leads, as before, to unbiased estimators satisfying the conditions and with minimum variance among linear estimators. It will be clear that with $p+1$ regression coefficients subject to $r+1$ independent linear restrictions, $r+1$ of the coefficients may be eliminated, so that the restricted regression is equivalent to one with $p-r$ coefficients. Thus, in principle there is a choice between expressing the model in terms of $p-r$ unrestricted coefficients or $p+1$ restricted ones; often the latter has advantages of symmetry and interpretability.

A simple example of restricted regression is one in which η is a weighted average of the x's but with unknown weights, $\beta_1, \cdots, \beta_p$. Here the side conditions would be $\beta_0 = 0$, $\beta_1 + \cdots + \beta_p = 1$.

As the introduction of side conditions effectively reduces the number of linearly independent coefficients, such conditions are useful in restoring estimability when the coefficients are nonestimable. In many problems these side conditions may be chosen to have practical significance. For example, where an over-all mean and a number of treatment "effects" are being estimated, it is conventional to specify the effects so that their mean vanishes; with this specification they represent deviations from the over-all mean.

When a restricted regression is being estimated, it will often be possible and of interest to estimate the unrestricted regression as well, in order to see the effect of the restrictions and to test whether the data are concordant with the conditions assumed. The test of significance consists of comparing the $(p+1)$-variable (unrestricted) regression with the $(p-r)$-variable (restricted) regression, in the manner described in the section on significance testing. This test of concordance is independent of the test of significance of any of the restricted coefficients.

Further details and examples of restricted regression are given by Rao (1965, p. 189) and Williams (1959, pp. 49–58). In the remainder of this article, the notation will presume unrestricted regression.

Missing values. When observations on some of the variables are missing, the simplest and usually the only practicable procedure is to ignore the corresponding values of the other variables—that is, to work only with complete sets of observations. However, it is sometimes possible to make use of the incomplete data, provided some additional assumptions are made. Methods have been developed under the assumption that (a) the missing values are in some sense randomly deleted, or the assumption that (b) the variables are all random and follow a multivariate normal distribution. Assumption (b) is treated by Anderson (1957) and Rao (1952, pp. 161–165). It is sometimes found, after the least squares equations for the constants in a regression relation have been set up, that some of the values of the dependent variable are unreliable or missing altogether. Rather than recalculate the equations it is often more convenient to replace the missing value by the value expected from the regression relation. This substitution conserves the form of the estimating equations, usually with little disturbance to the significance tests or the variances of the estimators.

The techniques of "fitting missing values" have been most fully developed for experiments designed in such a way that the estimators of various constants are either uncorrelated or have a symmetric pattern of correlations and the estimating equations have a symmetry of form that simplifies their solution. Missing values in such experiments destroy the symmetry and make estimation more difficult; it is therefore a great practical convenience to replace the missing values. Details of the method applied to designed experiments will be found in Cochran and Cox (1950). For applications to general regression models see Kruskal (1961).

The technique is itself an application of the method of least squares. To replace a missing value Y_j, a value $\hat{\eta}_j$ is chosen so as to minimize its contribution to the residual sum of squares. Thus, the estimate is equivalent to the one that would have been obtained by a fresh analysis; the calculation is simplified by the fact that estimates for only one or a few values are being calculated. The degrees of freedom for the residual sum of squares are reduced by the number of values thus fitted. For most practical purposes it is then sufficiently accurate to treat the fitted values as though they were original observations. The exact analysis is described by Yates (1933) and, in general terms, by Kruskal (1961).

Significance testing. In order to determine the standard errors of the regression coefficients and to test their significance, it is necessary to estimate the residual variance, σ^2. The sum of squares of deviations, $\sum(Y-\hat{\eta})^2$, which may readily be shown to satisfy

$$\sum(Y-\hat{\eta})^2 = \sum Y^2 - \boldsymbol{u}'\boldsymbol{T}^{-1}\boldsymbol{u} = \sum Y^2 - \boldsymbol{b}'\boldsymbol{u},$$

is found under $p+1$ constraints and so may be said to have $n-p-1$ degrees of freedom; if the model assumed is correct, so that the deviations are purely random, the expected value of the sum of squares is $(n-p-1)\sigma^2$. Accordingly, the *residual mean square*,

$$s^2 = \sum(Y-\hat{\eta})^2/(n-p-1),$$

is an unbiased estimator of the residual variance. The variances of the regression coefficients are estimated by

$$\text{est. var}\,(b_i) = t^{ii}s^2,$$

and the standard errors are the square roots of these quantities. The inverse matrix thus is used both in the calculation of the estimators and in the determination of their standard errors. From the off-diagonal elements t^{hi} of the inverse matrix are derived the estimated covariances between the estimators,

$$\text{est. cov}\,(b_h, b_i) = t^{hi}s^2.$$

The splitting of the total sum of squares of Y into two parts, a part associated with the regression effects and a residual part independent of them, is a particular example of what is known as the analysis of variance [*see* LINEAR HYPOTHESES, *article on* ANALYSIS OF VARIANCE].

Testing for regression effects. The regression sum of squares, being based on $p+1$ estimated quantities, will have $p+1$ degrees of freedom. When regression effects are nonexistent, the expected value of each part is proportional to its degrees of freedom. Accordingly, it is often convenient and informative to present these two parts, and their corresponding mean squares, in an analysis-of-variance table, such as Table 1.

In the table, the final column gives the expected values of the two mean squares; it shows that real regression effects inflate the regression sum of squares but not the residual sum of squares. This fact provides the basis for tests of significance of a calculated regression, since large values of the ratio of regression mean square to residual mean square give evidence for the existence of a regression relation.

Significance of a single coefficient. The question may arise whether one or more of the regression variables contribute to the relation anything that is not already provided by the other variables. In such circumstances the relevant hypothesis to be examined is that the β's corresponding to these variables are zero. A more general hypothesis that may sometimes need to be tested is that certain of the β's take assigned values.

The simplest test is that of the statistical significance of a single coefficient—say, b_i. The test will be of its departure from zero, if the contribution of x_i to the regression is in question. More generally, when β_i is specified, as, say, β_i^*, it will be relevant to test the significance of departure of b_i from β_i^*. The significance test in either case is the same; the squared difference between estimated and hypothesized values is compared with the estimated variance of that difference, which is s^2t^{ii}.

The ratio $F = (b_i - \beta_i^*)^2/(s^2t^{ii})$ has the F-distribution with 1 and $n-p-1$ degrees of freedom if the difference is in fact due to sampling fluctuations alone; in this case, the F-statistic is just the square of the usual t-statistic. When β_i differs

Table 1 — Analysis-of-variance table for testing regression effects

Source	Degrees of freedom	Sum of squares	Mean square	Expected mean square
Regression	$p+1$	$\sum b_i u_i$	$\dfrac{\sum b_i u_i}{p+1}$	$\sigma^2 + \dfrac{\boldsymbol{\beta}'\boldsymbol{T}\boldsymbol{\beta}}{p+1}$
Residual	$n-p-1$	$\sum Y^2 - \sum b_i u_i = (n-p-1)s^2$	s^2	σ^2
Total	n	$\sum Y^2$		

from β_i^* the F-statistic will tend to be larger, so that a right-tail test is indicated.

Testing several coefficients. To test a number of regression variables—or, more precisely, their regression coefficients—the method of least squares is equivalent to fitting a regression with and without the variables in question and testing the difference in the regression sums of squares against the estimated error variance. To choose a specific example, suppose the last q coefficients in a p-variable regression are to be tested. If the symbol S^2 is used to stand for sum of squares, the sum of squares for regression on all p variables may be written

$$S_p^2 = \boldsymbol{u}_p'\boldsymbol{T}_p^{-1}\boldsymbol{u}_p,$$

with $p+1$ degrees of freedom, and the corresponding sum of squares on the first $p-q$ variables as

$$S_{p-q}^2 = \boldsymbol{u}_{p-q}'\boldsymbol{T}_{p-q}^{-1}\boldsymbol{u}_{p-q}$$

with $p-q+1$ degrees of freedom. The difference, a sum of squares with q degrees of freedom, provides a criterion for testing the significance of the q regression coefficients. The ratio

$$F = (S_p^2 - S_{p-q}^2)/(qs^2)$$

has, under the null hypothesis that the last q coefficients are zero, the F-distribution with q and $n-p-1$ degrees of freedom. This simultaneous test of q coefficients may also be adapted to testing the departure of the q coefficients from theoretical values, not necessarily zero.

The significance test may be conveniently set out as in Table 2, where only the mean squares required for the significance test appear in the last column.

When $q = 1$, this test reduces to the test for a single regression coefficient, and the F-ratio

$$F = (S_p^2 - S_{p-1}^2)/s^2$$

is then identical with the F-ratio given above for making such a test.

Linear combinations of coefficients. Sometimes it is necessary to test the significance of one or more linear combinations of the coefficients—that is, to test hypotheses about linear combinations of the β's. A common example is the comparison of two coefficients, β_1 and β_2, say, for which the comparison $b_1 - b_2$ is relevant. The F-test applies to such comparisons also. Thus, for the difference $b_1 - b_2$, the estimated variance is $s^2(t^{11} - 2t^{12} + t^{22})$, and $F = (b_1 - b_2)^2/[s^2(t^{11} - 2t^{12} + t^{22})]$, with 1 and $n-p-1$ degrees of freedom.

In general, to test the departure from zero of k linear combinations of regression coefficients the procedure is as follows. Let the linear combinations (expressed in matrix notation) be

$$\boldsymbol{\Gamma}'\boldsymbol{b},$$

where $\boldsymbol{\Gamma}$ is a $(p+1)\times k$ matrix of known constants. Then the estimated covariance matrix of these linear combinations is

$$s^2\boldsymbol{\Gamma}'\boldsymbol{T}^{-1}\boldsymbol{\Gamma},$$

and the F-ratio is

$$F = \boldsymbol{b}'\boldsymbol{\Gamma}(\boldsymbol{\Gamma}'\boldsymbol{T}^{-1}\boldsymbol{\Gamma})^{-1}\boldsymbol{\Gamma}'\boldsymbol{b}/ks^2,$$

with k and $n-p-1$ degrees of freedom. Of course, this test can also be adapted to testing the departure of these linear combinations from preassigned values other than zero.

When the population coefficients β_i are in fact nonzero, the expected value of the regression mean square in the analysis of variance shown in Table 1 will be larger than σ^2 by a term that depends on both the magnitude of the coefficients and the accuracy with which they are estimated (see, for example, the last column of Table 1). Clearly, the greater this term, called the *noncentrality*, the greater the probability that the null hypothesis will be rejected at the adopted significance level. The F-test has certain optimum properties, but other tests may be preferred in special circumstances.

Table 2 — Analysis-of-variance table for testing several regression coefficients

Source	Degrees of freedom	Sum of squares	Mean square
Regression on p−q variables	$p-q+1$	S_{p-q}^2	...
Additional q variables	q	$S_p^2 - S_{p-q}^2$	$(S_p^2 - S_{p-q}^2)/q$
Regression on all p variables	$p+1$	S_p^2	...
Residual	$n-p-1$	$(n-p-1)s^2$	s^2
Total	n	$\sum Y^2$	

Multivariate analogues

Although hitherto only the regression of a single dependent variable Y on one or more regressors x_i has been discussed, it will be realized that often the simultaneous regressions of a number of random variables on the same regressors will be of importance. For instance, in a sociological study of immigrants the regressions of annual income and size of family on age, educational level, and period of residence in the country may be determined; here there are two dependent variables and three regressors.

Often the relations among the different dependent variables will also be of interest, or various linear combinations of the variables, rather than the original variables themselves, may be studied. The linear combination that is most highly correlated with the regressors may sometimes be relevant to the investigation, but the linear compounds will usually be chosen for their practical relevance rather than their statistical properties. [*For further discussion of multivariate analogues, see* MULTIVARIATE ANALYSIS, *especially the general article,* OVERVIEW, *and the article on* CLASSIFICATION AND DISCRIMINATION.]

Polynomial regression

When the relation between two variables, x_1 and Y, appears to be curvilinear, it is natural to fit some form of smooth curve to the data. For some purposes a freehand curve is adequate to represent the relation, but if the curve is to be used for prediction or estimation and standard errors are required, some mathematical method of fitting, such as the method of least squares, must be used. The freehand fitting of a curvilinear relation has all the disadvantages of freehand fitting of a straight line, with the added disadvantage that it is more difficult to distinguish real trends from random fluctuations.

The polynomial form is

$$E(Y) = \eta = \beta_0 + \beta_1 x_1 + \beta_2 x_1^2 + \cdots + \beta_p x_1^p .$$

Being a linear model, it has the advantages of simplicity, flexibility, and relative ease of calculation. It is for such reasons, not because it necessarily represents the theoretical form of the relation, that a polynomial regression is often fitted to data.

Orthogonal polynomials. The computations in polynomial regression are exactly the same as those in multiple regression, except that some simplification of the arithmetic may be introduced if the same values of x_1 are used repeatedly. Then instead of using the powers of x_1 as the regression variables, these are replaced by orthogonal polynomials of successively increasing degree, so defined that the sum of products of any pair of them, over their chosen values, is zero.

This procedure has the twofold advantage that, first, all the off-diagonal elements of the matrix $\boldsymbol{T}$ are zero, so the calculation of regression coefficients and their standard errors is much simplified, and, second, the regression coefficient on each polynomial and the corresponding sum of squares can be independently determined.

Because it is common for investigators to use data with values of the independent variables equally spaced, the orthogonal polynomials for this particular case have been extensively tabulated. Fisher and Yates (1938) tabulate these orthogonal polynomials up to those of fifth degree, for numbers of equally spaced points up to 75. However, if the data are not equally spaced the tabulated polynomials are not applicable, and the regression must be calculated directly.

Testing adequacy of fit. The question of what degree of polynomial is appropriate to fit to a set of data is discussed below (see "Considerations in regression model choice"). If for each value of x_1 there is an array of values for Y, the variation in the data can be analyzed into parts between and within arrays by the techniques of analysis of variance [*see* LINEAR HYPOTHESES, *article on* ANALYSIS OF VARIANCE]. The sum of squares between arrays can be further analyzed into that part accounted for by regression and that part not so accounted for (deviation from regression). The adequacy of a polynomial fitted to the data is indicated by nonsignificant deviation from regression.

When there is but one observation of Y for each value of x_1, such an analysis is not possible. To test the adequacy of a pth-degree polynomial regression, a common though not strictly defensible procedure is to fit a polynomial of degree $p + 1$ and test whether the coefficient b_{p+1} of x_1^{p+1} is significant. Anderson (1962) has treated this problem as a multiple decision problem and has provided optimal procedures that can readily be applied.

Estimation of maxima. Sometimes a polynomial regression is fitted in order to estimate the value of x_1 that yields a maximum value of η. A detailed discussion of the estimation of maxima is given by Hotelling (1941). To give an idea of the methods that are used, consider a quadratic regression of the form

$$\hat{\eta} = b_0 + b_1 x_1 + b_2 x_1^2 .$$

A maximum (or minimum) value of $\hat{\eta}$ occurs at the point $x_m = -b_1/2b_2$, and this value is taken as the estimated position of the maximum. Confidence limits for the position can be determined by means of the following device. If the position of the maximum of the true regression curve is ξ, then $\xi = -\beta_1/2\beta_2$, so that $\beta_1 + 2\beta_2\xi = 0$. Consequently the quantity

$$b_1 + 2b_2\xi$$

is distributed with mean zero and estimated variance

$$s^2(t^{11} + 4t^{12}\xi + 4t^{22}\xi^2).$$

The confidence limits for ξ with confidence coefficient $1 - \alpha$ are given by the roots of the equation

$$\frac{(b_1 + 2b_2\xi)^2}{s^2(t^{11} + 4t^{12}\xi + 4t^{22}\xi^2)} = F_{\alpha;1,n-3},$$

where $F_{\alpha;1,n-3}$ is the α-point of the F-distribution with 1 and $n - 3$ degrees of freedom, abbreviated below as F_α. The solution of this equation may be simplified by writing

$$g_{11} = \frac{F_\alpha s^2 t^{11}}{b_1^2}, \qquad g_{12} = \frac{F_\alpha s^2 t^{12}}{b_1 b_2}, \qquad g_{22} = \frac{F_\alpha s^2 t^{22}}{b_2^2},$$

so that the confidence limits become

$$X_L = x_m \frac{(1-g_{12}) \pm \sqrt{(1-g_{12})^2 - (1-g_{11})(1-g_{22})}}{1 - g_{22}}.$$

Note that these limits are not, in general, symmetrically placed about the estimated value $-b_1/2b_2$, since allowance is made for the skewness of the distribution of the ratio. Note also that the limits will include infinite values and will therefore not be of practical use, unless b_2 is significant at the α-level. In terms of the g-values, this means that g_{22} must not exceed 1.

When the regression model is a polynomial in two or more variables, investigation of maxima and other aspects of shape becomes more complex. [*A discussion of this problem appears in* EXPERIMENTAL DESIGN, *article on* RESPONSE SURFACES.]

Nonlinear models

In a nonlinear model the regression function is nonlinear in one or more of the parameters. Familiar examples are the exponential regression,

$$\eta = \beta_0 + \beta_1 e^{\beta_2 x_1},$$

and the logistic curve,

$$\eta = \frac{\beta_1}{1 + e^{-\beta_2 x_1}},$$

β_2 being the nonlinear parameter in each example. Such nonlinear models usually originate from theoretical considerations but nevertheless are often useful for applying to observational data.

Sometimes the model can be reduced to a linear form by a transformation of variables (and a corresponding change in the specification of the errors). The exponential regression with $\beta_0 = 0$ may thus be reduced by taking logarithms of the dependent variable and assuming that the errors of the logarithms, rather than the errors of the original values, are distributed about zero. If $Z = \log_e Y$ and $E(Z) = \xi$, the exponential model with $\beta_0 = 0$ reduces to $\xi = \log_e \beta_1 + \beta_2 x_1$, a linear model.

The general models shown above cannot be reduced to linear models in this way. For nonlinear models generally, the nonlinear parameters must be estimated by successive approximation. The following method is straightforward and of general applicability.

Suppose the model is

$$\eta = \beta_0 + \beta_1 f(x_1, \beta_2)$$

where $f(x_1, \beta_2)$ is a nonlinear function of β_2, and the estimated regression, determined by least squares, is

$$\hat{\eta} = b_0 + b_1 f(x_1, c).$$

If c_0 is a trial value of c (estimated by graphical or other means), the values of $f(x_1, c)$ and its first derivative with respect to c (denoted, for brevity, by f and f', respectively) are calculated for each value of x_1, with $c = c_0$. The regression of Y on f and f' is then determined in the usual way, yielding the regression equation

$$\hat{\eta} = b_0 + b_1 f + b_2 f'.$$

A first adjustment to c_0 is given by b_2/b_1, giving the new approximation

$$c_1 = c_0 + b_2/b_1.$$

The process of recalculating the regression on f and f' and determining successive approximations to c can be continued until the required accuracy is attained (for further details see Williams 1959).

The method is an adaptation of the *delta method*, which utilizes the principle of *propagation of error*. If a small change, $\delta\beta_2$, is made in a parameter β_2, the corresponding change in a function $f(\beta_2)$ is, to a first approximation, $f'(\beta_2)\delta\beta_2$. The use of this method allows the replacement of the nonlinear equations for the parameters by approximate linear equations for the adjustments. For a regression relation of the form

$$\eta = \beta_0 + \beta_1 e^{\beta_2 x_1},$$

Stevens (1951) provides a table to facilitate the calculation of the nonlinear parameter by a method similar to that described above, and Pimentel Gomes (1953) provides tables from which, with a few preliminary calculations, the least squares estimate of the nonlinear parameter can be read off easily.

Considerations in regression model choice

In deciding which of several alternative models shall be used to interpret a relationship, a number of factors must be taken into account. Other things being equal, the model which represents the predictands most closely (where "closeness" is measured in terms of some criterion such as minimum mean square error among linear estimators) will be used. However, questions of convenience and simplicity should also be considered. A regression equation that includes a large number of regression variables is not convenient to use, and an equation with fewer variables may be only slightly less accurate. In deciding between alternative models, the residual variance is therefore not the only factor to take into account.

In polynomial regression particularly, the assumed polynomial form of the model is usually chosen for convenience, so that a polynomial of given degree is not assumed to be the true regression model. Because of this, the testing of individual polynomial coefficients is little more than a guide in deciding on the degree of polynomial to be fitted. Of far more importance is a decision on what degree of variability about the regression model is acceptable, and this decision will be based on practical rather than merely statistical considerations.

Besides the question of including additional variables in a regression, for which significance tests have already been described, there is also the question of alternative regression variables. The alternatives for a regression relation could be different variables or different functions of the same variable—for instance, x_1 and $\log x_1$.

For comparison of two or more individual variables as predictors, a test devised by Hotelling (1940) is suitable, although not strictly accurate. It is based on the correlations between Y and the different predictors and of the predictors among themselves. For comparing two regression variables x_1 and x_2, the test statistic is

$$F = \frac{(u'_1/\sqrt{t'_{11}} - u'_2/\sqrt{t'_{22}})^2}{2s^2(1 - t'_{12}/\sqrt{t'_{11}t'_{22}})},$$

which is distributed approximately as F with 1 and $n-3$ degrees of freedom. Here, as before,

$$u'_i = \sum Y(x_i - \bar{x}_i),$$
$$t'_{hi} = \sum (x_h - \bar{x}_h)(x_i - \bar{x}_i),$$

and s^2 is the mean square of residuals from the regression of Y on x_1 and x_2, with $n-3$ degrees of freedom.

E. J. WILLIAMS

BIBLIOGRAPHY

ANDERSON, T. W. 1957 Maximum Likelihood Estimates for a Multivariate Normal Distribution When Some Observations Are Missing. *Journal of the American Statistical Association* 52:200–203.

ANDERSON, T. W. 1962 The Choice of the Degree of a Polynomial Regression as a Multiple Decision Problem. *Annals of Mathematical Statistics* 33:255–265.

BOX, GEORGE E. P.; and ANDERSEN, S. L. 1955 Permutation Theory in the Derivation of Robust Criteria and the Study of Departures From Assumption. *Journal of the Royal Statistical Society* Series B 17:1–26.

BOX, GEORGE E. P.; and WILSON, K. B. 1951 On the Experimental Attainment of Optimum Conditions. *Journal of the Royal Statistical Society* Series B 13:1–45. → Contains seven pages of discussion.

COCHRAN, WILLIAM G.; and CARROLL, SARAH P. 1953 A Sampling Investigation of the Efficiency of Weighting Inversely as the Estimated Variance. *Biometrics* 9: 447–459.

COCHRAN, WILLIAM G.; and COX, GERTRUDE M. (1950) 1957 *Experimental Designs.* 2d ed. New York: Wiley.

EZEKIEL, MORDECAI; and FOX, KARL A. (1930) 1961 *Methods of Correlation and Regression Analysis: Linear and Curvilinear.* New York: Wiley.

FISHER, R. A.; and YATES, FRANK (1938) 1963 *Statistical Tables for Biological, Agricultural and Medical Research.* 6th ed., rev. & enl. Edinburgh: Oliver & Boyd; New York: Hafner.

GAUSS, CARL F. 1855 *Méthode des moindres carrés: Mémoires sur la combinaison des observations.* Translated by J. Bertrand. Paris: Mallet-Bachelier. → An authorized translation of Carl Friedrich Gauss's works on least squares.

GEARY, R. C. 1963 Some Remarks About Relations Between Stochastic Variables: A Discussion Document. Institut International de Statistique, *Revue* 31:163–181.

HOTELLING, HAROLD 1940 The Selection of Variates for Use in Prediction With Some Comments on the General Problem of Nuisance Parameters. *Annals of Mathematical Statistics* 11:271–283.

HOTELLING, HAROLD 1941 Experimental Determination of the Maximum of a Function. *Annals of Mathematical Statistics* 12:20–45.

KENDALL, MAURICE G.; and STUART, ALAN (1943–1946) 1958–1966 *The Advanced Theory of Statistics.* New ed. 3 vols. New York: Hafner; London: Griffin. → Volume 1: *Distribution Theory*, 1958. Volume 2: *Inference and Relationship*, 1961. Volume 3: *Design and Analysis, and Time-series*, 1966. Kendall was the sole author of the 1943–1946 edition.

KRUSKAL, WILLIAM H. 1961 The Coordinate-free Approach to Gauss–Markov Estimation and Its Application to Missing and Extra Observations. Volume 1, pages 435–451 in Symposium on Mathematical Statistics and Probability, Fourth, Berkeley, *Proceedings.* Berkeley and Los Angeles: Univ. of California Press.

LEGENDRE, ADRIEN M. (1805) 1959 On a Method of Least Squares. Volume 2, pages 576–579 in David Eugene Smith, *A Source Book in Mathematics.* New York: Dover. → First published as "Sur la méthode des moindres carrés" in Legendre's *Nouvelles méthodes pour la détermination des orbites des comètes.*

MADANSKY, ALBERT 1959 The Fitting of Straight Lines When Both Variables Are Subject to Error. *Journal of the American Statistical Association* 54:173–205.

PIMENTEL GOMES, FREDERICO 1953 The Use of Mitscherlich's Regression Law in the Analysis of Experiments With Fertilizers. *Biometrics* 9:498–516.

PLACKETT, R. L. 1960 *Principles of Regression Analysis.* Oxford: Clarendon.

RAO, C. RADHAKRISHNA 1952 *Advanced Statistical Methods in Biometric Research.* New York: Wiley.

RAO, C. RADHAKRISHNA 1965 *Linear Statistical Inference and Its Applications.* New York: Wiley.

STEVENS, W. L. 1951 Asymptotic Regression. *Biometrics* 7:247–267.

STRODTBECK, FRED L.; MCDONALD, MARGARET R.; and ROSEN, BERNARD C. 1957 Evaluation of Occupations: A Reflection of Jewish and Italian Mobility Differences. *American Sociological Review* 22:546–553.

WILLIAMS, EVAN J. 1952 Use of Scores for the Analysis of Association in Contingency Tables. *Biometrika* 39: 274–289.

WILLIAMS, EVAN J. 1959 *Regression Analysis.* New York: Wiley.

WOLD, HERMAN 1953 *Demand Analysis: A Study in Econometrics.* New York: Wiley.

YATES, FRANK 1933 The Analysis of Replicated Experiments When the Field Results Are Incomplete. *Empire Journal of Experimental Agriculture* 1:129–142.

YATES, FRANK 1948 The Analysis of Contingency Tables With Groupings Based on Quantitative Characters. *Biometrika* 35:176–181.

II
ANALYSIS OF VARIANCE

Analysis of variance is a body of statistical procedures for analyzing observational data that may be regarded as satisfying certain broad assumptions about the structure of means, variances, and distributional form. The basic notion of analysis of variance (or ANOVA) is that of comparing and dissecting empirical dispersions in the data in order to understand underlying central values and dispersions.

This basic notion was early noted and developed in special cases by Lexis and von Bortkiewicz [*see* LEXIS; BORTKIEWICZ]. Not until the pioneering work of R. A. Fisher (1925; 1935), however, were the fundamental principles of analysis of variance and its most important techniques worked out and made public [*see* FISHER, R. A.]. Early applications of analysis of variance were primarily in agriculture and biology. The methodology is now used in every field of science and is one of the most important statistical areas for the social sciences. (For further historical material see Sampford 1964.)

Much basic material of analysis of variance may usefully be regarded as a special development of regression analysis [*see* LINEAR HYPOTHESES, *article on* REGRESSION]. Analysis of variance extends, however, to techniques and models that do not strictly fall under the regression rubric.

In analysis of variance all the standard general theories of statistics, such as point and set estimation and hypothesis testing, come into play. In the past there has sometimes been overemphasis on testing hypotheses.

One-factor analysis of variance

A simple experiment will now be described as an example of ANOVA. Suppose that the publisher of a junior-high-school textbook is considering styles of printing type for a new edition; there are three styles to investigate, and the same chapter of the book has been prepared in each of the three styles for the experiment. Junior-high-school pupils are to be chosen at random from an appropriate large population of such pupils, randomly assigned to read the chapter in one of the three styles, and then given a test that results in a reading-comprehension score for each pupil.

Suppose that the experiment is set up so that P_1, P_2, and P_3 pupils (where $P_1 = P_2 = P_3 = P$) read the chapter in styles 1, 2, and 3, respectively, and that X_{ps} denotes the comprehension score of the pth pupil reading style s. (Here $s = 1, 2, 3$; in general, $s = 1, 2, \cdots, S$.) There is a hypothetical mean, or expected, value of X_{ps}, μ_s, but X_{ps} differs from μ_s because, first, the pupils are chosen randomly from a population of pupils with different inherent means and, second, a given pupil, on hypothetical repetitions of the experiment, would not always obtain the same score. This is expressed by writing

$$(1) \qquad X_{ps} = \mu_s + e_{ps}.$$

Then the assumptions are made that the e_{ps} are all independent, that they are all normally distributed, and that they have a common (usually unknown) variance, σ^2. By definition, the expectation of e_{ps} is zero.

Because differences among the pupils reading a particular style of type are thrown into the random "error" terms (e_{ps}), μ_s, the expectation of X_{ps}, does not depend on p. It is convenient to rewrite (1) as

$$X_{ps} = \mu + (\mu_s - \mu) + e_{ps},$$

where $\mu = (\sum \mu_s)/S$, the average of the μ_s. For simplicity, set $\alpha_s = \mu_s - \mu$ (so that $\alpha_1 + \alpha_2 + \cdots + \alpha_S = 0$) and write the structural equation finally in the conventional form

$$(2) \qquad X_{ps} = \mu + \alpha_s + e_{ps}.$$

Here α_s is the differential effect on comprehension scores of style s for the relevant population of pupils. The unknowns are μ, the α_s, and σ^2.

Note that this structure falls under the linear regression hypothesis with coefficients 0 or 1. For example, if $E(X_{ps})$ represents the expected value of X_{ps},

$$E(X_{p1}) = 1 \cdot \mu + 1 \cdot \alpha_1 + 0 \cdot \alpha_2 + 0 \cdot \alpha_3 + \cdots + 0 \cdot \alpha_S,$$
$$E(X_{p2}) = 1 \cdot \mu + 0 \cdot \alpha_1 + 1 \cdot \alpha_2 + 0 \cdot \alpha_3 + \cdots + 0 \cdot \alpha_S.$$

Consider how this illustrative experiment might be conducted. After defining the population to which he wishes to generalize his findings, the experimenter would use a table of random numbers to choose pupils to read the chapter printed in the different styles. (Actually, he would probably have to sample intact school classes rather than individual pupils, so the observations analyzed might be class means instead of individual scores, but this does not change the analysis in principle.) After the three groups have read the same chapter under conditions that differ only in style of type, a single test covering comprehension of the material in the chapter would be administered to all pupils.

The experimenter's attention would be focused on differences between average scores of the three style groups (that is, $\bar{X}._1$ versus $\bar{X}._2$, $\bar{X}._2$ versus $\bar{X}._3$, and $\bar{X}._1$ versus $\bar{X}._3$) relative to the variability of the test scores within these groups. He estimates the μ_s via the $\bar{X}._s$, and he attempts to determine which of the three averages, if any, differ with statistical significance from the others. Eventually he hopes to help the publisher decide which style of type to use for his new edition.

ANOVA of random numbers—an example. An imaginary experiment of the kind outlined above will be analyzed here to illustrate how ANOVA is applied. Suppose that the three P_s are each 20, that in fact the μ_s are all exactly equal to 0, and that $\sigma^2 = 1$ (setting $\mu_s = 0$ is just a convenience corresponding to a conventional origin for the comprehension-score scale).

Sixty random normal deviates, with mean 0 and variance 1, were chosen by use of an appropriate table (RAND Corporation 1955). They are listed in Table 1, where the second column from the left should be disregarded for the moment—it will be used later, in a modified example. From the "data" of Table 1 the usual estimates of the μ_s are just the column averages, $\bar{X}._1 = -0.09$, $\bar{X}._2 = 0.10$, and $\bar{X}._3 = 0.08$. The estimate of μ is the over-all mean, $\bar{X}.. = 0.03$, and the estimates of the α_s are $-0.09 - 0.03 = -0.12$, $0.10 - 0.03 = 0.07$, and $0.08 - 0.03 = 0.05$. Note that these add to zero,

Table 1 — Data for hypothetical experiment; 60 random normal deviates

	X_{p1}	$X_{p1} + 1$*	X_{p2}	X_{p3}
	0.477	1.477	−0.987	1.158
	−0.017	0.983	2.313	0.879
	0.508	1.508	0.016	0.068
	−0.512	0.488	0.483	1.116
	−0.188	0.812	0.157	0.272
	−1.073	−0.073	1.107	−0.396
	−0.412	0.588	−0.023	−0.983
	1.201	2.201	0.898	−0.267
	−0.676	0.324	−1.404	0.327
	−1.012	−0.012	−0.080	0.929
	0.997	1.997	−1.258	−0.603
	−0.127	0.873	−0.017	0.493
	1.178	2.178	1.607	−1.243
	−1.507	−0.507	0.005	−0.145
	1.010	2.010	0.163	1.334
	−0.528	0.472	−0.771	−0.906
	−0.139	0.861	0.485	−1.633
	0.621	1.621	0.147	0.424
	−2.078	−1.078	−1.764	−0.433
	0.485	1.485	0.986	1.245
Mean	−0.09	0.91	0.10	0.08
Variance	0.83	0.83	1.03	0.78

* This column was obtained by adding 1 to each deviate of the first column.

as required. In ANOVA, for this case, two quantities are compared. The first is the dispersion of the three μ_s estimates—that is, the sum of the $(\bar{X}._s - \bar{X}..)^2$, conveniently multiplied by 20, the common sample size. This is called the between-styles dispersion or sum of squares. Here it is 0.4466. (These calculations, as well as those below, are made with the raw data of Table 1, not with the rounded means appearing there.) The second quantity is the within-sample dispersion, the sum of the three quantities $\sum_p (X_{ps} - \bar{X}._s)^2$. This is called the within-style dispersion or sum of squares. Here it is 50.1253.

This comparison corresponds to the decomposition

$$X_{ps} - \bar{X}.. = (\bar{X}._s - \bar{X}..) + (X_{ps} - \bar{X}._s)$$

and to the sum-of-squares identity

$$\begin{aligned}\sum_p \sum_s (X_{ps} - \bar{X}..)^2 &= \sum_p \sum_s (\bar{X}._s - \bar{X}..)^2 + \sum_p \sum_s (X_{ps} - \bar{X}._s)^2 \\ &= 20 \sum_s (\bar{X}._s - \bar{X}..)^2 + \sum_p \sum_s (X_{ps} - \bar{X}._s)^2,\end{aligned}$$

which shows how the factor of 20 arises. Such identities in sums of squares are basic in most elementary expositions of ANOVA.

The fundamental notion is that the within-style dispersion, divided by its so-called *degrees of freedom* (here, degrees of freedom for error), unbiasedly estimates σ^2. Here the degrees of freedom for error are 57 (equals 60 [for the total number of

Table 2 — Analysis-of-variance table for one-factor experiment

(a) ANOVA of 60 random normal deviates

Source of variation	df	SS	MS	F	Tabled $F_{.05;2,57}$
Between styles	$3-1=2$	0.4466	0.2233	0.25	3.16
Within styles	$60-3=57$	50.1253	0.8794*		
Total	$60-1=59$	50.5719			

* Actually, σ^2 here is known to be 1.

(b) ANOVA of general one-factor experiment with S treatments

Source of variation	df	MS	EMS
Between treatments	$S-1$	$\sum_{s=1}^{S} P_s(\bar{X}_{.s}-\bar{X}_{..})^2/(S-1)$	$\sigma^2+\sum_{s=1}^{S} P_s\alpha_s^2/(S-1)$
Within treatments	P_+-S*	$\sum_{s=1}^{S}\sum_{p=1}^{P_s}(X_{ps}-\bar{X}_{.s})^2/(P_+-S)$*	σ^2
Total	P_+-1*	$\sum_{s=1}^{S}\sum_{p=1}^{P_s}(X_{ps}-\bar{X}_{..})^2/(P_+-1)$*	

* Here P_+ is used for $\sum_{s=1}^{S} P_s$ for convenience.

observations] minus 3 [for the number of μ_s estimated]). On the other hand, the between-styles dispersion, divided by its degrees of freedom (here 2), estimates σ^2 unbiasedly if and only if the μ_s are equal; otherwise the estimate will tend to be larger than σ^2. Furthermore, the between-styles and within-style dispersions are statistically independent. Hence, it is natural to look at the ratio of the two dispersions, each divided by its degrees of freedom. The result is the F-statistic, here

$$\frac{0.4466/2}{50.1253/57}=0.25.$$

In repeated trials with the null hypothesis (that there are no differences between the μ_s) true, the F-statistic follows an F-distribution with (in this case) 2 and 57 degrees of freedom [*see* DISTRIBUTIONS, STATISTICAL, *article on* SPECIAL CONTINUOUS DISTRIBUTIONS]. Level of significance is denoted by "α" (which should not be confused with the totally unrelated "α_s," denoting style effect; the notational similarity stems from the juxtaposition of two terminological traditions and the finite number of Greek letters). The F-test at level of significance α of the null hypothesis that the styles are equivalent rejects that hypothesis when the F-statistic is too large, greater than its 100α percentage point, here $F_{\alpha;2,57}$. If $\alpha=0.05$, which is a conventional level, then $F_{.05;2,57}=3.16$, so 0.25 is much smaller than the cutoff point, and the null hypothesis is, of course, not rejected. This is consonant with the fact that the null hypothesis *is* true in the imaginary experiment under discussion.

Table 2 summarizes the above discussion in both algebraic and numerical form. The algebraic form is for S styles with P_s students at the sth style.

To reiterate, in an analysis of variance each kind of effect (treatment, factor, and others to be discussed later) is represented by two basic numbers. The first is the so-called *sum of squares* (SS), corresponding to the effect; it is random, depending upon the particular sample, and has two fundamental properties: (a) If the effect in question is wholly *absent*, its sum of squares behaves probabilistically like a sum of squared independent normal deviates with zero means. (b) If the effect in question is *present*, its sum of squares tends to be relatively large; in fact, it behaves probabilistically like a sum of squared independent normal deviates with *not* all means zero.

The second number is the so-called *degrees of freedom* (*df*). This quantity is not random but depends only on the structure of the experimental design. The *df* is the number of independent normal deviates in the description of sums of squares just given.

A third (derived) number is the so-called *mean square* (*MS*), which is computed by dividing the sum of squares by the degrees of freedom. When an effect is wholly absent, its mean square is an unbiased estimator of underlying variance, σ^2. When an effect is present, its mean square has an expectation greater than σ^2.

In the example considered here, each observation is regarded as the sum of (a) a grand mean, (b) a printing-style effect, and (c) error. It is conventional in analysis-of-variance tables not to have a line corresponding to the grand mean and to work with sample residuals centered on it; that convention is followed here. Printing-style effect and error differ in that the latter is assumed to be wholly random, whereas the former is not random but may be zero. The mean square for error estimates underlying variance unbiasedly and is a yardstick for judging other mean squares.

In the standard simple designs to which ANOVA is applied, it is customary to define effects so that the several sums of squares are statistically independent, from which additivity both of sums of squares and of degrees of freedom follows [*see* PROBABILITY, *article on* FORMAL PROBABILITY]. In the example, $SS_{\text{between}} + SS_{\text{within}} = SS_{\text{total}}$, and $df_b + df_w = df_{\text{total}}$. (Here, and often below, the subscripts "b" and "w" are used to stand for "between" and "within," respectively.) This additivity is computationally useful, either to save arithmetic or to verify it.

Analysis-of-variance tables, which, like Table 2, are convenient and compact summaries of both the relevant formulas and the computed numbers, usually also show *expected mean squares* (*EMS*), the average value of the mean squares over a (conceptually) infinite number of experiments. In fixed-effects models (such as the model of the example) these are always of the form σ^2 (the underlying variance) plus an additional term that is zero when the relevant effect is absent and positive when it is present. The additional term is a convenient measure of the magnitude of the effect.

Expected mean squares, such as those given by the two formulas in Table 2, provide a necessary condition for the F-statistic to have an F-distribution when the null hypothesis is true. (Other conditions, such as independence, must also be met.) Note that if the population mean of the sth treatment, μ_s, is the same for all treatments (that is, if $\alpha_s = 0$ for all s) then the expected value of MS_b will be σ^2, the same as the expected value of MS_w. If the null hypothesis is true, the average value of the F from a huge number of identical experiments employing fresh, randomly sampled experimental units will be $(P_+ - S)/(P_+ - S - 2)$, which is very nearly 1 when, as is usually the case, the total number of experimental units, P_+, is large compared with S. Expected mean squares become particularly important in analyses based on models of a nature somewhat different from the one illustrated in Tables 1 and 2, because in those cases it is not always easy to determine which mean square should be used as the denominator of F (see the discussion of some of these other models, below).

The simplest *t*-tests. It is worth digressing to show how the familiar one-sample and two-sample t-tests (or Student tests) fall under the analysis-of-variance rubric, at least for the symmetrical two-tail versions of these tests.

Single-sample t-test. In the single-sample t-test context, one considers a random sample, $X_1, X_2, \cdots, X_P$, of independent normal observations with the same unknown mean, μ, and the same unknown variance, σ^2. Another way of expressing this is to write

$$X_p = \mu + e_p, \qquad p = 1, \cdots, P,$$

where the e_p are independent normal random variables, with mean 0 and common variance σ^2. The usual estimator of μ is $\bar{X}.$, the average of the X_p, and this suggests the decomposition into average and deviation from average,

$$X_p = \bar{X}. + (X_p - \bar{X}.),$$

from which one obtains the sum-of-squares identity

$$\begin{aligned}\sum X_p^2 &= \sum (X_p - \bar{X}.)^2 + \sum \bar{X}.^2 + 2\bar{X}.\sum (X_p - \bar{X}.)\\ &= \sum (X_p - \bar{X}.)^2 + P\bar{X}.^2\end{aligned}$$

(since $\sum (X_p - \bar{X}.) = 0$), a familiar algebraic relationship. Since the usual unbiased estimator of σ^2 is $s^2 = \sum (X_p - \bar{X}.)^2/(P-1)$, the sum-of-squares identity may be written

$$\sum X_p^2 = (P-1)s^2 + P\bar{X}.^2\,.$$

Ordinarily the analysis-of-variance table is not written out for this simple case; it is, however, the one shown in Table 3. In Table 3 the total row is the actual total including all observations; it is of the essence that the row for mean is separated out.

Table 3

Effect	df	SS	EMS
Mean	1	$P\bar{X}.^2$	$\sigma^2 + P\mu^2$
Error	$P-1$	$\sum (X_p - \bar{X}.)^2$	σ^2
Total	P	$\sum X_p^2$	

The F-statistic for testing that $\mu = 0$ is the ratio of the mean squares for mean and error,

$$\frac{P\bar{X}.^2}{\sum (X_p - \bar{X}.)^2/(P-1)} = \frac{P\bar{X}.^2}{s^2},$$

which, under the null hypothesis, has an F-distribution with 1 and $P-1$ degrees of freedom. Notice that the above F-statistic is the square of

$$\frac{\bar{X}.}{s/\sqrt{P}},$$

which is the ordinary t-statistic (or Student statistic) for testing $\mu = 0$. If a symmetrical two-tail test is wanted, it is immaterial whether one deals with the t-statistic or its square. On the other hand, for a one-tail test the t-statistic would be referred to the t-distribution with $P - 1$ degrees of freedom [*see* DISTRIBUTIONS, STATISTICAL, *article on* SPECIAL CONTINUOUS DISTRIBUTIONS].

It is important to note that a confidence interval for μ may readily be established from the above discussion [*see* ESTIMATION, *article on* CONFIDENCE INTERVALS AND REGIONS]. The symmetrical form is

$$\bar{X}. - \sqrt{F_{\alpha;1,P-1}}\, s/\sqrt{P} \leqslant \mu \leqslant \bar{X}. + \sqrt{F_{\alpha;1,P-1}}\, s/\sqrt{P}.$$

Alternatively, $F_{\alpha;1,P-1}$ can be replaced by the upper $100(\alpha/2)$ per cent point for the t-distribution with $P - 1$ degrees of freedom, $t_{\alpha/2;P-1}$.

Suppose, for example, that from a normally distributed population there has been drawn a random sample of 25 observations for which the sample mean, $\bar{x}.$, is 34.213 and the sample variance, s^2, is 49.000. What is the population mean, μ? The usual point estimate from this sample is 34.213. How different from μ is this value likely to be? For $\alpha = .05$, a 95 per cent confidence interval is constructed by looking up $t_{.025;24} = 2.064$ in a table (for instance, McNemar [1949] 1962, p. 430) and substituting in the formula

$$\text{Confidence}\left[34.213 - 2.064\left(\frac{\sqrt{49.000}}{\sqrt{25}}\right) \leqslant \mu \leqslant 34.213 + 2.064\left(\frac{\sqrt{49.000}}{\sqrt{25}}\right)\right] = 0.95.$$

Thus,

$$\text{Confidence}\ [31.32 \leqslant \mu \leqslant 37.10] = 0.95.$$

This result means that if an infinite number of samples, each of size $P = 25$, were drawn randomly from a normally distributed population and a confidence interval for each sample were set up in the above way, only 5 per cent of the intervals would fail to cover the mean of the population (which is a certain fixed value).

Similarly, from this one sample the unbiased point estimate of σ^2 is the value of s^2, 49.000. Brownlee ([1960] 1965, page 282) shows how to find confidence intervals for σ^2 [*see also* VARIANCES, STATISTICAL STUDY OF].

Is it "reasonable" to suppose that the mean of the population from which this sample was randomly chosen is as large as, say, 40? No, because that number does not lie within even the 99 per cent confidence interval. Therefore it would be unreasonable to conclude that the sample was drawn from a population with a mean as great as 40. The relevant test of statistical significance is

$$t = \frac{34.213 - 40.000}{7/5} = \frac{-5.787(5)}{7} = -4.134,$$

the absolute magnitude of which lies beyond the 0.9995 percentile point (3.745) in the tabled t-distribution for 24 degrees of freedom. Therefore, the difference is statistically significant beyond the $0.0005 + 0.0005 = 0.001$ level. The null hypothesis being tested was H_0: $\mu = 40$, against the alternative hypothesis H_a: $\mu \neq 40$. Just as the confidence interval indicated that it is unreasonable to suppose the mean to be equal to 40, this test also shows that 40 will lie outside the 99 per cent confidence interval; however, of the two procedures, the confidence interval gives more information than the significance test.

Two-sample t-test. In the two-sample t-test context, there are two random samples from normal distributions assumed to have the same variance, σ^2, and to have means μ_1 and μ_2. Call the observations in the first sample $X_{11}, \cdots, X_{P_1 1}$ and the observations in the second sample $X_{12}, \cdots, X_{P_2 2}$. The most usual null hypothesis is $\mu_1 = \mu_2$, and for that the t-statistic is

$$\frac{\bar{X}._1 - \bar{X}._2}{s\sqrt{(1/P_1) + (1/P_2)}},$$

where the P's are the sample sizes, the $\bar{X}$'s are the sample means, and s^2 is the estimate of σ^2 based on the pooled within-sample sum of squares,

$$s^2 = \frac{1}{P_1 + P_2 - 2}\left\{\sum_p (X_{p1} - \bar{X}._1)^2 + \sum_p (X_{p2} - \bar{X}._2)^2\right\}.$$

Here $P_1 + P_2 - 2$ is the number of degrees of freedom for error, the total number of observations less the number of estimated means ($\bar{X}._1$ and $\bar{X}._2$ estimate μ_1 and μ_2, respectively). Under the null hypothesis, the t-statistic has the t-distribution with $P_1 + P_2 - 2$ degrees of freedom.

The basic decomposition is

$$X_{ps} - \bar{X}.. = (\bar{X}._s - \bar{X}..) + (X_{ps} - \bar{X}._s),$$

leading to the sum-of-squares decomposition

$$\sum_p\sum_s (X_{ps} - \bar{X}..)^2 = \sum_s P_s(\bar{X}._s - \bar{X}..)^2 + \sum_p\sum_s (X_{ps} - \bar{X}._s)^2.$$

Since s has only the values 1 and 2,

$$\bar{X}.. = \frac{P_1}{P_1 + P_2}\bar{X}._1 + \frac{P_2}{P_1 + P_2}\bar{X}._2,$$

Table 4

Effect	*df*	*SS*	*EMS**
Style	1	$\sum P_s(\bar{X}._s - \bar{X}..)^2 = \dfrac{(\bar{X}._1 - \bar{X}._2)^2}{(1/P_1)+(1/P_2)}$	$\sigma^2 + \dfrac{(\mu_1 - \mu_2)^2}{(1/P_1)+(1/P_2)}$
Error	$P_1 + P_2 - 2$	$(P_1 + P_2 - 2)s^2$	σ^2
Total	$P_1 + P_2 - 1$	$\sum\sum (X_{ps} - \bar{X}..)^2$	

* Note that the expected mean square for style is σ^2 plus what is obtained by formal substitution for the random variables ($\bar{X}._1$, $\bar{X}._2$) in the sum of squares of their respective expectations (divided by *df*, which here is 1). This relationship is a perfectly general one in the analysis-of-variance model now under discussion, but it must be changed for other models that will be mentioned later.

and therefore

$$\sum_s P_s(\bar{X}._s - \bar{X}..)^2 = \frac{P_1P_2}{P_1 + P_2}(\bar{X}._1 - \bar{X}._2)^2$$
$$= \frac{(\bar{X}._1 - \bar{X}._2)^2}{(P_1 + P_2)/P_1P_2}$$
$$= \frac{(\bar{X}._1 - \bar{X}._2)^2}{(1/P_1) + (1/P_2)}.$$

The analysis-of-variance table may be written as in Table 4. The F-statistic for the null hypothesis that $\mu_1 = \mu_2$ is

$$\frac{(\bar{X}._1 - \bar{X}._2)^2/(P_1^{-1} + P_2^{-1})}{s^2} = \frac{(\bar{X}._1 - \bar{X}._2)^2}{s^2[(1/P_1) + (1/P_2)]},$$

and this is exactly the square of the t-statistic for the two-sample problem.

Note that the two-sample problem as it is analyzed here is only a special case (with $S = 2$) of the S-sample problem presented earlier.

The numerical example continued. Returning to the numerical example of Table 1, add 1 to every number in the leftmost column to obtain the second column and consider the numbers in the second column as the observations for style 1. Now $\mu_1 = 1$ and $\mu_2 = \mu_3 = 0$. What happens to the analysis of variance and the F-test? Table 5 shows the result; the F-statistic is 5.41, which is of high statistical significance since $F_{.01;2,57} = 5.07$. Thus, one would correctly reject the null hypothesis of equality among the three μ_s.

The actual value of μ is $\frac{1}{3} \cong 0.33$, and that of α_1 is $\frac{2}{3} \cong 0.67$. The estimate of μ is 0.36, and that of α_1 is 0.55.

With three styles, one can consider many contrasts—for example, style 1 versus style 2, style 1 versus style 3, style 2 versus style 3, $\frac{1}{2}$(style 1 + style 2) versus style 3. There are special methods for dealing with several contrasts simultaneously [*see* LINEAR HYPOTHESES, *article on* MULTIPLE COMPARISONS].

ANOVA with more than one factor

In the illustrative example being considered here, suppose that the publisher had been interested not only in style of type but also in a second factor, such as the tint of the printing ink (t). If he had three styles and four tints, a complete "crossed" *factorial design* would require $3 \times 4 = 12$ experimental conditions ($s_1t_1, s_1t_2, \cdots, s_3t_4$). From $12P$ experimental units he would assign P units at random to each of the 12 conditions, conduct his experiment, and obtain outcome measures to analyze. The total variation between the $12P$ outcome measures can be partitioned into four sources rather than into the two found with one factor. The sources of variation are the following: between styles, between tints, *interaction* of styles with tints, and within style–tint combinations (error).

The usual model for the two-factor crossed design is

$$X_{pst} = \mu + \alpha_s + \beta_t + \gamma_{st} + e_{pst},$$

where $\sum_s \alpha_s = \sum_t \beta_t = \sum_s \gamma_{st} = \sum_t \gamma_{st} = 0$, and the e_{pst} are independent normally distributed random variables with mean 0 and equal variance σ^2 for each st combination. The analysis-of-variance procedure for this design appears in Table 6. The α_s and β_t represent *main effects* of the styles and tints; the γ_{st} denote (two-factor) *interactions*.

Table 5 — One-factor ANOVA of 60 transformed random normal deviates

Source of variation	*df*	*SS*	*MS*	*EMS*	*F*
Between styles	2	8.9246	4.4623	$\sigma^2 + 20\sum_{s=1}^{3}\alpha_s^2/2$	5.41
Within styles	57	50.1253	0.8794	σ^2	
Total	59	59.0499			

Table 6 — ANOVA of a complete, crossed-classification, two-factor factorial design with P experimental units for each factor-level combination

Source of variation	df	SS	EMS
Between styles	$S-1$	$PT\sum_{s=1}^{S}(\bar{X}_{\cdot s\cdot}-\bar{X}_{\cdots})^2$	$\sigma^2+PT\sum_s \alpha_s^2/(S-1)$
Between tints	$T-1$	$PS\sum_{t=1}^{T}(\bar{X}_{\cdot\cdot t}-\bar{X}_{\cdots})^2$	$\sigma^2+PS\sum_t \beta_t^2/(T-1)$
Styles × tints (interaction)	$(S-1)(T-1)$	$P\sum_{s=1}^{S}\sum_{t=1}^{T}(\bar{X}_{\cdot st}-\bar{X}_{\cdot s\cdot}-\bar{X}_{\cdot\cdot t}+\bar{X}_{\cdots})^2$	$\sigma^2+P\sum_s\sum_t \gamma_{st}^2/(S-1)(T-1)$
Within style–tint combinations	$ST(P-1)$	$\sum_{p=1}^{P}\sum_{s=1}^{S}\sum_{t=1}^{T}(X_{pst}-\bar{X}_{\cdot st})^2$	σ^2
Total	$PST-1$	$\sum_{p=1}^{P}\sum_{s=1}^{S}\sum_{t=1}^{T}(X_{pst}-\bar{X}_{\cdots})^2$	

Interaction. The two-factor design introduces interaction, a concept not relevant in one-factor experiments. It might be found, for example, that, although in general s_1 is an ineffective style and t_3 is an ineffective tint, the particular combination s_1t_3 produces rather good results. It is then said that style interacts with tint to produce nonadditive effects; if the effects were additive, an ineffective style combined with an ineffective tint would produce an ineffective combination.

Interaction is zero if $E(X_{pst})=\mu+\alpha_s+\beta_t$ for every st, because under this condition the population mean of the stth combination is the population grand mean plus the sum of the effects of the sth style and the tth tint. Then the interaction effect, γ_{st}, is zero for every combination. Table 7 contains hypothetical data showing population means, $\bar{\mu}_{st}$, for zero interaction (Lubin 1961 discusses types of interaction). Note tnat for every cell of Table 7, $\bar{\mu}_{st}-(\bar{\mu}_{s\cdot}-\mu)-(\bar{\mu}_{\cdot t}-\mu)=\mu=3$. (Here $\bar{\mu}_{\cdot\cdot}$ is written as μ for simplicity.) For example, for tint 1 and style 1, $3-(5-3)-(1-3)=3$.

One tests for interaction by computing F $MS_{\text{styles}\times\text{tints}}/MS_{\text{within style–tint}}$, comparing this F with the F's tabled at various significance levels for $(S-1)(T-1)$ and $ST(P-1)$ degrees of freedom.

Table 7 — Zero interaction of two factors (hypothetical population means $\bar{\mu}_{st}$)

Style \ Tint	1	2	3	4	Row means ($\bar{\mu}_{s\cdot}$)
1	3	4	5	8	5
2	0	1	2	5	2
3	0	1	2	5	2
Column means ($\bar{\mu}_{\cdot t}$)	1	2	3	6	$3=\mu$

If there were but one subject reading with each style–tint combination (that is, if there were no replication), further assumptions would have to be made to permit testing of hypotheses about main effects. In particular, it is commonly then assumed that the style × tint interaction is zero, so that the expected mean square for interaction in Table 6 reduces to the underlying variance, and the $MS_{\text{styles}\times\text{tints}}$ may be used in the denominator of the F's for testing main effects. No test of the assumption of additivity is possible through $MS_{\text{within style–tint}}$, because this quantity cannot be calculated. However, Tukey (1949; see also Winer 1962, pp. 216–220) has provided a one-degree-of-freedom test for interaction, or nonadditivity, of a special kind that can be used for testing the hypothesis of no interaction for these unreplicated experiments of the fixed-effects kind. (See Scheffé 1959, pp. 129–134.)

The factorial design may be extended to three or more factors. With three factors there are four sums of squares for interactions: one for the three-factor interaction (sometimes called a second-order interaction, because a one-factor "interaction" is a main effect) and one each for the three two-factor (that is, first-order) interactions. If the three factors are A, B, and C, their interactions might be represented as $A\times B\times C$, $A\times B$, $A\times C$, and $B\times C$. For example, a style of type that for the experiment as a whole yields excellent comprehension may, when combined with a generally effective size of type and a tint of paper that has over-all facilitative effect, yield rather poor results. One three-factor factorial experiment permits testing of the hypothesis that there is a no second-order interaction and permits the magnitude of such interaction to be estimated, whereas three one-factor experiments or a two-factor experiment and a one-factor experiment do not. Usually, three-factor nonadditivity is difficult to explain substantively.

A large number of more complex designs, most of them more or less incomplete in some respect as compared with factorial designs of the kind discussed above, have been proposed. [*See* EXPERIMENTAL DESIGN; *see also* Winer 1962; Fisher 1935.]

The analysis of covariance

Suppose that the publisher in the earlier, style-of-type example had known reading-test scores for his 60 pupils prior to the experiment. He could have used these antecedent scores in the analysis of the comprehension scores to reduce the magnitude of the mean square within styles, which, as the estimate of underlying variance, is the denominator of the computed F. At the same time he would adjust the subsequent style means to account for initial differences between reading-test-score means in the three groups. One way of carrying out this more refined analysis would be to perform an analysis of variance of the differences between final comprehension scores and initial reading scores—say, $X_{ps} - Y_{ps}$. A better prediction of the outcome measure, X_{ps}, might be secured by computing $\alpha + \beta Y_{ps}$, where α and β are constants to be estimated.

By a statistical procedure called the *analysis of covariance* one or more antecedent variables may be used to reduce the magnitude of the sum of squares within styles and also to adjust the observed style means for differences between groups in average initial reading scores. If $\beta \neq 0$, then the adjusted sum of squares within treatments (which provides the denominator of the F-ratio) will be less than the unadjusted SS_w of Table 2, thereby tending to increase the magnitude of F. For each independent antecedent variable one uses, one degree of freedom is lost for SS_w and none for SS_b; the loss of degrees of freedom for SS_w will usually be more than compensated for by the decrease in its magnitude.

A principal statistical condition needed for the usual analysis of covariance is that the regression of outcome scores on antecedent scores is the same for every style, because one computes a single within-style regression coefficient to use in adjusting the within-style sum of squares. Homogeneity of regression can be tested statistically; see Winer (1962, chapter 11). Some procedures to adopt in the case of heterogeneity of regression are given in Brownlee (1960).

The regression model chosen must be appropriate for the data if the use of one or more antecedent variables is to reduce MS_w appreciably. Usually the regression of outcome measures on antecedent measures is assumed to be linear.

The analysis of covariance can be extended to more than one antecedent variable and to more complex designs. (For further details see Cochran 1957; Smith 1957; Winer 1962; McNemar 1949.)

Models—fixed, finite, random, and mixed

In the example, the publisher's "target population" of styles of print consisted of just those 3 styles that he tried out, so he exhausted the population of styles of interest to him. Suppose that, instead, he had been considering 39 different styles and had drawn *at random* from these 39 the 3 styles he used in the experiment. His intention is to determine from the experiment based on these 3 styles whether it would make any difference which one of the 39 styles he used for the textbook (of course, in practice a larger sample of styles would be drawn). If the styles did seem to differ in effectiveness, he would estimate from his experimental data involving only 3 styles the variance of the 39 population means of the styles. Then he might perform further experiments to find the most effective styles.

Finite-effects models. Thus far in this article the model assumed has been the *fixed-effects* model, in which one uses in the experiment itself all the styles of type to which one wishes to generalize. The 3-out-of-39 experiment mentioned above illustrates a *finite-effects* model, with only a small percentage (8 per cent, in the example given) of the styles drawn at random for the experiment but where one has the intention of testing the null hypothesis

$$H_0: \mu_1 = \mu_2 = \cdots = \mu_{39}$$

against all alternative hypotheses and estimating the "variance," $\sigma^2_{\text{style}} = \sum_{s=1}^{39}(\mu_{.s} - \mu)^2/(39-1)$ from $MS_b = 20\sum_{s=1}^{3}(\bar{X}_{.s} - \bar{X}_{..})^2/(3-1)$ and $MS_w = \sum_{s=1}^{3}\sum_{p=1}^{20}(X_{ps} - \bar{X}_{.s})^2/[3(20-1)]$.

Random-effects models. If the number of "levels" of the factor is very large, so that the number of levels drawn randomly for the experiment is a negligible percentage of the total number, then one has a *random-effects* model, sometimes called a components-of-variance model or Model II. This model would apply if, for example, one drew 20 raters at random from an actual or hypothetical population of 100,000 raters and used those 20 to rate each of 25 subjects who had been chosen at random from a population of half a million. (Strictly speaking, the number of raters and the number of subjects in the respective populations would have to be infinite to produce the random-effects model, but for practical purposes 100,000/20 and 500,000/25 are sufficiently large.) If every rater rated every subject on one trait (say, gregariousness) there would be $20 \times 25 = 500$ ratings, one for each experimental combination—that is, one for each rater–subject combination.

This, then, would be a two-factor design without replication, that is, with just one rating per rater–subject combination. (Even if the experimenter had used available raters and subjects rather than drawing them randomly from any populations, he would probably want to generalize to other raters and subjects "like" them; see Cornfield & Tukey 1956, p. 913.)

The usual model for an experiment thus conceptualized is

$$X_{rs} = \mu + a_r + b_s + e_{rs},$$

where μ is a grand mean, the a's are the (random) rater effects, the b's are (random) subject effects, and the e's combine interaction and inherent measurement error. The $20 + 25 + (20 \times 25)$ random variables are supposed to be independent and assumed to have variances as follows:

$$\text{var } a_r = \sigma_r^2, \qquad \text{var } b_s = \sigma_s^2, \qquad \text{var } e_{rs} = \sigma_e^2.$$

For F-testing purposes, a, b, and e are supposed to be normally distributed.

The analysis-of-variance table in such a case is similar to those presented earlier, except that the expected mean square column is changed to the one shown in Table 8.

Table 8

Effect	EMS
Rater	$\sigma_e^2 + 25\,\sigma_r^2$
Subject	$\sigma_e^2 + 20\,\sigma_s^2$
Error	σ_e^2

The F-statistic for testing the hypothesis that the main effect of subjects is absent (that $\sigma_s^2 = 0$) is MS_s/MS_{error}, where

$$MS_{\text{error}} = \frac{1}{19 \times 24} \sum \sum (X_{rs} - \bar{X}_{r.} - \bar{X}_{.s} + \bar{X}_{..})^2.$$

Under the null hypothesis that $\sigma_s^2 = 0$, the F-statistic has an F-distribution with 24 and 19×24 degrees of freedom. (A similar F-statistic is used for testing $\sigma_r^2 = 0$.) An unbiased estimator of σ_s^2 is

$$\frac{1}{20}(MS_s - MS_{\text{error}})$$

with a similar estimator for σ_r^2. A serious difficulty with these estimators is that they may take negative values; perhaps the best resolution of that difficulty is to enlarge the model. See Nelder (1954), and for another approach and a bibliography, see Thompson (1962).

Note that here it appears impossible to separate random interaction from inherent variability, both of which contribute to σ_e^2, the variance of the e's; in the random-effects model, however, this does not jeopardize significance tests for main effects.

In more complex Model II situations, the F-tests used are inherently different from their Model I analogues; in particular, sample components of variance are often most reasonably compared, not with the "bottom" estimator of σ^2, but with some other—usually an interaction—component of variance. (See Hays 1963, pp. 356–489; Brownlee [1960] 1965, pp. 309–396, 467–529.)

Mixed models. If all the levels of one factor are used in an experiment while a random sample of the levels of another factor is used, a *mixed model* results. Mixed models present special problems of analysis that have been discussed by Scheffé (1959, pp. 261–290) and by Mood and Graybill (1963).

Other topics in ANOVA

Robustness of ANOVA. Fixed-effects models are better understood than the other models and therefore, *where appropriate*, can be used with considerable confidence. Fixed-effects ANOVA seems "robust" for type I errors to departures from certain mathematical assumptions underlying the F-test, provided that the number of experimental units is the same for each experimental combination. Two of these assumptions are that the e's are normally distributed and that they have common variance σ^2 for every one of the experimental combinations. In particular, the common-variance assumption can be relaxed without greatly affecting the probability values for computed F's. If the number of experimental units does not vary from one factor-level combination to another, then it may be unnecessary to test for heterogeneity of variances preliminary to performing an ANOVA, because ANOVA is robust to such heterogeneity. (In fact, it may be unwise to make such a test, because the usual test for heterogeneity of variance is more sensitive to nonnormality than is ANOVA.) For further discussion of this point see Lindquist (1953, pp. 78–86), Winer (1962, pp. 239–241), Brownlee ([1960] 1965, chapter 9), and Glass (1966). Brownlee (1960) and others have provided the finite-model expected mean squares for the complete three-factor factorial design, from which one can readily determine expected mean squares for three-factor fixed, mixed, and random models.

Analysis-of-variance F's are unaffected by linear transformation of the observations—that is, by changes in the X_{ps} of the form $a + bX_{ps}$, where a and b are constants ($b \neq 0$). Multiplying every observation by b multiplies every mean square by b^2. Adding a to every observation does not change the mean squares. Thus, if observations are two-decimal numbers running from, say, -1.22 upward, one could, to simplify calculations, drop the decimal (multiply each number by 100) and then add 122 to each observation. The lowest observation would become $100(-1.22) + 122 = 0$. Each mean square would become $100^2 = 10{,}000$ times as large as for the decimal fractions. With the increasing availability of high-speed digital computers, coding of data is becoming less important than it was formerly.

A brief classification of factors. The ANOVA "factors" considered thus far are style of printing type, tint of ink, rater, and subject. Styles differ from each other qualitatively, as do raters and subjects. Tint of ink might vary more quantitatively than do styles, raters, and subjects—as would, for example, size of printing type or temperature in a classroom. Thus, one basis for classifying factors is whether or not their levels are ordered and, if they are, whether meaningful numbers can be associated with the factor levels.

Another basis for classification is whether the variable is manipulated by the experimenter. In order to conduct a "true" experiment, one must assign his experimental units in some (simple or restrictive) random fashion to the levels of at least one manipulated factor. ANOVA may be applied to other types of data, such as the scores of Englishmen versus Americans on a certain test, but this is an associational study, not a stimulus–response experiment. Obviously, nationality is not an independent variable in the same sense that printing type is. The direct "causal" inference possible from a well-conducted style-of-type experiment differs from the associational information obtained from the comparison of Englishmen's scores with those of Americans (see Stanley 1961; 1965; 1966; Campbell & Stanley 1963). Some variables, such as national origin, are impossible to manipulate in meaningful ways, whereas others, such as "enrolls for Latin versus does not enroll for Latin," can in principle be manipulated, even though they usually are not.

Experimenters use nonmanipulated, classification variables for two chief reasons. First, they may wish to use a factor explicitly in a design in order to isolate the sum of squares for the main effect of that factor so that it will not inflate the estimate of underlying variance—that is, so it will not make the denominator mean square of F unnecessarily large. For example, if the experimental units available for experimentation are children in grades seven, eight, and nine, and if IQ scores are available, it is wise in studying the three styles of type to use the three (ordered) grades as one fixed-effects factor and a number of ordered IQ levels—say, four—as another fixed-effects factor. If the experimenter suspects that girls and boys may react differently to the styles, he will probably use this two-level, unordered classification (girls versus boys) as the third factor. This would produce $3 \times 4 \times 2 \times 3 = 72$ experimental combinations, so with at least 2 children per combination he needs not less than 144 children.

Probably most children in the higher grades read better, regardless of style, than do most children in the lower grades, and children with high IQ's tend to read better than children with lower IQ's, so the main effects of grade and of IQ should be large. Therefore, the variation within grade–IQ–sex–style groups should be considerably less than within styles alone.

A second reason for using such stratifying or leveling variables is to study their interactions with the manipulated variable. Ninth graders might do relatively better with one style of type and seventh graders relatively better with another style, for example. If so, the experimenter might decide to recommend one style of type for ninth graders and another for seventh graders. With the above design one can isolate and examine one four-factor interaction, four three-factor interactions, six two-factor interactions, and four main effects, a total of $2^4 - 1 = 15$ sources of variation across conditions. In the fixed-effects model all of these are tested against the variation within the experimental combinations, pooled from all combinations. Testing 15 sources of variation instead of 1 will tend to cause more apparently significant F's at a given tabled significance level than would be expected under the null hypothesis. For any one of the significance tests, given that the null hypothesis is true, one expects 5 spurious rejections of the true null hypothesis out of 100 tests; thus, if an analyst keeps making F-tests within an experiment, he has more than a .05 probability of securing at least one statistically significant F, even if no actual effects exist. There are systematic ways to guard against this (see, for example, Pearson & Hartley 1954, pp. 39–40). At least, one should be suspicious of higher-order interactions that seem to be significant at or near the .05 level. Many an experimenter utilizing a complex design has worked extremely hard trying to interpret a spuriously significant high-order interaction and in the process has introduced his fantasies into the journal literature.

Studies in which researchers do not manipulate any variables are common and important in the social sciences. These include opinion surveys, studies of variables related to injury in automobile accidents, and studies of the Hiroshima and Nagasaki survivors. ANOVA proves useful in many such investigations. [*See* Campbell & Stanley 1963; Lindzey 1954; *see also* EXPERIMENTAL DESIGN, *article on* QUASI-EXPERIMENTAL DESIGN.]

"Nesting" and repeated measurements. Many studies and experiments in the social sciences involve one or more factors whose levels do not "cross" the levels of certain other factors. Usually these occur in conjunction with repeated measurements taken on the same individuals. For example, if one classification is school and another is teacher within school, where each teacher teaches two classes within her school with different methods, then teachers are said to be "nested" within schools. Schools can interact with methods (a given method may work relatively better in one school than in another) and teachers can interact with methods *within schools* (a method that works relatively better for one teacher does not necessarily produce better results for another teacher in the same school), but schools cannot interact with teachers, because teachers do not "cross" schools—that is, the same teacher does not teach at more than one school.

This does not mean that a given teacher might not be more effective in another school but merely that the experiment provides no evidence on that point. One could, somewhat inconveniently, devise an experiment in which teachers did cross schools, teaching some classes in one school and some in another. But an experimenter could not, for example, have boys cross from delinquency to nondelinquency and vice versa, because delinquency–nondelinquency is a personal rather than an environmental characteristic. (For further discussion of nested designs see Brownlee [1960] 1965, chapters 13 and 15.)

If the order of repeated measurements on each individual is randomized, as when each person undergoes several treatments successively in random order, there is more likelihood that ANOVA will be appropriate than when the order cannot be randomized, as occurs, for instance, when the learning process is studied over a series of trials. Complications occur also if the successive treatments have differential residual effects; taking a difficult test first may discourage one person in his work on the easier test that follows but make another person try harder. These residual effects seem likely to be of less importance if enough time occurs between successive treatment levels for some of the immediate influence of the treatment to dissipate. Human beings cannot have their memories erased like calculating machines, however, so repeated-measurement designs, although they usually reduce certain error terms because intraindividual variability tends to be less than interindividual variability, should not be used indiscriminately when analogous designs without repeated measurements are experimentally and financially feasible. (For further discussion see Winer 1962; Hays 1963, pp. 455–456; Campbell & Stanley 1963.)

Missing observations. For two factors with levels $s = 1, 2, \cdots, S$ and $t = 1, 2, \cdots, T$ in the experiment, such that the number of experimental units for the *st*th experimental combination is n_{st}, one usually designs the experiment so that $n_{st} = n$, a constant for all *st*. A few missing observations at the end of the experiment do not rule out a slightly adjusted simple ANOVA, if they were not caused differentially by the treatments. If, for example, one treatment was to administer a severe shock on several occasions, and the other was to give ice cream each time, it would not be surprising to find that fewer shocked than fed experimental subjects come for the final session. The outcome measure might be arithmetical-reasoning score; but if only the more shock-resistant subjects take the final test, comparison of the two treatments may be biased. There would be even more difficulty with, say, a male–female by shocked–fed design, because shocking might drive away more women than men (or vice versa).

When attrition is not caused differentially by the factors one may, for one-factor ANOVA, perform the usual analysis. For two or more factors, adjustments in the analysis are required to compensate for the few missing observations. (See Winer 1962, pp. 281–283, for example, for appropriate techniques.)

The power of the *F*-test. There are two kinds of errors that one can make when testing a null hypothesis against alternative hypotheses: one can reject the null hypothesis when in fact it is true, or one can fail to reject the null hypothesis when in fact it is false. Rejecting a true null hypothesis is called an "error of the first kind," or a "type I error." Failing to reject an untrue null hypothesis is called an "error of the second kind" or "type II error." The probability of making an error of the first kind is called the *size* of the significance test and is usually signified by α. The probability of making an error of the second kind is usually signified by β. The quantity $1 - \beta$ is called the *power* of the significance test.

If there is no limitation on the number of experimental units available one can fix both α and β at any desired levels prior to the experiment. To do this some prior estimate of σ^2 is required, and it is also necessary to state what nonnull difference among the factor-level means is considered large enough to be worth detecting. This latter requirement is quite troublesome in many social science experiments, because a good scale of value (such as dollars) is seldom available. For example, how much is a one-point difference between the mean of style 1 and style 2 on a reading-comprehension test worth educationally? Intelligence quotients and averages of college grades are quasi-utility scales, although one seldom thinks of them in just that way. How much is a real increase in IQ from 65 to 70 worth? How much more utility for the college does a grade-point average of 2.75 (where C = 2 and B = 3) have than a grade-point average of 2.50? (For further discussion of this topic see Chernoff & Moses 1959.)

In the hypothetical printing-styles example (Tables 1 and 5) it is known that $\sigma^2 = 1$ and that the population mean of style 1 is one point greater than the population means of styles 2 and 3, so with this information it is simple to enter Winer's Table B.11 (1962, p. 657) with, for example, $\alpha = .05$ and $\beta = .10$ and to find that for each of the three styles $P = 20$ experimental units are needed.

In actual experiments, where σ^2 and the $\sum_{s=1}^{S} P_s \alpha_s^2$ of interest to the experimenter are usually not known, the situation is more difficult (see Brownlee [1960] 1965, pp. 97–111; McNemar [1949] 1962, pp. 63–69; Hays 1963; and especially Scheffé 1959, pp. 38–42, 62–65, 437–455).

Alternatives to analysis of variance

If one conducted an experiment to determine how well ten-year-old boys add two-digit numbers at five equally spaced atmospheric temperatures, he could use the techniques of regression analysis to determine the equation for the line that best fits the five means (in the sense of minimum squared discrepancies). This line might be of the simple form $\alpha + \beta T$ (that is, straight with slope β and intercept α) or it might be based on some other function of T. [*See* Winer 1962 *for further discussion of trend analysis; see also* LINEAR HYPOTHESES, *article on* REGRESSION.]

The symmetrical two-tail t-test is a special case of the F-test; $t_{df}^2 = F_{1,df}$. Likewise, the unit normal deviate (z), called "critical ratio" in old statistics textbooks when used for testing significance, is a special case of F: $z^2 = F_{1,\infty}$. The F-distribution is closely related to the chi-square distribution. [*For further discussion of these relationships, see* DISTRIBUTIONS, STATISTICAL, *article on* SPECIAL CONTINUOUS DISTRIBUTIONS.]

For speed and computational ease, or when assumptions of ANOVA are violated so badly that results would seem dubious even if the data were transformed, there are other procedures available (see Winer 1962). Some of these procedures involve consecutive, untied ranks, whose means and variances are parameters dependent only on the number of ranks; an important example is the Kruskal–Wallis analysis of variance for ranks (Winer 1962, pp. 622–623). Other procedures employ the binomial expansion $(p+q)^n$ or the chi-square approximation to it for "sign tests." Still others involve dichotomizing the values for each treatment at the median and computing χ^2. Range tests may be used also. [*See* Winer 1962, p. 77; McNemar (1949) 1962, chapter 19. *Some of these procedures are discussed in* NONPARAMETRIC STATISTICS.]

When the normal assumption is reasonable, there are often available testing and other procedures that are competitive with the F-test. The latter has factotum utility, and it has optimal properties when the alternatives of interest are symmetrically arranged relative to the null hypothesis. But when the alternatives are asymmetrically arranged, or in other special circumstances, competitors to F procedures may be preferable. Particularly worthy of mention are Studentized range tests (see Scheffé 1959, pp. 82–83) and half-normal plotting (see Daniel 1959).

Special procedures are useful when the alternatives specify an ordering. For example, in the style-of-type example it might be known before the experiment that if there *is* any difference between the styles, style 1 is better than style 2, and style 2 better than style 3 (see Bartholomew 1961; Chacko 1963).

It is also important to mention here the desirability of examining residuals (observations less the estimates of their expectations) as a check on the model and as a source of suggestions toward useful modifications. [*See* STATISTICAL ANALYSIS, SPECIAL PROBLEMS OF, *article on* TRANSFORMATIONS OF DATA; *see also* Anscombe & Tukey 1963.

Often an observed value appears to be so distant from the other values that the experimenter is tempted to discard it before performing an ANOVA. For a discussion of procedures in such cases, see STATISTICAL ANALYSIS, SPECIAL PROBLEMS OF, *article on* OUTLIERS.]

Multivariate analysis of variance. The analysis of variance is multivariate in the independent variables (the factors) but univariate in the dependent variables (the outcome measures). S. N. Roy (for example, see Roy & Gnanadesikan 1959) and others have developed a multivariate analysis of variance (MANOVA), multivariate with respect to both independent and dependent variables, of which ANOVA is a special case. A few social scientists (for example, Rodwan 1964; Bock 1963) have used MANOVA, but as yet it has not been used widely by workers in these disciplines.

JULIAN C. STANLEY

BIBLIOGRAPHY

ANSCOMBE, F. J.; and TUKEY, JOHN W. 1963 The Examination and Analysis of Residuals. *Technometrics* 5:141–160.

BARTHOLOMEW, D. J. 1961 Ordered Tests in the Analysis of Variance. *Biometrika* 48:325–332.

BOCK, R. DARRELL 1963 Programming Univariate and Multivariate Analysis of Variance. *Technometrics* 5: 95–117.

BROWNLEE, KENNETH A. (1960) 1965 *Statistical Theory and Methodology in Science and Engineering.* 2d ed. New York: Wiley.

CAMPBELL, DONALD T.; and STANLEY, J. S. 1963 Experimental and Quasi-experimental Designs for Research on Teaching. Pages 171–246 in Nathaniel L. Gage (editor), *Handbook of Research on Teaching.* Chicago: Rand McNally. → Republished in 1966 as a separate monograph titled *Experimental and Quasi-experimental Designs for Research.*

CHACKO, V. J. 1963 Testing Homogeneity Against Ordered Alternatives. *Annals of Mathematical Statistics* 34:945–956.

CHERNOFF, HERMAN; and MOSES, LINCOLN E. 1959 *Elementary Decision Theory.* New York: Wiley.

COCHRAN, WILLIAM G. 1957 Analysis of Covariance: Its Nature and Uses. *Biometrics* 13:261–281.

CORNFIELD, JEROME; and TUKEY, JOHN W. 1956 Average Values of Mean Squares in Factorials. *Annals of Mathematical Statistics* 27:907–949.

DANIEL, CUTHBERT 1959 Use of Half-normal Plots in Interpreting Factorial Two-level Experiments. *Technometrics* 1:311–341.

FISHER, R. A. (1925) 1958 *Statistical Methods for Research Workers.* 13th ed. New York: Hafner. → Previous editions were also published by Oliver & Boyd.

FISHER, R. A. (1935) 1960 *The Design of Experiments.* 7th ed. London: Oliver & Boyd; New York: Hafner.

GLASS, GENE V. 1966 Testing Homogeneity of Variances. *American Educational Research Journal* 3:187–190.

[GOSSET, WILLIAM S.] (1908) 1943 The Probable Error of a Mean. Pages 11–34 in William S. Gosset, *"Student's" Collected Papers.* London: University College, Biometrika Office. → First published in Volume 6 of *Biometrika.*

HAYS, WILLIAM L. 1963 *Statistics for Psychologists.* New York: Holt.

LINDQUIST, EVERET F. 1953 *Design and Analysis of Experiments in Psychology and Education.* Boston: Houghton Mifflin.

LINDZEY, GARDNER (editor) (1954) 1959 *Handbook of Social Psychology.* 2 vols. Cambridge, Mass.: Addison-Wesley. → Volume 1: *Theory and Method.* Volume 2: *Special Fields and Applications.* A second edition, edited by Gardner Lindzey and Elliot Aronson, is in preparation.

LUBIN, ARDIE 1961 The Interpretation of Significant Interaction. *Educational and Psychological Measurement* 21:807–817.

MCLEAN, LESLIE D. 1967 Some Important Principles for the Use of Incomplete Designs in Behavioral Research. Chapter 4 in Julian C. Stanley (editor), *Improving Experimental Design and Statistical Analysis.* Chicago: Rand McNally.

MCNEMAR, QUINN (1949) 1962 *Psychological Statistics.* 3d ed. New York: Wiley.

MOOD, ALEXANDER M.; and GRAYBILL, FRANKLIN A. 1963 *Introduction to the Theory of Statistics.* 2d ed. New York: McGraw-Hill. → The first edition was published in 1950.

NELDER, J. A. 1954 The Interpretation of Negative Components of Variance. *Biometrika* 41:544–548.

PEARSON, EGON S.; and HARTLEY, H. O. (editors) (1954) 1966 *Biometrika Tables for Statisticians.* Volume 1. 3d ed. Cambridge Univ. Press. → A revision of *Tables for Statisticians and Biometricians* (1914), edited by Karl Pearson.

RAND CORPORATION 1955 *A Million Random Digits With 100,000 Normal Deviates.* Glencoe, Ill.: Free Press.

RODWAN, ALBERT S. 1964 An Empirical Validation of the Concept of Coherence. *Journal of Experimental Psychology* 68:167–170.

ROY, S. N.; and GNANADESIKAN, R. 1959 Some Contributions to ANOVA in One or More Dimensions: I and II. *Annals of Mathematical Statistics* 30:304–317, 318–340.

SAMPFORD, MICHAEL R. (editor) 1964 In Memoriam Ronald Aylmer Fisher, 1890–1962. *Biometrics* 20, no. 2:237–373.

SCHEFFÉ, HENRY 1959 *The Analysis of Variance.* New York: Wiley.

SMITH, H. FAIRFIELD 1957 Interpretation of Adjusted Treatment Means and Regressions in Analysis of Covariance. *Biometrics* 13:282–308.

STANLEY, JULIAN C. 1961 Studying Status vs. Manipulating Variables. Phi Delta Kappa Symposium on Educational Research, *Annual Phi Delta Kappa Symposium on Educational Research:* [*Proceedings*] 2:173–208. → Published in Bloomington, Indiana.

STANLEY, JULIAN C. 1965 Quasi-experimentation. *School Review* 73:197–205.

STANLEY, JULIAN C. 1966 A Common Class of Pseudo-experiments. *American Educational Research Journal* 3:79–87.

THOMPSON, W. A. JR. 1962 The Problem of Negative Estimates of Variance Components. *Annals of Mathematical Statistics* 33:273–289.

TUKEY, JOHN W. 1949 One Degree of Freedom for Non-additivity. *Biometrics* 5:232–242.

WINER, B. J. 1962 *Statistical Principles in Experimental Design.* New York: McGraw-Hill.

III
MULTIPLE COMPARISONS

Multiple comparison methods deal with a dilemma arising in statistical analysis: On the one hand, it would be unfortunate not to analyze the data thoroughly in all its aspects; on the other hand, performing several significance tests, or constructing several confidence intervals, for the same data compounds the error rates (significance levels), and it is often difficult to compute the over-all error probability.

Multiple comparison and related methods are designed to give simple over-all error probabilities for analyses that examine several aspects of the data simultaneously. For example, some simultaneous tests examine all differences between several treatment means.

Cronbach (1949, especially pp. 399–403) describes the problem of inflation of error probabilities in multiple comparisons. The solutions now available are, for the most part, of a later date (see Ryan 1959; Miller 1966). Miller's book provides a comprehensive treatment of the major aspects of multiple comparisons.

Normal means—confidence regions, tests

1. Simultaneous limits for several means. As a simple example of a situation in which multiple comparison methods might be applied, suppose that independent random samples are drawn from three normal populations with unknown means, μ_1, μ_2, μ_3, but *known* variances, $\sigma_1^2, \sigma_2^2, \sigma_3^2$. If only the first sample were available, a 99 per cent confidence interval could be constructed for μ_1:

$$(1)\quad \bar{X}_1 - 2.58\sigma_1/\sqrt{n_1} < \mu_1 < \bar{X}_1 + 2.58\sigma_1/\sqrt{n_1},$$

where $\bar{X}_1$ is the sample mean, and n_1 the size, of the first sample. In hypothetical repetitions of the procedure, the confidence interval covers, or includes, the true value of μ_1 99 per cent of the time in the long run. [*See* ESTIMATION, *article on* CONFIDENCE INTERVALS AND REGIONS.]

If all three samples are used, three statements like (1) can be made, successively replacing the subscript "1" by "2" and "3." The probability that all three statements *together* are true, however, is not .99 but .99 × .99 × .99, or .9703.

In a coordinate system with three axes marked μ_1, μ_2, and μ_3, the three intervals together define a 97 per cent (approximately) confidence box. This confidence box is shown in Figure 1. In order to obtain a 99 per cent confidence box—that is, to have all three statements hold simultaneously with probability .99—the confidence levels for the three individual statements must be increased. One method would be to make each individual confidence level equal to .9967, the cube root of .99.

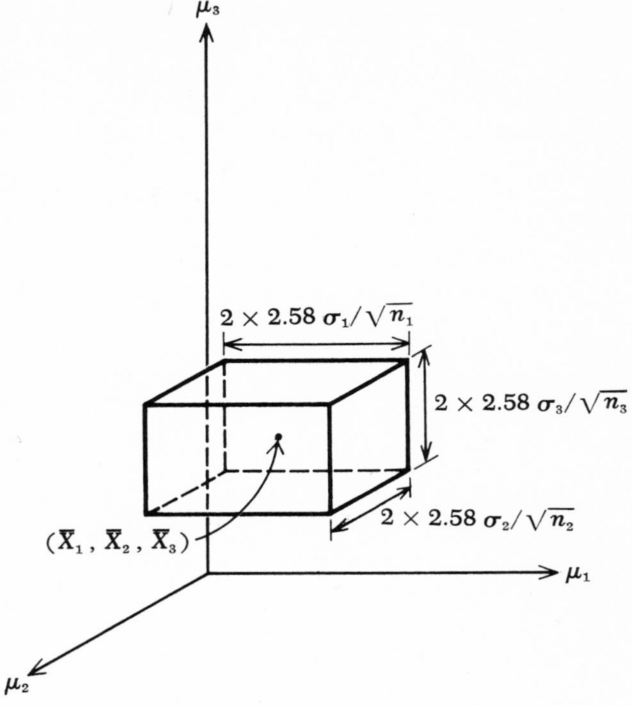

Figure 1 — A confidence box

The simple two-tail test of the null hypothesis (H_0) $\mu_1 = 0$ rejects it (at significance level .01) if the value 0 is not caught inside the confidence interval (1). It is natural to think of extending this test to the composite null hypothesis $\mu_1 = 0$ *and* $\mu_2 = 0$ *and* $\mu_3 = 0$ by rejecting the composite hypothesis if the point (0,0,0) is outside the confidence box corresponding to (1). The significance level of this procedure, however, is not .01 but 1 − .9703, almost .03. In order to reduce the significance level to .01, "2.58" in (1) must be replaced by a higher number. If this is done symmetrically, the significance level for each of the three individual statements like (1) must be .0033. In this argument any hypothetical values of the means, $\mu_1^*, \mu_2^*, \mu_3^*$, may be used in place of 0,0,0 to specify the null hypothesis; the point $(\mu_1^*, \mu_2^*, \mu_3^*)$ then takes the place of (0,0,0).

The same principles can be applied just as easily to the case where the three variances are not known but are estimated from the respective samples, in which case 1 per cent points of Student's *t*-distribution take the place of 2.58. Of course, any other significance levels may also be used instead of 1 per cent.

Pooled estimate of variance. The problem considered so far is atypically simple because the three intervals are statistically *independent*, so that probabilities can simply be multiplied. This is no longer true if the variances are unknown but are assumed to be equal and are estimated by a single *pooled* estimate of variance, $\hat{\sigma}^2$, which is the sum of the three within-sample sums of squares divided by $n_1 + n_2 + n_3 - 3$. This is equal to the mean square used in the denominator of an analysis-of-variance F [*see* LINEAR HYPOTHESES, *article on* ANALYSIS OF VARIANCE]. The conditions

$$\bar{X}_i - M\hat{\sigma}/\sqrt{n_i} < \mu_i < \bar{X}_i + M\hat{\sigma}/\sqrt{n_i}, \qquad i = 1,2,3$$

(where M is a constant to be chosen), use the same $\hat{\sigma}$ and hence are *not* statistically independent. Thus, the probability that all three hold simultaneously is not the product of the three separate probabilities, although this is still a surprisingly good approximation, adequate for most purposes.

Critical values, M_α, have, however, been computed for $\alpha = .05$ and $.01$ and for any number of degrees of freedom $(n_1 + n_2 + n_3 - 3)$ of $\hat{\sigma}^2$. If M_α is substituted for M in the three intervals, the probability that all three conditions simultaneously hold is $1 - \alpha$ (Tukey 1953).

Exactly the same principles described for the problem of estimating, or testing, three population means also apply to k means. A table providing critical values M_α for $k = 2, 3, \cdots, 10$ and for various numbers of degrees of freedom, $N - k$, has been computed by Pillai and Ramachandran (1954). Part of the table is reproduced in Miller (1966). The square of M_α was tabulated earlier by Nair (1948*a*) for use in another context (see Section 7, below). This table is reproduced in Pearson and Hartley ([1954] 1966, table 19).

Notation. In the following exposition, "$\bar{X}_i$" and "μ_i" represent sample and population means, respectively ($i = 1, \cdots, k$), "σ^2" the population variance, generally assumed to be common to all k populations, "$\hat{\sigma}^2$" the pooled sample estimate of σ^2, and "*SE*" the estimated standard error of a statistic (*SE* will depend on $\hat{\sigma}^2$, on the particular statistic, and on the sample sizes involved). The symbol "$\sum$" always denotes summation over i, from 1 to k, unless otherwise specified; N denotes $\sum n_i$, the total sample size, and "*ddf*" stands for "denominator degrees of freedom," the degrees of freedom of $\hat{\sigma}^2$.

2. Treatments versus control (Dunnett). Many studies are concerned with the *difference* between means rather than with the means themselves. For example, sample 1 may consist of *controls* (that is, observations taken under standard conditions) to be used for comparison with samples $2, 3, \cdots, k$ (taken under different treatments or nonstandard conditions), for the purpose of estimating the treatment effects, $\mu_2 - \mu_1, \cdots, \mu_k - \mu_1$. For $k = 3, 4, \cdots, 10$, for any number of denominator degrees of freedom, $N - k$, greater than 4, and for $\alpha = .05$ and $.01$, Dunnett (1955; also in Miller 1966) has tabulated critical values D_α such that with probability approximately equal to $1 - \alpha$, all $k - 1$ statements

$$|(\bar{X}_i - \bar{X}_1) - (\mu_i - \mu_1)| < D_\alpha SE, \qquad i = 2, 3, \cdots, k,$$

will be simultaneously true—that is, all $k - 1$ effects $\mu_i - \mu_1$ will be covered by confidence intervals centered at $\bar{X}_i - \bar{X}_1$ with half-lengths $D_\alpha SE$, where $SE = \sqrt{(1/n_i) + (1/n_1)}\,\hat{\sigma}$.

The over-all probability is exactly $1 - \alpha$ if all k sample sizes are equal. It is not the product of $k - 1$ probabilities (obtained from Student's *t*-distribution) of the separate confidence statements, because these are not statistically independent; dependence comes not only from the common estimator of σ in all statements but also from the correlation ($\rho \cong .5$ for sample sizes roughly the same) between any two differences $\bar{X}_i - \bar{X}_1$ with $\bar{X}_1$ in common. Surprisingly enough, the product rule gives a close approximation just the same.

Viewed as restrictions on the point (μ_1, μ_2, μ_3) in three-space, the two (pairs of) inequalities for $k = 3$ define a confidence region that is the intersection of the slab bounded by two parallel planes, $\mu_2 - \mu_1 = \bar{X}_2 - \bar{X}_1 \pm D_\alpha SE$, and another slab at 45° to the first slab. This is illustrated in Figure 2, where for simplicity all n_i are assumed to be equal. The region is a prism that is infinite in length, is parallel to the 45° line $\mu_1 = \mu_2 = \mu_3$, and has a rhombus as its cross section.

Dunnett's significance test rejects the null hypothesis, H_0: $\mu_2 = \cdots = \mu_k = \mu_1$, in favor of the alternative hypothesis that one or more of the μ_i differ from μ_1 if the $k - 1$ confidence intervals do not all contain the value 0 or, equivalently, if

$$(2) \qquad |t_{i1}| = |\bar{X}_i - \bar{X}_1|/SE \geqslant D_\alpha$$

for any i $(i = 2, \cdots, k)$. If the null hypothesis is of the less trivial form $\mu_i - \mu_1 = d_{i1}$, where the d_{i1} are any specified constants, then d_{i1} is subtracted from the differences of sample means in the numerators of t_{i1}.

The probability of rejecting H_0 if it is true, called the *error rate experimentwise*, is exactly the stated α if all sample sizes are equal, and is approximately α for unequal n_i, provided the inequality is not gross. Dunnett (1955) showed that a design using equal n_i, $i = 2, \cdots, k$, but with n_1 larger in about the proportion $\sqrt{k-1} : 1$ is most efficient. Unfortunately this leads to true error rates exceeding the stated α if Dunnett's table is used, and it is then safer to substitute a Bonferroni *t*-statistic for Dunnett's D_α if k is as big as 6 or 10 (for Bonferroni *t*,

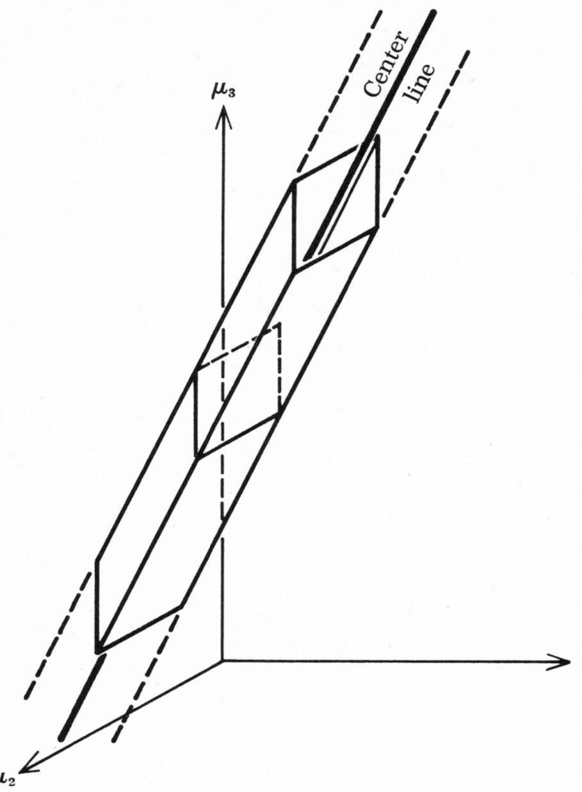

Figure 2 — Confidence region for Dunnett method

see Section 14, below; see also Miller 1966, table 2).

Simultaneous one-tail tests are of the same form as (2), above, except that the absolute-value signs are removed and an appropriate smaller critical value, D_α, also tabulated in Dunnett (1955), is used. The corresponding confidence intervals are one-sided, extending to infinity on the other side.

3. All differences—Tukey method. In order to compare several means with one another rather than only with a single control, a method of Tukey's (1953) is suitable. It provides simultaneous confidence intervals (or significance tests, if desired) for all $\binom{k}{2} = \frac{1}{2}k(k-1)$ differences, $\mu_i - \mu_j$, among k means.

A constant, T_α, is chosen so that the probability is at least $1-\alpha$ that all $\binom{k}{2}$ statements

$$|(\bar{X}_i - \bar{X}_j) - (\mu_i - \mu_j)| < T_\alpha SE,$$

or, equivalently,

$$|t_{ij}| = |(\bar{X}_i - \bar{X}_j) - (\mu_i - \mu_j)|/SE < T_\alpha,$$

will be simultaneously true. Here SE is equal to $\sqrt{(1/n_i) + (1/n_j)}\,\hat{\sigma}$. The probability is exactly $1-\alpha$ if the sample sizes are equal (Tukey 1953; Kurtz 1956; Kramer 1956).

Simultaneous confidence intervals for all the differences, $\mu_i - \mu_j$, are centered at $\bar{X}_i - \bar{X}_j$ with half-lengths $T_\alpha SE$. In a significance test of the null hypothesis, H_0, that the differences, $\mu_i - \mu_j$, have any specified (mutually consistent) values, d_{ij} (often 0), one substitutes d_{ij} for $\mu_i - \mu_j$ in the t-ratios and rejects H_0 if the largest ratio is not less than T_α.

The constant, T_α, is $R_\alpha/\sqrt{2} = .707R_\alpha$, where R_α is the upper α-point in the distribution of the Studentized range. Table 29 of Pearson and Hartley ([1954] 1966) shows R_α for $\alpha = .1$, .05, and .01, for values of k up to 20, and for any number of *ddf*. Briefer tables are found in Vianelli (1959) and in a number of textbooks—for example, Winer (1962). More extensive tables prepared by Harter (1960) can also be found in Miller (1966).

Geometrically, Tukey's $(1-\alpha)$-confidence region can be obtained, for $k=3$, by widening and thickening Dunnett's prism (Figure 2) in the proportion $T_\alpha : D_\alpha$ and then removing a pair of triangular prisms by intersection with a third slab. The cross section is hexagonal.

Tukey's multiple comparisons are frequently used after an F-test rejects H_0 but may also be used in place of F.

Simplified multiple t-tests. Simplified multiple t-tests, which were developed by Tukey, use the sum of sample ranges in place of σ and a critical value, T_α, adjusted accordingly. (See Kurtz et al. 1965.)

4. One outlying mean (slippage). In comparing k populations it may be desirable to find out whether one of them (which one is not specified in advance) is outstanding (has "slipped") relative to the others. Then using k independent treatment samples one may examine the differences, $\bar{X}_i - \bar{X}$, where $\bar{X} = \sum_{i=1}^{k}\sum_{j=1}^{n_i} X_{ij}/N = \sum n_i \bar{X}_i/N$. Let $\mu = \sum n_i \mu_i/N$.

Halperin provided critical values H_α such that with probability approximately $1-\alpha$,

$$|(\bar{X}_i - \bar{X}) - (\mu_i - \mu)| < H_\alpha \sqrt{\frac{k}{k-1}\left(\frac{1}{n_i} - \frac{1}{N}\right)}\,\hat{\sigma}$$

simultaneously for $i = 1, \cdots, k$ (Halperin et al. 1955). The probability is exactly $1-\alpha$ in the case of equal n_i. This provides two-sided tests for the null hypothesis that all $\mu_i = \mu$ and simultaneous confidence intervals for all the $\mu_i - \mu$, in the usual way. In case the table is not at hand, a good approximation to the right-hand side of the inequality is (upper $(\alpha/2k)$-point of Student's t) $\times$ $\sqrt{(1/n_i) - (1/N)}\,\hat{\sigma}$.

Critical values for the corresponding one-sided test, to ascertain whether one of the means has slipped in a specified direction (for example, whether it has slipped down), were first computed by Nair (1952). David (1962*a*; 1962*b*) provides improved tables. A refinement of Nair's test and of Halperin's is presented by Quesenberry and David (1961). In Pearson and Hartley ([1954] 1966), tables 26*a* and 26*b* (and the explanation on p. 51) pertain to these methods, whereas table 26 is Nair's statistic.

5. Contrasts—Scheffé method. A *contrast* in k population means is a linear combination, $\sum c_i \mu_i$, with coefficients adding up to zero, $\sum c_i = 0$. This is always equal to a multiple of the difference between weighted averages of two sets of means—that is, constant $\times (\sum_h a_h \mu_h - \sum_j b_j \mu_j)$ with summations running over two subsets of the subscripts $(1, \cdots, k)$ having no subscript in common and with $\sum_h a_h = 1, \sum_j b_j = 1$. The simple differences, $\mu_h - \mu_j$, are special contrasts. Some other examples include contrasts representing a difference between two *groups* of means (for example, $\frac{1}{3}[\mu_2 + \mu_3 + \mu_5] - \frac{1}{2}[\mu_1 + \mu_4]$) or slippage of one mean (for example, $\mu_2 - \bar{\mu}$, since this is equal to $\{[k-1]/k\}\mu_2 - [1/k][\mu_1 + \mu_3 + \mu_4 + \cdots + \mu_k]$), or trend (for example, $-3\mu_1 - \mu_2 + \mu_3 + 3\mu_4$).

In an exploratory study to compare k means when little is known to suggest a specific pattern of differences in advance, any and all striking contrasts revealed by the data will be of interest. Also, when looking for slippage or simple differences one may wish to take account of some other, unanticipated, pattern displayed by the data.

Any of the systems of multiple comparisons discussed in sections 1–4 can be adapted to obtain tests, or simultaneous intervals, for all contrasts. For example, the $k-1$ simultaneous conditions $|(\bar{X}_i - \bar{X}_1) - (\mu_i - \mu_1)| < D_\alpha \sqrt{(1/n_i) + (1/n_1)}\ \hat{\sigma}$, where D_α represents the critical value of the Dunnett statistic as defined in Section 2, above, imply that every contrast, $\sum c_i \mu_i$, falls into an interval of half-length $D_\alpha \sum_2^k (|c_i| \sqrt{2/n_i})\ \hat{\sigma}$, centered at $\sum c_i \bar{X}_i$, in the case of equal sample sizes.

The following method, developed by Scheffé, however, is more efficient for all-contrasts analyses, because it yields shorter intervals for most contrasts. Scheffé proved that

$$\sqrt{(k-1)F} = \max [\textstyle\sum c_i(\bar{X}_i - \mu_i)/SE],$$

the largest of all the (infinitely many) Studentized contrasts, where F is the analysis-of-variance F-ratio for testing equality of all the μ_i, and where $SE = \sqrt{\sum (c_i^2/n_i)}\ \hat{\sigma}$. Thus,

$$\begin{aligned} 1 - \alpha &= Pr\{F < F_\alpha\} \\ &= Pr\{\textit{all}\text{ Studentized contrasts} < \sqrt{(k-1)F_\alpha}\} \\ &= Pr\left\{\frac{\sum c_i(\bar{X}_i - \mu_i)}{SE} < \sqrt{(k-1)F_\alpha}\right. \\ &\qquad\qquad \left.\text{for } \textit{all} \text{ sets of } c_i \text{ with } \textstyle\sum c_i = 0\right\}. \end{aligned}$$

Simultaneous confidence intervals for all contrasts, $\sum c_i \mu_i$, are centered at $\sum c_i \bar{X}_i$ and have half-lengths $SE\sqrt{(k-1)F_\alpha}$. The confidence level is *exactly* the stated $1-\alpha$, regardless of whether sample sizes are equal.

For $k = 3$, any particular interval can be depicted in (μ_1, μ_2, μ_3)-space by a pair of parallel planes equidistant from the line given by $\mu_1 - \bar{X}_1 = \mu_2 - \bar{X}_2 = \mu_3 - \bar{X}_3$ through the point $(\bar{X}_1, \bar{X}_2, \bar{X}_3)$. Together these planes constitute all the tangent planes of the cylinder (in the "variables" μ_1, μ_2, μ_3),

$$\textstyle\sum n_i[(\bar{X}_i - \bar{X}) - (\mu_i - \mu)]^2 = (3-1)\hat{\sigma}^2 F_\alpha,$$

where F_α has degrees of freedom $3-1$ and $n-3$. This cylinder, like the prism of Figure 2, is infinite in length and equally inclined to the coordinate axes. (As in the case of the regions for Dunnett's and Tukey's procedures, the addition of the same constant to each of the coordinates X_1, X_2, X_3 of a point on the surface will move this point along the surface.) See Figure 3.

Significance test. A value of $F \geqslant F_\alpha$ implies $\sum c_i(\bar{X}_i - \mu_i) \geqslant SE\sqrt{(k-1)F_\alpha}$ for at least one contrast (namely, at least for the maximum Studentized contrast). Scheffé's multiple comparison test declares $\sum c_i \bar{X}_i$ to be statistically significant—that is, $\sum c_i \mu_i$ different from zero—for all those con-

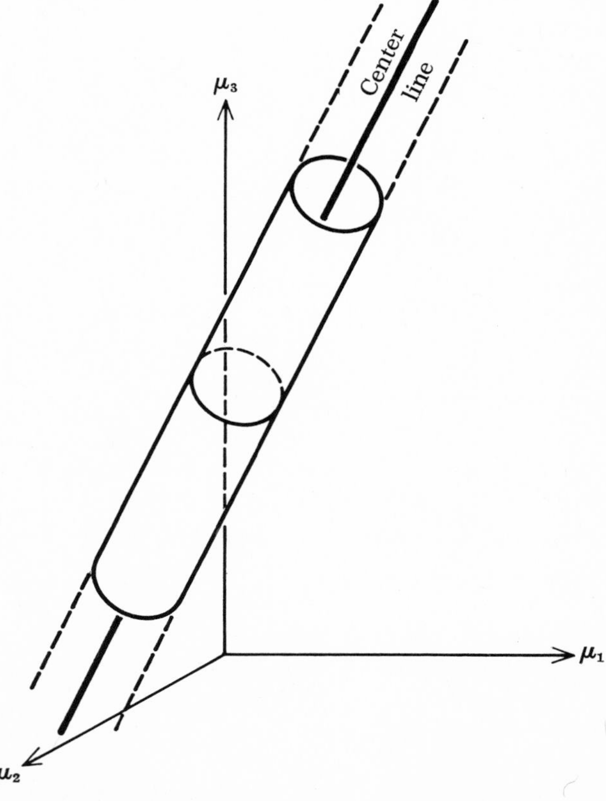

Figure 3 — Confidence region for all contrasts (Scheffé)

trasts for which the inequality is true. Thus, one may test every contrast of interest, or every contrast that looks promising, and incur a risk of just α of falsely declaring any $\sum c_i \mu_i$ whatsoever to be different from zero; in other words, the probability of making no false statement of the form $\sum c_i \mu_i \neq 0$ is $1 - \alpha$, the probability of making one or more such statements is α. Of course, the Scheffé approach gives a larger confidence interval (or decreased power) than the analogous procedure if only a single contrast is of interest.

General linear combinations. Simultaneous confidence intervals, or tests, can also be obtained for all possible linear combinations, $\sum c_i \mu_i$, with the restriction $\sum c_i = 0$ lifted. Then Scheffé's confidence and significance statements for contrasts remain applicable, except that $(k-1)F_\alpha$ is changed to kF_α and the numerator degrees of freedom of F are changed from $k-1$ to k. (See Miller 1966, chapter 2, sec. 2).

A confidence region for all (standardized) linear combinations consists of the ellipsoid in the k-dimensional space with axes labeled $\mu_1, \mu_2, \cdots, \mu_k$, $\sum n_i(\bar{X}_i - \mu_i)^2 < kF_\alpha \hat{\sigma}^2$. For $k = 3$, any particular interval can be depicted in (μ_1, μ_2, μ_3)-space by a pair of parallel planes equidistant from the point $(\bar{X}_1, \bar{X}_2, \bar{X}_3)$. Together these planes constitute all the tangent planes of the confidence ellipsoid (in the "variables" μ_1, μ_2, μ_3).

Tukey (1953) and Miller (1966) also discuss the generalization of the application of intervals based on the Studentized range (referred to in Section 3, above) to take care of all linear combinations. Simultaneous intervals for all linear combinations can also be based on the Studentized maximum modulus (Section 1); half-lengths become $M_\alpha \sqrt{1/n}\hat{\sigma} \cdot \sum |c_i|$ (Tukey 1953).

All of these methods dealing with contrasts and general linear combinations are described in Miller (1966).

Further discussion of normal populations

6. Newman–Keuls and Duncan procedures. The Newman–Keuls procedure is a multiple comparison test for all differences. It does not provide a confidence region. The sample means are arranged and renumbered in order of magnitude, so that $\bar{X}_1 < \bar{X}_2 < \cdots < \bar{X}_k$. The first step is the same as Tukey's test; the null hypothesis is rejected or accepted according as $\bar{X}_k - \bar{X}_1$, the range of the sample means, is $\geqslant$ or $< T_{\alpha;k} SE$, where $T_{\alpha;k}$ is the upper α-point of Tukey's statistic for k means and $N-k$ *ddf*.

Accepting H_0 means that there is not enough evidence to establish differences between any of the population means, and the analysis is complete (all k means are then called "homogeneous"). On the other hand, if the null hypothesis is rejected, so that μ_k, the population mean corresponding to the largest sample mean, is declared to be different from μ_1, the population mean corresponding to the smallest sample mean, the next step is to test $\bar{X}_{k-1} - \bar{X}_1$ and $\bar{X}_k - \bar{X}_2$ similarly, but with $T_{\alpha;k-1}$ in place of $T_{\alpha;k}$ (the original pooled variance estimator $\hat{\sigma}^2$ and $N-k$ *ddf* are used throughout). A subrange of means that is not found statistically significant is called homogeneous. As long as a subrange is statistically significant, the two subranges obtained by removing in one case its largest and in the other case its smallest $\bar{X}_i$ are tested, using a critical value $T_{\alpha;h}$, where h is only the number of means left in the new subranges—but testing is limited by the rule that every subrange contained in a homogeneous range of means is not tested but is automatically declared to be homogeneous. The result of the whole procedure is to group the means into homogeneous sets, which may also be represented diagrammatically by connecting lines, as in the example presented in Section 10, below.

Critics of the Newman–Keuls method object that the error probabilities, such as that of falsely declaring $\mu_2 \neq \mu_5$, are not even known in this test; its supporters, however, argue that power should not be wasted by judging subranges by the same stringent criterion used for the full range of all k sample means.

Duncan (1955) goes a step further, arguing that even $T_{\alpha;h}$ is too stringent a criterion because the $\frac{1}{2}h(h-1)$ differences between h means have only $h-1$ degrees of freedom. He concludes that $T_{\gamma;h}$ should be used instead, where $1-\gamma = (1-\alpha)^{h-1}$. This further increases the power—and the effective type I error probability. For a study of error rates of Tukey, Newman–Keuls, Duncan, and Student tests, see Harter (1957).

7. General Model I design. The F-test in the one-way analysis of variance and the multiple comparison methods already discussed are based on the fact that *ddf* times $\hat{\sigma}^2/\sigma^2$ has a chi-square distribution and is independent of the sample means. This condition is also satisfied by the residual variance used in randomized blocks, factorial designs, Latin squares, and all Model I designs. Therefore, all these designs permit the use of the methods, and tables, of sections 1–6, to compare the means defined by any one factor, provided that these are independent.

In certain instances of nonparametric multiple comparisons and in certain instances of multiple comparisons of interactions in balanced factorial designs, where the (adjusted or transformed) observations are not independent but equicorrelated, the multiple comparison methods of sections 2–6 still apply: The use of the adjusted error variance, $(1-\rho)\hat{\sigma}^2$, to compute standard errors fully compensates for the effect of equal correlations (see Tukey 1953; Scheffé 1953; Miller 1966, pp. 41–42, 46–47). Scheffé's method can also be adapted for use with unequal correlations (see Miller 1966, p. 53).

When several factors, and perhaps some interactions, are t-tested in the same experiment, the question arises whether extra adjustment should not be made for the resulting additional compounding of error probabilities. One method open to an experimenter willing to sacrifice power for strict experimentwise control of type I error is the conservative one of using error rates per t-test of α/(number of t-tests contemplated), that is, using Bonferroni t-statistics (see Section 14). For experimentwise control of error rates in the special case of a 2^r factorial design, Nair (1948a) has tabulated percentage points of the largest of r independent χ^2's with one degree of freedom, divided by an independent variance estimator (Pearson & Hartley [1954] 1966, table 19). The statistic is equal to the square of the Studentized maximum modulus introduced in Section 1.

8. An example—juxtaposition of methods. Three competing theories about how hostility evoked in people by willfully imposed frustration may be diminished led Rothaus and Worchel (1964) to goad 192 experimental subjects into hostility by unfair administration of a test of coordination and then to apply the following "treatments" to four groups, each composed of 48 subjects: (1) no treatment (control); (2) fair readministration of the test, seemingly as a result of a grievance procedure (instrumental communication); (3) an opportunity for verbal expression of hostility (catharsis); (4) conversation to the effect that the test was unfair and the result therefore not indicative of failure on the subjects' part (ego support). After treatment all subjects were given another—fair—test of coordination. Each treatment group was subdivided into three subgroups, a different experimenter working with each subgroup. All subjects had been given Behavioral Items for Hostility Scales (BIHS) three weeks before the experiment.

Table 1 — Analysis of variance of hostility scores

Source	*df*	*Mean square*	*F-ratio*
4 treatments	3	369.77	3.38*
3 subgroups	2	151.31	1.38
2 sexes	1	41.14	0.38
2 BIHS levels	1	2.68	0.02
All the interactions, none of them statistically significant	40		
4 replications (nested)	144	$109.54 = \hat{\sigma}^2$	

* Denotes statistical significance at the 5 per cent level.

The experimental plan was factorial: 4 treatments $\times$ 3 subgroups $\times$ 2 sexes $\times$ 2 BIHS score groups (high versus low) $\times$ 4 replications. The study variable, X, was hostility measured on the Social Sensitivity Scale at the end of the experiment.

The sample means (unordered) for the four treatment groups were $\bar{x}_1 = 47.08$, $\bar{x}_2 = 42.00$, $\bar{x}_3 = 48.53$, $\bar{x}_4 = 45.40$.

In fact, the numbers in Table 1 reflect an analysis of covariance. The mean squares shown are adjusted mean squares, the sample means are adjusted means, and $\hat{\sigma}^2$ has 143 df. But for the sake of simplicity of interpretation the data will be treated as if they had come from a $4 \times 3 \times 2 \times 2$ factorial analysis of variance. The estimated standard error for differences between two means, SE, is $\sqrt{[(1/48) + (1/48)] \times 109.54} = 2.136$.

Dunnett comparisons. The Dunnett method, with $\alpha = .05$, would be applied to the data of the experiment, as analyzed in Table 2. As indicated in Table 2, the one-tail test in the direction of the theory (H_1) under study declares μ_2 to be less than μ_1. Thus, the conclusion, if the one-sided Dunnett test and the 5 per cent significance level are adopted, is that instrumental communication reduces hostility but that the evidence does not confirm any reduction due to ego support or catharsis. If the two-tail test had been chosen, allowing for

Table 2 — Dunnett comparisons of control with three treatments, $\alpha = .05$

			DUNNETT METHOD: TWO-SIDED		*DUNNETT METHOD: ONE-SIDED*	
Pair	$\bar{x}_i - \bar{x}_j$	*t-ratio:* $\frac{\bar{x}_i - \bar{x}_j}{2.136}$	*Test:* $D_\alpha = 2.40$	*Confidence interval (half-length =* $2.136D_\alpha = 5.13$)	*Test:* $D_\alpha = 2.08$	*Confidence interval (lower length =* $2.136D_\alpha = 4.44$)
(1)–(2)	5.08	2.38	(near significance)	(−0.05,10.21)	*	(0.64,∞)
(1)–(3)	−1.45	−0.68	—	(−6.58,3.68)	—	(−5.89,∞)
(1)–(4)	1.68	0.79	—	(−3.45,6.81)	—	(−2.76,∞)

* Statistically significant at the 5 per cent level; all other comparisons do not reach statistical significance at the 5 per cent level.

Table 3 — All pairs, by Tukey and by Scheffé method, $\alpha = .05$

		TUKEY METHOD			SCHEFFÉ METHOD	
Pair	$\bar{x}_i - \bar{x}_j$	t-ratio: $\frac{\bar{x}_i - \bar{x}_j}{2.136}$	Test: $T_\alpha = 2.60$	Confidence interval (half-length = $2.136T_\alpha = 5.55$)	Test: $\sqrt{3F_\alpha} = 2.80$	Confidence interval (half-length = $2.136\sqrt{3F_\alpha} = 5.98$)
(1)–(2)	5.08	2.38	—	(−0.47,10.63)	—	(−0.90,11.06)
(1)–(3)	−1.45	−0.68	—	(−7.00,4.10)	—	(−7.43,4.53)
(1)–(4)	1.68	0.79	—	(−3.87,7.23)	—	(−4.30,7.66)
(2)–(3)	−6.53	−3.06	*	(−12.08,−0.98)	*	(−12.51,−0.55)
(2)–(4)	−3.40	−1.59	—	(−8.95,2.15)	—	(−9.38,2.58)
(3)–(4)	3.13	1.47	—	(−2.42,8.68)	—	(−2.85,9.11)

* Statistically significant at the 5 per cent level; all other pairs do not reach statistical significance at the 5 per cent level.

a possible *increase* in hostility due to treatment, the conclusion would be that there is insufficient evidence to reject.

All pairs—Tukey and Scheffé methods. A comparison of all possible pairs of means by the methods of Tukey and Scheffé is shown in Table 3. The tests of Tukey and Scheffé in this case both discount $\bar{x}_1 - \bar{x}_3$ but declare $\bar{x}_2 - \bar{x}_3$ "significant." The conclusion is that instrumental communication leaves the mean hostility of frustrated subjects lower than ego support does, but no other difference is established; specifically, neither test would conclude that instrumental communication actually reduces hostility as compared with no treatment or that ego support increases (or reduces) it.

In addition to the simple differences, the data suggest testing a contrast related to the alternate hypothesis $\mu_2 < \mu_4 < \mu_1 < \mu_3$, for example, the contrast $-3\mu_2 - \mu_4 + \mu_1 + 3\mu_3$. (It is legitimate, for these procedures, to choose such a contrast after inspecting the data.) For the present example, $-3\bar{x}_2 - \bar{x}_4 + \bar{x}_1 + 3\bar{x}_3 = 21.27$; the *SE* for a Scheffé test is $\sqrt{(3^2 + 1^2 + 1^2 + 3^2)/48}\hat{\sigma} = \sqrt{10} \times 2.136 = 6.755$, and $t = 21.27/6.755 = 3.15$, statistically significant at the 5 per cent level $(3.15 > 2.80)$. The conclusion is that $\mu_2 \leqslant \mu_4 \leqslant \mu_1 \leqslant \mu_3$ with at least one strict inequality holding. A Scheffé 95 per cent confidence interval for $-3\mu_2 - \mu_4 + \mu_1 + 3\mu_3$ is (1.36, 40.18). A Tukey test would not find this contrast statistically significant. For this analysis 2.136 is multiplied by $\frac{1}{2}(|-3| + |-1| + |1| + |3|) = 4$, instead of by $\sqrt{10}$, yielding 8.544. Thus, in this case $t = 21.27/8.544 = 2.49$, which is less than 2.60, and a confidence interval is (−0.94, +43.48).

The *SE* for individual $\bar{x}_i$, also used in slippage statistics, is $\sqrt{(1/48)\,\hat{\sigma}^2} = 2.136/\sqrt{2} = 1.510$. For $k = 4$, $M_{.05} = 2.50$, and simultaneous confidence intervals for the four μ_i are centered at the $\bar{x}_i$ and have half-lengths $2.50 \times 1.51 = 3.78$.

The 5 per cent critical value tabulated by Halperin et al. for two-sided slippage tests is 2.23; thus $(\bar{x}_2 - \bar{x})/1.51 = 2.48$ is statistically significant, whereas the other three *t*-ratios for slippage are not. The conclusion of this test would be that mean hostility after instrumental communication is low compared with that after other treatments; no other treatment can be singled out as leaving hostility either low or high compared with that after other treatments.

An example of Newman–Keuls and Duncan tests is given in Section 10, below.

Other multiple comparison methods

9. Nonparametric multiple comparisons. The multiple comparison approach has been articulated with nonparametric (or distribution-free) methods in several ways [*for background see* NONPARAMETRIC STATISTICS].

For example, one of the simplest nonparametric tests is the sign test. Suppose that an experiment concerning techniques for teaching reading deals with school classes and that each class is divided in half at random. One half is taught by method 1, the other by method 2, the methods being allocated at random. Suppose further that improvement in average score on a reading test after two months is the basic observation but that one chooses to consider only whether the pupils taught by method 1 gain more than the pupils taught by method 2, or vice versa, and not the magnitude of the difference. If C is the number of classes for which the pupils taught with method 1 have a larger average gain than those taught with method 2, then the (two-sided) sign test rejects the null hypothesis of equal method effect when the absolute value of C is larger than a critical value. The critical value comes simply from a symmetrical binomial distribution.

Suppose now that there are k teaching methods, where k might be 3 or 4, and the classes are each divided at random into k groups and assigned to methods. Let C_{ij} $(i \neq j)$ be the number of classes for which the average gain in reading-test score for the group taught by method i is greater than that for the group taught by method j. Each C_{ij} taken separately has (under the null hypothesis that the corresponding two methods are equally effective) a symmetric binomial distribution which is approximated asymptotically by $\frac{1}{2}n + z\frac{1}{2}\sqrt{n} + \frac{1}{2}$, where n is the number of classes, z is a standard normal variable, and $\frac{1}{2}$ is a continuity correction. But to test for the equality of all k methods, the largest $|C_{ij}|$ should be used. The critical values of this statistic may be approximated by $T_\alpha\frac{1}{2}\sqrt{n} + \frac{1}{2}$, where T_α is the upper α point for Tukey's statistic with k groups and $ddf = \infty$.

The same procedure is feasible for other two-sample test statistics—for example, rank sums. An analogous method works for comparing $k-1$ treatments with a control; in the teaching-method experiment, if method 1 were the control, this would mean using as the test statistic the maximum over $j \neq 1$ of $|C_{1j}|$ (or of C_{1j} in the one-sided case). For a discussion of this material, see Steel (1959).

Joint nonparametric confidence intervals may sometimes be obtained in a similar way. Given a confidence interval estimation procedure related to any two-sample test statistic with critical value S_α (see Moses 1953; 1965), the same procedure with S_α replaced by its multiple comparison analogue C_α yields confidence intervals with a joint confidence level of $1-\alpha$.

A second class of nonparametric multiple comparison tests arises by analogy with normal theory analysis of variance for the one-way classification and other simple designs [*see* LINEAR HYPOTHESES, *article on* ANALYSIS OF VARIANCE]. The procedures start by transforming the observations into ranks or other kinds of simplified scores (except that the so-called permutation tests leave the observations unaltered). The analysis is conditional on the totality of scores and uses as its null distribution that obtained from random allocations of the observed scores to treatments. The test statistic may be the ordinary F-ratio on the scores, but modified so that the denominator is the exact over-all variance of the given scores. This statistic's null distribution is approximately F, with $k-1$ and ∞ as degrees of freedom (where k is the number of treatments), or, equivalently, $k-1$ times the F-test statistic has as approximate null distribution the chi-square distribution with $k-1$ degrees of freedom. Similar adaptations hold for the Tukey test statistic and others. The approach may also be extended to randomized block designs; in another direction, the approach may be extended to compare dispersion, rather than location. Discussions of this material are given by Nemenyi (1963) and Miller (1966, chapter 2, sec. 1.4, and chapter 4, sec. 7.5).

A difficulty with these test procedures is that confidence sets cannot generally be obtained in a straightforward way.

A third nonparametric approach to multiple comparisons is described by Walsh (1965, pp. 535–536). The basic notion applies when there are a number of observations for each treatment or treatment combination. Such a set of observations is divided into several subsets; the average of each subset is taken. These averages are then treated by normal theory procedures of the kind discussed earlier.

For convenient reference, a few 5 per cent and 1 per cent critical points of multiple comparison statistics with $ddf = \infty$ are listed in Table 4.

Table 4 — Selected 5 per cent and 1 per cent critical points of multiple comparison statistics with ddf $= \infty$

	DUNNETT		TUKEY	NAIR–HALPERIN		SCHEFFÉ	DUNCAN
	k—1 versus one		*all pairs*	*outlier tests*			
k	*one-tail*	*two-tail*	*range/$\sqrt{2}$*	*one-tail*	*two-tail*	$\sqrt{\chi^2_{k-1}}$	
			5 per cent level				
2	1.64	1.96	1.96	1.39	1.39	1.96	1.96
3	1.92	2.21	2.34	1.74	1.91	2.45	2.06
4	2.06	2.35	2.57	1.94	2.14	2.80	2.13
5	2.16	2.44	2.73	2.08	2.28	3.08	2.18
6	2.23	2.51	2.85	2.18	2.39	3.23	2.23
			1 per cent level				
2	2.33	2.58	2.58	1.82	1.82	2.58	2.58
3	2.56	2.79	2.91	2.22	2.38	3.03	2.68
4	2.68	2.92	3.11	2.43	2.61	3.37	2.76
5	2.77	3.00	3.25	2.57	2.76	3.64	2.81
6	2.84	3.06	3.36	2.68	2.87	3.88	2.86

Table 5 — Frequency of church attendance of scientists in four different fields

Church attendance	(1) Chemical engineers	(2) Physicists	(3) Zoologists	(4) Geologists	Combined sample	Score u
Never	44	65	66	72	247	−1
Not often	38	19	21	30	108	0
Often	52	46	49	38	185	1
Very often	33	29	19	17	98	2
Sample size, n_i	167	159	155	157	$N = 638$	
$T_i = \sum$ Frequency $\cdot\, u$	74	39	21	0*	$T = 134$	
$\bar{u}_i = T_i/n_i$	0.443	0.245	0.136	0.000	$\bar{u} = 0.210$	
$1/n_i$	0.005988	0.006289	0.006452	0.006369	$1/N = 0.001567$	

* It is purely accidental that T_4 exactly equals 0.

Source: Vaughan et al. 1966.

10. An example. As an illustration of some distribution-free multiple comparison methods, consider the following data from Vaughan, Sjoberg, and Smith (1966), who sent questionnaires to a sample of scientists listed in *American Men of Science* in order to compare scientists in four different fields with respect to the role that traditional religion plays in their lives. Table 5 summarizes responses to the question about frequency of church attendance and shows some of the calculations.

Using the data of Table 5, illustrative significance tests of the null hypothesis of four identical population distributions, against various alternatives, will be performed at the 1 per cent level.

The method of Yates (1948) begins by assigning ascending numerical scores, u, to the four ordered categories; arithmetically convenient scores, as shown in the last column of Table 5, are −1, 0, 1, and 2. Sample totals of scores are calculated—for example, $T_1 = 44(-1) + 38(0) + 52(1) + 33(2) = 74$, and the average score for sample i is $\bar{u}_i = T_i/n_i$. From the combined sample (margin) Yates computes an average score, $\bar{u} = T/N = .210$, and the variance of scores,

$$\sigma^2 = \frac{N}{N-1}(\text{average square} - \bar{u}^2),$$

giving $(638/637)\{[247(1) + 108(0) + 185(1) + 98(4)]/638 - .210^2\} = 1.2494$.

Yates then computes a variance between means, $T_1^2/n_1 + \cdots + T_4^2/n_4 - T^2/N = 17.05$, and the critical ratio used is either $F = (17.05/3)/1.2494$ or $\chi^2 = 17.05/1.2494 = 13.7$. The second of these is referred to a table of chi-square with 3 df and found significant at the 1 per cent level (in fact, $P = .0034$).

It follows that some contrasts must be statistically significant. The almost linear progression of the sample mean scores suggests calculating $3\bar{u}_1 + \bar{u}_2 - \bar{u}_3 - 3\bar{u}_4 = 1.438$. For the denominator, $(3^2/167 + 1^2/159 + 1^2/155 + 3^2/157)\sigma^2 = .1240 \times 1.2494 = .1549$, so that $\chi^2 = 1.438^2/.1549 = 13.35$, or its square root, $z = 1.438/\sqrt{.1549} = 3.65$. (This comes close to the value $\sqrt{13.7} = 3.70$ of the largest standardized contrast—see Section 5.) When 3.65 is referred to the Scheffé table (in Table 4, above) for $k = 4$, or when 13.35 is referred to a table of chi-square with 3 df, each is found to be statistically significant (in fact, $P = .0040$). The conclusion that can be drawn from this one-sided test for trend is that the population mean scores are ordered $\tilde{\mu}_1 \geqslant \tilde{\mu}_2 \geqslant \mu_3 \geqslant \tilde{\mu}_4$ with at least one strict inequality holding. Had a trend in this particular order been predicted ahead of time and postulated as the sole alternative hypothesis to be considered, $z = 3.65$ could have been judged by the normal table, yielding $P = .00013$. The two-tail version of this test is Yates's one-degree-of-freedom chi-square for trend (1948).

Another contrast that may be tested is the simple difference $\bar{u}_1 - \bar{u}_4 = .443 - .000$. Here $SE = \sqrt{[(1/167) + (1/157)] \times 1.2494} = .1243$, and $z_{14} = .443/.1243 = 3.57$. Because it is greater than 3.37, this contrast is statistically significant. Similarly, $z_{13} = (.443 - .136)/.1239 = 2.48$, but this is not significant at the 1 per cent level, and the other simple differences are still smaller.

If Tukey's test had been adopted instead of Scheffé's, the same ratios would be compared with the critical value 3.11 ($k = 4$, $\alpha = .01$). The conclusions would be the same in the present case. Tukey's method could also be used to test other contrasts.

In the present example, the Newman–Keuls procedure would also have led to the same conclusions about simple differences: $z_{14} = 3.57$ is called significant because it is greater than 3.11; then z_{13} (which equals 2.48) and z_{24} (which is still smaller) are compared with 2.91 and found "not significant," and the procedure ends. The conclusions may be summarized as follows:

$$\underline{.443 \quad \underline{.245 \quad .136} \quad .000},$$

where the absence of a line connecting $\bar{u}_1$ with $\bar{u}_4$ signifies that $\bar{\mu}_1$ and $\bar{\mu}_4$ are declared unequal. It may be argued that a conclusion of the form "*A*, *B*, and *C* homogeneous, *B*, *C*, and *D* homogeneous, but *A*, *B*, *C*, and *D* not homogeneous" is self-contradictory. This is not necessarily the case if the interpretation is the usual one that *A*, *B*, and *C* *may* be equal (not enough evidence to prove them unequal) and *B*, *C*, and *D* may be equal, but *A* and *D* are not equal.

In Duncan's procedure the critical value 3.11 used in the first stage would be replaced by 2.76 (see Table 5), and the critical value 2.91 used at the second stage ($k = 3$) would be replaced by 2.68. Since $3.57 > 2.76$ but $2.48 < 2.68$, Duncan's test leads to the same conclusion in the present example as the Newman–Keuls procedure.

A Halperin outlier test would use max $|\bar{u}_i - \bar{u}|$, in this case $.443 - 2.10 = .233$, divide it by

$$\sqrt{4/3[(1/167) - (1/638)]\,1.2494} = .08582,$$

and compare the resulting ratio, 2.72, with the critical value, 2.61 ($k = 4$, 1 per cent level). The next largest ratio is $(.210 - .000)/.08944 = 2.35$. The conclusion is that chemical engineers tend to report more frequent church attendance than the other groups, but nothing can be said about geologists. If the outlier contrasts had been tested as part of a Scheffé test for all contrasts, none of them would have been found significant at the 1 per cent level (critical value 3.37) or even at the 5 per cent level.

What would happen if unequally spaced scores had been used instead of $-1, 0, 1, 2$ to quantify the four degrees of religious loyalty? In fact, Vaughan and his associates described the ordered categories not verbally but as frequency of church attendance per month grouped into 0, 1, 2–4, 5+. Although we do not know whether frequency of church attendance is a linear measure of the importance of religion in a person's life, the scores (0, 1, 3, 6) could reasonably have been assigned. In the present case this would lead to essentially the same conclusions that the other scoring led to: The mean scores become 2.35, 2.08, 1.82, and 1.57, Yates's χ^2 changes from 13.7 to 12.5, the standardized contrast for trend changes from $\sqrt{13.35}$ to very nearly $\sqrt{12.5}$, z_{14} changes from 3.57 to 3.36, and z_{13} and z_{24} again have values too small for statistical significance by Tukey's criterion or by Newman–Keuls'.

A fundamentally different assignment of scores —for example, 1, 0, 0, 1—would be used to test for differences in spread. It yields sample means, $\bar{u}_i$, of .461, .591, .548, .576, $\bar{u} = 0.541$ and a variance, σ^2, of .2484. Yates's analysis-of-variance χ^2 is 1.449/0.2484, that is, only 5.83, so $P = .12$. Thus, no contrast is called significant in a Scheffé test (or, it turns out, in any other multiple comparison test at the 1 per cent significance level). In the present example these tests for spread are unreliable, because the presence of sample location differences, noted above, can vitiate the results of the test for differences in spread.

Throughout the numerical calculations in this section, the continuity correction has been neglected. In the case of unequal sample sizes it is difficult to determine what continuity correction would yield the most accurate results, and the effect of the adjustment would be slight anyway. When sample sizes are equal, the use of $|T_i - T_j| - \frac{1}{2}$ in place of $|T_i - T_j|$ is recommended, as it frequently (although not invariably) improves the fit of the asymptotic approximation used.

11. Comparisons for differences in scale. Standand multiple comparisons of variances of k normal populations, by Cochran (1941), David (1952), and others, utilize ratios of the $\hat{\sigma}_i^2$. These methods should be used with caution, because they are ultrasensitive to slight nonnormality.

Distribution-free multiple comparison tests for scale differences are also available. Any rank test may be used with a Siegel–Tukey reranking [*see* NONPARAMETRIC STATISTICS, *article on* RANKING METHODS]. Such methods, too, require caution, because—especially in a joint ranking of all k samples—any sizable location differences may masquerade as differences in scale (Moses 1963).

Safer methods—but with efficiencies of only about 50 per cent for normal distributions—are adaptations of some tests by Moses (1963). In these tests a small integer, s, such as 2 or 3, is chosen, and each sample is randomly subdivided into subgroups of s observations. Let y be the range or variance of a subgroup. Then any multiple comparison tests may be applied to the k samples of y's (or $\log y$'s), at the sacrifice of between-subgroups information. The effective sample sizes have been reduced to $[n_i/s]$; if these are small (about 6), either a nonparametric test or, at any rate, $\log y$'s should be used. (Some nonparametric multiple comparison tests, such as the median test, have no power—that is, they cannot possibly reject the null hypothesis—at significance levels such as .05 with small samples. But rank tests can be used with several samples as small as 4 or 5.)

12. Multiple comparisons of proportions. A simultaneous test for all differences between k proportions $p_1, \cdots, p_k$, based on large samples, can be obtained by comparing

$$\text{Max}\frac{X_i/n_i - X_j/n_j}{\sqrt{\frac{N}{N-1}\left(\frac{1}{n_i}+\frac{1}{n_j}\right)\frac{X}{N}\left(1-\frac{X}{N}\right)}}$$

with a critical value of Tukey's statistic (Section 3), where X_i, $i = 1, \cdots, k$, denotes the number of "successes" in sample i and $X = \sum X_i$. Analogous asymptotic tests can be used for comparison of several treatments with a control and other forms of multiple comparisons. If X/N is small, the sample sizes must be very large for this asymptotic approximation to be adequate. (For a similar method see Ryan 1960.)

Small-sample multiple comparison tests of proportions may be carried out by transforming the counts into normal variables with known equal variances and then applying any test of sections 1–7 to these standardized variables (using ∞ *ddf*). [*See* STATISTICAL ANALYSIS, SPECIAL PROBLEMS OF, *article on* TRANSFORMATIONS OF DATA; *see also* Siotani & Ozawa 1958.]

A $(1-\alpha)$-confidence region for k population proportions is composed of a $\sqrt[k]{1-\alpha}$-confidence interval for each of them. Simultaneous confidence intervals for a set of differences of proportions may be approximated by using Bonferroni's inequality (see Section 14). For a discussion of confidence regions for multinomial proportions, see Goodman (1965).

Some discussion of multiple comparisons of proportions can be found in Walsh (1965, for example, pp. 536–537).

13. Selection and ranking. The approach called selection or ranking *assumes* a difference between populations and seeks to select the population(s) with the highest mean—or variance or proportion —or to arrange all k populations in order [*see* SCREENING AND SELECTION; *see also* Bechhofer 1958]. Bechhofer, Kiefer, and Sobel (1967) have written a monograph on the subject.

Error rates, choice of method, history

14. Error rates and choice of method. In a significance test comparing two populations, the significance level is defined as

$$a = \frac{\text{number of type I errors}}{\text{number of comparisons when } H_0 \text{ is true}}$$

in repeated use of the same criterion. This is termed the *error rate per comparison.* The corresponding confidence level for confidence intervals is $1 - a$.

For analyses of k-sample experiments one may instead define the *error rate per experiment,*

$$a' = \frac{\text{number of type I errors}}{\text{number of experiments analyzed, when } H_0 \text{ is true}}.$$

This is related to what Miller (1966) terms the "expected error rate." For m (computed or implied) comparisons per experiment, $a' = ma$; $a = a'/m$ (see Stanley 1957).

Standard multiple comparison tests specify an *error rate experimentwise* (or "familywise"):

$$\alpha = \frac{\text{number of experiments, when } H_0 \text{ is true, leading to any type I errors,}}{\text{number of experiments analyzed, when } H_0 \text{ is true}}.$$

Miller refers to this as the "probability of a nonzero family error rate" or "probability error rate."

The only difference between a' and α is that α counts multiple rejections in a single experiment as only one error whereas a' counts them as more than one. Hence, $\alpha \leqslant a'$; this is termed *Bonferroni's inequality.*

On the other hand, it is also true that unless a' is large, α is almost equal to a', so that α and a' may be used interchangeably for practical purposes. For example, D_α for 6 treatments and a control, M_α for $k = 6$, and T_α for $k = 4$ ($\binom{4}{2} = 6$), are all approximately equal to the two-tailed critical value $|t|_{\alpha/6} = t_{\alpha/12}$ of Student's t. More generally, m individual comparisons may safely be made using any statistic at significance level α/m per comparison when it is desired to avoid error rates greater than α experimentwise; this procedure may be applied to comparisons of several correlation coefficients or other quantities for which multiple comparison tables are not available. Only when α is about .10 or more, or when m is very big, does this lead to serious waste. Then a' grossly overstates α, power is lost, and confidence intervals are unnecessarily long (see Stanley 1957; Ryan 1959; Dunn 1961).

Some authors refer to (α/m)-points as Bonferroni statistics and to their use in multiple comparisons as the Bonferroni method. Table 2 in Miller (1966) shows Bonferroni t-statistics, $(.05/2m)$-points of Student's t for various m and various numbers of *ddf*.

Bonferroni's second inequality (see Halperin

et al. 1955, p. 191) may sometimes be used to obtain an upper limit for the discrepancy $a' - \alpha$ and a second approximation to critical values for error rates α experimentwise. This works best in the case of slippage statistics and was used by Halperin and his associates (1955), Doornbos and Prins (1958), Thompson and Willke (1963), and others.

The choice between "experimentwise" and "per comparison" is largely a matter of taste. An experimenter should make it consciously, aware of the implications: A given error probability, a, per comparison implies that the risk of at least one type I error in the analysis is much greater than a; indeed, about $a \times m$ such errors will probably occur.

Perhaps analyses reporting error rates experimentwise are generally the most honest, or transparent. However, too dogmatic an application of this principle would lead to all sorts of difficulties. Should not the researcher who in the course of his career analyzes 86 experiments involving 1,729 relevant contrasts control the error rate *lifetimewise*? If he does not, he is almost bound to make a false positive inference sooner or later.

Sterling (1959) discusses the related problem of concentration of type I errors in the literature that result from the habit of selecting significant findings for publication [*see* FALLACIES, STATISTICAL, *for further discussion of this problem*].

There is another context in which the problem of choosing error rates arises: If an experimenter laboriously sets up expensive apparatus for an experiment to compare two treatments or conditions in which he is especially interested, he often feels that it would be unfortunate to pass up the opportunity to obtain additional data of secondary interest at practically no extra cost or trouble; so he makes observations on populations 3, 4, $\cdots$, k as well. It is then possible that the results are such that a two-sample test on the data of primary interest would have shown statistical significance, but no "significant differences" are found in a multiple comparison test. If the bonus observations thus drown out, so to speak, the significant difference, was the experimenter wrong to read them? He was not—the opportunity to obtain extra information should not be wasted, but the analysis should be planned ahead of time with the experimenter's interests and priorities in mind. He could decide to analyze his primary and subsidiary results as if they had come from separate experiments, or he could conduct multiple comparisons with an overall error rate enlarged to avoid undue loss of power, or he could use a method of analysis which subdivides α, allocating a certain (large) part to the primary comparison and the rest to "data snooping" among the extra observations (Miller 1966, chapter 2, sec. 2.3).

Whenever it is decided to specify error rates experimentwise, a choice between different systems of multiple comparisons (different shapes of confidence regions) remains to be made. In order to study simple differences or slippage only, one of the methods of sections 2–4 above (or a nonparametric version of them) is best—that is, yields the shortest confidence intervals and most powerful tests, provided the n_i are (nearly) equal. But Scheffé's approach (see section 5) is better if a variety of contrasts may receive attention.

When sample sizes are grossly unequal, probability statements based on existing Tukey or Dunnett tables, computed for equal n's, become too inaccurate. Pending the appearance of appropriate new tables, it is better to use Scheffé's method, which furnishes exact probabilities. The Bonferroni statistics discussed above offer an alternative solution, preferable whenever attention is strictly limited to a few contrasts chosen ahead of time. Miller (1966, especially chapter 2, secs. 2.3 and 3.3) discusses these questions in some detail.

15. History of multiple comparisons. An early, isolated example of a multiple comparison method was one developed by Working and Hotelling (1929) to obtain a confidence belt for a regression line (see Miller 1966, chapter 3; Kerrich 1955). This region also corresponds to simultaneous confidence intervals for the intercept and slope [*see* LINEAR HYPOTHESES, *article on* REGRESSION]. Hotelling (1927) had already developed the idea of simultaneous confidence interval estimation earlier in connection with the fitting of logistic curves to population time series. In his famous paper introducing the T^2-statistic, Hotelling (1931) also introduced the idea of simultaneous tests and a confidence ellipsoid for the components of a multivariate normal mean.

The systematic development of multiple comparison methods and theory began later, in connection with the problem of comparing several normal means. The usual method had been the analysis-of-variance F-test, sometimes accompanied by t-tests at a stated significance level, a (usually 5 per cent), per comparison.

Fisher, in the 1935 edition of *The Design of Experiments*, pointed out the problem of inflation of error probabilities in such multiple t-tests and recommended the use of t-tests at a stated level a'

per experiment. Pearson and Chandra Sekar further discussed the problem (1936). Newman (1939), acting on an informal suggestion by Student, described a test for all differences based on tables of the Studentized range and furnished a table of approximate 5 per cent and 1 per cent points. Keuls formulated Newman's test more clearly much later (Keuls 1952).

Nair made two contributions in 1948, the one-sided test for slippage of means and a table for simultaneous *F*-tests in a 2^r factorial design. Also in the late 1940s, Duncan and Tukey experimented with various tests for normal means which were forerunners of the multiple comparison tests now associated with their names.

The standard methods for multiple comparisons of normal means were developed between 1952 and 1955 by Tukey, Scheffé, Dunnett, and Duncan. Tukey wrote a comprehensive volume on the subject which was widely circulated in duplicated form and extensively quoted but which has not been published (1953). The form of Tukey's method described in Section 3 for unequal n's was given independently by Kurtz and by Kramer in 1956. Also in the early and middle 1950s, some multiple comparison methods for normal *variances* were published, by Hartley, David, Truax, Krishnaiah, and others. Cochran's slippage test for normal variances was published, for use as a substitute for Bartlett's test for homogeneity of variances, as early as 1941 (see Cochran 1941).

Selection and ranking procedures for means, variances, and proportions have been developed since 1953 by Bechhofer and others.

An easy, distribution-free slippage test was proposed by Mosteller in 1948—simply count the number of observations in the most extreme sample lying beyond the most extreme value of all the other samples and refer to a table by Mosteller and Tukey (1950). Other distribution-free multiple comparison methods—although some of them can be viewed as applications of S. N. Roy's work of 1953—did not begin to appear until after 1958.

The most important applications of the very general methodology developed by the school of Roy and Bose since 1953 have been *multivariate* multiple comparison tests and confidence regions. Such work by Roy, Bose, Gnanadesikan, Krishnaiah, Gabriel, and others is generally recognizable by the word "simultaneous" in the title—for example, SMANOVA, that is, simultaneous multivariate analysis of variance (see Miller 1966, chapter 5).

Another recent development is the appearance of some Bayesian techniques for multiple comparisons. These are discussed by Duncan in the May 1965 issue of *Technometrics*, an issue which is devoted to articles on multiple comparison methods and theory and reflects a cross section of current trends in this field.

PETER NEMENYI

BIBLIOGRAPHY

The only comprehensive source for the subject of multiple comparisons to date is Miller 1966. *Multiple comparisons of normal means (and variances) are summarized by a number of authors, notably David* 1962*a and* 1962*b*. *Several textbooks on statistics—e.g.,* Winer 1962*—also cover some of this ground. Many of the relevant tables, for normal means and variances, can also be found in* David 1962*a and* 1962*b*; Vianelli 1959; *and* Pearson & Hartley 1954; *these volumes also provide explanations of the derivation and use of the tables.*

BECHHOFER, R. E. 1958 A Sequential Multiple-decision Procedure for Selecting the Best One of Several Normal Populations With a Common Unknown Variance, and Its Use With Various Experimental Designs. *Biometrics* 14:408–429.

BECHHOFER, R. E.; KIEFER, J.; and SOBEL, M. 1967 Sequential Ranking Procedures. Unpublished manuscript. → Projected for publication by the University of Chicago Press in association with the Institute of Mathematical Statistics.

COCHRAN, W. G. 1941 The Distribution of the Largest of a Set of Estimated Variances as a Fraction of Their Total. *Annals of Eugenics* 11:47–52.

CRONBACH, LEE J. 1949 Statistical Methods Applied to Rorschach Scores: A Review. *Psychological Bulletin* 46:393–429.

DAVID, H. A. 1952 Upper 5 and 1% Points of the Maximum *F*-ratio. *Biometrika* 39:422–424.

DAVID, H. A. 1962*a* Multiple Decisions and Multiple Comparisons. Pages 144–162 in Ahmed E. Sarhan and Bernard G. Greenberg (editors), *Contributions to Order Statistics*. New York: Wiley.

DAVID, H. A. 1962*b* Order Statistics in Shortcut Tests. Pages 94–128 in Ahmed E. Sarhan and Bernard G. Greenberg (editors), *Contributions to Order Statistics*. New York: Wiley.

DOORNBOS, R.; and PRINS, H. J. 1958 On Slippage Tests. Part 3: Two Distribution-free Slippage Tests and Two Tables. *Indagationes mathematicae* 20:438–447.

DUNCAN, DAVID B. 1955 Multiple Range and Multiple *F* Tests. *Biometrics* 11:1–42.

DUNCAN, DAVID B. 1965 A Bayesian Approach to Multiple Comparisons. *Technometrics* 7:171–222.

DUNN, OLIVE J. 1961 Multiple Comparisons Among Means. *Journal of the American Statistical Association* 56:52–64.

DUNNETT, CHARLES W. 1955 A Multiple Comparison Procedure for Comparing Several Treatments With a Control. *Journal of the American Statistical Association* 50:1096–1121.

FISHER, R. A. (1935) 1960 *The Design of Experiments*. 7th ed. London: Oliver & Boyd; New York: Hafner.

FISHER, R. A.; and YATES, FRANK (1938) 1963 *Statistical Tables for Biological, Agricultural, and Medical Research*. 6th ed., rev. & enl. Edinburgh: Oliver & Boyd; New York: Hafner.

GABRIEL, K. R. 1966 Simultaneous Test Procedures for Multiple Comparisons on Categorical Data. *Journal of the American Statistical Association* 61:1081–1096.

GOODMAN, LEO A. 1965 On Simultaneous Confidence Intervals for Multinomial Proportions. *Technometrics* 7:247–252.

HALPERIN, M.; GREENHOUSE, S.; CORNFIELD, J.; and ZALOKAR, J. 1955 Tables of Percentage Points for the Studentized Maximum Absolute Deviate in Normal Samples. *Journal of the American Statistical Association* 50:185–195.

HARTER, H. LEON 1957 Error Rates and Sample Sizes for Range Tests in Multiple Comparisons. *Biometrics* 13:511–536.

HARTER, H. LEON 1960 Tables of Range and Studentized Range. *Annals of Mathematical Statistics* 31: 1122–1147.

HARTLEY, H. O. 1950 The Maximum *F*-ratio as a Short-cut Test for Heterogeneity of Variance. *Biometrika* 37:308–312.

HOTELLING, HAROLD 1927 Differential Equations Subject to Error, and Population Estimates. *Journal of the American Statistical Association* 22:283–314.

HOTELLING, HAROLD 1931 The Generalization of Student's Ratio. *Annals of Mathematical Statistics* 2: 360–378.

KERRICH, J. E. 1955 Confidence Intervals Associated With a Straight Line Fitted by Least Squares. *Statistica neerlandica* 9:125–129.

KEULS, M. 1952 The Use of "Studentized Range" in Connection With an Analysis of Variance. *Euphytica* 1:112–122.

KRAMER, CLYDE Y. 1956 Extension of Multiple Range Tests to Group Means With Unequal Number of Replications. *Biometrics* 12:307–310.

KRAMER, CLYDE Y. 1957 Extension of Multiple Range Tests to Group Correlated Adjusted Means. *Biometrics* 13:13–18.

KRISHNAIAH, P. R. 1965*a* On a Multivariate Generalization of the Simultaneous Analysis of Variance Test. Institute of Statistical Mathematics (Tokyo), *Annals* 17, no. 2:167–173.

KRISHNAIAH, P. R. 1965*b* Simultaneous Tests for the Equality of Variance Against Certain Alternatives. *Australian Journal of Statistics* 7:105–109.

KURTZ, T. E. 1956 An Extension of a Method of Making Multiple Comparisons (Preliminary Report). *Annals of Mathematical Statistics* 27:547 only.

KURTZ, T. E.; LINK, R. F.; TUKEY, J. W.; and WALLACE, D. L. 1965 Short-cut Multiple Comparisons for Balanced Single and Double Classifications. Part 1: Results. *Technometrics* 7:95–169.

MCHUGH, RICHARD B.; and ELLIS, DOUGLAS S. 1955 The "Post Mortem" Testing of Experimental Comparisons. *Psychological Bulletin* 52:425–428.

MILLER, RUPERT G. 1966 *Simultaneous Statistical Inference.* New York: McGraw-Hill.

MOSES, LINCOLN E. 1953 Nonparametric Methods. Pages 426–450 in Helen M. Walker and Joseph Lev, *Statistical Inference.* New York: Holt.

MOSES, LINCOLN E. 1963 Rank Tests of Dispersion. *Annals of Mathematical Statistics* 34:973–983.

MOSES, LINCOLN E. 1965 Confidence Limits From Rank Tests (Reply to a Query). *Technometrics* 7:257–260.

MOSTELLER, FREDERICK W.; and TUKEY, JOHN W. 1950 Significance Levels for a *k*-sample Slippage Test. *Annals of Mathematical Statistics* 21:120–123.

NAIR, K. R. 1948*a* The Studentized Form of the Extreme Mean Square Test in the Analysis of Variance. *Biometrika* 35:16–31.

NAIR, K. R. 1948*b* The Distribution of the Extreme Deviate From the Sample Mean and Its Studentized Form. *Biometrika* 35:118–144.

NAIR, K. R. 1952 Tables of Percentage Points of the "Studentized" Extreme Deviate From the Sample Mean. *Biometrika* 39:189–191.

NEMENYI, PETER 1963 Distribution-free Multiple Comparisons. Ph.D. dissertation, Princeton Univ.

NEWMAN, D. 1939 The Distribution of the Range in Samples From a Normal Population, Expressed in Terms of an Independent Estimate of Standard Deviation. *Biometrika* 31:20–30.

PEARSON, EGON S.; and CHANDRA SEKAR, C. 1936 The Efficiency of Statistical Tools and a Criterion for the Rejection of Outlying Observations. *Biometrika* 28: 308–320.

PEARSON, EGON S.; and HARTLEY, H. O. (editors) (1954) 1966 *Biometrika Tables for Statisticians.* Vol. 1. 3d ed. Cambridge Univ. Press. → Only the first volume of this edition has as yet been published.

PILLAI, K. C. S.; and RAMACHANDRAN, K. V. 1954 On the Distribution of the Ratio of the *i*th Observation in an Ordered Sample From a Normal Population to an Independent Estimate of the Standard Deviation. *Annals of Mathematical Statistics* 25:565–572.

QUESENBERRY, C. P.; and DAVID, H. A. 1961 Some Tests for Outliers. *Biometrika* 48:379–390.

ROESSLER, R. G. 1946 Testing the Significance of Observations Compared With a Control. American Society for Horticultural Science, *Proceedings* 47:249–251.

ROTHAUS, PAUL; and WORCHEL, PHILIP 1964 Ego Support, Communication, Catharsis, and Hostility. *Journal of Personality* 32:296–312.

ROY, S. N.; and BOSE, R. C. 1953 Simultaneous Confidence Interval Estimation. *Annals of Mathematical Statistics* 24:513–536.

ROY, S. N.; and GNANADESIKAN, R. 1957 Further Contributions to Multivariate Confidence Bounds. *Biometrika* 44:399–410.

RYAN, THOMAS A. 1959 Multiple Comparisons in Psychological Research. *Psychological Bulletin* 56:26–47.

RYAN, THOMAS A. 1960 Significance Tests for Multiple Comparisons of Proportions, Variances, and Other Statistics. *Psychological Bulletin* 57:318–328.

SCHEFFÉ, HENRY 1953 A Method for Judging All Contrasts in the Analysis of Variance. *Biometrika* 40:87–104.

SIOTANI, M.; and OZAWA, MASARU 1958 Tables for Testing the Homogeneity of *k* Independent Binomial Experiments on a Certain Event Based on the Range. Institute of Statistical Mathematics (Tokyo), *Annals* 10:47–63.

STANLEY, JULIAN C. 1957 Additional "Post Mortem" Tests of Experimental Comparisons. *Psychological Bulletin* 54:128–130.

STEEL, ROBERT G. D. 1959 A Multiple Comparison Sign Test: Treatments vs. Control. *Journal of the American Statistical Association* 54:767–775.

STERLING, THEODORE D. 1959 Publication Decisions and Their Possible Effects on Inferences Drawn From Tests of Significance—or Vice Versa. *Journal of the American Statistical Association* 54:30–34.

THOMPSON, W. A. JR.; and WILLKE, T. A. 1963 On an Extreme Rank Sum Test for Outliers. *Biometrika* 50: 375–383.

Truax, Donald R. 1953 An Optimum Slippage Test for the Variances of *k* Normal Populations. *Annals of Mathematical Statistics* 24:669–674.

Tukey, J. W. 1953 The Problem of Multiple Comparisons. Unpublished manuscript, Princeton Univ.

Vaughan, Ted R.; Sjoberg, G.; and Smith, D. H. 1966 Religious Orientations of American Natural Scientists. *Social Forces* 44:519–526.

Vianelli, Silvio 1959 *Prontuari per calcoli statistici: Tavole numeriche e complementi.* Palermo: Abbaco.

Walsh, John E. 1965 *Handbook of Nonparametric Statistics.* Volume 2: Results for Two and Several Sample Problems, Symmetry, and Extremes. Princeton, N.J.: Van Nostrand.

Winer, B. J. 1962 *Statistical Principles in Experimental Design.* New York: McGraw-Hill.

Working, Holbrook; and Hotelling, Harold 1929 Application of the Theory of Error to the Interpretation of Trends. *Journal of the American Statistical Association* 24 (March Supplement): 73–85.

Yates, Frank 1948 The Analysis of Contingency Tables With Groupings Based on Quantitative Characters. *Biometrika* 35:176–181.

LINEAR PROGRAMMING

See Operations research *and* Programming.

LINGUISTICS

i. The Field	*Dell Hymes*
ii. Historical Linguistics	*Yakov Malkiel*
iii. The Speech Community	*John J. Gumperz*

I
THE FIELD

Linguistics has been called the science of language; but this definition begs the questions, What is scientific? What is language? Linguists themselves have not agreed; sometimes their answers have been quite narrow. If we are to consider the gamut of social science interests in language, we must adopt one of two approaches—either interpret "science of language" very broadly or conceive of it as part of some larger field.

In the first approach, "science" is taken in its broadest meaning, *Wissenschaft*, comprising all serious intellectual disciplines; "language" is taken as implicating all aspects of human speech. Linguistics is then truly the science of language, although as such it embraces work of both linguists and scholars in other disciplines. In the second approach, the "science of language" comprises only those kinds of knowledge for which linguists typically take responsibility. The science of language is then but part of a broader area of inquiry, the study of language; the science of language is linguistics proper, and the study of language may be called the field of linguistics.

The second approach is fairer to the present situation of linguistics. Linguistics is the indispensable basis for serious concern with any aspect of language, and its rapid growth is such that its effective scope may indeed come to equal the whole of the study of language. At present, the student of social science concerned with the place of language in human life must also consult other disciplines, perhaps including his own.

Our standpoint, then, will be that of the field of linguistics. We shall first sketch the development of linguistics within the context of the study of language, then characterize linguistics proper in terms of its scope and content today, and last discuss the import of its work with special reference to the social sciences.

Development of linguistics

The present expanding scope of linguistics is the outcome of a complex history. As a separately organized discipline, so named, linguistics is, however, quite young in English-speaking countries. The Linguistic Society of America was founded in 1924, and the Linguistics Association of Great Britain in 1965. Almost all of the independent departments of linguistics have appeared only since World War ii. Indeed, "linguistics" has only recently displaced "philology" as a general name for the study of language, and "linguist" is still widely used by laymen for "polyglot" rather than for a member of a scientific discipline.

Early periods. Behind modern linguistics lies an accumulation of insight and knowledge that reaches to the early stages of human history. No known language is without at least some terms for facts of language and hence an elementary metalanguage of a protolinguistic sort. Such terms sometimes show close analysis of structural features; for the most part, however, the internal structures of language remain unconsciously known, and it is terms for uses and varieties of language that are elaborated. Every society indeed has terms, beliefs, attitudes, and knowledge concerning language that may be singled out as its *folk linguistics*. The character and extent of this folk linguistics are of interest as conditioning linguistic change and as part of the subject matter of ethnoscience. Where a separate discipline of linguistic study has emerged, the interaction between it and the folk linguistics of its society may also set some of the limits and directions of the discipline and hence interest the historian of science and the sociologist of knowledge. Some 2,500 years ago there began to appear disciplined studies of language that can be taken as heralding a stage of *national philologies*. In China,

India, and Greece, valued texts (the cultural arm, as it were, of expanding civilizations and aspiring states) came to be given special attention intended to preserve accurate knowledge of them and to aid in their use. These philologies were preceded by systems of writing, themselves embodiments of analysis of language. In the philologies, techniques of analysis became explicit, if with different emphases and differential success. The greatest achievement occurred in the Indian tradition (independently of writing), culminating in the work of Pānini (c. 500 B.C.). (Pāṇini was to influence the development of linguistics in Europe, once his work was made known there at the start of the nineteenth century.)

The Western study of language was shaped through most of its history by a tradition of philosophic thought and pedagogic grammars. In the classical world, analysis of language began amid controversies over the regularity or irregularity of language (*analogia : anomalia*), over language as part of nature or culture (*physis : nomos*), over relations between language and other subjects; and amid the establishment of Sophistic training and of educational institutions generally (see Robins 1951; Sandys 1903–1908; Marrou 1948). Etymological curiosity played a prominent part. A system of grammatical categories was evolved, based on the nature of Greek and then Latin. A great merit of the classical work was that it treated language structure integrally with language use; indeed, in education the grammarian was subordinate to the rhetor. Exclusive attention to the language (or languages) of an empire was a great limitation, shared by all early philologies. Given the social role of language study, this restriction was perhaps inevitable, but it was crippling to a general knowledge of language itself.

Early modern period. In the medieval period of the West (during the intermittent periods of renaissance before that which bears the capitalized name) theoretical notions about the rational structure of language were elaborated and language's place in education and human life discussed (see Bolgar 1954; Robins 1951).

Skills that had begun in the classical world in the first renaissance of Greek literature—that of Alexandria—reached new heights in the Renaissance proper, and the tradition of classical philology which it founded provided the model for textual analysis and criticism in all fields, as well as models for grammars and dictionaries of the emerging national philologies in Europe. As the literary use and serious study of modern European languages grew, an empirical knowledge of languages from Asia, Africa, Oceania, and the New World slowly began to accumulate, especially through the field work of missionaries, history's first organized body of ethnographers. By the eighteenth century the growing body of information was considerable, and there were scientific expeditions whose mission included collection of linguistic data (see Gray 1939; Wonderly & Nida 1963).

Some criteria of relationship among languages had been sought earlier in attempts to harmonize the three great cultural languages (Hebrew, Greek, Latin) and to establish the origin of the peoples of the New World, as well as of modern European peoples. The search for relationships was abetted no doubt by the Biblical account of Babel, which (1) asserted original unity of all languages, and (2) left the details of differentiation open to discovery (see Borst 1957–1963; Metcalf 1964).

In this period the theoretical unity of human language was treated in the Cartesian rationalism of Leibniz and others, in British empiricism, Scottish "common sense," and French materialism. Indeed, as the intellectual foundations for the social sciences developed, the nature of language, posed as a problem of its origin in history and in the individual, engaged most major theorists—Hobbes, Locke, Rousseau, Adam Smith, Condillac, Herder, etc.—bearing as it did on the fundamental nature of man and the relationship between the natural and cultural worlds.

It is conventional to date the history of linguistics proper from the recognition of Sanskrit and the rise of diachronic linguistics, especially Indo-European studies, in the late eighteenth century and early nineteenth. This view (indeed, origin myth) preserves too much of the self-consciousness of an intellectual climate (romanticism, historicism) set off against the image of its predecessor, the Enlightenment. There was justice in the self-consciousness: in the study of language works were produced that became models and starting points for subsequent scholarship; with specialization, chairs, scholarly organizations, and journals increased quite dramatically. It is almost impossible, however, to fix any one point between the mid-eighteenth century and the mid-nineteenth century as decisive intellectually for the development of the successful methods of Indo-European study; Turgot, Rask, Bopp, Grimm, and Schleicher each has his claim to a contribution. Regarding theoretical views, some would now set aside much of the nineteenth-century effort, emphasizing the preceding rationalist inquiry as a more relevant predecessor. The work of Wilhelm von Humboldt thus comes to seem both an end point to developments of interest in the seventeenth and eighteenth centuries and a starting point for a strain of general linguistics in the nineteenth century.

No doubt the salience of periods of past linguistics will continue to change as modern linguistics changes. If we are to understand the history of linguistics, not for partisanship, but as a case in the comparative study of the general history of science and scholarship, one point is essential. Linguistic research, like social science research, proliferated as a sustained, organized, autonomous activity in the nineteenth century, but from an intellectual and empirical base in the general rise of scholarship and science in Europe as part of the expansion, at once intellectual and commercial, of its known world. With that rise began what can be truly called *general linguistics*, a linguistics which, while interdependent with the continued development of philologies and of specializations of other sorts, came to take as its compass all the languages of man. (On the place of linguistic thought in intellectual history, especially the place of language in human nature and culture, see Verburg 1952; Chomsky 1966; Cassirer 1923, chapter 1.)

Nineteenth century. The major study on nineteenth-century linguistics (actually a period approximately from the French Revolution to World War I) records it as the triumph of historical work, especially of comparative Indo-European (Pedersen 1924). From that standpoint the course of the century is one of increasing precision and power of historical method and of its very wide application. Indo-European studies held the center of the stage, partly because of their institutionalization in Prussia and subsequently elsewhere and partly because of the accident of cultural history that the languages prospective Indo-European specialists had to learn in school were the classical "languages of culture." Greek and Latin, together with their native languages and perhaps some other European language, gave these students intimacy with three or four branches of the language family they were to reconstruct. This cultural support and internal availability of data were not duplicated elsewhere. The Hungarian, Gyarmathai, had had the methodological insight to relate Hungarian and Finnish, in 1799 (see Pedersen [1924] 1962, pp. 105–106), but the languages of the family (Finno–Ugric) to which Hungarian belongs were scattered in Russia and the north, and scholars had to rely on cumulative field work. Moreover, there was no prestige in working out the relationship of one's mother tongue to the languages of poor "fish eaters" (the heroic Turkish conquerors were more attractive as linguistic kin, thus leading much research into a blind alley). Indo-European scholars worked amid the rise of Oriental philology and of interest in the "wisdom from the East" symbolized by Sanskrit.

Among the main accomplishments of the period were the pioneering comparisons of Rask (who was not adequately recognized in his own day); the comparative grammar of Bopp; the recognition of regular patterns of sound change in Germanic by Grimm (and Rask); the etymological dictionaries of Pott and Fick; the method of reconstruction and the family-tree model (*Stammbaum*) of relationship of Schleicher; the more exact specification of regularities in change in sound and of the role of grammatical analogy of the *Junggrammatiker* and others of the 1870s (Ascoli, Verner, de Saussure, Brugmann); the wave model of relationship (*Wellentheorie*) of Schmidt, complementing that of the family tree. The first basis was laid for the historical study of many language families, both within and outside Indo-European (e.g., comparative grammars of Romance, Celtic, Dravidian, Bantu, Athapaskan). Near the end of the period, the great comparativist Meillet, while calling for attention to regularities independent of specific histories, could rightfully state that the principles already developed for the handling of regular sound change, analogy, and borrowing could continue to be fruitfully extended to all the language families of the world.

The traditions of anthropological philology also became established in this period, beginning perhaps with Herder's thesis of the individuality and the scientific and humanistic value of the language and literature of every people, whatever its stage of development. This attitude was to be freshly stated many times, for example, by Boas, a century later. Much anthropological study of language has indeed been the philology of peoples without philology of their own. In this sense anthropology has been the third of the great philological enterprises of European civilization, following upon and complementing classical and Oriental philology.

A master term for the study of language was *philology*, a putative "queen of the sciences" to some, although "linguistics," *linguistique*, and *Sprachwissenschaft* also were in use. Historical linguistics, requiring interpretation of texts, was often termed "comparative philology" in English-speaking countries; and since philologists proper produced the needed grammars and dictionaries, descriptive work also was often identified as "philology." Analogous to "classical philology," the study of contemporary European languages was labeled part of "modern philology" (*Neuphilologie*), and study of a particular set would be, e.g., not "Romance linguistics," but "Romance philology." In American anthropology, "philology" remained the common term into this century (e.g., Boas was retained by the Bureau of American Ethnology as "philologist"). In British usage and some learned American usage "philology" continued to serve until very recently. After World War I the trend among practitioners themselves to distinguish sharply between "philology" and "linguistics" was well established, however favorably the relationship between the two might be viewed (Pedersen [1924] 1962, p. 79). Philology might range far, but it remained inseparable from the study of texts and history, and linguistics was being defined as a more general study of language.

Looking back from the standpoint of contemporary linguistics, one sees in the nineteenth century important strands, which were largely neglected in accounts of the triumph of historical work. One is well known and the progenitor of continuing lines of work—linguistic geography and dialectology. It emerged in a rising wave of interest in geographical distributions in all the human sciences during the half-century embracing the turn of the twentieth century as midpoint. [*See* LINGUISTICS, *article on* THE SPEECH COMMUNITY.]

A second major trend in general linguistics stemmed from von Humboldt and others and sought cognitive import in an evolutionary typology of languages. Carried on by Schleicher, Steinthal, and others in various forms, the effort was later discarded amid a general rejection of evolutionary sequences of stages in the cultural sciences. The whole-language labels, such as isolating, agglutinating, inflectional, polysynthetic, and incorporating, were retained only for individual traits that might be compresent within one language.

The concern with typology was the main source of the attention paid to the structural cut of languages and to its possible import (witness the joint launching of the first journal in social psychology by Steinthal and Lazarus in 1860); and the cognitive interest was retained, but associated with grammatical categories and processes of individual languages, quite divorced from broad classes and stages. (Through Boas the interest became an intrinsic part of American linguistic anthropology.)

Typology was thus part of a third trend, the preparation in the nineteenth century of the structural outlook that was to dominate the twentieth. In this outlook much was to depend on the approach taken to the sounds of speech. In the nineteenth century European languages often were taken as a norm, such that the sounds of "primitive" languages seemed odd and even to lack constant units—as so often, projection of a lack of structure here betrayed an inadequate understanding of the nature of the primitive language being studied. Speech sounds were studied officially by a phonetics conceived as a natural science (*Naturwissenschaft*), not as a part of linguistics. Seeking universal objectivity through finer physical observation, phonetics plumbed a pit of variation, failing to see that universal invariants in language can be attained only through recognition of a patterning within language itself, and that within a language, objectivity of units is in the first instance intersubjective and qualitative. In the 1880s such a cultural (or psychological) approach to speech sounds was worked out in Kazan by Baudoin de Courtenay and Kruszewski and was independently adumbrated by Boas. Their insights became effective only later—that of the Kazan school in the work of de Saussure, Trubetskoi, and Jakobson, the Boasian heritage in Sapir's great paper, "Sound Patterns in Language" (1925). Meanwhile, the comparativists, by establishing ever more precisely the principle of invariance in historical reconstruction, anticipated and aided application of this principle in nonhistorical contexts. De Saussure's brilliant reconstruction of a part of the proto-Indo-European vowel system, for example, was not only confirmed a generation later by the discovery in Hittite of a phonological feature postulated purely on internal evidence in the reconstruction, but its treatment of relationships within and between languages as manifestations of an underlying invariant feature earlier in time is also quite the same in form as the treatment of variants within a language as manifestations of an underlying invariant compresent in time, i.e., as manifestations not of an origin but of a present system.

Twentieth century. Modern synchronic, structural linguistics emerged essentially after World War I. Despite the groundwork that had preceded it, the participants in its emergence saw not continuity but conflict. De Saussure viewed synchronic and diachronic study as antithetical—the one dealing in systems, the other in atomistic traits; and many subsequent structuralists rejected historical work, at least as practiced. At the same time, many historical scholars rejected the new descriptive approaches. Even in American linguistics, where both history and structure have often been of common concern, as the work of Sapir and Bloomfield shows, the issue has been debated (Hockett 1948, p. 188; Hymes 1964*a*, p. 600). In some circles, especially in Europe, conflict over this issue is perhaps only ending now.

The new movement was part of a general upheaval of intellectual interests after World War I and of the general shift from a primarily historical perspective to an interest in structure and form. With it came the definite triumph of "linguistics" as the general name for the study of language and the development of several different orientations toward the proper tasks of linguistics, often enough excluding portions of the general study of language by way of self-definition.

The first text of structural linguistics, the posthumous *Cours de linguistique générale*, published from lecture notes by students of de Saussure, ends with the maxim that linguistics has for its true and only object language itself (i.e., not facts of history, psychology, sociology, or whatever). De Saussure introduced the distinction *la langue : la parole*. It subsumes a variety of contrasts and has been variously interpreted and used, but the main import has been that the linguist's task is the study of *la langue*, the underlying system and social fact (de Saussure was influenced by Durkheim, as was Meillet), rather than the various aspects of speech and other uses of language that were understood as *la parole*.

Saussurean linguistics as such was maintained in Switzerland by Sechehaye, Frei, Godel, and others. In Denmark Hjelmslev drew inspiration from de Saussure (and also from Sapir) and developed with Uldall a methodological algebra, *glossematics*, which postulated the immanence of language and made no assumption as to its empirical reality. In Czechoslovakia two Russian scholars, Trubetskoi and Jakobson, collaborated to lead in the development of a structural outlook uniting synchronic and diachronic work and giving attention both to internal and external functions of language. The accomplishments included a distinctive methodology for phonological and grammatical analysis; basic examination of phonological typology in connection with a search for general laws; new emphasis on the diffusion of linguistic features, structurally interpreted; and analyses of social and poetic varieties of language. In England J. R. Firth advocated a flexible, encompassing descriptive approach, one shaped partly by the English tradition of phonetic research and partly by Malinowski's notion of the "context of situation."

In the United States the matrix of structural linguistics was in large part anthropological. Boas had prepared the way by his critique of existing generalizations about the nature of language in the light of American Indian evidence and by his insistence on the description of each language *sui generis*. (The major statement of his contribution is the 1911 introduction to the *Handbook of American Indian Languages*.) His student, Sapir, put field work with a multitude of Amerindian language structures to brilliant account in his *Language* (1921) and in his 1925 study established the basic principle of structural analysis for both American linguistics and ethnography. Around Sapir and Bloomfield gathered the subsequent leaders of professional linguistics. In the United States Bloomfield's *Language* (1933) was the first systematic exposition of the new descriptive approach, and it became the standard reference for a generation. Both Sapir and Bloomfield stressed the autonomy of language and linguistics. Sapir's *Language* is a masterful set of variations on the theme of the autonomy of grammatical form, and Bloomfield's book declares that the study of language has many times been approached, but never properly begun, because of failure to focus on language in its own right. Granting this autonomy, both saw larger implications for the results of linguistics, and indeed an interdependence with other disciplines—especially Sapir; in this respect, Bloomfield remained the more austere.

Each of these strands of structuralism has been labeled—the Geneva school, the Copenhagen school, the Prague school, the London school, the Yale school (although the differences between Sapir and his successor Bloomfield perhaps require recognition of two Yale schools). It must be remembered that distinguished linguists worked in the Netherlands, France, and elsewhere, without acquiring separate names and images, and that the labels are poor predictors of the work of individual scholars in the places named. The labels do serve as markers of salient intellectual emphases and outlooks. Differing intellectual contexts and assumptions led to sometimes acerbic exchanges in the first years after World War II; in particular, the stringent behaviorism dominant in the United States was set in method and attitude against the more open-minded empiricism found in Britain and against those influenced by phenomenology, logic, and dialectic on the Continent. There was salient skepticism, if not outright rejection, of the study of meaning, and there was antipathy to statements in terms of process in the Neo-Bloomfieldian camp. In the United States, the effective scope of linguistics became especially narrow for a time (see Joos 1957), in contrast to European outlooks and, indeed, the outlook of Boas and Sapir.

Recent trends and structural models

Developments within structural linguistics continue to hold the center of the stage. The main trend has been away from primary concern with phonology (whose conquest by structural methods was a main achievement of the 1920s and 1930s and in terms of which the battles of the day were fought) to concern with morphology, syntax, semantics, and, to some extent, stylistics, or poetics. In the 1940s and early 1950s great attention was given to the analysis of grammar in terms of morphology, the identification and distribution of forms. Especially in the United States there was an attempt to analyze grammar in terms analogous to those used in phonology, and insofar as possible, on the basis of the results of phonological analysis. This strategy of working upward from phonology fitted an emphasis on overt data (rather a "decoding" one) and a reluctance to deal with imputed entities. In the words of Joos, the maxim was "text signals its own structure." European scholars had usually taken the psychological reality of linguistic structure into account, as had Boas and Sapir; and glossematics began with the higher levels of text and grammar, working downward to phonology. In the late 1950s and the 1960s Noam Chomsky has stressed the centrality of grammar and the underlying mental abilities of users of language. His central point has been that structure in text is largely recognized not because overt signals are perceived but because users of a language apply their knowledge of grammatical structure. Chomsky's work, along with a general revival of interest in semantic work, has been the major force in bringing general American opinion into agreement to this extent with European and earlier American interests.

Models of language structure current on the American scene can be noted cursorily as follows:

(1) The Trager–Smith–Joos model, dominant in the early 1950s, treats phonology, grammar, and semology as coordinate and parallel in organization. Relations of language to culture and society are treated as questions of "metalinguistics." Language is associated with other communicative systems, such as *kinesics* (gesture and body motion) and *paralinguistics* (nonlinguistic phenomena of voice), within a general framework for the analysis of culture (Hall 1959).

(2) The *tagmemic* model, devised by Pike and subsequently developed by Longacre and others, has become the framework for descriptions from many different parts of the world, used especially by the members of the Summer Institute of Linguistics (a group devoted to translating the Bible). It treats phonology, grammar, and lexicon as coordinate hierarchies, parallel in organization. The concept of *tagmeme* treats as central the relation in grammar between a position and the class of elements that can occur in it, thus reintroducing and generalizing the notion of paradigm. Inspired by Sapir, Pike has sought to generalize linguistic methodology to make it applicable to cultural behavior (see Pike 1954). In doing so he has coined the terms "emic" and "etic" (from "phonemic" and "phonetic") for the difference between classifications of phenomena that are based on features validated internally in terms of the structure in question and classifications that are based on externally devised or generalized criteria.

Recent descriptive work done by Pike has emphasized use of matrices; by Longacre, analysis of strings and inclusion of transformations (1964).

(3) The "means–ends" model, as Jakobson (1963) has dubbed the original Prague school approach, has diffused into several lines of American research, largely through Jakobson's presence since the early 1940s. There is widespread acceptance of the notion and importance of distinctive features in phonology: the "letter size" units, or phonemes, are not ultimate constituents but bundles of contrasting components (e.g., voicing, produced by vibration of the vocal chords, versus voicelessness, or absence of vibration, which distinguishes the otherwise identical series of English stops /p t k/ : /b d g/). But not all linguists follow Jakobson in defining phonological features acoustically (in terms of the physical properties of the speech signal), some retaining definition in terms of articulation (where and how the sounds are produced); neither do all linguists follow him in supposing a proposed set of 12 phonological features to be adequate for describing all languages or in regarding distinctive features as always forming oppositions of a binary sort. Jakobson's analyses of grammatical categories in terms of distinctive semantic features have helped shape componential analysis; his work has influenced literary scholarship, ethnography, and psychology as well. [*See* COMPONENTIAL ANALYSIS.]

An enduring importance of the Prague school is that it always keeps the true social complexity of language in view as an object of linguistic study. In its conception a language is a dynamic "system of systems." A language is never a static, homogeneous system, but a developing set of interdependent, imperfectly adjusted subsystems, some of whose items are disappearing, some emerging. A language, moreover, is a set of means specialized to a multiplicity of communicative and social ends; for example, there are referential, expressive, and directive functions in speech; and literary, standard, and other varieties of a language. (On the history and present development of the Prague school, see Vachek 1964; 1966*a*; 1966*b*.)

(4) The most influential model both in the United States and abroad is that of *transformational–generative grammar.* As first formulated in the early 1950s by Zellig Harris (codifier of much post-war American method), transformations were a technique for syntax and text analysis serving to account for relations between sentences. Particularly telling have been the ways in which transformational analyses can account for the ambiguity of a sentence in terms of its derivation from two different underlying sentences; uncover an underlying difference between two superficially quite similar sentences; and integrate the productive systematic relations between different forms of sentence (e.g., actives, passives, negatives).

In the work of Harris' student, Chomsky, transformations have become part of a new model of language as a whole and of a program for radical recasting of previously held assumptions and goals. Analysis of the underlying "deep structure" of grammar is stressed; much of what was treated by earlier descriptive linguistics is relegated to "surface structure." Grammar shapes phonology rather than the reverse, and the phonological output of a grammar is specified in terms of distinctive features. (For the first influential monograph, see Chomsky 1957; for subsequent views, see Chomsky 1964; 1965; 1966.) The program is one of attack on behaviorist and positivist outlooks from a standpoint of rationalism and recent philosophy of science. The Neo-Bloomfieldian goal of an algorithm, a mechanical procedure for the analysis of a language, is shown to be futile, and earlier models of syntax are found inadequate to account for the actual facts of languages and the abilities that users of languages must have. Indeed, the goal of accounting for observed data is defined as mere *observational adequacy* (in effect, merely reporting the data). At the least, linguistics must aim for *descriptive adequacy*, an account of the knowledge that a fluent user of a language has of its structure, and which he or she can apply in producing and interpreting the infinite set of sentences of which a language is normally capable. What is crucial is the agreement of a grammar not with a corpus but with users' judgments of acceptable and unacceptable sentences. The true goal of linguistics should be *explanatory adequacy*; that is, linguistics should characterize the nature of the equipment by means of which a child acquires such knowledge. To achieve the normal yet nearly miraculous result of an infinite capacity from a finite experience in but a few years, a child must be presumed to apply actively a native endowment, formulating theories to account for and go beyond the speech he hears. The rapidity and accuracy of a child's success, no matter what the language, indicate that all languages are of only one or a few fundamental types and that the contribution of the native endowment must be great. In this light the earlier emphasis in American linguistics on the diversity of languages is reversed in favor of an active search for universals.

The focus of linguistic theory is thus reformulated as *linguistic competence*, the knowledge of the ideally fluent user of language in an ideally homogeneous speech community. Theory is completed by an account of *linguistic performance*, comprising the various conditions—psychological, occasional, social—that modify and affect the expression of underlying competence. The critique of learning theory and behaviorism provides a new program for psychologists; the model of language stimulates new work in semantics and to some extent in stylistics and ethnography, although some lines of research into the social role of language are considered misguided or premature. It is fair to say that transformational–generative grammar has replaced Neo-Bloomfieldian work as the focus of attention today. Apart from the close-knit group centered about Chomsky and Halle, some linguists join transformational syntax with other approaches, especially in phonology; and some transformationalists abjure Chomsky's views of the psychological and philosophical import of the model (e.g., Harris, Henry Hiż).

(5) The *stratificational* model owes its name and central formulation to Sydney Lamb. It has attracted several leading linguists (e.g., Hockett, Gleason) and has affinities with the work of Halliday. Originating as a systematic explication of principles in earlier American descriptive work and as a response to needs in computer use, especially mechanical translation, the model treats language as four levels, or strata—semology, lexology, morphology, phonology. The elements of the several strata are related by realization rules, which may be traced either in speaking (semology to phonology) or in hearing (phonology to semology). The model thus is intended to represent the processes of a user of language in either activity (see Gleason 1964 and Lamb 1966 for other formalizations). As

with tagmemic analysis and the Harris–Hiż type of transformational analysis, there is interest in units larger than the sentence, such as whole narratives. The sememic analysis has close ties with work in componential analysis and ethnoscience.

(6) *System-structure* is a generic name for models derived from the Firthian heritage in Great Britain. The most notable of these models is what has come to be known as the "scale-and-category" grammar of M. A. K. Halliday and others (see Halliday et al. 1964; McIntosh & Halliday 1966). A special interest of the approach is its direct incorporation of questions of "institutional linguistics" (sociology of language) and its varied application to problems of language teaching, translation, analysis of style, and study of social dialect.

While models of the way grammars should best be written are the center of attention, other lines of linguistic work continue to develop, often revitalized in the light of structural principles; new interests emerge, often as applications and extensions of structural perspective; the concerns of the humanities and social sciences and of social institutions entail selective attention to the results and possible applications of linguistics. In short, controversy focused on structural models should not obscure the great variety of present-day linguistic activity. This variety can be grasped if one considers the three main ways, each cross-cutting the others, in which linguists may be grouped for purposes of congresses, journals, appointments, and so forth. There is affiliation with one or another of the structural approaches (some scholars affiliate with none); there are the subdisciplines, such as the phonetic sciences, lexicography, semantics, stylistics and poetics, onomastics, philology, dialectology, formal and mathematical linguistics, applied linguistics, anthropological linguistics, psycholinguistics, and sociolinguistics; and there are the groupings in terms of languages studied, whether in the sense of language family (Indo-European, Germanic, Algonquian linguistics) or area (African, Indian, Oceanic linguistics).

Distinctive constellations of approach, subdiscipline, and languages studied do occur, coupled with nationality or geographical region; but the overriding trends today are an internationalization and diffusion of interests and outlooks and a broadening and integration of them. Each major structural school, for example, has adherents in several countries, and a variety of links with subdisciplines and language families and areas. Moreover, each structural school has had a conception of structural linguistics as contributing to a larger enterprise, such as a general science of signs (semiology, or semiotics), and as a link in the integration of the natural and social sciences, or at least as a strategic sector of social science; and such contributions are increasingly being realized.

Like many histories, this of linguistics has been rather Hegelian, moving from place to place and topic to topic as the "spirit" of the main advances moved. The main outlines might be caricatured in a Hegelian manner, describing the successive stages as "no language is known" (folk linguistics); "one language is known" (early national philology); "few languages are known" (later philology); and "many languages are known" (general linguistics). Yet any period comprises both the new and emerging and the old and steadily continuing, in a variety of forms, as has been indicated for the present state of linguistics. The nineteenth century was not all historical; the twentieth century is not all structural grammar; and if future linguistics builds on both in pursuit of a dominant functional concern with the place of language in human life, it will be in a spirit not of disregard of other concerns but of their integration. (On current trends, see Mohrmann et al. 1962; International Congress . . . 1963; Ivić 1965; *Current Trends in Linguistics*; *Biennial Review of Anthropology.*)

Content of linguistics

We must now take stock more exactly of the present content of linguistics. Linguistics proper can be defined by tasks that remain constant and characteristic. These central tasks are to describe languages, to classify them, and to explain their differences and similarities.

Descriptions of linguistic data. The descriptive task (understood as equivalent to analysis) is primary. In pursuing it, linguists may use a variety of means for determining data and may place data in a variety of frames of reference. To grasp this variety a general framework is needed. We shall adapt and enlarge one put forward by Hockett (1948, pp. 188–190; Hymes 1964*a*, pp. 600–601), distinguishing four kinds of means by which data are determined (contact, philological, reconstructive, theoretical) and four major frames of reference within which data are placed (syn-

Table 1 — Means and frames of reference for linguistic data

FRAMES OF REFERENCE	MEANS: Contact	Philological	Reconstructive	Theoretical
Synchronic				
Diachronic				
Diatopic				
Syncritic				

chronic, diachronic, diatopic, syncritic; Table 1 outlines this descriptive mode.

Means for determining linguistic data. Of the four kinds of means, *contact* subsumes first-hand observation, interviews, surveys, and experimentation in direct contact with users of a language—in short, the various forms of field work and laboratory work, including introspection into one's own speech habits. Such work has been most characteristic of descriptive linguistics and dialectology, and of anthropology, but the expanding role of psychologists and sociologists in the study of language must be noted (see Lounsbury 1953; Hymes 1959; Samarin 1967; Berko & Brown 1960; Ervin-Tripp 1964).

The *philological* methods are those used in the interpretation of the nature and transmission of written records, especially texts. Such methods are not limited to the study of classical languages or the languages of civilizations with writing. In the narrower sense that philological methods have come to have for some linguists, a field worker may find himself later in a philological relationship to his own materials; and in areas such as the New World the interpretation of records left by earlier investigators is indispensable for many languages no longer spoken. In the broader, earlier sense of philology, the method leads on into the general interpretation of texts for their cultural content as well as their linguistic form (see Sandys [1903–1908] 1958, vol. 1, pp. 4–13; Bernardini & Righi 1947; Hymes 1965; Malkiel 1966).

By *reconstructive* methods are meant those methods that use systematic variation in known languages (or dialects) to infer the presence and perhaps the patterning of features unknown in some other. When the evidence is from one language (or dialect) and the inference is to an earlier stage of it, the work is known as *internal reconstruction.* When the evidence is from two or more dialects or languages and the inference is to an earlier ancestral language, one usually speaks of the *comparative method.* Notice that in linguistics the term "comparative method" has this specialized use. Scholars in other fields have sometimes been misled into taking it as designating a general method of comparison, or as equivalent to such other techniques as the method of controlled comparison in social anthropology or the comparative method of nineteenth-century social evolution. Analogues to these in the study of language fall within the syncritic frame of reference and are quite distinct from what linguists speak of as the "comparative method" (see Bloomfield 1933; Hoenigswald 1960).

A less common form is that in which the inference is from a series of geographically linked languages or dialects to an intermediate or adjacent one; such use may count as a sort of reconstruction in space rather than time.

Theoretical methods concern aspects of data that are postulated by a general theory or inferred on theoretical grounds. A theoretical component is present in any description, although the extent to which it is recognized, if at all, may vary. Some examples are: that dialects be described in terms of the elements of a fixed over-all pattern; that distinctive features be binary; that rules specifying the phonological shapes of words be ordered (or unordered); that of two differing accounts the shorter is to be accepted; that of two differing accounts the more intuitively persuasive is to be accepted; and so forth.

Frames of reference. As frames of reference, linguists commonly distinguish "structural," "descriptive," or "synchronic" from "historical," or "diachronic," linguistics; linguistic geography, or dialectology, and typological comparison, together with general linguistics, often are distinguished as well. The implicit logic is to separate the primary description of languages from concern with change (through time) and with variation (in space), and from contrast and generalization independently of space and time. In adopting this scheme (somewhat relabeled for symmetry's sake), we recognize that no concise grouping can be wholly satisfactory and that the names must be somewhat arbitrary, designating as they do gross clusters of work that overlap and are internally diverse.

Synchronic description treats features (dialects, a language) with respect to a particular time, and, by implication, with respect also to a particular place. ("Structural" is used as a surrogate, but descriptions of the sort intended developed long before modern structuralism, and analysis within any frame of reference may be methodologically structural.) While other kinds of work may be strictly speaking "synchronic," the common connotation of the term in linguistics is that for the purpose at hand, data can be treated as coming from a single source and as essentially homogeneous or unified; in effect, "synchronic" means an idealized single case. The classical presentation of such a synchronic analysis is in the form of a grammar, texts, and dictionary. (For treatments of grammatical description, see Harris 1951; Hockett 1958; Gleason 1955; Bach 1964; Katz & Postal 1964; Longacre 1964; Martinet 1960; Robins 1964; Chomsky 1965; McIntosh & Halliday 1966; and the several approaches represented in the *Monograph Series on Languages and Linguistics* [see "Report of the Fifteenth Annual . . ." 1964] and the journal *Language*. On texts, see references in Hymes 1964*a*, p. 365; on dictionaries, p. 209.)

A synchronic structural description must choose or assume a particular norm—say, the standard speech of educated persons or the informal patois of lifelong inhabitants of a village. That is, any serious description must specify its boundary conditions—for whom and when and where it holds. Questions of contexts, purposes, and modes of use must enter (a point most consistently made by Firth and other British linguists such as Robins 1964; Halliday et al. 1964; Dixon 1965). Such questions are often distinguished as "functional," "structural" serving for the internal make-up of language. This usage, with its internal–external dichotomy, is not happy, however, since use must itself be structurally analyzed and since the point of structural analysis of the make-up of language is to treat features in terms of their functional relationships (e.g., sounds in terms of the contrasts into which they enter to distinguish utterances; see Sapir 1925). Considerations of structure and function apply throughout linguistics, and the extension of this joint scope is of special importance to the social sciences. It is better to specify the exact kind of structure and function in question, rather than to rely on a usage that implies a false discontinuity.

What the classical presentation of a description of use might be like is not yet known. Models for the description of language use have been often postulated, but actual analyses are rare. As prolegomena to such descriptions one can cite the framework employed by Halliday (Halliday et al. 1964) and the concept of an "ethnography of speaking" (Hymes 1962; 1964*b*). Restricting attention here to an idealized single case, one can say that an ethnography of speaking would identify and describe the speech events and sequences of speech acts recognized in a community and their distribution; their purposes and interactional norms (e.g., formal/informal); the relationships within speech events—who can participate as speakers and hearers, with regard to what settings, topics, message forms, channels, and codes; the patterning of messages in exchanges and sequences (conversations, curses, narrations, etc.); the hierarchies of functions (referential, expressive, rhetorical, poetic, and other) in such events; and the role of language with respect to other codes. No full accounts yet exist.

Diachronic description treats features (dialects, languages) in terms of time. Often one is concerned with changes in a single line of development, but features that remain stable may be of interest too; and the tracing of borrowings and their etymologies into earlier periods of other languages may become an objective of study. Among products of diachronic description are historical grammars, etymological dictionaries, statements of sound laws connecting stages of languages (e.g., Grimm's law), depictions of innovations leading to the present vocabularies of members of language groups, and so forth. Diachronic descriptions need not draw a hard line between so-called internal and external aspects of language change, and, indeed, for many purposes cannot do so. Beyond the question of what has occurred, questions of when, where, how, and why arise, requiring reference to uses, contexts, and values for their answers. It is not unusual, however, for a distinction to be drawn between *historical linguistics*, internal change, and *language history*, external events. (See chapters on language change in Sapir 1921; Bloomfield 1933; Hockett 1958; Gleason 1955; Martinet 1960; 1962; Hymes 1964*a*, parts 8 and 9.)

Diatopic description treats features (dialects, languages) in terms of space; it is thus inseparably associated with dialectology. Two observations must be made. First, dialectology is often synchronic description; important early work in Europe, for example, was motivated by concern for local forms of speech as against standard languages. There is also a European tradition of local ethnography that includes community speech as well as objects and practices. Second, diatopic description proper has not usually been undertaken for its own sake. Interest in the distribution of phenomena has often derived from diachronic questions of origin, spread, and loss. For dialects and languages, one may seek to infer an earlier location, migration, dispersion, or particular processes of formation. For features, one may seek to infer a particular history and also to sharpen a theory of linguistic change.

It remains that dialectology and linguistic geography require separate recognition, both analytically and for their special traditions of work. Earlier diatopic work most familiarly focused on sounds and words and produced atlases and maps. Recently there has been much recasting of earlier work in structural terms—e.g., analyzing the distribution of sounds in terms of phonological patterns (Hymes 1964*a*, p. 481).

A second kind of diatopic description is concerned not with geographic space but with social space. Earlier work was most concerned with the social dimension as it "horizontally" tied together several communities. Current work stresses "vertical" relations within communities, talking more of *social dialect* than of geographical dialect.

Such study may focus on the distribution of specific linguistic variables within a community; in doing so it gives special attention to the social valuation and role of these variables, for the light shed on the community as well as on processes of origin and diffusion (see Fischer 1958; Labov 1963; 1964). Description of variation in social space may also focus on all the varieties of speech to be found in a community—speech levels, men's speech and women's, baby talk, argots, and the like. The features of such forms of speech are specifiable structurally, but they appear here as aspects of the use of language within a universe that is defined first of all in social, not linguistic, terms. From an internal linguistic standpoint, cases of, say, men's versus women's speech appear only when the differences intrude into the normal description of a language, e.g., as constant differences in the phonological shape of lexical items or as obligatory alternates for inflectional elements. The speech appropriate to men and women presumably is differentiated in every society, however; it should be possible to describe how to "talk like a man" and "talk like a woman" everywhere. From the present standpoint one would inquire into the nature of the differentiation—whether or not it could be ignored in an ordinary grammar.

Such diatopic work is closely linked with description of use within a community. Indeed, in the description of a single community a full diatopic account and a synchronic ethnography of speaking differ only by an element of definition. An idealized synchronic account would restrict itself to a single variety of a language; but in fact every speech community has at least three (formal, conversational, slang). At the level of relations among a series of communities, however, or of relationships within a unit such as the nation, new complexities and types of problems emerge, so that the community-linked perspective of an ethnography of speaking can be considered part of a more general enterprise, the construction of an integrated theory of sociolinguistic description for social units of whatever scale and size.

Syncritic description compares dialects, languages, or features without regard to relative position in space and time. Such work is often called "typological," especially when the purpose is structural classification of whole languages or their subsystems. "Comparative" would be a natural term, had it not been pre-empted for a reconstructive method and, by extension, the particular kind of work to which that method contributes. Some British linguists indeed seek to recapture "comparative" for comparison of languages generally, including comparison for purposes of translation and language teaching (often called "contrastive linguistics" in the United States; see Halliday et al. 1964, pp. 111–112). *Syncritic* (from the Greek *synkrisis*, meaning "comparison") seems useful as a term that is both general and unambiguous, and so we introduce it here.

Syncritic description is undertaken sometimes simply to exhibit what diversity of structure may exist among languages, perhaps also to devise a classificatory scheme or measures for a scheme. Two particular purposes can be distinguished as *contrastive* and *generic*. A contrastive study sets out to specify differences, as in the characterizations of French and German by Bally or in the setting of Hopi against "Standard Average European" done by Whorf. (Whorf introduced the term "contrastive" in this use.) A generic study seeks significant commonalties in order to establish universals of language—underlying principles either true of all languages or so widely true independently of relationship in time and space as to require a general, rather than a historical, explanation (see Conference on Language Universals 1963; Martinet 1962; Chomsky 1965; references in Hymes 1964*a*, p. 661).

Syncritic description of uses and contexts also has contrastive and generic purposes, the contrastive being more salient. A notable example is Bernstein's model of two types of code, elaborated and restricted, which are characterized by differences that include the signaling of subjective intent in verbally explicit form versus its transmission extraverbally; the focusing of attention on verbal versus extraverbal channels; reliance on verbal persuasion versus authority; orientation toward personal discretion within roles versus status relationships and shared assumptions. The model has been most discussed with regard to class differences in England and the United States, but it has a more general application. For members of any class some situations may call for restricted code behavior; and it seems likely that aspects of socialization pertaining to whole societies can be contrasted in these terms. Other examples of syncritic work of this sort contrast types of verbal interaction as transactional or personal; types of bilingualism as coordinate or compound; types of speech situation as formal or informal; and the like. (These examples and related ones are discussed in articles by Bernstein,

Ervin-Tripp, and Gumperz in Gumperz & Hymes 1964, and in articles by Bloomfield, Gumperz, Ferguson, Diebold, and Garvin in Hymes 1964*a*.)

Each of the contrastive analyses might be directed toward generic purposes. Thus one might have a systematic comparison of baby talk or of men's and women's speech with a view to generalizations as to their places in human society as a whole. A further step would be to analyze and compare ranges and uses for whole languages or speech communities, seeking to identify recurrent patterns of function (independent of historical connection) and to integrate such patterns with the results of the contrastive typologies. Such an approach entails a consideration of the place of language among other modes of human communication and the comparison of human communication with communication in other species, treating language as a resource differentially allocated and adapted in human societies on a certain generic base.

Comments. The sketch of kinds of means and frames of reference requires two comments. First, the broad categories of means and frameworks do not conflict or stand in isolation. A way of determining data may contribute to any frame of reference; a frame of reference may make use of any means. Field work, for example, is often thought of as a means to synchronic description, but its purpose may be to place a language genetically or to trace the process of acculturation; to study relations among geographical or social dialects; to determine the distinctive cognitive style of a language or to substantiate a proposed universal of grammar. Synchronic description is often based on contact work, but one may write grammatical rules for philologically interpreted texts or a reconstructed language or specify theoretically the universal parameters of grammar. Desirable as such interplay is in principle, in practice it may be obscured by specialization and controversy (as it has been on some occasions in synchronic and diachronic work); but in the long run interest in knowledge of languages prevails, especially in the work of great scholars. Every means that can contribute information is likely to find a place; frames of reference are likely to prove complementary. Such unity in diversity appears most often in work on a group of languages, be it Romance (see Malkiel 1964*b*), Dravidian, or Algonquian. Most linguists being specialists in some language group, such work is a source of stability and strength to the field.

Second, an exact analysis of kinds of work and their interrelationships would require a greater number of dimensions, accurately and systematically named. One set would distinguish study of syntactics (relations of signs within a code), semantics (relations of signs to referents), and pragmatics (relations of signs to their users). (The distinctions are those of Morris; see Greenberg 1948; Hymes 1964*a*, pp. 27–31.) Our discussion has, in fact, consistently noted study of use (pragmatics) as well as study of codes (syntactics, semantics). A second set of distinctions concerns the underlying dimensions of time, space, social group, system, and function. For these, one can use the Greek forms *-chronic, -topic, -gelic, -systemic, -telic* together with a prefix to specify in what way each dimension is taken into account. Useful prefixes include *a-* : without reference to the dimension; *mono-* : one reference point; *bi-, tri-,* etc.: two, three, etc., reference points; *poly-* : multiple reference points; *pan-* : all reference points; *syn-* : treatment as having common reference point; *dia-* : treatment as having continuum, or linked series of reference points. Such dimensions and terms make terminologically convenient a large number of necessary distinctions. Thus, studies that treat the history of a language in terms of discrete stages (e.g., bichronic) can be distinguished from studies that treat it as a continuous development (diachronic). Within the context of synchronic descriptive theory, one can distinguish the complex adequacy of Prague school theory (diatopic, diagelic, polysystemic, polytelic) from descriptive theory that implies a wholly homogeneous description (monotopic, monoagelic, monosystemic, monotelic).

We have broached something of the tasks of classification and explanation; more must now be said about each.

Classification of languages. Languages are often classified by their common internal features (phonological, grammatical, lexical) and in one or another of three ways: as belonging to the same family, the same area, the same type. Although each way implies a different sort of process and explanation, the three need not be mutually exclusive; in a limiting case, a set of languages may all belong to the same family, area, and type at once.

When languages belong to the same family they share a *genetic relationship.* Specific features of each are explained as due to retention (perhaps much changed) from a common ancestor of all. English, Frisian, Dutch, German, Icelandic, Norwegian, Danish, Swedish (and extinct Gothic), for example, belong to the same family, Germanic, in virtue of their descent from a common ancestor that is called Proto-Germanic. As it happens, that ancestor can be shown to belong to an older family, Indo-European, whose common ancestor, Proto-Indo-European, may itself someday be shown convincingly to belong in yet an older family. The proportion of features that attest the genetic connection of languages may be quite small; what is required is that the presence of the features be inexplicable by chance or borrowing.

When languages are said to belong to the same language area (German *Sprachbund*), or convergence area, they share an *areal relationship*. Continued compresence in the same area may enable genetically related languages to maintain great commonalty of content through shared innovations and mutual borrowing, despite long divergence from their joint ancestor; these languages may even increase their commonalty after an earlier period of differentiation (see Hoenigswald 1960, pp. 155–157; Malkiel 1964*a*; Kroeber 1955). The most salient cases of areal relationship are those in which the languages are genetically unrelated. Thus the languages of the subcontinent of India belong to three distinct families (Indo-Aryan branch of Indo-European, Dravidian, Munda), but they share significant traits through sustained contact (Emeneau 1956; Hymes 1964*a*, pp. 642–650).

When languages are said to belong to the same type, one must notice what portion of their features is concerned. A *typological relationship* may be defined by one or a few traits of interest or by a distinct system or level (phonology, morphology, syntax, lexicon). Attempts to assign languages as wholes to types (a *language type* proper) have focused on grammatical or semantic characteristics or both. When specific features are investigated, a given language may, of course, fall together in type with quite different sets of other languages, depending on the features in question. (On genetic, areal, and typological classification, see references in Hymes 1964*a*, pp. 659–661, 651–653, 661–663, respectively.)

Classification of languages in terms of context and use is less well developed, a fact reflected in the absence of a comprehensive conventional terminology. There exists a scattering of individual terms not yet systematized. The dimensions of the subject can be sketched, however, along lines corresponding to those just followed, taking the genetic as concerned primarily with origin, the areal with co-occurrence, the typological as independent of either.

Some terms focus attention on languages as marked by their origin in particular circumstances of use. A *koiné* is a language that has arisen as a lingua franca by a merging of traits among a group of related dialects, as in the Greek *koiné* of Hellenistic times (from which the term comes). A *pidgin* arises by drastic reduction of one language, typically with admixture of another; it is by definition a second language to all who use it. A *creole* arises if a pidgin becomes and remains the first language for a group, expanding into a normal range of use. (Thus, by definition a creole was once a pidgin.) By virtue of their common origin in conscious invention, constructed languages intended for international auxiliary use (Esperanto, Interlingua, etc.) belong here.

Some terms group languages according to their relationships within a community or larger population. Some groups of Sephardic Jews in Greece, for example, used Greek at work, Hebrew in religious observances, and Spanish in family conversation. Together the three languages formed their linguistic (or verbal) repertoire. One general classification of the varieties forming a verbal repertoire distinguishes those associated with geographic and social differences and those associated with differences of activity, as *dialectal* and *superposed*, respectively. [*On this and other aspects of use, see* LINGUISTICS, *article on* THE SPEECH COMMUNITY.] Terms often distinguish range of use; "standard language : dialect" and "world language : vernacular" are two such pairs. The use of "language : dialect" has varied and is still unresolved, but the two terms are always correlated in such a way that dialect is the subordinate term—language indicating a variety with higher status or wider use or a set of dialects as a whole.

An important kind of co-occurrence is that analyzed by Ferguson (1959; Hymes 1964*a*, pp. 429–438) as *diglossia*: two mutually unintelligible forms of language are in use—one for government, literature, formal religion, and the like (the "High" form) and one for informal conversation, the home, and the like (the "Low" form). The two are part of the verbal repertoire of some, but not all, members of a society, many knowing only the Low form. The general description of language co-occurrence within nations has begun to be studied as a nation's *sociolinguistic profile* (Ferguson 1966).

Some terms specify use without necessary reference either to origin or co-occurrence. One such term is *lingua franca*, a language that serves as a common medium throughout a linguistically diverse region. *Standard language*, as a consciously codified form of language, belongs here, considered in terms of its intrinsic characteristics and associated attitudes and functions (see Garvin 1959; Hymes 1964*a*, pp. 521–526, with references). Indeed, all terms that designate components of a verbal repertoire or sociolinguistic profile may be specified and studied syncritically: the High and Low forms of a diglossia situation, languages of religion, trade languages, languages of concealment, slang, etc., can all be studied both in terms of the social circumstances of their origin and in terms of their co-occurrence with other varieties of language.

The uses and imports of the modes of classification are varied but ultimately interrelated. Genetic classification has a certain priority, as a background against which to interpret relationships of area and use and from which to guarantee the historical independence of cases for typological generalizations. As a mode of explanation of resemblances among languages, genetic classification has sometimes been set off against areal classification, as in the Boas–Sapir controversy (see Swadesh 1951; Hymes 1964*a*, pp. 624–637) and in the earlier California work of Dixon and Kroeber (see Hymes 1961*a*; 1964*a*, pp. 689–707). But in fact, the logic underlying the historical modes of classification makes them interdependent. This logic is to determine if corresponding features are (1) of independent origin (universals, convergent, chance), or (2) due to historical connection, and, if historical, whether (*a*) genetic ("cognate"), due to retention from a common ancestor, or (*b*) diffusional ("borrowed"). Neither genetic nor diffusional origin can be assumed; each must be proved, and proof of one excludes the other. Actual historical work must thus attend to both. There remain questions concerning what explanation to assign to particular kinds and amounts of data. Well-integrated grammatical traits and basic vocabulary are the best, though not infallible, test of genetic connection. Despite a priori controversy, the work of the great students of linguistic prehistory is in practice one of cumulative inference from all the available evidence.

Although the languages of the world have been provisionally assigned to genetic groupings, such work is far from complete. For most parts of the world new and better descriptions of languages will permit deeper penetration of the past, as will reconstruction of protolanguages by the comparative method. Anthropologists (Swadesh, Greenberg, Haas, and others) have taken a leading role in this work, dealing with both proof of relationships and development of method for the great time depths and remote relationships that face students of linguistic prehistory. If data permit, beyond proof of relationship lies establishment of relative chronology (subgrouping) among the related languages and of the location and perhaps some of the cultural content of the ancestral language. Proof of borrowing may also lead to knowledge of relative chronology of relationship and the earlier location and cultural content of languages. Such work may provide a framework and hypotheses for prehistoric research with other lines of evidence, and of course it provides many precise examples of regularities and complexities of change, examples that have constantly been posed as problems for psychological and sociological explanation.

Studies of the American Indian languages of the Pacific Coast early revealed phonological areas where many distinct languages share systems containing few vowels and many consonants (including glottalized stops and voiceless laterals); and initial attempts to determine grammatical areas were made early in the century by Dixon and Kroeber. Neither in North America nor in the rest of the world outside Europe, however, has knowledge of areal connections gone beyond some notable individual studies. Increased interest in the structuring of interrelations of communities (such terms as "social field" and "intermediate societies") may stimulate increased attention to areal relationship as its linguistic counterpart (cf. Gumperz 1961).

Typological relationship may be linked to areal relationship, as when reconstruction of the Proto-Indo-European vowel system suggests a former areal tie with languages of the Caucasus or when it is proposed that proliferation of phonemes is correlated with fewness of speakers in areas of linguistic diversity, since persons in small communities learn the languages of their neighbors as a result either of accommodation or of exogamy, and in either way introduce among themselves phonetic habits that come to enlarge the phonological system of their language. Most typological classification points in one of two directions. It seeks to explain recurrent types in terms of the limited possibilities and internal interdependence of linguistic systems (e.g., laws of the sort, "If A, then B") and to relate such types to underlying generic properties of the human mind; or it seeks to delineate types in terms of the selective drift within a given culture history, as distinctive of a society or as characteristic of a sociocultural type. (Findings with regard to Hopi, Navajo, and Wintu, for example, may be seen as manifestations of an underlying outlook common to primitive society that Redfield dubbed "participant maintenance.") The two directions seem to alternate in attention, interest in distinctiveness having given way recently to interest in what is common, considered apart from sociocultural adaptation; but underlying commonalty does not level the projecting differences that show languages engaged in the histories and lives of those who use them. Both interests are required to explain language.

Classifications as to use (often dubbed functional classifications) are of obvious importance to any concern with the varying roles of languages in culture, society, and personality. Choice and role of language are particularly important in nationalism, political identity, state formation, economic development, and in literacy, education, international communication; and they are also important for changes in the valuation of language itself relative to other modes of experience and communication. New analyses and syntheses of what is known are greatly needed, but they are only slowly beginning to appear (see Weinreich 1953; Ferguson & Gumperz 1960; Fishman et al. 1966, pp. 424–458; Ferguson 1966).

Each principal mode of classification in terms of internal content may seem linked to a different frame of reference—genetic to diachronic, areal to diatopic, typological to syncritic—but something of their interconnection has appeared. Any instance of classification can be put into all frames of reference by asking: What are the underlying descriptions? How did the relevant features come about? Where do they occur? What are their defining characteristics? And in pursuit of historical explanation, the emergence, persistence, and sometimes extinction of families, areas, types, and modes of use are interwoven (see Hoenigswald 1960). Pidgins and creoles, for example, pose problems for theory of genetic and areal relationship and for generic interpretation of typological resemblances. In sum, each mode of classification is useful, indeed indispensable, for particular questions: the major questions of linguistic explanation join together all of the modes. To generalize what Boas once wrote (with genetic classification in mind): "the problem of the study of language is not one of classification. . . . Our task is to trace the history of the development of human speech" ([1920] 1955, p. 212).

For any one language, its features can in principle be explained in terms of a portion common to all languages as languages (typological–generic), a portion retained from an ancestral stage (genetic), a portion acquired from other languages with which it has come into contact (diffusional), all of these portions having adapted to each other along distinctive lines (typological–contrastive) in certain circumstances of use. In Sapir's words, "The formal configuration of speech at any particular time and place is the result of a long and complex historical development, which, in turn, is unintelligible without constant reference to functional factors" ([1924] 1949, p. 152).

Explanation and import. Descriptions and classifications go but part of the way in explaining linguistic data and their import. At the height of the historical approach to language the maxim was offered that the only explanation of a linguistic form is an earlier linguistic form. When the Neo-Bloomfieldian descriptive approach was dominant, some found it humorous to be asked to lecture on the nature of language. One asked of languages not "why" but "what." Such particularistic extremes set in relief the more common belief of linguists that in describing and classifying they also are illuminating something beyond the data in hand. How illumination is to come, what it should be, whether it is doggedly sought for or comfortably assumed—all yield much of the drama of the development of linguistics. The quest, most generally put, has been for meaning in particular texts and cultures, for the course of history, for characteristics of the human mind—in effect, for human nature as manifest in the concrete, in history, and in essence.

While the crucial role of language in human life makes its scientific study of perduring relevance to such goals, it remains true that most of the time most linguists seek the illumination of data within their own domain. "Why" questions, explicit or implicit, have a range of answers from the facts of a given language to general principles of structure, from facts of retention and borrowing to general processes of change. Each mode of description and classification implies explanation of some aspect of languages through the relationships it recognizes and discovers.

For our purpose, the critical point is reached when pursuit of explanation leads to relationships extending beyond language, when language is to explain or be explained in relation to other disciplines. Here questions of the unity and future of linguistics are most sharply posed. It is not that there are no questions of unity within linguistics proper, of the integration of different lines of purely linguistic work, but we can consider such questions only as they are entailed by the question of unity within the larger field of linguistics.

The field of linguistics

As must any discipline, linguistics proper must be master in its own house—literally, autonomous; but autonomy can be compatible with either isolation or integration. It is a striking fact that insistence on the independence of linguistics from other disciplines contributes to disunity within linguistics itself, for the independence is defined at the expense of some legitimate mode of studying linguistic data. Recognition of the unity of linguistics as a whole promotes recognition of its interdependence with other disciplines in the broader field of linguistics.

The many aspects of the import of linguistics and other disciplines for each other cannot be reviewed here; rather, we can consider what bases exist for integrating within a unified field of linguistics.

Unity and interdependence have long been recognized in principle, and often in practice, in the pursuit of historical explanation and philological interpretation, where one uses all there is to use. In the particular case, knowledge of customs, artifacts, social conditions, distributions, and environment plays a part inseparable from linguistic knowledge. The disciplines called upon to contribute include archeology, paleobotany, geography, folklore, comparative religion, numismatics, political and social history, and so forth. Where questions of the formation, movement, adaptation, specialization, obsolescence, and extinction of languages are concerned, dependence on social history is patent.

It is fair to say that the situation regarding unity is unclear outside the domain of historical explanation. A unity centered in structural analysis has gone far, integrating a great deal of work in linguistics proper, through recognition that structural formulations are prerequisite to many questions of history and use. There have been several efforts to base integration of a larger field on particular structural models (see references in Hymes 1964*a*, pp. 61–62), but none has prevailed. In other human sciences relevant to language one finds some use of linguistic models, some picking and choosing of linguistic results, some neglect of connection. The role of such disciplines in structural linguistics is similar; one finds some use of analytic models, some picking and choosing of results, some neglect or even denial of connection.

Such a situation may continue indefinitely. However, a larger unity within the field of linguistics can be attained; linguistic data must remain the focus, but the perspective brought to bear must encompass the gamut of relationships that determine the use of language.

The central requirement of such a perspective is that it focus on the integrity of the verbal message as an act. From such a focus there follows a series of consequences for conceptions of the object of analysis, consequences that have been partly indicated with regard to synchronic, diatopic, and syncritic description, but that must now be explicitly drawn.

(1) Linguistic description has focused on the form of languages, neglecting the structuring of their use (*la langue* as opposed to *la parole*). The social sciences, on the other hand, have usually been concerned with language use, neglecting form. Consequently, most attempts to integrate language with culture or society have inevitably failed, for the terms of the relationship have been conceived as disparate abstractions. A grammar and an ethnography both treat verbal messages as data, but, typically, neither studies messages as having an integral structuring of their own. The one abstracts certain aspects of form, the other certain aspects of content (other kinds of form), as if they were historically disjunct products. Having put asunder, one may try to join together, but the form and process of speech, wherein the relation of language to culture and society is mediated, the cambium, as it were, of both, has not been incorporated into either abstraction. A unified field of linguistics requires study of the patterning of speech as well as of codes.

(2) Structural description has usually defined its object synchronically as a single homogeneous code or the abilities of an ideally fluent user of such a code in an ideally homogeneous community. Such simplification is useful when models of internal structure are being devised and single codes are being described in their terms. Models of the structure of speech must allow for multiplicity of codes —quotation within messages and switching between messages (of bilinguals)—and specialization of codes in different topics, occasions, roles, and institutions. A unified field of linguistics should have as its natural unit of study the speech community rather than the individual code.

(3) Structuralists have usually considered the relation of language to other aspects of life as only supplementing what normally counts as language structure. One looks out from the linguistic account, seeing its features as subject to variation or additional rules and restrictions. The best models do envisage extension of structural description from sentences to larger units—paragraphs, narratives, even conversations, and the many recurrent routines that make daily speech so much more predictable than the infinite potential of language would suggest. Even so, much remains undiscerned until one looks at the linguistic account from the standpoint of its additional functions in social use. In general, one cannot predict such functions from

relations of structure as ordinarily described; rather, each level of organization (function) reveals new structural relationships among elements of those below it. Modal particles, for example, may show structural relationships only when seen to join with features of intonation to serve an expressive function. No internal linguistic relationship brings together greetings, terms of address, insults, curses, request forms, and so forth; only social rules can show each to be a set. Thus the lexicon and phrases of a language can be wholly analyzed structurally only from the standpoint of the social level, for some sets within the network of contrasts into which they enter are socially defined. Moreover, the usual structural account, normatively generalizing, omits as ungrammatical some sentences that specifically and acceptably do occur in a community.

In sum, social situations, relationships, and purposes bring into being and maintain linguistic (and nonlinguistic) features and relationships among them. A unified field of linguistics must consider the structures of languages from the standpoint of a description of their contexts of use.

(4) Structural descriptions have usually taken the functions of language for granted. They have focused on the organization of language in the service of reference. The latter term is used here as distinct from both denotation and meaning. One discovers the denotation of an expression in its application on particular occasions; its reference in a dictionary, which states criteria for its application; its meaning in the total import of the situation (see Firth 1935). In effect, most description has based itself on just those speech acts in which grammatical sentences are used with full referential force, neglecting the poetic or expressive facets of speech acts, for example, and the many messages in which (in Sapir's phrase) it is as if a powerful generator were hooked up to run an electric doorbell.

Descriptive theory has generally taken the social adaptation of language for granted as being everywhere the same. The images of one language per community and the infinite potential of any language (as well as the struggle against misconceptions of the adequacy of "primitive" languages) have led some to a militant egalitarianism that refuses to consider the obvious fact that the potentials of languages are not developed equally or in identical directions; that a language is often specialized in certain roles, not all; and that the valuation of even a native language may vary from community to community: free resource here, scarce good there; integral to unity here, easily abandoned there; an object of pride here, without prestige, even disvalued, there; and so forth.

Models of internal structure may ignore these variations in adaptation: reference is indeed the central function underlying grammatical structure. It remains that a unified field of linguistics must take the functions of language (both in speech acts and in communities) as problematic, and it must develop the concepts and methods for their study. (On functions in speech acts, see Jakobson 1960; Hymes 1962; 1964*b*; on functions of languages, see Hymes 1961*a*; 1966; Ferguson 1966.)

The patterning of speech, from the standpoint of communities and contexts of use and the gamut of functions that speech serves in particular acts and groups, as men enact and transcend their situations, is a dimension of a "totalizing" approach (Sartre 1960) that calls for case studies and analytic comparisons going beyond any line of work familiar to us now; yet the need for such an approach can be indicated readily with regard to several problems.

Understanding the acquisition of language by children is of both theoretical and practical importance. Some seek to account for linguistic competence as the process of a child's learning to use any and all grammatical sentences in a language; but such a conception of a child's competence at once omits and idealizes. It omits, in that a child competent in all sentences still would be master of none, not knowing when, where, and how to speak, and about what, to whom, not sharing the attitudes and valuations of the community toward language. It idealizes, in that mastery even of internal structure is a matter of degree, affected at its root by social environment. To explain and affect the communicative competence of children requires the totalizing approach just indicated.

The relation of language to thought is persistently of concern. While the two are far from identical, experience and experimental evidence demonstrate that features of a language do shape behavior and thought. In the long run a language is shaped by the needs of its users, but in the short run the acquisition of experience through a particular language and the need to call on ready linguistic categories partly shape men. All men potentially perceive and think much the same; actually, they notice, store, and recall information mainly in familiar verbal grooves, although the aspects of life for which this is true may vary from society to society. In a multilingual world, moreover, a given language may be the matrix of thought to one person but only its superficial, occasional garb to another. The effect of a language on thought and behavior cannot be inferred from the language alone, but on the basis of a sociolinguistic description of its place in social and personal life (see Hymes 1966).

Verbal art—poetry, narration, oratory, rhetoric, dialectic—is universally made possible by language. A language, indeed, may be viewed as an aesthetic product (Sapir 1921). The forms possible to a verbal art are conditioned by the language, which is also the indispensable means to their study. With the new interest in metrics, poetics, and stylistics as approached through structural linguistics, and with the aid of folklore and anthropology, a truly comparative literature, global in scope, may emerge. And, if seen as not a matter of forms and texts alone but of symbolic action as well, verbal art becomes of special interest to the human sciences generally [*see* DRAMA; INTERACTION, *article on* DRAMATISM]. The aspects of human nature that underlie the universality of verbal art; the extent to which abilities are cultivated or left dormant, and why; differences in the valuation of language as an aesthetic medium, relative to others (music, dance, ritual, plastic arts) and to other concerns; the structuring of performances and the possibilities that such structures show major areal groupings, express particular aspects of social life, and reflect particular conceptions of the uses of language—all such concerns require an approach through texts as situated in contexts.

The question of the origin of language has returned to prominence, even though theory in this field is in one sense a myth, a projection into time of assumptions on the essential nature of language and its meaning for man. Linguistics proper can prescribe the elements, generic to all languages, whose origins are to be accounted for. (There is the possibility also that some elements of the last stage of the emergence of true language might be recoverable genetically.) A theory of origin must draw on all possible lines of evidence—biological, psychological, archeological—within a theory of the evolution of man. Since language emerges within an ongoing communication system, it is crucial to specify the conditions of selection that would have been operative. Comparison of human communication systems with those of primates is indispensable; so also is comparison of human communication systems among themselves. Studies that analyze comparatively the uses of language are also necessary, in that they bring into view not only what language may be used for but also what it need not be used for in the transmission of culture and cooperative activity (e.g., some societies seem not to require language for hunting or transmission of tool-making traditions). It is likely that a very limited code, less than true language, sufficed in small homogeneous groups until relatively late in prehistory.

With regard to linguistic conceptions of the unity of man, three perspectives can be distinguished—one envisaging unity through a common origin in the past, one envisaging unity in terms of a common essential nature of language in every time and place, and one envisaging a prospective unity in the context of an emerging world society. The three perspectives are complementary, but the first was more prominent in the nineteenth century (although carried on today in the work of Swadesh and others); the second has been more prominent with the emergence of structural linguistics in this century; and the third is coming into prominence with the increased attention, theoretical and practical, to a sociolinguistic approach. For a long period of human history the differentiation and dispersion of languages was the dominant process, but reintegration and mutual adaptation of languages within more complex social systems have increasingly superseded it. Indeed, genetic differentiation may never occur again. The processes of reintegration and mutual adaptation have accelerated within the same period that general linguistics has emerged, and many of the varied phenomena that attract sociolinguistic attention are aspects of the development of a single modern world—the correlated standardization of national languages; acculturation of dialects and of whole languages; the emergence of pidgins and creoles at the frontiers of mercantile activity and colonization; the efforts to construct rational international languages; the growth of language academies and bourgeois notions of correctness; the cultivation of intertranslatability among the languages of Europe; the challenge to the stable diglossia of older philological civilizations by proponents of "Low" forms of speech; the extension of writing and literacy; and so forth. If these phenomena are to be related within linguistic theory, that theory must approach communities, functions, uses, and adaptations in a way that indeed takes on the character of an evolutionary perspective.

In one view, to be sure, the concept of evolution does not apply to language after its origin. Certainly no subsequent biological selection is apparent (although suggestions concerning a genetic basis for a few sounds have been made). From the standpoint of sociocultural evolution the matter is different. In their make-up, use, and survival, languages have been part of the specific adaptations of societies to environments, cultural contacts, and internal changes. And if all languages are equivalent in fundamental structure and potential capacity, languages as actually developed and available to their users have come to differ in ways that correspond, in part, to general stages of the cultural history of man. One mark is development in terms of the metalinguistic function (language about language), as seen in the development of linguistics itself. Some grammatical features and phonological characteristics seem present at one or another level of sociocultural integration and not at others. Most clearly, the differentiation of society is necessarily accompanied by technical elaboration and differentiation in vocabulary and syntax of a novel order. Recently, such development has been carried to the point of providing the linguistic tools for universal science and an incipient world civilization. Science itself is a key factor, for the languages in which it can be conducted (the small subset that may be called "world" languages) share the novel obligation that there be a name for everything in the universe: botany must leave no plant unnamed, ornithology no bird, ethnology no tribe, and so forth. While mathematics and logic have become what may be considered "postlanguage" developments, it remains true that they must be interpreted in natural languages and can be interpreted only in a few of them. The ideal of universal translatability is most nearly realized in these languages (as languages into which translation is made). These languages of course confer no necessary superiority or advantage on any individual. A user of English may be less able to master experience verbally and less skilled in language use than a user of a language quite local in scope. Even so, these observations must be controversial as they stand, offending as they do the widespread belief in the equivalence of all languages in complexity and function (see Hymes 1961*a*; 1964*c*). The practical importance of such observations is manifest, however, in many issues of education and language policy, both in industrialized and industrializing nations. It should be clear that a modern evolutionary approach to society and culture fails to be adequate, theoretically or practically, if it excludes language.

Linguistics will play a part in the social sciences in the future if only because language so often must be the means of access to other things. Interest in language for its own sake as an aspect of man and society will continue to be an integral part of anthropology and psychology, and, increasingly, of sociology. The novel contributions that linguistic results and linguistic methods can make will be a constant source of such interest, but if an integration within a larger field of linguistics is to be realized, the social sciences themselves will have to contribute results and methods to the study of language. The prominence of the terms "ethnolinguistics," "psycholinguistics," and "sociolinguistics" since World War II augurs such a trend. While each term mediates between linguistics and a particular discipline, the set in total mediates between linguistics and the social sciences as a whole, drawing the two together. The outcome of such a unity will be a linguistics that is truly the science of language.

DELL HYMES

BIBLIOGRAPHY

BACH, EMMON W. 1964 *An Introduction to Transformational Grammars.* New York: Holt.

BERKO, JEAN; and BROWN, ROGER W. 1960 Psycholinguistic Research Methods. Pages 517–557 in Paul Mussen (editor), *Handbook of Research Methods in Child Development.* New York: Wiley.

BERNARDINI, ANTONIO; and RIGHI, GAETANO (1947) 1953 *Il concetto di filologia e di cultura classica dal Rinascimento ad oggi.* 2d ed. Bari (Italy): Laterza.

Biennial Review of Anthropology. → Published since 1955.

BLOOMFIELD, LEONARD (1933) 1951 *Language.* Rev. ed. New York: Holt.

BOAS, FRANZ 1911 Introduction. Part 1, pages 1–83 in Franz Boas (editor), *Handbook of American Indian Languages.* U.S. Bureau of American Ethnology, Bulletin No. 40. Washington: Government Printing Office.

BOAS, FRANZ (1920) 1955 The Classification of American Languages. Pages 211–218 in Franz Boas, *Race, Language and Culture.* New York: Macmillan. → First published in Volume 22 of *American Anthropologist* New Series.

BOLGAR, R. R. 1954 *The Classical Heritage and Its Beneficiaries.* Cambridge Univ. Press. → A paperback edition was published in 1964 by Harper.

BORST, ARNO 1957–1963 *Der Turmbau von Babel: Geschichte der Meinungen über Ursprung und Vielfalt der Sprachen und Völker.* Vols. 1–4. Stuttgart (Germany): Hiersemann.

CASSIRER, ERNST (1923) 1953 *The Philosophy of Symbolic Forms.* Volume 1: Language. New Haven: Yale Univ. Press.

CHOMSKY, NOAM (1957) 1964 *Syntactic Structures.* The Hague: Mouton.

CHOMSKY, NOAM 1964 *Current Issues in Linguistic Theory.* Janua Linguarum, Series Minor, No. 38. The Hague: Mouton.

CHOMSKY, NOAM 1965 *Aspects of the Theory of Syntax.* Massachusetts Institute of Technology, Research Laboratory of Electronics, Special Technical Report, No. 11. Cambridge, Mass.: M.I.T. Press.

CHOMSKY, NOAM 1966 *Cartesian Linguistics: A Chapter in the History of Rationalist Thought.* New York: Harper.

CONFERENCE ON LANGUAGE UNIVERSALS, DOBBS FERRY, NEW YORK, *1961* 1963 *Universals of Language: Report of a Conference.* Edited by Joseph H. Greenberg. Cambridge, Mass.: M.I.T. Press.

Current Trends in Linguistics. → Published since 1963.

DIXON, ROBERT M. W. 1965 *What Is Language? A New Linguistic Approach to Linguistic Description.* London: Longmans.

EMENEAU, MURRAY B. 1956 India as a Linguistic Area. *Language* 32:3–16.

ERVIN-TRIPP, SUSAN 1964 An Analysis of the Interaction of Language, Topic, and Listener. Pages 86–102 in John Gumperz and Dell Hymes (editors), *The Ethnography of Communication.* American Anthropologist, New Series, Vol. 66, No. 6, Part 2. Menasha, Wisc.: American Anthropological Association.

FERGUSON, CHARLES A. 1959 Diglossia. *Word: Journal of the Linguistic Circle of New York* 15:325–340.

FERGUSON, CHARLES A. 1966 National Sociolinguistic Profile Formulas. Pages 309–315 in UCLA Sociolinguistics Conference, Los Angeles, 1964, *Sociolinguistics.* Edited by William Bright. Janua Linguarum, Series Maior, Vol. 20. The Hague: Mouton.

FERGUSON, CHARLES A.; and GUMPERZ, JOHN J. (editors) 1960 *Linguistic Diversity in South Asia: Studies in Regional, Social, and Functional Variation.* Indiana Univ., Research Center in Anthropology, Folklore, and Linguistics, Publications, Vol. 13. Bloomington, Ind.: The Center.

FIRTH, JOHN R. (1935) 1957 The Technique of Semantics. Pages 7–33 in John R. Firth, *Papers in Linguistics, 1934–1951.* Oxford Univ. Press.

FISCHER, JOHN L. 1958 Social Influence on the Choice of a Linguistic Variant. *Word: Journal of the Linguistic Circle of New York* 14:47–56.

FISHMAN, JOSHUA A. et al. 1966 *Language Loyalty in the United States: The Maintenance and Perpetuation of Non-English Mother Tongues by American Ethnic and Religious Groups.* Janua Linguarum, Series Maior, Vol. 21. The Hague: Mouton.

GARVIN, PAUL L. 1959 The Standard Language Problem: Concepts and Methods. *Anthropological Linguistics* 1, no. 3:28–31.

GLEASON, HENRY A. (1955) 1961 *An Introduction to Descriptive Linguistics.* Rev. ed. New York: Holt.

GLEASON, HENRY A. 1964 The Organization of Language: A Stratificational View. Georgetown University, Washington, D.C., Institute of Languages and Linguistics, *Monograph Series on Languages and Linguistics* 17:75–95.

GRAY, LOUIS H. 1939 *Foundations of Language.* New York: Macmillan.

GREENBERG, JOSEPH H. 1948 Linguistics and Ethnology. *Southwestern Journal of Anthropology* 4:140–147.

GUMPERZ, JOHN J. 1961 Speech Variation and the Study of Indian Civilization. *American Anthropologist* New Series 63:976–988.

GUMPERZ, JOHN J.; and HYMES, DELL (editors) 1964 *The Ethnography of Communication.* American Anthropologist, New Series, Vol. 66, No. 6, Part 2. Menasha, Wisc.: American Anthropological Association.

HALL, EDWARD T. 1959 *The Silent Language.* Garden City, N.Y.: Doubleday. → A paperback edition was published in 1961 by Fawcett.

HALLIDAY, MICHAEL A. K.; MCINTOSH, ANGUS; and STREVENS, PETER (1964) 1965 *The Linguistic Sciences and Language Teaching.* Bloomington: Indiana Univ. Press.

HARRIS, ZELLIG S. 1951 *Methods in Structural Linguistics.* Univ. of Chicago Press.

HOCKETT, CHARLES F. 1948 Implications of Bloomfield's Algonquian Studies. *Language* 24:117–131.

HOCKETT, CHARLES F. 1958 *A Course in Modern Linguistics.* New York: Macmillan.

HOENIGSWALD, HENRY M. 1960 *Language Change and Linguistic Reconstruction.* Univ. of Chicago Press.

HYMES, DELL 1959 Field Work in Linguistics and Anthropology. *Studies in Linguistics* 14:82–91.

HYMES, DELL 1961*a* Functions of Speech: An Evolutionary Approach. Pages 55–83 in Frederick C. Gruber (editor), *Anthropology and Education.* Philadelphia: Univ. of Pennsylvania Press.

HYMES, DELL 1961*b* Linguistic Aspects of Cross-cultural Personality Study. Pages 313–359 in Bert Kaplan (editor), *Studying Personality Cross-culturally.* New York: Harper.

HYMES, DELL 1961*c* Alfred Louis Kroeber. *Language* 37:1–28.

HYMES, DELL 1962 The Ethnography of Speaking. Pages 13–53 in Anthropological Society of Washington, *Anthropology and Human Behavior.* Washington: The Society.

HYMES, DELL (editor) 1964*a* *Language in Culture and Society: A Reader in Linguistics and Anthropology.* New York: Harper.

HYMES, DELL 1964*b* Directions in (Ethno-) Linguistic Theory. Pages 6–56 in A. Kimball Romney and Roy D'Andrade (editors), *Transcultural Studies of Cognition.* American Anthropologist, New Series, Vol. 66, No. 3, Part 2. Menasha, Wisc.: American Anthropological Association.

HYMES, DELL 1964*c* A Perspective for Linguistic Anthropology. Pages 92–107 in Sol Tax (editor), *Horizons of Anthropology.* Chicago: Aldine.

HYMES, DELL 1965 Methods and Tasks of Anthropological Philology (Illustrated with Clackamus Chinook). *Romance Philology* 19:325–340.

HYMES, DELL 1966 Two Types of Linguistic Relativity. Pages 114–158 in UCLA Sociolinguistics Conference, Los Angeles, 1964, *Sociolinguistics.* Edited by William Bright. Janua Linguarum, Series Maior, Vol. 20. The Hague: Mouton.

INTERNATIONAL CONGRESS OF LINGUISTS, NINTH, CAMBRIDGE, MASS., *1961* 1963 *Trends in Modern Linguistics.* Edited by Christine Mohrmann et al. Utrecht (Netherlands): Spectrum.

IVIĆ, MILKA 1965 *Trends in Linguistics.* Janua Linguarum, Series Minor, No. 42. The Hague: Mouton.

JAKOBSON, ROMAN 1960 Closing Statement: Linguistics and Poetics. Pages 350–373 in Conference on Style, Indiana University, 1958, *Style in Language.* Edited by Thomas A. Sebeok. Cambridge, Mass.: Technology Press of M.I.T.

JAKOBSON, ROMAN 1963 Efforts Towards a Means–Ends Model of Language in Inter-war Continental Linguistics. Pages 104–108 in International Congress of Linguists, 9th, Cambridge, Mass., 1961, *Trends in Modern Linguistics.* Edited by Christine Mohrmann et al. Utrecht (Netherlands): Spectrum.

JOOS, MARTIN (editor) 1957 *Readings in Linguistics: The Development of Descriptive Linguistics in Amer-*

ica Since 1925. Washington: American Council of Learned Societies.

KATZ, JERROLD J.; and POSTAL, PAUL M. 1964 *An Integrated Theory of Linguistic Descriptions.* Cambridge, Mass.: M.I.T. Press.

KROEBER, A. L. 1955 Linguistic Time Depth Results So Far and Their Meaning. *International Journal of American Linguistics* 21:91–104.

LABOV, WILLIAM 1963 The Social Motivation of a Sound Change. *Word: Journal of the Linguistic Circle of New York* 19:273–309.

LABOV, WILLIAM 1964 Phonological Correlates of Social Stratification. Pages 164–176 in John Gumperz and Dell Hymes (editors), *The Ethnography of Communication.* American Anthropologist, New Series, Vol. 66, No. 6, Part 2. Menasha, Wisc.: American Anthropological Association.

LAMB, SYDNEY M. 1966 An Outline of Stratificational Grammar. Unpublished manuscript.

LONGACRE, ROBERT E. 1964 *Grammar Discovery Procedure: A Field Manual.* Janua Linguarum, Series Minor, No. 33. The Hague: Mouton.

LOUNSBURY, FLOYD G. 1953 Field Methods and Techniques in Linguistics. Pages 401–416 in International Symposium on Anthropology, New York, 1952, *Anthropology Today: An Encyclopedic Inventory.* Univ. of Chicago Press.

MCINTOSH, ANGUS; and HALLIDAY, M. A. K. 1966 *Patterns of Language.* London: Longmans.

MALKIEL, YAKOV 1964*a* Some Diachronic Implications of Fluid Speech Communities. Pages 177–186 in John Gumperz and Dell Hymes (editors), *The Ethnography of Communication.* American Anthropologist, New Series, Vol. 66, No. 6, Part 2. Menasha, Wisc.: American Anthropological Association.

MALKIEL, YAKOV 1964*b* Distinctive Traits of Romance Linguistics. Pages 671–683 in Dell Hymes (editor), *Language in Culture and Society: A Reader in Linguistics and Anthropology.* New York: Harper.

MALKIEL, YAKOV 1966 Is There Room for "General Philology"? *Pacific Coast Philology* 1:3–11.

MARROU, HENRI I. (1948) 1956 *A History of Education in Antiquity.* London: Sheed & Ward. → First published in French.

MARTINET, ANDRÉ (1960) 1964 *Elements of General Linguistics.* Univ. of Chicago Press. → First published in French.

MARTINET, ANDRÉ 1962 *A Functional View of Language.* Oxford: Clarendon.

METCALF, GEORGE 1964 The Indo-European Hypothesis in the 16th and 17th Centuries. Paper prepared for Burg-Wartenstein Symposium, 25. Unpublished manuscript.

MOHRMANN, CHRISTINE et al. (editors) 1962 *Trends in European and American Linguistics, 1930–1960.* Utrecht (Netherlands): Spectrum.

PEDERSEN, HOLGER (1924) 1962 *The Discovery of Language: Linguistic Science in the Nineteenth Century.* Bloomington: Indiana Univ. Press. → First published in Danish.

PIKE, KENNETH L. 1954 *Language in Relation to a Unified Theory of the Structure of Human Behavior.* Part 1. Preliminary ed. Glendale, Calif.: Summer Institute of Linguistics.

[Report of the Fifteenth Annual Round Table Meeting on Linguistics and Language Studies.] 1964 Georgetown University, Washington, D.C., Institute of Languages and Linguistics, *Monograph Series on Languages and Linguistics* 17.

ROBINS, ROBERT H. 1951 *Ancient & Mediaeval Grammatical Theory in Europe With Particular Reference to Modern Linguistic Doctrine.* London: Bell.

ROBINS, ROBERT H. 1964 *General Linguistics: An Introductory Survey.* London: Longmans.

ROMNEY, A. KIMBALL; and D'ANDRADE, ROY GOODWIN (editors) 1964 *Transcultural Studies in Cognition.* American Anthropologist, New Series, Vol. 66, No. 3, Part 2. Menasha, Wisc.: American Anthropological Association.

SAMARIN, WILLIAM 1967 *Field Linguistics.* New York: Holt.

SANDYS, JOHN E. (1903–1908) 1958 *A History of Classical Scholarship.* 3 vols. New York: Hafner.

SAPIR, EDWARD A. 1921 *Language: An Introduction to the Study of Speech.* New York: Harcourt.

SAPIR, EDWARD A. (1924) 1949 The Grammarian and His Language. Pages 150–159 in Edward A. Sapir, *Selected Writings in Language, Culture and Personality.* Edited by David G. Mandelbaum. Berkeley: Univ. of California Press.

SAPIR, EDWARD A. 1925 Sound Patterns in Language. *Language* 1:37–51.

SAPIR, EDWARD A. 1929 The Status of Linguistics as a Science. *Language* 5:207–214.

SARTRE, JEAN PAUL (1960) 1963 *Search for a Method.* New York: Knopf. → First published in French. A British edition was published as *The Problem of Method.*

SWADESH, MORRIS 1951 Diffusional Cumulation and Archaic Residue as Historical Explanations. *Southwestern Journal of Anthropology* 7:1–21.

VACHEK, JOSEF (1964) 1966 *A Prague School Reader in Linguistics.* Bloomington: Indiana Univ. Press.

VACHEK, JOSEF 1966*a* *The Linguistic School of Prague: An Introduction to Its Theory and Practice.* Bloomington: Indiana Univ. Press.

VACHEK, JOSEF (editor) 1966*b* *Les problèmes du centre et de la périphérie du système de la langue.* Travaux linguistiques de Prague, 2. Prague: Éditions de l'Académie Tchécoslovaque des Sciences.

VERBURG, PIETR A. 1952 *Taal en functionaliteit: Een historisch-critische studie over de opvattingen aangaande de functies der taal vanaf de prae-humanistische philologie van Orleans tot de rationalistische linguistiek van Bopp.* Wageningen (Netherlands): Veenman.

WEINREICH, URIEL 1953 *Languages in Contact: Findings and Problems.* New York: Linguistic Circle of New York.

WONDERLY, WILLIAM L.; and NIDA, EUGENE A. 1963 Linguistics and Christian Missions. *Anthropological Linguistics* 5, no. 1:104–144.

II
HISTORICAL LINGUISTICS

Although consecrated by over a century and a half of use, the term "historical linguistics," as a designation of a discipline, is something of a misnomer, because the most exciting and controversial operations of that discipline concern the reconstruction of language, i.e., prehistory, rather than documented history. For this reason, perhaps,

Saussure, in his search for a label that would neatly contrast with the newly discovered "synchronic" perspective, suggested the qualifier "diachronic," which, possibly as a result of its paleness, later proved less than successful (1916). In the mid-twentieth century, it might be most apposite to speak of "genetic linguistics" in reference to the entire domain, reserving the alternative designation "glottodynamics" for the hard core of general doctrine governing the analyst's major operations.

Historical linguistics is very often equated with "comparative linguistics"; to the extent that the tracing of genetic relationships involves some confrontation of an earlier with a later stage of the same language (of Old English, say, with Middle or Modern English), a measure of overlap is indeed unavoidable. For practical purposes, however, it seems advisable to refer to comparative linguistics only where several cognate languages—ideally, they should be observed at the same time level—are jointly analyzed in an effort to arrive at the parental tongue, as when proto-Central Algonquian is reconstructed from available records of Sauk and Fox, Cree, Menomini, and Ojibwa. Of course, it is equally legitimate to engage in the typological comparison of languages with no thought of historical reconstruction and regardless of the presence of any kinship ties—see Bally's classic confrontation of Modern German and Modern French (1932) and the currently fashionable "contrastive" grammars.

Historical and comparative linguistics reached their first peak of development in the nineteenth century, although there were some rudimentary attempts in western and central Europe from 1500 to 1800. Language history, in contrast, represents a relatively new genre of research; its roots are in broad-gauged introductory chapters to technically worded historical grammars. In terms readily understandable to layman and beginner alike, language history interweaves austere linguistic analyses with discussions—rarely devoid of grace—of social, economic, broadly cultural, demographic, and literary conditions prevailing at the successive time levels, allowing also for remarks on the philological state of transmission. At its best, as in Migliorini's masterpiece (1960), language history excels at tracing the vicissitudes of a single language viewed within the matrix of the corresponding highly literate national culture.

The individual facts ascertainable through the various analyses devised by historical linguists lend themselves to two entirely unrelated kinds of synthesis. Certain language forms can be lifted out of their original philological context (which alone, in most instances, made their secure identification possible) and can be arranged on a higher plateau of abstraction so as to illustrate broad aspects of a specific linguistic transformation, e.g., the development of sounds, derivational molds, lexical meanings, or syntactic structures from stage A to stage B of the given language. Climbing to a still higher level of generalization, the analyst is at liberty to abandon even the context of the specific language at issue and to cite the modifications observed, for the sake of their illustrative value, in a general methodology of linguistic change. On the other hand, the slivers and nuggets of information obtained through stringent linguistic (in particular, etymological) analysis may be deftly inserted, as highly prized items, in the grandiose mosaics pieced together by patient and versatile historians. These items of information are similar to the fragmentary bits of knowledge collected by physical anthropologists, archeologists, folklorists, and others who attempt to recapture the elusive past.

Traditionally, from the days of such pioneers as the Germanist Jacob Grimm and the Romanist Friedrich Diez to that towering Indo-Europeanist of the early twentieth century, Antoine Meillet, the two conspicuously parallel tools of research in diachronic linguistics have been the manual of historical grammar and the etymological dictionary—the one providing a tightly ordered macrocosm and the other a loose kaleidoscopic array of microcosms. The full-sized historical grammar—not infrequently a multivolume venture—embraced phonology (with excursuses into prosody or accentology), inflection, "word formation" (i.e., affixal derivation and composition or their counterparts in non-Indo-European languages), and syntax. These centered, in ever widening circles, on the word, the phrase, and the sentence. An abridged version was limited to phonology and inflection. Inflection and the "syntax of the word" are so closely adjacent that they tend to merge, and a few scholars have gone so far as to consolidate all of morphology and syntax into the single domain of "morphosyntax," which forms the hard, inalienable kernel of linguistics. Excursions into semantics, metrics (also, through the inclusion of tropes, rhetoric, or poetics), and stylistics—the last-mentioned more loosely organized and defined in a variety of ways—have at all times been regarded as optional rather than obligatory. Only in recent decades have grammatical and lexical studies drifted apart so sharply in techniques and appeal as to render problematic any joint ventures in the immediate future.

The relative stabilization of historical linguistics in the period 1850–1925 had the advantage of producing a far-reaching standardization in its terminology; this, in turn, by virtue of the comparability achieved, has invited and furthered at every step the confrontation of older and more recent studies, a procedure that has become more difficult in the last three decades. The long-unchallenged preeminence of central European scholarship in this field is mirrored by the wide acceptance of such technical terms as "umlaut" (metaphony) and "ablaut" (apophony), while other German labels, potentially just as helpful (e.g., *Lehnwort* "assimilated borrowing" versus *Fremdwort* "unassimilated borrowing"), have enjoyed no such popularity. Early standardization was particularly beneficial in certain special types of nonverbal symbolization, e.g., quotation marks for meaning, italics for quoted forms, boldface for transliteration into another alphabet, small capitals for an ancestral language (e.g., Latin versus Romance vernaculars), large capitals for epigraphic material, square brackets for phonetic transcription, asterisks for hypothetical forms, and, above all, the two directional signs: > "changes into" and < "descends from."

Before long, the success of these symbols led to a temporary staleness, except where the stagnation was relieved by the introduction of signs manufactured by the more aggressively imaginative structuralist school (e.g., slanted lines for "phonemicization"). Thus, few historically oriented scholars have bothered to discriminate typographically between two logically distinguishable hypothetical forms: (a) those undocumented, yet assumed to have existed (*) and (b) those expressly presented as nonexistent ($_{*}$). Again, although few experts would deny the sharp cleavage between phonology and morphology, historical linguists have failed to capitalize on the possibility of contrastive symbolization of phonological versus morphological shifts.

To the extent that genetic linguists are concerned with historical situations, unique by definition, they can resort to the device of "model formation" only on a limited scale. In a way, any reconstruction of genetic relationship between languages or dialects involves a generous measure of schematization aimed at eliminating those details that would tend to blur the broad outline. One can visualize an entirely different kind of model: instead of focusing attention on concrete territories (at historical stages) or avoiding any commitment to the speakers' habitat (at prehistoric stages), the analyst may decide to invent imaginary countries with a sharply profiled distribution of coastlines, wastelands, mountain chains, ports of entry, emporia, cultural shrines, etc. He can further posit a certain succession of political, socioeconomic, and strictly linguistic events (say, invasions, retreats into the hilly inland, reconquest of coastal lowlands, splits into dialects) and project them onto the imaginary area, excogitating in abstract terms the likeliest concatenations of linguistic reactions to these pressures. By sharpening the analyst's alertness to possible and probable intricacies under artificial conditions that are relatively simplified, such schemata can prepare him for successful inquiries into real-life situations, incomparably more complex.

It should be emphasized that the postulate of historical uniqueness is not easy to reconcile with the search for evolutionary universals in the realm of language. However, the prospect of discovering such universals has for many decades been a source of constant titillation. One classic example is the often-observed correlation of word order (and comparable syntactic devices) with the available wealth of inflectional endings. Clarity and economy demand that, if relationships between members of a clause can no longer be expressed unequivocally by means of the endings (e.g., as a result of phonetic erosion), a stiffening of word order should provide an adequate substitute. Also, etymologists have discovered that, of all form classes, adjectives, on balance, tend to present lexical nuclei most resistant to identification. In addition, semanticists report that fluctuations and changes of meaning undergone by verbs exceed, as a rule, those to which a typical noun would be subject. The difficulty with trying to establish absolute universals is that each such attempt presupposes the testing of hundreds of languages. On the other hand, characteristic samples would suffice to identify tendential universals.

As in all evolutionary sciences, the question of purposeful, or oriented, change is at the heart of the philosophy underlying any genetic analysis of linguistic data. Linguists are sharply divided on this matter of teleology: the great Danish theorist Otto Jespersen and the founders of the Prague school categorically affirm the teleological principle (a few visualize a trend toward general improvement achieved through refinement, simplification, and economy); others, particularly Bloomfield (see 1933) and a whole generation of American linguists claiming allegiance to his doctrine, just as vehemently deny it. Discernibly different from the teleological approach, although occasionally confused with it, especially by opponents, is the idealistic slant (characteristic of Benedetto Croce's school in Italy and Karl Vossler's in Germany), which stresses the primacy of the speakers' thinking over their speech habits and grants them in the process a much wider margin of initiative and of control over linguistic change than would be accepted by believers in the pre-eminence of "blind forces" or those (such as Whorf) who view the configuration of a grammatical structure as a prime determinant of thinking and perception. The more literate the speaker and especially the writer, the stronger the case for the idealistic approach; in analyzing "graphemically" the comportment of ancient and medieval scribes, one can hardly fail to distinguish between what they aimed to achieve and what they actually accomplished.

Descriptive and historical linguistics

Basic to all operations in historical linguistics is the view which the analyst holds of the configuration of the speech community under study and of speech communities in general. This was clearly sensed by Bloomfield, who, in his influential book *Language* (1933), without disregarding the varying density of communication or denying the complexity of certain speech communities, impressed upon his readers the need to reckon with a far-reaching uniformity of speech habits. Similarly, in presenting the comparative method, he leaned toward favoring those situations that exhibit clear-cut dialect splits, without denying occasional alternatives. However, many younger scholars have recognized that the link holding together language communities is frequently mere similarity rather than actual homogeneity of speech habits, a point fraught with major implications for the geneticist. It is further held that bilingualism and even trilingualism are more widely disseminated the world over than is strict monolingualism, an assumption that demands flexibility in dealing with a multitude of diversified and changing situations. Thus, two groups speaking language X—one composed of members who have from infancy also mastered language Y and the other containing persons who happen to be constantly using language Z in certain social contexts—are unlikely to react identically to any incipient innovations spreading from a monolingual zone. (One also readily conceives of innovations arising at the intersection of languages.) One final argument in favor of fluidity in the object observed and elasticity in the method applied to its elucidation is the discovery that many areas commonly assigned *en bloc* to certain languages often lack such "natural boundaries" as might preserve a community of speakers in quasi-hermetic isolation. The emergence of such zones is due rather to conflation, i.e., to successive reapportionments of neighboring territories, each initially sheltering a different language or dialect. Therefore, unless perfect leveling subsequently ensues, one may detect beneath the present-day "roof" bracketing the dialects remnants and splinters of their original phonic, grammatical, and lexical systems in almost kaleidoscopic confusion.

In linguistics, the relation of the descriptive (or synchronic) to the historical (or diachronic) perspective has been the subject of considerable speculation and discussion, the consensus being that descriptive analysis bears preponderantly on simpler, less opaque situations. From this nearly unanimous opinion several discrepant conclusions may be drawn. Some experts maintain that new techniques, such as the structural method, should be tried out first on horizontal, later on vertical, slices of linguistic material. There are those who visualize a historical structure as a succession of descriptive structures superimposed on one another. The main difficulty in designing such an edifice lies in the fact that certain features structurally less than significant at one evolutionary stage may suddenly acquire conspicuous importance during transition to the next stage. Thus, the descriptivist is free to assert that in words like *danc-er*, *kill-er*, the ending *-er* as the carrier of an identifiably specific meaning ("agent") represents a derivational morpheme, while in *hamm-er*, *pinc-er*, *rudd-er* the same sequence of sounds plays no comparable role. But the historical linguist, while acknowledging this distinction on certain temporal plateaus, must at all times reckon with the strong possibility of joint actions, inextricably interwoven, by homonymous genuine suffixes (such as the *-er* of *kill-er*) and mere suffixoids (the *-er* of *rudd-er*). One consensus is worth mentioning: from the minute inspection of any given state of a single language the experienced analyst can tentatively extract almost as much information on its earlier stages ("internal reconstruction") as he can from comparing that language "externally" with its congeners.

One way of doing justice to both perspectives has been to engage in a "stairway projection"; among the practitioners of this novel approach one may count such seasoned experimenters as Otto Jespersen (for English), Antoine Meillet (for Latin), and Walther von Wartburg (for French). This particular method of intricate surgery affords glimpses of the consecutive periods of the chosen language, slanted alternately in the descriptive and in the historical direction. The implication of this design is clearly that one may distinguish between periods of relative rest and stability and others marked by spells of stress and strain.

One salient difference between the descriptive and the historical approach in linguistics is that the former in most instances enables the researcher to operate with a finite corpus, an intentional selection over whose scope he retains a modicum of control, while the latter often bears on an irremediably fragmentary volume of data. The ability to work with lacunary material and a certain flair for filling in gaps thus become important prerequisites for success in linguistic reconstruction, just as they are for research in geology, paleontology, and paleobotany. Developments are contrastively symbolized by solid lines (documented) or broken lines (hypothesized); however, the latter do not invariably represent initial, prehistoric segments of trajectories. An archaic stage A may very well owe its transparency to the realistic, readily adjustable spelling habits of the scribes concerned; conversely, stage B, although temporally closer to the beholder, may become nebulous, because the scribes of that period, plagued by conservatism, or subject to an inferiority complex, may have endeavored stubbornly to cling to the orthographic norms of their predecessors ("etymological spelling"), while the actual speech processes ran their course with unabated speed; then again, stage C may mark a vigorous return to graphic realism, entailing the relative translucency of actual speech events. A vivid illustration of these three phases is provided by early Latin, late Latin, certain varieties of "low" and medieval Latin, and, on an overwhelming scale, the budding Romance vernaculars.

It also happens that some word of unmistakably Latin provenience which, judging from its "normal" transformations, must have been in constant use over two millennia, disappears from written records in the fifth century, only to re-emerge a thousand years later. In cases of this kind, the literary genres of the extant texts act as prisms or filters, often seemingly capricious. They may long repress a word, keeping it submerged until there arises some opportunity—socially or aesthetically controlled—for its definitive surfacing into the standard language.

Trajectories of linguistic change

Systematic inquiry into the configuration of trajectories has not yet outgrown the stage of trial and error. Where regular phonological change occurs, older notions of strictly gradual transitions do not apply. Between, say, the Latin *ū*, as in *pūru*, and the French *ü*, as in *pur*, it is no longer admissible to posit an infinity of intermediate nuances of the stressed vowel without concurrently accepting some kind of cutoff point at which a vowel already markedly fronted, but still representing no more than an unusual variant within the phoneme /ū/, must have become a member, decreasingly erratic, of the sound family constituting the phoneme /ü/. In other words, structural thinking forces us to recognize the interaction of slow-working phonetic *rapprochements* and more or less sudden occasional jumps. This composite schema guarantees the semblance of a close-knit system to a language at any moment of its growth. Thus, the graduality of development—not superseded, but only qualified and hierarchized—remains a vitally important assumption. Significantly, the hypothesis that the shift *ū* > *ü*, eminently characteristic of the transformation of provincial Latin into French, is traceable to the contributing agency of Gaulish cannot be refuted by the argument that the Celtic language in question lacked a fully developed /ü/ in its own system. It would have sufficed for the local substratum language, at the start, to have slightly deflected the Latin *ū* from its original status of a high back vowel in the direction of *ü*, thus producing a kind of chain reaction or even an accelerated advance along a straight line.

In yet another context, the configuration of a trajectory of linguistic change, properly interpreted, may be revealing. If the changes due to associative interference were to be plotted on a chart, some of them might give the impression of a bizarre zigzagging curve. On such a chart a relatively level line may suddenly start climbing as a result of an outside pressure, a "disturbance," until it reaches a certain peak. Then the language's inner mechanism (e.g., the total weight of its inflectional paradigms) may begin to wipe out the irregularity, causing the line to drop until it reverts to its original direction. If in such an up-and-down movement, anteceding the advent of trustworthy written texts, the descending stage completely absorbs the effects of the ascending stage, it is quite impossible to detect the original disturbance. If the down movement falls short of counterbalancing the aberrancy or overcorrects it, there is bound to remain in its wake a residue of startling "exceptions." In case the irregularity happens to erupt at the very start of the written tradition, it may appear baffling in retrospect that the ancestral language and its eventual modern product should be in perfect mutual agreement while at such sharp variance with the intermediate step, which then, in fact, fails to perform any "mediation." Thus, the Latin third person singular imperfect ending *-ībat* (originally *-iēbat*) cast off in early Romance speech *-ía(t)*, which to this day survives in Spanish as *-ía*, a safely predictable form, but paradoxically it produced instead, in early Old Spanish, *-ié*, a variant difficult to reconcile either with its antecedent or with its sequel. Investigation (Malkiel 1959; 1964) has disclosed that the rise of *-ié* simply marks a minor temporary deflection (of ascertainable origin), ultimately neutralized, while the later form *-ía* represents far more faithfully the continuation of a basic trend.

Closely allied to the concern with the convolution of trajectories is the attempt, assuming a certain more or less steady rate of attrition in the core lexicon, to draw from parallel analyses tentative conclusions as to the degree of kinship between congeneric languages and the approximate date of their split. This approach, which rode the crest of a temporary vogue in the 1950s, has become known, broadly, as *lexicostatistics* and, with special application to dating, as *glottochronology*. Exaggerated claims, especially the attempt of some practitioners to place these techniques on the same pedestal as the rigorous study of sound correspondences, have led to quick disenchantment and virtual abandonment of the method.

Sound change

For better or worse, the vicissitudes of historical linguistics have been intimately linked with the theories of sound change. The recognition of regularity in these transmutations has been hailed as a milestone along the road to progress (cf. the radical programmatic statements of the "neogrammarians," or *Junggrammatiker*, circa 1870) or, more intransigently, as a touchstone of stringent scientific thinking. In the compressed classroom presentation of historical linguistics, lecturers have traditionally inclined toward concentrating on "regular sound changes" as the discipline's irreducible hard core. In the separate quarters of humanists and anthropologists alike, this rigid attitude has for decades contributed toward producing the impression of linguistics as a highly abstract subject, almost forbiddingly abstruse and, above all, divorced in its style and tone from cultural history, to say nothing of its aloofness from the realm of arts and letters. Moreover, because most provisional rules or "laws" admitted of a few exceptions and some of countless ones, there was for a while a widespread apprehension that the "regularists" were actually propounding some kind of mock science.

In reality, there exist several categories of sound change, each fairly autonomous—but not entirely so—and tied to diverse facets of human comportment and different levels of a speaker's consciousness. The immediate goal of linguists is to discover one workable formula for presenting these interconnections, however tenuous, and another for discovering the elusive ties of sound change categories to discrete mental processes.

The techniques of accurately circumscribing individual sound correspondences that are inherently limited in time and space can be traced to the nineteenth century. By contrasting the French *mer* ("sea") and *père* ("father") with their Latin prototypes *mare* and *patre*, the analyst learns that the Latin *a* tended, by and large, to yield *e* in French. Further refinement of this first approximation is within easy reach. The discrepant first vowels in *père* and *parrain* ("godfather") (originally *parrin*, from *patrīnus*) alert the observer to the possibility that the shift *a* > *e* hinges on a crucial accentual condition, while comparison of *père* < *pa-tre* with *part* < *par-te* dramatizes the share that the configuration of the stressed syllable may have had in an obvious bifurcation, depending on whether that syllable ended in a vowel or a consonant. By examining with scrupulous care all seemingly aberrant developments (amenable to observation with optimal results in Old French), the analyst isolates, step by step, the specific phonological ("internal") factors that must have presided over the evolution, erratic at first glance, of *(il)lāc* ("there") > *là; paupere* ("poor") > *povre* (modern *pauvre*); *clāuu* ("nail") > *clou; aqua* ("water") > *eaue* (modern *eau*); *palus* ("pole") > *pieus; caput* ("head") > *ch(i)ef*, etc. Comparably detailed breakdowns can be established for all other Latin sounds viewed in their transmission into a chosen "daughter language," and, by way of effective control, the linguist is free to reverse the perspective and select as a given the basic sound unit of the daughter language, assigning to himself the task of individuating its sources.

But this classification marks only a first step, yielding at best a tidily subdivided inventory of raw facts. The preliminary classification is nonexplicative, lacks statistical underpinning, fails to throw into bold relief parallels, convergences (including some that are partial or have been arrested), and, worse, concatenations of events, and does not begin to take into account other forms of sound shift. Such taxonomy disregards several broad or distinct categories of internal linguistic change. Moreover, it is not elastic enough to do justice to the various external pressures (demographic, social, educational) on evolutionary trends in speech and in the written word as well. It is in these directions—many of them affording fruitful contacts with a whole spectrum of other disciplines—that the chief advances of late-twentieth-century research are bound to lie.

The following are a few illustrations of research in progress and tempting prospects of investigation. Alongside regular phonetic change (akin to Sapir's "drift") scholars have placed sporadic shifts (also called spontaneous and saltatory), such as metathesis, the transposition of a sound or intermutation of two sounds, in contact or at a distance, haplology, the elimination of one or two successive segments partially identical, and certain dissimilatory processes. None of these, it has been argued, is confined to a specific locus or span of time, i.e., they are all, at least latently or tendentially, pantopic and panchronic. Granted the fundamental validity of this distinction, there arise several questions and second thoughts. Does the sound system of a language at a given stage—or, alternatively, its patterns of regular changes—typically stimulate or block sporadic shifts, or does it let them take their own course? Could it be true that, for all their uniqueness, regular sound changes, in any random selection, display such strong proclivities in a few characteristic directions that one discerns in them certain universals? Is it legitimate to grade the regularity of sound change (not as an ideal postulate, but as a bit of reality) and to contrast "strong" expectation of outcome, most likely to occur in monolithic societies, with "weak" predictability, attributable to, say, loose conflations of dialects, regional or social? Does such a state of prevalent weakness tend to intensify sporadic shifts and to invite even an excess of lexical contamination? Should frequency of lexical occurrence, or at least of incidence in actual speech, rank as a factor contributing to the degree of regularity, especially where a particularly unusual sequence of sounds falls into no broader pattern of immediate appeal? Can the exigencies of inflectional patterning slow down the pace of a sound change or counteract it to the point of weakening a phonetic "law"? Do other demands of this kind carry sufficient weight to set in motion or to accelerate potential and, especially, incipient sound changes? If the answer to the last two questions is affirmative, can one uphold the view that phonology operates in practically hermetic isolation? Specifically, is it still permissible to resolve the phenomena of genetic phonology into a neat interplay of sound relationships—to be precise, into an alternation of states of equilibrium and states of unrest or tension, to the virtual exclusion of all rival forces? Does it make sense to arrange sound changes in their presumed chronological succession (Richter 1934) without explicit forewarning that such sequences neither invariably presuppose nor necessarily imply the flow of one change from another or from the sum of all others already completed? Can one, in such contexts, ignore with impunity certain extraneous factors such as pressure of morphological paradigms and deflections from the straight course through associative lexical interference?

From earlier incidental mention it is clear that there are other kinds of change affecting linguistic form and, consequently, reflected in the sounds as the obligatory carriers of that form but not here caused by purely phonetic conditions. The most important of these supervenient categories of change is analogical. Speakers make adjustments bearing either on the configuration of a grammatical paradigm or on the shape of a single word; in the latter eventuality, both the radical and the affix are open to modification. Typically, such adjustments follow upon sound change; only by way of exception may one suspect them of impinging, as prime movers, upon sound development. Since analogical changes involve, by definition, associative interference, they seem to occur on a higher level of awareness than straight sound changes; thus they invite psycholinguistic analysis.

Sound symbolism constitutes yet another autonomous category, of slightly controversial status. To the extent that sounds, in symbolic context (and nowhere else), are credited with conveying messages of their own, this marginal category represents a tenuous bridge to semantic change, ordinarily removed from the realms of articulation, acoustics, and auditory perception. Sound symbolism may be absolute or relative. The former category prevails if the analyst attaches, cross-linguistically, an unvarying evocative value to, say, a high front vowel or to a hissing prepalatal consonant; the problem then is to ascertain whether speakers will allow words endowed with major connotative force, through such ingredients, to participate in normal sound shifts at the cost of heavy loss in suggestiveness. The effects of relative sound symbolism are conditioned by the given phonological system; thus, in a language generally averse to long consonants an occasional geminate may boast "expressive" value (which it would otherwise lack). Again, the language historian is curious to learn how speakers can maintain a word enhanced by such a feature in this privileged status amid the welter of pervasive transformations. At this juncture one welcomes contact with information theory.

Pressures for linguistic change

Entirely different from the classes of change are the categories of forces that are apt to produce changes of any kind. But the linguist's operational procedure in tackling this new problem remains essentially unaltered: again his dual task is first to isolate the forces in question and then to discover the closest available approximation to the formula for their interplay.

It is customary to divorce the internal from the external forces at the outset, notably because the separate inquiries into them seem to appeal to radically different minds. In the former group one can readily distinguish two drives, sometimes acting in polar opposition—one toward economy of effort, the other toward clarity. Economy, syntagmatically conceived, aims at the speech act; in paradigmatic perspective economy relates to the acquisition of, and sustained command over, neuromuscular skills. The former type determines the course of most assimilatory processes, contextual by definition (e.g., Latin *actu* > Italian *atto*) and governs the choice of those glides and buffer consonants that serve to smooth away troublesome contiguity (in Old Spanish viewed in its relation to Latin: *hōnōrāre* > *onrar* > *on-d-rar* versus *fēmina* > *femna* > *fem-b-ra*). The latter type precipitates mergers of phonemes in the system where continued distinction between them would produce only a meager yield (/ã/ and /ẽ/ in older Parisian, /ɛ̃/ and /œ̃/ with increasing momentum in present-day Parisian). It also dooms to extinction minute groups of words displaying an infrequent sound or combination of sounds.

A groping search for increased clarity may be behind most dissimilatory and haplologic processes. It accounts, as would no other supposition, for the speakers' readiness to augment their vocabulary (in an effort to reduce lexical polysemy) and to accept longer and more cumbersome syntactic structures (in a recoil from ambiguity). It is perhaps at this point that the newly achieved refinement of transformational grammar would most benefit the classic researches conducted by geneticists. The same urge for increased clarity ultimately justifies the sometimes successful flight from harmful homonymy or from its mere threat—the nearest escape routes being substitute words borrowed from neighboring dialects and reinterpreted within one's own cultural heritage, and words freely invented.

After one deducts the two-pronged quest for maximum economy and clarity, it is the residue left that threatens to cause serious difficulty; the wisdom of applying to it some such pleasing blanket term as "expressivism" remains to be demonstrated, especially since it is doubtful whether, in the last analysis, one can reduce the remaining forces to a single denominator. One nucleus that cannot by any stretch of the imagination be subsumed under either economy or clarity contains those formations associated with special moods—playful, tender, or festive. In contemporary English the colloquially flavored compositional types, such as *hush-hush, ping-pong, riffraff, wishy-washy, pribbles and prabbles, topsy-turvy, mumbo jumbo* —sometimes originating in the nursery and displaying a strong admixture of onomatopoeia—admirably fit this description. In Slavic and Romance languages, formations involving strings of hypocoristic suffixes would qualify as a counterpart. The Hebrew spoken in modern Israel, the twentieth century's linguistic melting pot par excellence, allows speakers the jocose lapse into the Ashkenazic rather than the officially favored Sephardic pronunciation for proper names affectionately uttered, thus proliferating doublets. On the other hand, one runs across a phenomenon such as hypercharacterization (i.e., the sharper, more explicit, even uneconomically generous marking of a major grammatical category—say, gender, number, or person). For instance, the Latin *socrus* ("mother-in-law"), hampered by its conspicuously uncharacteristic *-us*, is more neatly profiled with regard to gender (and sex) at the Romance stage through a new and far more appropriate ending (Italian, *suocera;* Spanish, *suegra*, etc.); cf. also the change of Latin *puppis* ("poop," "stern"), marred by an ending indeterminate as to gender, into the clear-cut Spanish *pop-a*. In such instances, the change is, of course, analogical, but the driving force behind it seems less easy to identify. It certainly can be neither economy nor any overflow of emotion, and one is hesitant, to say the least, to press into service a quest for heightened clarity. The propelling force, one suspects, is the speaker's endeavor to redesign selected portions of the language, to make the medium of transmission more pointed or so silhouetted as to be aesthetically more satisfying. Sapir's reference to the "cut" of a language comes to mind here—a fait accompli or a goal toward which speakers may strive.

The most familiar external forces whose impact will produce the various types of linguistic change are those resulting from contact between languages (occasionally one living and the other dead, but preserved in ritual or intensely studied) or regional and social dialects. Typically, a protracted transitional period of thoroughgoing bilingualism or plurilingualism is needed before the contact produces sizable results. In gauging any such impact on a specific language, the historian tries first to determine the principal layer of that language by inspecting the core structure of its grammar and those ingredients of its lexicon best known for their resistance, if not total immunity, to infiltration. Numerals, kinship terms, names of parts of the body, and grammatically functional words are typical examples of such elements. Once this frame of reference has been established, it becomes clear which layers, in the course of further study, will be labeled substrata and which superstrata—eloquent metaphors borrowed from geology and permitting a graphic projection of anteriority. Thus, vis-à-vis Great Russian, the numerous Finno–Ugric languages, now extinct or pushed back to the periphery of eastern Europe, constituted substrata; so did Coptic and, farther down the Nile valley in Egypt, the Greek *koinē* vis-à-vis Arabic, Frisian vis-à-vis Dutch in Holland, and French plus Canary Island Spanish vis-à-vis English in Louisiana. In the absence of any genuine symbiosis, it is doubtful whether American Indian languages may rank as substrata in relation to English in North America, as they indisputably do in relation to Spanish and Portuguese throughout Latin America. In the twilight hour between late Antiquity and the Middle Ages, Arabic in southern Spain and Frankish in northern Gaul represented superstrata in relation to divergent varieties of provincial Latin. To the extent that the Greeks tended to form independent cultural nuclei under the aegis of the expanding Roman Republic and later Roman Empire, their settlements qualify as examples of linguistic adstrata vis-à-vis Latin as well as the circum-Mediterranean indigenous languages.

Aside from such "vertical" relations, linguistic pressures operate "horizontally" across political borders and even at long distances through cultural diffusion. Thus, heavy clusters of Gallicisms are found not only in Spanish, Catalan, Italian, German, and Dutch, to say nothing of English, but also in languages occupying nonadjacent areas, such as Rumanian, Polish, Russian, and Swedish. Words are more easily borrowed than sounds, and affixes travel more rapidly than inflectional endings. A classic example of superimposed syntactic, semantic, and (probably) intonational patterns is provided by the multifarious Germanisms observable in eastern Switzerland's Romansh, a language descended from Raetian Latin.

Against the fairly trivial instances of direct, positive influence one may place the sorely neglected range of indirect or catalytic interferences. Thus, two early medieval Germanic kingdoms carved out of the ruins of the crumbling Roman Empire—that of the Suebi in Galician–Portuguese territory and that of the Burgundians in the Lyon–Geneva area—molded local Latin speech sparingly through loan words but exerted a powerful restraining influence by politically and culturally isolating their territories, at crucial junctures, from such centers of ceaseless linguistic innovation as Toledo and Paris.

An independent kind of external force comprises all sorts of nonlinguistic events potentially rich in linguistic reverberations. The invention of novel tools and machines may breathe new life into a moribund suffix serving to denote instruments. The emancipation of women the world over may develop dormant schemata (affixal, compositional, or otherwise derivational) for the designation of female agentials. A global vogue of formality or familiarity (in clothing, dwellings, human relations, etc.) could hardly fail to revolutionize the system of forms of address and to affect even personal pronouns and possessive adjectives. The sections of the linguistic edifice most vulnerable to these influences are, then, the vocabulary, the derivational machinery (at the midway point between lexicon and grammar), plus a few pieces from the morphosyntactic tool kit.

Far beyond this boundary, the "idealistic" school of thought, entrenched in Italy and Germany only a generation ago (Vossler 1925), tended to assess very liberally the impact of changing modes of thinking on linguistic forms, extending that impact to the foundations of sentence structure. While the consensus of most generations of scholars has ascribed the disappearance of case endings to attrition, recognizing the rise of prepositional paraphrases as a relatively smooth replacement, the "idealists" preferred to view as prime mover the emergence of a new way of thinking (such as analytic rather than synthetic), crediting it with the manufacture of appropriate substitutes which eventually eroded the older grammatical framework. The advent of Christianity figured in these interpretations (especially in H. F. Muller's) as another favorite determinant of linguistic evolution. The idealistic position is thus diametrically opposed to that of Whorf, who, following Sapir (1921), mused that patterns of thinking may, in the first place, be molded by pre-existent grammatical structures.

The complex interaction of all these isolable forces can be illustrated with the differing, if reconcilable, answers to the classic question: What dooms a word to extinction? Plausible explanations offered either separately or in any number of free combinations include an excess of paradigmatic intricacy or phonological oddity in the fated word; the peril besetting the weaker of two conflicting homonyms; an intolerable dosage of polysemy; a sudden general demand at all levels of the given society for lexical rejuvenation or large-scale overhaul; the obsolescence of a specific cultural element (say, some container or garment) heretofore designated by the word at issue; the ineluctable effect of some socially controlled restriction (taboo, etc.); acceptance, through borrowing from the local prestige language, of a more attractive equivalent, as when the imported *Cousine* dislodged the native *Base* in eighteenth-century German.

Theories of linguistic change

For the projection of major phases of linguistic growth, and especially for signaling the relationship between cognate languages, experts in reconstruction have resorted either to the somewhat older "family-tree theory" (*Stammbaumtheorie*) or to the wave hypothesis. The former is associated with the name of Schleicher, that contemporary and counterpart of the evolutionist Darwin, who actually refined rather than launched the "family-tree" concept (1861). It operates with a filiation chart reminiscent of those long favored in the life sciences. The filiation chart, germane in its verbalization and, even more, in its graphic suggestion to the physicists' and chemists' views of radiation, cannot be traced to any advocate earlier than Schuchardt (1866) and, in particular, Schmidt (1871). The inherently rigid family-tree diagram presupposes uniform speech communities and their sudden and clear-cut bifurcation. The more elastic wave diagram tends to dissolve any system (or, less orderly, any arsenal) of communication tools into its constituents, granting to each change, whether phonetic, morphosyntactic, or lexical, its own scope and history. Neither the lapse of time it demands nor the area it covers need be exactly identical with those involved in any comparable change. The latest thinking sees in these divergent hypotheses two complementary projections, neither satisfactory if applied in isolation. Regrettably, no theory apt to reconcile them and no technique capable of smoothly integrating their separate findings have so far been devised.

The wave theory has intrinsically tended to give unusual prominence to the territorial expansion of linguistic features, providing the logical justification for linguistic (*or* dialect) geography. The interest in dialect geography is now past its crest; for many decades it fed on its sentimental motivation, local patriotism, and its partisans' delight in open-air field work. Practitioners of this approach developed special methods for interviews, oral or written questionnaires, and the cartographic recording of field notes (linguistic atlases). Dialect geographers endowed with historical flair then proceeded to transform the geographic patterns laboriously established into bolder chronological sequences, calling themselves the geologists, paleontologists, or stratigraphers of human speech.

One extreme formulation of these assumptions, tastes, and techniques (the "age–area hypothesis") relies chiefly or even exclusively on territorial patterns in piecing together temporal successions. An attempt to schematize these procedures of "areal analysis" was undertaken by the small group of Italian "neolinguists," a school that produced a short flurry of activity from 1920 to 1950. A point that has hitherto not been satisfactorily investigated and yet clamors for imaginative inquiry is the wisdom of positing, alongside that "outer radiation" dear to dialect geographers and to diffusionists like Boas, some kind of "inner radiation" that might account in undulatory projections for the continuous restructuring of systems.

YAKOV MALKIEL

[*See also* HISTORY, *article on* CULTURE HISTORY; LINGUISTICS, *article on* THE SPEECH COMMUNITY; *and the biographies of* BLOOMFIELD; SAUSSURE; WHORF.]

BIBLIOGRAPHY

BALLY, CHARLES (1932) 1944 *Linguistique générale et linguistique française.* 2d ed. Bern: Francke.

BENVENISTE, ÉMILE 1966 *Problèmes de linguistique générale.* Paris: Gallimard.

BLOOMFIELD, LEONARD (1933) 1951 *Language.* Rev. ed. New York: Holt.

HYMES, DELL 1960 Lexicostatistics So Far. *Current Anthropology* 1:3–44. → Includes eight pages of "Comments" and "References."

KURYLOWICZ, JERZY 1960 *Esquisses linguistiques.* Wroclaw (Poland): Zakład Narodowy Imienia Ossolinskich.

LEROY, MAURICE 1963 *Les grands courants de la linguistique moderne.* 2d ed. Brussels, Université Libre, Faculté de Philosophie et Lettres, Travaux, Vol. 24. Presses Universitaires de Bruxelles. → Contains a reliable account of nineteenth-century research.

MALKIEL, YAKOV 1959 Toward a Reconsideration of the Old Spanish Imperfect in -ía ~ -ié. *Hispanic Review* 27:435–481.

MALKIEL, YAKOV 1964 Initial Points Versus Initial Segments of Linguistic Trajectories. Pages 402–405 in International Congress of Linguists, Ninth, Cambridge, Mass., 1962, *Proceedings.* Janua linguarum, Series Maior, Vol. 12. The Hague: Mouton.

MARTINET, ANDRÉ 1955 *Économie des changements phonétiques: Traité de phonologie diachronique.* Bern: Francke.

MIGLIORINI, BRUNO 1960 *Storia della lingua italiana.* Florence: Sansoni.

RICHTER, ELISE 1934 *Beiträge zur Geschichte der Romanismen.* Zeitschrift für romanische Philologie, Supplement 82. Halle (Germany): Niemeyer.

SAPIR, EDWARD A. 1921 *Language: An Introduction to the Study of Speech.* New York: Harcourt.

SAUSSURE, FERDINAND DE (1916) 1959 *Course in General Linguistics.* New York: Philosophical Library. → First published as *Cours de linguistique générale.* Published posthumously.

SCHLEICHER, AUGUST (1861) 1874–1877 *A Compendium of the Comparative Grammar of the Indo-European, Sanskrit, Greek and Latin Languages.* London: Trübner. → Selections from August Schleicher's *Compendium der vergleichenden Grammatik der indogermanischen Sprachen.*

SCHMIDT, JOHANNES 1871 *Die Verwantschaftsverhältnisse der indogermanischen Sprachen.* Weimar (Germany): Böhlau.

SCHUCHARDT, HUGO 1866 *Der Vokalismus des Vulgärlateins.* Volume 1. Leipzig: Teubner.

VOSSLER, KARL (1925) 1932 *The Spirit of Language in Civilization.* London: Routledge. → First published as *Geist und Kultur in der Sprache.*

III
THE SPEECH COMMUNITY

Although not all communication is linguistic, language is by far the most powerful and versatile medium of communication; all known human groups possess language. Unlike other sign systems, the verbal system can, through the minute refinement of its grammatical and semantic structure, be made to refer to a wide variety of objects and concepts. At the same time, verbal interaction is a social process in which utterances are selected in accordance with socially recognized norms and expectations. It follows that linguistic phenomena are analyzable both within the context of language itself and within the broader context of social behavior. In the formal analysis of language the object of attention is a particular body of linguistic data abstracted from the settings in which it occurs and studied primarily from the point of view of its referential function. In analyzing linguistic phenomena within a socially defined universe, however, the study is of language usage as it reflects more general behavior norms. This universe is the speech community: any human aggregate characterized by regular and frequent interaction by means of a shared body of verbal signs and set off from similar aggregates by significant differences in language usage.

Most groups of any permanence, be they small bands bounded by face-to-face contact, modern nations divisible into smaller subregions, or even occupational associations or neighborhood gangs, may be treated as speech communities, provided they show linguistic peculiarities that warrant special study. The verbal behavior of such groups always constitutes a system. It must be based on finite sets of grammatical rules that underlie the production of well-formed sentences, or else messages will not be intelligible. The description of such rules is a precondition for the study of all types of linguistic phenomena. But it is only the starting point in the sociolinguistic analysis of language behavior.

Grammatical rules define the bounds of the linguistically acceptable. For example, they enable us to identify "How do you do?" "How are you?" and "Hi" as proper American English sentences and to reject others like "How do you?" and "How you are?" Yet speech is not constrained by grammatical rules alone. An individual's choice from among permissible alternates in a particular speech event may reveal his family background and his social intent, may identify him as a Southerner, a Northerner, an urbanite, a rustic, a member of the educated or uneducated classes, and may even indicate whether he wishes to appear friendly or distant, familiar or deferential, superior or inferior.

Just as intelligibility presupposes underlying grammatical rules, the communication of social information presupposes the existence of regular relationships between language usage and social structure. Before we can judge a speaker's social intent, we must know something about the norms defining the appropriateness of linguistically acceptable alternates for particular types of speakers; these norms vary among subgroups and among social settings. Wherever the relationships between language choice and rules of social appropriateness can be formalized, they allow us to group relevant linguistic forms into distinct dialects, styles, and occupational or other special parlances. The sociolinguistic study of speech communities deals with the linguistic similarities and differences among these speech varieties.

In linguistically homogeneous societies the verbal markers of social distinctions tend to be confined to structurally marginal features of phonology, syntax, and lexicon. Elsewhere they may include both standard literary languages, and grammatically divergent local dialects. In many multilingual societies the choice of one language over another has the same signification as the selection among lexical alternates in linguistically homogeneous societies. In such cases, two or more grammars may be required to cover the entire scope of linguistically acceptable expressions that serve to convey social meanings.

Regardless of the linguistic differences among them, the speech varieties employed within a speech community form a system because they are related to a shared set of social norms. Hence, they can be classified according to their usage, their origins, and the relationship between speech and social action that they reflect. They become indices of social patterns of interaction in the speech community.

Historical orientation in early studies

Systematic linguistic field work began in the middle of the nineteenth century. Prior to 1940 the best-known studies were concerned with dialects, special parlances, national languages, and linguistic acculturation and diffusion.

Dialectology. Among the first students of speech communities were the dialectologists, who charted the distribution of colloquial speech forms in societies dominated by German, French, English, Polish, and other major standard literary tongues. Mapping relevant features of pronunciation, grammar, and lexicon in the form of *isoglosses*, they traced in detail the range and spread of historically documented changes in language habits. Isoglosses were grouped into bundles of two or more and then mapped; from the geographical shape of such isogloss bundles, it was possible to distinguish the *focal areas*, centers from which innovations radiate into the surrounding regions; *relic zones*, districts where forms previously known only from old texts were still current; and *transition zones*, areas of internal diversity marked by the coexistence of linguistic forms identified with competing centers of innovation.

Analysis along these lines clearly established the importance of social factors in language change. The distribution of rural speech patterns was found to be directly related to such factors as political boundaries during the preceding centuries, traditional market networks, the spread of important religious movements, etc. In this fashion dialectology became an important source of evidence for social history.

Special parlances, classical languages. Other scholars dealt with the languages of occupationally specialized minority groups, craft jargons, secret argots, and the like. In some cases, such as the Romany of the gypsies and the Yiddish of Jews, these parlances derive from foreign importations which survive as linguistic islands surrounded by other tongues. Their speakers tend to be bilinguals, using their own idiom for in-group communication and the majority language for interaction with outsiders.

Linguistic distinctness may also result from seemingly intentional processes of distortion. One very common form of secret language, found in a variety of tribal and complex societies, achieves unintelligibility by a process of verbal play with majority speech, in which phonetic or grammatical elements are systematically reordered. The pig Latin of English-speaking schoolchildren, in which initial consonants are transferred to the end of the word and followed by "-ay," is a relatively simple example of this process. Thieves' argots, the slang of youth gangs, and the jargon of traveling performers and other occupational groups obtain similar results by assigning special meanings to common nouns, verbs, and adjectives.

Despite their similarities, the classical administrative and liturgical languages—such as the Latin of medieval Europe, the Sanskrit of south Asia, and the Arabic of the Near East—are not ordinarily grouped with special parlances because of the prestige of the cultural traditions associated with them. They are quite distinct from and often unrelated to popular speech, and the elaborate ritual and etiquette that surround their use can be learned only through many years of special training. Instruction is available only through private tutors and is limited to a privileged few who command the necessary social status or financial resources. As a result, knowledge of these languages in the traditional societies where they are used is limited to relatively small elites, who tend to maintain control of their linguistic skills in somewhat the same way that craft guilds strive for exclusive control of their craft skills.

The standard literary languages of modern nation-states, on the other hand, tend to be representative of majority speech. As a rule they originated in rising urban centers, as a result of the free interaction of speakers of a variety of local dialects, became identified with new urban elites, and in time replaced older administrative languages. Codification of spelling and grammar by means of dictionaries and dissemination of this information through public school systems are characteristic of standard-language societies. Use of mass media and the prestige of their speakers tend to carry idioms far from their sources; such idioms eventually replace many pre-existing local dialects and special parlances.

Linguistic acculturation, language shift. Wherever two or more speech communities maintain prolonged contact within a broad field of communication, there are crosscurrents of diffusion. The result is the formation of a *Sprachbund*, comprising a group of varieties which coexist in social space as dialects, distinct neighboring languages, or special parlances. Persistent borrowing over long periods creates within such groups similarities in linguistic structure, which tend to obscure pre-existing genetic distinctions; a commonly cited example is the south Asian subcontinent, where speakers of Indo–Aryan, Dravidian, and Munda languages all show significant overlap in their linguistic habits.

It appears that single nouns, verbs, and adjectives are most readily diffused, often in response to a variety of technological innovations and cultural or religious trends. Pronunciation and word order are also frequently affected. The level of phonological and grammatical pattern (i.e., the structural core of a language), however, is more resistant to change, and loanwords tend to be adapted to the patterns of the recipient language. But linguistic barriers to diffusion are never absolute, and in situations of extensive bilingualism—

two or more languages being regularly used in the course of the daily routine—even the grammatical cores may be affected.

Cross-cultural influence reaches a maximum in the cases of pidgins and creoles, idioms combining elements of several distinct languages. These hybrids typically arise in colonial societies or in large trading centers where laborers torn out of their native language environments are forced to work in close cooperation with speakers of different tongues. Cross-cultural influence may also give rise to language shift, the abandonment of one native tongue in favor of another. This phenomenon most frequently occurs when two groups merge, as in tribal absorption, or when minority groups take on the culture of the surrounding majority.

Although the bulk of the research on speech communities that was conducted prior to 1940 is historically oriented, students of speech communities differ markedly from their colleagues who concentrate upon textual analysis. The latter tend to treat languages as independent wholes that branch off from uniform protolanguages in accordance with regular sound laws. The former, on the other hand, regard themselves primarily as students of behavior, interested in linguistic phenomena for their broader sociohistorical significance. By relating dialect boundaries to settlement history, to political and administrative boundaries, and to culture areas and by charting the itineraries of loanwords in relation to technical innovations or cultural movements, they established the primacy of social factors in language change, disproving earlier theories of environmental or biological determinism.

The study of language usage in social communities, furthermore, revealed little of the uniformity ordinarily ascribed to protolanguages and their descendants; many exceptions to the regularity of sound laws were found wherever speakers of genetically related languages were in regular contact. This led students of speech communities to challenge the "family-tree theory," associated with the neogrammarians of nineteenth-century Europe, who were concerned primarily with the genetic reconstruction of language history. Instead, they favored a theory of diffusion which postulates the spread of linguistic change in intersecting "waves" that emanate from different centers of innovation with an intensity proportionate to the prestige of their human carriers.

Thus, while geneticists regarded modern language distribution as the result of the segmentation of older entities into newer and smaller subgroups, diffusionists viewed the speech community as a dynamic field of action where phonetic change, borrowing, language mixture, and language shift all occur because of social forces, and where genetic origin is secondary to these forces. In recent years linguists have begun to see the two theories as complementary. The assumption of uniformity among protolanguages is regarded as an abstraction necessary to explain existing regularities of sound change and is considered extremely useful for the elucidation of long-term prehistoric relationships, especially since conflicting short-term diffusion currents tend to cancel each other. Speech-community studies, on the other hand, appear better adapted to the explanation of relatively recent changes.

Language behavior and social communication

The shift of emphasis from historical to synchronic problems during the last three decades has brought about some fundamental changes in our theories of language, resulting in the creation of a body of entirely new analytical techniques. Viewed in the light of these fresh insights, the earlier speech-community studies are subject to serious criticism on grounds of both linguistic and sociological methodology. For some time, therefore, linguists oriented toward formal analysis showed very little interest. More recent structural studies, however, show that this criticism does not affect the basic concept of the speech community as a field of action where the distribution of linguistic variants is a reflection of social facts. The relationship between such variants when they are classified in terms of usage rather than of their purely linguistic characteristics can be examined along two dimensions: the *dialectal* and the *superposed.*

Dialectal relationships are those in which differences set off the vernaculars of local groups (for example, the language of home and family) from those of other groups within the same, broader culture. Since this classification refers to usage rather than to inherent linguistic traits, relationships between minority languages and majority speech (e.g., between Welsh and English in Britain or French and English in Canada) and between distinct languages found in zones of intensive intertribal contact (e.g., in modern Africa) can also be considered dialectal, because they show characteristics similar to the relationship existing between dialects of the same language.

Whereas dialect variation relates to distinctions in geographical origin and social background, superposed variation refers to distinctions between different types of activities carried on within the same group. The special parlances described above form a linguistic extreme, but similar distinctions in usage are found in all speech communities. The language of formal speechmaking, religious ritual, or technical discussion, for example, is never the same as that employed in informal talk among friends, because each is a style fulfilling particular communicative needs. To some extent the linguistic markers of such activities are directly related to their different technical requirements. Scientific discussion, for instance, requires precisely defined terms and strict limitation on their usage. But in other cases, as in greetings, forms of address, or choosing between "isn't" and "ain't," the primary determinant is the social relationship between speakers rather than communicative necessity. Language choice in these cases is limited by social barriers; the existence of such barriers lends significance to the sociolinguistic study of superposed variation.

This distinction between dialectal and superposed varieties obviates the usual linguistic distinction between geographically and socially distributed varieties, since the evidence indicates that actual residence patterns are less important as determinants of distribution than social interaction patterns and usage. Thus, there seems to be little need to draw conceptual distinctions upon this basis.

Descriptions of dialectal and superposed variation relate primarily to social groups. Not all individuals within a speech community have equal control of the entire set of superposed variants current there. Control of communicative resources varies sharply with the individual's position within the social system. The more narrowly confined his sphere of activities, the more homogeneous the social environment within which he interacts, and the less his need for verbal facility. Thus, housewives, farmers, and laborers, who rarely meet outsiders, often make do with only a narrow range of speech styles, while actors, public speakers, and businessmen command the greatest range of styles. The fact that such individual distinctions are found in multilingual as well as in linguistically homogeneous societies suggests that the common assertion which identifies bilingualism with poor scores in intelligence testing is in urgent need of reexamination, based, as it is, primarily on work with underprivileged groups. Recent work, in fact, indicates that the failure of some self-contained groups to inculcate facility in verbal manipulation is a major factor in failures in their children's performances in public school systems.

Attitudes to language choice. Social norms of language choice vary from situation to situation and from community to community. Regularities in attitudes to particular speech varieties, however, recur in a number of societies and deserve special comment here. Thieves' argots, gang jargons, and the like serve typically as group boundary maintaining mechanisms, whose linguistic characteristics are the result of informal group consensus and are subject to continual change in response to changing attitudes. Individuals are accepted as members of the group to the extent that their usage conforms to the practices of the day. Similar attitudes of exclusiveness prevail in the case of many tribal languages spoken in areas of culture contact where other superposed idioms serve as media of public communication. The tribal language here is somewhat akin to a secret ritual, in that it is private knowledge to be kept from outsiders, an attitude which often makes it difficult for casual investigators to collect reliable information about language distribution in such areas.

Because of the elaborate linguistic etiquette and stylistic conventions that surround them, classical, liturgical, and administrative languages function somewhat like secret languages. Mastery of the conventions may be more important in gaining social success than substantive knowledge of the information dispensed through these languages. But unlike the varieties mentioned above, norms of appropriateness are explicit in classical languages; this permits them to remain unchanged over many generations.

In contrast, the attitude to pidgins, trade languages, and similar intergroup media of communication tends to be one of toleration. Here little attention is paid to linguistic markers of social appropriateness. It is the function of such languages to facilitate contact between groups without constituting their respective social cohesiveness; and, as a result, communication in these languages tends to be severely restricted to specific topics or types of interaction. They do not, as a rule, serve as vehicles for personal friendships.

We speak of *language loyalty* when a literary variety acquires prestige as a symbol of a particular nationality group or social movement. Language loyalty tends to unite diverse local groups and social classes, whose members may continue to speak their own vernaculars within the family circle. The literary idiom serves for reading and for public interaction and embodies the cultural tradition of a nation or a sector thereof. Individuals choose to employ it as a symbol of their allegiance to a broader set of political ideals than that embodied in the family or kin group.

Language loyalty may become a political issue in a modernizing society when hitherto socially isolated minority groups become mobilized. Their demands for closer participation in political affairs are often accompanied by demands for language reform or for the rewriting of the older, official code in their own literary idiom. Such demands often represent political and socioeconomic threats to the established elite, which may control the distribution of administrative positions through examination systems based upon the official code. The replacement of an older official code by another literary idiom in modernizing societies may thus represent the displacement of an established elite by a rising group.

The situation becomes still more complex when socioeconomic competition between several minority groups gives rise to several competing new literary standards, as in many parts of Asia and Africa, where language conflicts have led to civil disturbances and political instability. Although demands for language reform are usually verbalized in terms of communicative needs, it is interesting to observe that such demands do not necessarily reflect important linguistic differences between the idioms in question. Hindi and Urdu, the competing literary standards of north India, or Serbian and Croatian, in Yugoslavia, are grammatically almost identical. They differ in their writing systems, in their lexicons, and in minor aspects of syntax. Nevertheless, their proponents treat them as separate languages. The conflict in language loyalty may even affect mutual intelligibility, as when speakers' claims that they do not understand each other reflect primarily social attitudes rather than linguistic fact. In other cases serious linguistic differences may be disregarded when minority speakers pay language loyalty to a standard markedly different from their own vernacular. In many parts of Alsace-Lorraine, for example, speakers of German dialects seem to disregard linguistic fact and pay language loyalty to French rather than to German.

Varietal distribution. Superposed and dialectal varieties rarely coincide in their geographical extent. We find the greatest amount of linguistic diversity at the level of local, tribal, peasant, or lower-class urban populations. Tribal areas typically constitute a patchwork of distinct languages, while local speech distribution in many modern nations takes the form of a dialect chain in which the speech of each locality is similar to that of adjoining settlements and in which speech differences increase in proportion to geographical distance. Variety at the local level is bridged by the considerably broader spread of superposed varieties, serving as media of supralocal communication. The Latin of medieval Europe and the Arabic of the Near East form extreme examples of supralocal spread. Uniformity at the superposed level in their case, however, is achieved at the expense of large gaps in internal communication channels. Standard languages tend to be somewhat more restricted in geographical spread than classical languages, because of their relationship to local dialects. In contrast to a society in which classical languages are used as superposed varieties, however, a standard-language society possesses better developed channels of internal communication, partly because of its greater linguistic homogeneity and partly because of the internal language loyalty that it evokes.

In fact, wherever standard languages are well-established they act as the ultimate referent that determines the association of a given local dialect with one language or another. This may result in the anomalous situation in which two linguistically similar dialects spoken on different sides of a political boundary are regarded as belonging to different languages, not because of any inherent linguistic differences but because their speakers pay language loyalty to different standards. Language boundaries in such cases are defined partly by social and partly by linguistic criteria.

Verbal repertoires. The totality of dialectal and superposed variants regularly employed within a community make up the *verbal repertoire* of that community. Whereas the bounds of a language, as this term is ordinarily understood, may or may not coincide with that of a social group, verbal repertoires are always specific to particular populations. As an analytical concept the verbal repertoire allows us to establish direct relationships between its constituents and the socioeconomic complexity of the community.

We measure this relationship in terms of two concepts: *linguistic range* and *degree of compartmentalization*. Linguistic range refers to internal language distance between constituent varieties, that is, the total amount of purely linguistic differentiation that exists in a community, thus distinguishing among multilingual, multidialectal, and homogeneous communities. Compartmentalization refers to the sharpness with which varieties are set off from each other, either along the superposed or the dialectal dimension. We speak of compartmentalized repertoires, therefore, when several languages are spoken without their mixing, when dialects are set off from each other by sharp isogloss bundles, or when special parlances are sharply distinct from other forms of speech. We speak of fluid repertoires, on the other hand, when transitions between adjoining vernaculars are gradual or when one speech style merges into another in such a way that it is difficult to draw clear borderlines.

Initially, the linguistic range of a repertoire is a function of the languages and special parlances employed before contact. But given a certain period of contact, linguistic range becomes dependent upon the amount of internal interaction. The greater the frequency of internal interaction, the greater the tendency for innovations arising in one part of the speech community to diffuse throughout it. Thus, where the flow of communication is dominated by a single all-important center—for example, as Paris dominates central France—linguistic range is relatively small. Political fragmentation, on the other hand, is associated with diversity of languages or of dialects, as in southern Germany, long dominated by many small, semi-independent principalities.

Over-all frequency in interaction is not, however, the only determinant of uniformity. In highly stratified societies speakers of minority languages or dialects typically live side by side, trading, exchanging services, and often maintaining regular social contact as employer and employee or master and servant. Yet despite this contact, they tend to preserve their own languages, suggesting the existence of social norms that set limits to freedom of intercommunication. Compartmentalization reflects such social norms. The exact nature of these sociolinguistic barriers is not yet clearly understood, although some recent literature suggests new avenues for investigation.

We find, for example, that separate languages maintain themselves most readily in closed tribal systems, in which kinship dominates all activities. Linguistically distinct special parlances, on the other hand, appear most fully developed in highly stratified societies, where the division of labor is maintained by rigidly defined barriers of ascribed status. When social change causes the breakdown of traditional social structures and the formation of new ties, as in urbanization and colonialization, linguistic barriers between varieties also break down. Rapidly changing societies typically show either gradual transition between speech styles or, if the community is bilingual, a range of intermediate varieties bridging the transitions between extremes.

JOHN J. GUMPERZ

[*See also* LANGUAGE, *article on* LANGUAGE AND CULTURE; *and* LINGUISTICS, *article on* HISTORICAL LINGUISTICS.]

BIBLIOGRAPHY

BARTH, FREDERIK 1964 Ethnic Processes on the Pathan–Baluch Boundary. Pages 13–20 in *Indo-Iranica: Mélanges présentés à Georg Morgenstierne, à l'occasion de son soixante-dixième anniversaire.* Wiesbaden (Germany): Harrassowitz.

BERNSTEIN, BASIL (1958) 1961 Social Class and Linguistic Development: A Theory of Social Learning. Pages 288–314 in A. H. Halsey et al. (editors), *Education, Economy, and Society.* New York: Free Press. → First published in Volume 9 of the *British Journal of Sociology.*

BLOOMFIELD, LEONARD (1933) 1951 *Language.* Rev. ed New York: Holt.

BROWN, ROGER W. 1965 *Social Psychology.* New York: Free Press.

GUMPERZ, JOHN J.; and HYMES, DELL H. (editors) 1964 The Ethnography of Communication. *American Anthropologist* New Series 66, no. 6, part 2.

HALLIDAY, MICHAEL A. K.; McINTOSH, ANGUS; and STREVENS, PETER (1964) 1965 *The Linguistic Sciences and Language Teaching.* Bloomington: Indiana Univ. Press.

HAUGEN, EINAR I. 1956 *Bilingualism in the Americas: A Bibliography and Research Guide.* University, Ala.: American Dialect Society.

HAUGEN, EINAR I. 1966 *Language Conflict and Language Planning.* Cambridge, Mass.: Harvard Univ. Press.

HERTZLER, JOYCE O. 1965 *A Sociology of Language.* New York: Random House.

HYMES, DELL H. (editor) 1964 *Language in Culture and Society: A Reader in Linguistics and Anthropology.* New York: Harper.

JESPERSEN, OTTO (1925) 1964 *Mankind, Nation and the Individual, From a Linguistic Point of View.* Bloomington: Indiana Univ. Press. → First published as *Menneskehed, nasjon og individ i sproget.*

KURATH, HANS (editor) 1939–1943 *Linguistic Atlas of New England.* 3 vols. and a handbook. Providence, R.I.: Brown Univ. Press.

LABOV, WILLIAM 1966 The Social Stratification of English in New York City. Unpublished manuscript, Center for Applied Linguistics.

PASSIN, HERBERT 1963 Writer and Journalist in the Transitional Society. Pages 82–123 in Conference on Communication and Political Development, Dobbs Ferry, N.Y., 1961, *Communications and Political Development.* Edited by Lucian W. Pye. Princeton Univ. Press. → Contains a discussion of the relationship of national languages to political development.

WEINREICH, URIEL 1953 *Languages in Contact: Findings and Problems.* New York: Linguistic Circle of New York.

LINTON, RALPH

Ralph Linton (1893–1953), American cultural anthropologist, was one of the major contributors to the reconstruction of anthropology during the second quarter of the twentieth century. Trained in the traditions of the North American "historical school" of anthropology, Linton remained loyal throughout his career to the broad interests and general principles established by Franz Boas and other American anthropologists. But with the publication in 1936 of *The Study of Man*, which was quickly recognized by social scientists all over the world as a pioneering study of human behavior, he embarked on a series of creative and stimulating studies which provided new conceptions of social structure and cultural organization. He related these conceptions in a clear if somewhat simple manner to the biological individual and his personality and utilized them in his analyses of the processes of cultural change.

Linton belonged to the "third generation" of American academic anthropologists, succeeding such second-generation students of Putnam and Boas as Wissler, Dixon, Kroeber, Goldenweiser, Lowie, Sapir, and Radin. These academicians, together with a number of outstanding journeymen and masters involved more in field research than in teaching, had created a distinctive variety of anthropology. Like Tylor in England, they had a holistic approach to human studies which is still, thanks in part to Linton, a mark of American anthropology.

In the Americas much more than in Europe almost all anthropological study and training had been nurtured by experience in the field and disciplined by the empiricism required by field work on specific problems treating the temporal and spatial dimensions of culture. In dealing with the elements of local aboriginal development or culture history, most American anthropologists insisted that the combined skills of all the arts and sciences, as they may be relevant to the study of man, should be brought to bear on the task at hand. [*See* ETHNOGRAPHY.]

Linton's own teaching, writing, and research encompassed human biology, archeology, ethnography, ethnology, folklore, and regional and global cultural history. He contributed to all of these classical subfields of his discipline, although less significantly to physical anthropology, archeology, and folklore than to the others. He neglected technical developments in linguistics and approached the field with respectful diffidence, but he urged his students to become familiar with it, since he felt that it was the most scientific of the social disciplines. He did not emphasize statistical studies, nor did he use specialized mathematical methods in cultural or psychological anthropology, although he recognized these as legitimate activities. It was not any aversion to formalism or structuralism as such that made Linton shy away from these aspects of anthropology, for his approach to culture and to personality studies was essentially formalistic and structural.

Like many other American anthropologists who began as archeologists, Linton's professional career started with a focus on artifacts. As a boy he had systematically collected arrowheads, and his interests in artifacts continued throughout his life as he privately gathered outstanding examples of African textiles and masks, Peruvian ceramics, and Oceanic sculpture. Linton's eidetic memory and extraordinary capacity for visual imagery enabled him to identify and compare artifacts from all over the world; and he could retrieve data from the masses of material he had read, explaining that often he could simply "turn the pages" in his mind and reread them.

Linton did his undergraduate work at Swarthmore College, a liberal institution to which his Philadelphia Quaker background led him. The college offered no studies in anthropology, but Linton was a good student in the natural sciences and an omnivorous reader in history and literature, and he decided, as he later recalled, that anthropology provided the most promising opportunity for a synthesis of varied fields. In 1912 and 1913 Linton joined field expeditions working in the American southwest and in Guatemala; and in the summer of 1915, after receiving his B.A., he discovered in New Jersey a prehistoric site of controversial importance, which he described in his first professional publications in the two following years. His graduate training at the University of Pennsylvania, where he obtained an M.A. in 1916, at Columbia University, and finally at Harvard University, where he completed his PH.D. in 1925, was heavily weighted on the side of archeology and physical anthropology. Linton had two more summers of archeological experience in the southwestern United States, one in 1916 for the American Museum of Natural History and another in 1919 following his return from army service in France. He embarked in 1920 on his doctoral research on the archeology of the Marquesas Islands.

Linton's two years in Polynesia proved a turning point in his career, for he found work with living Marquesans more rewarding than his study of the meager remains of their ancestors. His concern for archeological problems continued—he was later active in excavations in Ohio and Wisconsin, and his posthumously published reconstruction of global cultural history demonstrates the mastery he always maintained over the data of world prehistory (see 1955)—but from the early 1920s on, his primary interest was the study of contemporary peoples.

On his return from Polynesia in 1922 he joined

the staff of the Field Museum of Natural History in Chicago, working on Oceanic and American Indian materials and conducting a one-man ethnographic expedition to Madagascar and adjacent parts of east Africa from 1925 to 1927. The publications he prepared during his years as a curator in Chicago indicate that for him the main task of ethnology was not far removed from that of archeology—the reconstruction of human history through careful descriptive studies of the development and distribution of cultural traits. Thus, when Linton began his own teaching career, accepting the first tenure position in anthropology at the University of Wisconsin, in 1928, he had moved little beyond the range of interests which had preoccupied the two preceding generations of American anthropologists.

His early years in the department of sociology at Wisconsin (soon the department of sociology and anthropology) marked the major turning point in Linton's intellectual and professional progress. He suddenly acquired wide interests in the many dimensions of human behavior. The competent fieldworker, museum archeologist, and ethnologist became in a few years a leading American social scientist.

Linton was an excellent lecturer and teacher. Almost as soon as he arrived at Wisconsin he acquired a following of young scholars who had done their undergraduate work at the university; John Dollard, J. P. Gillin, E. A. Hoebel, Clyde Kluckhohn, Lauriston Sharp, and Sol Tax were among them. Although none of these completed his graduate training under Linton, they were nonetheless widely identified with him. A number of colleagues had a marked influence on Linton's thinking during his early years at Wisconsin. He said that Kimball Young, the social psychologist, had perhaps helped him most in developing his view of social organization and its relation to individual personality formation; but he also acknowledged his debt to other members of the department, as well as to the psychologists Clark Hull and Harry Harlow, the geneticist Michael F. Guyer, the political scientist John Gauss, and the ethicists F. C. Sharp and Eliseo Vivas. Students in the university's newly established Experimental College, while dealing with the large problems of order and change in the civilizations of classical Greece and modern America, were reading a wide range of materials bearing on cultural anthropology, and Linton participated in sessions on the nature and organization of culture and civilization that were unlike most anthropology courses of the day.

For a few years during the early 1930s A. R. Radcliffe-Brown, then a leader of the British functionalist school of social anthropology, taught at the University of Chicago, where Linton maintained informal connections. At that time Radcliffe-Brown was claiming in a somewhat doctrinaire manner that history is irrelevant to the real task of social anthropology, which is to study societies synchronically and induce general sociological laws through a comparison of the forms and functions of the social organizations of particular living societies. To Linton, the rejection of history, however fragmentary and insecure our knowledge of it may be, was anathema. However, his own field work had convinced him that the task of determining the functions of segments or complexes of cultural behavior as well as the functional interdependence of parts within the totality of a culture is a legitimate and essential one (1933). Furthermore, Linton himself was seeking regularities and general principles in the varied array of cultural experience in different times and places. Thus, in their intellectual objectives the two scholars were close together, however they differed as to means. Linton's correspondence of the period indicates that he deplored Radcliffe-Brown's considerable influence on younger members of the profession as a threat to the larger traditional concerns of American anthropology and one which he felt personally obligated to combat. However, the discussions which took place between the two men sharpened Linton's perceptions of Radcliffe-Brown's own special field of social structure and led him to argue for improved functional analyses which would take into account historical factors. Eventually this point of view largely prevailed on both sides of the Atlantic.

In the 1930s the new developments in psychiatry, psychology, European sociology, and functionalism began to influence American anthropologists, particularly Sapir, Benedict, Margaret Mead, and Hallowell. Physical anthropology and archeology, which had links to the natural sciences, and linguistics were beginning to develop rapidly and even in America were showing a strong tendency to go their separate ways. However, Linton's eclectic and wide-ranging approach to the study of man and his behavior enabled him to bring together some of these radically diverging historical, sociological, psychological, and biological interests which were dividing the anthropologists. His contributions to unity were open-ended; he found it unnecessary to impose any single closed, elaborate, or wholly consistent theoretical system on the social sciences.

Concept of culture. The work which Linton always considered his major contribution to anthropology, *The Study of Man* (1936), was written in a simple but lively style which attracted layman and scientist alike. While intended as a text, it lacked the apparatus of a school book, containing only two footnotes and an almost irrelevant bibliography prepared hastily by a student. Except for the absence of sections on religion and the arts (originally intended for inclusion but not completed), the work was representative of the main areas of Linton's interests and foreshadowed the main thrusts of his later thinking.

Following a short opening section on human origins and the biological and primate backgrounds to cultural behavior, later elaborated in *The Tree of Culture* (1955), Linton turned directly to the individual as he interacts in defined social contexts with other individuals: the network of learned and shared behavior of individuals—their culture—creates or maintains a community or society. He conceived of culture as both overt, or open to observation, and covert, with an inferred content of meanings, emotions, values, attitudes, "and so on."

While Linton could speak of "the mind" without blushing, he failed to deal effectively with cognition and other epistemological problems, seeing the mind as a wholly internal private sense organ rather than as a process or a product of the transaction of social business between the external and the inner worlds. As he later became involved more explicitly with psychoanalytic theory, Linton increasingly dealt with the category of covert behavior as though emotion is the prime ingredient and almost the sole source of data for the inner workings of the human personality, thus almost entirely neglecting cognitive processes.

Status and role. Linton developed his concepts of "status" and "role" to deal with the discrete elements as well as the integrated aspects of society. By status he meant the place of an individual in society, defining it as a collection of rights and duties; by role he meant the dynamic aspect of behavior in a status, the putting into action of rights and duties (1936, pp. 113–114). Statuses and roles may be universal or specialized, depending on whether they are shared by all members of a society or only by a segment of the society. Roles appropriate to a given status are not necessarily performed in the same way by all those members of the society in that status, nor are they even performed identically by the same individual at different times. There may be recognized alternative ways of achieving particular customary goals: such alternative roles may arise within the society or they may be imported from without. Behavior in a role, according to Linton, is simply behavior appropriate to a particular recognized status.

Statuses or positions are, in Linton's view, either ascribed to the individual—that is, assigned at birth, on the basis of sex, caste, or other fixed characteristics—or they are achieved by the individual by virtue of his own effort. Roles also are of two kinds: "actual" roles—the way roles are in fact performed; and "ideal" roles—the normative patterns that serve as models for actual role performance. The total set of ideal roles constituted for Linton a social system. With this conception of roles, including child roles and those acquired as an adult, Linton laid the foundation of a theory of behavior that could bridge the gap between the individual and the cultural system.

Personality and culture. Instead of systematically refining these ideas or attempting a synthesis along the lines developed in social psychology, Linton pursued his interest in the nature of the relation between the individual personality and society. In 1937 he went to Columbia University and began there a period of collaboration in seminars and publications with Abram Kardiner, a psychoanalyst. Their views were published, with documentary ethnographic analyses, in *The Individual and His Society* (Kardiner 1939) and *The Psychological Frontiers of Society* (Kardiner 1945). From this work emerged the concept of basic personality structure, or modal personality type—

> . . . that personality configuration which is shared by the bulk of the society's members as a result of the early experiences which they have in common. It does not correspond to the total personality of the individual, but rather to the projective systems or, in different phraseology, the value–attitude systems which are basic to the individual's personality configuration. Thus the same basic personality types may be reflected in many different forms of behavior and may enter into many different total personality configurations. (Kardiner 1945, p. viii)

Somewhat disenchanted with the psychoanalytic approach, Linton expounded his own views in *The Cultural Background of Personality* (1945*a*), showing how each individual's experiences in a society—his performance of a particular set of more or less standardized cultural roles—produce what Linton then called the "status personality." The common elements of the status personalities found in a group of persons may be considered the basic personality type for a culture. Linton dealt with problems of deviation from type in a posthumously published volume, *Culture and Mental Disorders* (1956). While some anthropologists before Linton had been concerned with the individual, it was Linton's structural approach through status and role that did much to open the way for a retreat from the prevalent extreme reification of culture. [*See* AGE DIFFERENTIATION; CULTURE AND PERSON-

ALITY; INDIVIDUAL DIFFERENCES, *article on* SEX DIFFERENCES; NATIONAL CHARACTER; STATUS, SOCIAL.]

Hierarchy of interests. Related to Linton's concern with culture and personality and the character structure of ethnic groups was his work on the cultural interests, orientations, and values of groups. He was dissatisfied with Benedict's conclusion, in her popular *Patterns of Culture* (1934), that the total behavior of a society or of most of its members may express, through a dominant cultural pattern or configuration, a single mode of feeling or world view heavily biased in a particular direction. While agreeing that cultures are configurations, Linton suggested that any culture exhibits a whole range of patterned "interests," each of which has a "rating" reflecting its importance relative to other interests of the group. Only empirical investigation can reveal which particular interest or set of interests dominates the others in a given period and so provides the culture with an over-all orientation (1936, chapters 20, 24, 25). Morris Opler and others later refined this idea through the concept of "themes."

In his later years, and particularly after he accepted a Sterling professorship at Yale University in 1946, Linton returned to a problem which had engaged him at Wisconsin, the question of cultural relativity and the possibility that all cultures may exhibit certain universal ethical or other values. He asserted that there are common denominators of behavior among all cultures and that these support common values which then must be described at a rather abstract level (1952; 1954).

Cultural change. Linton's preoccupation with problems of culture history and culture change persisted from his first experience as an archeologist through his entire career; it even motivated his interest in the balanced relationships between the maturing individual and the changing culture in which he participates. Yet in his search for explanations of cultural change and transfer, Linton did not explore these relationships fully or systematically; rather, to explain the effective elements in change, acculturation, and social movements, he pointed to such general factors as the utility of the new, the compatibility of the new with the old, and the prestige of the innovator (1940). [*See* CULTURE, *article on* CULTURE CHANGE.]

Linton believed profoundly that the social sciences could become rigorous sciences and that their findings should inform the work of those dealing with current social problems (1945*b*, p. xiii). However, he was not optimistic about the immediate prospects of modern civilization. His own creative innovations were widely recognized and he received the highest academic and professional honors from colleagues both within and outside his discipline. But he felt that this recognition of his work had been won in a rare period of freedom, one which could not last and which was already threatened by the bigotries which had appeared abroad and at home in his own lifetime. Expecting a "dark age," he dedicated *The Study of Man* (1936) to "the next civilization"; and almost two decades later he concluded *The Tree of Culture* (1955) in the same vein, expressing the hope that the social sciences would use this period of unusual freedom to prepare some "solid platform from which the workers of the next civilization might go on."

LAURISTON SHARP

[*Other relevant material may be found in the biographies of* BENEDICT; RADCLIFFE-BROWN; SAPIR.]

WORKS BY LINTON

1933 *The Tanala: A Hill Tribe of Madagascar.* Field Museum of Natural History, Publication No. 317, Anthropological Series, No. 22. Chicago: The Museum.

1936 *The Study of Man: An Introduction.* New York: Appleton.

1940 LINTON, RALPH (editor) *Acculturation in Seven American Indian Tribes.* New York: Appleton.

1945*a* *The Cultural Background of Personality.* New York: Appleton.

1945*b* LINTON, RALPH (editor) *The Science of Man in the World Crisis.* New York: Columbia Univ. Press.

1952 Universal Ethical Principles: An Anthropological View. Pages 645–660 in Ruth N. Anshen (editor), *Moral Principles of Action: Man's Ethical Imperative.* New York: Harper.

1954 The Problem of Universal Values. Pages 145–168 in Robert F. Spencer (editor), *Method and Perspective in Anthropology.* Minneapolis: Univ. of Minnesota Press.

1955 *The Tree of Culture.* New York: Knopf.

1956 *Culture and Mental Disorders.* Edited by George Devereux. Springfield, Ill.: Thomas.

SUPPLEMENTARY BIBLIOGRAPHY

BENEDICT, RUTH (1934) 1959 *Patterns of Culture.* 2d ed. Boston: Houghton Mifflin. → A paperback edition was published in 1961.

GILLIN, JOHN 1954 Ralph Linton. *American Anthropologist* New Series 56:274–281.

KARDINER, ABRAM 1939 *The Individual and His Society.* With a foreword and two ethnological reports by Ralph Linton. New York: Columbia Univ. Press.

KARDINER, ABRAM 1945 *The Psychological Frontiers of Society.* With the cooperation of Ralph Linton, Cora DuBois, and James West. New York: Columbia Univ. Press.

KLUCKHOHN, CLYDE 1958 Ralph Linton. National Academy of Sciences, *Biographical Memoirs* 31:236–253. → Includes a bibliography.

LIPPMANN, WALTER

Walter Lippmann was born in 1889 in New York City. His upper-middle-class family exposed him early to art, music, and literature. He attended Harvard University, where he completed the requirements for the A.B. degree in three years. His fourth year at Harvard was spent as an assistant to the philosopher George Santayana; and he graduated formally with the celebrated class of 1910, which included many others who later became prominent in the arts, the sciences, and public affairs.

An early desire to write—he had published several pieces of social criticism in the *Harvard Monthly*—turned him to journalism as a career. His first opportunity came through Lincoln Steffens, who went to Harvard in search of "the ablest mind that could express itself in writing" to help him with a series of muckraking articles for *Everybody's Magazine*.

Lippmann's accomplishments as a writer rapidly attracted the attention of those intellectual circles which were influential in the progressive climate of the prewar years. A short and disappointing stint as secretary to the socialist mayor of a city in upstate New York was followed by a brief period of free-lance writing for several magazines. But it was an invitation from Herbert Croly to join the editorial board of a new liberal journal, the *New Republic*, that provided Lippmann with a congenial and more permanent environment for his talents. No longer a socialist, yet one of the young "movers and shakers" whose intellectual vitality made the period immediately prior to World War I a seedtime of new ideas and limitless hope for the future, Lippmann found in the pages of the *New Republic* an outlet for articles on almost any topic about which he chose to write.

The *New Republic* became increasingly identified with President Wilson's policies, and in 1917 Lippmann was appointed executive secretary of a postwar planning group, the so-called House Inquiry. The following year he received a commission as captain in military intelligence to conduct propaganda on the western front. At the end of the war he was attached to the American Commission to Negotiate the Peace. In this capacity he prepared, in collaboration with Frank Cobb, then editor of the New York *World*, an elaborate memorandum on Wilson's Fourteen Points which served the American delegation as a basis for the peace discussions.

Lippmann was disappointed at the commitments and concessions made by the United States at the Versailles Peace Conference and soon returned to the *New Republic*. But shortly thereafter he took leave from the magazine to write *Public Opinion* and, upon finishing the book in 1922, was invited to become an editorial writer for the *World*. After Cobb's death in 1923, Lippmann was placed in charge of the paper's editorial page, and in 1929 he became its editor. Although some critics castigated his measured direction of the editorial page as evasion and pusillanimity, the *World* remained, until its end in 1931, in the forefront of those fighting against social and political injustice and for liberal reforms, both within American society and in international relations.

In 1931 Lippmann surprised many of his admirers by accepting an offer to write an independent column for the conservative and traditionally Republican *New York Herald Tribune*. He was evidently given a free hand to write as he pleased, but from 1936 on, his affiliations and connections were no longer with those individuals and groups generally called liberal or progressive. He had become, more than any other columnist or commentator, a spokesman of the American "establishment."

Intellectual development. Lippmann's years at Harvard had a deep and lasting effect on his intellectual development. He had come in contact there with socialist ideas and, for a short time, had been active in the socialist movement. He had also met William James, whose philosophy of pragmatism provided a necessary foil for Santayana's humanist idealism. And most important, he had met the English social scientist and Fabian ideologue Graham Wallas, whose *Human Nature in Politics* (1908) gave direction to Lippmann's early writings.

The more indirect influence of Sigmund Freud was at least as important as any other for Lippmann's work on public opinion and public morality. He had read Freud while writing *A Preface to Politics* (1913), and Freud's ideas seem to have played a most important part in making Lippmann aware of the obstacles to that full rationality which he deemed the goal of intellectual effort.

Finally, one cannot ignore the intellectual impact that his colleagues on the *New Republic* probably had on Lippmann. The editors had divergent ideas which had to be related to one another in order to give the magazine a semblance of unity. There was the centralist, Hamiltonian nationalism that Croly had articulated in *The Promise of American Life* (1909); but there was also the decentralist, Jeffersonian radicalism that Walter E. Weyl, another editor, expressed in *The New Democracy* (1912). Lippmann surely learned at the *New Republic* the tolerance in the face of conflicting ideas that he called "disinterestedness" and which he cherished so much.

Lippmann's own basic intellectual position is extremely difficult to describe, especially since, until his more advanced years, his political outlook rarely remained the same for long. The key to his successive political shifts may lie in Lippmann's statement that "every truly civilized and enlightened man is conservative and liberal and progressive" (1962, p. 11). The best we can do is to examine Lippmann's major works and to distinguish the different stages in his intellectual development.

Major works. Two of Lippmann's early books —*A Preface to Politics* (1913) and *Drift and Mastery* (1914)—testify to his shift from socialism and progressivism to pragmatic liberalism. *A Preface to Politics* is the more important work, for it also contains a protest against the empty formalism and legalism of much political discussion. Lippmann described the book as "a preliminary sketch for a theory of politics, a preface to thinking," and it is not surprising, given his training in philosophy, that he should have begun his writings on this epistemological note. The problem of how to think about things political continued to be a theme throughout his writings.

His basic premises in *A Preface to Politics* are that government is not a routine to be administered but a problem to be solved and that the desires of man, rather than artificially contrived institutional mechanisms, are the proper study of politics. Reason, he felt, must serve the dual purpose of setting direction to human wants and providing the tools for their satisfaction.

The uses of reason as a tool is the main theme of *Drift and Mastery*. Not traditional authority but the method of science must be harnessed to attain human goals. Only this method will permit different persons to agree on what the facts are and to reach the same conclusions. It alone can replace passion with intelligence. The failure of progressivism was its inability to understand the changes that the new industrialism had brought about. Science is "the culture under which people can live forward in the midst of complexity, and treat life not as something given but as something to be shaped" (1914, p. 275).

After World War I Lippmann came to doubt that it is possible, and even that it is desirable, to create a rational society. In *Liberty and the News* (1920), he still expressed a belief that democracy can function, provided the public is supplied with reliable and relevant information. Two years later, however, in *Public Opinion* (1922), he came close to questioning whether citizens can possibly make rational, democratic decisions: the source of the difficulty in forming an intelligent public opinion is not man's irrationality but the necessity, inherent in the modern communications system, of condensing information into brief slogans. These slogans create a wall of stereotypes between the citizen and the issues to which he is expected to respond.

Lippmann's analysis of the public opinion process was remarkably advanced, considering that his contemporaries were still thinking in terms of such categories as "herd instinct" or "group mind." He recognized that both the external environment and man's own psyche are sources of errors that distort perceptions and opinions. Lippmann's use of the concept of stereotype in the analysis of public opinion was an original contribution and has remained a valuable one. Somewhat less original but very cogent was Lippmann's discussion of the role of the expert in public decision making. He did not consider the expert to be a mover and shaker in his own right; rather, he produces facts that may be helpful to those who do make decisions for the benefit of the mass. The mass, Lippmann concluded, is to all intents and purposes inarticulate—it does not decide issues; at most, it assents to or dissents from a proposition about a given issue.

While this denial of the possibility of genuine—in contrast with manipulated—democratic consensus is of course a prejudgment rather than a statement of fact, *Public Opinion* was predominantly analytical. Its sequel, *The Phantom Public* (1925), was frankly polemical. Here Lippmann asserted that the public's role in a democracy is a shadowy one, but he did not accept the conclusions of those conservative critics of democracy who celebrated the rule of an elite. However, his skepticism about the ability of the masses to decide on the merits of a question reflected his own disillusionment with the traditional theory of democracy. Unlike other critics, he became a skeptic moralist rather than an elitist. Morality is a relative, not an absolute, matter, determined at any given time by what men want rather than by what they know to be true, for "a code of the right and the wrong must wait upon a perception of the true and the false" (1925, p. 30). Since such perception is extraordinarily difficult, a code is virtually impossible to achieve.

Skeptic moralist though he had come to be, Lippmann could not accept a morality based on naked desires. Desires must be subjected to the moral test; and in the case of a humanistic morality appropriate to modern conditions, human experience rather than divine revelation must provide the criteria of good and evil. In his next major work, *A Preface to Morals* (1929), Lippmann sought to formulate a new public morality.

The moral test that Lippmann proposed for action was rationality and disinterestedness. Yet, having stated this moral imperative, he continued to doubt the multitude's ability to accept it. Statesmen and leaders would first have to re-educate the wants and desires of the many, and pending this outcome, these leaders must act on the basis of what the people will *in the end* consider good, rather than on the basis of their present desires.

A Preface to Morals in a sense reasserted Lippmann's faith in the rationality of man, tempered by psychological insight into man's volatility; it stated a belief in the possibility of responsible leadership but made the leaders subject to an ideal; and it excoriated current conditions as much as it expressed a new hope for the good society.

The appearance of the New Deal in America and of National Socialism in Germany presented a new challenge to Lippmann's thought. Initially his response to the New Deal was a favorable one, for the New Deal revived his old faith in the possibility of a rational ordering of society. In two small books, *The Method of Freedom* (1934) and *The New Imperative* (1935), his outlook was hopeful. But by 1937, in his *Inquiry Into the Principles of the Good Society*, his appraisal had changed. He identified the compensatory economy of the New Deal with the regimented economy of the totalitarian state, seeing both as evidence of the "collectivist heresy." Moreover, his old suspicion of irrational majorities was linked with a new fear of an irresponsible executive. Gradual collectivism, no less than any other collectivism, makes for arbitrary government.

True liberalism, he asserted in *The Good Society*, must insist on two social mechanisms that are threatened by the collectivist order—the free market and the law. With the market as the prime regulator of the division of labor, the state's function is limited to the administration of justice among men conducting their own affairs in terms of a common law of reciprocal rights and duties. Large public expenditures for education and public works are to be retained, as is protection against the hazards of a free economy, for liberalism is "radical in relation to the social order but conservative in relation to the division of labor in a market economy" (1937, p. 236). As to the role of the executive, society is so pluralistic and diversified that the statesman can only hope to reconcile social conflicts, but he cannot treat society as if it were an organization.

With the beginning of World War II, Lippmann's interest was diverted from problems of political theory to those of international affairs, and it was only with *Essays in the Public Philosophy* (1955) that he returned to his earlier concerns with the political order and democratic structure. The public philosophy, for Lippmann, is a set of positive precepts defining the law that is superior to arbitrary power. It can be discovered by any rational mind, and it is basic to Western institutions. It is the foundation of the good society and must be conscientiously cultivated and transmitted from generation to generation. The liberal democracies, Lippmann charged, have come dangerously close to ignoring the tradition of the public philosophy and accepting politics based on conflict and on interest as legitimate. But political conflict must have limits; and these, like the moral principles that must guide conduct, are to be discovered by reason.

If reason is sovereign, majority voting cannot be trusted, since the voters are too easily swept away by their passions and selfish interests. And their representatives are equally incapable of governing, for they are "insecure and intimidated men . . . [who] advance politically only as they placate, appease, bribe, seduce, or bamboozle, or otherwise manage to manipulate the demanding and threatening elements in their constituencies" (1955, p. 27). As in his first works, Lippmann turned to strong executive power as the practical way out—an executive power enlightened by rationality and constrained by natural law. Such an executive can rule in the interest of "the people"—namely, a "community of the entire living population, with their predecessors and successors" (1955, p. 32)—and not be subject to the whim of the voters.

Heinz Eulau

[*See also* Conservatism; Democracy; Liberalism; Political theory; Public opinion; *and the biographies of* Freud; James; Wallas.]

WORKS BY LIPPMANN

1913 *A Preface to Politics*. New York: Kennerley. → A paperback edition was published in 1962 by the University of Michigan Press.

1914 *Drift and Mastery: An Attempt to Diagnose the Current Unrest*. New York: Kennerley. → A paperback edition was published in 1961 by Prentice-Hall.

(1915) 1917 *The Stakes of Diplomacy*. 2d ed. New York: Holt.

1919 *The Political Scene: An Essay on the Victory of 1918*. New York: Holt.

1920 *Liberty and the News*. New York: Harcourt. → Reprinted in part from the *Atlantic Monthly*.

(1922) 1944 *Public Opinion*. New York: Macmillan. → A paperback edition was published in 1965 by the Free Press.

1925 *The Phantom Public*. New York: Harcourt.
1927 *Men of Destiny*. New York: Macmillan.
1928 *American Inquisitors: A Commentary on Dayton and Chicago*. New York: Macmillan.
(1929) 1952 *A Preface to Morals*. New York: Macmillan.
(1931–1932) 1932 *Interpretations: 1931–1932*. Edited by Allan Nevins. New York: Macmillan.
(1933–1935) 1936 *Interpretations: 1933–1935*. Edited by Allan Nevins. New York: Macmillan.
1934 *The Method of Freedom*. New York: Macmillan.
1935 *The New Imperative*. New York: Macmillan. → Contains two essays, "The Permanent New Deal" and "The New Imperative," both first published in 1935.
(1937) 1943 *Inquiry Into the Principles of the Good Society*. Rev. ed. Boston: Little.
1943 *U.S. Foreign Policy: Shield of the Republic*. Boston: Little.
1944 *U.S. War Aims*. Boston: Little.
1947 *The Cold War: A Study in U.S. Foreign Policy*. New York: Harper. → First appeared as a series of articles in the *New York Herald Tribune*.
1955 *Essays in the Public Philosophy*. Boston: Little.
1959 *The Communist World and Ours*. Boston: Little.
1962 Conservative, Liberal, Progressive. *New Republic* 146:10–11.

SUPPLEMENTARY BIBLIOGRAPHY

CHILDS, MARQUIS; and RESTON, JAMES (editors) 1959 *Walter Lippmann and His Times*. New York: Harcourt.
CROLY, HERBERT D. (1909) 1965 *The Promise of American Life*. Edited by Arthur M. Schlesinger, Jr. Cambridge, Mass.: Belknap Press.
EULAU, HEINZ 1951 Mover and Shaker: Walter Lippmann as a Young Man. *Antioch Review* 11:291–312.
EULAU, HEINZ 1952 Man Against Himself: Walter Lippmann's Years of Doubt. *American Quarterly* 4:291–304.
EULAU, HEINZ 1954 Wilsonian Idealist: Walter Lippmann Goes to War. *Antioch Review* 14:87–108.
EULAU, HEINZ 1956 From *Public Opinion* to *Public Philosophy*: Walter Lippmann's Classic Reexamined. *American Journal of Economics and Sociology* 15: 439–451.
WALLAS, GRAHAM (1908) 1962 *Human Nature in Politics*. 4th ed. Gloucester, Mass.: Smith.
WEINGAST, DAVID E. 1949 *Walter Lippmann: A Study in Personal Journalism*. New Brunswick, N.J.: Rutgers Univ. Press.
WEYL, WALTER E. (1912) 1920 *The New Democracy*. Rev. ed. New York: Macmillan. → A paperback edition was published in 1964 by Harper.

LIQUIDITY PREFERENCE

"Liquidity preference" is a term that was coined by John Maynard Keynes in *The General Theory of Employment, Interest and Money* to denote the functional relation between the quantity of money demanded and the variables determining it (1936, p. 166). He also used this term, or such variants of it as "liquidity preference function" and "liquidity function," to denote more narrowly the relation between the quantity of money demanded and the rate of interest (see, for example, p. 168). Since the *General Theory* the term "liquidity preference" has come to be used to refer to the hypothesis or theory that the aggregate quantity of money demanded by the economy will, *ceteris paribus*, tend to be smaller the higher the rate of interest.

Keynes's analysis of the systematic and intimate relation between the demand for money and interest rates and its implications is generally acknowledged to be one of his major contributions to economics. It is one of the two main pillars on which the edifice of the *General Theory* rests, the other being the hypothesis that in a contemporary monetary economy, money prices and especially money wages tend to be rigid in the downward direction (see "Liquidity preference, monetary theory and monetary management," below).

The demand for money

Pre-Keynesian theories. Information about the history of theories of the demand for money may be found elsewhere [*see especially* MONEY, *articles on* QUANTITY THEORY *and* VELOCITY OF CIRCULATION; *see also* Marget 1938 *and* Patinkin 1956, pp. 373–472]. It will suffice to recall here that although monetary theorists had long recognized that money is a "store of value" as well as a "medium of exchange," prevailing theories of the demand for money before the *General Theory* tended to stress the role of money as a medium of exchange and the "transaction demand." The two major, broadly accepted formulations before the *General Theory* were that of Irving Fisher and that of the Cambridge school. Fisher (1911) started from the now well-known identity called Fisher's equation of exchange: $MV \equiv PT$, where M is the quantity of money in circulation, T is the volume of transactions, P is the price level, and V is the "transaction velocity of circulation." This equation is also frequently restated as $MV_y \equiv PX \equiv Y$, where X is "real income," Y is money income, and V_y is the "income velocity of circulation." From these identities Fisher derived his theory by hypothesizing (1) that at a given point of time V can be taken as constant (or at least as largely independent of M) and (2) that V tends to change, at best, very slowly over time, being largely determined by institutional and technological factors with a high degree of inertia. The major factors of this kind include the frequency of receipts and disbursements (intimately related in turn to the so-called income period, which is the length of the interval between the dates at which various types of income, such as wages, salaries, and dividends, are typically paid), the degree of synchronization of receipts and expenditures, prevailing financial arrangements, the rapidity of transportation, and so on. [*See* MONEY, *article on* VELOCITY OF CIRCULATION.]

By contrast, the so-called Cambridge school tried to put the explanation of the demand for money into the more familiar format of value theory, i.e., in terms of a demand-for-money equation, $M^d = kY$, an exogenously given supply of money, M, and a clearing-of-market equation, $M^d = M$, implying $M = kY$ (see, e.g., Pigou 1917; Marshall 1923). By comparing this equation with Fisher's equation above, one can readily see that $k = 1/V_y$, i.e., that k is the reciprocal of the velocity of circulation. Indeed, in analyzing the determinants of k and the reasons for its hypothesized stability, the Cambridge school tended to stress largely the same forces on which Fisher's theory rests.

The Fisher and Cambridge models are generally regarded as providing the definitive basis for the so-called "quantity theory of money," a view of very old standing according to which the price level, P, tends to be directly proportional to M. In order for this relationship to follow logically from these models, not only must M not affect V (or k), as those models imply, but also one must suppose that money is "neutral" in the wider sense that it does not affect any of the "real" variables of the system—inputs, outputs, and relative prices, including interest rates. Under this assumption, which, as shown below (see "The significance of liquidity theory under wage flexibility"), might provide a reasonable approximation under conditions of perfect wage and price flexibility, real income, X, may be taken as fixed at the "full employment" level, say $\bar{X}$. From either the Fisher or the Cambridge equation it then follows that

$$P = \left(\frac{V_y}{\bar{X}}\right) M = \left(\frac{1}{k\bar{X}}\right) M,$$

that is, the price level is proportional to the quantity of money, M.

It should be acknowledged that some of the writers in the Cambridge tradition did at times suggest that the demand for money might depend on wealth and that they did make some occasional references to the possible influence of interest rates (see, for example, Pigou [1917] 1951, p. 166; Lavington 1921, p. 30; Marshall 1923, chapter 4; for still earlier references, see Eshag 1963, pp. 13–14). But they failed to explore systematically the effect of interest rates on the demand for money and the implications of this effect. This failure is even more conspicuous in Fisher. He makes no mention of interest rates in his list of factors affecting velocity, and although he makes fleeting mention of the "waste of interest" involved in holding money (1911, p. 152), one finds no reference to this passage in the index under the rubric "interest rates."

Two authors who anticipated Keynes in giving adequate recognition to the role of interest rates are Walras, in 1899, and Schlesinger, in 1914 (see Patinkin 1956, notes C and D), but their contributions were largely overlooked at the time. The most significant pre-Keynesian analysis of liquidity preference is generally acknowledged to be that of Hicks (1935), which, however, preceded the *General Theory* by but one year and was partly inspired by Keynes's earlier work, *A Treatise on Money*, published in 1930. This contribution to monetary theory, which in some respects has turned out to be even more influential for further developments than that of Keynes, will be touched upon below.

Keynes's theory. In chapters 13 and 15 of the *General Theory*, Keynes distinguished three "motives" for holding money. The first, the "transaction motive"—sometimes broken down into an income motive and a business motive—corresponds quite closely to the motives stressed by Fisher and the Cambridge school. Like his predecessors, Keynes did not regard transaction balances as being significantly affected by interest rates. The second motive is the "precautionary motive." Under this heading Keynes included balances not earmarked for some definite expenditure in the near future but held instead to "provide for contingencies requiring sudden expenditure and for unforeseen opportunities of advantageous purchases" (1936, p. 196). But why should these balances be kept in the form of idle cash instead of being invested in some kind of readily marketable securities, to be converted into cash if and when the contingency arises? The reason is that the market value of a debt instrument (or "bond"), if it is liquidated before its maturity, is uncertain, even if there is absolutely no risk of default. It depends on the market rate of interest prevailing at the future time of liquidation for loans having a duration equal to the remaining life of the bond: the higher this rate, the lower the market value. This uncertainty about the realization value of a bond would not by itself make bonds inferior to cash as a store of ready purchasing power if the sum of the uncertain liquidation value and the cash interest earned could be counted on to exceed the amount initially invested. However, there can be no such assurance, since between the times of purchase and liquidation interest rates could rise sufficiently to produce a capital loss in excess of the interest earned. Keynes suggested in particular that the likelihood of a net loss would be larger the smaller the yield of the bond originally acquired. This is because the smaller the yield, the smaller the rise in the rate of interest (in absolute as well as in percentage terms) that will produce a capital loss sufficient to wipe out the accrued interest earned. Furthermore, Keynes suggested that if the current rate is low by historical standards, it will usually be regarded as more likely to rise than to fall. He concluded that the lower the current rate, r, the stronger the incentive to hold precautionary reserves in the form of cash instead of securities. Therefore the (real) demand to hold money for precautionary reasons will tend to be inversely related to r. At the same time, somewhat surprisingly, Keynes did not appear to regard precautionary balances as very sensitive to r. Accordingly, much of the time he lumped together the demand for transaction and for precautionary reasons and regarded the sum, which he labeled M_1, as primarily controlled by—or a function of—current income. Thus, in his notation $M_1 = L_1(Y)$, where the function L_1 denotes the demand for money resulting from the transaction and precautionary motives.

The third and remaining source of demand for money is the speculative motive, a rather complex mechanism that Keynes had partly anticipated in *A Treatise on Money* (1930). In essence, speculative balances are balances held in cash rather than invested in (long-term) bonds, not just because of the risk that interest rates might rise but rather because of a definite expectation that the price of long-term bonds is likely to fall, and at a rate that more than offsets the interest earned by holding them. A person entertaining such an expectation would prefer to hold cash yielding nothing rather than invest it in what he regards as overpriced long-term bonds that would yield him a negative return. Since the price of long-term bonds varies inversely with long-term interest rates, we may equally well characterize speculative balances as those held by persons who regard the current long-term rate as untenably low and about to rise sufficiently rapidly.

The real significance of the speculative motive is that it may significantly impair, or even thwart altogether, efforts of the central bank to reduce long-term interest rates to the extent necessary to maintain investment at the level consistent with full utilization of resources (see "Liquidity preference, monetary theory, and monetary management," below). Normally, the central bank can expect to enforce lower long-term interest rates, or higher prices of long-term bonds, by buying such bonds with newly created money. Suppose, however, that a large portion of the market holds definite views about the minimum maintainable level of the long-term rate and hence the maximum maintainable level of bond prices. If, then, the bank attempts to bid up the price of bonds to that maximum or beyond, it will find the public prepared to dump a large portion of its long-term bond holding. The bank will therefore have very little success in lowering the long-term rate, even though it is prepared to acquire a large volume of bonds and to expand the money supply correspondingly. What happens in this situation is that the increase in the money supply is absorbed, not by an increased transaction demand, but by an offsetting increase in the speculative demand, with a resulting fall in the velocity of circulation. In other words, the expansion in M, instead of achieving the desired expansion in income, Y, that would occur if V_y, the velocity of circulation, remained constant, tends to generate an offsetting change in V_y, with little effect on Y. A situation of this type has come to be known in the Keynesian literature as a "liquidity trap."

Keynes denoted speculative balances by M_2 and wrote the demand function for such balances as $M_2 = L_2(r)$, where L_2 is a decreasing function of r (1936, p. 199). This formulation—that M_2 increases as r falls—is somewhat misleading, since presumably M_2 should depend not on r as such but only on r in relation to the prevailing market expectations about the maintainable rate, say r^e. Nor can r^e be supposed to stay constant through time or to be uniquely related to r itself. Keynes's formulation might be defended as a useful "short run" approximation: at a given point in time, r^e can be taken as a constant or, at least, as changing more slowly than r. Hence, a fall in r would necessarily imply a fall *relative* to r^e and thus a rise in M_2 (*ibid.*, pp. 201–202). Under this interpretation, however, one should be aware that L_2 may be subject to significant shifts through time as a result of shifts in market expectations.

The sum of the transaction and precautionary demand, M_1, and the speculative demand, M_2, is the total demand for money proposed by Keynes: $M = M_1 + M_2 = L_1(Y) + L_2(r)$ (*ibid.*, p. 199). The Keynesian literature has tended to de-emphasize the sharp distinction between the three motives for holding money and to write the demand for money in the more general form $M = L(r, Y)$. There has also been a tendency to minimize the role of interest expectations, r^e, and to associate the liquidity trap with a low *absolute* level of the interest rate.

The implied relation between M and r for a

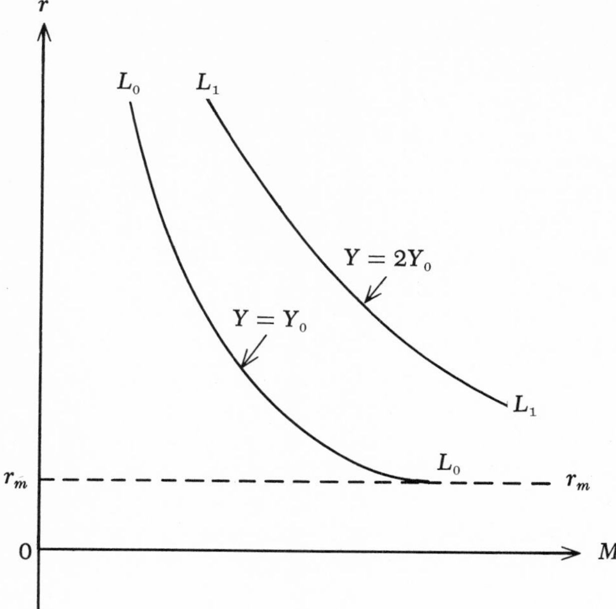

Figure 1 — Relation between the demand for money and the interest rate

given value of Y, say Y_0, is shown in Figure 1 by the curve labeled L_0L_0. (The choice of coordinates is dictated by the economists' peculiar convention, popularized by Marshall, of representing demand curves with the quantity demanded measured on the abscissa and the price on the ordinate.) The quantity of money demanded increases continuously as r falls, until, for some sufficiently low value, r_m, the liquidity trap is reached and the curve becomes horizontal (the demand becomes infinitely elastic). Alternatively, the demand curve might be drawn to approach the level r_m asymptotically. Just how low r_m may be depends somewhat on "institutional" factors and on whether r is understood to be the long-term or the short-term rate. But we can, with complete generality, place a lower bound on r_m: in a monetary economy, r_m can never be more negative than the (marginal) cost of storing money. In particular, when money is an intangible, the cost of storing it (at least in the form of bank deposits) is essentially zero, and therefore r_m cannot be (significantly) negative. Indeed, a negative r can be regarded as a premium paid by the lender to the borrower for carrying money over; for example, a short-term rate of -2 per cent per period means that the lender is willing to pay \$100 to receive only \$98 at the end of the period. If the cost of storing is less than 2 per cent, everybody would wish to borrow indefinitely large amounts, since by merely holding the money one would earn the excess of 2 per cent over storage costs. This implies in particular that with a zero (marginal) storage cost, at a negative rate of interest the demand for money must become indefinitely large—or, equivalently, that no matter how large the quantity of money, r can never be negative. Hence, the demand curve must tend to approach a horizontal asymptote, $r = r_m$ (or possibly reach it from above for some finite M and become discontinuous). Furthermore, r_m cannot be lower than zero (quite generally, it cannot be more negative than the marginal cost of storing money), although it may well be higher, as in Figure 1.

The curve labeled L_1L_1 illustrates the effect on the demand for money of increasing Y, say from Y_0 to $2Y_0$ in Figure 1. Clearly, the demand for money must then be greater at any given rate r; that is, LL must shift to the right. The relation between L_0L_0 and L_1L_1 becomes especially simple if the demand function $L(r, Y)$ takes a more specialized form, which was suggested, for example, by Pigou (1917) and tested by Latané (1954; 1960) and which has been gaining favor in recent writings—namely, $M = k(r)Y = Y/V(r)$. This formulation provides an obvious bridge between Keynes's original formulation and the received Fisher and Cambridge models. It implies that for a given r the fraction k (or the velocity of circulation, V) will be constant but that k will tend to fall (or V to rise) as the rate of interest rises. In terms of Figure 1, it implies that L_1L_1 is obtainable from L_0L_0 by multiplying by 2 the abscissa value of L_0L_0 corresponding to any given r. More generally, it implies that the LL curve corresponding to any given Y is simply the graph of $k(r)$, up to a proportionality factor, Y. Similarly, the graph of $V(r)$,

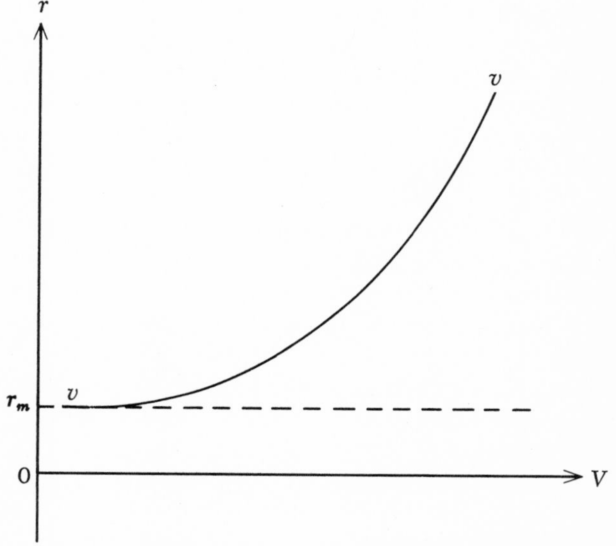

Figure 2 — Velocity of circulation and the interest rate

the velocity of circulation as a function of the interest rate, is the graph of the reciprocal of $L_0 L_0$ up to a proportionality factor, $1/Y_0$. The general shape of the graph of $V(r)$ is shown by the *vv* curve of Figure 2.

Post-Keynesian developments. As indicated earlier, post-Keynesian developments of liquidity theory were inspired not only by Keynes's *General Theory* but at least as much by two germinal ideas advanced by Hicks (1935). Hicks's first suggestion was that the major reason why transactors hold money balances having little or no yield when they could invest them in a large number of income-yielding assets, some at least not significantly less safe than money, is to be found in the costs and the "bother" of the transactions necessary to move from money into earning assets and back to money (p. 19).

The portfolio approach. Hicks's second suggestion was that the theory of the demand for money must be developed out of a more general theory of the allocation of wealth among various assets. This theory, Hicks suggested, should be analogous to the standard theory of consumers' choice, except that the object of choice, instead of being consumption flows, would be the various stocks appearing on the asset and liability side of the balance sheet, and prices would be replaced by expected yields. He saw this substitution as presenting a real challenge, since yields in contrast to prices would have to be recognized as uncertain, and this uncertainty in turn would have important implications for the nature of choices.

Both ideas have been extensively pursued with the help of the emergence of the theory of choice under uncertainty [*see* DECISION MAKING, *article on* ECONOMIC ASPECTS]. At present the major differences of view between monetary theorists (and they are not very major) seem related to the relative importance assigned to each of Hicks's two ideas.

Among those who have pursued the portfolio, or wealth, approach, the formulation of Friedman (1956), developed in numerous writings, has been particularly influential [*see* MONEY, *article on* QUANTITY THEORY]. Friedman views the demand for money as being determined by wealth (broadly understood as the present value of expected net future receipts from all sources), by the distribution of wealth between human and nonhuman (i.e., marketable) wealth, by the expected yield of all major types of assets that are alternatives to money as ways of holding wealth, and by the "utility attached to the services rendered by money" relative to other assets—namely, bonds, equities, and physical commodities. By combining this theory with his suggestion (1957) for ways of approximating wealth (or, more precisely, "permanent income," which is, however, essentially proportional to wealth as defined above) Friedman has endeavored to cast his theory in testable form and actually to test it (1959). He has concluded that his model fits the facts well, in that the demand for money increases with wealth and more than in proportion, although he can find little evidence that interest rates in fact play a significant role.

Other authors have been more concerned with developing and refining theoretical aspects of the Keynes–Hicks approach (see the very useful survey provided by Johnson 1962). Among their attempts, especially worth noting are the recent contribution of Turvey (1960) and the elegant formulation of the theory of choice between money and bonds of various maturities developed by Tobin (1958) along the lines of the modern theory of portfolio selection.

Transaction costs and the Neo-Fisherian approach. The portfolio approach suffers from one major inadequacy. As long as there exist any interest-bearing obligations that are issued by creditworthy borrowers and are of sufficiently short maturity—for example, redeemable on demand or on very short notice—it is impossible to explain why any portion of the portfolio should be held in the form of money, yielding less or nothing at all—except by explicit analysis of the role of transaction costs.

Even Keynes's stricture that, for sufficiently low interest rates, money may dominate bonds because of the uncertainty of the realization value cannot apply to short maturities or demand loans. These instruments dominate money in every possible dimension: they are equally safe, they yield an income, and they can be converted into the medium of exchange, if and when it is needed, at face value. Why, then, should anyone hold money, except for the very instant he receives a payment or is about to make one? The necessary and sufficient condition, as Hicks rightly pointed out, is that out-of-pocket costs and the effort required in moving from cash to bonds and back to cash exceed the yield. At first sight these transaction costs may appear too trivial to account for any substantial holding of cash, let alone for the observed cash holdings. (Aggregate cash holdings of U.S. consumers at the end of 1963 were estimated to represent slightly less than two months' income.) But this casual impression is misleading. It is well known, for instance, from the theory of optimum inventory holdings that transaction costs do account for a substantial portion of inventories held by business (which in the United States amount to some three months' sales). This parallel between business inventories and cash holdings is not fortuitous, for in many respects the holding of a stock of cash by transactors is closely analogous to the holding of a stock of goods by business. In fact, Allais (1947, chapter 8a) and Baumol (1952) pioneered in showing that the holding of cash balances could be analyzed by a straightforward application of the so-called lot-size formula of inventory theory: in order to avoid incurring too frequently the costs involved in transforming securities into cash, it pays to secure cash in a bulk or "lot" that will take care of expenditure requirements for a certain length of time, even though interest will be forgone on the amount withdrawn. Similarly, if a transactor is receiving money in a more or less continuous trickle, it will pay to accumulate a "lot" before investing it. The size of the lot, and hence the average cash balance held relative to the rate of outpayments (or receipts), which corresponds to the Cambridge k or to the reciprocal of the velocity of circulation, will be positively associated with the size of transaction costs and inversely associated with the rate of interest. Tobin (1956) refined and improved on this analysis, applying it more specifically to the consumer receiving his income in bulk at income-payment dates and spending it gradually over the income period.

Although these contributions are to be regarded as illustrative rather than as aimed at deriving an exact demand equation for money, they do point up one very fundamental principle. The amount that can be earned by investing an amount of cash, m, that will not be needed to meet expenditures for some span of time, t, in a security yielding r per cent per year, is approximately $m(tr - c)$, where c is the brokerage fee, if any, per dollar of investment. The investment will not be worthwhile unless this product exceeds the lump-sum cost of the two-way transaction, including both the out-of-pocket and the bother costs. To illustrate the order of magnitudes involved, suppose that a person earns $12,000 a year, paid monthly; he then receives $1,000 once a month. Suppose he spends these receipts at an even rate. He might then consider keeping half the sum for current expenditure and investing the remaining half, or $500, which he will not need until the first half is exhausted—that is, for half a month. Suppose the yield of a 15-day security, net of commissions, is 3 per cent per year; then all he stands to earn from the transaction is $\$500 \times .03/24$, or a mere 62.5 cents. If the two-way transaction cost and bother exceeds this, he will invest none of the monthly receipts and thus will end up holding, on this account, an average cash balance of $500, or 1/24 of his (annual) income. Note that if he were paid twice as frequently—that is, $500 every two weeks—it would a fortiori not pay him to bother, and he would be holding an average cash balance of $250, or 1/48 of his income.

The conclusion to be drawn from these illustrations can be summarized as follows: In a money-using economy, transactors are paid in money and in turn must pay in money; lack of synchronization between receipts and payments gives rise to pools of money that will not be needed for some length of time. Given the rate of return and the cost and effort of transactions, it will not pay to invest such pools unless the product of their size and the length of the "idle" time exceeds some critical threshold level. Thus, the basic reason for holding idle cash balances is not that they provide a useful service but simply that it does not pay to shed them. Obviously, given the rate of interest, the extent to which it does not pay to shed idle money, and thus the average cash balance held, will depend on such institutional–technological factors as (a) transaction costs—the higher the cost, the smaller the incentive to shed; (b) the size and nature of the transactor's business—large transactors may be confronted with pools so large that it pays to shed them even for very short periods, and they may also have an incentive to set themselves up so as to minimize marginal transaction costs; and (c) the frequency of income payment and settlement dates—the greater the frequency, the smaller the average cash balance. But these are, by and large, precisely the factors emphasized by Fisher in explaining the determinants of the velocity of circulation. The new element is the recognition that given all these factors, the average cash balance demanded will tend to fall with the rate of interest, which provides the incentive to shed.

How does the Keynesian liquidity trap fit into this model? The first point to be noted is that Keynes's theory of the speculative demand suffers from his excessive concentration on long-term bonds as the alternative to cash, to the neglect of short-term instruments. The proposition that people will flee from long-term bonds when the price of those bonds is deemed to be untenably high seems valid enough, but the obvious abode for the funds accruing from moving out of long-term bonds should be short-term ones, not cash.

However, a massive endeavor to move from long-term into short-term instruments will unavoidably depress short-term rates, perhaps to such an extent that for many investors the investment will no longer be worth the effort. Thus, they may eventually end up holding cash, but because of the low level of short-term rates, not directly in response to the low level of long-term rates. In short, the central bank's endeavor to depress long-term rates by buying bonds and increasing the money supply can always be counted on to depress short-term rates. However, it may not be very successful in depressing long-term rates to the desired extent, except insofar as a persistent low level of the short-term rate may eventually persuade the public that the long-term rate is really not unreasonably low. A good example of such a development is provided by the United States in the late 1930s. Because of a sizable monetary expansion after 1932, by 1939–1940 the short-term rate on government bills had been driven down very nearly to zero (below 2/10 of 1 per cent), but the long-term rate on high-grade bonds was still hovering around 3 per cent (down from about 4.7 per cent in 1929). In this sense the Keynesian liquidity trap must still be acknowledged as a possible serious hindrance to the effectiveness of monetary policy. And in any event, the proposition that no market rate—long or short—can ever be negative retains its validity.

The theory that emerges from the preceding discussion emphasizes the flow of transactions (and therefore income rather than wealth) and interest rates, especially the short rate and the rate on savings deposits, as the main arguments of the demand function for money. It further suggests that the parameters of this function are largely determined by the forces emphasized by Fisher and should therefore tend to change at best slowly through time. Because the model represents an obvious blend of the motives emphasized by Fisher and by Keynes and Hicks, we have referred to it as the Neo-Fisherian approach (although this terminology is not in general use).

Although the contrast between the "portfolio" approach and the "transaction" approach has deliberately been emphasized here, it is well to recognize that the difference between these two models is minor—largely a matter of relative emphasis—both in principle and in terms of practical implications. In particular, these models concur in the conclusion that the demand for money should be "homogeneous of first degree in current prices"—that is, that a change in the price level, other things being equal, should give rise to a proportional change in the demand for money while leaving unaffected "real demand" (demand measured in terms of purchasing power over commodities).

Empirical verification. Since the appearance of the *General Theory*, considerable effort has been devoted to assessing empirically the responsiveness of the demand for money to variations in interest rates and more generally to estimating demand functions for money and testing their stability (see, for the United States, Johnson 1962, pp. 354–357).

These investigations have tended to confirm that the demand for money is positively and closely associated with income or wealth or both and that a change in the price level tends to result in a proportional change in demand. They have also overwhelmingly tended to confirm that this demand is significantly responsive to changes in interest rates in the direction hypothesized by Keynes. The only significant exception in this regard is Friedman's results, cited in the section "The portfolio approach," above. His contrary conclusions, however, have been criticized for being very much dependent on the specific definition of money he uses (which includes means of payment and some, but not all, savings deposits), on the specific period chosen for his tests, and on his statistical techniques. They have also been criticized because his model, although it apparently fits the period from the second half of the last century to the late 1940s quite well, is not able to account for the very significant rise in velocity that has occurred since the beginning of the 1950s, concomitantly with the marked rise in interest rates. In particular, Meltzer (1963) and Brunner and Meltzer (1964), who otherwise fully sympathize with Friedman's basic theory, have found marked and significant interest-rate effects, whether one uses as additional variables income, or permanent income, or a measure of nonhuman wealth. The major novelty in their results is the strong showing of the nonhuman wealth variable as compared with current income, although these results contrast with those reported by other investigators using a different measure of wealth (e.g., Bronfenbrenner & Mayer 1960). On the whole, it seems fair to say that at the moment the evidence is not adequate for the fine discrimination between the wealth and the neo-Fisherian formulations of the demand for money.

Liquidity preference, monetary theory, and monetary management

The Keynesian revolution. As suggested earlier, the two major analytical contributions of the *Gen-*

eral Theory are the hypotheses of liquidity preference and of wage rigidity. The systematic analysis of the implications of these two highly fruitful hypotheses and their interaction was made more powerful and incisive by a third novelty, which is primarily methodological. This is the development of "aggregative analysis," or what has since come to be known as macroeconomic analysis. Economists had long before been used to analyzing economic variables as reflecting the interaction of simultaneous relations, and the notion of equilibrium was used precisely to denote the value of the variables simultaneously satisfying all the relevant relations. However, before the *General Theory* this method of analysis was generally applied in so-called "partial equilibrium analysis," that is, the study of some portion of the economy—say, the market for a particular commodity or a group of interrelated commodities. The method had also been applied with some success, largely by Walras, to the economy as a whole in "general equilibrium analysis," which formally recognizes the interactions of all possible markets, treating the economy as a very large scale closed system of simultaneous equations. The novelty of aggregative analysis consists in lumping together a large number of commodities having common characteristics for the problem at hand and treating the aggregate as a single commodity. This approach makes possible the approximation of the whole economy with a small system of simultaneous relations, and, by permitting closer scrutiny and understanding of the interactions, it has proved to be highly fruitful.

Analysts of Keynes's work have correctly pointed out that none of these basic ingredients of the *General Theory*—liquidity preference, wage rigidity, or the aggregative approach—was entirely new. We have documented this point above with respect to liquidity preference. The novelty consisted in the masterly way in which the ingredients were blended, which enabled Keynes to provide an analytical explanation of the phenomenon of unemployment and its possible persistence in an advanced capitalistic economy and to shed new light on the role and limitations of monetary and fiscal policy in controlling the level of employment and prices. It is this achievement, and its enormous impact on economics, that has since come to be known as the Keynesian revolution.

The rest of this section, relying largely on aggregative analysis, endeavors to sketch out the role of liquidity preference, first under the classical assumptions of perfect wage and price flexibility and then in combination with the empirically far more relevant hypothesis of downward wage rigidity. Our focus is primarily on the significance of liquidity preference as seen *today*, some thirty years after the appearance of the *General Theory*, rather than on summarizing or criticizing Keynes's original formulation. Accordingly, in what follows, the post-Keynesian elaborations are freely drawn upon.

The basic model. In Keynes's *General Theory* and, more particularly, in later endeavors by other authors to formalize its message (e.g., Hicks 1937; Lange 1938; Modigliani 1944; 1963; Patinkin 1956), the whole economy is reduced (explicitly or implicitly) to four aggregates: aggregate output, X; labor, N; money, M; and bonds, B. For each of these aggregate commodities there is a "market" characterized by supply conditions, demand conditions, and the "clearing-of-market" or equilibrium requirement that demand must equal supply. Demand and supply, in turn, are controlled by three prices or terms of trade between each commodity and money: P, the price of output (the "price level"); W, the price of labor (the "wage rate"); and $1 + r$, the number of dollars obtainable next period by lending a dollar today, where r is the rate of interest. To understand the mechanism determining the level of economic activity in a given short interval and the role of liquidity preference, we must examine the structure of the four markets and their interaction.

The demand for output in the commodity market, usually referred to in the literature as "aggregate demand" and denoted here by X^d, is a central construct of Keynesian analysis. It has given rise to a voluminous literature, both theoretical and empirical, which can be summarized here very briefly, since it is covered in other articles [*see in particular* INCOME AND EMPLOYMENT THEORY; CONSUMPTION FUNCTION; INVESTMENT, *article on* THE AGGREGATE INVESTMENT FUNCTION]. Two sources of demand are distinguished: current consumption, C, and investment demand, I—i.e., demand for current output destined to increase the stock of productive capital. Thus, $X^d = C + I$. Theoretical considerations, and the empirical evidence, suggest that consumption in turn is primarily controlled by (a) the level of real income that, disregarding for the moment the fiscal activity of the government sector, can be equated with aggregate output, X; (b) net real private wealth, A; and possibly (c) the rate of interest, r. This can be formalized by means of the "consumption function," $C = \mathcal{C}(X, A, r)$. Investment demand can be taken to be positively associated with aggregate output and negatively associated with the rate of interest and the pre-existing stock of capital, K_0; thus,

$I = \mathcal{I}(r_0, X, K_0)$. Finally, net private real wealth, A, the sum of all privately held assets minus private debt, can be expressed as $A = K_0 + G/P$; that is, it consists of the stock of capital plus the money value of the outstanding government debt, G, deflated by the price level, P, to express it in terms of purchasing power over output.

The four equations given above can be conveniently reduced to a single one by first substituting for A in the consumption function and then substituting this function and the investment function into the definition of aggregate demand:

$$(1) \qquad X^d = \mathcal{C}(X, K_0 + \frac{G}{P}, r) + \mathcal{I}(r_0, X, K_0).$$

Next, we observe that in equilibrium, aggregate demand X^d must equal aggregate supply, or

$$(2) \qquad X = X^d.$$

We use this property to replace X with X^d in the right hand side of (1). The resulting equation contains X^d on both sides of the equality. We can, however, "solve" the equation explicitly for X^d, obtaining finally an expression of the form

$$(1') \qquad X^d = D\left(r, K_0, \frac{G}{P}\right),$$

which will be referred to hereafter as the aggregate demand relation. Note that aggregate demand, X^d, may be expected to be negatively associated with r. This is because an increase in r will reduce investment demand directly, and this reduction, in turn, will reduce aggregate demand even further by means of its depressing effect on consumption demand, which depends on total output—this is the so-called multiplier effect [*see* CONSUMPTION FUNCTION]. Insofar as investment demand itself depends on output, X^d may in fact not decrease continuously as r rises, but this complication will be ignored here.

To complete the description of the output market, we also need an "aggregate supply function." Aggregate supply, X, may be expected to be positively associated with (a) the price, P, at which firms can sell their output relative to the wage rate, W, they must pay, or P/W, and (b) with the preexisting capital stock, K_0 (on the convenient approximation that the increment in the stock of capital resulting from current investment will not become productive until the next period); thus,

$$(3) \qquad X = S\left(\frac{P}{W}, K_0\right).$$

In the labor market, the aggregate demand for labor, N, can be inferred from the so-called aggregate production function, relating output, X, to the input of labor and the stock of capital, K_0. This function implies that N can be expressed in terms of X and K_0, say, $N = F(X, K_0)$. It is, however, more convenient to replace X in this equation with the right-hand side of (3), thus obtaining the "labor demand" equation

$$(4) \qquad N = \mathcal{N}\left(\frac{P}{W}, K_0\right).$$

The description of the supply side of the labor market is a somewhat more complex task, for it is here that we must formalize the Keynesian notion of "downward wage rigidity." In its broadest sense, this term connotes the absence of "wage flexibility," of a state of affairs in which money wages fall promptly whenever the supply of labor exceeds the demand for it and keep falling as long as the excess supply persists. In a narrower definition, it means that the current money wage will not be bid below some floor level, W_0 (reflecting the past history of the system), no matter how large the excess supply of labor—though it can be freely bid up in response to excess demand for labor. For present purposes, we shall rely on this narrower version, which we label "absolute" rigidity, because it is more readily formalized. However, the conclusion of the analysis below would not change qualitatively if the wage rate had some tendency to fall for sufficiently large unemployment and falling prices, as long as the reaction was sluggish and unsystematic. There can be little doubt that wage rigidity in this sense is, and has been for some time, a feature of free market economies.

To formalize the hypothesis of absolute wage rigidity we need to introduce the notion of a "potential supply of labor function," say, $\mathcal{E}(W/P)$, which gives the level of employment "desired," or labor force available, at any given real wage, W/P. Now, let E denote the actual level of employment. Then absolute wage rigidity can be expressed as follows:

$$(5) \qquad \begin{aligned} &(a)\ W = W_0, && \text{if } \mathcal{N}\left(\frac{P}{W_0}, K_0\right) < \mathcal{E}\left(\frac{W_0}{P}\right), \\ &(b)\ E = \mathcal{E}\left(\frac{W}{P}\right), && \text{if } \mathcal{N}\left(\frac{P}{W_0}, K_0\right) \geqslant \mathcal{E}\left(\frac{W_0}{P}\right), \end{aligned}$$

$$(6) \qquad E = N.$$

Line (a) of (5) states in essence that if at the rigid wage W_0 the demand for labor falls short of the potential supply, then the actual wage rate will coincide with W_0. Employment, being equal to the *demand* for labor as stated by (6), will then fall short of the potential supply, and the difference will represent the so-called involuntary unemployment. If, however, at W_0 the demand exceeds the potential supply, then line (b) of (5) becomes applicable: the floor level loses its relevance, and the actual wage will have to rise enough to equate the demand with the potential supply. This formulation of wage rigidity has the advantage that it can encompass wage flexibility as a limiting case, in which we assign to W_0 a value so small that the relevant portion of (5) will necessarily be line (b).

In the money market, the demand, M^d, can be expressed as $M^d = L(PX, PA, r)$, where L is, of course, the liquidity preference function that (in recognition of the two major points of view summarized in the section "Post-Keynesian developments" of liquidity preference) is written as a function of both money income (PX) and wealth (PA). By expressing A in terms of its components, K_0 and G, and using the property that a change in the price level should tend to give rise to a proportional change in the demand for money, the preceding equation can be rewritten as

$$M^d = PL(X, K_0 + G/P, r).$$

However, for the purpose of the graphical analysis that is developed below, we shall frequently find it convenient to rely on the specialized version $M^d = PX/V(r)$, where $V(r)$, it will be recalled, denotes the velocity of circulation as a function of the rate of interest. As to the supply side, unless otherwise specified, it will be assumed that money is created by the banking system in the process of purchasing debt instruments (bonds) issued either by the private sector or by the government, and that the total supply of money, M, is exogenously determined through central bank policy. Since in equilibrium we must have $M^d = M$, the description of the money market can be reduced to a single equation obtained by replacing M^d with M in the above equations:

(7) $$M = PL(X, K_0 + \frac{G}{P}, r),$$

or

(7′) $$M = \frac{PX}{V(r)}.$$

Equations (1) to (7) involve seven endogenous variables: X^d, X, N, E, P, W, r. They therefore form a closed system whose solution describes the short-run equilibrium of the economy. This solution also depends, of course, on the parameters of the various equations, on initial conditions, such as K_0 and G, and on policy variables, of which in the present case there is but one, the money supply, M. The demand and supply for the remaining commodity, namely, bonds, B, are not explicitly displayed in the system because, by a well-known principle called Walras's law, it can shown that the demand and supply for one commodity out of the set of all commodities are necessarily equal when all other markets are "cleared" (that is, when demand equals supply); we choose the bond market as the redundant one (Modigliani 1963).

With the help of this system we can now focus on the role of monetary forces, in particular that of liquidity preference, in the determination of equilibrium, beginning with the classical assumption of wage flexibility.

Wage flexibility. As already noted, under the assumption of wage flexibility the labor supply conditions are fully described by line (b) of equation (5). But this equation, together with that for labor demand, equation (4), and the equilibrium condition (6), turns out to involve only three variables: N, E, and P/W (or its reciprocal, the real wage). They therefore form a closed subsystem which can be solved independently of the rest. This solution yields the equilibrium real wage, $\widehat{W/P}$ (where "ˆ" denotes an equilibrium value), and employment, $\hat{N}$ (which is also "full employment" since it coincides with the labor supply). From (3) we can then infer the equilibrium or full-employment level of output, $\hat{X}$.

At this point it becomes useful to distinguish two possible cases, the one in which there is no national debt and the one in which there is.

No national debt. Referring back to the aggregate demand relation (1′), we observe that if G is zero, then the third argument of the aggregate demand function is necessarily zero, no matter what value P may take: in other words, *aggregate demand does not depend on the price level.* (This important implication, it should be noted, depends critically on the approximation implicit in the formulation of the consumption function, that aggregate consumption, C, depends only on *aggregate* net wealth, not on its distribution between households. Changes in the price level will of course affect the demand of individual consumers by causing redistributions of wealth between creditors and debtors, but our aggregative assumption implies that such redistributions will affect only the distribution of consumption between households, without affecting the total.) Since K_0 is a given initial condition, it can be seen that the right-hand side of (1′) contains only one variable, r. It follows that from (1′) we can infer the equilibrium value of r, $\hat{r}$, which makes the aggregate demand, X^d, equal to the aggregate supply, $\hat{X}$. Next, substituting $\hat{r}$ and $\hat{X}$ into the money-market equation

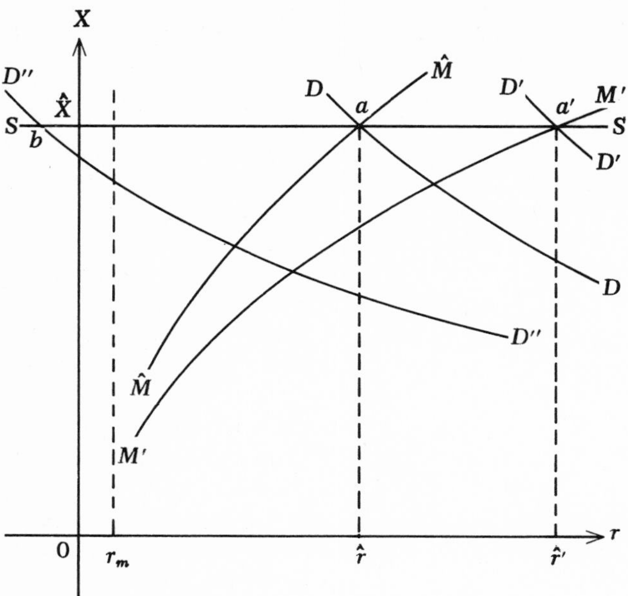

Figure 3 — Equilibrium under wage flexibility

(7), we can determine the price level $\hat{P}$ that equates the demand for money with the given supply (provided such a value of P exists; see below). Finally, from $\hat{P}$ and the equilibrium real wage, $\widehat{W/P}$, we can infer the equilibrium money wage, $\hat{W}$.

The nature of the solution can be clarified by means of Figure 3, in which X is measured on the ordinate and r on the abscissa. The horizontal line labeled SS, cutting the ordinate at $\hat{X}$, represents the aggregate supply consistent with full employment —that is, with the clearing of the labor market. It is a horizontal line because, as should be apparent from the derivation above, the value of $\hat{X}$ does not explicitly depend on r. The curve labeled DD is the graph of the aggregate demand relation (1′), which is shown falling from left to right for the reasons stated earlier. Equilibrium in the commodity (and labor) market is thus represented by the point of intersection of the demand and supply curves, namely, point a, with coordinates $(\hat{X},\hat{r})$.

There remains to be shown the role of money and the money market in the determination of equilibrium. For this we refer back to equation (7′) and note that for a given value of M/P this equation expresses a relation between the two variables X and r. It is therefore amenable to graphical representation in our figure. Indeed, the shape of this graph can be readily inferred by solving (7′) for X to obtain $X = V(r)(M/P)$. Given M/P, the graph of this equation is simply that of $V(r)$, already shown in Figure 2, except for a proportionality factor and for the fact that the axes are interchanged, r now being measured on the abscissa instead of the ordinate. The result is a curve such as $M'M'$, which represents the locus of (7′) for an arbitrarily chosen value of the "real" money supply, $(M/P)'$. It rises from left to right because, as r increases and transactors are induced to economize on their cash holdings, the velocity of circulation increases, and thus a given "real" money supply is capable of financing a larger and larger volume of transactions, X.

It should be readily apparent that the curve corresponding to some other value of M/P, say, a value m times larger, can be obtained from the $M'M'$ curve by multiplying by the factor m the ordinate of the $M'M'$ curve corresponding to any given value of r. It follows that provided $\hat{r}$ (the abscissa of point a) is to the right of r_m there will be some unique value of M/P, say, $\widehat{M/P}$, such that the corresponding MM curve will go through the point of intersection, a, of the other two curves. This unique curve is represented by $\hat{M}\hat{M}$ in the figure. Thus, with a real money supply $\widehat{M/P}$, the money market as well as the commodity and labor markets will all be simultaneously cleared with the output $\hat{X}$ and the rate of interest $\hat{r}$. But this in turn means that, given the actual money supply M, the price level must tend to the equilibrium level $\hat{P}$, such that $M/\hat{P} = (\widehat{M/P})$, or $\hat{P} = M/(\widehat{M/P})$. Similarly, $\hat{W} = \hat{P}(\widehat{W/P})$, where $(\widehat{W/P})$ is the full-employment equilibrium real wage. A higher value of W and P would make the money supply inadequate to transact the full-employment income, unless the rate of interest were higher than $\hat{r}$. But a higher r would reduce the aggregate demand below the full-employment supply. This in turn would cause unemployment which, with flexible wages, would lead to a fall of W and hence of P to the equilibrium levels $\hat{W}$ and $\hat{P}$; the converse would be true for values of P and W below the equilibrium levels.

There are three main implications of this analysis to which attention must be called:

(*a*) Provided $\hat{r} > r_m$, the only economic effect of M is to determine the price level $\hat{P}$; furthermore, it is apparent from the derivation of the last paragraph that $\hat{P}$ is proportional to M, so that, in this sense, the quantity theory of money holds.

(*b*) The equilibrium value of P corresponding to a given M depends, not only on full-employment output $\hat{X}$, which controls the position of SS, and on slowly changing institutional factors determining the shape of $V(r)$, but also on r. As can be seen from Figure 3, the larger $\hat{r}$ is, the smaller will be the equilibrium real money supply. But $\hat{r}$, for a given $\hat{X}$, is in turn associated with the position of the aggregate demand relation, *DD*. A rise in the aggregate demand relation—reflecting an increase in consumption or investment demand or both at each level of income and of the interest rate—will result in an upward shift of the *DD* curve, and this in turn will move to the right the point of intersection, *a*, of aggregate demand and supply, increasing its *r* coordinate. Such a shift is illustrated by the curve *D′D′* intersecting *SS* at *a′*. If in the face of such a shift the central bank does not force an appropriate contraction in *M*, excess demand will arise in the commodity and labor markets that will force wages and prices up. This will reduce the real money supply, lowering the *MM* curve, until a value of *P* is reached such that *MM* coincides with *M′M′*. If the price rise is to be avoided, the central bank must enforce an appropriate reduction in *M* (in the same proportion in which prices would rise otherwise). We deduce that once liquidity preference is recognized, if the monetary authority is concerned with maintaining the stability of the price level over time—as it must be if a monetary economy is to work smoothly—it must actively manage the money supply, enforcing a (relatively) larger money supply, and a smaller value of *r*, when demand tends to be slack and a relatively smaller supply, and higher *r*, when demand tends to be more active.

(*c*) Suppose, however, that in some period demand is slack and the *DD* curve is so depressed that it intersects *SS* at a value of *r* smaller than r_m, as illustrated by *D″D″* intersecting *SS* at *b* in Figure 3. It is then apparent that there can be no possible value of M/P such that the corresponding *MM* curve will go through *b*, since regardless of the value of M/P, every *MM* curve must lie entirely to the right of r_m. In this situation, sometimes referred to as "the Keynesian case" or "the special Keynesian case," the economic system will not have any equilibrium solution (a set of prices and interest rates that can simultaneously equate all demands and supplies). If prices and wages are flexible, they will both tend to fall indefinitely under the pressure of excess supplies. But this fall, which under normal conditions would re-establish equilibrium by shifting *MM* up, can now never prove sufficient. By the same token, monetary policy also breaks down: there is no feasible expansion of the money supply sufficient to eliminate the excess supply of goods and labor.

Thus, from liquidity preference Keynes was able to derive the important and novel result that under certain conditions an economy using a token money may simply break down, having no maintainable position of equilibrium (except through government fiscal policy or wage rigidity, which will be discussed below).

Positive national debt. The government debt, *G*, may consist of interest-bearing instruments (government bonds) or government fiat money or both, circulating along with or instead of the money created by the banking system. In any case, if *G* is positive, it is apparent from equation (1′) that aggregate demand depends not only on *r* but also on *P*. In terms of Figure 3, equation (1′) must now be represented by a *family* of curves, one for each value of *P*. For the sake of illustration, suppose that the curve *DD* in the figure corresponds to the received price level, P_0. It can readily be established that to a different value of *P*, say, $P_1 < P_0$, there will correspond a new *DD* curve higher and to the right, such as *D′D′*. This is because a fall in *P* will increase the real value of the government debt held by the public and hence the real net worth of the private sector. This in turn will tend to increase consumption demand, and hence total demand, for any given *r*. Conversely, a rise in *P* will shift *DD* downward and to the left.

This dependence of aggregate demand on *P* when *G* is not zero has come to be known in the literature as the "real-balance effect," and also as the "Pigou effect" because Pigou called attention to it in a very influential work (1947). However, the point had been made earlier by others, in particular by Scitovsky (1940). The main implication of the real-balance effect is that even with flexible wages the system *will* in general have a position of full-employment equilibrium. In other words, it rules out the possibility of the "Keynesian case" discussed above. To illustrate this point, suppose that corresponding to the received price, P_0, the aggregate demand function had the position *D″D″* in the figure, which could not possibly intersect an *MM* curve on *SS*. Since the position of *DD* now *depends* on *P*, as *P* falls under the pressure of excess supply the *DD* curve will keep shifting to the right at the same time that *MM* shifts upward. Except under very special *ad hoc* assumptions, *MM* and *DD* will eventually intersect on *SS* at some point to the right of r_m.

This demonstration that, provided *G* is positive, a system with flexible wages will possess a position of full-employment equilibrium, contrary to Keynes's conclusion, has been seized upon by some of Keynes's critics as disposing of one of his most significant and novel results. They have concluded that underemployment equilibrium can arise only from wage–price rigidities. This view must be regarded as unwarranted, mainly for the following reasons: (*a*) Keynes's conclusion stands when $G = 0$. (*b*) Even when $G > 0$, the conclusion that a full-employment solution would exist is valid only under the assumption, implicit in the model, that falling prices do not generate perverse expectations of further falls, which would reduce demand. Furthermore, it ignores the likelihood that a violent deflation, which might be necessary to produce a sufficient increase in the real value of the national debt, would severely disrupt a monetary economy by producing wholesale debtors' insolvency. In view of these considerations, Pigou's demonstration has little practical relevance, as Pigou himself acknowledged ([1947] 1951, p. 251). Even if full employment could be re-established by sufficient deflation of prices and wages, it would be preferable to avoid this outcome by relying on the kind of fiscal policy devices, discussed in the next section, that one would have to fall back on when $G = 0$. To look at the matter in a slightly different light, wage and price rigidity, instead of hindering the working of a monetary economy, may provide it with a degree of price stability that in the long run contributes to its smooth working, even though this rigidity makes the task of successful monetary management more challenging.

Downward wage rigidity. The working of the system when the level of the rigid wage W_0 is sufficiently high to be at least potentially effective can be illustrated by Figure 4, which is a simple variant of Figure 3. For this purpose it is convenient to

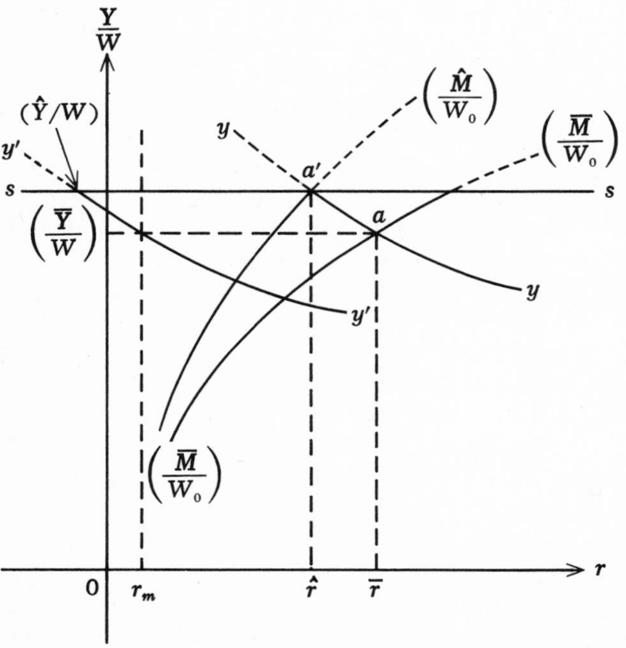

Figure 4 — Equilibrium with a rigid wage level (W_0)

introduce a new symbol to denote money income, Y, which is related to other variables of the system by the identity

$$(8) \qquad Y \equiv PX.$$

Also, for the sake of exposition we deal formally with the case $G = 0$, with some occasional reference to the (rather minor) modifications called for if this restriction is discarded.

We recall that with $G = 0$ the right-hand side of (1′) contains only the variable r. From (1′), (2), and (3) we can then derive a relation between Y/W and r. Here Y/W is income measured in what Keynes called wage units (that is, income measured in terms of labor as a *numéraire*). We first solve equation (3) for P/W in terms of X and write the solution as

$$(3') \qquad P/W = \mathcal{P}(X),$$

a "Marshallian" short-run supply function indicating the price—in terms of the cost of labor—needed to call forth a given supply, X. Next, using (1′) and (2), we can express X as a function of r. It follows that Y/W can itself be expressed as a function of r—say, $Y/W \equiv X(P/W) = X\mathcal{P}(X) = y(r)$. This equation is an obvious variant of the aggregate-demand relation (1′), shown as *DD* in Figure 3, except that output is expressed in wage units. Accordingly, its graph, shown by the *yy* curve of Figure 4, bears a close relation to that of *DD* in Figure 3, from which it differs only by the factor P/W. In particular, *yy* must fall from left to right if *DD* does, since P/W is an increasing function of X. The horizontal line *ss* again represents "full-employment output" in wage units, $(\widehat{P/W})\hat{X}$, where $\widehat{P/W}$ and $\hat{X}$ can be inferred from the solution of the system under flexible wages. The portion of *yy* above *ss* has been dashed to indicate that it can never be "effective," since real income there exceeds the full-employment level.

The curve rising from left to right and labeled $\bar{M}/W_0$ is again derived from the money market equation (7′), on the assumption that the given money supply is $\bar{M}$. First solve (7′) for PX, obtaining $PX = V(r)M$. Next replace M with $\bar{M}$ and divide both sides by W_0. This yields $Y/W_0 = V(r)(\bar{M}/W_0)$. Its graph must look like that of *MM* in Figure 3, for it is again the graph of $V(r)$ up to a proportionality factor M/W_0 (instead of M/P, as in Figure 3). It shows the level of income (in wage units) that can be transacted at each level of r, given the money supply in wage units.

If the *yy* curve and the money-market curve intersect in their effective range—below or on *ss*—as in Figure 4, then the coordinates of their point of intersection, labeled a, show the equilibrium value of income, $\bar{Y}/W$, and of the rate of interest, $\bar{r}$. If this intersection does not fall on ss, then the equilibrium is one of less than full employment. It is a position of *equilibrium* despite the presence of unemployment because, under wage rigidity, the excess supply of labor does not lead to any further adjustment (at least in the short run). By contrast, if wages were flexible, the excess supply would bid down W which, with $\bar{M}$ given, would raise $\bar{M}/W$, shifting the MM curve upward and moving its point of intersection with yy upward and to the left until it coincided with the full-employment point, a' in the figure. (If G is assumed to be positive, the fall in W will also tend to shift yy upward, moving a' to the right.)

Even under wage rigidity, output and employment could be increased by increasing the money supply, which, with W given at W_0, would raise M/W and hence the MM curve. In fact, provided that a' is to the right of r_m, there is an ideal money supply, $\hat{M}$, that produces an MM curve that intersects yy at a'. Alternatively, the goal of optimal monetary policy might be visualized as that of enforcing the rate of interest that would generate an aggregate demand equal to full-employment output, supplying whatever quantity of money is needed to enforce that rate. In terms of Figure 4, the rate of interest called for is, of course, $\hat{r}$ (which is the r coordinate of a'), and the corresponding quantity of money is again $\hat{M}$.

This analysis should help to show how the interaction of liquidity preference and wage rigidity makes the task of economic stabilization through monetary policy a highly complex and difficult one. In the absence of wage–price rigidities the concern of monetary policy would be reduced to the maintenance of price stability. And in the absence of liquidity preference the velocity of circulation could be counted upon to be sufficiently stable to make this task a relatively easy one. In a stationary economy it would call essentially for a stable money supply, whereas in an expanding economy it would call for a money supply that keeps pace with the growth of full-employment output, a growth that also appears to be characterized by a fair degree of stability.

But under wage rigidity, monetary policy has the double task of trying to achieve both price stability and full employment. Furthermore, because liquidity preference causes the velocity of circulation to vary with interest rates, the money supply needed to reach these goals will vary, relative to full-employment output, with variations in aggregate demand conditions. In terms of Figure 4, a rise in consumption or investment demand relative to income will shift the yy curve to the right; a corresponding fall will shift it to the left. These shifts have to be countered by contrary adjustments of the money supply relative to the level of full-employment output. Furthermore, failure to adjust the money supply properly will tend to have asymmetrical consequences. An excessive money supply will still give rise to increases in prices that could have been avoided and that are largely irreversible. But too small a money supply will result in an insufficient aggregate demand that, aside from deflationary effects on the price level, will result in the waste and social scourge of unemployment.

Note also that the central bank's control over the price level is at best partial and largely unidirectional. The price level is anchored to the wage rate, which monetary policy can readily push up by being too expansive but which it can hardly hope to force down, except possibly through the painful and wasteful route of prolonged and widespread unemployment. Furthermore, if the minimum money wage—the W_0 of equation (5)—tends to be pushed up even before full employment is reached, whether through powerful unions or through partial bottlenecks or both, and if the rise tends to exceed the rate of increase of productivity, then monetary (as well as fiscal) policy will be faced with the unsavory choice between "creeping inflation" and chronic unemployment. Whether this dilemma is in fact a serious and real one revolves around the issue of the determinants of the over-all level of money wages, an issue that the Keynesian analysis has opened up but that is still far from settled. [*See* INFLATION AND DEFLATION; *see also* Phillips 1958.]

One other implication of the Keynesian framework, which can be only touched upon in this survey dealing primarily with monetary aspects, is that fiscal policy provides an alternative approach to the control of aggregate demand for economic stabilization [*see* FISCAL POLICY]. Fiscal policy can be accommodated in our macroeconomic model by adding government expenditure on goods and services as a component of aggregate demand in equation (1′), making consumption (and possibly investment) depend on taxes as well as on income produced, and adding an equation relating tax collection to income and tax rates. Without attempting to pursue this line here we may indicate that, in terms of Figure 4, fiscal policy—defined as policy concerned with the level of government expenditure and taxation—will affect the position and shape of the aggregate demand relation yy. An increase in expenditure will shift it upward and to the right; an increase in tax rates will shift it in the opposite direction. Thus, given a position of less than full employment equilibrium such as *a* in Figure 4, output and employment could be raised toward or up to the full-employment level by increased government expenditure, tax reductions, or both, which would shift the *yy* curve to the right.

The possibility of affecting equilibrium output and employment through fiscal tools becomes of critical importance in the special "Keynesian case," in which the aggregate demand is so depressed that the *yy* curve intersects *ss* to the left of the minimum achievable interest rate, r_m. In this case (illustrated by the curve *y'y'* in Figure 4) full employment, as we have seen, is beyond the reach of monetary policy, for no money curve can have points to the left of r_m. Fiscal policy is then the only effective tool of stabilization policy, at least until the *yy* curve has been shifted rightward enough to cut *ss* to the right of r_m.

Beyond this point—and, more generally, whenever the intersection of *yy* and *ss* is to the right of r_m—either fiscal or monetary tools can be used in the pursuit of full employment and price stability. Of course, both tools can be used simultaneously and in coordinated fashion. This should be clear from the fact that, in terms of Figure 4, fiscal policy acts basically on *yy* whereas monetary policy acts basically on the money curve. (The graphical apparatus of Figure 4 was chosen to illustrate the working of the system partly because of its convenience in isolating the *modus operandi* of monetary and fiscal policy.)

There is a substantial literature concerned with the analysis of the relative advantages and shortcomings of monetary and fiscal policy in terms of such criteria as reliability, response delays, ease of implementation, and reversibility (for monetary policy, see Johnson 1962, pp. 365–377; for fiscal policy see, e.g., Keiser 1964, part 5), effects on long-run economic growth (e.g., Smith 1957; Modigliani 1961), and, more recently, differential impact on the balance of payments (e.g., Mundell 1962). Because of the complexity of the problem it is not surprising that there have been substantial differences in points of view between economists favoring the use of one tool, or of some specific mix, and those favoring others. These differences can be traced in part to differences in the subjective valuation of different goals. But in part they revolve around disagreement about the empirical importance of the "Keynesian case" in which monetary policy becomes powerless to maintain or reestablish full employment, either because it is ineffective in reducing interest rates any further (at least in the short run) or because the achievable reduction in interest rates is insufficient to induce the required expansion in investment and aggregate demand.

Liquidity preference, that is, the proposition that the demand for money is systematically and significantly affected by interest rates, has proved to be a major, lasting contribution to economic analysis, well supported by empirical evidence. From an analytical point of view its great significance lies in the implication that under certain conditions—the "special Keynesian case"—even an economy with flexible wages and prices might not possess a stable full-employment equilibrium. But beyond this fundamental theoretical contribution, the dramatic impact of the *General Theory* on economic theory and policy can be traced to its insightful analysis of the role of liquidity preference in a world of widespread wage and price rigidities. This analysis has led to a new understanding and fundamental reappraisal of the role of money and of the tasks and limitations of monetary and fiscal policy.

With downward wage rigidity (and even ignoring international trade) money cannot be regarded, even in first approximation, as "neutral," a mere veil having no effect on the economy other than the determination of the price level, except possibly when the money supply is excessive. Under conditions of less than full employment due to lack of demand, and barring the special Keynesian case, monetary policy plays a crucial role in the determination of income and employment. In the special Keynesian case, on the other hand, monetary policy breaks down, since it is incapable, at least in the short run, of affecting either output or prices.

FRANCO MODIGLIANI

BIBLIOGRAPHY

ALLAIS, MAURICE 1947 *Économie & intérêt: Présentation nouvelle des problèmes fondamentaux relatifs au rôle économique du taux de l'intérêt et de leurs solutions.* 2 vols. Paris: Librairie des Publications Officielles.

BAUMOL, WILLIAM J. 1952 The Transactions Demand for Cash: An Inventory Theoretic Approach. *Quarterly Journal of Economics* 66:545–556.

BRONFENBRENNER, MARTIN; and HOLZMAN, FRANKLYN D. 1963 Survey of Inflation Theory. *American Economic Review* 53:593–661.

BRONFENBRENNER, MARTIN; and MAYER, THOMAS 1960 Liquidity Functions in the American Economy. *Econometrica* 28:810–834.

BRUNNER, K.; and MELTZER, ALLAN H. 1964 Some Further Investigations of Demand and Supply Functions for Money. *Journal of Finance* 19:240–283.

ESHAG, EPRIME 1963 *From Marshall to Keynes: An Essay on the Monetary Theory of the Cambridge School.* Oxford: Blackwell.

FISHER, IRVING (1911) 1920 *The Purchasing Power of Money: Its Determination and Relation to Credit, Interest and Crises.* New ed., rev. New York: Macmillan.

FRIEDMAN, MILTON (editor) 1956 *Studies in the Quantity Theory of Money.* Univ. of Chicago Press. → See especially pages 5–21, "The Quantity Theory of Money—A Restatement," by Friedman.

FRIEDMAN, MILTON 1957 *A Theory of the Consumption Function.* National Bureau of Economic Research, General Series, No. 63. Princeton Univ. Press.

FRIEDMAN, MILTON 1959 The Demand for Money: Some Theoretical and Empirical Results. *Journal of Political Economy* 67:327–351.

HICKS, JOHN R. (1935) 1951 A Suggestion for Simplifying the Theory of Money. Pages 13–32 in American Economic Association, *Readings in Monetary Theory.* Philadelphia: Blakiston.

HICKS, JOHN R. 1937 Mr. Keynes and the "Classics": A Suggested Interpretation. *Econometrica* 5:147–159.

JOHNSON, H. G. 1962 Monetary Theory and Policy. *American Economic Review* 52:335–384.

KEISER, NORMAN F. 1964 *Macroeconomics, Fiscal Policy, and Economic Growth.* New York: Wiley.

KEYNES, JOHN MAYNARD (1930) 1958–1960 *A Treatise on Money.* 2 vols. London: Macmillan. → Volume 1: *The Pure Theory of Money.* Volume 2: *The Applied Theory of Money.*

KEYNES, JOHN MAYNARD 1936 *The General Theory of Employment, Interest and Money.* London: Macmillan. → A paperback edition was published in 1965 by Harcourt.

LANGE, OSKAR 1938 The Rate of Interest and the Optimum Propensity to Consume. *Economica* New Series 5:12–32.

LATANÉ, HENRY A. 1954 Cash Balances and the Interest Rate: A Pragmatic Approach. *Review of Economics and Statistics* 36:456–460.

LATANÉ, HENRY A. 1960 Income Velocity and Interest Rates: A Pragmatic Approach. *Review of Economics and Statistics* 42:445–449.

LAVINGTON, FREDERICK 1921 *The English Capital Market.* London: Methuen.

MARGET, ARTHUR W. 1938 *The Theory of Prices: A Re-examination of the Central Problems of Monetary Theory.* Vol. 1. Englewood Cliffs, N.J.: Prentice-Hall.

MARSHALL, ALFRED 1923 *Money, Credit and Commerce.* London: Macmillan.

MELTZER, ALLAN H. 1963 The Demand for Money: The Evidence From the Time Series. *Journal of Political Economy* 71:219–246.

MODIGLIANI, FRANCO (1944) 1951 Liquidity Preference and the Theory of Interest and Money. Pages 186–239 in American Economic Association, *Readings in Monetary Theory.* New York: Blakiston. → First published in Volume 12 of *Econometrica.*

MODIGLIANI, FRANCO 1961 Long Run Implications of Alternative Fiscal Policies and the Burden of the National Debt. *Economic Journal* 71:730–755.

MODIGLIANI, FRANCO 1963 The Monetary Mechanism and Its Interaction With Real Phenomena. *Review of Economics and Statistics* 45 (Supplement):79–107.

MUNDELL, ROBERT A. 1962 The Appropriate Use of Monetary and Fiscal Policy for Internal and External Stability. International Monetary Fund, *Staff Papers* 9:70–77.

PATINKIN, DON (1956) 1965 *Money, Interest, and Prices: An Integration of Monetary and Value Theory.* 2d ed. New York: Harper.

PHILLIPS, A. W. 1958 The Relation Between Unemployment and the Rate of Change of Money Wage Rates in the United Kingdom: 1861–1957. *Economica* New Series 25:283–299.

PIGOU, A. C. (1917) 1951 The Value of Money. Pages 162–183 in American Economic Association, *Readings in Monetary Theory.* Philadelphia: Blakiston.

PIGOU, A. C. (1947) 1951 Economic Progress in a Stable Environment. Pages 241–251 in American Economic Association, *Readings in Monetary Theory.* Philadelphia: Blakiston. → First published in Volume 14 of *Economica* New Series.

PIGOU, A. C. 1950 *Keynes's* General Theory: *A Retrospective View.* London: Macmillan.

SCITOVSKY, TIBOR 1940 Capital Accumulation, Employment and Price Rigidity. *Review of Economic Studies* 8:69–88.

SMITH, WARREN L. 1957 Monetary–Fiscal Policy and Economic Growth. *Quarterly Journal of Economics* 71:36–55.

TOBIN, JAMES 1956 The Interest-elasticity of Transactions Demand for Cash. *Review of Economics and Statistics* 38:241–247.

TOBIN, JAMES 1958 Liquidity Preference as Behavior Towards Risk. *Review of Economic Studies* 25, no. 2: 65–86.

TURVEY, RALPH (1960) 1961 *Interest Rates and Asset Prices.* New York: Macmillan.

LIST, FRIEDRICH

Friedrich List (1789–1846), German economist, was the son of a tanner from the free town of Reutlingen (Württemberg). Early in his life he absorbed the political ideas and doctrines of the Enlightenment, finding in them an excellent weapon against the rule of an arbitrary bureaucracy and the lingering restrictions of the age of the guilds. In the years following the defeat of Napoleon, he was able to give full scope to his liberal political ideas in his capacities as adviser to one of the leading statesmen of Württemberg, as professor of political economy at the University of Tübingen, and as editor of several periodicals.

With the rising tide of German reaction, however, his activity became suspect. When in 1819 he established an association of merchants and industrialists in Frankfurt am Main, the Handels- und Gewerbsverein, and advocated the abolition of internal German customs barriers, the officials of many German-speaking states, and especially Metternich, the Austrian chancellor, began to look upon him as a demagogue. In 1820 he was elected to the legislature of Württemberg. When he petitioned for an extension of local self-government and for publicity in judicial procedure, he was sentenced to ten months' imprisonment for attempting to undermine the stability of public institutions. He fled abroad in 1822 and led a wandering life for some years. In 1824 he returned to Germany and was promptly arrested. Released on the promise that he would emigrate to America—he had been invited by Lafayette—he sailed for New York in 1825.

In the United States, List engaged in various activities. He lived in Pennsylvania, first as an unsuccessful farmer, near Harrisburg, and then as the editor of a German newspaper, *Der Adler*, in Reading. He also discovered and successfully developed an anthracite coal mine near Tamaqua, Pennsylvania; the railroad he built to serve it—known as the Little Schuylkill Navigation Railroad and Canal Co.—was opened in November 1831 and was at the time the only railway line carrying both freight and passengers. At the same time he was a keen observer of the economic and political problems which beset the growing country; his entrepreneurial experiences confirmed his earlier doubts about the universal validity of Adam Smith's doctrines. He concluded that a protective tariff is indispensable for industrially underdeveloped countries. At the suggestion of Charles Ingersoll, vice-president of the Pennsylvania Society for the Promotion of Manufactures and the Mechanic Arts—the leading protectionist organization of the time—List wrote his "Outlines of American Political Economy" (1827). This was his first attempt at a systematic formulation of his views, and, indeed, it was the first attempt of any kind to draft a national system of political economy that was valid for early high capitalism. Copies of the "Outlines" were distributed to members of Congress, and the adoption of the Tariff Bill of 1828 was a direct consequence.

List supported the election campaign of Andrew Jackson in 1832 and was rewarded by being appointed American consul in Germany, serving first in Hamburg and then in Leipzig. While still American consul, he embarked on an ambitious plan to organize a German railway system. He contributed greatly to the development of the line between Leipzig and Dresden in 1837; it was one of the first railways on the Continent. The venture, although successful in itself, proved a source of personal and financial disappointment and even induced him to leave Germany for France.

It was in Paris in 1837 that List wrote his second systematic work, "Le système naturel de l'économie politique," which he submitted to the Académie des Sciences Morales et Politiques. The work was not rediscovered until 1925 and was published for the first time two years later in French and German (see *Schriften*, vol. 4). In this work, List deepened and expanded the theoretical system sketched in the "Outlines" and gave it, in addition, a historical basis. But the full results of his far-reaching studies and his international experiences were incorporated only in his best-known work on the subject of political economy, *The National System of Political Economy* (1841), which was written in Paris but appeared after List had finally returned to Germany in 1840. Beginning in 1843 he published *Das Zollvereinsblatt*, an influential review devoted to the dissemination of his ideas, which were by then both supported and confirmed by the rise of industrialism. He began to exercise an important influence on public opinion in Germany. However, financial worries, combined with the failure of his plan for an alliance between Germany and Great Britain, drove him to despair and led to his suicide.

In the nineteenth century List was the only economist, other than Karl Marx, who strongly emphasized the close interrelation of economic theory and political factors. He believed that economic doctrines have no abstract validity; he always examined accepted economic views and developed his own ideas in terms of concrete political areas at definite levels of economic development. He severely criticized the classical writers for not being aware of the great social and economic significance of the nation. For List, the nation is the most important link between the individual and mankind, whereas the economic principles of the classical school reflect the industrial and commercial supremacy of England in the nineteenth century and are inapplicable to the needs of underdeveloped but rising countries, such as nineteenth-century Germany, France, and the United States. Observing the destructive consequences of cheap British exports to the numerous small German states—consequences of the application of the English free-trade theory—List developed his countertheory of productive forces and of economic stages, related both to historical and cultural contexts. This was the basis of his later efforts to foster, by the development of railway systems, etc., the economic integration and industrial growth of the different German states that had been organized into the Zollverein (Customs Union) in 1834.

List's theory of protectionism, as presented in *The National System*, was actually only a small part of a much larger system in which he intended to deal with agricultural theory, the concept of balance between agriculture and industry within any economy, and the significance of the internal market. Unfortunately, his ideas were often not sufficiently clear, and his arguments were not always sound—the theoretical element in his basically historical approach was not adequate to the task he set himself. Consequently, his writings were often misunderstood. In the controversy over free trade, for example, some stressed List's argument that infant industries need protection if the nation's productive forces are to be developed, while others realized that free trade was List's ultimate goal. No one seemed to understand, however, that neither argument was central to List's concern. Rather, he wished to demonstrate that the growth of an economy is an organic process and that it is only because growth is organic that every nation has a temporary need for protection. Thus, List denied that the policy prescriptions of classical economic theory are absolute and asserted that a nation's best economic and commercial policy depends on its actual stage of development. The advisability of free trade is, therefore, a matter of politics and is not subject to a quasi-religious belief, as it was for the classical economists and as it is even today for many "neoliberals."

List's theory of economic stages is related to the pervasive eighteenth-century concept of harmony, for it is harmonic development that he saw realized in the *Normalnation*, the state of national development when productive forces are completely utilized. The fact that evolution proceeds from primitive conditions to the agricultural state, then to the agricultural-and-manufacturing state, and finally to the agricultural-manufacturing-and-commercial state may not only stimulate effort in underdeveloped nations but, if correctly interpreted, may also warn them against the dangers of underestimating the importance of agriculture and overestimating that of the most modern type of industry.

List was opposed to the individualistic–cosmopolitan orientation of classical economics, with its focus on value theory. He defended his organic doctrine of productive forces against the classical atomistic–materialistic approach, and he upheld his own concept of the cooperative aspects of the productive process against the classical stress on the division of labor. His dynamic approach and his consequent interest in the development of productive forces led him to his belief in the value of protective tariffs as a method whereby underdeveloped countries may exploit their natural resources and raise their economic level.

List's "Blicke in die Zukunft" (1846*a*), his vision of the political future, also manifests his concern for harmonic balance. He believed that the legal system of a developing nation should be preserved as a cultural prerequisite, as an ethical standard, and as a framework for political action both by individuals and by the people as a whole. Thus, the man who pioneered the Zollverein and heralded the politico–economic unity of the German nation had enough insight to anticipate the need to set limits to a possible German rise. Much more farsighted than other political thinkers of his time, he predicted the inevitable division of the world into a few mighty empires. He foresaw the enormous growth of American population, industry, and power in the twentieth century, and he even anticipated the great impetus that Russia's "conditions of culture, constitution, law and administration" would need in order for her to become a world power. He therefore consumed his last energies in fighting—without mandate or title—for an Anglo–German alliance. Such an alliance with a united Germany would preserve England's hegemony and would save Europe from being crushed politically between the two rising world powers, Russia and the United States.

For a hundred years List's system was generally accepted without really being understood, even in Germany. Free traders, for example, thought he was a reactionary, although he was the founder of the movement that consolidated Germany commercially and that eventually destroyed more customhouses and more obstacles to trade than were swept away by the political whirlwinds of the American and French revolutions. The efforts to integrate Europe in the years after World War II, however, led to a reappraisal of his statement: "Commercial union and political union are twins; the one cannot come to birth without the other following" ([1846*b*] 1931, p. 276). Many passages in *The National System* can be easily adapted to the post-World War II situation by changing only the names of the states. It is even possible to maintain that List foresaw, strove for, and advocated a European common market; the German economic and political union of the nineteenth century was simply a preliminary stage.

Since World War II the Anglo-Saxon world has also become interested in the ideas that concerned List. Streeten (1959), for example, has stated that in *The National System* List clearly formulated the now widely discussed problem of "balanced growth" in underdeveloped countries. It is also recognized that List was one of the first economists to emphasize the importance of so-called social overhead capital (especially the means of transportation) as a necessary precondition for any economic development, be it in Germany in the nineteenth century or in the many underdeveloped countries of the world in the twentieth. Paul Samuelson (1960) has even placed List among the really important American economists, not only because he began formulating his theory of economic development during his stay in the United States but also because—like the majority of American economists of the past—he can be characterized by a protectionist tendency and a nationalist attitude. Thus, for the practical questions of the integration of Europe and the industrialization of underdeveloped countries, List's work remains of utmost importance, while as a theorist, he is significant as the originator of the historical theory of economic growth.

EDGAR SALIN AND RENÉ L. FREY

[*For discussion of the subsequent development of List's ideas, see* ECONOMIC THOUGHT, *article on* THE HISTORICAL SCHOOL; INTERNATIONAL INTEGRATION, *article on* ECONOMIC UNIONS; INTERNATIONAL TRADE CONTROLS.]

WORKS BY LIST

(1827) 1931 Outlines of American Political Economy. Volume 2, pages 95–156 in Friedrich List, *Schriften, Reden, Briefe.* Berlin: Hobbing.

(1841) 1928 *The National System of Political Economy.* London: Longmans. → First published in German.

(1846*a*) 1931 Blicke in die Zukunft. Volume 7, pages 482–494 in Friedrich List, *Schriften, Reden, Briefe.* Berlin: Hobbing. → First published as "Politik der Zukunft."

(1846*b*) 1931 Über den Wert und die Bedingungen einer Allianz zwischen Grossbritannien und Deutschland. Volume 7, pages 267–296 in Friedrich List, *Schriften, Reden, Briefe.* Berlin: Hobbing. → Translation of extract in the text provided by the editors.

Schriften, Reden, Briefe. 10 vols. in 12. Edited by Erwin von Beckerath et al. Berlin: Hobbing, 1927–1936. → Volume 1: *Der Kampf um die politische und ökonomische Reform: 1815–1825,* 1932. Volume 2: *Grundlinien einer politischen Ökonomie und andere Beiträge der amerikanischen Zeit: 1825–1832,* 1931. Volume 3: *Schriften zum Verkehrswesen,* 1929–1931. Volume 4: *Das natürliche System der politischen Ökonomie,* written in French in 1837, first published in French and German in 1927. Volume 5: *Aufsätze und Abhandlungen aus den Jahren 1831–1844,* 1928. Volume 6: *Das nationale System der politischen Ökonomie,* 1930. Volume 7: *Die politisch-ökonomische Nationaleinheit der Deutschen: Aufsätze aus dem* Zollvereinsblatt *und andere Schriften der Spätzeit,* 1931. Volume 8: *Tagebücher und Briefe: 1812–1846,* 1932. Volume 9: *Lists Leben in Tag- und Jahresdaten,* 1935. Volume 10: *Verzeichnisse zur Gesamtausgabe,* 1936.

SUPPLEMENTARY BIBLIOGRAPHY

BRINKMANN, CARL 1949 *Friedrich List.* Berlin: Duncker & Humblot.

EHEBERG, KARL T. VON 1883 Historische und kritische Einleitung zu Friedrich Lists *Nationalem System der politischen Oekonomie.* Pages 1–249 in Friedrich List, *Das nationale System der politischen Oekonomie.* 7th ed. Stuttgart (Germany): Cotta.

GEHRING, PAUL 1964 *Friedrich List: Jugend- und Reifejahre 1789–1825.* Tübingen (Germany): Mohr.

HÄUSSER, LUDWIG 1850 Friedrich Lists Leben. Volume 1 in Friedrich List, *Gesammelte Schriften.* Stuttgart and Tübingen (Germany): Cotta.

HIRST, MARGARET E. 1909 *Life of Friedrich List and Selections From His Writings.* With an introduction by F. W. Hirst. London: Smith; New York: Scribner.

LENZ, FRIEDRICH 1930 *Friedrich List, "die Vulgärökonomie" und Karl Marx nebst einer unbekannten Denkschrift Lists zur Zollreform.* Jena (Germany): Fischer.

LENZ, FRIEDRICH 1936 *Friedrich List: Der Mann und das Werk.* Munich and Berlin: Oldenbourg.

MEUSEL, ALFRED 1928 *List und Marx: Eine vergleichende Betrachtung.* Jena (Germany): Fischer.

NOTZ, WILLIAM (1925) 1926 Frederick List in America. *American Economic Review* 16:249–265. → First published in German in *Weltwirtschaftliches Archiv.*

OLSHAUSEN, HANS P. 1935 *Friedrich List und der deutsche Handels- und Gewerbsverein.* Jena (Germany): Fischer.

RITSCHL, HANS 1947 *Friedrich Lists Leben und Lehre.* Tübingen and Stuttgart (Germany): Wunderlich.

SALIN, EDGAR (1921) 1963 Friedrich Lists Lehre von den Wirtschaftsstufen und die Bedeutung der Typik. Pages 301–309 in Edgar Salin, *Lynkeus: Gestalten und Probleme aus Wirtschaft und Politik.* Tübingen (Germany): Mohr. → First published in Volume 45 of *Schmollers Jahrbuch.*

SAMUELSON, PAUL A. 1960 American Economics. Pages 31–50 in Ralph E. Freeman (editor), *Postwar Economic Trends in the United States.* New York: Harper.

SOMMER, ARTUR 1927 *Friedrich Lists System der politischen Ökonomie.* Jena (Germany): Fischer.

STREETEN, PAUL 1959 Unbalanced Growth. *Oxford Economic Papers* New Series 11:167–190.

LITERACY

Whenever the term "literacy" is used, a context is always implied. If the context is archeological, anthropological, or ethnographic, literacy usually refers to the cultural fact that writing has been invented and that the society contains a class, a caste, or an occupational group whose members keep accounts or preserve religious and moral precepts in written form or use writing for some other specific purpose. So used, literacy implies also the contrasting idea of *preliteracy*—a cultural stage in which writing has not yet been invented. The change from preliteracy to literacy—the spread of literate societies throughout the world—probably began in ancient Sumer during the fourth millennium B.C., through a gradual transition from pictography to the use of an alphabet.

If literacy is used in a historical or modern comparative context, then the implied contrast is with *illiteracy.* Literacy then refers to the degree of dissemination among a society's population of the dual skills of reading and writing. Here a "literate" society is one in which most adult members can read and write at least a simple message. In this context, England, the United States, Sweden, Denmark, the U.S.S.R., and Japan are among the literate societies, whereas Iraq, Haiti, and Nigeria, for example, can be called illiterate—or, at least, not yet literate—societies, even though they contain many highly educated persons.

Extent of literacy

As the great variation between countries with respect to illiteracy (Table 1) has become better known, concern about its consequences has greatly increased. For some, the existence of high levels of illiteracy detracts from the dignity of man and constitutes evidence of immense numbers of personal tragedies for the illiterate adults who are thereby prevented from escaping poverty and mental isolation. To others, illiteracy is primarily an obstacle to peaceful and friendly international relations and to democratic processes within countries. Still others are aware that low levels of literacy act as brakes on the advance of countries along the paths of social and economic development and political power. These concerns have brought on a variety of efforts to gather detailed information on the extent of literacy in the world's countries and on the conditions under which the diffusion of literacy takes place.

From a world perspective, it is evident that in 1950, the latest date for which world-wide estimates are available, some 53 per cent of the world's population aged 10 and over were able to read and write a simple sentence; that is, in 1950 there were at least 800 million illiterates above the age of 10. The dissemination of literacy skills that has taken place since then is unlikely to have raised the per-

Table 1 — Illiteracy in selected census countries, by continent[a]

	PERCENTAGE OF ILLITERATES IN THE POPULATION AGED 10 AND OVER[b]	
	Year	Per cent
Africa		
Algeria	1948	82.1[c]
Egypt	1947	80.1[c]
Gold Coast (Ghana)	1948	92.0
Mozambique	1940	98.1
Nigeria	1952/3	88.3
Nyasaland	1945	91.1
Portuguese Guinea	1950	98.5
Union of South Africa	1946	55.3
South America		
Argentina	1947	12.6
Bolivia	1950	68.9
Brazil	1950	51.7
Chile	1952	19.9[c]
Colombia	1938	44.2
Ecuador	1950	43.7
Paraguay	1950	31.8
Peru	1940	56.6
Venezuela	1950	47.8[c]
Europe		
Bulgaria	1946	24.2[c]
Greece	1951	23.7
Italy	1951	14.4[c]
Poland	1931	23.1
Portugal	1950	41.7
Rumania	1948	23.2
Spain	1950	14.2
Yugoslavia	1948	25.4

	PERCENTAGE OF ILLITERATES IN THE POPULATION AGED 10 AND OVER[b]	
	Year	Per cent
North America		
Costa Rica	1950	21.2
Cuba	1953	22.1[c]
Dominican Republic	1950	56.8
El Salvador	1950	60.9
Guatemala	1950	72.0
Haiti	1950	89.5
Honduras	1950	64.8
Mexico	1950	43.2[d]
Nicaragua	1950	62.6
Panama	1950	28.3
Asia		
Burma	1953	30.1[e]
Ceylon	1946	42.2
India	1951	80.1
Indonesia	1930	90.1
Iraq	1947	89.1[f]
Korea	1930	68.6
Malaya (incl. Singapore)	1947	56.1
Pakistan	1951	77.3
Philippines	1948	40.2
Thailand	1947	46.3
Turkey	1950	66.1

a. The reader is cautioned against insisting too closely on comparisons between countries whose literacy rates fall within the same decile range. Moreover, rates taken from international sources such as UNESCO (1957) are not always identical with rates calculated from statistical compendia, because persons whose ages are unknown may be omitted or included in the age group 10 and over.

b. Only countries with rates above 10 per cent about 1950 have been included.

c. Population aged 15 and over.

d. Population aged 6 and over.

e. Data for 252 towns only, based on a 20 per cent sample; population aged 16 and over.

f. Population aged 5 and over.

Sources: Calculated from official data (census, statistical compendia, etc.) for each country, or from international sources such as UNESCO 1957 and *Demographic Yearbook* 1960, pp. 434 ff.

Table 2 — Illiteracy in the major world regions, 1930 and 1950, and in developed and underdeveloped countries, 1950

	PER CENT ILLITERATE OF ALL PERSONS AGED 10 AND OVER[a]			
	All countries		Developed countries[b]	Underdeveloped countries[b]
	1930	1950	1950	1950
World	59[c]	47	6	71
North America	4	2	2	
Europe	15	8	4	23
Oceania	14	11	1	88
U.S.S.R.	40	11	11	
South America	54	42	17	51
Middle America	59	48	22	53
Asia	81	70	2	75
Africa	88	88	56	91

a. The figures given in this table represent the weighted average obtained by combining the official and estimated rates for all the countries within the geographical division.

b. Developed countries are those with less than 50 per cent of their economically active males in agricultural pursuits, including hunting, fishing, and forestry; underdeveloped countries are those with 50 per cent or more of their economically active males in these pursuits. For a rationale of this division, see Davis (1951*b*, p. 8).

c. Abel and Bond (1929, p. 51) give a world average of 62 per cent for around 1920.

Sources: For 1930 Davis 1948, p. 614; for 1950 revisions have been made of Golden 1955, p. 2; for another set of 1950 estimates, see UNESCO 1957, p. 15.

centage to 60 or to have decreased the *number* of illiterates very much below 800 million, since population has grown very rapidly in this period. But, as Table 2 shows, the 1950 level represented a considerable *proportionate* gain over 1920 and 1930.

The literacy revolution. The world's transformation from largely illiterate to moderately literate began in the industrial nations of western Europe; the recent gains in world literacy reflect the entrance into this transition of an ever-increasing number of countries in many areas. As Table 1 shows, the differential spread of the literacy transition in 1950 suggests that today's countries can be arranged along a literacy scale that exhibits a definite pattern. The lowest rates exist in those areas that have completed the transition; the highest, in areas such as Ghana, Iraq, or Haiti, in which the transition has hardly begun; and between these two extremes fall all those countries, such as India, Pakistan, Bolivia, Paraguay, Mexico, and the Philippines, which are in the midst of the transformation.

The transformation from preponderantly illiterate to literate in the world's old industrial nations, which was accomplished in about 75 to 100 years, can be documented from official information and from estimates. At the beginning of the nineteenth century, although literacy and schooling were more general than is often realized (Anderson & Bowman 1965, p. 345), at least half the adult population of England and Wales was illiterate; in 1850 the proportion had probably dropped to about 45 per cent. By 1910 illiteracy had been largely eliminated, with perhaps 5 per cent of the adults still illiterate and these concentrated in the older age groups; in 1914 0.8 per cent of the men and 1.0 per cent of the women signed the marriage register by mark (for all these estimates, see UNESCO 1957, pp. 177 ff.).

The decline of illiteracy in countries entering the literacy transition later can be shown by information for the U.S.S.R., Italy, and Greece. In Russia illiteracy declined very rapidly—from about 76 per cent in 1897, according to official census figures, to about 2 per cent in the early 1960s in the population aged 9 and over (United Nations, Statistical Office 1963, p. 312). In Italy and Greece the transition has been slower. In Italy, illiteracy among marriage registrants declined from 65.8 per cent in 1872 to 3.3 per cent in 1951 (UNESCO 1957, p. 169); illiteracy among persons 10 and over fell from 75 per cent, according to the 1861 census, to about 8 per cent, according to the 1961 census. In Greece illiteracy in the population aged 8 years and over declined from 60 per cent in 1907 to about 25 per cent in 1951 (UNESCO 1957, p. 90).

Because the world's transformation from illiterate to moderately literate had its start in the West and has been completed primarily in the world's urban–industrial countries, these nations have a disproportionate share of the world's literate population (Table 2). In some major areas of the world, such as India, Pakistan, and Egypt, the proportion of the adult population that is illiterate is still very high. In India the illiteracy rate for the population aged 10 and over declined from 95 per cent in 1881 to about 70 per cent in 1961, according to the 1961 census (*Demographic Yearbook*, 1964, p. 698). Whereas the decline of illiteracy in Pakistan and Egypt has followed about the same pattern as in India, some areas, such as Haiti, Mozambique, and Ghana (Table 1) have hardly begun the transition. Even the breakdown by continents understates the concentration of the literate population, because within both Asia and Africa the literate population is mainly in a few countries or in cities. For example, in 1950 Japan—the major highly literate nation of Asia exclusive of the U.S.S.R.—had only 6 per cent to 7 per cent of Asia's total population but at least 20 per cent of its adult literates. Future literacy gains for the world as a whole depend, then, very heavily on the degree to which the highly illiterate countries of the world become involved in this educational transformation.

Evaluating literacy data

Official literacy information can often be obtained from enumerations of total populations (census counts), though sometimes it is based on marriage registers, on tests given to military recruits, or on sample surveys. The results of these enumerations are usually made available in official sources. While minor census inaccuracies can rarely be detected, major inaccuracies in literacy enumeration are discoverable through careful evaluation or by check through independent estimates. For example, because past school enrollment rates for all countries correlate moderately highly with present literacy rates, for a specific country past enrollment rates provide one means of checking the accuracy of census results on literacy.

Definitions of literacy. Census definitions of literacy usually refer to the minimum level of literacy skills; hence they are relatively simple and clear. Yet they still differ slightly from country to country because the instructions to enumerators incorporate somewhat different conceptions of what constitutes the minimum level. In India, for example, government statisticians have instructed enumerators to count as literate only those who have the ability to read and write a simple message in any language, a definition proposed by the United Nations Population Commission. When these instructions are carried out by local schoolteachers, few persons are likely to be counted as literate who do not have the minimum skills. In 1930 Finland applied perhaps the strictest minimum definition: only those persons were classified as literate who passed a rather difficult test. Those who failed were divided into two categories, the semiliterates, that is, persons who could read and write but made orthographic errors, and the illiterates, who could neither read nor write (UNESCO 1957, p. 29). By contrast, in the Hong Kong census of 1961 (as in many others) a person who *said* that he was able to read a language was assumed by inference also to be able to write it and was classified as literate. The acceptance of what the enumerator is told may result in inflating the percentage literate or, in some special cases, lowering this percentage (Davis 1951*a*, p. 151).

Literacy proportions. Because of differences in definition and in enumeration procedure, no actual figure or proportion can be accepted with complete certainty for any area; however, for word-wide comparisons and analyses of literacy, we can profitably use a given proportion as an indicator of the literacy level achieved by a country. The use of literacy proportions as indicators makes it easier to take advantage of literacy proportions available from enumerations of such segments of the population as marriage registrants or recruits. For example, in the 1930s the proportions obtained by each of these enumeration procedures placed France among the highly literate nations of the world (UNESCO 1957, p. 22).

Even when we treat literacy proportions as indicators, it is still desirable to eliminate children from the calculations of rates and to compare rates for the same age groups—preferably 10 and over or 15 and over. Underdeveloped countries frequently have a large proportion of their population under 10 years and cannot manage to teach even the minimum literacy skills until about that age. However, in some cases (see Table 1) it is necessary, for lack of more detailed information, to use the rates for age groups 5 and over, 9 and over, or 15 and over as *estimates* for the age group 10 and over.

Obviously, *illiteracy* rates for the total population, as well as for persons aged 5 and over, are higher than for any of the older age groups; in India, for example, the rate for the total population in 1951 was 83.4 per cent, whereas for the population aged 10 and over it was 80.1 per cent. The rates for the age groups 10 and over and 15 and over are usually quite close; for example, in 1948 in the Philippines the illiteracy rate for each of these age groups was about the same.

For detailed comparisons between two countries, age-group differences and other variations in enumeration results—as in the number of persons returned as "literacy status unknown" or "age status unknown"—must be carefully examined. When literacy proportions are used as indicators, these variations create problems only in rare cases.

Use of estimates. Since some countries have never taken censuses and others have not taken a census for many years, an appraisal of the world's literacy status at one time, 1950, must rely to some extent on estimates. The fact that estimates are used need not imply inaccuracy; some estimates are superior in accuracy to the average census. If, for example, the estimate is derived from reasonably accurate census returns on literacy or from valid statistical noncensus information, or from both, it may be quite reliable. For instance, on the basis of school enrollment information it was estimated that the illiteracy rate for Iraq in 1950 would be 85 per cent of the population aged 10 and over; the census returns for 1953 showed 89.1 per cent illiterate for the population aged 5 and over, or about 85 per cent for the population aged 10 and over.

China and Indonesia present perhaps the most difficult problems of estimating literacy rates. For China there are no national census figures on illiteracy available, and because of the paucity of other accurate information estimates range from 50–55 per cent illiterate for the population aged 15 and over (UNESCO 1957, pp. 16–17) to 70–75 per cent for the population aged 10 and over (Golden 1955, *passim*). The estimate for Indonesia also requires special comment. The census returns of 1930 gave Indonesia an illiteracy rate of 90 per cent for the population aged 10 and over; this figure is so high that it raises doubts about the official estimate of 39 per cent for the population aged 13 to 45 (United Nations 1963*c*, p. 15). Other estimates for Indonesia suggest an illiteracy level of 80–85 per cent for persons aged 15 and over (UNESCO 1957, p. 39) and 75–80 per cent for the population aged 10 and over (Golden 1955, *passim*). But despite such occasional anomalies and the general impossibility of absolute exactness, world-wide comparisons and analyses can most usefully be undertaken.

The meaning of literacy figures

The unequal distribution of literacy skills in the world stems from the fact that behind a given level of literacy lies the whole institutional structure of a society, particularly the occupational structure. Hence, the sharp contrasts in literacy levels between developed and underdeveloped countries (see Table 2) reflect the differential spread of industrialism through the world; the slighter differences among countries at about the same level of industrial development indicate other differences in the countries' institutional structure. Transition from illiteracy to literacy for a whole country is accompanied usually by differential rates of transition within the population. Literacy skills are acquired more readily by young adults than by the aged; by those aiming for skilled occupations for themselves or their children; and by those—such as city dwellers—who have relatively easy access to the means of learning. In general, then, throughout the transition some literacy differentials within countries are predictable.

Literacy and economic development. The close connection between the prevalence of literacy skills among the adult population of a society and the nature of the society's occupational skills has been demonstrated in several ways. In the first place, the invention of writing itself was clearly connected with other changes in human societies, such as increased occupational differentiation and the emergence of the first true cities. In general, the presence or absence of writing has been used as a criterion to distinguish between civilizations and tribal societies. Further, it should be emphasized that no country's adult population became *preponderantly* literate until after the industrial revolution. Statistically, the dissemination of literacy and the changes in the occupational structure in today's industrial nations are very closely linked; the coefficients of correlation for these time series are all above .9, where 1.0 would indicate perfect correspondence (UNESCO 1957, pp. 177 ff.; Golden 1955, p. 3). Indeed, not only is mass literacy a recent phenomenon in any society, but it is still confined to a relatively few countries. For 1950 literacy rates of the countries and territories of the world and indicators of the degree of industrial development correlated better than .8 on a scale, where 1.0 would have indicated perfect correspondence (Golden 1955, p. 3; United Nations 1961, p. 42).

The transformation from an illiterate to a literate society is triggered, so most authors suggest, by pressures exerted on governments, on special groups, and on individuals by the changing conditions accompanying industrialization. But it is not easily achieved; the transition usually has taken at least 75 years, though in some spectacular cases only about 50 years. Some societies have at times diverted large shares of their means toward the diffusion of literacy, and others, small shares; as a result, in 1950 literacy progress in some countries was advanced and in others retarded, as compared with industrial change. For example, in 1950 Brazil and Yugoslavia were about equally developed (if industrial development is measured by the proportion of the male labor force in nonagricultural pursuits), yet Brazil had an illiteracy rate of more than 50 per cent whereas Yugoslavia's rate was only about 25 per cent for the population aged 10 and over. This retardation or advance, so several authors have suggested, can prove to be a handicap or an asset for a country's future economic progress (Davis 1955; Golden 1955; Anderson & Bowman 1965). A government's assessment of its country's educational position requires not only a knowledge of the literacy level achieved but also an evaluation of the literacy position in relation to the level of economic development.

HILDA H. GOLDEN

[*See also* CAPITAL, HUMAN; EDUCATION; RURAL SOCIETY.]

BIBLIOGRAPHY

ABEL, JAMES F.; and BOND, NORMAN J. 1929 *Illiteracy in the Several Countries of the World.* Washington: Government Printing Office.

ANDERSON, C. ARNOLD; and BOWMAN, MARY J. (editors) 1965 *Education and Economic Development.* Chicago: Aldine.

DAVIS, KINGSLEY (1948) 1949 *Human Society.* New York: Macmillan. → See especially pages 595–617, "World Population in Transition."

DAVIS, KINGSLEY 1951*a* *The Population of India and Pakistan.* Princeton Univ. Press. → See especially pages 150–161, "Education, Language and Literacy."

DAVIS, KINGSLEY 1951*b* Population and the Further Spread of Industrial Society. American Philosophical Society, *Proceedings* 95:8–19.

DAVIS, KINGSLEY 1955 Social and Demographic Aspects of Economic Development in India. Pages 263–315 in Simon Kuznets, W. E. Moore, and J. J. Spengler (editors), *Economic Growth: Brazil, India, Japan.* Durham, N.C.: Duke Univ. Press.

Demographic Yearbook. → Issued annually by the United Nations since 1948. See especially the 1960 and 1964 volumes. Data in Table 1 extracted from *Demographic Yearbook* 1960, Copyright © United Nations 1961, are reproduced by permission.

GINSBURG, NORTON S. (editor) 1961 *Atlas of Economic Development.* Univ. of Chicago Press.

GOLDEN, HILDA H. 1955 Literacy and Social Change in Underdeveloped Countries. *Rural Sociology* 20:1–7.

HARBISON, FREDERICK; and MYERS, CHARLES A. 1964 *Education, Manpower, and Economic Growth.* New York: McGraw-Hill.

HAWKES, JACQUETTA; and WOOLLEY, LEONARD 1963 *Prehistory and the Beginnings of Civilization.* New York: Harper. → See especially Part 2, Chapter 6 on "Languages and Writing Systems: Education."

LORIMER, FRANK 1946 *The Population of the Soviet Union: History and Prospects.* Geneva: League of Nations. → See especially pages 79, 198–200.

MCCLELLAND, DAVID C. 1966 Does Education Accelerate Economic Growth? *Economic Development and Cultural Change* 24, no. 3:257–278.

RUSSETT, BRUCE et al. 1964 *World Handbook of Political and Social Indicators.* New Haven: Yale Univ. Press. → See especially pages 221–226.

SJOBERG, GIDEON 1960 *The Preindustrial City: Past and Present.* Glencoe, Ill.: Free Press. → See especially pages 285–320.

SULLIVAN, HELEN 1933 Literacy and Illiteracy. Volume 9, pages 511–523 in *Encyclopaedia of the Social Sciences.* New York: Macmillan.

UNESCO 1952 *Basic Facts and Figures.* Paris: UNESCO.

UNESCO 1953 *Progress of Literacy in Various Countries.* Paris: UNESCO.

UNESCO 1957 *World Illiteracy at Mid-century: A Statistical Study.* Paris: UNESCO.

UNESCO 1964 *Economic and Social Aspects of Educational Planning.* Paris: UNESCO.

UNITED NATIONS, DEPARTMENT OF ECONOMIC AND SOCIAL AFFAIRS 1961 *Report on the World Social Situation, 1961.* New York: United Nations.

UNITED NATIONS, DEPARTMENT OF ECONOMIC AND SOCIAL AFFAIRS 1963*a* *Report on the World Social Situation, 1963.* New York: United Nations.

UNITED NATIONS, ECONOMIC AND SOCIAL COUNCIL 1963*b* UNESCO World Campaign for Universal Literacy. Document E/3771. Unpublished manuscript.

UNITED NATIONS, STATISTICAL OFFICE 1963*c* *Compendium of Social Statistics: 1963.* Statistical Papers, Series K, No. 2. New York: United Nations.

WINSTON, SANFORD 1930 *Illiteracy in the United States.* Chapel Hill: Univ. of North Carolina Press.

WORLD CONGRESS OF MINISTERS OF EDUCATION ON THE ERADICATION OF ILLITERACY 1965 *Statistics of Illiteracy.* Paris: UNESCO.

LITERATURE

I
THE SOCIOLOGY OF LITERATURE

The sociological approach to literature is by no means an easy one. Like religion, sex, and art, literature is protected by taboos both numerous and powerful. To the cultured mind the study of the writer as a professional man, of the literary work as a means of communication, and of the reader as a consumer of cultural goods is vaguely sacrilegious.

Such a revulsion is all the more surprising, as the concept of literature first appeared to describe a sociocultural fact, not an aesthetic one. In Tertullian's Latin, as well as in eighteenth-century English or French, the word "literature" meant the distinctive culture of those who belonged to the social stratum of the *litterati*, "well-read people." It meant practically nothing else in Dr. Johnson's time and was still sporadically used in that sense as late as the end of the nineteenth century, notably by Sainte-Beuve and William Dean Howells.

Even when the Germans—particularly Lessing—evolved from their analysis of the written products of the human mind the objective notion of *Literatur* as the art of expressing one's thoughts in writing, on the one hand, and as the whole of the works thus produced and published in a definite community, on the other, they never separated the literary phenomenon from its social environment in time or space. For the group which gravitated around the brothers August Wilhelm and Friedrich von Schlegel and their pupil Madame de Staël, literature was, in fact as in value, strongly linked to, and even determined by, the two factors of *Zeitgeist*, "the spirit of the time," and *Volksgeist*, "the national spirit." Madame de Staël was among the first to use the French word *littérature* in the new sense, in her book *De la littérature considérée dans ses rapports avec les institutions sociales* (1800).

Such a clearly stated doctrine, which ultimately elicited Taine's positivist criticism, also stirred up a romantic reaction whose spokesmen individualized and even divinized what came to be called literary creation, while ignoring or denying the collective aspects of the literary phenomenon. Late romanticism established the still current notion of the divine solitude of the writer in the act of "creating." Alfred de Vigny was the prototype of the poet, throwing his poems into the anonymous crowd like a shipwrecked sailor entrusting a bottle carrying his message to the shoreless sea, or escaping the bondage of society by self-destruction.

In fact, social consciousness and a sense of solitude often coexisted in the literary attitude of the nineteenth century, but the contradiction between them was not obvious to the romantics, some of the greatest of whom—such as Byron and Hugo—were keenly aware of their moral solitude yet never ignored the strong ties which united them with society. Nevertheless, literary criticism more and more shifted its emphasis from a collective to an individual outlook. Carlyle, in 1840, did stress the effects of literary reputation on a writer, but his representation of the man of letters as a hero can be considered the turning point of the movement from presociological to psychological criticism. Although William Hazlitt, in the 1820s, tried to recapture the "spirit" of the great literary ages, Sainte-Beuve and after him Matthew Arnold, in the second half of the nineteenth century, strove to reconstruct the personality of writers as perceived through their works.

Meanwhile, in Germany the new science of philology had awakened an interest in form and style which eventually opened a new approach to literature through the aesthetic analysis of the work of art. In the early twentieth century, Wilhelm Dilthey concretized this tendency into a doctrine which gave birth to a strong antisociological current which reigned almost unchallenged in many countries under the various shapes of formalism, *Stilforschung*, and aesthetic structuralism. France, however, remained steadfastly committed to the historical positivism of Taine.

Early attempts

Sociology long avoided the difficult job of analyzing literature. When sociologists—most of them with a philosophical, not a literary turn of mind—touched on the subject, they included it in the wider categories of art, leisure, or communication, thus ignoring the specific characteristics of literature. Even Marx and Engels were extremely prudent in their handling of literary problems. Plekhanov, who was the first to offer a Marxist and a sociological theory of art (1899), did not treat literature satisfactorily.

There was a sociological tradition in Russian literary criticism. It was handed down from Belinski, a contemporary of Carlyle, through Pisarev, a contemporary of Taine, to the antiformalist critics of the Soviet era. But this "civic criticism," as it was called, merely rested on the assumption that a book must be judged by its revolutionary efficacy and by the degree of fidelity with which it represented historical reality. Most Marxists nowadays think this view much too simplistic to account for the complex nature of the literary phenomenon.

A true sociology of literature appeared only when literary critics and historians, starting from literature as a specific reality, tried to answer sociological questions by using current sociological methods. The difficulty was to formulate the questions. By the time an interest in sociology was awakened among literary specialists the habit had been formed of working on the writer as an individual or on the literary work as an isolated phenomenon but seldom on their relationship to the reading public.

As early as 1931 the German L. L. Schücking had tried to give an outline of a sociology of literary taste, but his attempt found little response. On the other hand, when the Hungarian György Lukács, after his conversion to a rather personal brand of Marxism, tried to base a method of critical analysis on a parallelism between the aesthetic patterns of the work of art and the contemporary economic structures of society, he certainly initiated a new type of sociological investigation in literary criticism (1961). The Lukácsian sociology of literature is widely followed in eastern and western Europe, particularly in France, where Lucien Goldmann may be said to have brought it to a high point of effectiveness (1950; 1964). It opened wide and numerous vistas on the social nature of literature, and no further studies on the subject can ignore it. Yet, although Lukács and his followers take into account society as the reality behind the appearances of literature, they still consider the work of art as an end in itself and neglect the part of the reader in literary communication. Indeed, they as much as ignore the very notion of literary communication.

Literary communication

Early sociological investigation in literature was stalemated by the antinomy between the ontological and phenomenological conceptions of literary criticism. Only when existentialism threw a new light on things was it possible to achieve a breakthrough. In that respect Jean-Paul Sartre's essay *What Is Literature?* (1948) may be considered a landmark. Sartre's idea, ostensibly very simple, was that the literary work—that is, the written product of the mind—only exists as such when it is read, since writing without reading is nonsense. An unread book is nothing but a handful of soiled paper. From this premise the inference is that the literary phenomenon cannot be the work of art itself, but rather the meeting and sometimes the clashing of two free acts, one of production and the other of consumption, with all their effects and side effects on moral and social relations. There is always another man in literature: a writer for a reader and a reader for a writer.

In fact, no fully satisfactory result may be obtained in investigating literature with sociological methods if one does not start from a clear idea of what in literary phenomena is fundamentally social.

There is danger in submitting the written product of the mind to purely aesthetic criteria. Although literature is an art, it is an impure one precisely because its main tools are language and writing. Whatever the aesthetic merits of a book may be, the sole fact that it is made up of words and letters—that is, of conventional symbols understood only in a given community, loaded with a semantic content and organized according to syntactic rules valid only for a definite body of population—provides it with an intellectual link to its society which far surpasses in strength if not in scope the links created by the purely sensuous, so-called language of art. The very nature of artistic values is thus inseparable from their actual or potential perception by a public. Instead of limiting the literary phenomenon to the isolated literary work, one should view it as an exchange between a writer and a reader through the medium of a book. Here again we find the familiar pattern of communication. But this pattern alone is insufficient for the needed sociological investigation.

As an instrument of communication the book does not work in a linear fashion. It does not go from one individual to another like a letter. The book appeared in the first millennium B.C., when new materials were found which were light enough to be carried about and smooth enough to allow quick and easy copying. However it is manufactured, a book is always defined by its two specific functions: multiplication and spatial dissemination of the written word. Although in some exceptional cases a book may have had only one reader, the mere fact that it *was* a book gave it an unlimited potential public. The writer may or may not imagine that public, which in turn may or may not be conscious of its own existence. We already know that the original notion of *litteratura* appeared in ancient Rome as a social characteristic when a highly educated reading public concentrated in a small area formed a community big enough to allow group consciousness. It fell into disuse at the beginning of the nineteenth century when many widely dispersed readers in all strata of society were unable to take stock of themselves as a community.

The literary milieu. Even in mass society the *litterati* of each ethnic, national, or social community still retain their group consciousness. Whether it is a motley and fast-changing *monde littéraire* as in France, a bright and sophisticated elite as in the United States, a pauperized intellectual aristocracy as in Spain, or a tight-knit union of writers or academy as in socialist countries, there is always a literary milieu in which ideas are exchanged, judgments passed, and values discussed.

The existence of such a milieu, the breeding ground of literary opinion, is and always has been inseparable from the very fact of literature. Other milieus are, of course, also touched by the literary work, but only the literary milieu has at its disposal the mental and verbal equipment, as well as the means of communication and expression, indispensable for fruitful and articulate intercourse.

In most cases the writer, who is also a reader, belongs to the literary milieu and takes part in the exchange of ideas and judgments. Even in the few cases when he lives apart from the literary world or belongs to an altogether different social set, he cannot escape being aware of the response of the literary milieu to his works and being influenced by it. Few writers are able to refrain from reading the reviews of their books, and those who do cannot ignore the reactions of their publishers, who in their turn are affected by literary opinion.

We are thus led to conceive of literature as a two-way communication in which an original message is broadcast by the writer to a community of readers, whose response to him takes the shape of thoughts, words, acts, and other messages, which react on one another and on the writer himself.

The pattern is made still more complicated by the fact that in normal circumstances many such messages are passed simultaneously to and fro and interfere with one another, while unsuspected readers or communities of readers beyond the social, educational, linguistic, or national borders may catch the message and unexpectedly add their own distortions to the jumble.

Last but not least, the literary milieu being part of a broader society and the writer being also a citizen, the whole network of literary intercourse is subject to all the conditions imposed by social life. In fact the amplitude, the significance, the richness—in short, the human worth—of literature depends to a large extent on the place occupied by the literary milieu and consequently by the writers in the society concerned, on their awareness of their situation, and on the assumption of the responsibilities implied by it. It was such a consideration which led Jean-Paul Sartre to make *engagement* the basis of all literary values.

Literary recognition and opinion

Since the writer exists as such only in the eyes of a reading community, the first problem to solve is that of recognition—that is, who is considered to be a writer by the reading public. The problem is easily understood from the following figures. If we count the names of all the writers retained by the historical memory of a given nation—that is, the writers mentioned in the histories of literature, the encyclopedias, the school or university curricula, the academic theses, the erudite articles published in specialized reviews, the papers read in symposia and congresses—we find that they represent about 1 per cent of the number who actually wrote and published literary books. (For example, in France between 1500 and 1900 about 1,000 out of 100,000 were remembered).

The severity of this elimination has been confirmed by the American psychologist Harvey C. Lehman, who conducted a poll among educated circles in the United States to find out which were the books of recognized importance. Out of the 733 "best books" by 488 authors named, Lehman found 337 books by 203 deceased authors and 396 books by 285 living authors (Lehman 1937). Many similar experiments have been conducted, and they all point to the fact that the historical image of literature in a given community includes a roughly equal number of contemporary and past writers. This means that the production of the more than 30 years which may be considered contemporary balances what remains of the production of several centuries. Furthermore, according to the findings of the Centre de Sociologie des Faits Littéraires in Bordeaux, France, 90 per cent of the books are eliminated after 1 year and 99 per cent after 20 years. Similar conclusions may be reached through a study of reprints (Schulz [1952] 1960, pp. 104–105).

How, by whom, and according to what criteria is the selection made? A certain amount of contemporary literary recognition is of course necessary. In spite of persistent legends, no book was ever reclaimed after *total* failure at its first appearance. Yet, immediate success is by no means a guarantee of survival. A best seller may be forgotten within a year and a low-sale book remembered for centuries. The picture of a given literature revealed by the contemporary comments of past critics is quite different from the historical picture later presented at school; all students of literature have been told time and again of the instances of "bad taste" displayed by their forefathers.

Education plays an important part in the selection. For example, a survey of French army recruits (Institut . . . 1966) showed that the type of education determines the choice of "noteworthy" authors. French elementary education, with its republican and rationalistic traditions, strongly stresses the eighteenth century, while high school education, with its more bourgeois and conservative leanings, gives the seventeenth century a predominant position. In all cases the number of contemporary and past writers is fairly equal. However, the choices of the recruits with a low educational level were largely stereotyped: their choice of past authors reflected school memories; their choice of present authors bore the stamp of modern mass media. In contrast the choices of the university students were widely differentiated. Moreover, the higher the level of education, the narrower the chronological gap between past and contemporary authors. While in the case of nearly illiterate recruits there may be a "no man's land" of fifty years between the last of the deceased and the first of the living authors, in the case of highly educated recruits there is no gap, but rather a continuously increasing number of choices.

The opinion-leading group is not simply defined by education and social status; age is also important. Lehman (1945) showed that 40 is a critical age for the literary survival of a writer: works published after a writer reaches 40 are more easily forgotten than those published before. The reason is that most writers are recognized as such between the ages of 20 and 30 by readers belonging to a similar age group. This is the average recognition age for novelists. It may come earlier for lyric poets, and it always comes later for philosophers, a fact which leads to the delusion that poets are short-lived and philosophers hard to kill. In any case a writer seldom changes the clientele which ensured his initial success. The age group which first recognized him carries him along his career and offers him a support in literary opinion until shortly after the group reaches 40, and its influence is superseded by that of younger and more numerous readers. Therefore, about fifteen years after recognition all writers have an appointment with oblivion unless, as sometimes happens, they are taken up by the new opinion leaders and start a career afresh.

Another element which determines the composition of the opinion-leading group is the existence of social and political structures that limit literary exchange. Social stratification is a permanent structure of this type. A society in which the bulk of production is regulated by the demands of a moneyed minority is characterized by a very narrow opinion-leading group, which imposes its taste in wholesale fashion on the masses. The phenomenon is less perceptible in literature than in *haute couture* or in gastronomy, for instance, because reading is a more serious occupation than designing clothing or preparing food and the hold of the higher classes on it is less strong. But the moneyed minority delegates its powers to the hybrid stratum of the intellectuals who in fact belong to the working class but live—at least culturally—on the same level as the wealthy.

Class structure and political structure are, of course, strongly linked to one another, and the state imposes even more demanding limits on literary exchange than does the stratification system. A calculation based on the average age of writers in France (Escarpit 1965, pp. 27–29) shows that the rhythm of the literary generations (Peyre 1948) is determined by the succession of the various regimes in that country. Great reigns like that of Louis XIV in France or Elizabeth I or Victoria in Great Britain and new political eras like those which began in 1792 for France, in 1865 for the United States, and in 1871 for Germany are always marked by the establishment of a powerful and comparatively young (25 to 35) team of writers. This team expresses the national literature and blocks the way to fresh recognitions until it in turn is eliminated by age or by a new historical change.

Political influence is also exerted through the existence of national borders, which partition literary life by erecting various obstacles to the free flow of books. However, a customs barrier, although its role must not be minimized, seems nowadays to be one of the least insurmountable obstacles. Furthermore, national markets tend to expand, and some countries like the Netherlands have a foreign book market quite disproportionate to their actual literary production: in 1961 it was equal to that of France or West Germany. Yet even internationally we find an opinion-leading minority based on economic power. The United Kingdom and the United States, with their huge industrial and financial machines and their almost universal language, account for nearly two-thirds of the Western book market. On the other hand, they import few books and translate still fewer, being practically self-sufficient (Escarpit 1965).

For most other countries language is a more effective barrier than customs. The 1,200 million potential readers in the world (probably no more than 200 to 300 million of whom are habitual readers) are distributed in more than a hundred linguistic enclosures. Yet five languages (English, Russian, Spanish, German, and French) account for 75 per cent of the world book production and 40 per cent of the readers. All the other language units suffer either from a scarcity of readers or from a scarcity of writers (the case of Communist China is passed over for want of verified data). Translation in its present form and organization is not adequate to remedy this disparity, since much fewer than 10 per cent of the books published in the world are translated into another language and nearly 75 per cent of these come from English, Russian, French, and German.

In sum, the minority responsible for the literary recognition of writers and for the elaboration of literary opinion can be defined as the university-educated intellectuals belonging to the influential circles (moneyed class, "upper crust," high political or technical strata) of the five highly developed economic powers with an important mass of population and a widely spread language: the United States, the United Kingdom, the Soviet Union, Germany, and France—a bare ten or fifteen million people.

Literature in mass civilization

The above may seem a pessimistic view and a difficult one to reconcile with contemporary mass culture.

The problem is not really new even if its dimensions are. Several times in the history of written culture the book, as well as the literature it spread, went through sudden mutations, under the pressure of fresh masses of readers. With the spread of Christian culture, the book evolved from the connoisseurs' *volumen* of ancient Rome to the easily handled *codex*; then to the hand-printed book when a comparatively well-educated urban upper class enjoyed enough leisure to afford the already flourishing bookseller a commercially workable field; then to the machine-printed hardbound volume of the nineteenth century, when the triumph of the bourgeoisie and the establishment of the capitalist system allowed the creation of an actual market for cultural productions; and finally, in our own time, to the paperback.

The scale of readership changed from the hundred to the thousand, from the hundred thousand to the million. But the change was qualitative as well as quantitative. At each stage, the form of the book met the specific demand of the leading minority and was conceived for one definite type of literature. All the rest—that is, the actual cultural material consumed by the masses of people—was considered as despicable subliterature until the pressure of social changes brought about a shift in the opinion-leading group. This shift was both cause and effect of each technical mutation of the book and led to total revisions of literary values.

In the eyes of the Latin-reading clerk of the Middle Ages the chivalric tales written in the vulgar Romance language (hence the word "romance") were frivolous and meaningless subliterature, but those tales were transformed into legitimate, even noble, literature when printing shifted the responsibility of literary opinion to the urban upper class. The same happened to the novel; despised as "female reading" at the beginning of the eighteenth century, it became the absolute sovereign of literature in the nineteenth, when mechanized printing allowed editions of 100,000 copies for the triumphant middle class, as against the average 2,000 or 3,000 copies of the previous century.

Marginal reading material for the consumption of the masses has always existed side by side with official literature. Long made up of broadsheets, almanacs, and chapbooks disseminated by itinerant storytellers and hawkers, it now takes the shape of illustrated magazines, comics, and photonovels. This literature must not be underestimated, since great works originate in it when it is accepted by the officialdom of a new literary milieu, but it lacks the essential of literary communication: the feedback from the reader to the writer through the medium of the literary milieu.

This feedback is normally ensured not only by the diffuse crosscurrents existing in the literary milieu but by a network of specific institutions, among which literary criticism and book selling are predominant.

There is no such thing as literary criticism for popular literature like comics now or chapbooks in past centuries. Even when the popular paperbacks are devoted to the publication of recognized works the professional critics hesitate to review them, a fact often lamented by publishers. The literary critic serves less as a guide than as a voice of the cultured public's taste. He is, so to speak, a sample of the literary milieu. His judgments may reflect a great variety of aesthetic, political, or religious opinions, but they all bear testimony to a particular culture and way of life.

In the case of the bookseller one must distinguish the real bookshops, characterized by an autonomous commercial policy based principally on the sale of books, from the mere book outlets, exercising little or no responsibility in the choice of literary goods offered for sale. These outlets may range from newspaper stands to specialized departments in general or chain stores or even huge "book cafeterias."

The part played by the true bookseller in literary communication is an important one. He has to make a responsible choice from the overwhelming literary production. The wrong choices could dangerously burden his stock and clutter up his window, since after one year 90 per cent of what is produced is unsalable. The choices he makes for his stock are influenced by his current sales to all kinds of occasional customers, but those he makes for his window reflect the cultural image that his opinion-leading clientele has of itself. The greater the discrepancy between the composition of the stock and the contents of the window, the higher the efficiency of the bookseller as an intermediary in literary communication, but the narrower his field of influence (Escarpit & Robine 1963).

At ordinary points of sale there is practically no difference between the stock and the window, and the salesman transmits no response from the people who buy reading material in his shop. Such is the case in most places where books are sold. Surveys on the topography of book distribution show that bookshops selling quality books in a responsible way are concentrated in districts of the cities which are rarely visited by working people, at least during business hours.

A commercial policy in the majority of sales points cannot therefore be based on an awareness of the readers' reactions. Books are sold like any other industrial product. Their contents, as well as their presentations, are elaborated according to proved specifications—some of them age-old—

simply enhanced or glamorized by modern techniques. Analysis shows that the difference between the almanacs of past centuries and contemporary magazines lies mainly in language, paper, printing, color, and advertising; the contents—a mixture of horoscopes, amusements, sentimental stories, and recipes—are practically unchanged.

The publisher of mass-circulation books is thus confronted with a difficult problem. "Creative" publishing demands that he make numerous and necessarily hazardous experiments, offering the output of new talents to a responsive public. Yet he must, in view of the substantial capital involved, reduce the risks of his operation either by limiting the experimental field to the cultured elite or by abandoning the idea of "creative" publishing and strictly programming his production—that is, making it conform to the functional needs of a preselected mass market.

The latter solution leads to the exclusive publication either of semitechnical works like cookbooks and "do-it-yourself" manuals or of stereotyped reading matter ranging from the lowest kind of subliterature—comics, photonovels—to mechanically produced biographies and historical novels based on standard popular themes.

The former solution may seem more constructive, but it has a twofold drawback. The stock of time-proved classics to be reprinted is not inexhaustible—a few thousand at most—and the supply of contemporary best sellers that can be successfully tried out in the cultured network is very limited. Furthermore, these best sellers have been recognized as such by a public socially and culturally different from the mass public, and this leads to an imposition of literary values from without; a situation quite contrary to a real literary exchange. Such a "bestowed" literature is doomed either to intellectual sclerosis or to the paralyzing conventionality of officialdom.

The mass-distribution book (paperback, *livre de poche*, *Taschenbuch*, etc.) affords the technical means of a fresh mutation of the book as a means of cultural communication. Based on a combination of mass production and industrial design, it makes possible a substantial reduction of price, combined with a convenient size, a pleasant appearance, and quality contents. The principle was first successfully applied by Allen Lane when, in 1935, he founded the British Penguin series. During World War II the need to supply the widely scattered Allied forces with handy and cheap reading material accelerated the diffusion of the paperback, which by 1950 had spread all over the world, upsetting the traditional patterns of publishing. In the United States the revolution was particularly spectacular. In the 1940s a sale of over 100,000 copies for a single title was considered exceptional, while twenty years later several paperbacks sold well over a million copies a year.

Yet the paperback is nothing but a tool. It cannot solve all problems, and indeed it may raise some fresh ones. As a tool, it is useless and might even become dangerous unless attention is paid to the reactions and needs of the reading public.

The sociology of reading

No sociology of literature is therefore possible without a sociology of reading and of cultural consumption in general. Much has been done in that direction since Schücking's pioneer work on the sociology of literary taste. Such men as R. D. Altick (1957) opened the way to a historical field of investigation which is now widely explored. On the other hand, methods for the study of reading, *in vivo* so to speak, were borrowed from economics by P. Meyer-Dohm (1957) and from the sociology of leisure by J. Dumazedier and J. Hassenforder (1963).

Although the consumption of drama is quite different from that of the book, John Lough's studies of early theater audiences (1957) and J. Duvignaud's later and more complete work (1965) are also relevant to the sociology of reading.

The main obstacle to a sociology of reading is that, unlike a theater audience, a reading public is not easily defined. One must not mistake the various social circles concerned about literary work for the mass of actual readers, whose size, composition, coherence, and group consciousness vary with each book.

Any writer, consciously or not, addresses prospective readers when he writes; any publisher directs his publication toward an expected public when he plans the manufacture and distribution of the volume; both the writer and the publisher more or less belong to a milieu of possible readers. Each of those publics plays an essential part in the birth and life of the literary work, although few or none of its members may ever read it. There are, of course, instances of books written for a hundred readers and published in a comparatively narrow milieu of a few thousand persons but ultimately read by millions; however, the opposite case is much more common.

The cases of books reaching unexpected and even unsuspected publics beyond social, national, linguistic, or temporal barriers are becoming more numerous. Of course there must always be an environment of contemporary readers to accept a book at the outset, but even though the existence of such an environment is indispensable, its size and composition may have nothing to do with those of the wider or later groups which will ultimately ensure the success of the book. Indeed, in most cases the later success of a book is due to causes quite foreign to those of the initial success. While the set of readers which was first responsible for the literary recognition of the work shared the historical and cultural experiences of the writer, spoke the same language, and thought according to similar patterns, groups which have no direct contact with the writer's world have no other recourse than to substitute their own keys for the original ones in order to decode the text which is handed down to them.

In fact, reading any work outside the immediate social or historical vicinity of the writer—and a fortiori reading it in translation—implies a betrayal of the writer's intentions, since absolute fidelity would imply a complete reconstruction of the writer's psychological and social environment, a condition which may be partly and painstakingly fulfilled by scholars, but which is in no way compatible with current literary reading.

We must then admit that a literary work, insofar as it survives its time, is permanently reinterpreted and redigested by various groups of readers. Those synchronic or diachronic layers of meaning which are added to it together form its true historical personality. The literary death of a book occurs when no further interpretation or misinterpretation of it can be given. We are thus led to consider "creative treason" as one of the main keys to the literary phenomenon (Escarpit 1961). By "creative treason" we mean an unconscious or deliberate misconstruction of the author's actual intentions when he wrote the book. This reinterpretation may bring out a latent significance of the work of which the author himself may not have been aware or add an unsuspected meaning that can even replace the original one. The most typical examples are Swift's *Gulliver's Travels* and Defoe's *Robinson Crusoe*, which were originally intended as serious works, with a philosophical message, and are now widely read as children's books.

Obviously many books which had a tremendous but short-lived and localized success were never "betrayed" and died soon. Others, in contrast, starting from a comparatively narrow acceptance, continued for centuries to call up wider, deeper, and stronger responses. The question may be raised whether the likelihood of being betrayed is due to some specific quality of the work and not the audience. Such a surmise is quite plausible and points to one of the ways in which the sociology of literature might help to found a system of literary values.

Such an objective is still beyond our grasp. We can for the time being only strive toward it along three lines of investigation. The first consists in studying the material conditions of reading so that its place in everyday life is clearly defined. According to the periods considered this may be done by historians or by sociologists. Applied to our time such a study may reveal the relationship of reading to the various forms of mass communication and cultural consumption like cinema, radio, television, records, etc. Another approach, mainly psychological or sociopsychological, tends to identify the various motivations and attitudes of readers according to sex, age, occupation, educational level, social class, IQ, etc. Typical patterns of behavior may thus be traced and linked to the factors that influence them. The third approach is through the study of the language of literary appreciation. A project for an international dictionary of literary terms was begun in 1962 by the International Comparative Literature Association. An effort is also being made—particularly in Bordeaux—to investigate the aesthetic vocabulary used by readers of the working class, in order to grasp the mechanism of literary appreciation among readers whose literary opinion is seldom voiced.

The aims and applications of the sociology of literature thus become clearer. Applied to past periods it may help to evolve a new type of historical criticism more directly linked to economic and social history than traditional formal criticism has been. Sociological criticism will never reveal the intimate nature of literary "creation" or supply a universal and eternal criterion of "beauty," but in spite of often stated ambitions, no criticism of any kind ever did or ever will.

More important still, the sociology of literature applied to contemporary problems may, on the one hand, help the persons or agencies responsible for book policy in the various regions of the world to take stock of the new problems raised by mass civilization and may, on the other hand, help the hitherto ignored masses of readers to gain aesthetic consciousness and claim their part of mankind's cultural heritage. It may ruffle a number of connoisseurs, comfortable in their minority culture, who would prefer to ignore what happens beyond their narrow intellectual circle. It may disturb more seriously and even revolt a number of writers who never wondered whence and whither the wind that blows through them. But no true lover of culture—

reader, critic, or writer—will suffer, in the long run, from a clear-sighted awareness of social realities.

ROBERT ESCARPIT

[*See also* COMMUNICATION, MASS; CREATIVITY; DRAMA; INTELLECTUALS; INTERACTION, *article on* DRAMATISM; SOCIAL SCIENCE FICTION; *and the biography of* LUKÁCS. *A guide to other relevant material may be found under* ART.]

BIBLIOGRAPHY

ALTICK, RICHARD D. 1957 *The English Common Reader: A Social History of the Mass Reading Public, 1800–1900.* Univ. of Chicago Press.

DUMAZEDIER, JOFFRE; and HASSENFORDER, JEAN 1963 *Éléments pour une sociologie comparée de la production, de la diffusion et de l'utilisation du livre.* Paris: Bibliographie de la France.

DUVIGNAUD, JEAN 1965 *Sociologie du théâtre.* Paris: Presses Universitaires de France.

ESCARPIT, ROBERT C. E. G. (1958) 1965 *Sociology of Literature.* Painesville, Ohio: Lake Erie College Press. → First published in French.

ESCARPIT, ROBERT C. E. G. 1961 "Creative Treason" as a Key to Literature. *Yearbook of Comparative and General Literature* 10:16–21.

ESCARPIT, ROBERT C. E. G. 1963 L'acte littéraire est-il un acte de communication? *Filološki pregled* (Belgrade) 1/2:17–21.

ESCARPIT, ROBERT C. E. G. (1965) 1966 *The Book Revolution.* Rev. ed. Paris: UNESCO; London: Harrap. → First published in French.

ESCARPIT, ROBERT C. E. G.; and ROBINE, NICOLE 1963 *Atlas de la lecture à Bordeaux.* Université de Bordeaux, Faculté des Lettres et Sciences Humaines, Centre de Sociologie des Faits Littéraires, Publications. Bordeaux: La Faculté.

GOLDMANN, LUCIEN 1950 Matérialisme dialectique et histoire de la littérature. *Revue de métaphysique et de morale* 55:283–301.

GOLDMANN, LUCIEN 1964 *Pour une sociologie du roman.* Paris: Gallimard.

HOGGART, RICHARD 1966 Literature and Society. *American Scholar* 35:277–289.

INSTITUT DE LITTÉRATURE ET DE TECHNIQUES ARTISTIQUES DE MASSE, UNIVERSITÉ DE BORDEAUX 1966 *Le livre et le conscrit: Les jeunes recrues devant la lecture.* → A survey of the reading habits of the recruits conducted by R. Escarpit and N. Robine at the Army Induction Center at Limoges.

LEHMAN, HARVEY C. 1937 The Creative Years: "Best Books." *Scientific Monthly* 45:65–75.

LEHMAN, HARVEY C. 1945 "Intellectual" Versus "Physical" Peak Performance: The Age Factor. *Scientific Monthly* 61:127–137.

LOUGH, JOHN 1957 *Paris Theatre Audiences in the 17th and 18th Centuries.* Oxford Univ. Press.

LUKÁCS, GYÖRGY 1961 *Schriften zur Literatursoziologie.* Edited by Peter Ludz. Berlin: Luchterhand.

MEYER-DOHM, PETER 1957 *Der westdeutsche Büchermarkt.* Stuttgart: Fischer.

PEYRE, HENRI 1948 *Les générations littéraires.* Paris: Boivin.

PICHOIS, CLAUDE 1961 En marge de l'histoire littéraire: Vers une sociologie historique des faits littéraires. *Revue d'histoire littéraire de la France* 61:48–57.

PLEKHANOV, GEORGII V. (1899) 1953 *Art and Social Life.* London: Lawrence & Wishart. → A collection of Plekhanov's principal writings on art and society. First published in Russian.

SARTRE, JEAN-PAUL (1948) 1949 *What Is Literature?* New York: Philosophical Library. → First published in French.

SCHÜCKING, LEVIN L. (1931) 1950 *The Sociology of Literary Taste.* London: Routledge. → First published in German.

SCHULZ, HANS FERDINAND (1952) 1960 *Das Schicksal der Bücher und der Buchhandel: System einer Vertriebskunde des Buches.* 2d ed., rev. & enl. Berlin: Gruyter.

STAËL-HOLSTEIN, GERMAINE DE (1800) 1959 *De la littérature considérée dans ses rapports avec les institutions sociales.* Edited by Paul van Tieghem. Geneva: Droz.

II
THE PSYCHOLOGY OF LITERATURE

The psychology of literature is an emerging, rather than an established, discipline. We can distinguish three aspects or stages in its development, although these are not sharply defined. First is the insertion of psychological questions and theories into the predominantly aesthetic or historical writing of students of literature. Second is the writing of psychologists who seek to explain and interpret literary works by means of theories and techniques developed in other contexts. Third is the psychological analysis of literature by those who try to adjust their method to the peculiar nature of the subject matter and who hope to make discoveries rather than to impose stock explanations. The present article, inevitably narrow in scope, will be organized loosely around these categories in an effort to sample the writings of the contemporary period.

As one of the most distinctive of human activities, literature would seem to be a natural focus of psychological inquiry. How it is produced, how it affects those who enjoy it, what it reveals concerning the author and his society—these are questions that have occupied major thinkers from early times. Psychology of literature is referred to in standard works on literary criticism, and a recent bibliography of the field lists thousands of relevant titles (Kiell 1963). Yet textbooks of psychology rarely mention either literature or psychology of literature. The paradox is partly explained by the positivistic restrictions of psychology and partly by the elusiveness of literature when approached by science.

Nature of literature. Some conception of literature necessarily precedes scientific study of it. Permanent material documents do exist that can be called repositories of literature, but these documents are simply a modern device for bringing author and reader together in the literary transaction. At an earlier time, essentially the same transaction took place by oral means, aided by gestures and pantomime and often by instrumental music, and nothing was stored in documents. Human memory and capacity for improvisation sufficed. The modern reader is a step removed from the early pantomime, but only a step. He can still turn the written words into spoken ones, and, if he is artistically sensitive, he is likely to do so. He can also, to some extent, experience the various kinds of imagery intended by the words, and, through the sound and imagery and temporal structure of the composition, participate in moods, attitudes, and values that may have acted as initiating and sustaining forces for the author. According to this view, literature is a process of expression by an author which induces a corresponding process of reception in a reader. The process in the reader is not necessarily equivalent to the process in the author, but it is such as to bind him to the author. Literature exists in that union. The author can, of course, be his own reader. This circular transaction, however, is typically not enough; the impulse of authorship moves toward communication.

Imperfect as this characterization of literature is, a scientific approach must be regulated by some such reflections; and since it appears that the literary process requires the scientific observer to be an intimate part of what he observes, it is evident that the methodological problem is grave.

Psychology in general discourse

The bulk of literary criticism falls in the first of the three categories mentioned above. Much of it does not pretend to be psychological. Some of it, however, consciously employs psychological language and theory to dress up, supplement, or govern the critical discussion. Rare are those works that are deeply imbued with psychology and are still, in the main, appreciative. An example is Bodkin's *Archetypal Patterns in Poetry* (1934). Exploring literature from a Jungian base, this book seeks to locate the meeting ground of author and reader in the universal symbols of the collective unconscious. The theory is not merely decorative; it controls the analysis throughout, although it is in turn controlled by mature literary taste.

The creative process. Lowes, in *The Road to Xanadu* (1927), an examination of Coleridge's vast reading as it contributed to the composition of his poetry, is more concerned with the author's part. The thesis that Lowes favors is that the poetic imagination is a variant of ordinary imagination, depending on the accumulation of miscellaneous images, the mingling and transformation of these in "the deep well of unconscious cerebration" (Henry James), their recovery in consciousness at the prompting of some stimulus, and their utilization in expression. Lowes's psychology is mainly British associationism. From Coleridge he draws such psychological phrases as "twilight realms of consciousness," "state of nascent existence in the twilight of imagination and just on the vestibule of consciousness," and "the streamy nature of associations, which thinking curbs and rudders." To this source of insight Lowes adds introspections of his own on dream and fantasy, and he acknowledges from personal experience that literary erudition and subliminal associative activity are not enough to produce a masterpiece of poetry. He does not explain the needed additional factor, but he refers to it under the terms "vision" and "will."

Lowes is not quite faithful to the author he admires. He reduces Coleridge's fundamental distinction between imagination and fancy to a mere intensity difference in the imaginative energy and ignores the distinction between primary and secondary imagination. For Coleridge, imagination is creative and esemplastic, making and shaping into organic unity, while fancy can only join together mechanically what imagination supplies. Fancy is thus removed some distance from the living I AM, "of imagination all compact," which stands at the source of all created things, whether universe (primary imagination) or poem (secondary). By the phrase "I AM" Coleridge designates the ultimate principle of God or the human soul. As the I AM of God creates the world, so the I AM of the human soul creates poetry. The poet's creative activity, "This light, this glory, this fair luminous mist, / This beautiful and beauty-making power," to use the words of his ode on "Dejection," is essentially joy, the joy of the soul in its own life. Coleridge's distinctions and the terms in which he makes them are the reaction of a poet to the inadequacy of Hartleian associationism for explaining poetry. In dwelling on association, Lowes, from Coleridge's point of view, would be regressing. From our point of view, Lowes may be seen as moving toward the new "associationism" of Freud, who has equally little room for the Coleridgean I AM but must agree with him that association depends more on recurring similar states of feeling than on ideas (Richards 1934, p. 68 in 1960 edition).

Poetry and dream. In agreement with Coleridge and Freud on the importance of feeling is Prescott, whose *The Poetic Mind* (1922) is an expansion of his earlier essays on the connection between poetry and dream. Prescott's agreement with Freud must not be overstressed. Like Freud he invokes the unconscious; distinguishes two modes of thought (practical and dreaming); closely identifies poetry with dream; emphasizes unfulfilled desire as the motive for both; makes use of the ideas of condensation, displacement, and projection; and otherwise shows an appreciation of Freudian principles. But, on the other hand, Prescott traces these principles to earlier sources, warns against the sterility of psychological science rigorously applied to literature, and takes particular exception to Freud's basic assumption that there is a latent dream content behind the manifest dream. For Prescott both literature and dream are direct, not cryptogrammic, expressions of the mind. He specifically compares poetic creation to sexual generation or the divine genesis of the universe.

Especially in his chapter on the formation of imaginary characters Prescott emphasizes the power of the mind to create. Fictional characters are held to be autogenous objectifications of the mind's tendencies. Although there are also exogenous characters, these exist in the literary composition because of their congruency with the author's desires. Prescott's emphasis has some relation to Coleridge's theory of the primacy of the I AM. That is, Prescott regards poetic creation as more than the concatenation and blending of ideas, whether in the Hartleian or the Freudian style—which would be what Coleridge calls "fancy"; it involves the vital participation of a real being, even to the extent of passing on to fictional characters a portion of real life. Thus it can happen that "the author divides himself to form characters" (Prescott 1922, p. 201 in 1959 edition).

Author types. One of Prescott's examples for the proposition that an author becomes divided into quasi-independent imaginary characters is the French dramatist François de Curel, studied by Binet. Unfortunately, Prescott does not consider Binet's later study of Paul Hervieu and his further reflections on this problem (Binet 1904).

Binet studied a number of contemporary authors by personal interview, including some formal testing, and by analysis of their lives and works. He attempted to sum up his impressions of the creative process by invoking two opposed mental forces, "imagination" and "critical function," the former tending to embody itself in more or less autonomous personal beings, the latter tending to inhibit or suppress this process. He put authors in three classes with respect to the relative strength of these tendencies. There are those like de Curel, in whom the critical function is suspended during the period of creative activity and the imagination-produced characters use the writer as an amanuensis or sort of trance medium. There are those like Victorien Sardou, in whom the opposition between the two mental forces continues, but the critical function itself becomes one or more of the autonomous persons, participating in the dramatic dialogue with other persons more charged with the imaginative force. (Perhaps, to use a modern analogy, the case would be like that of a social psychologist serving as a "participant–observer" in some passionate social organization and using the opportunity to undermine the fully engaged members.) Finally, there are those like Hervieu, in whom the critical function remains in control so completely that the imaginary characters never achieve full autonomy, being themselves rather the puppets through which the voice of the master speaks. In all three types, however, according to Binet, the literary work reveals the personality of the producer.

Psychoanalytic explanation

As is evident from the preceding discussion, the psychoanalytic influence has been felt everywhere in the study of literature. A varied collection of essays showing this influence at its best has been edited by Phillips (1957). Yet, as the first shock of Freud's innovations has worn off, it has become apparent that the general theory of an emotional, orectic, unconscious origin of literature was not new and that the distinctive psychoanalytic explanatory apparatus—the Oedipus complex, polymorphous-perverse infantile sexuality, the devious dream work—as employed in the interpretation of individual literary works and their authors has yielded dubious results. Long before Freud, Dowden was explicitly pursuing the aim of deducing Shakespeare's personality from his dramas (1875). The psychoanalytic studies in this genre, in comparison, often seem less judicious. Probably the best is the Ernest Jones study, *Hamlet and Oedipus* (1949), which soberly develops the idea proposed by Freud that Hamlet and his creator could be explained by the Oedipus complex.

The seeming arbitrariness of psychoanalytic explanation stems from Freud's theory of the dream (1900), and, by extension, of literature. The dream is supposed to be a coded message from the unconscious. The code consists of certain stereotyped, universal symbols, plus many individual symbols produced by very complex dreamwork. These individual symbols cannot be decoded accurately without the aid of the dreamer's free associations. It is a technical fault that in the application of psychoanalysis to literature this theoretical point has often been overlooked, the author's literary "dream" being decoded without benefit of the required associations. But there are other reasons for distrust. For one thing, the Freudian approach at times has an uncomfortable resemblance to the cryptographic approach of the Baconians searching through the plays of Shakespeare for hidden evidence that their candidate, Francis Bacon (Lord Verulam), was the real author.

A more general reason is that literature seems in its basic constitution the very opposite of a cryptogram. Authors on the whole strive to express, not to conceal. It is true, no doubt, that a great literary work is thick with meaning, layer upon layer, and that some layers are more sharply articulated than others; but authors are aware of this and welcome the depth of meaning, in exactly the spirit of an orator who is glad for his voice to take on tremors and intonations that do not seem to be called for by the logic of his argument or the matter-of-factness of his vocabulary. The richness and subtlety of a literary work may elude an ordinary reader, but it is doubtful that such deficiency in sensitivity is to be repaired by imputing conscious or unconscious concealment to the author.

These strictures are not meant to disparage the merit of psychoanalysis as a vivifying influence on the study of literature. Recognition of the depth of literature and its relevance to the concerns of the psychiatrist (and vice versa) cannot be regarded as mistaken. Furthermore, the expansion of outlook engendered by psychoanalysis holds much promise for the future. Too huge for consideration here, but an illustration of the promise, is Jung's study of the Miller fantasies in *Symbols of Transformation* (1912).

Studies concerned with method

Imagery analysis. To those who value simple and sharable method, the pioneer work of Spurgeon in *Shakespeare's Imagery* makes an instant appeal (1935). Definition of an image is difficult, but there can be practical agreement, she thinks, about these "word-pictures" in similes and metaphors, whether contained in a single word (as in "*ripeness* is all") or spread over a considerable portion of a dramatic scene. Once collected, the images can be classified and counted for the sake of answering various kinds of questions. Thus, she demonstrates that Shakespeare's imagery differs from Marlowe's and Bacon's; and she attempts to draw conclusions as to Shakespeare's favorite haunts (for example, gardens), particular experiences (for example, noticing an eddy in the Avon below the eighteenth arch of the Old Clopton Bridge), and general character. Undoubtedly, at times she pushes inference too far. For example, from Shakespeare's many references to blushing and other quick emotional changes in fair-skinned faces she concludes that his own face was fair-skinned and of a fresh color. It is questionable whether we have, or can have, principles that fully justify such an argument.

Armstrong has extended Spurgeon's method to the study of image clusters in *Shakespeare's Imagination* (1946). For example, he finds that the images clustering around the goose symbol in many of the plays commonly refer to disease and penal restraint, and somewhat less commonly to music, bitterness, and seasoning. Several such image clusters are studied in detail. There seems to be no doubt that certain images tended to cohere in groups in the dramatist's mind, so strongly indeed that the almost inevitable concatenation often results in surprising turns of thought. Armstrong presses his analysis into (1) hidden images and (2) submerged themes. By the first he means the unspoken image latent in a spoken one (as when reference to wax points to the legend of Icarus); by the second, the adumbration of an understory by the images used in telling the obvious one (as when the Hostess in *Henry IV*, Part II, charges Falstaff with unfaithfulness in terms suggesting the Passion of Christ and the betrayal by Judas). Here he touches on an aspect of method which can hardly be reduced to simple counting and cataloguing. The manifold allusiveness of literature makes for a "thickness" which contrasts with the "thinness" of scientific writing. It is this "thickness" which especially baffles the search for perfectly mechanical procedures. Although Armstrong is convincing at this deeper level of analysis, he does not prescribe the conditions that enable him to be. One condition is obviously possession of the right knowledge, for example, knowledge of the New Testament. Other conditions may be inherently less definable, such as that vague but real thing, literary sensitivity.

Armstrong attempts to state some of the organizing principles of Shakespeare's thought and advances a general theory of imagination. With regard to Shakespeare, he infers that a primitive dualism of the warring opposites of life and death, love and hatred, governs the associations; that the extremely free, rapid, fluent associative activity leads to extraordinary combinations but without loss of organic unity; and that, although the surface of the dramas is relatively bare of religious reference, the depths are often permeated with imagery that gives religious quality to the whole. With regard to imagination in general, he accepts Freud's scheme of unconscious energies working up from a primitive level through a preconscious censorship to produce conscious elements, but he wishes to add to this a reverse direction of work to explain literary creation. He argues that the creator, in directing his will toward a certain achievement, focuses consciousness on obscure points and thus induces processes below the threshold to respond with a solution. The mid-region of the Freudian preconscious censorship (a phrase that may suggest to strict Freudians a misunderstanding of Freud) becomes for Armstrong a region of selective subconscious association where liberating as well as restricting functions occur. His theory thus tries to overcome a one-sided emphasis on pathogenic defense, repression, and disguise, in order to accommodate the full, open, creative expressiveness of artistic imagination.

Analysis of plot and and character. Among American personality theorists, Murray has shown an unusual degree of interest in literature and has made a vital connection between literature and the clinic through his Thematic Apperception Test (TAT). The TAT stimuli (pictures) are used to elicit stories, and these are analyzed as revealing the personality of the storyteller, particularly his unconscious complexes (*Explorations* . . . 1938, esp. pp. 530–545). In an admirably concise paper Murray has drawn the parallel between TAT stories and literary masterpieces, as he argues from evidence that authors are reflected in their productions (1943). [*See* PROJECTIVE METHODS, *article on* THE THEMATIC APPERCEPTION TEST.]

Murray reports that experience with numerous college student subjects in the Harvard Psychological Clinic indicates that the personality revealed by analysis of major characters, repeated plots, etc., in TAT stories is consistent with what can be learned in other ways about an individual; for example, judges can successfully match autobiographies against corresponding TAT stories. He finds that TAT authors range from subjective egocentric to objective sociocentric, the former tending to identify consciously with their story heroes. His most definite examples of subjective egocentrism occurred most frequently among students majoring in English, but none of his TAT subjects exhibited the high degree of subjective egocentrism found in the literary geniuses Melville and Wolfe. From these facts it can be inferred that Melville and Wolfe must reveal themselves at least as fully as the students. Murray thinks that literary material can contain infantile complexes and Jungian archetypes but notes that such unconscious patternings have their support and fulfillment in objective realities. For example, he finds that the Ishmael or social outcast theme, prominent in Melville and Wolfe, is rooted simultaneously in an infantile sense of rejection by the mother (a complex), in the low status of the literary artist in our culture (a sociological fact), and in a long, continuous development of the rebel or Satan myth in the West (a historical fact). In his opinion, analysis of literary works has general validity for personality study, since objective sociocentric authors also reveal themselves as much as the others, although with less awareness.

McCurdy is another worker with a similar interest in analysis of literature as a mode of personality research, and in a series of papers on various authors and a book on Shakespeare (1953) he has attempted to refine method and reach theoretical conclusions. A brief summary of these studies may be found in his textbook on personality (1961, pp. 413–427). McCurdy is phenomenological in outlook, and he views personality as a changing structure of relations between a self and its objects, particularly person objects; or, in other words, as a dynamic social system constituting a personal world. He is therefore inclined to regard a literary work of imagination as a description of the author's world, or at least a significant portion of it, and in analysis to concentrate on such obvious features as the characters and their interactions. To some extent, analysis of plot and character can be quantitative, and McCurdy has explored the possibilities. For example, in his study of the Brontë novels, he quantified the degree of resemblance between the characters by determining the amount of trait overlap in order to be more precise about types of characters and kinship lines between them. In the Shakespeare study, he arrived at weights to represent the relative importance of the characters by counting their speech lines and utilized these weights in several ways. One analysis led to the discovery that the average relative weights of characters within plays follow a simple exponential formula; and this result, which he also obtained for other authors, seems to point to a basic principle of personality organization. In spite of his interest in quantitative procedures, McCurdy would be the last to deny the validity of an impressionistic approach. In fact, he would insist that quantification must be kept subordinate to a nonmetrical understanding capable of grasping wholes, appreciating qualities, and judging values. His persistent hope has been that the study of personality through literature, while leaving room for quantitative and even experimental procedures, might encourage psychologists to recognize important realities that cannot easily be measured.

One can foresee an era of computer research in the psychology of literature, as quantitative methods are clarified and large-scale comparative studies are undertaken. The danger in such a stepping-up of quantification is that it may divert attention even more from the unquantifiable fundamentals of literature. That direction of development is relatively easy. What is harder and more essential is to keep near and draw nearer to the delicate, passionate, living processes of literary creation and exchange. If we could somehow bind our scientific energies to this far more difficult task, we might grow toward a richer form of knowing than hitherto achieved. In the meantime, we may at least take note of the great, apparently unremovable diversity of reader reaction to any given piece of literature (Richards 1929) and consider the problem which that poses for scientific consensus.

HAROLD G. MCCURDY

[*See also* AESTHETICS; CREATIVITY; DREAMS; FANTASY; PSYCHOANALYSIS.]

BIBLIOGRAPHY

ARMSTRONG, EDWARD A. (1946) 1963 *Shakespeare's Imagination: A Study of the Psychology of Association and Inspiration.* Lincoln: Univ. of Nebraska Press.

BINET, ALFRED 1904 La création littéraire: Portrait psychologique de M. Paul Hervieu. *L'année psychologique* 10:1–62.

BODKIN, MAUD (1934) 1948 *Archetypal Patterns in Poetry: Psychological Studies of Imagination.* New York: Oxford Univ. Press. → A paperback edition was published in 1963.

DOWDEN, EDWARD (1875) 1957 *Shakespeare: A Critical Study of His Mind and Art.* London: Routledge.

Explorations in Personality: A Clinical and Experimental Study of Fifty Men of College Age. By Henry A. Murray et al. 1938 London and New York: Oxford Univ. Press.

FREUD, SIGMUND (1900) 1953 *The Interpretation of Dreams.* 2 vols. London: Hogarth; New York: Macmillan. → First published as *Die Traumdeutung.* Constitutes Volumes 4 and 5 of *The Standard Edition of the Complete Psychological Works of Sigmund Freud.* A paperback edition was published in 1962 by Science Editions.

GHISELIN, BREWSTER (editor) 1952 *The Creative Process: A Symposium.* Berkeley: Univ. of California Press. → A paperback edition was published in 1955 by the New American Library.

HYMAN, STANLEY E. 1948 *The Armed Vision: A Study in the Methods of Modern Literary Criticism.* New York: Knopf. → A paperback edition was published in 1955 by Vintage Books.

JONES, ERNEST 1949 *Hamlet and Oedipus.* London: Gollancz. → A paperback edition was published in 1954 by Doubleday.

JUNG, CARL G. (1912) 1956 *Collected Works.* Volume 5: Symbols of Transformation: An Analysis of the Prelude to a Case of Schizophrenia. New York: Pantheon. → First published in German.

KIELL, NORMAN 1963 *Psychoanalysis, Psychology, and Literature: A Bibliography.* Madison: Univ. of Wisconsin Press.

LOWES, JOHN L. 1927 *The Road to Xanadu: A Study in the Ways of the Imagination.* New York: Houghton Mifflin. → A revised paperback edition was published in 1964.

MCCURDY, HAROLD G. 1953 *The Personality of Shakespeare: A Venture in Psychological Method.* New Haven: Yale Univ. Press.

MCCURDY, HAROLD G. 1961 *The Personal World: An Introduction to the Study of Personality.* New York: Harcourt.

MAURON, CHARLES (1950) 1963 *Introduction to the Psychoanalysis of Mallarmé.* Berkeley: Univ. of California Press. → First published in French.

MURRAY, HENRY A. 1943 Personality and Creative Imagination. Pages 139–162 in English Institute, *Annual: 1942.* New York: Columbia Univ. Press.

PHILLIPS, WILLIAM (editor) 1957 *Art and Psychoanalysis.* New York: Criterion.

PRESCOTT, FREDERICK C. 1922 *The Poetic Mind.* Ithaca: Cornell Univ. Press. → A paperback edition was published in 1959.

RICHARDS, IVOR A. 1929 *Practical Criticism: A Study of Literary Judgment.* London: Routledge; New York: Harcourt. → A paperback edition was published in 1956.

RICHARDS, I. A. (1934) 1962 *Coleridge on Imagination.* 3d ed. London: Routledge.

SPURGEON, CAROLINE F. E. (1935) 1961 *Shakespeare's Imagery, and What It Tells Us.* Cambridge Univ. Press.

III
POLITICAL FICTION

Politics has to do with the public exercise of power; political fiction, with the understanding and appraisal of those who are the subjects or objects of this exercise of power. Some writers of political fiction emphasize understanding, others appraisal. In the first case their work, if successful, approaches scientific theory in its insightful understanding of the dynamics of political power. In the second, mere appraisal without systematic understanding produces polemic or diatribe, which may nevertheless contribute expressively to understanding problems of power.

Fiction, political and nonpolitical

As the line between understanding and judging is often indistinct, so also is the line between fiction that is political and fiction that is not. Ever since political leaders first exercised power over the rest of society, writers have had the elite as subject matter—as Sophocles had in *Antigone.* Ever since ordinary citizens began to exercise overt power, notably during and after the Protestant Reformation and later the industrial revolution, writers have had the additional task of understanding and judging the public exercise of power by both elite and nonelite. This inherent, reciprocal, ancient relationship between the leader and the led, each as the subject and object of power, had not been clearly stated, let alone understood, before the modern activation of ordinary citizens. The infusion of psychological knowledge into culture, notably starting in the twentieth century with Freud, has made it possible to understand and judge political power with a penetration previously rare. Several bold, and a few successful, fictional efforts have been made in this direction. Some of the bolder and more successful ones are discussed below.

Even fiction that is political only by the vaguest of connections, allegorical or otherwise, has had enormous political impact. A very long and rambling Chinese novel, dating from the fifteenth century or before, *Shui hu chuan* (translated in 1933 by Pearl S. Buck under the title *All Men Are Brothers*), has among its themes brigandage, corruption of kings and princes, and the unending effort of valiant, lawless men to destroy the rich and powerful so that the poor and impotent might live in decency and justice. Even before the 1949 revolution a leading Chinese communist called this medieval novel the first communist writing, and it became a kind of guiding light for the revolutionary leaders during the decades before they got full power.

"Ward No. 6," Anton Chekhov's late-nineteenth-century short story about corruption and inefficiency in a lousy Russian hospital, had profound influence on Lenin, epitomizing for him one of the central justifications for the revolutionary drive for power. Comparable in their influence have been the eighteenth-century satires of Jonathan Swift (the most savage, perhaps, being his *Modest Proposal* for solving the population problem in Ireland by selling yearling Irish children to be served as a delicacy on the tables of English gentlemen) and the portrayals of social stench by Charles Dickens in his novels of poverty in Victorian England and by Victor Hugo in France. Harriet Beecher Stowe's polemical novel on early-nineteenth-century slavery in the American South, *Uncle Tom's Cabin* (1852), was itself a contributing cause of the American Civil War and almost a century later infused some animus into the African drive against colonialism following World War II.

Such polemical social fiction, however strong its influence on the climate of political opinion among elite and nonelite, does not, except by portraying the social context, contribute much to understanding or judging political power. By the same token, some ostensibly political fiction, such as Anthony Trollope's *Phineas Finn* (1869), Émile Zola's *His Excellency* (1876), Edwin O'Connor's *The Last Hurrah* (1956), Allen Drury's *Advise and Consent* (1959), and Vladimir Dudintsev's *Not by Bread Alone* (1956), deals with rather peripheral aspects of power. João Guimarães Rosa's *The Devil to Pay in the Backlands* (1956), a Brazilian novel of backland banditry, is curiously reminiscent of the Chinese *All Men Are Brothers* in its preoccupation with primitive moral courage and the search for some justice in a lawless society.

Such fiction indeed involves political issues like corruption, personal integrity, and courage. But it relates these only peripherally to more central issues involved in the exercise of power. Or it only scratches the surface in areas where Dostoevski, Koestler, Orwell, and Mann have excavated deeply. There are books in running brooks, sermons in stones, and politics in everything, but there is also a continuous running babble of political fiction that signifies next to nothing.

The public exercise of power involves man in his relations with the state—that is, his relations with the government and with the citizenry, the public. These relations always include contact between individuals. The contact between one individual and another involves not only appraisal and understanding of the other individual but also appraisal and understanding of oneself.

The protest against unlimited power

The age-old questions of right and wrong, justice, and choice still endure. In recent decades they have been raised anew, in searching analyses of the individual himself, as the agent who chooses between right and wrong, just and unjust. The age-old rote exhortation to exercise power virtuously has in twentieth-century fiction been succeeded by a maturing comprehension of the intimate relations of one individual with others and with himself. Modern writers have boldly explored paths opened by psychologists of both intuitive and empirical orientation and with such modern knowledge have in effect analyzed ancient Greek and Judaic statements of the problem of political power. In the groping exploration of the nineteenth century the Russian Dostoevski had the Grand Inquisitor say in Spanish Seville that mankind wanted bread rather than liberty—wanted to survive but cared not for freedom. In the mid-twentieth century has come the rather antithetical observation that man and society can be enslaved and destroyed only (as Orwell seems to have said) if man, the social animal, is reduced to the point where his survival depends on the grace of an omnipotent Big Brother. To Dostoevski's assertion that men choose bread rather than liberty Orwell replies that this is so only in a tyranny and only when both are not available and choice is therefore impossible. As will be discussed, this thesis raises questions about the nature of man himelf.

Political fiction typically has been written in protest. It has originated not in abstract considerations of man's nature but in concrete appraisal of his circumstances. The protest, more often than not, has been against the social and political *status quo* and has favored some kind of utopia where the contemporary real and evil society and polity are replaced by the good. But with increasing frequency in the mid-twentieth century, the protest has radically criticized the good society envisioned by utopians. It has extrapolated from current developments to their logical conclusion in the polity that ends politics, when the exercise of power is unlimited and controls every human act. Orwell in *1984* finds the origin of this trend in the development of techniques of power by corrupt civilization. With a far more devastating analysis (which he seems to have abandoned in later writing), William Golding in *Lord of the Flies* (1955) finds it in the human soul, released from the restraints of civilization. Orwell says man is socially corrupted; Golding, in this novel, proclaims that man is innately corrupt. Each book is logical; each is equally incredible in its holistic analysis of political action as the product exclusively of either the environment or the organism. Both *1984* and *Lord of the Flies* have, however, set the focus of attention on the human psyche, the point where determining forces, external and internal, do their work and where choice—if the forces are not altogether determining—is made. And, as will appear later, Golding and others have proffered an explanation that is neither strictly environmental nor strictly organic but both.

The economic class struggle

Most political fiction involves status distinctions between people—differences of superiority and inferiority. In one major tributary of writing the status relation arising from economic inequality dominates the appraisal of political power.

A prototype is Thomas More's sixteenth-century *Utopia* (1516), a work of fiction that lacks two of the three classic ingredients of novels, plot and character, but expatiates on a setting that has since become a shibboleth. In Utopia the status distinctions of an England in transition from feudalism to an open society are eliminated in a classless egalitarianism where virtually everyone enjoys the simplest provision of goods. The few who enjoy a little more do so only in consequence of their feudal but acknowledged exercise of political power, which includes authority not only to maintain order and national defense but also to allocate work. To keep the citizens from becoming accustomed to killing, the slaughter of livestock is done by slaves. People are punished as readily for the intent to commit a crime as for its commission. There are few laws and treaties, men being bound together by love, not words.

Deeply troubled as More was by the misery produced when feudally common pasture lands were enclosed and anti-Catholicism was rampant, his future good society looks like a serene early Christian communism. And it employs supposedly popular coercive measures having the gray-brown drabness and uniformity of the totalitarian slave-labor camps that actually came into being in the twentieth century. The election of top princes by high officials, of high officials by lesser ones, and of lower officials by citizens voting in family units seems more like feudalism stood on its head than like representative democracy. Reacting against the atavism of his time (a breakdown of community and law that seems to occur in all societies in transition), More could propose only a reversion to humanized, equalized, coerced feudalism.

In Émile Zola's *Germinal* (1885) the exploitation theme of More, deriving from English rural poverty, appears in a French industrial setting. The exploiters are not landowners enclosing once-common lands, thereby causing sheep to devour men (as More put it), but mine operators who work their miners to death. One part of the problem is the class system. The other part is the selfishness of man, whether bourgeois or proletarian. Zola abhorred the state of affairs in which the strong devour the weak, in which the lawless aim of each is to acquire power for himself, and in which the ability to love, sexually or otherwise, becomes a means of exploitation. Without resolving the issues of egoism, power, and love, Zola, in Marxist fashion, trusted the power of the proletariat to lay the basis for utopia in the next century by an avenging destruction of the bourgeoisie.

Later novelists have likewise reacted to the class crisis after industrialization, and they have similarly described despair and longed for utopia. The American nineteenth-century Populist Ignatius Donnelly in *Caesar's Column* (1890) carried the injustices of class exploitation to a point, a hypothetical century later, when wealth and political power are joined in the same ruling elite. In *The Iron Heel* (1907), Jack London began the reign of plutocrats soon after the last free election, in 1912, and continued it for three centuries.

Donnelly's solution, following a crisis that arouses the innocent but beastly urban mob, is for the good people to escape to Africa, where they set up their utopia built on brotherly love and protected by a high wall that keeps the outside world out. London's solution arises within man himself, in his reaction against degradation. And it emerges out of the most depressed and ignored class of menial laborers, the "people of the abyss," who join forces with the kept class of skilled workers and with a few natural geniuses motivated by "sheer love of man." Both Donnelly and London were Marxist in their critiques and utopian in their solutions. But London precociously presented a dilemma that has persisted: the relation between unsophisticated, ordinary man and the cosmic superman whom he sees as necessary to salvation from political repression.

London's striking work, like Zola's, avoids a sentimental belief in the simple goodness of mankind and probes more deeply into the human psyche. London clarified the problem of power with a prescience that portended Orwell. In *The Iron Heel* he envisioned new techniques for controlling the minds of the "masses," including a bomb plot faked by the government. He asserted: "Power is not God, not Mammon, but Power." And he had one of his plutocratic "oligarchs" say, "We will grind you revolutionists down under our heel, and we shall walk upon your faces" ([1907] 1958, p. 83). Some forty years later Orwell wrote, in *1984*, "If you want a picture of the future, imagine a boot stamping on a human face—forever" (1949, p. 268).

In *Martin Eden* (1908), London came closest to examining the mind and motivation of his idealized leaders, with their "sheer love of man." In this book the ordinary citizen becomes less an object of sympathy than of pity, and the Nietzschean element in the leader becomes more explicit. London has Martin Eden, torn asunder by his love of both the downtrodden *and* the distinguished, reflect: "Perhaps Nietzsche had been right. Perhaps there was no truth in anything, no truth in truth—no such thing as truth." Eden says, "I am a sick man. . . . It is my soul, my brain. I seem to have lost all values. I care for nothing. . . . It is too late now." And he drowns himself at sea.

By comparison with his contemporaries London, however lost he was, was not lost in a fog. In *The Octopus* (1901), by Frank Norris, the destructive aspects of capitalism come into false focus. It is all a battle of the interests against the decent, hardworking, bravely risk-taking farmers. London was caught between Scylla and Charybdis and knew it. For his contemporaries, like Norris and Donnelly, power remained a murky mystery, and they wallowed in it exquisitely.

For Paul Leicester Ford, power was neither a murky sea nor a rocky shore. It was something that one simply seized and used—like an adolescent grasping a gyrocompass but not trigonometry. The hero of his *Honorable Peter Stirling* (1894) wins both the governorship and a fair young lady, almost simultaneously. Stirling, in his long, stolid, and solid evolution from a boor to the beloved and just champion of the poor, shuns demagogy and observes neither more nor less than a firm respect for the just interests of the rich. Like London's hero in *The Iron Heel*, Stirling is animated by a pure love of mankind, but he works in a simple, sweet, manageable world.

Writing in a fictional milieu that took class conflict as a given, Ford and Norris (and Anthony Trollope in *Phineas Finn*) remained not seriously dismayed by the problem of power. Like a mad mariner, London pointed in anguish toward the twentieth century, which people had entered but were not yet in, and foresaw the techniques and consequences of complete social control.

The racial conflict

Another major tributary of political fiction deals with the kind of status that is not a consequence of property differences but of race. Writers have appraised this political problem in both the colonial and the intranational context. The issue is indeed raised by Shakespeare in *Othello* (c. 1604), and Swift's *Modest Proposal* (1729) protests the infrahuman status to which Englishmen relegated their Irish subjects. But it was not until the twentieth century, when E. M. Forster wrote his *Passage to India* (1924), that a broad and deep statement was made of the consequences of the conjunction of one race that calls itself master and another that acknowledges and protests its own subordination. Forster analyzed hierarchy by observing the effects of racial status as it was superimposed by conquest on a culture where status was already indigenously and meticulously imposed by caste and religion. He probed intimately into the relations between individuals who try to see others and themselves as individuals but who cannot escape the differences of status and are not much helped by the abstract egalitarianism of Christianity and Islam.

The basic conflict is not oversimplified but is reduced by Forster to that of loyalty and affection between individuals as they are inhibited and restricted by the bonds of religious, social, and national status. In the novel, Forster implicitly argues for the greater value of individual ties of affection, basing this on his supreme valuation of individuality as more important than religion, caste, and nation. Forster also wrote: "If I had to choose between betraying my country and betraying my friend, I hope I should have the guts to betray my country."

Poignant statements of the problem in an African context have been made by Alan Paton, in *Cry, the Beloved Country* (1948) and *Too Late the Phalarope* (1953). In both, individuals try to reach each other across the chasm of racial distinction. In the second, the sexual aspect, clearly present but not dominant in *A Passage to India*, becomes a central theme—the fascination of forbidden fruit and the spontaneity of physical interpersonal love, which closes its eyes to skin color.

The etiology of the endemic disease of racial tension, as it affects both individuals and politics, is classically stated and explored in these three novels. The dynamics as they operate within a nation have been inevitably stated in America, with its centuries-old dilemma of relations between whites and Negroes. These writings have had little overt political content, from Stowe's *Uncle Tom's Cabin* to Lillian Smith's *Strange Fruit* (1944) and Robert Penn Warren's *Band of Angels* (1955) and his epic poem *Brother to Dragons* (1953). The more recent work of Negro authors, written with an intensity that cannot ever be attained by white writers, has also been largely apolitical.

What is remarkable is the enormous political influence such fiction has had. It is not true that any one book (or any other force) has by itself impelled a social or political movement, but these writings have at times helped raise the strong winds of opinion to hurricane force. Literary discussion from the 1850s to the 1950s of race relations, in intranational, colonial, and latterly in foreign-aid contexts—e.g., William J. Lederer and Eugene Burdick's *The Ugly American* (1958)—indicates the persistence of this politically explosive issue. [*See* HUMAN RIGHTS.]

Political equality and individual dignity

A common theme of social novels with status preoccupation—whether it be economic or racial in origin—is the equality and dignity of the individual human being. The criticism of discrimination on the basis of class or race rests implicitly or explicitly on the belief in equal dignity or equal worth, regardless of bodily or economic circumstances over which the individual has no control.

Another category of writings reverses this theme and looks at what can happen when the principle of equality as the only end is assumed and any means appropriate to its achievement is morally justified. From Dostoevski in *The Possessed* (1871) to Henry James in *The Princess Casamassima* (1886) and Joseph Conrad in *The Secret Agent* (1907) the antianarchic critique of amoral equality has stressed the need for decency, honor, and integrity on the grounds that monistic egalitarianism produces only the destruction of orderly society and ultimately the nihilistic negation of the individual himself.

The egalitarian context in which these three novels were written is socioeconomic. They say in effect: What you people like More, Trollope, Chekhov, Hugo, and Dickens are talking about is all very well, but if you altogether succeed, what then? Are you quite sure your poor, sat-upon, proletarian egg will not be hatched a hawk?

The theme of racial equality has undergone a similar attack more recently, in a pair of novels: Robert Ruark's *Something of Value* (1955) and Nicholas Monsarrat's *The Tribe That Lost Its Head* (1956). With a querulous, lascivious dwelling on the terrors of extreme brutality, these novels present at most, and only by implication, a ritualistic solution to the dilemma of inequality (return to the decent, humane virtues of the aristocratic race), but they do succeed in presenting the problem in a crude fashion. The recoil by such as Dostoievski, Conrad, and Ruark at some of the consequences of equality poses the question of the exercise of power without stint in a society dedicated solely to the proposition that all men are created equal. These writings are reactionary without being atavistic: indeed they radically criticize the atavism resulting from unconstrained equality.

Opposition to anarchy and tyranny

The dialogue between the proponents and opponents of socioeconomic and racial equality skirts but never directly enters the area of political power exercised for its own sake. It deals with the adjective rather than the noun, with wealthy or racist power in politics rather than power itself.

The moral problem of political power itself was posed as early as the fifth century B.C., in Sophocles' *Antigone*. In the more abstract form of a man's relation to his God the problem was posed in the Biblical story of Job (probably fifth or fourth century B.C.), who achieved no peace until he surrendered to the divine will and recognized the gracious omnipotence of his almighty Lord. In Shakespeare's *Macbeth* (c. 1606) the conscienceless pursuit of power at last pricks the conscience of its pursuer, but his destruction is at the hands of society. In Herman Melville's *Billy Budd* (1891) authority (that is, sanctioned power) and simple human virtue come into conflict, virtue bowing to power. A variation of the Billy Budd theme occurs in Herman Wouk's *The Caine Mutiny* (1951), the difference being that the story ends well: both authority and humane justice prevail and all's well. In C. Virgil Gheorghiu's *Twenty-fifth Hour* (1950), law, authority, order, chaos, and the machine combine to destroy the individual.

These direct statements of the power problem do not, however, bore into its origins and its portents. Starting in the 1930s, a brilliant succession of novels has probed man's soul, with a skill showing the enormous impact of Freudian depth psychology. The proliferation of these remarkable works and their failure to fit into a chronological development makes it necessary to consider them by type rather than time.

In his *Brave New World* (1932), Aldous Huxley portrays a 26th-century utopia (or an antiutopia, if More's Utopia is deemed a good society) where people have become truly contented as a result of the elimination of disunity and disorder through the use of both eugenics and childhood conditioning. Only in a genetic sport, a man who developed in a neglected portion of the earth to which conditioning has not yet made its way, is the serene pattern disturbed. Both frightening and at times hilarious, the novel lacks the somber quality of later penetration into individual and social psychology. Karel Čapek's *War With the Newts* (1936) continues the theme of a conformist utopia, portraying a primordial, slimy horror that Huxley's happy English background fails to elicit in print.

André Malraux's *Man's Fate* (1933) is a poignant portent of intensified horror, as the jungles of psyche and society are more deeply explored. Instead of setting his story in European "mass" society, Malraux placed his picture of the human condition in an Asian context, the naked power contest in 1927 between Chiang Kai-shek and the Chinese communists, a conflict Malraux himself had witnessed. In *Man's Hope* (1938) he continued the argument, now set in the Spanish Civil War—which he again saw firsthand. *Man's Fate* is an almost despairing account of cynicism, both individual and governmental, of egocentricity, and of a tiny, nearly extinct spark of human compassion that keeps man's fate from being quite hopeless. *Man's Hope*, in a kaleidoscopic, almost incomprehensible picture of air and land battles, seems to kindle the spark of compassion into a flickering flame that slightly warms both of the warring camps in Spanish society, and in human society in general.

Building at least systematically, if not actually, on the somewhat impersonal social accounts just discussed, the Italian writer Ignazio Silone increasingly personalized the power problem. In *Fontamara* (1934) and *Bread and Wine* (1937) the ordinary people are more fully drawn than are Malraux's. And a new feature—the top political leader, the chief of state—emerges somewhat dimly in the background. This character is absent or distant in the work of Huxley, Čapek, and Malraux. The dilemmas of ideology, utopia, simple affection among human beings (and its savage antithesis: sexual rape) are conjoined with a simple superstition among the peasantry that takes the form of fear of the leader combined with a feeling of his inevitability, his power, and his grace. Both the peasantry and the politically declassed members of the ruling elite are juxtaposed to the leader in passionate ambivalence.

Three later novels move the ruling class farther into the foreground and the ordinary citizenry into the background. Two of these are psychologically distinguished and logically brilliant; the other, with one or two exceptions, is unsurpassed in its psychological penetration. In *Animal Farm* (1946) and *1984*, George Orwell carries to their logical conclusions certain tendencies already well developed in modern industrial society. *Animal Farm*, the allegorical polity in which all animals are equal but the ruling elite of pigs is more equal than the other creatures, argues that ideology and social justice are trivial matters when they confront the lust for power. In *1984* simple, spontaneous, uncontrived, uninduced love, of course, loses the battle, and Winston Smith, mentally *in extremis*, betrays his beloved Julia and comes to love Big Brother himself.

The third of these three novels, Arthur Koestler's *Darkness at Noon* (1941), synthesizes the author's personal experiences in the Spanish Civil War, during which in 1937 he was in solitary confinement in a Seville prison for three months (two months incommunicado), and his earlier experiences as a communist and a newspaperman traveling as an honored guest in the Soviet Union.

The protagonist of the novel, Rubashov, is a composite of several Soviet leaders who were tried and executed during the Soviet purge trials of the late 1930s. He is a composite of ideologism, courage, intellectuality, opportunism, and atrophied compassion. His life deftly poses several fundamental questions of political power: What means justify what ends? What is truth? When may proximate falsehood be used in the interests of ultimate truth? What is the individual's usefulness, his dignity, and his value?

The book contains several tragedies: the destruction of love between man and woman, to serve party purposes; the exposure of a man's soul in ludicrous public display, to serve party purposes; and the destruction of a party faithful when his usefulness has passed. These tragedies are conjoined with two politically deeper ones: the growing compassion shown Rubashov by a never-seen fellow prisoner, an adherent of the old regime with whom he has nothing in common save uncultured humanity, and the inability of Rubashov to live outside the quite corrupt church of the Communist party, in which he has spent his life and the only thing to which he is dedicated aside from self. Neither the compassion of others nor fidelity to party saves him from destruction. In the end Rubashov can choose neither to stand with his fellow men nor to stand alone.

The early antiutopias of the 1930s and 1940s were relatively impersonal and dealt mainly with ordinary citizens. The more personal, and more real, accounts of Silone, Malraux, and Koestler move partially or completely from treatment of the ordinary to the extraordinary citizen, to the declassed member of the ruling elite. Two additional novels dealing with the same problems of unconstrained political power are fictionalized biographies of actual chiefs of state. Robert Penn Warren's *All the King's Men* (1946) follows closely the life of the American Huey P. Long, Louisiana's hypertrophied ruler without scruple in the 1930s. Peter Abrahams' *A Wreath for Udomo* (1956) fictionalizes the life of a prominent African chief of state whom Abrahams knew when both were in London as students and radical African nationalists.

Like Koestler's writing, *All the King's Men* juxtaposes a set of tragedies, the personal and political. There is the use and betrayal of people, the abuse of truth and the use of falsehood, the passionate sense of abstract justice combined with the enthusiasm for inducing a lawless personal dependency—revenge and grace without justice. The tragedy lies in the inability of the leader, Willie Stark, to extricate himself from the personal nest he has woven for himself and then befouled. Though lacking the somber quality of *Darkness at Noon, All the King's Men* ends in deeper tragedy, because instead of being entrapped by circumstance—a party and its ideology—Willie Stark, like Macbeth, is unable to escape himself and death at the hands of a close associate.

A Wreath for Udomo similarly conjoins the personal and the political. Udomo is beloved by and loves a mature Englishwoman he meets in London. He betrays her by having an affair with a mutual friend. When he later gets established as leader of his newly liberated African nation, he sacrifices the life of an old friend and devoted follower, as the price for getting technical aid from the hated, white-ruled nation of South Africa. He is at last killed by tribal atavism, the fear-driven reaction to the modern ways Udomo is introducing.

Most of these antianarchic novels (from Dostoevski to Conrad) and antityrannic novels, often mislabeled antiutopias (from Huxley to Abrahams), were written in western Europe. Out of eastern Europe, in the post-Stalin era, has come a series of novels that offer the promise, and no more as yet, of the re-emergence of intensely political writing in the land that produced Dostoevski and Gogol. The new books remain timid, uncrafted products, still too close to tyranny itself to be able to appraise it freely. Among these are Vladimir Dudintsev's *Not by Bread Alone*, more concerned with public administration than with public policy; Abram Tertz's *The Trial Begins* (1960), which deals directly if crudely with Stalinist tyranny; and Alexander Solzhenitsyn's *One Day in the Life of Ivan Denisovich* (1963), which considers the theme of selfishness and the platitude of the endurance of the human spirit, but otherwise is undistinguished. It nevertheless is a milestone in the public recognition it has accorded the author in the Soviet Union, where he was nominated in 1963 for the Lenin Prize.

Nietzschean and anti-Nietzschean themes

There remains still another category of political novels, incongruous among those that oppose either anarchy or tyranny. These are the writings that implicitly or explicitly espouse and justify—or reject and condemn—a Nietzschean, individualist anarchism divorced from any social or socialist commitment. In a sense, these are antipolitical works.

A prototype of this genre is Stendhal's *The Red and the Black* (1830). Its protagonist Julien moves through life and through people's lives with a moral dedication to self that rises above any less exalted purpose. He pushes into boudoirs and the bureaus of business and government with a purity of heart that beguiles. At the end he faces trial with a moral courage and a refusal to compromise his principle that makes it easy to overlook the principle to which he was dedicated. If the pure in heart ever are to see their God, Julien saw his in himself and was by himself blest.

The Red and the Black is indeed a pure novel, unbesmirched by the dilemma between individual distinction and social service. If the solution for Martin Eden was the escape of private suicide, Julien went to his public execution with the courage of Socrates and Christ, the sole difference being in the diverse principles for which Julien and Socrates and Christ died.

Two more-recent novels echo the *Red and Black* theme, in one case with several inklings of awareness of the dilemma and in the other with no more than an inkling. Hermann Hesse's *Steppenwolf* (1927) is the story of an individualist who moves from the writing desk to the dance hall, discovers affection for others, but does not swerve dangerously from his self-dedication. For a while, nevertheless, he enjoys warming and being warmed by others.

Not so Dr. Zhivago, in Boris Pasternak's novel by that name (1957). With a dedication to self that rivals Julien's, Zhivago moves endlessly across the well-limned Russian landscape during and after the great revolution, sloughing off those whom he has used and who have become attached to him. He does it all with a remarkable sense of high purpose, blaming only the chaos and the Soviet system for his faults, that is, his inability to succeed altogether in his self-service. The critical enthusiasm with which the book was received after its official Soviet condemnation and the awarding of the Nobel Prize to its author reflected a pharisaical condemnation of Soviet communism and no understanding of the refusal of Pasternak to face the dilemma confronted by London, Koestler, and Orwell. In *Dr. Zhivago*, Nietzsche is not problematical but axiomatic.

Two individualistic American novels throw this issue into relief: James Gould Cozzens' *The Last Adam* (1933) and Ernest Hemingway's *For Whom the Bell Tolls* (1940). Both emphasize individual values and candidly make their protagonists into heroes. Both clearly indicate a commitment of these heroes to their communities. There is a consequent warmth in Cozzens' and Hemingway's characters that contrasts with the vibrating chill of Julien and Zhivago.

A brilliantly madcap Italian drama on egocentricity, Luigi Pirandello's *Six Characters in Search of an Author* (1922), mixes tragedy and comedy as his protagonists step in and out of character as concupiscent egoists exploiting one another and protesting their altruism. Obviously nonpolitical, this pungent play deeply influenced Gamal Abdel Nasser, who viewed the same prurient egoism on the other side of the Mediterranean as a prime cause of Egyptian political impotence before and after the 1952 revolution.

Two French novelists have written on the theme, in works that replace Pirandello's mordant laughter with a moan from the wounds of egoism that rises to a cry of mortal despair. The existentialist Jean-Paul Sartre in *The Age of Reason* (1945) has his characters search for private freedom, after liberty has been publicly betrayed in the Spanish Civil War. They seek it in the paradox of uncommitted love that exploits others for their companionship and passion but ends in solitude. At the last the central character muses that he is "alone but no freer than before. . . . this life had been given him for nothing, he was nothing and yet he would not change: he was as he was made" ([1945] see 1959, p. 342). In Sartre's *Troubled Sleep* (1949), set in France during the Nazi occupation in 1940, the search for freedom is similarly fruitless. To personal egoism is conjoined national egoism: man cares neither for man nor woman nor *Vaterland* nor *patrie*—and vice versa. All one can do, Sartre seems to say, is endure, clutching the thin coin of existentialism whose other side is nihilism.

The cry of Albert Camus is even more piercing. In *The Plague* (1947) he seems to argue with Sartre's morbid description of man's isolation. In an allegory of France during the Nazi occupation, he finds individual men who dedicate themselves warmly to a solidary, compassionate succoring of the plague-stricken community. Fear of fatal infection and mistrust of one's neighbors are overcome by the "craving for human contacts" and the identification with the dying. Society must endure, and with individual compassion for individuals it can endure. "The Stranger" in Camus's 1942 novel by that name is an emotionally empty man who kills without feeling, without even hatred, an alien in a community whose members remain individually and collectively united against their asocial fellow citizen. But in *The Fall* (1956), Camus appears to have surrendered to despair. There can be no conjunction of freedom and society. Solitude is unbearable, and man cannot bear freedom, a court sentence imposed on oneself by oneself. Man must be a slave, in a society where all are slaves to their own inescapable egoism. Lacking love, men are dragged through life by their almost impotent hypersexuality. Their common guilt can hold them together, but it only delays the solitude of death.

And in Ingmar Bergman's screenplays the theme is repeated in Scandinavian settings, with the sharp skill of London, Sartre, and Camus but without their resignation or despair. In *Wild Strawberries* (1957), a distinguished septuagenarian scientist, about to be honored for his dedicated pursuit of reality, in his dreams sees himself as indifferent, unloving and unloved, living in deadly solitude. "I'm dead, although I live." In the triad of screenplays *Through a Glass Darkly* (1961), *Winter Light* (1963), and *The Silence* (1963), the theme is reinforced: psychoanalytic understanding, piety, and sexual passion without love do become deathly futile and impotent. But, Bergman insists, men are capable of compassion.

The problem of free choice

Political fiction, like political science, has always been a product of the developing stage of culture in which it was written. Both fiction and science have drawn from the same intellectual sources and appraised the dilemmas of the time. When the very idea of limited government was taking shape, Sophocles in *Antigone* raised the radical issue of civil disobedience. In the twentieth century, when tyranny underwent another revival—perhaps unequaled since the savage sixteenth century of the Reformation and Counter Reformation—the theme of tyranny again became central.

But political fiction now reflects the infusion of new knowledge, notably from psychology and physiology. It has consequently produced an inquiry into the causes and consequences of tyranny that is remarkable in depth and suggestiveness. In so doing, political fiction has articulated analyses of problems that in contemporary writing in political science have had largely disjointed treatment: the relationship between the individual, his fellow men, his fellow citizens, and government; the concept of justice in which government is more than an arbiter between citizens; the problem of moral choice and free choice; and above all, the criteria for choice.

Indeed, to a great extent the new political theory of the twentieth century has been written in fictional form. Some writings already discussed and some not yet discussed show this sharply.

In *1984* Orwell develops his story and his theory by employing an almost classic Freudian thesis. Government, to control individual political loyalty, must sever ties of loyalty between individuals. The basic tie, says Orwell, following Freud, is the erotic one—physical love with its attendant personal affection. To break this tie, government must destroy physical desire. To do this, government must, in turn, reactivate the primordial individual desire for sheer survival and replace love between real people with the childish dependent love for the never-seen omnipotence that graciously or tyrannically permits survival and provides the means for survival. Heterosexual love is replaced with asexual, childish, dependent love, and political autonomy is replaced with political infancy. Justice is controlled by what through "doublethink" is called the Ministry of Love, where men are reduced to impotence.

Koestler in *Darkness at Noon* offers a more complicated set of hypotheses. Love and loyalty between individuals are indeed deadened by tyranny. But the problem of justice gets a less stark, more subtle and realistic, consideration than Orwell's brutal statement that power is a boot stamping on a human face forever. Justice now relates to means and ends. As object and subject the individual is considered by Koestler to be a commodity to be valued quite apart from his usefulness to the polity. But can man choose? With a vague, attenuated humanitarianism that becomes entangled with the justification of any efficient means to humane ends, Rubashov chooses only to condemn himself. A socialized, collectivized Nietzschean, he can exercise his will only by conforming to the will of the political party, which has become identical with the will of the leader. Koestler seems to say that men can be aware but not choose.

The problem of free moral choice (a tautology, at least in politics) gets precocious emphasis in Joseph Conrad's *Under Western Eyes* (1911). With or without the benefit of psychoanalytic theory, Conrad poignantly refines the problem. He indicates that the consequence of choice, when it destroys other people, is to destroy the chooser.

The criteria for choice are considered in two of the first works which deeply explore political behavior. In the theoretical dialogue between sexual and nonsexual love (eros and agape), both these novels employ depth psychology and argue against a simplistic Freudian erotism.

Franz Kafka in *The Castle* (1926) has his protagonist, K., use sex to get ahead, to try to get the attention of the leader, the unseen chief in the castle. The wretch K. fails because, like Julien and Zhivago, he is concentered all in self and at last can only throw himself on the infinite mercy that accompanies infinite power.

William Golding in *Free Fall* (1959) evidently rejects his earlier thesis in *Lord of the Flies* that beneath man's enculturation crouches only a primordial beast. He now argues that man cannot live alone, that he must live with and for other individuals, and that the dilemma of living for oneself and for others will persist and is the basis for guilt, which also will persist. Man is not altogether formed by either his genes or his environs: he can choose, with inevitable guilt, but without guilt he could never make choices that are right —that is, moral. He can never help establish a free society or free himself without considering the consequences of his choices both for himself and for others.

In so stating the criteria for choice, Golding avoids the surrender to divine will implicit in the Biblical Job and the modern *Castle*, to the will of the party and leader explicit in *Darkness at Noon* and *1984*, and to individually uncontrollable forces as in *Martin Eden*. *Free Fall* thus implies there is choice, that forces within and without the individual are not altogether uncontrollable, and that anxiety and guilt will inevitably accompany the exercise of choice. To this extent Golding indicates a way out of the dilemma so poignantly posed by London.

All these factors have been integrated in unequaled, necessarily epigrammatic form in a political novella of classic proportions, *Mario and the Magician* (1929) by Thomas Mann. In *Mario* are fully presented the leader, the citizenry that is led, and the citizen who kills the tyrant. The roots of tyranny are exposed in the leader's envy, contempt, and hatred for the public and in the public's moral obtuseness that considers politics a game at which they are irresponsible spectators. And using the need for people to huddle together, the leader isolates potential dissenters. In a brilliantly contrived denouement, Mann has the leader exploit and pervert sexual love and be undone by a young man whose revulsion at the leader seems to stem from the depths of the untutored, natural man. Mann in this rather short story does not explicate other political fiction; he epitomizes it.

If the themes of private and public egoism, tyranny, and free choice had not recurred in Russian, English, Italian, French, German, and Swedish writing, in contexts scattered over centuries and over the globe, one might argue that the condition was not universal but parochial. In Malraux and Golding, the dying despair of Dostoevski, Orwell, Pirandello, Sartre, Camus, Koestler, and Kafka is quickened by hope. Man need not just exist and then cease: he can elicit his own compassion and can redeem himself and his fellow men. Deepened psychological understanding need not just witness or contribute to the destruction of men and society; it can help build both. Man is helpless neither against the tyranny of his own egoism nor against the tyranny of egoism in the general public and its leaders.

Political fiction and political science

One conclusion from a look at political fiction is that the lines between fiction, theory, and fact are very indistinct. *Darkness at Noon*, a fiction piece about the great Soviet purges of the late 1930s, portended not only the factual account of them in Beck and Godin's *Russian Purge and the Extraction of Confession* (1951) but also the profound study of brainwashing in Lifton's *Thought Reform and the Psychology of Totalism* (1961). In a sense fiction here was a decade ahead of published fact and two decades ahead of systematic theory and observation. Koestler in turn was building on fact. Bukharin, one of the most distinguished victims of the 1938 purge, said at his trial: "When you ask yourself: 'If you must die, what are you dying for?'—an absolute black vacuity suddenly rises before you with startling vividness. There was nothing to die for, if one wanted to die unrepentant" (quoted in Daniels 1960, p. 389).

In raising basic issues of power in its political manifestations and of the ability and responsibility to make choices, political fiction has been working in the same garden as have political theory and political research. The far from accidental consequence is that political fiction has posed problems and stated solutions that are rarely behind, and often ahead of, the statement and resolution of these problems by more prosaic investigators. There is a relationship between Job's argument with his God, Antigone's with her king, and Winston Smith's with his Big Brother. There is a tie between Freudian theory, Marxian socioeconomic theory, and the writings of Koestler, Golding, and Bergman. Each supports and facilitates the understanding of the other. One very notable distinction is that the fiction writer puts the reader on guard, since the reader of fiction realizes that what is being written is not necessarily ultimate truth or exact fact. The nonfiction theorist or researcher in politics seldom so protects the reader. In this sense writers of political fiction are exercising a responsible moral choice as to the canons of scientific method that is too infrequently faced by writers of political science.

JAMES C. DAVIES

[*See also* ALIENATION; IDEOLOGY; INTELLECTUALS; SOCIAL SCIENCE FICTION; UTOPIANISM.]

BIBLIOGRAPHY

The examples of political fiction cited in the text are not included in the bibliography.

BECK, F.; and GODIN, W. [pseudonyms] 1951 *Russian Purge and the Extraction of Confession.* London and New York: Hurst & Blackett; New York: Viking.

BLOTNER, JOSEPH L. 1955 *The Political Novel.* Garden City, N.Y.: Doubleday. → Contains a comprehensive list of political novels.

CROSSMAN, RICHARD H. S. (editor) (1949) 1959 *The God That Failed.* New York: Harper. → A paperback edition was published in 1963.

DANIELS, ROBERT V. 1960 *The Conscience of the Revolution: Communist Opposition in Soviet Russia.* Russian Research Center Studies, No. 40. Cambridge, Mass.: Harvard Univ. Press.

DONNER, JÖRN (1962) 1964 *The Personal Vision of Ingmar Bergman.* Bloomington: Indiana Univ. Press. → First published as *Djävulens ansikte: Ingmar Bergmans filmer.*

HOWE, IRVING 1957 *Politics and the Novel.* New York: World.

LIFTON, ROBERT J. 1961 *Thought Reform and the Psychology of Totalism: A Study of "Brainwashing" in China.* New York: Norton.

LLEWELLYN, KARL N.

Karl Nickerson Llewellyn (1893–1962) was a leading exponent of "realism" in the field of jurisprudence. Applying the realistic method to commercial law, he produced the Uniform Commercial Code, now effective law in the United States. He also wrote on legal education, emphasizing craft skills and law as a liberal art; on the professional responsibility and organization of the bar; and on the sociology of law. He analyzed law-government as an institution and demonstrated that dispute settlement is the most reliable indicator of the law and values of a group. In addition, he wrote poetry, painted, and composed songs.

At Yale, where he studied both as an undergraduate and as a law student, his exposure to the ideas of William Graham Sumner, through the lectures of A. G. Keller, aroused Llewellyn's interest in patterns of behavior as fundaments in societal structure. He was influenced by the fact-to-result analysis of cases used by Arthur L. Corbin and by the narrow-issue thinking of Wesley Hohfeld and Walter W. Cook. After teaching commercial law at Yale for two years, he went into practice in New York City, studying banking and business patterns as well as the crafts of counseling and advocacy. When he returned to Yale, his writings reflected his preoccupation with the relation of commercial practice and economics to law; his work also revealed his expanding interest in legal sociology. He admired Holmes, Pound, Cardozo, Max Weber, and Eugen Ehrlich. Starting in the 1920s, he drafted legislation for the Commissioners on Uniform State Laws; at the same time, he examined the process of rule making in its theoretical and practical aspects. Llewellyn's move to Columbia in 1924 coincided with the ferment there concerning the merits of fact research and of the integration of law with the other social sciences. His major study of commercial doctrine, factual patterns, and the ways in which cases reflect social conditions, business practices, and styles of judicial decision led to his *Cases and Materials on the Law of Sales* (1930*a*), a classic introduction to the study of law; *The Bramble Bush* (1930*b*); and a set of lectures delivered in Germany and entitled "Einführung in das amerikanische Präjudizienrechtswesen."

His publication of "A Realistic Jurisprudence—The Next Step" (1930*c*) precipitated a controversy about the nature of realism. Llewellyn saw realism as a method of attacking legal problems by first looking at what was in fact being done by courts and other officials. In this connection, he insisted on the importance of narrow, factual categories and the temporary divorce of "is" from "ought." He read cases for their narrow holdings (the facts, precise legal issue, and result), testing whether the courts were doing what doctrine seemingly required. The objectives of this analysis were, first, an accurate statement of the operative law; second, a testing of the relation between that law and the life situation it encompasses; third, an evaluation of the policy thus reflected; and finally, a decision as to what the law ought to be, and its statement in a well-drafted legislative or judicial rule. He saw legal rules as vital to the guidance and control of behavior and urged that these rules explicitly state their reason and that they be accompanied by explanation of the policy on which they rest. He believed that the Janus-faced nature of precedent forces courts to make policy choices and that courts cannot operate effectively in our society without such leeway of choice. He urged recognition of this fact as a first step to better decisions. Few scholars have been more interested and more active in the process of rule making and in relating law to values, and none has been more falsely accused of being concerned only with the "is."

Already active in the Legal Aid Society and the American Civil Liberties Union, in the 1930s he also helped plan strategy for the National Association for the Advancement of Colored People. His commercial-law articles became increasingly concerned with the relation of judicial method, institutional structure, and practice to the development of doctrine.

A study he made with E. A. Hoebel of the law-government of the Cheyenne Indians resulted in *The Cheyenne Way* (1941), which broke ground in anthropological method. In *The Cheyenne Way*, Llewellyn departed from the traditional procedure of inferring the character of the law from the statements of informants; his methodological innovation was to try to determine what the effective law of the group was—what happened in actual conflict situations.

His writings in jurisprudence reflected his view of law-government as an institution with its own functions, values, crafts, and traditions. He used "law-government" to designate the total legal component of society. It includes the mechanics of dispute settlement; the allocation of the power to decide particular types of issues; and the formulation of substantive rules, whether by legislation, executive action, or judicial decision. The concept of law-government rejects the view that the law is simply a body of rules; instead, the law is considered to be a set of institutions.

In the 1940s Llewellyn's theories of rule making and his perception of the appellate process bore fruit in the style of organization and drafting of the Uniform Commercial Code. His insistence on preliminary analysis in terms of narrow issues and narrow factual categories proved its value in the resulting clarification of the policy considerations involved in this legislation. He also studied the law-government of pueblo groups and drafted legal codes for the Santa Ana and Santo Domingo pueblos. In 1944, as chairman of the Curriculum Committee of the Association of American Law Schools, he made a report, which has become a classic, analyzing legal crafts and skills as they relate to legal education (see Association of American Law Schools 1944). His Storrs lectures at Yale Law School foreshadowed Llewellyn's *Common Law Tradition: Deciding Appeals* (1960), a definitive statement of the appellate process. In 1948/1949, while a visiting professor at Harvard, he prepared a jurisprudence syllabus incorporating his view of law-government.

In 1951 he moved to the University of Chicago, attracted by the ideas of Edward H. Levi, dean of the law school. At Chicago he concentrated on the development of his jurisprudence syllabus, the refinement of materials on legal argument that he had been collecting since 1934, and the completion of his study of the process of appellate judging. His writings in legal education deal more directly with questions of craft, scope, and responsibility, and he explored further the relationship of law to the humanities, as well as to the behavioral sciences.

SOIA MENTSCHIKOFF

[*See also* JURISPRUDENCE; PUBLIC LAW, *and the biographies of* CARDOZO; HOLMES; POUND; SUMNER; WEBER, MAX.]

WORKS BY LLEWELLYN

1930*a* *Cases and Materials on the Law of Sales.* Chicago: Callaghan.

(1930*b*) 1951 *The Bramble Bush: On Our Law and Its Study.* New York: Oceana.

1930*c* A Realistic Jurisprudence: The Next Step. *Columbia Law Review* 30:431–465.

1931 What Price Contract? An Essay in Perspective. *Yale Law Journal* 40:704–751.

1936–1937 On Warranty of Quality, and Society. *Columbia Law Review* 36:699–744; 37:341–409.

1938–1939 On Our Case Law of Contract: Offer and Acceptance. *Yale Law Journal* 48:1–36, 779–818.

1940 The Normative, the Legal and the Law-jobs: The Problem of Juristic Method. *Yale Law Journal* 49: 1355–1400.

1941*a* On the Problem of Teaching "Private" Law. *Harvard Law Review* 54:775–810.

1941*b* The Theory of Legal "Science." *North Carolina Law Review* 20:1–23.

1941 LLEWELLYN, KARL N.; and HOEBEL, E. ADAMSON *The Cheyenne Way: Conflict and Case Law in Primitive Jurisprudence.* Norman: Univ. of Oklahoma Press.

1944 Meet Negotiable Instruments. *Columbia Law Review* 44:299–329.

1960 *The Common Law Tradition: Deciding Appeals.* Boston: Little.

1962 The Study of Law as a Liberal Art. Pages 375–394 in Karl N. Llewellyn, *Jurisprudence: Realism in Theory and Practice.* Univ. of Chicago Press. → An address delivered on April 30, 1960.

Jurisprudence: Realism in Theory and Practice. Univ. of Chicago Press, 1962. → Contains essays first published between 1928 and 1960.

SUPPLEMENTARY BIBLIOGRAPHY

ASSOCIATION OF AMERICAN LAW SCHOOLS, COMMITTEE ON CURRICULUM 1944 The Place of Skills in Legal Education. *Columbia Law Review* 45:345–391. → Llewellyn served as chairman of the committee.

LOBBYING

If we had data on every government in every culture, we would probably find that lobbying in some form is an inevitable concomitant of government. The term originated in American governmental experience about 1830. Certain representatives of interest groups loitered in the lobbies off the assembly halls of the American Congress and state legislatures, hoping to get a chance to speak to legislators and thereby attempt to influence their decisions. As the term became part of the vernacular, it was broadened to include anyone who attempted to influence the decision of a governmental official. The term is currently used quite loosely, and often inappropriately, for all kinds of influence endeavors. Since it is popularly believed that lobbyists use improper methods in their attempts to influence officials, the term "lobbying" carries an unpleasant connotation to many minds.

Despite the imprecision of the current use of the term, some boundaries can be defined. (1) Lobbying occurs only in governmental decision making. Decisions made by private individuals, organizations, or corporations may be influenced by special interests, but the influence should not be called lobbying. (2) All lobbying is motivated by a desire to influence. Many actions and events may affect the outcome of governmental decisions, but if they are not accompanied by an intent to influence, there is no lobbying. (3) Lobbying implies the presence of an intermediary or representative as a communication link between citizens and governmental decision makers. A citizen who, of his own volition and by his own means, sends a message to a governmental decision maker is not considered a lobbyist even though he is attempting to influence governmental decisions. (4) All lobbying involves communication, for that is the only way that influence can be transmitted. Broadly defined, then, *lobbying is the stimulation and transmission of a communication, by someone other than a citizen acting on his own behalf, directed to a governmental decision maker with the hope of influencing his decision.*

Although most lobbyists do represent special-interest groups, or pressure groups, lobbying is not identical with interest-group behavior. For one thing, individuals as well as groups utilize lobbying. Second, interest groups engage in many activities in addition to lobbying; some groups, in fact, do not engage in lobbying at all. Third, individuals or groups with special interests may find direct representation without the intercession of lobbyists. Lobbying, then, is but one process or means of representation that individuals and groups might utilize.

Lobbying should be thought of as a process rather than as an organization. It is most helpful to think of it as a communication process by which lobbyists attempt to get governmental officials to accept the policy desires of lobbying clients. It is the lobbyist's job to create messages and to choose means of transmission that are most likely to ensure clear and favorable reception of the message by the intended receiver. This means that the lobbyist must anticipate the predispositions of his intended receiver(s) and so act that the message will be favorably received with as little distortion as possible. He must take care that the message is not intercepted or blocked. He must choose a transmission channel that is open (has access), is not likely to be overloaded, and has a low noise level.

The origin of the term "lobbying" and its legal definition in the United States statute, the Federal Regulation of Lobbying Act of 1946, leads many persons to believe that lobbying applies only to legislative decisions. The definition given above suggests, however, that lobbying occurs just as readily with executive-branch officials as with legislators, and even to a certain extent with judicial officials. Empirical data for the United States national government show that executive-branch lobbying is just as prevalent as legislative-branch lobbying (Milbrath 1963, pp. 319–320; Cherington & Gillen 1962).

Patterns of lobbying

Although there have been studies of interest groups in a number of countries, studies of the lobbying process are relatively rare and nearly always confined to the United States. Consequently, little is known about how lobbying is conducted outside of the United States. It does seem clear, however, that only in the United States are large numbers of special political actors designated to play the role of lobbyist on a full-time, professional basis. Most of the persons who perform lobbying functions in other national cultures probably do so as a part-time activity while maintaining a major role as an interest-group official, labor union official, attorney, or corporation executive.

For lack of empirical evidence, one can only speculate on reasons for the greater emphasis on lobbying in the United States as compared with other countries. One possible reason is that representation of interests is more clearly built into the governmental system of other Western countries than into the American governmental system. Interest groups, in these other countries, are given seats on advisory boards or are consulted as a matter of course by ministers or bureau chiefs. In addition, interest groups often succeed in electing one or more of their own men to seats in the legislative body. Of course, these things also occur in American government, but the difference in emphasis is substantial. American interest groups believe they must take the initiative if they hope to be heard at decision time.

Another possible reason for the difference in lobbying between America and other Western countries is the difference in centralization of decision making in the government. In most Western governments, decision making is highly concentrated in the cabinet executive, whereas in the United States it is divided between the executive and the legislature, and sometimes between the state and national governments. A diffuse decision process, one that has many decision points, more likely requires continuous scrutiny and pressure by special interests in order to get a policy moved past each of these points. In a sense, lobbying must be used in a diffuse decisional system to avoid degeneration of the system into inaction or stalemate.

Differences in the political-party system also seem to affect lobbying. European parties are more closely allied with and based on interest groups (especially in multiparty systems). Generally, they also are more "responsible" (able and required to carry out their program when given power) than American parties. American parties are so heterogeneous that they must compromise group interests rather than clearly speak for them. Furthermore, American parties cannot be counted on for firm policy leadership. Interest groups in the United States have almost abandoned working through parties and instead have hired lobbyists to secure policy representation (Milbrath 1963, p. 200). By way of contrast, European interest groups are more likely than American interest groups to find political parties a useful means of representation and to depend to a lesser extent on lobbying (Beer 1958, p. 138).

During the initial stages of lobbying's development in the United States, some groups sought competitive advantage over other groups by sending a personal envoy (a lobbyist) to the seat of government. Lobbying at this stage was very much a function of the direct personal relationship between lobbyists and official decision makers. Groups with more competent lobbyists were more likely to have their messages accepted by government officials. Groups at a competitive disadvantage because they had no lobbyist were stimulated also to send a lobbyist envoy. Eventually, the seat of the national government, and also the seats of some state governments, became crowded with lobbyists clamoring for an opportunity to deliver direct personal messages to officials. Easy access for direct communication between lobbyist and official, which had been possible with only a limited number of lobbyists, became very difficult. (Currently there are between eight hundred and one thousand registered lobbyists in Washington, D.C.)

Faced with a situation where the channels of direct communication with officials were constantly overloaded and seldom available, lobbyists turned to indirect communication methods. They sent messages through intermediaries who were thought to have better access, such as constituents or friends of the officials. They stimulated mass letter or telegram campaigns, hoping to impress officials with a ground swell of public sentiment for or against a policy. They launched massive public relations campaigns in the mass media, hoping to change (or maintain) political attitudes. This shift of tactics to indirect communication methods became known as "lobbying at the grass roots."

However, indirect methods also are limited in effectiveness. Grass-roots campaigns conducted by strong competitive groups often result in stalemate or *status quo*. Campaigns stimulated by lobbyists usually are detected as such by officials, and their potential impact is seriously discounted through knowledge of their nonspontaneous nature. Successful public relations campaigns require subtle management and are very expensive. As a result of these kinds of difficulties, the pendulum has begun to swing back from grass-roots lobbying.

Current lobbying methods in Washington, D.C. are a blend of direct and indirect methods of communication. Direct methods, such as personal presentation of viewpoints, are preferred by most lobbyists, but they cannot be relied on to get messages through to officials. Lobbyists turn to indirect methods when direct ones prove uncertain or unusable. In addition, lobbyists pay considerable attention to the problem of keeping their communication channels open. They employ various means of ingratiating themselves with officials to ensure that access will be speedy and direct when it is needed. Entertainment and bribery are not as widely used to ingratiate as is popularly supposed. They are not considered as rewards or favors by most officials, and bribery especially is dangerous to the careers of both officials and lobbyists (Milbrath 1963, chapter 13).

Lobbying occurs at all levels of government in the United States: city, county, and state as well as national. Research on state lobbying is scattered and uneven, while research on city and county lobbying is almost nonexistent. About three-fourths of the fifty states have a lobby-regulation or lobby-reporting law, but in most cases these laws are rather weakly enforced.

The scattered research evidence that exists on state lobbying suggests that lobbyists at the state level primarily employ direct methods of communication with officials. Competition for the time and attention of officials is less at the state level than at the national level. Consequently, state lobbyists do not find it so necessary to turn to the more expensive and less certain indirect methods that national lobbyists must employ.

Employing primarily direct methods, state lobbyists devote more time and resources to ingratiating themselves with officials and to keeping communication lines open. The reported incidence of entertainment and bribery is higher at the state level than at the national level. Furthermore, entertainment is considered more of a reward in state capitals than in Washington, D.C. Most state legislators do not establish residence at the seat of government, as most members of Congress do. Living in a hotel, the state legislator generally finds the prospect of spending an evening on a lobbyist's expense account much more appealing than does the overworked and overentertained member of Congress.

The study of lobbying

Lobbying is often studied within the context of some larger process. Four examples of such processes can be given. First, lobbying has been studied as a component of the legislative process (Herring 1929; Gross 1953). Second, it has been studied as a component of the process by which the total government arrives at a decision about a given bill or policy (Bailey 1950; Latham 1952; Bauer et al. 1963). Third, lobbying is a significant component of studies of the group process of politics (Bentley 1908; Truman 1951). Fourth, studies of the nature and activity of interest groups naturally incorporate lobbying activity as a part of total group activity (Garceau 1941; Kile 1948; Taft 1954; Eckstein 1960; Potter 1961).

A much smaller proportion of studies give direct and primary attention to lobbying per se; these fall into three categories. First, Congressional investigating committees have developed valuable information on lobbying in Washington, D.C., usually with a view to possible legislative changes in the regulation of lobbying. Two prominent examples are the House of Representatives Select Committee on Lobbying Activities, which was active in 1949 and 1950 and was chaired by Representative Frank Buchanan of Pennsylvania; and the Senate Special Committee to Investigate Political Activities, Lobbying, and Campaign Contributions, which was active in 1956 and 1957 and was chaired by Senator John McClellan of Arkansas. Second, some persons regard lobbying as a threat to free government and believe the process should be exposed from time to time to the glare of publicity. These journalistic exposés are usually more specific and polemical than general and scholarly; two book-length efforts are Crawford (1939) and Schriftgiesser (1951). Third, some recent scholarly work has focused directly on the lobbyist as political actor. Based on first-hand interview evidence, these studies describe the roles of lobbyists as mediators between groups and government and give detailed evaluations of methods and techniques used in the lobbying process (Milbrath 1963; Patterson 1963).

This last approach to the study of lobbying, deriving empirical data from the persons who practice lobbying, seems to shed most light on the subject. To date, such evidence is available only on Washington lobbyists and lobbyists in a few state governments such as Michigan (De Vries 1960) and Oklahoma (Patterson 1963). It is important that such evidence also be gathered in different national political systems. The role of lobbying in the policy-making process will be much better understood when comparisons using adequate and valid data are possible across national cultures.

Evaluation

The paucity of empirical data makes it difficult to give an adequate evaluation of the role of lobbying in the political process. It might be helpful, however, to list some of the utilities and disutilities of lobbying as a part of the political process.

One utility of lobbying is the service (primarily information) that lobbyists and lobby organizations provide to official decision makers. These services are often proclaimed as being free since they do not come directly out of the taxpayer's pocket. In another sense, however, the costs of lobbying are passed on to the public in the form of higher prices for goods and services. Since the public pays for the service in either case, the service should be evaluated according to its quality. The present system of lobbying services makes for considerable duplication and is clearly wasteful and time-consuming. Thus, even though officials make considerable use of this lobbying service, it probably could be obtained from alternative sources at a lower cost to the body politic.

On the other hand, there is something to be said for having alternative and duplicative sources of information and other services. An official who can turn to more than one source for information is less subservient to any one source. Dispensing with lobbying service probably would make Congress even more dependent on the executive, since Congress generally has fewer adequate information sources.

Perhaps the most useful service is the transmission and clash of viewpoints. This serves a creative function in alerting decision makers to all possible policy alternatives and mitigates a good deal of the waste and frustration involved in lobbying. Officials might find other sources for most services lobbyists provide, but they benefit quite clearly from the representational function that the lobbyist spokesmen for specific interests perform. Lobby groups and lobbyists were evolved as a part of government to fulfill this need for specific representation, a need that no other component of the political process is adapted to fill (Milbrath 1963, p. 313).

A major disutility of lobbying, in addition to waste, is its potential for corruption. Lobbyists usually represent persons seeking specific—therefore private—ends. Such private ends may coincide or be compatible with the public welfare, but, in many instances, they are not. An adequate political system reconciles these private ends to the public welfare, but it cannot do this if officials or lobbyists act corruptly. Corruption enters when the system responds to money or property instead of to votes alone; when personal pecuniary rewards are offered to or accepted by officials as they arrive at decisions; and when decisions are made in secret, thus foreclosing opportunity for dissent from the opposition.

Lobbying in Washington, D.C., has a relatively low incidence of corruption, not so much because of legal controls (which are relatively inadequate) but because of built-in systemic controls of the process. These systemic controls are integral to the total policy-making system. All of the actors in this system are interdependent; no man makes a governmental decision by himself. Furthermore, each actor is vulnerable; he can be punished by someone else if he does not perform according to expectations. Systems having interdependent, vulnerable actors naturally develop rules of the game so that actors may relate to one another with the least amount of friction. There is no room in the rules of such a system for corrupt or deceitful relationships between actors; the potential costs to other actors are too great. Actors who refuse to conform to these rules are readily ejected from the system (Milbrath 1963, part IV).

Lobbying is but one factor in the total policy-making process of any government. Seldom can the predominating influence on a policy decision be attributed to lobbying. Other influences—such as the desires of the voters, the cajolings of fellow officials, and the political philosophy of officials—generally outweigh the impact of lobbying. Yet lobbying makes a useful contribution by injecting the policy desires of special interests into the political system. The range of policy alternatives available to decision makers is probably broader, and the perceptions by officials of the potential impact of their decisions is probably clearer, because of lobbying activity. Assuming that this leads to better-informed and higher-quality decisions, the net contribution of lobbying to the political process is probably positive.

LESTER W. MILBRATH

[*See also* INTEREST GROUPS; LEGISLATION; POLITICAL FINANCING; POLITICAL GROUP ANALYSIS; REPRESENTATION; RULES OF THE GAME.]

BIBLIOGRAPHY

AMERICAN ACADEMY OF POLITICAL AND SOCIAL SCIENCE 1958 *Unofficial Government: Pressure Groups and Lobbies.* Edited by Donald C. Blaisdell. Annals, Vol. 319. Philadelphia: The Academy.

BAILEY, STEPHEN K. 1950 *Congress Makes a Law: The Story Behind the Employment Act of 1946.* New York: Columbia Univ. Press.

BAUER, RAYMOND A.; POOL, ITHIEL DE SOLA; and DEXTER, L. A. 1963 *American Business and Public Policy: The Politics of Foreign Trade.* New York: Atherton.

BEER, SAMUEL H. 1958 Group Representation in Britain and the United States. American Academy of Political and Social Science, *Annals* 319:130–140.

BENTLEY, ARTHUR F. (1908) 1949 *The Process of Government: A Study of Social Pressures.* Bloomington, Ind.: Principia.

CHERINGTON, PAUL W.; and GILLEN, RALPH L. 1962 *The Business Representative in Washington.* Washington: Brookings Institution.

CRAWFORD, KENNETH G. 1939 *The Pressure Boys: The Inside Story of Lobbying in America.* New York: Messner.

DE VRIES, WALTER D. 1960 The Michigan Lobbyist: A Study in the Bases and Perceptions of Effectiveness. Ph.D. dissertation, Michigan State Univ.

ECKSTEIN, HARRY H. 1960 *Pressure Group Politics: The Case of the British Medical Association.* London: Allen & Unwin; Stanford (Calif.) Univ. Press.

GARCEAU, OLIVER (1941) 1961 *The Political Life of the American Medical Association.* Hamden, Conn.: Shoe String Press.

GROSS, BERTRAM M. 1953 *The Legislative Struggle: A Study in Social Combat.* New York: McGraw-Hill.

HERRING, E. PENDLETON 1929 *Group Representation Before Congress.* Baltimore: Johns Hopkins Press.

KILE, ORVILLE M. 1948 *The Farm Bureau Through Three Decades.* Baltimore: Waverly.

LANE, EDGAR 1964 *Lobbying and the Law.* Berkeley: Univ. of California Press.

Latham, Earl 1952 *The Group Basis of Politics: A Study in Basing-point Legislation.* Ithaca, N.Y.: Cornell Univ. Press; Oxford Univ. Press.

Milbrath, Lester W. 1963 *The Washington Lobbyists.* Chicago: Rand McNally.

Patterson, Samuel C. 1963 The Role of the Lobbyist: The Case of Oklahoma. *Journal of Politics* 25:72–92.

Potter, Allen M. 1961 *Organized Groups in British National Politics.* London: Faber.

Schriftgiesser, Karl 1951 *The Lobbyists: The Art and Business of Influencing Lawmakers.* Boston: Little.

Taft, Philip 1954 *The Structure and Government of Labor Unions.* Cambridge, Mass.: Harvard Univ. Press.

Truman, David B. (1951) 1962 *The Governmental Process: Political Interests and Public Opinion.* New York: Knopf.

U.S. Congress, House, Select Committee on Lobbying Activities 1951 *Report and Recommendations on Federal Lobbying Act.* 81st Congress, 2d Session, House Report No. 3239. Washington: Government Printing Office.

U.S. Congress, Senate, Special Committee to Investigate Political Activities, Lobbying, and Campaign Contributions 1957 *Final Report.* 85th Congress, 1st Session, Senate Report No. 395. Washington: Government Printing Office.

Zeigler, Harmon 1964 *Interest Groups in American Society.* Englewood Cliffs, N.J.: Prentice-Hall.

LOCAL FINANCE

Local governments and their financial structures have been subjected to heavy strains by the rapid population growth, urbanization, industrialization, and centralization of the past century. A local government is usually constrained by limited territorial jurisdiction, restrictions on the functions it can perform, ceilings on the amount of permitted taxes and debt, and restrictions on sources of revenue. Not only is its freedom limited, but often most of its actions are ordered, and its behavior then supervised, by the central government. It is no surprise that under these conditions local governments have responded sluggishly to the great technological and institutional changes of the past century. Few generalizations can be made about local finance, since each nation has a different constitution and each has many types of local governments; but one statement which holds for most of the world is that local governments have become weak relative to central governments.

The most common argument explaining the relative decline of local government is a financial one. It is asserted that the most tax-productive bases are pre-empted by central governments and that it is not feasible for a local government to raise its taxes, since industry and persons will respond by moving to other locations. This is far too simple. Throughout the world, localities can be found with almost every type of tax, and the burden of local taxes is highly variable among nations. The tremendous variation in behavior casts doubt on statements of necessary relationship. Localities do have greater financial problems than do central governments, but solutions that enable the localities to be vigorous and relatively autonomous are available. The relative decline of local government has been accompanied by a refusal fully to exploit purely financial solutions to problems, and it indicates that nonfinancial factors are more significant.

Among nations, the United States has one of the most active sets of local governments, but even in the United States the ratio of federal expenditures on civilian activity to state and local expenditures doubled in the first half of the twentieth century. Despite this relative decline of local governments, in absolute terms local governments have grown greatly in importance. In 1902 local expenditures were less than $900 million, and by 1964 they were over $45,000 million in current dollars. State expenditures increased even more dramatically, from $134 million in 1902 to $24,275 million in 1964. Per capita state and local expenditures increased from under $13 in 1902 to over $360 in 1964. These growth figures are dramatic, but they are accompanied, though to a lesser degree, by the world-wide phenomena of an outright transfer of some functions to central governments and of a shift of financial support to central governments, with a consequent absorption of authority by the central governments.

Given the wide range of experiences in degrees of centralization, any simple set of hypotheses would most likely be wrong. Unfortunately, there has been very little research in comparative local finance, so that sophisticated arguments are not available; therefore, we will have to be satisfied with rather general explanations of the relative decline of local government and finance.

Local government, like the horse and the candle, has been the victim of technology. High among the list of significant technological breakthroughs have been the transportation and communication revolutions, which have greatly reduced spatial costs. While these innovations have completely changed industrial structures, have made markets national and international in scope, and have made resources, as well as production centers, highly mobile, local governments have remained fixed in spatial jurisdiction.

The increase in the size of input and product markets has resulted in a great increase in the number of local governments that can affect the efficient operations of the markets. A system of roads can be crippled by poor design of one part, or inadequate education in one area may mean a poor labor force for another area to which the population moves. Therefore, the supply of inputs or the market possibilities of a firm in a city may be strongly affected by the behavior of many distant local governments which it cannot directly influence. Mass-production, standardized industry expanded throughout the nation, while local governments remained fixed. It is not surprising that pressures were strong to create uniformity of tax treatment and of public services in the various parts of the nation—a reasonable uniformity which has been effected by transfer of functions to central governments and by central subventions to local governments.

The goal of uniform public service throughout the nation is not restricted to those services which are inputs to industry; it extends to products going directly to households. Uniformity in consumption of public services would not necessarily lead to centralization, were it not for a second major factor. Fiscal resources are not uniformly distributed among local jurisdictions. If localities were to apply similar tax structures to their economic bases, very different yields would result. If they sought to vary their tax systems in order to realize somewhat equal per capita yields and similar levels of public services, they would have highly variable tax systems. This would have the undesirable consequences of complexity in taxation and nonuniform treatment. The latter might encourage mobile resources to move elsewhere to find another structure that might not tax them as severely. Achievement of uniformity in service without too much variation in tax structure requires the transfer of financing to a central government.

The simplest and most adaptable response of government to the changing economy is the design of a central administrative agency which can establish operational rules independent of past conventions and responsive to the new set of needs. This response has been the most common. The transfer of functions to a central government means a centralization of authority, control, and finance; but administration may be as widely dispersed as the pattern of local governments, or it may take an entirely new organizational form. From the point of view of attaining the most effective government response to the need for public services, this total centralization may be best; but the less radical solution of attempting to work through existing local governments is often adopted. Despite the relatively greater growth of the central administration, local administration is still important and probably will remain so, especially in the United States, where the vitality of local government follows from the constitutionally imposed federal structure and from the structure of political parties, which have their strong base in state and local governments.

Types of arrangements

The nations of the world have invented many financial arrangements by which to support local governments; these arrangements can be ordered into a few categories.

Local taxes on differentiated bases. In the United States the major illustration of a separate tax base is the property tax. The federal government makes no use of the property tax, and state governments have been reducing their use of the tax. Some local governments, especially single-purpose districts like school districts and irrigation districts, are restricted to the property tax. Although the property tax is still the principal support of local government, it has declined in importance; its base has been progressively narrowed as more types of property have been removed from the base and other sources of support have been introduced.

Local reliance on the property tax is not uniform. The average property tax rate for the United States was estimated to be 1.4 per cent of market value of locally assessed property in 1962, but this varied from 2.7 per cent in Massachusetts to 0.5 per cent in South Carolina. Comparable variation exists in the percentage of local government revenues collected from property taxes.

Although property taxes have become relatively less important, their role as the distinctive local tax has resulted in extreme pressure to increase the property tax yield because of the increased demand for local services brought about by the rapid increase in urban population, especially in the number of school-age children. Although the demand for public services and property tax yields have increased, property tax payers have energetically sought to reduce their taxes through political action.

One way to reduce the property tax has been to introduce other financial sources, and these will be discussed below. Another way has been to limit the freedom of the local government in the use of the tax. This has taken the form of rate limits imposed by the state governments and of an erosion of the base through exemptions and poor administration. The property tax payer has been able to utilize his political power in the state capital to restrain local finance in one direction, but this has resulted in tax expansion in other directions.

Another political response to the increase in property taxes has been the adoption of fiscal profitability as a criterion for many local public policies, such as zoning, subdivision control, public facilities planning, and annexation.

In considering alternative land use developments, the local authority's analysts compute the property tax yields and the public expenditures associated with each alternative and then adopt the alternative with the maximum difference between property tax yields and public expenditures. Sometimes the analysis is more sophisticated, involving consideration of all the revenues to the local government and all the local expenditures requiring local finance. The results of the analysis almost always show low fiscal profitability in residential use by low-income families with school-age children and high fiscal profitability in industrial use requiring few transportation services, or in residential use by high-income families with few children. The outcome might be to encourage the development of clean industry and the residence of its executives and to discourage the workers employed in the plants from living in the area. Competitive behavior by all of the localities in the area would be self-defeating; on the other hand, if only a subset of the local governments adopted the criterion of fiscal profitability, then the entire area would develop inefficiently. Workers would travel longer distances, industry might not be optimally located, and so on.

The separate tax base does have the virtue of encouraging independent government, and certainly it has permitted American local government to be viable; but it has meant some loss in the efficiency of the operations of metropolitan areas. Although this separate (property) tax base is not likely to disappear, its role will decline because of the many defects of the tax per se and because of the endemic difficulties of independent financing of local governments. [*See* TAXATION, *article on* PROPERTY TAXES.]

Shared bases with separate levies. Two types of base sharing are practiced. One form is that of complete independence between the levels of government; the bases need not be identical and the rates are independently determined. In the second type the base is identical, although rates may be independently determined, and often there is common administration. Both types are common in all nations.

An illustration of complete independence is the income tax. Although this is usually considered a central tax, many localities use it as well. In the United States in 1964, it was used by two-thirds of the states and by 30 cities. Although the states may define their base so as to approximate the federal base, the local income taxes tend to be payroll taxes. Because its narrower base gives rise to charges of inequity, the local income tax is not likely to be used widely.

A more common form of sharing of bases is under some joint administration, either restricted to the definition of the base or extending to collection. The property tax takes this form within the structure of local governments and in some countries is shared by local and national governments.

In the United States property may be appraised by the state or county, and each of the hundreds of local governments may then independently determine the rate it requires to satisfy its revenue requirements. In some cases a common appraisal of the property is required, while in others it is simply economical for one community to accept the appraisal of another. In either event, the set of taxes may often be collected in one bill and then allocated among the governments.

Although this procedure does limit the power of the government to determine the base most advantageous to it, it has the advantages of uniformity and administrative efficiency while allowing each local government to determine the level and distribution of services it prefers.

A somewhat more centralized tax shared by state and local governments in the United States is the general retail sales tax. Over two-thirds of the states have retail sales taxes, and several thousand local governments add tax supplements onto the state tax. There is a marked trend to adopt this tax structure, with administration by the state or local government and local government option to share in the base. Generally there is a ceiling on the local supplement, and sometimes a specific amount is stipulated. Under this structure the local government has formal freedom, but the incentives for all local governments to develop a uniform policy are great.

The trend has been to move from overlapping taxation of a common base, with independent definition of the base and rates, to joint definition of the base and common administration, with independent rates, and then on to more restrictive rules about rates.

Shared taxes. A shared tax is simply the transformation of a local supplement to a national tax into a simple assessment of the tax by the national government, with some share going to the local governments. This scheme is fairly common throughout the world, though of relatively less importance in the United States. Generally the transformation has taken the form of extending state administration of the tax, returning some of the proceeds to the local government which had been using it, e.g., the development of state motor-vehicle license taxes out of local personal property taxes assessed against automobiles. The initial impetus to shared taxes was the desire to achieve simplification and uniformity, but rules of sharing have become increasingly complex. Issues of need have been introduced into the formulas, so that it is often difficult to distinguish between a shared tax and an intergovernmental grant. Although, in principle, these two forms of financing are very different, experience has shown that if the central government has authority over the sharing formula, it will exercise its discretionary power and the local government will lose control over the size of its budget and sometimes even over the use of these shared funds.

Intergovernmental grants. The most completely centralized form of local financing is tax assessment and collection by the central government, with a transfer of funds to local governments for financing their services. This type of finance has grown most rapidly. Control over finance does not logically entail authority over local public services, but experience has shown that this has been the usual result. Generally, the three preceding forms allow fairly complete freedom to the local government in the allocation of its budget and often in determining the size of its budget. But even if no financial controls are exercised by the central government, localities may not have autonomy, since in many nations local governments are required to provide specific services which sometimes are prescribed in detail.

There are two general types of financial transfers from central governments, basically distinguished by the amount of discretion which remains with the local government in the allocation of the funds at its disposal.

Unconditional grants. The free unconditional grant in its purest form would be a simple transfer of funds from the central government, which is considered the most efficient taxing body, to the local government, which is considered the best decision-making body. If the problem confronting local government were simply financial, one would expect to see these unconditional grants play a major role. In fact, their role is trivial. Few countries use them, and where they do exist, as in England, they are not a major factor in local finance.

Local government has long advocated that grants be made as unconditionally as possible, in order to retain as much local autonomy as possible. But even where only minimum conditions are accepted as desirable, redistribution objectives are introduced into the criteria by which the grants are allocated among communities; and these originally very broad redistributional objectives readily become more specific and thereby influence the quality and types of public services to be encouraged.

Conditional grants. Conditional grants to local governments carry with them specific requirements for local government behavior. Since the conditions must be policed, extensive audit procedures accompany the grants. Local governments generally oppose this form of support, since they dislike the administrative supervision by the central government and they oppose its direct control of their budget.

The motives behind conditional grants are many. In some cases, especially that of the United States, it is not politically feasible to establish a central administration, but the same results are sought through imposing very specific conditions. Two other important motives are the encouragement of specific services and financial equalization.

The encouragement of specific services is obvious when the grant does not require the local government to contribute to the support of the service. Some local governments might deplore that the grant is directed toward their less urgent needs, but at least it will not divert their resources. But often the condition of the grant requires matching outlays from the local government. Since the local dollar spent on the subsidized service will buy proportionately more of that service, it is clear that budgetary allocations will be affected. There will be incentives to expand local support of the subsidized services. This budgetary distortion has been resented by local authorities. The encouragement of specific services through local matching provisions has become less important.

Financial equalization has become more important. Although this objective was never absent, initial matching grants were more favorable to the wealthier communities. More complex formulas have since been devised to take into account local needs, local fiscal resources, and local fiscal effort. Despite the increasing sophistication and complexity of formulas, no consensus has developed about an optimal formula. Subsidies distort; their administration will be lax if there is no burden on the local government; and if a burden is imposed, then the localities may not have the appropriate incentive to expand the service or equity may not be served.

Financing of local debt

Another aspect of local finance which has dramatically changed in many countries is the financing of local debt. Even in the United States, where a local government usually goes to the capital markets very much as private firms do, changes have occurred. Not only have debt limits become common and referendums by the voters often required, but the approval of a state agency as to technical or financial feasibility of the project now is often required. A further change has been the growth of loans by the central government to the local governments. In some countries almost all loans are centralized; in the United States the loan program is one of the instruments of intergovernmental transfers. The loan is often administered by the agency which administers the grant program and which may be carrying on services as well. State governments also extend loans to local governments.

Although the centralization of government and finances has been the most important recent structural change, another reorganization, concerning metropolitan government, may be of comparable importance, especially in the United States. A typical metropolitan area is made up of hundreds of governments. Some are the residuals of an agricultural economy of a half-century past, others are the many new suburban cities, and still more are the special-function governments ranging from a small-area police district to a regional air-pollution control board. Most of them have taxing powers, while some can finance themselves only by user charges. The conflicts among these governments have focused on the suburban–central city rivalry for financial bases. Central cities have charged that suburbanites work in the central cities and use all of their amenities while living in the suburbs, where they pay their local property taxes. The suburbs charge that they bear the heavy burdens of education and residential services while the fiscally rich industrial and commercial properties are in the central cities or industrial enclaves. Issues of equity in finance and service have inhibited agreements about urban development programs, and meanwhile the government of the metropolitan area has deteriorated.

The problems of metropolitan government and finance have been elaborated in great detail. Solutions have been of an *ad hoc* nature, e.g., a federal subsidy for urban renewal, a new government for a mass rapid-transit system, or an additional tax base. Despite the muddling-through procedures, there has been a great deal of experimentation.

In the past decade, user charges have increased sharply at the state and local levels. The metering of water and on-street parking has expanded as a revenue source, and the value of user charges as rationing devices is beginning to be understood. User charges not only help to bring about an efficient rationing of limited public services, provide cues determining the scale at which services should be performed, and ease the financial plight of cities, but also lessen the conflict among governments. For example, if there is a charge on visiting the museum, it is irrelevant whether the school bus is discharging suburban or central city children: either school district would have to pay for cultural enrichment. Or it is unimportant if the parker is from the suburb or the central city if he pays the full incremental cost of making the street space available for his parked car. It is very likely that there will be a significant expansion of pricing of public services over a wide range of activities. [*See* PRICES, *article on* PRICING POLICIES.]

Innovations in local government arrangements have occurred in response to crises: many special authorities without taxing powers, or districts with taxing powers which move freely across old jurisdictional lines, have been created. From one perspective the *ad hoc* responses to crises have generated another layer of bureaucracies and assessing agencies, complicating still further the problems of rational management. But these governments are very fluid, their political bases are weak, and the possibilities of a more deliberative reshuffling of government and financial structures are not trivial. Metropolitan governments may develop out of the array of municipal governments and overlapping special districts and authorities, but it is likely that the state and federal governments will be the prime movers in metropolitan development and that the financial base of the metropolitan government may look very different from that of a mere composite of existing local governments.

JULIUS MARGOLIS

[*See also* LOCAL GOVERNMENT; TAXATION.]

BIBLIOGRAPHY

BRAZER, HARVEY E. 1962 Some Fiscal Aspects of Metropolitanism. Pages 61–82 in Guthrie S. Birkhead (editor), *Metropolitan Issues: Social, Governmental, Fiscal.* Syracuse Univ., Maxwell Graduate School of Citizenship and Public Affairs.

BURKHEAD, JESSE 1963 *State and Local Taxes for Public Education.* Syracuse Univ. Press.

DUE, JOHN F. 1963 *Taxation and Economic Development in Tropical Africa.* Cambridge, Mass.: M.I.T. Press.

Federalism and Economic Growth in Underdeveloped Countries: A Symposium, by Ursula K. Hicks et al. 1961 New York: Oxford Univ. Press.

HUMES, SAMUEL; and MARTIN, EILEEN M. 1961 *The Structure of Local Governments Throughout the World.* The Hague: Nijhoff.

MARGOLIS, JULIUS 1961 Metropolitan Finance Problems: Territories, Functions, and Growth. Pages 229–293 in Universities–National Bureau Committee for

Economic Research, *Public Finances: Needs, Sources, and Utilization*. Princeton Univ. Press.

MAXWELL, JAMES A. 1965 *Financing State and Local Governments*. Washington: Brookings Institution.

NETZER, DICK 1966 *Economics of the Property Tax*. Washington: Brookings Institution.

PHILIP, KJELD 1954 *Intergovernmental Fiscal Relations*. Copenhagen: Institute of Economics and History.

PREST, ALAN R. 1962 *Public Finance in Under-developed Countries*. London: Weidenfeld & Nicolson.

SIMON, HERBERT A. 1943 *Fiscal Aspects of Metropolitan Consolidation*. Berkeley: Univ. of California, Bureau of Public Administration.

U.S. ADVISORY COMMISSION ON INTERGOVERNMENTAL RELATIONS 1962 *Measures of State and Local Fiscal Capacity and Tax Effort*. Washington: Government Printing Office.

U.S. ADVISORY COMMISSION ON INTERGOVERNMENTAL RELATIONS 1964 *The Role of Equalization in Federal Grants*. Washington: Government Printing Office.

U.S. ADVISORY COMMISSION ON INTERGOVERNMENTAL RELATIONS 1965 *Metropolitan Social and Economic Disparities: Implications for Intergovernmental Relations in Central Cities and Suburbs*. Washington: Government Printing Office.

U.S. BUREAU OF THE CENSUS 1964 *Census of Governments: 1962*. Washington: Government Printing Office. → See especially Volume 5, *Local Government in Metropolitan Areas*, and Volume 6, No. 4, *Historical Statistics on Governmental Finances and Employment*.

LOCAL GOVERNMENT

Local government may be loosely defined as a public organization authorized to decide and administer a limited range of public policies within a relatively small territory which is a subdivision of a regional or national government. Local government is at the bottom of a pyramid of governmental institutions, with the national government at the top and intermediate governments (states, regions, provinces) occupying the middle range. Normally, local government has general jurisdiction and is not confined to the performance of one specific function or service.

This simple definition obscures wide variations in local governmental systems and operational patterns, and it should be supplemented by a system of classification for both description and analysis. In the past, local governments have been classified largely in terms of their formal structures. Thus, in the United States great stress was laid on the question of whether a local government had a mayor with broad executive powers or a mayor who was little more than a presiding officer of the city council (the strong versus the weak mayor "plans"); whether the council members divided among themselves administrative responsibility for the several aspects of local government (the commission plan); or whether the council employed a professional executive agent to administer the city's affairs and be accountable to the council (the city manager plan). Similar emphasis was placed on form and structure by authors attempting cross-national comparisons of local governmental systems. A perusal of the publications of the International Union of Local Authorities (e.g., *The Structure of Local Governments* . . . , Humes and Martin 1961) or of the contents of *The Municipal Yearbook* will indicate the dominant concern for structure. The *Yearbook*, for example, provides details on the organization of local government, but only in 1963 did it begin to provide data on local elections.

The formal structure of local government, important as it can be to the character of a system, is not the only nor even the most significant determinant of the style of local government. The quality and character of a local government are determined by a multiplicity of factors—for example, national and local traditions, customary deference patterns, political pressures, party influence and discipline, bureaucratic professionalism, economic resource controls, and social organization and beliefs. That a local government is located in a nation controlled by a communist party may be an infinitely more important fact than the structural forms it has. That an American city is located in the South, where Negroes occupy an inferior social position, may explain far more about the local government than its structure. The existence of a huge economic enterprise within a given municipality may be more determinative of the style and policies of a local government than its organization. And, it might be added, this may be as true in a totalitarian regime as in a democratic one.

There are hundreds of thousands of local governments in the world, and we lack sufficient information about their operational characteristics to make completely confident generalizations about the nature of local government or to isolate the most critical variables that shape it. In the process of moving toward surer understanding of the phenomenon it is useful to pursue answers to three basic questions about any local government. First, to what extent is there local self-government? For example, do the people of the community have an opportunity to participate in government through meaningful elections and to have access to public officials to express their opinions by organized and individual activity? Second, to what extent does the municipality have relative autonomy and discretionary authority to act? That is, is there a *deconcentration* of authority from the central government to the locality with little or no local discretion, or is there *decentralization* of authority with relative discretion to undertake programs on local initiative and with relative freedom from strict supervision and restriction from the central government? Third, is the local government a vital and significant force in the lives of the people? Is the government an institution with the will and the authority to undertake activities that deeply affect the lives of people, or is it so marginal an aspect of life that the citizenry is scarcely aware that it exists?

To facilitate discussion of local government in terms of these broad questions, five broad categories of local governmental systems may be postulated: (1) federal–decentralized, (2) unitary–decentralized, (3) Napoleonic–prefect, (4) communist, and (5) postcolonial. The meaning of each category will become clear in the discussion.

Federal–decentralized systems

Those federal systems which decentralize much authority to the regional governments that compose the federation also tend to be the nations that allow the broadest range of discretionary authority to local government. This is not true of all systems that are called federal, however, but only of those with actual decentralization. The Soviet government is formally organized along federal lines, but such decentralization of authority to the districts as exists occurs under strict central government controls; it is made abundantly clear that the subunits of the Soviet system (the "republics" and their subdivisions) are in reality agents of the central government and the Communist party. In federal systems with much decentralization (for example, Australia, Canada, Germany, Switzerland, and the United States) the degree of autonomy of local government varies considerably from country to country, but in all cases a considerable degree of local independence prevails.

This variation extends deeper than the country-by-country comparison, for there is often much variation among individual states or provincial–regional governments as to the forms and authority of local government. For example, the closeness of supervision by administrative agencies of regional governments varies widely from fairly extensive reporting and oversight to almost none, except in cases of flagrant corruption. Likewise, certain states in the United States grant "home rule" to municipalities by statutory or state constitutional provisions that permit municipalities to alter their forms of government at will and that grant local authority to "make all laws and ordinances relating to municipal concerns," or broadly the "powers of local self-government," while in other states the municipality has to appeal to the state legislature for specific permission to undertake a particular program.

The idea of "home rule" as local independence is an ancient doctrine, but as a legal concept it originated in the late nineteenth century when American state legislatures interfered, often corruptly, with the functioning of local government. Gradually, home rule has extended, with varying degrees of effectiveness, to most of the states. Home rule does not grant total autonomy by any means, since legislatures through general law and the courts through interpretation still restrain local government. Nevertheless, the concept contradicts the principle of municipal inferiority that previously stood as a basic rule of law. In the late nineteenth century Judge John F. Dillon stated the classic principle of the status of the local government by saying that municipal corporations were completely creatures of the legislature which could control or even destroy municipalities at will. In the famous Dillon's Rule he stated:

> It is a general and undisputed proposition of law that a *municipal corporation possesses and can exercise the following powers, and no others:* First, those granted in *express words;* second, those *necessarily or fairly implied* in or *incident* to the powers expressly granted; third, those essential to the accomplishment of the declared objects and purposes of the corporation—not simply convenient, but indispensable. Any fair, reasonable, substantial doubt concerning the existence of power is resolved by the courts against the corporation, and the power is denied. (Dillon [1872] 1911, vol. 1, sec. 237)

American courts no longer follow Dillon's Rule rigidly, although its fundamental precepts are still frequently drawn upon even in home rule states, when local and state jurisdictions are in conflict. Litigation and the threat of litigation are important restraints upon local independence.

In the United States all local legislative bodies and most chief executives are directly elected. Local government organization varies enormously —from the town meeting, where all registered voters may participate in basic decision making, to the highly bureaucratized governments of many large cities where mayors combat the inertia of professionalism and pluralistic stasis (see Sayre & Kaufman 1960; Dahl 1961; Banfield 1961). In some cities powerful political party machines control decision making by the formal officeholders; in others business elites have great power; in still others authority is widely dispersed to independent boards and commissions which are relatively invisible to the voters and partially beyond the control of the council or the mayor (for example, Los Angeles). Although it has commonly been thought that American small communities are highly democratic in the sense that the public has easy access to and much control over their representatives, research on local governmental operation suggests that this is not necessarily true (see Vidich & Bensman 1958; Presthus 1964). For example, survey research in American cities concerning the citizen's "subjective competence" (that is, a person's belief that he can exert significant influence upon his local government) indicated that two-thirds of the respondents felt a high degree of confidence in their political effectiveness, but there was no evidence of significant variation in terms of the size of the community from which the respondent came. Indeed, insofar as there was a variation, it favored the larger as opposed to the smallest cities (see Almond & Verba 1963, p. 235).

Swiss municipalities also have a wide area of local autonomy, although there are variations among the Swiss cantons (states) in this respect. The German-speaking cantons usually permit more discretion than do the Italian- and French-speaking ones. A high degree of local self-government prevails, particularly in the rural communities; in nine out of ten communes the municipal deliberative body is an assembly of all electors. In larger municipalities elective councils are employed, and under certain conditions a referendum may be used to submit questions to the vote of the people.

Other federal systems permit somewhat less local autonomy. In Australia, for example, local actions are subject to review by the state governor and ordinances are effective only after their approval by the governor, although there remains a general autonomy for the locality within the limitations of its local charter and the supervision of the state departments of local government. In Canada a considerable sphere of local autonomy exists, but not as much as traditionally prevails in the United States or Switzerland. An illustration of this is found in the decision of the provincial legislature of Ontario to form a new unit of metropolitan government in the Toronto area in 1953. The premier of Ontario warned that the legislature would act if the local communities failed to create some orderly method of coping with the problems of the metropolitan area, and when no action followed the legislature created a new governmental unit covering both the center city and its suburbs. While such action would be legally feasible in most (although not all) states in the United States, American political traditions of local independence make it nearly impossible to do this.

The local government system of the West German Federal Republic also has variations in local powers and procedures among the provincial governments (*Länder*), yet the over-all independence of local governments is considerable. The degree of independence does not match that in the United States or Switzerland, however. The burgomaster (roughly equivalent to a mayor) is a professional administrator and occupies a very strong position in the local government; significantly, he is not only a local official but a federal and state official as well, since the city performs certain functions for the higher jurisdictions. The supervision of local government from higher echelons is also fairly rigorous, and this has increased as the practice of the state's delegating certain functions for local performance has grown. It is perhaps suggestive of the representativeness of German local government that a far higher proportion of German respondents to an opinion survey indicated that they believed they could "do something about an unjust local law or regulation" than those who felt any competence to correct an unjust national law (Almond & Verba 1963, p. 185).

The vitality of local government in the federal–decentralized countries varies both within and among countries. In the United States the role of local government expanded greatly with the maturation of industrial society in the first half of the twentieth century; protective, regulatory, welfare, planning, economic promotion, cultural, and other activities were initiated or expanded. But the extent of expansion varies greatly with the size of the city, the area of the country, and even for adjacent cities. In the largest cities, where the functional expansion has been greatest, the hugeness and impersonal nature of the government probably make government appear to impinge less on the lives of the citizens than it does in fact. In smaller rural or suburban communities, local government ranges from the moribund to the fairly vital. Likewise in other nations the degree of vitality and impact of government varies widely. In the Swiss communities where a town-meeting style of government prevails, the sense of involvement and the level of participation are high. The English-speaking Commonwealth federal systems appear to have a range of variation in the vitality of local government that compares generally with that in the United States. [*See* FEDERALISM.]

Unitary–decentralized systems

Great Britain and the Scandinavian countries are examples of nations with unitary (that is, nonfederal) governments which have a considerable degree of decentralization of autonomous power to localities. Although in all cases there is supervision by the central government, and although localities can take only such actions as authorized by the central government, local governments in these nations do have fairly wide responsibilities and make independent decisions about them. The independent status of the English city has a long history, as evidenced by ancient royal charters of cities. The first charters were just agreements by the king to recognize certain concessions that local leaders had bought or bargained for, but in time the charters became regularized and the basis of a considerable area of local discretion. As early as the fifteenth century merchant guilds and borough councils originated the rudiments of local self-government. Parliament remains the supreme source of local authority, but the practice of permitting local prerogatives is so firmly established that curtailment is always resisted and comes only after great deliberation. Nevertheless, there has been a considerable diminution of local independence since the nineteenth century. Although the functions of the municipality have in some respects been enlarged with the coming of new problems and public policies to meet them (for example, public housing), an extension of the central government's concern for formerly purely local matters has taken place simultaneously. Particularly in the fields where the central government has provided a percentage of the cost of programs through grants-in-aid, central government departments have greatly extended their control over local decisions. Centrally established minimum standards of performance have unquestionably raised the efficiency of local government, but at the same time they have curtailed the independence that once existed.

British local government is representative self-government. The local council is directly elected, although the local executive is not. The mayor (or chairman in certain local bodies) is chosen from among the council members, but he is not the chief executive in the same way that an American mayor is. The British mayor is more a ceremonial and presiding official than an active executive leader, and to the extent that he is the latter it is the result of his personal qualities or his political position. The major operating element of the British local council is the committee system, into which noncouncil members are co-opted as experts on aspects of policy covered by the particular committee. Although the council must ratify all committee actions before they are valid, the committees are the active elements in the process rather than the council as a whole. The town (or county) clerk also plays a significant role in local government in his relationship to the committees. It is he who prepares information for the committee and sets the agenda, but he is not a British parallel to the American city manager, for he is not directly given the function of overseeing administration. Traditionally clerks are not trained in administrative management but in the law, although their apprenticeship in local government necessarily emphasizes administrative matters, and as the problems of local government become more complex it increasingly falls to the clerk to provide expertise and to coordinate the diverse elements of local government.

Since the early nineteenth century local governments in the Scandinavian nations have been allowed a fair degree of autonomy. The list of powers for local government is extensive, and while regional appointees of the central government who are in some respects similar to the French prefect oversee local operations, the actual supervision is not strict and does not compare with that in nations with prefectoral systems. In Norway all actions involving expenditures must be cleared with the provincial governor before they can be carried out, which on the surface suggests that Norwegian local government may be less autonomous than that of Britain. In fact, however, Norwegian municipalities have somewhat more discretion, since the supervision is not strict. Norwegian local government is vital, has broad scope, and is a very important aspect of the nation's political–governmental system. Local government is a common recruiting ground for higher political office, and local forms and practices have been used as modes for creating regional institutions and practices. Denmark also has close supervision of fiscal matters, but the check on local government that this might imply is not apparently onerous. Local government is democratic, has a fairly wide range of discretion, but is somewhat less autonomous and vital than Norwegian local government. In Sweden local government activities are divided between those that are "free" of supervision, except on legal challenge, and those that are "regulated." Generally speaking, the free functions are those concerned with municipally provided utilities and cultural–recreational activities, whereas the regulated ones include a long list of functions extending from welfare services to town planning, local courts, and school administration. As in Norway and England there is extensive use of committees of the council for conduct of business. Finland's local governments have somewhat less discretionary authority and are subject to closer supervision, but the general pattern appears to be not markedly different from that in other Scandinavian nations. [*See* PARLIAMENTARY GOVERNMENT.]

Napoleonic–prefect systems

The peculiarity of this style of local government is that the central government places in subregions of the nation an agent of the national government to oversee, and if necessary to countermand, suspend, or replace local governments. The system is a direct survivor of the ancient institutions by which France attempted to create a centralized nation out of a scattered system of feudal fiefs, small cities, and ecclesiastical domains. The office of *intendant*, conceived by Richelieu in the early seventeenth century, was a means of extending the king's authority into the hinterland, where the thirty *intendants* were known as the "thirty tyrants." Animosity toward the office resulted in its dissolution in the French Revolution, but Napoleon restored it as the office of prefect, and it still flourishes in France today. In varying forms the office is commonly found in southern Europe and in Latin America, just as British forms are found in English-speaking nations.

In France the basic unit of local government is the commune, of which there are some 38,000, and each is under the supervision of a prefect of a *département* (of which there are 90) or under the intermediate control of a subprefect of an *arrondissement* (more than 300). (In some areas superprefects also provide regional supervision.) The commune is typically a small community, since most of France is rural, although cities are also organized as communes. There is a high degree of local interest in commune politics, and council elections are often heatedly contested. The mayor, who is chosen from the ranks of the council, has a wide range of executive authority; and although he is legally accountable to the council, he nevertheless is a powerful political force in the municipality. Initiative in fiscal matters and other policy issues is in the mayor's hands. The mayor and the council operate under the eye of the prefect or subprefect, however; and all commune actions are subject to review by the prefect, who may refuse to approve or may even dissolve the local council or remove the mayor. There are, on the average, some three hundred dissolutions per year, although a major cause of this is irreconcilable disagreement within the council rather than conflict with the prefect.

It should not be assumed, however, that French local government is actually controlled from Paris. Prefects and subprefects have a considerable area of discretion, and they often find it wise to strike a political balance between themselves and the mayors, who are not entirely without weapons to deploy against a demanding prefect, for national political forces are often just barely beneath the surface of local politics. Many mayors are influential national political figures, and local politics is a common basis for a political career. Despite this countervailing force against centralization, local government in France remains far more subordinate and dependent than in such countries as the United States and England. Police and education, for example, are largely beyond local control; fiscal controls and subventions are deployed by prefects to bring commune policy in line. Interest and participation, however, run high in France. A British observer, granting that in England local government had more autonomy than it does in France, nevertheless found in France more interest in local matters and more vitality in local government (Chapman 1953, p. 221).

In other Mediterranean countries and in Latin America, where the prefectoral system prevails, there are many variations on the French pattern. In Spain and Italy, for example, there is considerably more centralization than in France. In Spain central government controls are rigorously applied to the more than nine thousand municipalities; the mayor is appointed by the central government, and he is the strongest force in local affairs. Portugal has a similar system of central control. In Italy the prefectoral system was a convenient device for extending the powers of the fascist system into the hinterland, and interestingly one of the consequences of the fascist interlude is that the prefect has greater power today than in the prefascist era (Fried 1963, p. 261). Local councils are popularly elected, but the mayor and the councils are well aware of the power of the prefect, who uses his position not only to provide general administrative supervision but to pursue political objectives as well —such as the curbing of the power of communists when they take over a local government. In rural areas particularly, local government is not a vital or popular institution; it is often considered by the people to be an element of nature to be endured—like drought or disease—not something from which benefits are likely to be derived.

In Latin America extensive supervision of local

government by officials similar to the prefect is common. In some countries the local mayor is appointed by the central government, and in others he is elected, but his actions and those of locally elective councils are subjected to extremely close control by the central government. Brazil, with its federal system, does not conform to this, however, and it has relatively little central or state government oversight of the details of local government operations. An essentially prefectoral system is also used in Japan, where, significantly, a large measure of the authority of the supervising administrator lies in his discretionary authority to grant subsidies to local government.

Communist systems

The local governmental systems of communist nations are, in general, examples of deconcentration of authority rather than decentralization. That is, the local governmental unit is an agency of the central government, and it functions as an integral element of the hierarchical administrative system of the state. The area of local independence is narrow and extends only to minor matters, whereas control devices are extensive and are rigorously applied. Local officials are well aware that their decisions must conform to an over-all design of higher authorities, and they know, too, that to divert budget funds to other purposes without permission may mean dismissal or even imprisonment. These systems are unique in that local governments are given a role in economic activities infinitely more extensive than in capitalist nations. Finally the discipline of the Communist party is a means of controlling policy in detail. As a supplement to and a check on the administrative system, the Communist party with its rigid discipline controls the key positions in government. Indeed, the Communist party's role is remarkably similar to that of the classic American local government party machine. Where a classic American machine acquired complete control, the formal distribution of authority was unimportant; what mattered was the internal discipline of the party through which decisions were made from the top to the bottom of the government (McKean 1940). The critical difference between the two situations is that the American boss system depends upon local insularity to maintain control, whereas the communist system utilizes the local party to carry out the program of the national party leaders.

Local government in the Soviet Union is subject to very intensive control, but the minute and stifling controls of the Stalin era are no longer used. The ponderous apparatus needed for detailed supervision of local operations from Moscow became so expensive and inefficient that in the 1950s efforts were made to decentralize to a limited extent. In the 1930s the rigidity of controls was such that a local bakery's request for a supplemental flour allotment was passed to higher and higher authority until it finally reached the desk of the premier, and he approved the request himself (Granick 1960, p. 162). Documents captured by the Germans in 1941, in the town of Smolensk, also reveal the manner in which the party was used to assert tight control by Moscow over local operations (Fainsod 1958).

The decentralizing tendencies of the 1950s and 1960s did not necessarily increase the degree of local self-government. As before, the locality elects large local soviets in which there is much discussion of local affairs, but apparently the decision-making power remains with the executive committee of the soviet rather than with the soviet members themselves. Local leaders are, however, permitted a wider range of discretion for which ultimately they are held responsible to their superiors. Evidence that the new policies did not involve a total change is the story in *Pravda* following the departure of Khrushchev from power. Khrushchev favored reinforced concrete blocks over bricks for construction and, as word of his attitude filtered down the hierarchy, local managers shut down brickworks regardless of local demand. Khrushchev's successors promised in *Pravda* to grant to local soviets power to "decide all local issues"; if this becomes a reality it will involve an enormous change in the traditional balance of political power in the U.S.S.R. [*See* COMMUNISM, *article on* SOVIET COMMUNISM.]

The Chinese commune is a striking experiment in devising local institutions to serve the purposes of a dedicated communist regime. The communes are at once instruments of economic planning, educational and cultural activity, and governmental control. In order to increase manpower, women are freed from child care and household work through provision of nurseries, common eating facilities, and "service centers" for clothing repair and other household chores. Millions of Chinese eat in public mess halls in both agricultural and urban communes. Local marginal industries are organized and operated by the commune. It is claimed that more than 500 million Chinese were in communes in 1960, but this probably includes many paper organizations. Nevertheless, the commune is potentially an impressive device in its totality of involvement of the citizen's life, the opportunities it offers for political control through propaganda, police, and tight party discipline, and its potential for economic production where man power so greatly exceeds all other forms of capital. It is an attempt to resolve China's age-old problem of balancing local initiative and central control—this time consistent with the requirements of an industrial revolution under rigid totalitarian control.

Yugoslavia offers a significantly different kind of communist local governmental system. Although the party and its discipline remain an important control factor, it is evident that a great degree of decentralization has been introduced. The Yugoslav commune has a bicameral council, one house being a political body elected by area and the other concerned with economic matters and representative of workers and farmers in their respective work units. The economic chamber is somewhat less powerful than the political one, since it acts on a more restricted range of issues; but on all basic economic questions, including the budget, the two chambers must agree. The central government has basic responsibility for the economic growth of the nation, and it grants funds for economic investment; yet the locality has some discretion about the form of development it desires and relative independence in the conduct of local enterprises once established. The municipal council sets basic standards of operation for all municipal economic organizations, and it appoints their managers; but the workers in the enterprises and their elected representatives have control over some aspects of operations. In addition to the workers councils, numerous other elected bodies deal with a broad range of subjects from education to social security. Periodic meetings of all voters who wish to participate allow for discussion of current questions, and under certain circumstances a referendum is possible, although it has been little used. In comparison with other communist systems, Yugoslavia has a high degree of decentralization and vitality. Local discretion and self government are, however, circumscribed by the existence of the party as a "guide" for local action. Yugoslavian leaders stress the importance of local self-government but at the same time emphasize the importance of the Leninist principle of "democratic centralism," which holds that minority views should give way to strict party discipline when basic decisions have been made. [*See* COMMUNISM, *article on* NATIONAL COMMUNISM.]

Postcolonial systems

The creation of new nations from former colonies involves varying degrees of change in local government. In some cases the imposition of a strong single-party political system subverts old patterns almost entirely; in others, where adjustment more than revolutionary change has been the theme, local government patterns have not altered drastically. The legacy of colonialism is omnipresent, however much the new leaders strive for complete breaks with the colonial past [*see* COLONIALISM]. The pre-existing systems of local government, closely supervised by colonial officials and native subordinate administrators, have often remained as the general pattern of local–central government relationships. The terminology and basic structures of the colonial local government system frequently persist for reasons of habituation and convenience, if no other. Some leaders of postcolonial nations do not have a simple alternative of returning to a precolonial local government system, both because the colonial powers undermined or abolished the old ways and because the old systems were incapable of dealing with the conditions of Westernized and modernized life. The original tribal and village systems or bureaucratized empires of the past were appropriate to a rural, self-sufficient, and isolated kind of social life or to conditions of minimal central control; but as these nations become urbanized and begin to develop integrated economies, the simple forms of the past are inappropriate. Although some of the ancient forms of tribal rulership were allowed to continue by some colonial powers, it was apparent to local residents that the real authority rested not with the traditional chiefs and elders councils but with the administrators, both native and colonial, who supervised local operations. Not the least important of the remnants of colonialism, then, is the simple continuance of the great authority of the outside supervisor; the creation of active local democracy is difficult under any circumstances but the more so when habits of central supervision are generations old.

Local government in these nations is beset by staggering social and economic problems. In the first place, many of the cities of Asia and Africa are not cities in the European sense; they lack the technology, organization, resources, and slowly developed institutions of the Western city and are often massive accumulations of squatters. Also, as new regimes the central governments tend to be politically unstable. Extraordinary poverty, severe difficulties associated with economic growth, and chronic overcrowding in the cities all produce a range of problems not faced in more modernized nations. For example, many Indian cities face a serious problem in dealing with the tens of thousands who perforce must sleep in the streets at night, and a common problem of the local Indian city corporation is the prevalence of beggars who are organized into self-protective groups to defend their rights. Interestingly, in certain African cities the analogue of the American boss system seems to have developed, where local politicians cater to ethnic minorities and attempt to provide assistance to the city newcomers in exchange for voting support. Remoteness of local communities where transportation is difficult means that many parts of the postcolonial nations have a high degree of local independence through default—the central government being unable to assert its potential authority. A few Near Eastern nations have suffered for long periods from a breakdown in local and national bureaucracy so that local services are not rendered and a semianarchic confusion prevails.

Although modernization is gradually prevailing over traditionalism throughout the postcolonial world, conflict between modernists and traditionalists is endemic [*see* MODERNIZATION]. Tradition in religion and in social organization is the enemy of rational bureaucratization and the extension of power by the new political parties of the developing nations; it is a battle between an old man in a gilded chair (the tribal chieftain) and a young man in a swivel chair (Cowan 1958, p. vi). The virtual elimination of the tribal chief as a man of authority, as in Ghana, is one pattern; whereas the retention of chiefs as significant factors, as in parts of Uganda, is another (Burke 1964). Where political parties are extremely powerful, for example, in Tunisia and Ghana, the forces of traditionalism have been hardest hit—although traditional forms have a way of surviving, partly because they tend to rest on kinship relations that are basic elements of the social fabric. In Morocco, for example, orders from the central government to establish local councils to direct local affairs meant that a few dominant families selected their leaders as the new ruling body. Likewise, commands by the Israeli government to resident Arab communities to create local governing councils produced a council of family elders based on kinship patterns.

There is much conscious effort in the postcolonial nations to improve the quality of local government performance, but much of this involves assertion of controls from above to get local action. In Pakistan, for example, the central government in its Basic Democracies Order of 1959 established a system of local government for all of Pakistan and, outwardly at least, encouraged the growth of local democracy. Yet the control of local operations by the central government is very close, and one observer has found that in a given area no less than 85 per cent of all issues on local council agendas were put there by communications from the central government (Rahman 1962, p. 31). Inevitably the patterns of local governmental development in the postcolonial societies differ greatly, but the needs for economic growth and the extension of new national power to the hinterlands and in the rapidly growing cities have the tendency to produce as much central control as the regime finds possible. As a general rule the patterns are more like those of Richelieu's France than of Jefferson's United States.

The role of local government

Paradoxically, local government in the twentieth century seems to expand the number of functions it performs at the same time that it faces increasing central government supervision and a narrowing of its independence. As the problems of large and complicated cities and metropolitan areas grow, at least to the extent that financial means to cope with the problems exist, the city has greatly extended its role. Cultural activities expand simultaneously with programs on housing, redevelopment, air pollution control, and the recruitment of business enterprises. Many of the most dramatic and important of these functions are financed in good part by grants-in-aid from higher level governments, thereby decreasing local discretion at least to some extent. Also the expansion occurs simultaneously with a narrowing of distances between the central government and the municipality as the means of communication develop and as areas once isolated economically and politically become an integral part of a national economy and political system. It is therefore sometimes difficult to say whether local governments in a particular nation are now more or less significant agencies of government than they were in a simpler age.

In the case of the smaller communities there is not much doubt that increasing centralization has affected their range of discretion negatively. Although the capacity of a central government to control tends to dwindle with distance for the simple reason that remoteness prevents control, the growth of rapid communication tends to undercut this source of independence. Likewise, smaller communities caught up in the sprawl of metropolitan growth suddenly cease to be independent units and become entangled in the complications of over-all metropolitan areas. This leads to the development of regional institutions that in some degree may supplant or at least supplement local government, and it also tends to force local officials into governing in part through negotiation with officials from higher levels of government and with those of neighboring municipalities (Wood & Almendinger 1961).

Finally, it is important to note that the role of the municipal executive has grown greatly in the present century, owing to the same forces that have heightened the role of the executive in national government. The technological complexity of the problems being dealt with increases the power of the bureaucracy; and the diversity and diffusion of modern life also tend to lead to a stronger executive since, especially in larger cities, the chief executive seems to be the only functionary capable of controlling the bureaucracy, focusing public attention on key issues, and pressuring the various actors on the city scene to respond to the challenges a city faces.

DUANE LOCKARD

[*Directly related are the entries* CENTRALIZATION AND DECENTRALIZATION; CITY, *especially the article on* METROPOLITAN GOVERNMENT; LOCAL FINANCE; LOCAL POLITICS. *Other relevant material may be found under* COMMUNITY.]

BIBLIOGRAPHY

ADRIAN, CHARLES R. (1955) 1961 *Governing Urban America.* 2d ed. New York: McGraw-Hill.

ALDERFER, HAROLD F. 1964 *Local Government in Developing Countries.* New York: McGraw-Hill.

ALMOND, GABRIEL A.; and VERBA, SIDNEY 1963 *The Civic Culture: Political Attitudes and Democracy in Five Nations.* Princeton Univ. Press.

BANFIELD, EDWARD C. (1961) 1965 *Political Influence.* New York: Free Press.

BURKE, FRED G. 1964 *Local Government and Politics in Uganda.* Syracuse Univ. Press.

CHAPMAN, BRIAN LAING 1953 *Introduction to French Local Government.* London: Allen & Unwin.

CHAPMAN, BRIAN LAING 1955 *The Prefects and Provincial France.* London: Allen & Unwin.

COWAN, L. GRAY 1958 *Local Government in West Africa.* New York: Columbia Univ. Press.

DAHL, ROBERT A. (1961) 1963 *Who Governs? Democracy and Power in an American City.* New Haven: Yale Univ. Press.

DILLON, JOHN F. (1872) 1911 *Commentaries on the Law of Municipal Corporations.* 5 vols., 5th ed. Boston: Little.

FAINSOD, MERLE 1958 *Smolensk Under Soviet Rule.* Cambridge, Mass.: Harvard Univ. Press. → A paperback edition was published in 1963 by Random House.

FINER, HERMAN (1933) 1950 *English Local Government.* 4th ed. London: Methuen.

FRIED, ROBERT C. 1963 *The Italian Prefects: A Study in Administrative Politics.* Yale Studies in Political Science, Vol. 6. New Haven: Yale Univ. Press.

GOTTMANN, JEAN (1961) 1964 *Megalopolis: The Urbanized Northeastern Seaboard of the United States.* Cambridge: Massachusetts Institute of Technology Press.

GRANICK, DAVID 1960 *The Red Executive.* Garden City, N.Y.: Doubleday.

GREER, SCOTT A. 1962 *Governing the Metropolis.* New York: Wiley.

HUMES, SAMUEL; and MARTIN, EILEEN M. 1961 *The Structure of Local Governments Throughout the World.* The Hague: Nijhoff.

LETHBRIDGE, HENRY J. 1961 *China's Urban Communes.* Hong Kong: Dragonfly Books.

Local Government in the Twentieth Century. International Union of Local Authorities, Publication No. 72. 1963 The Hague: Nijhoff.

LOCKARD, DUANE 1963 *The Politics of State and Local Government.* New York: Macmillan.

MCKEAN, DAYTON D. 1940 *The Boss: The Hague Machine in Action.* Boston: Houghton Mifflin.

The Municipal Yearbook. 1963 Chicago: International City Managers' Association.

PRESTHUS, ROBERT V. 1964 *Men at the Top: A Study in Community Power.* New York: Oxford Univ. Press.

RAHMAN, A. T. RAFIQUR 1962 *Basic Democracy at the Grass Roots.* Comilla: Pakistan Academy for Village Development.

RAO, V. VENKATA 1960 *A Hundred Years of Local Self-government and Administration in the Andhra and Madras States 1850 to 1950.* Bombay: Local Self-government Institute.

ROBSON, WILLIAM A. 1954 *Great Cities of the World: Their Government, Politics, and Planning.* 2d ed., rev. & enl. London: Allen & Unwin.

SAYRE, WALLACE S.; and KAUFMAN, HERBERT 1960 *Governing New York City: Politics in the Metropolis.* New York: Russell Sage Foundation.

TINKER, HUGH 1954 *The Foundations of Local Self-government in India, Pakistan and Burma.* London: Athlone.

VIDICH, ARTHUR J.; and BENSMAN, JOSEPH 1958 *Small Town in Mass Society: Class, Power and Religion in a Rural Community.* Princeton Univ. Press.

VRATUŠA, ANTON et al. 1961 The Yugoslav Commune. *International Social Science Journal* 13:379–450.

WOOD, ROBERT C.; and ALMENDINGER, VLADIMIR V. 1961 *1400 Governments: The Political Economy of the New York Metropolitan Region.* New York Metropolitan Region Study, No. 8. Cambridge, Mass.: Harvard Univ. Press.

WRAITH, RONALD E. 1964 *Local Government in West Africa.* London: Allen & Unwin.

LOCAL POLITICS

Politics consists of the process by which goods, services, and privileges are allocated by government or the rules are established for their allocation by other social institutions. Local government is a political subdivision of a national or regional government which performs functions that are culturally defined as being "local" in character, which in nearly all cases receives its legal powers from the national or regional government but possesses some degree of discretion in the making of decisions and which normally has some taxing powers. Local politics, therefore, consists not merely of local activities which relate to national political matters, but it involves a degree of choice to be made within the boundaries of the local unit of government relative to the selection of office holders and the making and execution of public policy. These decisions are not necessarily made unilaterally through a local political system and its institutions. Often decisions are shared with other governments, and local political institutions and processes are commonly interwoven with those of neighboring localities and with regional and national political systems.

The patterns of politics at the local level are greatly varied. They assume a particular character in a particular locality according to the prevailing influences of ideology, social structure, and technology in the society. In primitive social systems there may be little in the way of recognized political institutions, but of those that do exist, the local political systems are often more important than the national so far as the typical citizen is concerned. In more complex societies, where governmental bureaucracies are specialized, where much is expected in the way of governmental functions, and where rapid means of transportation and communication exist, the activities and relative importance of local government become largely a function of ideology—the belief systems and traditions that condition the minds of a politically significant portion of the population. In some cases, as in Nazi Germany from 1933 to 1945, local government is of little importance; in others, as in the United States throughout its history, local government has been important in theory and quite important in practice.

In societies in which the concepts of change, "progress," specialization, or economic interdependence are little developed, local government is dominated by a politics of consensus. Traditional functions are accepted and honored. Politics may center largely on particular politicians, with the size and importance of personal followings determining political power. One of the functions of politics may be that of entertainment for the ordinary citizen who has little else to amuse him. Innovation is not expected from the local political process. The notions of ameliorating social problems or elevating the standard of living may be unrecognized or unaccepted concepts. African, Asian, and Latin American village societies tend to follow this pattern. Even in fairly complex, industrially developed societies, the dominant ideology in rural areas may call for this kind of function to be performed by local government. The village, in all societies, tends to have a politics based on face-to-face relationships, with the behavior of politicians tempered by considerations of the expectations of friends and neighbors.

In complex industrialized societies, local politics may be analyzed according to (1) images of the ideal function or goals of local government, (2) the degree to which local government is integrated with or insulated from the national political process, (3) the degree of autonomy of local government in relation to the national government in terms of discretionary powers in policy making, or (4) the distribution of power within the community.

Images of local government. The leaders in each community, irrespective of the amount of discretionary power vested in local government, seem to have an image of what the ideal community would be like and they seek to convert the image into reality. No one has attempted to develop a world-wide typology of such images, but some information concerning them is available. In primitive societies, the image is generally well established by a prevailing set of values and an absence of a desire for change: that which is—if uncorrupted by outside influences—is right.

In the United States, three types of images have been identified by Williams and Adrian (1963):

(1) Those designed to utilize government for specific policy goals constitute the first type; they can be divided into two subcategories, those with (*a*) production goals and (*b*) consumption goals. In the case of production goals, the common one in the United States is expressed in terms of "boosterism." The emphasis is upon public support for extending water supply, sewer lines, and other services into areas where industry or large commercial enterprises might locate, so as to help attract new jobs and broaden tax bases in the community. Land-use planning and controls designed to reserve sites for industrial parks, efforts to annex new territory suitable for industrial development, and special tax inducements for new industry are among the other attempts to lure new sources of wealth to the area and keep them there.

One special version of the production-oriented community is the "company town." This institution (in which the owners of a mine, lumber company, or factory own all property and businesses in the community) is disappearing in the United States. It so exclusively emphasized production goals or interests that it became unacceptable to the contemporary American culture. In some communities a single firm still dominates the local economy and takes a large part in social and political life. With the decline of locally owned industry and the dispersion of members of high-status "old" families, this pattern of *noblesse oblige* (and the development by these elites of a unique community and one attractive to live in) has become much less common.

Since the end of World War II the residential suburb has been more likely to emphasize consumption goals, i.e., more of life's amenities provided by local government than by the central city; these include effective sewage systems, palatable water supplies, beautiful parks, quiet traffic, good schools, imaginative recreation programs, and ornamental street lights. To maintain life styles desired by the politically dominant, there is likely to be interest in a comprehensive community plan to help clarify and program goals, as well as in effective land-use controls. Emphasis is generally upon the professional administration of these activities, with the council–manager plan often the preferred urban structure.

(2) A second type of community image calls for local government to perform, at a minimum level, only those traditional functions that are viewed as strictly necessary for the community, such as education, police, fire, and water services. This approach, sometimes called the "caretaker" image, is often associated in the United States with a low-tax ideology. All over the world it is associated with traditionalism and opposition to industrialism and the breaking down of established life styles.

(3) A third image of the proper role of local government, never dominant in the United States, is that of an instrument for the administration of central government policy with no local policy making. This is the prevailing image in countries where strong central control over local government is traditional, as it is in France and in many Asian nations.

Probably no single image is held exclusively in any given community of a complex society, although in some cases one is clearly dominant. Where images compete for acceptance, compromise seems to be the ordinary result, with some concessions to each of them.

Insulation or integration. The politics of local government may be closely tied to that of national politics or may be quite independent. In many democratic (e.g., Great Britain) and nondemocratic nations (e.g., the Soviet Union), national parties are active at the local level. On the other hand, in some democratic nations (e.g., the United States) or nondemocratic ones (e.g., some African states), national political party activity may be sharply separated from local.

In European democracies national parties commonly include in their platforms proposals relative to local government policies (although national and local elections do not necessarily coincide). It is assumed that politicians active at the local level are also committed to work for a national party. Whereas this is normal in European democracies, in the United States the pattern has been more complex. The American political arrangement in the last half of the nineteenth century was similar to that of European democracies. Political machines of that period were closely linked to national politics, and this remained the case past the mid-twentieth century in some cities, particularly in the East and in Chicago. But the reform movement that affected many communities, beginning in the 1880s or thereabouts, placed emphasis upon the separation of local from state and national politics. The result was a nonpartisan movement, based on the assumptions that local government issues are unrelated to the activities of national political parties and that the political aspects of recruitment for local offices should be reduced as much as possible. In the 1960s, even where party labels continue to appear on the ballot, it is common for local elections to be largely separated from other elections in terms of election dates, issues, and personnel. Parties continue to be important in most non-school-board and nonmunicipal elections and particularly in county and township elections. But because relatively few counties in the United States have meaningful two-party competition, even where the office seekers are active in a party, the real competition for office is often within a single party [*see* PARTIES, POLITICAL].

The amount of organization for politics at the local level has been declining in the twentieth-century United States and elsewhere. The great urban political machines that emerged during the period of rapid urbanization following the American Civil War were examples of near-complete political organization in a democracy. With their well-financed, ably led, city-wide party structure, they had ward, precinct, and block workers who looked after the party's interests and provided welfare services for party adherents. These machines achieved an intimacy concerning the problems, expectations, and political mood of constituents that rivaled that of the rural county and township machines, which also flourished during this period. [*See* POLITICAL MACHINES.]

The machines declined with the coming of alternative group associations (e.g., trade unions and ethnic and racial social and benevolent societies), middle-class reform efforts (especially to provide a secret ballot and accurate election results and to mobilize those who once believed it was unavailing to "fight city hall"), a higher living standard for a greater portion of the working class, and the professionalization of welfare services, particularly after 1933. Local politics in the United States is today characterized by the presence of few professional politicians. Candidates are commonly amateurs, recruited (sometimes self-recruited) from business, labor, or the professions, often by groups of lay citizens who have banded together into a part-time political-action group. Some candidates are clearly the choice of, and spokesmen for, particular interests (realtors, builders, merchants, labor unions), and the current pattern seems to encourage such candidates more than did the political machines. The boss's brokerage concept of the role of the councilman or mayor was broader than the concept of the guardianship of some specific interest. Political communication at the local level remains more on a face-to-face basis than it does for politics in general, but radio and television have become important, especially in the larger urban areas. Much communication is through associations that are only in part political, such as labor union locals, neighborhood associations, chambers of commerce, farm organizations, church lay groups, and community councils. The leaders of these organizations are also important opinion leaders, for many ordinary citizens rely upon them as sources of political guidance [*see* INTEREST GROUPS; POLITICAL CLUBS].

Discretionary decision-making powers. The variety of local politics is accounted for in part by the political stakes involved in local decisions, and these vary according to the social significance of decisions that can be made at the local level. In some traditional societies local politics may involve no expectation that the actors will make decisions affecting the allocation of goods, services, and privileges. In nations such as France through much of its modern history, where powers are centralized but political parties cannot provide effective leadership, or many Asian nations where innovation is encouraged by the central government, local politics may center on actors who seek to protect traditional local standards and values against the views and policies of the professional national bureaucracy.

In some countries, such as Great Britain and those of Scandinavia, where political parties seek to tie the various levels of government together in a common move toward agreed-upon governmental service goals, local politics tends to be oriented toward the activities of national parties. Political actives, rather than civil service specialists, provide the principal coordination in programs. In countries with a strong tradition of decentralized decision making, such as the United States, local politics combines showmanship, questions of relationships with national parties and state and national bureaucracies, and the settlement of many policy questions which are left to local governments by the states. Although the process of cooperative federalism, which has been developing for many decades in the United States, has reduced local autonomy in decision making, many decisions that affect the allocation of goods, services, and privileges are still made by actors in local political roles. As a result, the viewpoints of those who occupy particular offices are often important. But local politics is not necessarily on a higher plane in the United States because local government is a power center. The patterns of recruitment and contesting for office and of decision making may depend chiefly on whether or not there is consensus regarding the image of the proper policies for local government [*see* FEDERALISM].

The distribution of community power. A central problem in the analysis of local politics has been that of identifying the power holders. Studies designed to do this have generally ignored the question of how much power local governments actually are able to allocate (the amount available may, in theory at least, bear some relationship to the status levels of persons who become involved in the local political process). The concentration has been on identifying those who are wielders of power over whatever decisions can be made locally. By the mid-1960s questions of power were still of keen interest to social scientists, but many questions concerning its character remained unanswered. Among the issues the following were of critical importance:

(1) Is power deliberately used by an elite in a conspiracy to control society or is it essentially a socially useful device serving to provide an orderly social system? The conspiratorial theory stems from Marxian ideology and holds that a relatively few persons dominate local decision making for the benefit of the business and industrial leaders and middle-class citizens generally. In contrast, another theory holds that in a pluralistic democracy power may be distributed widely among various classes and groups in the community, with a variety of resources (e.g., money, votes, status, intensity of concern) as a basis for power. In support of the latter position, some have argued that the rising importance and numbers of functions of government have made the formal holders of elective office and the professional civil servants

powerful in their own right and not mere satraps for hidden leaders.

(2) Is the power structure monolithic or internally competitive? Early studies tended to find a monolithic pattern in which power holders met informally to decide policy relative to major items on the community agenda and to compromise any differences within the group. More recent studies indicate that power holders compete with one another, posing power against power, and negotiate with one another as diplomats and politicians. The concept of a "power structure," or simple pyramid of relatively powerful persons ranged in hierarchical order, is being replaced by that of a "power complex" of often competing persons from downtown businesses, neighborhood businesses, industry, organized labor, religion, education, politics, and sometimes other areas.

(3) Is power integrated or multinucleated? That is, are the power holders all in communication with one another, ordered in a single hierarchy, concerned with all major issues, and equally powerful in relation to all major issues? Or is power distributed functionally, so that those who have much to do with decisions about education policy, for example, overlap little or not at all with those in the fields of transportation, parks, or sewage disposal? Early studies (Robert and Helen Lynd in the 1920s, W. Lloyd Warner in the 1930s, and Floyd Hunter in the 1940s) tended to see an integrated structure. More recently, research reports indicate functional specialization, but whether the differences result from improved research techniques or from a changing distribution of power is not known.

(4) How are power holders to be distinguished from power users? A number of problems have arisen in efforts to identify those who are powerful in local politics. Some of these are problems of theory construction (Is a person powerful if his wants are anticipated and met even though he does not directly participate in a decision?); others are those of method (Can the powerful be identified more accurately by collecting and classifying the opinions of the supposedly knowledgeable or by observing the actors in particular decisions?). The study of local political power is complicated by the efforts of decision makers to anticipate the wants of those who are believed to be important or potentially powerful. It is also complicated, among other ways, by the fact that respondents and researchers have varying definitions and concepts of power and by the probability that a person asked to name the powerful cannot accurately identify them all and may overdiscount (or alternatively, exaggerate) the power of persons he disapproves of or regards as lacking a *legitimate right* to be powerful. In the 1960s research was continuing on the problem of analyzing local political power. Some of the most productive work in sociology and political science was taking place in this area [*see* COMMUNITY, *article on* THE STUDY OF COMMUNITY POWER; *see also* POWER].

Liberalism and conservatism. The concepts of liberalism and conservatism common in the Western world do not necessarily have the same meaning when applied to local politics as they do at the national level. The socialist, labor, and other reasonably well-disciplined parties of European democracies have tried to give the terms equivalent meanings at all levels of government. American national parties have not seriously attempted to bring local issues into their platforms or campaigns, and they have not themselves been clearly identified along a liberal–conservative continuum. In the twentieth century liberalism has become identified with the involvement of government in coping with a large variety of economic and social issues financed through a progressive tax system. While the social-service state has become the established pattern in the United States, home ownership has also become increasingly widespread. As a result studies have shown that persons who vote for liberal candidates for state and national offices may vote for conservatives at the local level, and vice versa. In particular, working-class homeowners with modest incomes sometimes oppose bond issues for capital outlays that would benefit them and vote for advocates of "caretaker" government, apparently because the cost of local government so clearly falls on the property owner. Sometimes they do this despite strong appeals for support of an issue or candidate by labor or other liberal leaders. Working-class persons have not pressed for social-service state and liberal reform programs (such as public housing or urban renewal) at the local level. Upper-middle-class persons, on the other hand, frequently are willing to spend local tax monies and subscribe to the images of "boosterism" and "amenities." As a result the terms liberal and conservative are often quite meaningless when applied to local government.

Local politics and democracy. Studies of local politics since the end of World War II indicate that the bulk of citizens in American democracy do not exert much individual influence, even at the local level. In fact, the pattern at the local level appears to be not much different from that at the national, despite the prevalence of nonpartisanship and the supposed significance of physical proximity to the decision makers. The level of information possessed by the typical citizen is low, citizens take their cues from various political leaders, and decisions seem to be largely the product of bargaining among leaders. Voter participation at the local level is typically lower than it is for national and state elections, and some scholars have been concerned about the high level of alienation at the local level, although evidence as to the significance of this, if it exists at all, is inconclusive. The indifferent do, however, seem to move toward the extremes of the political spectrum when they become activated, just as is the case in national elections. In the 1960s, then, the study of local politics leaves unanswered some questions that are important for democracy. Particularly, it is still uncertain how much citizen participation is necessary for healthy democracy at the local level, what form this participation should take for the viability of democracy, or to what degree present systems of local government provide adequate or satisfying representation and access to decision makers by all segments of the local population.

CHARLES R. ADRIAN

[*See also* CENTRALIZATION AND DECENTRALIZATION; CITY; COMMUNITY; LOCAL GOVERNMENT; POLITICAL MACHINES; POLITICAL PARTICIPATION.]

BIBLIOGRAPHY

AGGER, ROBERT E.; GOLDRICH, DANIEL; and SWANSON, BERT 1964 *The Rulers and the Ruled: Political Power and Impotence in American Communities.* New York: Wiley.

BANFIELD, EDWARD C. (1961) 1965 *Political Influence.* New York: Free Press.

DAHL, ROBERT A. (1961) 1963 *Who Governs? Democracy and Power in an American City.* New Haven: Yale Univ. Press.

Decisions in Syracuse, by Roscoe C. Martin et al. Metropolitan Action Studies, No. 1. 1961 Bloomington: Indiana Univ. Press.

FORM, WILLIAM H.; and MILLER, DELBERT C. 1960 *Industry, Labor and Community.* New York: Harper.

HUNTER, FLOYD 1953 *Community Power Structure: A Study of Decision Makers.* Chapel Hill: Univ. of North Carolina Press. → A paperback edition was published in 1963 by Doubleday.

JANOWITZ, MORRIS (editor) 1961 *Community Political Systems.* New York: Free Press.

LONG, NORTON E. 1958 The Local Community as an Ecology of Games. *American Journal of Sociology* 64: 251–261.

LYND, ROBERT S.; and LYND, HELEN M. (1929) 1959 *Middletown: A Study in American Culture.* New York: Harcourt.

MARTIN, ROSCOE C. 1957 *Grass Roots.* University: Univ. of Alabama Press.

MICHIGAN STATE UNIVERSITY OF AGRICULTURE AND APPLIED SCIENCE, INSTITUTE FOR COMMUNITY DEVELOPMENT AND SERVICES 1962 *Main Street Politics: Policy-making at the Local Level, a Survey of the Periodical Literature Since 1950.* East Lansing, Mich.: The University.

PARSONS, TALCOTT 1957 The Distribution of Power in American Society. *World Politics* 10:123–143.

PYE, LUCIAN W. 1958 The Non-Western Political Process. *Journal of Politics* 20:468–486.

SAYRE, WALLACE S.; and KAUFMAN, HERBERT 1960 *Governing New York City: Politics in the Metropolis.* New York: Russell Sage Foundation.

SEELEY, JOHN R. et al. 1956 *Crestwood Heights: A Study of the Culture of Suburban Life.* New York: Basic Books.

VIDICH, ARTHUR J.; and BENSMAN, JOSEPH 1958 *Small Town in Mass Society: Class, Power and Religion in a Rural Community.* Princeton Univ. Press.

WARNER, W. LLOYD; and LUNT, PAUL S. 1942 *The Status System of a Modern Community.* New Haven: Yale Univ. Press.

WILLIAMS, OLIVER P.; and ADRIAN, CHARLES R. 1963 *Four Cities: A Study in Comparative Policy Making.* Philadelphia: Univ. of Pennsylvania Press.

WOOD, ROBERT C. 1959 *Suburbia: Its People and Their Politics.* Boston: Houghton Mifflin.

LOCATION AND DISPERSION

See under STATISTICS, DESCRIPTIVE.

LOCATION THEORY

See SPATIAL ECONOMICS. *Related material may be found in* CENTRAL PLACE; GEOGRAPHY, *article on* STATISTICAL GEOGRAPHY.

LOCKE, JOHN

John Locke made important contributions in the areas of epistemology, political theory, education, toleration theory, and theology; he also wrote on natural law and on various economic topics.

Born in 1632 in a Somerset village, he was the eldest and ultimately the only surviving child of a family of tradesmen and small landholders. His grandfather had been a tanner and clothier; his father was a notary with landholdings later inherited by his son. He kept his connections with his ramified west-country family and friends, most of whom were Whigs throughout the turbulent years of the later Stuart rule. After living for many years at Oxford and on the Continent, Locke made his headquarters in Essex in 1691 with his friend Lady Masham; in 1704 he was buried among the Mashams in the village church at High Laver.

Intellectual development. Locke studied at the Westminster School and Christ Church, Oxford, where in 1658 he was elected senior student (the equivalent of a fellow in other colleges) and taught moral philosophy. His academic duties were always light, and he consistently sought to lighten them still more, especially after 1666, when he met Lord Ashley (later Lord Shaftesbury), the great Whig leader; thenceforth Locke spent more time in London than at Oxford.

The political parliamentarianism of Locke's father may have influenced Locke's own ultimate Whiggery, which was strengthened by his association with Shaftesbury. Many west-country families, like Locke himself, became part of the "Shaftesbury connection" of Whigs, later supporting William of Orange in his successful coup. By all odds the most influential connection of Locke's life was with Shaftesbury, who quickened his early, though latent, interest in questions of political philosophy and practice. During his Shaftesbury years Locke sat on the Council of Trade and Plantations, an overseeing body for crown colonies, Ireland, and proprietary holdings in the New World. His interest in economic problems can be dated from that experience. Although he had been only on the fringes of the complicated politics of the late reign of Charles II, in 1683 Locke had to leave Oxford for good, a political refugee in Shaftesbury's wake.

Locke's intellectual development was marked by autonomy and autodidacticism. Evidently bored by his studies, he independently followed the medical curriculum at Oxford; though he never took his doctor's degree, he was qualified to practice medicine and did so, largely for the Shaftesbury family. He also studied chemistry in Robert Boyle's laboratory; in this way he came to know Boyle and eventually became an executor of his will. Other scientific friends were Richard Lower, Thomas Willis, and David Thomas; in 1688 he was elected a fellow of the Royal Society. Locke's "corpuscularianism," or atomic theory of matter, had much in common with Boyle's; his general curiosity and interest in "things" rather than in their names, as well as his experimental approach to social and scientific matters, can all be connected with his serious interest in the biological sciences. His medical empiricism was much like that of his associate Thomas Sydenham, one of the major experimental physicians of his day, who was especially interested in public health; both Sydenham and Locke voiced their awareness of the "unknowing," the "probabilism" involved in medical practice, notions which later influenced Locke's epistemology.

Locke's fear of Catholicism and absolutism had its roots in the English political scene and was deepened by several journeys to France, where persecution of the Huguenots was then intense. His Dutch sojourn, from 1683 to 1689, was voluntarily undertaken as a prudential flight from a government increasingly hostile to men of his political association and views: he was deprived of his studentship at Christ Church and even put on a proscription list of James II's real and supposed enemies hidden in Holland. During that time, Locke met many congenial thinkers who in different ways reflected his own biases and concerns: among others, Arminian broad-church theologians, all theorists of toleration; medical men interested in experiment and learned in a tradition other than his own, that of Cartesian medicine; publicists dedicated to the diffusion of both learning and information.

When Locke returned to England in 1689, it was to a government of which he could approve; by that time he himself had become an honored man and was recognized as a major thinker. Thenceforward, he devoted himself to studying and writing, while holding minor government offices and occasionally conferring with political leaders

Writings. From the early 1660s Locke had written many short essays, evidently for his own clarification, on natural law, on the civil magistrate, on toleration. In 1669 these preoccupations fed into Lord Shaftesbury's *Fundamental Constitutions of Carolina*, written with the aid of Locke. (Although this item appears in Locke's collected works—see *The Works . . .*, vol. 10, pp. 175–199—it has been established that Shaftesbury was the principal author.) Locke's *Two Treatises* (1690*a*) were written, as we now know, at the time of the Exclusion crisis of 1679–1681, when Shaftesbury unsuccessfully attempted to exclude the duke of York from succession to the throne because he was a Catholic.

While Locke was in Holland, one of his publicist friends, Jean Le Clerc, persuaded him to write for his periodical: thus, in the *Bibliothèque universelle et historique*, a fortnightly review of issues and books of international interest, Locke published some book reviews—among others, one of Newton's *Principia*—as well as original works of his own, the chief of which was his abridgment of the then unpublished *Essay Concerning Human Understanding* (1690*b*).

In 1689–1690 Locke began his serious publishing career: *A Letter Concerning Toleration, Being the Translation of the* "Epistola de tolerantia" appeared in 1689 (*The Works . . .*, vol. 6, pp. 1–58); the *Two Treatises of Government* in 1689, bearing the date 1690; the *Essay Concerning Human Understanding* in the same year. From then on, Locke never ceased publishing: he continually revised and republished his *Essay*, also supervising its translation into French; between 1690 and 1704 he wrote three more letters on toleration (*The Works . . .*, vol. 6, pp. 59–574); in 1690, *Some Thoughts on Education* (*ibid.*, vol. 9, pp. 1–210);

in 1695, *The Reasonableness of Christianity* (*ibid.*, vol. 7, pp. 1–158); various defenses of the *Essay*; economic tracts; and paraphrases of Paul's Epistles. Much of the immediate stimulus to this work was topical: his study of education grew out of private letters to his friend Edward Clarke; the economic tracts all sprang from fiscal and commercial problems of the government; the later writings on toleration were called forth by attacks on his ideas and on William's efforts to solve the problem of dissent in England. Characteristically, however, even his topical writings contain elements of "philosophy," generalizations not required by the work's immediate polemical purpose.

Major contributions

Locke has often seemed a singularly disconnected thinker, an asystematic philosopher with occasional brilliant insights. Since the acquisition by the Bodleian Library of many Locke manuscripts from the Lovelace Collection, the development of Locke's interests and of his thinking can be more accurately traced than before; further, the ways in which his ideas, apparently so disparate, hang together has become clearer from study of the manuscripts. His earliest work was on natural law, which led him ultimately into his serious work on two branches of that large subject, political theory and human understanding. Though these two interests branched widely apart from one another and seemed far removed from his initial concern with the "covering" aspect of natural law, his friends expected, in vain, that he would eventually write a treatise about natural law, after he had completed his *Essay*. His early natural-law essays were written between 1660 and 1664 and deal with both the epistemological problem of knowing in natural law and with the natural law as a binding moral and social force; the essays show clear signs of Locke's later full-scale attack upon innateness and *consensus gentium*, as well as his incipient psychological sensationalism. As for moral natural law, Locke assumed it as a *donnée* from God, binding upon man's reason; this view remains rudimentary both in the *Second Treatise* ([1690*a*] 1960, pp. 283–446) and in Locke's other writings. In his manuscript treatises on the civil magistrate and on toleration, dating from the early years of the Restoration, Locke moved from a restrictive position to a more tolerant one, at first insisting on public order as a primary value and then stressing the irenic power of the civil magistrate, particularly in the regulation of religious practices. From these early works Locke's philosophical investigations emerged. They will be treated under several headings, with stress laid upon those elements of his thought most significant for the development of the social sciences: political theory, religious ideas, economic ideas, epistemology, psychology, educational theory.

Political thought. Locke's major contributions to political thought are in his *Second Treatise*, a document notoriously lacking in system, partly because of its remnant character, partly because of its connection with contemporary events, partly because of Locke's failure to rewrite it substantially for publication in 1689, ten years after its completion. Within its own time the work contained "dangerous" doctrines, some anathematized by decree in 1683, when Locke fled his country. By the time of its publication, however, it expressed the parliamentarian ideals of mixed government and separation of powers established in England by the political settlement reached after William's invasion. The origins of the tract seem to have been in the Exclusion crisis; it was designed to justify constitutional change, for which Locke undertook to investigate the origins and structure of civil (political) society. His polemical aim was to diminish popular acceptance of the patriarchalism which gave authority to much of the contemporary argument for absolutism; to do so, he postulated an original, direct relation of every man to God rather than to or through any political intermediary. Each man was in some sense God's "property": bypassing the notion of Adam as a model ruler of the social group, Locke postulated a state of nature regulated by laws derived from God, a state of nature in which men were equal and free before the Lord and each other. Paradoxically, the rule of law (in this case, the rule of the law of nature) was requisite for freedom; without such natural law man's "freedom" would have been anarchy. In this sense Locke's conception approached the anarchic state of nature postulated by Hobbes, although his insistence upon fundamental natural law saved him from Hobbes's pessimism about the lawlessness of basic human nature. From this natural condition, Locke inferred both a "law of reason," by which individuals reach and assent to social consensus, and the practical laws requisite to permit, even to insure, personal freedom [*see* NATURAL LAW]. Originally, in the state of nature, executive power of the natural law was vested in every individual; subsequently—whether suddenly or gradually is not made clear—men consented to live in a common society regulated by the communal executive power of the law of nature. Locke divided this communal power into three—the legislative, executive, and federative powers—with judicial decision a general power of the political commonwealth.

To effect the passage from the state of nature

to "civil society," Locke developed his important variation on the idea of property, which in turn graded into his theory of labor. From the natural-law postulate that a man has property in his own life, Locke derived the view that a man has property in the things necessary to the preservation of that life, so long as those things are rightfully his (that is, taken from the commonwealth at a point when the specific acquisition harmed or deprived no one else). A man has a right in himself and thus in his own labor; in turn, he has a right to what "he hath mixed his labor with," or a right to his property. A corollary of this is Locke's formulation of the labor theory of value, almost incidental to his argument: the value and the price of commodities in any society reflect the labor that has gone into them.

There are two sorts of relations between men, the first a natural social contract, entered into by the exercise of rational considerations of self-preservation, the second defined by rights in property. The function and end of government are the preservation of life, liberty, and property. One corollary of this formulation is that political rights derive from property and that the propertyless are either without political rights or are slaves. Such a conception of the commonwealth permits emphasis both on the common interest and on private holdings, which in Locke's essay (in line with seventeenth-century usage and notions of value) generally means land.

Without in any sense denying the importance and validity of a familial organization of society, Locke demonstrated that the power over children and dependents vested in the father (who shares it with the mother, interestingly enough) is simply a form of trusteeship: the guardian–father has certain obligations toward his children, especially to educate them; when the children reach full exercise of their reason, they are free "from subjection to the will and command of the father." The family was, for Locke, important in his theory of the origins of civil society, the conjunction of male and female being both a symbol of a wider assent and obligation and a primary stage in the voluntary community of mankind. Thus, even in families, arbitrary government is "impossible"; in commonwealths the necessary consent of each individual to enter into the bond of civil society (the social contract) eventuates in election, the choice of representatives charged to exercise legislative power. Legislative power is supreme in Locke's mixed government of separate legislative, executive, and federative powers. His assumption is that a man with political rights (by reason of his property in himself) enters into political life, inheriting with his property his obligations to the government that represents him. In turn, the government may not touch his property (i.e., levy taxes) without his consent through his representative. One implication of this formulation is a doctrine of resistance, or revolution, as expressed in the last chapter of the *Second Treatise*, the chapter which, above all others, made Locke objectionable to the government before 1688 and valuable to the government thereafter. Unlike the Protestant resistance-theorists of the sixteenth century, Locke did not base his revolutionary theory upon sanctions of conscience or religion; unlike the English parliamentarians of the 1640s, he did not base it on precedents in English law; unlike Algernon Sidney, he did not base it on a metaphysical and metapsychological natural right to liberty; rather, he advocated a restrained and considered revolution for the restoration of proper balance in the body politic. [*See* SOCIAL CONTRACT.]

Locke's theory of government emphasizes process, both the hypothetical process of human development from a state of nature to civil society and the processes of self-government. He therefore limited the number of specifiable elements in the proper commonwealth and was careful to leave ample room for adjustments to changing social needs. He was, in short, indicating a successful process of representative majority rule rather than setting up an exclusive structure for one. Hence, there are large areas of his thought which seem blank, either because he was unconcerned with total consistency or because he was concerned with leaving social alternatives open, especially in "matters of indifference."

Views on religion. His toleration theory, taken in conjunction with his religious views, demonstrates his appreciation of practical approaches. Thus, his *Letter Concerning Toleration* of 1689, Locke dealt with Christian toleration, "the chief characteristical mark of the true church." Since every man appears orthodox to himself, no one in his right or his wrong mind will accept as just the persecution of himself; furthermore, since in any case persecution cannot touch a man's inmost conviction, regardless of what he may say under stress, there is no practical merit in persecution. Locke politicized the problem of religious pluralism, assigning to the civil magistrate the protection of various rights (here defined as "life, liberty, and indolency of body") of members of a commonwealth. The care of souls was no more committed by God to the civil magistrate than the care of one man's conscience was committed to any other member of society. The magistrate's power consists only in civil force, which is irrelevant to any church (defined as "a voluntary society of men").

From the privileges of toleration, Locke excluded some—he excluded atheists from the benefits of the law, because they refuse to acknowledge its source—but he included idolators, men simply given to erroneous worship. Toleration is to be withheld from religious groups who deny it to others, a view supported by Locke's experiences in France, where persecution of Huguenots reached extremes between 1679 and 1685. Whenever religious assemblies endanger the public peace, then the civil magistrate, on civil grounds, may intervene against them; even then, however, he is not to interfere with their belief, which remains in the category of "things indifferent" and is therefore irrelevant to questions of public order. Although in this work Locke did not justify resistance, rebellion, or revolution for religion's sake, he made it plain that oppression of any kind naturally impels men toward sedition.

In *The Reasonableness of Christianity* Locke defended the Christian revelation against atheism and against natural religion without revelation, demonstrating by scriptural and historical authority the fact of Christ's messiahship. The tract defends the necessity of revelation against the idea of a sufficient natural religion, but at the same time it treats Christ's teachings as the fulfillment and explanation of the moral law of nature. Man's reason cannot by itself discover the full moral law of nature, but it can confirm it. Nowhere in the tract did Locke sanction a particular form of worship, but instead he endorsed a general scriptural Christianity to which, as it were, all Christians could subscribe. (For this, he was roundly attacked as being a deist.) In ways connected with his toleration theory and his epistemology, he adduced the uncertainties of man's perceptions and knowledge to support his minimal articles of faith, drawn from scriptural revelation and corroborated by the action of reason. [*See* CHRISTIANITY.]

Economic ideas. Locke's economic interests, stimulated during his early association with Shaftesbury, emerged long after in 1691 in *Some Considerations of the Consequences of the Lowering of Interest, and Raising the Value of Money* (*The Works* . . ., vol. 5, pp. 1–130) and in 1695 in *Further Considerations* . . . (*ibid.*, vol. 5, pp. 131–206). In these works, he advocated maintaining the interest rate and not devaluing the currency, on grounds of natural law. His economic laws were (1) that the intrinsic value of any piece of goods is not necessarily reflected in its price; (2) that its market value depends upon the proportion of supply and demand (which he called "quantity" and "vent"); (3) that price is determined by the amount of money relative to the supply and demand for a piece of goods. These laws permit prices to be set with some flexibility, according to varying conditions, and they rely upon a controlling notion in Locke's thought, that of self-regulation toward equilibrium. When it came to practice, as in the cases of the poor and of Irish manufactures, Locke advocated government intervention in economic affairs.

Psychology. The aim of Locke's *Essay* (1690*b*) was to determine the limits of human knowledge, so that men might address themselves to problems within their power to solve. He set out to describe the process of human understanding, to inquire into probable knowledge, and to determine the nature of ideas. He concluded, very simply, that ideas have two sources, sensation and reflection upon ideas produced by sensation. It turns out, however, in the course of the book, that knowledge can also be intuitional and demonstrative, though in the discussion intuition tends to be assimilated to sensation and demonstration to reflection. Ideas may be either simple or complex: simple ideas are the result of sensation and reflection and are compounded of simple parts which can be found by analysis. Locke attributed reality to the external world and relied upon intuition to explain the relation between an idea and its referent in the external world. Knowledge derived by intuition (such as that of revelation) is "certain"; certain knowledge can also be derived from demonstration but less reliably than from intuition, since errors in reason and in memory may distort the result of demonstration. Locke's ontological proof of God's existence, much like Descartes's, is an example of the fusion of demonstration with intuition: that is, one's own existence is intuited, and from one's own existence God's can be demonstrated. He relied upon the skeptical provisionalism inherent in empirical investigations, both in his recognition of the role probability plays in human understanding and assessment of life and in his recognition of the idiosyncratic formation of each man's personal set of ideas. As in so much of his work, Locke took a middle position in the *Essay*, incorporating elements of skepticism and elements of idealism, combining what we now call behaviorism with gestalt principles. His empiricism embraced both the particular and the consensual: in the ongoing search for true knowledge individual men are required to check their ideas against those of the group, and the group does so against those of any given individual. [*See* GESTALT THEORY; THINKING.]

Locke's psychological principles are a by-product

of his effort to describe human understanding. His major hypothesis, that the mind is not equipped with innate ideas or principles but is at its formation a "white paper" (his translation of *tabula rasa*), was reached in part through his own empirical observation of children. He concluded that there are only two ways of human understanding, by sensation and by reflection on ideas derived from sensation. His whole notion of "understanding" is developmental; throughout the *Essay* he cited examples from his observation of the successive stages of men's lives. From his observation of children, he demonstrated that their understanding derives from their experience of the external and social world. Approximating modern notions of "control," Locke cited a great deal of evidence from his observation of human beings who were exceptional in that they lacked some "normal" element of apprehension or reflection—children, not yet developed to full powers; idiots; men born blind (including the famous philosophical example of a man who by an operation got his sight); men suffering from amnesia because their heads had been kicked by horses. In spite of their deficiencies, all such people entertained ideas that seemed to them as authentic as those "clear and distinct" ideas that are the hallmark of proper understanding. Madness, drunkenness, and dreaming interested Locke: the Cartesian criterion for human existence, consciousness, seemed to him too narrow to account for the existence of faultily conscious minds. His solution to the problem of identity turned on assumptions now associated with gestalt psychology: on the continuous existence of an organized body whose parts (including its intellectual store) shift over time in relation to one another. So "the night man" and "the day man," the drunken man and the sober man, the madman and the sane man may coexist in the same person, even though their control over consciousness may be intermittent or interrupted. To this notion may be connected Locke's idea of what are nowadays called "roles," the multiple relations, psychological and social (father, brother, son, son-in-law, servant, master, older, younger, etc.), possible and even inevitable in every man's experience. Memory (retention), the operation of which was never altogether accounted for in the Lockean philosophy or psychology, plays a major part in maintaining continuous personal identity. One of Locke's major psychological insights, that arbitrary mental connections are "stamped" on men's minds by the chance conjunctions of their experience, appears in the famous chapter on the association of ideas, an afterthought in his organization. There he demonstrated, by a kind of negative example, the supremacy of experience over rational powers: a man taught to dance in a room containing a trunk could never dance in the absence of a similar trunk; a man nearly axed in a doorway by a berserk village idiot could never go through a door without glancing behind him. So by experience, governing intellectual and emotional constellations are induced in individual minds. This doctrine and that of the *tabula rasa* underlie Locke's precepts for education. [*See* Developmental psychology; Learning; Role; Senses.]

In the sense that he postulated ideas as originating in sensation, Locke's psychology is certainly mechanistic. His general concern, however, to establish the same organic interrelationship for the contents of the mind as for the members of the body or the state, tempers his mechanism with organic and developmental notions. Although he conceived of the body as made up of elements in a mechanistic organization, he saw that mechanism as having considerable feedback into its own individual, even idiosyncratic, development. Feedback is in turn not automatic, in his view, since the mind's judgment, the faculty which selects and arranges ideas in relation to one another, is also constantly at work during consciousness.

Locke's social conception of language may serve as a partial model for his ideas of how men understand as well as of how society functions: Although the designation of words is established by consensus, each man may alter it privately for himself alone, according to his individual associations of words and experience. Furthermore, though encountered as datum in each man's life, language is not rigid but is subject to modification over time by the social needs of the group using it.

Pedagogy. Locke's ideas of education follow from his psychology. The child inevitably grows into the man and should grow into as healthy a man as possible. Since each child is strongly individuated, no fixed regime works for all children, but Locke laid down general rules of education, chiefly applicable (as he wrote) to gentry sons whose duty was to undertake public service. Boys were to be educated at home, carefully fed, clothed, and taught to build and preserve good health. The father was to "imprint" obedience on his son but with such care and tact as to turn the child–subject naturally into his friend. Rewards and punishments were to be systematic but moderate (Locke outlawed beating, as making a child slavish). The father, tutor, and governor, charged with educating the child, were to be his moral exemplars; therefore, it was necessary for parents both to regulate themselves and to choose their surrogates with care. Though children must learn self-denial, some cravings may be gratified, especially since "craving" is so closely allied to "curiosity," nature's instrument to correct ignorance. So the child must be allowed to learn whenever ready and can often be cozened into learning by means of games and toys. Children's questions must always be answered truthfully, and conversation with them must be free of condescension. Instruction in the nature of reality —including the idea of God, excluding the idea of goblins—was to be undertaken early.

As for learning itself, Locke's program was practical: reading, writing, French, then Latin (for use, chiefly); geography, arithmetic, astronomy, geometry, chronology, history, ethics, civil law, rhetoric and logic, natural philosophy; then Greek and Latin as cultural subjects and, last of all, method. For learning by rote Locke had no use; he also advocated learning such practical subjects as trade and accountancy as well as recreations such as music, dancing, gardening, joinery—all useful to young men of property. Finally, the young man should travel, first at home and later abroad, before settling down to matrimony and his social and political obligations at the age of one and twenty.

Locke's originality and influence

In its day Locke's thought seemed strikingly "new," cast in a new language for any literate man to read; it had, naturally, many sources and analogues in ancient and contemporary thought. His skepticism and empiricism came from deep within the medical tradition; his attitude, and even the words he used, recall Sextus Empiricus and, more often, Montaigne, another essayist concerned with knowing, education, understanding, nescience, and probability. Locke had, too, a recognizably British stoicism, a preference for directness and plainness in morality and rhetoric; he often cited Seneca and the stoical writings of Cicero. His toleration theory derived from a long line of Protestant writers going back to Servetus and Erastus and exemplified by his Arminian friends; there are affinities between his view of church–state relations and the thought of Chillingworth, Falkland, and John Owen. His citations of natural law are to Hooker and Grotius, whose books he certainly knew, though he seems to have referred to them more out of piety and the need for authorities than from any desire to analyze their thought in relation to his own. Although he was a notable revisionist of the Cartesian epistemology and psychology, Locke's doctrine of ideas owes something to Descartes, his psychological theory of sensationalism shares elements of Cartesian mechanism, and his ontological proof of God's existence is brief and efficient partly because Descartes's similar proof was so thoroughly argued. Locke's nominalism had many sources: Greek empiricism, the Scotist tradition in scholasticism, and chiefly Francis Bacon and his followers in contemporary England.

However connected to other strands in the history of thought, Locke was characteristically original in pattern and device. His empirically argued rejection of innate ideas and principles, for example, in the first book of the *Essay* ran counter to traditional epistemologies ancient and modern. Among his contemporaries, both Cartesians and Cambridge Platonists, as well as most divines, postulated innateness as the basis of human knowing, relying on both Platonic and Stoical authorities. In psychology and epistemology a major contribution was his concept of the association of ideas, an involuntary experiential formation in the thought of individual men caused by the linkage of their simultaneous experiences. In economic thought his is the first full argument for the labor theory of value; his notions of property, revolution, and the social contract, though deriving from natural-law theory and resistance theory, are combined in a new interrelation and based upon assumptions of the rule of law that are neither narrowly legalistic nor generally metaphysical.

Across the range of Locke's topics of investigation his preoccupations are clear: his constant interest in the relation of thought to behavior, his concern for the balance of individual right and social obligation, his provisional attitudes to solutions, his distrust of dogmatism, his emphasis on equilibrium and self-stabilization. The last emphasis governs his notion of "power," according to which, even though a man is limited in his finite existence by certain conditional restraints, he is nonetheless free to exercise his mind and even his will. Notions of stabilization and equilibrium operate in his epistemology too, where individual understanding is, among other things, conceived as a constant altering of the balance and relationship between different experiences and ideas. Connected with this, one of Locke's personal behavior patterns makes some sense: from the 1650s until the 1690s Locke, wherever he was, joined or organized discussion groups in which ideas could be cooperatively investigated and idiosyncrasies modulated into a permissive consensus.

Locke's influence can hardly be overestimated; nor can it be accurately measured. His idealism, his concentration upon the autonomy of inward life found an extreme, though corrective, disciple in

Berkeley; his skepticism, in Hume. At first his *Essay* was fiercely attacked. Later, except for such idealists as Leibniz and his own pupil, the third earl of Shaftesbury, for most educated people the book seemed to provide as comprehensive a description and explanation of the mind's workings as Newton's of the workings of the cosmos. Locke's influence on deist thought, perceptible in his lifetime and deplored by him, was considerable both in England and in France; his notions of private education were often cited by eighteenth-century English gentlemen at home and in the colonies; his psychological principles were gradually absorbed into accepted belief and can be traced particularly in the work of eighteenth-century novelists (e.g., Richardson, Sterne, and Diderot). Voltaire's enthusiasm for Locke's ideas had considerable effect in popularizing them in prerevolutionary France. As for political thought, the American and French revolutions have been laid at his door: unquestionably his work was widely read in both countries by men concerned for their political rights, but how deeply they read it remains an open question. His epistemology inaugurated a "new way of ideas," his psychology certainly bore fruit in nineteenth- and twentieth-century psychological theory. Locke's works turn up in many auction lists of eighteenth-century private libraries and are found in the libraries of ancient educational institutions in England and America: Trinity College, Dublin, incorporated the doctrines of the *Essay* into its basic curriculum at an early stage, and Locke's influence at colonial Harvard has also been attested.

ROSALIE L. COLIE

[*See also* CIVIL DISOBEDIENCE; CONSENSUS; CONSERVATISM; CONSTITUTIONS AND CONSTITUTIONALISM; LEGITIMACY; NATURAL LAW; POLITICAL THEORY; SOCIAL CONTRACT; *and the biographies of* BACON; BURKE; HARTLEY; HOBBES; HUME.]

WORKS BY LOCKE

(1690*a*) 1960 *Two Treatises of Government*. Edited by Peter Laslett. Cambridge Univ. Press.

(1690*b*) 1959 *An Essay Concerning Human Understanding*. 2 vols. Edited by Alexander C. Fraser. New York: Dover.

Essays on the Law of Nature. Edited by Wolfgang von Leyden. Oxford: Clarendon, 1954. → Contains the Latin text with a translation.

The Works of John Locke. 10 vols. Aalen (Germany): Scientia Verlag, 1963. → A reprint of the 1823 edition.

SUPPLEMENTARY BIBLIOGRAPHY

AARON, RICHARD I. (1937) 1955 *John Locke*. 2d ed. Oxford: Clarendon.

BOURNE, HENRY R. FOX 1876 *The Life of John Locke*. 2 vols. London: King; New York: Harper.

CHRISTOPHERSEN, HANS O. 1930 *A Bibliographical Introduction to the Study of John Locke*. Norske-videnskaps-akademi i Oslo, Historisk-filosofisk Klasse, Skrifter, 1930: no. 8. Oslo: Dybwad.

CRANSTON, MAURICE W. 1957 *John Locke: A Biography*. New York: Macmillan.

DEWHURST, KENNETH 1963 *John Locke (1632–1704), Physician and Philosopher: A Medical Biography*. London: Wellcome Historical Medical Library.

GIBSON, JAMES (1917) 1960 *Locke's Theory of Knowledge and Its Historical Relations*. Cambridge Univ. Press.

GIVNER, DAVID A. 1962 Scientific Preconceptions in Locke's Philosophy of Language. *Journal of the History of Ideas* 23:340–354.

KING, PETER (1829) 1884 *Life and Letters of John Locke, With Extracts From His Journals and Common-place Books*. London: Bell.

LARKIN, PASCHAL 1930 *Property in the Eighteenth Century: With Special Reference to England and Locke*. London and New York: Longmans.

LOCKE, JOHN 1965 *The Library of John Locke*. Edited by John Harrison and Peter Laslett. Oxford Univ. Press.

MACPHERSON, CRAWFORD B. 1962 *The Political Theory of Possessive Individualism: Hobbes to Locke*. Oxford: Clarendon.

MANDELBAUM, MAURICE 1964 *Philosophy, Science, and Sense Perception: Historical and Critical Studies*. Baltimore: Johns Hopkins Press. → See especially Chapters 1 and 2 on John Locke.

OXFORD UNIVERSITY, BODLEIAN LIBRARY 1959 *A Summary Catalogue of the Lovelace Collection of the Papers of John Locke in the Bodleian Library*, by P. Long. Oxford Bibliographical Society, Publications, New Series, Vol. 8. Oxford Univ. Press.

POLIN, RAYMOND 1960 *La politique morale de John Locke*. Paris: Presses Universitaires de France.

SIMON, WALTER M. 1951 John Locke, Philosophy, and Political Theory. *American Political Science Review* 45:386–399.

TUVESON, ERNEST L. 1955 Locke and the Dissolution of the Ego. *Modern Philology* 52:159–174.

VIANO, CARLO A. 1960 *John Locke: Dal razionalismo all' illuminismo*. Turin (Italy): Einaudi.

YOLTON, JOHN W. 1956 *John Locke and the Way of Ideas*. Oxford Univ. Press.

LOGIC

See REASONING AND LOGIC.

LOGICAL POSITIVISM

See POSITIVISM.

LOMBROSO, CESARE

Born of Jewish parents in Verona, Cesare Lombroso (1835–1909), the Italian criminologist, was educated by the Jesuits; he received a degree in medicine from the University of Pavia in 1858 and a degree in surgery from the University of Genoa in 1859. At various times he was an army physician and in charge of the insane at several hospitals, but his major positions, all at the University of Turin, were those of professor of legal medicine and public hygiene, 1876; professor of psychiatry and clinical psychiatry, 1896; and professor of criminal anthropology, 1906. Although he wrote extensively about such diverse subjects as pellagra, the nervous system, and genius, he came into prominence with his major work, *L'uomo delinquente*, first published in 1876. The book went through five editions in Italy and was translated into various European languages, although never into English.

Lombroso was influenced by French positivism, German materialism, and English evolutionism. In particular, he was influenced by Auguste Comte; Charles Darwin; Bénédict Morel, the French alienist who developed a theory of degeneracy; Bartolomeo Panizza, the Pavian comparative anatomist; Carl Rokitanski, the Viennese pathologist; and Enrico Ferri, his principal younger colleague, who suggested to him the term "the born criminal."

Although Lombroso was aware of the importance of social and psychological factors in the causation of crime, his primary emphasis was on the concept of the atavistic criminal. He believed the atavistic criminal to be a biological throwback to an earlier stage of evolution, since inborn delinquency was not natural to contemporary mankind but peculiar to primitive races. The atavistic criminal could be identified by various anatomical, physiological, and psychic stigmata, different kinds of inborn delinquency being identifiable by different patterns of stigmata.

Lombroso later modified his ideas about criminal typology. Because in the first edition of *L'uomo delinquente* he had focused his attention so exclusively on such anatomical and anthropometric data as skull measurements and facial asymmetries, he had been led to an excessive emphasis on one type of criminal and one theory of criminal causation, atavistic criminality. In later editions he expanded his investigations and consequently his theory, adding degeneracy as a cause of criminality and considering atavism to be a form of degeneracy. Although his theoretical linking of atavism and degeneracy was challenged by biologists, it did widen his original narrow concept of the born criminal, which had been the primary point of attack of his critics. Lombroso's investigations also revealed that the born criminal had pathological symptoms in common with the moral imbecile and the epileptic, and this led him to expand his typology to include the insane criminal and the epileptic criminal. The insane criminal type includes the alcoholic, the mattoid, and the hysterical criminal. Further additions to the typology include the criminaloid—a criminal qualitatively similar to the born criminal but differing quantitatively from him—who had become a criminal more from precipitating external factors than from predisposing internal ones; the pseudocriminal; the habitual criminal; and the person who commits a crime of passion.

Although Lombroso did not believe that all criminal behavior is of organic origin, there is no doubt that he never completely relinquished his belief in the existence of the born criminal type. However, in the fifth and last edition of *L'uomo delinquente* in 1896–1897 reduced his estimate of the proportion of this type to 40 per cent of the total criminal population, and in his introduction to his daughter Gina's summary of his work, *Criminal Man* (1911), he reduced it still further. In response to suggestions by friends and attacks by critics he also came to give more attention to factors in the physical and social environment of the offender. For example, in *Crime: Its Causes and Remedies* (1899) he not only revised the estimate of the born criminal to 33 per cent of the criminal population but also discussed social circumstances which might be partially responsible for encouraging a variety of transmissible biological anomalies that in turn would function within and affect the social structure.

Lombroso was not entirely opposed to the death penalty but believed it should be used only as a last resort. He favored attempts to readjust the criminal and suggested a doctrine of symbiosis of crime, whereby society would make use of the labor and aptitudes of offenders. Included in this doctrine is the idea of the compensation of the victims of crime from the proceeds of work done by prisoners.

Lombroso's work influenced criminological thinking principally by redirecting emphasis from a legalistic concern for crime to a scientific study of the criminal. His approach is most evident in the clinical criminology of Benigno Di Tullio and his associates in Italy.

MARVIN E. WOLFGANG

[*See also* CRIMINOLOGY; DELINQUENCY, *article on* PSYCHOLOGICAL ASPECTS; PENOLOGY; PSYCHOLOGY, *article on* CONSTITUTIONAL PSYCHOLOGY; *and* PSYCHOPATHIC PERSONALITY.]

WORKS BY LOMBROSO

(1876) 1896–1897 *L'uomo delinquente in rapporto all'antropologia, alla giurisprudenza ed alle discipline carcerarie.* 5th ed., 3 vols. Turin (Italy): Bocca.

(1893) 1927 LOMBROSO, CESARE; and FERRERO, GUGLIELMO *La donna delinquente, la prostituta e la donna normale.* 5th ed. Turin (Italy): Bocca. → Partly translated as *The Female Offender* and published in 1958 by Philosophical Library.

(1897) 1907 *Genio e degenerazione: Nuovi studî e nuove battaglie.* Palermo (Italy): Sandron.

(1899) 1911 *Crime: Its Causes and Remedies.* Boston: Little. → First published in Italian. A bibliography of the writings of Lombroso on criminal anthropology appears on pages 453–464.

SUPPLEMENTARY BIBLIOGRAPHY

DI TULLIO, BENIGNO 1959 Cesare Lombroso e la politica criminale moderna. *La scuola positiva* Series 4th 1:495–508.

KURELLA, HANS G. (1910) 1911 *Cesare Lombroso: A Modern Man of Science.* London: Rebman. → First published in German.

LOMBROSO-FERRERO, GINA 1911 *Criminal Man According to the Classification of Cesare Lombroso.* New York and London: Putnam.

LOMBROSO-FERRERO, GINA (1915) 1921 *Cesare Lombroso: Storia della vita e delle opere.* 2d ed. Bologna (Italy): Zanichelli. → A short biography and a bibliography appear on pages 447–476.

MANNHEIM, HERMANN 1936 Lombroso and His Place in Modern Criminology. *Sociological Review* 28:31–49.

WOLFGANG, MARVIN E. 1960 Cesare Lombroso. Pages 168–227 in Hermann Mannheim (editor), *Pioneers in Criminology.* London: Stevens.

LONGFIELD, SAMUEL MOUNTIFORT

Samuel Mountifort Longfield (1802–1884), the Irish jurist, had only a brief career as a professional economist; he was the first occupant of the chair of political economy at Trinity College, Dublin, that Richard Whately founded when he was made archbishop of Dublin. Longfield held this professorship from 1832 to 1836 and then resigned to pursue a legal career.

It was in 1903 that Edwin R. A. Seligman (1915) drew attention to Longfield by referring to him as a "neglected" economist, and indeed he appears to have been virtually unread outside Ireland until then. His work certainly deserved belated recognition, even though it had not become part of the mainstream of economic thought, for in some aspects of that work, he was thirty—even sixty—years ahead of his time.

In establishing the determinants of value, Longfield emphasized cost of production as one determinant, and had a rudimentary conception of the importance of diminishing marginal utility of demand as the other determinant. Thus he spoke of price as indicating what the buyer with the least intense demand was willing to pay. The distribution of income, like diminishing marginal utility, was for Longfield a marginal problem—that of productivity. He enunciated a nicely symmetrical theory of factor payments, in the course of which he denied the importance of the cost of subsistence for the level of wages. He asserted that the wage rate was governed instead by that unit of labor applied least efficiently in the production of any given quantity of a commodity. Nonetheless, like most of his contemporaries, Longfield rejected Malthusian population theory as determining the necessary cost of production of labor, asserting that ". . . to find out what is the cost of production of common labourers, appears to be a trifling with a serious subject" (1834*b*, pp. 202–203).

The cost of capital is the cost of sacrificing present commodities for future ones, and in suggesting the idea of the productivity of roundabout production, Longfield may well, as Seligman points out (1915, p. 113), have sketched a theory of interest that combined time preference and the productivity of capital. But again it was the most disadvantageously used machine—that is to say, the least productive—that determined the rate of interest. In the area of allocation theory Longfield did interesting work in the concept of comparative advantage. This and, even more, the marginalist aspects of his economic analysis may well be connected with the fact that Longfield had always been an able mathematician and in 1872 even published *An Elementary Treatise on Series* (Black 1947, p. 53).

It was consistent with his rejection of Malthus that Longfield did not share the gloom of some of the English classical school concerning economic evolution, and believed that technological improvements in agriculture could more than offset the effects of population increase. He not only advocated that Ireland be industrialized but also predicted that industrialization would over time result in such an increase in capital that the rate of profits would fall and the productivity, hence the real wage, of labor would rise.

Longfield was president of the Statistical and Social Inquiry Society of Ireland from 1863 to 1867, but made few contributions to its proceedings. In a paper to the society (1872*b*), he appears to have supported the idea of government intervention in economic matters, advocating pensions for the blind and the aged, state education, medical care regardless of demonstration of need, housing control, and state-provided clubrooms for workers.

ERSKINE MCKINLEY

[*For the historical context of Longfield's work, see the biography of* MALTHUS. *For discussion of the subsequent development of his ideas, see especially* WAGES, *article on* THEORY; *see also* CAPITAL.]

WORKS BY LONGFIELD

1834*a* *Four Lectures on Poor Laws.* Dublin: Curry.

(1834*b*) 1931 *Lectures on Political Economy.* Series of

Reprints of Scarce Tracts on Economic and Political Science, No. 8. London School of Economics and Political Science.

(1835) 1938 *Three Lectures on Commerce and One on Absenteeism.* Series of Reprints of Scarce Works on Political Economy, No. 4. London School of Economics and Political Science.

1872*a* *An Elementary Treatise on Series.* Dublin.

1872*b* The Limits of State Interference with the Distribution of Wealth, in Applying Taxation to the Assistance of the Public. *Journal of the Statistical and Social Inquiry Society of Ireland* 6:105.

SUPPLEMENTARY BIBLIOGRAPHY

BLACK, R. D. COLLISON 1945 Trinity College, Dublin, and the Theory of Value, 1832–1863. *Economica* New Series 12:140–148.

BLACK, R. D. COLLISON 1947 A History of the Society. Pages 1–47 in the Statistical and Social Inquiry Society of Ireland, Dublin, *Centenary Volume, 1847–1947.* Dublin: Eason.

SCHUMPETER, JOSEPH A. 1954 *History of Economic Analysis.* Edited by E. B. Schumpeter. New York: Oxford Univ. Press.

SELIGMAN, EDWIN R. A. (1915) 1925 An Economic Interpretation of the War. Pages 161–179 in Edwin R. A. Seligman (editor), *Essays in Economics.* New York: Macmillan. → First published in Seligman's *Problems of Readjustment After the War,* 1915.

VINER, JACOB 1932 The Doctrine of Comparative Costs. *Weltwirtschaftliches Archiv* 36:356–414.

VINER, JACOB 1933 Samuel Mountifort Longfield. Volume 9, pages 605–606 in *Encyclopaedia of the Social Sciences.* New York: Macmillan.

LONGITUDINAL STUDIES

See DEVELOPMENTAL PSYCHOLOGY; PANEL STUDIES; TIME SERIES.

LORIA, ACHILLE

Achille Loria (1857–1943), Italian economic theorist, was born and raised in Mantua and received his *laurea* in law at Bologna in 1877. Subsequently he came under the influence of Luigi Cossa at Pavia, Angelo Messedaglia at Rome, and Adolf Wagner at Berlin. In 1881 he was named professor of political economy at Siena, where he remained for ten years. In 1891 he moved to the University of Padua and in 1903 to the University of Turin, where he taught until his retirement in 1932. He was elected to the Accademia dei Lincei in 1901 and was appointed to the Senate in 1919.

Loria developed his theory from a wide range of predecessors—the English classical school, Marx, Darwin, the German historical school, and Luigi Cossa, a specialist in the history of economic theory. Loria was not, however, a simple eclectic, for he used borrowed ideas to formulate an original deterministic and mechanistic theory of economic development and social history. From an intensive and extensive reading on landholding in the British Museum in 1882, when land reform in Ireland and England was being very earnestly debated, he came to the conclusion that the key to the historical process is the relationship between the productivity of land and the density of population. Loria contended that the relative scarcity of land leads to the subjugation of some members of society by others. Different forms of subjugation produce stages in the historical process: slavery, feudalism, high capitalism, and late capitalism. Thus, social and political phenomena are determined at each stage by basic economic and demographic circumstances.

This fundamental concept was developed in a large number of books, many of which were translated into foreign languages. In these works an effort was made to substantiate the theoretical statement by presenting empirical evidence, especially that derived from the experience of colonial countries like America. Loria placed great emphasis upon the importance of free land in the history of the United States. Reviews and discussions of his work in the *Political Science Quarterly* of Columbia University introduced his work to many historians and political scientists. Clearly his views had an impact upon Frederick Jackson Turner in the formulation of his theory regarding the role of the frontier in American life and upon Charles A. Beard in his investigations of the place of economic interests in American political behavior (Benson 1950). The wide interest in the works of Turner and Beard has meant that Loria has had a considerable indirect influence on the interpretation of American history.

SHEPARD B. CLOUGH

[*See also the biographies of* BEARD; TURNER.]

WORKS BY LORIA

1880 *La rendita fondiaria e la sua elisione naturale.* Milan: Hoepli.

1882 *La legge di popolazione ed il sistema sociale.* Siena: Sordomuti.

1884 *Carlo Darwin e l'economia politica.* Milan: Dumolard.

(1886) 1904 *The Economic Foundations of Society.* London: Sonnenschein; New York: Scribner. → First published as *La teoria economica della costituzione politica.*

1889 *Analisi della proprietà capitalista.* 2 vols. Turin: Bocca.

(1890) 1891 *Studi sul valore della moneta.* Turin: Bocca.

1892 *La terra ed il sistema sociale.* Verona and Padua: Drucker.

(1894) 1911 *Contemporary Social Problems.* London: Sonnenschein; New York: Scribner. → First published in Italian.

1899 *La costituzione economica odierna.* Turin: Bocca.

1900 *La sociologia, il suo compito, le sue scuole, i suoi recenti progressi.* Conferenze tenute all'Università di Padova, gennaio-maggio, 1900. Verona and Padua: Drucker.

1901 *Il capitalismo e la scienza: Studi e polemiche.* Turin: Bocca.

1902 *Marx e la sua dottrina.* Milan: Sandron.

1903 *Il movimento operaio: Origini, forme, sviluppo.* Milan: Sandron.

(1904) 1915–1920 *Verso la giustizia sociale (idee, battaglie ed apostoli).* 2 vols. Milan: Società Editrice Libraria.

1905 *La morphologie sociale.* Conférences tenues à l'Université Nouvelle de Bruxelles au mois de mars 1905. Brussels: Larcier; Paris: Giard & Brière.

(1909) 1914 *The Economic Synthesis: A Study of the Laws of Income.* London: Allen & Unwin. → First published in Italian.

(1910) 1934 *Corso di economia politica.* 4th ed., rev. Turin: Unione Tipografico–Editrice Torinese.

(1912) 1918 *The Economic Causes of War.* Chicago: Kerr. → First published as *Les bases économiques de la justice internationale.*

1921 *Aspetti sociali ed economici della guerra mondiale.* Milan: Vallardi.

1922 *I fondamenti scientifici della riforma economica: Studio sulle leggi della produzione.* Turin: Bocca.

1926 *Davide Ricardo.* Rome: Formíggini.

1927 *Ricordi di uno studente settuagenario.* Bologna: Zanichelli.

1935 *Dinamica economica: Studio sulle leggi delle variazioni.* Turin: Unione Tipografico–Editrice Torinese.

SUPPLEMENTARY BIBLIOGRAPHY

BENSON, LEE (1950) 1960 *Turner and Beard: American Historical Writing Reconsidered.* Glencoe, Ill.: Free Press. → See pages 2–40 on "Achille Loria's Influence on American Economic Thought."

EINAUDI, LUIGI 1932 *Bibliografia di Achille Loria.* Turin: La Riforma Sociale. → Published as a Supplement to Volume 43, no. 5 of *La Riforma Sociale.*

EINAUDI, LUIGI 1946 Achille Loria 1857–1943. *Economic Journal* 56:147–150.

RICCI, UMBERTO 1939 *Tre economisti italiani: Pantaleoni, Pareto, Loria.* Bari: Laterza.

LOTKA, ALFRED J.

Alfred James Lotka (1880–1949) anticipated many of the ideas of cybernetics and did original work in demography, evolutionary processes, and self-renewing aggregates. Born in Austria of American parentage, he spent his boyhood in France and acquired his advanced education in England, Germany, and the United States. He was employed as a chemist, physicist, mathematician, and biologist until 1924, when he joined the Metropolitan Life Insurance Company. There he worked on tasks that made heavy demands upon his actuarial and demographic skills. Lotka's 95 technical papers and 6 books reflect his deductive acumen, imagination, pragmatism, precision, and erudition. These works, as well as his magazine articles, also manifest a deep appreciation of the arts and humanities. He held the office of president of the Population Association of America and of the American Statistical Association and several posts in the International Union for the Scientific Study of Population.

His key concern was the set of processes underlying self-renewing aggregates and systems undergoing change, especially irreversible change; this interest prompted the work to which "the field of demography owes virtually its entire central core of analytical development" (Notestein 1950, p. 23). Having shown in 1907 how a closed population with fixed age distribution grows, Lotka (with F. R. Sharpe 1911) demonstrated how a closed population develops a stable age distribution and a characteristic rate of increase, thereby supplying the most powerful of the modern demographer's analytical tools, the stable population model. Building on this and later work, Lotka (with L. I. Dublin 1925) showed how to compute a stable age distribution and the "intrinsic" (or "true") rate of increase, a discovery meriting for him the title "father of demographic analysis" (Vincent 1950, p. 14). This study revealed how misleading crude rates of natural increase can be. Lotka subsequently published many studies of self-renewing aggregates, evolution of age distributions, indices of reproductivity, progeny of population elements, orphanhood, changes in fertility and family size, family extinction, mortality, and so on. Some of this work appeared in the revised editions of Dublin and Lotka's *The Money Value of a Man* and *Length of Life: A Study of the Life Table*, and a great deal was summarized in Lotka's *Théorie analytique des associations biologiques* (1934–1939).

Probably most representative of Lotka's thought is *Elements of Physical Biology* (1925). Appearing when few social scientists used mathematics, it informed some of them of the uses of differential equations, the mechanics of systems and subsystems and the uses of systemic theory, and an essentially cybernetic view of organismic behavior (Simon 1959, p. 494). The book was the source of certain central modern ideas, and it demonstrates Lotka's ability to discover significance in diverse phenomena. Even today it contributes to the understanding of statics and dynamics. The book focuses upon the mechanics of one of the "systems undergoing irreversible changes in the distribution of matter" among its several components, namely, the evolving "life-bearing system," which is made up of an assembly of biological species, among them man, and collections of certain inorganic materials. Having defined irreversibility and conceived of evolution as the redistribution of matter, Lotka described the fundamental equations of the kinetics of evolving systems, along with growth functions and constraints. Under "statics" he treated steady states and diverse equilibria (e.g., chemical, interspecies, moving); Le Châtelier's principle, displacement of equilibrium, homeostasis, stability conditions, and what is now called "comparative statics"; and the role of parameters which define the state of systems. Under "dynamics" he discussed "the progressive redistribution of the matter of the system" among "aggregations of living organisms" or "energy transformers," together with the inorganic background within which substance circulated and parameters could change, albeit very slowly. He described in detail the elements composing the apparatus which energy transformers use in coping with their external environments, among them depictors, receptors (including communicators), elaborators, epictors, effectors, adjusters, and "consciousness" involved in depictors and adjustors [*see* INFORMATION THEORY]. This nonteleological apparatus enables some organisms, especially man, to discriminate, select, and in some environments stem that increase in entropy which dominates irreversible systems; its influence may be accentuated by favorable orthogenesis.

JOSEPH J. SPENGLER

[*For discussion of the subsequent development of Lotka's ideas, see* COMPUTATION; CYBERNETICS; LIFE TABLES; POPULATION.]

WORKS BY LOTKA

1911 LOTKA, ALFRED J.; and SHARPE, F. R. A Problem in Age Distribution. *Philosophical Magazine* 21:435–438.

(1925) 1957 *Elements of Mathematical Biology.* New York: Dover. → First published as *Elements of Physical Biology.*

1925 LOTKA, ALFRED J.; and DUBLIN, LOUIS I. On the True Rate of Natural Increase. *Journal of the American Statistical Association* 20:305–339.

(1930) 1946 DUBLIN, LOUIS I.; and LOTKA, ALFRED J. *The Money Value of a Man.* Rev. ed. New York: Ronald.

1934–1939 *Théorie analytique des associations biologiques.* 2 vols. Paris: Hermann. → Volume 1: *Principes.* Volume 2: *Analyse démographique avec application particulière à l'espèce humaine.*

(1936) 1949 DUBLIN, LOUIS I.; LOTKA, ALFRED J.; and SPIEGELMAN, M. *Length of Life: A Study of the Life Table.* Rev. ed. New York: Ronald. → Spiegelman is a joint author of the revised edition only.

SUPPLEMENTARY BIBLIOGRAPHY

LOPEZ, ALVARO 1961 *Problems in Stable Population Theory.* Princeton Univ., Office of Population Research.

NOTESTEIN, FRANK W. 1950 Alfred James Lotka. *Population Index* 16:22–29. → Contains a bibliography.

SIMON, HERBERT A. 1959 [A Book Review of] *Elements of Mathematical Biology,* by Alfred J. Lotka. *Econometrica* 27:493–495.

VINCENT, PAUL 1950 Alfred J. Lotka: 1880–1949. *Population* 5:13–14.

LOTZE, HERMANN

Rudolf Hermann Lotze (1817–1881), German psychologist and philosopher, was born in Bautzen, Upper Lusatia. His father was a surgeon in the army of Saxony. In the confusion of the Napoleonic Wars, his family moved frequently, finding a permanent home only in 1818 in Zittau. There, in 1828, Lotze entered the excellent classical Gymnasium, graduating cum laude in 1834. In his last years at the Gymnasium, he wrote poetry, as well as a novelistic essay along the lines of Goethe's *Wilhelm Meister.* Strongly influenced by Goethe, and as yet unaware of the works of other thinkers, he began to develop what were to remain the essentials of his philosophy.

Lotze's lack of funds forced him to abandon his literary and other interests and prepare himself for a profession. Following in his father's footsteps, he began, in 1834, to study medicine at the University of Leipzig. He also studied philosophy under Christian H. Weisse, a friend of Fechner's and an adherent of the idealist philosophy of Schelling and Hegel. Lotze's later work was decisively influenced both by his medical and scientific training and by Weisse's idealist teaching.

He completed his study of medicine in 1838 with a dissertation entitled *De futurae biologiae principiis philosophicis.* As a scientist he vigorously opposed the medical mysticism implied in the concept of "vitality," replacing it with mechanistic explanations; as a philosopher, however, he denied that a mechanistic system of explanation is necessarily based on a materialist philosophy. He obtained a master's degree in philosophy at the same time as his medical degree.

Lotze practiced medicine in Zittau for a year, but he soon found the town too confining. Encouraged by his former professor, Weisse, he returned to Leipzig as an instructor in medicine and philosophy; he was appointed associate professor in 1843. While he was at Leipzig he produced the outlines of his scientific life work: the *Metaphysik* (1841), in which he broke with Hegelian idealism; the *Allgemeine Pathologie und Therapie als mechanische Naturwissenschaften* (1842); the *Logik* (1843*a*); and three articles for Rudolf Wagner's *Handwörterbuch der Physiologie,* "Leben, Lebenskraft" (1843*b*), "Instinct" (1844), and "Seele und

Seelenleben" (1846). In 1844 he accepted an appointment as full professor at Göttingen, occupying what had been Johann Friedrich Herbart's chair. He remained at Göttingen for 37 years until, at the urging of Eduard Zeller and Helmholtz, he accepted the chair vacated by Harms in Berlin. He died soon after his move to Berlin.

Lotze always remained both a scientist and a philosopher. His works are characterized, first, by his efforts to eliminate mysticism from science by using the causal–mechanistic method and, second, by his concern to dissociate mechanistic systematization from materialist–atheist philosophy. To Lotze intellectual achievement without faith was a *caput mortuum*, and science without causal–mechanistic systematization was not a science. Ultimately, to be sure, what concerned him was the ideal—what *ought* to be—and he saw the understanding of causal relationships simply as a condition for the realization of the ideal. Thus, mechanistic processes are indispensable to the existence of a phenomenon, but they are not its *raison d'être*. In this way Lotze tried to combine mechanistic systematization with ethical freedom, with what he called the dignity of subjectivity. In his own time his postulate of freedom, which went counter to the anti-idealist *Zeitgeist*, was not understood; his contemporaries availed themselves, instead, of the mass of physiological facts he cited —which clearly confirmed the dependence of the psychical on the physical—to support their materialist philosophy.

Lotze's *Allgemeine Physiologie des koerperlichen Lebens* appeared in 1851, and his *Medicinische Psychologie: Oder, Physiologie der Seele* in 1852. The latter is the first physiological psychology, the prototype of all later works bearing similar titles. In contrast to Fechner's parallelism, Lotze's psychology is a theory of interaction: sensation is produced by the mind "at the initiative of a neural state." Space is a mode of perception peculiar to the mind. A corollary to this theory of space perception is Lotze's theory of "local signs," which asserts that the world of external space is never simply perceived but rather reproduced by the mind.

His two-volume magnum opus, *Microcosmus* (1856–1864), has two aspects: it is both a polemic against materialist philosophy and an expansion of Lotze's psychology into a comprehensive anthropology. (Its German subtitle is "Versuch einer Anthropologie.") Exploring what he called education (*Bildung*), that is, the conditions under which a human being becomes human, he dealt with such subjects as national temperament, the evolution of customs and morals, and the influences of home, family, division of labor, and so forth. He regarded the history of mankind as the history of the evolution of the human mind.

Lotze founded no school; he had no disciples. Yet he was a pioneer with some influence, for the friends and pupils he did have were men of scientific importance: Teichmüller, Stumpf, Konrad Langenbeck, and Georg E. Müller. Stumpf studied with Lotze in 1867–1868, and, after working with Franz Brentano in Würzburg for two years, he returned to Göttingen as an instructor. Müller took his doctorate with Lotze in 1873, became an instructor at Göttingen in 1876, and succeeded Lotze as professor there in 1881.

It is unlikely that anyone with an empirical, problem-oriented approach to psychology will find Lotze's work of direct relevance. But if he does not dismiss Lotze's work too readily as obsolete, he may find fertile suggestions there.

WILHELM J. REVERS

[*For discussion of the subsequent development of Lotze's ideas, see* PERCEPTION, *articles on* DEPTH PERCEPTION *and* PERCEPTUAL DEVELOPMENT.]

WORKS BY LOTZE

(1838) 1885 De futurae biologiae principiis philosophicis: Dissertatio inauguralis medica. Volume 1, pages 1–25 in Hermann Lotze, *Kleine Schriften*. Leipzig: Hirzel.

(1838–1881) 1885–1891 *Kleine Schriften*. 3 vols. Edited with an introduction by David Peipers. Leipzig: Hirzel.

1840 *Gedichte*. Leipzig: Weidmann.

1841 *Metaphysik*. Leipzig: Weidmann.

(1842) 1848 *Allgemeine Pathologie und Therapie als mechanische Naturwissenschaften*. 2d ed. Leipzig: Hirzel.

1843*a* *Logik*. Leipzig: Weidmann.

(1843*b*) 1885 Leben, Lebenskraft. Volume 1, pages 139–220 in Hermann Lotze, *Kleine Schriften*. Leipzig: Hirzel.

(1844) 1885 Instinct. Volume 1, pages 221–250 in Hermann Lotze, *Kleine Schriften*. Leipzig: Hirzel.

(1846) 1886 Seele und Seelenleben. Volume 2, pages 1–204 in Hermann Lotze, *Kleine Schriften*. Leipzig: Hirzel.

1851 *Allgemeine Physiologie des koerperlichen Lebens*. Leipzig: Weidmann.

1852 *Medicinische Psychologie: Oder, Physiologie der Seele*. Leipzig: Weidmann.

(1856–1864) 1894 *Microcosmus: An Essay Concerning Man and His Relation to the World*. 4th ed., 2 vols. Edinburgh: Clark. → First published as *Mikrokosmus: Ideen zur Naturgeschichte und Geschichte der Menschheit: Versuch einer Anthropologie*, in 3 volumes.

1857 *Streitschriften*. Volume 1: In Bezug auf Prof. I. H. Fichte's *Anthropologie*. Leipzig: Hirzel.

1868 *Geschichte der Aesthetik in Deutschland*. Akademie der Wissenschaft, Munich, Geschichte der Wissenschaften in Deutschland, Vol. 7. Munich: Cotta.

(1874) 1888 *Logic, in Three Books: Of Thought, of Investigation, and of Knowledge.* 2d ed., 2 vols. Oxford: Clarendon Press. → First published in German. Part 1 of Lotze's "System of Philosophy."

(1879) 1887 *Metaphysic, in Three Books: Ontology, Cosmology and Psychology.* 2d ed., 2 vols. Oxford: Clarendon Press. → First published in German. Part 2 of Lotze's "System of Philosophy."

(1881) 1886 *Outlines of Psychology.* Boston: Ginn. → First published in German.

SUPPLEMENTARY BIBLIOGRAPHY

BORING, EDWIN G. (1929) 1957 *A History of Experimental Psychology.* 2d ed. New York: Appleton. → See especially pages 261–270 on "Hermann Lotze."

BRETT, GEORGE S. (1912–1921) 1962 *Brett's History of Psychology.* Edited and abridged by R. S. Peters. London: Allen & Unwin; New York: Macmillan. → An abridged edition of the original three-volume publication, *A History of Psychology.* See especially pages 591–600 on Lotze's soul psychology.

FALCKENBERG, RICHARD F. O. 1901 *Hermann Lotze.* Stuttgart: Fromann.

HALL, G. STANLEY 1912 *Founders of Modern Psychology.* New York: Appleton. → See especially pages 65–121 on "Rudolph Hermann Lotze."

HARTMANN, EDUARD VON 1888 *Lotze's Philosophie.* Leipzig: Friedrich.

MURPHY, GARDNER (1929) 1949 *Historical Introduction to Modern Psychology.* Rev. ed. New York: Harcourt.

WENTSCHER, MAX 1925 *Fechner und Lotze.* Munich: Reinhardt.

LOUIS, P. C. A.

Pierre Charles Alexandre Louis (1787–1872), who did much to introduce the use of statistics into medicine, was born the son of a vineyard proprietor in the small town of Ay (Marne) in Champagne. Although his father died when Louis was six, his mother saw to her son's primary education. After his schooling was over he was sent to a law office to prepare for a legal career. In 1807, deciding that the law was not to his liking, Louis began to study medicine. He spent a year at Reims with a surgeon and then went to Paris to pursue his studies, graduating in 1813 with a medical degree.

A chance encounter during a brief vacation in his native town had an important effect on his career. The comte de Saint-Priest, an emigré noble in whose family Louis's aunt had been a governess, was friendly with the Louis family and paid them a visit. As governor of Podolia, Saint-Priest was in the service of the tsar and persuaded Louis to accompany him to Russia. After traveling about that country for three years Louis settled in Odessa, where he acquired a substantial practice and even received a titular appointment as physician to the tsar. In 1820 Odessa experienced a diphtheria epidemic, an event which led Louis not only to realize the shortcomings in his knowledge of disease but to give up his practice and return to Paris for further study.

Six months in the Paris hospitals convinced Louis that clinical medicine required a more precise basis than it had and that this could be achieved by what he called the numerical method. A.-F. Chomel, his friend and fellow student, was attending physician at the Charité Hospital and gave Louis the run of two wards of his service, as well as the privilege of performing all the autopsies on the patients who died there. For six years Louis worked at the hospital from three to five hours a day, devoting at least two hours to each autopsy and collecting over two thousand observations. In 1827 he retired to Brussels, where the cost of living was lower, and spent a year tabulating and analyzing his statistical data.

Some of his observations had been published while he was still in Paris, and in 1825 Louis had brought out his *Recherches anatomico-pathologiques sur la phthisie*, based on 123 cases. (Some eighty were added to the second edition of 1843.) By the time he returned to Paris in 1828 he had acquired a reputation in medical circles. That year he was sent, together with Armand Trousseau and Nicolas Chervin, to investigate a yellow fever epidemic at Gibraltar. In 1828 his work on typhoid fever was published and he became attending physician at La Pitié Hospital. Subsequently he was also appointed to the Hôtel-Dieu; he served in these institutions for many years. Louis's last important publication was his critical analysis of the alleged therapeutic effects of bloodletting, *Recherches sur les effets de la saignée dans quelques maladies inflammatoires* (1835). In this book he employed the numerical method to refute the views of François Broussais on copious bloodletting in pneumonia and other inflammatory diseases.

Louis married a daughter of the marquis de Montferrier in 1832, when he was 45. For some twenty years he carried on an ample consultation practice in Paris. His only son, Armand, died of tuberculosis in 1854, a loss from which Louis never recovered.

The numerical method. Louis's major contribution resides in his efforts to apply statistical analysis to problems of clinical medicine. His advocacy and use of the *numerical method* served this end. What Louis did was to study each patient as thoroughly as possible at the bedside and at autopsy, employing rigorously the methodology already established by G. L. Bayle, René Th. H. Laënnec, and others of the Paris school of clinicians and pathologists. Having carefully collected his observations he then grouped them in tabular form. From these grouped and tabulated data inferences might be drawn concerning the relations between diverse clinical phenomena, the probability of their occurrence, the value of a given therapy, and other items. Although he had used his approach in his earlier publications on phthisis and typhoid fever, the numerical method was first fully presented in 1835 in Louis's therapeutic study, *Recherches sur les effets de la saignée . . .*, and in a special memoir *De l'examen des malades et de la recherche des faits généraux* (1837).

Essentially, Louis's numerical method was not new. The procedure had been employed some three decades earlier by Philippe Pinel to prove the value of his "moral treatment" of mental patients. It was also being employed in the 1820s and 1830s by physicians concerned with such public health problems as the causes of differential mortality and the effect on health of such factors as economic and social class, occupation, race, imprisonment, intemperance, or lack of proper sanitation. Furthermore, Louis's handling of numerical data was basically simple. If, as it is said, Louis was familiar with the work of Laplace on probability, there is no evidence that he ever used such knowledge in his statistical thinking. Like so many of his contemporaries he dealt with small numbers of observations and had no knowledge of how to establish the precision or validity of his results. There is no doubt that Louis was himself conscious of these difficulties; yet he did not seek statistical criteria of reliability, nor did he try to decide when the number of observations was large enough to avoid error.

Nevertheless, Louis has a significant place in the evolving application of statistical analysis to health problems. First of all, he recognized the basic importance of accurate observations. His insistence on good clinical records established a fundamental principle for statistical work in clinical medicine. Second, Louis made an important contribution as a teacher and a propagandist. Through his students, of whom a considerable proportion were foreigners (among them Americans), through the Société Médicale d'Observation (which several of his students founded in 1832), and through his writings Louis advocated and spread the idea of the numerical method, in spite of vigorous opposition. He envisaged the goal of a science of clinical medicine and pointed to the road that would lead to it.

GEORGE ROSEN

WORKS BY LOUIS

(1825) 1843 *Recherches anatomico-pathologiques sur la phthisie.* 2d ed. Paris: Baillière.

(1828) 1841 *Recherches anatomiques, pathologiques . . . sur la maladie connue sous les noms de fièvre typhoïde . . .* 2 vols., 2d ed. Paris: Baillière.

1835 *Recherches sur les effets de la saignée dans quelques maladies inflammatoires.* Paris: Baillière.

1837 De l'examen des malades et de la recherche des faits généraux. Société Médicale d'Observation, *Mémoires* 1:1–63.

SUPPLEMENTARY BIBLIOGRAPHY

ASTRUC, PIERRE 1932 Le centenaire de la Société Médicale d'Observation. *Progrès médical,* supplément illustré 9:73–87.

BÉCLARD, JULES-AUGUSTE 1878 *Notices et portraits: Éloges lus à l'Académie de Médecine.* Paris: Masson. → See especially pages 228–257.

GREENWOOD, MAJOR (the younger) 1936 *The Medical Dictator and Other Biographical Studies.* London: Williams & Norgate. → See especially pages 123–142.

OSLER, WILLIAM 1908 *An Alabama Student and Other Biographical Essays.* Oxford Univ. Press. → See especially pages 189–210.

ROSEN, GEORGE 1955 Problems in the Application of Statistical Analysis to Questions of Health: 1700–1800. *Bulletin of the History of Medicine* 29:27–45.

WOILLEZ, EUGÈNE J. 1873 *Le docteur Pierre Charles Alexandre Louis: Sa vie—ses oeuvres (1787–1872).* Paris: Dupont.

LOVE

See AFFECTION.

LOWELL, A. LAWRENCE

Abbott Lawrence Lowell (1856–1943), political scientist and president of Harvard University, was born into one of the great families of Boston society. The Lowells had been established in Massachusetts since 1639 and had contributed to American life a distinguished line of ministers, merchants, industrialists, philanthropists, jurists, and poets. Much of their philanthropy supported education, especially Harvard University, the Massachusetts Institute of Technology, and the Lowell Institute. When he graduated from Harvard College in 1877, A. Lawrence Lowell was the sixth in an unbroken series of generations of alumni.

After receiving an LL.B. from the Harvard Law School in 1880, Lowell opened a law office in Boston. When his practice proved unsuccessful, he began to write in his spare time, soon turning from legal topics to political science. A series of magazine articles, collected as *Essays on Government* (1889), received sufficient recognition to encourage him to begin work on a major study in comparative government, the two-volume *Governments and Parties in Continental Europe* (1896). From 1897 to 1900 he was a part-time lecturer at Harvard, and in 1900 he received a permanent appointment as professor of the science of government. His book *The Government of England* (1908) won praise on both sides of the Atlantic. Lowell was active in university affairs, and this led to his selection as president of Harvard in 1909, a post he held until 1933.

His basic approach to political science is stated on the opening page of *Essays on Government:* "The real mechanism of a government can be understood only by examining it in action." Studies were needed, therefore, to provide detailed descriptions of the actual operation of contemporary political structures. He observed, furthermore, that political parties, more than formal institutions, determine political practice.

Lowell's two major books were based on these themes. The one on continental Europe (1896) carefully described the formal political institutions of France, Italy, Germany, Austria–Hungary, and Switzerland and the way that the specific party system dominated the institutions of each country. The book on England (1908) provided a detailed review of the political life of that country, based on extensive interviews with political leaders as well as printed source material. These and less ambitious works discussing the management of legislation by parties and the impact of public opinion on party operations aroused contemporary enthusiasm. In the *English Historical Review* it was said that Lowell "has done for England what Mr. Bryce has done for the American Commonwealth" (Raleigh 1908, p. 809). Although succeeding generations may not rate Lowell's insights this highly, they will still find useful his precise portraits of how governments operated at the beginning of the twentieth century.

In his 24 years as president of Harvard, Lowell was particularly eager to enhance the stature of the undergraduate college. He modified the undergraduate curriculum by curtailing freedom in the choice of courses and by introducing the tutorial system to encourage individual work. He altered the structure of the college by the inauguration, in 1930, of the "house system," which split the undergraduate body into smaller residential and social units, on the model of the English universities. And despite his great identification with New England, he supported changes in admission rules and scholarship eligibility that opened Harvard to public school graduates from the entire country and transformed the college into a national institution.

Although Lowell aroused considerable liberal hostility when he supported the convictions of Sacco and Vanzetti, he was keenly sensitive to any encroachments on academic freedom. He strongly defended faculty members under attack by the public and by alumni for unpopular opinions—Hugo Münsterberg for pro-German attitudes during World War I, Zechariah Chaffee for liberal views during the "Red Scare" of the 1920s, and Harold Laski for his support of the police in the Boston police strike of 1919.

MILTON BERMAN

[*Other relevant material may be found in* PARTIES, POLITICAL; *and in the biographies of* BRYCE *and* MICHELS.]

WORKS BY LOWELL

1889 *Essays on Government.* Boston: Houghton Mifflin.

1896 *Governments and Parties in Continental Europe.* 2 vols. Boston: Houghton Mifflin.

1902 The Influence of Party Upon Legislation in England and America. American Historical Association, *Annual Report* [1901] no. 1:319–542.

(1908) 1912 *The Government of England.* 2 vols., new ed. New York: Macmillan.

(1913) 1926 *Public Opinion and Popular Government.* New ed. New York: Longmans.

1923 *Public Opinion in War and Peace.* Cambridge, Mass.: Harvard Univ. Press.

1934 *At War With Academic Traditions in America.* Cambridge, Mass.: Harvard Univ. Press.

1938 *What a University President Has Learned.* New York: Macmillan.

SUPPLEMENTARY BIBLIOGRAPHY

GREENSLET, FERRIS 1946 *The Lowells and Their Seven Worlds.* Boston: Houghton Mifflin.

MORISON, SAMUEL E. (editor) 1930 *The Development of Harvard University Since the Inauguration of President Eliot: 1869–1929.* Cambridge, Mass.: Harvard Univ. Press.

MORISON, SAMUEL E. 1936 The Lowell Administration. Pages 439–481 in Samuel E. Morison, *Three Centuries of Harvard: 1636–1936.* Cambridge, Mass.: Harvard Univ. Press.

RALEIGH, T. 1908 [A Book Review of] *The Government of England,* by A. Lawrence Lowell. *English Historical Review* 23:809–810.

YEOMANS, HENRY A. 1948 *Abbott Lawrence Lowell: 1856–1943.* Cambridge, Mass.: Harvard Univ. Press.

LOWIE, ROBERT H.

Robert H. Lowie (1883–1957), American anthropologist, was born in Vienna of a German mother and a Hungarian father. From the time he was ten he lived in New York City. In 1897 he entered City College, concentrating on Latin and Greek for the first two years and then on science. After he received his B.A. in 1901 he taught for three years in the New York public schools. Then he began graduate work in anthropology at Columbia University, studying primarily with Franz Boas; his minor field was psychology. He volunteered his services to Clark Wissler at the American Museum of Natural History and was sent by Wissler on his first field trip, to the Lemhi Shoshone, in 1906. In 1908 he received his PH.D. from Columbia, with a thesis on a subject in comparative mythology. Lowie spent most of his active professional life at two institutions: at the American Museum, from 1907 to 1917, and at the University of California at Berkeley, from 1917 until 1950. He married Luella Cole, a psychologist, in 1933. His last teaching position was at Harvard in the summer of 1955.

Lowie was exceedingly productive: his bibliography totals about four hundred separate pieces of writing—14 books, 18 monographs, 3 translations of monographs, 203 reviews, and numerous articles. Nearly all his works were on ethnology, but he did include some archeology in his *Introduction to Cultural Anthropology* (1934) and collected three volumes of texts in the Crow language. His many honors attest to the recognition of his contributions: he served as president of several major professional societies (the American Folklore Society, 1916–1917, the American Ethnological Society, 1920–1921, and the American Anthropological Association, 1935–1936); he was elected to the National Academy of Sciences in 1931; he received an honorary doctorate from the University of Chicago in 1941; he gave the Huxley lecture at the Royal Anthropological Institute in 1948; and he was awarded the Viking medal in the same year. He also served his profession as editor of the *American Anthropologist* from 1924 to 1933.

Approach to theory. Lowie's theoretical position was, in his own words, middle-of-the-road (*Selected Papers*, p. 13); for example, on the subject of the correlation of semantic categories in kinship terminologies, on the one hand, and social structure and behavior, on the other, he took a position somewhere in between Kroeber's historical one and the functional view propounded by Radcliffe-Brown. He refused to accept theories when he considered the supporting evidence to be weak, as in the case of Freudian interpretations of cultural behavior, for he insisted that ethnology is a science and that its theories must be supported by facts.

Of all Lowie's books, *Primitive Society* (1920) had the greatest impact on anthropology. Although Kroeber criticized the book for being too destructive of old theories and too little concerned with replacing them (Kroeber 1920), and although White repeatedly berated Lowie for being too harsh with L. H. Morgan (White 1943; 1944; 1945), *Primitive Society* dominated social organization theory until the almost simultaneous appearance of three new books, one by Lowie himself (1948), one by Murdock that appeared in 1949, and one by Lévi-Strauss, also in 1949. Lowie's 1920 book would have been great even if it had done nothing more than clarify terminology, but it contained so much more that graduate students reading it for the first time are often surprised to find that it anticipates much of current teaching.

Although Lowie used no explicit sampling technique, he was familiar with so wide a range of ethnographies that many of his global generalizations have since been confirmed by more refined methods. The broad scope of the book, which includes chapters on property, associations, rank, government, and justice, in addition to the discussion of kinship, is paralleled most closely by Hoebel's general textbook, published in 1949. Lowie's theoretical position in *Primitive Society* reflects that of the Boas historical school. While not denying independent invention and parallel and convergent evolution, especially in the field of economics, Lowie did reject the evolution of social organization proposed by L. H. Morgan and emphasized the dominant role of diffusion: "Creating nothing, this factor [diffusion], nevertheless makes all other agencies taper almost into nothingness beside it in its effect on the total growth of human civilization" ([1920] 1947, p. 434).

Lowie's *History of Ethnological Theory* (1937) shows more tolerance of the opinions of others than does *Primitive Society*. Although Lowie regarded many of the extreme diffusionist views and evolutionary sequences of the German *Kulturkreis* school as being undemonstrable, he nevertheless conceded (1937, p. 190) that the correlations the German anthropologists had obtained between feminine tillage, matrilocal residence, matrilineal descent, bride service, and monogamy were correct. These correlations have been confirmed statistically in recent years. Similarly, although Lowie had little use for Radcliffe-Brown's more general laws, he accepted the correlations Radcliffe-Brown had established among specific variables of kinship terminology and social organization. For instance, Radcliffe-Brown (1913) was the first to point out that in Australia four-section systems of social organization and marriage with a first cross-cousin were associated with one kind of kinship terminology, while eight-section systems and marriage with a second cross-cousin went with a different kind of kinship terminology.

Psychology and anthropology. Lowie maintained an interest in psychology throughout his life, mentioned it in many of his writings, and devoted a section of his *History of Ethnological*

Theory (1937, pp. 262–274) to it. He regarded psychology as the study of innate behavior, in contrast to the learned behavior of culture, and he pointed out that ethnological studies had shown that many kinds of behavior are in fact culturally determined, although they had previously been thought to be of genetic origin. At the same time he suggested that mythology and religion have common elements across cultures which are derived from dreams, and that these dreams may have some sort of biological basis. Lowie accepted Galton's notion that individual differences between members of the same society may be in part genetically determined, and even that there might be significant genetic differences between races, not in over-all ability but in special abilities, such as aptitude for music. He was among the first anthropologists to point out that cultural selection is a part of natural selection (1937, p. 267) and that it can in part determine which genes will be advantageous and which will be deleterious. He tended to distrust the sweeping Freudian generalizations of the early personality studies by ethnologists and never fully endorsed personality as an important subdiscipline within ethnology.

During World War II, Lowie taught an "area course" on Germany and the Balkans at Berkeley. This led to a book on Germany (1945), a field trip to Germany, Switzerland, and Austria in 1950/1951, and a second book on Germany in 1954. Lowie did a considerable amount of interviewing on the field trip, and he read a large amount of material on Germany, including self-evaluations by Germans. The 1954 book was concerned principally with describing the impact of the war on the personalities of German people.

Anthropological analysis. Lowie's many monographs on North American Indians, which were written for the most part while he was connected with the American Museum, are excellent. His field work on the Crow Indians goes far beyond the kind of cultural inventory that was common at the time and includes many insights into functional relationships. Take his description of the chaos that would result from an endogamous marriage within a single sib (or clan):

> A Crow in such circumstances loses his bearings and perplexes his tribesmen. For he owes specific obligations to his father's relatives and others to his mother's, who are now hopelessly confounded. The sons of his father's clansmen ought to be his censors, whereas his mother's are bound to shield him from criticism; but now the very same persons are his joking-relatives and his clansmen. The dilemma affects others as well as himself. ([1948] 1960, p. 237)

The historical and comparative summaries at the end of his work on Plains Indian age-societies (1916*a*) were praised even by Boas, who was critical of so many historical reconstructions. They are still cited as among the best examples of the kind of comparative and historical interpretation produced by the Boas school.

It was in one of his early articles (1916*b*) that Lowie showed how well a balance can be preserved between historical and "sociological" (i.e. functional) interpretation of such data as kinship terminologies. Indeed, since more recent cross-cultural studies of kinship terminologies have largely ignored historical explanations, they have in this respect retrogressed from Lowie's position of 1916. However, in works by Naroll (1961; 1964), Naroll and D'Andrade (1963), and Driver (1966), Lowie's dual interpretation has been confirmed in applications to geographical distributions. It is an interpretation that can, in fact, be applied to almost all anthropological data.

Lowie wrote a number of articles in which he drew on more than one academic discipline (see *Selected Papers*, pp. 189–290) and in which he reached, among others, the following conclusions: that oral traditions are not reliable history and that a more accurate history can be inferred from careful comparative study in ethnology, archeology, linguistics, and physical anthropology; that all races are not necessarily equal in all inherited mental abilities just because they have not been proven to differ; that the concept of incorporeal property is common in primitive societies; that economic factors can explain only a minor part of cultural behavior; and that the progression from American Indian societies with the simplest form of government to the totalitarian state of the Inca was not a simple one. There was no unilineal development toward ever greater centralization of authority; for example, the Iroquois avoided military despotism because it would have conflicted with the separatism of their matricentered kinship organization.

Lowie's theory of evolution acknowledged the general increase in culture complexity through time and the increase in the efficiency of economic productivity, but it denied the inevitability of any universal increase in complexity and efficiency: particular races, languages, or cultures may either level off, retrogress, or become extinct rather than evolve toward greater complexity. Lowie also denied the inevitability of moral progress.

Lowie was early aware of the possibility and desirability of applying correlation techniques to cross-cultural variables, and in a book published in 1948 he also discussed the relation of correlation to the laws of evolution. Although he himself never applied the method of correlation to cross-cultural data, he praised Murdock's 1949 book for doing so. He was well aware of the essentials of scientific method in cross-cultural comparisons, such as the necessity of basing generalizations on representative samples. He pointed out also the lack of precise definition of the ethnic unit (society) and the equally vague definition of some of the variables (culture traits) being correlated. Rather than abandon quantitative methods entirely, Lowie argued for refinement of such definitions and caution in inferring time sequence or causality from correlations. In his books of world-wide scope he consistently cited sufficient evidence from every major world area, so that the generalizations he made have never been invalidated by statistics or even been challenged. In his comparative writings he made use of all the major explanations of resemblances in the culture inventories of ethnic units: universals, parallels, convergences, diffusions, and heritages from a common protoculture.

Most of Lowie's field work was done under the supervision of Clark Wissler of the American Museum of Natural History, who directed him to do reconnaissance in central Canada and the entire Great Basin area in the United States. When he was permitted to remain with the Crow Indians for a relatively long period of time, Lowie's field work was superb. His modest appraisal that his descriptions of material culture were not as competent as Wissler's may be correct, but his work on social organization and religion surely excelled that of his mentor and became a model for those who followed. He obtained most of his information from a small number of informants, but he occasionally used a larger number when he suspected significant individual differences, as in reports of visionary experiences. In addition to collecting material in English from competent bilinguals, he obtained three volumes of texts in the Crow language, thus preserving for the future a large amount of primary data.

HAROLD E. DRIVER

[*See also* ETHNOGRAPHY; INDIANS, NORTH AMERICAN; POLITICAL ANTHROPOLOGY; SOCIAL STRUCTURE; *and the biographies of* BOAS; KROEBER; MORGAN, LEWIS HENRY; RADCLIFFE-BROWN; WISSLER.]

WORKS BY LOWIE

1916*a* Plains Indian Age-societies: Historical and Comparative Summary. Volume 11, pages 881–1031 in American Museum of Natural History, *Anthropological Papers*. New York: The Museum.

(1916*b*) 1960 Historical and Sociological Interpretations of Kinship Terminologies. Pages 65–74 in Robert H. Lowie, *Selected Papers in Anthropology*. Edited by Cora DuBois. Berkeley: Univ. of California Press.

(1920) 1947 *Primitive Society*. New York: Liveright. → A paperback edition was published in 1961 by Harper.

(1921) 1960 A Note on Aesthetics. Pages 137–142 in Robert H. Lowie, *Selected Papers in Anthropology*. Edited by Cora DuBois. Berkeley: Univ. of California Press.

(1934) 1952 *An Introduction to Cultural Anthropology*. Rev. ed. New York: Farrar.

1937 *The History of Ethnological Theory*. New York: Farrar.

1942 *Studies in Plains Indian Folklore*. California, University of, Publications in American Archaeology and Ethnology, Vol. 40, no. 1. Berkeley: Univ. of California Press.

1945 *The German People: A Social Portrait to 1914*. New York and Toronto: Farrar.

(1948) 1960 *Social Organization*. New York: Holt.

1954 *Toward Understanding Germany*. Univ. of Chicago Press.

1959 *Robert H. Lowie, Ethnologist: A Personal Record*. Berkeley: Univ. of California Press.

Selected Papers in Anthropology. Edited by Cora DuBois. Berkeley: Univ. of California Press, 1960. → Thirty-three papers written or published between 1911 and 1957.

SUPPLEMENTARY BIBLIOGRAPHY

Bibliography of Robert H. Lowie. 1958 *American Anthropologist* New Series 60:362–375.

DRIVER, HAROLD E. 1966 Geographical–Historical versus Psycho–Functional Explanations of Kin Avoidances. *Current Anthropology* 7:131–182.

HOEBEL, E. ADAMSON (1949) 1958 *Man in the Primitive World: An Introduction to Anthropology*. 2d ed. New York: McGraw-Hill.

KROEBER, A. L. 1920 [A Book Review of] *Primitive Society*, by Robert H. Lowie. *American Anthropologist* New Series 22:377–381.

LÉVI-STRAUSS, CLAUDE 1949 *Les structures élémentaires de la parenté*. Paris: Presses Universitaires de France.

MURDOCK, GEORGE P. 1949 *Social Structure*. New York: Macmillan. → A paperback edition was published in 1965 by the Free Press.

NAROLL, RAOUL S. 1961 Two Solutions to Galton's Problem. *Philosophy of Science* 28:16–39.

NAROLL, RAOUL S.; and D'ANDRADE, ROY G. 1963 Two Further Solutions to Galton's Problem. *American Anthropologist* New Series 65:1053–1067.

NAROLL, RAOUL S. 1964 Fifth Solution to Galton's Problem. *American Anthropologist* New Series 66: 863–867.

RADCLIFFE-BROWN, A. R. 1913 Three Tribes of Western Australia. *Journal of the Royal Anthropological Institute of Great Britain and Ireland* 43:143–194.

RADIN, PAUL 1958 Robert H. Lowie: 1883–1957. *American Anthropologist* New Series 60:358–361.

WHITE, LESLIE A. 1943 Energy and the Evolution of Culture. *American Anthropologist* New Series 45:335–356.

WHITE, LESLIE A. 1944 Morgan's Attitude Toward Religion and Science. *American Anthropologist* New Series 46:218–230.

WHITE, LESLIE A. 1945 Diffusion vs. Evolution: An Anti-evolutionist Fallacy. *American Anthropologist* New Series 47:339–356.

LOYALTY

Loyalty can be defined as a feeling of attachment to something outside of the self, such as a group, an institution, a cause, or an ideal. The sentiment carries with it a willingness to support and act in behalf of the objects of one's loyalty and to persist in that support over an extended period of time and under conditions which exact a degree of moral, emotional, or material sacrifice from the individual. Josiah Royce captured most of the connotations of the term when he defined it as "the willing and practical and thorough going devotion of a person to a cause" (1908, pp. 16–17).

As used in political discourse, the concept of loyalty occupies the ground between patriotism and obligation. It is something less than the typically uncritical adulation of one's own political group, often accompanied by rejective attitudes toward outsiders, which is the heart of patriotism. It is something more than the formal, rationally justified duty to obey law, which is the essence of obligation. Loyalty is cooler in emotional tone, more rational in its bases, and less comprehensive in its object than patriotism; and it is warmer, less rational, and more comprehensive than obligation.

Since loyalty is an attitude, it varies along the same dimensions as any other attitude: intensity, specificity, endurance, direction, content, and so forth. Loyalties emerge out of a social matrix, and the processes of loyalty formation, growth, and change are closely akin to those involved in the process of identification. When one is said to be loyal to a group, for example, it is tantamount to saying that he has identified himself with the group, that his membership in the group forms part of his own self-definition, and that he perceives his own interests and purposes as integrally connected with those of the group. Loyalty thus has both instrumental and affective components.

Political loyalties are those directed toward political objects that are of importance in the life of the political community. These objects include formal institutions, parties, interest groups, political leaders, social and economic classes, military organizations, constitutions, traditions, and symbols and myths which a population perceives as embodying or representing the community, history, and destiny which make them a distinct people. Political loyalties form part of a system's political culture—that particular constellation of normative, practical, and emotional orientations toward political things shared by the population of a political system (Almond & Verba 1963, chapter 1). Loyalties can be directed toward a variety of objects within the political system, and systems can easily and usefully be classified according to the strength, incidence, objects, and patterns of loyalties among the citizenry. [*See* POLITICAL CULTURE.]

Patterns of loyalty. Since loyalties sustain both the individual and the polity by laying the groundwork necessary for shared effort and unity of purpose, loyalty is a very old subject of political discourse, and virtually "all serious political writing regards the quality of loyalty as a good thing" (H. B. White, quoted in Grodzins 1956, p. 16). Classical Greek and Roman writers regarded loyalty as the supreme political virtue, and while few persons in the ancient states enjoyed the status of citizenship, those who did were taught to regard the role of citizen as the noblest of all roles. Duty to the state was the highest duty, and loyalty was the highest value. This evaluation of political loyalty and citizenship permeates the writings of Plato, Aristotle, Thucydides, and Plutarch. Early Christian writers, however, placed little value on loyalty to city or state; for them, religious salvation was the supreme goal, and loyalty to the church and creed that held the keys to that kingdom the highest loyalty. Between the fall of the Roman Empire and the rise of the nation-state, political loyalty, except in the form of the local and semipersonal loyalties of feudalism, mattered little to individuals. Machiavelli's reassertion of the primacy of political loyalty—his statement that he preferred his country to the safety of his soul—was considered blasphemous in the opinion of his time. The modern idea of mass political loyalty and the conception of the nation as the capstone and most comprehensive object of loyalty are really no older than the eighteenth century. They appeared with the French Revolution and reached their most passionate expression in Rousseau's plea for a "civil religion" (*Social Contract*, especially book 4, chapter 8).

Patterns of thought and behavior involving loyalty have been complex and contradictory since the end of the eighteenth century. On the one hand, a number of liberal internationalist thinkers have attacked loyalty to the nation-state as an outmoded and dangerous conception. They argue that increasing national interdependence requires a shift of loyalty away from the nation-state to the institutions and symbols of the international community. On the other hand, the totalitarian states of the twentieth century have demanded of their subjects a degree of concentrated loyalty toward national political leaders, institutions, and policies which is without precedent. Also, the creation of many new states in the underdeveloped areas of the world has meant a renewed growth of national loyalties at a time when such loyalties may be on the wane in the highly developed states.

It is characteristic of the advanced, complex, highly industrialized states that the loyalties of individuals tend to be numerous, segmental, and increasingly instrumental. The individual yields partial loyalty to many objects instead of giving all his devotion and allegiance to one or a very few objects. Similarly, peer-group loyalties increasingly supplant hierarchical affiliations. This is part of the meaning of the movement from "status to contract" [*see the biography of* MAINE] or from *Gemeinschaft* to *Gesellschaft* [*see the biography of* TÖNNIES]. One strand of modern social criticism laments this transformation in loyalty patterns as the "decline of community," while another welcomes it as the advent of an era of increased individual liberty.

Over and above these matters stands the dominant fact that no political system can long endure or enjoy much stability unless its citizens, and especially the elites, place a high value on political loyalty. Among the emerging nations, the development of sentiments of national loyalty and identification is a task of the highest priority (Pye 1962). Many of the emerging nations are riddled by tribal, ethnic, linguistic, and regional divisions. The inhabitants must be urged to abandon their parochial loyalties, and they must be imbued with a sense of affiliation with the national community and a willingness to obey the directives of central authority. Links must be forged in the minds of individuals between their personal interests and joys and the policies and institutions of the state. In order to do this, governments employ all the resources of propaganda and communication to reach the masses. Promoting nationalist ideologies, publicizing the activities and words of charismatic leaders, fomenting antagonism toward foreign governments and peoples, and developing programs of mass action and ritual participation are among the standard methods used in these attempts to build national loyalties. [*See* MODERNIZATION.]

In a political system that has existed longer as an entity and reached a higher stage of political and economic development, the problem is not to create national loyalties but to maintain them. There, loyalty is both a product of the individual's direct identification with and involvement in the nation's history, symbols, institutions, and destiny and, indirectly, a product of the individual's private satisfactions. Rewards and satisfactions gained in the private sphere have a kind of spillover effect, and political objects receive the benefits of the individual's gratitude for the joys of personal life. In addition, the level of communication and integration is higher in such states, and inhabitants are frequently exposed to political symbols and messages. The public schools carry the message of patriotism and loyalty to millions of children: after an extensive review of European and American experience, Merriam (1931) concluded that the public school had become the dominant agency for transmitting the themes of loyalty and "civil religion," having largely replaced the army, the church, the family, and patriotic rhetoric in performing this function. In such polities, through the processes of political socialization, attitudes of loyalty toward the nation are widely shared. The national political community forms a common reference point for nearly all citizens. [*See* SOCIALIZATION, *article on* POLITICAL SOCIALIZATION.]

Thus, loyalty is the ordinary condition. Although political loyalties are not prominent for most people most of the time, they are there in the background and can be evoked by the appropriate stimuli. Since loyalty is the ordinary condition—the atmospheric condition—active disloyalty is very difficult: custom, the climate of opinion, informal and formal sanctions, inertia, fear, the lack of clear alternative objects of loyalty—all these forces work to assure that even those who are not actively and intensely loyal are at least not *dis*loyal. Ordinarily, political authorities do not ask for more than that, for it is enough.

Multiple loyalties. Few persons are loyal to just one object. Most men move within a network of loyalties—to primary group, party, occupational group, clubs, and so forth. In the liberal–democratic states, these partial loyalties are not regarded as incompatible with a larger, comprehensive loyalty to the political community. In fact, these circles of particular loyalties are held to be the very foundation for firm loyalty to the nation (Grodzins 1956). This view, which is widely held among modern pluralistic theorists, is really a rediscovery of Burke's insistence that what holds society together and gives it meaning and richness is the multiplicity of its "little platoons," its primary associations of individuals. Individuals, then, are tied to the central symbols and agencies of the political system through a series of linkages formed by loyalties to smaller groups [*see* IDENTIFICATION, POLITICAL].

In an important study, Shils and Janowitz (1948) found that while goals and policies might be set by central political authorities, individuals acted in accordance with those policies not so much out of direct loyalty to the nation as in response to the smaller, primary groups in which they were involved. This was found to be the case within the German army during the Nazi period. The finding thus runs counter to the whole totalitarian conception of loyalty, which insists that all loyalty must be concentrated directly around one political center. As Mussolini stated the totalitarian conception of loyalty, "Fascism takes a man from his family at six, and gives him back to it at sixty." Contrary to this conception, it seems clear that lesser loyalties must exist even in totalitarian states and that these lesser loyalties constitute the individual's primary attachments. It is through them that he is tied to the state, and it is largely in response to them that he loyally accepts and executes his duties to the state.

The existence of multiple loyalties implies the constant possibility of conflicting loyalties. Hence, conflict of loyalties is a theme that entered political writing along with the subject of loyalty itself, and it is already present in the story of Abraham and Isaac and in the tragedy of Antigone. Conflicts of loyalty are especially important during times of rapid social change and when the state feels threatened from within and without. During such times, individuals are uncertain of the intentions and the reliability of others, and the old patterns of belief and affiliation conflict with the new patterns that are emerging. Governments are then likely to require formal professions of loyalty, to undertake investigations of loyalty, and to insist on public adherence to official ideology (see Brown 1958; Schaar 1957). Loyalty is equated with conformity, criticism with disloyalty. The concept of "loyal opposition," one of the supreme achievements of the liberal–democratic regimes, is placed in jeopardy.

Still, while conflicts of loyalty are dramatic and painful, it must be repeated that loyalty is the normal condition. Individuals, by processes similar to those subsumed under the theory of cognitive dissonance, tend to perceive their loyalties as mutually consistent, even when they might appear inconsistent to an observer. Or they tend to rationalize incompatible loyalty imperatives as not really incompatible after all.

In most political systems there is a measure of ambiguity as to just what one must be loyal to in order to be regarded as loyal. Does one owe loyalty to the nation? The government? Traditions and ideals? A mission? Rulers? Hence, actions which seem to be disloyal by one standard may be justified as entirely loyal by another. In all these ways, individuals are able to "save the appearances," to regard themselves as loyal and to defend themselves against charges of disloyalty.

Political loyalty is supremely important both for individuals and for political communities, and many psychological mechanisms and social processes work to build and maintain it and to assure that loyalty rather than disloyalty or conflicts of loyalty will be the rule.

JOHN H. SCHAAR

[*See also* DUTY; IDENTIFICATION, POLITICAL; NATIONALISM. *Other relevant material may be found in* INTERNMENT AND CUSTODY; PERSONALITY, POLITICAL; SOCIAL CONTROL; *and in the guide to the reader and the articles under* COMMUNITY.]

BIBLIOGRAPHY

ALMOND, GABRIEL A.; and VERBA, SIDNEY 1963 *The Civic Culture: Political Attitudes and Democracy in Five Nations.* Princeton Univ. Press.

BLOCH, HERBERT A. 1934 *The Concept of Our Changing Loyalties: An Introductory Study Into the Nature of the Social Individual.* New York: Columbia Univ. Press.

BROWN, RALPH S. 1958 *Loyalty and Security: Employment Tests in the United States.* Yale Law School Studies, No. 3. New Haven: Yale Univ. Press.

CURTI, MERLE 1946 *The Roots of American Loyalty.* New York: Columbia Univ. Press.

DEWEY, JOHN (1922) 1950 *Human Nature and Conduct: An Introduction to Social Psychology.* New York: Modern Library.

DICKS, HENRY V. 1950 Personality Traits and National Socialist Ideology. *Human Relations* 3:111–154.

FREUD, SIGMUND (1921) 1955 Group Psychology and the Analysis of the Ego. Volume 18, pages 67–143 in *The Standard Edition of the Complete Psychological Works of Sigmund Freud.* London: Hogarth; New York: Macmillan. → First published in German.

GRODZINS, MORTON 1956 *The Loyal and the Disloyal: Social Boundaries of Patriotism and Treason.* Univ. of Chicago Press.

HOFFER, ERIC 1951 *The True Believer: Thoughts on the Nature of Mass Movements.* New York: Harper. → A paperback edition was published in 1958 by New American Library.

MEERLOO, JOOST A. M. 1954 The Psychology of Treason and Loyalty. *American Journal of Psychotherapy* 8: 648–666.

MERRIAM, CHARLES E. 1931 *The Making of Citizens: A Comparative Study of Methods of Civic Training.* Univ. of Chicago Press.

PYE, LUCIAN W. 1962 *Politics, Personality, and Nation Building: Burma's Search for Identity.* New Haven: Yale Univ. Press.

ROYCE, JOSIAH (1908) 1936 *The Philosophy of Loyalty.* New York: Macmillan.

SCHAAR, JOHN H. 1957 *Loyalty in America.* Berkeley: Univ. of California Press.

SCHACHTER, STANLEY 1959 *The Psychology of Affiliation: Experimental Studies of the Sources of Gregariousness.* Stanford Studies in Psychology, No. 1. Stanford Univ. Press.

SHERIF, MUZAFER; and CANTRIL, HADLEY 1947 *The Psychology of Ego-involvements, Social Attitudes and Identifications.* New York: Wiley; London: Chapman.

Shils, Edward 1956 *The Torment of Secrecy: The Background and Consequences of American Security Policies.* Glencoe, Ill.: Free Press.

Shils, Edward; and Janowitz, Morris 1948 Cohesion and Disintegration in the Wehrmacht in World War II. *Public Opinion Quarterly* 12:280–315.

West, R. G. Ranyard (1945) 1951 *Conscience and Society: A Study of the Psychological Prerequisites of Law and Order.* 2d ed. London: Methuen.

West, Rebecca (1947) 1964 *The New Meaning of Treason.* Rev. & enl. ed. New York: Viking. → First published as *The Meaning of Treason.*

LUBBOCK, JOHN

Sir John Lubbock (1834–1913) was an English biologist, anthropologist, and popular writer on science. His father, Sir John William Lubbock, was for forty years a distinguished member of the English scientific community and at the same time the successful head of the family banking establishment. The son achieved a similar kind of dual identity, adding to his scientific achievements a successful career in government.

Lubbock was essentially self-taught, although he did receive a certain amount of classical education. After entering the family banking business at the age of 14, he began to study natural history, following a program he had prepared himself. In the mid-nineteenth century the renaissance of natural history was an important event on the English intellectual scene; as a participant in this renaissance Lubbock was one of the first to investigate the social behavior of animals, and he published important studies in zoology and botany.

Apart from the mathematical and scientific interests of his father, the most compelling influence on Lubbock's development as a scientist was the relationship he established, while still an adolescent, with Charles Darwin. Darwin was then already a distinguished naturalist; he was also a friend of the elder Lubbock and his neighbor at Down. Darwin left no students and only a few protégés, of whom Lubbock was the first. Lubbock became an ardent supporter of Darwin's evolutionism when the *Origin of Species* was published in 1859. He was the youngest of that small articulate band whose reasoned and informed defense of the new doctrine led to its general acceptance within a decade; and all of his subsequent work was infused with the excitement of applying the theory of evolution.

Basic to all of his work was the underlying point of view that a science of human society is both necessary and possible: like other phenomena in nature, human society may be subjected to objective description leading to the formulation of general principles.

The discovery of man's great antiquity and the almost simultaneous publication of the principles of organic evolution by Darwin, in 1859, provided the essential theoretical elements for all of Lubbock's subsequent work in anthropology. Drawing upon an increasing body of data concerning the variation in human behavior, he constructed an over-all theory of cultural evolution that came to be the mainstay as well as the hallmark of English anthropology for almost half a century, even though his extreme position was rejected by more objective scholars. In *The Origin of Civilization and the Primitive Condition of Man* (1870) he developed a theory of the evolution of man and culture that rested on his equation of primeval man and the contemporary primitives. His extreme emphasis on the ideas of "natural progress" led him to arrange his materials (social, ethical, and technological) along a slowly ascending line leading to modern (nineteenth-century) perfection.

Lubbock's deserved reputation as a popularizer of developments in biology and anthropology, and the occasional innocence with which he approached fundamental problems in these fields, should not be permitted to conceal the significance of his own original contributions to both fields, especially to the nascent field of anthropology. He was the first to compile and synthesize the scattered data concerning the prehistory of Europe and North America, in a series of articles that formed the basis of his *Prehistoric Times* of 1865. But he believed that archeology is more than description and that it forms the link between geology and history. He clearly defined prehistoric archeology as a concern of anthropology and saw the reconstruction of past cultures as part of the evolutionary history of the continuous past rather than as the simple collection of monuments and antiquities. Prehistory was established as a science of man rather than an adjunct of classics or art history.

Lubbock drew upon ethnographic descriptions of contemporary "savages" to discover the use and cultural context of archeological materials. In reclassifying the stone tool categories formulated by Danish archeologists he coined the term "paleolithic" to designate the chipped tools found in caves and glacial gravels. He further suggested that these tools preceded a stage of development that he called "neolithic," characterized by the polished stone implements found in Danish peat bogs. Lubbock never accepted the revision of this scheme that was proposed by Mortillet.

On a practical level Lubbock used his parliamentary position and his private means to instigate the passage of the Ancient Monuments Act in order to protect the ancient monuments of Britain against destruction.

JACOB W. GRUBER

[*For the historical context of Lubbock's work, see* ANTHROPOLOGY, *article on* THE FIELD; *and the biographies of* DARWIN *and* TYLOR.]

WORKS BY LUBBOCK

(1865) 1913 *Prehistoric Times as Illustrated by Ancient Remains and the Manners and Customs of Modern Savages.* 7th ed., rev. London: Williams & Norgate.

(1870) 1912 *The Origin of Civilization and the Primitive Condition of Man: Mental and Social Conditions of Savages.* 7th ed. New York: Longmans.

WORKS ABOUT LUBBOCK

GRANT-DUFF, URSULA [Lubbock] (editor) (1924) 1934 *The Life Work of Lord Avebury (Sir John Lubbock): 1834–1913.* London: Watts.

HUTCHINSON, HORACE G. 1914 *Life of Sir John Lubbock, Lord Avebury.* 2 vols. London: Macmillan.

PUMPHREY, R. J. (1958) 1959 The Forgotten Man: Sir John Lubbock. *Science* 129:1087–1092. → First published in *Notes and Records of the Royal Society of London.*

LUKÁCS, GYÖRGY

György Lukács, literary critic and Marxist social theorist, was born in 1885 of wealthy Jewish parents in Budapest, then the second capital of the Austro–Hungarian monarchy. His father was a director of the Budapest Kreditanstalt, the leading bank in Hungary. A member of a remarkable generation of Hungarian Jewish intellectuals, many of whom later emigrated to Western countries and made their mark in the sciences and the humanities, Lukács received a cosmopolitan education. From adolescence he displayed a lively interest in European literature and a talent for literary criticism. His earliest critical writings date back to 1903 (when he was 18), and a two-volume study of the modern drama, written in Hungarian in 1908–1909, was published in 1911. In the same year Lukács issued the first German-language edition of any of his works, *Die Seele und die Formen,* which had been published in Hungarian in 1910, and from this time onward he partly abandoned his native Hungarian in favor of German as a medium of public and private discourse. (He came to be known widely by the German form of his name, Georg Lukacs.)

Early intellectual experience. A complex intellectual development carried Lukács from early involvement with the aestheticism fashionable before 1914 to a prominent role in the German and east European communist movements after 1918. Prior to the outbreak of World War I, he shared with other central European intellectuals of his generation a pronounced distaste for politics and a commitment to the autonomy of art, not merely as an aesthetic principle but as a way of life. This attitude implied a criticism of bourgeois society, albeit its criteria were derived from Nietzsche and the aestheticism of the 1890s rather than from Marx. Like Thomas Mann, for whom, even in later years, he retained an admiration which Mann to some degree reciprocated, the youthful Lukács considered bourgeois society inherently hostile to the arts and specifically to the aesthetic claim to possession of certain intuitively apprehended truths about the nature of reality.

After early studies in Budapest, Lukács moved to Berlin and later to Heidelberg, where he stayed until 1916. During these prerevolutionary years he studied social science and philosophy, and in particular came under the influence of Max Weber and Georg Simmel, who introduced him to sociology. He was likewise influenced by the philosopher Emil Lask, who had constructed a logical bridge leading from the then dominant Neo-Kantianism to the phenomenological school founded by Edmund Husserl. At the same time, Lukács became acquainted with the literary critic Friedrich Gundolf, a member of the esoteric circle around the poet Stefan George, in which both the Nietzschean contempt for democracy and the aestheticist cult of the individual sensibility had been pushed to their farthest limits. The residual influences of this period were to plague Lukács in later years, when (after first going through a Hegelian phase) he had become a more or less orthodox Marxist.

Lukács's own account of this transformation, while not wholly trustworthy, lends due emphasis to the impact of the 1914–1918 war upon the generation of central European intellectuals to which he belonged and whose concerns he shared. In the preface (dated July 1962) to the new edition of his *Theorie des Romans* (an essay on the novel, drafted in 1914–1915, first published in a literary journal in 1916 and, expanded, in book form in 1920), he describes his wartime mood as one of despair, from which he was eventually rescued by the events of 1917—that is, by the Russian Revolution. Prior to this he had been tormented by the —as it seemed to him—depressing choice between the prospect of a German victory and the triumph of "Western civilization," which as a youthful Nietzschean he had learned to identify with soulless commercialism and materialism. This was also how the issue presented itself to conservative German intellectuals like Thomas Mann (see the latter's *Unpolitical Reflections*), but Mann gradually and hesitantly accepted Western democracy as the lesser evil, if not as a positive good, while Lukács opted for Lenin.

Heterodox Marxism. Lukács's return to Budapest and his subsequent involvement in the Hungarian revolution of 1918–1919 coincided with a major change in his philosophical and political orientation: his acceptance first of Hegelianism and later of Marxism. Philosophically, the way for this conversion had been paved by his earlier rejection of Neo-Kantian epistemology insofar as it applied to the aesthetic realm, where, it appeared to him, intuitive apprehension of absolute truth is possible. Even as a youthful Neo-Kantian around 1910, he had not quite accepted the doctrine that knowledge of the empirical world does not extend to the nature of ultimate reality but is confined to phenomenal appearances, which in the last resort are the product of human understanding. He was not satisfied with this positivist interpretation of Kant, which Weber accepted, and for a while found solace in the belief that—in the arts at least—ultimate reality is cognizable through intuition of "pure essences." From about 1916 onward he came to believe that Hegel offered a way out of the impasse created by positivist science. The solution seemed to lie in treating the moral and aesthetic values (deemed by Weber and others to be wholly subjective) as entities located in the structure of reality and as such cognizable by philosophy, although not by empirical science. To this fundamental belief Lukács has adhered, with the necessary consequence that his Hegelianized Marxism has always appeared heretical to the adherents of Soviet orthodoxy, although not to Marxists faithful to the tradition of German idealism.

After brief involvement, as commissar for education, in the short-lived Hungarian communist regime of 1919, Lukács moved to Vienna, where as editor of the official party journal, *Kommunismus*, he came into conflict with the dominant faction. A dispute within the Hungarian Communist party over political tactics culminated in 1923 in the publication by Lukács of a collection of essays best known under the original, German title, *Geschichte und Klassenbewusstsein*. The appearance of this work initiated his new career as a semiheretical exponent of Marxism–Leninism, while at the same time it effectively ended his position as an official party spokesman. In later years he was to be an influential figure in the intellectual life of the Hungarian Communist party, but he never again held an official party position, and his utterances on literary and philosophical topics were henceforth regarded with suspicion by those Hungarian communist theoreticians (some of them his former pupils) who in 1923–1924 had committed themselves to the official Soviet interpretation of Marxism–Leninism.

Without going into the details of this controversy (a succinct account of which may be found in Watnick 1962) it can be said that Lukács's general orientation clashed with Lenin's pre-Hegelian (indeed, pre-Kantian) understanding of philosophy, while at the same time he pushed Lenin's implicitly elitist view of the Communist party's role to the point of paradox. In recovering the Hegelian dimension of Marx's own thought, Lukács had unwittingly transgressed upon Lenin's version of Engels' "dialectical materialism," with its naively pictorial interpretation of the role of consciousness. Philosophically speaking, he appeared to his Leninist critics as a left-wing Hegelian rather than a materialist. At the same time he allotted to the role of revolutionary "consciousness" an importance quite consonant with Lenin's own conception of the "vanguard." The consequences of this contradictory commitment were to pursue Lukács for years, down to the abortive Hungarian rebellion of 1956, which resulted in his temporary banishment and forced withdrawal from public life.

Acceptance of orthodoxy. From 1933 to 1945 Lukács, like most other leading Hungarian communists, lived in Moscow, where he somehow escaped the great purge of 1936–1938. Those Hungarian communists who had sided against him in 1923–1924 (principally József Révai and László Rudas) had meanwhile become orthodox Stalinists, while Lukács himself—although from about 1932 the most doctrinaire of Leninists—paid only lip service to Stalin's "theoretical" contributions. He did, however, purge himself of his idealist errors by solemnly denouncing (in an address to the philosophical section of the Communist Academy in 1934) his 1923 work *Geschichte und Klassenbewusstsein* as an unwitting departure from Marxist–Leninist orthodoxy. After recalling the early influence upon him of Simmel and Max Weber, he named Georges Sorel as one of the pre-1914 writers who had reinforced his leanings toward what in 1934 he termed "romantic anticapitalism." Having stigmatized his earlier views as "objectively" counterrevolutionary, he paid a special tribute to the significance of Lenin's philosophical work, *Materialism and Empiriocriticism*.

This self-abasement set the tone for the literary productions of the following two decades, culminating in *Die Zerstörung der Vernunft* (1953*a*), a bulky 700-page diatribe against modern philosophy, couched in propagandist, indeed abusive, language. Its central thesis—the ideological decay of "bourgeois irrationalism," from Schelling via Nietzsche to the philosophers of the Third Reich—was worked out at such a primitive level that even some of his sympathizers in the West began to despair of Lukács.

Sociology of knowledge. An assessment of Lukács's significance as a forerunner of what is currently known as the sociology of knowledge must proceed from the recognition that as a theorist he has been primarily concerned with other than sociological topics. The "class consciousness" which appears in the title of his 1923 collection of essays (his only sustained excursion into sociopolitical theory) is not the empirical consciousness of the actual working class, but a political consciousness "imputed" to it (*zugerechnet*, to use his term) on extraempirical grounds. Lukács thus is not a sociologist, not even a Marxist sociologist. He took over from Marx the notion of social development through class conflict, culminating in a new type of society without classes, but did not attempt to apply it to the new postbourgeois reality around him. In particular he remained indifferent to the problem of social stratification in industrial society, as distinct from the issue of class relations in bourgeois society. As a critic of bourgeois culture he was content to rely on the Marxist analysis of capitalism. This furnished him with the assurance that industrialism could provide the economic basis for an organization of social life in which human labor would recover the dignity it had lost, and that human "alienation" (a term not explicitly employed by him in 1923, but inherent in his critique of "objectification") would be overcome.

Culture. The area where Lukács nonetheless has come to grips with genuinely sociological issues is that of culture. According to the Marxist hypothesis, a class with a genuine historical role is, among other things, the bearer of a new world view and ultimately of a new civilization. Lukács has tried to employ this concept in his voluminous writings on aesthetics. Basing his work on the principle that a particular outlook (variously described as "materialist" or "realist") has been shared by the bourgeoisie in its early revolutionary phase and the working class in its subsequent effort to build a higher culture, he has tried to safeguard the heritage of classical bourgeois realism. The antithesis of this classical realism is manifest, according to Lukács, in the various forms of modernism, which (in common with Soviet orthodoxy, although in more sophisticated terms) he has denounced as "decadent."

Ideology. The ascription to the labor movement (and in particular to the Communist party as the supposed "vanguard" of this movement) of a viewpoint radically different from that of the collapsing bourgeois society furnished Lukács with a criterion for his definition of ideology. He attributed "false consciousness" (ideology) uniquely to the self-definition of the ruling class, while crediting the submerged revolutionary class with the possession of a "true consciousness," albeit imperfectly articulated and thus necessitating the separate existence of a "vanguard" of theorists in the shape of the Communist party. In principle the working class is held by Lukács to possess a theoretical insight into the historical situation superior to that of the bourgeoisie, although in the actual waging of political conflict this insight needs to be supplemented by the intellectual efforts of the Marxist party.

Objective knowledge. Dissatisfaction with this approach subsequently led Karl Mannheim (who in 1918–1919 had been acquainted with Lukács in Budapest but had not joined the communists) to develop the notion of the intelligentsia as a privileged floating stratum. Mannheim, like Lukács, had originally been induced by his reading of Weber and Simmel to question the possibility of objective truth in historical and social matters. As he saw it, all sociological statements were hopelessly compromised by sectional and party standpoints. Unlike Lukács, he did not seek a solution by identifying a particular standpoint (that of the rising proletarian class) with the attainment of absolute or objective insight. Rather, he contented himself with allotting to the intellectuals as a group the task of criticizing the sectional viewpoints of the major social classes. Lukács's work provided the chief stimulus for Mannheim's *Ideology and Utopia*, and in this sense he may be said to have been an important link between the sociology of Weber and Simmel and what later became known as *Wissenssoziologie.* But whereas Mannheim's "relational" doctrine seemed to issue in a species of relativism, Lukács retained the notion of a privileged intellectual standpoint, historically conditioned indeed (as all forms of thought must be), yet certifying its superiority over rival standpoints by virtue of its unique possession of insights enabling it to comprehend both its epoch and itself. Here we see the Hegelian heritage which had originally attracted the youthful Lukács to Marxism and subsequently to Leninism as the contemporary form of Marxism.

All of this was too Hegelian for Soviet Marxists

and their east European followers, yet it was also incompatible with what Lukács termed "bourgeois empiricism." Mannheim and others, although personally and doctrinally sympathetic to socialism, rejected the Hegelian–Marxist notion of a truth about history independent of, and superior to, the insights available to empirical sociology. The Marxian rejoinder (anticipated by Lukács in 1923) was to assert that, in thus rejecting philosophy, the sociology of knowledge had also relinquished the notion of an objective truth about history and society, leaving only partial truths relative to the standpoint of the observer and therewith seemingly opening the road toward a skepticism as boundless as it was hopeless. This theme was revived in the West after 1945, when impatience with the prospect of endless and pointless data accumulation carried a number of writers at least halfway toward the Hegelianized Marxism of the early Lukács—a tendency particularly marked among the Neo-Hegelian and Neo-Marxist schools in France and Italy.

In the central European context, the passions stirred by the 1923 controversy continued to be felt in the writings of Lukács's fellow heretic, Karl Korsch. They have likewise echoed in the historical and sociological studies published before and after the Hitler era by the scholars associated with the Frankfurt Institut für Sozialforschung—notably Max Horkheimer, T. W. Adorno, and Herbert Marcuse. The influence of the early Lukács is also discernible in the writings of such a noted literary critic of the Weimar period as Walter Benjamin, while a more distant echo may be discerned in the work of *émigré* scholars such as Leo Lowenthal of the University of California at Berkeley. From central Europe, the message of Lukács's Hegelianized Marxism was carried to France by the Rumanian-born scholar and literary critic Lucien Goldmann, whose studies of Pascal and Racine acquainted the French academic world with a new manner of treating literary subjects. Some of Goldmann's conclusions had been anticipated in 1934 by the Vienna-born scholar Franz Borkenau in an important, although neglected, work, *Der Übergang vom feudalen zum bürgerlichen Weltbild*. In contrast, Lukács paradoxically has not exercised any profound influence upon the younger generation of Marxist writers in central and eastern Europe since 1956. In general they have found him too orthodox for their taste and in particular too deeply wedded to the Leninist notions current in Soviet literature. These "revisionist" writers (e.g., the Austrian Ernst Fischer) tended to go beyond Lukács in trying to construct a specifically Marxist doctrine of the social relevance of art. In philosophy, too, it was the existentialism of Sartre rather than the work of Lukács which, after the post-Stalin "thaw" of 1956, enabled the younger east European Marxists (e.g., the Polish writer Leszek Kolakowski) to free themselves from the ideological trammels of Leninism.

GEORGE LICHTHEIM

[*See also* LITERATURE, *article on* THE SOCIOLOGY OF LITERATURE; MARXIST SOCIOLOGY; *and the biographies of* HEGEL; LENIN; MANNHEIM.]

WORKS BY LUKÁCS

1903 Az új Hauptmann (The New Hauptmann). *Jövendő* [1903], August 23:29–32.

1906 A dráma formája (The Form of the Drama). *Szerda* [1906]:340–343.

1907 Gaugin. *Huszadik század* [1907]:559–562.

1908 Stefan George. *Nyugat* 2:202–211.

(1910) 1911 *Die Seele und die Formen*. Berlin: Fleischel. → First published as *A lélek és a formák (kisérletek)*.

1911 *A modern dráma fejlödésének története* (The History of the Development of the Modern Drama). 2 vols. Budapest: Kisfaludy Társaság.

1914 Soziologie des modernen Drama. *Archiv für Sozialwissenschaft und Sozialpolitik* 38:303–345, 662–706.

(1920) 1963 *Die Theorie des Romans*. New ed., enl. Neuwied am Rhein (Germany): Luchterhand.

1923 *Geschichte und Klassenbewusstsein*. Berlin: Malik. → Contains essays first published between 1919 and 1922.

(1933) 1955 Mein Weg zu Marx. Pages 225–231 in *Georg Lukacs zum siebzigsten Geburtstag*. Berlin: Aufbau.

1934 Znachenie *Materializma i empiriokrititsizma* dlia bol'shevizatsii kommunisticheskikh partii (The Significance of *Materialism and Empiriocriticism* for the Bolshevization of Communist Parties). *Pod znamenem marksizma* 4:143–148.

(1935–1939) 1964 *Studies in European Realism*. New York: Grosset & Dunlap. → Contains essays first published in Hungarian and German.

(1946*a*) 1955 *Goethe und seine Zeit*. Berlin: Aufbau. → First published in Hungarian.

1946*b* *Nietzsche és a fasizmus* (Nietzsche and Fascism). Budapest: Hungaria.

(1947) 1965 *The Historical Novel*. New York: Humanities. → First published in book form as *A történelmi regény*. Parts 1 and 2 first appeared in Russian in 1937 in Volumes 7, 9, and 12 of *Literaturnyi kritik*. A paperback edition was published in 1963 by Beacon.

1948 *Der junge Hegel: Über die Beziehungen von Dialektik und Ökonomie*. Zurich and Vienna: Europa.

(1953*a*) 1954 *Die Zerstörung der Vernunft*. Berlin: Aufbau. → First published as *Az ész trónfosztása*. A third Hungarian edition was published in 1965.

(1953*b*) 1954 *Beiträge zur Geschichte der Ästhetik*. Berlin: Aufbau. → First published as *Adalékok az esztétika történetéhez*.

(1958) 1963 *The Meaning of Contemporary Realism*. London: Merlin. → First published as *Zur Gegenwartsbedeutung des kritischen Realismus*.

1961 *Schriften zur Literatursoziologie*. Edited by Peter Ludz. Berlin: Luchterhand.

Werke. Vol. 1—. Neuwied am Rhein (Germany): Luchterhand, 1963—. → A projected 12-volume work. Volumes 5, 6, 7, 9, 11, and 12 had appeared by 1966.

SUPPLEMENTARY BIBLIOGRAPHY

ADORNO, T. W. (1961) 1963 Erpresste Versöhnung: Zu Georg Lukacs "Wider den missverstandenen Realismus." Volume 2, pages 152–187 in T. W. Adorno, *Noten zur Literatur*. Frankfurt am Main (Germany): Suhrkamp. → First published in Volume 11 of *Der Monat*.

Georg Lukacs und der Revisionismus: Eine Sammlung von Aufsätzen. 1960 Berlin: Aufbau.

Georg Lukacs zum siebzigsten Geburtstag. 1955 Berlin: Aufbau.

GOLDMANN, LUCIEN (1958) 1963 *Recherches dialectiques.* 3d ed. Paris: Gallimard. → See especially the essay "Georg Lukacs: L'essayiste."

OLTVÁNYI, AMBRUS (compiler) 1955 Lukács György irói munkássága (The Literary Works of György Lukács). *Irodalomtörténet* (Budapest) 43:402–420. → A comprehensive bibliography of Lukács's writings from 1903 to 1955.

RÉVAI, JÓZSEF (1950) 1956 *Literarische Studien.* Berlin: Dietz. → First published as *Irodalmi tanulmányok.*

RÉVAI, JÓZSEF 1951 *La littérature et la démocratie populaire: À propos de Georg Lukacs.* Paris: Les Éditions de la Nouvelle Critique.

WATNICK, MORRIS 1962 Relativism and Class Consciousness: Georg Lukacs. Pages 142–165 in Leopold Labedz (editor), *Revisionism: Essays on the History of Marxist Ideas.* New York: Praeger.

LUNDBERG, GEORGE

George Andrew Lundberg (1895–1966) was a vigorous and influential advocate of the pursuit of sociological knowledge by the method of natural science. Much of his writing was devoted to stating and clarifying the postulates of scientific thought, the fundamental attributes of objective research, and the applicability of such principles to sociological inquiry. He dedicated his academic career to the view that there are no characteristics of social phenomena and no features of scientific method that would preclude rigorous adherence to that method in the investigation of those phenomena. He gave particular emphasis to two implications of this position. First, he insisted that quantification of sociological concepts is possible and that great effort should be devoted to it. Second, he consistently argued that the achievement of scientific competence requires that sociologists learn to abandon traditional moralistic orientations toward their subject matter (Lundberg et al. 1929, pp. 403–404).

During his lifetime great strides toward quantification were taken which Lundberg credited chiefly to the impact of successful empirical work, such as demographic studies, rather than to any methodological arguments (1944*a*, p. 7). He was far from sanguine in his last years, however, regarding the emancipation of contemporary sociologists from a legalistic–moralistic mode of thought, and this alleged bondage became the central issue of his final polemics.

Lundberg's positivism

Lundberg asserted that not all words have empirical referents but that people have responded to them as if they did. The alleged distinction between the "tangible" subject matter of the physical sciences and the supposedly "intangible" subject matter of the social sciences is merely a reflection of the differential advancement of observational and symbolizing techniques in the two fields; it is not an intrinsic difference in the respective classes of events being observed. Nothing essential is "left out" when we study societal phenomena objectively, although we often mourn the loss of feelings that were associated with familiar but ambiguous terms we have had to abandon. The operations by which we measure characteristics of the phenomena we study constitute definitions of those characteristics. The same phenomena may be studied according to various frames of reference, but these will lead to different conclusions.

Exclusion of value judgments. Lundberg's conceptual approach was similar to that of the Vienna circle, but he arrived at it independently. He attempted to show that all too many of the familiar-sounding terms in the sociological vocabulary were the sociological equivalent of the early chemist's phlogiston—no more necessary to describe or explain social phenomena than phlogiston was to account for combustion.

The sociologist's central task, he said, is to gather reliable data and from them to state principles—i.e., predictable sequences of behavior within highly standardized situations. Such principles can then be used to explain events in other situations whose significant departures from the standardized situation can be measured.

To be scientific, our analysis must be nonteleological. The physical sciences do very well without the concept of values, Lundberg said, but social scientists persist in transforming the verb "valuating" (which refers to discriminal or selective responding) into a noun, "values," and then they hunt in vain for its ostensible referent (1941*a*, p. 351). When critics accused him of "leaving out" what is essentially human, Lundberg replied that he was not denying the occurrence or importance of value judgments but only insisting that they are a kind of behavior and that standards of value are inferences from behavior. Thus defined, values are not inaccessible to scientific study (1941*b*, p. 84). Men have always had visions of the good life, and these have helped to shape human actions. Reliable assessment of the changing content of such visions is a prerequisite to their effective public implementation, and there now exist scientific procedures by which one can do this assessing better than it is done by traditional methods (1950*a*, pp. 110–111). Lundberg offered specific proposals for the study of human values (*ibid.*, p. 105), but he continued to be accused of advocating a sociology that would "omit" this indispensable concept.

For some, this accusation gained plausibility from his perennial insistence that no science tells us what to do with the knowledge it creates. Scientific conclusions are statements of the probability of certain occurrences under clearly specified conditions, but they do not contain assessments of the "goodness or badness of the sequences described, *apart from specified standards.* The crucial point is that these standards are not themselves set by the scientific methods that result in the conditional scientific statements" (1950*b*, p. 265).

Social science and citizenship. In his presidential address to the American Sociological Society during World War II, Lundberg adamantly maintained that "it is more important than ever that we should not let the priority of our duties as citizens blind us to our functions as scientists" (1943*a*, p. 69). As a means of winning the war it was probably necessary, he conceded, to fabricate seriously distorted pictures of the world and of the nature of the enemy. Unfortunately, such pictures would persist, at least in part, for some time after the war and would influence the structure of the peace settlement. With a peace founded on illusion, another war was rendered likely (1944*b*, p. 89). It was vital that *social scientists themselves* not mistake the distortion for truth. Some of his statements illustrating this point were offensive to certain members of his audience and may have obscured his main message—that social scientists could hope to command public respect and thus be effective in an advisory role in regard to the peace settlement only if they were to demonstrate their scientific competence and objectivity (1944*a*, pp. 1–2).

Mindful of the impatience of others, Lundberg responded to the cliché that objective pursuit of abstract knowledge in such a crisis was like "lecturing on navigation while the ship goes down." Because some men were content to keep on studying while their personal ships sank, he said, we have today some accumulated knowledge of navigation. We would not, had they joined the clamor for "short cuts to salvation whenever a storm occurred" (1943*b*, p. 199).

What bothered Lundberg most was the superficiality of the commitment of so many social scientists to the thoughtways of science. He lamented that in times of crisis many of us easily slip back "into the familiar personalistic–dramatic pattern of theology in which the forces of Good and Evil under their respective personal leaders again struggle for mastery" (1941*b*, p. 93). Not all scholars agreed with him when he spoke of the "theological and metaphysical nonsense" characterizing wartime discussions of "a highly subjective and relative concept called freedom." He held that "men are free when they feel free. They feel free when they are thoroughly habituated to their way of life" (1944*a*, p. 4). But some of his audience apparently felt dissatisfied with such a relativistic notion of freedom.

His unconventional views—for example, he had the temerity to argue that the understandable Jewish hostility to the German government exacerbated that government's hostility toward Jews—led to accusations that Lundberg had an anti-Semitic and profascist outlook, a product of his sociological positivism (Hartung 1944, pp. 340–341). If fascism means government by a self-appointed elite that suppresses all expressions of opposition, the accusation was clearly contradicted by Lundberg's lifelong insistence on the importance of distinguishing the role of scientist from the role of citizen and giving the scientist, in his role as citizen, no greater voice in public policy making than might be assented to by other citizens (1949, p. 10).

There is some indication that the accusation of anti-Semitism may have influenced Lundberg's subsequent choice of research topics, for although he had studied patterns of status differentiation and preferential association in the prewar years, he had not done previous research on minority groups as such or on ethnocentrism (Lundberg & Steele 1938; Larsen 1965*a*). He turned to these topics after the war, as if to substantiate his contention that moralistic and legalistic biases had heretofore tended to limit social science inquiry into these matters. As Lundberg saw it, numerous Jewish organizations striving to combat anti-Semitism pursue policies which actually aggravate it (1944*c*). The preventive for such ill-conceived programs is more adequate and more reliable knowledge, to which

Lundberg proposed to contribute (Lundberg & Dickson 1952).

Career and influence

Lundberg's polemics, less than persuasive to his accusers, were not his sole preoccupation in the postwar years. He also coauthored one of the leading introductory sociology textbooks (in its third edition at the time of his death), and he served as chairman of the department of sociology at the University of Washington during a period of rapid expansion of its faculty, its graduate program, and its research activities. Other facets of his postwar activities included writing the popular book *Can Science Save Us?* (1947) and editing a sociology series for a book publisher. Lundberg lectured on, and helped to promote, sociology in the Scandinavian countries, and, after concluding his administrative role at the University of Washington, he continued to teach there for a number of years before he retired. He was in demand as a lecturer at various universities and before nonacademic groups as well.

Before assuming the chairmanship at Washington, Lundberg had been on the faculties of the University of Pittsburgh, Columbia University, and Bennington College and had held appointments at Stanford, Brigham Young, and Minnesota. He had held research positions with federal and local welfare agencies and had been elected president of the Sociological Research Association and two regional sociological societies, as well as the American Sociological Society.

Lundberg was a graduate of the University of North Dakota, which also awarded him an LL.D. in 1958. He held the M.A. degree from Wisconsin and the PH.D. from Minnesota, which also awarded him its Distinguished Achievement Medal in 1951. He was editor of *Sociometry* from 1941 to 1947 and wrote some seventy articles, as well as several influential books.

At the time of Lundberg's retirement, Paul H. Furfey, one of his stanchest intellectual adversaries, paid him this tribute: "He has always made it seem obvious that winning an argument is unimportant, but that arriving at the truth is supremely important" (Larsen 1965*a*, p. 26).

WILLIAM R. CATTON, JR.

[*See also* LEISURE; POSITIVISM; VALUES.]

WORKS BY LUNDBERG

1929 LUNDBERG, GEORGE A.; BAIN, READ; and ANDERSON, NELS (editors) *Trends in American Sociology.* New York: Harper.

1934 LUNDBERG, GEORGE A. et al. *Leisure: A Suburban Study.* New York: Columbia Univ. Press.

1938 LUNDBERG, GEORGE A.; and STEELE, MARY Social Attraction-patterns in a Village. *Sociometry* 1:375–419.

1939 *Foundations of Sociology.* New York: Macmillan. → A revised and abridged paperback edition was published in 1964 by McKay.

1941*a* The Future of the Social Sciences. *Scientific Monthly* 53:346–359.

1941*b* Societal Pathology and Sociometry. *Sociometry* 4:78–97.

1941*c* What Are Sociological Problems? *American Sociological Review* 6:357–369.

1943*a* A Message From the President of the American Sociological Society. *American Sociological Review* 8:69–70.

1943*b* Introductory Note. *Sociometry* 6:199 only.

1944*a* Sociologists and the Peace. *American Sociological Review* 9:1–13.

1944*b* Scientists in Wartime. *Scientific Monthly* 58:85–95.

1944*c* Letter of March 1, 1944, to Dr. Zvi Cahn of the Nascent American Jewish Sociological Society. Unpublished manuscript.

(1947) 1961 *Can Science Save Us?* 2d ed. London: Longmans.

1949 Applying the Scientific Method to Social Phenomena. *Sociology and Social Research* 34:3–12.

1950*a* Human Values: A Research Program. Washington State University, Pullman, *Research Studies* 18:103–111.

1950*b* Can Science Validate Ethics? American Association of University Professors, *Bulletin* 36:262–275.

1952 LUNDBERG, GEORGE A.; and DICKSON, LENORE Selective Association Among Ethnic Groups in a High School Population. *American Sociological Review* 17:23–35.

(1958) 1963 LUNDBERG, GEORGE A.; SCHRAG, CLARENCE C.; and LARSEN, OTTO N. *Sociology.* 3d ed. New York: Harper.

SUPPLEMENTARY BIBLIOGRAPHY

HARTUNG, FRANK E. 1944 The Sociology of Positivism: Proto-fascist Aspects. *Science and Society* 8:328–341.

LARSEN, OTTO N. 1965*a* The Art of George A. Lundberg as a Teacher. *Sociologiske meddelelser* 10:19–28.

LARSEN, OTTO N. 1965*b* Publications of George A. Lundberg. *Sociologiske meddelelser* 10:6–18.

LUTHER, MARTIN

Although the Reformation was in its purest essence a religious movement, from the outset it also involved social, political, and economic forces and effected fundamental changes in many areas of life. The first of the magisterial reformers, Martin Luther (1483–1546), was pre-eminently concerned with theological matters, but his evangelical insight into the deepest meaning of the Christian gospel had tremendous implications for all aspects of social life and theory. Throughout his life he gave evidence of his concern for social action.

The operative principle of Luther's social ethics,

as expressed in his treatise entitled *Christian Liberty* (1520), was that religious faith must be active in love. The person precedes the action, for, as he asserted, "good works do not make a good man, but a good man does good works." The new spiritual life of a man who has come to a trusting faith in the gracious God revealed in Christ produces in him a spontaneous outflowing love for his fellow man. This love far transcends a mere prudential desire for the highest good and, like God's love, should not be dependent upon the worthiness or lovableness of the object. This ethical principle intensifies the force of conscience and the inner-directedness of the Christian in society, minimizing heteronomous controls.

Luther believed that all reality belongs to God's realm, for in the church God works through the Word of the Gospel for the spiritual good of man, and in the secular orders God works through men for the temporal good of man. Thus, such natural orders as the family, the various vocations, the state, and the organization of society in general are also divine orders. While historically they have shown development and are structurally subject to change, these natural orders have their origin in the divine will and are divinely ordained. This view allowed Luther to transcend the negative assessment of secular institutions characteristic of much medieval thought. Institutions such as marriage and state authority had been viewed merely as restraints necessitated by sin or as systems whose legality depended upon the sanction of the church. He viewed them positively as instruments of God's love and urged men to be thankful for them and to sustain them.

Luther held natural law to be the basis of the natural orders and of all secular authority, including that of non-Christian rulers. He understood this natural law to be the law of love implanted in man's consciousness and more clearly revealed in the Decalogue and refined in the Sermon on the Mount. Since communities are of divine ordinance, their good positive laws cannot be contrary to God's will; these laws are rooted in natural law and have a theonomous, or divinely obligating, character. Luther stressed emphatically the need to keep separate the secular and spiritual authorities, for the state is an authority that wields power and is exclusively concerned with the temporal order, while the church is a communion or priesthood of all believers responding to the gospel of God's love.

Luther's view of society and of man's culture, then, was dialectical. On the one hand, culture and society are theonomous insofar as they are sustained by the ever-present creative action of God, who initiates all, encompasses all, and rules over men. On the other hand, they are autonomous insofar as they are the product of man's own free, rational, responsible, cooperative action. Christians moved by love should participate in the social order and mend and improve it for the good of mankind. Because of his own foreshortened eschatology and preoccupation with ecclesiastical concerns, Luther did not invest effort in the systematic renovation or reorganization of society, as Calvin did, but his thought contained the basic elements for a constructive social philosophy.

In addressing himself to specific social issues, Luther at times reflected conservative views of long standing and at other times expressed novel ideas, which were ahead of his time and which found echoes in subsequent theorists. Although he was himself the son of a rising middle-class mining entrepreneur, he believed in the superior virtues of agrarian life over commerce. He opposed usury with vehemence and flayed the monopolies of ruthless large capitalists like the Fuggers and Medicis. He argued for the just-price theory and accepted the labor theory of value. He stressed the value of vocation to the active life and raised the *ordo naturalis* to the dignity of the *ordo spiritualis*. He opposed the mere giving of alms to beggars and urged that people sunk in poverty be given the means to help themselves. While encouraging support of the government and military service in the case of a just war of defense against an aggressor or an international lawbreaker, he insisted that under absolutely no circumstances could a Christian serve in an unjust cause or against his own conscience. It would seem that the highly organized and welfare-oriented social philosophies of such Lutheran lands as Denmark, Sweden, Norway, and Finland reflect generically the basic social thought of Luther. His pivotal faith in God gave him a certain detachment toward material wealth and a courageous attitude in the face of hostile political power and military threats—qualities that perhaps retain a basic relevance for modern social thought.

LEWIS W. SPITZ

[*See also* PROTESTANT POLITICAL THOUGHT; *and the biography of* CALVIN.]

BIBLIOGRAPHY

ERIKSON, ERIK H. (1958) 1962 *Young Man Luther: A Study in Psychoanalysis and History.* Austin Riggs Monograph No. 4. New York: Norton.

FORELL, GEORGE W. 1954 *Faith Active in Love.* New York: American Press.

HOLL, KARL (1911) 1959 *The Cultural Significance of the Reformation.* New York: Meridian. → First published as *Kulturbedeutung der Reformation.*

HUEGLI, ALBERT G. (editor) 1964 *Church and State Under God.* St. Louis, Mo.: Concordia.
LUTHER, MARTIN (1520) 192? *Christian Liberty.* Philadelphia: United Lutheran Publication House. → No date appears on the title page.
Luther's Works. 56 vols. St. Louis, Mo.: Concordia; Philadelphia: Muhlenberg, 1955–1965.
PAUCK, WILHELM (1950) 1961 *The Heritage of the Reformation.* Rev. & enl. ed. Glencoe, Ill.: Free Press.
RUPP, ERNEST G. 1953 *The Righteousness of God: Luther Studies.* London: Hodder & Stoughton.

LUXEMBURG, ROSA

Rosa Luxemburg (1870–1919) was one of the founders of the Social Democratic party of Poland and Lithuania, the leader of the left wing of the Social Democratic party (SPD) in Germany, and a prominent Marxist economic theorist. She was born in Zamosc but spent her childhood and youth in Warsaw. She came from a family of Polish-speaking Jewish merchants, and her mother brought her up in a liberal atmosphere, instilling in her a love of classical German culture. She grew up in a period when the tsarist government was increasing its political and religious oppression and when socialist activity was beginning in Poland.

While still in high school Rosa Luxemburg became active in the socialist movement, and in 1889 she was forced to flee abroad. She entered the University of Zurich with the intention of studying natural sciences but soon shifted to political economy. In addition to the university program, she studied the works of Adam Smith, Ricardo, Rodbertus, and, above all, Marx. In her doctoral thesis, *Die industrielle Entwicklung Polens* (1898; "The Industrial Development of Poland"), she argued that the development of industrial capitalism in the Polish kingdom depended heavily on the Russian market and that the economy of the Polish kingdom would never be more than a part of the tsarist economy. The analysis in this book formed the basis upon which the Polish Social Democratic party built its political program.

In order to be able to take part in the German socialist movement, she acquired German citizenship through a fictitious marriage with a German emigrant. From 1897 until her death she lived, except for short intervals, in Berlin.

Immediately upon her arrival in Germany she joined Karl Kautsky in the fight against Eduard Bernstein and his revisionist followers. Bernstein's thesis, "The movement is everything, the aim nothing," was incompatible with her belief that the struggle for political power was a necessary aim of the socialist movement. Her essays criticizing Bernstein's economic and political doctrines were collected in *Reform or Revolution* (1899).

In 1905 she returned to Warsaw under an assumed name to help the revolutionary movement there but was soon arrested. After her release from jail she went first to St. Petersburg and then to Finland, where she wrote the pamphlet *Massenstreik, Partei und Gewerkschaften* (1906; "General Strike, Party and Trade Unions"). The work contains a sociological analysis of the driving forces of social revolution and its mechanism—an analysis, on the one hand, of the role of the masses and, on the other hand, of the organization and role of the leaders. In this pamphlet she also developed the view that the general strike is the fundamental instrument in the struggle of the working class for power.

As the orthodox Marxists discussed their revolutionary experiences, particularly their experiences with political strikes, essential differences among them emerged. This led to a break between Luxemburg and Kautsky, which meant that the German Social Democratic party became divided into three groups: a right wing led by Bernstein, a center group led by Kautsky, and a left wing led by Luxemburg.

Beginning in 1907 she lectured at the Berlin school of the Social Democratic party. Both her earlier lectures on political economy and her later ones on economic history were published posthumously from her manuscripts, with the title *Einführung in die Nationalökonomie* (1925). Her most famous economic work, *The Accumulation of Capital* (1913), also grew out of these lectures.

The Accumulation of Capital may well be Luxemburg's most important contribution to the social sciences. The book has as its main theme the conditions of economic growth under capitalism, and its original contribution lies, therefore, in the field of economic theory. In Luxemburg's opinion, pure capitalism cannot create conditions adequate to maintain its own development. The main factor that gives capitalist production its dynamic power is the expansion toward noncapitalist areas, both underdeveloped countries and spheres of noncapitalist production within capitalist countries. This expansion comes about because capital accumulates, while at the same time demand within the capitalist society does not increase fast enough to absorb the increasing supply of goods.

During the imperialist phase of capitalism this difficulty is solved by the production of arms. The arms not only absorb domestic capital but also help create new markets in the colonies. The state's customs and tax policies also play an important part in the economic development of capitalism, especially in the period of imperialism. Luxemburg saw free international trade as only an episode in the history of capitalism and criticized Marx for disregarding the historical conditions that affected the accumulation of capital; she charged Marx with considering historical conditions important only in relation to the birth of capitalism and exclusively with reference to private accumulation. Luxemburg believed instead that the relations between capitalism and its precapitalist surroundings constitute a source of tension and international conflict. These lead to a series of wars and social revolutions that in turn start the process of the decline of capitalism. In the history of Marxist economic theory Luxemburg's work on the accumulation of capital has produced much theoretical and political polemics.

Initially, the reactions to *The Accumulation of Capital* were negative. Such theorists as Karl Kautsky, Otto Bauer, and Nikolai Bukharin not only rejected the major theory of the book but even questioned whether the problems investigated by Luxemburg were important ones. The first work in the literature of economics seriously to consider as well as to extend Luxemburg's theory of accumulation was Fritz Sternberg's *Der Imperialismus* (1926). Only with the Keynesian revolution was Luxemburg's theory, that lack of purchasing power causes a breakdown in the capitalist system, rehabilitated.

Luxemburg was again imprisoned during World War I, this time for her antimilitary activities. She devoted the three years she spent in jail to theoretical and journalistic writing. She wrote a book answering the critics of *The Accumulation of Capital*, a brief work on the crisis of social democracy (known as the "Junius Pamphlet"; see Luxemburg 1916), and the unfinished manuscript from which the posthumously published *Russian Revolution* (see in 1904–1922) was drawn. *The Russian Revolution* is one of the most controversial works in socialist political literature, where it occupies a position similar to that of *The Accumulation of Capital* in economic literature. Luxemburg acclaimed the October Revolution as the most important result of World War I, but this did not prevent her from criticizing Bolshevik practice. Thus, she deplored the fact that the postrevolutionary political system was a dictatorship not *of* the masses, but *over* the masses. She was disappointed that the large landholdings had been divided among the peasants, for she felt that this created a new and powerful class of proprietors, i.e., enemies of socialism. She also disapproved of Bolshevik policy toward nationalities.

Upon her release from prison at the end of 1918, Luxemburg immediately joined the German revolution. Late that year she and Karl Liebknecht together founded the German Communist party and wrote its program. They were both arrested early in 1919 and were both assassinated by the soldiers in whose custody they had been placed.

TADEUSZ KOWALIK

[*For the historical context of Luxemburg's work, see* ECONOMIC THOUGHT, *article on* SOCIALIST THOUGHT; IMPERIALISM; MARXISM; SOCIALISM; *and the biographies of* BERNSTEIN; KAUTSKY; MARX.]

WORKS BY LUXEMBURG

(1894–1925) 1951 *Ausgewählte Reden und Schriften.* 2 vols. With a preface by Wilhelm Pieck. Berlin: Dietz.

1898 *Die industrielle Entwicklung Polens: Inaugural-Dissertation.* Leipzig: Duncker & Humblot.

(1899) 1951 *Reform or Revolution.* With an introduction by Hector Abhayavardhan. Bombay: Modern India Publications. → First published as *Sozialreform oder Revolution?*

(1904–1922) 1961 *The Russian Revolution* and *Leninism or Marxism?* With an introduction by Bertram D. Wolfe. Ann Arbor: Univ. of Michigan Press. → Two pamphlets, first published in German. *Leninism or Marxism?* was first published in 1904; *Die russische Revolution* was published posthumously in 1922, edited by P. Levi.

(1906) 1951 Massenstreik, Partei und Gewerkschaften. Volume 1, pages 157–257 in Rosa Luxemburg, *Ausgewählte Reden und Schriften.* Berlin: Dietz.

(1913) 1964 *The Accumulation of Capital.* New York: Monthly Review Press. → First published in German.

(1916) 1951 Die Krise der Sozialdemokratie (Junius-Broschüre). Volume 1, pages 258–399 in Rosa Luxemburg, *Ausgewählte Reden und Schriften.* Berlin: Dietz. → The 1916 edition was published under the pseudonym Junius.

1922–1928 *Gesammelte Werke.* Vols. 3, 4, and 6. Berlin: Vereinigung Internationaler Verlags-Anstalten. → Volumes 1, 2, and 5 were never published.

(1925) 1951 Einführung in die Nationalökonomie. Volume 1, pages 411–741 in Rosa Luxemburg, *Ausgewählte Reden und Schriften.* Berlin: Dietz.

SUPPLEMENTARY BIBLIOGRAPHY

ARENDT, HANNAH 1966 A Heroine of Revolution: [A Book Review of] *Rosa Luxemburg,* by J. P. Nettl. *New York Review of Books* 8, no. 5:21–27.

BUKHARIN, NIKOLAI I. (1926) 1927 *Der Imperialismus und die Akkumulation des Kapitals.* Berlin: Verlag für Literatur und Politik. → First published as *Imperialism i nakoplenie kapitala.*

CLIFF, TONY 1959 Rosa Luxemburg: A Study. *International Socialism: Quarterly for Marxist Theory* [1959]: no. 2–3.

FRÖLICH, PAUL (1939) 1940 *Rosa Luxemburg: Her Life and Work.* Translated by Edward Fitzgerald. London: Gollancz. → First published in German.

GROSSMANN, HENRYK 1929 *Das Akkumulations- und Zusammenbruchsgesetz des kapitalistischen Systems (Zugleich eine Krisentheorie)*. Leipzig: Hirschfeld.

LAURAT, LUCIEN 1930 *L'accumulation du capital d'après Rosa Luxembourg, suivi d'un aperçu sur la discussion du problème depuis la mort de Rosa Luxembourg.* Paris: Rivière.

LENIN, VLADIMIR I. (1916) 1964 The Junius Pamphlet. Pages 305–319 in Vladimir I. Lenin, *Collected Works.* 4th ed. Volume 22: December 1915–July 1916. London: Lawrence & Wishart.

NETTL, JOHN P. 1966 *Rosa Luxemburg.* 2 vols. Oxford Univ. Press.

OELSSNER, FRED 1951 *Rosa Luxemburg: Eine kritische biographische Skizze.* Berlin: Dietz.

STERNBERG, FRITZ 1926 *Der Imperialismus.* Berlin: Malik.

STERNBERG, FRITZ 1929 Der Imperialismus *und seine Kritiker.* Berlin: Soziologische Verlagsanstalt.

M

MACAULAY, THOMAS BABINGTON

Thomas Babington Macaulay (1800–1859), English historian, essayist, and politician, was born at Rothley Temple, Leicestershire. His father, Zachary, one of the leading members of the "Clapham sect," was a stern evangelical who fought unremittingly for the abolition first of the slave trade and then of slavery itself. Macaulay's mother was the daughter of a Quaker bookseller and herself a devout evangelical. Thus, the young Macaulay, an astonishingly precocious boy, grew up in an atmosphere of piety, introspection, and humanitarian endeavor. He absorbed and retained the moral and ethical imperatives inculcated upon him; but much to the chagrin of his father, he never underwent a conversion experience and always remained wary of the emotional excesses, cant, and hypocrisy to which an experiential religion so easily lends itself.

At Trinity College, Cambridge, he distinguished himself as a classicist and a poet. He became a fellow of the college in 1824. While at the university, he triumphed as an orator in the Union Debating Society and began his brilliant career as an essayist. In the latter role, he first made his mark with his essay "Milton," which appeared in the *Edinburgh Review* of October 1825 ([1825–1844] 1963, vol. 1, pp. 150–194). It was indeed appropriate that in that essay, which made him famous overnight, he should have taken his place on the libertarian side of seventeenth-century English politics. Although Macaulay had been a mild Tory when he entered the university, he was a staunch Whig when he left, and in many ways his political stance was derived from his study of the constitutional conflicts of the seventeenth century. In "Milton" and subsequent writings he transferred the theme of those conflicts to the decade of struggle between Whig and Tory before the passage of the Reform Act of 1832.

His early essays in the *Edinburgh Review* are richly caparisoned with wit, paradox, and antithesis, but as Bagehot justly remarked, "Macaulay is anything but a mere rhetorical writer, there is a very hard kernel of business in him." What gave his writings this "kernel of business" was his sturdy common sense, his fondness for Baconian induction, his suspicion of system making and *idées reçues,* and his ability to get to the root of the matter. These characteristics led him on occasion to anticipate some of the insights of twentieth-century social science; the results are still well worth sampling in some of his articles: "Thoughts on the Advancement of Academic Education in England" (1826), in which he presented a well-argued case against the collegiate system of Oxford and Cambridge and for a nonresidential university in an urban setting; "Social and Industrial Capacities of Negroes" (1827), in which Macaulay saw the roots of the Negro problem as fundamentally social and economic rather than in any sense innately "racial"; "Machiavelli" (*The Works of Lord Macaulay,* vol. 7, pp. 63–113), which, as Paul Lazarsfeld has pointed out (1957), contains an account of what is probably the first projective test recorded in the literature; "History" (*Works,* vol. 7, pp. 167–220), which makes an excellent case for writing the history of societies as a whole, rather than of wars, battles, diplomacy, and politics; "Mill on Government" (*Works,* vol. 7, pp. 327–371), which argues against the utilitarian theory of government persuasively enough to have convinced John Stuart Mill himself; and "Civil Disabilities of the Jews" (*Works*, vol. 8, pp. 1–17), which brilliantly places the problem of anti-Semitism into a historical context.

Macaulay was elected to Parliament in 1830. His speeches in favor of the Reform Bill in 1831 and 1832 gained him immense repute as an orator and secured for him, an outsider who lacked both wealth and noble birth, entry into the strongholds of Whig society. For him parliamentary reform was not merely a matter of expediency, although, to be sure, he emphasized that the aristocracy had better make timely political concessions to the middle classes if it wanted to avoid revolution. Reform was, rather, the latest inevitable stage in a series of historical developments that had resulted in a more widespread distribution of property, great increase of wealth, ever greater triumphs of science and industry, and a steady progress from rudeness to refinement. In other words, the Reform Act was merely one way of bringing political arrangements into alignment with an advancing state of society.

In 1834 Macaulay went to India as a member of the governor's Supreme Council. His personal motive for going was to make himself financially independent. In India he made two significant contributions. In 1835 he wrote the historic and still controversial "Minute on Indian Education" ([1831–1853] 1935, pp. 345–361), which proposed English as the principal language of instruction for any national system of education in India, so that Western science, culture, and technology could more easily be transmitted. And he was largely responsible for drawing up a uniform Indian penal code in 1837. Its substance was the English criminal law. Revised by Sir Barnes Peacock, it went into operation in 1862.

In 1838 Macaulay returned to England, and it was in the course of that year that he began seriously to plan his major literary work, which eventually appeared under the title *The History of England, From the Accession of James the Second, . . .* (1848–1861). He remained active in politics, was Secretary at War from 1839 to 1841, and sat in Parliament for most of the rest of his life.

The first two volumes of the *History* came out late in 1848, and it was appropriate that a work celebrating the bloodless revolution of 1688 and the establishment of English constitutional stability should make its appearance in the course of a year that had seen revolutionary violence on the continent of Europe, but not in England. In his *History* Macaulay showed himself to be a master of historical narrative.

The tour de force of the *History* is undoubtedly "England in 1685," the first volume's famous third chapter which in the space of 150 pages surveys the nation's geography, population, resources, means of transport, and varied social classes and their occupations, as well as its army, navy, science, literature, and press. It is descriptive rather than analytical social history. Still, of its kind and of its time it remains a magnificent achievement.

The *History of England* is not without its defects. Macaulay's historical imagination was strong but limited. He approached the past from the vantage point of a more glorious present. He was, as S. R. Gardiner pointed out, a better judge of situations than of character. There are some distortions. But those who expect to find in the *History* a naively stated *parti pris* will look in vain.

The popular success of the *History* (volumes 3 and 4 appeared in 1855, a fifth volume posthumously in 1861) was immense and constituted a unique publishing phenomenon in nineteenth-century England. It appealed to the pride as well as the prejudices of its purchasers and was read with both pleasure and profit by an ever-growing literate public. In historiographical terms it marked, as Leopold von Ranke observed, the triumph of the Whig view of seventeenth-century English history over the Tory view, articulated by David Hume. But the recent tendency to categorize and then dismiss Macaulay as a "mere" Whig historian is giving way to a more balanced sense of his achievement.

Macaulay was awarded a peerage in 1857, the first English historian to be so honored.

John Clive

[*For the historical context of Macaulay's work, see* History, *article on* social history.]

WORKS BY MACAULAY

(1825–1844) 1963 *Critical and Historical Essays.* 2 vols. New York: Dutton.

1826 Thoughts on the Advancement of Academic Education in England. *Edinburgh Review* 43:315–341. → Published anonymously.

1827 [Social and Industrial Capacities of Negroes.] *Edinburgh Review* 45:383–423. → An anonymously published review of four papers.

(1831–1853) 1935 *Speeches by Lord Macaulay, With His "Minute on Indian Education."* Selected with an introduction and notes by G. M. Young. Oxford Univ. Press.

(1835–1837) 1946 *Lord Macaulay's Legislative Minutes.* Selected with a historical introduction by C. D. Dhaker. Oxford Univ. Press.

(1848–1861) 1913–1915 *The History of England, From the Accession of James the Second, ...* Edited by Charles Harding Firth. 6 vols. London: Macmillan.

The Works of Lord Macaulay. Albany edition, 12 vols London: Longmans, 1898. → Volumes 1–6: *History of*

England. Volumes 7–10: *Essays and Biographies.* Volumes 11–12: *Speeches, Poems and Miscellaneous Writings.*

WORKS ABOUT MACAULAY

BAGEHOT, WALTER (1856) 1950 Thomas Babington Macaulay. Volume 2, pages 198–232 in Walter Bagehot, *Literary Studies.* New York: Dutton.

BEATTY, RICHMOND C. 1938 *Lord Macaulay: Victorian Liberal.* Norman: Univ. of Oklahoma Press.

BRYANT, ARTHUR 1933 *Macaulay.* London: Davies.

CLIVE, JOHN 1960 Macaulay's Historical Imagination. *Review of English Literature* 1, no. 4:20–28.

FIRTH, CHARLES H. (1938) 1964 *A Commentary on Macaulay's* History of England. New York: Barnes & Noble.

GLADSTONE, WILLIAM E. (1876) 1879 Macaulay. Pages 265–341 in William E. Gladstone, *Gleanings of Past Years: 1843–1878.* Volume 1: Personal and Literary. London: Murray.

LAZARSFELD, PAUL F. 1957 The Historian and the Pollster. Pages 242–262 in Mirra Komarovsky (editor), *Common Frontiers of the Social Sciences.* Glencoe, Ill.: Free Press.

PAGET, JOHN 1861 *The New "Examen": Or, an Inquiry Into the Evidence Relating to Certain Passages in Lord Macaulay's* History *Concerning I. The Duke of Marlborough; II. The Massacre of Glencoe; III. The Highlands of Scotland; IV. Viscount Dundee; V. William Penn.* Edinburgh and London: Blackwood.

STEPHEN, LESLIE (1876) 1904 Macaulay. Volume 3, pages 227–271 in Leslie Stephen, *Hours in a Library.* New York and London: Putnam.

TREVELYAN, GEORGE O. (1876) 1932 *The Life and Letters of Lord Macaulay.* Oxford Univ. Press.

McCULLOCH, JOHN RAMSAY

John Ramsay McCulloch (1789–1864), economist and statistician, was born in Scotland, the son of a small landowner. He studied law in Edinburgh but soon abandoned that field in favor of political economy. His first publication, which appeared in 1816, called for a reduction of the rate of interest on the national debt on both theoretical and practical grounds and led to a correspondence with Ricardo. When Ricardo's *Principles* appeared in 1817, McCulloch immediately supplied a masterful digest of the book to the *Edinburgh Review,* the most popular quarterly of the day. For the next twenty years almost every issue of the *Review* carried an article by him. At the same time, he contributed to the *Scotsman,* and from 1818 to 1820 he edited this famous liberal paper.

In 1820 he went to London, where he taught economics privately. After Ricardo died in 1823, his friends and admirers chose McCulloch to deliver the Ricardo memorial lectures at a privately rented hall. These lectures were expanded into an outline of basic principles in the article on political economy for the new edition of the *Encyclopaedia Britannica* (1824*a*); in this article McCulloch equates Ricardo's brand of economics with the science itself. It was succeeded by a formal treatise, *The Principles of Political Economy* (1825), a work which had considerable vogue until J. S. Mill's work of the same title (1848) supplanted it. There followed *A Treatise on the Circumstances Which Determine the Rate of Wages* (1826), to which the Webbs later drew attention by calling McCulloch "the inventor of the wages fund doctrine" (Webb & Webb 1897). However, this doctrine is to be found in Adam Smith's writings, as well as in Ricardo's, and McCulloch did not contribute anything new to its presentation.

Academic security eluded him all his life. In 1828 he was appointed to an unendowed chair at the newly founded University College in London. He resigned the position in 1832 because no donor had come forward to endow the chair. Earlier an attempt to make him the first incumbent of a new chair of political economy at the University of Edinburgh had also been unsuccessful. At last, in 1838 he obtained a lifetime sinecure as comptroller of Her Majesty's Stationery Office. He took little part in the activities of the department and, although he had by then abandoned journalism, he continued to publish books and pamphlets on economic subjects.

It was McCulloch, more than any other man, who was responsible for Ricardo's enormous influence upon the economic thinking of the times. He was, however, more than Ricardo's spokesman; he was the greatest economic publicist of his day—so much so that all those who detested political economy invariably selected him as their whipping boy. He appears, Scots accent and all, as "McGroudy" in Carlyle; as "MacFungus" expounding "ecoonoomical science" in Peacock; and as "The Scot" in that old Victorian favorite *Noctes Ambrosianae,* by Christopher North. Today he is chiefly remembered as a prime example of the zealous, dogmatic disciple. But devoted disciple though he was, he did not endorse all of Ricardo's opinions: he condemned Ricardo's *volte face* on the question of technological unemployment; he never fully accepted the theory of comparative advantage; and he always qualified Ricardo's theory of profit. In later years he openly admitted defects in the Ricardian system.

An indifferent theorist, McCulloch appears at his best in his statistical and descriptive compendia rather than in his theoretical writings. His *Dictionary . . . of Commerce and Commercial Navigation* (1832), much of which was embodied in his later treatise *A Descriptive and Statistical Account of the British Empire* (1837), demonstrated his encyclopedic knowledge of the British economy, and it remains to this day an authoritative reference work. Moreover, he deserves to be regarded as the first professional historian of economic thought. *A Discourse on the Rise . . . of Political Economy*, first published in 1824 and then appended to his *Principles*, was the first attempt in any language to project a formal history of this subject. Later contributions to the historiography of economics consisted of an edition of Adam Smith's *Wealth of Nations* in 1828, with copious notes; an edition of the works of Ricardo in 1846, with a famous biography; numerous reprints of scarce tracts; and a celebrated *catalogue raisonné*, *The Literature of Political Economy* (1845*a*), based upon his own magnificent collection of economic works.

Unlike other members of Ricardo's circle, McCulloch did not subscribe to radicalism in politics, nor did he share the utilitarian enthusiasm for land reform. His outlook was that of a liberal Tory, optimistic but conservative. He always took exception to the gloomy implications of the Malthusian theory of population. He hesitated to condemn the poor laws entirely and, in contrast to most other economists of the day, disapproved of the Poor Law Amendment Act of 1834. Although a convinced free trader, he never joined Richard Cobden and John Bright in demanding immediate and total repeal of the corn laws. In his days as a journalist, he achieved notoriety as an apologist for the new factory system, but in later years he grew increasingly uneasy about the consequences of the industrial revolution.

MARK BLAUG

[*For the historical context of McCulloch's work, see the biography of* RICARDO.]

WORKS BY MC CULLOCH

1824*a* Political Economy. Supplement, Volume 6, pages 216–278 in *Encyclopaedia Britannica*. Edinburgh: Constable.

1824*b* *A Discourse on the Rise, Progress, Peculiar Objects, and Importance, of Political Economy: Containing an Outline of a Course of Lectures on the Principles and Doctrines of That Science*. Edinburgh: Constable. → Later appended to McCulloch 1825.

(1824*c*) 1921 The Founding of the Political Economy Club. Volume 6, page 41 in Political Economy Club of London, *Minutes of Proceedings, 1899–1920; Roll of Members and Questions Discussed, 1821–1920; With Documents Bearing on the History of the Club*. Centenary Volume. London: Macmillan. → The Johnsonian flavor of McCulloch's mind is best conveyed by his impromptu observations at the Political Economy Club and by letters in Ricardo 1817–1823.

(1825) 1886 *The Principles of Political Economy*. London: Ward.

(1826) 1868 *A Treatise on the Circumstances Which Determine the Rate of Wages, and the Conditions of the Labouring Classes. . . .* London: Longmans. → First published as *An Essay on the Circumstances. . . .*

(1832) 1882 *A Dictionary, Practical, Theoretical, and Historical, of Commerce and Commercial Navigation*. London: Longmans.

(1837) 1854 *A Descriptive and Statistical Account of the British Empire*. 4th ed., rev., 2 vols. London: Longmans. → First published as *A Statistical Account of the British Empire*.

(1845*a*) 1938 *The Literature of Political Economy*. London School of Economics and Political Science Series of Reprints of Scarce Works on Political Economy, No. 5. London School of Economics and Political Science.

(1845*b*) 1863 *A Treatise on the Principles and Practical Influence of Taxation and the Funding System*. 3d ed. Edinburgh: Black.

1848 *A Treatise on the Succession to Property Vacant by Death*. London: Longmans.

SUPPLEMENTARY BIBLIOGRAPHY

BLAUG, MARK 1958 *Ricardian Economics: A Historical Study*. Yale University Studies in Economics, No. 8. New Haven: Yale Univ. Press.

BONAR, JAMES 1895 John Ramsay McCulloch. Part 6, pages 1–5 in Bernard Quaritch (editor), *Contributions Towards a Dictionary of English Book-collectors*. London: Quaritch.

CANNAN, EDWIN (1893) 1953 *A History of the Theories of Production and Distribution in English Political Economy, From 1776 to 1848*. 3d ed. London and New York: Staples.

HALÉVY, ÉLIE (1901–1904) 1952 *The Growth of Philosophic Radicalism*. New ed. London: Faber. → First published in French.

MILL, JOHN STUART (1848) 1961 *Principles of Political Economy, With Some of Their Applications to Social Philosophy*. 7th ed. Edited by W. J. Ashley. New York: Kelley.

RICARDO, DAVID (1809–1823) 1951–1955 *Works and Correspondence*. Edited by Piero Sraffa. 10 vols. Cambridge Univ. Press. → Volumes 6 through 9 contain Ricardo's correspondence.

SMITH, ADAM (1776) 1950 *An Inquiry Into the Nature and Causes of the Wealth of Nations*. 6th ed., 2 vols. Edited, with an introduction, notes, marginal summary, and an enlarged index, by Edwin Cannan. London: Methuen. → A paperback edition was published in 1963 by Irwin.

TAUSSIG, FRANK W. (1896) 1932 *Wages and Capital: An Examination of the Wages Fund Doctrine*. London School of Economics and Political Science.

WEBB, SIDNEY; and WEBB, BEATRICE (1897) 1920 *Industrial Democracy*. New ed. 2 vols. in 1. London and New York: Longmans.

McDOUGALL, WILLIAM

William McDougall (1871–1938) occupies a position in the history of psychology that is not easy to define. During the earlier part of his working life he was a central figure, in touch not only with all that was going on in psychology but also with anthropology and physiology as well. As time went on certain qualities of character and intellect tended to isolate him, and before he died he had moved to the fringes of the academic world, writing largely for laymen and associated in the minds of his fellow scientists with a discredited instinct theory, Lamarckian genetics, and parapsychology. He was aware of this and felt it deeply. "Similar abilities, energy, and sustained effort, applied in any other line of work, might well have brought considerable reward," he wrote in his autobiography. "The more I write, the more antagonism I seem to provoke" (1930, p. 223).

McDougall was born in Lancashire, England. A precocious student, he graduated from the University of Manchester at age 17. Two years later he went to Cambridge to study physiology, then as now a common approach to a medical qualification. His M.B., which he took in London in 1898, was not intended to lead to work as a physician. He had a few months of physiological research with Sherrington before returning to Cambridge, where his brilliant academic record had brought him a fellowship at St. John's College.

Almost immediately he was involved in a scientific expedition to the Torres Strait. W. H. R. Rivers, who was to influence so many Cambridge men, asked him to carry out psychological observations on the natives, and his wide-ranging mind was soon at home in the anthropological literature of his day. Darwin's influence at that time must have been so pervasive as to be unrecognizable, yet looking back we can see that it was the primary source of McDougall's thinking in many fields. On an expedition such as that to the Torres Strait the zoologists and botanists must have had the *Voyage of the Beagle* very much in mind, and the direction of their work was to identify the part played by various structures and activities in the adaptive economy of the species in which they occurred. This kind of interest, when it arises in psychology, forms part of the viewpoint which has been called functionalism to distinguish it from the psychological structuralism of Wundt and the quasi-physiological theories of behaviorism. It dominated the Anglo-Saxon world for a time and received its clearest expression in William James's great *Principles of Psychology*.

Returning to Cambridge, McDougall sampled the German and British philosophical psychologists of his period. Lotze attracted him but Wundt did not. The former was philosophical and tentative in his approach, with a bias against mechanism and an interest in psychological functioning; the latter was dogmatic in his claim that mental content is the only valid subject matter for psychology. On the advice of James Ward, professor of moral philosophy at Cambridge, McDougall went to Göttingen and studied under Georg E. Müller. He did not become a disciple but was attracted to color vision research. His work led him to reject the theories both of Hering and of Helmholtz, but his own theory did not constitute a major departure. Rather it was an attempt to supplement the views of Helmholtz so as to accommodate Hering's findings, by adding an evolutionary footnote. If McDougall had formulated his suggestion somewhat differently, as others did at the time, it would be acceptable today. [*See* VISION, *article on* COLOR VISION AND COLOR BLINDNESS.] At the same time he was concerned with the general nature of cerebral activity; here his views tended toward the theory, first put forward by Flourens, that the brain does not function as an enormous collection of individual pathways but is a unitary organ acting as a whole. This "mass action" theory may best be thought of as a protest against oversimplification. McDougall also displayed an interest in the relationship between mind and body which persisted throughout his life. He took a dualistic line and suggested that mental events as such may influence bodily processes. His views were unfashionable then, and, despite the rise of psychosomatic medicine, they have remained so. [*See* NERVOUS SYSTEM; PSYCHOSOMATIC ILLNESS.] They were also undoubtedly linked with his emerging interest in psychical research. He related his views in this connection to his "uncompromising arrogance" and to his inclination to support a theory merely because it was unpopular.

In 1904 McDougall went to Oxford as Wilde reader in mental philosophy. He had to give some forty lectures a year on topics of his own choosing, and the rest of the time was his own for research and writing. He did not feel at home in the Oxford atmosphere, but he did have a small laboratory in the department of physiology and some outstanding research students, including Cyril Burt and J. C. Flugel.

Some of his best work belongs to this period. His little *Physiological Psychology* appeared in 1905. It is not read now because later techniques and theories have dated it, but within its scope it was an admirably clear and objective piece of work, and its qualities highlight the diversity of McDougall's talents at this stage of his career. [*See* PSYCHOLOGY, *article on* PHYSIOLOGICAL PSYCHOLOGY.]

An Introduction to Social Psychology was published in 1908, and in it McDougall first propounded his influential instinct theory. The book ran through more than twenty editions in as many years and is perhaps as much undervalued today as it was overvalued then. In ethology and elsewhere, aspects of McDougall's position are now widely current, although restatement has done much to disguise them. To McDougall the fact that anthropologists could identify the adaptive role of social organizations and that zoologists could do the same for inherited patterns of behavior meant that at the human level also there is a mediating mechanism through which complex adaptive ways of behaving, both social and individual, can be transmitted, and that mechanism is instinct. An instinct, for McDougall, was not a built-in response pattern specified in detail—such as we see in the repertoire of solitary insects—but merely a tendency, under given conditions, to notice certain kinds of stimuli, to respond to them in ways that can best be specified by reference to some goal, and to experience a particular emotion if the response is delayed. Learning plays a great part in this mechanism both by diversifying and stabilizing the response. McDougall's later critics, using a much more limited definition of instinct, often did him an injustice by failing to give due weight to this last point.

The work was written rather quickly and was based on reading and reflection rather than actual research, but the argument was so persuasive that it soon established itself as one of the most widely read texts on either side of the Atlantic. The early acclaim for this vulnerable piece of work probably accounts in part for the vehemence with which it was later denounced. There also occurred during McDougall's lifetime, however, a change in the climate of opinion, which more than anything else was responsible for the curiously inverted nature of his career, with its early fame and later comparative obscurity. The functionalist approach, which derived from Darwin, became replaced by a more analytic and objective attitude. In psychology, the rise of behaviorism and associationist learning theory marked this change. McDougall found himself more and more out of step with his colleagues and, being the man he was, reacted polemically rather than creatively to the challenge.

Body and Mind, with its revealing subtitle, *A History and a Defense of Animism*, came out in 1911 and showed clearly that even before the rise of behaviorism there were expressions of hostility to mechanistic theories in the biological field. McDougall himself, who was not without insight into his own foibles, described the work as another characteristic championship of an unpopular view just because it was unpopular. Yet even then his reputation as a scientist must have been very high. In 1912 he was elected a fellow of the Royal Society, one of the small number of psychologists ever to receive this honor.

World War I brought about some shift in the direction of McDougall's interests from pure research and speculation toward applied and clinical problems. Since he was medically qualified, it was natural that he should serve as a psychiatrist. Neither psychologist nor psychiatrist had much in the way of professional training in those days, and demarcation disputes did not arise. Many of the psychiatric casualties of World War I suffered from the hysterical condition known as shell shock. The methods which McDougall found most useful in treating psychiatric casualties confirmed his earlier belief in the value of Jung's work. He did not find it necessary to trace a breakdown to events in the early childhood of a patient but treated it as an inadequate reaction to an immediate situation. After the war he went to Jung in Zurich and underwent analysis. Writing of it later he said that his personality was so "hopelessly normal" that the process made very little difference to him. He remained, however, well disposed toward Jung.

In 1920 there appeared *The Group Mind*, a study in which the Darwinian ideas of the *Introduction to Social Psychology* were supplemented and elaborated by other ideas from analytic psychology and anthropology. It was conceived by its author to be the first part of his masterwork, and he had high hopes of being able to work out a single systematic treatment of his subject from its social and anthropological to its biological frontiers. His ideas, however, were far too speculative and his statement of them far too discursive to make what he had to say widely acceptable to his contemporaries. This seems to have been the turning point. Although McDougall was still to contribute much of value to psychology, the setback that he suffered at this stage seems to have done more than anything else to drive him into the byways. Although the size of his output remained considerable, its scientific content tended to decline.

It was perhaps a symptom of his unsettled state that he felt it would be a good idea to move from Oxford to Harvard. Münsterberg he had found congenial, and William James was probably, of all psychologists, the one he admired with fewest reservations. These were the names that represented Harvard to him, and he felt that he would find there a more sympathetic environment than anywhere else. It was an ill-judged move in many ways. The atmosphere had changed since the days of James and Münsterberg, the administrative arrangements were not what he had supposed, and in his frustration he may well have alienated some of his colleagues.

He began some animal experiments to test the Lamarckian hypothesis, and he published during this period two considerable but little read books—*Outline of Psychology* (1923) and *Outline of Abnormal Psychology* (1926). In a few years, however, the difficulties of Harvard became oppressive, and he made his final move, to Duke University in North Carolina. Duke had been recently founded and richly endowed, and it seemed to promise the independence and financial support required by a research scientist and something of the isolation demanded by a prophet. At any rate the change was a happy one, and McDougall settled down in his new home as contentedly as he could anywhere. He carried on his Lamarckian work, he supported psychical research, he built up a good psychology department, and he published extensively on a wide range of topics. It is not unfair to say, however, that judged by contemporary standards nothing of this later work is of first-rate importance.

McDougall's dogmatism and impatience are partly responsible, no doubt, for the fact that despite his brilliant gifts and tremendous industry he felt himself to have been a failure. He did arouse hostility where he need not have done, and, as has been pointed out, he lived through a period of rapid change in biological science and was out of step with events. More basic, however, as a reason for his difficulties seems to have been an emotionally toned refusal to look at human beings with the detachment and objectivity of the scientist. He was always a moralist and sometimes a metaphysician, so that his conclusions were as often a function of his personality as of his data.

JAMES DREVER

[*For the historical context of McDougall's work, see the biographies of* DARWIN; FLOURENS; HELMHOLTZ; HERING; JAMES; JUNG; LOTZE; MÜNSTERBERG; *for discussion of the subsequent development of his ideas, see* EMOTION; ETHOLOGY; INSTINCT; PARAPSYCHOLOGY; SOCIAL PSYCHOLOGY.]

WORKS BY MC DOUGALL

1905 *Physiological Psychology.* London: Dent.

(1908) 1950 *An Introduction to Social Psychology.* 30th ed., enl. London: Methuen. → A paperback edition was published in 1960 by Barnes and Noble.

(1911) 1938 *Body and Mind.* 8th ed. London: Methuen. → Previously published as *Body and Mind: A History and a Defense of Animism.*

1920 *The Group Mind: A Sketch of the Principles of Collective Psychology, With Some Attempt to Apply Them to the Interpretation of National Life and Character.* New York and London: Putnam. → A sequel to McDougall's *Introduction to Social Psychology.*

1923 *Outline of Psychology.* New York: Scribner.

1926 *Outline of Abnormal Psychology.* New York: Scribner.

1930 Autobiography. Volume 1, pages 191–223 in *A History of Psychology in Autobiography.* Worcester, Mass.: Clark Univ. Press.

SUPPLEMENTARY BIBLIOGRAPHY

ROBINSON, ANTHONY L. 1943 *William McDougall, M.B., D.Sc., F.R.S.: A Bibliography, Together With a Brief Outline of His Life.* Durham, N.C.: Duke Univ. Press.

SMITH, MAY 1939 William McDougall: Bibliography. *Character and Personality* 7:184–191.

MACHIAVELLI, NICCOLÒ

Niccolò Machiavelli (1469–1527) was an Italian political and military theorist, civil servant, historian, playwright, and poet.

The Machiavellis, an ancient middle-class family of Florence whose income came from landed property, had been reduced to near poverty at the time of Machiavelli's birth. His father was a doctor of law. Machiavelli seems to have been carefully educated in humanistic studies, although he never learned Greek. He entered Florentine government service in 1498, at the age of 29, as second chancellor and secretary of the Ten of Liberty and Peace, an executive committee concerned with domestic as well as military and foreign affairs. During his 14-year tenure he was engaged in numerous and sometimes lengthy diplomatic missions which took him to France, Switzerland, and Germany. His dispatches and reports contain ideas that anticipate many of the doctrines of his later works.

Military affairs were a continuing preoccupation of Machiavelli's. Not only was the famous militia ordinance of 1506 his, but also the responsibility for implementing it, in the capacity of secretary of the specially constituted Nine of the Militia. When the Florentine government was threatened in 1512 with the restoration of the Medici by Spanish forces, Machiavelli skillfully mobilized an army of twelve thousand conscripts to withstand the invasion; however, the amateur citizen-soldiers proved ineffectual before seasoned troops.

With the restoration of the Medici, Machiavelli was briefly imprisoned and tortured. Upon release he was banished from Florence to live in impoverished retirement on the small estate his family owned at Sant'Andrea. After 13 years of political inactivity he was recalled to government service by the Medici in 1525, but two years later the Medici were overthrown, and the new republic again excluded Machiavelli from office. He died in 1527, receiving the last rites of the church.

Machiavelli was a good father and an affectionate if unfaithful husband. Scrupulously honest, he was also generous and tolerant and had unusual courage and integrity. He excelled in witty conversation and storytelling. As much a poet as a man of practical affairs, he was a dedicated republican who desired only to serve Florence rather than any particular party. He was an extraordinary literary artist and has long been recognized for his masterful prose style; as the author of the comedy *Mandragola* (see 1509–1527) he has been acclaimed the equal of Molière.

Method. Machiavelli was neither a system builder nor a philosopher in a technical sense. In no single treatise did he rigorously expound his theory of man and government. His views are presented in a diffuse and impressionistic fashion, scattered through a number of different works. At the same time, there is system and remarkable consistency to his ideas, even if the coherence is not the most obvious and depends to a degree upon imaginative reconstruction by the sensitive reader.

Among Machiavelli's particular achievements was his attempt to discover an order in political activity itself, not in some external standard or cause. He examined politics in a detached, rational manner, analyzing the ways power can be acquired and maintained. He showed the kinds of actions that in varying situations will lead to political success or failure. Although he was not concerned with moral and political obligation or with the analysis of moral and political concepts, a conception of a good society does inform most of his political writings.

The sources of his approach are a matter of conjecture. He probably owed less to the traditional philosophers than to nonphilosophical classical writers—in particular, to Livy, Tacitus, Plutarch, Xenophon, Polybius, Vegetius, and Frontinus. Machiavelli was not alone among his contemporaries in abandoning a moralistic approach to human behavior for a rational and objective one: the influence of Platonism resulted generally in increasing efforts to reduce activity to an inherent order and these efforts in turn led to the scientific revolution of the seventeenth century (Cassirer 1927). That Machiavelli lived in a city whose very life was finance and commerce may also help to explain his method, which had some of the characteristics of a business calculation of profit and loss. Another possible influence was the increasing conceptualization of government policy, since the thirteenth century, in terms of a notion of public utility: the Holy Roman Emperor Frederick II (1194–1250), Philip IV of France (1268–1314), and some Italian legalists held that the security and well-being of the state at times necessitated official acts which under ordinary circumstances would be considered morally reprehensible. Machiavelli was heir to this late medieval tradition.

Machiavelli was essentially concerned with ascertaining the conditions of political success, and he sought to do so by determining what kinds of acts have proved beneficial and what kinds detrimental to the (political) actors who performed them. In *The Prince* and the *Discourses*, written between 1513 and 1521 (see 1532*a*), he demonstrated the soundness of certain political precepts by using a kind of calculus: he cited numerous examples, drawn from history and from the events of his own time, that would support a particular proposition about the conditions of political success, and he then searched for further examples that would appear to negate the same maxim; only after careful scrutiny of the "negative" cases did he decide whether they really were in fact negative or only appeared to be so because of very different circumstances. He used this method for military precepts, in these works and in *The Art of War* (1521). Again, his penchant for discovering general patterns is evident in his *History of Florence*, completed in 1525 (1532*b*), in which he sought to establish causal relationships in place of mere chronology. It is a pioneer work in modern western European historical writing.

The inspiration for the method may well have been two books with which he was familiar—the *Dictorum factorumque memorabilium* of Valerius Maximus, a compendium of ancient examples to illustrate human behavior, which was dedicated to the first century emperor Tiberius, and the *Strategemata* of Frontinus, a catalogue of military stratagems of the latter part of the same century. Whatever the sources, the method differs markedly from that of classical and medieval political theory. In a way, Machiavelli's approach anticipates the inductive method of Francis Bacon, which, much like an adversary proceeding, entails the collection of positive and negative examples and their resolution.

Theory of man. Crucial to Machiavelli's political theory is his concept of man's nature. From his own shrewd observation and omnivorous reading of history, he concluded that man's nature is changeless—were it not changeless, generalizations about politics could not be made—and that it is essentially evil. (Unlike Plato and Aristotle, Machiavelli used the concept of human nature in a descriptive rather than a normative sense.)

Man's innate evil qualities are such, however, that they do not preclude the possibility of cooperative human endeavor; indeed, some of these very qualities facilitate social cooperation. Man's basic traits are the following: he is a creature of insatiable desires and limitless ambition, and his primary desire is for self-preservation; he is shortsighted, judging most commonly by the immediacy of reward rather than the remote consequences of his actions; he is imitative, inclined to follow the example of authority figures; and he is inflexible, so that behavior patterns established through imitation can be changed only to a limited extent.

Given these traits, the outlook for social cooperation may appear dim, but this is not so: men's desire for self-preservation and their very shortsightedness make them peculiarly susceptible to manipulation by civic leaders, and as stated above, their imitativeness predisposes them to accept the conditioning provided by leadership and organization. Furthermore, under conditions of necessity, when their lives are threatened by a hostile physical environment or by an act of aggression, men's desire for self-preservation moves them to act cooperatively and even virtuously: they prove to be industrious, courageous, and self-denying. Even after an immediate threat to survival has been overcome, social virtues can be maintained by astute leadership and rational social organization. In other words, Machiavelli differentiated between an original (evil) and a second (socially benevolent) nature, between natural and socially acquired characteristics.

Man's essentially evil nature, then, is raw material that may be molded or conditioned by leadership and organization; although, to be sure, the original nature of the material limits its malleability. Man is capable of socialization, and more or less desirable characteristics can be imprinted on his original nature by education, in the sense of conditioning. Civil society is the great school of mankind. Human behavior can be vitally affected by the structure of the social environment, by the socially established ends that canalize human desire. All men are to some extent creatures of convention rather than merely natural men; indeed, neither an absolutely natural nor an absolutely conventional man can exist, any more than either an absolutely evil or an absolutely good man is possible. All men fall somewhere along a scale between these extremes. It seemed plausible to Machiavelli that good and evil are roughly in equilibrium in the world, although their distribution may vary from age to age, each quality being in some periods concentrated in particular societies, and in other periods dispersed.

Values. The supreme end of politics, in Machiavelli's view, is the public utility, the security and well-being of the community rather than the moral goal imputed to politics by previous thinkers. When he assessed the validity of political precepts by examining the consequences of particular political acts, he treated moral acts like any other kind, from a strictly instrumental point of view. The social and political consequences of acts always interested him more than the moral intent of the actors, and he argued that in human affairs the consequences of acts are bound to be both good and evil. Basically, he was not concerned with the problems of moral philosophy, and he accepted the fact that a life of action is necessarily one of moral dilemma and paradox. Perhaps Machiavelli's one important moral insight, never explicitly articulated, is that the very conditions of personal morality are dependent upon the security afforded by the immorality of the state.

This does not mean that Machiavelli condoned violations of personal morality or that he was himself immoral. He did distinguish between moral and immoral acts in the conventional sense. He never suggested that some people are innately superior to others, thereby having a right to dominate and enslave. He was usually careful to affirm that the common good upon occasion excuses rather than justifies immoral means. Violation of the standards of personal morality is excusable only when necessary for the public utility. Statesmen must know how to act iniquitously for the sake of the common good; but violence, cruelty, and deception should never become ends in themselves, and they should always be rationally controlled.

While Machiavelli himself was not above moral reproach, he was born and died a Christian and was neither depraved nor unprincipled. His attacks on the church were anticlerical rather than antireligious, being directed against the scandalous lives of the popes and their political activities. He did compare contemporary Christianity unfavorably with the paganism of the ancients, but he criticized Christianity primarily because it had become the means to socially undesirable ends—the subjection of the many to an avaricious minority—and called for a return to some kind of original creed. While he dwelt upon the socially pragmatic value of religion he did not view it from this standpoint alone.

The highest end to be pursued by man, according

to Machiavelli, is glory. Glory is conferred by acts that are remembered and cherished by mankind. The brief but glorious life of an individual or commonwealth is worth far more to Machiavelli than a lengthy mediocre existence. Mere success or reputation arising from great power or wealth has far less value than true glory. The greatest glory is to be won (in order of decreasing importance) by founding religions, by establishing commonwealths, by commanding armies, and by creating literature.

True glory depends upon the *virtù* of an individual or a people. Machiavelli's term is ambiguous, but what he seems most often to have had in mind is the pattern of conduct of the soldier in battle who displays foresight, self-discipline, constancy, determination, purposefulness, decisiveness, bravery, boldness, and vigor. War is only the archetypal struggle between *virtù* (the manly) and *fortuna* (the changeable, unpredictable, and capricious), for in fact all of life is such a contest. Rational control over the physical and social environments, so essential for human survival and well-being, depends upon the opposition of *virtù* to *fortuna*. By virtuous action men can control at least some part of their lives and limit the whims of chance.

Machiavelli again studied history to discover the conditions that produced the greatest possible amount of *virtù* in a commonwealth and the consequent achievement of glory. He decided that the most virtuous leaders and peoples were those of classical antiquity, particularly of republican Rome. The *virtù* of a people, he believed, depends entirely on education, while that of a prince or leader tends to be inborn but shaped by education. A republicanism in which liberty flourishes, defended by a citizens' army, is the atmosphere most conducive to the exercise of *virtù;* under these conditions political power will be the greatest and most durable, and the political order will be the most stable. The basic elements in Machiavelli's conception of political success, then, are glory, *virtù*, and liberty. Machiavelli lamented the decline of *virtù* in his own age; he condemned its luxurious, commercial life and directed his efforts to the problem of restoring the conditions of glory.

Conflict and corruption. Conflict is a vital concept in Machiavelli's political thought. He accepted conflict as a universal and permanent condition of society, stemming from human nature. The traditional classical and medieval view had been that social conflict is not a natural condition, and many classical and medieval thinkers had tried to design a type of social organization that would eliminate contention. The conception of social conflict as unnatural ran parallel to the Aristotelian concept that matter at rest is more natural than matter in motion. Machiavelli abandoned the former of these ancient modes of thought with his notion of the naturalness of social conflict, although the latter was not discarded until the next century with Galileo's revolutionary insight that the natural state of matter is motion.

The basic manifestation of social conflict, according to Machiavelli, is the perennial struggle between the common people and the great and powerful. While this is clearly a notion of class struggle involving economic factors, Machiavelli's explanation of the struggle is not couched in economic terms. The primary cause of domestic strife and of war between states is, as he saw it, a lust for power and domination. Within any state, the overwhelming majority seek security for their persons and possessions, while a handful, either a hereditary aristocracy or a commercial oligarchy, desire to dominate the masses.

Inspired by Polybius, Machiavelli believed that such conflict is not only natural but that it may be turned to socially useful ends. Virtuous commonwealths exhibit this kind of conflict no less than do corrupt ones. The difference lies not in the presence of conflict in the one and the absence in the other, or even in the degree of conflict, but in the quality of conflict in each.

Conflict in a virtuous commonwealth takes place within certain bounds: it is limited by a patriotic dedication to the common good that supersedes narrow self-interest, by a willingness to respect law and authority, and by an aversion to the use of violence and nonlegal activity. Republican Rome, Machiavelli's ideal of the virtuous commonwealth as described in the *Discourses*, exemplified this kind of limited conflict in that the struggle between patricians and plebeians was institutionalized through the Senate and the popular assemblies with their tribunes. The very strength and unity of the republic together with the citizens' liberties depended upon the continued contest.

By contrast, Florence, as analyzed in the *History of Florence*, is Machiavelli's prototype of the corrupt state. In such a state, society becomes atomized; each man is for himself. Religious sentiment declines, and with it civic honesty, the spirit of civic duty, and respect for authority. Factionalism and conspiracy are rife, and government is the successive captive of the most powerful cliques. *Virtù* decays; avarice proliferates; indolence, luxury, and economic inequalities rend the social fabric. Corruption is likely to develop in an overly successful society that knows peace and prosperity for a lengthy period. With the lack of challenge to survive, with well-being and leisure, men turn to private advantage; laws are no longer vigorously observed and enforced or adjusted to compensate for new conditions. Prevention of corruption requires a return to first principles, a periodic renovation of the civic order. Even the greatest vigilance and most prudent statesmanship, however, will not stem the tide of decay forever. Change is the way of all things, and the best-ordered commonwealths —for example, Rome and Sparta—are bound to decline.

Government and politics. The most important contrivance at man's command for containing and canalizing man's egoistic nature toward socially desirable ends is, according to Machiavelli, the state. By means of the state man can create the conditions for security and well-being.

Although Machiavelli frequently used medical imagery to describe the state, his conception of it actually resembles a mechanism more than an organism. The state has no higher end or spiritual purpose, nor does it have a life or personality apart from the people who constitute it. What has come to be called "reason of state," an expression Machiavelli himself never employed, is the calculated and prudent policy of statesmen to advance the secular aims of the governed, not a superrationality.

In *The Prince* and the *Discourses* Machiavelli presented a twofold classification of states based on the number who rule—the polar types being monarchies and republics. Monarchies may be limited (France), despotic (Turkey), or tyrannical (Syracuse); republics may be mass (Athens) or balanced (Rome). Of the balanced republics, in turn, two principal types exist—aristocratic (Venice) and democratic (Rome). On the basis of the Florentine experience Machiavelli distinguished two unstable forms intermediate between monarchies and republics, which might best be called oligarchy and plebiscitary monarchy. Machiavelli also classified states in other respects: according to the way power is acquired; according to their tendencies to expansion (Rome) or preservation (Sparta), to corruption (Florence) or *virtù* (Roman Republic); and according to whether the constitution originates with a single lawgiver (Sparta) or develops over time and with experience (Rome).

Machiavelli had, of course, elaborate prescriptions for successful government. Good government rests upon the foundation of a strong military establishment for protection against the external enemy. The life, property, family, and honor of each citizen must be safeguarded against interference from other citizens. General economic prosperity should be encouraged, individual economic aggrandizement prevented, and luxury strictly regulated. Adequate recognition must be given to the meritorious among the citizens, and advancement in the service of the state should be open to those who seek honor and glory. The best government draws upon and utilizes the skills of the governed, and the best state is one in which rank corresponds to ability.

These ends can be realized most fully in a republic patterned after the Roman one, which had a mixed constitution and such institutions as dictatorship in times of emergency, censorship, public accusations, popular assemblies, sumptuary laws, and a citizens' army. Republics, however, cannot be established everywhere; the form of the state should be suited to the conditions of a particular society. Moreover, the successful founding of any commonwealth depends on the presence of a single individual of the greatest *virtù* and prudence.

Any well-ordered state is, according to Machiavelli, a rational organization in which citizens know with a high degree of certainty the legal consequences of their actions, i.e., what they can and cannot do with impunity. Hence, central to Machiavelli's proposals for successful government is a rational system of law that will eliminate arbitrary rule by guaranteeing legal equality, by providing regularized procedures for the redress of grievances, by prohibiting retroactive laws, and by executing all laws vigorously and efficiently. Civil law should establish a state religion for the inculcation and maintenance of civic virtue. Law should also institute a citizens' army that will have a genuine stake in the common good and that will serve as a prime means of civic education, instilling citizens with a respect for authority, patriotism, and martial virtues.

Machiavelli's description of the model army in *The Art of War* gives a clearer picture of his concept of a rational society than does the *Discourses*. Since he viewed domestic politics as a kind of warfare and dealt with political matters as a general might deal with the problem of defeating an enemy, it is not surprising that he wrote about politics as classical military theorists wrote about war. Military stratagems are translated into political maxims of the same calculating objectivity, and a rationally organized and commanded army serves as a model of a rational social organization.

Most political situations, Machiavelli believed, are conspiratorial or counterconspiratorial, and conspiracy is primarily of a military character. The political art is akin to the military art with its premium upon secrecy, planning and preparedness, estimation of factors, flexibility, rapidity and decisiveness of execution, surprise, and deception.

These qualities characterize the conspiratorial methods necessary for founding or radically reforming a state and the counterconspiratorial methods required for maintaining a state (since conspiracy must be prevented by avoiding the hatred and contempt of the governed). Prior to Machiavelli, only military theorists had dealt in detail with the problems of conspiracy; in the *Discourses* (see III, vi), he formulated the West's first general theory of political conspiracy.

Not only did Machiavelli liken political situations to military ones and the art of politics to the military art, but he also considered political and military leadership to be similar. Political leadership resembles the creative activity of the general who organizes, disciplines, trains, and leads an army to victory. That *virtù* is the cardinal quality of political leadership as well as of successful generalship is significant. The political virtuoso is rational, calculating, and eminently self-controlled, plays many roles with aplomb, and is prudent enough to identify his own interest with the well-being of those he seeks to manage. Machiavelli's heroes are the ancient founders and the soldier-statesmen of the Roman Republic. He particularly admired the moderate, liberal-minded, and humane military genius Scipio Africanus Major.

Good internal government and successful foreign policy are carried on essentially in the same way. A state's foreign policy is advanced either by diplomacy or war. The familiar roster of necessary qualities is attached to skillful diplomacy—foresight, initiative, decisiveness, flexibility, and deception. Negotiation is the technique of the ambassador, who must be ready to persuade, temporize, or intimidate, as occasion demands. If negotiation fails, war may well be unavoidable. Careful military preparations must be made in peacetime because sooner or later war is inevitable, given man's nature. Machiavelli preferred a war with limited objectives and gains to total war.

Significance and influence. Although few would deny Machiavelli a foremost place among Western political thinkers, his reputation, all too often based on *The Prince* alone, has long rested on his description of the stratagems by which political power can be seized and conserved without regard for moral ends. Consequently, for centuries he has been vilified as devil's disciple and despots' tutor. More favorable appraisals have appeared in recent years: he is being discovered as the first political scientist, the first modern political theorist, or the first liberal. But these positive labels again contain only half-truths. One does find in Machiavelli's thought harbingers of science, modernity, and liberalism. Yet it must not be forgotten that he had one foot firmly planted in the classical world, and this classical aspect of his work has had a considerable influence. The seventeenth-century English classical republicans—Harrington, Neville, and Sidney—found in Machiavelli theories of limited republican government and of a citizens' militia, and bequeathed them to the American constitutional fathers. Montesquieu came upon the Machiavelli of the *Discourses* in England, and his imprint is seen throughout the *Considérations sur les causes de la grandeur des Romains et de leur décadence* and also in *L'esprit des lois*, which in turn fired the radical Rousseau, the conservative Burke, and the liberal Tocqueville. Bodin, Hobbes, Spinoza, and Hegel all recognized Machiavelli's genius.

Machiavelli has also been vitally important as a military thinker. Because of his revival in *The Art of War* of the classical stress upon military training, discipline, and organization, he is unquestionably the father of modern military science, who directly or indirectly influenced practitioners and theorists from Maurice of Nassau to Clausewitz.

Today, Machiavelli is of importance as a forerunner of the rationalism of the Enlightenment. Notwithstanding his pessimism about human nature and cynicism about human behavior, he was not without hope. He never lost his vision of a good society and his faith that men could in part shape their destinies. Relevant to the social scientific concerns of our own time are his views on the integrative function of conflict, the instrumental value of law and ideology in shaping society, the role of conspiracy, and the political craft in general. A careful study of his military image of politics may help us to perceive more readily the inadequacy of our own comparable image of the political.

NEAL WOOD

[*See also* LEADERSHIP; POWER; SOCIAL CONTRACT; STATE; *and the biographies of* BODIN; CLAUSEWITZ; HARRINGTON; HEGEL; HOBBES; KAUṬILYA; MONTESQUIEU; ROUSSEAU; SHANG YANG; SPINOZA.]

WORKS BY MACHIAVELLI

(1504–1549) 1965 *Chief Works and Others.* 3 vols. Durham, N.C.: Duke Univ. Press.

(1506–1549) 1963 *Lust and Liberty: The Poems of Machiavelli.* With notes and introduction by Joseph Tusani. New York: Obolensky.

(1509–1527) 1961 *Literary Works: Mandragola; Clizia; A Dialogue on Language; Belfagor; With Selections From the Private Correspondence.* Edited and translated by J. R. Hale. Oxford Univ. Press.

(1521) 1965 *The Art of War.* Edited with an introduction by Neal Wood. Indianapolis: Bobbs-Merrill.

(1532*a*) 1950 *The Prince* and *The Discourses*. With an introduction by Max Lerner. New York: Modern Library.

(1532*b*) 1960 *History of Florence and of the Affairs of Italy, From the Earliest Times to the Death of Lorenzo the Magnificent.* With an introduction by Felix Gilbert. New York: Harper.

(1532*c*) 1950 *Discourses.* With an introduction and notes by Leslie J. Walker. 2 vols. New Haven: Yale Univ. Press.

The Historical, Political, and Diplomatic Writings. 4 vols. Boston: Osgood, 1882.

SUPPLEMENTARY BIBLIOGRAPHY

BARON, HANS 1955 *The Crisis of the Early Italian Renaissance: Civic Humanism and Republican Liberty in an Age of Classicism and Tyranny.* 2 vols. Princeton Univ. Press.

BAYLEY, CHARLES C. 1961 *War and Society in Renaissance Florence: The* De militia *of Leonardo Bruni.* Univ. of Toronto Press.

CASSIRER, ERNST (1927) 1964 *The Individual and the Cosmos in Renaissance Philosophy.* Translated and with an introduction by Mario Domandi. New York: Barnes & Noble. → First published as *Individuum und Kosmos in der Philosophie der Renaissance.*

CHABOD, FEDERICO (1924–1955) 1958 *Machiavelli and the Renaissance: Essays.* London: Bowes & Bowes. → First published in Italian.

GILBERT, ALLAN H. 1938 *Machiavelli's* Prince *and Its Forerunners:* The Prince *as a Typical Book de Regime Principum.* Durham, N.C.: Duke Univ. Press.

GILBERT, FELIX 1965 *Machiavelli and Guicciardini: Politics and History in Sixteenth-century Florence.* Princeton Univ. Press.

HEXTER, J. H. 1964 The Loom of Language and the Fabric of Imperatives: The Case of *Il principe* and *Utopia. American Historical Review* 69:945–968. → See especially Hexter's discussion of the concept of "*lo stato*" in Machiavelli's work.

MEINECKE, FRIEDRICH (1924) 1962 *Machiavellism: The Doctrine of Raison d'État and Its Place in Modern History.* New York: Praeger. → First published as *Die Idee der Staatsräson in der neueren Geschichte.*

POST, GAINES 1964 *Studies in Medieval Legal Thought: Public Law and the State, 1100–1322.* Princeton Univ. Press.

RAAB, FELIX 1964 *The English Face of Machiavelli: A Changing Interpretation, 1500–1700.* With a foreword by Hugh Trevor-Roper. London: Routledge.

RIDOLFI, ROBERTO (1954) 1963 *The Life of Niccolò Machiavelli.* Univ. of Chicago Press. → First published in Italian.

STRAUSS, LEO 1959 *Thoughts on Machiavelli.* Glencoe, Ill.: Free Press.

VILLARI, PASQUALE (1877–1882) 1892 *The Life and Times of Niccolò Machiavelli.* 2 vols. New ed., rev. & enl. London: Unwin. → First published in Italian.

WHITFIELD, JOHN H. 1947 *Machiavelli.* Oxford: Blackwell.

MACHINE TABULATION

See COMPUTATION.

MACHINES, POLITICAL

See POLITICAL MACHINES.

McILWAIN, CHARLES H.

Charles Howard McIlwain, political scientist and historian, was born in Saltsburg, Pennsylvania, in 1871. He received a B.A. degree from Princeton in 1894. Three years later he was admitted to the Pennsylvania bar, but shortly thereafter he accepted a post as teacher of Latin and history in a private school. His knowledge and interest in the fields of Latin, history, and law, which later found expression in his writings on English constitutional development and ancient and medieval political thought, were sharpened and refined during his study for the doctorate at Harvard from 1901 to 1903. In 1911 McIlwain was appointed assistant professor of history and government at Harvard and was promoted to a full professorship only five years later, which was quite extraordinary at the time. In 1927 he was named Eaton professor of the science of government, and he held this chair until his retirement in 1946. During an active teaching career which spanned almost half a century, he lectured at numerous universities, including Oxford. In 1936 he was elected president of the American Historical Association.

McIlwain was profoundly disturbed by the divorce of political science and history. The disciplines were brought together, especially at Harvard, through the force and originality of McIlwain's scholarship. The dominance of political theory, and its historical orientation, in the Harvard department of government is in large measure a legacy from McIlwain. His influence was strongly felt by scholars of his own day—Edward Corwin and George Sabine, to name but two—and the work of more recent theorists, such as Louis Hartz and Leonard Levy, reflects the continuing impact of McIlwain's approach to the study of political thought.

Historical roots of judicial activism. Avoiding the pitfall of reading the present into the past, McIlwain justly prided himself on his ability to interpret medieval writers such as Henry de Bracton and John Fortescue in terms of their own thinking and experience. His insight into juristic thought in England during the Middle Ages greatly contributed not only to a general understanding of the period but also to a clarification of political concepts such as constitutionalism and sovereignty. The unique and phenomenal discretionary power enjoyed by the American judiciary cannot be explained in the absence of an understanding of its historical roots in English jurisprudence. Addressing himself to this problem, McIlwain argued in *The High Court of Parliament* (1910) that medieval English courts exercised similar powers. He hammered home the point that medieval judicial activism was due to a *fusion*, not a *division*, of governmental powers. It is therefore a misconception to regard the High Court of Parliament as a court of justice which, in addition to its judicial function, exercised legislative powers. The distinction between legislation and adjudication was simply not recognized, thereby allowing the lower courts, as well as Parliament, to exercise both types of powers.

The fusion of powers in governmental institutions spawned not only judicial activism but also what might well be considered its natural outgrowth, judicial review. It is only within the context of McIlwain's interpretation of the character of governmental powers in seventeenth-century England that Sir Edward Coke's famous statement that "in many cases the common law will controul acts of Parliament" ([1610] 1826, p. 375) is reconcilable with his earlier declarations that Parliament's power is absolute (in [1644] 1817, pp. 28–36). The apparent paradox vanishes when one realizes that Coke was not invoking judicial authority against legislative sovereignty, but holding that common law, as higher law, is binding upon the ordinary courts and the High Court of Parliament alike.

Constitutionalism. The crux of McIlwain's concern was the true meaning of constitutionalism. Throughout his writings he championed the principles of medieval constitutionalism, perhaps most effectively in a thin volume which has become a classic, *Constitutionalism: Ancient and Modern* (1940). He defined constitutional government as government limited by law. It embodies the basic distinction, so clearly drawn by Bracton, between *gubernaculum* and *jurisdictio*, between discretion and law. The same concept was echoed by Coke in his famous Case of Proclamations. "It is a grand prerogative of the King," Coke declared, "to make proclamation . . . [yet] the King hath no prerogative but that which the law of the land allows him" ([1656] 1826, p. 299). In a word, within the bounds of higher law, the king is supreme. Bodin, too, developed views of sovereignty that recognized both the absolute power of the sovereign to make ordinary laws and the limitation of the sovereign by fundamental law; McIlwain therefore regarded Bodin as a constitutionalist [*see* BODIN].

Against this concept, McIlwain critically posed the more modern view of constitutionalism, that is, that constitutional government must be founded upon a division of powers which effectively restrains governmental action. This view—which is, in McIlwain's opinion, historically unsound—obscures the distinction between control and limitation. Constitutional government must be strengthened to survive in the modern world, not enfeebled by checks and balances which dissipate its powers and render it ineffectual. While McIlwain believed that responsible and effective constitutional government necessitates the removal of balances, he emphasized that the limits beyond which no government can legally go must be strengthened. In a vein strikingly similar to the legal absolutists' position in the United States today, McIlwain declared, "I frankly want to rely on the earlier, the sounder, yes the medieval principle, that there are some individual rights that even a people's government can never touch" (1917–1937, p. 263). He placed complete reliance upon the judiciary to hold the line.

Viewed from a functional approach, McIlwain's juristic concept of constitutionalism is subject to major criticism. Intent upon demonstrating that the medieval *idea* of supreme, limited government embodied the true principle of constitutionalism, McIlwain was little concerned with the problem of the power relations necessary *actually* to limit government. Clearly, a balance of power within government may hamper governmental responsibility and effectiveness; however, it appears to be equally true that government cannot be effectively limited if it does not reflect a division of power among groups and classes within the community. Indeed, during the Middle Ages constitutionalism was actually operative only in those periods when the king was restrained by the power of the ecclesiastical authorities and the feudal landowners.

Convinced of the merits of the medieval distinction between control and limitation of government, McIlwain was naturally critical of the doctrine of separation of powers and the doctrine of checks and balances, both of which clearly violate this distinction. His argument would have been on firmer ground if he had not ignored the important question of whether government can be effectively limited in the absence of institutionalized controls.

PETER BACHRACH

[*For the historical context of McIlwain's work, see* CONSTITUTIONS AND CONSTITUTIONALISM; *and the biography of* COKE.]

WORKS BY MC ILWAIN

1910 *The High Court of Parliament and Its Supremacy: An Historical Essay on the Boundaries Between Legislation and Adjudication in England.* New Haven: Yale Univ. Press.

(1917–1937) 1939 *Constitutionalism and the Changing World: Collected Papers.* Cambridge Univ. Press.

1918 Introduction. In James I, King of England, *The Political Works of James I.* Cambridge, Mass.: Harvard Univ. Press.

1923 *The American Revolution: A Constitutional Interpretation.* New York: Macmillan. → A paperback edition was published in 1958 by Cornell University Press.

(1932) 1959 *The Growth of Political Thought in the West, From the Greeks to the End of the Middle Ages.* New York: Macmillan.

(1940) 1947 *Constitutionalism: Ancient and Modern.* Rev. ed. Ithaca, N.Y.: Cornell Univ. Press. → A paperback edition was published in 1958.

SUPPLEMENTARY BIBLIOGRAPHY

Coke, Edward (1610) 1826 Dr. Bonham's Case. Volume 4, part 8, pages 355–383 in Great Britain, Courts, *The Reports of Sir Edward Coke.* London: Butterworth.

Coke, Edward (1644) 1817 *The Fourth Part of the Institutes of the Laws of England Concerning the Jurisdiction of the Courts. . . .* London: Clarke. → Published posthumously.

Coke, Edward (1656) 1826 Proclamations. Volume 6, part 12, pages 297–299 in Great Britain, Courts, *The Reports of Sir Edward Coke.* London: Butterworth. → Published posthumously.

MacIVER, ROBERT M.

Sociologist, political theorist, philosopher, university administrator, and humanist, Robert Morrison MacIver was born in Stornoway, Scotland, in 1882. He will be remembered in the history of Western thought for having set forth systematically the fundamental moral, sociological, and philosophical principles of democratic institutions and processes.

Although he sought answers to the perennial theoretical problems of social, political, and moral philosophy that seem to defy ultimate solution, MacIver did not eschew concern for the mitigation of immediate social problems. He attempted to demonstrate by precept that sociological insights can be practicably applied to such pressing problems as labor relations, economic reconstruction, internationalism and peace, intergroup conflicts, religion, academic freedom, social work, juvenile delinquency, and effective utilization of manpower resources. He was vice-chairman of the Canadian War Labor Board in World War I and director of the City of New York Juvenile Delinquency Evaluation Project from 1956 to 1961, and he contributed effectively to the leadership of the Social Science Research Council, the Russell Sage Foundation, and the National Manpower Council.

MacIver's very important contribution to political theory is his view of the state as an agency of human purpose. The state, he argued, is an association established by the community for the regulation of the external conditions of the social order. It is thus an instrumentality within a more inclusive unity. Its essential tasks are to establish order and to respect personality, but it is a creature of society and is bound by the value systems that men live by and for. MacIver revealed the intimate relations between political structures and processes, on the one hand, and human values, on the other.

MacIver's contributions to sociology may be viewed as fourfold. First, he systematically developed and fruitfully exploited an impressive network of fundamental sociological concepts. Second, he helped stem the tide of excessive positivism and raw empiricism in American sociology, especially through his insistence on theory as a methodological tool. The progress of science, he suggested, is the progress of thought. Every scholar should be at the same time a specialist in his own field and a thinker about a larger one (1960, p. 30). Third, he reaffirmed the view of man as a creative human being with subjective hopes, feelings, aspirations, motives, ideals, and values. Life, he insisted, is expansively creative. Finally, he demonstrated that sociological writing can be clear, artistic, and literate. To an area of confusion and literary and intellectual chaos, MacIver brought both clarity of thought and felicity of expression.

Especially important in MacIver's sociological system are his classification of social interests, the distinction between community and association, the concept of social evolution, the harmony theory of the relation between society and individuality, and the differentiation between the institutions concerned with means (civilization) and the world of ends (culture).

The classification of social interests, particularly the distinction between like and common interests, has proved of immense value in clarifying the nature of interindividual relationships, the bases of group organization, and the nature of the social bond. The distinction between community as the matrix of social organization and associations as specific organizations which grow and develop within that matrix is the keystone of MacIver's political doctrines. To sociologists the distinction has proved significant in permitting a more precise definition of the problem of social solidarity and in providing a framework for a deeper understanding of the nature of a pluralistic or multigroup society.

MacIver's reaffirmation of the validity of the concept of social evolution, in the face of the bitter attacks upon it by anthropologists such as Goldenweiser, anticipated by many years the resurgence of interest in and the defense of the concept by Julian Steward and other American anthropologists, as well as by sociologists such as Talcott Parsons (1964), Robert Bellah (1964), S. N. Eisenstadt (1964). Numerous insights have stemmed from MacIver's tracing of a pattern of social change from the primitive type of functionally undifferentiated society, wherein life is of a communal nature, to the more evolved, functionally diverse, and institutionally and associationally differentiated social entity, wherein the basis of individual relationships is less communal and more associational and wherein personality becomes more developed and more expansive.

Important, too, is MacIver's resolution of the timeworn controversy of the relationship between the individual and society. Rejecting both social contract theories and organismic theories, he stressed the fundamental harmony between individuality and society, recognizing, at the same time, that this harmony is far from perfect. Sociality and individuality, he asserted in one of his most successful formulations, develop *pari passu*.

Also significant is the distinction between the world of means (civilization) and the world of ends (culture). The terms are unfortunate because of the more traditional connotations of "civilization" and "culture," but the emphasis on the difference between means and ends provides numerous analytical insights into the processes of social change and a better understanding of the functions of various social institutions. It indicates the areas of social life to which one may properly apply the concept of progress.

MacIver was an inspiring teacher. He had an impact on students at Aberdeen University, the University of Toronto, Barnard College, and Columbia University. At Columbia he held for more than twenty years the chair of Lieber professor of political philosophy and sociology. He served as president of the New School for Social Research in 1963/1964. He received advanced degrees from the universities of Edinburgh and Oxford and numerous honorary degrees.

In his Kurt Lewin memorial award address of 1961, MacIver stated: "In every area of scientific research we have often to depend on degrees of probability, on approximations, on indirect approaches, and such procedures can yield results of considerable importance. There are many ranges between certitude and ignorance, and nearly all we know about human beings and human activities lie within these ranges" (1962*a*, pp. 89–90). He has not been afraid to face "the paradox of knowledge," namely, that "the only things we know as immutable truths are the things we do not understand," while "the only things we understand are mutable and never fully known" (1938, p. 124).

HARRY ALPERT

[*See also* ACADEMIC FREEDOM; CAUSATION; NEIGHBORHOOD; PREJUDICE, *article on* SOCIAL DISCRIMINATION; PUBLIC INTEREST; STATE.]

WORKS BY MAC IVER

(1917) 1935 *Community: A Sociological Study; Being an Attempt to Set Out the Nature and Fundamental Laws of Social Life.* 3d ed. London: Macmillan.

1919 *Labor in the Changing World.* New York: Dutton.

(1921) 1956 *The Elements of Social Science.* 9th ed., rev. London: Methuen.

(1926) 1955 *The Modern State.* Oxford Univ. Press.

1930*a* Jean Bodin. Volume 2, pages 614–616 in *Encyclopaedia of the Social Sciences.* New York: Macmillan.

1930*b* The Trend to Internationalism. Volume 1, pages 172–188 in *Encyclopaedia of the Social Sciences.* New York: Macmillan.

1931*a* *The Contribution of Sociology to Social Work.* New York: Columbia Univ. Press.

1931*b* *Society: Its Structure and Changes.* New York: Long & Smith.

1932 Interests. Volume 8, pages 144–148 in *Encyclopaedia of the Social Sciences.* New York: Macmillan.

1933 Maladjustment. Volume 10, pages 60–63 in *Encyclopaedia of the Social Sciences.* New York: Macmillan.

1934*a* Social Pressures. Volume 12, pages 344–348 in *Encyclopaedia of the Social Sciences.* New York: Macmillan.

1934*b* Sociology. Volume 14, pages 232–246 in *Encyclopaedia of the Social Sciences.* New York: Macmillan.

1935 Graham Wallas. Volume 15, pages 326–327 in *Encyclopaedia of the Social Sciences.* New York: Macmillan.

1937 *Society: A Textbook of Sociology.* New York: Farrar & Rinehart. → A rewriting of MacIver 1931*b*.

1938 The Social Sciences. Pages 121–140 in *On Going to College: A Symposium.* New York: Oxford Univ. Press.

1939 *Leviathan and the People.* University: Louisiana State Univ. Press.

1942 *Social Causation.* Boston: Ginn. → A paperback edition was published in 1964 by Harper.

(1947) 1961 *The Web of Government.* New York: Macmillan.

1948 *The More Perfect Union: A Program for the Control of Inter-group Discrimination in the United States.* New York: Macmillan.

(1949) 1961 MACIVER, ROBERT M.; and PAGE, CHARLES H. *Society: An Introductory Analysis.* New York: Holt. → Book 3 (Chapters 22–29) is an unusually extensive treatment of social change in a general textbook.

1952 *Democracy and the Economic Challenge.* New York: Knopf.

1955*a* *Academic Freedom in Our Time.* New York: Columbia Univ. Press.

1955*b* *The Pursuit of Happiness: A Philosophy for Modern Living.* New York: Simon & Schuster.

1960 *Life: Its Dimensions and Its Bounds.* New York: Harper.

1962*a* Disturbed Youth and the Agencies. *Journal of Social Issues* 18, no. 2:88–96.

1962*b* *The Challenge of the Passing Years: My Encounter With Time.* New York: Simon & Schuster. → A paperback edition was published in 1963 by Pocket Books.

1964 *Power Transformed.* New York: Macmillan.

1966 *The Prevention and Control of Delinquency: A Strategic Approach.* New York: Atherton.

SUPPLEMENTARY BIBLIOGRAPHY

ALPERT, HARRY (editor) 1953 *Robert M. MacIver: Teacher and Sociologist.* Northampton, Mass.: Metcalf Printing and Publishing Company. → An evaluation by eight former students.

ALPERT, HARRY (1954) 1964 Robert M. MacIver's Contributions to Sociological Theory. Pages 286–292 in Morroe Berger, T. Abel, and C. H. Page (editors), *Freedom and Control in Modern Society.* New York: Octagon Books.

BELLAH, ROBERT N. 1964 Religious Evolution. *American Sociological Review* 29:358–374.

COLUMBIA UNIVERSITY, COMMISSION ON ECONOMIC RECONSTRUCTION 1934 *Economic Reconstruction: Report.* Robert M. MacIver, Chairman. New York: Columbia Univ. Press.

EISENSTADT, S. N. 1964 Social Change, Differentiation and Evolution. *American Sociological Review* 29:375–386.

PARSONS, TALCOTT 1964 Evolutionary Universals in Society. *American Sociological Review* 29:339–357.

SPITZ, DAVID (1954) 1964 Robert M. MacIver's Contributions to Political Theory. Pages 293–313 in Morroe Berger, T. Abel, and C. H. Page (editors), *Freedom and Control in Modern Society.* New York: Octagon Books.

MACKINDER, HALFORD

Sir Halford John Mackinder (1861–1947) was both an academic geographer and a practicing politician. After reading physical science and modern history at Oxford, he served that university's pioneer extension scheme for adult education. He was deeply convinced of the value of this missionary effort to spread knowledge more widely in England. He lectured up and down the country between 1885 and 1893 on what he called "the new geography." He was a natural orator, and he preached his geographical gospel with zeal and fervor.

At that time the subject of geography did not occupy a high place in British or American education; it had little or no prestige in the universities. The fame of Mackinder's Oxford extension lectures reached the Royal Geographical Society of London. In January 1887 he was invited to lecture to the society on the scope and methods of geography. In the discussion after the lecture he defined geography as "the science of distribution, the science, that is, which traces the arrangement of things in general on the earth's surface" (1887, p. 160) and urged that physical and political geography be combined. An examination of the lecture shows that many notions that are now commonplace in geographical teaching were first enunciated by Mackinder.

Mackinder had a special mission for geography that still has considerable importance: in the 1887 lecture he said that "one of the greatest of all gaps lies between the natural sciences and the study of humanity. It is the duty of the geographer to build one bridge over an abyss which in the opinion of many is upsetting the equilibrium of our culture" (p. 145). In the same year that he gave this lecture Mackinder was appointed to a readership in geography at Oxford; he claimed that he was the first Oxford reader in geography since Hakluyt, the Elizabethan. As a result of Mackinder's efforts, the school of geography was established at Oxford in 1899; this was the first British university department of geography.

The idea of the region was an implicit part of Mackinder's argument for geography as an academic discipline. At Oxford one of his regular annual courses was always concerned with the analysis of a particular region. His *Britain and the British Seas* (1902) is one of the few classics of modern geographical literature. This book was the first of a series planned by Mackinder to present "a picture of the physical features and condition of a great natural region, and to trace their influence upon human societies" (1902, p. 7). By their efforts at Oxford both Mackinder and his successor, A. J. Herbertson, placed the study of regions in the forefront of geographical work. Mackinder also taught that geography is a unity which should not be split into fragments. These ideas about the unity of geography as a subject and the necessity for basing it on integrated studies of regions are the foundations upon which modern British academic geography has been built.

In January 1904 Mackinder read a paper entitled "The Geographical Pivot of History" to the Royal Geographical Society. He was then still teaching at Oxford but had just been elected director of the London School of Economics. Mackinder described a central part of Eurasia as "the pivot area," a term he later changed to "heartland." In his lecture he laid down two principles. The first was that since the modern improvement of steam navigation, the world had become one and, in so doing, had also become one closed political system. The second and main point of his argument concerned the importance to the world of the modern expansion of Russia. He asserted that "the pivot region of the world's politics" is "that area of Euro-Asia which is inaccessible to ships," and is controlled by Russia (1904, p. 434). If the world is regarded as a unit, he argued, combinations of power "are likely to rotate round the pivot state, which is always likely to be great, but with limited mobility as compared with the surrounding marginal and insular powers" (pp. 436–437). In the discussion after the lecture Mackinder bluntly asserted that the development for the first time in recorded history of a great stationary population in the steppes constituted a revolution in the world (p. 442). In 1919 Mackinder expanded his paper into a book, *Democratic Ideals and Reality*, which was described by J. Russell Smith as "a tract addressed to the Peace Conference at Versailles" (1945, p. 148). It contains the famous warning: "When our Statesmen [at Versailles] are in conversation with the defeated enemy, some airy cherub should whisper to them from time to time saying: 'Who rules East Europe commands the Heartland: Who rules the Heartland commands the World-Island: Who rules the World-Island commands the World" ([1919] 1942, p. 150).

Between the two world wars Mackinder's theory of the heartland received little attention in the English-speaking world; but it was closely examined in Germany, where it became a basic idea among the students of geopolitics (*Zeitschrift für Geopolitik, passim*). General Karl Haushofer (1937) described Mackinder's 1904 paper as the greatest of all geographical world views. During World War II, Mackinder's idea of the heartland received considerable attention in both Britain and America. In 1943 Mackinder, then 82 years of age, restated his heartland theory, with modifications, in an article in *Foreign Affairs*. He believed that his concept of the heartland was even more valid than it had been forty years earlier, and he boldly asserted that ". . . if the Soviet Union emerges from this war as conqueror of Germany, she must rank as the greatest land Power on the Globe. Moreover, she will be the Power in the strategically strongest defensive position. The Heartland is the greatest natural fortress on earth. For the first time in history it is manned by a garrison sufficient both in number and quality" (1943, p. 601).

Mackinder's writings on land power can be compared with those of Mahan on the influence of sea power [*see the biography of* MAHAN]. It has been suggested that modern air power destroyed the validity of the arguments of both Mahan and Mackinder. But Mackinder in 1919, and again in 1943, used the coming of air power to support his older thesis. He also stated his conviction that the conquest of the air gave the world's unity a new significance for all mankind. W. Gordon East, in a reasoned commentary of Mackinder's theories in the light of more recent events, similarly insisted that Mackinder's "geopolitical thinking is still relevant to the task of winning the peace" (1950, p. 93).

Mackinder's interest in politics led him to become a practicing politician, and he was a member of Parliament from 1910 to 1922. He also served as British high commissioner for South Russia in 1919–1920. But his achievements in politics are not as memorable as his pioneer research in the field of applied geography. He created modern British geography as a university subject. He can be regarded as a founder of several of its branches, especially that of political geography, but he steadfastly believed in the unity of the subject as a whole. He wanted geography to enlighten the practical affairs of daily life. In his own words, "geography must underlie the strategy of peace if you would not have it subserve the strategy of war" (1931, p. 335).

EDMUND W. GILBERT

[*See also* GEOGRAPHY, *article on* POLITICAL GEOGRAPHY.]

WORKS BY MACKINDER

1887 On the Scope and Methods of Geography. Royal Geographical Society, *Proceedings* 9:141–174. → Includes 14 pages of discussion.

(1902) 1930 *Britain and the British Seas*. 2d ed. Oxford: Clarendon.

1904 The Geographical Pivot of History. *Geographical Journal* 23:421–444. → Includes seven pages of discussion.

(1919) 1942 *Democratic Ideals and Reality: A Study in the Politics of Reconstruction*. London: Constable; New York: Holt.

1931 The Human Habitat. *Scottish Geographical Magazine* 47:321–335.

1935 Progress of Geography in the Field and in the Study During the Reign of His Majesty King George the Fifth. *Geographical Journal* 86:1–12.

1943 The Round World and the Winning of the Peace. *Foreign Affairs* 21:595–605.

SUPPLEMENTARY BIBLIOGRAPHY

EAST, W. GORDON 1950 How Strong Is the Heartland? *Foreign Affairs* 29:78–93.

GILBERT, EDMUND W. 1951 Seven Lamps of Geography: An Appreciation of the Teaching of Sir Halford J. Mackinder. *Geography* 36:21–43. → Contains a bibliography.

GILBERT, EDMUND W. 1961 *Sir Halford Mackinder, 1861–1947: An Appreciation of His Life and Work*. London: Bell.

HAUSHOFER, KARL 1937 *Weltmeere und Weltmächte*. Berlin: Zeitgeschichte Verlag.

SMITH, J. RUSSELL 1945 Heartland, Grassland, and Farmland. Pages 148–160 in Hans W. Weigert and Vilhjalmur Stefansson (editors), *Compass of the World: A Symposium on Political Geography.* New York: Macmillan.

UNSTEAD, J. F. 1949 H. J. Mackinder and the New Geography. *Geographical Journal* 113:47–57.

McLENNAN, JOHN FERGUSON

John Ferguson McLennan (1827–1881), Scottish lawyer and theorist of social evolution, was born in Inverness and died in Hayes Common in Kent. He was educated at King's College, Aberdeen, graduating with distinction in 1849. He went on to Cambridge, where he stayed until 1855 without taking a degree. In 1857 he was called to the Scottish bar, and in 1871 he was made parliamentary draughtsman for Scotland. In 1874 Aberdeen University conferred on him an honorary doctor of laws degree. McLennan's later life was marred by continual ill health, and much of his work was published posthumously, edited first by his brother Donald and then by W. Robertson Smith. After these two had died, the remaining manuscripts were edited by McLennan's widow, Eleanora, and a friend, Arthur Platt.

McLennan's legal studies led him to an interest in "symbols," i.e., survivals in contemporary cultures of previous legal and customary behavior. He noted, for example, that even as late as the nineteenth century Scottish law was replete with feudal concepts. Another of the striking survivals that McLennan described and elaborated upon was the custom of simulated bride capture: as it occurred in ancient Rome, he suggested, it was a symbol of the actual practice of earlier times.

His attempt to account for such survivals led to a theory of the evolution of social forms. In this context he proposed a sequence of familial development in which matrilineal kinship preceded patrilineal. He suggested this sequence independently of J. J. Bachofen, who first proposed it. He defended his theories, sometimes acrimoniously, against the views of Maine, Morgan, Lubbock, Spencer, and even of Mr. Gladstone. Because McLennan saw contemporary primitive peoples as representing various stages of arrested social development, he believed that historical reconstruction consists in noting trait survivals and discovering functional explanations for them. Thus, when customs appeared to be nonfunctional, he attempted to deduce the earlier context in which they had arisen and in which they *had* been functional. When, for example, the levirate—wherein a man inherits his brother's widow—was found to coexist with polyandry in any society, one could conclude that polyandry was a necessary precondition for the levirate. McLennan developed his entire scheme of social evolution on this principle.

McLennan is chiefly remembered for his invention of the terms *exogamy* and *endogamy*, and for his analysis of totemism. These concepts emerged from his general scheme of evolution, which ran as follows: Originally, tribes were promiscuous, children being affiliated with the social group rather than with their biological parents. Harsh conditions of existence led to female infanticide. Because of the resulting sex imbalance, and also because these early tribes were always warring, capture came to be the prevailing method of obtaining wives. The corollary of bride capture was exogamy, which obliged men to seek marriage partners outside of their own social group. Such marriages were of the archaic polyandrous type, where no regulated relationship existed among the male partners of one woman. Since paternity could not be biologically determined, kinship was traced through females only.

According to McLennan's scheme, the capture of foreign women and matrilineal kinship furthered the recognition of subtribal divisions. These new social units continued to be exogamous, while for the larger tribal group, endogamy became possible. It should be noted that McLennan never clarified the identity of the social units involved; Morgan, in rebuttal of McLennan, insisted that the subtribal units were clans. Nevertheless, McLennan's conception of this early stage of polyandry did take cognizance of what later ethnologists have called local exogamy and the rules of residence attending upon marriage.

As the archaic form of polyandry was transformed into fraternal polyandry, the levirate became common practice. Kinship could then be established through males, and the way was paved for monogamy and polygyny. The thread of functional reasoning runs through all of this deductive reconstruction, but the ethnographic information on which McLennan based his evolutionary scheme was inadequate and resulted, therefore, in incorrect deductions. Moreover, the assumption of universal stages of social evolution based on no criteria other than kinship rendered his arguments circular. It is fair to say that McLennan was not unique in his faults, which stemmed not so much from his own inadequacies as from the currently accepted mode of evolutionary analysis. His critics were guilty of the same errors.

Of his debates with these critics, the only one

that retains its significance is that with Morgan, on the meaning of kinship terms. McLennan (1876) argued—against the views of Morgan in his *Systems of Consanguinity and Affinity of the Human Family* (1871)—that kinship terms are not indicative of consanguineous relationships but express "degrees of respect" based on "age and station." This point—that the terms refer to statuses and not to blood relationships—is now accepted; but anthropologists are still divided into those who follow Morgan and attach great significance to terminology and those who, perhaps unwittingly, follow McLennan in thinking that its importance is overrated.

McLennan's ideas concerning totemism were also part of his parallelist emphasis. He saw the totemic symbols attached to kinship groups as survivals of an earlier, localized worship of fetishes, and the worship of animals, plants, and eventually, of anthropomorphic gods was seen in terms of survivals derived from totemism. Exogamy caused totemic identifications to be dispersed, because they were transmitted through the female line. According to McLennan, totems became gods—often associated with a particular locality—when patrilineal descent groups were formed. His idea of totemism as the most primitive form of religion had wide influence. It is echoed in the work of Freud and Durkheim, and it directly influenced the thinking of Frazer (1887), Jevons (1896), and Robertson Smith (1885; 1889). Robertson Smith, a close friend and collaborator, interpreted the religious and social evolution of the Semitic peoples in accordance with McLennan's theories. Tylor (1899) was one of the first of many to criticize McLennan's totemic theories of the origins of religion. He insisted that totemism is of "far greater importance in sociology than religion, connected as it is with the alliance between clans which ensues from the law of exogamy." This, together with Tylor's opinion that totemism is an expression of man's tendency to classify the universe, represents the most influential modern view (see Lévi-Strauss 1962).

J. R. Fox

[*For the historical context of McLennan's work, see* KINSHIP; *and the biographies of* BACHOFEN; LUBBOCK; MAINE; MORGAN, LEWIS HENRY; SPENCER; TYLOR. *For discussion of the subsequent development of his ideas, see the biographies of* DURKHEIM; FRAZER; FREUD; SMITH, WILLIAM ROBERTSON; WESTERMARCK.]

WORKS BY MC LENNAN

1857 Law. Volume 13, pages 253–279 in *Encyclopaedia Britannica*. 8th ed. Edinburgh: Black.

1865 *Primitive Marriage: An Inquiry Into the Origin of the Form of Capture in Marriage Ceremonies*. Edinburgh: Black.

(1865–1876) 1886 *Studies in Ancient History*. New York: Macmillan. → Includes McLennan 1865, 1866*b*; and 1876.

1866*a* Bride Catching. *Argosy* 2:31–42.

1866*b* Kinship in Ancient Greece. *Fortnightly Review* 4:569–588, 682–691.

1867 *Memoir of Thomas Drummond. . . .* Edinburgh: Edmonston & Douglas.

1868 Totem. Supplement, pages 753–754 in *Chamber's Encyclopedia*. London: Chambers.

1869–1870 The Worship of Animals and Plants. *Fortnightly Review* New Series 4:407–427, 562–582; 7: 194–216.

(1876) 1886 Classificatory System of Relationship. Pages 247–315 in John Ferguson McLennan, *Studies in Ancient History*. New York: Macmillan.

1877*a* Exogamy and Endogamy. *Fortnightly Review* New Series 21:884–895. → A rejoinder by Herbert Spencer appears on pages 895–902.

1877*b* The Levirate and Polyandry. *Fortnightly Review* New Series 21:694–707.

1885 *The Patriarchal Theory*. Edited and completed by Donald McLennan. London: Macmillan. → Published posthumously.

1896 *Studies in Ancient History: Second Series*. Edited and completed by Eleanora A. McLennan and A. Platt. London: Macmillan. → Published posthumously.

SUPPLEMENTARY BIBLIOGRAPHY

BACHOFEN, JOHANN J. (1861) 1948 *Das Mutterrecht*. 2 vols. Basel: Schwabe.

DURKHEIM, ÉMILE (1912) 1954 *The Elementary Forms of the Religious Life*. London: Allen & Unwin; New York: Macmillian. → First published as *Les formes élémentaires de la vie religieuse, le système totémique en Australie*. A paperback edition was published in 1961 by Collier.

FRAZER, JAMES G. (1887) 1910 *Totemism and Exogamy*. 4 vols. London: Macmillan. → See especially "Totemism" in Volume 1, pages 1–87.

FREUD, SIGMUND (1913) 1959 Totem and Taboo. Volume 13, pages ix–162 in *The Standard Edition of the Complete Psychological Works of Sigmund Freud*. London: Hogarth; New York: Macmillan. → First published in German.

JEVONS, FRANK B. (1896) 1914 *An Introduction to the History of Religion*. 6th ed. London: Methuen.

LEACH, EDMUND R. 1961 *Rethinking Anthropology*. London School of Economics and Political Science Monographs on Social Anthropology, No. 22. London: Athlone. → See especially Chapter 1.

LÉVI-STRAUSS, CLAUDE (1962) 1963 *Totemism*. Boston: Beacon. → First published as *Le totémisme aujourd'hui*.

LOWIE, ROBERT H. 1937 *The History of Ethnological Theory*. New York: Farrar & Rinehart. → See especially Chapter 5.

LUBBOCK, JOHN (1870) 1912 *The Origin of Civilization and the Primitive Condition of Man: Mental and Social Conditions of Savages*. 7th ed. New York: Longmans. → Chapter 3 is devoted almost entirely to McLennan's theories.

MAINE, HENRY SUMNER (1861) 1960 *Ancient Law: Its Connection With the Early History of Society, and Its Relations to Modern Ideas*. Rev. ed. New York: Dutton; London and Toronto: Dent. → A paperback edition was published in 1963 by Beacon.

Maine, Henry Sumner (1875) 1893 *Lectures on the Early History of Institutions.* 6th ed. London: Murray.

Morgan, Lewis H. 1871 *Systems of Consanguinity and Affinity of the Human Family.* Smithsonian Contributions to Knowledge, Vol. 17, art. 2, Publication No. 218. Washington: Smithsonian Institution.

Morgan, Lewis H. (1877) 1964 *Ancient Society.* Cambridge, Mass.: Belknap. → A long note to Chapter 6 deals with McLennan.

Smith, William Robertson (1885) 1903 *Kinship and Marriage in Early Arabia.* New ed. London: Black.

Smith, William Robertson (1889) 1959 *The Religion of the Semites.* New York: Meridian. → First published as *Lectures on the Religion of the Semites.*

Spencer, Herbert (1876) 1925 *The Principles of Sociology.* New York: Appleton. → Volume 1, Part 3, "Domestic Institutions," is a long dialogue with McLennan.

Tylor, Edward B. 1899 Remarks on Totemism, With Especial Reference to Some Modern Theories Respecting It. *Journal of the Royal Anthropological Institute of Great Britain and Ireland* 28:138–148.

Westermarck, Edward A. (1889) 1922 *The History of Human Marriage.* 5th ed., rev. New York: Allerton. → Criticizes McLennan's notion of "primitive promiscuity."

MACROECONOMICS

See Income and employment theory; Interest; Liquidity preference; Money.

MADISON, JAMES

James Madison (1751–1836), fourth president of the United States, from 1809 to 1817, was the principal framer of the constitution of 1787. It was Madison who made the first preliminary move toward the drafting of the constitution by sponsoring the Annapolis Convention of 1786. The constitution embodied his conviction that liberty and the rights of property could best be harmonized and secured in a federal republic, with powers divided between subordinate states and a supreme federal government, each with internal checks and balances to prevent the rise of arbitrary power. According to Madison, republican government required that representatives be elected directly (or, perhaps, in one house, indirectly) by the great body of the people; otherwise the republic would degenerate into an aristocracy or an oligarchy. Government so organized, he believed (relying to some extent on Hume), would be progressively safer to liberty and property as the territorial area was enlarged, since diversity of regional interests and of population would prevent any national majority—whether moved by a common property interest, by political or religious passion, or swayed by an ambitious leader—from gaining power and oppressing the minority. He believed that the acquisition and protection of property is the ruling force in political faction and that the need to protect liberty and restrain power is a pressing one. These concepts, which he presented to the Philadelphia Convention of 1787, persuaded delegates fearful of the excesses of democracy to place their trust in democratic self-government. His voluminous notes of debates furnish the principal record of the convention.

In Congress Madison introduced the first ten amendments to the constitution, designed to enlarge its libertarian provisions into a bill of rights. In presenting these amendments he placed heaviest emphasis on freedom of religion, speech, and press. The religious guarantee was based on his modification of the 1776 Virginia Declaration of Rights, which discarded "toleration" and affirmed absolute rights of conscience, and on his successful "Memorial and Remonstrance Against Religious Assessments" (1785) for support of teachers of religion; such assessments, he asserted, were tantamount to an establishment of religion. His expectation that "independent tribunals of justice" would form "an impenetrable bulwark" against every encroachment on constitutional liberties was dashed by the enactment and savage enforcement of the Sedition Act of 1798. Consequently he wrote the Virginia Resolutions of 1798, which asserted the right of the states, in case of a deliberate and dangerous violation of the federal compact, to interpose collectively "for arresting the progress of the evil." Widespread interpretation of this as an assertion of the right to nullify acts of Congress led to his "Report on the Resolutions" (1799–1800), likewise adopted by the Virginia legislature, which defined interposition as an exertion of influence within the terms of the constitution but denied interposition any judicial force. The "Report" was notable for its assertion that freedom of the press exempted the press from punishment for licentiousness and its denial that the federal government had power to punish crimes under the common law of England.

In the famous *Federalist* No. 10, Madison systematized his earlier discussions of political faction. By that term he did not refer to political parties of the modern type but to the united activities of a majority or minority of the people "actuated by some common impulse of passion, or of interest, adverse to the rights of other citizens, or to the permanent and aggregate interests of the community" (Hamilton, Madison & Jay [1787–1788] 1961, p. 57). The unsteadiness and injustice of state governments, resulting from a factious spirit, had led to the breakdown of public trust and increasing alarm for private rights. The latent causes of faction, he believed, lie in the nature of man, especially men's varying capacities for acquiring property and its consequent unequal distribution. Liberty feeds faction, but limiting liberty is a greater evil than faction. The remedy, therefore, lies in controlling the effects of passion through checks and divisions of governments.

Madison had a deterministic view of human conduct and was essentially a pragmatist, committed to no particular school of political thought but intensely devoted to preserving the Union, maintaining a broadly based republican government, and protecting human rights. In the furtherance of national policy, his tendency was to rely upon coercive measures. In the first Congress, he sponsored a moderate protective tariff (though generally preferring free trade), advocated counterdiscrimination against British navigation acts injurious to American shipping, and worked unofficially to help repel senatorial encroachments on the president's powers. Madison and Hamilton were equally committed to full payment of depreciated Revolutionary War claims, but Madison resisted Hamilton's policy of full payment to speculators who purchased claims, urging that a share should go to the original holders, mostly impoverished veterans. This initiated the political alignment that developed into Hamiltonian federalism and Jeffersonian democracy. Hamilton's sweeping interpretation of the power to spend for the general welfare likewise prevailed over Madison's attempt to limit spending to subjects covered by the other enumerated powers—a view which did not prevent him, as president, from inaugurating government distribution of smallpox vaccine.

Jay's 1794 treaty with England blocked Madison's counterdiscrimination policy, but maritime restrictions continued and the Napoleonic Wars provoked wholesale seizures of American ships by both belligerents. In striking contrast with President Jefferson's defensive shipping embargo, Madison in his first month as president made identical offers to England and France: that if the power addressed would cease its aggressions against American commerce, and the other continued them, he would ask Congress to declare war against the continuing offender. Without knowing of these offers, Congress in effect gave them legal force by the Macon Bill No. 2 of 1810, leading to the War of 1812 with England.

Except during his student days at Princeton and the major portion of his years in public office, Madison spent his entire life on his extensive estate, Montpelier, in the Virginia Piedmont. He pioneered in modern scientific agriculture and warned of the future dangers from world-wide overpopulation and man's upsetting of the balance of nature. Although strongly opposed to slavery, he lived by its fruits. The apparent happiness of his slaves, he told Harriet Martineau, was an illusion, concealing the degradation inherent in the institution. Believing that white Americans would permanently deny rights to which freedmen were entitled, he advocated the freeing of all slaves through government purchase—to be financed by western land sales—and voluntary resettlement in Liberia and other separate communities. The final years of his life were devoted to his work as rector of the University of Virginia and to preparing polemical articles combating South Carolina's nullification doctrine.

IRVING BRANT

[*See also* REPRESENTATION, *article on* REPRESENTATIONAL SYSTEMS; *and the biographies of* HAMILTON *and* JEFFERSON.]

WORKS BY MADISON

(1751–1836) 1962– *Papers*. Edited by William T. Hutchinson and William M. E. Rachal. Univ. of Chicago Press. → The first of a projected series of volumes.

(1769–1836) 1900–1910 *The Writings of James Madison, Comprising His Public Papers and His Private Correspondence, . . .* 9 vols. Edited by Gaillard Hunt. New York: Putnam.

(1785) 1904 Memorial and Remonstrance Against Religious Assessments. Pages 183–191 in James Madison, *The Writings of James Madison, Comprising His Public Papers and His Private Correspondence, . . .* Volume 2: 1783–1787. New York: Putnam.

(1787–1788) 1961 HAMILTON, ALEXANDER; MADISON, JAMES; and JAY, JOHN *The Federalist*. Edited with introduction and notes by Jacob E. Cooke. Middletown, Conn.: Wesleyan Univ. Press. → See also the 1961 John Harvard Library edition, under the editorship of Benjamin F. Wright and Irving Brant, for assignment of authorship.

(1789) 1904 June 8: Amendments to the Constitution. Pages 370–389 in James Madison, *The Writings of James Madison, Comprising His Public Papers and His Private Correspondence, . . .* Volume 5: 1787–1790. New York: Putnam.

(1799–1800) 1906 Report on the Resolutions. Pages 341–406 in James Madison, *The Writings of James Madison, Comprising His Public Papers and His Private Correspondence, . . .* Volume 6: 1790–1802. New York: Putnam.

1966 *Notes of Debates in the Federal Convention of 1787*. With an introduction by Adrienne Koch. Athens: Ohio Univ. Press.

SUPPLEMENTARY BIBLIOGRAPHY

BRANT, IRVING 1941–1961 *James Madison*. 6 vols. Indianapolis, Ind.: Bobbs-Merrill. → Volume 1: *The Virginia Revolutionist*. Volume 2: *The Nationalist:*

1780–1787. Volume 3: *Father of the Constitution: 1787–1800.* Volume 4: *Secretary of State: 1800–1809.* Volume 5: *The President: 1809–1812.* Volume 6: *Commander in Chief: 1812–1836.*

BRANT, IRVING 1961 Settling the Authorship of *The Federalist. American Historical Review* 67:71–75.

BURNS, EDWARD M. 1938 *James Madison: Philosopher of the Constitution.* Studies in History, Vol. 1. New Brunswick, N.J.: Rutgers Univ. Press.

MOSTELLER, FREDERICK; and WALLACE, DAVID L. 1963 Inference in an Authorship Problem: A Comparative Study of Discrimination Methods Applied to the Authorship of the Disputed Federalist Papers. *Journal of the American Statistical Association* 58:275–309.

U.S. CONSTITUTIONAL CONVENTION, *1787* (1911) 1937 *The Records of the Federal Convention of 1787.* 4 vols., rev. ed. Edited by Max Farrand. New Haven: Yale Univ. Press.

MAGIC

The article under this heading discusses witchcraft and sorcery as well as magic. Related material will be found under POLLUTION; RITUAL; *and in the articles mentioned in the guide to* RELIGION. *The biographies of* DURKHEIM; FRAZER; KLUCKHOHN; MALINOWSKI; MAUSS; *and* NADEL *should also be consulted.*

The relation of magic to religion and to science provided fuel for early anthropological speculation. All students of primitive religion have had to face the question in some form or other. It has proved difficult to circumscribe the subject of magic with any degree of precision. If, as is often the case, the subjects of *mana*, taboo, totemism, and ritual are included, the discussion of magic easily dissolves into comparative religion.

In recent years, apart from a notable work on taboo (Steiner 1956), there has been a lack of interest in magic, although the work of Lévi-Strauss on primitive thought (1962; 1964) promises to revive discussion. In the past 30 years anthropologists have concentrated on describing and analyzing the moral and religious ideas and institutions of particular peoples in great detail. In these studies the great philosophical issues of magic, science, and religion, which exercised thinkers in the nineteenth and early twentieth centuries, have receded into the background. There has been great interest in specific institutions, such as sorcery and witchcraft, which may be regarded as the social dimensions of magic. Although theoretical formulations in these fields have not kept pace with the greatly increased area of knowledge, such contributions as those of Evans-Pritchard (1937), Kluckhohn (1944), and Nadel (1952) have had important repercussions.

In historical terms, there can be seen a development from attempts to single out isolated and exotic instances of belief or practice in order to buttress a highly abstract philosophical position (such as Frazer's work) to an effort to place all magical acts in their proper context within the totality of moral and religious ideas, institutions, and practices of a culture.

For nineteenth-century thinkers like Tylor (1871), McLennan (1865–1876), Spencer (1876–1896), and Lang (1901), the question of greatest interest was the origins of magic as related to the origins of religion. Their works were attempts to understand how early man was led in the direction of superstition by faulty observation and reasoning. This line of inquiry led to Lévy-Bruhl's famous work on primitive mentality (1910). Frazer (1890) was also working on evolutionary premises. Theories regarding the evolution of religion or science from magic are no longer in vogue, but Frazer's work will remain one of the most sustained efforts to penetrate the difficulties of the subject. Frazer regarded magic as an earlier, primitive form of both religion and science. He observed rightly that primitive practice is often based on excellent observation of natural phenomena and involves a theory of causality. He therefore felt that there was a basic similarity between magic and science. The only difference was that for a variety of reasons the mistaken assumptions and erroneous conclusions of magic were veiled from the observer and did not shake his beliefs.

The basic principles of magic, according to Frazer, were two: the law of similarity and the law of contagion. According to the first principle, like produces like, so that sticking pins into a doll is like sticking arrows into the enemy; and according to the law of contagion, prolonged or intimate contact produces identity, so that the enemy's nail parings and hair can be treated as if they represented him.

Evans-Pritchard (1933) has remarked that if Frazer had observed what the natives did rather than what they thought, he would have been less inclined to draw similarities between scientists and witch doctors. He would also have seen the difference between scientific methods and traditional arts.

While anthropologists were skeptical about the attempt to reduce the exuberant complexity of primitive ritual and magic to two principles of thought, the initial impact of Frazer's ideas was considerable, especially beyond the circles of academic anthropology. In retrospect, Frazer's work is generally regarded as having one crippling difficulty: similar customs and practices from all cultures of the world were collected and examined under common labels. Since the labels and their relations exemplified Frazer's own thinking on the subject, the data merely filled the preconceived receptacles and did not add to the analysis of the phenomena in any one culture (Leach 1961).

Since Frazer, every major writer on primitive religion has struggled with "magic," and every major monograph has provided more material on this elusive subject. Durkheim (1912), for instance, distinguished magic and religion on the assumption that religion presupposed a church or a *congregation*, while the magician worked alone and merely had a *clientele*.

Malinowski wrote in a different vein. In his article "Magic, Science and Religion" (1925), he argued, in Frazerian terms, for the necessity of distinguishing among these fields, but on a nonevolutionary basis. Magic, he suggested, is related to anxiety. In ordinary, everyday economic pursuits there is no magic. But when the outcome of the enterprise is uncertain and there is danger involved, the native has recourse to magic. Moreover, magic is directed to specific ends and differs from religion in not being concerned with the worship of spiritual beings.

As Malinowski pointed out, the natives of the Trobriand Islands are perfectly able to distinguish the sphere of magic from that of technology. Thus, although every step of the cultivation process is marked by magical rites, there is no question of giving up one's own efforts to cultivate gardens and attempting to grow the food by magic alone. On the contrary, they know that even after having spent their best efforts on cultivation, some unpredictable act of nature may destroy their crops. Thus, argued Malinowski, the native has his "scientific technology" clearly distinguished from the sphere of magic. It is against the unpredictable that magic is utilized. Natives would consider it laughable to do otherwise.

This pragmatic point of view expressed by Malinowski has had many supporters. (We may observe also that the relation which he posits between anxiety and ritual harks back to psychoanalytic theory.) But the utilitarian basis of these theories has recently been severely questioned. It has become clear that the facts of ethnography do not fall into place as neatly as Malinowski had thought. Some features of magic, of Australian increase ceremonies, or of totemism don't make sense in simple utilitarian terms. Malinowski wrote, for instance, that ". . . food is the primary link between the primitive and providence. . . . The road from the wilderness to the savage's belly and consequently to his mind is very short" ([1925] 1948, pp. 26–27). But in the magical repertoire of aboriginal Australians there are "increase ceremonies" for all kinds of nonutilitarian categories—for instance, mosquitoes—and simple pragmatic explanations for such complicated facts would be naive.

Malinowski had specifically dismissed the views of Mauss, who had argued (see Lévi-Strauss 1950) that magic is a special application of the forces of sacred powers, like *mana*, some conception of which is found in every society. For Mauss, *mana* was, in fact, a connection between religion and magic. Magic comes from religion into the realm of everyday life, where its end is action.

Malinowski, in denying the role of *mana*, attempted to place the emphasis again on pragmatic functions. He asked, ". . . what is *mana*, this impersonal force of magic supposed to dominate all forms of early belief? Is it a fundamental idea, an innate category of the primitive mind, or can it be explained by still simpler and more fundamental elements of human psychology . . . ?" These fundamental elements turn out to be merely "a blend of utilitarian anxiety about the most necessary objects of his surroundings. . . . With our knowledge of what could be called the totemic attitude of mind, primitive religion is seen to be nearer to reality and to the immediate practical life interests of the savage" ([1925] 1948, pp. 4–5).

Lévi-Strauss (1950) upholds Mauss and is concerned to redress the balance in favor of an argument that the inner logic of religious ideas is not utilitarian and that their logic has to be understood in their own terms. Features of primitive belief must be examined not by imputing our materialist viewpoint to the idealized native but in terms of the position of such ideas and symbols in the total tapestry of customary belief and practice. Thus, Lévi-Strauss agrees with Mauss and notes that the concept of *mana* is truly like a common denominator for concepts of the "sacred" and is, indeed, intimately related to magic. The conclusion here is that to understand magic, we must understand the refractions of the concept of the sacred in the culture.

Magic, then, is not a uniform class of practices and beliefs which can be immediately discerned in every society. On the contrary, it is best regarded as an aspect of religious belief and practice that takes its special force from the antecedent and deeply rooted recognition in many societies of supernatural or divine power. The place given to the practical use of such powers for everyday purposes such as healing or assuring luck and fertility—which in very general terms we may refer to as magic—differs from society to society.

Witchcraft and sorcery also involve the belief in supernatural powers, and sorcery in particular may be regarded as a specialized branch of offensive magic. What is said about magic and religion holds true for witchcraft and sorcery as well: it is imperative to place these beliefs and practices within the context of the total supernatural belief system of the culture in question. It will then be feasible to raise the question of whether there is logic in this madness and to what extent the different parts of the supernatural system show structure, division of labor, and specialization of function.

Sorcery and witchcraft

The terms "sorcery" and "witchcraft" refer to practices and supernatural beings which are part and parcel of the European Christian tradition. Their use in anthropology involves an essential widening of their meaning to cover a great many beliefs and practices from other cultures which have proved difficult to classify. The conceptual categories involved in such supernatural beings and practices are sometimes so unique to particular peoples that the translation of concepts from one cultural idiom into another becomes a difficulty of the first magnitude. Is "witchcraft" similar to the "evil eye"? Is a European witch the "same" as an Islamic djinn or a Hindu *yakṣa*? These questions about the similarities and differences between belief systems of different cultures remain largely unresolved.

With the above general reservations, it may be noted that in the area of witchcraft and sorcery, the empirical and theoretical distinctions made by Evans-Pritchard (1937) in his analysis of the ideas of the Azande have won general acceptance. The conceptual distinction made by the Azande has been observed in numerous other African cultures. The distinction turns on the nature of witches. According to Azande theories, "witches" are ordinary members of society who have inherited special supernatural powers to harm others and who may be completely unconscious of their evil potentialities. The Azande have consistent and developed physiological theories to explain just where in the human body such powers lie. They also have their special ways of consulting oracles to discover who among them carries the power, the reason for the attack, and how the danger is to be averted. Among the Azande these witches who are singled out by their fellow men are sharply distinguished from "sorcerers." Sorcerers are men who have learned the particular techniques of handling special substances and charms whereby they can affect others. While the witches' supernatural powers are innate and unconscious, sorcery is an acquired technique and is conscious. In one case a person fully unconscious of his guilt may be publicly accused as a "witch" and by the use of oracles may be confirmed as such, whereas in the other case, at least in theory, there is a conscious agent responsible for certain incidents who may or may not be accused of evil intentions.

These distinctions have thrown light upon anthropological field information beyond the Azande material from which they were developed. Sorcery theory and practice are evidently very widespread on all continents; but witchcraft, with its direct accusations of certain individuals who may be totally unaware of what they are accused of, is a more remarkable and less widespread phenomenon. Apart from the celebrated medieval European and New England examples, cases of witchcraft accusation from parts of Middle America (Nash 1960) and central and east Africa also have been described. On the whole, the term "witchcraft," in the narrow sense, has not been used to describe related phenomena in the Near East and south Asia.

The above definitions make it possible to distinguish a gradation of witchcraft belief ranging from the fully developed dogmas that certain people become witches in some form (which may be embellished with detailed stories of their secret meetings and activities) to vague feelings that certain people might possess occult powers (such as the evil eye) to cause some harm, even though they may not be directly accused. The latter fear, in various degrees, is very widespread in the Mediterranean region as well as the Near East and south Asia, even though these powers are not usually described as "witchcraft."

It should be underlined that this distinction between sorcery and witchcraft lies entirely within the region of ideas and that there may be no "objective" basis to either set of beliefs. In other words, although it should be theoretically possible to observe the sorcerer at his work, and although external evidence could be produced in the form of magical substances, special bundles, and the like, it is also quite possible that while there may be widespread fear of sorcery, it may in fact never be practiced by anybody. In this sense, in the study of both sorcery and witchcraft we are almost entirely concerned with the analysis of supernatural beliefs.

Cultural and structural approaches

Although descriptive works of high quality are now numerous, little progress has been made by anthropologists into the systematic analysis of customary belief systems. The dilemma has remained: how far are belief systems to be related to and analyzed in terms of the economic and social structures of the groups in question? Or if such systems are not directly related to economic and social structures, are there internal logical and categorical features which produce consistency and form in belief systems? The differences between these approaches have made themselves felt in the emphasis placed on the cultural or structural aspects of these phenomena.

Internal features of belief systems. The cultural approach to witchcraft and sorcery has underlined the consistency or logical closure of such systems: thus witchcraft and sorcery ideas are theories of causation concerning good and evil in human society. When a misfortune takes place, it can be explained by witchcraft or sorcery. This explanation in turn involves the necessity of discovering the agents of causation, i.e., those witches and sorcerers responsible. Thus, beginning with a theory of causation, one is led to techniques of divination. These, in turn, necessitate the development of the arts of healing and defense. Hence, ideas regarding witchcraft and sorcery become part of a coherent and consistent set of ideas regarding the nature of events in the world. Since these ideas have very wide ramifications and are inextricably related to the thought, language, and customary behavior of the societies in question, convictions regarding witches, sorcerers, and magic cannot be contradicted on simple rational or empirical grounds. They are rooted deep in the nature of social life.

There has been little analysis of the total "design" of supernatural belief systems, even though witnesses in the field have generally taken their coherence for granted. The "design" means here the characteristics, roles, rights, and obligations of supernatural beings, their organization and relations with each other and with human society at large. It also includes the methods whereby they may be approached, communicated with, appeased, angered, or utilized. It seems clear that all societies have a design of this nature whereby a division of labor between different sections of the supernatural is effected.

An example of the operation of such a system is to be seen among the Sinhalese villagers of Ceylon. In these communities the world of supernatural beings has both Buddhist and Hindu features. The Buddha and his monks, who are held in high esteem, are seen to help man's prospects in the next existence or in eternity, whereas the Hindu-influenced pantheon of supernatural beings is seen to hold sway over the present life and worldly prospects of men. Within this general framework, however, the supernatural beings who deal with this world are divided into gods and goddesses who are thought to ensure long life, well-being, and fertility, on the one hand, and demons and demonesses who are thought to wreak havoc and to bring infertility, suffering, and death, on the other. Oversimplifying, their relations can be seen as the forces of light and darkness, or those of good and evil.

The place of magic in this picture becomes clear when we observe the elaborate precautions which are taken on the threshing floors at harvest time. The threshing floor is treated as the temple–residence of the gods and goddesses who try to increase the yield. The small circle becomes the battleground for the gods and demons over the fertility of the lands and the yield of the harvest. The demons and demonesses are feared to be hovering outside its borders, aiming to attack the grain on the threshing floor and to steal it. Special magical precautions are taken to please the gods and repulse the demons. Indeed, until recently Sinhalese peasants in the interior spoke a special language, which the demons could not comprehend, when they entered the sacred precincts of their threshing floors.

It is in this context that the role of sorcery is also seen most clearly. Just as there are elaborately developed techniques of communicating with the supernatural in the threshing floor to appease the gods and hold the demons at bay, there are also techniques, said to be very dangerous, to achieve the opposite. Logically, if the achievement of the good is within the bounds of human influence, so is the working of evil. Hence, Sinhalese villagers fully believe that some people can activate the demons against them by special offerings and incantations. Thus, sorcery is part of the very foundations of the total belief system of the villagers. And further, if there is sorcery, and if there are demons who are active, then men must seek magical protection. Indeed, the great theatrical art of ritual healing—directed specifically against sorcery—is one of the most noteworthy and developed aspects of folk culture among the Sinhalese (Wirz 1954; Yalman 1964).

Such precise linking of supernatural cause and effect, white magic and sorcery, sorcery and ritual healing is not always clearly visible in the detailed description of supernatural designs, but it appears likely that further analysis will reveal similar logical interlinkages in most primitive religions. As Evans-Pritchard observes for the Azande, "witchcraft, oracles and magic are like three sides of a triangle" (1937, p. 387).

The attempt to understand fully the inner workings of the mind of even the most primitive peoples is an obvious prerequisite to the analysis of their supernatural beliefs, behavior, and rituals. Without such penetration into what appear to be irrational and alien mentalities, all observations are bound to be superficial, rash, or wrong. The process of understanding the minds of others is partly a matter of insight and freedom from prejudice, and although the discipline of anthropology has gone far in this direction, there is much room for improvement. In any case, the objective and respectful attempt to understand the inner logic in what superficially appears meaningless or illogical cannot be taken for granted. But the further question must also be raised of whether the linked and orderly system of ideas presented to us is really that of the native, or whether the order is artificially imposed on the phenomena by the mind of the anthropological observer. This issue is a difficult one, resting near the precipice of metaphysics, but its difficulty does not prevent the observation that the heuristic assumption of "system" in primitive ideologies has proved to be very fruitful. The claim regarding the systematic nature of primitive ideas is always open to further verification, but as yet no anthropologist has been able to sustain an argument based on the senselessness or illogicality of primitive beliefs.

In the meantime, further developments toward the understanding of belief systems have derived from structural linguistics. These are based on the desire not only to understand belief systems in a general way but also to go beyond the generalities and analyze the detailed features of belief systems on the model of communication systems (Lévi-Strauss 1964). Proponents of this approach maintain that belief and ritual systems have elements of order and internal structure because they form the framework for human communication. Lévi-Strauss (1955) has recommended examining the most minute details of primitive myths, as if they were literary texts. Other anthropologists have suggested that the sequences of ritual may be susceptible to the type of analysis that is applied to sequences of sounds in modern linguistics (Yalman 1964). These developments in the fields of mythology and ritual have an important bearing on magic, witchcraft, and sorcery; but as yet they remain promising methods rather than well-rounded and well-supported theoretical and analytic positions (Leach 1964). Their aim is the clarification of the structure of the language of mythology and ritual. Thus, they are formal analyses divorced both from Marxist opinions regarding the primacy of the social structure over systems of ideas and from the Freudian assumptions concerning the effects of the unconscious. Whether this line of inquiry will prove effective remains to be seen (Lévi-Strauss 1963).

Structural aspects. We turn now to the effect of the beliefs in sorcery and witchcraft on social relations. The direct or veiled accusation of a person or a group is a critical element in the sorcery and witchcraft complex. Wherever these beliefs occur, we may expect a great elaboration of supernatural weapons of offense and defense against sorcerers and witches and these accusations.

There have been attempts to relate overt accusations of witchcraft and sorcery to the morphology of kinship or social groups. It is suggested that such accusation of evil intent of one person by another must run along the lines of stress in the structure of social groups. There is undoubtedly much truth in this statement, and it is confirmed by the widespread feeling among people of many cultures that institutions such as the evil eye, witches, and sorcery spring directly from one of the most powerful human sentiments, jealousy. This is merely a different way of expressing the strained social relations between the accuser and the accused. This is why jealousy and envy are so often given as the reason for the supernatural attack (Wilson 1951*a*). Witchcraft accusations that reveal both secret and unconscious envy as well as overt suspicions may be regarded as particularly clear symptoms of strain in the social structure.

One of the most interesting studies of this problem is by Nadel (1952). For purposes of precise comparison he selects two pairs of societies: the Nupe and Gwari of Nigeria, and the Korongo and Mesakin of the Sudan. Each pair is similar in most cultural respects but differs in a few critical structural features. Thus, in the Nigerian pair Nupe women are often traders, and their economic interest and activities put a well-recognized strain on husband–wife relations. Among the Gwari, the economic problems do not exist, and the strains are absent. Accordingly, although both cultures firmly believe in witchcraft, among the Nupe witches are conceived of as women, and witch associations are said to resemble women's trade associations. The Gwari, on the other hand, conceive of their witches as being both male and female.

In the second pair there is greater contrast. According to Nadel, the Korongo have no witchcraft beliefs at all, whereas the Mesakin are said to be totally obsessed by witchcraft. In general structural form the two groups are similar, except for some critical features which are singled out by Nadel. Both groups are matrilineal. Among the Korongo the age-class system permits easy mobility through the numerous classes for young men, whereas among the Mesakin there are fewer grades and they remain closed and rigid. Among the latter, mobility is curtailed and is replaced by competition and hostility between the generations. The Korongo have no witch problems, whereas among the Mesakin most witchcraft accusations occur among maternal kin—more specifically, between mother's brother and sister's son, who are placed in positions of the most intense competition in the age-grade system.

In such theories the ideology and practice of witchcraft are related with some precision to areas of anxiety and stress in the social fabric. All these theories are based on the incidence of witchcraft accusations between individuals in certain specific social roles. But, for obvious reasons, statistical evidence of sufficient depth and range in connection with such highly charged issues is difficult to collect and evaluate.

Middleton and Winter (1963) have raised some important questions regarding both the coherence of dogma and the structural aspects of witchcraft and sorcery. Accepting the notion that witchcraft and sorcery have coherent doctrines which explain events in social life, they argue that sorcery and witchcraft beliefs are exhaustive systems of supernatural explanation. When found in the same society, moreover, they are opposed explanations. Theoretically, then, one set should be redundant; but in fact most African societies, they argue, have both systems of dogma. If so, they suggest, witchcraft and sorcery must fit in with different aspects of the social structure, and this hypothesis is related to the different natures of witchcraft and sorcery.

Since sorcery is a voluntary matter and merely a technique which can be learned, anybody may be in a position to use it for offense or defense. Moreover, depending upon the motives of the sorcerer, it is not innately evil. On the other hand, witchcraft is by definition an innate matter, usually evil, in which the alleged witch has no choice. For this reason Middleton and Winter suggest that witchcraft accusations are more characteristically made against persons who are in *ascribed* roles, such as involuntary membership in unilineal descent groups where the individual acquires his position by virtue of his birth, whereas sorcery accusations tend to be made against persons in *achieved* statuses and are more characteristic of the nonunilineal aspects of societies.

Thus, among Lugbara lineages, the women who come in as wives are incorporated into their husbands' patrilineages and become full members. Even if they leave the husband, their future children legally continue to belong to his patrilineage. In this context the elaborate ideology of witchcraft is linked to women, and witches are always said to be females. Among the Nyoro, on the other hand, people live in mixed nonunilineal neighborhoods, the women are not incorporated into patrilineages, most social positions are voluntary, and there is a developed technology of sorcery rather than witchcraft.

Even though the specific application of these ideas is illuminating, it is difficult to generalize from them to witchcraft beliefs at large. For there is always an ascribed aspect to social status, and it appears difficult to evaluate the witchcraft of complex communities in early New England, medieval Europe, or present-day Indian communities of Middle America and South America in these terms.

Apart from the question of tension in social relations, the psychological aspects of witchcraft beliefs are another dimension of the facts. If witchcraft beliefs are regarded as unrealistic fantasies—a weak theoretical position from the point of view of anthropology—then some similarity and connection may be seen between witchcraft, sorcery, and infantile fantasies. But since these ideas, however unrealistic, are collective fantasies, their explanation can be related in any meaningful fashion only to collective infantile experiences. The question remains interesting but open.

The dogmas of witchcraft, sorcery, and magic are also relevant to the social control and inheritance systems of certain societies. Among the Trobriand Islanders the power of sorcery was an important weapon which buttressed the position of the chief. Although commoners had access to sorcerers, the chief could call upon the services of many in different districts and thereby extend his authority. Frazer has reported similar instances of the use of supernatural means to secure extensive reinforcement of traditional political organizations. The divine kingship of the Shilluk is one of the well-known instances (Evans-Pritchard 1948).

In some societies where witchcraft is regarded as an innate quality in certain individuals, there are theories of its inheritance. In some cases when the main line of descent, for purposes of family organization, is in the male line, witchcraft is thought to run in the female line.

Magic and social change

Ideas about magic and supernatural creatures play a vital explanatory role as organized and institutionalized systems of public belief in traditional societies. They explain disease, injustice, misfortune, and death. Social reformers often feel that education may be used as the most potent weapon against such superstitions. It is true that modern education attacks these customary systems by providing alternative explanations for events and, probably more important, by undermining the authority of the spokesmen for the traditional system.

However, it is ironic that the fundamental changes in traditional society which permit the establishment of modern educational systems also bring about greater insecurity and increased tensions in social relations. Under such conditions, there is an even greater urge to turn to such supernatural weapons and beliefs as are available. It is notorious that modern governments in parts of Africa which have forbidden such practices as divination, the poison oracles, and similar traditional observances as being mere superstitions have naturally been seen as aligned with the forces of evil. For if the government prevents the use of appropriate traditional antiwitchcraft defensive weapons, they in effect frustrate the witch hunters and thereby materially contribute to the increase of witches. Hence, at least for parts of Africa, observers note that notwithstanding modernization, witches are felt to be more active and there is increased interest in modern movements of witch finders.

Magic, witchcraft, and sorcery are rooted in traditional customary ideas whereby cultures categorize and order the universe around them. As such, they not only are intertwined with every aspect of culture, thought, and language but also provide coherent and systematic means to influence the world in which man lives. For the anthropologist such belief systems provide essential material for the understanding of the metaphysics of non-Western cultures. They may also lead to a better understanding of the structured aspects of customary thought.

Ideas regarding witchcraft and sorcery appear strange in a rationalist period such as ours, but we should recall what immense sway such beliefs have held over very sophisticated and highly intelligent men. We must be guarded in our haste to dismiss these ideas of the supernatural. Rather, we must understand the very roots which provide the strength of conviction for such beliefs.

All knowledge rests on some degree of trust and respect. In modern societies the specialized task of developing knowledge and examining the basis of knowledge is given to thinkers and scientists in institutions of learning. Those not directly involved with a particular branch of investigation—if they understand its language at all—take their conclusions on trust. The respect in which the institution is held is an important aspect of this trust. Similarly, the knowledge of supernatural powers, of gods and goddesses, of demons and demonesses, of sorcerers and witches in all primitive societies derives from respected traditions and institutions and from men who have proved themselves worthy of trust. Commonly shared beliefs are at the basis of communal sentiments, and hence beliefs which appear primitive and totally illogical to the Western observer not only rest on dogma but also take added strength from the fact that they are part of the moral foundations of the society in which they are found.

NUR YALMAN

BIBLIOGRAPHY

DURKHEIM, ÉMILE (1912) 1954 *The Elementary Forms of the Religious Life*. London: Allen & Unwin; New York: Macmillan. → A paperback edition was published in 1961 by Collier.

EVANS-PRITCHARD, E. E. 1933 The Intellectualist (English) Interpretation of Magic. Cairo, Jāmi'at al-Qāhirah, Kullīyat al-Ādāb, *Bulletin of the Faculty of Arts* 1:282–311.

EVANS-PRITCHARD, E. E. (1937) 1965 *Witchcraft, Oracles and Magic Among the Azande*. Oxford: Clarendon.

EVANS-PRITCHARD, E. E. 1948 *The Divine Kingship of the Shilluk of the Nilotic Sudan*. Cambridge Univ. Press.

FORTUNE, REO F. (1932) 1963 *Sorcerers of Dobu: The Social Anthropology of the Dobu Islanders of the Western Pacific*. Rev. ed. London: Routledge.

FRAZER, JAMES (1890) 1955 *The Golden Bough: A Study in Magic and Religion*. 3d ed., rev. & enl. 13 vols. New York: St. Martins; London: Macmillan. → An abridged edition was published in 1922 and reprinted in 1955.

GUITERAS-HOLMES, CALIXTA 1961 *Perils of the Soul: The World View of a Tzotzil Indian*. New York: Free Press.

HUBERT, HENRI; and MAUSS, MARCEL (1904) 1960 Esquisse d'une théorie générale de la magie. Pages 1–141 in Marcel Mauss, *Sociologie et anthropologie*. 2d ed. Paris: Presses Universitaires de France. → First published in Volume 7 of *Année sociologique*.

KLUCKHOHN, CLYDE 1944 *Navaho Witchcraft*. Harvard University, Peabody Museum of American Archaeology and Ethnology, Papers, Vol. 22, No. 2. Cambridge, Mass.: The Museum.

KLUCKHOHN, CLYDE; and LEIGHTON, DOROTHEA [CROSS] (1946) 1951 *The Navaho*. Oxford Univ. Press.

LANG, ANDREW 1901 *Magic and Religion*. London: Longmans.

LEACH, EDMUND R. 1961 Golden Bough or Gilded Twig? *Dædalus* 90:371–387.

LEACH, EDMUND R. 1964 Telstar et les aborigènes, ou *La pensée sauvage*. *Annales; économies, sociétés, civilisations* 19:1100–1116.

Lévi-Strauss, Claude (1950) 1960 Introduction à l'oeuvre de Marcel Mauss. Pages ix–lii in Marcel Mauss, *Sociologie et anthropologie.* 2d ed. Paris: Presses Universitaires de France.

Lévi-Strauss, Claude (1955) 1963 The Structural Study of Myth. Pages 206–231 in Claude Lévi-Strauss, *Structural Anthropology.* New York: Basic Books. → A revision of an article first published in English in Volume 68 of the *Journal of American Folklore.*

Lévi-Strauss, Claude (1962) 1966 *The Savage Mind.* Univ. of Chicago Press. → First published in French.

Lévi-Strauss, Claude 1963 Réponse à quelques questions. *Esprit* 31:628–653.

Lévi-Strauss, Claude 1964 *Le cru et le cuit.* Paris: Plon.

Lévy-Bruhl, Lucien (1910) 1951 *Les fonctions mentales dans les sociétés inférieures.* 9th ed. Paris: Presses Universitaires de France.

McLennan, John Ferguson (1865–1876) 1886 *Studies in Ancient History.* New York: Macmillan. → Includes *Primitive Marriage* (1865).

Malinowski, Bronislaw (1925) 1948 Magic, Science and Religion. Pages 1–71 in Bronislaw Malinowski, *Magic, Science and Religion, and Other Essays.* Glencoe, Ill.: Free Press.

Marwick, M. G. 1950 Another Modern Anti-witchcraft Movement in East Central Africa. *Africa* 20:100–112.

Marwick, M. G. 1952 The Social Context of Cewa Witch Beliefs. *Africa* 22:120–135, 215–233.

Métraux, Alfred (1958) 1959 *Voodoo in Haiti.* New York: Oxford Univ. Press. → First published as *Le voudou haïtien.*

Middleton, John; and Winter, Edward H. (editors) 1963 *Witchcraft and Sorcery in East Africa.* London: Routledge.

Nadel, S. F. 1952 Witchcraft in Four African Societies: An Essay in Comparison. *American Anthropologist* New Series 54:18–29.

Nash, Manning 1960 Witchcraft as Social Process in a Tzeltal Community. *América indígena* 20:121–126.

Smith, William Robertson (1889) 1956 *The Religion of the Semites: The Fundamental Institutions.* New York: Meridian. → First published as the first series of *Lectures on the Religion of the Semites.*

Spencer, Herbert (1876–1896) 1925–1929 *The Principles of Sociology.* 3 vols. New York: Appleton.

Steiner, Franz 1956 *Taboo.* New York: Philosophical Library.

Thomas, Northcote W. 1926 Witchcraft. Volume 28, pages 755–758 in *Encyclopaedia Britannica.* 13th ed. Chicago: Benton.

Tylor, Edward B. (1871) 1958 *Primitive Culture: Researches Into the Development of Mythology, Philosophy, Religion, Art and Custom.* 2 vols. Gloucester, Mass.: Smith. → Volume 1: *Origins of Culture.* Volume 2: *Religion in Primitive Culture.*

Wilson, Monica H. 1951*a* *Good Company: A Study of Nyakyusa Age-villages.* Published for the International African Institute. Oxford Univ. Press.

Wilson, Monica H. 1951*b* Witch Beliefs and Social Structure. *American Journal of Sociology* 56:307–313.

Wirz, Paul 1954 *Exorcism and the Art of Healing in Ceylon.* Leiden (Netherlands): Brill.

Yalman, Nur 1964 The Structure of Sinhalese Healing Rituals. Pages 115–150 in Conference on Religion in South Asia, University of California, Berkeley, 1961, *Religion in South Asia.* Edited by Edward B. Harper. Seattle: Univ. of Washington Press.

MAHAN, ALFRED THAYER

Alfred Thayer Mahan (1840–1914) was an American naval officer who wrote extensively on naval strategy and the history of sea power. From his studies of naval warfare he drew principles of strategy that greatly influenced the development and employment of naval forces during the first half of the twentieth century. As a historian he studied the relations of sea power and history, and he developed a philosophy of history in which the concept of force played a major role.

Mahan was born at West Point, New York, where his father was a professor of military engineering at the United States Military Academy. Mahan chose the navy for his profession and, graduating from the United States Naval Academy in 1859, saw active service in the American Civil War. At its conclusion, he continued his navy career and traveled widely. There was little indication during these years of the intellectual importance he was to attain.

Mahan was selected in 1885 to lecture on naval strategy, tactics, and history at the newly established Naval War College. He probably received the assignment because he wrote "The Gulf and Inland Waters," a competent volume appearing in 1883 as a part of a larger history of the American Civil War. His duties at the war college forced him to crystallize his thoughts on sea power and history. It was not his intention to do original research but rather to use the best historical works available to investigate his chosen field. From his lectures came the basis for his most important work, *The Influence of Sea Power Upon History: 1660–1783*, which appeared in 1890. There followed in 1892 *The Influence of Sea Power Upon the French Revolution and Empire: 1793–1812* and in 1905 *Sea Power in its Relations to the War of 1812.* He also wrote biographies and biographical sketches, as well as several interpretative articles upon events of his time.

A large number of his professional colleagues in the United States Navy did not recognize the importance of the task Mahan had set for himself. By his own choice, he retired from the navy in 1896 to pursue his literary career. He was a member of the naval war board that provided advice on strategy during the Spanish–American War. As a representative at the First International Conference at The Hague, he spoke against prohibiting poison gas, because he thought it inconsistent with permitting the use of the submarine torpedo. He was also instrumental in persuading American delegates not to sign the convention establishing the Hague Permanent Court of Arbitration until a reservation was added safeguarding the traditional position of the United States against European involvement in the Americas and American involvement in Europe.

Concepts of naval strategy. Mahan defined sea power as the ability of a nation to control movement across the sea. He claimed that this control is the most potent factor in national prosperity and in the course of history. The components of a nation's sea power are geographical factors and national resources, the character of its people and its government, and its diplomatic and naval policies.

From his studies Mahan derived several strategic principles, having to do with the concentration of force, the choice of the correct objective, and the importance of lines of communications. Reduced to more concrete terms these principles mean that a nation should construct a battle fleet that has as its main objective the ability to destroy an enemy battle fleet. French naval history in the seventeenth and eighteenth centuries and the American experience during the War of 1812 led him to believe that cruiser warfare and raids against merchant shipping were of secondary importance. Until Mahan, however, such warfare had been the basic naval strategy of the United States.

Mahan's works appeared at a time when national rivalries were producing the international crises that culminated in World War I and when technological developments made possible the *Dreadnought*-type battleship which had only big guns. His works were avidly read by the British, the Japanese, and the Germans. In his own nation, he exerted influence in part by his writings and in part by his close friendship with such leaders as Theodore Roosevelt and Henry Cabot Lodge.

Mahan's theories of sea power remained cogent in naval strategy until the middle of the twentieth century. After World War II his concepts of sea power required modification. He had studied naval rivalries and fleet actions; consequently, his theories were applicable primarily when two or more powers were contesting the control of the sea. His principles did not easily fit the post-World War II situation in which the United States, controlling the sea, confronted the Soviet Union, controlling a large land mass. Nonetheless, his principles are still valuable in military analyses.

Military power and theory of history. It was perhaps inevitable that Mahan, with his background and professional concerns, should see military force as playing a dominant role in history. To him history was the revelation of the plan of Providence. An integral part of this plan was the use of military force to preserve civilization and to right moral wrongs. It followed, therefore, that a nation could not blindly accept arbitration on all questions, for such arbitration might involve compromises on moral issues. Although Mahan saw history as a plan, he did not deny the individual a role: a military leader or a statesman can, by correct decision and action, shape events, but his power is limited by the materials with which he must work. Mahan, in his presidential address to the American Historical Association in 1902, issued a warning against too much research on detail, urging instead a careful grouping of facts and parts that would yield the truth of the whole.

Mahan was widely read in his own day. His emphasis on the role of the military and his call for expansion found resonance in the nationalism and imperialism of his time. While the basis of his philosophy was an orthodox, and even fundamentalist, Protestantism, the results of his thoughts were acceptable to the evolutionists of "the survival of the fittest" school. Historians feel that Mahan overstressed sea power and neglected the importance of other factors, but Mahan's contributions have not been erased. The strategic value of his principles has declined with the advent of the missile age and the nuclear weapon. Yet as both a historian and a strategist, Mahan influenced his own age and left a legacy of value to the future.

FRANCIS DUNCAN

[*For discussion of the subsequent development of Mahan's ideas, see* MILITARY POLICY *and* STRATEGY; *and the biography of* DOUHET.]

WORKS BY MAHAN

1883 *The Navy in the Civil War.* Volume 3: The Gulf and Inland Waters. New York: Scribner.

(1890) 1963 *The Influence of Sea Power Upon History: 1660–1783.* New York: Hill & Wang.

(1892) 1898 *The Influence of Sea Power Upon the French Revolution and Empire: 1793–1812.* 10th ed. Boston: Little.

(1897) 1899 *The Life of Nelson: The Embodiment of the Sea Power of Great Britain.* 2d ed., rev. Boston: Little.

(1897) 1918 *The Interest of America in Sea Power: Present and Future.* Boston: Little.

1899 *Lessons of the War With Spain, and Other Articles.* Boston: Little.

(1900) 1905 *The Problem of Asia and Its Effect Upon International Policies.* Boston: Little.

1902 *Retrospect and Prospect: Studies in International Relations, Naval and Political.* Boston: Little.

(1905) 1919 *Sea Power in Its Relations to the War of 1812.* Boston: Little.

1907 *From Sail to Steam: Recollections of Naval Life.* New York: Harper.

1909 *The Harvest Within: Thoughts on thc Life of the Christian.* Boston: Little.

(1910) 1919 *The Interest of America in International Conditions.* Boston: Little.

1912 *Armaments and Arbitration: Or, the Place of Force in the International Relations of States.* New York: Harper.

SUPPLEMENTARY BIBLIOGRAPHY

DUNCAN, FRANCIS 1957 Mahan: Historian With a Purpose. United States Naval Institute, *Proceedings* 83: 498–503.

HUNTINGTON, SAMUEL P. 1954 National Policy and the Transoceanic Navy. United States Naval Institute, *Proceedings* 80:483–493.

LIVEZEY, WILLIAM E. 1947 *Mahan on Sea Power.* Norman: Univ. of Oklahoma Press. → Contains a comprehensive bibliography.

MAINE, HENRY SUMNER

Sir Henry Sumner Maine (1822–1888) was a lecturer on jurisprudence at Oxford and Cambridge, the founder of anthropological jurisprudence as an aspect of comparative law, a legal historian, and a colonial statesman. His enduring contribution to the social sciences is to be found in his formulation of the concept of ideal polar types and its uses in the comparative analysis of social phenomena.

Status and contract. In his works, especially in *Ancient Law* (1861), Maine contrasted early societies in which social relations are dominated by *status* with "progressive" (complex) societies in which social relations are predominantly determined by *contract.* By status Maine meant "a condition of society in which all the relations of Persons are summed up in the relations of Family" ([1861] 1960, p. 99). These relations are ascribed to the individual as a member of a kinship group. By contract Maine meant individual obligation arising "from the free agreement of individuals."

Although Maine explicitly declared that he could recognize no evidence that proved any society to be entirely destitute of the concept of contract, his major proposition was that in early societies the individual creates few or no rights for himself and few or no duties. Rather, he is subject to the traditional rules that govern his status and to new rules which are issued as commands by the head of his household.

Maine held that the primitive kinship group is patrilineal and autocratic. The commands of the household headman are the authoritative expression of the *patria potestas.* "In truth, in the primitive view, Relationship is exactly limited by Patria Potestas. Where the Potestas begins, Kinship begins; . . . here we have the reason why the descendants of females are outside the limits of archaic kinship" (*ibid.*, p. 88).

The polar opposite to the patriarchally dominated, kinship-determined condition of status is the kind of social system exemplified by the complex Roman society during the time of Justinian. This kind of system is marked by contract-determined relations wherein the first person promises to perform acts or to observe certain forbearances and wherein a second person signifies his expectation that the first party will fulfill the proffered promise. The mental act of consensus is theoretically separated from the external formality of the ritual of the pact or convention (e.g., in transfers of possessions), and an obligation has been added which receives the full support of legal enforcement. This is true contract.

Maine wrote in the intellectual climate of eighteenth-century and nineteenth-century social evolutionism, and accordingly he set his model in an evolutionary mold. His polar types were designed not only to represent extremes in a range of variable social forms but also to describe development in the dimension of time. Hence the famous formula: ". . . we may say that the movement of the progressive societies has hitherto been a movement *from Status to Contract*" (*ibid.*, p. 100).

Because Maine worked exclusively with written historical records, his documentation of the evolutionary process was limited almost entirely to the Greco–Roman juridical experience. He judiciously defended this on the grounds that data on other ancient civilizations were scanty or altogether missing and that in any event Roman notions have so permeated most later systems as to preclude comparative study of crucial variations. Maine anticipated the concept of multilinear evolution when he expressed his belief that there can be no theory that accounts universally for the evolution of all social phenomena. Nonetheless, Maine concluded that "it may be reasonably believed that the history of ancient Roman Contracts is, up to a certain point, typical of the history of this class of legal conceptions in other ancient societies" (*ibid.*, p. 199).

In accordance with the concept of multilinear evolution, Maine proceeded to describe the steps by which the transformation from status to contract occurred. The life of ancient man in its earliest phases knew no custom, Maine believed, but was controlled by a regimen of caprice—the commanding judgments of the patriarchal family head or the king. These took the form of themistes—judgments on the individual case under the directive of divine inspiration. ". . . It must be distinctly understood," Maine held, "that they are not laws, but judgments . . . they cannot be supposed to be connected by any thread of principle; they are separate, isolated judgments" (*ibid.*, p. 3).

Subsequently, in the process of social evolution the heroic king lost his sacred power and was politically displaced by a class of aristocrats who were not themselves royalty. In Maine's account, the early councils of aristocrats, although they abjured the claim to divine inspiration (except in Asia), nonetheless established the claim that they alone knew the body of principles in accordance with which quarrels were to be settled. In short, they became the repositories and administrators of *law*. Theirs was the "epoch of customary law."

The next phase, called by Maine the "Era of Codes," followed the invention of writing. The reduction of law to the written word ended the "spontaneous" growth of law, and all subsequent legal development was the product of deliberate effort to close the gap between changing society and frozen codes.

Maine was not content to assert the idea of social evolution; he undertook to demonstrate evolutionary mechanisms. The instruments of legal change, which permitted the modification of the forms of archaic law and the growth of modern law, were examined by him in great detail, under the rubrics of fictions, equity, and legislation.

Particularly significant is Maine's treatment of legal fiction, defined as any assumption which conceals, or affects to conceal, the fact that a rule of law has undergone alteration, its letter remaining unchanged while its operation is modified. Fiction makes legal change possible at a time when it cannot be overtly admitted that change is possible. Maine considered fiction to be a more primitive device than equity, which followed. Equity is distinguished by the fact that there is recourse to a new body of principles which are believed to have universal validity (as in *jus gentium* and natural law). It exists alongside the pre-existing civil law but supersedes it. The last mechanism of change to be developed was legislation. It differs from all previous sources of law, in Maine's view, because its obligatory force is independent of its principles. Its authority derives from an external body, existing as fiat.

In early twentieth-century social science, particularly in anthropology, Maine's theory of comparative law fared rather badly. Although he enjoyed some first-hand knowledge of the village community in India, there are no references in his *Ancient Law* to contemporary nonliterate tribal society. Maine was content to interpolate a hypothetical state of universal social organization from the materials of ancient Greece and Rome. He had nothing to say about customs and law in any known primitive society.

To the modern social scientist, Maine's customless society is not only empirically nonexistent but theoretically impossible. It has not been difficult for ethnographers to prove invalid Maine's assumption of the initial universality of patrilineal, patriarchal social organization, characterized by absolute submergence of the individual within the corporate whole. Of 564 nonliterate societies in G. P. Murdock's "World Ethnographic Sample" (1957), less than half (44 per cent) are patrilineal, one-third are bilateral, and one-sixth are matrilineal (Aberle 1961, p. 665). The very simplest of these primitive societies tend to be neither patrilineal nor matrilineal. Furthermore, detailed examination of actual primitive systems has demonstrated that the patriarchal authoritarianism of the *patria potestas*, as it was known in early Rome, is not a common characteristic of primitive patrilineality.

Recent empirical anthropology, following R. H. Lowie (1920), has demonstrated also the extent of nonkinship groupings (clubs, fraternities, voluntary associations) and relationships in primitive society. Anthropologists have thoroughly established that Maine was wrong in his dogmatic assumption that the kin bond was the sole initial basis of political union and that its later subversion by the establishment of local contiguity as the basis of common political action was an antipathetic revolution. Geography as well as kinship is now known to be a more or less important factor in all sociopolitical systems.

Tort and crime. A second major formulation of polar opposites advanced by Maine was the contrast between the law of tort and the law of crime. "If therefore," he wrote, "the criterion of a *delict, wrong,* or *tort* be that the person who suffers it, and not the State, is conceived to be wronged, it may be asserted that in the infancy of jurisprudence the citizen depends for protection against violence or fraud not on the Law of Crime but on the Law of Tort" ([1861] 1960, p. 218). The test is the law of responsibility for initiation and carrying through of legal action; it is a test of procedure. Although there is a good deal more of criminal law in the law of primitive societies than Maine imagined, Maine's contrast is essentially correct. The general trend of the law, from primitive to civilized, is toward an increasing shift of procedural responsibility from the individual as a member of a kinship group to the public officer as representative of the society at large.

Maine's influence. In spite of the antievolutionary reaction that almost submerged Maine, along with Lewis Henry Morgan, Tylor, and other social evolutionists of the late nineteenth century, Maine's working tool of ideal polar types was never wholly lost. Morgan used it to formulate his contrast of *societas* and *civitas*. Émile Durkheim used it to contrast the hypothetical isolated society of absolute homogeneity, bound by "mechanical solidarity," with the interdependent community ("the social organ") bound by the "organic solidarity" of interrelated, differentiated units. Through Durkheim, and through Tönnies' contrast of *Gemeinschaft* and *Gesellschaft*, Maine's influence on current French, German, and American sociology is clear.

As anthropology extends its interests beyond the illiterate tribe to the peasant community in the setting of civilization, interest in Maine is being renewed. The folk–urban continuum of Redfield and his followers is Maine's model with a new content. The extensive study of village communities in India and elsewhere, which burgeoned in the years following World War II, has revived Maine's work of comparative contrast, *Village-communities in the East and West* (1871).

In like manner, the current revival of interest in social evolution among anthropologists, as expressed in the writings of V. Gordon Childe, Leslie White, Julian H. Steward, and Marshall Sahlins, lends new vitality to Maine's work.

Above all, the problem of the economic and social development of recently independent underdeveloped nations has forced Maine's basic ideas once more to the fore. Economists, anthropologists, and sociologists have written extensively and emphatically to impress administrators of economic-development programs that African and Asian economic systems function as by-products of noneconomic institutions.

The most vigorous response to Maine's thought, relating to mid-twentieth century interests, is found in the writings of F. S. C. Northrop and his associates. Northrop goes beyond Maine, to hold that the concept of contract is a unique Roman invention, the product of Stoic lawyers creating, in the tradition of Greek mathematics, an imageless, logical–realistic universal concept. He attributes to the concept of contract the same significance for Western politico–legal development that the imageless constructs of Western scientific thought have for technical advancement and considers modernization possible only if status-type social systems are replaced with universal contract relations.

In contrast, such men as Roscoe Pound and Morris Cohen, in their work earlier in this century with reference to trends within Western society, stressed countercontract developments in social and labor legislation that limit individual freedom of contract. Examples are workmen's compensation and minimum wage acts. Similarly, the standardization of contract terms in landlord–tenant, mortgage, insurance and other contracts is seen by some writers as substituting a group status-determinant for self-determination. Thus, when applied empirically to modern society, Maine's model is no more adequate than it proved to be when applied to actual primitive societies. In other words, contemporary empiricists have demonstrated that Maine's concept taken as absolute historical dogma will not stand up in detail; however, this does not mean that it may not be highly useful as a model of ideal types.

E. ADAMSON HOEBEL

[*For the historical context of Maine's work, see* EVOLUTION, *article on* CULTURAL EVOLUTION; JURISPRUDENCE; LAW; MODERNIZATION. *For discussion of the subsequent development of his ideas, see the biographies of* DURKHEIM; POUND; REDFIELD; TÖNNIES.]

WORKS BY MAINE

(1861) 1960 *Ancient Law: Its Connection With the Early History of Society, and Its Relations to Modern Ideas.* Rev. ed. New York: Dutton; London and Toronto: Dent. → A paperback edition was published in 1963 by Beacon.

(1871) 1890 *Village-communities in the East and West, to Which Are Added Other Lectures, Addresses, and Essays.* New ed. London: Murray.

(1875) 1897 *Lectures on the Early History of Institutions.* 7th ed. London: Murray. → A sequel to the author's *Ancient Law.*

SUPPLEMENTARY BIBLIOGRAPHY

ABERLE, DAVID F. 1961 Matrilineal Descent in Cross-cultural Perspective. Pages 655–727 in David M. Schneider and Kathleen Gough (editors), *Matrilineal Kinship.* Berkeley: Univ. of California Press.

BOHANNAN, PAUL 1963 *Social Anthropology.* New York: Holt.

GRANT DUFF, MOUNTSTUART E. 1892 *Sir Henry Maine: A Brief Memoir of His Life.* New York: Holt.

GRAVESON, R. H. 1940/1941 The Movement From Status to Contract. *Modern Law Review* 4:261–272.

HOEBEL, E. ADAMSON 1964 Status and Contract in Primitive Law. Pages 284–294 in F. S. C. Northrop and Helen H. Livingston (editors), *Cross-cultural Understanding: Epistemology in Anthropology.* New York: Harper.

LOWIE, ROBERT H. (1920) 1947 *Primitive Society.* New York: Liveright. → A paperback edition was published in 1961 by Harper.

MURDOCK, GEORGE P. 1957 World Ethnographic Sample. *American Anthropologist* New Series 59:664–687.

NORTHROP, F. S. C. 1964 Toward a Deductively Formulated and Operationally Verifiable Comparative Cultural Anthropology. Pages 194–222 in F. S. C. Northrop and Helen H. Livingston (editors), *Cross-cultural Understanding: Epistemology in Anthropology.* New York: Harper.

REDFIELD, ROBERT 1955 *The Little Community: Viewpoints for the Study of a Human Whole.* Univ. of Chicago Press. → A paperback edition was published in 1962.

SEAGLE, WILLIAM (1941) 1946 *The History of Law.* 2d ed. New York: Tudor. → First published as *The Quest for Law.* See especially pages 252–277 in the 1941 edition, "The Omnipotence of Contract."

SMITH, JOSEPH C. 1964 The Theoretical Constructs of Western Contractual Law. Pages 254–283 in F. S. C. Northrop and Helen H. Livingston (editors), *Cross-cultural Understanding: Epistemology in Anthropology.* New York: Harper.

STONE, JULIUS (1946) 1950 *The Province and Function of Law: Law as Logic, Justice, and Social Control; a Study in Jurisprudence.* Cambridge, Mass.: Harvard Univ. Press. → See especially pages 451–484 on "Social Types and Legal Types."

MAITLAND, FREDERIC WILLIAM

Frederic William Maitland (1850–1906), English legal historian and jurist, was born in London and died at Las Palmas in the Canary Islands, where ill-health had compelled him to winter since 1898. He was born into a family of intellectual distinction: his father was successively a fellow of Trinity College, Cambridge, a barrister, and secretary to the civil service commissioners; his mother was a daughter of a physicist, J. F. Daniell, a fellow of the Royal Society; his paternal grandfather, Samuel Roffey Maitland, barrister, clergyman, and for a short time the Archbishop of Canterbury's librarian at Lambeth Palace, London, was the author of 37 works, among them a remarkable book on medieval heresies (1832) that, in its skeptical attitude to accepted beliefs and its insistence on documentary proof, curiously anticipates the salient characteristics of his grandson's approach to history. From this grandparent, Maitland inherited, at the age of 16, a small property at Brookthorpe in Gloucestershire, which made him financially independent. In 1886 he married a niece by marriage of Sir Leslie Stephen (whom he commemorated in *The Life and Letters of Leslie Stephen* 1906), who was also the sister of H. A. L. Fisher, the historian and politician.

Education and academic career. With an excellent grounding in German from his governesses that was to serve him well in later life, Maitland went to Eton College in 1863, where his school life was unremarkable and unremarked, and then in 1869 to Trinity College, Cambridge. There he abandoned his first interest, mathematics, in favor of moral and mental sciences, in which he was bracketed first in the final examination in 1872. A long-distance runner for his university and a skilled oarsman for his college, he was also president of the Union Society and already noted for his fluent and witty speech. Called to the bar as a member of Lincoln's Inn in 1876, he was professionally engaged for eight years afterward in the work of conveyancing and equity; his first publication, in 1879, "The Law of Real Property" (see *Collected Papers*, vol. 1, pp. 162–201), entered a sardonic plea for the abolition of cumbrous procedures, however sacrosanct the passage of time had apparently made them. Not until 1926 was this reform belatedly accomplished.

Maitland was slow to find his true vocation and to realize that to him the history of the law was much more attractive than its practice. Nevertheless, his course was being set by three essays: "The Laws of Wales: The Kindred and the Blood Feud" in 1881, "The Criminal Liability of the Hundred" in 1882, and "The Early History of Malice Aforethought" in 1883 (*ibid.*, pp. 202–229, 230–246, 304–328). Furthermore, he had in these years taken the momentous step of reading legal records in the Latin shorthand of the original manuscripts at the Public Record Office in London and as a result edited his first book, *Pleas of the Crown for the County of Gloucester Before the Abbot of Reading . . . 1221* (1884). Seeking entrance to academic life, he was rejected by Oxford but accepted by Cambridge in 1884 as reader in English law. He produced a magnificent three-volume edition of *Bracton's Note Book* (1887), defraying the cost of publication himself. It contained a collection of some two thousand legal actions between 1217 and 1240 that had been made for the great thirteenth-century judge Henri de Bracton to use in writing his monumental treatise *De legibus et consuetudinibus Angliae* (1569). This scholarly achievement led to Maitland's appointment as Downing professor of the laws of England at Cambridge in 1888.

The legal historian. Before Maitland's time, the history of English law had suffered from three main defects: its expositors, among whom the most worthy was John Reeves (*History of the English Law* 1783–1829), were overwhelmed by the austere technicalities of the law as it existed in their day and in consequence produced quite unreadable factual surveys; they isolated the subject from all other departments of learning; and they saw no need to place it against its European background. Maitland wrought the great metamorphosis. Although he mastered the facts with infinite patience and used them constantly to provide concrete illustrations for his generalizations, he was interested above all else in the pattern of legal thought, particularly as it revealed itself in the origin and development of legal institutions. He insisted that the study of law, far from being a narrow, specialized discipline, provides the indispensable means of understanding the political, constitutional, social, economic, and religious history of the English people; he emphasized the value of comparative law, whether Roman and Germanic, Norman and French, Welsh and Scandinavian, and he placed the law of England firmly in the mainstream of European jurisprudence. In sharp contrast to William Stubbs, Maitland possessed the rare quality of mind that could free itself from the fetters of traditional concepts, whether about church or state, and reveal the way people of past eras defined the truth, thus making "the thoughts of men of the past thinkable to us."

Common law. To advance the knowledge of the history of English law, in 1887 he helped to found the Selden Society in London, and he sustained the burden of editing its early volumes until it had firmly established itself. Thus, he edited volume 1 of *Select Pleas of the Crown* (1888), *Select Pleas in Manorial and Other Seignorial Courts* (1889), and *The Court Baron* (1891*a*), and he provided the introduction to *The Mirror of Justices* (1895). These volumes helped to prepare the way for the incomparable *History of English Law Before the Time of Edward I* (1895). Though ostensibly a joint work with Sir Frederick Pollock, this work was written entirely by Maitland except for a section on Anglo-Saxon law. Soon after, Maitland made his own investigations into the dark terrain of pre-Conquest England in his *Domesday Book and Beyond* (1897). In 1903 he committed the Selden Society to the formidable task of printing the Year Books, which recounted the arguments of counsel in the king's courts from the first years of Edward I's reign until the time of the early Tudors, and he himself edited three of them and coedited three (1903–1951). To assist the reader, Maitland made an elaborate study of the complicated accidence of law French and this has ever since elicited the praise of grammarians. Whether discussing the knotty problem of law enforcement (1885) or the obdurate persistence of custom (1898*a*) or compiling the charters of the borough of Cambridge (1901*a*), he never failed to focus a new and brilliant light upon the many facets of English society in the Middle Ages. [*See* LEGAL SYSTEMS, *article on* COMMON LAW SYSTEMS.]

Canon law. Although not anticlerical, Maitland was, in his own words, "a dissenter from all churches" and remarkably free from ecclesiastical presuppositions. His *Roman Canon Law in the Church of England* (1898*b*) revealed a whole library of theological books as invalid: it controverted the Anglican legend of the Reformation, which had been espoused by Stubbs, by showing that English ecclesiastical courts had regarded papal law as authoritative and had failed to observe it in practice only because of state intervention. [*See* CANON LAW.]

Comparative law. To discover the interplay between English common law and Roman law before the fourteenth century, Maitland examined in minute detail, in *Select Passages From the Works of Bracton and Azo* (1895), how much the English judge was indebted to the jurist of Bologna. At Cambridge in his Rede lecture, *English Law and the Renaissance* (1901), he looked again at the influence of Roman law, this time in Tudor England. To support his distinction between the concept of the trust and what was known abroad as the legal corporation, he translated part of the third volume of Otto Friedrich von Gierke's *Das deutsche Genossenschaftsrecht* under the title of *Political Theories of the Middle Age* (1900) [*see* GIERKE].

The history of Parliament. Although unappreciated at the time, it is now beyond question that Maitland's introduction to the parliament rolls of 1305, printed as *Records of the Parliament Holden at Westminster* (1893), abandoned the long-hallowed belief that the early parliament was a "national assembly of estates" and introduced the modern conception that it was essentially "the king's council" in one of its many forms. Maitland here achieved another breakthrough, another destruction of old habits of thought, and his brilliant essay has formed the starting point of a whole series of parliamentary studies, still vigorously pursued.

Literary style. As an artist in words, Maitland followed no conventions and is himself inimitable. The severity of the subject matter and the vast erudition needed to cope with it did not prevent him from attaining a beautiful clarity in exposition. He seems to take the reader into his confidence and to converse with him, charming him with his exquisite sense of the perfect word and phrase, his happy epigrams, his gay humor. Yet he has been termed the "historian's historian," and it is true that it was not simply literary merit that made him known to a wide circle: he probed deep below the surface in his preoccupation with analysis and rarely committed himself to writing narrative, although he did this with felicity in his chapter, "The Anglican Settlement and the Scottish Reformation" (1903).

Recognition. In the range of his interests, the fineness of his intellect, and the considerable bulk of what he wrote in barely twenty-five years, Maitland has no match among English historians. He was honored in his lifetime with doctorates from Cambridge (at the age of 41, while still serving that university), Oxford, Glasgow, Moscow, and Cracow; he was one of the first fellows of the British Academy; he was elected an honorary fellow of Trinity College, Cambridge, and a bencher of Lincoln's Inn; he was awarded the James Barr Ames medal by the Harvard law faculty. So highly was he revered that after his death, notes of his lectures were reassembled and published as *The Constitutional History of England* (1908), *Equity* (1909*a*), and *The Forms of Action at Common Law* (1909*b*).

Not all his views have been beyond dispute—for example, those on the garrison theory of borough origins, the superficiality of Bracton's knowledge of Roman law, the nature of corporations, the stability of the common law at the time of the Renaissance, and the Elizabethan religious settlement. Nevertheless, his reputation has increased, not dwindled, during the last sixty years: a historian can be paid no higher compliment.

G. O. SAYLES

[*See also* PARLIAMENTARY GOVERNMENT *and* PLURALISM.]

WORKS WRITTEN, EDITED, OR TRANSLATED BY MAITLAND

1884 GREAT BRITAIN, CURIA REGIS *Pleas of the Crown for the County of Gloucester Before the Abbot of Reading . . . 1221.* Edited by Frederic W. Maitland. London: Macmillan. → Text in Latin.

1885 *Justice and Police.* London: Macmillan.

1887 GREAT BRITAIN, COURTS *Bracton's Note Book.* Edited by Frederic W. Maitland, 3 vols. London: Clay. → A collection of cases decided in the reign of Henry III, annotated by a lawyer of that time, seemingly Henri de Bracton. Text in Latin.

1888 GREAT BRITAIN, CURIA REGIS *Select Pleas of the Crown.* Volume 1: A.D. 1200–1225. Edited for the Selden Society by Frederic W. Maitland. London: Quaritch. → Latin text and English translation on opposite pages.

1889 MAITLAND, FREDERIC W. (editor) *Select Pleas in Manorial and Other Seignorial Courts.* Volume 1: Reigns of Henry III. and Edward I. Edited for the Selden Society. London: Quaritch. → Latin text and English translation on opposite pages.

1891*a* MAITLAND, FREDERIC W.; and BAILDON, WILLIAM P. (editors) *The Court Baron: Being Precedents for Use in Seignorial and Other Local Courts . . .* Edited for the Selden Society. London: Quaritch.

1891*b* GREAT BRITAIN, CURIA REGIS *Three Rolls of the King's Court in the Reign of King Richard the First: A.D. 1194–1195.* Pipe Roll Society, London, Publications, vol. 14. With an introduction and notes by Frederic W. Maitland. London: Wyman.

(1893) 1964 GREAT BRITAIN, PARLIAMENT *Records of the Parliament Holden at Westminster on the Twenty-eighth Day of February, in the Thirty-third Year of the Reign of King Edward the First (A.D. 1305).* Edited by Frederic W. Maitland. New York: Kraus.

1895 Introduction. In Andrew Horn, *The Mirror of Justices.* London: Quaritch.

(1895) 1952 POLLOCK, FREDERICK; and MAITLAND, FREDERIC W. *The History of English Law Before the Time of Edward I.* 2 vols., 2d ed. Boston: Little.

1895 BRACTON, HENRI DE; and AZZO OF BOLOGNA *Select Passages From the Works of Bracton and Azo.* Edited for the Selden Society by Frederic W. Maitland. London: Quaritch.

1897 *Domesday Book and Beyond: Three Essays on the Early History of England.* Cambridge Univ. Press.

1898*a* *Township and Borough.* Cambridge Univ. Press.

1898*b* *Roman Canon Law in the Church of England: Six Essays.* London: Methuen.

(1900) 1958 Introduction. In Otto von Gierke, *Political Theories of the Middle Age.* Translated with an introduction by Frederic W. Maitland. Cambridge Univ. Press. → Gierke's work was first published in 1881 as "Die publicistischen Lehren des Mittelalters," a section of Volume 3 of Gierke's *Das deutsche Genossenschaftsrecht.*

1901*a* CAMBRIDGE (ENGLAND), CHARTERS *The Charters of the Borough of Cambridge.* Edited by Frederic W. Maitland and Mary Bateson. Cambridge Univ. Press.

(1901*b*) 1957 English Law and the Renaissance. Pages 135–151 in Frederic W. Maitland, *Selected Historical Essays.* Cambridge Univ. Press.

(1903) 1934 The Anglican Settlement and the Scottish Reformation. Pages 550–598 in *Cambridge Modern History.* Volume 2: The Reformation. New York: Macmillan.

1903–1951 GREAT BRITAIN, YEAR BOOKS, 1307–1327 *Year Books of Edward II.* 24 vols. Edited for the Selden Society. London: Quaritch. → Volumes 1–3 were edited by Frederic W. Maitland, Volume 4 by F. W. Maitland and G. J. Turner, and Volumes 5 and 7 by W. C. Bolland, F. W. Maitland, and L. W. Vernon Harcourt.

1906 *The Life and Letters of Leslie Stephen.* London: Duckworth.

1908 *The Constitutional History of England.* Cambridge Univ. Press.

(1909*a*) 1936 *Equity.* Cambridge Univ. Press.

(1909*b*) 1936 *The Forms of Action at Common Law.* Cambridge Univ. Press.

The Collected Papers of Frederic William Maitland. 3 vols. Edited by H. A. L. Fisher. Cambridge Univ. Press, 1911.

The Letters of Frederic William Maitland. Edited by C. H. S. Fifoot. Cambridge, Mass.: Harvard Univ. Press, 1965.

Selected Essays. Edited by H. D. Hazeltine, G. Lapsley, and P. H. Winfield. Cambridge Univ. Press, 1936.

Selected Historical Essays. Chosen and introduced by Helen M. Cam. Cambridge Univ. Press, 1957.

SUPPLEMENTARY BIBLIOGRAPHY

BELL, H. E. 1965 *Maitland: A Critical Examination and Assessment.* London: Black; Cambridge, Mass.: Harvard Univ. Press.

BRACTON, HENRI DE (1569) 1915–1942 *De legibus et consuetudinibus Angliae.* 2 vols. New Haven: Yale Univ. Press.

DELANY, VINCENT T. H. (editor) 1957 *Frederic William Maitland Reader.* Dobbs Ferry, N.Y.: Oceana.

FISHER, HERBERT A. L. 1910 *Frederic William Maitland, Downing Professor of Laws of England: A Biographical Sketch.* Cambridge Univ. Press.

MAITLAND, SAMUEL R. 1832 *Facts and Documents Illustrative of the History, Doctrine and Rites of the Ancient Albigenses and Waldenses.* London: Rivington.

PLUCKNETT, T. F. T. 1958 *Early English Legal Literature.* Cambridge Univ. Press. → See especially "Maitland's View of Law and History" on pages 1–18.

REEVES, JOHN (1783–1829) 1880 *Reeves' History of the English Law, From the Time of the Romans to the End of the Reign of Elizabeth* [1603]. 5 vols. Philadelphia: Murphy.

SCHUYLER, ROBERT L. 1952 The Historical Spirit Incarnate: Frederic William Maitland. *American Historical Review* 57:303–322.

SMITH, ARTHUR LIONEL 1908 *Frederic William Maitland.* Oxford: Clarendon.

MAJORITY RULE

The term "majority rule" stands for a rule of decision making within a specified group. At its simplest, the rule requires that the vote of each member shall be counted as equal to that of every other and that no vote or decision by a minority may override that of a majority. By extension, majority rule is sometimes contrasted with any rule requiring that decisions be unanimous or by any number larger than a simple majority. According to this extended version, then, not only may a minority never override a majority but also it can never *check* a majority: a majority vote is conclusive for the whole group. It is common to distinguish this usage by referring to it as "bare majority" rule, rule by "simple majority," or "strict majoritarianism." Within democratic regimes most of the controversies about majority rule relate to whether it is desirable to apply the "bare majority" rule at some particular stage of the political process, or even whether the ethical premises of democracy demand its application. For electoral purposes it is common, especially where a two-party system prevails, to permit choice (election) by a plurality that is less than a majority. Strictly speaking, this procedure violates the majority principle, and such devices as run-off elections are often used to increase the probability that the elected candidate will have majority support.

History of theory and practice

Among the ancient Greeks, democracy entailed rule by majority vote of a popular assembly, of which all adult male citizens were members. Even in democratic Athens, however, there were institutional as well as practical limits on the power of majorities. A select group determined the agenda of the assembly, thus playing a significant role in framing the issues. Moreover, many important officials were selected by lot rather than by vote. This practice tended to limit the power of an organized majority or of a class or interest that comprised a majority, because in accordance with the laws of chance it gave proportionate representation to minority groups, as simple majority rule fails to do.

During the medieval period, whether in the great council of the church, in abbey chapter, or in secular parliament, decision by a bare or simple majority was slow to gain acceptance in practice and even slower to be vindicated in principle. The concurrence of all, the unanimity principle, seems universally to have been considered the ideal for positive action. It was common, however, to recognize that action could not be taken *against* the expressed wishes of a majority. (In this basic sense, majority rule prevailed.) The result was a kind of rule by "concurrent majorities" (Calhoun [1851] 1953, pp. 16–31). Typically, there was no fixed, mechanical formula for determining when a decision could be made, but unanimity was sought even if it could be obtained only by the process of wearing down and shouting down the dissenters—or by resort to threats or physical force. It was not until the sixteenth century that the ideal of unanimity and the practice of "veto groups" (the requirement of concurrence of the representatives of each town, county, etc.) gave way to the rule that the vote of a majority of individual representatives should prevail for positive as well as for negative action. Doubtless the rising individualism of this period, reinforced by the practical necessities of a state in which legislation was playing a far more important role than it had in the medieval period, led to this development.

The doctrine that the state should be based upon the consent of the majority of the people and that the specific acts of government should express the will of the majority (of adult males) was most systematically expounded and justified in the writings of John Locke (1690). Locke's fundamental position was founded upon the equality principle, which he assumed to be self-evident and which seemed to him to dictate the majority principle as opposed to any form of minority rule. Popular acceptance of this decision-making rule, he felt, was based upon both convenience and the superior strength of a majority.

This theory spread rapidly and became the foundation of political liberalism. Rousseau adopted it, with the important refinement that he specifically indicated that the support of more than a bare majority for all important political decisions should be insisted upon, unless the urgency of reaching a decision dictated otherwise [*see* ROUSSEAU]. In England, Jeremy Bentham and the Utilitarian school accepted the equalitarian principle unquestioningly and, as a corollary, accepted also the rule that for all political decisions the concurrence of a majority should be a sufficient as well as a necessary condition [*see* BENTHAM]. The theory and practice of constitutional democracy, however, as it spread throughout most of the Western world in the nineteenth and twentieth centuries, generally recognized certain individual and minority rights and gave them some form of constitutional protection, thus placing limitations on bare majorities. [*See* CONSTITUTIONS AND CONSTITUTIONALISM.]

Contemporary issues

Today, within the context of democratic principles, majority rule as the rule for decision making is the subject of continuing analysis and discussion from two points of view. One debate relates to whether it is legitimate, from the point of view of the democratic ethic, to require more than a bare majority for certain decisions. The other area of discussion deals with the question of whether majority rule is, in any sense of that difficult word, the best, most "rational" technique for expressing the equality principle, maximizing satisfaction, or attaining any other posited objective of democratic government.

Merits of majoritarianism. Various writers have argued that the essence of the democratic ethic requires that the will (vote) of a simple majority should always prevail over the opposition. Any other rule, they urge, places a minority in a position to frustrate a majority and thus, in a sense, to rule. Accordingly, the logical and only legitimate derivative of the equalitarian, democratic assumption is held to entail bare majority rule.

Others defend the same decision-making rule on more pragmatic grounds. They maintain that a requirement, for any purpose, of more than a simple majority places undesirable obstacles in the way of government. The dice are sufficiently loaded against progressive change without placing in the hands of self-interested or traditionally oriented minorities a powerful instrument of obstructionism. As long as opportunity for free association, discussion, and deliberation prevails, they argue, the rights of minorities will not be trampled upon. In a fluid and pluralistic society, a majority will not consist of a solid, fixed interest but will be made up of shifting coalitions of groups well aware of the fact that tomorrow they may be part of a minority and, therefore, sensitive to the interests and rights of minorities.

Opponents of strict majoritarianism advance numerous arguments. First, they point out that the majoritarian principle might be used to destroy the conditions of its own existence, such as freedom of association and expression. Moreover, other individual rights widely accepted as fundamental, such as the right to freedom of religion, the protection of fair procedure ("due process"), or property rights, might not always be respected by the majority. They also contend that bare majority rule is potentially unfair: it does not really institutionalize the equality principle, for instead of giving to the minority its rightful proportionate weight, it gives it none at all. The strict majoritarian position is questioned on still another ground: not only does it fail to give weight to minorities; it also takes no account of the intensity of interest or demand. Finally, quite apart from the equality principle, the desirability of rule by a bare majority may be challenged on purely pragmatic grounds. Where feelings are intense, a decision to override a large minority poses a serious threat to basic consensus. On the question of racial segregation in United States public schools, for instance, the minority feels so intensely that the basis for law and order itself is threatened when the attempt is made to compel complete integration.

Majoritarians have frequently argued in an abstract manner that renders at least part of their position so unrealistic as to be inapplicable in real life. If it is the majority that should in all situations and at every turn rule, because of the principle of political equality, presumably it is the majority of the electorate who should rule. In other words, nothing short of direct democracy could satisfy this condition, for representatives do not always express the will of the majority of their constituents. Even if each representative did always vote the wishes of a majority of his constituents and if all constituencies contained exactly the same number of voters, the majority might not rule because minorities might be unevenly dispersed among the electoral districts. Moreover, on most questions that confront legislatures, many or most of the voters have no opinion, as opinion surveys are continually showing. The majority principle under these circumstances leads to pursuit of a will-o'-the-wisp. From these and similar considerations emerges the conclusion that the principle of political equality cannot lead to any clear and invariable rule for decision making. What institutional and voting arrangements should be adopted becomes a pragmatic matter, whether the goal is to reflect the desires of the greatest number of voters or whether different objectives, such as preservation of consensus and other conditions for continuing democracy and giving effect to intensity as well as numbers of opinions or desires, are taken into account.

Rational decision making. The other approach from which the problem of majority rule is currently being studied is a refinement of one of the arguments enumerated above, using the techniques of mathematics and of game theory. Even with models assuming rational men (defined as men who know what they want and pursue their ends by the most efficient means available), it appears that majority rule is not always an optimal decision-making process—that is, it does not maximize satisfaction. In particular, where the problem is one of allocation of goods, the results of majority decisions may be quite fortuitous, because everything depends upon the procedure adopted for proposing alternatives and submitting them for decision. Moreover, under certain circumstances, majority decisions may consistently lead to results that are less satisfactory (e.g., by the standard of the "Pareto optimum") than decisions arrived at in some other way (Buchanan & Tullock 1962, chapter 12; Ward 1961).

Serious problems could arise where voters' preferences are socially intransitive—that is, where the ways in which different voters would rank a series of possible choices are scrambled rather than patterned. For example: X prefers A to B, B to C, and A to C. Y prefers B to C, C to A, and B to A. Z prefers C to A, A to B, and C to B. It will be seen that a majority prefer A to B and B to C. It would seem, then, that the community, if it is rational, prefers A to C. But in fact a majority prefer C to A; and this result (known as the "voters' paradox") would be arrived at by the normal legislative procedure of voting on each of the possible pairs in turn (Arrow 1951, p. 3). This analysis suggests an important question: How often are preferences affecting political decisions in fact distributed in this socially intransitive fashion? Currently data bearing on this question are almost wholly lacking [*see* DECISION MAKING].

Evaluation

It has been shown that it would be impossible to carry majority rule to its logical conclusion—to insist that all public policies be determined by majority will. Further, many arguments have been adduced that suggest serious ethical and practical limitations to the principle. Although the shortcomings of the principle are increasingly recognized, disagreement and sheer puzzlement as to desirable substitutes still prevail. Clearly no single alternative is acceptable. Beyond this point, generalization becomes difficult. Liberal democrats are widely agreed that individual and minority rights should have some protection against tyrannous majorities. Most constitutional democracies today seek to give a special status to some of these rights, protecting them from infringement by simple majorities. The government of Great Britain comes closer than most to enthroning simple majorities, yet even there the House of Lords remains as a slight check upon pure majoritarianism, while strong traditions of constitutional morality, fair play, and respect for minority rights place even more effective checks upon majorities. Many contend that informal checks are enough and that legal checks, whether in the form of requirements for extraordinary majorities or of the concurrence of different branches of a government responsible to separate constituencies, are unnecessary and undesirable. Some would cite the British experience in support of this position, but others would maintain that all depends upon the conditions of the country in question. In France under the Fourth Republic, for instance, institutional arrangements not very different from those that prevail in Britain permitted (and some would say encouraged) a degree of governmental instability that eroded consensus and respect for government to the point that the regime collapsed.

Granted, however, that constitutional devices to limit majorities may be desirable, it is difficult to show what devices are best, even under a given set of circumstances. Protection for the freedoms necessary for the continued effective functioning of majority rule are easily defended, but even here there is room for dispute as to means. It is difficult to determine whether requirements for extraordinary majorities, for bicameralism, or for the separation of powers are more or less likely to give proper weight to intense desires and to maximize satisfaction. Such devices do, however, have one important virtue, from the democratic point of view: they compel delay, giving time for deliberation; they force the majority, or those who are seeking governmental action, to try to win support for their proposal. This process is likely to contribute to the dissemination of information, to analysis of the probable effects of alternative courses of action, and to considered judgment of the various values and disvalues that may be involved. On such questions, however, one must rely at best on highly qualitative judgments. The need for research in this area is great.

Since modern industrial societies are typically highly pluralistic, majorities for any course of action can normally be obtained only by aggregating the support of a number of powerful groups. This process requires educational campaigns, argumentation, and deliberation. In itself it may meet the needs pointed out in the criticisms of majoritarianism, and it may do so without offering minority interests the opportunities for obstructionism provided by the numerous constitutional restraints embodied in, say, the constitution of the United States.

With respect to the shortcomings of the majority principle as a means for solving allocation problems in a way that maximizes satisfaction, a similar dilemma appears. It is easier to criticize the principle than to offer a better one. Here, again, the need for research and speculative imagination is great. Can ways be found to obtain fairer results without sacrificing the protection that majority rule provides against a consolidated and tyrannous minority? Can this be done without also giving up the values of popular interest and participation in the policy-making process? Ideally, different decision-making rules would be demanded for different situations, depending upon such variables as the type of question to be decided and the nature of the prevailing party and pressure-group systems.

One concluding point helps place the subject in perspective. Relatively small groups whose members view each other with respect and as equals tend to make their decisions unanimously, especially on important matters and, where unanimity is impracticable, to approach it as closely as possible. At the other extreme, small groups whose consensus is low are also likely to insist upon unanimity, more from mutual distrust than from mutual respect. In large groups unanimity is impracticable. If consensus is high, as in Great Britain, the polity may tolerate rule by simple majority. Where the society is more heterogeneous, or the divisions are sharper, concurrence by more than a simple majority will often be required and will, in fact, be essential for the preservation of a viable polity.

J. Roland Pennock

[*See also* Consensus; Democracy; Elections; Equality; Liberalism; Representation.]

BIBLIOGRAPHY

Arrow, Kenneth J. (1951) 1963 *Social Choice and Individual Values.* 2d ed. New York: Wiley.

Baty, Thomas 1912 The History of Majority Rule. *Quarterly Review* 216:1–28.

Black, Duncan 1958 *The Theory of Committees and Elections.* Cambridge Univ. Press.

Buchanan, James M.; and Tullock, Gordon 1962 *The Calculus of Consent: Logical Foundations of Constitutional Democracy.* Ann Arbor: Univ. of Michigan Press.

Calhoun, John C. (1851) 1953 *A Disquisition on Government, and Selections From the Discourse.* New York: Liberal Arts Press. → Published posthumously.

Clarke, Maude V. (1936) 1964 *Medieval Representation and Consent: A Study of Early Parliaments in England and Ireland With Special Reference to the Modus Tenendi Parliamentum.* New York: Russell.

de Grazia, Alfred 1963 *Apportionment and Representative Government.* New York: Praeger. → A paperback edition was published in 1963 by the American Enterprise Institute.

Friedrich, Carl J. 1942 *The New Belief in the Common Man.* Boston: Little. → See especially Chapter 4.

Heinberg, John G. 1932 Theories of Majority Rule. *American Political Science Review* 26:452–469.

Kendall, Willmoore 1939 The Majority Principle and the Scientific Elite. *Southern Review* 4:463–473.

Kendall, Willmoore 1950 Prolegomena to Any Future Work in Majority Rule. *Journal of Politics* 12:694–713.

Lindblom, Charles E. 1965 *The Intelligence of Democracy: Decision Making Through Mutual Adjustment.* New York: Free Press.

Locke, John (1690) 1964 The Second Treatise of Government: An Essay Concerning the True Original, Extent, and End of Civil Government. Pages 283–446 in John Locke, *Two Treatises of Government.* Cambridge Univ. Press.

McClosky, Herbert 1949 The Fallacy of Absolute Majority Rule. *Journal of Politics* 11:637–654.

Mims, Edwin Jr. 1941 *The Majority of the People.* New York: Modern Age.

Pennock, J. Roland 1952 Responsiveness, Responsibility and Majority Rule. *American Political Science Review* 46:790–807.

Ranney, J. Austin; and Kendall, Willmoore 1951 Democracy: Confusion and Agreement. *Western Political Quarterly* 4:430–439.

Riemer, Neal 1951 The Case for Bare Majority Rule. *Ethics* 62:16–32.

Rousseau, Jean Jacques (1762) 1962 *The Social Contract.* New York: Oxford Univ. Press. → First published in French. See especially Book 4, Chapter 2.

Ward, Benjamin 1961 Majority Rule and Allocation. *Journal of Conflict Resolution* 5:379–389.

MAJUMDAR, D. N.

D. N. Majumdar (1903–1960) was born of Bengali parents. He obtained a first-class master's degree in anthropology from the University of Calcutta in 1924. The training that he received there was in both cultural and physical anthropology, and to the end of his life he retained a broad interest in both the physical and the cultural aspects of the science of man. A large number of his papers and two of his books deal with anthropometric and serological studies among the tribes and castes of Uttar Pradesh, Gujarat, and Bengal.

"General anthropology" was not a mere slogan for Majumdar; it reflected his firm conviction that a unified science of man is not only desirable but also possible. Thus, in his analyses of social stratification in India, he emphasized the need to examine racial factors. Earlier H. H. Risley, in *The Tribes and Castes of Bengal* (1891*a;* 1891*b*) and *The People of India* (1908), had asserted a relationship between race and social groups in India; Majumdar gave further support to this view by his own extensive investigations. He showed that in Uttar Pradesh those castes which constitute "clusters," being close to each other in the hierarchy of castes, also fall within a narrow range of biometric variation (1949). Similarly, in his unpublished studies of growth among the schoolchildren of Uttar Pradesh, he included a sociocultural factor as a significant variable.

The greater part of Majumdar's published work is ethnographic in nature and consists of accounts of the Ho (Bihar), the Khasa, the Korwa, the Tharu, and the so-called criminal tribes (all of Uttar Pradesh), the Gond (Madhya Pradesh), and the Bhil (Gujarat). He published monographic studies of both the Ho (1937) and the Khasa (1962). He knew the Khasa best and spent 22 summers doing field work among them.

Majumdar considered these studies to be contributions to cultural anthropology; he regarded social anthropology as a subdiscipline within cultural anthropology and not as an alternative frame of reference for the study of human social behavior. His approach to the study of culture was that of a functionalist. He went to England in 1933 to work for his doctorate at Cambridge, and he was awarded his degree in 1935. While in England he attended Malinowski's seminar at the London School of Economics and came under his abiding influence. Majumdar was also much influenced by the writings of Ruth Benedict (e.g., Majumdar 1944*a*). He stressed the integrated character of culture and maintained that cultural stresses and strains are the outcome of a disturbance in a culture's "base." The "base" of a culture, he wrote (1937), is a function of four variables, namely, man, area, resources, and cooperation. If the disturbance is not of too fundamental a nature, a culture has a tendency to absorb the shock and revert to its original character; if otherwise, it changes to attain a new equilibrium (1958). His view of culture was thus essentially "integrationist," though not static.

Majumdar was the first formally trained Indian anthropologist to study the impact of nontribal cultures upon the ways of life of Indian tribes. This early interest in cultural change led him, in the 1950s, to welcome the emergence in India of rural anthropology. He played a notable part in this new field of research and produced one of the first book-length village studies in India (1958).

He also pleaded for the application of the findings of social science to the task of national reconstruction. As a member of the Research Programmes Committee of the National Planning Commission, he emphasized the help which anthropologists and sociologists could give to the administration by studying the problems of backward communities and by assessing the impact of government-sponsored projects of community development. His posthumous book on the Khasa (1962) contains a detailed discussion of the community development program in Jaunsar-Bawar (Uttar Pradesh).

It was Majumdar's deep belief in the utility of applied sociological research which made him undertake, in 1954, a survey of the industrial city of Kanpur in Uttar Pradesh (1960*a*). In this, as in many other personal and academic attitudes, he reflected the strong influence of Western social science. Although he did not visit the United States until 1952–1953, when he attended a Wenner–Gren Foundation symposium on anthropology and lectured at Cornell University, from quite early in his life he was receptive to ideas emanating from American universities. Thus, in his very first book (1937) he underscored the importance of studying the psychological dimension of human behavior, particularly in the acceptance and rejection of innovations.

Majumdar's ethnographic works are characterized by a richness and precision of detail, but they lack theoretical sophistication. This is probably due to the fact that almost the whole of his work in physical as well as in cultural anthropology was of a pioneering nature. More than any other individual of his generation, he endeavored to place anthropological studies in India on a scientific footing. The success he achieved, considering the circumstances, was considerable.

At the time of his death, Majumdar was professor of anthropology and dean of the faculty of arts at the University of Lucknow. When he died, a book on polyandry among the Khasa was about to be published; at least one more (a village study) was ready for the publisher; and a research project on growth among schoolchildren in Uttar Pradesh was in progress. He was editor of the *Eastern Anthropologist*, a journal he founded in 1947. All these activities bear testimony to the breadth of his academic interests.

T. N. MADAN

[*Directly related are the entries* ASIAN SOCIETY, *article on* SOUTH ASIA; CASTE; *and the biographies of* BENEDICT *and* MALINOWSKI.]

WORKS BY MAJUMDAR

(1937) 1950 *The Affairs of a Tribe: A Study in Tribal Dynamics*. New & enl. ed. Lucknow: Universal Publishers. → First published as *A Tribe in Transition: A Study in Culture Patterns*.

1944*a* *The Fortunes of Primitive Tribes*. Lucknow: Universal Publishers.

(1944*b*) 1961 *Races and Cultures of India*. 4th ed., rev. & enl. New York and Bombay: Asia Pub. House.

1947 *The Matrix of Indian Culture*. Lucknow: Universal Publishers.

1949 MAHALANOBIS, P. C.; MAJUMDAR, D. N.; and RAO, C. R. Anthropometric Survey of the United Provinces, 1941: A Statistical Study. *Sankhyā: The Indian Journal of Statistics* 9:89–324.

1950 *Race Realities in Cultural Gujarat: Report on the Anthropometric, Serological and Health Survey of Maha Gujarat*. Bombay: Gujarat Research Society.

(1956) 1960 MAJUMDAR, DHIRENDRA N.; and MADAN, T. N. *An Introduction to Social Anthropology*. New York and Bombay: Asia Pub. House.

1958 *Caste and Communication in an Indian Village*. Bombay: Asia Pub. House.

1960*a* *Social Contours of an Industrial City: Social Survey of Kanpur; 1954–1956*. New York and Bombay: Asia Pub. House.

1960*b* MAJUMDAR, DHIRENDRA N.; and RAO, CALYAMPUDI R. *Race Elements in Bengal: A Quantitative Study*. With a foreword by P. C. Mahalanobis. New York and Bombay: Asia Pub. House.

1962 *Himalayan Polyandry: Structure, Functioning and Culture Change; A Field-study of Jaunsar-Bawar*. New York and Bombay: Asia Pub. House. → Published posthumously.

SUPPLEMENTARY BIBLIOGRAPHY

RISLEY, HERBERT H. 1891*a* *The Tribes and Castes of Bengal: Ethnographic Glossary*. 2 vols. Calcutta: Bengal Secretariat Press.

RISLEY, HERBERT H. 1891*b* *The Tribes and Castes of Bengal: Anthropometric Data*. 2 vols. Calcutta: Bengal Secretariat Press.

RISLEY, HERBERT H. (1908) 1915 *The People of India*. 2d ed. Calcutta: Thacker.

MALINOWSKI, BRONISLAW

Bronislaw Kaspar Malinowski (1884–1942) was a Polish-born social anthropologist whose professional training and career, beginning in 1910, were based in England. Through his scientific activities, especially his methodological innovations, he was a major contributor to the transformation of nineteenth-century speculative anthropology into a modern science of man. As a fieldworker, a scholar, a theorist, and above all, a brilliant and controversial teacher and lecturer, he played a decisive part in the formation of the contemporary British school of social anthropology. An accomplished polemicist, he also attracted a wide audience to anthropology as a field of knowledge. Early in his own development he came to view anthropology as a field-oriented science, in which theory and the search for general laws must be based on intensive empirical research involving systematic observation and detailed analyses of actual behavior in living, ongoing societies. His principal field work was carried out among the Papuo-Melanesian people of the Trobriand Islands, located off the coast of New Guinea.

Malinowski's primary scientific interest was in the study of culture as a universal phenomenon and in the development of a methodological framework that would permit the systematic study of specific cultures in all their particularities and open the way to systematic cross-cultural comparison. He reacted strongly against the speculative reconstructions of both evolutionists and diffusionists and against the atomistic treatment of traits and trait complexes torn from their cultural contexts (1926*a*; 1929*a*; 1931*a*). In *The Dynamics of Culture Change* (1945) he insisted that culture change must be subjected to observation and analysis of the total interactive situation. [*See* CULTURE, *article on* CULTURE CHANGE.]

Malinowski was the originator of a functionalist approach to the study of culture. Although the idea of "function" is a key concept throughout his work—from his early scholarly research on the Australian aboriginal family (1913) to his final theoretical statement in *A Scientific Theory of Culture* (1944*a*)—his use of the term was open-ended, exploratory, and subject to continual modification. He treated culture as the assemblage of artifacts and organized traditions through which the individual is molded and the organized social group maintains its integration and achieves continuity. But he also treated culture as an instrumental reality and emphasized its derivation from human needs, from the basic universal needs of the individual organism to the highly elaborated and often specialized needs of a complex society. In his view functionalism was a research tool, "the prerequisite for field-work and for the comparative analysis of phenomena in various cultures" (1944*a*, p. 175), that permitted the study of aspects of culture and the analysis of culture in depth. Through the intermediate analysis of institutions, a functionalist approach revealed the multilevel relationships between man as a psychobiological organism and man's creation, culture. [*See* FUNCTIONAL ANALYSIS.]

For purposes of research and exposition, Malinowski treated each culture as a closed system and all cultures as essentially comparable. However, he made little use of the comparative method, except illustratively. Rather, he treated the empirical study of a specific culture as a contribution to the understanding of the universal phenomenon of culture. In *Argonauts of the Western Pacific* he stated that the ethnographer's final goal must be

> to grasp the native's point of view, his relation to life, to realize *his* vision of *his* world. We have to study man, and we must study what concerns him most intimately, that is, the hold which life has on him. . . . In each culture we find different institutions. . . . To study the institutions, customs, and codes or to study the behaviour and mentality without the subjective desire of feeling by what these people live, of realising the substance of their happiness—is, in my opinion, to miss the greatest reward which we can hope to obtain from the study of man. . . . Perhaps as we read the account of these remote customs there may emerge a feeling of solidarity with the endeavours and ambitions of these natives. Perhaps man's mentality will be revealed to us, and brought near, along some lines which we never have followed before. Perhaps through realising human nature in a shape very distant and foreign to us, we shall have some light shed on our own. (1922*a*, p. 25 in the 1961 edition)

Malinowski regarded residence among the people under study, competent use of the native language, observation of the small events of daily life as well as the large events affecting the community, sensitivity to conflict and shades of opinion, and a consideration of each aspect within the context of the whole culture as indispensable conditions to ethnographic work and, indirectly, to the sound development of theory. His demands on the fieldworker are very high; what is continually captivating is his expectation of the ethnographer's involvement simultaneously with "these natives" and with "man." [*See* ETHNOGRAPHY.]

Intellectual background. Malinowski was born in Cracow in the region of Poland that was then politically part of the Austro–Hungarian empire. His father, Lucyan Malinowski, 1839–1898, an eminent Slavic philologist, was instrumental in bringing modern linguistic studies to Poland and also did work in ethnography and folklore (Symmons-Symonolewicz 1959). Bronislaw Malinowski grew up at a time and in a setting in which central European intellectuals were deeply aware not only of their special cultural heritage (which led many to an intense political nationalism) but also of the multilingual, multicultural milieu in which they moved. Malinowski had a gift for language, and like many intellectuals of his background, he had a wide command of modern languages, including Polish, Russian, German, French, English, Italian, and Spanish. In terms of his background, it is illuminating that his scientific interest in language centered on language as a mode of behavior and on problems of culturally determined meaning. In the same period that Franz Boas returned to the field to study types of speech, using new recording devices, Malinowski predicted the use of sound film for the study of "fully contextualized utterances" (1935*a*, vol. 1, p. 26).

His early experience certainly contributed to his assumptions about cultural uniqueness and the comparability of all cultures, assumptions that are not fully spelled out or tested in his work. They are, of course, crucial to his use of a single primitive culture, that of the Trobriands, as his vehicle of methodological exploration and analysis. However, in seminar discussions he drew—and encouraged his students to draw—on a wide range of complex cultures for contrast and comparison. Both forms of exposition delighted him.

Malinowski's initial training was in physics and mathematics, in which he took his PH.D. in 1908 at the Jagellonian University in Cracow. Ill health, which pursued him all his life, forced him to terminate work in these fields. Then, "as the only solace to his troubles," he began to read, in English, the three-volume edition of Frazer's *The Golden Bough* and discovered that "anthropology . . . is a great science, worthy of as much devotion as any of her elder and more exact sister studies" (1925*a*, pp. 93–94 in the 1954 edition).

For a brief period he studied at the University of Leipzig (where his father had earlier received his doctorate) and, working under Wilhelm Wundt and Karl Bücher, came in contact with current ideas of experimental psychology and historical economics. But in 1910, when he went to England as a postgraduate student at the London School of Economics, he already had his research on Australian aboriginal culture under way (Barnes 1963, p. xii) and probably his book on primitive religion and forms of social structure, later published in Poland (1915*a*).

Work on kinship. British anthropology was lively and contentious then, and Malinowski's work was responsive to the crosscurrents of thought. *The Family Among the Australian Aborigines* (1913) is a magnificent tour de force in its use of a vast patchwork of source materials to make the point (doubtful to those who looked upon the peoples of Australia as the living exemplars of an earlier stage of man) that these peoples had "individual marriage." Characteristically, Malinowski had another aim: "It is not *the* actual relationship, or *the* individual family, or 'family in the European sense'. . . . It is the aboriginal Australian individual family, with all its peculiarities and characteristic features, which must be constructed from the evidence" ([1913] 1963, p. 8). Westermarck's influence on his thinking is clear [*see the biography of* WESTERMARCK]. But he also raised the question of how to "find in all this complexity the structural features, the really essential facts, the knowledge of which in any given society would enable us to give a scientifically valid description of kinship" (*ibid.*, p. 198). Family and kinship, the unique culture and the universally applicable method, these are constant themes in his work.

This study is chiefly valuable today as a period piece and as a source book on Malinowski's thinking at the outset of his career. However, his handling of the data and choice of subject matter are measures of his virtuosity and unerring ability to select as the carrier of his own ideas a problem attractive to fellow scientists and a wider audience as well. [*See* KINSHIP.]

Field research. His interest now shifted to field research in New Guinea, an area that was being opened up by A. C. Haddon, W. H. R. Rivers, C. G. Seligman, and others who influenced his thinking. His training in scientific method and the fine detail of his scholarly work peculiarly fitted him for a part in developing the new techniques of intensive field research. Mainly through Seligman's efforts, he obtained a Robert Mond Travelling Studentship (University of London) and a Constance Hutchinson Scholarship (London School of Economics). Thus equipped, he went out to New Guinea via Australia, where he attended a meeting of the British Association as a guest of the Commonwealth government (which later made him a supplementary grant). In view of the cost of modern field research, it is enlightening to realize that over the six-year period 1914–1920, he had available for field work, data collection, and writing "little more than £250 a year" (1922*a*, p. xix in the 1961 edition).

His first expedition, September 1914 to February 1915, was to the Mailu of Toulon Island. Already familiar with the structure of Melanesian languages—in *Coral Gardens and Their Magic* (1935*a*, vol. 1, p. 453), Malinowski described his progress in learning these languages—he spent four weeks in Port Moresby working on pidgin English and Motu, the lingua franca used by the Mailu. His report on the Mailu (1915*b*), together with his Australian researches, earned him his D.SC. in 1916. But in later years he discounted this first field work. He found the Mailu "coarse and dull" (1922*a*, p. 34 in the 1961 edition). What excited his interest were their accounts of the Massim, to the east, from whom came handsome objects, lively songs and dances, and fearful tales of sorcery and cannibalism. Yet his report on the Mailu is of interest, since it documents not only his use of a conventional framework but also his attempt to use new kinds of ethnographic subject matter (for example, his observations of daily life), his difficulties in coming to grips with the problems of working in an ongoing society, and his leap ahead in recognizing essential conditions for field work. The necessity of working through an interpreter and an intermediate language was a particular source of frustration.

Returning to Australia, he paused briefly on Woodlark Island, where he hoped to work later. Instead, his second expedition, from June 1915 to May 1916, took him to the Trobriand Islands. He set up his tent in Omarakana, the village in which he began his work. By September he had dispensed with an interpreter and was using Kiriwinian, the Trobriand language. But he could follow fast conversation and take notes in the language only on his second Trobriand field trip, from October 1917 to October 1918, after he had organized his first year's notes (1935*a*, vol. 1, p. 453).

Between field trips he wrote his first account of the culture, "Baloma: The Spirits of the Dead in the Trobriand Islands" (1916). In retrospect, it is clear that he had now found his subject, his style of work, and his characteristic mode of presentation. In this essay he described in vivid detail the afterlife of the spirits (*baloma*), their relations to the living, their return visits at feasts in their honor, and their reincarnation. In one digression he discussed magic spells, the use of ancestral names in magic, and the inheritance of magic in this matrilineal, patrilocal society. Another dealt with Trobriand ignorance of physiological paternity and his struggle in the field to clarify Trobriand belief. In the final section he discussed the fieldworker's problem of bringing order into the "chaos of facts"—here referring to the diversity of views, the different levels of knowledge, and the various types of emotional response among different individuals. Fresh from the field, he was convinced that "no 'natives' [in the plural] have ever any belief or any idea; each one has his own ideas and his own beliefs" (1925*a*, p. 240 in the 1954 edition). The ethnographer, studying the "social dimension" in all its complexity, must find ways of systematizing the diversity of formulations and of extricating ideas and beliefs from native behavior and the institutions in which they are embedded. He wrote that "field work consists only and exclusively in the interpretation of the chaotic social reality, in subordinating it to general rules" (*ibid.*, p. 238). [*See* FIELD WORK.] Finally, he defined the opposition between "individual ideas" and "the dogmas of native belief, or the social ideas of a community" that must be "treated as invariably fixed items" (*ibid.*, p. 244), and so he laid the groundwork for his later discussions of myth, magic, and religion. But even as he acknowledged his indebtedness to Durkheim and his school, he rejected the concept of "collective ideas" as incompatible with the reality of the "aggregate of individual souls" in a community (*ibid.*, pp. 273–274, n. 77). This highly selective way of handling the theories of his predecessors, in which he transformed what he accepted, was characteristic of Malinowski's approach, especially in his polemical writings.

This essay exhibits the mosaic quality that is typical of Malinowski's exposition. He stated a theme, he developed it in narrative form around an institution, a set of institutions, or the activities relevant to an aspect of the culture, and at different stages, he interpolated data on other aspects, other activities. Thus, step by step he progressed toward abstraction. On a larger scale the whole of the work on the Trobriands forms a very elaborate mosaic, no part of which stands wholly alone. The successive discussions are not serially linked; instead, his analysis grows by expansion and elaboration, over time, with the elaboration of his own thinking in the process of organizing the data. Yet each work, like this first long essay on the spirits of the dead, is characteristic of the whole.

A large part of Malinowski's work consists in the attempt to develop principles and create models for just this intermediate stage of interpretation, using Trobriand culture as his laboratory. One of the persistent criticisms of his work is that it is "overloaded with reality" (Gluckman 1947, p. 15). But it is with the ordering of this reality that he was concerned.

Career in London. In October 1918 Malinowski returned from the field to Australia. There he married Elsie Masson. He did not immediately go back to London but for reasons of health spent a period on Tenerife in the Canary Islands, where he worked on *Argonauts of the Western Pacific*.

He had first begun to lecture at the London School of Economics in 1913; in the early 1920s he again began to give short courses. In 1924 he was appointed to a readership in anthropology and in 1927 to the first chair in anthropology at the University of London. With the publication of *Argonauts* (1922*a*) his position as a scientist was secure, and he began to acquire an international reputation. The next 15 years, 1923–1938, were his most productive ones as a writer and as a teacher who drew into his seminars an ever-increasing number of talented and mature students, research workers, and professionals from various fields.

Describing Malinowski's relations to his students, Audrey I. Richards wrote:

> He tended to regard them rather as a team engaged on a joint battle than as a number of individuals with different interests and needs. They learnt a particular method of work and a particular theoretical interest, rather than a body of detailed facts. . . . It was in seminars that his teaching gifts were best displayed. These weekly discussions became famous, and attracted students of the most different types. Colonial officers on leave valued Malinowski's live approach. . . . Senior research students came from many parts of the world, and Malinowski would often flash retorts in four or five different languages. University lecturers sat side by side with the veriest amateurs. . . . There was a curious kindling touch in all he did, and a rare power of evoking ideas in others. (1943, p. 3)

Malinowski's teaching methods reflected his own quick responsiveness and his need for response in others. Intellectual pretense he treated with caustic contempt, but he had unexpected resources of patience and gentleness in his relations with able, still inexperienced and self-doubting students. As more mature students progressively measured themselves against his standards of intellectual complexity, skill, and originality, he could be in turn ruthlessly witty at their expense, provocative, and devastatingly critical of what he valued most in them, their capacity for independent judgment. His most able students in time responded with anger and self-assertion mixed with admiration and devotion, a complex of attitudes that is evident in their later, very careful assessments of his work (Firth 1957; Gluckman 1947).

Malinowski's publications in his London years fall into several groups which, while overlapping, indicate his varied interests.

First, there are his major works on the Trobriand Islanders. *Argonauts of the Western Pacific* is an analysis of Trobriand economics through the study of overseas trading expeditions in the highly formalized *kula* ring, in which the circular exchange of "valuables" provided a setting for trade and communication [*see* ECONOMIC ANTHROPOLOGY]. *The Sexual Life of Savages in Northwestern Melanesia* (1929*b*) is an exposition of the individual's induction into the adult life of marriage and the family. Here Malinowski worked out in the field what he had glimpsed through his study of the Australian aboriginal family, and even today it is one of the most detailed and acute analyses of how, in one primitive society, cultural tradition molds individual behavior in the most highly emotionally charged aspect of personal life. *Coral Gardens* (1935*a*), Malinowski's most sophisticated and self-critical work, deals with the organization of Trobriand social life through activities related to horticulture, the place of magic in the belief system, and the integrative aspects of gardening. In this work Malinowski also presented the most sustained exposition of his linguistic approach through analyses of gardening spells.

In a second group of publications, including "Magic, Science and Religion" (1925*a*), *Crime and Custom in Savage Society* (1926*b*), *Myth in Primitive Psychology* (1926*c*), and *The Foundations of Faith and Morals* (1936*a*), he took up, and on several occasions returned to, topics that had long provided controversial issues. Each statement is, among other things, a demonstration of the transforming effect of detailed field work on the criteria of what is relevant to the delineation of a problem. Perhaps in no other context does Malinowski give such clear evidence of his position as a transition figure in social science. For in these essays he breaks new ground not in his choice of topic but in his dazzling use of field data. Yet, though he looks forward in this, he remains linked to the past in his use of very limited data to generalize about primitive culture and man.

Magic, science, and religion. In his handling of science, magic, and religion, Malinowski essentially accepted the traditional Western conception of a dual reality—the reality of the natural world, grounded in observation and rational procedures that lead to mastery, and supernatural reality, grounded in emotional needs that give rise to faith. Unlike Frazer, for example, Malinowski derived science not from magic but from man's capacity to organize knowledge, as demonstrated by Trobriand technical skills in gardening, shipbuilding, etc. In contrast, he treated magic, which coexisted with these skills, as an organized response to a sense of limitation and impotence in the face of danger, difficulty, and frustration. Again, he differentiated between magic and religion in defining magical systems as essentially pragmatic in their aims and religious systems as self-fulfilling rituals organized, for example, around life crises. Significantly, he differentiated between the individual character of religious experience and the social character of religious ritual. In his analysis he linked myth to magic and religion, not as an explanation but as evidence of the authenticity of the magical act and the religious dogma. Particularly illuminating is his discussion of the use of public magic in the Trobriands as an initiating act in the organization of stages of work. *The Foundations of Faith and Morals* represents an attempt to apply hypotheses based on primitive cultures to the problems of European societies [*see* MAGIC; *see also* Nadel 1957].

Anthropology and psychology. Throughout his career Malinowski sought for a systematic psychology on which he could draw in establishing a dynamic relationship between man and culture. In the 1920s Freudian theory had a profound, if somewhat diffuse, influence on his thinking. As Meyer Fortes has pointed out (Firth 1957, pp. 157–188 *passim*), Freud's hypothesis about the Oedipal situation provided Malinowski with a psychological framework for developing his own analysis of the relationship of father, son, and maternal uncle in Trobriand culture. Although he later turned against psychoanalysis, such publications as "The Psychology of Sex" (1923*a*), "Psycho-analysis and Anthropology" (1924), *The Father in Primitive Psychology* (1927*a*), and *The Sexual Life of Savages* (1929*b*), in which he incorporated much of the earlier material, indicate the creative use he made of psychoanalytic concepts and some of the difficulties he faced in trying to transform psychological into cultural process. Even though Malinowski derived culture ultimately from man's needs, he eventually gave precedence to cultural tradition as the primary influence in the molding of the individual. In his last years at Yale he was attracted by Hullian learning theory (1944*a*); in fact, however, it had little effect on the core of his thinking. [*See* CULTURE AND PERSONALITY.]

Culture change. In the late 1920s Malinowski began to turn his attention to problems of culture change and the development of a "practical anthropology" as a field tool. Although he himself was called on for expert advice and his students, working in Africa, were brought face to face with the difficulties of research in rapidly changing societies, his approach was essentially schematic and exploratory (1945). Aside from a four-month trip in 1934 to visit his students' field sites in Africa, he lacked the crucial experience of relevant field work.

Career in the United States. In 1938 Malinowski came to the United States on sabbatical leave. The death of his wife in 1935 after a long illness had broken the thread of his personal life in London. This was not his first visit to America. In 1926 he spent some months there at the invitation of Lawrence K. Frank of the Laura Spelman Rockefeller Memorial. At that time he traveled, taught briefly at the University of California, and visited the Hopi Indians in the Southwest. In 1933 he delivered the Messenger lectures at Cornell University. In 1936 he came as a delegate of the University of London to the Harvard Tercentenary celebration, at which he delivered an address on culture as a determinant of behavior (1936*b*; 1937) and was awarded an honorary D.SC.

After October 1939 he was at Yale University, first as visiting professor, from 1939 to 1940, and then as Bishop Museum visiting professor, from 1940 to 1942. His marriage to Valetta Swann, the painter, in 1940 opened the way to new companionship and happiness.

Nevertheless, the years at Yale were very difficult ones. In the United States he was a stranger, celebrated and sometimes lionized, but a man in exile. For the most part, his Yale students were far less mature than his students in London. They were unfamiliar with his work, and his European point of view seemed no less exotic to most of them than American manners seemed to him. The necessity of beginning his teaching from the beginning again did not stimulate him. The simplified form in which he presented his theoretical system in *A Scientific Theory of Culture* (1944*a*) reflects his detachment. His strictly theoretical presentations (1926*a*; 1929*a*; 1929*c*; 1929*d*; 1931*a*), though elegant, are somewhat bare in comparison with those in which he was arguing or working toward abstraction, but his last and most extended statement is also curiously tentative.

In the 1930s he had become progressively alarmed at the dangers presented by totalitarianism. Like many intellectuals, he worked unsparingly to alert people to the possibility of "a period of dark ages, indeed the darkest ages of human history" (1944*a*, p. 15). Advised not to return to wartime England, he worked passionately on behalf of the democratic cause and a postwar international world order.

In 1940, in spite of ill health, he began a new field project, a study of marketing among the Zapotec of Oaxaca. He planned a series of studies, each from a special stance, and made two field trips in the summers of 1940 and 1941. In between, he worked closely with a young Mexican colleague, Julio de la Fuente, an experienced and accomplished fieldworker. The work promised methodological innovations. In 1942 he received a permanent appointment at Yale, effective in October. He died on May 16 of that year, in the midst of ongoing work.

Assessment. Malinowski's place in anthropology is as yet exceedingly difficult to assess. In the years since his death, much of his theoretical work has been bypassed. Certain of his ideas that made him a storm center in the 1920s have been so fully incorporated into anthropological thinking that his exposition now appears unnecessarily didactic. He was an innovator, but the very necessity of breaking through older conceptions kept his attention focused on issues and problems that were absorbed or transformed by the new methods of observation and analysis and the new theoretical formulations that developed out of his own work and that of his students. Nadel pointed out that "at some stage, someone must ask, and attempt to answer, those 'big' questions if empirical work is to proceed systematically and fruitfully" (1957, p. 190). The necessity of doing so in ways that were relevant to a field-oriented science kept Malinowski a generalist even as he trained his students to become specialists. Nadel spoke for others among Malinowski's students when he said, "Today, we have grown much more modest, but also more conscious of the need for precision and solid empirical evidence" (*ibid.*, p. 189). It was Malinowski's breadth of vision that made this advance possible.

The contribution which his students, even the most critical of them, value is his comprehension of the total field situation and his ability to communicate to others the complex interplay of problem and reality. The actual period of time Malinowski spent in the field was astonishingly brief —only two and one-half years in New Guinea. But in one sense his lifework was a continual renewal and re-creation of this experience.

His method of institutional analysis made it possible for him to express, through a model, certain core ideas of his theory: the integrity of each culture; the complex interrelationship of the society, the culture, and the individual; the grounding of culture in the human organism (in man's needs and capacities and in the individual as the carrier of culture); and the systematic nature of culture as a phenomenon. He treated the institution as the unit of analysis; whatever its difficulties in application, it indicates how complex any "unit" of analysis must be.

Malinowski's theoretical framework is a major contribution. However, no anthropologist today is prepared to make the dizzying leap from the particular to the universal that characterized his attempt to create an effective methodology. There are essential intermediate steps. These involve, for example, intensive studies of process within and across cultures and over time. We require also fine-grained systematic comparison of intensively studied cultures and cultural process. Today we are acquiring the tools (for example, the sound-film recording devices Malinowski himself foresaw as necessary in studies of communication) that are making more delicate and systematic research feasible. Malinowski's search for an adequate psychology was a step toward broadening the base of empirical research. But collaboration among all the relevant sciences will be necessary. The study of culture is crucial to, but not in itself sufficient for, the development of a science of man.

Malinowski's attempt to formulate theory on the basis of limited data places him in extreme contrast with his older contemporary Franz Boas, as does his almost exclusive preoccupation with a theory of culture. Boas had a very broad experience, beginning early in his career, in planning for and administrating research, in much of which he was personally involved, in the whole field of anthropology. Necessarily, he worked within a comparative framework in space and time, and with full awareness of the importance of carefully recorded detail. Like Malinowski, he had the natural scientist's commitment to the formulation of general laws, but in his case, concern for long-term gains made him extremely dubious of the value of theoretical formulations based on partial evidence.

In the history of a science it is necessary to take into account the temperamental as well as the experiential differences among innovators. It is possible that the tensions necessary for the development of new thinking arise from just such differences. Malinowski's impact on a whole generation of anthropologists—like that of Boas—was a measure of his capacity as a thinker and a teacher to evoke in others a clear perception of the state of the science and confidence in the value of their own work. It remains to be seen whether their successors can resolve these tensions through research that will shape new aims.

RHODA MÉTRAUX

WORKS BY MALINOWSKI

1912*a* The Economic Aspect of the Intichiuma Ceremonies. Pages 81–108 in *Festskrift tillegnad Edvard Westermarck i Anledning av hans femtioårsdag den 20 november 1912.* Helsingfors (Finland): Simelli.

1912*b* Plemienne zwiazki w Australii (Tribal Male Associations of the Australian Aborigines). Akademja Umiejetnosci, Krakow, Wydział Filologiczny, Wydział Historycznofilozoficzny, *Bulletin international* . . . [1912]:56–63.

(1913) 1963 *The Family Among the Australian Aborigines: A Sociological Study.* New York: Schocken.

1915*a* *Wierzenia pierwotne i formy ustroju społecznego* (Primitive Religion and Forms of Social Structure). Cracow (Poland): Akademja Umiejetnosci.

1915*b* The Natives of Mailu: Preliminary Results of the Robert Mond Research Work in British New Guinea. Royal Society of South Australia, *Transactions* 39: 494–706.

(1916) 1948 Baloma: The Spirits of the Dead in the Trobriand Islands. Pages 125–227 in Bronislaw Malinowski, *Magic, Science and Religion, and Other Essays.* Glencoe, Ill.: Free Press. → First published in Volume 46 of the *Journal of the Royal Anthropological Institute of Great Britain and Ireland.*

1918 Fishing in the Trobriand Islands. *Man* 18:87–92.

1920*a* Classificatory Particles in the Language of Kiriwina. London, University of, School of Oriental and African Studies, *Bulletin* 1, no. 4:33–78.

1920*b* Kula: The Circulating Exchange of Valuables in the Archipelagoes of Eastern New Guinea. *Man* 20: 97–105.

1920*c* War and Weapons Among the Natives of the Trobriand Islands. *Man* 20:10–12.

1921 The Primitive Economics of the Trobriand Islanders. *Economic Journal* 31:1–16.

(1922*a*) 1960 *Argonauts of the Western Pacific: An Account of Native Enterprise and Adventure in the Archipelagoes of Melanesian New Guinea.* London School of Economics and Political Science, Studies, No. 65. London: Routledge; New York: Dutton. → A paperback edition was published in 1961 by Dutton.

1922*b* Ethnology and the Study of Society. *Economica* 2:208–219.

1923*a* The Psychology of Sex in Primitive Societies. *Psyche* 4:98–128.

(1923*b*) 1948 The Problem of Meaning in Primitive Languages. Pages 228–276 in Bronislaw Malinowski, *Magic, Science and Religion, and Other Essays.* Glencoe, Ill.: Free Press.

1923*c* Psycho-analysis and Anthropology [Letter to the Editor]. *Nature* 112:650–651.

1924 Psycho-analysis and Anthropology. *Psyche* 4:293–332.

(1925*a*) 1948 Magic, Science and Religion. Pages 1–71 in Bronislaw Malinowski, *Magic, Science and Religion, and Other Essays.* Glencoe, Ill.: Free Press. → A paperback edition was published in 1954 by Doubleday; citations in the article are to this edition.

1925*b* Complex and Myth in Mother-right. *Psyche* 5: 194–216.

1925*c* The Forces of Law and Order in a Primitive Community. Royal Institution of Great Britain, London, *Proceedings* 24:529–547.

1925*d* Forschungen in einer mutterrechtlichen Gemeinschaft (Auf den Trobriand-Inseln, östlich von Neu-Guinea, Südsee). *Zeitschrift für Völkerpsychologie und Soziologie* 1:45–53.

1926*a* Anthropology. Supplementary volume 1, pages 131–140 in *Encyclopaedia Britannica.* 13th ed. Chicago: Benton.

(1926*b*) 1961 *Crime and Custom in Savage Society.* London: Routledge.

1926*c* *Myth in Primitive Psychology.* London: Routledge; New York: Norton.

1926*d* Anthropology and Administration [Letter to the Editor]. *Nature* 118:768.

1926*e* The Life of Culture. *Psyche* 7, no. 2: 37–44.

1926*f* Primitive Law and Order. *Nature* 117 (Supplement):9–16.

1926*g* The Role of Myth in Life. *Psyche* 6, no. 4:29–39.

1927*a* *The Father in Primitive Psychology.* London: Routledge.

(1927*b*) 1928 The Life of Culture. Pages 26–46 in Grafton Elliot Smith et al., *Culture: The Diffusion Controversy.* London: Routledge.

1927*c* Lunar and Seasonal Calendar in the Trobriands. *Journal of the Royal Anthropological Institute of Great Britain and Ireland* 57:203–215.

1927*d* Prenuptial Intercourse Between the Sexes in the Trobriand Islands, N.W. Melanesia. *Psychoanalytic Review* 14:20–35.

(1927*e*) 1953 *Sex and Repression in Savage Society.* London: Routledge; New York: Harcourt. → A paperback edition was published in 1955 by Meridian.

1928 The Anthropological Study of Sex. Volume 5, pages 92–108 in International Congress for Sex Research, First, Berlin, 1926, *Verhandlungen.* Berlin: Marcus & Weber.

1929*a* Social Anthropology. Volume 20, pages 862–870 in *Encyclopaedia Britannica.* 14th ed. Chicago: Benton.

(1929*b*) 1962 *The Sexual Life of Savages in Northwestern Melanesia: An Ethnographic Account of Courtship, Marriage, and Family Life Among the Natives of the Trobriand Islands, British New Guinea.* New York: Harcourt.

(1929*c*) 1962 Kinship. Pages 132–150 in Bronislaw Malinowski, *Sex, Culture and Myth.* New York: Harcourt.

(1929*d*) 1962 Marriage. Pages 1–35 in Bronislaw Malinowski, *Sex, Culture and Myth.* New York: Harcourt.

1929*e* Practical Anthropology. *Africa* 2:22–38.

1930*a* Kinship. *Man* 30:19–29.

1930*b* Parenthood: The Basis of Social Structure. Pages 113–168 in Victor F. Calverton and Samuel D. Schmalhausen (editors), *The New Generation: The Intimate Problems of Modern Parents and Children.* New York: Macaulay.

1930*c* Race and Labour. *Listener* 4, Supplement no. 8.

1930*d* The Rationalization of Anthropology and Administration. *Africa* 3:405–430. → Includes a résumé in French.

1931*a* Culture. Volume 4, pages 621–645 in *Encyclopaedia of the Social Sciences.* New York: Macmillan.

1931*b* The Relations Between the Sexes in Tribal Life. Pages 565–585 in Victor F. Calverton (editor), *The Making of Man: An Outline of Anthropology.* New York: Modern Library.

1931*c* Science and Religion. Pages 65–81 in *Science & Religion: A Symposium.* London: Howe.

1932 Pigs, Papuans, and Police Court Perspective. *Man* 32:33–38.

1933 The Work and Magic of Prosperity in the Trobriand Islands. *Mensch en maatschappij* 9:154–174.

1934 Stone Implements in Eastern New Guinea. Pages 189–196 in *Essays Presented to C. G. Seligman.* London: Routledge.

(1935*a*) 1965 *Coral Gardens and Their Magic.* 2 vols. Bloomington: Indiana Univ. Press.

1935*b* Preface. In Friedrich Lorentz et al., *The Cassubian Civilization.* London: Faber.

1936*a* *The Foundations of Faith and Morals: An Anthropological Analysis of Primitive Beliefs and Conduct With Special Reference to the Fundamental Problems of Religion and Ethics.* Oxford Univ. Press.

1936*b* Culture as a Determinant of Behavior. *Scientific Monthly* 43:440–449.

1936*c* The Deadly Issue. *Atlantic Monthly* 158:659–669.

1936*d* Native Education and Culture Contact. *International Review of Missions* 25:480–515.

1937 Culture as a Determinant of Behavior. Pages 133–168 in Harvard Tercentenary Conference of Arts and Sciences, Cambridge, Mass., 1936, *Factors Determining Human Behavior.* Cambridge, Mass.: Harvard Univ. Press.

1938*a* The Anthropology of Changing African Cultures. Pages vii–xxxviii in *Methods of Study of Culture Contact in Africa.* International Institute of African Languages and Cultures, Memorandum 15. Oxford Univ. Press.

1938*b* A Nation-wide Intelligence Service. Pages 81–121 in Charles Madge and Tom Harrisson (editors), *First Year's Work, 1937–1938, by Mass-observation.* London: Drummond.

1939*a* The Group and the Individual in Functional Analysis. *American Journal of Sociology* 44:938–964.

1939*b* The Present State of Studies in Culture Contact: Some Comments on an American Approach. *Africa* 12:27–47.

(1941*a*) 1948 An Anthropological Analysis of War. Pages 277–309 in Bronislaw Malinowski, *Magic, Science and Religion, and Other Essays.* Glencoe, Ill.: Free Press. → First published in Volume 46 of the *American Journal of Sociology.*

1941*b* War—Past, Present and Future. Pages 21–31 in American Historical Association, *War as a Social Institution: The Historian's Perspective.* Edited by Jesse D. Clarkson and Thomas C. Cochran. New York: Columbia Univ. Press.

1941–1942 Man's Culture and Man's Behavior. *Sigma Xi Quarterly* 29:182–196; 30:66–78.

1942 The Scientific Approach to the Study of Man. Pages 207–242 in Ruth N. Anshen (editor), *Science and Man: Twenty-four Original Essays.* New York: Harcourt.

1944*a* *A Scientific Theory of Culture, and Other Essays.* Chapel Hill: Univ. of North Carolina Press. → A paperback edition was published in 1960 by Oxford Univ. Press.

1944*b* *Freedom and Civilization.* With a preface by Valetta Malinowska. New York: Roy.

(1945) 1949 *The Dynamics of Culture Change: An Inquiry Into Race Relations in Africa.* New Haven: Yale Univ. Press. → A paperback edition was published in 1961.

1957 MALINOWSKI, BRONISLAW; and FUENTE, JULIO DE LA *"La economía de un sistema de mercados en México": Un ensayo de ethnografía contemporánea y cambio social en un valle Mexicano.* Acta anthropologica, Epoca 2, Vol. 1, no. 2. Mexico City: Escuela Nacional de Anthropología e Historia, Sociedad de Alumnos.

Magic, Science and Religion, and Other Essays. Glencoe, Ill.: Free Press, 1948. → Contains essays published between 1916 and 1941. An abridged paperback edition was published in 1954 by Doubleday.

Sex, Culture and Myth. New York: Harcourt, 1962. → Contains essays first published between 1913 and 1941.

SUPPLEMENTARY BIBLIOGRAPHY

BARNES, J. A. 1963 Introduction. In Bronislaw Malinowski, *The Family Among the Australian Aborigines: A Sociological Study.* New York: Schocken.

FIRTH, RAYMOND (editor) (1957) 1964 *Man and Culture: An Evaluation of the Work of Bronislaw Malinowski.* New York: Harper.

GLUCKMAN, MAX (1947) 1949 *An Analysis of the Sociological Theories of Bronislaw Malinowski.* Rhodes-Livingstone Papers, No. 16. Oxford Univ. Press.

KABERRY, PHYLLIS M. (1945) 1958 Introduction. In Bronislaw Malinowski, *The Dynamics of Culture Change: An Inquiry Into Race Relations in Africa.* New Haven: Yale Univ. Press.

LEACH, EDMUND R. 1965 Frazer and Malinowski. *Encounter* 25, no. 5:24–36.

LEE, DOROTHY D. 1940 A Primitive System of Values. *Philosophy of Science* 7:355–378.

LEE, DOROTHY D. (1949) 1959 Being and Value in a Primitive Culture. Pages 89–104 in Dorothy D. Lee, *Freedom and Culture: Essays.* Englewood Cliffs, N.J.: Prentice-Hall. → First published in the *Journal of Philosophy.*

LEE, DOROTHY D. (1950) 1959 Codifications of Reality: Lineal and Nonlineal. Pages 105–120 in Dorothy D. Lee, *Freedom and Culture: Essays.* Englewood Cliffs, N.J.: Prentice-Hall. → First published in *Psychosomatic Medicine.*

LOWIE, ROBERT H. 1937 *The History of Ethnological Theory.* New York: Farrar & Rinehart.

LOWIE, ROBERT H. 1947 Biographical Memoir of Franz Boas: 1858–1942. National Academy of Sciences, Washington, D.C., *Biographical Memoirs* 24:303–322.

MURDOCK, GEORGE P. 1943 Bronislaw Malinowski. *American Anthropologist* New Series 45:441–451.

NADEL, S. F. 1957 Malinowski on Magic and Religion. Pages 189–208 in Raymond Firth (editor), *Man and Culture: An Evaluation of the Work of Bronislaw Malinowski.* London: Routledge.

RADCLIFFE-BROWN, A. R. 1946 A Note on Functional Anthropology. *Man* 46:38–41.

RICHARDS, AUDREY I. 1943 Bronislaw Kaspar Malinowski: Born 1884–Died 1942. *Man* 43:1–4.

SYMMONS-SYMONOLEWICZ, KONSTANTIN 1958 Bronislaw Malinowski: An Intellectual Profile. *Polish Review* 3, no. 4:55–76.

SYMMONS-SYMONOLEWICZ, KONSTANTIN 1959 Bronislaw Malinowski: Formative Influences and Theoretical Evolution. *Polish Review* 4, no. 4:17–45.

SYMMONS-SYMONOLEWICZ, KONSTANTIN 1960 Bronislaw Malinowski: Individuality as a Theorist. *Polish Review* 5, no. 1:53–65.

MALNUTRITION

See FAMINE *and* FOOD.

MALTHUS, THOMAS ROBERT

Thomas Robert Malthus (1766–1834) was born ten years before the publication of Adam Smith's *Wealth of Nations,* and his work as an economist belongs to the broad tradition established by Smith's treatise. After being privately educated, Malthus entered Jesus College, Cambridge, where he was elected to a fellowship at the age of 27. He took orders in 1797 and held a curacy for a short period. He married in 1805 and shortly thereafter was appointed professor of modern history and political economy at the East India Company's college at Haileybury, the first appointment of its kind in England. He died at Haileybury in 1834, the year that saw the passage of a new poor law inspired by his writings.

Malthus' father was a friend of Rousseau and shared the optimistic belief of Condorcet and William Godwin that nothing stood in the way of a regime of ideal equality but private ignorance and public inertia: propaganda and education were therefore the means for bringing about perfect happiness. The younger Malthus disagreed and argued that the effort to realize the perfect human society would always founder on the tendency of population to outrun the food supply. His father urged him to put his ideas on paper, and in 1798 Malthus published a long pamphet entitled *An Essay on the Principle of Population, as It Affects the Future Improvement of Society; With Remarks on the Speculations of Mr. Godwin, M. Condorcet, and Other Writers.* There was nothing original in Malthus' argument. It had all been said before, albeit with less force. Nevertheless, Malthus was attacking the dominant contemporary view, which saw underpopulation rather than overpopulation as a problem. When the first census, in 1801, produced evidence of a sharp rise in population growth in recent decades, Malthus decided to take advantage of the change in the climate of opinion by turning his pamphlet into a book (published in 1803) with a new subtitle that implied a change in emphasis: *A View of Its Past and Present Effects on Human Happiness With an Inquiry Into Our Prospects Respecting the Future Removal or Mitigation of the Evils Which It Occasions.* What had started out as an occasional tract against certain dangerous ideas held by some contemporary thinkers had become a full-scale treatise on the subject of demography. Further revised editions of the book were published at regular intervals during his lifetime, the sixth edition appearing in 1826.

Although Malthus' fame in the nineteenth century was based squarely on his theory of population, his modern reputation with economists rests rather on his prescient opposition to the Ricardian doctrine of the impossibility of "general gluts." As Keynes put it in *The General Theory*: "Ricardo conquered England as completely as the Holy Inquisition conquered Spain," in consequence of which, "The great puzzle of Effective Demand with which Malthus had wrestled vanished from economic literature" (1936, p. 32). Malthus' ideas on gluts, or, as we would now say, business depressions, were embodied in his *Principles of Political Economy*, first published in 1820. Other minor but significant publications on strictly economic questions are *An Inquiry Into the Nature and Progress of Rent* (1815); *The Measure of Value Stated and Illustrated* (1823); and *Definitions in Political Economy* (1827).

Demographic ideas. Malthus' theory of population is baldly stated in the first two chapters of the *Essay*. These pages are brilliantly written in terse phrases and striking images, and they help us to understand why the book captured the imagination of its first readers, rousing a storm of controversy that never died down during Malthus' lifetime. The thesis itself is familiar enough, although all of its implications are not immediately evident: population, *when unchecked*, increases in a geometrical ratio, while the food supply at best increases in an arithmetical ratio; hence, population tends to increase up to the limits of "the means of subsistence." This is *the* principle of population that Malthus maintained against all his critics. He realized, of course, that in the real world there are checks that prevent population from increasing beyond the food supply. The checks are of two kinds: "positive" checks that show up in the death rate, such as war, famine, and pestilence; and "preventive checks" that show up in the birth rate, such as abortions, infanticide, and birth control. Both checks are the consequences of lack of food, which may, indeed, be regarded as the ultimate check on population growth that is always in operation.

Such was Malthus' argument in the first edition of the *Essay*. Its weakness was quickly discovered by Godwin, who pointed out that the working classes in the richer countries seemed to be maintaining themselves at a level considerably above the physical minimum of existence, without benefit of either the positive or the preventive checks. Malthus, realizing that he had trapped himself by denying the possibility of any rise in the standard of living, quietly gave way in the second edition of the *Essay* by recognizing the existence of a new preventive check, namely, "moral restraint." He defined "moral restraint" as postponement of the age of marriage accompanied by strict sexual continence before marriage, and, while the other checks were frequently described as "misery" or "vice," the new preventive check was allowed to stand alone without any pejorative tag attached to it. For the first time a hopeful note crept into the argument, although Malthus himself always remained profoundly pessimistic about the capacity of mankind to regulate its numbers by the exercise of prudential restraint. Few readers realized that he had really abandoned his original thesis, and Malthus did nothing to help them appreciate the escape clause that had now been built into the doctrine.

Any critic who produced evidence of subsistence increasing faster than population without signs of "misery" or "vice" was silenced by the logical implication that the working class must be practicing "moral restraint," a phenomenon included in the theory. This left the critic with no reply other than to show that the average age of marriage had not increased or that the rate of illegitimate births had not fallen. Since contemporary population statistics were not adequate to verify such assertions, Malthus had furnished himself with an impregnable defense. There were a few critics who attacked the theory by questioning the notion that birth control constitutes "vice." Malthus' argument here was simply that birth control must be wrong, since man, being naturally indolent, could hardly be expected to work or save if it were made so easy for him to escape the consequences of his "natural passions." He was confident of the support of contemporary opinion in lightly dismissing what were later called neo-Malthusian checks, "both on account of their immorality and their tendency to remove a necessary stimulus to industry" ([1798] page 512 in 1878 edition).

Some hostile critics realized the futility of denying that unchecked populations tend to increase at a geometrical rate, inasmuch as no one had ever observed the growth of an unchecked population. Instead, they attacked the idea that the food supply could not possibly keep pace with the irrepressible tide of population. Here Malthus had recourse to the principle of diminishing returns in agriculture —in fact, he was one of the first to state this general principle in so many words. Since this principle soon became an integral part of orthodox political economy via Ricardo's theory of rent, it was difficult to criticize Malthus on this score [*see* RICARDO]. We realize now that Malthus was actually appealing not to the impeccable Ricardian law of diminishing returns to variable factor increments in a situation of given technical knowledge, but to a questionable historical law of diminishing returns from technical progress in agriculture. But the distinction between statics and dynamics was so little understood in those days—even Ricardo switched easily from static analysis to historical generalization, sometimes in the same sentence—that Malthus had no difficulty in meeting criticism along these lines.

The utter simplicity and familiarity of the ideas involved, calling neither for new concepts nor for new facts, was the essence of Malthus' popular appeal. All he seemed to be doing was to bring together a few familiar facts of life and to deduce the necessary consequences of these facts. Surely it was true that population nearly always multiplied up to the limits of the available food supply. And surely, where living standards had improved, the gain was necessarily precarious and always liable to disappear in a new spurt of population growth. Was it not self-evident that an unchecked multiplication of human beings must quickly lead to an impossible situation, whatever the plausible rate of increase of the means of subsistence? The contrast that Malthus drew between the two kinds of mathematical progression carried the hypnotic persuasive power of an advertising slogan. It was easy to see—"a slight acquaintance with numbers will show," as Malthus said—that even the smallest finite sum growing at the smallest *compound* rate must eventually overwhelm even the largest possible finite sum growing at the highest *simple* rate, so that, whatever the initial situation, there must soon be "standing room only." *Quod erat demonstrandum!*

It did not hurt the Malthusian theory that it justified the resistance of the upper classes to all efforts to reform existing social and political institutions: for if poverty had its roots in the unequal race between population and subsistence, only the working class itself, by practicing prudential restraint, could improve its own conditions. Even the working-class newspapers of the day accepted the desirability of prudential restraint and condemned birth control devices. The Malthusian theory of population was widely appealing: it neatly explained the existence of poverty; it exposed the visionary panaceas of reformers; it enabled everyone to pontificate on questions of public policy; it rationalized the subsistence theory of wages, to which all contemporary economists subscribed; lastly, it underlay Ricardo's preoccupation with the land-using bias of economic progress, and Ricardo was the foremost economist of the day. Any one of these factors would have been enough to make a theory influential. Put together, they fully account for Malthus' astonishing success, a success that has few parallels in the history of ideas.

Despite all the attractive features of the Malthusian theory, it is doubtful, however, whether it would have received so wide a hearing if there had not also been a population explosion in the last two decades of the eighteenth century. Strangely enough, when Malthus published the first edition of the *Essay* in 1798, he shared the general belief of his day that the population of England had actually increased little in the eighteenth century. The census of 1801 showed how wrong everyone had been, and later generations credited Malthus with prophetic foresight in warning of the dangers of overpopulation as early as 1798. But, in fact, Malthus made no effort, nor was it his intention, to explain the unprecedented population explosion, even in the later versions of the *Essay*. Furthermore, it is evident that he did not provide the tools for such an explanation. The Malthusian theory emphasizes birth and marriage rates, whereas the population explosion of the 1780s was a more complicated phenomenon of rising birth rates in new factory districts and falling death rates in rural areas and congested towns. Unfortunately, the demographic data of the period, based as they are on defective registration of baptisms and burials, are so unreliable that modern authorities are still not agreed on whether the industrial revolution largely created its own labor force by a demand pull on births or whether improved sanitation, nutrition, and housing produced a supply push through a fall in the death rate. The fact remains, however, that Malthus makes a poor guide to the causes of the population explosion that gave such prominence to his views.

Permanent influence. Malthus' magisterial influence on public opinion lasted until the last decades of the nineteenth century. By that time, the record of sustained economic growth, the rise in the standard of living, and the decline in fertility in Western countries made disparagement of the Malthusian doctrine as common as praise had been before. Every schoolboy at the turn of the twentieth century could prove that Malthus had gone wrong by underestimating both the potentialities of technical progress and the possibility of family limitation by birth control devices. As far as it goes, of course, this is a perfectly valid refutation of the Malthusian theory, but it is so obvious now that it is hardly worth stating. One can make a much stronger case against Malthus.

The Malthusian theory of population is a perfect example of metaphysics masquerading as science. So long as we hold with Malthus that birth control is morally reprehensible, the history of population growth in the last two centuries proves him right: nothing has stemmed the tide of human numbers but "misery" and "vice." If, on the other hand, we consider birth control morally defensible, Malthus is vindicated again: "moral restraint" in the larger sense of the phrase is one of the checks that has limited the tendency of population to outstrip the food supply. The Malthusian theory cannot be refuted because it can be applied to any actual or any conceivable population change: it purports to say something about the real world, and what it says must be true by definition of its own terms.

By the 1920s, the Malthusian theory had lost almost all of its earlier prestige. Indeed, the Malthusian specter of overpopulation had given way to the Keynesian specter of underpopulation. But since World War II, the problem of underdeveloped countries has brought Malthus back into favor. Most underdeveloped countries today have the worst of both worlds: the typical high birth rates of agrarian economies and the typical low death rates of urbanized industrialized economies. Economic development will in time cure these difficulties, as they were cured in industrial Europe, but for the next few generations these countries face the alternative of the Malthusian checks of famine and disease or voluntary family limitation in opposition to prevailing religious mores. The name of Malthus is still bandied about in debates on population policies in Asia, Africa, and Latin America, although it is difficult to believe that the Malthusian theory has much relevance to the discussion of modern population problems. It sheds no light on the causes of declining fertility in developing societies; it tells us little about the demographic relationship between fertility and mortality; it is silent on the economic and social consequences of changes in the age distribution of a population; and it is of no help in framing policies for areas of heavy population pressure. Be that as it may, there is no doubt that the revival of interest in the Malthusian doctrine in our own day makes it one of the longest-lived social theories of all times. And, popular interest apart, demographers can never ignore him or forget him, for, with all his errors, Malthus put the problem of population growth on the map.

MARK BLAUG

[*For the historical context of Malthus' work, see* INCOME AND EMPLOYMENT THEORY; POPULATION, *article on* POPULATION THEORIES; *and the biography of* CONDORCET. *For discussion of the subsequent development of Malthus' ideas, see* POPULATION, *articles on* OPTIMUM POPULATION THEORY *and* POPULATION POLICIES; *and the biographies of* RICARDO *and* MARX.]

WORKS BY MALTHUS

(1798) 1960 *On Population.* New York: Modern Library. → First published in pamphlet form as *An Essay on the Principle of Population.* A paperback edition was published in 1963 by Irwin.

1815 *An Inquiry Into the Nature and Progress of Rent, and the Principles by Which It Is Regulated.* London: Murray.

(1820) 1964 *Principles of Political Economy Considered With a View to Their Practical Application.* 2d ed. New York: Kelley.

1823 *The Measure of Value Stated and Illustrated, With an Application of It to the Alterations in the Value of the English Currency Since 1790.* London: Murray.

1827 *Definitions in Political Economy.* London: Murray.

SUPPLEMENTARY BIBLIOGRAPHY

BLAUG, MARK 1962 *Economic Theory in Retrospect.* Homewood, Ill.: Irwin. → Reviews the theoretical issues in the inconclusive debate between Ricardo and Malthus, and lists additional readings on both sides of the question. Also considers Malthus' employment theory.

BONAR, JAMES (1885) 1924 *Malthus and His Work.* 2d ed. London: Allen & Unwin; New York: Macmillan.

BONER, H. A. 1955 *Hungry Generations: The 19th-Century Case Against Malthusianism.* New York: King's Crown Press; Oxford Univ. Press.

CANNAN, EDWIN (1893) 1953 *A History of the Theories of Production and Distribution in English Political Economy From 1776 to 1848.* 3d ed. London and New York: Staples.

GLASS, D. V. (editor) 1953 *Introduction to Malthus.* London: Watts; New York: Wiley. → Contains useful background material, as well as a reprint of Malthus' "Summary View of the Principle of Population," which he contributed to the *Encyclopaedia Britannica* in 1830.

KEYNES, JOHN MAYNARD 1936 *The General Theory of Employment, Interest and Money.* London: Macmillan.

MCCLEARY, GEORGE F. 1953 *The Malthusian Population Theory.* London: Faber. → Contains a spirited defense of Malthus' ideas on population.

NEWMAN, JAMES R. 1956 Commentary on Thomas Robert Malthus. Volume 2, pages 1189–1191 in James R. Newman (editor), *The World of Mathematics: A Small Library of the Literature of Mathematics From A'h-mosé the Scribe to Albert Einstein.* New York: Simon & Schuster.

SMITH, KENNETH 1951 *The Malthusian Controversy.* London: Routledge. → Reviews the great nineteenth-century debate on the Malthusian doctrine.

UNITED NATIONS, DEPARTMENT OF SOCIAL AFFAIRS, POPULATION DIVISION 1953 *The Determinants and Consequences of Population Trends.* Population Studies, No. 17. New York: United Nations. → Covers succinctly the history of population theory before and after Malthus.

MAN

See ANTHROPOLOGY; EVOLUTION; RACE.

MAN, HENDRIK (HENRI) DE

Hendrik (Henri) de Man (1885–1953), a Flemish-born socialist militant, was led by his long and disheartening experience with the stultified proletariat and bureaucratized socialist movements of Belgium, Germany, and England to question the doctrinal and pragmatic adequacy of that radical Marxism to which he had early subscribed. His searing experience during World War I of man's capacity for self-sacrifice and of the role of national identity precipitated a major reformulation of socialist ideology, presented in his works *Psychology of Socialism* (1926) and *Die sozialistische Idee* (1933). This critique from the left could not be dismissed as mere bourgeois propaganda and, moreover, answered to the radical discontent with socialist practice reflected at that time in the defection of militants to the communist movement.

De Man's essential argument concerned the inadequacy of Marxist theory to account for contemporary trends within the socialist movement—above all, the unacknowledged collapse of chiliastic expectations that a socialist society would be ensured by means of the proletarian conquest of power. In political reality, the widening split between socialist practice and theory was leading to the covert sanctioning of reformist accommodation to the Western bourgeois order, a process that was merely veiled by the increasingly unrealistic revolutionary ideology. At the same time, the Russian experience demonstrated that orthodox Marxism could engender a tyrannical and Philistine sham egalitarianism.

The basic cause of the discrepancy between theory and practice was, de Man argued, the utilitarian explanation of behavior, which Marxism had inherited from classical economics. In interpreting all significant human action as the product of the maximization of advantages, "scientific socialism" had misinterpreted its own nature. This was strikingly demonstrated by its failure to explain such an anomaly as the absence of a class-conscious socialist movement in America and by the interpretation of the European movement as a response to economic conditions per se rather than to the conjunction of these conditions with invidious social distinctions.

De Man believed that if the autonomous role of values were recognized, it would also become evident that the development of a socialist society involved not only revolutionizing outward relations to the means of production but also infusing the work role itself with socialist values. This insight informed de Man's pioneer study in industrial sociology, *Joy in Work* (1927). Further, he held that an ideology that justified socialism in terms of values rather than class interests would more clearly establish the manifold goals of the socialist movement and would facilitate its coming to political power by furnishing a cogent basis for rallying nonproletarian support.

These ideological considerations received concrete political expression in the form of the *plan du travail* with which de Man returned to Belgium in 1933 from the University of Frankfurt, shaken by the overthrow of that *Sozialdemokratie* in which he had invested his greatest hope of reformation. The new plan of action, which defined a minimal program necessary to resuscitate the economy—essentially a substantial public works program and public control of the principal credit institutions—and which called for political support from all segments of the population suffering from the hegemony of finance capitalism, revived the *élan* of the Belgian socialist party. But with the onset of a financial crisis in 1935 the party, in effect, sacrificed integral *planisme* in order to participate in progressive coalition governments, in which de Man occupied strategic ministerial positions.

In the late 1930s de Man, frustrated by the evanescence of "structural reform" and unsuited by temperament to the compromises of political practice, called for radical revision of parliamentary government in the direction of what he termed authoritarian democracy, capable of sustained and resolute action. He also diverged from his fellow socialists in his fidelity to the appeasement policy; upon the Nazi conquest, he issued a manifesto in which he celebrated the cessation of the ineffective political role of the socialist movement and recommended a rigidly neutralist policy toward the occupying power (1940). Within a year de Man had to acknowledge the bankruptcy of his desperate attempt to construe Nazism in the image of socialism, and he thereupon completely withdrew from public life. He found ultimate refuge in Switzerland and after the war was convicted *in absentia* for treason. Generalizing from the ruin of his life's ambitions, he concluded that the socialist movement could not transcend its capitalist environment; in the general decadence the responsible individual could hope only that it would be possible to preserve the patrimony of the ages despite the convulsions of the historical "zone of catastrophe."

If the political circumstances of the 1930s robbed de Man's ideological reformulation of its force, the folly of the war years guaranteed that none thereafter would speak in his name. Yet postwar developments have moved socialism in the direction he indicated, and perhaps the perspicacity of this sociological socialist is best indicated by his insistence that responsible socialism must make ideological provision for the positive implementation of the rights of man in industrial society.

PETER DODGE

[*For the historical context of de Man's work, see* MARXISM *and* SOCIALISM; *for discussion of the subsequent development of his ideas, see* INDUSTRIAL RELATIONS *and* MARXIST SOCIOLOGY.]

WORKS BY DE MAN

(1926) 1928 *Psychology of Socialism.* London: Allen & Unwin. → First published as *Zur Psychologie des Sozialismus.*

(1927) 1929 *Joy in Work.* London: Allen & Unwin. → First published as *Der Kampf um die Arbeitsfreude.*

1933 *Die sozialistische Idee.* Jena (Germany): Diederich.

1940 Manifesto. *Gazette de Charleroi* [1940], July 3.

1941 *Après coup: Mémoires.* Brussels and Paris: Toison d'Or.

1948 *Cavalier seul: Quarante-cinq années de socialisme européen.* Geneva: Cheval Ailé. → A significantly rewritten and enlarged version of de Man 1941.

1951 *Vermassung und Kulturverfall: Eine Diagnose unserer Zeit.* Bern: Francke.

SUPPLEMENTARY BIBLIOGRAPHY

DODGE, PETER 1966 *Beyond Marxism: The Faith and Works of Hendrik de Man.* The Hague: Nijhoff. → Includes a bibliography.

JONG, FRITS DE 1952 Aanvaardbare vernieuwing? *Socialisme en democratie* 9:187–200.

KÄHLER, OTTO H. 1929 *Determinismus und Voluntarismus in der* Psychologie des Sozialismus *Hendrik de Mans.* Dillingen an der Donau (Germany): Schwäbische Verlagsdruckerei.

PESKI, ADRIAAN M. VAN 1963 Hendrik de Man: Ein Wille zum Sozialismus. *Hamburger Jahrbuch für Wirtschafts- und Gesellschaftspolitik* 8:183–204.

PFAFF, A. A. J. 1956 *Hendrik de Man: Zijn wijsgerige fundering van het moderne socialisme.* Antwerp and Amsterdam: Standaard Boekhandel.

MANAGEMENT

See ADMINISTRATION, *article on* THE ADMINISTRATIVE FUNCTION; BUSINESS MANAGEMENT; INDUSTRIAL RELATIONS; OPERATIONS RESEARCH.

MANDATE

See REPRESENTATION *and* TRUSTEESHIP.

MANDEVILLE, BERNARD

Bernard Mandeville (1670?–1733), English political satirist, was born in (or near) Rotterdam. He was educated there at the Erasmian School and, at the age of 15, matriculated at the University of Leiden. There his studies included medicine and philosophy. The early influence on Mandeville of mechanistic philosophy—Descartes and Gassendi—was later reinforced by a reading of Hobbes. The fourth generation of a medical family, Mandeville took his M.D. in 1691 and followed his father's specialization in nervous and digestive disorders. By 1699 he had moved this practice to England, settled, and married there. He published a dialogue on his speciality, *A Treatise of the Hypocondriack and Hysterick Diseases* (1711; enlarged in 1730), but even before this work appeared he had begun a second career as a satirist and wit, an anatomist of individual and social behavior.

Among Mandeville's early poems, translations, and dialogues—all published anonymously—was *The Grumbling Hive: Or, Knaves Turn'd Honest* (1705), a pamphlet describing in verse a thriving, vicious beehive: "Millions endeavouring to supply / Each other's Lust and Vanity" ([1714–1729] 1957, volume 1, p. 18). Each part is vicious, but the whole hive is wealthy and powerful. It is a dissatisfied, grumbling hive until, miraculously reformed, it becomes virtuous, contented, and, consequently, impoverished and depopulated. Since vice is as much a cause of greatness as hunger is of eating, "fools only strive / To make a Great an Honest Hive"; proponents of the Golden Age "must be as free, / For Acorns, as for Honesty" (*ibid.*, volume 1, pp. 36–37). In 1714 Mandeville explained the poem in "An Enquiry Into the Origin of Moral Virtue" and twenty "Remarks," entitling the now substantial work *The Fable of the Bees: Or, Private Vices, Publick Benefits.* In 1723 he expanded the work again, enlarging the "Remarks" and adding "An Essay on Charity and Charity-schools" and "A Search Into the Nature of Society." A second volume, *The Fable of the Bees, Part II* (a series of explanatory dialogues), appeared in 1729. Mandeville reiterated and corrected his views in *An Enquiry Into the Origin of Honour, and the Usefulness of Christianity in War* (1732).

Mandeville's outrageous paradox—"private vices, publick benefits"—involves a series of suggestive explanations. The vices of luxury (unnecessary consumption), pride (vain and fashionable display), greed, envy, and avarice (self-interest in various forms) all contribute to prosperity. To supply the luxury of a scarlet coat requires many manufacturing and trading operations—an extensive division of labor (see [1714] 1957, volume 1, pp. 356–358; volume 2, pp. 142, 284). A nation that restricts the consumption of foreign luxuries to achieve frugality will instead reduce its own prosperity because the countries that export those luxuries will no longer be able to import its own goods (*ibid.*, volume 1, pp. 107–116). Mandeville's descriptions of the economic benefits of vice, crime, and (limited) natural disaster approach the modern concept of a self-regulating economic system (*ibid.*, volume 1, pp. 85–89, 359–364). Among the benefits of the scheme proposed in *A Modest Defence of Publick Stews* is a self-regulating supply of prostitutes (1724, pp. 64–65).

Although his objections to meddling with trade make Mandeville a forerunner of laissez-faire

([1714] 1957, volume 1, pp. 299–300; volume 2, p. 353), he advocated not only that private property be secured, justice be impartially administered, and trade, agriculture, and fishery be promoted but also that the government manage taxes and prohibitions to maintain a favorable balance of trade (*ibid.*, volume 1, pp. 115–117, 197, 248–249). Private vices may be made public benefits through skillful management by a wise politician (*ibid.*, volume 1, p. 169).

Mandeville's argument was annoying because he insisted that vices are not the consequences of social decadence but rather the very motives on which a flourishing, civilized, powerful society depends; simultaneously, he insisted that these vices are obviously incompatible with virtue (or Christianity), which requires a self-denying endeavor to benefit others or to be good (*ibid.*, volume 1, pp. 48–49; volume 2, pp. 16–19, 109–110). Not only is virtue contrary to human instinct; but society is not, as Shaftesbury had argued, based on man's natural sociability. Society is founded on the difficulty men have in gratifying their appetites (self-preservation) and is made possible by their susceptibility to praise (self-love) and their capacity for hypocrisy. Men have been socialized by politicians and moralists who, by flattery, have produced the moral virtues, especially honor and shame, and thus induced men to conform to the fashionable social code, profess virtue, and disguise their passions even though they cannot conquer them. But Mandeville's functional analysis of social institutions does not depend upon the existence of mythical dexterous politicians, for, as he explains, morality, language, government, arts, and sciences—all social institutions—are "the joynt Labour of many Ages" (*ibid.*, volume 2, pp. 128, 238–243, 266–269, 285–290, 318–323; 1732, p. 41).

The *Fable*'s vigorous wit and social satire, like the similar mockery of Erasmus and La Rochefoucauld, was intended to encourage men to examine their own motives instead of censuring others. Especially in his *Free Thoughts on Religion* (1720), Mandeville followed Bayle in skeptically arguing for toleration and against priestcraft, in particular clerical politics. He pointed out that most men believe about God what they have been taught from infancy, but few men live according to their professed beliefs. Atheists, whether abstruse philosophers or aristocratic libertines, are few and harmless (1720, pp. 4–6).

Mandeville's *Fable of the Bees* was widely read in the eighteenth century. Berkeley denounced it for libertinism and atheism; Francis Hutcheson objected to its egoistic reduction of morality. Hutcheson's pupil Adam Smith rejected Mandeville's moral theory but was influenced by the general tendencies of the *Fable* toward laissez-faire economics and the description of the division of labor. Luxury was a widely discussed eighteenth-century problem; Voltaire's treatment of it is derived from the *Fable*. Both Hume and Rousseau mention Mandeville; both are indebted to him.

M. M. GOLDSMITH

[*For the historical context of Mandeville's work, see the biographies of* DESCARTES *and* HOBBES; *for discussion of the subsequent development of his ideas, see* LAISSEZ-FAIRE; *and the biographies of* HUME; ROUSSEAU; SMITH, ADAM.]

WORKS BY MANDEVILLE

1705 *The Grumbling Hive: Or, Knaves Turn'd Honest.* London: Ballard. → Later incorporated into *The Fable of the Bees.*

(1711) 1730 *A Treatise of the Hypocondriack and Hysterick Diseases.* 3d ed. London: Tonson. → First published as *A Treatise of the Hypocondriack and Hysterick Passions.*

(1714) 1957 *The Fable of the Bees: Or, Private Vices, Publick Benefits.* Edited by F. B. Kaye. 2 vols. Oxford: Clarendon. → The introduction and notes by Kaye include a biography, a critical and historical evaluation, and an annotated bibliography.

(1720) 1723 *Free Thoughts on Religion, the Church, and National Happiness.* London: Brotherton.

(1724) 1740 *A Modest Defence of Publick Stews: Or, an Essay Upon Whoring, as It Is Now Practis'd in These Kingdoms.* London: Scott & Browne.

1732 *An Enquiry Into the Origin of Honour, and the Usefulness of Christianity in War.* London: Brotherton.

SUPPLEMENTARY BIBLIOGRAPHY

MAXWELL, J. C. 1951 Ethics and Politics in Mandeville. *Philosophy* 26:242–252.

ROBERTSON, JOHN M. 1907 *Pioneer Humanists.* London: Watts. → See especially pages 230–270 on "Mandeville."

ROSENBERG, NATHAN 1963 Mandeville and Laissez-faire. *Journal of the History of Ideas* 24:183–196.

STEPHEN, LESLIE (1876) 1949 *History of English Thought in the Eighteenth Century.* 3d ed. 2 vols. New York: Smith. → A paperback edition was published in 1962 by Harcourt.

VINER, JACOB 1958 Introduction to Bernard de Mandeville, *A Letter to Dion (1732).* Pages 332–342 in Jacob Viner, *The Long View and the Short: Studies in Economic Theory and Policy.* Glencoe, Ill.: Free Press.

MANGOLDT, HANS KARL EMIL VON

Hans Karl Emil von Mangoldt (1824–1868), German economist, was born in Dresden. After studying law and political science at the universities of Leipzig and Geneva, he took his doctorate in political science at the University of Tübingen with a dissertation entitled "Über die Aufgabe,

Stellung und Einrichtung der Sparkassen" (1847; "On the Purpose, Position, and Establishment of Savings Banks"). He returned to Dresden after obtaining his doctorate.

It was some years before Mangoldt entered upon an academic career. Between 1847 and 1850 he held a post in the ministry of foreign affairs but had to resign for political reasons. After spending two years in Leipzig studying political economy, he became editor of the *Weimarer Zeitung* in 1852. However, his political convictions again made it necessary for him to resign his position. The publication of his *Lehre vom Unternehmergewinn* in 1855 won him an appointment as *Privatdozent* of political economy at the University of Göttingen, and in 1858 he was promoted to associate professor. In 1862 he was appointed professor of political science and political economy at the University of Freiburg (Breisgau). Only four years after he moved there he died of a heart attack.

Mangoldt's principal works, *Die Lehre vom Unternehmergewinn* (1855) and *Grundriss der Volkswirthschaftslehre* (1863), are outstanding works of nineteenth-century German economics. Yet at the time that he wrote, the significance of his contributions was more fully appreciated in England than in Germany. The neglect and even rejection of economic theory that prevailed in Germany after the rise of the historical school diminished the impact of Mangoldt's ideas on economists in German universities, who lacked the well-grounded theoretical tradition of their Anglo-Saxon colleagues.

In England, Mangoldt's theory of international values—a highly original extension of Ricardo's theory of comparative costs—aroused the interest of F. Y. Edgeworth, who discussed it at length in the *Economic Journal* (1894); and his doctrine of entrepreneurial profit was mentioned approvingly by Alfred Marshall in the latter's exposition of his theory of quasi-rent: "It has indeed been shown by a long series of writers, among whom Senior and Mill, Hermann and Mangoldt are conspicuous, that much of what is commonly called profits ought rather to be regarded as belonging to a special class of income derived from 'a differential advantage in producing a commodity'; that is, the possession by one or more persons of facilities for production that are not accessible to all" ([1890] 1961, vol. 2, p. 462). Indeed, Mangoldt was one of the first economists who endeavored to establish entrepreneurial profit as a special category of income alongside wages, interest, and rent.

Mangoldt's theory of prices, as expounded in the first edition of the *Grundriss*, is truly a pioneer achievement of lasting value. With a precision not attained by any other author prior to 1863, he set forth the static theory of price formation on the assumption of free atomistic competition in supply and demand; the form of his presentation remains valid today. Cournot had employed curves of supply and demand as far back as 1838, but there is no reason to assume that Mangoldt was acquainted with Cournot's work; Edgeworth was probably right when he described Mangoldt as "one of the independent discoverers of the mathematical theory of Demand and Supply" (see 1891–1921, pp. 52–53). Yet Mangoldt went far beyond Cournot, and this is his truly original contribution. He did not confine himself to determining the existence of an equilibrium price but set forth the special features of price formation that arise from various forms of the supply curve and the demand curve and pointed out that there may be several equilibrium prices. He also described the process of transition from disequilibrium to an equilibrium price. Yet Mangoldt's most significant contribution to price theory is, no doubt, the analysis of price formation for the case of joint demands or for the case of joint supplies or for the case of both. Ideas and modes of thought initiated here were not developed further until Alfred Marshall took them up.

Mangoldt's important pioneering achievements were not appreciated in Germany. Although the second edition of the *Grundriss*, edited by F. Kleinwächter in 1871, after Mangoldt's death, appeared without any of the geometrical apparatus of the first edition, the book failed to gain a wider market. Only today do we begin to realize the significance of Mangoldt's contribution as an important link in the chain of great German theoretical achievements of the nineteenth century.

ERICH SCHNEIDER

[*For the historical context of Mangoldt's work, see the biographies of* COURNOT; EDGEWORTH; MARSHALL.]

WORKS BY MANGOLDT

1847 Über die Aufgabe, Stellung und Einrichtung der Sparkassen. Dissertation, Univ. of Tübingen.

1855 *Die Lehre vom Unternehmergewinn: Ein Beitrag zur Volkswirthschaftslehre.* Leipzig: Teubner.

(1863) 1871 *Grundriss der Volkswirthschaftslehre.* 2d ed. Stuttgart (Germany): Maier. → A chapter of this work, "Das Tauschverhältniss der Güter im allgemein," was translated as "The Exchange Ratio of Goods" and published in Volume 11 of the *International Economic Papers.*

SUPPLEMENTARY BIBLIOGRAPHY

EDGEWORTH, FRANCIS Y. (1891–1921) 1963 *Papers Relating to Political Economy.* New York: Franklin. → Contains and reviews articles which appeared in the *Economic Journal* from 1891 to 1921.

Edgeworth, Francis Y. 1894 The Theory of International Values. *Economic Journal* 4:35–50, 424–443, 603–638. → Reprinted in Edgeworth 1891–1921.

Hutchison, Terence W. (1953) 1962 *A Review of Economic Doctrines, 1870–1929*. 2d ed. Oxford: Clarendon.

Marshall, Alfred (1890) 1961 *Principles of Economics*. 9th ed., 2 vols. New York and London: Macmillan.

MANIC–DEPRESSIVE DISORDERS

See Depressive disorders.

MANNHEIM, KARL

Karl Mannheim (1893–1947), German sociologist, was born in Budapest. He attended school in that city and then studied at the universities of Berlin, Budapest, Paris, and Freiburg before going to the University of Heidelberg, where he habilitated as a *Privatdozent* in 1926. At that time Heidelberg was still the major intellectual center of the German academic world. Alfred Weber, Heinrich Rickert, Marianne Weber, Friedrich Gundolf, Ernst Kantorowicz, and Emil Lederer were among its major personalities. The spirit of Max Weber, who had died in 1920, dominated the atmosphere, and the youthful brilliance of György Lukács in his pre-Marxist period had not been forgotten. Mannheim lived and worked in Heidelberg until he was called to the professorship of sociology at the University of Frankfurt in 1930. He remained at that post until the spring of 1933, when, following the coming to power of the National Socialists, he took refuge in Great Britain. There he was lecturer in sociology at the University of London (London School of Economics) from 1933 to 1945; and from 1945 until his death, he was professor of the sociology and philosophy of education in the Institute of Education at the same university.

Mannheim's work falls into two main phases, which correspond approximately to his German and his British careers. In the first phase the sociology of knowledge—its methodological legitimation, its epistemological implications, and its substantive application—formed his main field of work. In the second phase the study of the structure of modern society came to the fore. In these latter studies he combined macrosociological and microsociological concerns with an explicit interest in social policy.

Sociology of knowledge

Mannheim's early writings expressed his struggle against the inheritance of German idealism. They were attempts to revise its epistemology in an instrumentalist direction and constituted a critique of its conception of intellectual history as an autonomously developing sequence of ideas. In this first phase of his work Mannheim was much influenced by the tradition of historicism and by the Marxist model of society; no less fundamental to his thought was his interest, derived from the classics of German sociological thought and from Marxism, in the structure and determinants of agreement and disagreement, of consensus and dissensus.

Mannheim went further than Marx and Tönnies: they saw society split by class conflict and class interest or by mutual distrust; Mannheim thought that the cleavages existed at deeper levels as well. Mannheim saw social cleavages not merely as divergences of interest but as divergences of modes of thought, of the categories in which events are conceived, and even, indeed, of the very criteria of validity. In "Competition as a Cultural Phenomenon" (1929) and *Ideology and Utopia* (1929–1931) he set forth his views on the profundity of the cleavages in styles of thought which had developed in modern times.

The profundity of these cleavages led Mannheim to formulate the distinction between "particular" and "total" conceptions of ideology. He was always concerned with the re-establishment of consensus: believing that the disintegration of the social order had penetrated into the epistemological and ontological spheres, he desired to lay the foundations for a comprehensive "perspective" which would transcend the partial perspectives associated with particular social positions. In *Ideology and Utopia* and in his article "Wissenssoziologie" he sought an epistemological solution (the article is incorporated in the English and American editions). Independently of Durkheim's and Lévy-Bruhl's relativization and "sociologization" of the categories of thought, Mannheim asserted that the fundamental categories are functions of divergent interests, aspirations, and *Weltanschauungen*, which are in turn related to social status, role, and position; he sought a way out in what he called "relationism." He insisted that the truth of a proposition cannot be assessed without regard for the "values and position of the subject . . . and the social content"; he did not take seriously the possibility of autonomous, disinterested, and disciplined intellectual action. The historicist view that each age has its own distinctive problems, views of the world, and conceptions of the good and true; the Marxist view that there are "bourgeois" and "proletarian" truths; and the idea of *Weltanschauung*, developed in the writings of Dilthey and Spranger, all came together in Mannheim's thought in the 1920s.

Mannheim's earliest formulation of relationism, in "On the Interpretations of 'Weltanschauung'" (1923), prefigured the whole concern and intellectual position of his German period. This essay represents an effort to legitimate a mode of understanding intellectual works as manifestations, expressions, or parts of something else. He regarded the *Weltanschauung* of an individual, school, or epoch as the nonrational matrix from which every particular work was an emanation. A major task of the analysis of particular works was, therefore, to discern their "style." According to this approach, style consists of features which a work shares with other works, which each part of a work shares with each other part of the work, and which intellectual works share with nonintellectual manifestations of a *Weltanschauung*. Thus, the problem with which Mannheim was concerned was the subsumption of a particular work under the pattern of other works like it and of the style of the *Weltanschauung* as a whole. Each particular intellectual work was treated —and *accounted for*—as related to or derived from something else.

Although Mannheim first applied this conception to art history, its implications for the next stage of his thought were patent. In two essays, "The Problem of a Sociology of Knowledge" (1925) and "Ideologische und soziologische Interpretation der geistigen Gebilde" (1926), he advanced to the treatment of moral works, mainly works of political and social philosophy, and to the "sociological approach." Whereas the "ideological" interpretation of intellectual works treated them simply as derivable from other intellectual works which preceded them and as generated by a process internal to the mind, the sociological approach purported to go further. It claimed that intellectual works are generated in response to the needs of the class or group to which their creators belong, as it is confronted with "practical" tasks and challenges to its position by other classes or groups. However much he sought to distinguish his own view from Marxism, he never fully escaped from the Marxist categories of *Unterbau* and *Überbau*.

The question may be asked, Did he really succeed, in this first phase of his work, in freeing himself from the ideological interpretation he tried to transcend? Much of his subsequent sociological analysis of political and cultural beliefs, not least that in his major substantive work, "Conservative Thought" (1927), consisted in relating particular beliefs to more general patterns of belief or *Weltanschauungen*. His work became sociological through scattered assertions that particular views are correlated with particular value orientations, characteristic of particular roles or statuses—for example, membership in particular social classes or the practice of particular occupations or styles of life. In this period he attempted fewer correlations with social structural variables than with the culture or value orientations of classes or occupational strata. His "sociological" interpretations of political and social beliefs remained ideological. Nonetheless, the specification of the social group which possesses a particular culture or *Weltanschauung* did represent a genuinely sociological extension of the ideological approach, rather than its replacement or negation.

The sociological variables Mannheim used in this phase of his career were largely derived from Marxism, e.g., "declining classes," "ascendant classes," "threatened classes," "newly self-conscious classes," etc., although he also cited generations, sects, and parties as the structural bearers of different *Weltanschauungen*. In *Ideology and Utopia* he asserted, for example, that "uprooted" and "unintegrated" revolutionary groups think intuitively and lay little or no stress on historical development; that conservative groups think morphologically; that liberal–humanitarian strata stress the openness of the future and the progressive realization of ethical values; and that oppressed strata, which are chiliastic, expect immediate and sharply disjunctive changes.

The correlations were at best no more than correlations. Mannheim avoided the task of causal imputation and of a differentiated analysis of the process or mechanism through which ideas and social position are connected. In the main he committed himself to nothing more than the assertion that thought is "existentially connected" (*seinsverbunden*) with social position. His work was characterized by insights of great penetration, both into the interconnections between diverse elements in a given *Weltanschauung* and also, if more rarely, into the correlations of these elements with "positions" in society.

The contradictory combination of a persistent idealism with the Marxist negation of idealism by "standing it on its head" remained basic in Mannheim's thought throughout his German period. It was a contradiction which he did not overcome and of which he was unaware. His continuous insistence that the "internalist" (ideological) view is wrong and his failure to recognize how much of it he himself retained led to his failure to perceive the partial autonomy of intellectual traditions and the institutional structure in which autonomous intellectual activity is effectuated. By constantly stressing that intellectual activities are responses to current practical–political situations, which are "nonintellectual," he was precluded from a sociological analysis of the institutional structures of intellectual activity, which make possible the continuity of intellectual traditions. (His one effort to study the social processes that are immanent in intellectual continuity and change, "The Problem of Generations" [1928], remained very general and vague and was never assimilated into his sociology of knowledge.)

There were other reasons why Mannheim's sociology of knowledge failed. What he meant by "knowledge" was largely normative and metaphysical beliefs, ideas about the nature and right organization of society, and interpretations of history. He never came to grips with the natural sciences, that is, with science as that term is understood in English-speaking countries. Scientific knowledge as a body of systematically verified beliefs remained at the margin of his interests. The influence of science and of scientific, research-based technology on social structure passed unnoticed before him. This omission made it easier for him to neglect the element of continuity and the processes of internally instigated innovation within an intellectual pattern. His denial that there is anything like a "self-contained intellect which evolves by and from itself" and his equal insistence that every change in a pattern of thought corresponds to "a change in the position of the group" required that intellectual interest and criteria of truth other than the successful mastery of life situations also be denied.

In the three years between the publication of *Ideology and Utopia* and his departure from Germany, Mannheim's transition from the sociology of knowledge to the macrosociological and microsociological study of social structure began to become visible. Much influenced by Max Weber's ideas about bureaucracy, he wrote an essay, "Über das Wesen und die Bedeutung des wirtschaftlichen Erfolgsstrebens" (1930), in which he analyzed the psychological correlates of the bureaucratic career and the bureaucratization of modern society and adumbrated his later interest in a pragmatic educational policy. His interest in personality and culture and in the "planning of personality" also appeared here for the first time. He also wrote a book on the intelligentsia, which was unpublished in his lifetime. (It was published posthumously in 1956, as *Essays on the Sociology of Culture.*) In the final section of that book, entitled "The Democratization of Culture," he presented an original analysis of the postulates of the democratic outlook, setting forth for the first time his later more fully developed views about fundamental democratization and the deterioration of the rationality and solidarity of elites.

The structure of modern society

After Mannheim went to England, he ceased almost entirely to study doctrinal beliefs and their social correlates. His epistemological interests, which had foundered in inconclusiveness, were largely discontinued. (For example, his distinction, in *Man and Society in an Age of Reconstruction* [1935], of three modes of thought—thought at the level of discovery, at the level of invention, and at the level of planning—avoided all questions of epistemological validity.) Nonetheless, certain earlier themes continued to preoccupy him in this second stage of his career; dissensus, the conflict of classes, the disagreements of doctrines, and the irreconcilability of political movements still engaged his mind, although the particular contexts changed in which these phenomena were seen. While in his first phase his attention was preponderantly directed to the reconciliation of contending and antithetical interpretations of events and criteria of truth, the main aim of the macrosociology of his second period was the delineation of the contemporary dissensus, the disclosure of its causes, and the discovery of the means of its displacement by a new consensus.

Another line of continuity may be seen in his attitude toward sociology. Although in his second phase he came much closer to the scientific aspirations of empirical sociology, he never fully resigned himself to them. He became more sympathetic to the largely ahistorical, sociological, and social-psychological research of the period, but he never ceased to insist on the necessity of a "dynamic" and "historical" sociology. The natural-science model of knowledge remained alien to him and was never integrated into his thought.

In both periods he looked upon sociology as a potential cure for the ills of society. Just as the sociology of knowledge had been intended to emancipate intellectuals from extreme partisanship and from particularistic perspectives ([1929–1931] 1954, pp. 97–104), so a sociologically oriented education and sociologically oriented planning became the means, in his second phase, of overcoming dissensus and of avoiding the dangers of totalitarianism. His historicism led him to underemphasize the elements of identity between various societies, and he therefore believed that modern mass society is afflicted with a degree of dissensus such as no other society had ever suffered. But instead of focusing his attention on the dissensus of the intellectuals, he now stressed the dissensus of social strata and political groups.

Mannheim added some variants of his own to the German sociological tradition which derived from Tönnies and Simmel and which emphasized the disintegration of modern urban society. Unlike his predecessors, who characterized bourgeois society as uniform throughout its history, Mannheim distinguished between the stages of minority democracy and mass democracy. Several elements, not previously considered in the older diagnosis of the perpetual crisis resulting from unbridled conflicts of individual and collective desires, were added by him: the concentration of authority, the bureaucratization of work, "functional rationalization," increased integration ("increasing interdependence"), and "fundamental democratization." The concomitance of these major processes resulted in the democratization of access to positions within elites. Through these processes individuals who lacked practical and experienced judgment moved into the political elites at the very time that more and more of social life had become dependent on the decisions of these elites.

Mannheim stressed the intensification of demands which accompanied the democratization of political participation and the consequent increase in the frequency of unrealistic and unfulfillable demands. Yet the first years of his sojourn in Great Britain changed the accent of his thought. His outlook became more optimistic and more concrete. The increased optimism was manifested in his effort to promulgate a pattern of democratic planning. The enhanced concreteness arose in part from his increased interest in empirical sociological and social-psychological research. It was also related to the much greater matter-of-factness of discussions of social and political problems in Great Britain, where political differences were not invariably reduced to metaphysical and *weltanschauliche* differences. He became more sympathetic to psychoanalysis and better acquainted with it. He also became increasingly interested in educational techniques—that is, the possibility of transforming conduct through scientifically based educational techniques. This interest, encouraged by Sir Fred Clarke, the director of the University of London Institute of Education, brought him into a greater intimacy with the practical problems of education. His dislike of the prototype of the generally educated man espoused by German idealism had already, in his German period, caused him to reach out toward more practical types of education, which would be concerned with fitting individuals for differentiated social roles. His growing interest in planning strengthened his interest in education as preparation for participation in a democratic consensus.

His membership in an unusual group called the Moot, which met quarterly and which included Joseph Oldham, long active in Church of England affairs and social reform; Alec Vidler, a notable Anglican theologian and historian, then dean of Windsor Chapel; T. S. Eliot; J. Middleton Murry; and other literary and academic men, civil servants and theologians, made him more sensitive to religious belief and its possible role in the planned democracy of the future than he had ever been before. It was to this group that he presented a long paper, "Towards a New Social Philosophy: A Challenge to Christian Thinkers by a Sociologist" (1943). Mannheim argued that laissez-faire has exhausted its possibilities; as a result of fundamental democratization and the process of functional rationalization, the free play of forces in the economy has lost its powers of self-equilibration. Man's capacity for autonomous and responsible individual judgment has weakened at the very time that greater demands for such judgment are being placed on him. The irrationality generated by these two processes has increased the danger of totalitarianism. The "primordial images" which have directed the life experiences of men through the ages have vanished, and nothing has taken their place. Conduct, in consequence, "falls to pieces," and only "disconnected fragments of unintegrated behaviour patterns" remain.

In the final product of his constructive imagination, *Freedom, Power, and Democratic Planning* (1950), Mannheim defined the principal task as the creation of a society-wide "spontaneous" consensus, which would permit planning to be carried out effectively. In Germany he had shared many of the general views of democratic socialism, and in the 1930s he came to accept the inevitability and desirability of planning. To prevent planning from becoming totalitarian, self-restraint in collective demands and confinement of popular participation in the exercise of power to specific occasions were necessary. The indispensable condition for such restraint and limitation was consensus, and the two paths to consensus were, first, pedagogy, and, second, a readiness to accept and even to arouse religious sensibility and the moral attitudes called forth by religious experience. He saw the function of religion as helping man to restrain himself through spontaneously experienced moral norms and therewith to stabilize a social framework which would permit a modicum of freedom in a society that had to be planned in order to exist. Society in its latest phase needed a spiritual purpose, to avoid having a purpose imposed on it by a totalitarian elite. Thus, it became necessary to plan religion—not by prescribing a theology, but by the planned provision of institutional settings in which religious experience could flourish.

Mannheim's influence

Although he was an extraordinarily stimulating teacher, Mannheim had few intellectual descendants: his Frankfurt students were scattered and their incipient careers broken; at the London School of Economics, students interested in empirical research found him insufficiently at home in the then prevailing techniques, and there were very few equipped to do the kind of historical and macrosociological work that was Mannheim's forte. During World War II the teaching of sociology ceased in England, and Mannheim was thereby deprived of the opportunity to influence the new generation of sociologists. In Germany the long suspension of social scientific work resulted in an attrition of the culture required to sustain Mannheim's kind of sociology, and when social scientific work was resumed after the war, the older tradition had been lost and Mannheim's prewar macrosociological writings did not appear relevant to current interests.

The sociology of knowledge as practiced by Mannheim has found no succession. Its only manifestations are Ernst Kohn Bramstedt's dissertation, *Aristocracy and Middle-classes in Germany* (1937), Hans Gerth's "Die sozialgeschichtliche Lage der bürgerlichen Intelligenz um die Wende des 18. Jahrhunderts" (1935), and Hans Speier's "Die Geschichtsphilosophie Lassalle's" (1929). Much work has been done since World War II which may be said to fall within the jurisdiction of the sociology of knowledge broadly conceived, yet very little of it bears the impress of Mannheim's thought.

More recent works like Thomas S. Kuhn's *Structure of Scientific Revolutions* (1962) and Michael Polanyi's *Personal Knowledge* (1958), which have carried very far the systematic analysis of patterns of thought and their modes of change, owe nothing to Mannheim's analyses of *Weltanschauungen*. Similarly, Mircea Eliade and Claude Lévi-Strauss, in work on the fundamental categories of thought, owe much to Jung, Durkheim, and Mauss; they owe practically nothing to Mannheim. Latent-structure analysis, which was developed by Paul F. Lazarsfeld and others for the analysis of attitude-survey data and which offers great possibilities of development for the analysis of the structure of beliefs, is also independent of Mannheim's influence.

The situation is somewhat different with regard to the study of ideologies: there can be little doubt that the prominent place which this kind of work is now beginning to occupy in sociological analysis owes something to the fact that Mannheim brought the term "ideology" to the attention of sociologists. His influence in this area is a product less of anything specific he said about the problems of ideology than of the fact that he dwelt on them long and seriously. Similarly, the study of the political and social role of intellectuals and of the institutional systems of intellectual life, as carried on by Theodor Geiger, Robert K. Merton, Joseph Ben-David, Talcott Parsons, Helmuth Plessner, Martin Trow, Lewis Coser, A. H. Halsey, and others, owes some of its impetus to Mannheim's concern with these subjects.

Mannheim's macrosociological views of contemporary large-scale society have had a more receptive audience and a more enduring influence. They were in harmony with an already established tradition in the analysis of modern urban society, and their appearance coincided with the emergence of the influence on sociology of Marxism and of Max Weber's writings on bureaucracy and capitalism. Also, they appeared at a time of troubled interest in the causes of the breakdown of liberal societies and the emergence of populistic totalitarian regimes and movements. Mannheim's very term "mass society" focused attention on certain unique features of modern large-scale societies, and his emphasis on the significance of bureaucratization and democratization in government, industry, commerce, and culture created one of the major themes of contemporary sociological thought.

Mannheim's "morphological" approach, derived partly from German historicism, partly from Marxism, and partly from Weber's broad categories and comparative studies, made him one of the first proponents of the macrosociological approach in the world of English-language sociology. Here again, it was his inclination to think of society as a whole, rather than his specific hypotheses, which led to macrosociology. He was vague in his formulations, and there is a tantalizing ambiguity in nearly everything he wrote. Yet, he dealt with very important subjects. The adage which asserts that the mistakes of a distinguished mind are more interesting than the truths of a mediocre one was true of Mannheim. He had in large measure the rare gift of touching on vital and enigmatic things.

EDWARD SHILS

[*Directly related are the entries* IDEOLOGY; INTEGRATION, *article on* CULTURAL INTEGRATION; INTELLECTUALS; KNOWLEDGE, SOCIOLOGY OF; MASS SOCIETY; POLITICAL SOCIOLOGY; SOCIAL MOVEMENTS. *Other relevant material may be found in* CONSERVATISM; EDUCATION, *article on* THE STUDY OF EDUCATIONAL SYSTEMS; ELITES; GENERATIONS; HISTORY, *articles on* THE PHILOSOPHY OF HISTORY *and* INTELLECTUAL HISTORY; MARXIST SOCIOLOGY; PLANNING, SOCIAL; REVOLUTION; *and in the biographies of* DILTHEY; GEIGER; LUKÁCS; MARX; SCHELER; SIMMEL; TÖNNIES; WEBER, ALFRED; WEBER, MAX.]

WORKS BY MANNHEIM

(1922–1940) 1953 *Essays on Sociology and Social Psychology*. Edited by Paul Kecskemeti. London: Routledge; New York: Oxford Univ. Press.

(1923) 1952 On the Interpretations of "Weltanschauung." Pages 33–83 in Karl Mannheim, *Essays on the Sociology of Knowledge*. New York: Oxford Univ. Press. → First published as "Beiträge zur Theorie der Weltanschauungsinterpretation."

(1923–1929) 1952 *Essays on the Sociology of Knowledge*. Edited by Paul Kecskemeti. New York: Oxford Univ. Press.

(1925) 1952 The Problem of a Sociology of Knowledge. Pages 134–190 in Karl Mannheim, *Essays on the Sociology of Knowledge*. New York: Oxford Univ. Press.

1926 Ideologische und soziologische Interpretation der geistigen Gebilde. *Jahrbuch für Soziologie* 2:424–440.

(1927) 1953 Conservative Thought. Pages 77–164 in Karl Mannheim, *Essays on Sociology and Social Psychology*. London: Routledge; New York: Oxford Univ. Press. → First published as "Das konservative Denken."

(1928) 1952 The Problem of Generations. Pages 276–320 in Karl Mannheim, *Essays on the Sociology of Knowledge*. New York: Oxford Univ. Press. → First published as "Das Problem der Generationen."

(1929) 1952 Competition as a Cultural Phenomenon. Pages 191–229 in Karl Mannheim, *Essays on the Sociology of Knowledge*. New York: Oxford Univ. Press. → First published as "Die Bedeutung der Konkurrenz im Gebiete des Geistigen."

(1929–1931) 1954 *Ideology and Utopia: An Introduction to the Sociology of Knowledge*. New York: Harcourt; London: Routledge. → A paperback edition was published in 1955 by Harcourt. Part 1 is an introductory essay. Parts 2–4 are a translation of *Ideologie und Utopie* (1929); Part 5 is a translation of "Wissenssoziologie" (1931).

1930 Über das Wesen und die Bedeutung des wirtschaftlichen Erfolgsstrebens: Ein Beitrag zur Wirtschaftssoziologie. *Archiv für Sozialwissenschaft und Sozialpolitik* 63:449–512.

(1935) 1940 *Man and Society in an Age of Reconstruction: Studies in Modern Social Structure*. Revised and considerably enlarged by the author. New York: Harcourt. → First published as *Mensch und Gesellschaft im Zeitalter des Umbaus*.

(1939–1943) 1950 *Diagnosis of Our Time: Wartime Essays of a Sociologist*. London: Routledge.

(1943) 1950 Towards a New Social Philosophy: A Challenge to Christian Thinkers by a Sociologist. Pages 100–165 in Karl Mannheim, *Diagnosis of Our Time: Wartime Essays of a Sociologist*. London: Routledge.

1950 *Freedom, Power, and Democratic Planning*. New York: Oxford Univ. Press. → Published posthumously.

1956 *Essays on the Sociology of Culture*. Oxford Univ. Press. → Published posthumously.

SUPPLEMENTARY BIBLIOGRAPHY

BRAMSTEDT, ERNST KOHN (1937) 1964 *Aristocracy and Middle-classes in Germany: Social Types in German Literature, 1830–1900*. Rev. ed. Univ. of Chicago Press.

GERTH, HANS H. 1935 Die sozialgeschichtliche Lage der bürgerlichen Intelligenz um die Wende des 18. Jahrhunderts. Unpublished manuscript.

KUHN, THOMAS S. 1962 *The Structure of Scientific Revolutions*. Univ. of Chicago Press. → A paperback edition was published in 1964.

LENK, KURT 1963 Die Rolle der Intelligenzsoziologie in der Theorie Mannheims. *Kölner Zeitschrift für Soziologie und Sozialpsychologie* 15:323–337.

MERTON, ROBERT K. (1941) 1957 Karl Mannheim and the Sociology of Knowledge. Pages 489–508 in Robert K. Merton, *Social Theory and Social Structure*. Rev. ed. New York: Free Press.

MILLS, C. WRIGHT (1940) 1963 Methodological Consequences of the Sociology of Knowledge. Pages 453–468 in C. Wright Mills, *Power, Politics and People: The Collected Essays of C. Wright Mills*. New York: Oxford Univ. Press.

POLANYI, MICHAEL 1958 *Personal Knowledge: Towards a Post-critical Philosophy*. Univ. of Chicago Press.

SPEIER, HANS 1929 Die Geschichtsphilosophie Lassalle's. *Archiv für Sozialwissenschaft und Sozialpolitik* 61: 103–127, 360–388.

MANORIAL ECONOMY

The word *manoir* was used in Normandy in the eleventh century to designate the residence of a lord, the point of concentration of his economic and social power, and the place where the products of his lands were collected and where his men performed the services they owed him. In 1086, when Norman clerks drew up the inventory known as the *Domesday Book* for William the Conqueror, they used the word *manoir* as the key term in their descriptions of English estates. The word became part of the vocabulary of England. The expression "manorial economy" thus signifies, for Anglo-Saxon historians, a certain mode of economic organization of men and the land that developed during the feudal period. Continental historians usually employ the term "seignorial economy."

Earliest manifestations. The first clear image of the manorial system appears from documents drawn up in the ninth century in northern France, western Germany, and Lombardy describing the landed estates of large monasteries and the way in which they were managed. The French scholar Benjamin Guérard published the oldest and most complete of these inventories, which was drawn up before 829 for the monastery of Saint-Germain-des-Prés in Paris. He made the first analysis of manorial economy at that period; the work of subsequent medievalists has added precision to his analysis.

These immense monastic estates were divided for management purposes into large units known as *villae;* their centers (*curtis*) corresponded exactly to the *manoir* in the Anglo-Norman vocabulary of the eleventh century. A more or less compact assemblage of cultivated and uncultivated land, covering hundreds and often thousands of hectares, was attached to the residence of the lord. This enormous landed estate was divided into two portions, each having entirely different economic functions.

The larger part, which comprised all the woods and pastures, most of the meadows and vineyards, and large tracts of arable land, formed the domain proper (*terra indominicata*). The master of the *villa* kept direct operation of this in his own hands and received all its produce.

The rest of the land was broken up into a number of operating units of much smaller size. Each of these, containing only a few hectares of plowland and sometimes a bit of meadow and vineyard, was attached to the lot where the family of the peasant lived (*mansus*). Each family of workers managed this farm and took what it produced, in exchange for certain obligations to the lord. This was a holding. The oldest inventories make a distinction between two types of *mansi:* one called free, the other servile. There were also two large legal categories among the peasant population: the freemen and the slaves. However, no perfect agreement existed between the status of the tenure and that of the peasants who operated it: some freeholdings were occupied by households of slaves and vice versa.

This division of the lord's land into two parts, the domain and the individual holdings, was in response to operating requirements. The central problem of management was a problem of manpower. The very low level of farming technique and the wretched inefficiency of farm tools made it necessary to employ a large number of laborers to make the fields and vineyards sufficiently productive. But the rural regions of Europe were very sparsely inhabited in the ninth century and there was insufficient money in circulation to permit regular use of wage labor. On the other hand, the reduction in traffic in slaves had made it impossible, by the ninth century, to base the operation of great aristocratic domains on the employment of human chattels, as had been done in previous epochs.

A set of domestic slaves was still maintained at the lord's residence at the center of the *villa*, but they were too few to farm the vast cultivated fields of the reservation at the time of major operations: haymaking, harvesting, vintage, ditching and fencing, cultivating the vineyards and, above all, plowing. Moreover, this team of domestics had to be re-formed periodically. The chief function of the holdings was to ensure periodical renewal of this group of domestics and provide it with supplementary unpaid labor services. The tenures known as servile were probably originally set up by the lord in order that some of his slaves might lead a family life on each such *mansus*. This separate settlement had two advantages.

The slave family had to get its food from its own holding. The lord was thus relieved of its maintenance. To be sure, this meant the loss of a part of the productive power of the family, but only a part. The tenant slaves continued to work for him without pay. The women were employed in the domestic workshops of the *villa* and produced pieces of cloth at home. The head of the family had to do any tasks given him during three days a week. The first function of the tenure was to provide the master with unpaid, half-time domestics.

Further, the married slaves, established by pairs in family homes, begot children and raised them until they were of an age to work. From these children the lord recruited the servants for full-time service in his house. Thus, the existence of servile tenures promoted the operation of a type of slave economy in an economic and social *ambiance* in which the slave markets were no longer regularly supplied.

As for the tenures known as free, whether they too had been set up by the lord on his own lands or were peasant farms that had once been independent and had been annexed to the *villa* in one way or another, they were generally more extensive than the servile tenures, for the peasant families holding them had a larger proportion of their time available for working their farms and usually kept work animals. The economic function of these freeholdings was a different one. To some extent they provided income, delivering a portion of their produce to the lord in the form of dues—in kind or in money. Their main contribution to the economy of the *villa*, however, was likewise labor. This took two forms: (1) a piece of land from the domain, assigned each year to each holding, had to be cultivated and its entire produce turned in; (2) at fixed times, for a certain number of days, the tenants, with their teams, had to be at the service of the lord and help the household servants in the work of plowing and cartage.

The system described above seems to have been fairly widespread in the ninth century in the regions between the Loire and the Rhine, and in the Po Valley. There it represented a developed form of the great aristocratic estates of the Roman era. From that time on, it seems to have spread gradually in the Germanic regions and in England. It was, in fact, perfectly adapted to a social structure in which slavery was in the process of dissolution but in which a sharp distinction was maintained in the peasant world between the free and the unfree, and in which a strong aristocracy, religious or secular, held huge tracts of land and completely dominated those who labored on the land. The economy was certainly not entirely closed (the existence of regular dues in money proves that the tenures, as well as the great estates, were normally engaged on the market), but labor productivity was low, population sparse, and the circulation of money very slow. The manorial system, whose basic nexus was the association of the holdings to the work of the domain, made possible the operation of the great grain-producing estates on which the power of the aristocracy rested.

Development under feudalism. Between the tenth and thirteenth centuries, in the rural regions of western Europe, the political power of the landholding aristocracy was strengthened and the old forms of slavery disappeared. The peasants were still divided into two legal categories: (1) the "free" peasants, subject only to the territorial lord's powers of justice and police; and (2) the personal dependents—serfs, *hommes de corps*, *Leibeigene*, villeins—hereditarily attached to a private master. The most significant changes took place in production. Great progress in rural techniques brought about a sharp improvement in the yield of human labor, and, as a result, a continual growth of population and acceleration in exchange and in the circulation of money. The manorial economy adapted to this evolution in the environment.

England. The new forms of the manorial economy appear most clearly in thirteenth-century England. An abundance of documents, well exploited by economic historians, gives us the following picture of the structure of the manor on the landed estates of the great English religious foundations.

The heart of the manor was the domain, a large unit whose production was to a great extent intended for sale, for at that time there were large markets for grain and wool. The peasant holdings ranged around the domain. Some of them were free, and their obligations consisted almost exclusively of dues. The others, which were closely associated in the work of the domain, fell into two groups. (1) Some, granted to men known as *bordarii*, were too small to provide full sustenance for the family that occupied them. Their holders were required to give one or more days of unpaid labor on the domain of the manor; additional days were worked for payment. (2) The tenures granted to *villani*, on the other hand, corresponded in size to the labor power and needs of a peasant household having a plow and team. Their obligations were much heavier. There was a multiplicity of dues which transferred a large portion of the produce of the land to the seignorial house. Above all, there were various kinds of *corvée*, or forced labor: the tenant and his livestock were summoned to perform both definite tasks and what was called "week work"—the obligation to go to work on the domain a certain number of days each week. On some manors, during the heaviest work of harvesting and haymaking, this duty could extend to all the people living on the holding and to every working day. In addition, in the thirteenth century *villani* and *bordarii* were held to have no liberty. Accordingly, they were excluded from the jurisdiction of the public courts and subject to the private justice of the manor. They paid a number of personal taxes, by means of which the lord appropriated a part of the money they earned.

On these manors, therefore, the association for work between the domain and the individual holdings remained unbroken. On the contrary, during the thirteenth century the link seems to have become tighter: the managers of the great monastic estates, eager to increase production on the domains in order to have more to sell, were stricter in exacting the *corvée* and tried to extend such work. However, the *corvée* never was sufficient to get the work of the domain done. Part, often the major part, of the labor was done by a set of full-time servants and by workers for wages. The *bordarii* were regularly hired on the days they were not required to do unpaid work, and so were the poor peasants of the village, who were looking for supplementary resources. The growth of this rural proletariat in the thirteenth century favored recourse to paid labor; it kept the level of wages very low while the price of food rose, thus increasing the profits of the large estates.

It should be added that the manorial organization described in the ecclesiastical documents did not by any means characterize all seignorial lands. On most English manors the part played by statute laborers in working the domain was very slight or nonexistent; servants and wage laborers constituted the entire labor force.

The Continent. On the Continent—in France, the Low Countries, Germany, and Italy—the statute labor required from tenants diminished during the eleventh and twelfth centuries. By the thirteenth century, it had very often disappeared completely or was only two, three, or four days a year. Dues, collected in money for the most part, had taken its place. The old tenures, many of which had broken up and disintegrated, thus yielded only money income. The very large number of new holdings set up on the vast expanses of newly cultivated land had for the most part been exempted from *corvées* since their inception. Further, changes in the price level had in effect reduced the money dues, the most common obligation. By the thirteenth century, the obligations of the tenures had become trifling. Finally, emancipations had greatly reduced the number and cost of personal dependents.

But although the old manorial system was no longer very profitable to the aristocracy, they gained by other means. By taxes on inheritances and sales of tenures, by tithes on harvests, by tallage (*taille*, a periodical tapping of the capital in chattels of the peasant households), the lords took virtually all the money earned by a more numerous and more productive peasantry. Further, great investment operations—extensions of vineyards and cattle raising and, in Italy, of the *coltura promiscua*—introduced contracts of a new type binding the rural laborers to the lords. The latter contributed the land and the capital but kept the greater part of the profits.

However, the lords had not turned into mere passive receivers of income from the land. The almost complete disappearance of forced labor had not diminished the economic importance of the management of their domains, whose value had been considerably increased by the advances in rural production. But this large-scale seignorial farming was now based on the use of domestics and hired labor; it was furthered by the opening of the market for agricultural products and by the growth of the rural proletariat.

Final forms of the manorial economy. The last parts of the framework of manorial organizations were gradually destroyed in Europe during the thirteenth and fourteenth centuries by the extension of leaseholding (contracts of *fermage*). Under this system certain economic powers were ceded for short periods to an intermediary in exchange for payments fixed in advance. It was employed very early for the collection of certain seignorial rents. On the Continent it was employed by the greatest lords in the operation of their domains from the end of the twelfth century on. For an annual payment the lands of the domain, all the means for cultivating them, and, in particular, what was left of statute labor, were granted for some years, under certain guarantees, to a farming entrepreneur—the community of the peasants of the village, the former bailiff, a bourgeois capitalist, or even an ordinary peasant who had enough ability to take over the operation of all the great domain. Use of this procedure spread very widely during the fourteenth century and soon got to England.

At that time, the dominant tendencies in rural economy were reversed almost everywhere. Rural population was rapidly decreasing. The resultant rise in agricultural wages, coupled with the fall in grain prices, tolled the knell of the large-scale agricultural operation based on wage labor. From that time on, the extension of leaseholdings was accompanied by division of the great domains into small holdings. Leaseholds and farm contracts calling for payment in kind (*métayage*) were for much smaller tracts, corresponding to the means of production of a family helped by a few domestics. At the same time, political and social disorders did away with almost all survivals of personal servitude. In eastern Germany, however, certain political conditions, producing a re-formation of serfdom, intervened to promote the rise of large estates based on the *corvée*, namely, the *Gutsherrschaften*, the longest-lasting form of manorial economy.

GEORGES M. DUBY

[*See also* FEUDALISM. *Other relevant material may be found in* LAND TENURE.]

BIBLIOGRAPHY

ABEL, WILHELM 1962 *Geschichte der deutschen Landwirtschaft vom frühen Mittelalter bis zum 19. Jahrhundert.* Stuttgart (Germany): Ulmer.

BLOCH, MARC (1931) 1952–1956 *Les caractères originaux de l'histoire rurale française.* New ed. 2 vols. Paris: Colin. → Volume 2, *Supplément établi d'après les travaux de l'auteur (1931–1944),* was written by Robert Dauvergne.

The Cambridge Economic History of Europe From the Decline of the Roman Empire. Volume 1: The Agrarian Life of the Middle Ages. 1941 Cambridge Univ. Press.

DUBY, GEORGES 1962 *L'économie rurale et la vie des campagnes dans l'occident médiéval (France, Angleterre, Empire, IX–XV siècles): Essai de synthèse et perspectives de recherches.* 2 vols. Paris: Aubier.

SLICHER VAN BATH, BERNARD H. (1960) 1963 *The Agrarian History of Western Europe: A.D. 500–1850.* London: Arnold. → First published in Dutch.

MANPOWER

See LABOR FORCE; WORKERS; *see also* CAPITAL, HUMAN.

MAPS

See CARTOGRAPHY *and* GRAPHIC PRESENTATION.

MARETT, ROBERT RANULPH

Robert Ranulph Marett (1866–1943) was one of a number of classically trained scholars in England (Frazer, Andrew Lang, and Myres were others) who at the end of the nineteenth century were attracted to the then developing subject of anthropology. Marett's own interest in anthropology was originally stimulated by his preparations for the Oxford University Green moral philosophy prize, which in 1893 was to be given to an essay on the ethics of savage races. At the time a tutor in philosophy at Exeter College, Marett won the prize, and so came into the orbit of E. B. Tylor. Marett was to spend almost his entire academic life at Oxford (from 1928 until his death he occupied the post of rector of Exeter College).

He remained essentially an "armchair" anthropologist, although he conducted some archeological excavations on his native island of Jersey. His major interests lay in the field of primitive religion. His theories of a "preanimistic" stage of religion were a development of Tylor's concept of "animism," but he insisted also upon the psychological component of religious belief. Unlike the heavy, comparative treatises of many of his contemporaries, most of Marett's books were initially lectures and addresses. He excelled in the nicely illustrated argument which examines in brief compass a new idea, approach, or observation. Marett's initial reputation was acquired through one such paper, delivered to the British Association for the Advancement of Science in 1899, "Pre-animistic Religion." Coming at a time when the psychological component of behavior was receiving growing recognition, the central idea—that a diffuse religious feeling probably preceded Tylor's postulated creed of "belief in spiritual beings"—was accepted by a number of English and German scholars and received the distinction of a lengthy discussion in Wundt's *Völkerpsychologie*, where it was translated as "der Marettische Präanimismus." The paper was included in Marett's first collection of essays, *The Threshold of Religion* (1900), which contains many of his key and most original ideas.

Anthropology, a popular general account reprinted many times in the following decades, was published in 1912, and a second collection of essays and addresses, *Psychology and Folk-lore*, in 1920. Marett was invited to give the Gifford lectures at St. Andrew's University in 1931/1932, and these were published in two volumes—the first, *Faith, Hope and Charity in Primitive Religion* (1932), dealing with religious sentiment in primitive societies, and the second, *Sacraments of Simple Folk* (1933), with primitive rituals. A final collection of essays, *Head, Heart & Hands in Human Evolution*, appeared in 1935, followed the next year by a biography of Tylor.

Marett viewed anthropology as a broad, coordinated study centrally concerned with "man in evolution." He stated many times that anthropology is based on Darwinian theory, but his was a humanized Darwinism, which insisted upon the unity of human nature that underlies the diversity of behavior: "Darwinism is the touch of nature that makes the whole world kin" (1912, p. 11). In view of the importance which is generally ascribed to Tylor's introduction into anthropology of the concept of "culture," it is interesting to observe that Marett, Tylor's pupil and great admirer, did not begin to make any distinctive use of this concept before he wrote the papers published in *Psychology and Folk-lore* (1920), by which time it was also being developed by other writers, notably in the United States. The methodologically more diffuse concept "custom" was, for Marett, more important; he viewed behavior in primitive society as essentially "custom-bound," and primitive religion as "mobbish."

Marett criticized Tylor's and Frazer's theories concerning religion and magic for their "intellectualism" and pointed out the absurdity of regarding the "savage" as a kind of "primitive philosopher"; yet, in his own theories he perhaps did little more than substitute notions of primitive faith or religious "feeling" for their notions of primitive creed or their postulated theories about nature. For Marett, the original "stuff" of religion was "supernaturalism," a matter of emotion rather than of intellect; "that basic feeling of Awe, which drives a man ere he can think or theorise upon it, into personal relations with the Supernatural" ([1900] 1929, p. 15). Both magic and religion spring from this original, undifferentiated category of experience (which he called "magico–religious"), the former in practices antithetical to the common good, the latter in practices or beliefs in harmony with it. The concepts of taboo and mana gave Marett ethnographic evidence for such elemental apprehension of the supernatural, "mana" referring to it in a positive mode, "taboo" in a negative mode. This taboo–mana formula, delineating a belief in impersonal forces, Marett adopted for his own minimum definition of religion. He also referred to this wider category of belief by the term "animatism," in order to distinguish it from Tylor's "animism," defining it as "the attribution of life and personality to things, but not of a separate apparitional soul" (British Association . . . 1912, p. 262).

The teaching of anthropology in Oxford had started in 1884, with Tylor's appointment as reader, but he had extremely few pupils, and it was not until 1905, with the setting up of a committee for anthropology and the inauguration of a diploma in anthropology (in which Marett was actively concerned), that the subject obtained wider recognition in the university and a regular flow of students began. Marett held the post of reader in social anthropology from 1908 until 1934, when a chair was created, which Marett occupied for one year, until Radcliffe-Brown, who had already been appointed, was able to take up his duties. Despite his own lack of field experience, Marett held that the teaching of anthropology should be directed toward field work; the teaching of prospective colonial administrators was started at Oxford shortly after the diploma course was inaugurated, and a number of the students (including A. C. Hollis, R. S. Rattray and C. K. Meek) later made important contributions to anthropology while holding appointments in the colonial service.

M. J. RUEL

[*Other relevant material may be found in* MAGIC; RELIGION; *and in the biographies of* FRAZER; MAUSS; TYLOR.]

WORKS BY MARETT

(1900) 1929 *The Threshold of Religion.* 4th ed. London: Methuen.

1912 *Anthropology.* New York: Holt.

1915 Magic. Volume 8, pages 245–252 in *Encyclopaedia of Religion and Ethics.* Edited by James Hastings. Edinburgh: Clark.

1920 *Psychology and Folk-lore.* London: Methuen.

1932 *Faith, Hope and Charity in Primitive Religion.* Oxford: Clarendon.

1933 *Sacraments of Simple Folk.* Oxford: Clarendon.

1935 *Head, Heart & Hands in Human Evolution.* London: Hutchinson.

1936 *Tylor.* New York: Wiley.

1941 *A Jerseyman at Oxford.* Oxford Univ. Press. → An autobiography.

SUPPLEMENTARY BIBLIOGRAPHY

BRITISH ASSOCIATION FOR THE ADVANCEMENT OF SCIENCE 1912 *Notes and Queries on Anthropology.* 4th ed. Edited by Barbara Freire-Marreco and J. L. Myres. London: Routledge. → The first edition was published in 1874; a sixth and revised edition in 1954.

Custom Is King: Essays Presented to R. R. Marett on His Seventieth Birthday, June 13, 1936. 1936 Edited by L. H. Dudley Buxton. London: Hutchinson. → Includes a bibliography of Marett's scientific writings.

EVANS-PRITCHARD, E. E. 1965 *Theories of Primitive Religion.* Oxford: Clarendon.

ROSE, HERBERT J. 1943 Robert Ranulph Marett, 1866–1943. British Academy, London, *Proceedings* 29:357–370.

WUNDT, WILHELM (1900–1909) 1911–1929 *Völkerpsychologie: Eine Untersuchung der Entwicklungsgesetze von Sprache, Mythus und Sitte.* 10 vols. Leipzig: Engelmann.

MARGINAL PRODUCTIVITY

See PRODUCTION; PRODUCTIVITY; WAGES.

MARKET RESEARCH

I
MARKET ANALYSIS

Market analysis is concerned with predicting the size and location of markets as measured by sales. The term is sometimes used as a synonym for "market research," which is more accurately defined to include the entire range of methods and techniques employed not only for the delineation of the sizes and shapes of markets but also for the evaluation of tactics and strategies useful for developing and exploiting markets.

While market analysis and advanced methods of sales forecasting derive from the relatively young fields of statistics, survey methodology, and econometrics, the practice of prediction—commercial prediction no less than any other kind—has a very long history. Before the Delphic liturgy was defined, the auguries were divined from the livers of bulls and the entrails of doves; and the ambiguities of the oracle may not have been less than some of the forecasts that today trumpet tomorrow's fortunes.

The process and the outcome of sales forecasting command general interest among business managers, since sales volume constitutes the most important source of income for all but a narrow class of (financial) enterprises; and it is basic for corporate planning with respect to plant, personnel, and investment. Marketing plans and the allocation of promotional budgets are, of course, importantly influenced by expectations of the level and distribution of market opportunities.

The methods of market measurement. In measuring markets, one is concerned with both industry and enterprise concepts—total generic product sales in an area, loosely referred to as "market potential," and enterprise or brand sales, which are some proportion of industry sales. This is the "market share" of the firm or brand. The sales forecasts of particular companies normally depend on estimates of market potential (itself sometimes an inference from a general economic forecast), which are then adjusted for the firm's expected market share.

Methodological discussions of market analysis usually focus on sales or market potential. In practice, of course, it is not always obvious what the most appropriate definition of "market" or "product" is. One speaks of markets in various contexts: the "gasoline market," for example, of which the "high octane market" is a segment. The "petroleum market" and the "liquid fuels market" are broader concepts—but narrower than the "energy sources market." Similarly, one often hears of the "high price" and "low price" markets, the "New York," the "west coast," and the "export" market. In estimating market potentials it is important to choose the relevant definition, but this choice is often influenced by the data available. [*See* MARKETS AND INDUSTRIES.]

While successful forecasting depends on gauging the effects of changes in the firm's marketing policy, on competitive behavior, and on the consequences of future events that may transform the environment, business planning often starts from estimates of present (recent) sales. It is common practice to estimate potential market size by taking recent industry volume as the first approximation to the measure of expected market size. Even this is not always easy. Not only are there difficulties in establishing a relevant definition of "industry," but data on recent industry sales are not as readily available as one might expect. Census data of various sorts offer authoritative figures on production and sales volume of fairly broadly defined product classes in the United States, but these tabulations do not appear at frequent intervals. More frequent compilations of industry statistics are by-products of excise taxes (e.g., gasoline and tobacco in the United States) and/or import duties. Other sources of industry sales-volume data are sometimes found in the publications and the archives of trade associations and of advertising media. Many firms find it useful to subscribe to one or more of the commercial subscription services that collect panel data from households and/or dealers for certain kinds of products. These panels provide much more detailed information on product movement—by brand, price level, and type of outlet, for example—than is available by other means. Finally, of course, it is possible to undertake special surveys of product volume and use.

In the absence of industry sales figures, and in order to avoid the expense of direct data collection, corollary or proxy data may be used to estimate market potentials. Data on complementary goods, for example, can serve this purpose—the market potential of automobile batteries for replacement can be estimated from data on the distribution of cars, sales of electrical appliances will be related to and limited by the number and location of wired homes.

Whatever the data sources of the market potential estimates, they are often available only on a national basis. One of the tasks of market analysis is to make the conversion to local and regional estimates. The conversion is characteristically made by distributing national figures in proportion to such measures as population, income, number of employees, and value added by manufacture, which are available for smaller geographic units.

The technology of sales forecasting. It is customary in the literature of forecasting to distinguish between short-term and long-term forecasting, although there is only rough agreement on definitions. "Short term" clearly refers to the monthly or quarterly outlook and many practitioners would include the annual forecast. "Long term" can safely be attached to 10-year forecasts, but many technicians would so classify any predictions whose horizon is greater than one year. Forecasts for three years and five years are sometimes categorized as "intermediate range." Much (most) of the technology of forecasting is common to predictions of the various planning horizons, although truly long-range forecasts (e.g., for 10 and 15 years) depend heavily on trend analysis of such fundamental variables as population, productivity, income distribution, political developments, and leisure—all of which change slowly and are assumed to be stable in forecasts for any period up to a few years.

While few analysts would enthusiastically endorse Alphonse de Lamartine's observation that "History teaches everything, even the future," the fact is that the experience of yesterday and today constitutes all we know about tomorrow. The technology of forecasting includes methods for identifying relevant historical data and for manipulating them in ways which may make the record more meaningful and illuminating. The art of forecasting largely consists in interpreting historical data and in specifying those future events that will condition tomorrow's performance.

There are numerous ways of categorizing sales forecasting methods. It is convenient here to distinguish among the following: "judgment forecasts," including sales-force estimates; market surveys; market tests; time series analysis, including curve fitting; and regression analysis. While these various techniques are sometimes presented as mutually exclusive and alternative analytical tools, in practice full reliance is seldom placed on any single method; two or more approaches often supplement each other. Certainly, the forecast ultimately accepted as the basis for company planning almost always will reflect the intuitive estimates of senior management.

Judgmental approaches. Hardly anyone will quarrel with the assertion that intuition and judgment dominate the practice of sales forecasting. Ease, cheapness, and flexibility all combine to support the use of predictions of sales volume which rest unabashedly on the judgment of one or more persons in the firm. Judgment forecasts, whether made by individuals or committees, are dominated by the experience, perception, and intuition of the forecasters. The process cannot be separated from the performer(s) and replication is impossible. However inelegant the method may appear, impressionistic evidence suggests that the more rigorous statistical forecasting methods continue to play a subsidiary role in business planning.

Judgment forecasts are sometimes based on

sales-force estimates of future sales. It is hoped that sales personnel (and their managers) are familiar with the needs and circumstances of customers and the relative strength of competitive offerings. In some companies sales representatives systematically interview customers concerning their spending plans. Rarely, however, are sales-force estimates the sole basis of a company's forecast. Substantial editing is generally contributed by corporate staff and senior management.

While it is often claimed that salesmen (and their supervisors) are unduly optimistic and therefore generate faulty forecasts, evidence is hard to come by. It is not obvious that such a bias should consistently attach to their estimates, since the estimators' interest will be a function both of the character of the compensation plan and the particular use to be made of the forecast.

Market surveys. Whereas sales-force estimates rely on a survey of the forecasts of sales personnel, a more recent development has been that of the survey of buyer intentions. The market survey rests on a sample of potential buyers whose attitudes and/or intentions to purchase are solicited in person or by mail or telephone.

The survey has enormous appeal as a forecasting aid. It seems plausible that buyers should know (and be able and willing to say) what and whether they plan to buy in the future—especially if the future is not too distant. But this view assumes that consumers can predict what the future will be like as well as what they will choose to do if the future is as they expect it to be. Evidence on the validity of these assumptions is uncertain.

The Survey of Consumer Finances was initiated in 1946 by the Board of Governors of the Federal Reserve System (Juster 1964). These surveys, covering intentions to purchase durable goods (e.g., houses, automobiles, and major household appliances), are among the best-known and most thoroughly analyzed materials in the literature of forecasting. They are in many respects models of methodological nicety and generally far surpass ordinary commercial standards—and costs—of market investigation. Despite the relatively long history of these surveys and the superior methods and skills of the investigators, one must still characterize the method as more promising than certain. What does seem clear is that the survey method is best adapted to products involving relatively large expenditures and a fairly high degree of planning for purchase. In the case of family expenditures, homes and automobiles most clearly meet these conditions. In the case of industrial markets, expenditures for capital goods (e.g., expensive machinery and new plant construction) obviously qualify. Indeed, surveys of spending plans for industrial capital goods have tended to yield more accurate forecasts than those for consumer goods.

Market testing. Another method used to estimate market potential is the market test. Employed primarily for new products and invading brands, the market test is essentially an "experiment" which eschews direct questioning of respondents in favor of measuring their behavior. Market experiments are not feasible for all product categories, and they are expensive even when confined, as they usually are, to one or a few markets. The test is most commonly employed for packaged consumer goods items—the frequently purchased branded food, drug, and household supply products of relatively low price and high turnover. Market tests by and large amount to "tryouts" in one or a few markets—typically cities or metropolitan areas—which are selected as test locations because they are considered to be representative and relatively self-contained and have trade outlets and advertising media which are amenable to experimentation.

Virtually nothing is publicly available on the predictive value of the test market as a forecasting method. Test marketing is above all else a private affair. One infers that it provides useful, if not precise, information from the fact that successful and sophisticated enterprises continue to employ the method. At the same time, some conspicuous commercial failures suggest that test marketing is far from infallible as a basis for estimating market potential. In an article on the predictive power of test marketing, the author concluded:

> Despite its shortcomings, test marketing has provided a certain degree of service to marketing management. It has, without question, considerably narrowed the range of new product sales prediction error over forecasts arrived at by judgment, even experienced judgment. From a management point of view, however, for a technique as expensive as test marketing, and one that exposes the company's future hand to competitors, it would seem that we have a right to expect a much greater measure of reliability and accuracy. (Gold 1964, p. 16)

Time series analysis. Among the most frequently employed statistical forecasting techniques is that of time series analysis, which probes the record of past sales behavior in search of patterns that may be extrapolated. Historical sales, economic, and social data constitute time series which can be analyzed by statistical techniques of various kinds. But when measured against the task, the statistical tools are rudimentary and, some statisticians believe, of dubious value. One persistent approach seeks indicating or "leading" series which signal the direction and, hopefully, the extent of movement in the "following" or "lagging" series. While experience has dampened the hope that many companies can find consistently reliable lead–lag relationships, the search has not abated and empiricism rules.

Past sales patterns are sometimes mechanically projected by methods of curve fitting and trend analysis. The results are extremely sensitive to the particular formulas chosen and are perhaps most often used in combination with the forecasters' best guesses about the state of key variables in the future and often with a substantial dash of reasoning by analogy.

Forecasting for the month or the quarter ahead is frequently characterized by relatively mechanical projections of recent sales, usually "smoothed" by one statistical device or another. The availability of computers and developments such as exponentially weighted projections of past sales, the weights declining as one incorporates earlier and earlier data, promise better short-term forecasts and improved inventory control in situations of highly complex inventory assortments and relatively strong seasonal demand.

In all forecasting it is well to have some criterion of success and, particularly, a measure of the extent to which forecasts do little but exploit the tendency for sales figures to show inertia, each period tending to be close to the experience of the immediately preceding period. This interest in a criterion underlies the so-called "naive models." The simplest of such models is the "no-change" model, that is, the forecasted sales for the period ahead will equal the sales of the current period. A somewhat more complex formulation would be that the direction and rate of change, rather than the absolute value, will persist. (These are, of course, simple methods of extrapolation.) Naive models have been used mainly as standards for evaluating alternative forecasting methods. Nonetheless, the notion underlying naive models can be expressed in various autoregressive statistical methods that have some promise of improving judgmental forecasts, even for periods as long as a year.

Regression analysis. Regression analysis, in its many forms, attracts increasing interest and use. The underlying idea is to exploit the statistical relationship evidenced in the past between the variable to be forecast and the so-called independent variables (e.g., income, population, prices) that may be related to it. There are numerous regression analyses "explaining" the sales of various products, in the sense of showing a statistical relationship between sales and the independent variables. The prediction problem is then shifted from the dependent variables (sales) to the independent variable(s). Occasionally, of course, a lagged relationship can be shown to exist. Predicting from a regression analysis assumes stability of the past statistical relationships. As in all other statistical forecasting techniques, intuition and judgment are required to allow for changes in basic conditions that are neither reflected in historical data nor embraced by the statistical model.

The advent of the computer has made it possible to undertake more sophisticated (complex) manipulations of data than ever before. Computer programs make feasible the exponential smoothing of time series, stepwise multiple regression, the solution of systems of multiple regression equations, and simulation. But while the contributions of the computer promise wider use of complex forecasting techniques and offer improved opportunities for experimenting and testing alternative methods, the millennium is not yet.

Status and prospect. Despite the enthusiasm for sales forecasting and the exhortations that it constitutes the basis if not, indeed, the essence of business planning, the record is neither clear nor impressive. Accurate forecasting is still a wish rather than a fact. Distressingly little published information is available on the degree to which actual sales conform to forecast sales. One survey in the United States reported that there was an average deviation of 8 per cent between forecasts and actuals in 1955, but the average performance masks a wide range of deviations within and between industry groups (American Management Association 1956, p. 148).

In an English study Carter and Williams suggest some of the difficulty of making accurate sales predictions in the case of new ventures. In 57 per cent of the cases examined where expected and actual yields were at variance, the explanation was associated with "unforeseen changes of demand, or changes in the price of competing product." They properly observed:

> The importance of changes in demand can be seen. Many of these were changes in the demand for an intermediate product, deriving from a change in the nature of, or the demand for, some final products of other industries. Given the long period which must often elapse between the final decision to go ahead with a new plant and the sale of its first product, it is clearly unreasonable to expect many of these com-

plex changes in demand to be foreseen; market research is not an answer to everything. (1958, pp. 90–91)

Limited information on European experience indicates mixed results, although the record of the "Munich Business Test" on quarterly forecasts of turning points is encouraging (see Theil 1958, chapters 4, 5).

There is an extensive literature on market analysis and sales forecasting, but most of it is preoccupied with technique and much of it is hortatory. And as Lorie observed a few years ago:

> Progress comes most rapidly in any pragmatic discipline when adequate testing devices are available for measuring the success of current theories and procedures. Only by such testing is it possible to discard what has not succeeded and to cling to what has succeeded, for the purposes of further elaboration and refinement. These facts are considered self-evident in the field of meteorology, where most of the practitioners make their living by forecasting. As a consequence, a very extensive literature devoted to problems of evaluation has developed during the last seventy-five years. (1957, p. 177)

Unfortunately, the evaluation of sales forecasts is not general in the literature, and it is not common in industrial practice. Much too little is known about the predictive value of alternative techniques. The most sanguine would agree that there is much to be learned and that the task of prediction is to be approached with humility. Performance offers ample opportunity for improvement. The recording of methods and specific quantified forecasts with subsequent comparison with experience is certainly to be encouraged, not only as a means of educating technicians, but also as an opportunity for evaluating them.

JOHN E. JEUCK

BIBLIOGRAPHY

AMERICAN MANAGEMENT ASSOCIATION, MARKETING DIVISION 1956 *Sales Forecasting: Uses, Techniques, and Trends.* Special Report No. 16. New York: The Association.

CARTER, CHARLES F.; and WILLIAMS, BRUCE R. 1958 *Investment in Innovation.* Oxford Univ. Press.

FERBER, ROBERT 1960 The Railroad Shippers' Forecasts and the Illinois Employers' Labor Force Anticipations: A Study in Comparative Experience. Pages 181–199 in Universities–National Bureau Committee for Economic Research, *The Quality and Economic Significance of Anticipations Data.* National Bureau of Economic Research, Special Conference Series, No. 10. Princeton Univ. Press.

GOLD, JACK A. 1964 Testing Test Market Predictions. *Journal of Marketing Research* 1, no. 3:8–16.

HUMMEL, FRANCIS E. 1961 *Market and Sales Potentials.* New York: Ronald Press.

JUSTER, FRANCIS T. 1964 *Anticipations and Purchases: An Analysis of Consumer Behavior.* Princeton Univ. Press.

LORIE, JAMES H. 1957 Two Important Problems in Sales Forecasting. *Journal of Business* 30:172–179.

MCLAUGHLIN, ROBERT L. 1962 *Time Series Forecasting: A New Computer Technique for Company Sales Forecasting.* Chicago: American Marketing Association.

NATIONAL INDUSTRIAL CONFERENCE BOARD 1964 *Forecasting Sales.* Studies in Business Policy, No. 106. New York: The Board.

SPENCER, MILTON H.; CLARK, COLIN G.; and HOGUET, PETER W. 1961 *Business and Economic Forecasting: An Econometric Approach.* Homewood, Ill.: Irwin.

THEIL, HENRI (1958) 1961 *Economic Forecasts and Policy.* 2d ed., rev. Amsterdam: North-Holland Publishing.

II
CONSUMER RESEARCH

Consumer research, or marketing research, is the systematic gathering, recording, and analyzing of data and problems related to the marketing of goods and services. The "first law" of marketing has been expressed as "Make what people want to buy; don't merely try to sell what you happen to make." This dictum reflects the existence of a society in which consumers can and do exercise considerable freedom of choice in purchasing.

Present interest in the consumer can be viewed against a historical background of concern with two other factors: production and sales. Concern with production grew in importance during the industrial revolution and reached a peak in the most advanced countries in the early part of the twentieth century with the introduction of assembly lines and mass production methods. Then, as manufacturing efficiency increased and unit costs decreased, the need to dispose of the fruits of mass production gradually shifted management's attention to sales. Later, with the increase in competition for the buyer's dollar within the market, sellers found that they had to take an interest in the consumer and, thus, turned to marketing research to find out what it is that people want to buy. By telling the seller what people want to buy, the researcher helps him plan more efficiently, avoid failures (thus lowering costs to consumers), and provide consumers with a much wider choice of products.

Definition. The first and most important step in any marketing research undertaking is to define the problem. A clear statement of the problem is sometimes more than half the answer. Sometimes, too, after the problem is clearly outlined, it becomes obvious that the answer is already known or may cost too much to obtain. However, the cost of *not* having the answer must also be considered. If it is high, research may pay off. But if the price of being without the answer is minimal, marketing research may be uneconomical.

Once the problem has been defined and agreement has been reached as to what kinds of measurement will yield acceptable answers, the researcher designs his experiment. There are two basic ways of obtaining information about consumers: one is to ask them directly about their awareness, attitudes, and *opinions;* the other is to observe their actual *behavior* (other than verbal behavior). Depending upon the problem and the need for a precise answer, the opinion test (sometimes called "consumer jury") may be entirely adequate. This approach is often used because it is quick, relatively inexpensive, and often provides useful guidance for marketing decisions. Its major drawback is that consumers do not always do what they say they will, for a variety of reasons.

Motivation research. In an attempt to obtain better answers about why consumers act as they do, marketing researchers sometimes engage in motivation research (MR). The basic assumptions of MR are that people often have unconscious motivations and that indirect questioning and various projective devices may be more effective than direct questions.

In a study by Haire, for example, women were asked to describe a hypothetical individual solely on the basis of reading a grocery list prepared by that individual. There were two such lists, differing only in one item. One list included a reference to "regular grind coffee," and the other list referred to "instant coffee." Reactions to the second list showed that a significant number of women believed that the use of instant coffee characterized its user as "lazy." Once the reason for the product's lack of acceptance had been identified, the next step was to conduct an educational campaign, pointing out to housewives that by reducing food-preparation time, they could be with their families more—a use of the saved time that the experimenter assumed was consistent with the housewives' values (Haire 1950).

Other examples of such techniques include:

(*a*) *Word association.* ("Tell me the first word that comes into your mind when I say 'margarine.'")

(*b*) *Incomplete sentences.* (The respondent is asked to complete a sentence such as "The main reason my family doesn't have soup more often is ______.")

(*c*) *Balloon cartoons.* (An example would be a comic strip drawing of two men in conversation. The balloon above one of the men might read: "John, I've been thinking about buying a station wagon." The balloon above John's head is blank, and the respondent is asked to suggest John's response.)

(*d*) *Narrative projection.* (Character descriptions are followed by questions about the kinds of attitudes or purchasing behavior that might be expected from the individuals described.)

(*e*) *Involuntary attention tests.* (The respondent is asked to look at one of two stimuli, and the one he picks up and examines first is assumed to be more interesting.)

There is little doubt that for certain kinds of problems, and particularly for certain kinds of products and services about which people are sensitive (such as personal-care items or small loans), the techniques of motivation research are appropriate and even necessary. But to claim, as some proponents did during the 1950s, that these techniques are the only way to measure attitudes properly is to go to extremes. The violent arguments of that era between the quality-oriented, small-sample MR specialists and the more traditional, quantity-oriented, big-sample researchers (dubbed "mere nose counters" by the MR group) have largely ceased. It became clear that MR, although it contributed many lasting insights and methods that eventually influenced even the most traditional researchers, was not the ultimate key to a complete understanding of human behavior.

Sampling. In most marketing research projects, once the problem has been defined, the next step is to decide how the sample of respondents is to be selected and how large the sample should be. It is important that the sample be free from systematic bias that could influence the conclusions. For example, a pre-election political survey of voter preference in upper-income suburbs would very probably be biased in favor of one political party; hence the sample findings could be quite different from the outcome of the actual election [*see* SAMPLE SURVEYS].

In marketing research it is not always desirable to sample from the total population. For example, if we wish to study reactions to a brand of hair tonic, we would be wise to qualify respondents as tonic users before proceeding to interview them about their reactions. Going still further, we might want to talk only to heavy users. For a wide variety of frequently purchased products it has been shown that the 50 per cent of buyers who are heavy buyers account for 80 to 90 per cent of total sales volume (Twedt 1964).

Since about half the population uses hair tonic, a fourth of the total population (the top half of users) accounts for nearly 90 per cent of all hair tonic consumption. There is increasing evidence that this relationship is not limited to packaged goods; the same basic pattern of purchase concentration is shown in sales of gasoline to credit card customers, in tolls for residential long-distance telephone calls, and even in sales of fractional horsepower motors to industrial buyers.

Since consumption varies by individual and by household, it seems appropriate to let each respondent "vote with his pocketbook" by weighting his response according to the amount of the given product he consumes. Suppose, for example, that research has been conducted to determine whether a package for cake mix should have a red or a blue background for package illustration. From hypothetical data in Table 1, one sees that although the total sample gives a majority vote to the package with the red background, the correct marketing decision would be to choose the blue background, since it is clearly more appealing to the heavy users, who account for about 85 per cent of total cake mix purchased.

Table 1 — Package-background preferences of cake-mix users*

	PREFERENCE	
	Red background	*Blue background*
Light users	450	50
Heavy users	150	350
Total	600	400

* Based on a sample of 1,000 cake-mix users (500 heavy users and 500 light users).

Questionnaires. After the necessary decisions have been made as to the purpose of the survey and who the respondents will be, it is necessary to make up a questionnaire. Questionnaires are often designed with a few general, bland questions at the beginning in order to establish rapport between interviewer and respondent. It is essential to ask the questions in such a way that the answer to a given question does not bias succeeding questions. For this reason many researchers build questionnaires by writing each question on a separate card, moving the cards around until a smooth sequence is achieved, and then transferring the questions to a regular questionnaire format. In major surveys the questions are "pretested" on a small group of 25 to 50 respondents, whose answers are not included in the final tabulations but are analyzed to see if the questions are clear and unambiguous. Revisions are made, and the questionnaire is again pretested. It is not unusual for a survey to go through as many as a dozen revisions before the questionnaire is finally approved (Payne 1951).

Precoding and tabulation. The next step is to precode the questionnaires by assigning to, and printing next to, each question the appropriate code for machine tabulation of responses. Questionnaires can now be designed for optical scanning by machine, with the answers converted directly to either punched cards or magnetic tape; the cards or tape can be programmed to produce a page of "print-out" that is used as photographic copy for the final research report. The enormous economies in human time and the accompanying error reduction through elimination of tedious copying and hand tabulation and computing make it obvious that these developments will continue. The great potential economies of the computer in marketing research are not its only value; a beneficial side effect is that in order to use the computer to its maximum efficiency, the entire research project, including the final tabulations, must be thought through in advance, and this usually results in uncovering mistakes in planning at a time when they can be more easily corrected.

Quality control in field interviewing. Questionnaire surveys are usually made by interviewing organizations that specialize in this type of work. A list of such firms, and of others that offer a broader variety of services, including consulting, experimental design, and preparation of the final report with recommendations for action, is contained in *Bradford's Directory of Marketing Research Agencies*, which lists 350 firms in the United States and abroad (Bradford 1965–1966).

After the interviewing organization has been selected, it is customary to hold a briefing session with the project leader, the interviewing supervisors, and the interviewers in order to give detailed instructions on how the interview is to be conducted. Any questions the interviewers have should be answered at this time. Often they will be told not to proceed after the first day of interviewing until the field supervisor has had an opportunity to review the quality of work done during that day.

As the field work is progressing, or immediately after it is completed, 10 to 20 per cent of the interviews are validated in one of several ways: reinterview, a telephone call, or by mail. During these follow-up procedures, the supervisor verifies that the interview actually took place, and a few key questions may be repeated to check for report consistency. When the work of a given interviewer seems irregular, all the interviews turned in by that person are rechecked. If, as occasionally happens, it develops that the interview was not made and that the questionnaire has been faked, the interviewer is not employed again by the same organization. One of the weakest links in the entire data-gathering and data-processing chain is the failure to validate questionnaires properly [*see* QUALITY CONTROL, STATISTICAL].

Recommendations for action. If the objectives of a research survey have been clearly defined, the right questions asked of the right people in order to answer these objectives, and the field work properly supervised, the two remaining tasks—tabulation and analysis, and report preparation—should be fairly routine. There are, however, two major conflicting viewpoints about the extent to which the researcher should make firm recommendations for marketing action.

One group of marketing executives tends to regard the researcher primarily as a technician from whom only "the facts" are wanted, with no interpretation or conclusions about appropriate courses of action. The other viewpoint is reflected by Theodore Levitt of Harvard University, who says,

> Expertness [in marketing research] encompasses much more than the elaboration and use of formal techniques in research and analysis. More than anything else it should be viewed as involving imaginative audacity in the interpretation of data and events and in formulating positive action-oriented proposals for management's consideration. . . . Too often nothing is permissible in the way of making policy or entertaining ideas unless the data are so unambiguously in favor of proposed policies or ideas that even the elevator operator can see their merit. (1962, pp. 187–190)

Observing behavior. Most of the discussion up to this point relates to the gathering of opinions through survey research. There are many other ways in which marketing research can be conducted. Observing and recording consumer behavior takes many forms. Legibility tests of an advertisement, for example, can be made by determining the amount of illumination or length of exposure required to allow reading of the sales message. It is even possible to measure behavior which the respondent is not consciously aware of, such as pupillary dilation while viewing a product or an advertising stimulus. Or suppose that we wish to determine the proportion of consumers that will read the statement of ingredients on the package label of a new food product. It is a simple matter to observe shoppers at the moment of buying and record the number of seconds they examine each package before selecting it.

Another major method of behavioral research in marketing is to conduct controlled advertising and sales tests in selected areas. Two cities may be matched, for example, on the basis of their previous sales of a given product. An advertising campaign may then be undertaken in one city, and a different campaign (or perhaps no advertising) employed in the other city. After a predetermined time period sales results are compared for the two cities. Variations of this method may include much more complex statistical procedures and may involve factorial and Latin-square experimental designs, with many cities or retail outlets included in the test. The measures may be actual sales, the proportion of consumers who are aware of a given brand name, or the proportion who can recall specific sales points about the product. [*See* EXPERIMENTAL DESIGN.]

Subjects for marketing research. The most common research activities of 1,660 companies are shown in Table 2.

Table 2 — Market research activities*

Activity	*Companies involved (per cent)*
Sales and market research:	
Development of market potentials	68
Market share analysis	67
Determination of market characteristics	67
Sales analyses	66
Establishment of sales quotas	57
Distribution and costs studies	52
Test markets, store audits	37
Consumer panel operations	27
Sales compensation studies	44
Studies of premiums, coupons, sampling, deals	29
Product research:	
New product acceptance	63
Competitive product studies	65
Product testing	57
Packaging research	45
Business economics and corporate research:	
Short-range forecasting (to 1 year)	62
Long-range forecasting (over 1 year)	59
Studies of business trends	58
Profit and/or value analysis	53
Plant and warehouse locational studies	44
Diversification studies	49
Purchase of companies, sales of divisions	44
Export and international studies	39
Linear programming	35
Operations research	29
Program evaluation review technique studies	18
Employee morale studies	32
Advertising research:	
Motivation research	30
Copy research	37
Media research	47
Evaluation of advertising effectiveness	48

* Based on activities of 1,660 companies.

Source: American Marketing Association 1963.

Advertising research. Advertising research is a special application of marketing research but employs many of the same techniques and methods. The task of advertising research usually is to find answers to one or more of the following questions: (1) What shall we say? (2) How shall we say it? (3) Where, when, and how often shall we say it? (4) How well did we communicate the intended message? These questions are investigated, respectively, in motivation research, copy research, media research, and evaluation research [*see* ADVERTISING, *article on* ADVERTISING RESEARCH].

Growth of marketing research departments. Of 1,660 companies surveyed more than half reported having a marketing research department (American Marketing Association 1963). Research departments are most common among companies that manufacture consumer goods (62 per cent have them), industrial companies (60 per cent), and publishers and broadcasters (57 per cent). The bigger the company, the more likely it is to have a research department. The research department is a fairly recent addition to corporate staffs; more than half of the departments in the survey had been formed since 1955. Even the companies that do not have formal marketing research departments carry on such research, either through their own personnel or through outside consulting firms. Between 1960 and 1965 marketing research budgets as a percentage of sales increased for both consumer and industrial companies.

It is clear that marketing research has matured greatly since 1955 and that it has gained increased acceptance from business management. It is also true that marketing research has not yet reached its full potential.

DIK TWEDT

[*Directly related are the entries* ADVERTISING *and* CONSUMERS. *Other relevant material may be found in* INTERVIEWING, *article on* SOCIAL RESEARCH.]

BIBLIOGRAPHY

Readers interested in more detailed consideration of the various aspects of marketing research are referred to Wales & Ferber 1956, *an annotated bibliography of more than 1,600 references covering 28 major areas. For current developments in the United States and abroad, see the three leading professional journals:* Journal of Marketing, Journal of Marketing Research, *and* Journal of Advertising Research.

AMERICAN MARKETING ASSOCIATION 1963 *A Survey of Marketing Research: Organization, Functions, Budget, Compensation.* Edited by Dik W. Twedt. Chicago: The Association.

BRADFORD, ERNEST S. (editor) 1965–1966 *Bradford's Directory of Marketing Research Agencies and Management Consultants in the United States and the World.* 11th ed. Middleburg, Va.: Bradford.

HAIRE, MASON 1950 Projective Techniques in Marketing Research. *Journal of Marketing* 14:649–656.

Journal of Advertising Research. → Published since 1960.

Journal of Marketing. → Published since 1936.

Journal of Marketing Research. → Published since 1964.

LEVITT, THEODORE 1962 *Innovation in Marketing: New Perspectives for Profit and Growth.* New York: McGraw-Hill.

PAYNE, STANLEY L. 1951 *The Art of Asking Questions.* Studies in Public Opinion, No. 3. Princeton Univ. Press.

TWEDT, DIK W. 1964 How Important to Marketing Strategy Is the "Heavy User"? *Journal of Marketing* 28, no. 1:71–72.

WALES, HUGH G.; and FERBER, ROBERT (1956) 1963 *A Basic Bibliography on Marketing Research.* Chicago: American Marketing Association.

MARKETS AND INDUSTRIES

The market is the stage on which economic actors—firms, households, and unions—meet and make key economic decisions for society. Out of the process of market exchange come the prices, wages, and profits that serve to determine the allocation of the economy's resources and the distribution of the national income.

The market is thus a central concept in economics. It is, however, an elusive concept. It may mean merely the geographical place where exchange takes place—a nodal point where buyers and sellers meet to exchange goods and services. But the concept of the market as economists use it also embraces the whole set of circumstances that surround the process of exchange, and indeed it concerns as well the outcomes of the process of exchange. Thus we speak of market structure and market behavior and market price. Firms and households may take conditions in the market as external to them, and such conditions affect their behavior. But this behavior in turn affects market results and, indeed, may determine what is the market.

The market in the most general sense is the entire web of interrelationships between buyers, sellers, and products that is involved in exchange. The appropriate definition of the market depends upon which aspects of this web are of interest at the time; for different problems there are different appropriate definitions.

Historically and in much of common usage "the market" means a place where buyers and sellers meet to buy and sell goods. But while this usage serves well enough to identify the Fulton Fish Market, it provides little insight into what is meant by the used-car market, the stock market, the labor market, the mortgage market, or the black market in Japanese yen. Within the market, however defined, buyers and sellers negotiate the exchange of goods or services. A market definition may focus upon what the products are, as the market for cement, aluminum cable, or wheat. In this usage it is common to speak of the market as an industry. Alternatively, however, it may focus upon who the buyers are, as, for example, the market for loans to Chicago borrowers. It may focus upon who the sellers are, as the market for engineers or the market in which the integrated oil companies operate. Market definition may focus upon the rules by which the market is run, as in an auction market, or upon when goods are to be exchanged, as in the distinction between a present and a futures market. Finally, geographical definition may concern where buyers or sellers reside or do business as well as where they meet to exchange. In this sense the New York Stock Exchange is often regarded as an international securities market.

None of these bases for definition is without interest some of the time. In general, differences in focus will lead to differences in designation of which transactions belong in a market. The market is a concept with many dimensions.

The market in economic theory

Economists use the word "market" in two substantially different senses. While they have etymological precedent for this—the Latin root *mercatus* means either the place of *or* the method of contact between buyers and sellers—the result is often confusion.

The first sense in which economists use the word concerns the general conditions under which buyers and sellers exchange goods and services. The conditions may be summarized in a series of alternative theoretical market structures, such as "perfect competition," "monopoly," "oligopoly," and "monopolistic competition." [*See* COMPETITION; MONOPOLY; OLIGOPOLY.] These theoretical structures, or models, make assumptions about such things as the number of sellers and buyers and their perceptions of each other and yield predictions about market behavior. In turn this predicted behavior leads to predictions about market results: what will be the prices, quantities, and qualities of outputs that emerge from the market. Market structure is not one-dimensional, but it is often convenient to think of different market structures as differing from one another in terms of the kind and degree of competition that they lead to.

The second sense in which the word is used is to delineate the boundaries (usually geographic) that identify specific groups of buyers, sellers, and commodities. This concept of the market is designated *extent of the market.* In this sense we define the fluid-milk market for the New York City area or the upper Midwest cement market by an appropriate map.

Up to a point these two usages are both separate and separable. One does not need geographic boundaries to derive predictions about how, for example, a perfectly competitive market works in equating demand and supply, nor does one need theoretical models of market structure to describe or delimit the Fulton Fish Market. The need to confront these separate aspects of a market arises whenever economists wish to use economic theories of market structure to make predictions about the behavior or performance of real-world markets; it arises as well if they wish to use observed data about real-world markets to test the predictions of their theories; it arises, further, if one wishes to use economic conclusions about market behavior and performance in establishing or enforcing public policies that relate to the behavior of actual industries or firms. Since these are among the important uses of economics, it arises often.

The number of participants in the market is held to be a key factor in market structure, and thus in market behavior and in market results. The number of participants in a market will, however, vary as we change the boundaries of the market. Market structure and market extent are thus interrelated in applications. The great hazard in analyses of economic markets is the circular, or prediction-determining, definition.

Defining market extent by its structure. Most well-defined theories of market structure contain implicit rules for delineating which transactions belong in the market. Using such implicit rules is superficially an appealing way to solve a difficult problem. Except in rare cases it proves quite unsatisfactory. Consider market definitions under perfect competition and under monopoly.

Under perfect competition. A central prediction of the theory of perfect competition is that the price of all transactions will tend to uniformity, allowing for differences in transportation costs. Empirically, the boundaries of a *perfectly competitive market* may be established by searching for the area over which transactions occur at common prices. This definition of a market has an honored past and a wide range of contemporary acceptance. It is the definition used by Cournot (1838, chapter 4), popularized by Alfred Marshall (1890, p. 327 in 1920 edition), and repeated in leading contemporary texts (Stigler 1942, p. 92 in 1947 edition).

One drawback of this definition is that actual price behavior in such a market cannot be used to test the prediction of uniformity of prices. A more serious difficulty concerns the interpretation of transactions that occur at other than the adjusted common price. Do they represent transactions in a different market or do they provide evidence that this market is in fact not a perfectly competitive one? The implications of these two possibilities are totally different. In U.S. law, for example, the merger of two firms is legal if they are in quite separate markets but may be illegal if they are in the same, imperfectly competitive market. Using uniform price behavior to define market extent would be satisfactory if such behavior were a common implication of all theories of market structure; this, however, is not the case.

Under monopoly. The theoretical model of monopoly comprehends a situation in which there is but a single seller of the commodity (or a group of sellers who act as if they were under a single coordinated management). The implicit market for a monopolized product consists of all transactions in the commodity in which the monopolist is the seller. It is *not* a prediction of the theory that the price need be uniform among all customers, since the monopolist can discriminate among buyers. It is a prediction of the theory of discriminating monopoly that prices will be uniform only among subgroups of customers who can resell the commodity or among whom demand elasticities are approximately equal. Were we to apply the implicit competitive definition of a market in a situation that is, in fact, that of a discriminating monopolist, the group of transactions which occur at a common price would represent only a small part of the total relevant market.

The major deficiency of defining a market on the basis of theories of market structure is that different market structures contain different implicit rules for definition of the market. Indeed, their reason for being is that they make different predictions about market results. To define the market according to the price behavior exhibited destroys any possibility of using the market so defined to say anything about price behavior, and it prejudges the question of which market structure is the relevant one for making predictions. An empirically useful market definition must be independent of the alternative theoretical models of market structure, if we wish to test or to apply those theories.

Defining market extent by demand and supply alternatives. Any particular buyer or seller has a definable set of alternative sources of supply or demand which he considers available to him. From his point of view the relevant market is the set of these alternatives. This kind of individualized definition of a market would be of little general use if there were not important clusters of buyers and sellers for whom the relevant market was approximately the same; suppose there are such groups and that it is thus feasible to define markets that apply to significant numbers of transactions.

As a logical matter, market extent defined in this way may also be circular. The perceptions of, for example, a buyer as to which are the real alternative sources of supply depend upon the prices that prevail. A housewife who says she will never go across town to shop for food means it only within limits. A big enough "sale" will change her view. Thus if prices are, in fact, uniform as among sellers, the radius of the market extent around a customer will be much smaller than the market to which he might turn if prices were not uniform. Some Californians buy cars in Detroit if prices on the west coast get too far out of line.

Empirical approximations to definition

While as a logical matter there is no satisfactory definition of a market that identifies the relevant transactions independent of the market results, reasonable markets do exist in many commodities. While everything in principle depends upon everything else, in many cases the interactions and feedbacks are small enough to be negligible. Bicycles and sports cars are not in the same market, although there conceivably exists a set of prices that would lead to large-scale substitution of one for the other. As a practical matter cement is so rarely sold outside of a radius of 200 miles from the factory that a regional cement market may be defined.

The basic empirical problem of market definition is to define the range of alternatives to which a buyer or seller may *practicably* turn and to identify the sets of transactions whose outcomes are sufficiently interrelated that to subdivide them further invites error. One definition of an industry is as "a gap in the chain of substitutes"; a parallel definition of a market is as "a gap in the chain of alternatives." As a logical matter it has been argued that industries do not exist (Triffin 1940) and that all firms must be viewed either alone or as part of a generally interdependent network. Most economists reject this nihilistic view and believe the industry is a useful aggregate concept. Similarly, the market is a useful aggregation of sets of related transactions.

Suppose we seek an empirical approximation of the set of real, practicable alternatives. We must ask: "Real alternatives to whom?" One may focus upon the products or the sellers that are real alternatives to a particular group of buyers, one may instead ask what are the alternative sources of demand to a group of sellers, or one may ask what are the products that are effective substitutes for a particular product. There are, indeed, many aspects of each of these different ways of looking at the set of alternatives. Consider the producer of a given product: he may at one time be concerned with the group of other sellers of this product; at another time he may be concerned with other products that are technologically similar so that they represent real alternatives to him in production; at still another time he may be concerned with different products that his customers may regard as substitutes for his product. Of the hundreds of possible ways of defining sets of alternatives, two are of major interest to students of economic markets and how they work.

The first is *the real alternative sources of supply available to a defined group of buyers*. We may ask, for example, what are the sources of supply of credit available to the small businessman; we may be concerned with the sources of supply of safety glass to automobile manufacturers; or we may be concerned with the sources of supply of automobiles in the $1,500–$2,500 price range to buyers living in Peoria. Much of the public concern with competition is concerned with preserving a sufficient number of independent sources of supply so that every group of customers has genuine alternative sources of supply. The legislative concern evidenced in the major antitrust laws is centrally concerned with preserving effective competition in markets defined in this way.

The second is *the group of relevant rivals to a particular seller*. This concept of the market is crucial to understanding the market behavior of sellers. The number of rivals that a seller has and the nature of the interactions between them are hypothesized to be major determinants of the price and product patterns that emerge in an industry. Indeed, the very concept of an industry rests upon the identification of a group of sellers in substantial rivalry (actual or potential) with one another. Economists largely concerned with industrial structure and behavior regard this focus as central to the definition of the market.

Implicit in each of these definitions is the notion that a distinct "product" or group of products exists. The classification of products into meaningful "industries" is a major concern of the U.S. Bureau of the Census and other statistical agencies. The recognition that for different purposes different clusters of products are relevant has led to the development in the United States of a Standard Industrial Classification (SIC) at several levels of aggregation. There are seventy-eight "2-digit" industries, hundreds of "3-digit" industries, and several thousand "4-digit" industries. By appropriate recombinations of the 4-digit industries a very much larger number of industries may be defined. The focus of the SIC is on the supply side rather than the demand side, and SIC industries are more nearly appropriate to the identification of interrelated sellers than of alternatives to buyers.

Markets defined in these ways overlap but do not coincide. Every transaction involves a buyer, a seller, and a well-defined product. It may, however, be a transaction in several different markets. Consider, for example, the purchase of a new compact Chevrolet by an individual living in St. Louis. From the buyer's point of view the relevant alternative products may have been any of four or five models of new cars or any of a number of used cars in the same price range. (The list of alternatives will certainly not include a truck or a tractor and almost certainly will not include a new Cadillac.) The relevant sellers will be the new- and used-automobile dealers in a definable geographic region centered largely on St. Louis, as well as private sellers with whom the buyer may make contact.

To the General Motors Company the transaction appears in a very different light. Its rivalry with Ford and Chrysler and American Motors for the new-car dollar is nation-wide and includes Buicks and Cadillacs as well as Chevrolets. At the same time, the compact-car market—in which the various American manufacturers are in open competition with certain foreign manufacturers, particularly Volkswagen—involves a different set of rivalries.

From the product point of view, the transaction occurred in SIC industry 37, Transportation Equipment; in industry 371, Motor Vehicles and Motor Vehicle Equipment; and in industry 3717, Motor Vehicles and Parts. Even the smallest of these is a substantially comprehensive classification including the manufacturing or assembling of (among other things) passenger automobiles, trucks, ambulances, and fire engines and also including the parts that make up such motor vehicles, such as axles, radiators, drive shafts, exhaust systems, universal joints, and automobile bumpers. For many purposes SIC 3717 is much too broad; an automobile muffler and an automobile bumper are not in any sense substitute products. The statistical problem of industry definition is made complex by the fact that some firms make a large variety of such component products and others specialize. For other purposes the definition of industries in the SIC is too narrow. Multiproduct firms may operate in many industries, and their wage policies and their labor market negotiations may extend across industry lines. All production workers of American Motors, whether they are making cars or refrigerators, are covered by contract negotiations with the United Automobile Workers.

The market to buyers. Major impetus to empirical definition of markets in the United States has been a by-product of the Anti-merger Act of 1950 (the so-called Celler–Kefauver Act). It made very general a prohibition on mergers "where in any line of commerce in any section of the country, the effect of such acquisition may be substantially to lessen competition, or to tend to create a monopoly."

A first step in every one of the cases involving this statute is the definition of the relevant market. Pathbreaking opinions in a series of antitrust decisions have sharpened the notion of what is a relevant market, as well as defining the legal issues involved. It is clear that one can always define a sufficiently localized geographical area in such a way that there is but one seller of a particular product; conversely, one can usually define an area so broadly as to make the effect on competition appear trivial. Every merger leads to the disappearance of one seller. But one out of how many? For example, the 1961 merger of the Continental Illinois National Bank and the City National Bank reduced the number of banks in the 200 S. block of LaSalle Street, Chicago, from 2 to 1, the number of business district banks from 16 to 15, and the number of banks in the Chicago Metropolitan Area from 219 to 218. For the whole United States there were about 14,000 commercial banks. After the merger there was one less.

Recent court opinions have established guidelines:

> . . . the boundaries of the relevant market must be drawn with sufficient breadth to include competing products . . . to recognize competition where, in fact, competition exists. (*Brown Shoe Co.* v. *U.S.*, 370 U.S. 294, 326, 1962)

> The relevant market is the area to which customers *can* practicably turn for supplies. (Paraphrase of *U.S.* v. *Philadelphia National Bank*, 374 U.S. 321, 1963)

> The proper question, . . . is not where is the customer located, but what is the geographic area of effective competition for his patronage. (*U.S.* v. *Manufacturers Hanover Trust Co.*, CCH Trade Cases 71,708, pp. 80,744, 1965)

> A relevant geographic market cannot be defined, however, solely on the basis of where . . . banks have actually done business, or even where customers have actually turned for their banking needs. The market must be drawn also on the basis of potential competition. . . . Where could customers practically turn for alternative sources of supply? (*ibid.*, pp. 80,746)

These are sensible guidelines; implementing them is hard. The problem is in relating observation to guideline. A customer buys from a particular seller for any or all of a number of reasons: it may be habitual, it may be convenient, it may be a matter of some indifference, or, importantly, it may be necessary. Defining the relevant choices of the buyer is in fact defining the group of sellers from one of whom it is necessary that he buy. Put differently, if we can define sellers from whom it is impracticable to buy, we have defined sellers outside of the relevant market. If one is to base empirical delineation of the extent of a market upon observations of which sellers are in fact utilized by buyers, the key problem is to differentiate the factor of necessity from that of convenience.

A housewife in a moderate-sized city will in general have a dozen or more supermarkets at which she may conveniently shop, and another dozen at which she might shop if there were any real reason to do so. In fact she will usually tend to shop at two or three, because, other things being equal, she has certain preferences. Indeed she may only shop at one. But this one is an explicit or an implicit choice from the larger set of practicable choices. It is the larger group that constitutes her real opportunities and that defines the market.

The determinants of a customer's choice of a supplier may in general be several. Some of these are (1) portability of the product, (2) cost of transportation of the product, (3) information about the availability and conditions of supply of the product, (4) acceptability of the customer to the seller, (5) price of the product, (6) convenience, and (7) chance and habit. These factors may be related to one another: for example, while there are limits to the geographic range over which fresh milk and live lobsters can be transported without spoiling, these limits may be extended by increasing costs of delivery. Refrigerated trucks and railroad cars extend the markets for fresh produce, some Maine lobsters are shipped to the Midwest by air (but none are shipped to San Francisco), and so on. Similarly, information can be gathered, but at some cost and some inconvenience. What is of concern in defining markets is the distinction between the first four listed factors (singly or in interaction), which represent real limits on practicable alternatives, and the last three, which represent instead the bases of choices among real alternative sources of supply.

As a practical matter geographic market definition becomes relatively easy when one of the first four considerations exercises a dominant limitation on sources of supply. Consider a few examples. For commodities such as cement, for which transportation cost per unit is a high fraction of unit value, the geographic limits on choice of suppliers is very clear. It is easy to define the relevant cement market for a given customer. The relevant housing market for an individual is delimited by distance from his work, by his income, and in some cases, additionally, by his race. The market for a business loan for a small business is effectively limited to those financial institutions that will accept local credit evaluations. Such a small borrower is typically limited to his home city or a portion thereof. Purchase of a used car tends to be limited more by available information than by anything else. On the other hand, well-organized markets in securities make the supplier from whom one buys 100 shares of General Motors stock a matter of substantial indifference. The borrowing of $1 million for working capital by a national corporation is not practicably limited to any small geographic region.

Observing from whom each of the individual members of a large group purchases will tend to define the relevant geographic market if transportation cost, portability of product, information, or acceptability provides a binding constraint on available alternatives. Chance, convenience, and habit will average out over a large group, and over time variations in price will average out as well. The fact that over 90 per cent of all loans to businesses with assets of less than $50,000 are made by banks in the same city, county, or metropolitan area strongly suggests that the relevant geographic market is limited. Of customers with assets of over $100 million, only one-third borrow from local banks. (As this example suggests, one can perhaps *infer* geographic limitation by observed behavior. This is a complex matter of statistical estimation, discussion of which is inappropriate to this article.) Where no binding limitations of these kinds can be identified, geographical delineation of market extent is virtually impossible.

The market to the seller. Identifying the relevant rivals to a particular seller is typically a very much easier matter than identifying markets for customer groups, particularly for manufacturers of major commodities. But not always. Some forty firms in the United States manufacture electrical equipment, but only six of them manufacture turbine generators, only four manufacture meters, about a dozen manufacture industrial control equipment. And General Electric and Westinghouse are clearly in rivalry with General Motors in the manufacture and sale of refrigerators, though they are no part of the automotive industry.

In practice the relevant group of rivals has to be defined in the context of a particular problem. With respect to price determination, of primary concern in many cases, sellers who regard each other's commodities as close substitutes and employ consciously parallel price policies clearly are in the same market. Products whose prices move closely together over a sufficient period of time to permit other influences to vary are usually regarded as in the same market, and the suppliers of them are considered to form an industry. Again, difficulties in precise definition exist but need not prevent reasonable estimation of related groups of suppliers who sell in the same market.

The many markets for a commodity. Consider the market(s) for business loans. A Federal Reserve Board survey in 1955 revealed over 1.2 million outstanding loans by some 7,000 U.S. member banks, amounting in aggregate to over $30,000 million. Most of these loans were very small: over 1 million were for less than $25,000, and they accounted for only one-sixth of the dollar total. On the other hand, 42,000 of these loans were for over $100,000, and they accounted for two-thirds of the total dollars of outstanding loans. There is no doubt that there is a national market for very large loans. There is also little doubt that small loans are largely limited to local markets. There are thus hundreds of local markets and a national market as well. (There may be regional markets in addition.) Let us consider the definition of one such local market, that for the Chicago Metropolitan Area (CMA).

In a total of 20,500 loans representing about

Table 1 — Loans involving CMA bank or borrower (millions of dollars)*

Location of bank \ Location of borrower	In CMA	Not in CMA	All
In CMA	1,125 (16.5)	1,224 (2.5)	2,349 (19.0)
Not in CMA	756 (1.5)		
All	1,881 (18.0)		

* Number of loans in thousands in parentheses.

Source: Special unpublished tabulation from Federal Reserve Board 1955 loan survey.

Table 2 — Loans under $100,000 involving CMA bank or borrower (millions of dollars)*

Location of bank \ Location of borrower	In CMA	Not in CMA	All
In CMA	215 (14.8)	36 (2.3)	251 (17.1)
Not in CMA	20 (0.8)		
All	235 (15.6)		

* Number of loans in thousands in parentheses.

Source: Special unpublished tabulation from Federal Reserve Board 1955 loan survey.

$3,105 million in value, either borrower or bank was located in the CMA. What fraction of this business was in the CMA "local loan" market? Table 1 shows this total business classified by location of bank and borrower. For only $1,125 million were both bank and borrower in the CMA. Chicago-located borrowers borrowed $756 million from other banks, and Chicago banks loaned $1,224 million to other borrowers. Some of the loans for which both bank and borrower were located in the CMA were very large loans, in which dealing with a local bank was a matter of convenience rather than necessity. Table 2 presents all loans with an outstanding balance of less than $100,000. Of these about 15,000 loans, representing $215 million, were between CMA banks and CMA borrowers. Judge MacMahon (in the Manufacturers Hanover case) suggested that only business loans under $100,000 should be considered limited to the local market. If he is correct, then the transactions in the CMA local market of $215 million are but a small fraction of the total transactions involving Chicago banks or Chicago customers.

Definition of a local market for loans no doubt requires more sophisticated measures than merely the address and size of loan used here. One would wish to pay attention to the size of the borrower, the nature of his business, his other sources of funds, and so on. Further, one would wish to consider nonbank suppliers of funds as well. But the illustration is suggestive.

Does it really matter how one defines a market? In some cases it matters very much. For example, in the CMA bank illustration the share of the market of the four largest suppliers (called the 4-firm concentration ratio) varies enormously as the definition of the market is changed. For 1955, the four largest Chicago banks made 84 per cent of the dollar volume of business loans of banks in the CMA, 42 per cent of the dollar volume of loans to CMA located borrowers, but only 25 per cent of the dollar volume of loans of under $100,000 to CMA borrowers. These are major differences in terms of the relevant theoretical model to apply: 84 per cent is in the range where monopolistic models are often invoked; 25 per cent is near the competitive level. These differences are also important in terms of the legal status under antitrust laws. To take a different example, failure to recognize the geographical limits to the economical shipment of cement would lead to the conclusion that the U.S. cement industry has dozens of small sellers. In fact regional cement markets are highly concentrated and in some cases have but a single supplier.

The concept of a market is multidimensional and it is complex, but reasonably accurate delineation of markets is required if economic theory is to be brought into contact with economic observation. No single definition serves the many uses to which the concept is put; the relevant definition must be suited to the particular application required. Logical difficulties exist in attempting to define market extent independent of market behavior and market performance. Notwithstanding these difficulties, there is scope for approximations to the extent of relevant markets. These require both care in formulation and sophistication in empirical estimation. No greater barrier exists to the fruitful application of economic theory than the failure to forge the links to observable data. The operational definition of economic markets is such a link.

PETER O. STEINER

[*See also* ANTITRUST LEGISLATION.]

BIBLIOGRAPHY

COURNOT, ANTOINE AUGUSTIN (1838) 1960 *Researches Into the Mathematical Principles of the Theory of Wealth.* New York: Kelley. → First published in French.

MARSHALL, ALFRED (1890) 1936 *Principles of Economics.* 8th ed. New York and London: Macmillan. → A two-volume variorum edition was published in 1961.

STIGLER, GEORGE J. (1942) 1960 *The Theory of Price.* Rev. ed. New York: Macmillan.

TRIFFIN, ROBERT 1940 *Monopolistic Competition and General Equilibrium Theory.* Harvard Economic Studies, Vol. 67. Cambridge, Mass.: Harvard Univ. Press.

MARKOV CHAINS

A Markov chain is a chance process having the special property that one can predict its future just as accurately from a knowledge of the present state of affairs as from a knowledge of the present together with the entire past history.

The theory of social mobility illustrates the idea. Considering only eldest sons, note the status of successive generations of a particular male line in a society divided into three classes: upper, middle, and lower. If we assume the movement of a family among the three social classes is a chance process —governed by probabilistic laws rather than deterministic ones—several possibilities present themselves. An independent process represents a perfectly mobile society: the probability that a man is in a particular class depends in no way on the class of his father. At the other extreme is a society in which the probability that a man is in a particular class depends on the class of his father, that of his grandfather, that of his great-grandfather, etc.

A Markov chain is a process of intermediate complexity: the probability that a man is in a given class may depend on the class of his father, but it does not further depend on the classes of his earlier antecedents. For instance, while upper-class and middle-class fathers may have different probabilities of producing sons of a given class, an upper-class father whose own father was also upper class must have the same probability of producing a son of a given class as does an upper-class father whose father was, say, lower class. (This example will be used to illustrate each concept introduced below.)

No chance process encountered in applications is truly independent—in particular, no society is perfectly mobile. While in the same way no natural process exactly satisfies the Markov chain condition, many of them come close enough to make a Markov chain model useful.

Formal definitions. For an exact formulation of the Markov chain concept, introduced in 1907 by the Russian mathematician A. A. Markov, imagine a system (family, society, person, organism) that passes with each unit of time (minute, hour, generation) from one to another of the s *states* $E_1, E_2, \cdots, E_s$. (Upper class, E_1, middle class, E_2, and lower class, E_3, are the states in the social mobility example.) Assume that a chance process governs the evolution of the system; the chance process is the collection of probability laws describing the way in which the system changes with time. The system is that which undergoes change; a particular analysis may involve many systems of the same kind (many families, or many societies, etc.), all obeying the same process or set of probability laws.

Since the system passes through various states in sequence, time moves in jumps, rather than continuously; hence the integers 1, 2, 3, $\cdots$ provide a natural time index. Denote by $P(E_k|E_i, E_j)$ the conditional probability that at time $n+2$ the system is in state E_k, given that at times n and $n+1$ it was in states E_i and E_j in that order; and similarly for longer or shorter conditioning sequences of states. We make the usual assumption that the conditional probabilities just defined do not depend on n (that is, the conditional probabilities do not change as time passes). The process is a Markov chain if $P(E_k|E_i, E_j) = P(E_k|E_j)$, $P(E_l|E_i, E_j, E_k) = P(E_l|E_k)$, $P(E_m|E_i, E_j, E_k, E_l) = P(E_m|E_l)$, etc.

The *transition probabilities* $p_{ij} = P(E_j|E_i)$ determine the fundamental properties of the Markov chain; they form an s by s *transition matrix* $\boldsymbol{P} = (p_{ij})$, the basic datum of the process. (A matrix such as $\boldsymbol{P}$ that has only nonnegative entries and has rows summing to 1 is called a stochastic matrix.)

An independent process can be considered a special sort of Markov chain for which $p_{ij} = p_j$ (that is, the p_{ij} do not depend on i): the rows of $\boldsymbol{P}$ are all the same in this case. The *second-order transition probabilities* provide a second example of information contained in $\boldsymbol{P}$. If the system is presently in state E_i, then the conditional probability that it will pass to E_j and then to E_k in the next two steps is $P(E_j|E_i)P(E_k|E_i, E_j) = p_{ij}p_{jk}$; hence the conditional probability that the system will occupy E_k two time units later is

$$p_{ik}^{(2)} = \sum_{j=1}^{s} p_{ij}p_{jk}.$$

(Summing over the index j accounts for all the possible intermediate states.) But this second-order transition probability $p_{ik}^{(2)}$ is just the (i,k)th entry in $\boldsymbol{P}^2$ (the matrix $\boldsymbol{P}$ times itself in the sense of matrix multiplication).

Table 1

	E_1	E_2	E_3
E_1 (upper class)	.448	.484	.068
E_2 (middle class)	.054	.699	.247
E_3 (lower class)	.011	.503	.486

Social mobility in England and Wales is approximately described by a Markov chain with transition matrix shown in Table 1. (These numbers must, of course, be arrived at empirically. The problem of estimation of transition probabilities is discussed later.) For example, a middle-class man has chance .054 of producing a son (recall that only eldest sons are considered here) who enters the upper class. Now the chance that a man in the upper class has a middle-class grandson is $p_{12}^{(2)} = (.448 \times .484) + (.484 \times .699) + (.068 \times .503) = .589$, while the chance that a man in the middle class has a middle-class grandson is $p_{22}^{(2)} = .639$.

Notice that these last two probabilities are different, which raises a point often misunderstood. The Markov chain definition prescribes that an upper-class man with upper-class antecedents must have the same chance of producing a middle-class son as an upper-class man with lower-class antecedents has. But influence—stochastic influence, so to speak—of a man on his grandson, which does exist if $p_{12}^{(2)} \neq p_{22}^{(2)}$, is entirely consistent with the definition, which requires only that the grandfather exert this influence exclusively through the intermediate generation (the father).

To describe natural phenomena by Markov chains requires idealization; the social mobility example carried through here makes this obvious. Since Markov chains allow for dependence, however, they can with satisfactory accuracy account for the evolution of diverse social, psychological, biological, and physical systems for which an independent chance process would make too crude a model. On the other hand, Markov chains have simple enough structure to be mathematically tractable.

As another example of an approximate Markov chain, consider sociological panel studies. A potential voter is asked his party preference each month for six months preceding an election; his answer places him in state E_1 (Republican), E_2 (Democrat), or E_3 (undecided). The voter's progress among these states (approximately) obeys the Markov rule if, in predicting his August preference on the basis of his previous ones, one can without (essential) loss disregard them all except the most recent one, namely that for July (and similarly for the other predictions). In learning theory, Markov models have proved fruitful for describing organisms that change state from trial to trial in response to reinforcement in a learning process. (See Bibliography for applications in such areas as industrial inspection, industrial mobility, sickness and accident statistics, and economics.)

Mathematical analysis. The transition matrix $\boldsymbol{P}$ determines many of the characteristics of a Markov chain. We have seen that the (i,j)th entry $p_{ij}^{(2)}$ of $\boldsymbol{P}^2$ is the conditional probability, given that the system is in E_i, that it will be in E_j two steps later. In the same way, the nth *order transition probability* $p_{ij}^{(n)}$, the conditional probability that the system will occupy E_j after n steps if it is now in E_i, is the (i,j)th entry in $\boldsymbol{P}^n$. But $\boldsymbol{P}$ alone does not determine the absolute probability $a_i^{(n)}$ that at time n the system is in state E_i. For this we need $\boldsymbol{P}$ and the *initial probabilities* $a_i^{(1)}$.

The probability that the system occupies states E_i and E_j respectively at times n and $n+1$ is $a_i^{(n)}p_{ij}$; adding over the states possible at time n, we conclude that $\sum_i a_i^{(n)} p_{ij} = a_j^{(n+1)}$, or, if $\boldsymbol{a}^{(n)}$ denotes the row vector $(a_1^{(n)}, \cdots, a_s^{(n)})$, $\boldsymbol{a}^{(n)} \boldsymbol{P} = \boldsymbol{a}^{(n+1)}$. More generally, the mth order transition probabilities link the absolute probabilities for time $n+m$ to those for time n: $\sum_i a_i^{(n)} p_{ij}^{(m)} = a_j^{(n+m)}$ or $\boldsymbol{a}^{(n)}\boldsymbol{P}^m = \boldsymbol{a}^{(n+m)}$. Thus the absolute probabilities $a_i^{(n)}$ are completely determined, via the relation $\boldsymbol{a}^{(n)} = \boldsymbol{a}^{(1)}\boldsymbol{P}^{n-1}$, by the transition probabilities p_{ij} and the initial probabilities $a_i^{(1)}$. In other words, $\boldsymbol{P}$ and $\boldsymbol{a}^{(1)}$ completely specify the probability laws of the Markov chain.

Chains with all $p_{ij} > 0$. The most important mathematical results about Markov chains concern the stability of the $a_i^{(n)}$ and the behavior of $p_{ij}^{(n)}$ for large n. Although some of the p_{ij} may be zero, suppose they are all strictly greater than zero. (Later this restriction will be lifted and other chains considered.) One expects that for large n, $p_{ij}^{(n)}$ should not depend much on i—the effect of the initial state should wear off. This is indeed true: there exist positive numbers $p_1, \cdots, p_s$ such that $p_{ij}^{(n)}$ is close to p_j for large n ($\lim_{n\to\infty} p_{ij}^{(n)} = p_j$ for all i and j). It follows that $a_i^{(n)} = \sum_k a_k^{(1)} p_{ki}^{(n-1)}$ approaches $\sum_k a_k^{(1)} p_i = p_i$ as n becomes large, so that the absolute probabilities $a_i^{(n)}$ stabilize near the p_i, no matter what the initial probabilities $a_i^{(1)}$ are.

The numbers p_i have several important mathematical properties, which in turn have probability interpretations. Clearly they sum to one: $\sum_i p_i = 1$. Moreover, if n is large, $\sum_i p_{ki}^{(n)} p_{ij}$ is near $\sum_i p_i p_{ij}$, while $p_{kj}^{(n+1)}$ is near p_j. Since $\sum_i p_{ki}^{(n)} p_{ij} = p_{kj}^{(n+1)}$, we have $\sum_i p_i p_{ij} = p_j$, or, with $\boldsymbol{p} = (p_1, \cdots, p_s)$, $\boldsymbol{pP} = \boldsymbol{p}$. Therefore the p_j solve the system

$$(1) \qquad \begin{aligned} \sum_{i=1}^{s} p_i p_{ij} &= p_j, \qquad j = 1, 2, \cdots, s, \\ \sum_{i=1}^{s} p_i &= 1 \end{aligned}$$

of $s+1$ equations in s unknowns. Since it turns out that this system has but one solution, the limits p_j can be found by solving it, and this is the method used in practice. The vector $\boldsymbol{p}$ for the social mobility example is (.067, .624, .309). Whatever a man's class, there is probability near .309 that a descendant a great many generations later is in the lower class.

The quantities p_j connect up with the absolute probabilities $a_j^{(n)}$. If $\boldsymbol{a}^{(n)} = \boldsymbol{p}$, then $\boldsymbol{a}^{(n+1)} = \boldsymbol{a}^{(n)}\boldsymbol{P} = \boldsymbol{pP} = \boldsymbol{p}$, and similarly $\boldsymbol{a}^{(m)} = \boldsymbol{p}$ for all m beyond n. In other words, if the system has at a given time probability exactly p_j of being in state E_j (for each j) then the same holds ever after. For this reason, the p_j are called a set of *stationary probabilities;*

since the solution to (1) is unique, they form the only such set.

Thus a system evolving according to the laws of the Markov chain has long-range probability approximately p_j of being in E_j; and if the probability of being in E_j at a particular time is exactly p_j, this relationship is preserved in the future. The law of large numbers gives a complementary way of interpreting these facts. Imagine a large number of systems evolving independently of one another, each according to the laws of a common Markov chain. No matter what the initial states of the many systems may be, after a long time the numbers of systems in the various states will become approximately proportional to the p_j. And once this state of affairs is achieved, it will persist, except for fluctuations that are proportionately small if the number of systems involved is large. In the social mobility example, the proportions in the three classes of a large number of family lines will eventually be nearly 067:624:309.

A system setting out from state E_i is certain to return again to E_i after one or more steps; the expected value of the number of steps until first return turns out to be $1/p_i$, a result that agrees qualitatively with intuition: the lower the probability of a state the longer the average time between successive passages through it. There exist also formulas for the expected number of steps to reach E_j for a system starting in E_i. In the example from mobility theory, the mean time to pass from the lower class to the upper class is 26.5 generations, while the mean for the return trip is but 5.6 generations (which should be a lesson to us all).

Other Markov chains. In the analysis sketched above, it was assumed that the p_{ij} were all strictly greater than zero. More generally, the same results hold even if some of the p_{ij} equal zero, provided the Markov chain has the property that the states all communicate (for each i and j there is an n for which $p_{ij}^{(n)} > 0$) and provided also that there is no periodicity (no integer m exceeding 1 exists such that a passage from E_i back to E_i is possible in n steps only if n is divisible by m). Such a chain is called ergodic. The results can also be reformulated to cover nonergodic chains.

The theory extends in still other useful ways. (a) A chance process is a Markov chain of second order if the probability distribution of future states depends only on the two most recently visited states: $P(E_l|E_i,E_j,E_k) = P(E_l|E_j,E_k)$, $P(E_m|E_i,E_j,E_k,E_l) = P(E_m|E_k,E_l)$, etc. These processes contain ordinary Markov chains as a special case and make possible a more precise description of some phenomena. The properties derived above carry over to chains of second (and higher) order. (b) If, for instance, the system is a population and the state is its size, there are then infinitely many possible states. The theory generalizes to cover such examples, but the mathematics becomes more difficult; for example (1) becomes a system of infinitely many equations in infinitely many unknowns. (c) Continuous time, rather than time that goes in jumps, is appropriate for the description of some systems—for example, populations that change state (size) because of births and deaths that can occur at any instant of time. Such processes in principle admit an approximate description within the discrete-time theory: one observes the system periodically (every year or minute or microsecond) and ignores the state occupied at other time points. However, since such an analysis is often unnatural, an extensive theory of continuous-time processes has grown up.

Statistical analysis. One may believe a given process to be a Markov chain—or approximately a Markov chain—because of his knowledge of the underlying mechanism. Or he may hypothesize that it is a Markov chain, hoping to check this assumption against actual data. Under the Markov assumption, he may want to draw from actual data conclusions about the transition probabilities p_{ij}, which are the basic parameters of the model. In other words, statistical problems of estimation and hypothesis testing arise for Markov chains just as they do for independent processes [*see* ESTIMATION; HYPOTHESIS TESTING].

Suppose one observes n systems (governed by a common Markov chain), of which n_i start in state E_i, and follows each of them through one transition. If n_{ij} is the number that step from E_i to E_j, so that $\sum_j n_{ij} = n_i$, then the log-likelihood function is $\sum_{i,j} n_{ij} \log p_{ij}$; maximizing this function with the s constraints $\sum_j p_{ij} = 1$ gives the natural ratios n_{ij}/n_i as the maximum likelihood estimators of the p_{ij}. The numerical matrix given for the social mobility example was obtained in this way from a sample of some 3,500 father–son pairs in England and Wales. If the n_i are large, the estimators are approximately normally distributed about their mean values p_{ij}. By seeing how far the n_{ij}/n_i differ from putative transition probabilities p_{ij}, one can test the null hypothesis that these p_{ij} are the true parameter values. The statistic appropriate for this problem is $\sum_{i,j}(n_{ij} - n_i p_{ij})^2/n_i p_{ij}$; it has approximately a chi-square distribution with $s(s-1)$ degrees of freedom if the n_i are large.

Other tests are possible if the systems under observation are traced for more than one step. Suppose n_{ijk} is the number of the systems that start in E_i, step to E_j, and then step to E_k. If the process is a Markov chain, then (*a*) the chance that the second step carries the system from E_j to E_k does not depend on the initial state E_i and (*b*) the transition probabilities for the second step are the same as those for the first.

Let a dot indicate an index that has been summed out; for example, $n_{\cdot ij} = \sum_k n_{kij}$ is the number of systems that are in states E_i and E_j at times 2 and 3, respectively (with the state at time 1 completely unspecified). Assuming (*a*), one can test (*b*) by comparing the estimators $n_{ij\cdot}/n_{i\cdot\cdot}$ of the transition probabilities for the first step with the estimators $n_{\cdot ij}/n_{\cdot i\cdot}$ of the transition probabilities for the second step. And one can test (*a*) itself by comparing the ratios $n_{\cdot jk}/n_{\cdot j\cdot}$ (the estimated second-step transition probabilities) with the ratios $n_{ijk}/n_{\cdot jk}$ (the estimated second-step transition probabilities, allowing for possible further influence of the initial state); if (*a*) holds, $n_{ijk}/n_{ij\cdot}$ should, independently of *i*, be near $n_{\cdot jk}/n_{\cdot j\cdot}$; thus one can check on the Markov chain assumption itself.

This statistical analysis, based on following a large number of independently evolving systems through a small number of steps, really falls under the classical chi-square and maximum likelihood theory. There is also a statistical theory for the opposite case, following a small number of systems (perhaps just one) through many steps. Although the estimates and tests for this case have forms similar to those for the first case, the derivation of their asymptotic properties is more involved.

The statistical analysis of Markov chains may be extended in various directions. For example, a mode of analysis in which *times of stay* in the states are considered, together with transition probabilities, is discussed by Weiss and Zelen (1965).

PATRICK BILLINGSLEY

[*Other relevant material may be found in* PANEL STUDIES; SOCIAL MOBILITY.]

BIBLIOGRAPHY

ANDERSON, T. W.; and GOODMAN, LEO A. 1957 Statistical Inference About Markov Chains. *Annals of Mathematical Statistics* 28:89–110. → A detailed treatment of the problem of many short samples.

BILLINGSLEY, PATRICK 1961 Statistical Methods in Markov Chains. *Annals of Mathematical Statistics* 32:12–40. → A review paper covering the problem of one long sample from a Markov chain. Contains a large bibliography.

BLUMEN, ISADORE; KOGAN, MARVIN; and MCCARTHY, PHILIP 1955 *The Industrial Mobility of Labor as a Probability Process.* Cornell Studies in Industrial and Labor Relations, Vol. 6. Ithaca, N.Y.: Cornell Univ. Press. → A detailed empirical study of mobility problems.

FELLER, WILLIAM 1950–1966 *An Introduction to Probability Theory and Its Applications.* 2 vols. New York: Wiley. → A classic text covering continuous-time processes as well as chains with infinitely many states. Excellent examples. The second edition of the first volume was published in 1957.

GLASS, D. V.; and HALL, J. R. 1954 Social Mobility in Great Britain: A Study in Inter-generation Changes in Status. In D. V. Glass (editor), *Social Mobility in Britain.* London: Routledge. → This is the source of the original data for the social mobility example.

GOODMAN, LEO A. 1961 Statistical Methods for the Mover–Stayer Model. *Journal of the American Statistical Association* 56:841–868.

GOODMAN, LEO A. 1962 Statistical Methods for Analyzing Processes of Change. *American Journal of Sociology* 68:57–78. → This and the preceding paper treat modifications of the Markov model for mobility problems.

JAFFE, JOSEPH; CASSOTTA, LOUIS; and FELDSTEIN, STANLEY 1964 Markovian Model of Time Patterns of Speech. *Science* 144:884–886.

KEMENY, JOHN G.; and SNELL, J. LAURIE 1960 *Finite Markov Chains.* Princeton, N.J.: Van Nostrand. → Contains both theory and examples. This is the source of the figures for the social mobility example.

PRAIS, S. J. 1955 Measuring Social Mobility. *Journal of the Royal Statistical Society* Series A 118:56–66. → This is the source of the analysis of the social mobility example.

WEISS, GEORGE H.; and ZELEN, MARVIN 1965 A Semi-Markov Model for Clinical Trials. *Journal of Applied Probability* 2:269–285.